CW01206636

1,000,000 Books
are available to read at
Forgotten Books

www.ForgottenBooks.com

Read online
Download PDF
Purchase in print

ISBN 978-1-5284-3249-8
PIBN 10927165

This book is a reproduction of an important historical work. Forgotten Books uses state-of-the-art technology to digitally reconstruct the work, preserving the original format whilst repairing imperfections present in the aged copy. In rare cases, an imperfection in the original, such as a blemish or missing page, may be replicated in our edition. We do, however, repair the vast majority of imperfections successfully; any imperfections that remain are intentionally left to preserve the state of such historical works.

Forgotten Books is a registered trademark of FB &c Ltd.
Copyright © 2018 FB &c Ltd.
FB &c Ltd, Dalton House, 60 Windsor Avenue, London, SW19 2RR.
Company number 08720141. Registered in England and Wales.

For support please visit www.forgottenbooks.com

1 MONTH OF
FREE
READING

at

www.ForgottenBooks.com

By purchasing this book you are eligible for one month membership to ForgottenBooks.com, giving you unlimited access to our entire collection of over 1,000,000 titles via our web site and mobile apps.

To claim your free month visit:

www.forgottenbooks.com/free927165

* Offer is valid for 45 days from date of purchase. Terms and conditions apply.

English
Français
Deutsche
Italiano
Español
Português

www.forgottenbooks.com

Mythology Photography **Fiction**
Fishing Christianity **Art** Cooking
Essays Buddhism Freemasonry
Medicine **Biology** Music **Ancient**
Egypt Evolution Carpentry Physics
Dance Geology **Mathematics** Fitness
Shakespeare **Folklore** Yoga Marketing
Confidence Immortality Biographies
Poetry **Psychology** Witchcraft
Electronics Chemistry History **Law**
Accounting **Philosophy** Anthropology
Alchemy Drama Quantum Mechanics
Atheism Sexual Health **Ancient History**
Entrepreneurship Languages Sport
Paleontology Needlework Islam
Metaphysics Investment Archaeology
Parenting Statistics Criminology
Motivational

P Med M

THE MEDICO-LEGAL JOURNAL.

Published under the Auspices of the Medico-Legal Society of New York.

CLARK BELL, Esq.,
EDITOR-IN-CHIEF.

ASSOCIATE EDITORS:

LEGAL.

Prof. W. L. BURNAP, Vermont.
Judge ABRAM H. DAILEY, Brooklyn.
Judge JOHN F. DILLON, New York.
T. GOLD FROST, Esq., New York.
Judge C. G. GARRISON, Camden, N.Y.
F. L. HOFFMAN, Esq., Newark, N. J.
SAMUEL BELL THOMAS, Esu., N.Y.
W. H. S. MONCK, Esq , Dublin.
A. WOOD RENTON, Esq., London.

MEDICAL.

Judge CONWAY W. NOBLE, Cleveland, O.
Dr. HAVELOCK ELLIS, London.
Prof. J. T. ESKRIDGE, Denver, Colo.
W. W. IRELAND, M. D., Scotland.
HERMAN KORNFELD, M. D., Silesia.
GEORGE B. MILLER, M. D., Phila.
JULES MOREL, M. D., Belgium.
WM. ORANGE, M. D., London.
H. EDWIN LEWIS, M. D., Burlington, Vt.

SCIENTIFIC.

C. VAN D. CHENOWETH, Mass.
Prof. R. O. DOREMUS, New York.
MORITZ ELLINGER, Esq., N. Y.
Prof. W. B. MACVEY, Boston.
Prof. W. XAVIER SUDDUTH, Chicago.
Prof. VICTOR C. VAUGHAN, Mich.

RAILWAY SURGERY.

LEGAL.

C. H. BLACKBURN, Esq., Cincinnati.
Judge WILLIAM H. FRANCIS, N.Y. City
C. A. LIGHTNER, Esq., Detroit.
Judge CONWAY W. NOBLE, Cleveland.
Hon. J. M. THURSTON, Nebraska.

MEDICAL.

CHARLES K. COLE, M. D., Montana.
GRANVILLE P. CONN, M.D. Concord.
Prof. A. P. GRINNELL, Burlington, Vt.
DWIGHT J. KELLY, M. D., Ohio.
R. HARVEY REED, M.D., Rock Spring, Wy
NICHOLAS SENN, M. D., Chicago.

VOL. XIX.—No. 1.

NEW YORK:
MEDICO-LEGAL JOURNAL.

1901.

42475
3.7.4

MEDICO-LEGAL SOCIETY.

OFFICERS FOR 1901.

President,
CLARK BELL, Esq., of New York.

1st Vice-President,
JUDGE CHARLES G. GARRISON, of N. J.

2nd Vice-President,
T. D. CROTHERS, M. D., of Conn.

Vice-Presidents for the States, Territories and Provinces.

Alabama—JudgeThos W.Coleman,Montgomery.
Alaska—Clarence Thwing, M. D., Sitka.
Arizona—D. M. Purman, M. D., Phoenix.
Arkansas—H. C. Dunavant, M. D., Osceola.
Austria—Prof. R. Krafft-Ebing, Vienna.
Belgium—Dr. Jules Morel, Mons.
Brazil—Prof. Nina Rodrigues, M. D , Bahia.
British Honduras—Ada M Chevaillier, Balize
California—A. E. Osborne, M. D., Glen Ellen.
Colorado—Prof. J. T. Eskridge, Denver.
Connecticut—Judge A.M.Tallmadge, Bridgeport.
China—Harold Browett, Esq., Shanghai.
Cuba—Chief Justice Hechavarria, of Santiago.
Dakota, N.—Dr. Dwight S. Moore, Jamestown.
Dakota, S.—John M. Harcourt, Steele.
Delaware—Judge Ignatius C. Grubb, Wilm'gt'n.
Denmark—Prof. Godeken, Copenhagen.
Dist. of Columbia—Irving C. Rosse, M. D ,Wash.
Dom of Canada—Hon. A. G. Blair, Ottawa.
England—William L. Orange. M. D., London.
Ecuador—Senor J. M. P. Cammano, Wash. D. C.
Florida—N. de V. Howard, M. D., Sanford.
France—Victor Parent, M. D., Toulouse.
Georgia—Richard J. Nunn, M. D., Savannah.
Germany—Dr. H. Laehr, Berlin.
Guatemala—Senor Rafael Montufar.
Hawai—J. W. Wangbop M. D., Koloa.
Hayti.—Genl. J. A. Bordes, Jeremie.
Holland—Dr. P. A. H. Sueeus, Vucht.
Hungary—Staatsanwalt Em.V.Havas,BudaPesth
Illinois—J. E. Owens, M. D., Chicago.
India—P. S. Sivaswamy Aiyar, Madras.
Indiana—W. B. Fletcher, M. D., Indianapolis.
Indian Territory—I. H. Bailey, M. D., Dexter.
Iowa—Jennie McCowen, M. D., Davenport.
Ireland—Conolly Norman, M. D., Dublin.
Italy—Enrico Ferri, M. D., Rome.
Japan—Dr. J. Hashimoto, Tokio.
Kansas—Judge Albert H. Horton, Topeka
Kentucky—F. H. Clark, M. D., Lexington.
Louisiana—I. J. Scott, M. D., Shreveport.
Maine—Judge L. A. Emery, Ellsworth.
Manitoba—D. Young, M. D., Selkirk.
Maryland—Wm. Lee Howard, M. D., Baltimore.
Massachusetts—Theo. H. Tyndale, Boston.
Mexico—Leon Lewis, M. D., Ozuluama.
Michigan—Clarence A. Lightner, Detroit.
Minnesota—C. K. Bartlett, M. D., Minneapoli
Missouri—W. B. Outten, M. D., St. Louis.
Montana—C. K. Cole, M. D., Helena.
Nebraska—Hon. John M. Thurston, Omaha.
Nevada—S. M. Bishop, M. D., Reno.
New Brunswick—
Newfoundland—Dr. K. D. McKenzie, St. John
New Hampshire—Gran. P. Conn, M.D.,Concor
New Jersey—Judge C. G. Garrison, Camden.
New Mexico—Gov. Bradford L. Prince,Santa F
New South Wales—George A. Tucker, M. D.
New York—Mrs. M. Louise Thomas, N. Y. Cit
New Zealand—Prof. Frank G. Ogston, Dunedi
North Carolina—E. C. Smith, Esq., Raleigh.
Norway—Dr. Harold Smedal, Christiania.
Nova Scotia—Hon. Wm. S. Fielding, Ottawa.
Ohio—Judge H. C. White. Cleveland.
Oklahoma Ter.—A. H. Simonton, M. D.,Okla.C
Ontario—Daniel Clark, M. D., Toronto.
Oregon—Ex-Chief Just. Hon. Wm.P.Lord, Sale
Pennsylvania—Geo. B. Miller, M. D., of Phila.
Peru—Senor F. C. C. Zegarro, Washington, D. C
Portugal—Bettincourt Rodriguez, M. D., Lisbon
Quebec—Wyatt Johnson, M. D., Montreal.
Rhode Island—Judge P. E. Tillinghast, Provid'
Russia—Prof.Dr.Mierzejewski, St. Petersburgh
San Domingo—A. Wei Yos Gil, San Domingo.
Saxony—Judge de Alinge, Oberkotzon Hof.
Scotland—W.W. Ireland, Edinburgh.
Servia—Hon. Paul Savitch, Belgrade.
Sicily—Prof. Dr. Fernando Puglia, Messina.
Silesia—H. Kornfeld, M. D., Grotkau.
South Carolina—S. W. Babcock, M. D., Columbia
Spain—Sig. A. M. Alv. Taladriz, M.D.,Valladolid
Sweden—Prof. Dr. A. Winroth, Lund.
Switzerland—Prof. Dr. L. Wille, Basle.
Tennessee—Michael Campbell, M. D., Nashville
Texas—Dr. D. R. Wallace, Terrell.
Tonga—Dr. Donald McClennen, Tonga.
Utah—Frederick Clifft, M. D., St. George.
Vermont—Prof. A. P. Grinnell, Burlington.
Virginia—William F. Drewry, Petersburg.
Washington—Jas. C. Waugh, M. D., Mt. Verno
West Virginia—F. M. Hood, M. D., Weston.
Wisconsin—Dr. U. O. B. Wingate, Milwaukee.
Wyoming—R. Harvey Reed, M. D., Rock Spring

Secretary,
H. GERALD CHAPIN, Esq., of N. Y.

Corresponding Secretary,
MORITZ ELLINGER, Esq., of N. Y.

Assistant Secretary,
SAMUEL BELL THOMAS, Esq of N. Y.

Pathologist,
F. B. DOWNS, M. D., Conn.

Treasurer,
CAROLINE J. TAYLOR
Bridgeport, Conn.

Chemist,
PROF. C. A. DOREMUS, M. D. N.

Curator,
J. MOUNT BLEYER, M. D., New York.

Toxicologist,
PROF. W. B. McVEY, of Boston.

Librarian,
FRED. L. HOFFMAN, Esq., of N. J.

Assistant Librarian,
THOS. G. FROST, Esq , of N. Y.

Bacteriologist,
G. BETTINI DI MOISE, M. D., of N. Y.

Microscopist,
DR. ERNEST J. LEDERLE, of N. Y.

TRUSTEES:
for 3 yea s.

Legal,
JUDGE A. J. DITTENHOEFER, of N. Y.
JUDGE WM. H. FRANCIS, of N. J.

Medical,
G. STANLEY HEFFT, M. D., of Conn.
P. M. WISE, M. D., of N. Y.

ISAAC N. LOVE, M. D., of N. Y.

COUNSELLORS,
For 3 years.

Legal.
STILES JUDSON, JR., of Conn.
HENRY WOLLMAN, Esq., of N, Y.
FRED. E. CRANE, Esq., of Brooklyn.

Medical.
RALCY HUSTED BELL, M. D., of N. Y.
ISAAC N. LOVE, M. D., of N. Y.
CARLETON SIMON, M. D., of N. Y.

PERMANENT COMMISSION:
For 3 years.

Legal,
HON L. A. EMERY of Maine.
HON. JOHN M. THURSTON, of Neb.
CLARK BELL, Esq., of N. Y.

Medical,
GEO. L. PORTER, M. D., of Conn.
VICTOR C. VAUGHAN, Esq., of Mich
NICHOLAS SENN, M. D., of Chicago.

The following are the EXCHANGE JOURNALS.

Archives Italian,
Archivio Giuridico,
Archives d'Anthropologie Criminalle,
Alienist and Neurologist,
American Journal of Insanity,
American Law Register,
Archives of Pediatrics,
Archives de la Psychiatrie Clinique et Legale et de Neurologie,
Academie de Medicine de Paris,
American Journal of Psychology,
American Chemical Journal,
American Law Review,
Atlanta Medical and Surgical,
Annales Medico-Psychologique,
Archivio di Psi Sci pen et antro crim.,
Archievs de Neurologie,
Annales Societe Medico-Legal, ed Belge,
Albany Law Journal,
American Microscopical Journal,
Amer. Med. Review.
Annals Univ. Med. Science,
Aerzliche Sachverstandingen-Zeitung.
American Medical Journalist,
Amer. Monthly Retrospect,
Amer. Journal of Med. Science,
Applied Microscopy,
American Economist.
American Lawyer,
Astrological Journal.

Buffalo Medical Journal,
Boston Medical and Surgical Journal,
Bulletin Societie de Medicine Mentale Belgique,
Bulletin of the Iowa State Institutions

Case and Comment,
Canadian Practitioner,
Central Law Journal,
Connecticut State Board of Health,
Courier of Medicine,
Centralblatt fur Nerv.,
Canadian Law Times,
Charlotte Med. Journal,
Cape Law Journal,
Chicago Law Journal,
Chicago Legal News,
Columbus Med. Journal,
Canadian Journal Med. Surgery,
Cleveland Journal of Medicine,
Chicago Clinic,
Charities,

Der Irrenfreund,
Der Gerichtssaal,
Del Kongelige Sundhedskollegiums,
Davenport Acad. of Nat. Sci.
Detroit Legal News,
Dietetic and Hygiene Gazette,
Dunglisan Col. & Clin. Record.

English Lunacy Commission.

Fordhand Svensta Lakare Sallskapts,
Fort Wayne Med. Jour.,
Fishing Gazette,

Guy's Hospital Reports,
Gazette del Tribunal,
Giornale di Neuropatalogia,
Gerichtl Zeitung, Vienna,
Gazette des Hopitaux,

Hygiea,
Harvard Law Review,
Holstein Friestin Register,
Hot Springs Med. Journal,

Illinois State Board of Health,
International Journal of Surgery,
Index Medicus,
Iowa Law Bulletin,
Il Pisania Gazetta Secula,
Indian Review.
Ideal Review.

Johns Hopkins University,
Journal of Inebriety,
Journal of Medical Sci.,
Journal of Nervous and Mental Diseases,
Journal de Medicine,
Jahrbucher fur Psychiatrie,
Journal of Electro Therapeutics,
Journal of Tuberculosis.

Kansas City Med. Inde

La. Psi. la Neurol e Sci
Lippincott's Magazine,
L'Anthropologie,
London Lancet,
Littell's Living Age,
Law Quarterly Review,
Le Progress Medicale,
Louisville Medical New,
Lunacy and Charity,
Literary Digest,
Legal Intelligencer,
Lancet Pub. Co.,
La Habana Medica.
Law Students Journal
Literature,

Mass. State Board Health,
Medico Legal Society Massachusetts,
Medical Review of Views,
Medical Annales,
Medical News,
Messenger of Neurolog and Forensic Psy pathology, St. Peterburg.
Medicine,
Menorah Monthly.
Madras Law Journal,
Medical Fortnightly,
Medical Mirror,
Modattscarfft fur Unfal heilkunde,
Medical Herald,
Mind,
Medical Sentinel.
Med. and Surg. Bulleti
Medical Bulletin,
Medical Register.
Medicus.

North American Reive
New Orleans Med. ar Surg.
New York Med. Record
Nordisk Medicinskt Ark
N. Amer. Journal of D agnosis and Practice,
N. C. Med. Journal,
Occidental Med. Times,
Our Animal Friends,

Philadelphia Times an Register,

Pacific Medical Journal,
Pacific Record of Medicine and Surgery,
Personal Rights,
Phrenological Journal,
Psychological Review,
Penn Yan Democrat,
Pa. State Com. of Lunacy,
Public Opinion,
Psy and Nerve Path. Kharkoff, Russia,
Public Health Journal,
Printer's Ink.
Penny Magazine.
Perry's Magazine.
Providence Medical Journal.
Psychiatrische en Neuralgische Bladen.

Revue De Medicine,
Revue Medicale,
Repertorie de Pharmacie,
Review of Reviews,
Railway Surgeon,
Railway Age,
Revue de la Hypnotisme,
Revista Ciencas Medicas,
Revista Penale,
Revista Medico-Legal,
Revista de Neuralogie Psychiatra,
Revista de Antropologie Criminella of Sciencias Medico-Legales,
Revista de Neurol, and Phy. (Lisbon),
Revista de 'Neurologie

Scotch Board of Lunacy,
Sanitarian,
Sanitary Record,
Smithsonian Institute,
Societe Medicine Legale de France,
Society D'Anthropologie, Brussels,
Society for Psychical Research,
Society for Promoting the Welfare of the Insane,
Scienza Italiana,
St Louis Courier of Med.,
Sei-I Kwai Med. Journal,
Spirit of the Times,
Suggestive Therapeutics.
Suggester and Thinker.
Spectator.

The Southern Law Review.
The Journal of Mental Pathology.
The Southern Medical Journal
The Hannemanian,
Tennessee State Board of Health,
The Journal of Miss. State Med. Ass.
The Cape Law Journal,
The American Journal of Psychology,
The Green Bag,
The Open Court,
The Freeman,
The Arena,
The Monist
The Cosmopolital Osteopath,
Texas Sanitarian,
Texas Medical Journal,
Interstate Med. Journal,
Turf, Field and Farm,
The Legal Adviser,
The Philistine,
The Sheep Breeder,
The Therapist,
The Physician and Surgeon.
The Public,
The Texas Clinic,
The Flaming Sword,
The Raven.
The Coming Age,
The Stylus.
The Legal Gazette.
The Surgical and Dent News.
The Colorado Medi Journal.

Union Industrial Dre Penale,
Universal Med. Science

Vermont Medical Monthly.
Virginia Law Register,
Virginia Medical Sem Monthly,

Woman's Med. Journal
Western Reserve La Journal,
Weekly Law Journal,
West Virginia Bar,

X-Ray Journal.

Yale Law Journal.
Youth's Companion.

Zeitschrift fur Schwei Strafrecht,
Zeitschrift fur Psychiat

OFFICERS, AUTHORS AND PROMINENT MEMBERS OF THE AMERICAN CONGRESS ON TUBERCULOSIS.

. E. P. LACHAPELLE, Vice President.
Montreal, Canada.

DR. E. J. BARRICK, Vice President
Toronto, Ontario.

DR. A. N. BELL, Honorary President.
Brooklyn, N. Y.

)R. GEO. BROWN, Vice President.
Atlanta, Ga.

DR. E. CHANCELLOR, Vice Preside
St. Louis, Mo.

DR. HENRY D. HOLTON, President.
Brattleboro, Vt,

LOUIS J. ROSENBERG, State Delegate,
Detroit, Mich.

DR. W. F. DREWEY, Superintendent, &c.
Petersburg, Va.

THE MEDICAL EXPERT EVIDENCE IN THE CASE OF THE DAVIS BELLEVUE HOSPITAL HOMICIDE CASE.

BY R. L. PRITCHARD, ESQ., M. D., OF THE NEW YORK BAR.

This case, recently tried in this city, has brought the question of medical expert evidence once more prominently before the public. The accused was a nurse in charge of the Insane Pavilion, and he was charged with having caused the death of a patient through violence. Three witnesses testified for the prosecution that they saw the accused nurse strike the patient Hilliard, and pull on a sheet which he had placed around Hilliard's throat. The accused nurse, Davis, as a witness in his own behalf, admitted that he had used restraining force upon Hilliard, and that he had slapped him. The defense was that Hilliard did not die from the effects of the violence.

In no recent case has the issue of the defendant's guilt been so entirely dependent on medical expert evidence as in this case. The defence examined eight medical witnesses, and amongst them were men of the highest standing in the medical profession. The prosecution, not to be left too far in the number of medical expert witnesses, examined five experts, and amongst them were also men in the front rank of the medical profession. The experts on one side differed from those on the other—this is not unusual; but to emphasize their differences, the District attorney described the testimony of the expert witnesses as a race of liars.

The question which concerns the student of legal medi-

Read before the Medico-Legal Society, March 20, 1901.

cine, is whether the science of medicine is still so for speculative, that five prominent physicians can testify that death resulted from strangulation, induced by fracture of the hyoid as a consequence of violence used; whilst with equal certainty, eight prominent physicians can testify that death was due to dilatation of the heart, and that the violence could not have fractured the hyoid bone. With all respect to the District Attorney, neither the experts on one side of the case nor on the other can be charged with wilful mis-statements. The medical issues in this case, upon which the medical experts diametrically differed, were not of a subtle nature, dependent on microscopic bodies one-ten thousandth of an inch in diameter, but upon lesions of a gross nature.

These lesions were the *post mortem* appearances of strangulation, and the fracture of the hyoid bone, as a result of pulling on a sheet around the throat. With differences in the evidence so striking as they were in this case, and the expert witnesses so eminent, it would be pertinent to inquire whether the District Attorney, and the able counsel for the defendant, had presented the medical facts in the case, so as to make the differences of the expert witnesses almost impossible? In other words, whether the differences are not due to counsel, who were wading in a science to which they were strangers, rather than hold responsible thirteen members of acknowledged ability in the science under investigation?

The legal profession refuses to assume any responsibility for the differences of medical opinion, on the ground that it is the duty of the lawyer to present the best side of his client's case. This is doubtless true of this lawyer's duty, but when the result of long drawn out medical expert testimony is negatived by a mass of contradictory opinions; has counsel done his full duty to his client, when he has barricaded his case with favorable expert opinions? What he has done his opponent on the other side of the case can accomplish by arranging the facts so as to elicit opinions favorable to his side. Criticism of expert evidence regards the difference in the opinions, but seldom compares the facts upon which the opposite opinions were given. Counsel can hardly be content because his expert concluded favorably to his side of the case. If his expert opinions are founded on a full and fair statement of facts, the same statement of facts ought to submitted to the opposing expert in cross-examination. The expert, when cross-examined, may cross-examine his cross-examiner, if permitted to do so, but the field is the lawyer's, if he will hold to an absolute statement of facts. By doing so, the opposing expert testimony will lose in weight by the qualifications added to answers already given, or by evasion of material questions.

Was the expert medical evidence in this case of the People against Davis brought out on a full statement of facts? Counsel for the defendant may not think that this was necessary on his part, as he has secured an acquittal of his client. But how far was his success a fortuitous accident, which could not be trusted to on other occasions? As the medical issues were framed by the District Attorney, did he make clear all the evidence of Hilliard's death, so that reasonable men could only read in them Strangulation? The facts of the post-mortem examination were mainly congestion of the inner organs and imperfect æration of the blood. These are symptoms of strangulation, but they are also symptoms caused by dilatation of the heart. If the District Attorney knew as much about strangulation as he does about law, he would not have sought a verdict implying death from strangulation on the facts presented by him. How then did the people's expert wit nesses testify that death was caused by strangulation? Not by relying on the *post-mortem* appearances, but by taking into consideration extraneous facts, along with the morbid evidences presented by the people. On the other hand, the defendant's experts excluded from their consideration the same extraneous facts, and found the morbid evidences insufficient to constitute strangulation. The medical differences were actually made upon the weight given by each on other than medical data. The District Attorney was deficient on a statement of facts pointing to strangulation; and the defendant's counsel—though successful—was deficient in not confronting the people's experts with the absence of these evidences. As defendant's counsel was, however, successful, the deficiencies will sit lightly upon him. And yet, as a scientific man, he must realize that he has achieved a result for which circumstances must be largely credited.

On the question of the fracture of the hyoid bone by means of a sheet around the neck, the people's experts did not go far enough when giving their opinion that it could be produced in this manner. The fact that eminent surgeons and pathologists doubted it, should have called from them such explanation of its probability as would have carried conviction. Not to have done so left a reasonable doubt, which the jury properly gave to the defendant. The hyoid bone is no part of the skeleton. This bone does not articulate with any other bone, and on this account its mobility is only limited by the soft structures through which it runs. This bone is a ridge acting as a centre for a large number of muscles. When compression is applied over this bone by means of a sheet, which is to some extent yielding, the pressure will bear more upon the muscles above and the musculo-membranous space between the hyoid bone and thyroid cartilage. The direct pressure capable of breaking the bone, must be such as will fully grasp it, and compress it more from side to side than from before backwards. Still, compression over and about the hyoid bone is not without serious results to the bone itself, only in that the effect is not direct. The result of the pressure is to interfere with the free entrance of air, and this interference with respiration causes spasmodic contraction of the muscles which act upon the hyoid bone. The muscles acting upon the bone from below are six, and those acting from above are ten. The hyoid bone is subjected to violent and irregular contraction of the muscles inserted into it, with the effect of the bone breaking, as a result of this muscular contraction. Fracture of the hyoid bone caused by muscular action is recognized in all surgical works which treat of this subject. The attention of the experts having been directed to the direct force of the compressing sheet, when from the rarity of the accident it was fairly open to doubt whether the injury could follow directly from this violence. Even the defendant's experts would have admitted the possibility of the bone breaking from muscular action. It is too much to expect of the expert witness that he should take into consideration every possibility, indirect as well as direct. That is impossible, as the mind, however honest, decides on facts placed before it. It is counsel's duty to marshal the facts and submit them fully.

Medical expert testimony is not a race among liars. Medical expert testimony, as this case demonstrates, is more often defective from the manner of its presentation than an assumed yielding of the expert witness to whatever opinion is desired of him. Medical expert evidence has the indifferent witness who makes the possibilities of medical science his excuse for almost any opinion demanded of him. That medical witness exists, and it behooves the medical profession to brand him as a canker eating into their body professional. They alone can do it, as they are the only ones capable of weighing an opinion sanctioned by the medical diploma. But this last class of medical expert evidence is not found in a trial of great public interest, and where the medical witnesses are the foremost members of the medical profession.

RAILWAY SURGEONS AND HOSPITALS.

BY JUDGE WILLIAM H. FRANCIS.

The practice of medicine is one of the most useful and ancient vocations, and, from the crude usages of the "medicine man" of savage and untutored tribes, to the efficient treatment of the trained physician of enlightened countries, more closely touches and affects man in his actual physical personality, than any other calling.

The physician deals with the intricate problems of corporeal structure, the laws of birth, existence and health, the cunning mechanism constituting the machinery set and kept in motion by the invisible force or principle, called life, plots against the threatened approach of disease, assists nature in resisting it when it comes, says to the life force, "Stay! You shall not go forth;" plans battles and conducts campaigns against death, or crosses weapons with him in close combat, and with the command "Hold!" "Away!" "Not now!" drives him from the field, although he cannot kill him, for his time has not come.

The history of the practice of medicine is one long and illustrious record of devotion, patience, skill, heroism, self-sacrifice and serviceable attainment.

The, physician, regarded solely as the dispenser of medicine, is largely the applier of theory, and, of necessity, often an experimenter; he reasons from cause to effect, from effect to cause, from diagnosis to remedy; he watches for symptoms with discriminating eye, carefully notes "the course of the disease," and anticipates its "turn." He

---

Read before the Section of Medico-Legal Surgery and the Medico-Legal Society, April 17, 1901.

plays a game of skill, in which there is an element of chance, with the malady, and the waits between moves are often long and the game extended.

The work of the surgeon is more direct; the crisis he has to meet is often more imminent, his time for action limited. With steady nerve, unwavering eye, dextrous hand and disciplined judgment, he plies his instruments in the very citadel of human life, saves the shattered body, binds up its wounds, and with his knife or probe, in place of the warrior's blade, stands forth the victor.

The surgeon has, also, his theory, but his highest skill consists in intelligent, prompt and effective action. Instead of administering a drug or potion, as his means of relief, (although he may make it his efficient aid), and deliberately waiting for its effect upon one of the organs of the body, he lays open the organ, handles the artery, fingers the throbbing courses of life, lops off deformity or excrescence, removes the actual physical force, the cause of disturbance, deftly manipulates muscle, ligament or bone, patches up the disfigured human frame, and renders it again as good, or almost as good, as the original work of the Almighty.

No department or phase of man's varied callings and activities has shown more astounding development than that of surgery. Operations are now performed, almost as a matter of course, that fifty years ago were thought to be impossible, and every day, in metropolitan hospitals, work is successfully done that would have made the old time surgeon, himself no tyro, thrill with amazement.

It is possible, however, that in reality the modern practitioner is not, after all, so much wiser than the ancients, and that some things in medicine and surgery may now be among the "lost arts" (wherever they are) which would, if discovered by us, challenge our admiration and wonder.

The New York Times states, that "the science of medicine was in great favor in Mexico before the discovery of America. The primitive Mexicans recognized and classified the principal diseases and their principal remedies, and each one had its system of treatment. They understood the virtues of cold water and of vapor baths, both being favorite remedies for a number of diseases. They also practiced blood-letting, and used as lancets the sharp pointed ends of the maguey plant, from which pulque is made. The setting of fractured limbs was done with skill, and surgeons even ventured with success upon trepanning, and when their surgeons made painful operations they gave narcotic and stupefying herbs to deaden the pain. This, notwithstanding the fact, that in Europe no anæsthetic was known until 1840, when ether was discovered. Thus it is seen that in medical knowledge the ancient Mexicans were superior to their conquerors."

Not alone in city hospitals are the highest illustrations of surgical skill to be witnessed. The railway surgeon takes high rank among operators, and the department of surgery and hospital service of our great railway corporations is one of the most useful and interesting features calling for observation in the ever onward march of practical and humane science.

For some years connected with one of our leading railroads (Northern Pacific) in a legal capacity, I had good opportunity for learning the value of such a department.

A beneficial association, to which the officials and employees of the road contribute certain stated dues, rated in accordance with their respective salary or wages, furnishes, or goes far in furnishing, hospitals supplied with a corps of good surgeons, and with the "up-to-date" appliances for surgical and medical work, and the care of the injured and the sick, and all employees, wounded or ill, in the service of the company, receive as good care and treatment, for instance in the hospital at Brainerd, Minnesota, or at Missoula, Montana, as could be extended to them in the excellent hospitals of Greater New York, and all connected with the corporation, from the president to the humblest workman, are proud of this hospital equipment and service, and cheerfully contribute to its maintenance. In addition to the surgeons and physicians directly connected with the hospitals, there are local physicians and surgeons at many places along the line, and when accident occurs their service is usually promptly available for passengers or employees, and these local physicians and surgeons, as well as those in attendance at the hospitals, are selected for their experience and skill.

Other extensive railroad lines have efficient hospital service, creditable to the wise management under which they are operated.

A detailed description of one of these modern railroad hospitals would make an interesting paper, and disclose some striking features of the wonderful improvement made in medicine and in surgery, and in appliances for the care and cure of the sick and the injured.

In such service, however, many, if not the greater number, of our railroads are deficient, and no railway corporation is fully modern, or comes up to the measure of its duty to its servants and the traveling public, that is not provided with adequate hospital service and appliances for the care of the sick and the injured, in proportion to the extent of its operation.

In the numerous actions against railway corporations, brought for the recovery of damages for personal injury or for loss of life, the railway surgeon is an essential factor, and the counsel of the company relies upon him for important assistance. The liability of the company once admitted, or established as the result of the application of settled law to ascertained facts, the existence, nature and extent of the injury complained of becomes important as the basis for fixing the amount to be allowed as compensation, and here the significance of the skill, experience and opinion of the railway surgeon becomes apparent.

Nor is the company alone benefitted by the examination and care of the injured on the part of the railway surgeon, or the post-mortem made by him. These surgeons, as a rule, are not only skillful, but high minded, and their testimony is in the line of truth and unadulterated science, not distorted in an attempt to aid the company at the expense of fact, and so the court, counsel on both sides, and the jury are enlightened by their dispassionate and lucid discourse concerning the disease or the injury, and its cause and effect, and the tendency now is to give such testimony in simple and plain terms, without unnecessarily interjecting words or phrases hard to be understood by the layman, or as is sometimes the case, utterly unintelligible to him.

Expert, as well as other witnesses, too often testify falsely or carelessly,—not so often, perhaps, as is popularly supposed,—but the cases are very rare in which a railway surgeon has deliberately distorted the truth or falsified science, or equivocated in the use or explanation of technical terms or conclusions, in the interest of his company, and the surgeon who should thus sin would become a leprous medical outcast.

We should also not forget, that in many railroad and other cases, nice distinctions arise in science, in theory and in practice, where difference in opinion may well exist, and expert witnesses are, at times, unjustly charged with false swearing, or credited with bias in favor of those employing them, when, in fact, the circumstances of the case, or the legal or scientific principles involved, give ground for reasonable doubt or candid difference of opinion.

The opinion of the expert (for much of expert testimony is enlightened opinion merely) to be trusworthy must be based upon, or deduced from, actual knowledge of relevant principles and things, investigation, experience and well supported theory, and as no two persons, although having normal eyes, see, or having normal ears, hear the same thing precisely alike, so no two minds view the same question, transaction or problem in exactly the same light, especially if it be complicated or delicate, or rests upon the discernment and application of principles or elements only to be understood and applied after careful and intelligent examination, comparison and test.

So let us not lightly charge the expert witness, particularly the experienced surgeon, with the crime of perjury.

Ignorance on the part of judges, lawyers and jurymen, concerning matters covered by expert testimony, notably such testimony as is necessarily given by physicians and surgeons in railroad and other cases, and their consequent failure to properly or fully understand and apply such testimony, is not at all uncommon, and, not infrequently, is the cause of the failure of justice.

Lawyers at the bar, judges and jurors could well become better versed in the elementary principles of medicine and chemistry, and other branches of science, and some of them in the ordinary rules of business affairs.

Neither the judge nor the lawyer should be compelled to rely blindly upon the testimony of an expert.

When judges and lawyers have better qualifications in such matters, the alliance between medicine and law will be even more effective, and expert testimony, given by physicians and surgeons, chemists and alienists, will become more and more useful in the trial of causes in which the correct and just application of the law, and humane enforcement of its penalties, depends upon the ascertainment of certain facts, principles or results which ordinary testimony is utterly inadequate to point out, explain or prove.

The railway surgeon must cover a wide range, and becomes, in fact, a medical detective, for the results of accidents. as shown in injuries to the human body are varied, and the alleged injury may be one that gives no outward sign; shamming injury or disease is also an accomplishment not readily unmasked.

It was recently noticed that a western woman (the western air is good for the nerves) had sued a railroad company to recover damages for the loss of her appetite, or liking for cucumbers, asserted as the result of her injury.

While the railway surgeon has accomplished much, he can do more. Let us wish for him, and for the fraternity of physicians and surgeons in general, even greater achievement than the splendid success in the past.

Our Medico-Legal Society, founded upon the beneficent and efficient alliance of medicine and law, has a useful section in that of Medico-Legal Surgery. Let us strive to make it and the other sections, and the Society in general, more extended and useful, remembering that not mere research to satisfy, if I may say so, an epicurean mental curiosity, but research for some good and practical end should be ours. Let us seek to let light in upon darkness; to remove barriers that should no longer be tolerated; to replace despair with hope, and failure with success; to crowd out the false and establish the true; pull down the wrong and exalt the right; let us be sincere advocates of true science, which may be termed Orderly Knowledge.

We are only on the threshold of many things. A great

expanse still stretches before us, countless labyrinths await invasion, countless peaks of truth tower, countless avenues of thought invite entrance, countless seas of knowledge allure our crafts, countless stars of intelligence still hide from our telescopes. and countless problems await solution.

Life is too brief, mind too precious, to be used wantonly, or for ignoble or useless purpose. The gems of wisdom are only found by laborious digging, and not among the common pebbles rolling under our feet on every hand. Men die, principles live. Material things perish, mind work stays. Truth ascertained shines evermore. A vital principle established sits on an enduring throne. Error is evil—an enemy—and will inevitably be overthrown. Every wrong righted stands upon the prostrate body of an evil overcome. Only that which is truly good in man and in thought, in work and in deed will survive. "The last enemy that shall be destroyed is Death." And when, ultimately, the Angel of Death, himself dead, shall be hurled from shining battlements into Oblivion's abyss, then Life and Truth will alone remain and occupy the Kingdom that shall have no end.

FIRST AID AND TRANSPORTATION OF THE INJURED.

BY GEO. CHAFFEE, M. D., OF BROOKLYN, N. Y.

The two subjects which I have selected for discussion are of deep interest to railway surgeons. They are distinct and separate subjects and I have purposely written upon both in one paper, not with the idea of covering them, but more for the purpose of separating and clearly defining the limits of each. By first aid we mean to give to the sick or injured temporary relief by simple means, or to make them as comfortable as possible by position of body or limb, until a doctor can reach them or until they can reach a doctor, according to the nature of the case. Such aid may vary from the giving of a glass of water or placing of a person in a recumbent position in a case of fainting, to the dressing of an injured part, the splinting and bandaging of a broken limb, or the checking of a hemorrhage. To understand and appreciate the value of first aid work one should be in a position where the results from many cases of injury may be observed and compared. Such good results have followed modern, clean work in surgery and proper attention to the first dressing ot wounds, that a system of first aid work, which has become very popular, is the result. Of course, first of all, the humane feature of first aid work stands out most prominently, but as surgeons we must also consider all cases from a surgical and bacteriological standpoint.

Experience has shown that when a clean dressing is promptly and correctly applied to an injured part, the per

Read before the Section of Railway Surgeons in Joint Session with the Medico-Legal Society, April 17, 1901.

cent. of cases infected will not only be very low, but also serious and painful sickness and even loss of life may be prevented.

The benefits of the first aid packet have become so apparent that many corporations, factories and shops where many people are employed, consider it necessary to provide first aid packets for immediate use when needed. The first aid packet should be small. All that is really necessary for it to contain is two ribbon bandages, a triangular bandage, a small pad of lintine (felted cotton), and safety pins.

The idea should be, not to see how many useful articles may be crowded into a small packet, but to see how few we may complete the packet with and make it practical so as to meet the needs of first aid work. Medicines have no place in a first aid packet. I would not consider the placing of any narcotic in the packet safe or wise. In regard to splint material, that also in my opinion, has no place in a first aid packet. When required, suitable splint material may be found in most places. Newspapers properly folded make a very efficient first aid splint for many cases of fracture.

It has with propriety been pointed out that employees might possibly feel so well satisfied with their first aid dressing that they might neglect to have the case seen by a surgeon, and so raise the question of liability in case of serious results following. In any accident where the skin is broken, however slight it may be, if not properly dressed with clean material at first, it is liable to become infected. Employees should be instructed on this point, also on the limits of first aid, and made to understand the necessity of consulting a surgeon at once, and failing to do so, they should be made to assume the responsibility. The practice, when compelled to do so, of using unclean dressing material in first aid and emergency work, is very dangerous indeed, and one case so dressed may cost a corporation a hundred times what it would cost to equip an entire line with first aid packets and emergency boxes.

The following shows, that dangerous as it certainly is, the practice is still often resorted to on lines where no provision has been made for relief.

"The accident occurred at the end of the tunnel, about one-half a mile from the station. Several physicians who were passengers on the local went to work with a will aiding the injured. Handkerchiefs were used for bandages, and when they were exhausted clothing was torn into strips and used to bind up cuts and close wounds."

Even in far off Siberia, on the Great Siberian Railway, recently opened to traffic, they have provided for first aid. In his article "Russia of To-day," in Scribner's for November, 1900, Henry Norman says: "At every station there is a medicine chest, and an official corresponding to a dresser in one of our hospitals, called a *Felscher*, capable of treating simple ailments and rendering first aid to the injured. For his services and medicine no charge is permitted to be made." * * * *

Instructions to employees should be brief but practical. In this, as in the matter of filling the packet, one should be inclined to be very sparing indeed. Teach them as little as possible, but let it be so practical, plain and simple that they cannot help but understand aud apply it. The idea of selecting one competent man as dresser, with perhaps one or two assistants, is the proper course to follow. It is a question if we as surgeons associated have the right, if we so desired, of giving as complete a course of instruction to employees in first aid as has been recommended by the national body.

Instruction to railway employees should be given by

railway surgeons only, and is not supposed to cover a course in minor surgery. The tendency is to teach too much and the result may be confusion and failure. We should remember that "A little knowledge is a dangerous thing," also the saying, " Beware of an axe in the hands of a child."

It is a fact that the adoption of first aid work insures close relations between officials and employees, and that cleanliness, personal purity and religious work go hand in hand with this great work of relief and first aid to the injured. It is very important that the first aid service adopted by a corporation should be uniform over the entire line or system, and to secure uniformity on all first aid points, a complete surgical service with a chief surgeon, is a necessity.

TRANSPORTATION OF THE INJURED.

Transportation consists in removing people from the place where they are injured to a place of shelter and comfort, to their homes or to the hospital. They may be carried in various ways with or without stretchers, and by from one to four persons, in the city ambulance, and in railway accidents, by the relief car.

Relief cars are now in operation on five lines of railways, These relief cars are baggage cars or day coaches remodelid and have a transportation room with cots, beds and stretchers, and an operating room well equipped for emergency work. The car is not intended for first aid work, but to follow up and supplement it where such service is found necessary, and to furnish humane, up-to-date transportation and treatment *enroute* to the sick and injured.

To the medical profession and to the majority of railway officials no argument should be necessary in support of the humane feature of the hospital car. Certainly we should neglect no particular whereby the horrors of railway accidents may be palliated. Naturally this would seem to be the very first duty of those in charge of the relief department of a railway. Is it not far better to be fully prepared for half a dozen wrecks along the line, than to have even one occur with no preparation whatever? A railway corporation would present an interesting spectacle whenever a wreck occurs if it were obliged to improvise a wreck train before the line could be cleared, and yet that is exactly what most lines are doing to-day in regard to relief trains and the transportation of injured human beings. The records of the hospital ships will be the brightest pages in the history of the Spanish and Boer wars. The fact is, the hospital car is practically an unknown quantity so far as the public is concerned. In its outside appearance it does not differ from the ordinary passenger coach. It stands on a side track in the yards or train sheds, and is seen by but very few people. To know what it is equipped with and used for one must go inside the car and inspect it, and if people were allowed that privilege they would patronize the lines having most hospital cars. A car equipped and ready for use costs only from $2,500 to $3,500. One car is sufficient for the Long Island Railway, and from three to six or eight would equip much longer lines. If, say even ten cars were required for the longest lines, at a cost of $3,000 each making a total cost of $30,000, to ease the pangs of suffering humanity, would it not be money well spent and for a most worthy purpose? The hospital car is not extravagance, it is a necessity and a splendid investment.

The following note from Chief Surgeon C. W. P. Brock shows what the C. & O. Ry. is doing in the way of transportation of the injured:

RICHMOND, VA.

DR. GEO. CHAFFEE,
226 47th Street, Brooklyn Borough, N. Y.

Dear Sir.—Replying to your letter of inquiry in regard to hospital car recently equipped for service on the C. & O. Ry., I beg to state that we took a baggage car and had it fitted up so as to convey patients to our hospitals more comfortably. No special design was used. Yours truly.

C. W. BROCK, Chief Surgeon.

As one short straw, Dr. Brock's note plainly indicates in which direction the wind is blowing around the chief surgeon's office of the C. & O. Ry. Evidently the officials of the C. &. O. are believers in the saying, "in time of peace prepare for war," even at the risk of possibly frightening the public. In regard to the matter of expense of placing a hospital car in service on the C. & O., Dr. Brock's note does not give one the impression that a terrible outlay of cash was necessary. These cars are already the property of the corporation and the cost of equipping them with surgical supplies, cots, etc., which may vary from $300 to $1,000, is all that should be directly charged to the expense of placing a hospital car in service.

In '92 I began to advocate the adoption of hospital cars for our railways, for I could plainly foresee what a great blessing and comfort they would be to all concerned, and often they may become life savers. At that time there was not to my knowledge, one hospital car in service. To-day there are hospital cars on at least five railway systems; viz., on the Lehigh and Susquehanna Branch of the New Jersey Central, Plant System, Long Island Ry., M. K. & T. and the C. &. O. Ry. * Whatever objections there may formerly have been to the adoption of hospital cars they are certainly wearing away, and it is pleasing to note that one by one, our railway corporations are falling in line in this matter of furnishing comfortable and humane transportation to sick and injured people.

I believe absolutely in the many benefits and blessings

* I have been told to-night, that the Lehigh Valley Railroad is now placing a hospital car in service.

of a complete surgical service on railways, and also that the hospital car is easily the most humane and popular feature of such a service.

A company having one or more hospital cars will find them to be a mighty fine piece of property, and one they will not be ashamed to use whenever occasion requires. It is difficult to imagine that an enterprising corporation, composed of intelligent business men, could long delay the adoption of hospital cars after the subject has been properly brought to their notice. If an injured person is transported in comfort in the hospital car, with as little jolting and pain as possible to his injured member his feelings toward the company will certainly be very much different from those of a person who has been injured and cared for on the old style of transportation on a freight car, or even a passenger coach.

A good thing is all right anywhere. The hospital car is a good thing and it is all right. The fact that the car costs a few dollars, and that it is not, and could not possibly be on hand within a very few minutes from the time when a wreck may occur, is a very weak argument indeed against its adoption. I believe that a company that is humane and enterprising enough to adopt the hospital car, will prosper sufficiently to be able to pay for it, and I also believe that the officials of such a line will find a way of getting that car to the scene of a wreck without delay.

ANKLE SPRAINS—SO CALLED.

BY WEBB J. KELLY, M. D., GALION, OHIO.

In the domain of railway surgery there is possibly no one injury that occurs more frequently, nor one that causes the surgeon so much grief, as this "ankle sprain," so called.

I have never been pleased with the word "sprain," in this connection, as I do not believe it expresses, in the least, the extent of injury. Foster gives the definition of a sprain as "the condition of pain and swelling produced in the soft parts about a joint, by a violent wrenching or straining of them without dislocation of the articular surfaces; also the lameness that follows." I believe that when we are describing these injuries, we should, when practical, designate it as a subcutaneous laceration of the ligaments, fascia, tendons, muscles or vessels, and indicate the extent of injury by prefixing the degree partial or complete. An example would be—"a partial laceration of the Anterior Annular Ligament, sustained subcutaneously." If it was thought advisable we might add—by too much violence being brought to bear on the tendon of the Tibialis Anticus. This at once indicates the exact location, nature and extent of injury.

To many this may seem unnecessary and even frivolous—and I readily agree with them that "sprained ankle" is short, saves time in making reports, and covers up all mistakes in diagnosis—but at the same time when the

Read before the Section of Medico-Legal Surgery, Medico-Legal Society, April 17, 1901.

Read before the Big Fuor Surgeon's Association at Chicago. 1500.

patient comes to your company for a settlement of his claim, and the papers are referred to the chief surgeon to give an opinion as to the extent of injury, your report will aid him very little.

Let us for a moment take up the anatomy of the ankle joint. It is a ginglymus joint—capable of extension and flexion, but very little lateral movement. It is made up by the lower extremity of the tibia and its malleolus and the malleolus of the fibulae being united to form an arch which receives the upper convex surfaces of the astragalas and its two lateral facets.

The protection that is thus afforded the joint by the malleoli renders lateral dislocation without fracture of the malleolus of that side almost an utter impossibility.

Ligaments are composed of bundles of white fibrous tissue placed parallel. They are strong, tough and inextensile, but at the same time pliant and flexible.

Now if we turn the foot inward, violently, suddenly, and with sufficient force to almost produce a dislocation, what, as a rule, is the result? A fracture of the external malleolus. This being caused by the action of the middle fasciculus of the external lateral ligament, which is attached to the apex of the external malleolus, pulling downward and inward toward the lower attachment at the oscalcis. Knowledge of the attachment and action of this ligament shonld aid us in our outline of treatment. To dress the fracture to aid union, erect the foot as much as possible and encase the foot and joint in a light plaster of paris dressing, which should not be removed nnder five or six weeks.

The inner malleolus is not so frequently the seat of fracture for the reason that the lower end of the tibia protects it somewhat. This injury is only sustained by great violence. Here the internal lateral ligament assumes the responsibility. The attachment being to the apex, anterior and posterior borders of the internal malleolus; and the lower attachment to the scaphoid, os celeis and astragalas. The treatment would be the same with the exception that the position of the foot would be reversed.

It sometimes happens that the violence in the first case will only be sufficient to either partially or completely rupture the external lateral ligament, and in the second case tear loose or rupture one or the other of the attachments of the internal lateral ligament. My recommendation in treatment would be the same in both instances as in the case of fracture of the malleolus, with the exception that I would moderately flex the foot. The laceration and contusion of the soft parts is certainly benefitted by the sweating immediately following the application of the plaster dressing, and certainly no one can object to fixation in these cases. My rule as to the amount of plaster to use is simply enough to fix the joint. While the plaster is still soft I always use my thumb to press in just below the malleolus, causing thereby a support from below. Occasionly you will meet with a case where you have a little swelling and still have considerable injury to the soft parts, which require some support. Again a case where plaster of paris is not well tolerated. With these cases I use the rubber adhesive plaster, doing a basket strapping from the toes to above the ankle. Years ago, before the time of rubber adhesive plaster and when plaster of paris was still a novelty, I used the moleskin plaster in the same way.

Another injury requiring the application of the plaster of paris dressing is a complete rupture of the anterior annular ligament. This ligament binding down the exterior tendons is liable to receive serious injury in cases of violent falls where the foot is extended suddenly. The position of the foot, in dressing, would most rationally be in extreme flexion.

In dislocations of the joint and in serious injury to the synovial membrane it has always been my practice to immediately encase the joint in plaster of paris dressing.

We now come to those injuries of the ankle which may be classed as sprains. An injury to the soft parts, in which the smallest vessels may have been ruptured in connection with severe sprains or stretching of tendons and other soft parts. In this class of cases the violence, as a rule, has been moderate in a degree. The parts swell quickly, eckymose, and become very painful. This class of cases yield to treatment readily. Place the foot in as warm water as can be born, leaving it there for at least thirty minutes, adding from time to time sufficient warm water to keep up the temperature. After removing the foot encase it neatly in a soft roller bandage, preferably flannel. Do this twice a day. Between baths it has been my custom to keep the bandage saturated with a liniment composed of equal parts of Tincture of Arnica, Camphor Opium and Olive Oil. I find this greatly aids the reduction of the swelling and tenderness. The oil acts nicely on the skin and prevents the pain usually attendant in these cases.

TUBERCULOSIS.

SOME SUGGESTIONS FOR THE PREVENTION OF TUBERCULOSIS.

Written From Personal Observation.

BY C. F. ULRICH, A. M., M. D., WHEELING, W. VA.

It is generally acknowledged that tuberculosis, usually called consumption, is one of the worst, the most destructive enemies of human life. Many efforts have been made by intelligent, laborious and benevolent physicians to put an end to the ravages of this fearful foe of man. Many so-called specifics have been offered for sale by manufacturers of patent medicines as a sure cure for this death-dealing disease. But, so far very little has been accomplished in this direction. However, while medicine has failed, it has fallen to the lot of hygiene and sanitation to do much in relieving suffering humanity from the attacks of this relentless foe. It is not the province of this paper to discuss the character, the origin and the development of this disease. But in order to make my suggestions for its prevention clear and intelligible I must advance some kind of a theory of its evolution. I do not claim infallibility for my explanation; but merely say that it is plausible, and will make my hints for the prevention of tuberculosis and the treatment of the incipient stage of the disease more easily understood. When we go into close examination of the evolution of the human race, we find that heredity lies at the foundation of the process. Not only the physical form, mode of motion and other characteristics, but also the psychical peculiarities of man are inherited from his ancestors. Even acquired traits pass to the next generation and go on increasing in strength until they become part of the individual. The same is true in the development of disease; a child will inherit the strength or weakness of one or both of its parents. By weakness, in this connection, I mean a tendency to acquire certain diseases, or deficient power of resistance to repel their attacks. Then, when the surroundings

Presented to the American Congress of Tuberculosis May 15 and 16, 1901.

are unfavorable to health in general, or favorable to the production of a certain disease, the individual gradually succumbs, unless he can be removed from the unhealthy environments, or the evil influences can be driven away.

It is well known that the food taken by man undergoes certain changes in the stomach and intestines, called digestion; after which it is assimilated and forms part of the tissues. There is a certain power possessed by all matter of attracting other matter. In the planetary system it is called gravity or centripetal force and the mutual attraction of the planets to each other. In chemistry, magnetism and electricity it is known as attraction, with its opposite, repulsion. Darwin, in his "Origin of Species," calls it natural selection. Haeckel, in his "Evolution of Man," characterizes it as adaptation. This same force within the alimentary canal, the chylopoietic and vascular systems, produces what we call assimilation; i. e., the selection by each organ and tissue of such a portion of the digested food as is necessary to its growth or repair; at the same time repelling what is not needed, that it may find its way to the emunctories to be carried out of the body. Now when an individual has inherited a deficiency of this force of attraction, of selection, adaptation or assimilation. what is the result? There is not a proper selection of material from the nutrient ingesta. Substances not appropriate to the organ or tissue to be built up are deposited and form the tubercles. These, besides occupying the place of the true tissue, set up inflammation, break down, causing ulceration and suppuration. If this takes place in the intestines we have miliary tubercles, giving rise to all sorts of intestinal diseases; if in the stomach, there arises a variety of lesions appropriate to that organ, among which I include all forms of gastric carcinoma. If this deficiency exists in the lungs, they are filled with those unhealthy deposits which interfere with natural respiration. Thus the blood fails to be relieved of the waste which should have passed out by means of expiration, and flows back to the heart unpurified, whence this polluted stream is sent back into the general circulation, carrying this poison, increased by the addition of the new waste of worn tissue to all the organs; which, if long continued, soon puts an end to a miserable life; or in the milder cases entails years of suffering and unhappiness. Now, what is to be done in such cases? Can we relieve the suffering by the free use of drugs, absorbents, detergents, antiseptics, nutrients, or by whatever name the infinite variety of articles of the pharmacopoeia may be called? Past experience has taught us that very little can be accomplished by stuffing the patient with the contents of a drug store. In most cases more harm is done than good. Of course, the doctor receives his fee; i. e., sometimes, but he does not add much to his reputation: for his patients of that class seldom recover. The druggist, especially he who deals extensively in patent medicines, is the man who derives the greatest profit from those unhappy beings. Sanitation and hygiene alone are of any avail here. The Vis Medicatrix Naturae is the proper physician for treating such patients. But they must betaken in hand early; otherwise even that great physician will fail. Because, in consumptive cases there is great emaciation, it was suggested that fatty food should be given to fill up the interstices in the muscular fiibers thus rounding up the figure. But even if this fat were assimilated it would add nothing to the strength. Cod liver oil was introduced because, beside supplying fat, it contains iodine, bromine and other antiseptics. But, although it benefits some who are deficient in fat, I have seldom seen those who have that peculiar lack of assimilative force which I have described as pathognomonic of tuberculosis, receive any appreciable benefit from its administration. There is, perhaps, some advantage in the use of the hypophosphites, because phosphorus enters largely into the composition of nerve tissue, but even this is a weak prop to lean upon. My obesrvation has taught me, that, for a case of tendency to tuberculosis, or one in the incipiency of the disease, an abundance of fresh, pure air, charged with ozone; moderate but regular exercise in the open air, where that is possible; a proper development of the muscular system by what is called callisthenics or free gymnastics; also the moderate and judicious use of the gymnastic apparatus, avoiding the break-neck feats, which are only fit for professionals; abundant pedestrian exercise, daily and hourly expansion of the chest, filling the lungs with air at every inspiration, at the same time throwing the shoulders back, thus permitting the lungs to grow. As to food, great care should be exercised, not using any one class of diet exclusively, but judiciously combining a variety of articles. A reasonable amount of farinaceous diet, with abundant fruits and vegetables will be beneficial. Although many of our modern physicians are vegetarians and condemn flesh diet in toto, I cannot agree with them, believing that a certain amount of flesh is not only useful, but absolutely necessary. Of course, a reasonable discretion must be exhibited as to the kind, the quality and the quantity of the meat to be consumed. The food question may be summed up in a few words; they want no food containing much useless material, unfit to make tissue. They require such as abounds in nutrient substances that will strengthen the muscles, the nerves, and especially the ganglionic system, which promotes nutrition. The specifications I will leave to those who make a special study of dietetics. Since a large percentage of the body consists of water the question confronts the physician, and the parents of the children under observation; what shall they drink? Many doctors in the good old times, thinking that the weakness incident to the disease must be combatted by strong drinks, ordered brandy, whisky, wines, etc. Our modern medical faculty is inclined to put an interdict on all adcoholic beverages. Although I think both are somewhat on the extreme, I will not discuss the question here. On one point we are all agreed, that an abundance of pure water should be consumed by all, both in sickness and in health. The main object in the preventive treatment is to counteract that inherited weakness, which interferes with assimilation. This seems to be principally accomplished by nerve force. In the strengthening of the nerves the chief agent is ozone,which imparts to the blood increased activity, adding power to the nerves through its electric element. This increases the attractive force of the tissues, enabling them to draw sustenance from the nutrients in the blood. It also increases the power of the muscular system which promotes motion throughout the body, carrying nutritive substances to their proper places and moving the waste and surplus out of the body by way of the emunctories. Ozone is found in the greatest abundance in rural districts, in elevated regions, where the air is free from the contamination of a dense population and from the noisome exhalations of miasmatic swamps. Therefore the most favorable resort for those with consumptive tendency is in mountainous regions with their pure air and clear, sparkling water.

Of these advantages, however, only a few, comparatively, could avail themselves, for financial and business reasons.

They must therefore do the next best thing that can be done; try to live in houses constructed on sanitary principles, arranged for the free admission of light and air and for the egress of the waste, which latter is accomplished by sanitary plumbing. The children should have a large, light and airy room, with no obstruction of the light by heavy curtains, and satisfactory ventilation. Capitalists and manufacturers could contribute much to this by building that class of tenement houses and renting them for a reasonable sum; for it is as much to their advantage to have healthy operatives in their employ as it is to the employees themselves. The intellectual training of such children should not be neglected, but should never be pushed beyond their physical powers. Consumptive children are sometimes very precocious in intellect. Such should be held back rather than urged forward, and more attention paid to their physical training, letting the mind, for the time being, take care of itself. I became cognizant of a very pathetic incident, illustrating this idea, while engaged in teaching school in Ohio, during my youthful days. A little girl of six years was an intellectual prodigy: being an excellent reader, beside exhibiting a remarkable familiarity with grammar, geography and history. Her parents were so proud of her attainments that they exhibited her on all occasions and continually urged her to learn more. The poor little creature died at the age of eight. In regard to confirmed consumptives who have passed the years of childhood and for whom there is no hope of recovery, with nothing before them but a life of misery, I am going to say something that may be stigmatized as unfeeling and cruel. But, on the principle of the greatest good to the greatest number, I regard the idea as humane. I do not refer to what was at one time strongly advocated by many prominent physicians, under the title of "Euthanasia," because in this age of exaggerated humanity, it would not be permitted, even if its utility and general benefit to mankind were proved beyond the shadow of a doubt. What I wish to speak of is this. In every case of confirmed tuberculosis, cease your efforts to prolong life, devoting your entire energy to the endeavor to make your patient as comfortable as possible, even though the means employed should have a tendency to shorten life. For, if you lengthen out the span of a miserable existance, permitting the unhappy being to marry and send an infected progeny out into the world to increase the aggregate of suffering in a geometrical progression until the earth is filled with pale, emaciated, unhappy, useless, life-marring men and women; do you feel that you have accomplished a humanitarian work? or do you rather know that you have contributed your share to the task of converting this beautiful earth, that ought to be the abode of joy and happiness, into a vale of tears and sorrow, a pandemonium of suffering and misery? Every young incurable victim of tuberculosis that dies before he or she has had an opportunity to bring into the world other infected beings, lessens by that death, the amount of human suffering. Of course, if such afflicted persons would refrain from marrying, or otherwise propagating their race, these words need not be spoken and this apparently cruel course need not be pursued. But we know that the sexual instinct and passion are strong in the human race; even stronger in the degenerate and diseased than in the sound and healthy. Therefore, legislation for the regulation of marriage to prevent the propagation of a diseased offspring would only be partially effective. As an example of what may be accomplished by being placed in hygienic conditions, in preventing tuberculosis; and even in some rare cases bringing about a recovery, I will briefly relate two cases. One was told me by a medical friend of mine in Kentucky. He had a tuberculous patient, aged 25, of whose recovery he despaired. He discharged him, advising him to live as pleased him best, since he had but a short time to live. The man departed and the doctor lost sight of him for five years. One day a hale, healthy, sun-browned man stepped into his office and introduced himself as the consumptive patient of five years ago. He related that he had lived the life of a wild man of the woods, being out of doors most of the time, hunting, fishing, frequently sleeping in the forest. In very bad weather he sought shelter in some woodman's hut or farmer's dwelling, doing light work to reward them for their hospitality. But when the weather permitted he was always in the open air, wandering in the forest, or on the banks of a stream; sometimes wading across it to reach some desired locality. The doctor said the result seemed to him almost miraculous, as he would never have recognized the pale, sickly consumptive of five years ago in the robust man, fairly strutting with health, that stood before him. The other case has been under my observation very many years.

A boy was born, descended from a grandmother who died of tuberculosis, and a mother who was delicate all her life and finally died of asthma and pericarditis. He was so weak that he was condemned to an early death by his physician and all the family. Four children preceding him died when only a few months' old. He was three years old before he gathered strength enough to learn to walk. His father was healthy and lived to a good old age. The mother was an intelligent woman, knowing something of hygiene. She placed his cradle in a place where he could inhale the fresh air. After he learned to walk he was sent out for a walk several times a day in charge of his sister. When he was nearly ten, the family emigrated to America. A sea voyage of ten weeks in a two-master, and a tramp on foot of about four hundred miles, partly through primeval forests and a sparsely settled country, with a very primitive mode of living, invigorated him and greatly improved his health. Being declared unfit to making his living by manual labor, he managed to acquire a collegiate education, and later studied medicine. At the age of thirty-five, he entered the army, during the Civil War, in the capacity of surgeon. Being an ardent student of hygiene he managed to make his military life amid the hardships of war, contributed greatly to the improvement of his health; so that, from a pale, delicate man who, although not suffering from any disease, was by no means robust or strong, he became hale and hearty. With the growth of his physical constitution, his intellectual faculties expanded, and he has been able to be of some use to his fellowmen, with a very fair prospect of living to a ripe old age. I cite these two cases to show that the germs of consumption can be eradicated by a hygienic mode of living; and that even now and then a well advanced case may recover by adopting a similar course when the circumstances are favorable. I can vouch for the truth of the latter example; for it is my own history I have related, having learned the history of the first four years from my mother; while from that period my recollection is clear and distinct to the present time. The result of my observations, both of myself and of many others, is that but little benefit follows the administration of drugs; but that the salvation of the unhappy child, born with the germs of tuberculosis in its constitution, and thus doomed from its very birth to a life of suffering and an early death, depends upon a strict adherence to the laws of health; giving the poor sufferer every advantage that bountiful nature affords; keeping from it, as far as possible, all that might retard the development of vital force and a healthy organization. Especially let the child enjoy the pure air with its life giving oxygen, its invigorating ozone; as well as regular and systematic motions of the body and limbs to promote and increase the circulation of the blood, to expand the lungs, enabling them to take in more air, thus increasing the activity of all the organs. Let me right here give a word of caution to the fond parents of the weak and delicate child, not to coddle it for fear of its taking cold; but to give the powers of nature full sway, only exercising reasonable caution to avoid extremes of temperature and to shelter its tender body against too rough winds. It is by such treatmnet, by such watchful care that many children, born of tuberculous parents, or who have inherited this tendency from more distant ancestors, can be saved from the unhappy fate of the miserable, sickly, useless life of the victims of tuberculosis. Every life, thus saved, rescued from pain and suffering and added to the army of the useful workers who are contributing to the progress of civilization, not hothouse civilization, but one of strong life, health and happiness, will be a brilliant star in the crown of every one who has been instrumental in accomplishing that glorious work.

TUBERCULOSIS—A RETROSPECT.

BY HENEAGE GIBBES, M. D., DELEGATE FROM THE DETROIT ACADEMY OF MEDICINE TO THE AMERICAN CONGRESS OF TUCERCULOSIS.

Looking back over the last twenty years at the varying conditions in our knowledge of tuberculosis, an interesting problem is presented to the thoughtful mind.

We are now in a transitional stage, and I am convinced that in a few years the views now held by a large majority of the medical profession will undergo some radical changes. The first statement made by a recent Congress at Berlin, that "tuberculosis is a communicable disease due to Koch's tubercle bacillus acting on an organism prepared to receive it" is the keynote to the situation. Here is an admission that a primary morbid condition is necessary before the tubercle bacillus can produce the characteristic lesions.

First as to this lesion, it was found necessary to establish the unity of phthisis, that the pathological picture presented by the disease should be entirely disregarded and the presence of the bacillus should be deemed sufficient to establish the diagnosis. In acute miliary tuberculosis the lesions occur in both lungs from apex to base. Dr. Klein and Prof. Hamilton had shown, before Koch discovered the tubercle bacillus, that these lesions were of two distinct forms, the one a new growth, the other a mass of inflammatory change. In 1882, in a paper read before the Medical Society of London, I showed that these two forms did not occur in the same lungs, and that the relation of the tubercle bacillus to them was entirely different. Since then I have never missed an opportunity to examine the lungs in this disease and have seen nothing to make me modify the opinion I then formed. Neither have I seen or heard of any work done on this subject, Acute Miliary Tuberculosis, which disproves the position I took so long ago.

Read before the American Congress of Tuberculosis in joint session with Medico-Legal Society May 15, 16. 1901.

In regard to chronic tuberculosis and pulmonary phthisis, as they were formerly called, and now included under the head of tuberculosis, the question is a more complex one owing to the difficulty experienced in getting an opportunity to examine the initial lesions.

But an important fact has been demonstrated by numerous observers in different parts of the world, in such a manner and by men so well know that it cannot be disputed, and that is that cases occur in which the clinical diagnosis is one of tuberculosis and yet no tubercle bacilli can be found in the sputum, while after death the lungs are found to be full of cavities, neither the walls of which or the contained pus have any tubercle bacilli in them.

This condition is explained in various ways by some of the latest writers, but after all their explanations are merely theoretical.

I made a number of experiments to try and throw some light on this condition, I obtained pus from various sources, which were, as far as it was possible to ascertain, non-tubercular and which subsequent cultures proved to be so. With this I inoculated a number of animals, mostly guinea pigs, without producing any tubercular lesion. I also inoculated susceptible animals with caseous material from human cases of tuberculosis, where extended observation had failed to show any tubercle bacilli in the sputum during life, or in the lungs after death. In every case the inoculated animals died after the usual time had elapsed, with all the tubercular conditions found in the same animals (guinea pigs), when inoculated with tubercular material, but in no case were there any tubercle bacilli to be found in the lesions after death. Other observers have obtained similar results.

The tubercle bacillus, as we first knew it on Koch's discovery in 1882, was supposed to have certain characteristics which gave it an almost unique position.

First, Its reaction to staining agents, the only other bacillus with the same reaction at that time was that of leprosy. Now we have the smegma bacillus, others found in Timothy grass and in the droppings of domestic cattle. I have found bacilli in the liver of Rhea, the South American ostrich, and in cold-blooded animals, such as the Indian Python and Boas. I have also recently found in the sputum from three tubercular cases a large bacillus having the same reaction, but differing morphologically from that of tuberculosis.

Secondly, It was considered to be a bona fide parasite as it would only grow at the temperature of the human body. I have numerous cultures growing luxuriantly which have never known any heat beyond that of an ordinary room. This has been abundantly proved by other observers.

There have been numerous observations made all over the world which show that, as I said before, we are in a transitional state, as regards tuberculosis.

Every year adds to the number of qualified men who do not agree with the present views.

Haeppe, Professor of Hygiene in the University of Prague, says: "I have arrived at the definite opinion that the tubercle bacillus is the parasitic growth form of a pleomorphic mould and is not a true bacterium at all, but in respect to its morphology is closely related to the ray fungus."

Number of other observers have expressed their opinions as being antagonistic to the doctrine of Koch and his followers, and I think Dr. C. F. McClintock, in a paper read at the annual meeting of the Michigan State Medical Society last year, has put the matter very happily, he says: "In the laboratory we find the germ rather exacting in its food requirements, and I am inclined to believe that we shall eventually find some certain chemical constitution of tissue, a diathesis if you please, is essential in the production of tuberculosis; that back of the tubercle germ lies the essential cause of tuberculosis."

The Berlin Congress decided that heredity played but a small part in the production of tuberculosis. This is an improvement on the condition existing a few years ago, when the influence of heredity was denied entirely by many bacteriologists. We have to go not so very far back to find tuberculosis given as the absolute proof of the heredity of disease, and this by men of vast clinical experience. Were they all wrong in their deductions from their own experience and careful observation of cases with which they were thoroughly familiar? Of one thing I feel sure, and that is we shall have to separate the cavitation in the lungs following bronchopneumonia from that produced by the breaking down of tubercular lesions, and pertinent to this, has anyone seen a case of tubercular laryngitis occuring in the course of a breaking down of the lung tissue in broncho-pneumonia? I mean where the conditions were verified by microscopical examination post-mortem. Whatever may be the cause of consumption, we have to face a very present evil and one which the community at large is getting keenly alive to, and some radical measures will have to be adopted. I do not believe that the establishment of consumption hospitals or sanitaria in such a climate as that of Michigan would be of the slightest use. It would be simply herding the affected and concentrating the disease. The expense would be so great that all the people suffering from the disease could not be included, and the only possible good would be from withdrawing all those affected from contact with their fellows. As a matter of fact, consumption is one of the most easily handled diseases we have to cope with, as far as infection is concerned. There are two conditions which would in the course of time stamp out the disease. Take the health of the people out of the hands of the politicians, and take as much care in mating human beings as you do with blooded stock.

A PLEA FOR STRICTER ATTENTION TO TUBERCULODERMATA.

BY NOAH E. ARONSTAM, M. D., PH. G., ASSISTANT TO CHEMISTRY AND CLINICAL DERMATOLOGY, MICHIGAN COLLEGE OF MEDICINE AND SURGERY, DETROIT, MICH., MEMBER WAYNE COUNTY MEDICAL SOCIETY, DETROIT MEDICAL SOCIETY, ETC.

To battle with an enemy in an open field; to exterminate an invading foe by a previous timely knowledge of his force, velocity of approach and strategem, is by no means a difficult nor hazardous task. To carry on warfare, however, with a hidden host, who will insiduously attack us from behind, and give us no opportunity for preparation, but mercilessly slaughter and decimate our ranks, is a task, which demands the keenest efforts of our senses, all our alertness and assiduous labor to resist and combat any sudden ingression of such a foe within our midst.

We are well acquainted with some of the most important phases of microorganic life; we possess sufficient knowledge of the mode of invasion of some microorganisms; we are familiar with the ravages they may produce, and we have also at our command the measures which are likely to prove effective in their eradication. Notwithstanding this, there is a legion of undiscovered foes, whose nature is unknown to us, whose life history is but a matter of presumption, and whose activities are wrapped up in obscurity. True, we some times *do* gain a glimpse of their mysterious existence, but what of it? Either the facts accompanying it are so meagre and fluctuating, as to warrant circumspection, or else we become totally discouraged of ever attaining the desired aim.

This has been the case in the domains of dermatology. Few investigators have had the boldness to assert, that a number of cutaneous affections are solely due to the action of microorganisms. The assertions of these few were unfortunately plucked in the bud, and their ardent attempts at further systematic research, were silenced and checked through the unjust and bitter opposition, offered by the adherers of the so-called "intrinsic school" of dermatology. Even the extrinsists themselves, did not at first accede to these plausible assumptions. Still the greater part of the achievements obtained, belongs to the latter, and due credit must be given to them. Without their timely intervention and valuable support, cutaneous bacteriology would have been sneered at, and regarded as a mere outgrowth of a vivid imagination.

Modern dermatologists attribute almost all dermatoses to the invasion of microorganisms, which may either occur on the body surface, or be caused by bacterial toxins within. This view prevails almost universally among the French and Italian physicians. To put it tersely, it may be stated, *that all skin diseases with but few exceptions, are due to the action of micro-organisms.* Thus, psoriasis, which has hitherto been regarded as a neurotic dermatosis, is now known to be the result of a special parasite. So, too, ezcema, which has been attributed to the combined action of some local and constitutional factors, has been proven to be the result of microbism. The same holds good of the various forms of dermatitis, not to speak of the many cutaneous affections, the parasitic nature of which has long been known to us. We refer to the several varities of tinea.

Furthermore, clinical experience teaches us, that the trychophytic diseases can easily be combated by the diligent application of parasiticides. This, however, is not the case with a certain other class of skin diseases, the nature of which we shall presently discuss.

Every competent observer will admit that eczema, lupus, echthyma, lichen, and even leprosy have something in common. Clinicians and bacteriologists unanimously agree, that (a) lupus is always due to the bacillus tuberculosis; (b) eczema is but an attenuated form of a general tuberculosis: the tubercle bacillus and other microorganisms have at times been detected within its multiple and manifold lesions, as well as in its secretion: (c) that the tubercle bacillus bears a close resemblance to the bacillus of leprosy, and (d), that echthyma and lichen are the result of mixed infection, in which the bacillus tuberculosis may be found.

To argue from this, it would seem that the diseases enumerated are related to each other, at any rate, have a common origin. This origin is nothing else but tuberculosis. In a word, *the majority of dermatoses are of a tubercular nature.*

Pulmonary phthisis, may manifest symptoms, which would put us on our guard. A progressive anaemia, a continuous, hacking, irritable and distressing cough, a poor digestion and assimilation, a rapid emaciation, a peculiar pinched and sallow countenance, a hectic fever of vespertive exacerbations, are symptoms, any one of which would strongly suggest the presence of a pulmonary tuberculosis, or of a systematic tubercular dyscrasia. This is the foe in the open field, which could be met with sufficient alertness. But think of an echthyma of the leg, of a lichen of the thigh, of the incipient stage of leprosy invading those portions of the body which are covered by clothing, and escape the notice of our neighbors. Think again, of an insignificant infantile eczema, which is disregarded by loving parents and slighted by the doctor. Think again of a recurring desquamation of the skin of the face, accompanied by a stationary, wine colored area of the same region, which either is so trivial as to escape our notice, or else is entirely disregarded, but harbors the tubercle bacilli. Think of all this; think of their immediate and remote consequence, and tremble!

What, if the one afflicted with leprosy was in the same bath tub, before you were in? What if small flakes of scales of lupus detach themselves from the face of an individual, and cling to your skin, and clothing? What if you neglect an insignificant eczema and permit it to develope into a general tubercular tendency, let alone its infectiveness to others? What of all this?

Can we afford to let individuals afflicted with these diseases wander broadcast without attempting their segregation, or at least, their disinfection? What is the ratio of pulmonary tuberculosis, contracted from tubercular skin diseases? Again, what is the ratio of those diseases contracted from patients afflicted with them? Unfortunately, statistics do not give the exact proportion of the foregoing. We are altogether too lenient to those suffering from tuberculodermata. We think, we would only undeservedly inflict misery upon those, whose malady does not call for such strict measures. But this is very erroneous. The cutaneous maladies heretofore mentioned are just as much infectious as ordinary pulmonary tuberculosis. In fact, we think, they are much more so, for the reason, that in these instances we have to battle with a hidden enemy.

We plea, therefore,—being cognizant of the contagious character of a great majority of skin diseases, many of which are tubercular in nature,—to adopt the following measures:

(1) That every physician or dermatologist report cases of tubercular skin diseases, especially those five enumerated, to the local health authorities.

(2) Immediate segregation of those suffering from leprosy and lupus.

(3) Eczema, ecthyma and lichen should receive thorough and prompt disinfection and appropriate treatment without isolation.

By the enforcement of these measures, it is hoped that not only tuberculosis, but tuberculodermata will gradually vanish and become things of the past.

PREVENTION OF TUBERCULOSIS.

BY W. BAYARD, M. D., LL. D., CHAIRMAN OF THE PROVINCIAL BOARD OF HEALTH OF NEW BRUNSWICK, CANADA. VICE-PRESIDENT AMERICAN CONGRESS OF TUBERCULOSIS FOR THE PROVINCE OF NEW BRUNSWICK.

Mr. President, Ladies and Gentlemen:

When I received your request to read a paper before your Association, I felt it a duty, as a well-wisher of my race, to acpuiesce and contribute my mite towards the noble work before us. But there is another motive prompting me, in fact, that the compliment comes from my cousins—if I may be allowed to call you such—on this side of the imaginary line that divides our countries. It is true the same blood flows in our veins, we speak the same language, we are governed by the same laws, and our aspirations are similar. Hence may I express the hope that the line will ever remain a shadow, obstructing none. Also accept my sincere thanks for electing me as one of your vice presidents.

Let me now claim the privilege of bringing under your notice that widespread disease tuberculosis, the history, the symptoms, and the treatment of which I well know you are perfectly familiar. My object in doing so, is to enlist your aid in educating the masses as to the best mode of preventing its ravages. To do this, we must obtain the confidence and the co-operation of the victim, disabuse his mind of the too prevalent belief that his disease is incurable. Impress upon him that it is contagious, and that by the non-observance of certain rules he may not only increase his own disease, but transmit it to his family or his neighbor.

The disease is always with us, stealing upon its victim like a thief in the night, leaving death and desolation in its path, and causing more deaths than any other three diseases combined. It has occupied the master minds of the medical profession, from the time of Hippocrates to the present cen-

Read before the joint session of the American Congress of Tuberculosis and the Medico Legal Society, New York, May 15-16, 1901.

tury, yielding various opinions and theories, some supporting its contagious character, others that it is transmitted from parent to child; all admitting its deadly character, but none arriving at any positive conclusion as to its cause. This knowledge was reserved for Robert Koch, a German bacteriologist, who in March, 1882, announced to the world, his discovery of the bacillus tuberculosis, a rod-like germ as the cause, and declaring the disease to be contagious. Other investigators have established the correctness of his statements. Armed with this information, it is now the universal belief that the disease is transmitted from man to man by the germs contained in the expectoration of a consumptive; by drinking the milk from a tuberculous cow; by eating the meat of a diseased animal when not properly cooked, and possibly by several other modes of conveyance.

There are many problems in this disease. It may be asked why are the Jews far less susceptible to it than any other race? Why is the death rate of the Negro and the Indian double that of his white brother? Why do goats, rats and mice possess immunity, while cats, rabbits, field mice, pigs and fowls are susceptible? Why is the disease common in cattle, and rare in horses and sheep? Why do apes and monkeys so readily contract tuberculosis in confinement, and seldom in their native wilds? And why do measles, whooping-cough and diabetes predispose to the disease? These are questions we are unable to answer.

It is needless for me to say to you that the bacillus tuberculosis is one of the smallest living beings known to science, made up of a single cell, each growing and multiplying entirely by itself; each cell multiplies by its division into two,reaching its adult age in less than half an hour. This subdivision continuing, it is a simple arithmetical calculation to show that starting from a single cell, there will be in twenty-four hours, no less than seventeen million descendants of that original cell, and so light are they, that it would take five hundred million of them to weigh one grain. And it has been estimated that the expectoration from a consumptive would yield in twenty-four hours seven billion. These bacilli are possessed of great vitality, light and air not having the same effect upon them as they do uoon other bacilli.

The germs are not transmitted by the breath, the expectoration must become dry and pulverized, when it is disseminated through the air and inhaled. Having obtained access to the lungs, if the soil is suitable, and if they are not destroyed by existing organisms, they block up the air passages and ultimately form pin-head solid bodies, which again change their character and become cavities, when consumption is established. They may enter the system by ingestion, as by the use of tuberculous milk and meat, by the saliva of a consumptive, as by kissing, the common use of the communion cup, caressing domestic animals having the disease, as dogs, cats, birds, etc. They may also be conveyed by inoculation, as by inserting the hand with an abrasion on it, into water polluted with tuberculous expectoration, and by ritual circumcision, tattooing, etc.

Carswell, Goodhart, Charcot, Bourdell and many others, have established the fact that consumption is curable. And the post-mortem table has afforded ample proof of spontaneous recovery by the existence of cicatrized lung lesions in persons killed by accident, and in whom tuberculosis was not suspected. It has been claimed that the proportion of such recoveries range from 25 to 30 per cent.

Hippocrates wrote that "The greatest and most dangerous disease, and the one proved the most fatal to the greatest number, was consumption." And while its mortality has decreased very nearly 50 per cent. during the last sixty years, at this day it is generally conceded that one-seventh of all deaths are due to consumption, and that one-sixth of all mankind is tuberculous. This decrease may be largely attributed to general sanitary improvements in house construction, and ventilation, and better housing of the poor, as so ably urged by your townsman, A. S. Knopf.

From what has been said regarding the inhalation of the germs, it is quite evident that the destruction of the sputa before it becomes dry is the best preventive against the spread of consumption. The victim should be made to understand that he is a standing menace to his family, to his friends, and to the public generally, unless he follows strictly the precautions advised. What are they? When in his house, he should always expectorate in a vessel containing some fluid disinfectant. When out, he should invariably carry and use a receptacle for it; this will prevent the filthy habit of expectorating on the floors of rooms, railway cars, sidewalks, etc. And the contents of the vessel should be burned daily or oftener, NEVER thrown on the ash-heap, garden, street or field. Then the vessel should be placed in boiling water, and allowed to remain there twenty minutes. The expectoration may become dry on his hands, clothes and beard, hence he should be smooth shaven, and keep himself scrupuously clean. If he allows the sputa in his room to become dry and pulverized—while nature is helping him by throwing off the germs,—he is keeping up his disease by re-inhaling them.

All the good advice that can be given will not eradicate the universal habit of spitting on the sidewalks. Therefore dame fashion makes a grave mistake when she decrees that they shall be swept by the skirts of our ladies, regardless of the germs they carry into the household. Again dame fashion errs when she destroys the grace of a lady's walk, by making it imperative that one hand shall be inelegantly occupied by keeping their skirts from performing that filthy work. In aid of the above precepts laws should be enacted to enforce them. The use of cuspadores containing some fluid disinfectant should be enforced in all hotels, shops and places of public resort.

Those who are compelled to live in the company of consumptives, should live in the open air as much as circumstances permit. The atmosphere of their bedrooms cannot be too fresh and pure, they need not fear loose windows, summer or winter. In mild weather, the windows in his room should be lowered a few inches from the top, day and night. When there is no fire in the room, a lighted lamp in the fire-place will create an upward draught.

The room in which a consumptive patient has lived or died should on no account be occupied by another, without being thoroughly disinfected. To do this the ceiling should be lime washed, the wall paper removed, in default of that, well rubbed with fresh bread, and the debris burned, the floors and wood work well washed with a solution of corrosive sublimate and permanganate of potash. All furniture in the room should receive the same treatment, and all clothes worn by the patient should be disinfected by steam or fumigation.

I need not say to you that the germs may infest various

parts of the body, but between the ages of 15 and 35 they are most often found in the lungs. Let us suppose an individual with a narrow chest, anaemic, nervous, bad eater, averse to exercise, losing flesh, strength and color, with oppressed breathing upon ascending a hill or stair, chilly in the morning, feverish in the evening, perhaps followed by perspiration at night, with occasional cough in the morning. With such symptoms, he should without fail consult his physician, who will perhaps find slight dullness over the apex of one or both lungs, and bacilli in his expectoration. When he will direct his patient to have his room thoroughly purified—should it not already be in that state—kept day and night, at a temperature of about 55 F. by abundance of fresh and pure air. If this can not be accomplished in the house in which he lives he should immediately place himself in a sanatorium. I need not say that wherever he may be placed, he should faithfully carry out the directions given, regarding the care of his expectoration and cleanliness. It is not contended that pure air alone will cure consumption. His physician will order appropriate medicine and food for the different stages of his disease.

Time will not permit my going into detail regarding the therapeutic treatment of the various symptoms that often accompany this disease, but I may say that Dr. Coghill, physician to the Ventnor Hospital in England, in his address at the Berlin Congress in 1899, claimed that in his hands Guaicol given hypodermically has produced better results than any other remedy. He gave 5 minims of solution of strychnia combined with from 5 to 15 minims of pure guaiacol once or twice a day. He also recommends the inhalation of one part of mixture of chloroform with three parts of guaiacol. I have used it on several occasions with marked benefit. I may also say that good nourishing food forms an important part of the treatment of this disease.

Tuberculosis may be properly called the "scourge of man and beast." It has been estimated that from 5 to 20 per cent. of all milch cows are tuberculous, and among the high bred cattle it often ranges at 50 per cent. The milk from diseased cows generally contains the germs in proportion to the extent of the disease in the animal. Those who drink such milk, may—and often do—contract the disease.

Dr. Martin of the Royal Commission in England, says "The milk from cows with tuberculous udders possesses a virulence which can only be described as extraordinary." Hence as milk is used by man from his cradle to his grave, the first step towards prophylaxis in man is to stamp out the disease in cattle. How is this to be accomplished? By the universal inspection of all milch cows, and by the application of the tuberculin test by a veterinary surgeon, not by the owner, the isolation of all diseased cattle, and by the destruction of all meat containing germs.

To have wholesome milk, the animal yielding it must be in perfect health. To secure this she should be carefully fed, groomed, and the stable in which she is kept, clean, light, and affording not less than 2000 cubic feet of air space. Milk taken from the udder of a healthy animal contains no germs, and if hermetically sealed will keep indefinitely. But its power of absorption is such, that in the process of milking—when in an impure atmosphere—it will absorb thousands. If exposed over night in the atmosphere of a room containing patients with scarlet fever, or any other contagious disease, a person drinking it may and probably will take the disease. As an illustration I may state that in the year 1892, 294 cases of scarlet fever existed in one of the most healthy districts in London. Each family was supplied with milk from the same dairy; upon investigation it was found that the disease had existed at the time in the house of the dairyman. The house was purified, and no more cases appeared in the district.

The cow should be milked outside of the barn, standing on a clean spot. The udder washed before the milking is commenced, the hands of the milker thoroughly clean, and his body clothing covered with a washable sack. The milk taken in sterilized glass vessels, and rapidly cooled.

While the tuberculin test is not infallible it is so nearly so, as to make it a crime in a mother to feed her child with milk from a doubtful animal. Indeed the most prudent course will be to invariably sterilize it, for dairymen too often neglect having their cattle tested, rather than pay the fee for having it done. All milk for sale in railway stations and public places should be kept in closed vessels.

General sanitary improvements have reduced the mortality

from consumption nearly two-thirds since 1838. England was. the first country to establish special hospitals for the treatment of the disease, but the percentage of improvement in them being only 20 to 30 per cent. as compared with 50 to 90 per cent. in sanatoria, where the aerotherapeutic treatment is pursued. Hence sanatoria have become a necessity, and are being established in all civilized countries. It is hard to arrive at correct conclusions regarding the mortality in them, so much depends upon the stage of the disease existing in the patient at the time he enters the institution.

Dr. Walters asserts that "generally speaking one may say that from one-fourth to one-third of the patients treated in sanatoria are practically cured, or a still greater proportion if they are treated in the early stage of the disease. Probably systematic and prolonged treatment from an early stage would restore to health from one-half to two-thirds of our consumptive patients.

The sick, as a rule, will not submit to more than a few months' treatment in a sanatorium, so that we must trust to the educational influence of the sanatorium to complete the recovery of those treated in it. One argument in favor of sanatoria, is that they are the best educators regarding prevention and treatment. General hospitals necessarily claim few recoveries from consumption. Patients seldom seek admission to them during the early stage of the disease, and their sojourn averages about 15 months, costing about one dollar per day, while the sojourn in a sanatorium rarely exceeds six months, and oftener much less, costing very little more per day. Again it is cruel to place consumptives among those laboring under various other diseases, the aerotherapeutic treatment and surroundings will not suit both. The value of sanatoria in the treatment of consumption is ably illustrated by Knopf, who informs us that upwards of 150 are in existence in various parts of Europe and America, and they are daily increasing.

A sanatorium should be located within easy reach of the centre of population, say not more than 4 or 5 hours by rail, in a region free from malarial influences, fog, smoke, dust and cold winds; on elevated porous ground, capable of being drained, with a southern exposure, having a good water supply, with acreage sufficient to afford ample walks and shade·

trees. Climate is not considered of such importance as was once supposed.

It is beyond the region of doubt that the ever present "tuberculosis" is the cause of a vast number of deaths in every community. Recent investigations have demonstrated that the disease is transmitted from man to man, by the germs contained in the expectoration, thrown—as it is—broad cast in all directions, rendering it impossible to guard against its ravages. Such being the cause, remove it, and the disease will follow. Can this be accomplished without State assistance? I answer No. Laws must be enacted to enforce the care and destruction of the cause before it can produce its mischief. No law can be enforced without the co-operation and will of the people. It is our duty to educate them to that necessity. It is the imperative duty, as it is the interest of the State to protect the welfare of its people. To do this the State should enact and enforce all laws urged by those who have made the subject a study, and whose status is such as to give weight to their opinion. The State should build and support hospitals for incurable consumptives, thereby largely preventing the cause of contagion The State should build and support sanatoria for the cure of the disease. It is idle to require or to expect philanthropists to furnish them, they have enough on their shoulders when they furnish general hospitals. All are to reap benefit from the suppression of the plague, and all should pay their proportion, for no man can say when it may not visit his fireside. I do not mean to convey the impression that all who enter hospitals, shall do so at State expense.

With our present knowledge, it is criminal when a State does not enact and enforce laws for performing the tuberculin test upon all milch cows, and preventing the use of tuberculous meat.

Throwing aside its moral responsibility, the State has a pecuniary interest in the life of every individual belonging to it. The Registrar General of England values the life of every individual, old and young, of both sexes, at 149 pounds sterling. In this country the value is greater. The State does not hesitate to pay for the introduction of immigrants, fine horses, cattle, etc. It may be asked why should it not as willingly pay for the saving of the lives of its subjects.

In conclusion, Mr. President, ladies and gentlemen, let me say that one of the problems agitating the public mind at the present day, is the possibility of combating that great scourge of humanity, Consumption. The laity look to the medical world for aid in the matter, and it is our duty to afford it. I well know that when I appeal to my "confreres," I am appealing to a body of gentlemen who are ever foremost in philanthropic work, and who perform more charitable labor than all other professions combined. We all know that the disease is largely preventable, and largely curable; let us impress this fact upon the mind of all. Man is prone to neglect health, until he begins to lose it. Let us teach him the nature, the cause, and the prevention of the disease, in fact teach him all we know about it, when he will realize the advantage of applying for aid in the early stage of the disease. Let us seek the co-operation of the philanthropist the statesman, and the sanitarian, when I have no doubt we will succeed in curing the curable, and making harmless the incurable.

TUBERCULOSIS AND LEGISLATION.

BY CLARK BELL, ESQ., LL. D., PRESIDENT OF THE MEDICO-LEGAL SOCIETY.

Tuberculosis has been aptly termed "The Scourge of the Human Race."

The most important subject at the opening of the new century, the one that directly threatens the lives of the largest number of human beings on the globe, is that dread spectre which faces the race from the cradle to the grave, that terrible, devastating,and merciless disease, which wastes mankind by a slow lingering death; that has increased in volume until it now heads the list of mortality among many of the races that people the earth· No other one cause sweeps from life such a large number as does consumption· We have stood as a race until the very recent past, waiting and wondering on whom its summons would fall, and not unlike the prisoners in the French Revolution, awaiting in turn the selection of the victim, to a more terrible death than that of the guillotine; because that was more merciful, in that it was swift and instantaneous. Until recently the medical faculties of all the world, however they may have differed on other questions, have been united in this: that consumption could not be cured. Save the voice of "the retired clergyman whose sands of life had nearly run out," of which we heard in our childhood days, medical science has offered no panacea, no cure for this fell destroyer.

The question of all questions in the interest of the human race; the question of the hour is : How can the ravages of tuberculosis be stayed? How can it be averted? From any standpoint from which it can be viewed, the most important factor in the solution of this grave and important problem, rests on preventive legislation. The ablest thinkers in the world, in all countries, are coming to the conclusion that no other means are so full of hope and success as this. It becomes, then, the most stupenduous question in legal medicine that has ever been brought to the consideration of the professions of law and medicine.

His Excellency, the Earl of Minto, Governor General of the Dominion of Canada, at Ottawa, on February 14th, last, in opening a conference on the "Prevention of Tuberculosis," at which the ablest men of the bar and in the medical profession from every Canadian Province were represented, said:

He hoped the expert information brought to bear at the discussions, might not only assist the public to some knowledge of the dread disease which besets them, but would encourage the public to unite in one body to try and repel its ravages. Success must to a very large extent depend upon the assurance and the goodwill of the public at large. Ten years ago the annual deaths from consumption in Ontario numbered 2400. In 1889 they had gone up to 3405. Of course, allowance must be made for the increase of the population, but even allowing for this, it was a very considerable increase. From 1887 to 1898 the total deaths from consumptive causes were 31,699, while the annual estimate for the Dominion was now between seven and eight thousand deaths a year. In the period from 1887 to 1898 the total deaths from small-pox were only twenty-one. The small mortality from small-pox was very encouraging, as showing what can be done by preventive measures.

Sir James A. Grant, M. D., the eminent physician, suggested and selected by general acclamation to preside over that conference, and who was chosen president of the "Canadian Association for the Prevention of Tuberculosis," as a result of that conference, with vice-presidents selected from the ablest jurists and medical men, two from each province, in taking the chair at the opening of that Congress, said:—

That this was the twentieth year of the discovery of the tuberculosis germ. The yearly death rate in this country was estimated at between seven and eight thousand, and in the neighboring republic about 150,000 annually. In Great Britain and the Continent of Europe, the results from this malady were not encouraging.

Sir William Hingston offered the first resolution, which had been sent out for discussion. It was as follows:—

Whereas, in view of the general prevalence of tuberculosis in Canada, and of the very high mortality caused by the disease; in view of the communicable nature of the same, and of the constant and continued dangers caused by its chronic and unusually prolonged course, during which a patient may infect not only one house, but many other places of temporary or permanent abode; and especially in view of scientific facts going to show the curability as well as the moderately contagious character of the disease in its early stages.

Resolved, that in the opinion of this conference, which represents the governments and people of every part of Canada, it is the duty of every government, municipality and individual citizen, to adopt organized methods for lessening the spread of a disease which is causing directly or indirectly, probably one-fifth of the total deaths in the Dominion.

He supported it and in the course of his remarks, said:—

He took strong grounds that consumption is not an hereditary disease. Consumption is not confined to the lungs; we may have it in the liver, in the kidneys, the bones, in the knee-joints. He had seen it on the lips of a young lady teacher who scratched her lip with a pencil. The baccilus enters the lungs from the air. people are not careful. They spit indiscriminately. The germ in the sputum lives for months, and is disseminated by the atmosphere. It is scattered by ladies with long skirts, by much handled bank bills, etc. It is not hereditary; it is preventable; it is curable; not in the last stages, but in the early stages. For the consolation of those who could not afford it, he said change of climate was not so important, and friends should never consent to people going to Florida, and afar off, to die away from home.

The motion was seconded by Dr. Lafferty, of Calgary. He said:—

The disease is curable, and emphasized the importance of the duty devolving on governments to establish sanitariums properly located in parts of the country where the climatic conditions were favorable. The Alberta district, where he came from, was being over-run by outsiders suffering from this disease looking for health, and unlesss restrictive measures were taken by the government, the district would have to take strong measures to protect itself. He thought the Dominion government should pay for the erection and controlling of sanitoriums.

The resolution, after extended discussion from the ablest jurists, as well as medical men from every Province of Canada, was unanimously adopted.

The leading men of England, realizing the magnitude of the danger of the dread disease to the British nation, have announced a congress to be held in London in July next, at which the then Prince of Wales had consented to preside, and which will receive his cordial support now that he has come to the English throne. This congress will embrace the ablest statesmen, publicists, and medical men of Great Britain, and it is announced that the governments of several nations, beside our own, are to be invited to send delegates to that convocation, where the same question will be the uppermost one for discussion.

The Medico-Legal Society has felt that it was a neglect of duty on its part, not to bring this subject up for action and discussion; and the congress to be held by the American Congress of Tuberculosis, in joint session with the Medico-Legal

Society on the 15th and 16th of May, proximo, at the metropolis of the nation; was the result of what has seemed to be a public necessity, in an hour of great pubic urgency, and in the performance of a duty that could not be ignored.

The officers of the American Congress of Tuberculosis, which had been organized in February, 1900, on invitation from the Medico-Legal Society, consented to this joint congress, and the preliminary announcement was ordered to be sent out by the officers of both organizations, of which the following is a copy:

New York, Feb. 6. 1901.

It is announced that the Second Annual Meeting of the American Congress of Tuberculosis will be held at the Grand Central Palace, in the City of New York, on the 15th and 16th days of May, 1901, in joint session with the Medico-Legal Society of New York. That a dinner will be given to the members and guests. It is proposed to open a Museum of Pathology, Bacteriology and Public Health, with an exposition of electrical and other instruments; with the use of the power furnished at the building, which it is intended to be made most complete, educating and attractive; of all appliances used in any way in arrest or treatment of the disease.

The leading maunfacturers have enlisted already, many of them, and the display will be on an extensive scale. The objects of the Congress will be to exchange the information and experience gained throughout the world, as to forces and methods most available for the extermination of consumption, which at the present moment is a disease, the most destructive of human life of any that now afflicts humanity.

The medical profession of all countries will be invited to contribute papers to be read before this Congress, in their behalf by a committee selected for that purpose; in case of the inability of the author to attend; and to enable those who could not hope or expect to be present, to participate in the work and usefulness of the body. As the questions to be discussed involved remedial legislation, legislators, lawyers, judges, and all publicists, who take an interest in the subject, are also invited, both to enroll and contribute papers.

The papers should be forwarded to the secretary on or before the 15th day of April, and the title of the papers forthwith, to facilitate clasification, as the time is short. The enrolling fee will be $3, entitling the member to the Bulletin of the Transactions free.

The complete list of officers and committees will be announced as early as possible. The preliminary announcement is now made to obtain the names of those who will co-operate in the Congress, and an early clasification of the subjects and titles.

The Medico-Legal Society directed that the governors of

the several states and territories and of the provinces of the Dominion of Canada, should be invited to send at least three delgates from each state and province, which has been done.

The following letter has been sent to the governors of the states and provinces:

Medico-Legal Society Office of the President, 39 Broadway,
New York, Feb. 20, 1901.

Honored Sir:—Preventative legislation against the spread of tuberculosis seems to be a grand factor if not the most effective of all means left at our command in averting what has come to be "The Scourge of the Race."

In many of the states and provinces legislation favorable to the construction of state hospitals and sanitariums for the care, treatment and cure of its victims, has been secured. In many more it has been considered, and is now under contemplation.

It has arrested the public attention. It is a fruitful, a terribly pathetic, even tragic question. It is the problem of the hour.

I enclose you the preliminary announcement of the American Congress of Tuberculosis to be held in the City of New York, on the 15th and 16th of May proximo, at the Grand Central Palace, in 43rd street.

I am authorized by the Medico-Legal Society at its meeting held on the 20 inst., to invite the governors of the several American states and territories, and the governments of the Central and South American States The State Medical Societies of the United States and the Canadian provinces, of the Dominion of Canada, to name three or more delegates to attend that congress; and to present their views in regard to the best legislative means of prevention.

Will you kindly advise me of the name and address of such delegates as you may name, as early as possible, so that correspondence may be opened with them, as the time is short.

Very faithfully yours, CLARK BELL.

Invitations have been sent also to a large number of eminent men in our own and foreign countries, to attend and participate in the congress, or to contribute papers to be read and discussed at the session.

The invitation has been made to the entire medical and legal professions to co-operate, and to the officers of the state boards of health throughout the United States and the Dominion of Canada.

The following letter has been sent to a large number of prominent men of all the professions, with the intention to publish such replies as are received in time to accompany this address before the congress not only, but to have it sent, with such replies as are received; a time sufficiently long to enable the same to reach the most careful and competent students of the science in all professions:

Medico-Legal Society, Office of the President, 39 Broadway, New York, March 6, 1901.

Dear Colleague:—I have the honor to mail you herewith the preliminary anouncement of the American Congress of Tuberculosis for its session, May 15th and 16th, to be held at the Grand Central Palace, in this city.

I assume that you are advised of the action of the conference held at Ottawa, Canada, February 14th, 1901, and of the organization of the "Canadian Association for the Prevention of Tuberculosis" at that time, and its action; if not, and you advise me, I will forward to you a copy of its transactions. I also assume that your attention has ben called to the "British Congress of Tuberculosis," to be held in London, July next.

Dr. Bryce, Secretary of the Board of Health of Ontario, has sent me the programme of the Ottawa conference, of February 14, 1901; and of the Ontario act respecting "Municipal Sanitoria for Consumptives," (Cap. 57 Stat. 1900), and the action of the Ottawa Provincial Board of Health of June 15th, 1900.

I have the honor to invite you to co-operate in the work proposed for May 15th and 16th, next, and to enroll you in this congress and to contribute a paper to be read before that body.

Invitation have been sent to the governors of the several American states and territories, to send each three or more delegates to this congress, and to the governors of the Canadian provinces also. Those who have as yet replied, say that they will comply with our wishes.

The most ihmportant factor in the solution of the problems that confront us, seems to be: how to utilize preventive legislation, and how to frame it so as to be most practical and effective on the one hand, and least objectionable on the other.

It is, or seems to be as necessary, to have an intelligent and strong public sentiment, to secure the passage of preventive meaures, as it is to enforce them when adopted.

It may be wise to ask for an expression of your views as to some of the subjects that are to be discussed before this congress, and that some preliminary questions shall be sent out relating to the vital questions of the hour, and I will feel obliged for your opinion for the benefit of those who desire the aid of advanced thinkers and experienced observers.

1st.—What importance do you attach to preventive legislation as a factor in diminshing the spread of Tuberculosis?

2nd.—Assuming the importance, necessity and utility of preventive legislation, how can the public be best educated and its sentiment aroused sufficiently, to secure the passage of preventive laws, and their enforcement after they are pased?

3rd.—Which would you regard as for the best interest of the people.

(1) Legislation authorizing the employment of drastic measures for the enforcement of the necessary regulations, or,

(2) A broad policy of education of the masses, as to the cause, the danger and the remedy for a factor in diminishing the spread of Tuberculosis?

Kindly reply to this letter at once, because the time is so short; and if you will contribute a paper and enroll in the congress, do so.

Please send your reply to the questions as early as possible, so that I can publish your anwer as a part of my contribution to the Congress, to be sent at least a month before its session to delegates, and in time, to awaken interest, and arouse discussion upon the subject at the Congress itself. Very faithfully yours,

CLARK BELL.

The government of the United States has been advised of the contemplated congress, and its co-operation solicited, and a request that the government and its army and navy departments, especially the surgeon generals of both, and their attaches and offices, be represented at the congress.

As to the legal propositions involved in what may be considered as of the greateat practical force and effect, in the matter of preventive legislation; the question rests strongly upon the proposition, upon which the medical world is now substantially in accord.

Is tuberculosis an infectious or communicable disease? Can it be communicated from one person to another?

How far can legislation avert it, framed with a view of arresting the spread of the disease, by regulations, the enforcement of which would result in diminishing the opportunities and the facilities for its being communicated from one person to another?

The police power of the government has been held to exist, and it no doubt does in all cases, where a communicable disease is liable to, or is in danger of spreading; and this liability or danger can be averted, lessened, or diminished by stringent regulations.

To obtain the consent of the people to the adoption of stringent and drastic laws in such cases, requires the education of the public sentiment among the more thoughtful and influential members of the community.

Preventive legislation must, to secure its enforcement, be sustained also by a strong and educated public sentiment.

The action of the congress will not be limited to the subjects presented by this paper alone.

The programme of work will be broad enough to consider

all questions relating to tuberculosis, its cause, cure, treatment, climatic influence, and every question in any way related to it.

The programme will be a classification of its subjects, and a large number of enrolled members will take part in the discussion, and this paper is sent out in advance to awaken arouse and incite to that discussion.

The following are some of the earliest replies received in response to the questions sent out, the remainder of which will be submitted later, if received after the Congress adjourns:—

Sir James A. Grant, M. D., President of "The Canadian Association for the Prevention of Tuberculosis," one of the most progressive of the medical men of the Dominion of Canada, on the Legislation of Tubercuosis, says:—

150 Elgin Street, Ottawa Canada, March 28, 1901.

"Clark Bell, Esq.,

My Dear Sir—In reply to your kind communication of March 12th inst. in reference to the "Preventive Legilation," I would recommend, that a Bureau of Public Health be established at Washington, under the Government, and that specific directions, in keeping with the progress of science, be circulated throughout the "various States of the Union," for the guidance of the public in all points with reference to Tuberculosis, also, that from the "Educational Department," a small work, containing, in a succinct and comprehensive form, all information on consumption, should be circulated, and in fact taught in every school and college, for the guidance of the people as a whole.

A system of general information, such as defined, would be productive of practical results, and tend towards a marked reduction, in the present fatality from consumption, in your great Republic.

Sincerely yours,

J. A. GRANT.

P. S.—

My Dear Sir—I feel that as a British subject, I have no right to dictate advice to your Government, but if, by your Tuberculosis Conference, you can bring about so progressive a move, the advantage to the Republic would be great indeed.

Sincerely yours,

J. A. GRANT."

Dr. E. P. Lachapelle, is one of the most experienced of observers in the Dominion of Canada. He is the President of the Board of Health of the Province of Quebec. He resides at Montreal. He replies:—

Board of Health of the Province of Quebec.
76 St. Gabriel, Montreal, April 1, 1901.

"Clark Bell, Esq., Secretary of the American Congress of Tuberculosis, 39 Broadway, New York.

Dear Sir.—I have received only Saturday last your circular letter bearing date of March 9th, it having been addressed to "Quebec," instead of "Montreal" where I reside.

"The legislative measures I am prepared to advocate as I attach great importance to their being enacted, are: compulsory notification of all cases of tuberculosis which have reached the suppuration and expectoration stage, disinfection of dwellings after the removal or death of a consumptive, regulating the cubic space and other sanitary conditions in public buildings, (school, factories, etc.) exclusion from dairies of all cows presenting a tuberculous disease of the udder, fixing a minimum air space for cow sheds, control of slaughter-houses and markets, in cities and towns at least. None of the above constitute what I would call drastic measures.

"Other desiderata will have, I think, to be secured by persuasion. Notification of advanced tuberculosis and disinfection after the death of a consumptive are now law in the Province of Quebec.

"The best way of securing the co-operation of the public would be to begin its education at the schools, (I have advocated this at our recent Ottawa Conference), to multiply leagues which would publish literature for free distribution and give popular conferences, etc.

Sanitoria also, especially those where the poor would be admitted free are, in my opinion, an efficient means of checking the propagation of the disease by decreasing the number of foci among the population. Moreover, patients coming out of these establishments with improved health, spread wide and large practical notions about the rational and preventive care of the tuberculous, and stand as a living proof of the usefulness of these establishments. These patients would certainly help to convince affected people that they get something in return for taking health officers into their confidence.

"I always intend to be present at your meeting on the 15th of May, and to take part in the discussions which will undoubtedly arise, and if needed, I will more fully explain my views on the matter.

Yours sincerely,
E. P. LACHAPELLE."

Dr. T. D. Crothers, of Hartford, Conn., the editor of the Journal of Inebriety,is a trained observer of Sanitary subjects. He is one of the Vice Presidents of the Medico-Legal Society, and of the American Congress of Tuberculosis. He writes:—

WALNUT LODGE HOSPITAL.

Hartford, Conn., April 1, 1901'

T. D. Crothers, M. D., President and Superintendent.

"My Dear Mr. Bell.—In answer to your first question I would say that the time has not come to inaugurate drastic preventive legislation. The public is not yet ready for preventive laws. Second, the passage of general laws calling attention to the subject and the enforcing isolation of persons who are diseased would be a good measure. In the second list of questions, the broad policy of education pointing out the danger of such cases and the remedy by isolation, treatment, etc., is that which is most needed at present. The action of the Congress should call special attention to the sanitary side of the question and the possibility of removing the cause by intelligent co-operation of the public as well as police regulations. I shall hope to see you some time this month. With thanks, believe me,

Very truly yours,
T. D. CROTHERS."

Hon. Moritz Ellinger, Ex-Coroner of New York, Corresponding Secretary of the Medico-Legal Society, and one of the most erudite students of Sociological and Psychological questions of our time, a member and contributor to the present American Congress of Tuberculosis, replies as follows:

New York, April 1, 1901.

"Clark Bell, Esq., st;mea sureseS

"Dear Sir.—In answer to the questions propounded by you in your circular of the 9h ult., I beg to state briefly my opinion without entering into lengthy arguments.

"I. Preventive legislation can only refer to the possible cure, and therefore diminshment of the cause of infection of Tuberculosis. It is no longer held that Tuberculosis is incurable; on the contrary it yields to rational treatment such as the inhalation of pure air; living in an atmosphere which is not loaded with the microbes of tenement house effluvia, and nursing with pure air, healthy food, and the evasion of nostrums offered by charlatan quacks, of patent medicine. Sanatariums for the poor, should therefore be established in every State, with sanitary surroundings, and these can only be accomplshed by the Legislatures in every State.

"2. Drastic measures are of no avail, and will do no good. Proper education as to the danger which lurks in the streets of all large cities, by the disregard of provisions in public conveyances for the deposit of the patient's expectorations; and of the observance in the house of such measures as may be prescribed, would be much more effective than punitive measures. It is well for the Board of Health to prohibit expectoration in public conveyances, useless if not accompanied by the compulsion of the companies to furnish receptacles for the sputum. It is generally agreed that the sputum of the patient is the most prolific source of the infection.

"I think for the present this would answer as to the main reforms to be needed. In Europe a great impetus has been given to the last Congress of Tuberculosis, held in Vienna, to the building of Public Sanitariums, and to this measure our efforts might be confined for the present. Stamp out the prevailing sickness, as far as you can, and you will strike at the source of the infection.

Yours truly,

M. ELLINGER."

Dr. U. O. B. Wingate, one of the most active members of the Medico-Legal Society; and a Vice Chairman of the Psychological Section of that body; the executive office of the Wisconsin State Board of Health, and a close and careful student of Sanitary Science, replies as follows:—

Milwaukee, April 3, 1901.

"Hon. Clark Bell, 39 Broadway, New York.

My Dear Sir.—Replying to the questions in your circular letter, I have to state as follows:

"1st. What importance do you attach to preventive legislation as a factor in diminishing the spread of Tuberculosis?' Ans.—"I think a certain amount of legislation relative to the control of Bovine Tuberculosis and milk supplies of very great importance, and laws relative to this matter should be enacted requiring all milch cows to be tested, so that the meat supply and public milk supply can be relied upon as safe. I do not think that legislation relative to the spread of consumption among the human family of much importance. I do not see the necessity of reporting cases of consumption to local boards of health, and in this State especially, it would be impossible to enforce a law prohibiting spitting in public places. In some localities, however, where there is a great deal of consumption, I believe that such a law should be enacted.

'2nd. Assuming the importance, necessity and utility of preventive legislation, how can the public best be educated and its sentiments aroused sufficiently, to secure the passage of preventive laws, and their enforcement after they are passed?'

Ans. "By the circulation of literature on the subject; by public lectures and public meetings of boards of health, and by securing the co-operation of newspapers in presenting to the public the actual situation and the importance of necessary steps in the prevention of the disease. About two years ago, the State Board of Wisconsin issued a circular, through the local health officers throughout the State, to the dairymen, calling their attention to the importance of having their herds tested with tuberculine, with a view of weeding out tuberculosis in their herds. As a result of these circulars the calls for the State Veterinarian to make these tests, became so great that it was utterly impossible for him to comply with the requests made, and much work has been accomplished resulting from this, which goes to show that it does not require a great deal of effort to interest the public in this matter, and especially where commercial interests are involved, as in the sale of stock and milk. I believe that the public at the present time, especially in this State, are well on the way to a pretty thorough information of the necessi of taking steps to prevent the disease.

"3rd. Which would you regard as or the best interests of the people?"

(a). "Legislation authorizing the employment of drastic measures for the enforcement of the necessary regulations, or

(b). "A broad policy of the eduction of the masses, as to the cause, danger and the remedy for berculosis?"

Ans. "By all means a broad polic of education of the masses."

Trusting these answers may be ceived in time, and to your satisfaction, I remain,

aithfully yours,

U. O. B. WINGATE.

A. P. Reid, M. D., a Sanitaria of high standing and Secretary of the Provincial Boardof Health of Middletown, Nova Scotia, answers as follows

Midetown, N. S., April 3, 1901.

Clark Bell, Esq., New York.

"Dear Sir.—Your favors received and contents noted. I would wish very much to take part and hve tried to interest "the powers that be," (but I cannot get a resonse). As to the questions I have a hesitation in giving opinion that are not based on experience.

1st. "Go slow."—Only legislate a tile ahead of public opinion.

2nd. "Moral suasion."—The press, the pulpit, and by association.

3rd. "Suggestion (b) more nearly fills the bill. We have now in some places legislation that canno be carried out.

For instance, you will see in street cars, notice—"NO SPITTING ON FLOORS," etc., but there are no spittoons furnished, and what can a man do: he can't carry it in his mouth for half an hour; he should not swallow it, and a handkerchief may not be available.

incerely yours,

A. P. REID, M. D.

Dr. George Ben Johnston of Richmond, Virginia, replies as follows:

Richmond, Va., April 9, 1901.

"Clark Bell, Esq., New York.

My Dear Mr. Bell.—"I have not been able to respond earlier to your recent letter for many reasons. I regret this extremely. However, I hope, I am not too late for your purpose.

"No legislation has been enacted in Virginia towards the prevention of Tuberculosis or looking to the establishment of a State Hospital for consumptives, nor is any in contemplation. The truth is, we have been so occupied with many economical question that, we have not given as much attention to State medicine as the subject deserves. The time is near at hand, however, when all of this will be changed, and I hope that Virginia will fall into line.

with the most advanced States of the Union on all questions pertaining to public health.

"In replying to your questions, I would make these responses:

"First. I consider preventive legislation based upon a healthy public sentiment as the most competent factor in diminishing the spread of Tuberculosis.

"Second. The best method of educating the masses in matters relating to public health is for the leading men of every community to form themselves into associations which shall discuss these questions publicly, and disseminate their views through the public prints, thus reaching the people and enlightening them in regard to preventive measures.

"Third. (a). Legislation authorizing employment of drastic measures for the enforcement of necessary legislation at this juncture would be unwise.

(b). "A broad policy of education of the masses as to the cause of danger and the remedy for diminishing the spread of Tuberculosis is the only method that could succeed. This requires time and great effort on the part of the intelligent men of the community who are interested in the public health.

Yours very cordially,

GEORGE BEN. JOHNSTON.

Dr. Dwight S. Moore is one of our alienists who has made thorough studies of Tuberculosis. His reply is as follows:—

NORTH DAKOTA HOSPITAL FOR INSANE.

Clark Bell, Esq., New York City.

Dear Sir.—In reply to your letter of inquiry of the 9th ult.,:—

1st. Preventive legislation as a factor in diminishing the spread of Tuberculosis deserves the chief consideration, but will be difficult of attainment, and the way to it must be paved by thorough public instruction on this and kindred topics.

2nd. By systematic presentation of the knowledge which it is desired to impart through the medium of the daily and weekly press, the expense to be defrayed by assessments levied upon the members of the association, text-books and popular lectures not to be neglected.

3rd. Measures must not be too stringent at first. Martyrs must not be made, nor the "antis" excited to organization. I think (b). the latter, is preferable.

Very truly,

D. S. MOORE."

Dr. J. W. Kime, editor of the Iowa Medical Journal, who has made studies of this disease, says:—

"Ft. Dodge, Iowa, April 5, 1901.

Hon. Clark Bell, Esq., New York. N. Y.

"Dear Sir.—I am just in receipt of your kind invitation to be present at the Congress of Tuberculosis in May, and shall take pleasure in meeting with you. In reply to your questions, I beg to say:

"1st. I hold that legislative action is of the first importance. I am fully convinced that a very large factor in the causation of Tuberculosis is the presence of the disease in the bovine species, and that milk is especially dangerous. We have a tremendous task on hand, however, when we attack this problem, as the dairy and live stock interests are immediately arrayed againt us. I think it almost useless to try to rid the human race of the disease, while we permit our dairymen to carry it into our kitchens each day.

2nd. This question is very difficult. The public is densely ignorant, upon this subject, and, in my experience, the man who seeks to enlighten it receives scant consideration for his pains. No man can accomplish much single-handed and alone, but the official acts and declarations of a Congress, that is world-wide in its character, will have much weight with the better class of the public. A simple statement of the mind of this Congress on the various phases of the subject—the contagiousness of the disease, its non-heredity, its specific cause and the best manner of dealing with it, the relation of human and bovine tuberculosis, the climatic factors, the part which hygienic conditions play in its treatment, and the many other important phases of the question,—will be productive of great good in an educational way. If these points can be made clear and be properly brought before the people, we will accomplish much. Preventive laws will be difficult of passage until work along this line has been done. The average legislator is but little in advance of his constituents.

"Drastic measures cannot be passed with us. So far we have not been able to even get the word "tuberculosis" inserted into our laws. It must be a campaign of education and not a little of this must be within the ranks of the medical profession, itself.

"Our work will be slow and we will die before we reap the harvest which we are attempting to sow.

"Trusting that the meeting may be a success in every sense, I am

Sincerely yours,

J. W. KIME."

Dr. Eduardo Liceaga is one of the most prominent names in the medical profession in the Republic of Mexico, especially in the Department of Public Health and Sanitary Science. He is President of the Board of Health of Mexico, and was recommended to me by His Excellency, the Mexican Minister at Washington. His reply is as follows:—

Mexico, April 17, 1901.

Dr. Clark Bell, President of the Medico-Legal Society, New York, N. Y.

My Esteemed Colleague :—In answer to your favor of the 22nd of March last, I have to state as follows :

1st. That I consider preventative legislation an important factor in the diminishing or preventing the propagation of tuberculosis.

2nd. I recognize that its action is slow and tardy, and, consequently, that the same thing may be said of the education which it is necessary to give the public in order to prepare it for the conversion of the preventative into effective legislation, and making its precepts binding on the general public.

3rd. As a general rule, I consider that a system founded on the complete education of the masses is more efficacious and places them in a position to understand the dangers of tuberculosis, the causes of its propagation and the measures to be taken to avoid it, and such general education will always do more good than the enactment of laws which would authorize the employment of drastic measures.

Nevertheless, I cannot fail to recognize that, under certain circumstances, these drastic measures may be of great utility, but it is necessary to act with great tact in order to find the opportune moment for their employment.

I take great pleasure in promising you a paper for the Congress which is about to meet in New York, to which I will in due time forward the paper I have lately presented in the Third Pan-American Medical Congress, which met in Havana during the month of February last, as well as a new one on some subject. In the one I have already presented you will find a full answer to your questions, and you will also see that I propose that the whole of the Associations which have been formed in different countries of the world, to defend the public against tuberculosis, should organize in one single Central Association, somewhat similar to the International Association of the Red Cross, which through the unification of its organization, under a central committee, has rendered the most important services to the cause of humanity.

I remain yours very respectfully,

E. LICEAGA.

Dr. V. Podstata is Vice President of the American Association of Assistant Physicians of Hospitals for the Insane, and a thoughtful student of the subject. He writes:—

Eastern Hospital for the Insane. Hospital, Illinois.
New York, April 28th, 1901.

Clark Bell, Esq., 39 Broadway, New York City.

Dear Sir:—My answers to your questions, pertaining to tuberculosis, are as follows:

1st. Wise preventive legislation could undoubtedly be made an important factor in diminishing the spread of tuberculosis.

2nd. The help of the newspapers, the public schools, and, possibly, the clergy, can be secured, popular lectures given, when and where effective; it appears to me that the public might be aroused to the proper understanding of the terrible disease.

3rd. (1) I am not in sympathy with any drastic measures. (2) The education of the masses appears to me the most effectual means of doing good to the people.

Respectfully,

V. PODSTATA. M. D., Pathologist.

Dr. F. Powers, a leading physician of Connecticut, writes:—

Westport, Conn., May 2, 1901.

Clark Bell, Esq., President Medico-Legal Society, New York City.

Dear Sir:—While the exact role of the tubercle bacillus may not be fully determined, it seems to be an established fact that consumption is contagious. I would advocate further teaching the public the most simple truths regarding this matter before invoking the law in the employment of drastic measures. Very sincerely yours,

F. POWERS, M. D.

Dr. R. F. Graham is one of the delegates to the American Congress of Tuberculosis, appointed by the Governor of Colorado, and one of the foremost physicians of that state. He says:

Greely. Colorado, April 9, 1901.

Clark Bell, Secretary and Treasurer, New York City.

Dear Sir:—My vote on the questions propounded, in your letter of March 9th, is as follows:

1. The value of preventive legislation would depend largely on what part heredity played in causing tuberculosis. There seems to be no reason to doubt thal the germs must be taken on from the outside, when one acquires tuberculosis; but it appears quite important that the germs be deposited in proper soil if they grow. I am still unable to disabuse my mind entirely of the old (but not necessarily incorrect because old) idea of hereditary tendency of tuberculosis.

However, even if heredity plays a strong role, the public should be protected as far as possible against infection.

2. Educate the mdeical profession and the public through it. It has been demonstrated, time and again, that without a united profession we can get nothing sustained by the people in the way of legislation.

3. I have already answered this question under 2.

Stringent legislation, without the public sentiment aroused to the importance of it, would only excite antagonism and thwart its own purpose.

Very truly, B. F. GRAHAM.

One of the most aggressive and strenuous of those medical men who take an advanced stand in medical legislation, is the able physician, Dr. Henry B. Baker, Secretary of the State Board of Health of Michigan, and a Vice President of the Congress. Dr. Baker says:

State Board of Health, Michigan, Lansing, April 17, 1901.

Clark Bell, President, Medico-Legal Society, No. 39 Broadway, New York City, N. Y.

Dear Sir:—In reponse to your questiou,

"1st. What importance do you attach to preventive legislation as a factor in diminishing the spread of tuberculosis?" I reply: Very great importance. A good law is a powerful educator.

"2d. Assuming the importance, necessity and utility of preventive legislation, how can the public best be educated and its sentiment aroused sufficiently, to secure the passage of preventive laws, and their enforcement after they are passed?" I reply: I know of no way so effective as through the systematic labors of a state board of health, which should be one of the most important educational institutions of every state. One principle of action, which should be thoroughly complied with, is: People can be educated on a subject if definite information on that subject is put before them, in concise form, at such time as they are especially interested in that subject. People can best be taught relative to tuberculosis when that disease is present in their own household, or among those persons with whom they associate. In order that a state board of health may most successfully carry on a "campaign of education," it is essential that the state board shall have for distribution concise pamphlets, leaflets, diagrams, or slips, containing reliable information relative to the subject to be taught—tuberculosis. It is essential that the state board shall have knowledge of just where there are persons sufficiently interested in the subject to be willing to read the pamphlets, leaflets, diagrams, or slips. Therefore, the first essential is official notice of cases of well-developed tuberculosis, so that the instructions may be supplied either direct from the state board of health, or indirectly through the action of the local health officials, possibly aided by the attending physician. It thus seems plain that the first requisite for progress toward the restriction or prevention of tuberculosis, is *notification* of every case of well-developed tuberculosis in such form as to be communicable, as, for instance, what is commonly known as "consumption of the lungs."

3d. "Which would you regard as for the best interest of the people:

"(a.) Legislation authoriziug the employment of drastic measures for the enforcement of the necessary regulations, or,

"(b.) A broad policy of education of the masses, as to the cause, danger, and the remedy for tuberculosis?" I reply: the latter policy. It is not possible to restrict or prevent any communicable disease without the co-cperation of all classes of people; that co-operation cannot be obtained except through the intelligence of the people generally on that special subject; therefore, the first legislation should be for notification of cases to the local health officers, and by them to the central office of the state board of health, which should be prepared, and can then act for the further education of the masses.

Very respectfully, HENRY B. BAKER.
Secretary.

R. Harvey Reed, M. D.,is the Surgeon General of the State, and was formerly the editor of the Columbus Medical Journal. He has a wide field of observation. His reply to my letter is as follows:—

Rock Springs, Wyo., May 6th, 1901.

Hon. Clark Bell, New York, N. Y.,

Dear Doctor:—In answer to your esteemed favor of 3d inst., and to your guestions, as to what Wyoming has done as to legislation regarding tuberculosis, I desire to say that Wyoming has done nothing except pass a very stringent health law, which gives the Secretary of the State Board of Health power to quarantine all contagious diseases, so as to prevent its spreading among the people. In this connection, I desire to say that tuberculosis is an unknown disease among the natives of this state, in fact with the large number of patients that we have to treat every year, comprising over forty nationalities, from different parts of the state and country, I am confident I have not known of a dozen cases of tuberculosis during the three and one-half years that I have been here in Roc Springs, Wyoming, and each and every one of these cases have been imported from without the state on account of their ill health, and did not contract the disease here in this state, to the best of my knowledge and belief.

In answer to the question on the enclosed slip, I beg leave to say, first, that proper preventative legislation, with the view of diminishing the spread of tuberculosis is important to every state, and should, in my judgment, be regulated by proper federal laws in addition to the state laws; second, by proper instruction in the public schools, and proper public meetings for the discussion of these very important questions with a view of creating public sentiment that will favor such legislation. Third: (1) By no means through drastic measures; (2) By all means through a broad policy of education, backed up by proper laws for the enforcement of well defined, practical principles for the prevention of tuberculosis. Very respectfully submitted.

R. HARVEY REED.

Major Geo. H. Torney, of the Army, who is one of the ablest men in sanitary matters; is in charge of the Army and Navy General Hospital of the Government at Hot Springs, Arkansas. His name was suggested to me by Surgeon General Sternberg, of the Army. In reply to the question, Major Torney writes:—

Army and Navy General Hospital,
Hot Springs, Ark., May 4th, 1901.

Mr. Clark Bell, Secretary American Congress of Tuberculosis,
39 Broadway, New York, N. Y.

Dear Sir:—In reply to your request for an expression of my views as to some of the subjects that are to be discussed at the meeting of the American Congress of Tuberculosis, on May 15th and 16th, 1901, I desire to submit the following replies in answer to the several questions:

1. I consider preventive legislation a factor of great importance in diminishing the spread of tuberculosis.

2. By persistent and intelligent dissemination of facts relative to the danger of contagion in this disease.

3. (1) Assuredly no drastic measures for the enforcement of regulations, (2) until the mass of the people have been educated as to the cause, the danger, and the remedy for a factor in diminishing tke spread of tuberculosis. Respectfully submitted,

GEO. H. TORNEY,
Major and Surgeon, U. S. Army.

Major A. Havard is Chief Surgeon of the United States Army in Cuba, through the courtesy of General Sternberg, Chief Surgeon of the Army of the United States, the questions were referred to him on his post of duty in Cuba. His reply was as follows:

Headquartets Department of Cuba,
Office of the Chief Surgeon,
Havana, Cuba, May 4, 1901.

Many thanks for the announcement of American Congress of Tuberculosis which I have just received. In answer to your questions I would state in a very genèral way not having time to enter into details. The employment of drastic measures should *be cordial*; the best results to be obtained by policy of education of the masses.

Let each State provide sanitariums where individuals may be induced to go and where they shall be treated gratuitously or according to their means. Patients preferring to stay at home should observe prescribed regularions and be subject to official inspection. It is my belief that after a general campaign of education there will be no difficulty in procuring the necessary legislation and inducing the great majority of the people to submit to it.

Yours very sincerely,
V. HAVARD, Surgeon U. S. A.

[*To be continued.*]

CONTRIBUTION ON THE CURING OF TUBERCULOSIS IN SANITARIA.

BY PROF. SCHROTTER, OF VIENNA, AUSTRIA.

The question of treatment of Tuberculosis in Sanataria, to which I have devoted myself since 1883, has become at this moment one of the most actual in the whole world. It requires particular attention on two points.

1. Stating cases of real success, which we call curing.

2. Making a special study and an accurate analysis of every case in which the treatment in the sanitarium failed.

a. In the medical reports of our Sanitarium at Alland, near Vienna, we are very careful in pronouncing the word "cured," and do not rubricate the cases dismissed from the sanitarium as healed or ameliorated, but speak only of essentially ameliorated, etc. Keeping all cases in continual evidence so that we may be able to say after some years what the real state of the patient is. The patients are compelled to show themselves regularly either in the sanitarium at Alland, or in our Central Bureau in Vienna, where the same medical men who made the first examination on which depended the admission of the patient (or not), continues to observe the patient, not from his memory alone, but with the assistance of the exact dates in the protocolls. So we hope to be able to give in some years reliable statistics of real cures. At this moment we have every reason to be contented with good results. They are better even than we expected them to be, and we hope not to be obliged in the future to alter this good opinion.

b. What can be the causes supposing that we had accepted quite a favorable case for the Sanitarium, that instead of the expected amelioration, exactly the contrary finis lethalis, takes place? In the first volume of Zeitschrift fur Tuberculose und Heilstattenwesen, Leipzig, 1900, described from the above point of view, a case of very severe Tuberculosis, in

Read before the New York Medico-Legal Society and American Congress of Tuberculosis in joint session, May 15-16, 1901.

which it advanced to our great astonishment, not only to a progradient amelioration in the general state of health, but to a complete cicatrisation of the extended ulcerations of the larnyx, so far that it came even to a stenosis; and also of proceedings of induration in the lungs; but unfortunately destroyed all good effects, and Tuberculosis in the intestinal tract took place to which the patient finally succumbed.

Now I will show another case which at first promised to turn out well and then unfortunately turned out badly. Why? I shall try to be as brief as possible.

The patient, a delicate girl of twenty-six years of age, whose disease began in January, 1898, with coughing sometimes blood-tinged sputa, in Galy pleurisy, was admitted into Alland in September of the same year. We found a slight infiltration of the right apex as far as the second rib and the rest of a pleuritic inflation lower down. After a considerable amelioration, which was only interrupted by intercurrent pleuritis, she showed on the 26th of November, 1898, every symptom of a pneumothoray, which was on account of the pleuritic effusion, pneumopyothoray. Yet we were lucky enough to be able to state that after the pleuritic condition had spread entirely over the right side, on the 26th of February, 1899, every sign of pneum•thoray together with the effusion had disappeared, and the weight of the patient had increased 3. 3k. She was so well that the medical men were on the point of dismissing her from the sanitarium, and took the trouble of looking for a place for her where only light work was required. The patient followed from the middle of October, 1899, to March, 1900, a treatment with acid cinnamylicum and increased in weight. Under continuing good health the second incident arrived. On the 21st of June, 1900, the symptoms of pneumothoray could be again stated. On the 9th of December, 1900, she suddenly coughed up 350 An. 3 purulent sputum. Now there are two things possible, either the second pneumothoray was caused by perforation of the lung with very slow increasings of the plueritic effusion till it reached finally on the 9th of December, the opening of the lung, with the result of the abundant expectoration; or the opening in the lungs was again shut up, the effusion increased slowly to a certain degree and then a new larger, but now permanent perforation took place. In this state the patient came into my clinic. She was constantly feverish, complained of pains in the right side and of an abominable taste in her mouth, caused by the above mentioned purulent expectoration. As different gargles and inhalations brought no relief, we performed on the 20th of January, 1901, the thoracotomy with a large incision at the back in the eighth intercostal space, following which, about half a liter of foetid purulent fluid flowed away. We continued washing the pleural cavity with kali hypermangan. The abominable expectoration ceased. This is all we could do for the real relief of the poor patient, for it was soon clear that the continuation of fever was not caused by the disease in the right side, but by the increasing of Tuberuclosis in the left lung. She died on the 1st of February, 1901, and the post mortem showed a plum-sized cavity with an opening about the size of a lentil, in the compressed right lung with subacute tuberculosis in the left.

We see in this case the event of pneumothoray took place twice, perhaps three times; we see an energetic struggle even against so serious an occurrence, with good effect and only at the entrance of open pneumothoray was the fate of the poor patient sealed. We could do nothing but bring her relief, and the subacute tuberculosis of the left lung accelerated the fatal end.

What we learn by this case is that the treatment of sanataria will not be able in every case to prevent the advancement of Tuberculosis and with that the entrance of severe complications, but this treatment can give the body such a resistance as certainly the patient did not possess before and may be able to a certain degree to overcome such serious incidents.

I must mention the possibility that injections of acid cimen. had some good effect.

LUPUS—A TUBERCULAR AFFECTION OF THE SKIN.

BY W. A. HACKETT, M. B., M. C. P. S.,
Professor of Dermatology and Venereal Diseases in the Michigan College of Medicine and Surgery.

The different cutaneous affections in which the bacillus of tuberculosis has been found, may be divided into four chief varieties:True tuberculosis, miliary tuberculosis, lupus vulgaris, and lupus erythematosus.

TRUE TUBERCULOSIS.

This is a form of primary tuberculosis due to contact with tubercular ulceration and is usually found on the lips, the vulva, or anus. Small tubercular growths are present, which soften gradually and become the foci of round or oval ulcerations, with clear-cut edges. The ulcers are usually cov ered with sanious purulent discharge, which soon changes into a grayish crust. If the discharge be removed, the bottom of the ulcer will be a red color.

MILIARY TUBERCULOSIS OF THE SKIN.

This disease is more often met with than one would be led to suppose from the publications upon the subject. It occurs nearly always in individuals suffering from some other form of tuberculosis, usually of the lungs.

Many of the cases are traceable to auto-inoculation, while in some the inoculation seems to have originated from without. The intense itching of the skin causes the tuberculous patient to scratch and thus inoculate himself.

Papillomatous granulations soon appear which spread superficially and become ulcerated

LUPUS VULGARIS.

This is now recognized as a tuberculous affection of the skin, or mucous membrane, which may proceed to ulceration or not. The form resulting in ulceration, is known as lupus exedens, and occurs in persons under thirty (30) years of age, while in the other variety, thin scales are thrown off from the lesion and it is known as lupus exfoliativus.

Read before the Medico-Legal Society in joint session with the Ameri-Congress of Tuberculosis, May 15-16, 1901.

SYMPTOMS.

In both varieties, lupus begins in the form of yellowish-red blotches, varying from the size of a millet-seed to that of a pea. Nodules form slowly, and later on break down and ulcerate, becoming covered with scabs. Beneath the scabs is a bed of bloody pus and the ulceration gradually extends, eating away in all directions. The deeper structures become involved after a time, and the muscular, tendinous and cartilaginous tissues are gradually invaded. The nose, mouth, pharynx and conjunctiva are often included in the destructive process and deformities of these parts result. This awful disease unfortunately attacks the face oftener than any other region.

Lupus takes a number of different forms, hence many names have been applied, as papillomatous, vorax, hypertrophied, etc.

All the forms of lupus, with the exception of lupus vorax, progress slowly, and sometimes become stationary, or even recede. Such complications as adenitis, erysipelas, cancer, etc., are apt to occur.

LUPUS ERYTHEMATOSUS.

This form of lupus is not believed by some to be tuberculous, but the tubercle bacillus has been found in a great many cases. It is more common in females than males, and the eruption can sometimes be traced to exposure, to great heat, or to cold.

The skin does not offer to the tubercle bacillus a fertile ground, and its infectious properties often remain limited to the skin, without showing general infectious symptoms. The infectious power of the germ, when capsulated in the tissues, may remain latent for years, ready to break out at any time in the form of lupus from old scars.

TREATMENT.

It is not my intention to go thoroughly into the treatment of lupus, but rather to enter a plea for isolation of these unfortunate patients. They should not be allowed tb come into close contact with other members of the family, should sleep in separate rooms, and use different towels, combs, brushes, dishes, etc. Of course, complete isolation would be impossible in many cases, but should be advised as far as possible.

An important feature of the treatment of lupus vulgaris is

attention to the general health. Being a tuberculous affection, it is therefore associated with general vital depravity.

Out-of-door exercise, wholesome food, tonics, etc., tend to assist the local measures by increasing the powers of resistance of the tissues to bacillary invasion.

Excision, Tuberculin, the Roentgen rays, and the Finsen rays are warmly recommended by different dermatologists.

ETIOLOGICAL FACTORS OF TUBERCULOSIS OTHER THAN THE BACILLUS OF TUBERCULOSIS.

BY U. O. B. WINGATE, M. D., MILWAUKEE.

Secretary Wisconsin State Board of Health.

Since the discovery of the bacillus of tuberculosis by Koch in 1882 there has been a general belief in the minds of many, apparently, that the cause of the disease known as pulmonary tuberculosis or consumption is fully known and the means of its prevention necessarily a simple problem; the question of how best to put into operation such means has been the chief topic for consideration.

It is evident, however, to one after a very little study and observation that there are other factors in the causation of pulmonary consumption than the bacillus of tuberculosis.

That the bacillus of tuberculosis is the seed of the diseased process must be admitted, but seed will not take root and develop unless planted in proper soil and in a favorable environment, and in the study of how best to prevent tuberculosis we must consider the individual and the various influences which may affect his general health. It is true that if there were no such thing in existence as the bacillus of tuberculosis there would be no pulmonary consumption. On the other hand, if there were no proper soil (certain conditions of the body) and certain favorable conditions for their development, there would be no bacilli of tuberculosis. Is it not more important, then, to endeavor to prevent the growth and development of the germ than to try to destroy the germ after it has an existence? Or in other words, is it not a wiser course, or a more strictly scientific sanitation, to prevent the entrance of the germ than to attempt to drive him out after he has gained an entrance? This principle of secondary action on the part of the sanitarian—the waiting until infection becomes established before attempting to prevent its ravages—is one of the most conspicuous and

Read before the Medico-Legal Society and American Congress of Tuberculosis in joint session. May 15-16, 1901.

dangerous defects in sanitary administration of the present age. Especially is the evil of this principle observed in the legal provisions of public health in our various states, as for instance, power given to establish quarantine after the disease has made its appearance, but power and means withheld to establish sanitary conditions which will prevent the first appearance of the disease and thereby render quarantine unnecessary.

As early as 1862, that erudite and keen observer, Dr. Henry I. Bowditch, called attention to the condition of the soil as a cause of consumption. He said that "Damp soil, whether that dampness be inherent in the soil itself or caused by percolation from adjacent ponds, rivers, meadows, marshes, or springy soils, is one of the principal causes of consumption." He laid this down as a law, and also claimed that the disease could be checked in its career, and probably prevented, by attention to this law. He relates a number of cases of patients who recovered after changing their place of residence from low, damp locations to elevated and dry ones.

Every physician who has studied the etiology of consumption must recognize the inherited conditions that predispose to tuberculosis. Perhaps the most conspicuous of these inherited tendencies is a depressed state of the nervous system—a state in which nutrition is easily impaired, a low depressed state in which stimulants are craved and their victims often fall a prey to the habit of alcoholism, and I have several times met with individuals, whose ancestors were tuberculous, who have told me that they never experienced a well moment in their lives, except when under the influence of some artificial stimulant. While I do not go so far as has been claimed by one writer on the subject, that tuberculosis is invariably caused by a diseased condition of the vagus nerve, I do recognize the fact that an inherited condition of the nervous system is a prominent factor in the causation of this disease.

In the prevention of tuberculosis, it would seem that we should give more attention to the actual natural condition of the individual, and his environment, and less to the germ of the disease. To render the individual immuned is of the greatest importance, not only in tuberculosis but in all other infectious diseases, and to accomplish this desirable end the sanitarian must give more attention to the fundamental principles of hygiene. Ideal sanitary surroundings, such as the location of habitation on high, well-drained land, must be the first principle. Then the early correction of any physical defects, either hereditary or acquired, must receive our most careful attention. By such means we will be able to produce a generation of individuals who are far above the invasion of germ foes, and to render the individual capable of resisting the invasion of infection should be the first work of the future sanitarian.

The germs of disease cannot exist without favorable sustenance, and to cut off the conditions which favor their life and growth is more important work than their destruction after they have gained an existence. There are many individuals who will not contract tuberculosis, even though they take large numbers of bacilli into their systems. It should be the endeavor of the sanitarian to establish such conditions that all persons may possess such immunity. Fruitless indeed will be our efforts until we proceed along these lines as well as along the lines of germ destruction.

THE INFLUENCE OF THE BACILLUS IN PULMONARY TUBERCULOSIS.

BY HUBBARD WINSLOW MITCHELL, D. D.,
EX-PRESIDENT MEDICO LEGAL SOCIETY.

The special object of this paper is to inquire what specific function the tubercle bacillus plays in the disease known as Pulmonary Tuberculosis, and what influence it has, if any, in inducing this disease in a lung, which was previously healthy.

Prior to the year 1882 many observers in our own country and in Europe, suspected that this disease was produced by the introduction of a germ into the cellular tissue of the lung, and setting up an ulcerative process of the lung, known as tuberculosis.

After considerable research, Prof. Koch, of Berlin, stated that he had discovered the long looked for germ, and announced his discovery to the medical profession. Since his time it is universally believed that the bacillus is the active and only agent in setting this disease into activity, and so thoroughly is his idea fixed in the medical mind, that when a case of ulcerative disease of the lung presents itself, if the sputum shows the presence of the bacillus, it is regarded absolutely as a case of Pulmonary Tuberculosis, and if a case identical with it in all respects is presented, and the sputum contains no bacilli, then it is not regarded as a case of tuberculosis.

No case of lung disease can be called tuberculosis, unless it shows the presence of the bacillus of Koch, and this idea seems to be everywhere accepted, but if we accept it, then a great number of cases of lung disease in which the sputum shows no bacilli from first to last, are not tuberculosis. My own belief for a long time, was that held by the general profession, namely, that tuberculosis, per se, could not exist without the presence of the bacillus.

Read before the Medico-Legal Society and American Congress of Tuberculosis in joint session, May 15–16, 1901.

During the past five years 675 cases of Pulmonary Tuberculosis have come under my personal observation, and in every case without exception the sputum was examined one or more times by the most competent and experienced microscopist in this city, and it was found after most careful search, that a considerable percentage of cases contained no bacilli whatever, and yet every symptom during the course of the disease was identical in character with those cases of the disease which contained bacilli.

I have selected from my own practice 102 cases of pulmonary disease that I regarded as typical cases. All of them were under my care for considerable periods of time, namely, from one to three years, and I had an opportunity of seeing them at short intervals, and of treating them myself.

The microscopical examinations of the sputum in these 102 cases revealed the following facts:

Cases where no bacilli existed........................	25
Cases where few bacilli existed......................	44
Cases where numerous bacilli existed..................	22
One case contained only one single bacillus during the entire progress of the disease......................	1
Cases that had few bacilli in the beginning and increased in number later..................................	2
Cases where few bacilli existed and disappeared soon afterwards	4
Cases where none existed at first and few appeared afterwards	4
	102

It will be asked at once what methods were followed in the examination of the sputum, and some will question the accuracy of these examinations, but precision of method cannot be called into question when I mention the care with which these examinations were made.

All of them, namely, the 102 cases, were examined at the Department of Health of this city, in the Division of Bacteriology, and the very accurate and scientific methods employed by the Board of Health, are too well known to admit of any doubt. Some of these cases were examined several times by the Board of Health, and all of them were secondarily examined by a Microscopist of deservedly high reputation above mentioned, who employed the methylene blue stain, and used a 1-12 objective lens in oil immersion, and the results of his examinations in every case agreed with those made at the Board of Health, so that there is absolutely no question as to the accuracy of the methods of examination employed.

The results of these examinations in the above mentioned 102 cases, as well as the examinations of all the cases, have led me to divide cases of Pulmonary Tuberculosis so called, into the following divisions:

First. Cases in which no bacilli were found at any time.

Second. Cases in which few bacilli were found and continued during the progress of the disease.

(By few bacilli, I adopt the significance of the term employed by the Board of Health, namely, "where bacilli are not present in every field, but only one or more are to be found in the entire preparation.")

Third. Where numerous bacilli are found and persist during the continuance of the disease.

(By the term numerous I again follow the Board of Health which says "that the bacilli are present in every field, and that each field contains more than five bacilli.")

Fourth. Cases where few bacilli are found at first, and afterwards that is, during the end of the term of treatment, no bacilli whatever are found. In these cases the bacilli disappear during the active treatment of the disease.

Fifth.—Cases where no bacilli are found at first but appear several months afterwards, during active treatment. These sometimes persist until recovery.

The above five divisions are not arbitrary, but are based upon practical and careful observations of this disease.

As regards severity of symptoms I have found that cases containing no bacilli, or few, differ very little from each other, not only do they not differ in severity of symptoms, but they maintain a very close parallelism as they proceed to recovery or death.

If then, say about one-third of the cases of pulmonary disease do not contain bacilli at any stage of the disease, and yet resemble those cases which do contain bacilli, in every symptom and detail, what influence does the bacilli exert upon cases of ulceration of the lung, for, after all, the term Pulmonary Tuberculosis is not as good a term as ulceration of the lung, if we could prove that the bacillus does not set up the dicase. If the disease is not induced by the introduction of a germ, the bacillus, what does induce it?

In a paper I had the honor to read before the Medico-Legal Society on October 17th, 1900, I suggested the idea that perhaps the pus-cell was the carrier of the special toxic principle of this disease and that it, and not the bacillus, was the exciting cause. For it is seen that cases where no bacilli or few bacilli were present, were identical, then the cases where they did not exist could not be induced by the bacillus. It must be produced by some other cause. We know that the pus-cell is never absent. In an ulcerative and supperative disease like this, the pus-cell is of necessity formed, else there would be no supperative process.

Now it seems to me that the pus-cell which is the carrier of disease in other maladies, must be the carrier of the disease in Pulmonary Tuberculosis. I still use the term Pulmonary Tuberculosis, because it is generally and better understood, but if the views I here advance are correct, that the bacillus may not be the mischievous element, then the term ulceration of the lung is the more correct.

If we will look through the microscope at a properly stained specimen of tuberculous sputum, we see one or more or no bacilli. When met they are very minute in size and seem incapable of setting up the mischief we find in a diseased lung, but the same field under the microscope is always crowded with pus-cells.

The significance of all this is as follows:

If a case of lung disease presents itself, and no bacilli are found, it is usually dismissed as a simple case with little heed paid to it, and herein lies the mischief

Every observer of experience will agree with me that a given case of lung disease whether it contains bacilli or not is a very severe and protracted and often fatal disease.

As stated at the outset of this paper the object is to inquire whether the bacillus is the disseminator of the disease or whether the pus-cell is the active agent, and when we consider that the pus-cells are thrown off by the million, and the minute bacillus in fewer numbers or not at all, we are forced to the conclusion that the real carrier of the disease is the pus-cell and not the bacillus.

LEGAL ACTION TO PREVENT THE SPREAD OF TUBERCULOSIS.

BY LOUIS J. ROSENBERG LL. B., DETROIT, MICH.,

Associate of the "Victoria Institute," London, Eng., (Philosophical Society of Great Britain); Member of the Historical Society of Lancashire and Cheshire, Liverpool, Eng., etc , etc.

Legislation seeks to protect man against the assault and encroachment of his neighbor. It is because of that, that we continually find it necessary to swell the volume of our criminal code. Legislation seeks to protect man against himself. It is because of that, that we enact laws regulating or repressing the liquor traffic. But legislation goes farther than that. It seeks to protect the public against the individual. It is because of *that*, that we enact laws regarding public health.

That sanitary legislation is of cardinal importance, will not be denied by any one. But, perhaps, no branch of sanitary legislation is so important as that regarding that terrible disease, the disease of diseases,—Tuberculosis. Indeed, if wise and skilled legislators are needed in any branch of legislation, it is in that of legislating against the spread of the "White Plague." Truly said Surgeon General Walter Wyman, in his remarkable address on "Sanitation and Progress" at the Pan-American Medical Congress, held at Havana, February 7th, 1901: "In the sanitary progress of the new century, it has occurred to me, there must be developed new classes of individuals in sanitary affairs. Today every physician is considered, in a sense, a sanitarian; then there are the professional sanitarians, represented chiefly by those holding sanitary offices; but there are very few men today engaged in legislation who give any thought to sanitary legislation. We need a class of men who are versed in the law, *who are skilled in framing laws*, and who are familiar with the difficulties and methods of securing their enactment."

Read before the Medico-Legal Society in joint session with the Ameri- Congress of Tuberculosis, May 15-16, 1901.

The basis of any legislative work directed to prevent the spread, of this disease among human beings, should be, "the elimination of bovine tuberculosis." There ought to be state appropriations for the preparation of efficient tuberculin: and the latter, as well as the service of competent veterinary surgeons should be granted by the state gratis, to all cattle owners who will give their cattle a sanitary rearing in well constructed stables, and isolate those animals which react to tuberculin tests.

As to the danger of tuberculosis incurred by drinking milk from consumptive cows, it seems to me, that although the peril can be avoided by boiling it, the public, nevertheless, has an absolute right to demand pure, unadulterated and non-diseased milk. "Milk, if it is pure," said President Loudon at the inaugural meeting of the Toronto Association for the Prevention and Treatment of Consumption and other forms of Tuberculosis," is perhaps the best product we have. If it is not pure, it is perhaps, the most dangerous thing we have. Our health inspectors have done much for us in this matter, but let them remember that continued success depends on eternal vigilance." For general rules, I would suggest the following measures:

(1.) First, compulsory notification of every disease of the bovine udder.

(2.) Second, report of every milk dealer as to how and where he gets his milk.

(3.) Third, regulations as to cow-sheds and dairies.

As to regulations regarding meat, I would suggest these measures:

(1.) First, to slaughter only in abbattoirs.

(2.) Second, inspection to be conducted immediately after the slaughter of animals.

(3.) Third, stamping of joints of all carcasses passed as sound.

These measures would necessarily call for well-qualified inspectors, which should be at least six in number, and divided as follows: (2) Two veterinary surgeons, (1) one physician, (1) one microscopist, (1) one first class cattle salesman, and (1) one butcher.

The report of a French commission appointed to consider the "Notification of Pthithsis" positively asserted that this is a matter which cannot, for the present time, be done. In

America too, it has frequently been said, that where notifications cannot be obtained voluntarily it should not be forced. But I think otherwise. While I would be slow in making the disease of the person under treatment, public,—I am inclined to think, that in a good many cases it is by far the best thing, to report. While voluntary notification should be encouraged, I would, nevertheless, insist on having a law *compelling* notification where it cannot be obtained voluntarily, because through notification we are at least enabled to give the sufferer specific instructions as to the precautions necessary for his own safety and for that of the public.

Certain regulations, also, regarding the sputum ought to be made; such, for instance, as its disinfection, prevention of expectoration in public conveyances, thoroughfares, etc. Doctor Rodick at the meeting of the Canadian Association for the Prevention of Tuberculosis was certainly right in condemning "the laxity of existing regulations respecting expectoration on the asphalt pavement, in the streets, and in railway cars."

The danger of contracting tuberculosis may also be greatly obviated by the introduction of sanitary house building; that is to say, the walls of the interior should never be allowed to be covered with wall paper, which is always a favorable medium for the tubercle germ. Instead, we should have calcimined or painted walls, so that when necessary they could be easily cleansed by mopping them over with a disinfecting solution. Regulations on this subject seems to me, comes just as much within the scope of legislation as sanitary plumbing, and is perhaps of more public importance than the latter.

In addition to all these regulations, the government ought also to take a strong hand in the establishment of sanitoria. It is now universally acknowledged that the best kind of treatment is sanitorium treatment, and to erect such sanitoria we need the aid of the respective municipalities. Each state —and where practical each municipality—ought to have an appropriation fund for the purpose of helping the establishment of such institutions. I am glad to notice, that the State Board of Health of Illinois is about to recommend the construction of a State Sanitarium, and that the Governor of New Hampshire is to name a commission to inquire into the propriety of constructing such an institution for the consumptives of his state.

Finally, I would suggest that local boards should provide the sufferers with the necessary leaflets instructing them as to the requisite precautions by them to be taken. The display of such instructions, may be made compulsory upon public institutions.

These are the most vital points for legislators to consider. No doubt there are many more. This essay certainly does not give a complete expose of all the legislative measures in respect to this disease, but enough has been said, to indicate to what extent and in what manner legal action may be exercised in the prevention of that awful, menacing and direful disease—Tuberculosis.

TUBERCULOSIS DUE TO TOXAEMIC STATE.

T. D. CROTHERS, M. D., HARTFORD, CONN.,

Vice President American Congress of Tuberculosis.

There are two facts which I wish to make prominent in this paper: One, that tuberculosis is dependent on states of toxaemia where the poisons are introduced from without. and, second, formed within the body. The other is that the bacillus of tuberculosis is only active and dangerous when the favoring soils and conditions are present for its development and growth.

The widespread diffusion of the germs of tuberculosis in the air, water, food, and surroundings, and wherever human beings congregate, has attracted attention and indicated the posibility of in some way destroying them and breaking up their habitat..

Thus, efforts to prevent the sputa from drying up and floating about in the air and so being inhaled again into the lungs, are carried out with more or less rigor in cities and towns.

Wherever consumptives are found, the destruction of the sputa is considered a prophylactic measure of great importance.

The dust-laden air of our northern cities and the large number of tuberculous patients seem to make it impossible to thoroughly destroy these germs which are often carried in the clothing and must, of necessity, exist in the surroundings of consumptives.

Notwithstanding the widespread diffusion of these germs comparatively few persons become infected by them.

A recent writer thinks that all persons in the northern climates and in the consumptive belts, are exposed to this infection, and that sometime during their life these germs have effectd a lodgment but for various reasons have been thrown off and prevented from full development. He cites

Read before the New York Medico-Legal Society and American Congress of Tuberculosis in joint session, May 15-16, 1901.

as proof the common experience of nearly every person who at some time has had severe attacks of bronchitis or debilities, with symptoms of disturbance of nutrition, high temperture and night sweats. After a time these symptoms disappear and long after when such persons die cicatrices in the lungs point to a previous deposit which has been overcome.

The records of the post mortem examinations in large hospitals show the same facts and indicate that tuberculosis has existed at some previous time but had been checked.

These and similar facts show conclusively that an early infection is not only possible but probable in many persons but for some reason it is checked in its growth, and does not go on to full development.

The extreme fatality of tuberculosis has been diminishing, and there is a strong probability that more exact medical care and study will reduce it to a minimum and practically stamp out "this white plague."

This change is due not so much to the medicines used as to the hygienic conditions and early recognition of the cause and the means for prevention.

The removal of these causes and the cultivation of conditions which tend to increase and strengthen the vital forces are the directions in which preventive measures are leading.

One of the active causes which seem to precede and favor the growth of tuberculosis is faulty nutrition.

Recently it has been recognized that failures of nutrition result in the formation of poisons which have a very marked influence over states of health and disease. Some facts of the physiology of food wil make this more clear..

The fact is well established that the vigor of the body depends upon the nutrition which it receives.

This in a general way must be albumeniod material, which is furnished by fish, meat, and eggs, and which must constitute about one-fifth of the weight of the entire food.

The hydrocarbons or fats required are about the same proportion, and the carbohydrates, containing starch and sugar, must form about three-fifths. These foods in about the same proportions are necessary for full health and vigor.

There will be some variation due to occupation and climate but the general average will hold good.

If too much of one and too little of another is used there will be disproportion and derangement, and if continued long enough, there must be degrees of starvation, and at all events, material introduced into the body which cannot be used, and hence, will become waste; and, therefore, a source of infection.

As a common example, the ordinary meals taken by persons who live in hotels and who travel will suggest this source of danger. The breakfast at such places includes meat and eggs in quantity over one-half albumenoid matter; and the dinner is the most unhygienic of all. Such dinners consist of oysters or clams, with soup, fish and roast meat, and various kinds of entrees. These are served with vegetables and belong largely to the proteid foods which should not exceed one-fifth of the total amount taken. When there is added bread and the common dessert, the proteids may be brought down to a half, but not less. Then come the carbohydrates consisting of starch and sugar in large quantities, which taken into a normal stomach will seriously impair the salivary digestion and destroy the power of the pancreatic juice.

The sugar and starch in the dessert is injurious to all persons in whom there is a tendency to fermentation.

In addition to these come sauces, and condiments, which produce by overstimulation of the glands a large flow of gastric and other juices, so that the desire to eat is increased far beyond the ability to properly digest the foods. The digestive glands are exhausted and cannot do the work required. Often, along with this excess alcoholic beverages are used. Alcohols impair the digestive processes and lessen the function of the stomach and produce equally serious damage with that of the large proportion of proteids which can neither be broken up nor assimilated.

Under the direction of ignorant cooks and caterers, foods are served to every one, from childhood to old age, as if the peptic glands were disabled and in constant need of the most energetic stimulation.

Also, as if three-fifths or four-fifths of all food should be nitrogenous instead of one-fifth.

As a result, the daily diet of all persons is irrational, unreasonable and disease-producing. The digestive functions suffer from toxaemia produced by decomposition of foods which cannot be used. Also from irritants taken as condiments and peptic stimulants.

The secretory organs are overtaxed, the liver is burdened, the intestines and kidneys have an increased amount of secretory work to do, which is followed by early exhaustion.

These are the conditions which provoke many maladies, of which the terms lithaemia, uricacidaemia, and other obscure forms of auto-intoxication describe.

Probably no one substance in common use disturbs the nutrition and impairs the vigor of the body more positively than alcohol.

Statistics of consumptives show that a very large proportion of these were spirit and beer drinkers in the early stages, with marked symptoms of dyspepsia, faulty nutrition and exhaustion.

Spirit and beer drinkers are practically starved, and suffer from poisoned states through derangement of nutrition and foods taken which cannot be utilized.

One author claims that eighty per cent. of all consumptives have used spirits or beer in excess before consumption appeared.

From such inquiries it would appear that fully fifty per cent. of spirit and beer drinkers in northern climates die of consumption.

The relation between consumption and drinking is very close.

The subsidence of the drink craze is often followed by acute tuberculosis and death.

The use of spirits to excess not infrequently masks and covers up the symptoms of tuberculosis but it is quite certain that it never cures the disease.

Both spirit drinking and consumption seem to be dependent upon exhaustion, imperfect nutrition, and poisoned states.

Alcohol seems to have a specific power to change and destroy the normal metabolism of the body.

All users of spirits suffer from the presence of waste products which accumulate in the system and seriously interfere with the normal metabolism essential to health.

A great variety of elements sustain these theories and point out the specific causes with great exactness.

A careful study of the history of many cases of tuberculosis shows a period of faulty nutrition from irregular habits of eating, bad foods badly cooked, associated with beer, spirits, and other substances damaging to the vigor and health of the body.

Faulty surroundings is another very active cause of pathological conditions which favor the growth of the tuberculosis germ.

Thus, in an examination of the homes of a large number of persons having consumption in villages and country towns in assachusetts, it was found that more than half of the number of homes contained wells or springs in the cellars under the sleeping and living rooms. Also that these rooms were badly ventilated and wanting in proper supply of sunlight.

In many instances trees and vines shut out both light and air.

Homes on streams and in valleys exposed to the dampness and screened from sunlight showed a larger proportion of consumptives than dwellings situated in better conditions.

The well-known fact has been confirmed over and over again that dark alleys, ill-ventilated back rooms, prison cells, factories and dark homes furnish a large number of consumptives.

These are the contributory causes, by lessening the vigor and force of the body to throw off the poisons of the system and creating states of starvation, defective nutrition and auto-intoxications, which favor the development and growth of the bacillus.

The common neglects of the body are other causes of tuberculosis. These, of course, include a great variety of injuries and faults, the more common of which may be mentioned, as, want of rest, both mental and physical.

In our high-wrought civilization the nervous system is so far kept on a continual strain, and soon the power of recovery is so far diminished that exhaustion and starvation follows.

Neurasthenic states are said to be the direct result of poisons which follow from imperfect nutrition and the formation of poisons which the system is unable to throw off, and along with the incessant mental strain is often neglect of proper bathing. The waste from mental and nervous activity is not eliminated and becomes a source of further exhaustion. The kidneys and excretory organs are overworked in the effort to remove these poisons, and as a result Bright's disease, diabetes and other troubles follow.

The opposite of overwork, underwork, is also a prolific cause of the same general disturbance and faulty elimination.

Irregular work with excessive strains and long periods of rest break up the normal rhythm of the body and provoke congestion and irritation.

One writer affirms that the excessive perspiration which is a common symptom of tuberculosis is simply an effort of nature to throw off the poison states which exist in the body; also that the nerve centers which control this function take on a paroxysmal period of activity in their efforts to eliminate the toxins.

Practically it is found that great care is necessary to remove the poison from the body by washing and rubbing with dry towels, treating the patient very much in the same way that we remove the sputum and destroy it to prevent its being absorbed. In night sweats the change of underclothing and frequent bathing of the body secures the same thing.

These sources of disease are very active, and in some instances are beyond all question.

The toxaemias which follow from these conditions are due to disturbances within the body.

Where spirits are taken, the toxins seem to be introduced from without, and form active sources of still further depressing conditions with enfeebled resisting powers of both the blood and nervous centers.

After the disease has been discovered, another source of danger comes from overmedication.

Formerly spirits entered largely into all early remedies; now they are found to be injurious.

The depression and paralysis which follow from their use are a continuous series of shocks to the nerve centers as well as introducing other toxins which disturb and further depress the vitality of the body.

Remedies given for the purpose of destroying the bacteria, or chemical agents to throw off the germ growths are exceedingly doubtful in their practical value.

It is evident that spirits conceal the progress of the disease by their anaesthetic action and encourage degenerative states favoring an early and sudden collapse.

An exceedingly dangerous advice is not infrequently given by thoughtless physicians to use all the spirits possible. This is usually fatal.

When the diagnosis is clear the conditions present should indicate the medical means most essential.

First, the toxins formed in the body should be neutralized and removed.

The danger of reinfection from the germs should be reduced to a minimum by removing the patient to some condition of surroundings where reinfection would be difficult.

Cod liver oil and emulsive mixtures may be in many cases most dangerous vehicles for the formation of toxins by further destroying the nutritive balance and increasing the waste.

The old theory to feed the patient to excess, assumes a normal digestive capacity, which very rarely or never exists. and is a fallacy.

Foods unfitted for the conditions present are far more dangerous than helpful because they may impair and increase the conditions of faulty nutrition already existing.

Foods containing a disproportion of the normal demands are also disturbing.

A study of the nutrition is the most essential thing in the early treatment or the possible prevention of consumption.

Change of surroundings and conditions of life and living are not more important than the study of nutrition.

Albuminous foods or carbohydrates in excess in a debilitated impaired digestion furnish new sources of infection and diminish the power of restoration.

The modern trend of public opinion in the most advanced treatment is a recognition of these great principles of poisoning and their removal.

Public hospitals in mountain regions and regulation of diet, removal of sources of reinfection and auto-intoxications, are thoroughy preventative as well as curative.

Some of the conclusions I wish to make prominent are:

First. Tuberculosis in this climate follows auto-intoxications and poison states of the body.

Second. After tuberculosis has been established, numerous and complex toxaemias follow which not only intensify but increase the rapidity and fatality of the disease.

Third. Toxaemias following overwork, bad nutrition, and various other and allied causes are very common, and can be prevented by a larger knowledge of the more common hygienic measures essential to good health.

Fourth. Alcohol in all forms is a very potent cause of toxaemia, and the disease inebriety is very closely allied to tuberculosis. It not only precedes this disease but increases its growth by lessening the vigor of the body, and intensifying the degenerations which tuberculosis produces.

Fifth. Both of these diseases depend on toxaemias formed in the body poisons introduced from without.

With both are associated defective nutrition, defective elimination and faulty metabolism.

Sixth. In the treatment of tuberculosis, the most important danger to be corrected is that of poisons generated within the body. Also the elimination of these toxins, and the avoidance of all food and fluids which act as media and nidus for growth of the toxins and germs.

Seventh. Reinfection from the tuberculosis germ in the air, in the clothing, and from other sources can in a large measure be prevented by isolation and correction of the sources from which they spring.

Eighth. The restoration of the vigor and the lost resisting power of the organism can be obtained best from a study of nutrition and the application of such foods whose digestion can be perfected without damage from the waste of overfeeding.

Ninth. The scientific treatment of tuberculosis and its studies of nutrition and surroundings and the means and measures to break up the sources of poison which perpetuate the disease.

THE DEVELOPMENT OF TUBERCULOSIS IN THE INDIVIDUAL.

BY H. EDWIN LEWIS, M. D., BURLINGTON, VT.

Philanthropy properly concerns itself with the afflictions of the multitude, but the humanitarianism of true medical science prescribes that its usefulness should begin with a consideration of disease as it affects the unit of society—the individual.

The medical professon owing its existence to the needs of individual mankind should therefore in the study of tuberculosis, preface all consideration of the disease by a due investigation of the factors and changes involved in the development of tubercular conditions in the individual.

It is not necessary to speak of the fearful ravages of tuberculosis. All men recognize the serious character of the problem that has long confronted us, and the mighty efforts that will be needed to effect its solution.

The pessimist in retrospection finds small results from the labors of those great students who have devoted their lives and their fortunes to the study of the disease. He is prone to claim that the slight lowering of the death rate from tuberculosis during the last decade has resulted solely from greater accuracy in diagnosis and a universal tendency towards decrease of the general mortality rate.

But the optimist, God bless him, sees in the priceless labors of Buehl, Villemin, Cohnheim, Klebs, Koch, Virchow, Roux, Dieulafoy and countless other toilers in the field of experimental medicine great promise for the future. From statistics and clinical observation he recognizes the assailability of tuberculosis through hygienic and sanitary measures, and from the post mortem table he is awakening to the significant fact that tubercular lesions are non-fatal in a fair majority of instances. On every hand, therefore, he sees abundant signs to foster the hope —yea, the confident expectation that sooner or later the treatment of tuberculosis will be as specifically defined as that of syphilis, diptheria or malaria.

Read at joint session of the Medico-Legal Society and American Congress of Tuberculosis, May 15th and 16th, 1901.

It is true that at present we are groping in the dark, but every observer, great and small, is helping to dispel the shadows by adding his particular ray of light. Soon the accumulated discoveries and facts will be sufficient to illumine the whole field of our work, and then at last we will find that boon for which we seek, the means of mastering tuberculosis, closer perhaps than we ever thought.

In order, however, to make our study of tuberculosis most effective let me reiterate that we must begin at first principles. It is the rankest of empiricism and the most illogic of procedures to seek hither and thither for a specific remedy, trying this thing and that thing, without first acquiring accurate information concerning the etiology and pathology of tubercular processes. Yet to the shame of the medical profession, we are witnessing this very spectacle every day. Here are men and there are men, legitimate members of the profession, who are flaunting specific drugs and remedies, even urging them on an eager but innocent public, without themselves possessing any adequate idea of the real pathologic changes involved in the development of tuberculosis. Is this science? Certainly not, and can never produce the result so zealously sought.

But thinking men, honest in every sense of the word, realize that the facts essential to the ultimate conquest of tuberculosis, lie behind the phenomena which occur when the tubercle bacillus enters the living organism—and perhaps before. More plainly expressed, the successful treatment and cure of tubercular conditions must be based on a more accurate knowledge of the infective agent, and the development and progress of its characteristic lesions in the human body.

For years the hereditary factor in the development of tuberculosis has held great importance. But latter day investigation and more intimate knowledge of cause and effect has modified the theory of heredity to a marked degree. To-day we know that direct transmission of tuberculosis from parents to offspring is a rare occurrence, and never takes place except by infection during prenatal life, through the maternal blood supply to the fetus. This, then, is the only tenable remnant of the theory of the direct hereditary transmission of the disease.

We de recognize, however, the possibility of handing down certain stigmata of degeneration. Not necessarily to the extent of physical characteristics, like marked increase or decrease of the cephalic index, or changes in the helix of the ear, the teeth, the palatal vault, mental condition, etc., but in certain histologic depreciations in the vitality and resistance of the cellular structures. Briefly stated, this theory which has ample verification in clinical experience, is that any disease or degenerative change which vitiates the parental cellular elements may give rise to degenerative tendencies in similar histologic structurs of the offspring, thus increasing susceptibility to any disease. The lymphatic system probably shows the influence of hereditary vitiation more often than any other bodily tissue, and since the rise or fall of this particular portion of the human organism has the greatest importance on the development of tuberculosis, as I will endeavor to show later on, we can readily understand how easy it has been in the past to superficially consider pulmonary tuberculosis a hereditary disease.

Of 176 cases of tubercular phthisis I have been able to collect reliable data from, and whose family history I have been able to trace back two generations, I have found tuberculosis or other respiratory disease that might have been tubercular in only 71 parents, or grandparents of 42 cases.

The following table of the diseases that either caused death or prominently occurred in the parents or grandparents of the above 176 cases of pulmonary tuberculosis is interesting:

Tubercular phthisis or other disease that might have been tubercular	71
Epilepsy	16
Apoplexy	46
Bright's Disease	39
Cancer, or Malignant Growths	60
Heart Disease	148
Insanity	28
Chronic Alcoholism	84
Diabetes	14
Syphilis	11
Miscellaneous disease of chronic character	157
Negatie history of chronic ailment	382
Total parents and grandparents	1056

From the foregoing it would seem fairly evident that the hereditary role of pulmonary tuberculosis is hardly so important a factor in the development of the disease as has been claimed in the past. It would also seem to have no more causative bearing on the production of a fertile soil than many other chronic ailments tending to histologic vitiation.

Another premise that should modify statistics of heredity is the fact that the offspring of tubercular parents are much more exposed to infection from the intimacy of family relations, hence acquirement of the disease in many seemingly hereditary cases must be atributed, not to heredity, but to direct infection.

The discovery of the specific germ of tuberculosis in 1882 cleared up many mooted points in regard to the disease. The infectivity of tubercular material had long been recognized, but the exact agent was unknown. Koch's discovery settled the matter once and for all, and medical science profited wonderfully as a consequence of the marked impetus given the study of bacteriology.

The recognition of a definite causative agent more or less constant in its results, stimulated further research of tubercular phenomena, and with the advent of more accurate information, many old theories were proven fallacious. The doctrine of heredity sank back to an unimportant place, and close clinical observers awoke to the fact that while tubercle bacilli were the cause of tuberculosis, certain other factors modified their pathogenic action. In other words certain conditions of the human organism must be favorable to the growth and perpetuation of the tubercle bacillus, or the disease is not produced,—that is the soil must be adapted to the seed. It seems to me that study of this question will bring us very close to the correct solution of all the varied problems presented by the development or non-development of tubercular lesions.

But first we must study the seed. What factors or conditions increase or decrease virulence of tubercle bacilli? The answer to this question is as yet unknown, but there is abundand proof to indicate that tubercle bacilli do show variation in pathogenic intensity. Thus bacilli from manifest disease in the cow, the horse or in man are markedly different in their degree of virulence as shown by the experiments of Theobald Smith.* Likewise tubercle bacilli from different lesions in the human body also show decided pathogenic variation. The experiments of Arloing and Lingard conclusively indicate this fact, for they have demonstrated that tubercular material from lesion in the lungs killed guinea pigs and rabbits much quicker

* Journal of Boston Society of New Science, 1900 iv, 95.

than that taken from caseous glands or other parts of the body.

Every observer of clinical phenomena recognizes variations in the progress and duration of tubercular processes in general, but more particularly those occurring in the lung. Such variations may, it is true, result from special susceptibility of the infected tissue in many instances, but in many others there are abundant signs to point to a varying degree of virulence of the infective material. One class of cases may begin abruptly in individuals comparatively robust and give rise to all the symptoms of an acute pneumonic process constituting the well known "galloping consumption," or "phthisis florida," which frequently proves fatal in four to eight weeks. In still another class of cases composed of individuals recognized as physically weak, the tubercular condition may be so insidious in onset, and with a prodromal stage so protracted that the distinct lesions of the disease cannot be defined until far advanced. Periods of seeming resolution and recovery may occur, and yet the patient finally succumb years after the initial onset of the disease. As I have previously said, the natural deduction from these two types of the same disease is that they owe their variance to different degrees of susceptibility of the individual. In a measure this may be true in every case. Certainly we cannot controvert such a deduction for we have no means of guaging vital resistance. But I have been able to demonstrate that infective material from widely different types of pulmonary tuberculosis does show marked variation in virulence for the lower animals. My experiments, while not so complete nor so skillfully conducted as might have been possible, in a well equipped laboratory, were as follows:

One group of five guinea pigs and four rabbits, after aseptic preparation, were inoculated with sputum from two cases of rapidly fatal acute pneumonic phthisis; and a second group of same number of animals with sputum from two chronic cases, both of over one year's duration, but with slight invasion of the lung substance. Of the first group the guinea pigs all showed extensive lesions in five to fourteen days, and all but one died inside of eight weeks. All of the rabbits also showed comparatively rapid extension of the tubercular infection. But the results in the second group were quite different. In the same number of animals the extension of the disease from the inoculated area was delayed two or three times as long, and only one of the guinea pigs died inside of three months. Of the second group of rabbits only two gave any reaction to the inoculations whatsoever.

The quantity of tubercle bacilli in the specimens of sputum used, did not enter into the result, for the comparative number of bacilli judged from seven or eight microscopic slides was greater in one of the chronic cases than both of the acute and rapidly fatal ones. The Vermont State Bacteriologist confirmed this fact, reporting for the same specimens of sputum that the number of bacilli in both of the acute and one of the chronic cases was "moderate," while in the other chronic case the bacilli were "numerous."

Again, it is my belief, that the tubercle bacilli found in late stages of pulmonary tuberculosis are more virulent than those found at the onset. To adequately prove this the necessary experiments will have to extend over long periods, and though I have several such under investigation, I have not as yet been able to accumulate sufficient evidence to prove my belief. However, during the progress of my experiménts, I have obtained one or two striking results.

A little over two and one-half years ago I inoculated three rabbits with sputum from a case of early, but positive pulmonary tuberculosis. The tubercle bacilli were easily demonstrable in the sputum. All of the rabbits showed characteristic lymphatic enlargement after several weeks, but when killed and examined three months later only one gave indications of advanced pulmonary or general involvement. The case from whom the sputum used was obtained, drifted out of my sight, and I did not see him again for one year and nine months, when he again applied to me for treatment. His disease had been progressive, and he was evidently in the last stages. Both lungs were extensively involved, as was the larynx. Expectoration was profuse, but did not contain relatively any more bacilli than the sputum obtained at the first examination. I inoculated several rabbits and was astonished in a few days by the reaction produced. The point of inoculation in all of the rabbits in from four to twelve days showed marked evidence of suppuration and extension to the lymphatics. In two of the rabbits a zone of extensive ulceration occurred around the inoculated point. All of the animals were profoundly affected, in contra-distinction to those inoculated with the same man's sputum one year and nine months before. Indeed, the rabbits first experimented with were apparently not affected at all, for the atrium of inoculation healed in a few days and never amounted to more than a slight nodule that could be felt under the skin. Suppuration never took place.

I came to the conclusion that the second group of rabbits were suffering from a mixed or additional pyogenic infection, and considered that this nullified the experiment so far as determining the relative virulence of bacilli in different stages of the disease was concerned. On the thirty-ninth day one of the rabbits died. Autopsy showed very evident tubercular lesions in the lungs, kidney, liver and mesenteric glands. I killed the other rabbits on the forty-fourth day, and they too gave gross evidence of tubercular disease of glands, lungs, kidneys and other organs.

The fact, then, that of the first group of rabbits none should die, and only one after three months time give evidence of microscopic lesions, while of the second group one should die, and all show inside of two months such marked progress of the disease, certainly seems significant. Of course, I realize that this single experiment will not justify and hard and fast conclusions, but no one can deny that it is suggestive. Some reason must have existed to hasten or increase the pathogenetic action of the tubercle bacilli in the last specimen of sputum. Whether it was the presence of the mixed infection or not, I am not prepared to say. I am inclined to believe so, however, since certain experiments with the lower animals have demonstrated that some germs that alone are comparatively non-pathogenic to individual animals, become decidedly so when combined with some other. For instance, Roger found that when animals immune to malignant edema were simultaneously injected with one to two c. cm. of a culture of the bacillus prodigiosus and a culture of malignant edema, they would speedily contract the latter disease. Giarre also found that adult guinea pigs, which ordinarily resist infection with the pneumococcus succumb readily to septicemia when pneumococci are combined with the diptheria bacilli.

Some recent observers, notably Sata and Ophuls,* have

* American Journal of Medical Sciences, 1900 cxx 56.

been studying the presence of other bacteria in pulmonary tuberculosis, and their research and investigations point to the importance of mixed infection in producing the pathologic conditions and symptoms considered characteristic of the disease. It would seem that pulmonary tuberculosis is a pure tuberculosis only in the beginning, that advance of the disease is coincident with the establishing of a new factor which in itself is largely responsible for the destructive process, or else greatly augments the action of the tubercle bacilli. More extended study is needed on this subject, but from my own clinical and microscopic observations I am convinced that the fatal character and progress of pulmonary tuberculosis is invariably hastened and may possibly be largely due to the presence of a secondary or mixed infection.

Another phase of the study of tubercle bacilli and their action is the investigation of certain pseudo-tubercular conditions. Flexner* has described a pathologic condition characterized by a caseous pneumonia and a nodular condition of the peritoneum which he has called pseudo-tuberculosis-hominis-streptothrica. A streptothrix which was found in the lesions was very different from ordinary forms of tubercle bacilli or streptothrix. The fact that small branched forms of tubercle bacilli are occasionally found in tubercular lesions resembling the actinomyces, to which the above streptothrix probably belongs, may show that these pseudo forms of tuberculosis bear some relation to the real disease after all.

Moller** has recently described a grass bacillus which he found in barn dust. This germ forms rods in fluid media and in its morphologic aspect closely resembles the tubercle bacillus. It is pathogenic to guinea pigs, the lesions being almost microscopically identical with those of true tuberculosis. Histologically the process also closely resembles tuberculosis. It is an interesting fact that Moller while studying this grass bacillus was taken ill with a sore throat, and in certain masses which he expectorated he was able to demonstrate this germ. Therefore such organisms might readily be mistaken for potent tubercle bacilli.

Then again may it not be possible for this so-called grass

*4 Centralt f. Baht Ablt. 1899. 369-373. **3 Jour. of Exper. Med. 1898;

bacillus to acquire the identical pathogenic properties of the real tubercle bacilli by continued passage through bovines or susceptible human beings just as it has been demonstrated that the virulence of weakly potent tubercle bacilli is increased in intensity by passing through a series of highly susceptible animals like the guinea pig?

Now the question arises from all the varied mass of evidence resulting from investigation of the tubercle bacillus and its allied forms what deductions can be drawn?

Just this: From clinical and laboratory study there are substantial grounds for the belief that the tubercle bacillus is evolutionary in character, which evolution is evidenced by certain variations and gradations in a morphology and virulence modified by the chemic or biochemic conditions of different environments.

This brings us up to a consideration of the soil or those conditions within the human body which favor development of tubercle bacilli and their characteristic lesions. From Hippocrates down medical men have recognized a predisposition to tuberculosis in certain individuals. In the main this predisposition has been considered a lowering of vital resistance, a weakness of the defensive forces opposed to the attack of bacterial hordes.

But this so-called vital resistance is an unknown quantity and the real nature of immunity and susceptibility is at best only conjective. Until the solution of these mysteries is wrested from the fastness of the human body the cause of tuberculosis will remain just as chimerical as it has always been. To find the truths we seek, back to the ultimate cell we must go and carefully study these phenomena, chemic or histologic, which either arrest or permit the march of the bacterial executioner.

A careful study of the lymphatic system of the human body points to the fact that this portion of the animal organism has an important bearing on the development of tuberculosis. As early as 1695 Sylvius recognized a weakness of the lymphatic vessels in scrofulous conditions,and later observers confirmed his views. More recently Fox attributed defects of the lymphatics, while Virchow has laid the cause of scrofula to a weakness or imperfection in the arrangement of individual lymphatic systems.

Histologic investigation teaches us that the lymph "glands" or more properly the "lymph nodes" act as filters of all foreign material that gains entrance to the body. Whether this property of attracting and storing up, as it were, foreign microscopic bodies is a phase of chemotaxis or simply a mechanical phenomenon no one can say, but the fact remains.

Experiments on animals and numerous clinical facts prove conclusively that the first brunt of an invading infection, and the first attempt at bodily resistance is borne by the lymphatic tissue. And still further clinical observation, substantiated by post mortem examinations, demonstrates that the lymphatics successfully overcome and resist tubercular infection in a fair proportion of cases.

Considerable discussion has arisen in regard to the exact nature of the protective forces resident in the lymphatic tissue. Defensive proteid substances called alexins have been shown to normally exist in the blood, their presence conferring certain forms of immunity. It is probable, therefore, that like substances are present, or produced when needed, in the cells of the lymph nodes. It is an important fact furthermore, that physiologically the lymphatic system has an important influence on the chemic phenomena which we are pleased to call the process of nutrition or tissue metabolism.

It should be remembered that every cell of the body is having its own struggle for existence, a struggle which consists of assimilating nutritive material, transforming the same into complex tissue elements necessary for a maintenance of cell identity and the production of cell energy, and getting rid of superfluous end products unnecessary for these functions. Any time during the life of a cell or an aggregation of cells the metabolic equilibrium may be destroyed from several causes:—By variation in the supply or quality of the nutritive pabula, by mechanical injury, or by toxic influence. The result in a cell metamorphosis or a cyto-degeneration, and through resulting inability of the cell to throw off chemic substances inimical to the preservation of its original identity and existence, the degeneration continues and finally ends in necrobiosis.

Now it may properly be asked what relation does cyto-degeneration bear to the development of tuberculosis? A rational deduction is just this: If substances analogous to the alexins of the blood, or other factors in the lymphatic system whose function is to arrest or destroy the influence of tubercle bacilli, are insufficient for this purpose, then the germs gain entrance to the circulation in a potent form and are scattered throughout the body. Should cyto-degenerative changes be general and extensive the tubercle bacilli will find many locations presenting favorable conditions for their growth and destructive influence. A disease, therefore, of which acute miliary tuberculosis presents a typical picture, is the result.

But if the cyto-degenerative areas are few and small, no matter how many bacilli gain entrance to the system, the conditions will be unfavorable for the development and destructive influence of all but a small number, and the tubercular process will be limited, just as it is seen to be in the insignificant tubercular nodules found in many lungs on post mortem examinations.

It should not be understood that all physical weakness or degeneration induces tuberculosis. Conditions of marked vitiation or depravity of the bodily structures may exist quite generally throughout the body and yet tuberculosis never occur, even when external conditions are extremely favorable to infection. If this was not so nearly every injury or disintegration of tissue would become tubercular at the point of solution. But we know from clinical investigation and experiments on animals that the point where tubercular infection enters the organism rarely shows progressive tubercular lesions. The typical tubercular process usually becomes evident in some organ more or less remote from the atrium of infection.

The more frequent occurrence of tuberculosis of the lung would seem to militate against the theory that cellular degeneration per se does not induce tubercular disease, for it has been pretty thoroughly demonstrated that tubercle bacilli enter the body more frequently by inhalation than otherwise. But under normal conditions the anatomic arrangement of the air passages, their irregularities, and the moisture of the lining membranes thoroughly arrests foreign particles and clarifies the inspired air before it reaches the air vesicles. Furthermore, foreign material which does reach the bronchial tubes is rapidly carried to the nearest lymph tissue, the bronchial "glands" and there left, as is shown by the post mortem appearance of the bronchial glands of those whose work requires the constant inhalation of air laden with soot or coal dust.

There is also ample proof that tubercle bacilli do infect the bronchial and other lymph nodes without extension to the lung tissue, but there is nothing to show that tubercular lesions of the lung are not preceded by glandular infection. It is not strange that the lungs should most frequently present definite tubercular lesions. When the other factors that prevent the systemic ingress of active tubercle bacilli are removed, the nature of the respiratory process, the extreme and constant tax that is placed on the cellular structure of the lung by atmospheric variation, and the trophic and circulatory changes it is subjected to by internal conditions, make cyto-degeneration of the lung more common than in any other part of the body.

In conclusion let me emphasize this fact. The development of tuberculosis in the individual is the result of a coincidence of not one but of several conditions. Those conditions are first a potent tubercular infection depending for its potency on a certain degree of virulence; second, a certain negative chemic or histologic condition of the lymph nodes, resulting from hereditary tendencies or circumstances of environment, which fails to arrest or inhibit the growth and systemic ingress of potent tubercle bacilli; and third, a retrograde metamorphosis of structural cells in some part of the body, (more particularly in the lung), from trophic traumatic or toxic influence which favors the local growth of the invading germ.

It can be readily understood that the first two conditions are relative, that is, a particularly large amount or a specially virulent tubercular infection might overcome resistent conditions of the lymphatic system that ordinarily would be effective against a less virulent or smaller amount of infective material. And conversely a weakened lymphatic system might prove vulnerable to what under ordinary conditions would be non-potent tubercular material. In other words, the success of tubercle bacilli in making a systemic ingress depends upon a bacterial power, toxic or vegetative, which is numerically or through special potency greater than the chemic or histologic forces of the lymph nodes which tend to resist or prevent such ingress.

In leaving my subject I realize that there is much in the foregoing that may be open to question and difficult of proof. But as contradiction or affirmation of any statement requires new facts or a more accurate presentation of old ones, my humble deductions may prove of some slight value after all.

TREATMENT OF TUBERCULOSIS.

BY GEORGE BROWN, M. D., ATLANTA, GA.

If free discussion tends to the development of truth, then the treatment of tubercular cases ought to be well on the way to solution. And yet, since the Astral worshippers were out-talked by the Phallic-riters, down to the present day religion has been pretty generally discussed to no apparent purpose. Truth seems never to reveal more than here and there a bald aspect. Let us trust that, since the treatment of tuberculosis should contain a modicum of scientific consideration, its fate may be less protracted than that of religion which has engaged the thought and tongue of all races for vast stretches of time.

It seems to me, and I make the assertion with all modesty that we, of the medical profession, are too prone to submit to intellectual emasculation by "schools" and "ethics." When a physician, as a rule, enters into discussion self-consciousness gives way to school-consciousness, and "ethics" bind like iron bands. We try so hard to be accurate that in our struggles we become as slaves to words and are free only to the extent that we are vague. The virility of common sense is sapped by a stupid indulgence in the lore of senseless text-books, until our wisdom bears the owl trademark. If that were the extent of our sinning against mother-wit, we might yet find some small cause for self-congratulation. But, unfortunately, our dogmatism is a menace in the hands of tyros and a positive danger to the lives of a vast number of the passive laity.

Now, so far as I know, the sins of omission, however great and divers, are yet less than those of commission. And if we fail to insist upon that of which we are ignorant, surely it were better than an iron foot of insistence let fall in the dark; for destruction, after all, is a blind giant. And if there be disgrace in agnosticism, let us out with it and live it down.

Read before the Medico-Legal Society and American Congress of Tuberculosis in joint session. May 15-16, 1901.

I make no hesitancy in acknowledging the very little I know of the subject which is engaging our attention today. And while I am fairly familiar with the work done by my colleagues in this particular field, I still feel the want of that which precise knowledge should grant. But nevertheless, I can see no reason for approaching the matter in other than commonsense ways.

The question of legislative prophylaxis may consistently be left to our legal brethren whose well-known partiality for enactment of laws affords them a vocation in life and I trust a meet reward in death.

Climate, doubtless, has much to do with the course of the disease—and the kind of climate most favorable to recovery of the patient has so long been determined by common consent that I will forbear to dwell upon it here and now.

That brings me up to the consideration of Habit, Food and Medication:

Generally speaking, regular habits under hygienic regime, which of course includes fresh air, exercise, and wholesome, nutritious diet, roughly disposes of the two former questions. It remains, therefore, to speak of medication in the treatment of what my colleague, Mr. Clark Bell, calls "the scourge of the human race."

Up to the present time the use of many and diverse drugs has been recommended by able doctors; but the numerical aspect of these remedies has argued rather strongly against their efficiency. I have recently, however, through the courtesy of one of our best known chemical houses, had my attention called to a new preparation in the form of a watery solution of $CHFI_3$. I became interested in this, which is one of the organic combinations of fluorine, because, in my judgment, the therapeutic value of the fluorine compounds has been strangely neglected while much valuable time and life have been uselessly sacrificed to experimentation with drugs bearing no rational relation to the basic and allied conditions of tuberculosis.

It has been demonstrated that the fourth element of the halogen group—fluorine—has a physiological action far in excess of the other halogen compounds. When we consider, therefore, what the physiological action of this group is, it requires no very great feat of imagination—and with very little danger of a leap in the dark—to seriously consider fluoroformol, or as it is also known aqua flouroformii, invaluable in the rational treatment of tuberculosis. Prof. Stepp, this observer cites more than fifty cases in which the fluoroform water in a number of cases of tubercular infiltration, particularly in local lesions like arthritis, anal ulcer and lupus. In acute pneumonia both in children and in adults, this observer cites more than fifty cases in which the fluoroform treatment apparently moderated the severity of the symptoms, shortened the duration of the disease and certainly caused a truly remarkable condition of comfort and euphoria in the patient.

My work with this fluorine combination so far has necessarily been too limited to warrant any broad statement based on purely clinical ground. But so far as I have gone I feel eminently justified in calling the attention of this body to this particular fluorine compound in the treatment of tuberculosis. The effect of CHFl3 in this aqueous solution upon metabolism,—primarily the hypnotic action on the sensory and vaso-motor nerves, and consequently its effect upon micro-organisms apart from its purely antisceptic action, cannot, it would seem, be attended with other than startling results when administered in tubercular cases. But, as I have said, it remains, gentlemen, for you and me to see if the clinical facts tally with the pretty theory. Certainly, nothing so far has been given to the profession that augurs so well for the victims of tuberculosis.

THE NEED OF A NATIONAL SOCIETY FOR THE PREVENTION OF TUBERCULOSIS.

BY JOHN A. ROBISON, A. M., M. D.,

Secretary of Illinois Society for the Prevention of Consumption ; Delegate of the Illinois State Medical Society, Chicago.

The financial world has demonstrated that the so-called trusts are operated at less expense and produce greater dividends, than the individual corporations. The same principle may be applied to the problem of the prevention of tuberculosis. There are various state organizations endeavoring to control the spread of the disease by educational and legislative methods. Each organization is working independently, and according to its own ideas. But it is quite apparent to me that the work would be greatly facilitated if we had a national organization, a trust as it were, whose object would be to secure the passage of uniform laws concerning the prevention of tuberculosis in all the states, secure appropriations in all the states for the erection of sanitoria, distribute pamphlets gratuitously to educate the public, and also secure funds for the care of the tuberculous poor.

The difficulty of securing a live interest in the problem has been demonstrated to me by my work as Secretary of the Illinois Society during the past three years. The difficulties are three fold: 1. An apathy to the subject on the part of the medical profession, coupled with an inexcusable ignorance of the curability and preventabilitv of the disease. This apathy and ignorance exists among the urban as well as the rural profession, but is perhaps not quite so well marked in the former. A national organization, by means of universal agitation of the subject, might arouse a more general interest in the work among physicians, and by having large quantities of literature published and distributed more cheaply than state organizations could afford would do a great work in dispelling this cloud of ignorance.

Read before the joint session of the American Congress of Tuberculosis and the Medico-Legal Society, New York, May 15-16, 1901.

2. The lack of knowledge on the part of the laity as to the causes and modes of prevention of tuberculosis. Ten years ago I organized and incorporated a society for the establishing of a private sanitorium for the cure of the tuberculous. My work of education then commenced, and I found it was sadly needed, for not only the average man, but the professional man was ignorant concerning the subject. This ignorance, of course, was due principally to lack of interest in the subject and lack of investigation. When I quoted the possibilities of infection, lawyers, ministers, and other intelligent men were amazed, and said I would alarm the people if I came before them with such information. I replied, that the people needed alarming, and I still am sounding the alarm, but it is for the purpose of rescue. The press has been of great help in the past few years in popularizing the knowledge concerning tuberculosis, and a national organization would enlist the co-ordination of the press throughout the United States, and it would be only a short time when all the people would have a complete understanding of the success which attends properly directed efforts to eradicate the disease.

3. The most difficult problem in the way of successful inauguration of preventive measures is to interest our legislators. I framed a bill for the establishment of a state sanitarium for consumptives and asked for an appropriation of $200,000, and it passed the house of representatives, and the legislators seemed to think it was a good bill and should be passed, but after passing appropriations of $250,000 for the St. Louis exposition, and many hundreds of thousands for numerous other objects, they discovered they had no money left, and, forsooth, the appropriations for a sanatorium for consumptives, a colony for epileptics, et cetera, must be pigeon-holed. It is difficult to get our legislators to realize that when they appropriate money for the prevention of disease, they are saving the state many times the amount appropriated, indirectly.

A national organization, by endeavoring to have passed uniform laws on the notification of the disease, the sanitary conduct of cases, and the care of cases which become a public charge, would be a powerful body in securing proper recognition in all the state legislative bodies.

My recommendation would be, the organization of a state

society for the prevention of tuberculosis in each state, with a national central body composed of delegates from all the state organizations, with executive officers and an office in some centrally located city. A certain per cent. of the membership funds of the state organizations should be set aside for the maintenance of the central organization, and all publications of the central organization should be furnished the state organizations at a small per cent. of profit, say 2 per cent., thus enabling the state organizations to obtain literature for distribution at a much less rate than it would be possible in smaller quantities. The national organization could enlist the co-operation of physicians all over the United States when legislative measures were to be considered, and popular opinion would force the enactment of proper preventive laws, and the proper provision for the care of the tuberculous. Congress could be memorialized, and a widespread national interest in the work aroused. Instead of the widely separated skirmishes against the foe that are taking place now, let us mass our army, and move with irresistible force against the foe. Let us sweep the entire country, and arouse an interest which cannot fail in its object.

I trust this short paper will arouse a discussion as to the best plan of a national organization, as my experience leads me to believe such an organization is sadly needed in the United States.

THE TREATMENT OF CONSUMPTION.

BY W. L. BULLARD, A. M., M. D., COLUMBUS, GA., VICE PRESIDENT AMERICAN CONGRESS OF TUBERCULOSIS.

The advance guard of progress seems to move in even rank. As we look back over the past we are astonished at the uncertain lines of development. In some directions there is rapid progress while others of apparently equal importance seem to lag. But in this aspect of change there is no real ground for pessimistic view. Civilization taken in its entirety makes for the better—its fruits, on the whole is good. And so, while it seems strange that so little has been accomplished by science for the prophylaxis and cure of tuberculosis, it is yet a matter of sincere congratulation that assemblages of learned men, such as this, are meeting or arranging to meet in all the great countries of earth for the purpose of lessening by every means known to man the tragic and wasteful effects of this insidious and terrible disease, I will not attempt to discuss legislative means to this much desired end. The gentlemen learned in the law and practiced in the art of lawmaking will I am sure meet the question as fully and as satisfactorily as may be done with the light that is to be had on the subject. And while I feel that the burden of prevention and cure of tuberculosis must ever rest most heavily on the medical fraternity I am is no sense, I hope, oblivious to the great aid which may be expected from the legal profession and the State boards of health. To my mind prevention offers greater assurances than any known means of cure. Hygienic environment, cleanly habits, careful selection of food, abundance of open air exercise with free and assured exercise of lung under suitable climatic conditions, my judgment tells me, are of more importance than all the medicines that have so far engaged the thought of physicians. I think the concensus of medical opinion bears me out in this view. Still the impor-

Read before the American Congress of Tuberculosis in joint session with the Medico-Legal Society, May 15, 16, 1901.

tance of the proper use of right drugs is not to be gainsaid; nor indeed would I so far forget myself as to neglect their consideration in the prevention, treatment and amelioration of this dread scourge. So far as I know there has been no specific claimed by the scientific world. I have tried the various preparations of creosote I regret to say with little success. Local treatment seems largely out of the question, though the needle has been pressed into thisservice with I fear but indifferent success.

But there are many unhappy symptoms which obtain in tubercular cases that do yield to the timely administration of certain drugs. I may mention pain, fever, insomnia, gastric disturbances, profuse "night sweats" pleuritic phenomena and a host of others. Surely, it is the duty of the medical practioner to relieve these even if the relief per se be very far from cure. When the highly excited condition of the nervous centres becomes manifest in the various phenomena of pyrexia, pain or profuse prespiration, treatment looking to removal of the basic cause of the disturbance is often best conserved by removal of symptoms of distress. but whether or no this be in strict accordance with the theory and logic of treatment, it is nevertheless assured by clinical experience.

That drug which tends by its physiological action on systemic metabolism to readjust the molecular interplay of nervous structure and reestablish the equilibrium of the organism such as for instance the judicious administration of some such synthetic product of the coal tar derivatives in combination with Codea sulphate, why beyond all question such are the drugs to receive our careful attention. For by the use of it we work along the lines of least resistance which is nature's habitual method and thereby conserve the vis vitae most happily. I mention this drug because in my hands in this class of cases I have secured most pronounced and favorable results.

There are yet many preconceived notions which we adhere to in the handling of cases of this kind, and which should be excluded from practice. Too great reliance on drugs, is, in my opinion, a hindrance to the best interests of the patient which we seek to protect and favor. If we would place greater stress on the importance of hygiene, cleanly habit, wholesome food, lung gymnastics under conservative regulation, fresh air, moderate exercise and climatic conditions, we would I think, find a much greater per cent of cures and less reason for despair in the treatment of tuberculosis cases.

SURGERY IN THE TREATMENT OF TUBERCULOSIS.

BY M. M. JOHNSON, M. D., OF HARTFORD, CONN.

Every tissue in the human organism is liable to be invaded by the bacillus tuberculosis. It is not only found in the respiratory organs, but the brain and the entire nervous system may be involved. The alimentary canal and the reproductive organs are favorite localities, while the lymphatic and glandular organs are especially chosen points of infection. All the natural openings into the system are known for highways of tubercular infection.

Osler states that, "In adults, the lungs may be regarded as the seat of election; in children, the lymph glands, bones and joints." The preventive treatment of tuberculosis by surgical interference is most conspicuous where the lymphatic tracts are involved leading to tubercular adenitis, peritonitis, nephretis and affections of the genital organs, as the early removal of the infected parts will prevent the further invasion of the disease in the system and prove curative in tubercular affections of the joints, peritonitis and indirect lung surgery. Cervical tubercular adenitis is usually secondary to a previous eczema of the scalp, or ears, or a catarrhal or tubercular inflammation of the mucous membrane of the nose, or pharynx, and it may be a decayed tooth, or any abration of the mucous membrane.

Any or all these conditions may afford an easy portal of entrance for bacilli into the lymphatic channels. Or, as Senn states, "what is more probable, that which has been regarded as a catarrhal inflammation is, in reality, a mild tubercular inflammation, that may disappear after the infection of the lymph glands has occurred." Osler also states that "A special predisposing factor in lymphatic tuberculosis is a catarrhal inflammation of the mucous membrane, which in itself excites a slight adenitis of the neighboring glands." Usually the first glands to be infected are the submaxillary

Read before the American Congress of Tuberculosis in joint session with Medico-Legal Society, May 15, 16, 1901.

and from these the progress is, gland by gland,until the whole chain is infected. This condition is alarming and should receive prompt attention to prevent general infection. Senn insists that "Early operative interference is as necessary in the treatment of tubercular adenitis, as in the treatment of malignant tumors, and holds out more encouragement, so far as a cure is concerned." He further states "That by prompt removal of the primary foci of infection, successive infection of proximal glands and a general miliary tuberculosis are prevented almost to a certainty if the operation is performed before the disease has extended beyond the capsule of the glands." Great thoroughness is demanded in this operation; the surgeon should remove all the glands in a connected chain, as this avoids the chance of leaving infection behind. In like manner a kidney, or ovary, or any other organ should be removed when it is the focus of infection.

Tubercular Peritonitis. That the peritoneum is especially susceptible to tubercular infection has been established by experimental inoculations. This is admirably stated by Senn (Principals of Surgery, p. 480) when he says,"The peritoneum can, under favorable conditions, dispose of a large dose of a pure culture of pus-microbes, but the implantation of a minute fragment of tubercular tissue, in animals susceptible to tuberculosis, is almost certain to be followed by genuine local and general tuberculosis."

Tuberculosis may be primary in the peritoneum, but is more frequently secondary to a general tubercular condition or to some infected foci, as in the genito-urinary, or intestinal tract, in the mesenteric nodes, or by the circulation. In males the infection is more frequently by the intestinal tract—more rarely by the genito-urinary; while in females the prevalence of the infection among the cases which have been reported points to the Fallopian tubes as a primary seat of infection, with a secondary invasion of the peritoneum from this source.

Quoting from Sacks' statistics: "In 2600 autopsies 25 per cent of tubercular peritonitis were found to be secondary to tubercular disease of the genital tract in comparison with 65 per cent from the intestinal tract." In children the main sources of infection are the mesenteric glands themselves,usually through absorption. In this connection Senn furnished an interesting illustration from the "Implantation experiments in animals" of the manner in which the process becomes diffuse. At the point of implantation a granulation mass forms around the graft, and from here innumerable tubercle-nodules take their starting point, forming every where new centres of infection. The movement of abdominal walls during respiration and the peristaltic action of the intestines are potent factors in the local dissemination of tubercular infection. He further states "that in primary tuberculosis of the peritoneum, infection takes place by floating bacilli becoming arrested in the capillary vessels of the membrane."

In recent years the frequent appendical operations have revealed the fact that a diseased appendix affords an easy entrance for tubercular infection to the peritoneum. It is not frequent that the nodules of infected exudate extending over the caecum and involving the peritoneum are filled with miliary tubercules.

Tubercular peritonitis manifests itself in three forms: (1) The ascitic, or tubercular ascites; (2) The dry fibro-plastic form, adhesive tubercular peritonitis; (3) The ulcerative or suppurative forms. We will only consider tubercular ascites, as it is the only form amenable to surgical treatment. It is by far the most common; the peritoneum is studded with tubercles; the ascitic fluid is very abundant and is rarely purulent.

The first surgical treatment for this condition was performed by Sir Spencer Wells in 1862, when he opened the abdominal cavity under a mistaken diagnosis, tubercular peritonitis was found and the incision was closed. The patient made an excellent recovery. From this time on the operation was successfully performed. The operation consists in opening the abdominal cavity, draining the serum and washing out the cavity with a saline solution. Some surgeons close the abdomen at once and others treat it openly and drain. Richardson claims that prolonged drainage and irrigation is unnecessary, as he gets good results by closing the abdomen at once.

Robert T. Morris, appreciating the fact that patients made a rapid recovery from tubercular peritonitis when the abdomen was opened and irrigated, reasoned that "When tuberculosis comes to a stop, we presume that the tubercle bacilli have been killed." He instituted a series of experiments to ascertain what should bring about this result. He removed several ounces of fluid from the abdominal cavity in a typical case of tubercular peritonitis, and exposed them to the air for twenty-four hours, when the fluid was swarming with saprophytes, and the toxines which they produced were separated from it. Small portions of these toxines proved fatal to virulent test tube-cultures of tubercle bacilli: this result was corroborated by a series of experiments on rabbits. His conclusions are that, when the abdomen is opened and drained, saprophytes, which enter through the drainage, produce toxines, which are either fatal to, or which inhibit the growth of the bacilli. Dr. Morris considers this a rational explanation why patients recover from tubercular peritonitis after operations; but, on this theory he claims that the abdomen should be treated openly and drained, so as to allow the saprophytes to enter through the drainage. His theory is quite applicable to the case in hand and has all the conditions of a rational explanation, but in Sir Spencer Wells' case, the abdomen was closed at once and a good result followed. Maurice H. Richardson also claims that he gets equally good results when he closes the abdomen at once. This does not destroy the theory of Dr. Morris, as the saprophytes may enter when the abdomen is opened and drained. The fact remains, however, that the surgical treatment of this form of peritoneal tuberculosis is highly successful.

One of the cases which occurred in the practice of the writer is of interest, as illustrating this phase of the subject. A boy thirteen years of age was sent me for an operation for appendicitis. The abdomen was distended with fluid. The patient had been running a low fever for three weeks, and had suffered considerable abdominal pain. An incision was made over the caecum followed by a flow of fluid. The appendix was highly inflamed; the peritoneum and intestines were studded full of miliary tubercules. The appendix was removed and the cavity thoroughly irrigated with a saline solution and a wick drainage inserted. The fever subsided and the patient made a good recovery. His family history was excellent with no trace of tuberculosis on either side. There is no doubt that the inflamed appendix was the food of tubercular infection and the operation resulted in a radical cure.

Lung Surgery. The most advanced phase of the subject

is embodied in the paper read before the section of Surgery and Anatomy, of the American Medical Association, at its meeting last June at Atlantic City, by Dr. LeMoyne Wills, from Los Angeles, California, under the title of External Drainage of Lung Cavities. In this article, published in the first number of the Journal, in the present year, Dr. Wills relates his investigations and experiments, by which he was convinced that surgical procedures would be of value in the case of lung cavities. He states the difficulties he had in inducing a patient to submit to an operation. His patient was a man who had formerly been strong and vigorous, but had become the victim of pulmonary tuberculosis with all the degenerative conditions which had resulted in a large cavity in the lower lobe of the left lung. The doctor's idea was to establish a free drainage of this cavity, which he accomplished be resecting 1½ inches of the 6th rib in the anterior axillary line. Free drainage and irrigation were the main treatment, which finally resulted in the entire recovery of the patient, so that he was able to work as well as ever. His second case was similarly treated and although not so favorable a case, yet the result of the operation was quite satisfactory.

It is fair to state that the surgery of the lung has not received the attention its importance is entitled to. When the necrotic process has gone so far as to cause a cavity, there is little hope of saving life by medical treatment. the patient is practically doomed. From the success that has already been achieved by the drainage of lung cavities, it opens up a new and interesting field for the surgical treatment of this army of hopeless sufferers.

The views of Dr. Fred. S. Dennis are important when he says, "The results of pneumotomy for abscess of the lung are most encouraging since there have been 15 cases of complete recovery, which I have collected in two years, and to this number it is safe to say, that several have been added. This is most remarkable for a new operation designed to relieve a class of cases, which hitherto were almost uniformly fatal." The technique is not complicated, neither are the dangers great: it is safe to say that, when the operation of pneumotomy has received the attention that its importance deserves, it will be as frequent and as successful as appendectomy now is.

THE NEED OF A SEPARATE PRISON FOR CONSUMPTIVE CONVICTS.

BY W. H. BLAKE, M. D., PHYSICIAN ON THE BOARD OF INSPECTORS OF CONVICTS FOR ALABAMA.

Sheffield, Ala., April 31st, 1901.

Clark Bell, Esq., President Medico-Legal Society of New York, Secretary American Congress of Tuberculosis, 39 Broadway, New York.

Dear Sir—It is with much regret that I must inform you that I cannot attend the American Congress ot Tuberculosis which convenes in New York, May 15th, and to which I have been appointed a delegate from Alabama.

For four years, beginning March 1st, 1897, I was physician member ot the Convict Commission of Alabama. The high death rate from consumption among the convicts caused me to make an effort to have a law enacted requiring the isolation of consumptive prisoners. After persistent work such a law was passed, a copy of which I herewith inclose. I beg to call your attention to the enclosed reprint of "The need of a separate prison for consumptive convicts." The real object in writing this pamphlet was to reach the members ot legislature. To each member of the legislature, I wrote a personal letter and sent him one ot the pamphlets.

There were many discouraging difficulties to overcome in procuring the enactment of this law.

Yours respectfully,

W. H. BLAKE, M. D.

No. 1045. AN ACT. S. 520.

To provide for the isolation of convicts suffering with tuberculosis.

Section 1. Be it enacted by the General Assembly of Alabama, That the inspectors of convicts in this State, be and they are hereby required to establish a separate camp or place for all convicts in this State suffering fzom tuberculosis, at which all convicts, whether State or county, shall be sent and there kept at such labor as they may be able to perform, under the superintendence and direction of said Board of Inspectors.

Sec. 2 Be it iurther enacted, That said Board of Inspeotors shall prescribe such rules and regulations as may be necessary to ascertain what convicts are suffering from tuberculosls, and to provide for the removal of the same to the camp or place provided for in the first section of this act.

Approved March 5, 1901-

(Official) ROBERT F. McDAVID,

Secretary of State.

The importance of this subject, I am sure, justifies me in repeatedly bringing it before this association. The housing of large bodies of men, whether they be workmen in factories, soldiers in barracks or prisoners in confinement requires the best thought and the most careful attention. If any class need more consideration in regard to the hygiene of his dwelling than another, it assuredly is the inmate of our prisons. He is compelled to occupy whatever accommodations the authorities provide him, and to endure whatever condition they may determine.

Dr. Rohe in his work on Hygiene says: "The mortality of convicts, even in the best regulated prisons where special attention is paid to sanitary requirements of such buildings, is three times as great as among workmen in mines, confessedly one of the most dangerous occupations." Confinement lowers the vital force and causes the system to yield more readily to disease. That disease which brings death to more convicts than all others combined is consumption. Rohe says it causes from 40 to 80 per cent. of these deaths. His estimate is for the United States as a whole. Animals placed in captivity die rapidly of this disease, which, in their native state, is unknown to them.

Among the convicts of Alabama consumption prevails to an alarming degree and the death rate from this cause is on the increase.

In Alabama the record of deaths for State convicts covers a period of eighteen years. For the first half of this period consumption caused 20.3 per cent. of the total mortality; for the last half it caused 42 per cent. In the penitentiaries of different States, of the total deaths, the per cent. caused by consumption is as follows:

These figures are from recent reports:

Mississippi, 20 per cent.; Arkansas, 20 per cent.; Florida, 30 per cent.; Ohio, 31 per cent.; Michigan, 33 per cent.; Allegheny County Work House, Penn'a, 33⅓ per cent.; Virginia, 41 per cent.; Kentucky, 42 per cent.; Joliet, Illinois, 70 per cent.; Huntsville Penitentiary, Texas, 66 per cent.; Rusk Penitentiary, Texas, 33 per cent.; Washington, 16 per cent.; Connecticut, 1898, 60 per cent.; Tennessee, 65 per cent.

In 1897 every death that occurred in the penitentiary of Connecticut was caused by consumption. According to the last national census, consumption causes 11 per cent. of all deaths among our free population.

In regard to the propagation of this disease, our present knowledge justifies the following statements: Every new case of tuberculosis must be derived from another case. The disease can only be transmitted from parent to offspring by transmission of the tubercle bacilli. The offspring of consumptive parents under favorable environments, are less liable to have the disease than are men and women of healthy parentage who marry consumptives.

Flick says with regard to this disease: "The history of tuberculosis in all times and in all countries is a broad demonstration of its contagiousness, and by inference of its preventability."

Osler recounts observations made under Koch's supervision, where dust was gathered from buildings in which consumptives were confined, and out of 118 samples, forty were infective and produced the disease in animals. Strauss performed the following experiment: In the nostrils of twenty-nine nurses and hospital attendants, he placed plugs of cotton wool to collect the dust of the wards. In nine of the twenty-nine cases the cotton contained the tubercle bacilli and proved infective to animals. Prison management in Alabama furnishes conditions specially favorable to the propagation of consumption. Convicts are not kept in separate cells, but from fifty to one hundred are confined together in a single large cell. Consumptive convicts, unless acutely ill, are confined in the same cells with the well convicts.

An effort is made to cause those expectorating to spit into cuspidors containing a disinfectant, but this cannot be enforced. The results are, a prison atmosphere full of the germs of consumption, an alarming death rate from that disease, and this death rate on the increase.

There is only one remedy for this condition, and that is to separate the consumptive convicts from the non-consumptive. We need something more than separate wards in the same building or separate buildings on the same grounds. We need a separate camp for consumptive convicts, the further from the other prisons the better, in order to give the non-tuberculosis prisoners the greatest possible immunity from this disease. With the organization of such a camp, and the exercise of painstaking care in detecting consumption in its early stages, and the prompt removal of such convicts to said camps; in doing this, we shall have accomplished all that our present knowledge of this disease points out as our duty in the premises. This would give the consumptive better treatment, and the well men a chance to remain well. In this matter, the duty of the State is plain. It has the right to deprive the offender of his liberty, but it has not the right to deprive him of his health. Think of the horrible fate of continuous confinement in the same rooom with a contagious and deadly disease. Such is the fate of every convict in Alabama to-day. To organize a separate camp for consumptives is the one great object I have sought to bring about during my term as director of the medical department of the State convict system, so far without success.

Our law makers are not fully alive to the gravity of the situation. It behooves us as physicians to continue to agitate this subject. I am sure Alabama is due this much to its prison population, whose labor is turning large revenues into her treasury. I am also sure that a humane and intelligent citizenship will endorse the administration that carries out the prison reform suggested in this paper.

MEDICO-LEGAL SURGERY.

ASSOCIATE EDITORS.

Medical.

Granville P. Conn, M. D., Concord, N. H.
R. Harvey Reed, M. D., Wyoming.
Nicholas Senn, M. D., Chicago, Ill.
Webb J. Kelley, M. D., Galion, Ohio.

Legal.

Clarence A. Lightner, Esq., Detroit, Mich
Judge Wm. H. Francis, New York.
Prof. A. P. Grinnell, M. D., Burlington, Vt.

This department is conducted as the organ of the Section of the Medical Jurisprudence of Surgery of the Medico-Legal Society. Its officers for 1901 are as follows:

Chairman.

Chief Surgeon Charles K. Cole, M.D., of Helena, Montana.

LEGAL. Vice-Chairmen.

Clark Bell, Esq., of New York.
Judge W. H. Francis, of New York.
Hon. J. W. Fellows, of N. H.
Hon. W. C. Howell, of Iowa.
Prof. A. P. Grinnell, M. D., of Vermont.
Hon. A. R. Parmenter, of Troy, N. Y.
Hon. George R. Peck, of Illinois.
Hon. J. M. Thurston, of Nebraska.
Judge A. H. Dailey, of Brooklyn, N. Y.
Hon. Allen Zollers, of Indiana.

SURGICAL. Vice-Chairmen.

Ch. Surg W. A. Adams, of Ft. Worth. Tex.
Ch. Surg. F. H. Caldwell, M. D., of Fla.
Ch. Sur. Granville P. Conn, M. D., of N. H.
Ch. Surg. W. B. Outten, M. D., of Missouri.
Surgeon Geo. Chaffee, M. D., of Brooklyn.
Ch. Surg. B. F. Eads, M. D., of Texas.
Ch. Surg. John E. Owen, M. D., of Chicago.
Surg. Gen. R. Harvey Reed, M. D., of Wy.
Surg. Gen. Nicholas Senn, M. D., of Ill.
Ch. Surg. S. S. Thorne, M. D., of Ohio.

Secretary.

Clark Bell, Esq., 39 Broadway, N. Y.

Treasurer.

Judge Wm. H. Francis, New York City.
39 Broadway, N. Y.

Executive Committee.

Clark Bell, Esq., Chairman.

Surg. Thomas Darlington, M. D., of N. Y.
L. L. Gilbert, Esq., Pittsburg, Pa.
Ex-Ch. Sur. Geo. Goodfellow, M. D., Cal.
Surgeon J. N. Hall, of Denver, Colo.
Chief Surg. A. C. Scott, M. D., of Texas.
Judge A. H. Dailey, of Brooklyn, N. Y.
Sur. R. S. Parkhill, M.D., of Hornelsville, N.Y.
Sur. Fayette H. Peck, M. D., of Utica, N. Y.
Chief Sur. T. I. Pritchard, of Wis.
R. C. Richards, Esq., of Chicago, Ill.
Ch. Surg. F. A. Stillings, M. D., of N. H.
Ch. Surg. J. J. Buckley, Missoula, Montana

To Railway Surgeons and Railway Counsel:

We take occasion to advise you to unite with the Section of Medico-Legal Surgery, which can now be done by an annual subscription of $1.50, entitling each member to the *Medico-Legal Journal* free.

G. P. CONN, M. D.,
Ex-Chairman Section Med.-Leg. Surgery.

ABRAM H. DAILEY,
Ex-President Medico-Legal Society of New York.

SAMUEL S. THORN, M. D.,
Chief Surgeon T., St. L. & K. C. Railway Co., Ex-President National Association Railway Surgeons.

J. B. MURDOCH, M. D.,
Surgeon and Ex-President National Association of Railway Surgeons.

R. HARVEY REED, M. D.,
Surgeon General of State of Wyoming.

R. S. HARNDEN, M. D.,
Ex-President New York State Association Railway Surgeons. Ex-President Erie Railway Surgeons.

HUBBARD W. MITCHEL, M. D.,
Ex-President Medico-Legal Society of New York.

Members of the Section on Medico-Legal Surgery, who have not remitted their annual subscription to the Section, will please send same to Judge Wm. H. Francis, No. 39 Broadway, N. Y., and members will please not confound the Section Dues with the Annual Dues of the Society, which should be remitted to Caroline J. Taylor, Treasurer, Bridgeport, Conn. Members of the Society or Section will please propose names for membership in this Section.

It is proposed that members of the Society and Section each donate one bound volume annually to the Library of the Medico-Legal Society, by action of the Executive Committee.

The following new members of the Section are announced: J. P. Webster, M. D., Ex-Pres. Erie Railway Surgeons, Chicago, Ills.; W. L. Cuddebuck, M. D., Pres. Erie Railway Surgeons, Port Jervis, N. Y.; Dr. A. E. Ellingwood, Attica, N, Y.; Chief Surgeon J. J. Buckley, N. P. Ry. Co., Missoula, Montana.

SECTION OF MEDIGO-LEGAL SURGERY.

The most important action respecting Medico-Legal Surgery, since our last issue, was the April meeting of that body in joint session with the Medico-Legal Society, on the 3rd Wednesday of April, 1901.

The following papers were contributed and appear in the June number, 1901 :

1. "Railway Surgeons and Hospitals." By Judge Wm. H. Francis, of New York City.

2. "First Aid to the Injured." By Geo. Chaffee, M. D., of Brooklyn, N. Y.

3. "Ankle Sprains." By Webb J. Kelley, M. D., of Galion, Ohio.

THE INTERNATIONAL ASSOCIATION OF RAILWAY SURGEONS.

This body meets at Milwaukee, Wisconsin, on June 10th, 11th and 12th, 1901.

As the American Medico-Psychological Association meets at the same time, and as Milwaukee has made great preparations to receive these bodies, an interesting meeting is expected.

PSYCHOLOGICAL.

This Department is conducted with the following Associate Editors:

Judge Abram H. Dailey, Brooklyn, N. Y.	Wm. Lee Howard, M. D., Baltimore, Md.
Prof. A. A. D'Ancona, San Francisco, Cal.	R. J. Nunn, M. D., Savannah, Ga.
H. S. Drayton, M. D., N. Y	A. E. Osborne, M. D., Cal.
M. Ellinger, Esq., N. Y. City.	Jas. T. Searcey, M. D., Tuscaloosa, Ala.
Dr. Havelock Ellis, London.	U. O. B. Wingate, M. D., Milwaukee, Wis.
Thomson Jay Hudson, Esq., Wash., D. C.	Prof. W. Xavier Sudduth, Chicago, Ill.

as the organ of the Psychological Section.

The Psychological Section of the Medico-Legal Society has been organized, to which any member, Active, Corresponding or Honorary, is eligible on payment of an annual enrollment fee or dues of $1.50.

Any student of Psychological Science is eligible to unite with the Section without joining the Medico Legal Society on an annual subscription of $1.50. payable in advance and receive the MEDICO-LEGAL JOURNAL free. The officers for 1900 are as follows:

Chairman,
PROF. W. XAVIER SUDDUTH, OF CHICAGO, ILL.

LEGAL AND SCIENTIFIC.	*MEDICAL.*
Vice-Chairmen.	*Vice-Chairmen.*
Clark Bell, Esq., of New York.	T. D. Crothers, M. D., of Hartford, Conn.
Rev. Antoinette B. Blackwell, of N. Y.	F. E. Daniel, M. D., of Austin, Texas.
Harold Browett, Esq., Shanghai, China.	H. S. Drayton, M. D., of New York.
C. Van D. Chenoweth, Worcester, Mass.	Wm. Lee Howard, M. D., of Baltimore, Md.
Judge Abram H Dailey, of Brooklyn.	Henry Hulst, M. D., Grand Rapids, Mich.
Moritz Ellinger, Esq., of New York.	Prof. Thomas Bassett Keyes, of Chicago.
Rev. Phebe A. Hanaford, of New York.	R. J. Nunn, M. D., of Savannah, Ga.
Thomson Jay Hudson, Esq., Wash'n, D. C.	A. E. Osborne, M. D., of Glen Ellen, Cal.
Sophia McClelland, of New York.	Jas T. Searcy, M. D., Tuscaloosa, Ala.
Mrs. Jacob F. Miller, of New York.	U. O. B. Wingate, M. D., Milwaukee, Wis.

Mrs. Mary Louise Thomas, of New York.

Secretary and Treasurer.
CLARK BELL, ESQ., OF NEW YORK.

Executive Committee.
CLARK BELL, ESQ., Chairman.
SAMUEL BELL THOMAS, OF NEW YORK CITY, Secretary.

M. Ellinger, Esq.	Judge A. H. Dailey.	Geo. W. Grover, M. D.
Carleton Simon, M. D.	Ida Trafford Bell.	H. W. Mitchell, M. D.

The work of the past quarter has greatly centered on tuberculosis, its cause, prevention, treatment, etc., and the American Congress of Tuberculosis held at the Hotel Majestie, May 15th and 16th, 1901.

The Congress was a great success and resulted in effecting a permanent organization for the year 1901–2.

The following officers were elected :

HONORARY PRESIDENT:

A. N. BELL, M. D., Brooklyn, N. Y.

PRESIDENT:

HENRY D. HOLTON, M. D., of Vermont,
Secretary State Board of Health, Brattleboro, Vt.

VICE PRESIDENTS:

HENRY B. BAKER, M. D., Lansing, Mich.
E. T. BARRICK, M. D., Toronto, Ont.
WM. BAYARD, M. D., St. John, N. B.
RALCY HUSTED BELL, M. D., New York City.
A. C. BERNAYS, M. D., St. Louis, Mo.
J. MOUNT BLEYER, M. D., New York City.
GEO. BROWN, M. D., Atlanta, Ga.
W. L. BULLARD, M. D., Columbus, Ga.
COL. E. CHANCELLOR, M. D., St. Louis, Mo.
C. K. COLE, M. D., Helena, Mont.
T. D. CROTHERS, M. D., Hartford Conn.
JUDGE ABRAM H. DAILEY, Brooklyn, N. Y.
HOM. MORITZ ELLINGER, New York City.
JUAN A. FORTICH, M. D., Cartagena, Colombia, S. A.
R. F, GRAHAM, M. D., Greely, Colorado.
A. P. GRINNELL, M. D., Burlington, Vt.
MAJOR A. HAVARD, U. S. A., Vice-Pres., Havana, Cuba.
THOS. BASSETT KEYES, M. D. Chicago, Ill.
LUIS H. LABAYLE, M, D., Leon, Nicaragua.
E. P. LACHAPELLE, M. D., Montreal, Canada.
LOUIS LEROY, M. D., Nashville, Tenn.
DR. EDOUARD LICEAGA, City of Mexico.
DWIGHT S. MOORE, M. D., Jamestown, S. Dak.
WM. H. MURRAY, M. D., Plainfield, N. J.
J. A. MCNEVEN, Gibbonsville, Idaho.
A. E. OSBORNE, M. D., Glen Ellen, Cal.
JOHN H. PRYOR, M. D., Buffalo, N. Y.
J. C. SHRADER, M. D., Iowa City, Iowa.
J. H. TYNDALE, M. D., Lincoln, Nebraska.
C. S. WARD, M. D., Warren, Ohio.
PROF. S. H. WEEKS, M. D., Portland, Maine.
CRESSY L. WILBUR, M. D., Lansing, Mich.
U. O. B. WINGATE, M. D., Milwaukee, Wis.
C. F. ULRICH, M. D., Wheeling, W. Va.

SECRETARY AND TREASURER:

CLARK BELL, Esq., City of New York.

The transactions of this body will appear elsewhere in our columns.

Some of the papers read appear in the current number, and the whole will be published in the Bulletin of the American Congress of Tuberculosis, and a copy sent to every enrolled member.

A large number of delegates were appointed by the Governors of the several States of the American Union, and delegates were in attendance from Canada and many of the Central and South American States.

The time being too short to obtain delegates from all, the time of enrolling was extended and papers solicited to August 15th, 1901, which will appear in the Bulletin, if received by that date.

Delegates were authorized to be named to the British Congress of Tuberculosis in London next July, and the Executive officers authorized and empowered to name two or more Vice-Presidents from every State, Territory or dependency of the United States, the Dominion of Canada and of each country in Central and South America.

The Vice-Presidents, from States under the authorization of the Congress, up to the time of going to press, will, if possible, be given later.

The Congress was closed by a dinner at the Hotel Majestie on the evening of the 16th of May, which was well attended, and was a credit to that excellent hotel, at which Mr. Clark Bell presided and speeches were made by prominent members.

The delegates to the British Congress of Tuberculosis, in July, have not yet been fully selected, but the following delegates have already been named:

Clark Bell, Esq., LL.D., of New York City, President of the Medico-Legal Society and Secretary of the American Congress of Tuberculosis; H. Edwin Lewis, M. D., of Burlington, Vt., Editor *Vermont Medical Monthly;* Dr. Aug. C. Bernays, of St. Louis, Mo.; Dr. Geo. Brown, of Atlanta, Ga., and Dr. J. C. Shrader, President Iowa State Board of Health, of Iowa City.

AMERICAN MEDICO-PSYCHOLOGICAL ASSOCIATION.

The fifty-seventh annual session of the American Medico-Psychological Association was held in Milwaukee, on June 11-14. The President. Dr. P. M. Wise, of New York, reviewed in his presidential address, the recent progress of psychology and psychiatry, and appealed for a closer co-operation of these two sciences. He briefly pointed out the probable course of the psychical sciences, and predicted the removal of the judicial features necessary, at the present time, for the treatment of of the insane, especially in its early stages. He also appealed to the Association for a greater conservatism on the question of psychics, which presents no evidence to human sense outside of individual experience, but he maintained that such experience was plentiful enough to demand respect. He also believed that in time to come the development of the sixth sense would make psychic manifestations clear to us, which now seems obscure. He criticised mildly all revolutionary methods for lunacy reform, and claimed that in this respect statutory changes should be graduated. He made a strong appeal to superintendents to maintain the scientific department of the hospitals and to not permit the fiscal duties pertaining to their office to wean them from the more important professional work.

A number of papers were presented having a medico-legal aspect, and worthy of careful reading and attention. The transactions are annually published in book form and can be had from the secretary of the Association The officers elected for the ensuing year were, for president; Dr. R. J. Preston, of Virginia; for vice-president, Dr. G. Alder Blumer, of Rhode Island, and for secretary and treasurer, Dr. C. B. Burr, of Michigan.

Many members of the Association gave particular attention to the Wisconsin system of caring for the insane, which is peculiar to Wisconsin, and involves a copartnership between the counties and the State.

EDITORIAL.

PREMATURE BURIAL.

The consciousness of a certain silently approaching inevitable death, from which there is no escape, reprieve or rescue, is perhaps the concentration of human mental agony.

Perhaps in the case of one who in the last stages of a protracted struggle for life with an incurable disease, like cancer or tuberculosis, where physical pain lends its additional agony to the sufferer, we might hesitate; but is there any fate more terrible to contemplate or consider than that of being buried alive?

The imprisoned one in a burning building from which there is no escape, when death literally stares him in the face and reaches out flaming fingers and a scorching breath, is horrible to think of, and terrible to realize.

If on a vessel at sea it is none the less terrible, because it has often a ray of hope, that the conflagration may attract some one to come to succor, but when hope has gone and the last dread moments or remaining life have fled, still there can be little doubt that the acme of mental anguish and agony exceeds all physical pain to the imprisoned one in the silence of the grave.

But what even are all these, compared to the horrible mental suffering that comes to him, who awakening from unconsciousness finds himself in his coffin in the grave, and who must face a death which is so slow, sure and terrible that madness and insanity would be merciful, in that it ended mental depths of anguish, despairing, indescribable, unendurable and beyond the capacity of the human mind to adequately realize, much less to endure.

The contemplation even of such an ending of life, is heart rending, and it stirs every depth of the soul to strictly describe or even consider it.

It is a charitable and philosophic view of the actuality of life, that the hopeful optimist takes, who agrees with certain medical men that such a fate is an impossibility and such an ending need not be either dreaded or feared.

If we could accept such a view it would comfort many who have an overwhelming fear and terrible dread of such a fate.

It is argued that such instances as are generally believed to occur occasionally under the head of narrow escapes, are all that need be feared or guarded against.

That the time elapsing between death and burial and decomposition itself is in the way of any view that would leave such circumstance possible.

On the other hand a large number of people are terribly afflicted by the awful fear of such a fate, and the welfare of even such, should enlist our attention and compel our sympathy, as well as our aid.

I have often thought the heroic measures adopted by the modern undertaker was to some extent an adjunct to prevent premature burial.

The practice of so called embalming when the abdomen is opened to have the cavity filled with a poisonous fluid would seem at first as a safeguard against premature burial.

The insertion of the knife to open the body for such a purpose would of course break the spell of unconsciousness from catalepsy or any other causes.

The danger of this process of embalming the body, which has come into very general recognition, has one side to it, that is so objectionable and such a menace to the citizen that it should be strictly prohibited by law.

Its greatest objection, that as now practiced by the ordinary undertaker, is, that it affords a certain protection to conceal crime in cases where the death was due to poisoning. The murderer escapes by having the body treated by the undertaker, as there is no means now known by toxicologists to discriminate between poisons administered before death or after death by the absorption from filling the abdominal cavity.

A strong objection to the whole process of so called embalming is that it impregnates a great many cemeteries with aresnic, especially on hill sides by infiltration from one grave to another. So that the finding of arsenic in a grave now would not be positive evidence in a case where death was caused by arsenical poisoning.

The so-called embalming as practiced by undertakers is now a menace to the public safety, in preventing the detection of crime and it is used by poisoners to conceal their crime.

The fear of premature burial, while not universal, is much more extensive than is generally supposed.

Any action that would dispel this fear would be a great public boon.

More people would be thus benefitted than could by any reasonable possibility ever be the subject of premature burial.

That premature burial occurs must be conceded, as the evidence of its occurrence are undoubted, but we may safely assert that it is of rare occurrence.

Many cases have been authentically reported, where the danger was imminent and some accident only has prevented.

As a public evil, the fear of premature burial far exceeds the actual occurrence by many thousand fold, and the greatest value to the race of a certain preventive against premature burial, would be in banishing the fear of it from all minds.

TRUTH VS. ERROR.

There are two methods in vogue in the world and more especially in the medical profession, relative to error and how to combat, meet and overthrow it.

One is by intrigue and management to suppress the discussion of subjects, deemed to be improper, and to prevent full discussion; the other is to meet error face to face and vanquish it in a fair fight and open contest.

The most striking instance of recent days is when a physician, whose name was on the programme of enrolled members, read a paper at the recent session of the American Congress of Tuberculosis in New York, attacking the view that consumption was infectious, and denying the existence of the bacilli of tuberculosis, with propositions and statements, at variance with the universal opinions of members. He was allowed to occupy his whole time.

Then objection was made to his being heard farther, when Dr. C. K. Cole, of Montana, moved and obtained general consent that he be heard in full.

The Congress then by vote on division:

1. Refused to receive his paper, or allow it to be published in its transactions, and

2. Placed itself squarely as in opposition to the views of the author, and on division squelched the author and his paper by an overwhelming vote, not one member of the Congress sustaining the author or his paper, although three members of the large audience who had been invited by the chair to vote, voted with him.

The incident places the Congress square on the record:

1. That tuberculosis is an infectious disease.

2. That as such it was the proper subject of preventive legislation. The truth need never fear the outcome of a fair open, square, stand up fight with error.

It is not the wiser policy to avoid such a conflict when the issue is crucial. There can be found no proposition, however absurd, that will not find some voting to support it.

The medical profession have not until very recently agreed that tuberculosis was infectious. It is not united now as to whether the baccillis is the cause or the result of the disease.

The writer of the paper assailed the motives of medical men in the strongest and most reprehensible language and was squelched because of his want of *savoir faire.*

The officers were criticised for permitting such a paper to be read. None of the papers were under censorship. There should be no muzzle on the discussion of scientific questions. The same principle that lighted the fires at Smithfield, and inspired the massacre of the innocent in the struggle for opinion, is at stake in scientific questions.

The American Congress of Tuberculosis stands on much higher ground, since it allowed a member to express views in conflict with those of every one of his colleagues, rather than to suppress or avoid the full discussion of the subject.

If tuberculosis is not infectious there would be no safe ground on which to base preventive legislation and the incident, although a surprise to the whole body, forced an expression on vital questions on which the unanimity of opinion was remarkable, which could not have been made apparent but for the extraordinary occasion and its surroundings.

THE PREVENTION OF TUBERCULOSIS.

The most prominent question in Forensic Medicine of the present hour, the one to which thoughtful minds in all nations are now turning with deepest interest, is how far can legislation avail to prevent the spread of this terrible disease among all the people of the human race.

During the past four or five months this question has been foremost in the councils and work of the Medico-Legal Society. The conference in Canada, at Ottawa, in February last, following the opening meeting of the American Congress of Tuberculosis held at the instigation and under the auspices of the Medicol-Legal Society, in February, 1900, in the City of New York, indicate the intense interest felt in the subject by the great masses of the people of many countries.

In Great Britain, the government has strongly supported and led in public demonstrations on the subject, and men of both professions in law and medicine, have actively supported it. In the forthcoming Congress announced to be held in London in July next, the sympathy of the English Government will be strongly manifested, and a great public demonstration will be made.

In Sweden there is public interest in the question, and in Italy and Germany.

The Dominion of Canada is also in strong sympathy with the movement in that portion of America.

In contrast, in the United States of America, is the remarkable apathy of the medical profession. There is now no great name in the American metropolis in the medical profession identified with the cure of consumption. Perhaps half a dozen medical men in the great army of physicians of the metropolis treat it as a specialty. The stronger men, the medical specialists, do not treat it. It is not a desirable practice.

It falls to the lot of family physicians to grapple with this enemy of the race, and so far as we have learned, no responsive echo has been found among medical men in any of the States of the American Union, save the praiseworthy efforts of a few good men in a few States, towards the organization of State societies for the prevention of tuberculosis.

It will be conceded, in the near future, that the action of the Medico-Legal Society in initiating the movement which resulted in the organization of the American Congress of Tuberculosis, was laudable, praiseworthy and deserving of public praise. The second annual meeting, which has just been held with wonderful success at the Hotel Majestic, in New

York City, has crystallized its work with a body that can properly be called American in the broadest and most comprehensive sense.

It embraces all the countries and peoples on the continent of both North and South America. Time and distance prevented the South American and some of the Central American States from being represented at the May meeting, but every government and country in South and Central America was invited, and it is only a question of time when every one of them will be officially represented.

The action of that body on the first day will appear in detail in our columns, and its labors will be published in a bulletin after the summer vacation.

More than 200 delegates were appointed by the Governors of the States and Territories of the American Union and by the Governments of other countries in response to the invitations of the officers, although the time was so short that in many of the distant States it was impossible to have the responses reach the delegates in time to attend the Congress.

Action was taken, beside the list of officers chosen which appears in our columns, for the election of two or more vice presidents, selected from both legal and medical men from every State and Territory in the United States, every province in the Dominion of Canada, and every State and country in Central and South America.

The invitation from the British Congress of Tuberculosis, at London, to send delegates was accepted, and a delegation from this body will attend the London Congress.

It will, as a result of its labors already, solidify and crystalize the abler and more aggressive men in both professions of law and medicine to co-operate along lines of usefulness in affecting legislation in aid of the construction of sanitaria for the consumptive in the American States, and to consider and devise the best methods of awakening a pronounced and advanced public sentiment in favor of such preventive legislation against the causes and spread of tuberculosis, as will we trust, result in the welfare and good of the race.

THE GOSPEL ACCORDING TO ELBERT HUBBARD.

Mr. Elbert Hubbard has a wonderful and exceedingly engaging personality.

He is tall, and lithe, and sinewey, slender, with a winning captivating smile.

He resembles more than any other man that I can recall the great artist George Inness.

The resemblance is as much in manner and facial expression, gesture, command of language, as in complexion personal traits, and indescribable little things which bring back to you the dead artist, when you look at Fra Elberto.

Compare their photographs and they might not even resemble each other, but the Elbert Hubbard speaking on the platform in action on his theme, brings up the figure of Inness in later life, when he was describing a painting that he admired, or speaking of the faith which governed his life. Both wore the hair alike, both black and flowing, black, piercing eyes, both a captivating smile, a little more cynicism in the artist, and more of tenderness and emotion and love in the Philistine.

Hubbard is the most picturesque, take him all in all: of any of the men of the platform today, and few that I have heard can hold an audience so intently, and keep them so entranced as he for over an hour.

He speaks on a theme that dominates his life, governs all his action; along lines that he has walked arm and arm with the conviction of his soul, toward an end that, regardless of the applause or censure of others, lies nearest his heart, and which has refreshed him constantly by the blessings he gives others, coming back like sunshine and rain and flowers to make his soul jubilant and strong. No one has more profoundly the courage of his own convictions than he; and it is doubtful if any human soul has felt more profound blessing at the early realization of his dreams for the uplifting of others, or for good to his kind than the pastor of the Philistines. His life and career and the school he has created, and example that has seen fruition under his own eye, will be an object lesson for the race, when he has passed into the unknown. It is as unique as it is successful if we are to measure men by the good they do, in their lives, taking into account their environment, their opportunities and their limitations, when they have had to create not only their opportunities, but the means of obtaining their realization; it does not need an orator to say that the historian of his life must place his name high in the scale of those who have succeeded best.

NUGGETS FROM ELBERT HUBBARD.

Art is the expression of our love for our work.

The soul never dies: its growth is as constant as it is eternal.

That worker is respectable at the Roycroft shop who does his work as well as he can.

To live each day for itself, doing always the best we can, is the highest human ideal of high excellence.

It is the crowning glory of our country that it has no leisure class, and no place for such a class.

The Duke of Manchester said recently: "Why you know you have no leisure class in your country." "Yes," was the American reply, "We call such here Hoboes."

"If you should put ten graduates of Harvard on a foundered vessel and shipwrecked all would perish, because none of them would know how to build a raft."

"Harvard in its education is no worse than the other colleges. They are all equally bad alike."

What the world needs now is not more sincerity but more kindness. To be kind—just that old divine emotion of pity—just the simple act of being kind! And above all, let us not forget how to laugh.

The dark brooding night is as necessary for our life as the garish day. Great crops of wheat that feed the nations grow only when the winter's snow covers all as with a garment.

Every man of genius the world has ever produced has come from a little belt of land in the North Temperate Zone.

To have a full stomach and a fixed income are no small things. However, one may set his ambition higher.

A bird in the bush is worth two on a woman's hat.

Had Thomas Edison lived a few hundred years ago and pressed the button the clergy would have done the rest.

I sing paeans to the man who minds his own business.

People who take pains never to do any more than they get paid for, never get paid for any more than they do.

Every preacher who preaches has two doors to his church: one where he leaves people in and the other through which he preaches them out.

Contemplation is usually safer than hustling, and when you are in doubt what to do take the advice of Seneca and do nothing.

Good people are only half as good, and bad people are only half as bad as others regard them.

When you see something new to you in art or hear a proposition in philosophy you never heard before, do not make hot haste to ridicule, deny, or refute: possibly the trouble is with yourself—who knows!

Most generally, when I travel, I go alone—this is to insure being in good company.- To travel with another is a terrible risk; it puts a great strain on the affections.

MEDICINE AMONG THE HINDOS.

B. Suryanarain Row, B. A., F. R. H. S., & M. A. S. B., Editor of the Astrological Magazine of Madras, India, writes me in regard to medical knowledge among the Hindos as follows:

Madras, 3, 4, 1901.

Dear Sir. Your kind letter of the 24th December to hand, and I thank you very much for getting me elected as a member of your learned society.

Please let me know what are the duties and liabilities of your members and what the society expects from them. I shall send my subscription after I hear from you fully on this subject.

I shall insert a futl page advertisement of yours from my May magazine. I would have done so from February last but for my absence at head quarters on account of my son's marriage. With best regards, and thanking you for kindness,

Yours very respectfully.

B. SURYANARAIN ROW.

P. S.—I do not know whether you are aware of the existence of a very elaborate and thorough system of hygiene and medicine among the Hindoos.

I shall be very glad to help you in the publication of the medical system in your journal. I have got splendid native medical gentlemen who are thorough experts in all the branches of medicine. The Hindoo knowledge of medicine three thousand years ago elicited the highest admiration of the Greeks and Arabs. I may assure you that a very large amount of the most useful information regarding the diagnosing of the diseases and their treatment successfully with simple remedies, can be obtained by a little encouragement given to the best adepts in the land who are most shamefully neglected through shere prejudice and pride of the authorities concerned. Most of the cases pronounced hopeless by the most eminent surgeons in India are often treated with remarkable success by the humble native pundits with very simple remedies.

If you you like you can publish this letter in your journal with such comments as you please. If you can see your way, either individually or as representing the interests of the Medico-Legal Society, to pay reasonable sums to encourage Indian Pundits I shall be able to furnish you with very valuable information which may be quite new to your people. Please reply.

B. S. R.

NEW HAMPSHIRE SANATORIA FOR TUBERCULOSIS.

The following action was taken last winter:

A joint resolution in favor of a committee to consider the question of a state sanitarium for consumptives, was passed, viz:

Resolved by the senate and house of representatives in general court convened:

That the governor be, and is, hereby authorized and instructed to appoint a committee consisting of three, or five, members, one of whom shall be a member of the State Board of Health, to consider the question of a state sanitarium for consumptives; and who shall report to the next legislature the best location for, and probable cost of erection and maintenance of, such an institution, together with such recommendations as they deem proper; (the report to be submitted to the legislature sometime during the first six days of the session); the committee to serve without pay, except for actual necessary expenses, which shall be paid from money in the treasury not otherwise appropriated, and the governor is hereby authorized to draw his warrant for the same.

Approved February 15, 1901.

Gov. Jordan, of New Hampshire, has appointed the following Commissioners under the Act:

Irving A. Watson, M. D., of Concord, of the State Board of Health.

Nathaniel G. Brooks, M. D., of Charleston.

Ezra Mitchell, M. D., of Charleston.

THE LONDON CONGRESS OF TUBERCULOSIS.

The following have been named as delegates from the American Congress of Tuberculosis to the British Congress of Tuberculosis, to be held in London in July next:

Clark Bell, Esq., LL. D., of New York, General Secretary of the American Congress of Tuberculosis and Editor Medico-Legal Journal.

H. Edwin Lewis, M. D., Editor Vermont Medical Monthly, Burlington, Vermont.

Augustus C. Bernays, M. D., of St. Louis, Mo., Delegate appointed by the Governor of Missouri.

Geo. Brown, M. D., of Augusta, Georgia, Military Surgeon on the Governor's Staff.

J. C. Shrader, M. D., Iowa City Delegate appointed by the Governor of Iowa, President State Board of Health.

The Board has empowered Clark Bell, Esq., General Secretary,to make additional appointments of delegates to the British Congress of Tuberculosis. All members of the Congress or of the Medico-Legal Society or its Sections, who intend going to London in July, will please communicate with Mr. Bell in respect to this Congress, as well as other foreign bodies with whom the Medico-Legal Society is in correspondence, to whom the Society usually sends delegates.

AMERICAN MEDICO-PSYCHOLOGICAL ASSOCIATION.

This body holds its 57th Annual meeting at Milwaukee, June 11th, 12th, 13th and 14th, 1901, under the Presidency of Dr. P. M. Wise, with an attractive programme, and the following Committee of Arrangements:

Richard Dewey, M. D., Wauwatosa, Wis.; W. A. Gordon, Supt. N. H. Hospital for Insane, Winnebago, Wis.; W. B. Lyman, M. D., Eau Claire, Wis.; W. J. White, M. D., Supt., Wauwatosa, Wis.; W. F. Beulter, M. D., Supt. of Chase Asylum for Insane, Wauwatosa, Wis.

PAN-AMERICAN EXPOSITION—THE MIDWAY STAR ROUTE—E. W. McCONNELL, GEN'L MANAGER.

None who visit the Exposition must miss the Midway Red Star Route. Col. McConnell has brought the wonders and marvels of the Islands of the Pacific Ocean, where our flag now floats, to help that Exposition of parts of our country.

Those who suppose that Pan-American related only to the two continents of North and South America will learn that the Stars and Stripes have extended the blessings of the freedom we enjoy, to the Islands of the distant seas.

Col. McConnell has made one of the wonderful spectacles of the Exposition. What the *Midway Plaissance* was to Chicago "The Red Star Route" is to Buffalo. It will be an object lesson, to our people, of the natives of our new possessions and the role they are to play in the America of the 20th Century.

GEO. H. DANIELS, General Passenger Agent of the New York Central and Hudson River Railroad Company, writes that if any one sends a postage stamp to him at the Grand Central Station, New York, he will send a copy of "*Saratoga the Beautiful*," and to show his opinion of the merits of this delightful resort, the genial George adds:

"AMERICA'S GREATEST WATERING PLACE—SARATOGA SPRINGS.

"No person who comes east this year from a distant point of the country, should go home without seeing SARATOGA SPRINGS, the most beautiful, as well as the most popular, watering place on this continent.

"The Annual Grand Floral Festival will be held at Saratoga the first week in September.

"Saratoga Springs is only 3¾ hours from New York; 6¾ hours from Boston; 7½ hours from Buffalo, by the NEW YORK CENTRAL."

What about the Foreign travel, the Canadians, and the New England and Seaboard, who travel west, George?

THE RHODE ISLAND MEDICAL SOCIETY.

The following officers were elected at its annual meeting on June 6, 1901.

President, George F. Keene.

Vice Presidents, Wm. R. White, and Christopher H. Banker.

DELEWARE STATE HOSPITAL FOR THE INSANE.

The officers elected June 7th, 1901, for ensuing year were:

President. Dr. John J. Black, re-elected.

Secretary, Dr. Paris T. Carlisle.

PERSONAL.

DR. FRANK W. DRAPER, of Boston, as President of the Mass. State Medical Society distinguished his official service by presenting some eminent men of letters in other professions at the 120th anniversary, June 12th, President Elliote, of

Harvard, President Capen, of Tufts. The delegates from the sister New England States, among whom we noted Dr. F. A. Stillings, of Concord, Dr. C. V. Chapen, of Providence.

Dr. R. J. PASTON, Superintendent of the South Western Hospital for the insane, of Marion Vt., has been elect President of "The American Psychological Society."

SELECTIONS.

TREATMENT OF SOME SEPTIC CONDITIONS.

To Professor Crede belongs the credit of having shown that in metallic silver of the colloid form we possess an agent which not only destroys pathogenic organisms, but renders their toxins inert and harmless. In an article, recently published in the *Medical Summary*, Dr. Max Staller, Surgeon Mt. Sinai Hospital, Philadelphia, related his experience with the unguentum Crete, a 15 per cent. preparation of soluble silver, and this report serves well to illustrate the wide range of utility of this remedy in affections of bacterial origin. During the past two years the author has treated 25 cases of erysipelas with unguentum Crete. The ointment was rubbed gently into the inflamed area for 20 to 25 minutes, by which time the greater portion had been absorbed. Any case, if seen early, was cured in 3 to 5 days. Improvement was noticeable within 5 to 6 hours, the skin losing its parchment-like appearance, becoming softer, and the burning sensations also subsiding. A case of cellultis phlegmonosa of the leg in a patient suffering with nephritis was cured within 3 days by four applications of unguentum Crete of 2 drachms each at intervals of 5 hours. In gonnorrhea at the first threatening symptoms of bubo, two or three inunctions of one-half drachm over the affected area, with rest for 24 hours, always aborted pus formation. Remarkably successful results were obtained in mammary abscess from the use of the ointment in connection with the ice bag. Even when it failed to prevent suppuration, it located the process and completely relieved the pain and discomfort. An inunction of 2 drachms, repeated at intervals of 4 hours, usually prevented pus formation if the case was seen early enough. During an epidemic of cerebro-spinal fever the author employed unguentum Crete in 7 cases, with only one death, each patient receiving 6 inunctions, besides the routine treatment. In 50 cases of scarlet fever, some of marked severity, the remedy also exerted a pronounced beneficial effect. A mixture of unguentum Crete 2 drachms, to 2 ounces of ung. aqu. rosæ, was rubbed into the body, and in none of these cases was the least trace of albumen observed in the urine.—*International Journal of Surgery.*

ALL THE GREAT RESORTS

are reached by the *New York Central Lines* and their connections. You will get a deal of valuable information in regard to the great resorts of America and how best to reach them from the now famous "FOUR TRACK SERIES," the New York Central's books of travel and education.

An Illustrated Catalogue will be sent free, prepaid, to any address, on receipt of a postage stamp, by George H. Daniels, General Passenger Agent, Grand Central Station, New York.

TRANSACTIONS.

AMERICAN CONGRESS OF TUBERCULOSIS

IN JOINT SESSION WITH

THE MEDICO-LEGAL SOCIETY.

WEDNESDAY, MAY 15, 1901, 10 A. M.

OPENING SESSION.

In the Chair:

For the Medico-Legal Society, Clark Bell, Esq., President, of New York.

For the American Congress of Tuberculosis, A. N. Bell, M. D., President, of Brooklyn.

In Joint Session.

This body met in joint session, with the Medico-Legal Society on the morning of May 15th, 1901, at the Hotel Majestic, in the city of New York, at 10 o'clock A. M., pursuant to an announcement made by the Presidents of the two organizations, under the authority and direction of the executive officers and committees of each.

The chair was occupied by Hon. Clark Bell, Esq., L L. D., President of the Medico-Legal Society, presiding for that body; and by A. N. Bell, M. D., Editor of the Sanitarian, President of the American Congress of Tuberculosis, with a large attendance of members and delegates from all parts of the American Union, the Canadas, and Central and South American States.

Mr. Clark Bell, as President of the Medico-Legal Society, called the meeting to order and made an address of welcome.

Mr. Clark Bell then introduced Dr. A. N. Bell, President of the American Congress of Tubercuosis, who made an address on "The Prevention of Tuberculosis."

On motion, carried unanimously, the following Committee on Nomination of Permanent Officers of the Congress, was appointed by the chair:

Dr. J. C. Shrader, of Iowa.

Dr. E. Beecher Hooker, of Connecticut.

Dr. J. A. McNeven, of Idaho.

Dr. A. Myers, of New York City.

Dr. Geo. Brown, of Alabama.

Dr. John A. Donavan, of Montana.

Mr. Clark Bell, in the chair, then introduced the following gentlemen, who made addresses:

Dr. E. P. Lachapelle, of Montreal, President of the Provincial Board of Health, of Montreal, Canada.

OFFICERS AND PROMINENT MEMBERS OF THE AMERICAN CONGRESS OF TUBERCULOSIS.

DR. AUGUSTUS C. BERNAYS, Vice President.
St. Louis, Mo.

DR. C. S WARD. Vice President.
Warren, Ohio.

DR. W. L. BULLARD, Vice President.
Columbus, Ga.

DR. W. E. WOODWARD,
Health Officer
Washington, D. C,

DR. H. EDWIN LEWIS,
Editor Vermont Medical Monthly.
Burlington, Vt.

DR. JOAQUIN YELA.

DR. A. E. OSBORNE,

Dr. Joaquin Yela, Consul General at New York, who presented credentials as a delegate from the Government of Guatemala.

Dr. Luis Debayle, of Leon, Nicaragua, who presented credentials from the Government of the Central American States, Nicaragua, Honduras and Ecuador.

Dr. J. A. Fortich, of Cartagena, Colombia, South America.

Dr. Henry D. Holton, of Brattleboro, Vermont, Secretary State Board of Health, and delegate appointed by the Governor of Vt.

Dr. C. F. Ulrich, of Wheeling, West Virginia, delegate appointed by the Governor of West Virginia, and Vice-President of the American Congress of Tuberculosis.

Dr. T. D. Crothers, of Hartford, Conn., Editor of the Journal of Inebriety, and Vice-President of the American Congress of Tuberculosis.

Dr. J. C. Shrader, of Iowa City, Iowa, President of the State Board of Health, and delegate appointed by the Governor of Iowa.

Dr. John H. Pryor, of Buffalo, N. Y., delegate appointed by the Governor of New York.

Dr. Cressy L. Wilbur, of Lansing, Mich., of the Department of Vital Statistics, of Michigan.

Dr. E. Beecher Hooker, of Hartford, Conn., delegate from a State Society.

Dr. J. M. Emmert, of Atlantic, Iowa; State Senator and delegate appointed by the Governor of Iowa.

Dr. R. F. Graham, of Greely, Colorado; a delegate appointed by the Governor of Colorado.

Dr. T. V. Hubbard, of Atlanta, Georgia, delegate appointed by the Governor of Georgia.

Dr. Louis LeRoy, of Nashville, Tenn., Pathologist to the State Board of Health, and delegate appointed by the Governor of Tenn.

Prof. S. H. Weeks, of Portland, Maine; delegate appointed by the Governor of Maine.

Dr. Henry Mitchell, of Trenton, N. J., Sec. of the State Board of Health, of New Jersey.

Dr. J. A. McNeven, delegate appointed by the Governor of Idaho.

Dr. Alonzo E. Austin, delegate appointed by the Governor of Alaska.

Wm. E. Woodward, Esq., M. D., Health Officer of Washington, D. C.

Dr. John A. Donovan, of Butte, Montana; a delegate appointed by the Governor of Montana. The Congress took a recess.

WEDNESDAY, MAY 15, 1901, 2 P. M.

AFTERNOON SESSION.

In the Chair:

For Medico-Legal Society, Clark Bell, Esq., President Medico-Legal Society.

For the American Congress of Tuberculosis, C. F. Ulrich, Vice-President, of West Va., and Dr. E. L. Lachapelle, of Montreal.

In Joint Session.

The report of the Nominating Committee was presented by the Chairman, Dr. J. C. Shrader, of Iowa. On motion the report was received and unanimously approved.

The following officers were then duly elected on recommendation of the Committee:

HONORARY PRESIDENT:

A. N. BELL, M. D., Brooklyn, N. Y.

PRESIDENT:

HENRY D. HOLTON, M. D., of Vermont,
Secretary State Board of Health, Brattleboro, Vt.

VICE PRESIDENTS:

HENRY B. BAKER, M. D., Lansing, Mich.
E. T. BARRICK, M. D., Toronto, Ont.
WM. BAYARD, M. D., St. John, N. B.
RALCY HUSTED BELL, M. D., New York City.
A. C. BERNAYS, M. D., St. Louis, Mo.
J. MOUNT BLEYER, M. D., New York City.
GEO. BROWN, M. D., Atlanta, Ga.
W. L. BULLARD, M. D., Columbus, Ga.
COL. E. CHANCELLOR, M. D., St. Louis, Mo.
C. K. COLE, M. D., Helena, Mont.
T. D. CROTHERS, M. D., Hartford Conn.
JUDGE ABRAM H. DAILEY, Brooklyn, N. Y.
HOM. MORITZ ELLINGER, New York City.
JUAN A. FORTICH, M. D., Cartagena, Colombia, S. A.
R. F. GRAHAM, M. D., Greely, Colorado.
A. P. GRINNELL, M. D., Burlington, Vt.
MAJOR A. HAVARD, U. S. A., Vice-Pres., Havana, Cuba.
THOS. BASSETT KEYES, M. D. Chicago, Ill.
LUIS H. LABAYLE, M, D., Leon, Nicaragua.
E. P. LACHAPELLE, M. D., Montreal, Canada.
LOUIS LEROY, M. D., Nashville, Tenn.
DR. EDOUARD LICEAGA, City of Mexico.
DWIGHT S. MOORE, M. D., Jamestown, S. Dak.
WM. H. MURRAY, M. D., Plainfield, N. J.
J. A. MCNEVEN, Gibbonsville, Idaho.
A. E. OSBORNE, M. D., Glen Ellen, Cal.
JOHN H. PRYOR, M. D., Buffalo, N. Y.
J. C. SHRADER, M. D., Iowa City, Iowa.
J. H. TYNDALE, M. D., Lincoln, Nebraska.
C. S. WARD, M. D., Warren, Ohio.
PROF. S. H. WEEKS, M. D., Portland, Maine.
CRESSY L. WILBUR, M. D., Lansing, Mich.
U. O. B. WINGATE, M. D., Milwaukee, Wis.
C. F. ULRICH, M. D., Wheeling, W. Va.

SECRETARY AND TREASURER:

CLARK BELL, Esq., City of New York.

The Nominating Committee recommended that Vice-Presidents from each State, Territory, Province or country be named hereafter, at least two from each, and selected as far as practicable from both professions of law and medicine.

It was on this recommendation, on motion, unanimously

Resolved, That the Executive Officers, or the Executive Committee, have the authority to name and appoint Vice-Presidents from States, Territories, Provinces, or foreign Countries, selected from the professions of Law and Medicine, with a view of securing representation in each country on the American Continents, of both North and South America.

The chair then introduced Dr. Henry D. Holton in a short address.

Dr. Holton took the chair of the American Congress of Tuberculosis and made a brief address, accepting the office and expressing his appreciation of the honor, and thanks for the distinction.

Dr. Holton said:

Gentlemen of the Congress:—

I have to thank you for the honor you have conferred in asking me to preside over your deliberations.

You are here for a great philanthropic purpose. Tuberculosis for a long period stood at the head as a cause of mortality, and is only second now in some localities to pneumonia. It is for you in connection with the Medico-Legal Society of New York to consider what legislation can properly be asked for, that will prevent its spread and to discuss other means of arresting its progress. Without further delay we will proceed with the work of the Congress.

On motion the Congress proceeded to the reading of papers as named on the programme:

TUBERCULOSIS AND LEGISLATION.

Paper by Clark Bell, Esq., LL.D., of New York, was read by the author; "Tuerculosis and Legislation," with symposium of replies from observers, viz:

Sir James A. Grant, M. D., of Ottawa, President of the Canadian Association for the Prevention of Tuberculosis; Dr. E. P. Lachapelle, President of the Board of Health of the Province of Quebec, Montreal, Canada; T. D. Crothers, M. D., of Hartford, Conn., Vice-President Medico-Legal Society, and of the American Congress of Tuberculosis; Hon. Moritz Ellinger, Ex-Coroner of New York City, Cor. Secretary Medico- Legal Society and Vice-President of the Amercian Congress of Tuberculosis; U. O. B. Wingate, M. D., of Milwaukee, Wis., executive officer of the State Board of Heatlh, and President of the Congress; A. P. Reid, M. D., of Middletown, Nova Scotia, Secretary of the Provincial Board of Health; George Ben Johnston, a distinguished physician of Virginia, and a delegate named by he Governor of Virginia; Dwight Shumway Moore, M. D., Supt. of North Dakota Hospital for Insane; Dr. J. W. Kime, Editor of the Iowa Medical Journal; Dr. Edward Liceaga, City of Mexico, President of the Mexican Board of Health; Dr. V. Podstata, of Illinois Hospital, Vice-President of the American Association of Assistant Physicians of Hospitals for the Insane; Dr. F. Powers, a prominent physician of Westport, Conn.; R. F. Graham,

M. D., of Greely, Colorado, a delegate appointed by the Governor of Colorado, and a Vice-President of the Congress; Henry B. Baker, Secretary of the Michigan Board of Health, and Vice-President of this Congress; General R. Harvey Reid, of Rock Springs, Surgeon Gen. of Wyoming; Major Geo. H. Torney, M. D., U. S. A., in charge of the Army and Navy General Hospital of the U. S. Government at Hot Springs, Ark., and Major A. Havard, M. D., U. S. A., Chief geon of the Army Department of Cuba.

Paper by Ex-Judge Abram H. Dailey, of Brooklyn,
"Medical Legislation from a Legal Standpoint."

Dr. C. F. Ulrich, of Wheeling, W. Va.,
"Suggestions for the Prevention of Tuberculosis from Personal Observation."

Louis J. Rosenbergh, Esq., of Detroit,
"Legal Action to Prevent the Spread of Tuberculosis."

Dr. William Bayard, of St. John, N. B.,
"The Prevention of Tuberculosis."

Dr. Edward Liceaga,
President of the Board of Health of Mexico, City of Mexico,
"The Prevention of Tuberculosis."

TREATMENT OF CONSUMPTION.

Prof. Schrotter, of Vienna,
"Contribution to the Cure of Tuberculosis in Sanitoria."
Was read in the absence of the author, by Dr. E. T. Bowers, of N. Y.

Dr. W. S. Bullard, of Columbia, Ga.,
"The Treatment of Consumption."

Dr. Geo. W. Brown, of Atlanta, Ga.,
"Treatment of Tuberculosis."

Prof. Thos. Bassett Keyes, M. D., of Chicago,
"Camp and Outdoor Life in Northern Wisconsin."

Dr. P. H. Dunlap, Battle Creek, Mich.,
"Vapor Massage in the Prevention and Cure of Tuberculosis."

Dr. J. Leffingwell Hatch, of New York City,
"Clinical Report of Cases under Dr. Crotte's Treatment."

Dr. J. F. Labadie, of New York,
"Treatment by Static Electricity."

Dr. A. E. Aronstam, of Detroit, Mich.,
"A Plea for Stricter Attention to Tuberculosis."

Carleton Simon, M. D., of New York,
"The Case of Hammenn."

In the absence of Dr. H. W. Mitchell, who was reported ill, Dr. T. D. Crothers was called to the chair of the Medico-Legal Society; and Dr. H. D. Holton, President, was in the chair of the Congress supported by Dr. E. P. Lachapelle, of Montreal.

It was moved and carried that the reading of the paper by Judge Abram H. Daily be passed on account of his engagement in Court, and that it be read later in the session.

After the reading of the paper by Vice-President C. F. Ulrich it was moved and carried that owing to the large number of papers on the programme, that it be made a standing order of the Congress, that in the absence of an author when his paper was reached on the programme, that it be read by title, unless otherwise voted by the Congress.

The paper of Dr. Edward Liceaga on the "Prevention of Tuberculosis," was read by title, to enable him to complete it more in detail, at his request, and the Secretary read a communication from him contributing an English translation of the paper he had sent to the Pan-American Congress in February, 1901, entitled, "The Treatment of Incipient Pulmonary Tuberculosis." On motion the thanks of the body was extended to Dr. Liceagua for this contribution, which was ordered printed in the transactions.

The papers under Legislation by

Capt. Upper, U. S. A., in charge of Hospital for Consumptives, Fort Bayard, New Mexico, "Prevention of Tuberculosis."

A. A. Jakoby, Esq., of New York, "Prevention of Tuberculosis."

were read by title at the request of authors, to enable them to be completed later, in time for the Bulletin.

It was suggested that discussion on these papers be deferred until the latter part of the session.

On the reading of the paper by Dr. Carleton Simon, on "The Case of Hammenn,"—the paper was discussed by Dr. C. C. Carroll, of New York, J. Mount Bleyer and others. Dr. Simon closed the debate. The Congress took a recess at 6:30 P. M.

WEDNESDAY, MAY, 15, 1901, 8 P. M.

EVENING SESSION.

In the Chair:

For the Medico-Legal Society, Ex-President, Judge Abram H. Dailey, of Brooklyn.

For the American Congress of Tuberculosis, Dr. E. P. Lachapelle, of Montreal; Dr. C. F. Ulrich, of Wheeling, W. Va., supported by Dr. H. D. Holton, President.

The following papers were read by title:

J. A. Fortich, M. D., of Cartagina, Colombia, South America; "Variety of Forms of Tuberculosis in the Mountains and the Valleys of Colombia."

Louis W. Shrading, M. D., delegate from Tenn., "Why Not Educate Against Tuberculosis."

LIGHT AND ELECTRICITY IN TREATMENT.

This order not having been completed at the afternoon session, was now taken up and, the following papers were read:

J. W. Kime, M. D., of Des Moines, Iowa, "The Role of Light in the Treatment of Tuberculosis." by title in the absence of the author.

Dr. J. Mount Bleyer, M. D., of New York,
"Light in the Treatment of Tuberculosis."
Dr. H. L. Mason, E. E., of New York,
"The Actinic Ray in the Nature of Tuberculosis."
which papers were illustrated by instruments.

SURGICAL TREATMENT OF TUBERCULOSIS.

Dr. Augustus C. Bernays, M. D., of St. Louis, not being present his paper was read by the title.
"The Results of Treatment of Tuberculosis by Surgical Entirpation."
Dr. M. M. Johnson, of Hartford, Conn., then read his paper on
"On the Surgical Treatment of Tuberculosis."
Dr. J. B. Sacasa, of Nicaragua,
"A Contribution to the Surgical Treatment of Tubercular Peritonitis." The paper was read by title at author's request.

THE ETIOLOGY OF TUBERCULOSIS.

The Order of the Etiology of Tuberculosis was then taken up and the following papers read:

By Dr. U. O. B. Wingate, of Milwaukee, Secretary State Board of Health, "Etiological Factors of Tuberculosis, other than Bacillus Tuberculosis."

By Hubbard W. Mitchell, M. D., ex-President Medico-Legal Society, "The Bacillus of Tuberculosis."

By T. D. Crothers, M. D., of Hartford, "Tuberculosis Due to Toxaemic States."

By Edwin F. Bowers, M. D., of New York, "Bioplasm in Tuberculosis."

Paper by Dr. Nils R. Finsen, of Copenhagen, Denmark, "Photo-Theraphy of Lupus Vulgaris," was read by title.

Paper by Dr. W. J. Stapleton, of Detroit, Mich., was read by title, "Symptoms of Tuberculosis."

By Dr. Albert Strauss, of San Francisco, Cal., was read by title, "The Heart in Pulmonary Tuberculosis."

By Prof. W. A. Hackett, M. D., of Detroit, Mich., was read by title, "Lupus—A Tubercular Affection of the Skin."

By Dr. Edwin Leonard, Jr., M. D., "The Basophilic Leucocyte vs. The Tubercular Bacilli," was read by the author.

Paper by Col. E. Chancellor, M. D., of St. Louis, Mo., "The Significance of Certain Physical Signs in Incipient Phytamosis—Their Diagonis Value," was read by title at author's request.

The paper by Ex-Judge Abram H. Dailey, of Brooklyn, "Medical Legislation from a Legal Standpoint," that had been passed in its order was then read. A demonstration of the papers on Light and Electricity was then reached. The Congress took a recess to 10 A. M., of May 16.

ROLL OF DELEGATES.

Appointed by Governors of States.

ALABAMA.

W. H. Blake, M. D.,
Sheffield, Ala.
Dr. C. H. Jernigan,
Birmingham, Ala.
Dr. W. J. Kernahan,
Florence, Ala.
Dr. E S. Johnson,
Troy, Ala.
Dr. R. F. Michael,
Montgomery, Ala.
Dr. J. B. Kelly,
Anniston, Ala.
Dr. J. P. Furman,
Selma, Ala.
Dr. H. A. Moody,
Mobile, Ala.
Dr. E. L. Marechal,
Mobile, Ala.
Dr. R. M. Cunningham,
Ensley, Ala.
Dr. S. J. Gay,
Lineville, Ala.
Dr. J. A. Howle,
Eclectic, Ala.
Dr. F. A. Gillespie,
Hanceville, Ala.
Dr. W. G. Somerville,
Tuscaloosa, Ala.
Dr. M. C. Schooler,
Centerville, Ala.

ALASKA.

Dr. C. D. Rogers,
Juneau, Alaska.
Dr. A. E. Austin,
17 E. 66th St., N. Y.
Dr. B. K. Wilbur,
Sitka. Alaska.

COLORADO.

Dr. J. N. Hall,
Denver, Col.
Dr. B. P. Anderson,
Colorado Springs.
Dr. R. F. Graham,
Greely, Col.
Dr. Will B. Davies,
Pueblo. Col.
Dr. J. T. Mellvin,
Saguache, Col.
Mrs W. S. Decker,
Denver, Col.

CONNECTICUT.

Dr. M. M. Johnson,
Hartford, Conn.
Dr. J. H. Townsend,
New Haven, Conn.
Dr. Elias Pratt,
Torrington, Conn.

GEORGIA.

Dr. Howard Williams,
Macon, Ga.
Dr. Geo. Brown,
Atlanta, Ga.
Dr. R. E. L. Burford,
Waynesboro, Ga.
Dr. J. B. Graham,
Atlanta, Ga.
Dr. M. F. Carson,
Griffan, Ga.
Dr. T. V. Hubbard,
Atlanta, Ga.
Dr. L. P. Hammond,
Rome, Ga.
Dr. W. F. Westmoreland,
Atlanta, Ga.
Dr. W. B. McMaster,
Waynesboro, Ga.
Dr. Jefferson Herman,
Eastman, Ga.
Dr. J. B. Morgan,
Augusta, Ga.
Dr. S. C. Benedict,
Athens, Ga.
Dr. R. Lattimore,
Savannah, Ga.
Dr. Geo. Grimes,
Columbus, Ga.
Dr. T. S. Hopkins,
Thomasville, Ga.
Dr. Arthur H. Van Dyke,
Atlanta, Ga.

IDAHO.

Dr. J. A. McNevin,
Gibbonsville. Idaho.
Dr. W. W. Watkins,
Moscow, Idaho.
Dr. W. F. Smith,
Mountain Home, Idaho.
Dr. L. P. McCalla,
Boise, Idaho.

IOWA.

Dr. J. C. Shrader,
Iowa City, Iowa.
Dr. J. M. Emmert,
Atlantic, Iowa.
Dr. Arthur Wright,
Carroll, Iowa.
Dr. Chas. M. Bowen,
Atlantic, Iowa.
Dr. J. J. Gibson,
Denison, Iowa.
Dr. Chas. S. James,
Centerville, Iowa.
Dr. Robert E. Conniff,
Sioux City, Iowa.

Dr. Donald McRae.
Council Bluffs, Iowa.
Dr. Frank J. Newberry,
Iowa City, Iowa.

KENTUCKY.

Dr. J. N. McCormick.
Bowling Green, Ky.
Dr. Chester Mayer,
Louisville, Ky.
Dr. M. K. Allen,
Louisville, Ky.

LOUISIANA.

Dr. T. E. Schumpert.
Shreveport, La.
Dr. T. S. Debayle,
New Orleans, La.
Dr. W. G. Owen,
White Castle, La.

MAINE.

Prof. S. H. Weeks.
Portland, Maine.
Dr. A. G. Young.
Augusta, Me.
Dr. F. C. Thayer,
Waterville, Me.

MICHIGAN.

Louis Rosenberg, Esq.,
Detroit, Mich.
Dr. Cressey L. Wilbur,
Lansing.

MINNESOTA.

Dr. H. L. Taylor,
St. Paul, Minn.
Dr. E. W. Buckley,
St. Paul, Minn.
Dr. J. C. Markoe,
St. Paul, Minn.
Prof. Wm. A. Hall.
Minneapolis, Minn.
Dr. Dunn,
Minneapolis, Minn.
Dr. G. S. Wattam,
Warren, Minn.
Dr. J. C. Boenm.
St. Cloud, Minn.
Dr. John F. Baker,
St. Paul, Minn.
Dr. Burnside Foster,
St. Paul, Minn.
Dr. C. K. Barlett,
Minneapolis, Minn.
Dr. J. E. Bell.
Minneapolis. Minn.
Dr. J. L. Camp,
Brainerd. Minn.
Dr. J. B. McGaughtey,
Winona, Minn.
Dr. C. E. Caine,
Morris, Minn.

MISSOURI.

Dr. Frank J. Lutz.
St. Louis, Mo.
Dr. E. L. Priest.
Nevada, Mo.
Dr. J. Martin,
Kahota, Mo.
Dr. S. A. Proctor.
Donipan, Mo.
Dr. C. H. Rigg.
Middletown, Mo.
Dr. S. O. Davis.
Warsaw, Mo.
Dr. E. H. Chinn.
Rocheport, Mo.
Dr. R. L. Hamilton.
Richmond, Mo.
Dr. U. S. Wright.
Fayette, Mo.
Dr. J. L. Eaton,
Irondale, Mo.
Dr. J. Pettijohn.
Brookfield, Mo.
Dr. A. C. Bernays.
St. Louis, Mo.
Dr. R. L. Willis,
Neosho, Mo.
Dr. William F. Kuhn,
Kansas City, Mo.
Dr. J. T. McClanahan,
Booneville, Mo.
Dr. G. A. Goben,
Kirksville, Mo.
Dr. C. H. Fulbright.
St. James, Mo.
Dr. W. E. Shelton,
Appleton, Mo.
Dr. C. W. Chastine,
Plattsburg, Mo.
Dr. W. L. Ray.
Fulton, Mo.
Dr. L. T. Hall.
Potosi, Mo.
Dr. Wm. H. Grandall.
Birch Tree, Mo.
Dr. W. L. Crawford,
Sedalia, Mo.
Dr. J. P. Porth,
Jefferson City, Mo.

MONTANA.

Dr. Ernest Crutcher,
Great Falls, Mon.
Dr. L. C. Bruning.
Miles City, Mon.
Dr. W. D. Tuttle,
Helena, Mon.

NEBRASKA.

Dr. J. H. Tyndale,
Lincoln.

NEW HAMPSHIRE.

Dr. J. W. Fellows.
Manchester, N. H.

Dr. G. P. Conn,
Concord, N. H.
F. A. Stillings, M. D.,
Concord, N. H.
Henry Marble, M. D.,
Gorham, N. H.

NEW JERSEY.

Dr. Lucius F. Donohue,
Bayonne.
Dr. E. J. Marsh,
Patterson.
Dr. Henry M. Mitchell,
Trenton.
Dr. W. H. Newton,
Patterson.
Dr. Thos. H. McLean,
Elizabeth.
Dr. W. H. Murray,
Plainfield.

NEW MEXICO.

Dr. Geo. W. Harrison.
Albuquerque, N. M.
Dr. Geo. C. Bryan,
Alamagorda, N. M.
Dr. E. B. Shaw,
Las Vegas, N. M.
Dr. J. J. Shuler,
Raton, N. M.
Dr. Francis Crosson,
Albuquerque, N. M.
Dr. J. H. Sloan,
Santa Fe, N. M.
Dr. G. G. Cruikshank,
San Marcial, N. M.

NEW YORK.

Dr. Frederick C. Curtis,
Albany, N. Y.
Dr. John H. Pryor,
Buffalo, N. Y.
Dr. Alfred Meyer,
New York City.

SOUTH CAROLINA.

Dr. F. Barker,
Medical College,
Charleston, S. C.
Dr. Charles F. McGahan,
Aiken, S. C.
Dr. W. R. Lowman.
Orangeburg, S. C.
Dr. R. G. De Sassure,
Pres. Medical Society
of Charleston, S. C.
Dr. B. W. Taylor,
Columbia, S. C.
Dr. T. Grange Simons,
Charleston, S. C.
Dr. J. W. Babcock,
Columbia, S. C.
Dr. George R. Dean.
Spartanburg, S. C.

SOUTH DAKOTA.

Dr. E. L. Diefendorf.
Aberdeen, S. Dak.
Dr. Robinson,
Pierre, S. Dak.
Dr. F. A. Spofford,
Flandrau, S. Dak.

TENNESSEE.

Dr. Louis Leroy,
Nashville.

VERMONT.

Dr. Charles S. Caverly,
Rutland, Vt.
Dr. Truman Stiles,
St. Johnsburg, Vt.
Dr. Henry D. Holton,
Battleboro, Vt.

VIRGINIA.

Dr. W. F. Drewrey,
Petersburg, Va.
Dr. Geo. Ben Johnson,
Richmond, Va.
Prof. E. G. Williams,
Richmond, Va.

WASHINGTON.

Dr. Ralcy Husted Bell,
New York City.
Edward H. Thomas, Esq.,
Whatcome, Wash'n.
Hon. Watson C. Squire,
Ex-Senator from Wash.
New York City.

WEST VIRGINIA.

Dr. C. F. Ulrich,
718 Main St., Wheeling, W. Va.
Dr. H. D. Hatfield,
Thacker, W. Va.
Dr. J. P. Fitch,
Morgantown, W. Va.
Dr. T. L. Barber,
Charleston, W. Va.
Dr. D. Hatfield,
Parkersburg, W. Va.

WISCONSIN.

Dr. Solon Marks,
Milwaukee, Wis.
G. W. Harrison,
Ashland, Wis.
Dr. F. C. Suiter,
La Crosse, Wis.
Dr. W. O. B. Wingate,
Milwaukee, Wis.
Dr. Q. O. Sutherland,
Janesville, Wis.
Wm. F. Whyte,
Watertown, Wis.
Dr. J. H. McNeel,
Fond du Lac, Wis.

DELEGATES

Appointed by State and local Societies who were present or represented:

Dr. Henneage Gibbes,
Detroit, Mich.
From Detroit Academy of Medicine.
Dr. W. E. Woodward,
of Washington.
From the Medical Society of the District of Columbia.
Dr. John A. Robinson,
Illinois State Medical Society
Dr. M. R. Crain,
Rutland, Vt.
State Medical Society of Vermont.
John A. Donavan, M. D.,
Butte, Mont., Montana State Medical Society.
H. Edwin Lewis, M. D.,
Burlington, Vt., Vermont State Medical Society.
E. P. Lachapelle, M. D.,
Montreal, Union Medicale de Canada.
E. P. Benoit, M. D.,
Montreal, Union Medicale de Canada.
Jas. E. Newcome, M. D.,
N. Y. City, American Laryngolical Assoc'n.

(Delegates of this class not present will be named later in the Bulletin.)

Note by Secretary:—We are unable to give complete list of State Delegates because some of the Governors did not report their lists delegates. The same with State and other societies.

The Bulletin will contain as full a list as possible and also the roll of members:

The following have been appointed Executive Committee:
Clark Bell, Esq., of New York, Chairman.
Henry B. Baker, M. D., of Lansing Mich.
T. D. Crothers, M. D., Hartford, Conn.
Judge Abram H. Dailey, of Brooklyn, N. Y.
Moritz Ellinger, Esq., New York City.
E. P. Lachepelle, M. D., of Montreal.
J. C. Shroeder, M. D., of Iowa City, Iowa.

EX-OFFICIO

Dr. A. N. Bell, of Brooklyn, honorary president.
Dr. Henry D. Holton, president.
Four shall constitute a quorum or any three with the chairman.

[*To be continued.*]

AMERICAN CONGRESS OF TUBERCULOSIS.

ADDRESS OF WELCOME.

BY CLARK BELL, ESQ., LL. D., PRESIDENT MEDICO LEGAL SOCIETY.

The Second American Congress of Tuberculosis convened in conjunction with the New York Medico-Legal Society as per announcement, on the morning of May 15, 1901, at the Hotel Majestic, in the city of New York.

There was an audience of about fifty members of the society and delegates to the Congress from several States of the Union, from Canada and other Central and South American nationalities present, representative of the interest in the purpose of the Congress, by the civil authorities from whom they presented credentials.

The convention was called to order and welcomed by Clark Bell, Esq., President of the Medico-Legal Society.

My Dear Colleagues of the Medico-Legal Society, Officers and Members of and Delegates to the American Congress of Tuberculosis: It is due to you and through you to not alone the professions of Law and Medicine, but to the great mass of people, who are so deeply afflicted by the dread disease, which is so terribly destructive to human life, that some reasons and perhaps explanations should be made for the organization of this Congress.

The Medico-Legal Society, which long ago ceased to be a local body, is not only National but International in its scope, influence and action, has come to consider the question of appropriate legislation to prevent the spread of tuberculosis as one of the supreme and most profoundly important questions of forensic medicine that is likely to come under the examination of lawyers, physicians, law-makers and statesmen, who study the welfare of the race.

You meet to consider tuberculosis in all its aspects, but above all the means for its prevention. Its nature, characteristics, extent and results are and should be fruitful themes for your careful examination and most scrutinizing study, but the overpowering, all-important and crucial question of all is, from a medico-legal view point, can its spread be averted by legislation, or can legislation aid in its prevention?

The most thoughtful men in Great Britain, three years since, organized a movement for the United Kingdom, in which the ablest lawyers, physicians and statesmen united for the consideration of this great question, over which the Prince of Wales presided, and in which he was deeply interested. It set in motion a world-wide question along lines of the broadest statesmanship.

Italy followed with a similar movement, in which the evil wa recognized and its enormous interest conceded. The scholars of that country also asked what was the duty of the race in such a peril, and how could the ravages of that dread devastation be even diminished?

There seemed to be no action contemplated by the great medical bodies in our country to organize any movement for the prevention of tuberculosis. The lamentable death of Dr. A. L. Loomis appeared to be on the eve of such a movement, and had his life been prolonged there is good reason to think that ere now he would have aroused the medical profession of our country to a united effort for the prevention of consumption.

In default of any such effort by the medical profession in this country, the Medico-Legal Society, following example of the united professions and men of affairs who organized the British association, before referred to, obtained the co-operation of the professions. The Medico-Legal Society initiated the movement in February, 1900, and organized the body which to-day holds its second annual session.

The report of last year's Congress, with its printed Part I of its Bulletin, was presented to the 13th International Medical Congress at Paris in August, 1900, by a select committee of the American Congress.

The most remarkable, and to my mind the most important, action co-ordinate was organized in the Canadian provinces last February. At a conference among the best lawyers, statesmen and physicians of the Dominion of Canada held at Ottawa, the Society for the Prevention of Tuberculosis was formed. His Excellency Earl Minto presided, the Lieutenant-Governors of the several provinces were made vice-presidents, and the management intrusted to Sir James Grant, M.

D., as president, and two officials from each province, one a physician and one a lawyer or member of the Dominion or Provincial Parliament.

This body is most distinctly under the authority and protection of the Government, and I predict for it a marked success in the Dominion of Canada.

It would not be proper or right for me in this place or on this occasion to omit to notice the organization of a society at Toronto, in Ontario, which has already made itself felt in the legislation of that province under the presidency of Dr. E. J. Barrick, of Toronto, a member of this Congress, and who will address you on a phase of this question, and to the labors of his colleague, Dr. Bryce, of the Board of Health of Ontario, who have placed that Province in the vanguard of practical legislative action, looking towards the arrest and spread of consumption.

It is also worthy of mention that a society has been organized in the State of Illinois, entitled "The Illinois Society for the Prevention of Tuberculosis," of which Dr. John A. Robinson, an eminent physician of Illinois, is secretary, who is a member of this congress, and who will present a paper "On the Need of a National Interstate Society for the Prevention of Tuberculosis."

A second session of the British Association has been called to meet next July in London, and invitations have been sent to foreign countries, to send delegates to its meeting, at which the then Prince of Wales had consented to preside before he came to the throne.

That body has sent an invitation to the American Congress of Tuberculosis to send delegates there at the July session of 1901.

In order that the medical profession might be fully represented throughout the nation, all the State medical societies and all the academies of medicine have been invited to enroll and co-operate, and to send delegates to this session, some of whom have done so.

The question of the construction of sanatoria in the States is attracting great attention, and the most important feature of this conference is that the Governors of all the States and Territories of the Union and of Canada, and of the States of South and Central America were invited to send delegates here. The Governors have very generally made the appointments, only two Governors in the Union declining, and the illness of one and absence of others has prevented their selection in a few states; but the nature of other delegates selected have not reached the officers of this body.

The shortness of the time prevents many of the Central and South American States from being represented, but notice has been given that all papers contributed to this Congress, which reach its officers after the session and prior to August 15th will still be embraced in its Bulletin.

This, gentlemen, brings me to a more agreeable duty, that of presenting the President of the American Congress of Tuberculosis, Dr. A. N. Bell, the veteran sanitarian, who for more than a quarter of a century has been at the head of sanitary science in our country, but who, on account of deafness, desires to vacate the chair on your election of a successor.

As two bodies are here meeting in joint session, I hope that the selection of his successor and of permanent officers of this American Congress will be deferred until after the opening exercises are concluded, except the appointment of a nominating committee, whose report can be accepted at the afternoon session of 2 p. m.

THE PREVENTION OF TUBERCULOSIS.

By A. N. Bell, A. M., M. D., President of the American Congress of Tuberculosis, New York, May 15, 1901.

This Congress is in perpetuation of the first American Congress of Tuberculosis, held here in February, last year, which as you have already been informed, was prompted by the organization of the National Association for the Prevention of Consumption, in London, the year before. The striking similarity of the membership of that organization to that of the New York Medico-Legal Society, inasmuch as it was composed of physicians and lawyers, and of the most intelligent and progressive persons of other pursuits, eminently available for the promotion of the objects of the organization, was promptly grasped by the ever vigilant and aggressive altruist who has just addressed you, and it is to him especially that this organization owes its existence.

The nature of Tuberculosis is now common knowledge. All intelligent persons now know that it is contagious and that it is the most universally prevalent and fatal disease that afflicts the human race. Yet it is known to be preventible; and the prevention of Tuberculosis is the now leading thought of sanitarians everywhere. The purpose of this Congress is to aid in the practical application of this thought.

Tuberculosis in all its forms is the work of a microbe, the tubercle bacillus, a living organism, which when it once gains foothold in a susceptible subject, multiplies in countless millions. It is by the transmission of these bacilli from person to person and from animals to persons that tuberculosis is communicated. The chief way by which they are transmitted is by means of the expectoration of affected persons, which contains them in myriads, and when the expectorated matter becomes dry, the germs are disseminated in the form of dust round about and liable to be inhaled by persons or animals in the vicinity. And, unfortunately, consumption is so prevalent and insidious that progressive health authorities have recognized the danger of expectoration in all places where the sputum is likely to dry and leave its residue to be disseminated in the air and become the means of spreading consumption, and have instituted measures for its prevention. Such efforts are praiseworthy and should be enforced to the utmost extent, as should be also the kindred practice of collecting and destroying the sputum of known consumptives everywhere; but such efforts are essentially of small scope when considered in relation to the universal distribution of tubercle bacilli, whose maintenance everywhere evidently depends upon susceptible subjects among the lower animals as well as mankind.

Tuberculosis has been long known to be no less universal and fatal among domestic animals, especially those of the bovine species, than among mankind; and for the most part the conditions of its prevalence are the same in both.

That consumption is not everywhere and in all places correspondingly prevalent with the germs round about is because persons in sound health possess the physiological power of resisting and destroying them. The natural secretions of the respiratory organs of healthy persons arrest and devour them by oxidation, and they are cast off.

There must be besides the seed the soil adapted to their planting and nutrition, otherwise they cannot obtain foothold. But the cosmopolitan nature, various propensities, occupations and habits of mankind are such as to always present a more or less fruitful soil for the maintenance of tubercle bacilli. And no community, to our knowledge, surpasses New York in the display of the predisposing conditions. Moreover, it is an old story to some of us who have taken notice of its rehearsal for many years.

Indeed, it may be said of the health department of this city from the time of its first organization on a scientific basis thirty-five years ago to the present time, it has constantly exhibited the predisposing conditions of tuberculosis in the community.

The exceeding prevalence of consumption in the crowded and filthy tenement houses among the stifled, poorly nourished and badly clad occupants, the relative prevalence of the disease in the different wards of the city with relation to density of population, and the Factory Inspector's display of the disease-distributing sweatshops are not new revelations.

OFFICERS, AUTHORS AND PROMINENT MEMBERS OF THE AMERICAN CONGRESS OF TUBERCULOSIS.

J. B. CLAYBERG, ESQ.,
'ice-President for State of Montana,
Helena, Mont.

SAMUEL BELL THOMAS, ESQ.,
Assistant Secretary Medico-Legal Society
of New York City.

DR C. C. CARROLL,
New York City.

MORITZ ELLINGER, ESQ.,
of New York Vice-Pres.
Am. Congress of Tuberculosis.

DR. J. HILDEGARDE TYNDALE,
Lincoln, Neb., Vice-Pres.
Am. Congress of Tuberculosis.

. W. P. SMITHWICK, M. D.,
e-President from N. Carolina,
La Grange, N. C.

J. A McNEVEN, M D.,
V. P. Am. Cong Tuberculosis,
Gibbonsville, Idaho.

M. M. SMITH, M. D.,
of Austin Tex., Vice-Pres. for
Texas, Am Cong. of Tuberculosis.

Some of us have had familiar knowledge of these cultures for more than forty years. But it is only just now, as it were, that they have been intelligently recognized by the law-makers. The new tenement house law and the establishment of sanatoria for the poor victims of the preventible conditions referred to, are encouraging indications. But approximate conditions pervade the community and society at large. It is for the promotion of efforts to overcome such conditions wherever they exist, that this Congress has been organized.

From a physiological standpoint, all observers appreciate the important difference which exists in regard to the requirements of nutrition between the young of all animals and those of mature growth, and in none is it more marked than in the human species. In infancy, and throughout the growing period of life, not only is it necessary to repair the waste of tissues constantly going on in the young as well as in the old, but the frame has to be built up to the degree of development it is destined to reach. To meet this demand on the part of the animal economy, is the foundation of the enormous appetites and rapid digestion common to the young of all animals. Every organ of the body, in addition to sustenance, appropriates the additional amount of nutriment necessary to give it required bulk. The current of nutritive life in the young is, therefore, an exceedingly rapid one, and the especially remarkable feature of it is that the blood itself, from which the organism is built up, receives its impressions and modifications—its constitutional predisposition—chiefly from the nature of the food during the growing period of life. Such, indeed, is the main foundation of the so-called "hereditary" diseases, for it is well known that the offspring of progenitors with well-marked constitutional tendencies may often have their hereditary tendencies wholly overcome, and a radical change effected, by a change in the quality of the nutriment and the physical surroundings; and, on the contrary, the offspring of those possessed of the highest degree of physical organization may be dwarfed to the lowest degree of degeneracy by withholding the necessary conditions of healthy development, or by subjecting them to poor food and a vitiated atmosphere deprived of sunlight.

That city cow-stable milk, is peculiarly liable to produce diarrhoea, debility and marrasmus in infants has been long known; and recent knowledge shows that intestinal tuberculosis is communicated by the same means.

Other food, of adults as well as of children, is liable to tuberculous contamination by exposure to the germs afloat as dust in the atmosphere, and particularly in rooms that have been or are occupied by consumptives, or to the dust shaken from clothing and bedding that has been so exposed. This danger is the greater, since facts demonstrate that the tubercle bacillus preserves its virulence through three or four removes, and that successful inoculations have been made with tubercular matter from a patient who had been dead for thirty-six hours, and with sputum which had been in a dried condition for twenty days. In experiments on animals, it has been found to produce no effect after having been boiled, provided the boiling was thorough. Some veterinarians believe that it is communicated by forage, soiled by the expectorations of diseased animals and consumed by the healthy.

It is notable, in this respect, that in the marked progress of practical sanitation in recent years veterinarians are in the vanguard, and chiefly because people are wont to respond with more alacrity and with greater liberality for the suppression of an epizootic among their horses or a pleuropneumonia among the horned cattle than for the arrest of small-pox or the prevention of consumption. Individuals, communities and States will make liberal appropriations to improve the breed of stock or contribute to the contest for a prize at a dog-show, while they will refuse assistance or oppose a tax for the admission of air and sunlight into a stunting school, or for the drainage of a marsh which by its emanations and cultivation of mosquitoes is a perennial source of human degeneracy, disease and death. It is, therefore, fortunate, that in the progress of veterinary sanitary science, it has been discovered that many of the most fatal and loathsome diseases which afflict the human race are equally common to—if, indeed, they do not actually take their rise from—domestic animals. Tuberculosis, scrofula, small-pox, syphilis, malignant pustule, hydrophobia and trichinosis are examples. Veterinary sanitary science, therefore, may well be regarded as the right arm of public hygiene.

In conclusion, it has been my purpose rather to display the field of labor for the prevention of tuberculosis than to attempt any detail of the procedures. It is sufficiently comprehensive and, I think, sufficiently perspicuous to enlist the co-operation of all intelligent people.

But it is incumbent for me to no longer be an obstacle to the work of the congress by my incompetency for this chair. The imperfection of my hearing is such as to make it impossible for me to keep the run of the proceedings. I, therefore, resign the honor of longer presiding, and request that you proceed to elect a successor.

ROENTGEN SOCIEMY OF THE. U S.

This body announces its second annual meeting at the University of Buffalo, on September 10-11, 1901. The following are its officers:

Dr. Heber Robarts, President, Editor of the American X-Ray Journal, 301 Chemical Building, St. Louis, Mo.

Dr. G. P. Girdwood, First Vice-President, Montreal, Canada.

Dr. H. P. Bender, Second Vice-President, Brooklyn, N. Y.

Dr. J. Rud'is-Jicinsky, Secretary, Cedar Rapids, Iowa.

W. A. Price, D. D. S. M. E., Assistant Secretary, Cleveland, O.

Dr. E. A. Florentine, Treasurer, 507 So. Washington St., Saginaw, Mich.

Its committee on Medico-Legal matters is as follows:

Dr. Mihran K. Kassabian, Chairman, 1808 Green St., Philadelphia, Pa.

Dr. F. Wessley Sells, Murray, Iowa.

Dr. Constantine V. S. Boettger, Ottawa, Ont., Canada.

Dr. Frank Ring, 612 Chemical Building, St. Louis, Mo.

Mrs. E. Fleischman-Aschhiem, 611 Sutter St., San Francisco, Cal.

Dr. S. D. Brooks, Surgeon, U. S. Marine Hospital, Portland, Oregon.

C. Edmund Kells, Jr., D. D. S., Medical Building, New Orleans, La.

The society solicits members. Price of admission $5, and its programme will be completed and mailed to members by August 25, 1901.

JOURNALS AND BOOKS.

RECOLLECTIONS OF A REBEL SURGEON. By Dr. F. A. Daniel, Austin, Texas.

There is a medical journal published at Austin, Texas, which rejoices and blossoms monthly, in the wondertul climate of that luxuriant State of the Lone Star, in a cover as brightly red as the Chinaman's deepest vermilion.

Its editor, originator and publisher is as genial a specimen of a Doctor as any one would wish to see, Dr. F. E. Daniel, and he is the author, when his hair has grown gray, of the reminiscences of the War of the Rebellion in 1861, when he was in his salad days, a soldier in the army of the Great Rebellion.

He calls his journal "*The Redback*," and he goes to his office and writes his reminiscences of the war, when he was a boy, with a gusto impossible to either imitate or excel.

To those who have seen this Doctor in his den in Austin, this Douglass in his hall, who have been warmed by his hospitable wine, and tasted of all the sweets of life as it is lived in Austin, under the inspiration of his voice and smile, the book will recall the genial Doctor, whom he dubs as "Fat Philosopher," "Jolly old Doctor" and "Our Genial Friend." Daniel always did draw on a lively imagination, but never more so than when he calls himself a "Fat Philosopher."

But to read this book brought recollections of one of the pleasant *red letter* visits of my life, at the Texas capital, of that "Texas Daniel," who was not he of the "Lion's Den" and was always spelling his name without an "s," or else "cursing" the other fellow who did.

There was a deal of good stuff ie this same "Daniel" of the "Texas Journal," who was, in his youth, "a rebel surgeon," and who had two weaknesses—he was "fond of fishing" and fond of "Swearingin."

To his passion for the rod and his worship of Isaac Walton he devoted much of a useful life. Fishing was all in all to Dr. Daniel. Then to his love of his friends, and among them all "Swearingin." His love was like that of David and Jonathan.

I knew Swearingin and Daniel's affection was well bestowed. If it was a weakness, it was a human, a touching, a beautiful one.

The sweetest thing between the covers of the Doctor's book, that I read with delight, is his dedication of it to the memory of his old friend, to whom his heart clung all the more tenderly and lovingly when the Doctor had come back to his children from the grave of their mother.

THE NEW YORK INSTITUTION FOR THE DEAF AND DUMB. Dr. E. H. Currier sends the 82nd Annual Report of the oldest institution for the deaf and dumb on this continent.

It is splendidly illustrated and shows the value of this superb work for this unfortunate class of men, to whom Dr. Isaac L. Peet gave so many years of his loving and devoted life.

But in a work so profusely illustrated we wondered that it contained no portrait nor a more compfete record of the life of Judge Enoch L. Fancher, who was for more than forty years a Director and for the past fourteen years President of that institution, which was deeply indebted to his laborious and painstaking labor throughout a long and useful life.

ALLGEMEINE ZEITSCHRIFT FÜR PSYCHIATRIE, PSYCHISCH-GERICHTLICHE MEDIZINE. H. Lachs, Editor, Berlin.

The May number, 1901, contains the following articles:

"Clinical Contributions to Katatonie." By Von Schule.

"On the Prognosis of Epilepsie" By Dr. Habermaas.

"Tetania and Psychose." By Dr. Luther. [inger.

"Kretinical Psychose in the Institution at Zürich." By Dr. Bertsch-

"On so-called Menstrual Psychoses." By. Aug. Heger-Illenau.

"Ætiology of Progressive Paralysis in the Tyrol." By Dr. Geo. Eisath.

"Hysterical Stupor with Prisoners." By Dr. Raecke.

"Clinical Forms of Prison Psychoses." By Ernst Rüden.

"On the Relations between Neurology and Transitory Psychoses." By R. V. Krafft-Ebing.

Congress of Southwest German Alienists, at Karlsruhe, of the Psychiatrical Society of the Rhine Province, and the Psychiatrical Society at Berlin.

ZEITSCHRIFT FÜR MEDIZINALBEAMTE. Dr. Otto Raxmund, Editor, Minden on the Weser.

No. 10, of May, 1901, contains the following articles:

Original Contributions. Guardianship by Reason of Mental Disability. By Court Counsellor Hahn.

From Meetings and Societies. Report on the Tenth Session of the Society of the Medical Officers of the District of Gumbirmen.

Minor Contributions and Clippings from Periodicals.

A *Judicial Medicine and Psychiatry:*

Pinoy: Experimental Study of the Effect of the Kalium Kantharidate upon the Placenta of the Guinea Pig.

Pinoy and Miss Densusian: Effect of the Kantharidine sour Kali upon the Nerve Cell.

Ch. Achard and M. Lœper: The White Blood Corpuscles in Some Poison Cases.

M. Nicloux: Does the Blood of Normal or Narcotic Animals Contain Coal Oxyd?

Dr. H. Kreuser: Late Reconvalescences in Mental Diseases.

Dr. Paul Steffans: On three cases of Hysteria Magna.

Dr. E. Myers: Contribution to the Science of the Induced Irrationality and the Querulous Delusion.

B. *Bacteriology, Infectious Diseases, Hygiene and Public Sanitary Matters:*

G. Hayem and R. Bensande: Peculiarity of the Blood Corpuscle and Blood Serum in the Primary Variola Hæmorrhagica - Mechanism of Hemorrhages.

Dr. Lahmer: On the treatment of the Melaena Neonatorum.

Dr. Norbert Scoobada: Is there a Melaena Vera?

L. Nattan-Larrier: Experimental Mastitistuberculosis of the Guinea Pig.

J. Mitchell Wilson, J. Wright Mason and F. W. Martin: On the seizing and condemnation of meat containing tuberculosis.

Dr. Geo. Frank. On the effect of disinfection of alcohol, especially of alcoholic vapors.

Dr. M. L. J. S. Lœblowitz: Women Asylums. A Hygienical Study.

THE JOURNAL OF MENTAL PATHOLOGY. Louise Robinovitch, Editor. New York.

The first number, devoted to mental medicine, is on our table. It has an extraordinary array of talent in its "Editorial Board," Drs Magnan Joffroy and Raymond, of Paris; Dr. Jul. Morel, of Belgium, and E. Regis, of Bordeaux, from the Continent, and Profs. C. H. Huges and C. K. Mills, of our leading Psychiatrists.

Dr. Louise G. Robinovitch, the Editor, was a pupil of Magnan and has had a valuable training at St. Anne, Paris.

She was a delegate from the Medico-Legal Society to the Psychological Section, and that of Mental Medicine of the Paris International Congress of 1900, and arranged there for a corps of contributors from the Continent, of exceptional strength and ability, for her Journal.

The leading article of the opening number is by the Editor, on "Idiot and Imbecile Children," based on her personal observation.

Dr. A. Marie contributes an article on "Psycho-Motor Hallucinations in General Paralysis."

Dr. G. C. Ferrari, Editor of the Italian Journal, "Revista Sperimentale de Freniatria," contributes a short paper, being a clinical study of seven cases of "Circular Insanity," made in 1898 and 1899, and contrasting results with similar studies in 1893 and 1894.

Dr. Paul Parez, of Paris, gives a short paper, entitled "Suggestion During Natural Sleep."

Drs. Paul Serieux and F. Farnarier report on a case of verbal blindness and deafness with an autopsy.

Dr. Robinovitch has had suitable training and education to fit her for the role she has assumed.

She has aimed high in her ideals. There is abundant room for such a journal, and if she has the aid of a tithe of the talent she places on her list, she will make a journal of the first rank in the whole realm of Mental Medicine.

THE SANITARIAN. Dr. A. N. Bell, Editor.

The June number contains the opening addresses made at the American Congress of Tuberculosis, and a list of the officers elected at the second session. It promises a more complete account of that body and its important papers in future numbers.

An important abstract is made from the Bulletin of the Chicago Health Department for March, 1901, on "Influenza as a factor of recent mortality in the city of Chicago," showing that pneumonia, in that city, has advanced to the first place as to causes of death, usurping the position that pulmonary consumption had occupied for many years.

We extract this data :	1889	1890	1891.
Total deaths from all causes.............	16,496	21,856	27,754
Rated as to 1,000 of population, per cent..	18.11	19.87	23.92
Deaths from pneumonia...................	1,170	2,073	2,898
Ratio per 10,000 of population, per cent...	12.05	18.8	25.0
Deaths from consumption................	1,489	1,927	2,120
Ratio per 10,000 of population, per cent...	15.9	17.9	18.3

R. S. Guernsey, of the New York Bar, continues his article on "Taxation and Altruism."

The veteran Editor, Dr. A. N. Bell, shows the same virility and strength in his work that has characterized his labor for the past twenty years. He has valuable collaborators and stands at the head of the front of Sanitary Science in this country.

He has occupied a central and commanding figure in the enormous work of organizing the American Congress of Tuberculosis, and declined a re-lection to the Presidency of that body on account of his disability of hearing, which interfered with his duties as a presiding officer.

He was honored with the Emeritus well-earned position of Honorary President.

We publish his portrait in the current number with pride and pleasure, as he has pulled a strong stroke oar in the preliminary work

Dr. Henry D. Holton, who succeeds him as President of the American Congress of Tuberculosis, is perhaps one of the best equipped men on the western hemisphere for the work laid out for the future of that organization.

As Secretary of the State Board of Health of Vermont he is in close touch with the work, in this direction, throughout the United States and the Canadas.

He is an admirable presiding officer and will have a large influence in bringing into the work of the body members of the local and State Boards of Health, throughout the Union. His portrait appears in our current number, in the group with Dr. A. N. Bell.

EDWARD BOK, in LADIES' HOME JOURNAL, advises mothers to take their children to a farm for their summer vacation and to "avoid the Summer Hotel." He says:

"It is the essence of the lives that are lived in the country that we need so much in our lives: the essence of simplicity, of sincerity, of freedom from things which are external and not worth while. We cannot, of course, live in the city and live as do country folk. What we can do, however, is to go to the country in the summertime and live with them and extract some of the wholesome lessons of simple living which their lives can teach us. The love of Nature is implanted in all of us to a more or less degree: the crime to ourselves is that we give it so little chance of development or expression. And the crime is doubled when we withhold the expressions of Nature's workings in our children."

REVIEW OF REVIEWS. Albert Shaw, Editor.

This splendid journal maintains its high standard. It has a fine presentation of the Pan-American Exposition at Buffalo, with illustrations and a fair notice of the Exposition at Glasgow; a fine notice of the Southern Educational Conference, at Salem, North Carolina, in April.

The comment on the career of the late Prof. Henry A. Rowlands is well placed and well deserved.

Sylvester Baxter contributes a disappointing article on "The Winning War Against Consumption," a subject of great public interest, which the writer seems not to have studied critically. There is nothing new in the article, and its statements of statistical knowledge are not carefully made. The splendid work done in the Dominion of Canada this year, in the line of preventive legislation, is ignored, and it is doubtful if the writer knew of it. The article seems to have been more in the nature of an advertisement of Dr. Knopf's book than a serious article on an important subject.

He is of the opinion that "It is now definitely established that consumption is a curable disease," and he asserts that "With the new methods it is no longer necessary for the patient to seek a climate of the kind that has been supposed to possess some specific property against the disease."

ANNALES DE LA SOCIETE DE MEDICINE LEGALE DE BELGIQUE CHARLEROI. Dr. de Nobele, Editor. Ghent. 1901.

No. 4 of the 12th year is on our table. The number contains the transactions of the session of January 26, 1901, of the Medico Legal Society of Belgium, under the presidency of Dr. Le Brun.

M. Busschere and Dr. Berer were elected 1st and 2nd Vice-Presidents of the Society,

The Report of Drs. Corin and De Ryckere upon the question: "At What Time May the Medico-Legal Jurist Perform an Autopsy?" was then taken up and the question discussed by Drs. Vleninckx, De Ryckere, Hendrix, Le Brun, Corin, and the question laid over for further discussion.

THE SOUTHERN LAW REVIEW Hon. W. R. Hammond, Editor, Atlanta, Ga.

No. 1 of Vol. 1 is before us Mr. Hammond certainly presents his initial number of a new Law Journal under more than ordinarily favorable auspices.

The late Chief Justice Bleckley, of the Supreme Bench of Georgia, makes a personal appeal to the profession, in which he endorses Hon W. R Hammond as the Editor of the Journal.

Judge Samuel Lumpkin, of the Supreme Bench, contributes the leading article on "The Power of the Trial Courts of Georgia, as compared with that of the Supreme Court."

Wm. J. Curtis contributes an excellent historical sketch of James Kent, and the masterly oration of Hon. Joseph R. Lamar, President of the Bar

Association of Georgia, pronounced before that body in July, 1900, is a splendid paper for all time.

The editorial work shows that Mr. Hammond can pull a good stroke oar. We predict a succesful future for the Journal.

There is no reason why Georgia should not furnish for the Bar of the Southeastern and Southern States a Journal of high character.

Georgia, as it seemed to me in passing through that State, has felt the impulse of the business energies of the nation more than any Southern State of the seaboard or the South, save Texas.

Atlanta had all the characteristics of a thriving western city, and was not in any respect like other Southern cities. Birmingham was as lively a town as any in the nation. The Cotton Mill has gone to Georgia and awakened a new interest and a new life. Why should not the Law Journal follow and keep pace with the Cotton Mill?

Die Entmündung Geistesgestörten — für Juristen und Sachverstændige. By Prof. Dr. Herman Kornfeld, Privy Councillor and Government Physician at Gleiwitz, Silecia. Published by Ferdinand Enke, Stuttgart. 1901,

This eminent Alienist has been lately appointed Gen. Sanitätsrath at Gleiwitz, and Physician to the Royal Court, a place to which his high talents and rich experience has eminently qualified him.

He has received this recognition from the Government, which will give his many friends in all countries great pleasure to learn.

In return he has published this work upon the commitment to guardianship of the feebleminded and insane.

Dr. Kornfeld, in his preface, refers to his previous works, especially the annotations of Blandford on Insanity, in Berlin in 1878; Borderlines of Insanity; and various brochures, in medical and scientific publications, and as an introduction to his present contribution.

It is very properly dedicated to Jurists and to Experts.

The treatise, containing 64 pages, is divided into five Divisions. The 1st relates to their rights under the law of August 18, 1896; The 2nd, to the ordinary proceedings, under the act, for commitment; the 3rd, as to proceedings in cases of voluntary commitments; the 4th, proceedings under the law of November 28, 1899, as to the manner of commitment of the insane and feebleminded.

The brochure sheds a new light on this procedure in this part of Germany.

The position Dr. Kornfeld now holds, the rich experience of his past life, the studies he has made into the higher realms of psychiatry and neurology, will make his work all the more valuable to the alienists of his own and of other lands.

We congratulate the scientific world that Prof. Kornfeld has taken up his pen in this domain, and predict for his future work still greater success than he has achieved in the past.

Vermont Medical Monthly. H. Edwin Lewis, M. D , Editor.

This is one of the leading New England Medical Monthlies. Its account of the American Congress of Tuberculosis, in the June number, was by far the best of any we saw, and we quote from it with pride and pleasure. We have taken occasion to look up Dr. Lewis, and following is the result of our enquiries.

H. Edwin Lewis, M. D., Physician and Editor, was born in Providence, R. I., in 1872; son of Charles E. and Alla M. (Clark) Lewis; maternal great-grandfather was a member of General Washington's staff in the War of the Revolution. His father is of Scotch ancestry.

His early education was received in the public schools of Providence, R. I., and he is a graduate from the Providence High School; entered Brown University in 1892, completed a two-years' course of special study in biology, chemistry and the languages, and then entered the Medical Department of the University of Vermont, graduating in 1897. Following graduation he served as Resident Physician of the Fanny Allen Hospital, Burlington, Vt., for one year, and engaged in special study in New

York and Montreal Previous to graduation he taught with success in the public schools of Woodstock, Vt., a town noted for its culture and educational advantages.

Dr. Lewis was connected with the *Atlantic Medical Weekly* until the opportunity was offered him, in 1895, to assume the management of the *Vermont Medical Monthly*, a position he has since filled with success. He has made the *Monthly* one of the leading local medical journals in the country.

At present Dr. Lewis is Consulting Surgeon on the General Staff of the Fanny Allen Hospital and Surgeon in charge of the Eye, Ear, Nose and Throat Department of the same institution. He also is Opthalmologist, Aurist and Rheumologist to the Providence Hospital and Orphan Asylum, of Burlington, Vt., Medical Examiner of the Connecticut General Life Insurance Company, and other insurance companies.

He is a member of the American Congress of Tuberculosis, the Medico-Legal Society of New York, the Vermont State Medical Society, the American Editors' Association, and the Burlington Clinical Society. While in college he was a member of the R. I. Alpha of Phi Delta Theta, of Brown, and of the Delta Mu Fraternity of the Medical Department of the University of Vermont, and is a member of the Ethan Allen Club, one of the oldest and leading organizations in Vermont.

Dr. Lewis, although a zealous student, does not ignore every-day pursuits. He is especially fond of horses and dogs, being a Director of the Champlain Kennel Club.

Although a young man. Dr. Lewis has made several interesting and important contributions to literature and science. He is the author of "Lights and Other Poems," a small, unpretentious volume, published while in college; "The Philosophy of Sex," a small work which has received commendation from all parts of the world, and a lengthy article written in collaboration with Dr. A. P. Grinnell, on the "History of Medicine in Vermont," published in Heards' History of New England. Dr. Lewis has written several important articles on the therapeutic uses of certain drugs, one on "*Cannabis Indica*" in Meicks' Archives for April, 1900, being awarded a prize of $75 for special merit. In his editorial work Dr. Lewis has been very successful, his writings being characterized by candor and comprehensiveness. He has a large and lucrative practice and the confidence of his friends.

He is one of the delegates to the British Congress of Tuberculosis from the American Congress of Tuberculosis, and a delegate from the Medico-Legal Society to the Medico-Legal Society of France.

LE BULLETIN MEDICAL DE QUEBEC. No. 10· *Travaux Originaux:* Absces sous-periostique de l' apophyse mastoide, par le Dr. N. A. Dussault. *Revue Analitique des Journeax:* Traitement preventif des coliques opatiques; La Pretendue fievre ganglionnaire de la compression suhle par la tete fœtale dans les applications de forceps; Du Traitement des fractures des jambes; Catherisme et lavage urethral; Traitement du delirium tremenas. *Arthritisme:* De la laparatomie vaginale conservtrice comparee a la laparate mie abdominale; Apropos de l' e mploie de l' eau oxygenee, pour le decolement des pansements adherents. *Extraits:* Glaucome aige; Dentologie medicale. *Reproduction:* Les savons et l'antisepsie en obstetrique; L'epreuve du visicatoire.

BOOKS, PAMPHLETS AND JOURNALS RECEIVED.

HENRY J. GARRIGUES, A. M., M. D. "The Legislation Needed in Regard to Apparent Death."

THE THIRTEEN CLUB, New York City. 18th Annual Report. 1901.

KINAHAN CORNWALLIS, New York. "The War for the Union, prefaced by The Song of America and Columbus, or The Story of the New World." 1899.

PROF. DR. LEO WACHHOLZ, University of Krakow, Russia. Sonderabdruck aus der Vierteljahrsschrift. Gerichtl. Medicin. u. öffent liches Sanitäts-Wesen.

LOUIS LEROY, B. S., M. D., Nashville, Tenn., State Bactiriologist, and Professor of Pathology and Bacteriology in Vanderbilt University. "Smallpox; its Diagnosis, Treatment, Reduction and Prevention." Published by the Tennessee Board of Health.

BENCH AND BAR. Vol. I. No. 6. New Law Journal. Chicago, Ill.

MAGAZINES.

POPULAR SCIENCE MONTHLY. Edited by J. McKeen Cattell.

The May number of this journal contains an interesting article by Havelock Ellis, entitled "A Study of British Genius," relating to the month of their birth, and the date of their conception.

The writer has traced these, by months and quarters, with interesting incidents in the lives and characters of many of the most eminent English names.

Dr. W. J. Holland, LL.D., Director of the Carnegie museum at Pittsburgh, contributes an interesting account of the history of that Museum, beautifully illustrated with an admirable portrait of Mr. Carnegie.

THE NORTH AMERICAN REVIEW. Edited by George B. M. Harvey.

This journal has held a commanding position for some years, but since the change of management to Franklin Square it has still further advanced.

Mr. Harvey proves to be the right man in the right place. The June number contains an article by Sir Norman Lockyer on "Sunspots and Rainfall." By Sidney Webster, on "Revelations of a Senate Document." By Dr. W. A. P. Martin, on "Poetry of the Chinese" By Goldwin Smith, on "The Irish Question." W. D. Howells writes the biography of Wm. J. Stillman, journalist.

THE ASTROLOGICAL MAGAZINE. B. Suryanarain Row, B. A., M. R. A. S., Editor. Madras, India.

The May number, 1901, contains an interesting article on "Sun, Air and Water Baths," in which the editor gives high praise to Dr. J. Mount Bleyer's article on Light, read last year before the American Congress of Tuberculosis, and shows that it is in accord with ancient Hindu lore, as related to cases of consumption.

It contains a horoscope of King Edward VII, Emperor of India, and an interesting article on "Hindu Psychic Development," quoting from the *Star of Magi*, of Chicago; an article entitled "Mystic Hindu Parchments;" as to the statements of Robert Williams, an electrical engineer, regarding "The White Horse Mine" at or near Boulder City.

Dr. Geo. S. Goodspeed, Professor of Hebrew, failed in an attempt to decipher the parchments.

The author says: "In the Hata, Raga, and Laya Yogas, various processes of psychic development are recorded, and if practiced under the instructions of a proper *Guru*, they reveal a world of energies at which the ordinary mind reels in bewilderment." "Knowledge is not an ordinary; that divine *knowledge* is the greatest of known energies.

CURRENT LITERATURE. Current Literature Publishing Company, 55 Liberty Street, New York.

The June number of this periodical, which we have just received, illustrates its peculiar excellence. It completes its 30th valume with this number. It is admirably edited and its selections from the cotemporary journals are choice, interesting and chosen with great skill.

Let any one read this excellent number, and they will get a taste of the best bits of the current literature of the hour.

INTERSTATE MEDICAL JOURNAL, June, 1901. *Editorials:* The Parasite of Cancer; Curious Cases of Auto Sectio Cæsarea; Concentration in Scientific Work; Treatment of Eclampsia; Medical Library Building; The Sero-Diagnosis of Tuberculosis; The Treatment of Abdominal Gunshot Wounds; The Interstate Medical Journal; The Interstate Medical

Laboratory. *Clinical Lectures:* Lecture on Surgery, by George Boody, M. D., of Independence, Iowa; Clinical Lectures on Surgery, by N. Senn, M. D., Ph. D., LL.D., of Chicago, Ill. *Original Articles:* Katatonia, by George Boody, M. D., of Independence, Iowa; Some of the Uses of Electricity in Gynecological Practice, by W. H. Walling, A. M., M. D., of Philadelphia; Anæmia, with special consideration of the pernicious forms, by Dr. W. S. Lessinger, of Mt. Pleasant, Iowa; Morbid Anatomy and Blood Pathology, by Dr. Charles Hoffman, A. M., Ph. D., of Mt. Pleasant, Iowa; Otomycosis, by Robert M. Lapsley, of Keokuk, Iowa; Scientific Miscellany, Personal Comment, Medical Societies, Medical Treatment, Surgical Suggestions, Our Book Table, New Remedies.

THE TEXAS MEDICAL JOURNAL. F. E. Daniel, M. D., Editor. June number, 1901. *Original Aiticies:* Pelvic Abscess, by Dr. R. M. Ddunn, Palestine, Texas. *Society Notes:* Meeting of the Brazos Valley Medical Association; South Texas Medical Association; East Texas Medico-Chirurgical Society; Tenth Semi-Annual Meeting of the South Texas Medical Association. *Editorial:* San Antonio's New Hospital; Against Substitution. Abstracts and Selections, News and Miscellany, Publisher's Notes.

LA REVUE MEDICALE DU CANADA. June 12. *Travaux Originaux:* Medicine: L' ærophagie (fáusse flatulence ærophagique); Chirurgie: Des Differentes formes de la' septicemie buccale. *Traitement du Cancroide:* Gynecologie: Le deciduome malin; Obstetrique: Dequeampiegrion du perinee et de la vulve en obstetrique; Maladies Veneriennes: Retrecissement mitral et syphilis. Le salicya; Pediatrie: Traitement du muguet par lesucon borique. Traitement de la coqueluche par les insufflations d'orthoforme; Note sde pharmacie pratique, Bibliographie, Formulaire, Nouvelles et varietes.

THE MEDICAL HERALD. June, 1901. *Original Articles:* Antepartum Diagnosis; Association, in Women, of Pelvic and Hepatic Diseases. Philbrick; An Improved Introducer for Intubating the Larynx. Dean; Chorea. Kiny; Report of Three Cases of Malaria. Pritchard. *Correspondence:* Surgery on Europe. Lord. *Editor's Forum:* Inspection of Public and Private Schools; Death of Dr. Frank C. Hoyt; American Medical Assocsation; Medical Association of Missouri; Change in Date of Meeting of the Mississippi Valley Medical Association; The Use of Heroin in Morphinism; Throat, Nose, Ear; Chicago's Missouri Club. *The Doctor's Library:* Diseases of the Eye. Foltz; Infant Feeding in Health—Nursing. Davis Fischer; Pulmonary Consumption. Mays; Progressive Medicine, Vol. 1. Hare; A Handbook of Materia Medica, Pharmacy and Therapeutics. Potter. *Notes on Reliable Remedies:* Automatic Safety Valve Stopper—a device for preventing the bursting of Peroxide of Hydrogen bottles; Scientific and Practical Facts, Laxation in Constipation, The Ideal Hemagogue and Emenagogue, Colchi-Sal in Obscure Gouty Manifestations.

DETROIT MEDICAL JOURNAL. June, 1901. *Original Articles:* Ectopic Pregnac. Longyear. *Correspondence:* Journal of a Naval Surgeon. *Editorial:* Calomel Administration and Ptyalism; Army Canteen Endorsed; A Modern Snob. *Editorial Notes:* Items and News, Book Reviews, Therapeutic Brevities, Medical Progress.

MEDICAL SENTINEL. June, 1901. *Original Articles:* Reciprocity Between State Medical and Licensing Boards, by C. E. Worthington, M. D., of Mullen, Idaho; Report of Dynamic Ileus, by L. P. McCalla, M. D., of Boise, Idaho; Post-Graduate Study in London, by Warren Brown, M. D., of Tacoma, Wash. *Extracts:* Automatic Safety Valve Stopper—a device for preventing the bursting of Peroxide of Hydrogen bottles; Alum in Food; Laxation in Constipation, by J. A. Rene, M. D., West Superior, Wis.; The Effect of Codeine. *Editorial:* Smallpox in Alaska. *Notes:* Expansion in Medical Teachiag, The Washington State Medical Society, Marchand's Peroxide, Oregon State Medical Society, Doctor Worden Warning, American Medical Association.

RIVISTA DI MEDICINA LEGALE E DI GIURISPRUDENZA MEDIC A CON RIGUARDO ALLE QUESTIONI DEGLI. INFORTUNI SUL LAVORO. Diretta Dàl Prof. A. Severi. February, 1901. *Communicationi Originali:* A. Severi. Per la conoscenza di alcune cause che favoriscono dell' acqua nell' apparechio respiratoreo dei cadaveri somersi. *Reviste:* Anatomia patologica e Patologica sperimentale; Tossicologa sperimentale; Traumatologia ed Unfortuni sul lavoro; Antropologia criminale; Science penali; Guirisprudenza sugli Infortuni del lavoro. *Bibliografia:* Pieraccini A. L' assistenza dei pazzi nel manicomio:e nella famiglia. *Letteratura:* Tossicologia sperimentale e Chimica tossocologia; Trumatologia e Infortuna sul lavoro. *Siena:* Tip. E. Lit. Sordo; Muti Di D. Lazzeri, 1901.

THE ARENA. The Alliance Publishing Company, 569 Fifth Avenue, New York.

The July number opens the twenty-sixth volume of that "twentieth century review of vital thought." It contains many up-to-date articles from the pens of distinguished writers. Miss Kellor's sixth article on "The Criminal Negro" is devoted to psychological tests of females.

Editor McClean announces a symposium on "The Curse of Inebriety" for the August number.

THE MEDICO-LEGAL JOURNAL.

Published under the Auspices of the Medico-Legal Society of New York.

CLARK BELL, ESQ.,
EDITOR-IN-CHIEF.

ASSOCIATE EDITORS:

LEGAL.

Prof. W. L. BURNAP, Vermont.
Judge ABRAM H. DAILEY, Brooklyn.
Judge JOHN F. DILLON, New York.
T. GOLD FROST, Esq., New York.
Judge C. G. GARRISON, Camden, N.Y.
F. L. HOFFMAN, Esq., Newark, N. J.
SAMUEL BELL THOMAS, Esq N.Y.
W. H. S. MONCK, Esq , Dublin.
A. WOOD RENTON, Esq., London.

MEDICAL.

Dr. HAVELOCK ELLIS, London.
Prof. Dr. J. T. ESKRIDGE, Denver, Colo.
W. W. IRELAND, M. D., Scotland.
HERMAN KORNFELD, M. D., Silesia.
GEORGE B. MILLER, M. D., Phila.
JULES MOREL, M. D., Belgium.
T. F. SUTHERLAND, M. D., Edinburgh, Scotland.
H. EDWIN LEWIS, M. D , Burlington, Vt.

SCIENTIFIC.

C. VAN D. CHENOWETH, Mass.
Prof. R. O. DOREMUS, New York.
MORITZ ELLINGER, Esq., N. Y.
Prof. W. B. MACVEY, Boston.
Prof. W. XAVIER SUDDUTH, Chicago.
Prof. VICTOR C. VAUGHAN, Mich.

RAILWAY SURGERY.

LEGAL.

C. H. BLACKBURN, Esq., Cincinnati.
Judge WILLIAM H. FRANCIS, N.Y. City
C. A. LIGHTNER, Esq., Detroit.
Judge CONWAY W. NOBLE, Cleveland.
Hon. J. M. THURSTON, Nebraska.

MEDICAL.

CHARLES K. COLE, M. D., Montana.
GRANVILLE P. CONN, M. D. Concord.
A. P. GRINNELL, M. D., Burlington, Vt.
DWIGHT J. KELLY, M. D., Ohio
R. HARVEY REED, M. D., Rock Spring, Wy
NICHOLAS SENN, M. D., Chicago.

VOL. XIX.—No. 2.

NEW YORK:
MEDICO-LEGAL JOURNAL.
1901.

MEDICO-LEGAL SOCIETY.

OFFICERS FOR 1901.

President,
CLARK BELL, Esq., of New York.

1st Vice-President
JUDGE CHARLES G. GARRISON, of N. J.

2nd Vice-President,
T. D. CROTHERS, M. D., of Conn.

Vice-Presidents for the States, Territories and Provinces.

Alabama—Judge Thos. W. Coleman, Montgomery.
Alaska—Clarence Thwing, M. D., Sitka.
Arizona—D. M. Purman, M. D., Phoenix.
Arkansas—H. C. Dunavant, M. D., Osceola.
Austria—Prof. R. Krafft-Ebing, Vienna.
Belgium—Dr. Jules Morel, Mons.
Brazil—Prof Nina Rodrigues, M. D, Bahia.
British Honduras-Ada M Chevaillier, M.D., Balize
California—A. E. Osborne, M. D., Glen Ellen.
Colorado—Prof. J T Eskridge, M. D., Denver.
Connecticut—Judge A. M. Tallmadge, Bridgeport.
China—Harold Browett, Esq., Shanghai.
Cuba—Chief Justice Hechavarria, of Santiago.
Dakota, N.—Dr. Dwight S. Moore, Jamestown.
Dakota, S.—John M. Harcourt, Steele.
Delaware—Judge Ignatius C. Grubb, Wilm'gt'n.
Denmark—Prof. Godeken, Copenhagen.
Dist. of Columbia—Irving C. Rosse, M. D., Wash.
Dom of Canada—Hon A. G. Blair, Ottawa.
England—William L. Orange. M. D., London.
Ecuador—Senor J. M. P. Cammano, Wash. D. C.
Florida—N. de V. Howard. M. D., Sanford.
France—Victor Parent, M. D., Toulouse.
Georgia—Richard J Nunn, M. D., Savannah.
Germany—Dr. H. Laehr, Berlin.
Guatemala—Senor Rafael Montufar.
Hawaii—J. W. Waughop M D., Kealia Kauai
Hayti.—Genl. J. A. Bordes, Jeremie.
Holland—Dr. P. A. H. Sueens, Vucht.
Hungary—Staatsanwalt Em V. Havas, Buda Pesth
Illinois—J. E. Owens, M. D, Chicago.
India—P. S. Sivaswamy Aiyar, Madras.
Indiana—W. B. Fletcher, M. D., Indianapolis.
Indian Territory—I. H. Bailey, M. D, Dexter.
Iowa—Jennie McCowen, M D., Davenport
Ireland—Conolly Norman, M. D., Dublin
Italy—Enrico Ferri, M. D, Rome.
Japan—Dr J. Hashimoto, Tokio
Kansas—Judge Albert H Horton, Topeka
Kentucky—F. H. Clark, M. D, Lexington.
Louisiana—I. J. Scott, M. D., Shreveport.
Maine—Judge L. A Emery, Ellsworth.
Manitoba—D. Young, M. D., Selkirk
Maryland—Wm. Lee Howard, M. D., Baltimore.
Massachusetts—Theo. H. Tyndale, Boston.
Mexico—Leon Lewis, M. D., Ozuluama
Michigan—Clarence A. Lightner, Detroit.
Minnesota—C K. Bartlett, M. D., Minneapolis.
Missouri—W. B. Outten, M. D., St. Louis.
Montana—C. K. Cole, M. D., Helena.
Nebraska—Hon. John M. Thurston, Omaha.
Nevada—S. M. Bishop, M. D., Reno.
New Brunswick—
Newfoundland—Dr. K. D. McKenzie, St. Johns.
New Hampshire—Gran. P. Conn, M.D., Concord.
New Jersey—Judge C. G. Garrison, Camden.
New Mexico—Gov. Bradford L. Prince, Santa Fe.
New South Wales—George A. Tucker, M. D.
New York—Mrs. M. Louise Thomas, N. Y. City.
New Zealand—Prof. Frank G. Ogston, Dunedin.
North Carolina—E. C. Smith, Esq., Raleigh.
Norway—Dr. Harold Smedal, Christiana.
Nova Scotia—Hon. Wm. S. Fielding, Ottawa.
Ohio—Judge H. C. White. Cleveland.
Oklahoma Ter.—A. H. Simonton, M. D., Okla. Cy.
Ontario—Daniel Clark, M. D., Toronto.
Oregon—Ex-Chief Just. Hon. Wm. P. Lord, Salem.
Pennsylvania—Geo. B. Miller, M. D., of Phila.
Peru—Senor F. C. C. Zegarro, Washington, D. C.
Portugal—Bettincourt Rodriguez, M. D., Lisbon.
Quebec—Wyatt Johnson, M. D., Montreal.
Rhode Island—Judge P. E. Tillinghast, Provid'e
Russia—Prof. Dr. Mierzejewski, St. Petersburgh.
San Domingo—A. Wei Yos Gil, San Domingo.
Saxony—Judge de Alinge, Oberkotzon Hof.
Scotland—W. W. Ireland, Edinburgh.
Servia—Hon. Paul Savitch, Belgrade.
Sicily—Prof. Dr. Fernando Puglia, Messina.
Silesia—H. Kornfeld, M. D., Grotkau.
South Carolina—S W. Babcock, M. D, Columbia.
Spain—Sig A. M. Alv. Taladriz, M.D., Valladolid.
Sweden—Prof. Dr. A. Winroth, Lund.
Switzerland—Prof. Dr. L. Wille, Basle.
Tennessee—Michael Campbell, M. D., Nashville.
Texas—Dr. D. R. Wallace, Terrell.
Tonga—Dr. Donald McClennen, Tonga.
Utah—Frederick Clifft, M. D., St. George.
Vermont—A. P. Grinnell, M. D, Burlington.
Virginia—William F. Drewry, Petersburg.
Washington—Jas C. Waugh, M. D., Mt. Vernon.
West Virginia—F. M. Hood, M. D., Weston.
Wisconsin—Dr. U O B. Wingate, Milwaukee.
Wyoming—R. Harvey Reed, M. D., Rock Springs

Secretary,
H. GERALD CHAPIN, Esq., of N. Y.

Corresponding Secretary,
MORITZ ELLINGER Esq. of N. Y.

Assistant Secretary,
SAMUEL BELL THOMAS, Esq., of N. Y.

Pathologist,
F. B. DOWNS, M. D., Conn.

Treasurer,
CAROLINE J. TAYLOR
Bridgeport, Conn.

Chemist,
PROF. C. A. DOREMUS, M. D. N. Y.

Curator,
J. MOUNT BLEYER, M. D., New York.

Toxicologist,
PROF. W. B. McVEY, of Boston.

Librarian
FRED. L. HOFFMAN, Esq., of N. J.

Assistant Librarian,
THOS. G FROST, Esq., of N. Y.

Bacteriologist,
G. BETTINI DI MOISE, M. D., of N. Y.

Microscopist,
DR. ERNEST J. LEDERLE, of N. Y.

TRUSTEES:
for 3 years.

Legal,
JUDGE A. J. DITTENHOEFER, of N. Y.
JUDGE WM. H FRANCIS, of N. J.

Medical,
G. STANLEY HEFFT, M. D., of Conn.
P M. WISE, M. D., of N Y.

ISAAC N. LOVE, M D., of N. Y.

COUNSELLORS,
For 3 years.

Legal.
STILES JUDSON, JR., of Conn
HENRY WOLLMAN, Esq., of N. Y
FRED. E. CRANE, Esq., of Brooklyn

Medical.
RALCY HUSTED BELL, M D., of N. Y.
ISAAC N. LOVE, M. D., of N. Y
CARLETON SIMON, M. D, of N. Y.

PERMANENT COMMISSION:
For 3 years.

Legal,
HON L. A. EMERY of Maine.
HON. JOHN M. THURSTON, of Neb.
CLARK BELL, Esq., of N. Y.

Medical.
GEO. L. PORTER, M. D., of Conn.
VICTOR C. VAUGHAN, Esq., of Mich.
NICHOLAS SENN, M. D., of Chicago.

THE FOLLOWING ARE THE EXCHANGE JOURNALS.

Archives Italian,
Archivie Giuridico,
Archives d'Amthropologie Criminalie,
Alienist and Neurologist,
American Journal of Insanity,
American Law Register,
Archives of Pediatries,
Archives de la Psychiatrie Clinique et Legale et de Neurologie,
Academie de Medicine de Paris,
American Journal of Psychology,
American Chemical Journal,
American Law Review,
Atlanta Medical and Surgical,
Annales Medico-Psychologique,
Archivio di Psi Sci pen et antro crim.,
Archives de Neurologie,
Annales Societe Medico-Legal, ed Belge,
Albany Law Journal,
American Microscopical Journal,
Amer. Med. Review,
Annals Univ Med. Science
Aerztliche Sachverstandingen-Zeitung,
American Medical Journalist,
Amer. Monthly Retrospect,
Amer Journal of Med-Science,
Applied Microscopy,
American Economist,
American Lawyer,
Astrological Journal,

Buffalo Medical Journal,
Boston Medical and Surgical Journal,
Bulletion Societe de Medicine Mentale Belgique,
Bulletin of the Iowa State Institutions,

Case and Comment,
Canadian Practitioner,
Central Law Journal,
Connecticut State Board of Health,
Courier of Medicine.
Centralblatt fur Nerv.,
Canadian Law Times,
Charlotte Med. Journal,
Cape Law Journal,
Chicago Law Journal,
Chicago Legal News,
Columbus Med. Journal,
Canadian Journal Med. Surgery,
Cleveland Journal of Medicine,
Chicago Clinic,
Charities,

Der Irrenfreund,
Der Gerichtssaal,
Del Kongelige Sundhedskollegiums,
Davenport Acad. of Nat. Sci.
Detroit Legal News,
Dietetic and Hygiene Gazette,
Dunglisan Col. & Clin. Record.

English Lunacy Commission

Fordhand Svensia Lakare Sallskapts,
Fort Wayne Med. Jour.,
Fishing Gazette,

Guy's Hospital Reports,
Gazette del Tribunal,
Giornale di Neuropatalogia,
Gerichtl Zeitung, Vienna,
Gazette des Hopitaux,

Hygiea,
Harvard Law Review
Holstein Friestin Register,
Hot Springs Med. Journal,

Illinois State Board of Health,
International Journal of Surgery,
Index Medicus,
Iowa Law Bulletin,
Il Pisania Gazette Secula,
Indian Review,
Ideal Review,

Johns Hopkins University,
Journal of Inebriety,
Journal of Medical Sci.,
Journal of Nervous and Menfal Diseases,
Journal de Medicine,
Jahrbucher fur Psychiatrie,
Journal of Electro Therapeutics,
Journal of Tuberculosis

Kansas City Med. Index

La. Psi. la Neurol e Sci
Lippincott's Magazine,
L'Anthropologie,
London Lancet,
Littell's Living Age,
Law Quarterly Review,
La Progress Medicale,
Louisville Medical News
Lunacy and Charity,
Literary Digest,
Legal Intelligencer,
Lancet Pub. Co..
La Habana Medica,
Law Students Journal,
Literature,

Mass. State Board o Health,
Medico-Legal Society o Massachusetts,
Medical Review of Reviews,
Medical Annales
Medical News,
Messeger of Neurolog and Forensic Psycopathology, St. Petersburg,
Medicine,
Menorah Monthly,
Madras Law Journal,
Medical Fortnightly,
Medical Mirror,
Modattscarfft fur Unfallheilkunde,
Medical Herald,
Mind,
Medical Sentinel,
Med. and Surg. Bulletir
Medical Bulletin,
Medical Register,
Medicus,

North American Review
New Orleans Med. an Surg.,
New York Med. Record,
Nordisk Medicinski Arki
N. Amer. Journal of Diagnosis and Practice,
N C. Med Journal,

Occidental Med. Times,

EXCHANGE JOURNALS—Continued.

Our Animal Friends,

Philadelphia Times and Register.
Pacific Medical Journal,
Pacific Record of Medicine and Surgery,
Personal Rights.
Phrenological Journal,
Psychological Review,
Penn Yan Democrat,
Pa. State Com.of Lunacy,
Public Opinion,
Psi and Nerve Path, Kharkoff, Russia.
Public Health Journal,
Printer's Ink.
Penny Magazine,
Perry's Magazine,
Providence Medical Journal,
Psychiatrische en Neuralgische Bladen,

Revue De Medicine,
Revue Medicale,
Repertorie de Pharmacie,
Review of Reviews,
Railway Surgeon,
Railway Age,
Revue de la Hypnotisms,
Revista Ciencas Medicas,
Revista Penals,
Revista Medico-Legal,
Revista de Neuralogie, Psychiatre,
Revista de Antropologie, Criminella of Sciencias Medico-Legales,
Revista de Neurol, and Phy. (Lisbon),
Revista de Neurologie,

Scotch Board of Lunacy,
Sanitarian,
Sanitary Record,
Smithsonian Institute,
Societe Medicine Legale de France,
Society D'Anthropodogie, Brussels,
Society for Psychical Research,
Society for Promoting the Welfare of the Insane,
Scienza Italiana,
St.Louis Courier of Med.,
Sei-I Kwai Med Journal,
Spirit of the Times,
Suggestive Therapeutics,
Suggester and Thinker,
Spectator,

The Southern Law Review,
The Journal of Mental Pathology,
The Southern Medical Journal,
The Hannemanian,
Tennessee State Board of Health,
The Journal of Miss. State Med. Ass.
The Cape Law Journal,
The American Journal of Psychology,
The Green Bag,
The Open Court,
The Freeman
The Arena,
The Monist,
The Cosmopolitan Osteopath,
Texas Sanitarian,

Texas Medical Journal
Interstate Med. Journa
Turf, Field and Farm,
The Legal Adviser,
The Philistine,
The Sheep Breeder,,
The Therapist,
The Physician and Sur geon,
The Public,
The Texas Clinic,
The Flaming Sword,
The Raven,
The Coming Age,
The Stylus,
The Legal Gazette,
The Surgical and Dent News,
The Colorado Medic Journal,

Union Industrial Dro Penale,
Universal Med. Science

Vermont Medical Monthl
Virginia Law Register,
Virginia Medical Sem Monthly,

Woman's Med. Journal
Western Reserve La Journal,
Weekly Law Journal,
West Virginia Bar,

X-Ray Journal,

Yale Law Journal,
Youth's Companion.

Zeitschrift fur Schweiz Strafetcht,
Zeitschrift fur Psychistr

PROMINENT SANITARIANS IN FAVOR OF LEGISLATION TO PREVENT SPREAD OF TUBERCULOSIS.

HON. ABRAM H. DAILEY,
of Brooklyn, N. Y.,
Vice Pres. American Congress of Tuberculosis.

DR. T. D. CROTHERS,
of Hartford, Conn.,
Vice Pres. American Congress of Tuberculosis.

ROF. THOS. BASSETT KEYES
of Chicago,
Vice Pres. Am. Congress of
Tuberculosis.

SIR JAMES A. GRANT,
of Ottawa,
Pres. of the Canadian Society for the
Prevention of Tuberculosis.

DR. J. J. GIBSON,
State Veterinarian, Iowa,
Vice Pres. Am. Congress of
Tuberculosis.

R GEO. G. VERBRYCK,
e President for Wyoming,
Cambria, Wyoming.

MIHRAN K. KASSALIAN, M. D.,
of Philadelphia, Pa.

DR. T. B. LACEY,
Vice President for Iowa,
Council Bluffs, Iowa.

SANITORIA FOR CONSUMPTIVES IN THE UNITED STATES AND THE CANADAS.

BY CLARK BELL, ESQ., LL. D., OF N. Y., PRESIDENT MEDICO-LEGAL SOCIETY, SECRETARY AMERICAN CONGRESS OF TUBERCULOSIS.

The great public interest in the questions involved in the value and utility of sanitorium treatment of the consumptive, is my reason for contributing such few facts and data as I have been able to gather since the adjournment of the American Congress of Tuberculosis on May 16 last, and especially since it was suggested to me to prepare this brief paper in season to present it before the London Congress of Tuberculosis, which met July 22, 1901, in the British metropolis.

IN THE UNITED STATES OF AMERICA

The question of sanatoria for the General Government is under the charge of the War and the Navy Departments. These are for the benefit of the soldiers and sailors of the army and navy of the United States, and are in charge of the surgeon generals of the army and navy, respectively.

The enclosed letter from the Surgeon General of the Army gives the location and officers in command of the government hospitals for the army:

Clark Bell, Esq., 39 Broadway, New York.

Dear Sir:—Replying to your letter of April 27th I would say that the following named medical officers are in charge of the U. S. General Hospitals in this country:

Lieut. Col. Alfred C. Girard, Commanding U. S. General Hospital, Presidio, San Francisco, California.

Major George H. Torney, Commanding Army and Navy General Hospital, Hot Springs, Ark.

Major A. H. Appel, Commanding U. S. General Hospital (for tuberculosis), Fort Bayard, New Mexico.

Major Wm. C. Borden, Commanding U. S. General Hospital, Washington Barracks, D. C.

For information with reference to the Marine Hospital Service you should address Dr. Walter Wyman, Supervising Surgeon General, Marine Hospital Service, Washington, D. C.

Very truly yours,
GEO. M. STERNBERG,
Surgeon General, U. S. Army.

The U. S. General Hospital for the Treatment of Pulmonary Tuberculosis at Fort Bayard, New Mexico.

Major D. M. Appel, M. D., Surgeon U. S. Army, Commanding this Hospital sends me advance sheets of a copy of his report to the Surgeon General of the United States for the year ending December 31, 1900, which I received July 9th, almost the last possible moment to utilize the same as a whole.

The report shows the treatment of 283 tubercular patients during the year; a detailed illustrated discription of the buildings and structures, treatment and clinical work and I much regret I cannot now include it.

Walter Wyman, M. D., Supervising Surgeon General of the United States Marine Hospital Service at Washington, D. C., in response to my letter for information on the Sanataria of the government in relation to tuberculosis in the navy, forwarded the official list of government marine hospitals and quarantine stations issued January 1, 1891, with a list of all his assistants and officers in the hospital service of the government in the naval service. He reports:

In the North Atlantic District, Hospitals.............. 3
At Boston, Mass.; Portland, Me.; Vineyard Haven, Mass.

In the Middle Atlantic District, Hospitals............. 2
At New York City; Delaware Breakwater (Lewes, Del.)

In the South Atlantic District, Hospitals.............. 2
Baltimore, Md.; Wilmington, N. C.

In the District of the Gulf, Hospitals.................. 3
Key West, Fla.; Mobile, Ala.; New Orleans, La.

In the District of the Ohio, Hospitals................. 3
At Louisville, Ky.; Cincinnati; Evansville, Ind.

In the District of the Mississippi, Hospitals............ 3
At St. Louis; Memphis; Cairo, Ills.

In the District of the Great Lakes, Hospitals.......... 3
At Chicago; Cleveland; Detroit.

In the District of the Pacific, Hospitals.............. 3

Total Hospitals 22

The hospital at Fort Stanton, New Mexico, is devoted to the care of the consumptive patients, among the sailors, and he refers to its report which is too voluminous for even an abstract, in a paper like the present.

The report of Dr. M. J. Rosenau, Past Assistant Surgeon, to the American Congress of Tuberculosis of 1900, which is published in the Bulletin of that Congress, part I of vol. II at page 48, to which I refer:

Dr. Rosenau says that the death rate among the 100,000 sailors which compose the clientele of the Marine Hospital Service, has been for the past ten years from tuberculosis, one-fourth of all the deaths or 25 per cent., many times exceeding the death rate from any other single disease. That the Marine Hospital Service treats from 800 to 1200 cases of tuberculosis annually.

Assuming that the ratio of deaths by tuberculosis in the United States, is as claimed, seven per cent. of all deaths, Dr. Rosenau claims, that the mortality among sailors is three and a half times larger than the average.

Dr. W. D. Bratton, under direction of the Surgeon General, prepared a report in favor of New Mexico as a suitable place for a sanitarium for consumptives.

Secretary L. J. Gage detailed Past Assistant Surgeon J. O. Cobb to examine the abandoned military reservations, for a suitable site, and he reported in favor of Fort Stanton, New Mexico. President McKinley, April 1, 1899, transferred this reservation and devoted it to the Marine Hospital Service, and cases of tuberculosis may now be sent from any of the marine hospitals to the Fort Stanton Sanitary Ranch for treatment.

The Fort Stanton Hospital now isolates the tubercular sailor at this hospital, so that all the inmates at other hospitals are no longer exposed to infection, and probably places the consumptive sailor in the most favorable position for recovery now existing anywhere in the world.

STATE HOSPITALS.

In the United States the questions relating to the construction of hospitals by the government under the American autonomy is under the jurisdiction and authority of the several States and rests upon action by the State legislatures.

The question of sanitoria for consumptives is practically in its infancy, or at its inception and in the majority of the States of the American Union no provision has been made by State legislatures.

The extreme shortness of time beyond which my data could reach the London Congress before its session on the 22d, decided me to apply to the governors of the several States for the copies of acts of legislation on this subject or facts at their command, as the best method of obtaining and communicating reliable data on this subject. I shall confine myself to reporting from each State in the order in which the information comes to me, from governors, or State Boards of Health to whom the governors frequently refere for the data, without reference to alphabetical order.

ARIZONA.

Governor N. O. Murphy, of Arizona, replies as follows:—

Phoenix Arizona, July1, 1901.

Clark Bell, Esq., Secretary and Treasurer American Congress of Tuberculosis, 39 Broadway, New York.

Dear Sir.—In reply to your inquiry of June 25th, 1901, I have to inform you that there has been no legislation in this Territory on the subject of the construction of sanatoria for consumptives.

Yours respectfully,
N. O. MURPHY,
Governor.

CALIFORNIA.

The Hon. Henry T. Gage, Governor of California, referred my letter to Dr. W. P. Mathews, the Secretary of the State Board of Health of that State, who replies as follows:

Sacramento, July 6, 1901.

Mr. Clark Bell.

Dear Sir.—Your letter to the executive department of the State of California asking for copies of acts of legislation providing for sanitoria for consumptives has been referred to me.

I regret to say that our legislature has not taken any steps in that direction, and therefore, no sanitoria for consumptives, authorized by law and under the control of the State, exists here.

Very truly yours.
W. P. MATHEWS,
Secretary.

COLORADO.

Hon. J. B. Orman, Governor of Colorado, replies as follows:

Denver, June 29, 1901.

Clark Bell, Esq., 39 Broadway, New York, N. Y.

Dear Sir.—Your letter of the 23rd instant, in regard to legislation enacted in this state regarding the construction of sanitoria for consumptives is before me, and I beg to say that no legislation of this character has been enacted in this state.

I have referred your letter to Dr. G. E. Tyler, Secretary of the State Board of Health, with the request that he give you such information as he may have that would be useful to you.

Very truly yours,
JAMES B. ORMAN,
Governor.

ILLINOIS.

Governor Yates referred my communication to the State Board of Health of that State.

James J. Egan, M. D., Secretary and Executive Officer, replied as follows:—

July 12, 1901.

Clark Bell, Esq., 39 Broadway, New York, N. Y.

Dear Sir.—In reply to your letter of the 26th ult., to Governor Yates, I beg to inform you that there has been no legislation enacted in this state regarding the construction of a sanatorium for consumptives. The enclosed bill was introduced during the last session of the legislature, but failed to pass. (House Bill 339.)

Very truly yours,
JAMES A. EGAN,
Secretary.

The Act referred to is too lengthy to embrace it here. It was an Act to provide for the location, erection, organization and management of a State Sanitorium for persons affected by tuberculosis and making an appropriaiton for the purchase of land and the construction of the necessary buildings and the maintenance of the sanitorium.

The bill was introduced by Mr. Rankin, of Warren county, February 14, 1901, in the Lower House, and was House Bill 339.

IOWA.

Hon. Lester M. Shaw, Governor of Iowa, replies as follows:—

Des Moines, Iowa, June 29, 1901.

Mr. Clark Bell, Sec. and Treas. American Congress of Tuberculosis, 39 Broadway, New York, N. Y.

Sir.—Your communication has been received by the Governor of Iowa. In respect of the information desired, I can only say that there has been no enactment by the general assembly of this state regarding the construction of a sanitoria for consumptives; nor, as the Governor is advised, has such legislation been proposed at any time.

Yours,
WM. H. FLEMING,
Private Secretary.

KANSAS.

Hon. W. E. Stanley, Governor of Kansas, responds as follows:

Topeka, June 29, 1901.

Mr. Clark Bell, New York City.

Dear Sir.—Your favor of the 25th to Governor Stanley has been received, and in reply I beg to say that there has been no legislation enacted in this state relative to the construction of sanitoria for consumptives. If any such laws had been enacted, the Gov would have been pleased to send you copies of the same.

Yours very truly,
LUTHER BURNS,
Secretary to the Governor.

KENTUCKY.

Governor Beckham, of Kentuck, makes the following reply:

Frankfort, July 1, 1901.

Mr. Clark Bell, New York.

Dear Sir.—Replying to yours of recent date, I am directed by the Governor to say that there is not now in this state a public sanitarium for consumptives, nor does he know of any movement to that effect.

Very truly,
EDW. O. LEIGH,
Private Secretary.

LOUISIANA.

Hon. W. W. Heard, Governor of Louisiana, replies as follows:—

Baton Rouge, June, 29, 1901.

Dr. Clark Bell, Secretary American Congress of Tuberculosis, 39 Broadway, N. Y.

Dear Sir.—The Governor has directed me to acknowledge receipt of your inquiry of the 25th instant, and in reply to inform you that the General Assembly of Louisiana has taken no step as yet towards the construction of a sanitaria for consumptives, nor has any law upon this subject been passed. The subject has, however, received the strong advocacy of the Times-Democrat, of New Orleans, also of influential medical authorities in the State.

Very respectfully,
LEON JASBREMSKI,
Private Secretary.

MAINE.

A. G. Young, M. D., of Augusta, Maine, Secetary of the State Board of Health, whom I addessed, replied as follows:

Augusta, July 10, 1901.

Clark Bell, Esq., Sec. American Congress of Tuberculosis, 39 Broadway, New York.

Dear Sir.—Answering yours of July 1st, which was received yesterday, I would say that there is no sanatorium for consumptives in the State of Maine. The circular which I herewith enclose is one which has been sent out by the Maine State Sanatorium Association. We have no laws bearing directly upon sanatoriums. Tuberculosis is, however, under the law, a notifiable disease in this state, as you will see by referring to page 7 of "Abstract of Health Laws," a copy of which I send in the same mail with this. Under the general provisions of the law relating to the care of infectious diseases, local boards of health may may require the disinfection of rooms which have been occupied by consumptives and of things that have been used by them. Yours truly,

A. G. YOUNG,
Secretary.

The State Sanatorium Association to which Dr. Young refers, is a duly organized body under the laws of the State, its pupose and object stated as "To establish and maintain a public institution or institutions for the isolation, treatment and cure of persons affected with pulmonary disease and to exert its influence toward the lessening of the prevalence of tuberculosis."

It was organized in December, 1900. Its officers are:—

President—Hon. John F. Hill, Governor.

Vice President—General Selden Conn, Lieut. Governor.

Secretary—Dr. A. G. Young.

Treasurer—Ireby Johnson, Augusta.

The Board of Trustees is Dr. C. F. Thayer, Waterville; Hon. P. O. Vickery, Augusta; Hiram W. Ricker, Poland Springs; A. W. Hall, Caribou; Hon. F. C. Whitehouse, Topsham; Hon. F. O. Beal, Bangor; Hon. Waldo Pettengill, Rumford Falls; Dr. S. H. Weeks, Portland; George Bliss, Waldoboro.

It is in its infancy, but has a membership of over 260 persons.

Prof. D. H. Weeks, of Portland, Maine, Vice President of the American Congress of Tuberculosis of Portland, Maine, a high sanitary authority writes as follows:—

Portland, Maine, July 8, 1901.

Clark Bell, Esq., LL D.

My Dear Sir.—We have no such law in our State, but hope to have one soon. Sincerely yours,

S. H. WEEKS.

MARYLAND.

Hon. John W. Smith, Governor of Maryland, referred the

subject to the Secretary of State Board of Health of that State, Dr. John S. Fulton, who replied as follows:—

Baltimore, July 3rd, 1901.

Mr. Clark Bell, Sec. American Congress of Tuberculosis, 39 Broadway, New York.

Dear Sir —Yours to his Excellency, Governor Smith, referred to me, and in reply thereto I have to say that there is no law in Maryland on the subject of human tuberculosis, and no plans for State sanatoria have received legislative sanction.

Yours very truly,
JOHN S. FULTON,
Secretary.

MICHIGAN.

Governor Aaron T. Bliss, of that State, writes as follows:

June 13, 1901.

Mr. Clark Bell, Secretary, New York City, N. Y.

My Dear Sir.—Governor Bliss is in receipt of your favor of date, June 7th, and directs me to inform you that there has been no recent legisltion relative to tuberculosis or the construction of sanitaria. A bill providing for the establishment of a state sanitarium was introduced during the last session but failed to pass. A copy of the same is herewith enclosed.

Your very truly,
HERBERT E. JOHNSON,
Secretary to the Governor.

SECTION 1. That a State sanitarium for the care and treatment of incipient pulmonary tuberculosis patients, in some suitable locality, be and hereby is established.

SEC. 2. The Governor, by and with the advice and consent of the Senate, shall appoint five citizens of this State, three of whom shall be physicians legally registered as required by the laws of this State, who shall constitute the board of trustees of the Michigan State Sanitarium for the treatment of incipient pulmonary tuberculosis. The full term of office of each trustee shall be five years, one of such board retiring from office through expiration of his term each year, and his successor appointed for the full term. To effect such order of expiration of term of office, the first appointments shall be made for the respective terms of one, two, three, four and five years. Any such trustee may be removed by the Governor with the consent of the Senate, for such cause as they may deem sufficient, after an opportunity to be heard in his own defense has been granted him. Any vacancy arising in said board by reason of removal, accepted resignation or by death, shall be filled for the unexpired term by appointment in like manner as in first instance. A majority of the board shall constitute a quorum, but no business shall be transacted except by the affirmative vote of at least three members of said board.

SEC. 3. The lands to be held for the purposes herein mentioned shall in no instance be taken under the power of eminent domain except as expressly designated by the Legislature.

SEC. 4. For the purposes of this act, the board of trustees and their successors in office shall be a body corporate, with all the powers necessary to carry into effect this act.

SEC. 5. Said board of trustees shall have the general control of the property and concerns of the institution, and shall take charge of its general interests, and see that its designs be carried into effect, and everything therewith connected be faithfully performed according to the requirements of the Legislature.

SEC. 6. There shall be a thorough visitation of said sanitarium by two members of the board of trustees monthly, and by a majority of them quarterly, and by the whole board semi-annually, at each of which monthly visitations at least one of the board who is a physician shall be in attendance. At each visitation of said board of trustees, or portion thereof, a written report of the state of the institution shall be drawn up, all of which reports shall be presented at the annual meeting which shall be held between the first day of October and the first day of November. At the annual meeting the board of trustees shall make a detailed report and shall examine and audit the report of the treasurer, which shall be presented at said annual meeting, and shall transmit it with their annual report to the Governor and Senate.

SEC. 7. The board of trustees shall appoint a medical superintendent, not a member of said board, who shall be a graduate of a recognized medical college, of six years' experience in the practice of his profession, at least one year of which shall have been in the service of a general hospital, and who shall be chosen with special view to his skill and experience in the care and treatment of diseases of a tubercular nature. Such medical superintendent shall in all matters pertaining to the institution be under the general supervision of the board of trustees, who may remove him for cause which they deem sufficient, and appoint his successor.

SEC. 8. Said board of trustees shall appoint a treasurer, not a member of said board, who shall give an undertaking to the people of the State for the faithful performance of his trust, in such penal sum and form and with such sureties as the board of trustees shall approve. Such treasurer may at any time be removed, and his successor appointed, by said board of trustees in its discretion.

SEC. 9. The board of trustees shall appoint, upon the nomination of the medical superintendent, such other officers, assistants and employes in and for the sanitarium as may be, from time to time, necessary to carry into effect this act: Provided, however, That all medical officers and assistants shall be well educated physicians. All such officers, assistants and employes shall be under the direct supervision of the medical superintendent, and may be removed for cause by him. In case of removal by the medical superintendent of any such officers, assistants or employes, said medical superintendent shall forthwith report the same to the said board of trustees, together with his nomination of a successor.

SEC. 10. The board of trustees shall, from time to time as it may become necessary, determine the annual salaries and allowances of the officers, assistants and employes of said sanitarium: Provided, however, That the aggregate of such salaries and allowances shall not in any one year exceed the sum of $7,500.

SEC. 11. The board of trustees is hereby empowered and expressly directed to establish such by-laws as it may deem necessary and expedient for regulating the appointments and duties of officers, assistants, employes and attendants; for fixing the conditions of admission, support and discharge of patients; and for conducting in a proper manner the business of the institution; also to ordain and enforce a suitable system of rules and regulations for the internal government, discipline and management of the sanitarium.

SEC. 12. The board of trustees shall have authority to purchase on behalf of the State, real estate as a site for said sanitarium, and to cause to be erected thereon suitable buildings for said sanitarium, which shall furnish suitable accommodations for not less than two hundred patients, exclusive of the officers, assistants and employes, and to provide for the equipment of said buildings: Provided, however, That the expenditure for carrying out this act shall not exceed one hundred and fifty thousand dollars: And provided further, That no expenditure shall be made for the erection of buildings, except for plans therefor, until said plans have been approved by the Governor and Senate. The trustees shall have power to make all contracts and employ all agents necessary to carry into effect this act.

SEC. 13. The board of trustees shall receive no compensation for their services, but their actual and reasonable expenses incurred in the performance of their duties shall be paid by the State Treasurer on the warrant of the Auditor General on th rendering of their accounts, out of any money to the credit of the general fund not otherwise appropriated.

SEC. 14. The medical superintendent shall be the chief executive officer of the sanitarium. He shall have the general superintendence of the buildings, grounds, together with the furniture, fixtures and stock, and the direction and control of all persons therein, subject to the by-laws and regulations established by the board of trustees. He shall daily ascertain the condition of all the patients, and prescribe their treatment in the manner directed in the by-laws. He shall cause full and fair accounts and records of all his doings, and the entire business and operation of the institution, to be kept regularly, from day to day, in books provided for that purpose, in the manner and to the extent prescribed in the by-laws; and he shall see that all the accounts and records are fully made up to the last day of September and present the same to the board of trustees at their annual meeting. It shall be the duty of the medical superintendent to admit any of the board of trustees into every part of the sanitarium, and to exhibit to him or them on demand all the books, papers and accounts, and writings belonging to the institution, or pertaining to its business, management, discipline or government; also to furnish copies, abstracts and reports whenever required so to do by said board. The medical supeirntendent shall make in a book kept for that purpose, at the time of reception, a minute, with the date of the same, of the name, age, residence, occupation and such other statistics in regard to patients admitted to the sanitarium as the by-laws may require.

SEC. 15. The treasurer shall have the custody of all monies, bonds, notes, mortgages and other securities and obligations belonging to the sanitarium. Said monies shall be disbursed only for the uses and benefit of the sanitarium, and in the manner prescribed by the by-laws, upon the written order of the medical superintendent, specifying the object of the payment. He shall keep full and accurate accounts of the receipts and payments, in the manner directed in the by-laws, and such other accounts as the board of trustees shall prescribe. He shall further render an account of the state of the books, and of the funds and other property in his custody, whenever required so to do by the board of trustees. He shall have all accounts and records pertaining to his office fully made up to the last day of September and present the same to the board of trustees at their annual meeting.

SEC. 16. The charges for the support of the patients of said sanitarium as are of sufficient ability to pay for same, or have persons or kindred bound by law to maintain them, shall be paid by such patients, such persons, or such kindred, at a rate to be determined by the board of trustees of said sanitarium. The board of such patients as have a legal settlement in some city or town shall be paid by such city or town, if such patients are received at said sanitarium at the request of the overseer of the poor of such city or town. The trustees may receive, at their discretion, other patients who may be without means to defray their expenses, and the board of all such patients shall be paid out of the treasury of the State.

SEC. 17. The sum of one hundred and fifty thousand dollars is hereby appropriated for the purpose of purchasing a site and of erecting, constructing and equipping the sanitarium and buildings as are herein provided for. The treasurer of the State shall, on the warrant of the Auditor General and on the certificate of the State architect, pay over to the treasurer of said sanitarium the above named sum in such amounts as may, from time to time, in the judgment of the board of trustees be necessary.

Dr. Henry B. Baker, Secretary State Board of Health, Vice President American Congress of Tuberculosis, writes as follows in response to inquiry:

Lansing, Mich., June 25, 1901.

Clark Bell Esq., Sec. American Congress of Tuberculosis, 39 Broadway, N. Y.

Dear Sir.—Replying to your letter of June 24th, permit me to state that there are no laws in this state regarding sanatoria for consumptives, nor any relating specifically to the prevention of tubercluosis. I enclose herewith a copy of the law requiring the notification of cases of any "disease dangerous to the public health." A case is now in the Michigan courts to determine whether or not consumption is such a disease within the meaning of that statute.

Very Respectfully,
HENRY B. BAKER,
Secretary.

Sections 4452, 4453 and 4454, Compiled Laws 1897 (Secs. 87, 88 and 89, Public Health Laws 1899), are as follows:

(4452.) Sec. 43. Whenever any householder, hotel keeper, keeper of a boarding house, or tenant, shall know, or shall be informed by a physician, or shall have reason to believe that any person in his family, hotel, boarding house or premises, is taken sick with smallpox, cholera, diphtheria, scarlet fever, or any other disease dangerous to the public health, he shall immediately give notice, in writing, thereof to the health officer of the township, city or village in which he resides. Said notice shall state the name of the person sick, the name of the disease, if known, the name of the householder, hotel keeper, keeper of boarding house or tenant giving the notice, and shall, by street and number, or otherwise, sufficiently designate the house in which he resides or the room in which the sick person may be; and if he shall refuse or wilfully neglect immediately to give such notice, he shall be deemed guilty of a misdemeanor, and upon conviction thereof he shall be punished by a fine of not exceeding one hundred dollars and costs of prosecution; or in default of payment thereof, by imprisonment not exceeding ninety days in the county jail, in the discretion of the court: Provided, That such fine or imprisonment shall not be enforced if the physician in attendance has given to the health officer or other officer hereinbefore mentioned an immediate notice of said sick person and true name of the disease, in accordance with the requirements of this section.—Sec. 1675, Howell's Statutes.—As amended by Act 37, Laws of 1889, and by Act 158, approved May 18, 1895; Sec. 87, Public Health Laws 1899.

(4453.) Sec. 44. Whenever, any physician shall know that any person whom he is called to visit, or who is brought to him for examination, is infected with smallpox, cholera, diphtheria, scarlet fever, or any other disease dangerous to the public health, he shall immediately give notice thereof to the health officer of the township, city or village, in which the sick person may be; and to the householder, hotel keeper, keeper of a boarding house, or tenant within whose house or rooms the sick person may be. The notice to the officer of the board of health shall state the name of the disease, the name, age and sex of the person sick, also the name of the physician giving the notice; and shall, by street and number, or otherwise, sufficiently designate the houes or room in which said sick person may be. And every physician and person acting as a physician, who shall refuse or neglect immediately to give such notice shall forfeit for each such offense a sum not less than ten nor more than fifty dollars.* Provided, That this penalty shall not be enforced against a physician if another physician in attendance has given to the health officer, or other officer hereinbefore mentioned, an immediate notice of said sick person, and the true name of the disease, in accordance with the requirment of this section.—Sec. 1676, Howell's Statutes.—As amended by Act 11, Laws of 1883, and by Act 158, approved May 18, 1895; Sec. 88, Public Health Laws 1899.

(4454.) Sec. 50. For each complete notice in writing to an officer of the board of health, in full compliance with the preceding section, requiring from physicians, or other person, notices of diseases dangerous to the public health, the physician who gave the notice shall be entitled, on duly certifying that each notice was correct, and when the bill has been duly audited by the board of health, to receive from the township, city or village, in which the notice was given, the sum of ten cents.—Sec. 1681a Howell's Supplement; Sec. 89, Public Health Laws, 1899.

Minnesota.

Hon. S. A. Van Sant, Governor of Minnesota, responds as follows:—

Clark Bell, Esq., New York.

Dear Sir.—Answering your communication of recent date, permit me to say that a sanatorium for consumptives has not as yet been constructed. You will observe by an examination of the inclosed bill, that a commission has been named to select a suitable location. The commission, of which Dr. Rogers, of St. Paul, is chairman, are now considering the matter of a suitable location for such an institution.

Respectfully,

S. R. VAN SANT,

Governor.

Chapter 300—S. F. No. 502.— Laws of Minnesota for 1901.

An act to appoint a commission to investigate the advisability of establishing a state sanatorium for consumpitves, and to appropriate money therefor.

Be it enacted by the Legislature of the State of Minnesota:

Sec. 1. That within thirty (30) days after the passage of this act, the governor shall appoint three (3) persons, residents and freeholders of this state, whose duty it shall be to investigate into the advisability of establishing a state sanatorium for consumptives.

Sec. 2. Should said commission deem it advisable for the state to establish such an institution, then it shall become their duty to ascertain what location would be the most desirable and what building or buildings would be most suitable for such sanatorium.

Sec. 3. Such commission shall render a full report of their investigations and doings under this act to the Legislature of the state, to convene in the year 1903.

Sec. 4. Each member of said commission shall, before entering upon the performance of his duties as such member, take and subscribe an oath that he will faithfully perform his duties as member of said commission, which said oath, with the certificate of the officer administering the same, shall be filed in the office of the secretary of state.

Sec. 5. Said commission shall receive no salary or compensation for their services, but they shall receive their necessary expenses incurred in their performance of their duties under this act.

Sec. 6. To carry into effect the purpose specified in this act, there is hereby appropriated out of any money in the state treasury not otherwise appropriated, the sum of one thousand dollars. ($1,-000).

SEC. 7. This act shall take effect and be in force from and after its passage.

Approved April 13, 1901.

MISSISSIPPI.

Governor A. H. Lengino referred my letter to the State Board of Health of that State, which elicited the following reply from Dr. J. F. Hunter, the Secretary and Chief Executive officer of that Board:—

Jackson, Miss., July 11, 1901.

Mr. Clark Bell, 39 Broadway, New York, N. Y.

Dear Sir.—Your letter of the 25th ult. to Governor A. H. Longino has been referred to me, and I will state for your information that no act or legislation has been enacted by this State regarding the construction of a sanatoria for consumptives. It is a shame that the State of Mississippi has no established sanatoria for this purpose. A recommendation will be made to the next Legislature by the State Board of Health requesting an appropriation for this purpose.

Yours truly,

J. F. HUNTER.

MISSOURI.

Governor Alexander M. Dockery, of that State, replies as follows:

Jefferson, Mo., June 28, 1901.

Clark Bell, Esq., New York, N. Y.

Dear Sir.—The State of Missouri has passed no such law as the one to which you refer.

Very truly yours,

A. M. DOCKERY.

MONTANA.

Hon. Joseph K. Toole, Governor of Montana, responds as follows:—

Helena, Montana, July 1, 1901.

Mr. Clark Bell, Secretary, 39 Broadway, New York, N. Y.

My Dear Sir.—I am directed by the governor to acknowledge receipt of your communication under date of June 25, 1901, in which you ask for any laws that the State of Montana might have, bearing upon the construction of a sanitoria for consumptives, and to reply saying that Montana has no such laws, and that he regrets that he is unable to give you the information asked for.

Very respectfully,

LON. R. HASS,
Private Secretary.

NEBRASKA.

Hon. C. H. Dietrich, Governor of Nebraska, who has been elected Senator of the United States, replies to my letter as follows:—

Lincoln, Nebr, July 2, 1901.

Clark Bell, 39 Broadway, New York City.

Dear Sir.—Answering your favor of June 25th, will say that there has been no legislation in this state regarding the construction of sanitoria for consumptives. Very respectfully,

C. H. DIETRICH.

NEBRASKA.

The change in the office of the Governor of Nebraska, on the occasion of electing Governor Dietrich to the Senate of the United States, was perhaps the reason why we were not officially informed of the names and addresses of the delegates from that State, and explains why they were omitted.

In answer to our inquiries and also for the list of the delegates, the following reply came from the successor to that chair:

Lincoln, Neb., July 8, 1901.

Mr. Clark Bell, Sec'y American Congress of Tuberculosis, 39 Broadway, New York City.

Dear Sir.—Attached please find a list of delegates appointed by ex-Governor Dietrich to the Tuberculosis Congress held in New York City last May.

No legislation has ever been enacted in this State providing for the establishment of sanitaria for consumptives, nor has there been any legislation particularly directed to that subject. The fact is that our State Board of Health, which is composed of the Governor, Attorney General and Superintendent of Public Instruction, which is authorized to appoint three secretaries who shall be physicians, is almost wholly without power or authority to carry out any measures for the prevention of contagious diseases. We take care of our live stock all right, but have not progressed so far as to look after the welfare of the human family. We hope to improve.

Yours very truly,

H. C. LINDSAY,
Secretary to the Governor.

Dr. J. Hiddegand Tyndale, of Lincoln, Nebraska, a Vice President of the American Congress of Tuberculosis, replies as follows to my letter:—

Lincoln, Neb., July 8, 1901.

Hon. Clark Bell, Dundee, N. Y.

My Dear Sir.—There are no laws in Nebraska respecting sanitoria or any legislation in reference to same.

A state hospital for poor consumptives is contemplated and plans are being pushed. It is to be located three miles from Lincoln—once the Western Normal College. Cordially yours,

J. H. TYNDALE.

NEW HAMPSHIRE.

Governor Chester B. Jordan reports that the following action was taken last winter:

A joint resolution in favor of a committee to consider the question of a state sanitarium for consumptives, was passed, viz:

Resolved by the senate and house of representatives in general court convened:

That the governor be, and is, hereby authorized and instructed to appoint a committee consisting of three, or five, members, one of whom shall be a member of the State Board of Health, to consider the question of a state sanitarium for consumptives; and who shall report to the next legislature the best location for, and probable cost of erection and maintenance of, such an institution, together with such recommendations as they deem proper; (the report to be submitted to the legislature sometime during the first six days of the session); the committee to serve without pay, except for actual necessary expenses, which shall be paid from money in the treasury not otherwise appropriated, and the governor is hereby authorized to draw his warrant for the same.

Approved February 15, 1901.

Gov. Jordan, of New Hampshire, has appointed the following Commissioners under the Act:

Irving A. Watson, M. D., of Concord, of the State Board of Health.

Nathaniel G. Brooks, M. D., of Charleston.

Ezra Mitchell, M. D., of Charleston.

NEW JERSEY.

Gov. Foster M. Voorhees, replies as follows:

June 28, 1901.

Mr. Clark Bell, 39 Broadway, New York City.

Dear Sir.—In answer to your letter of the 25th inst., to Governor Voorhees, I beg to enclose you herewith, a copy of a bill introduced at the last session of the legislature. No action was taken thereon, however, and hence the bill failed to become a law.

Yours truly,
HOBART TUTTLE,
Private Secretary.

Be it enacted by the Senate and General Assembly of the State of New Jersey.

1. The governor, with the advice and consent of the senate, shall appoint six persons, who shall constitute the board of trustees of the New Jersey sanitarium for tubercular patients, and who shall hold office for the terms of one, two, three, four, five and six years respectively, beginning with the first day of April in the present year, and until their respective successors are appointed and qualified; and previous to the first day of April in each year thereafter the governor shall, in like manner, appoint one such trustee, to hold office for the term of six years, beginning with the first day of April in the year of his appointment, and until his successor is appointed and qualified; any such trustee may be removed by the governor for such cause as he may deem sufficient and as shall be assigned in the order of removal; any vacancy occuring in said board shall be filled in like manner for the unexpired term; the said board of trustees shall serve without compensation, and shall immediately organize by electing a president, secretary and treasurer.

2. The lands held by said trustees in trust for the state, for the use of said sanitarium, as hereinafter provided, shall not be taken for street, highway or railroad without leave of the legislature specially obtained.

3. As soon as may be, after organization, said board of trustees shall procure offers of sites for the location of said sanitarium, with the prices thereof, and shall procure plans for the said sanitarium building or buildings to be made, with estimates of the cost thereof, necessary to properly fit said building or buildings for the purposes of said sanitarium, and report the same to the governor with their recommendation thereon, and upon his approval, are authorized to enter into contracts for the purchase of such site, and the erection and equipment of said sanitarium; provided, however, that the expenditure for carrying out the purposes of this act shall not exceed fifty thousand dollars.

4. No member of the board of trustees shall be directly or indirectly interested in any contract in connection with said sanitarium, or with the furnishing of supplies for said sanitarium, and the violation of this section shall be a misdemeanor.

5. The board of trustees shall not order the expenditure of any money, or make any contract or contracts except by a majority vote of all its members, which vote shall be taken by ayes and nays and entered on the minutes of said board of trustees.

6. Said board of trustees shall have the general direction and control of all the property and concerns of said sanitarium, not otherwise provided by law, and shall take charge of the general interests of said sanitarium, and see that the objects and designs thereof are carried into effect, and everything done faithfully according to the requirements of the legislature and the by-laws, rules and regulations of said sanitarium.

7. The said board of trustees shall make rules and regulations for the government of said sanitarium; they shall make all needful by-law, rules and regulations for the government of the proceedings of said board of trustees, and shall fix the terms for care and board upon which all persons who are able to pay their board shall be admitted to said sanitarium; but no person shall be refused admission to said sanitarium because of his or her inability to pay; they shall appoint all medical directors and assistant physicians, employes, nurses and servants and fix their compensation; all rules and regulations made by said board of trustees in pursuance of this section shall be made subject to the approval of the governor.

8. Said board of trustees shall have authority to recover for the use of said sanitarium, any and all sums which may be due upon any note or bond in their hands belonging thereto; also, any and all sums which may be charged and due, according to the by-laws, for the support of any patient therein, or who may have been therein, in which action the declaration may be in a general indebitatus assumpsit, and judgment shall be rendered for such as may be found due, with interest from the time of the demand made by the treasurer of such payment; said board of trustees may also, upon the receipt of the money due upon any mortgage belonging to said sanitarium, execute and acknowledge, or cause to be executed and acknowledged, a release thereof, so that the same may be discharged of record.

9. It shall be the duty of said board of trustees to visit said sanitarium at least twice in each year, and to inspect said sanitarium and management, and to make, in their annual report, such recommendations as they may deem necessary concerning said sanitarium.

10. This act shall take effect immediately.

NEW MEXICO.

The Governor of New Mexico replies to my inquiry as follows:—

Santa Fe, July 6, 1901.

Clark Bell, Esq., Secy American Congress of Tuberculosis, 39 Broadway, New York.

Dear Sir.—We are in receipt of your letter of the 25th ult. We do not have any law in this territory regarding the construction of sanitariums for consumptives. Yours very truly,

MIGUEL A. OTERO,
Governor of New Mexico.

NEW YORK.

The Governor of New York in reply sends me a copy of the act passed in that State for the establishment of a State Hospital in the Adirondacks, passed April 12, 1900.

Chapter 416, Laws of 1900, of which the following is a copy:

The People of the State of New York, represented in Senate and Assembly, do enact as follows:

SECTION 1. Establishment and objects of hospital.—A state hospital in some suitable locality in the Adirondacks, for the treatment of incipient pulmonary tuberculosis is hereby established.

§ 2. Trustees.—The governor, by and with the advice and consent of the senate, shall appoint five citizens of this state, of whom two shall be physicians, who shall constitute the board of trustees of the New York state hospital for the treatment of incipient pulmonary tuberculosis. The full term of office of each trustee shall be five years, and the term of office of one of such trustees shall expire annually. To effect such order of expiration of terms of trustees, the first appointments shall be made for the respective terms of five, four, three, two and one years. Appointments of successors shall be for the full term of five years, except that appointment of persons to fill vacancies occurring by death, resignation or other cause, shall be made for the unexpired term. Failure of any trustee to attend in each year two stated meetings of the board shall cause a vacancy in his office, unless said absence be excused by formal action of the board. The trustees shall receive no compensation for their services, but shall be allowed their actual and necessary traveling and other expenses, to be paid on the audit and warrant of the comptroller. Any of said trustees may at any time be removed from office by the governor by and with the consent of the senate for any cause they may deem sufficient after an opportunity to be heard in his or her defense, and others may be appointed in their places as herein provided. Three members of the board of trustees shall constitute a quorum, but no business involving expenditure shall be transacted except by the affirmative vote of at least three members.

§ 3. Lands.—The lands to be held for the purposes herein mentioned shall not be taken for any street, highway or railway without leave of the legislature.

§ 4. Powers and duties of trustees.—For the purposes of this act the said trustee and their successors shall be a body corporate with all the powers necesary to carry into effect the purposes of this act, together with the following powers, duties and obligations. They shall,

1. Take care of the general interests of the hospital and see that its design is carried into effect, according to law, and its by-laws, rules and regulations.

2. Establish such by-laws, rules and regulations as they may deem necessary and expedient for regulating the appointment and duties of officers and employees of the hospital, and for the internal government, discipline and management of the same.

3. Maintain an effective inspection of the affairs and management of the hospital, for which purpose the board shall meet at the hospital at least once in every three months, and at such other times as may be prescribed in the by-laws. The annual meeting of the board of trustees shall be held on the second Saturday of January.

4. Keep in a book provided for that purpose, a fair and full record of the doings of the board, which shall be open at all times to the inspection of its members, the governor of this state, and officers of the state board of charities, or any person appointed by the governor or either house of the legislature to examine the same.

5. Cause to be typewritten within ten day after each meeting of such trustees or of a committee thereof, the minutes and proceedings of such meeting, and cause a copy thereof to be sent to each member of such board.

6. Enter in a book kept by them for that purpose, the date of each of their visits, and the condition of the hospital and patients and all such trustees present shall sign the same.

7. Make to the legislature in January of each year, a detailed report of the results of their visits and inspection, with suitable suggestions and such other matter as may be required of them by the governor, for the year ending on the thirty-first day of December, preceding the date of such report. The resident officers shall admit such trustees into every part of the hospital and its buildings, and exhibit to them on demand all the books, papers, accounts and writings belonging to the hospital or pertaining to its business management, discipline or government, and furnish copies, abstracts and reports whenever required by them.

§ 5. Annual report; state board of charities.—The board of trustees of the hospital shall annually, on or before the first day of November, for the preceding fiscal year, report to the state board of charities the affairs and conditions of the hospital, with full and detailed estimates of the next appropriation required for maintenance and ordinary uses and repairs, and of special appropriations, if any, needed for extraordinary repairs, renewals, extensions, improvement, betterments or other necessary objects, as also for the erection of additional buildings; and the state board of charities shall, in its annual report to the legislature, certify what appropriations are, in its opinion, necessary and proper. The said hospital shall be subject to the visitation and to the general powers of the state board of charities.

§ 6. Donations in trust.—The trustees may take and hold in trust for the state any grant or devise of land, or any gift or bequest of money or other personal property, or any donation, to be applied principal or income, or both, to the maintenance and the general uses of the hospital.

§ 7. Site of hospital.—The said trustees are hereby empowered to select a site for the establishment of said hospital, such site to be subject to the approval of the state board of health and the Forest preserve board. The said trustees are empowered to contract for the purchase of, to acquire title to and to hold a tract of land not exceeding one thousand acres in extent for the establishment of such hospital, or at the request of the said trustees, subject to the approval of the state board of health, the Forest preserve board may set apart a like amount of land owned by the state for the purposes of said hospital.

§ 8. Buildings and improvements.—The trustees to be appointed under the provisions of this act are authorized, empowerd and required as soon as the site for such hospital is selected and approved to proceed with the construction and equipment of all necessary and suitable buildings including heating, lighting, plumbing, laundry fixtures and water supply therefor, and with the construction of roads thereto, upon plans adopted by them, to be approved by the state architect, and the state board of charities at an expense not to exceed one hundred and fifty thousand dollars, which buildings shall furnish accommodations for at least two hundred patients beside the officers, employees and attendants of said institution. The said trustees shall have power to select plans approved as above and to make and award contracts for the erection and construction of said buildings, and the equipment above provided; but no part of the several sums herein appropriated shall be available for any construction, improvement or purchase unless a contract or contracts shall have first been made for the completion or purchase within the appropriation therefor and the performance thereof secured by a satisfactory bond approved by the comptroler.

§ 9. Superintendent and treasurer.—The trustees shall also have power to appoint a superintendent of the hospital, who shall be a well-educated physician, not a member of the board of trustees, a graduate of a legally chartered medical college, with an experience of at least six years in the actual practice of his profession, including at least one year's actual experience in a general hospital, and a treasurer, who shall give an undertaking to the people of the state for the faithful performance of his trust in such penal sum and form and with such sureties as the comptroller shall approve. Said officers may be discharged or suspended at any time by the said board of trustees in its discretion.

§ 10. Duties of superintendent.—The superintendent shall

1. Appoint such employees as are necessary and proper for the due administration of the affairs of such institution, prescribe their duties and places and, subject to the approval of the trustees, fix their compenation, within the appropriation fixed therefor.

2. Oversee and secure the individual treatment and personal care of each and every patient of the hospital while resident therein, and keep a proper oversight over all the inhabitants thereof.

3. Have the general superintendence of the buildings and grounds with their furniture and fixtures and the direction and control of all persons employed in and about the same.

4. Give from time to time such orders and instructions as he may deem best calculated to induce good conduct, fidelity and economy in any department for the treatment of patients.

5. Maintain salutary discipline among all employees, patients and inmates of the hospital, and enforce strict compliance with his instructions, and obedience to all the rules and regulations of the hospital. He shall, under the supervision and control of the board, discharge such patients as are sufficiently restored to health, or such as are found to be unsuitable patients for the hospital.

6. Cause full and fair accounts and records of the conditions and prospects of the patients to be kept regularly, from day to day, in books provided for that purpose.

7. See that such accounts and records shall be fully made up to the first days of January, April, July and October, in each year, and that the principal facts and results with the report thereon be presented to the trustees at their regular meetings.

8. Conduct the official correspondence of the hospital, and keep a record or copy of all letters written, and files of all letters received.

9. Prepare and present to the board, at its annual meeting, a true and perfect inventory of all the personal property and effects belonging to the hospital, and account, when required by the board, for the careful keeping and economical use of all furniture, stores and other articles furnished for the hospital.

§ 11. Duties of treasurer.—The treasurer, among his other duties, shall

1. Have the custody of all moneys received and all money, notes, mortgages and other securities and obligations belonging to the hospital.

2. Keep a full and accurate account of all receipts and payments, in the form prescribed by the by-laws, and such other accounts as shall be required of him by the trustees.

3. Balance all the accounts on his books on the first day of each January, and make a statement thereof, and an abstract of all the receipts and payments of the past year; and within five days thereafter deliver the same to the auditing committee of the trustees, who shall compare the same with his books and vouchers, and verify the same by a comparison with the books of the superintendent, and certify the correctness thereof to the trustees at their annual meeting.

4. Render a quarterly statement of his receipts and payments to such auditing committee who shall, in like manner as above, compare, verify, report and certify the result thereof, to the trustees at their annual meeting, who shall cause the same to be recorded in one of the books of the hospital.

5. Render a further account of the state of his books, and of the funds and other property in his custody, whenever required by the trustees.

6. Receive for the use of the hospital, money which may be paid upon obligations or securities in his hands belonging to the hospital; and all sums paid to the hospital for the support of any patient therein or for actual disbursements made in said patient's behalf for necessary clothing and traveling expenses; and money paid to the hospital from any other source.

7. Prosecute an action in the name of the hospital to recover money due or owing to the hospital, from any source; including the bringing of suit for breach of contract between private patients or their representative and the trustees of the hospital.

8. Execute a release and satisfaction of a mortgage judgment, lien or other debt when paid.

9. Pay the salaries of the superintendent and of all employees of the hospital, and the disbursements of the officers and members of the board as aforesaid. The treasurer shall have power to employ counsel, subject to the approval of the board of trustees.

10. Deposit all moneys received for the care of private patients and all other revenues of the hospital, in a bank designated by the comptroller, and as often as the comptroller may require, transmit to the comptroller a statement showing the amount so received and deposited and from whom, and for what received, and the dates on which such deposits were made. Such statement of deposit shall be certified by the proper officer of the bank receiving such deposit or deposits. The treasurer shall make affidavit that the sum so deposited is all the money received by him from any source of income for the hospital up to the date of the latest deposit appearing on such statement. A bank designated by the comptroller to receive such deposits shall, before any deposit be made, execute a bond to the people of the state in a sum and with sureties to be approved by the comptroller, for the safe keeping of such deposits.

§ 12. Medical assistants and examining physicians.—All medical assistants shall be appointed by the superintendent. No medical assistant shall be appointed who is not a well-educated physician and a graduate of a legally chartered medical college, and with an experience of at least two years in the actual practice of his profession, including at least one year's actual experience in a general hospital. Said trustees shall also appoint in all the cities of the state reputable physicians, citizens of the state of New York, who shall examine all persons applying for admission to said hospital for treatment. There shall be not less than two or more than four of such examining physicians appointed in cities of the first class, and two each in cities of the second and third class. Said examining physicians shall have been in the regular practice of their profession for at least five years, and shall be skilled in the diagnosis and treatment of pulmonary diseases. Their fee or compensation for each patient examined shall be three dollars. Not more than one-half of all the physicians to be appointed under this section shall belong to the same school of medicine or practice.

§ 13. Free patients.—The trustees of said hospital to be appointed under and pursuant to the provisions of this act, and their successors, are hereby given power and authority to receive therein patients who have no ability to pay, but no person shall be admitted to the hospital who has not been a citizen of this state for at least one year preceding the date of application. Every person desiring free treatment in said hospital shall apply to the local authorities of his or her town, city or county having charge of the relief of the poor, who shall thereupon issue a written request to the superintendent of said hospital for the admission and treatment of such person. Such request shall state in writing whether the person is able to pay for his or her care and treatment while at the hospital, which request and statement shall be kept on file by the superintendent in a book kept for that purpose in the order of their receipt by him. When said hospital is completed and ready for the treatment of patients, or whenever thereafter there are vacancies caused by the death or removal, the said superintendent shall thereupon issue a request to an examining physician, appointed as provided for in section twelve, in the same city or county, and if there be no such examining physician in said city or county then to the nearest examining physician, for the examination by him of said patient. Upon the request of such superintendent said examining physician shall examine all persons applying for free admission and treatment in said institution, and determine whether such persons applying are suffering from incipient pulmonray tuberculosis. No person shall be admitted as a patient in said institution without the certificate of one of said examining physicians certifying that such applicant is suffering from incipient pulmonary tuberculosis. Admissions to said hospital shall be made in the order in which the names of applicants shall appear upon the application book to be kept as above provided by the superintendent of said hospital, in so far as such applicants are subsequently certified by the said examining physician to be suffering from incipient pulmonary tuberculosis. Every person who is declared as herein provided to be unable to pay for his or her care or treatment, shall be transported to and from the hospital at the expense of said local authorities.

§14. Private patients.—Applicants for admission to this institution who are able to pay for their care and treatment are not required to obtain a written request from the local authorities having charge of the relief of the poor, but shall apply in person to the superintendent who shall enter the name of such applicant in the book to be kept by him, for that purpose, as provided in section thirteen; and when there is room in said hospital for the admission of such applicant, without interfering with the preference in the selection of patients, which shall always be given to the indigent, such patient shall be admitted to the hospital upon the certificate of one of the examining physicians, which certificate shall be kept on file by the said superintendent.

§ 15. Support of free patients.—At least once in each month the superintendent of the hospital shall furnish to the comptroller a list countersigned by the treasurer of the hospital of all the free patients in the hospital, together with sufficient facts to enable the comptroller to collect from the proper local official having charge of the relief of the poor such sums as may be owing to the state for the examination, care and treatment of the patients who hve been received by the hospital and who are shown by the statement of such local official to be unable to pay for their care and treatment. The comptroller shall thereupon collect from the said local official the sums due for the care and treatment of each such patient at a rate not exceeding five dollars per week for each patient.

§ 16. Support of private patients.—The trustees shall have power and authority to fix the charges to be paid by patients who are able to pay for their care and treatment in said hospital, or who have relatives bound by law to support them, who are able to pay therefor.

§ 17. Appropriation.—The sum of fifty thousand dollars is hereby appropriated for the purpose of purchasing a site and of erecting, constructing and equipping the hospital and buildings as herein provided. The treasurer of the state shall, on the warrant of the comptroller, and on the certificate of the state architect pay to the treasurer of the trustees of said hospital the above named sums in such amounts as may, from time to time, in the judgment of the trustees, be necessary.

§ 18. When to take effect.—This act shall take effect immediately.

State of New York,
Office of the Secretary of State. ....

I have compared the preceding with the original law on file in this office, and do hereby certify that the same is a correct transcript therefrom and of the whole of said original law.

JOHN T. McDONOUGH,
Secretary of State.

NEW YORK.

Dr. Daniel Lewis, one of the leading physicians of the State, and a sanatarian of great ability, is President of the State Board of Health. His reply to my inquiry is as follows:—

252 Madison Av., New York, July 13th, 1901.

Hon. Clark Bell, 39 Broadway, City.

Dear Mr. Bell.—We have no laws in this state concerning sanatoria of the character to which you refer in your letter of the 1st.

The only thing the state has done was to pass an act last year appointing a commission to locate and erect a consumptive hospital in the Adirondacks, for which $50,000 was appropriated, and another appropriation for the same commission at the session of 1901, for $100,000. The question of a site for this hospital is still open. The Governor, Senator Ellsworth, President pro tem of the Senate, and Mr. Nixon, Speaker of the Assembly, were appointed to review the location which had been decided upon by the commission at Ray Brook.

This special committee has thus far taken no action, so far as I know, and nothing of course has been commenced looking to the erection of the buildings. Very truly yours,

• DANIEL LEWIS.

NEW YORK CITY.

The following is the reply of Hon. John B. Sexton, President of the Board of Health of the City of New York in reply to my letter of inquiry to which the reply alludes:—

Department of Health, City of New York,
S. W. Cor. 55th Street and Sixth Avenue,
Borough of Brooklyn, Manhattan,
New York, July 24, 1901.

Dr. Clark Bell, Secretary American Congress of Tuberculosis, 39 Broadway, New York City.

Dear Sir:—I beg to acknowledge the receipt of your communication to the President of this Board, requesting to be furnished with copies of the Sanitary Code of this Department, and information relating to the mehods employed by the Board of Health in respect to tuberculosis, for the American Congress of Tuberculosis, to be published in its transactions, and to inform you I have this day mailed to you all the literature we have in this Department upon that subject, also a copy of the Sanitary Code.

In reply to your request to be informed how far the ravages of tuberculosis can be averted and the best methods for the attainment of such results, I beg to say this information will be prepared and submitted to you by Dr. H. M. Biggs, the Chief of the Division of Bacteriology of this Department.

Very Respectfully,

C. GOLDENNAU,
Secretary pro tem.

The following is a list of the several reports, articles and printed matter accompanying the letter of the Hon. John B. Sexton, President of the Board of Health of the Department of Health of the City of New York:

1. Sanitary Code of the Board of Health of the Department of Health, New York City. (1900).
2. Report of the Board of Health to the Mayor of New York City on "Pulmonary Tuberculosis." (1897).
3. Circular to Physicians as to Restriction and Prevention from Health Department, New York City. (1897).
4. Circular to Farmers relating to the Collection and care of milk from New York Health Department. (May, 1901).
5. Circular from New York Health Department, regarding "Reporting Cases of Tuberculosis," with set of blank forms for (1901).
6. Circular of Information as to the growth of Bacteria in milk. (1901).
7. Circular as to Bacteriaological Examinations of Pulmonary Tuberculosis. (1897).
8. Circular to Physicians on, "Prevention of Tuberculosis."
9. Circular of Physicians to Consumptives. (1899).
10. Report on Tuberculosis by Herman Biggs, M. D., Chief Inspector of Pathology Bacterological and Disinfection.
11. Forms used by Medical Inspectors.
12. Forms of Notice to Superintendents of Institutions.

13. Form of Report of Medical Inspectors.
14. Paper by Herman Biggs, M. D., entitled "The Regulation of Tuberculosis."
15. Paper by Herman M. Biggs, M. D., and Arthur R. Greenard, M. D., on "Antitoxin Serum in Diphtheria."

NORTH CAROLINA.

Hon. Charles B. Aycock, Governor of North Carolina, replies as follows:

State of North Carolina, Executive Department, Raleigh, July 1.
Clark Bell, Esq., 39 Broadway, New York.

Dear Sir.—There is no legislation in this State regarding the construction of a Sanitoria for consumptives. Dr. Westry Battle, of Asheville, N. C., will furnish any information which you may desire in reference to Sanitoria for consumptives in this State.

Very Truly Yours,
CHARLES B. AYCOCK, Governor.

NORTH DAKOTA.

Hon. Frank White, Governor of North Dakota, replies as follows:

June 29, 1901.
Clark Bell, Esq., 39 Broadway, New York, N. Y.

Dear Sir.—I beg to acknowledge receipt of your favor of June 25th to Governor White, and in reply will state that we have no legislation regarding the construction of sanitoria for consumptives in this State.

Very respectfully,
C. W. GEDCHEY,
Private Secretary.

OHIO.

The letter enclosed from Governor Geo. K. Nash, of that State, is as follows:

Columbus, Ohio, June 27, 1901.
Mr. Clark Bell, 39 Broadway, New York City.

Dear Sir.—Replying to your favor of the 25th instant, the Governor directs me to say that there has been no legislation in this State concerning the construction of sanitoria for consumptives; therefore, there is no data he can furnish you.

Very truly yours,
FREDERICK L. LINKS,
Private Secretary.

PENNSYLVANIA.

The following is the reply from that State:

1420 Chestnut St., Philadelphia, June 29, 1901.
Clark Bell, Esq., Sec. American Congress of Tuberculosis, 39 Broadway, New York, N. Y.

Dear Sir.—His Excellency, the Governor of Pennsylvania, has referred to me for reply your communication of the 25th inst., in which you request a copy of any act or legislation enacted in our state regarding the construction of sanatoria for consumptives.

I would say in reply that no such legislation has as yet been proposed in this State. An application was made, however, to the legislature for an appropriation in aid of a movement known as the

"Free Hospital for the Consumptive Poor," and the legislature included an item of $110,000 for this purpose in the general appropriation act. This has not yet received the sanction of the Governor, and it is possible that the amount may be either cut down or stricken out altogether. The Commissoner of Forestry of the state, Dr. J. T. Rothrock, whose office is in Harrisburg, is considering the possibility of establishing sanitary camps for those in the early stages of this disease on certain of the forestry reservations, and has invited me to make a visit of inspection to the different reservations in order to determine on appropriate sites for such camps.

I shall be glad to let you know if this movement takes definite shape.

Yours very truly,

BENJAMIN LEE,
Secretary.

Dic. to D. V. D.

Rhode Island.

Dr. Jay Perkins, of Providence, is a close student of the subject, with a fine experience in the treatentm.

I wrote him, and the following is is his reply:—

July 11, 1901.

Clark Bell, Esq., New York.

Dear Sir.— Your letter in reference to sanatoria in Rhode Island was received and then mislaid until to-day, and I regret not having answered it before.

We have, as yet, in Rhode Island no provision for taking care of tuberculous patients in separate institutions. In connection with the State's Almshouse, there is a separate pavilion where the consumptives are isolated and given excellent care, but this is open only to inmates of the Almshouse. In St. Joseph's Hospital they take a certain number of tuberculous patients and have a separate ward for them; their accomodations for these patients are quite limited, however.

At the Rhode Island Hospital I have charge of an out-patient department devoted exclusively to cases of pulmonary tuberculosis; this has been established one year.

At the last session of the legislature a committee was appointed to inquire into and report upon the advisability of establishing a State sanatorium for curable cases. This committee is at work upon the subject and will make a favorable report, and as there is a favorable sentiment in the legislature we hope to see something done. This is all I can report for you for Rhode Island.

Yours sincerely,

JAY PERKINS.

The Governor of Rhode Island sent no delegates to the Congress, and I wrote the Secretary of the State Board of Health of that State, Dr. Gardner T. Swarts, of Providence, who replied as follows:—

Providence, July 11, 1901.

Mr. Clark Bell, Esq., 39 Broadway, New York City, N. Y.

Dear Sir.—In reply to your circular letter concerning sanitoria for consumptives, I will state that our present condition is that we have no laws governing sanitoria for consumptives, but at the last January session of the Legislature I succeeded in having a commission appointed to investigate the needs of a sanatoria and to ascertain the location of a suitable site in the state.. The commission has commenced its labors and I expect it will be able to report to the next session. Sentiment in favor of such an institution seems to be very strong and we hope to obtain an appropriation for the purpose.

Yours truly,

GARDNER T. SWARTS,
Secretary.

South Carolina.

Governor M. B. McSweeny, of South Carolina, referred my letter of inquiry to the Secretary of the State Board of Health, who makes the following reply:

State of South Carolina, State Board of Health,
Florence, S. C., July 1, 1901.

Clark Bell, Esq.

Dear Sir.—Your letter of June 25th inst., to Gov. M. B. McSweeney has been referred to me for reply. There is no law in this state in regard to the construction of Sanitoria for consumptives, nor have any such buildings been erected, or in contemplation of construction, so far as I am aware.

Yours truly,

JAMES EVANS, M. D.,
Sec. State Board of Health.

South Dakota.

Governor Herreid, of South Dakota, replies as follows:—

Pierre, S. D., July 2nd, 1901.

Clark Bell, Esq., New York.

My Dear Sir.—South Dakota has had no legislation on the proposition you refer to in your letter of the 25th inst., looking towards the construction of sanitoria for consumptives.

Very Respectfully,

E. A. WARNER,
Private Secretary.

CHARLES N. HERREID,
Governor.

Tennessee.

Governor Benton McMillan, of Tennessee, referred my letter to Dr. J. A. Albright, Secretary of the State Board of Health, who sent me the following reply:—

Nashville, July 2nd, 1901.

Dr. Clark Bell, Sec. and Treasurer Am. Congress of Tuberculosis, 39 Broadway, New York City, N. Y.

Dear Doctor.—Yours of the 25th instant, addressed to Governor Benton McMillin, has been referred to this office for attention, and in reply will say that Tennessee has no state institution for the care of consumptives. The Tennessee Board of Health, however, has had under consideration for some time and hope, during the next session of our State legislature, to present such proposition in tangible form with a view to securing necessary legislation.

Very respectfully,

J. A. ALBRIGHT, M. D.,
Secretary State Board of Health and Executive Officer.

TEXAS.

Hon. Joseph D. Sayres, Governor of Texas, replies as follows:—

Austin, July 2, 1901.

Clark Bell, Esq., 39 Broadway, New York City.

Dear Sir.—Yours of the 25th ultimo has been received and contents noted. There has been no legislation in this State regarding the construction of a sanitorium for consumptives.

Yours truly,
JOSEPH D. SAYERS.

UTAH.

Hon. Heber M. Wells, Governor of Utah, replies as follows:—

Salt Lake City, July 2, 1901.

Clark Bell, Secretary American Congress of Tuberculosis, 39 Broadway, New York.

Dear Sir.—Your letter of the 25th ultimo to Governor Wells reached in the absence of the Governor from the State. Replying to same I beg to advise you that there is no legislation whatever upon our statute books upon the subject of construction of sanitoria for consumptives.

Very respectfully,
GERSHOM B. WELLS,
Private Secretary.

VIRGINIA.

Governor J. Hoge Tyler, of Virginia, referred the subject to the Secretary of the State Board of Health of that State, who writes as follows:

State Board of Health of Virginia, Secretary's Office, July 1, 1901.

Hon. Clark Bell, Sec. and Treasurer American Congress of Tuberculosis, 39 Broadway, New York.

My Dear Sir.—Your letter, addressed to the Hon. J. Hoge Tyler, Governor of Virginia, has been forwarded to me to answer.

I regret to say that our State Board is still an infant, though growing finely. We have had a great deal to contend with, our people not being enlightened on health laws and sanitation, but are yielding to its influence more and more each year. We have been able to do nothing as yet toward establishing sanitoria for consumptives, for which we have an ideal climate.

I have read with interest the proceedings of your Congress, sent me by Gov. Tyler. Assuring you of my esteem and best wishes, believe me

Very truly yours,
PAULUS A. IRVING, Secretary.

Dr. Henry D. Holton, Secretary of the State Board of Health, and President of the American Congress of Tuberculosis, is thoroughly familiar with the laws of that state. In reply to my inquiry he says:

We have no hospital for tuberculosis in the State of Vermont, although we are talking of such things.

WASHINGTON.

Governor J. B. Rogers, of Washington referred the subject of my letter to the Secretary of the State Board of Health, the secretary of which replies as follows:—

Spokane, Wash., July 4, 1901.

Clark Bell, Esq., Sec. American Congress of Tuberculosis, New York City, N. Y.

Dear Sir.—Replying to your favor of the 26th inst., addressed to Governor Rodgers would say that this State has no sanitoria for consumptives, and none have so far been provided for.

Yours very truly,

D. C. NEWMAN,
Secretary State Board of Health.

WEST VIRGINIA.

Dr. C. F. Ulrich, of West Virginia, one of the vice presidents of the American Congress of Tuberculosis, replies as follows to my letter:—

Wheeling, W. Va., July 11, 1901.

Clark Bell, Esq.

Dear Colleague.—According to your request I have made diligent inquiry and find no sanatoria for consumptives in West Virginia. A number of years ago Dr. Blum, of this city, established, at his own expense, a sanatorium for that and similar diseases in the mountains of this state at a place called Helvetia. It ruined him financially and he died of what is usually called a broken heart. There was some talk of having it purchased and rehabilitated by the state, but nothing was ever done and it has gone to decay. I will do what I can to stir up an interest before the next meeting of the legislature to get something done in that direction.

Respectfully yours,

C. F. ULRICH.
July 11, 1901.

There is not time left me to attempt to enumerate and describe in this article the sanitaria not under the control of the governments of the nation or states.

There are none yet under the management of the Dominion Government in Canada.

The time required to have this paper before the London Congress of Tuberculosis, which meets July 22-25, renders it impossible to embrace them.

To enumerate the Private Sanitoria or describe them would require a treatise.

The answers that come after I close this paper for the London Congress from the Governors of States, or members of Boards of Health can be published as an addenda in my Journal.

If I shall have thrown any light on this branch of the question, to which the Congress of Tuberculosis will open a discussion, I shall feel content.

West Virginia.

Hon. Geo. W. Atkinson, Governor of West Virginia, referred my letter to his successor, who replied as follows:—

Charleston W. Va., July 5, 1901.

Clark Bell, Esq., Secretary, 39 Broadway, New York, N. Y.

Dear Sir.—Your favor of June 25th to ex-Governor Geo. W. Atkinson has been referred to this office.

As far as we are advised there is no legislation in this State for the construction of sanatoria for consumptives.

Respectfully yours,
..E. S. BOGGS,
Private Secretary.

Wyoming.

Governor Richards, of Wyoming, replies as follows:—

Cheyenne, July 2, 1901.

Clark Bell, Esq., Sec'y Am. Congress of Tuberculosis, 39 Broadway, N. Y. City.

Dear Sir.—Your circular letter of the 25th ult., enclosing a copy of the first day's proceedings of your congress is received and in reply will say that no act has ever been passed by a Wyoming legislature regarding the construction of sanitoria for consumptives.

Yours very truly,
DeF. RICHARDS.

THE PROVINCE OF QUEBEC, DOMINION OF CANADA.

Dr. E. P. Lachapelle, President of the Board of Health of the Province of Quebec, has sent me the Quebec Public Health act of 1891. 1 Edward vii chapter xix, entitled "An Act to amend and consolidate the law respecting public health," assented to 26th March, 1901. This act is too long for this paper. I submit an abstract of the act or synopsis which is entitled, Table of Contents:

Nuisances: power to define them, art. 28; verification, arts. 29 to 31; suppression, arts. 32 to 40.
Approval of plans for aqueducts and drainage works: arts. 41 to 43.
Penalty for polluting water-supplies: art. 44.
Food and drink: shall be wholesome, art. 45; confiscation, art. 46; suspension of operations in dairies and food factories for cause of unsanitary condition, arts. 47 and 48; Board of Health of the Province may intervene directly, art. 49.
Contagious diseases: notification, arts. 50 to 53; duty of municipalities to take measures to check them, art. 54; maintainance of hospitals, etc., art. 55; sick or suspects found in public conveyances or moving about, arts. 56 and 57; removal to hospital in certain cases, art. 58; taking possession of properties in urgent cases, art. 59; disinfection, art. 60; jurisdiction of municipalities over infected vessels, art. 61; venereal diseases, art. 62.
Inspections, etc.,. arts. 63 to 64.
Penalties and prosecutions: art. 65.
Section II. Sanitary conditions of Industrial Establishments...17
Regulations by the Board of Health of the Province and their execution, arts. 66 to 70.
Section III. Special Provisions in cases of Epidemic—The Board of Health of the Province, in becoming "Central Board," may enact special by-laws 18
Interpretation, art. 71; Present section put in force by a proclamation, art. 72; Organization of the Central Board of Health, art. 73; By-laws of the Central Board, art. 74 and 75; Expenses of Central Board, art. 76; Local board of health, their organization, duties and powers, arts. 77 to 81; Central Board may substitute its action to that of local boards, when the latter prove themselves incompetent, art. 82; Expenses of local boards, art. 83; Penalties and prosecutions, arts. 84 to 87.
Section IV. Inoculation with small-pox virus and anti-variolic vaccination 23
Inoculation with small-pox virus prohibited, arts. 88 and 89; all municipalities may render vaccination compulsory, art. 90; vaccination in municipalities having over 300 inhabitants, arts. 91 and 92; duties of parents re vaccination, arts. 93 and 94; certificates of vaccination, arts. 95 and 97; fee for certain vaccination, art. 98; vaccination in schools, arts. 99 and 100; penalties and prosecutions, arts. 101 to 104.
Section V. Collection of Vital Statistics, arts. 105 to 114.... 28
Temporary provisions, etc., arts. 115 to 120................ 30
Forms, re vaccination and re statistics................... 31

I also make same citations from the act bearing on the questions we are interested in. Section 9, page 5, provides in certain of its sections as follows:

The Board of Health of the Province may make, amend, repeal and replace by-laws for the following purposes:
To insure the good sanitary condition of educational institutions, workshops, hospitals, asylums for the insane, charitable institutions, barracks, prisons and asylums.

Sub-division 5 of section 9, provides as follows:

To regulate the sanitary condition of houses, dairies, cow-sheds, places where milk is sold, butter factories, cheese factories, slaughter-houses, stables, pig-sties and yards, and insure the sanitary condition thereof.

Sub-division 8 and 9 of same section 9, provides as follows:

To define the diseases and lesions which render animals, meat and other alimentary animal products, unsuitable for consumption or prejudicial to health.

To prevent as much as possible epidemic, endemic and contagious diseases of men and animals.

Section 45 of such act provides as follows:

Only such food or drink as is of wholesome and of healthy origin shall be sold or otherwise disposed of by onerous title.

Every infringement of this provision renders the person found guilty thereof liable to a fine not exceeding fifty dollars.

Sections 46 and 47 of said act provide as follows:

Every executive officer of the municipal sanitary authority or every other officer appointed by it for that purpose, may inspect all animals, dead or alive, meat, fowl, game, fish, fruit, vegetables, grease, bread, flour, milk or other liquid and food intended for human consumption and offered for sale or deposited in a place or transported in a vehicle for the purpose of being afterwards sold or offered for sale, or delivered after being sold; and, if upon inspection, such animals, liquids or food appear to be unwholesome, putrid, damaged or infected with the germs of disease, or otherwise injurious to health, he may seize the same, carry them off, and dispose of them so that they shall not be offered for sale or serve as food for man.

The burden of proof that the animals, liquids or food are not intended to be sold, or to be delivered after having been sold, or to serve as food for man lies upon the owner or person who had possession thereof.

Every executive officer of the municipal sanitary authority or every other officer authorized by it for that purpose may inspect the dairies, stables and cow-sheds situated within or without the limits of the municipality, whence is supplied the milk sold in the municipality, as well as the places in the municipality where milk is sold, and, if he finds that such dairies, table, cow-sheds or places are not kept in the condition required by the by-laws of the Board of Health of the Province, he shall give an order in writing to the proprietor or the person in possession to discontinue the sale and distribution of the milk from such dairies, stables or cow-sheds or to suspend the sale in such places until they shall be placed in the condition required by such by-laws.

Every sale or delivery of milk in contravention of the notice prescribed by this article renders the persons guilty thereof liable to a fine not exceeding twenty-five dollars.

Section 50 of said act provides in part as follows:

Whenever the head of any household or of any establishment whatever ascertains that any person dwelling in his home or in the establishment under his control, has small-pox, asiatic cholera, plague, typhus, diphtheria, croup, scarlatina, typhoid fever, measles, tuberculosis which has reached the stage of suppuration and expectoration, leprosy or any other disease which the Board of Health of the Province has designated by by-law, he shall within twenty-four hours notify the same to the municipal sanitary authority of the locality in which he resides or has his establishment

Section 55 provides in part as follows:

Every municipal council may establish and maintain:

1.Temporary or permanent hospitals or houses for the reception and treatment of persons suffering from contagious diseases.

The act is divided into four sections. The first 65 sub-divisions or sections compose what is called the section I of the act.

Section II relates to the public health in industrial establishments.

Sub-division or section 66 of the act is the first sub-division of section II. It provides in part as follows:

The Board of Health of the Province of Quebec, called in this section the "Board of Health," may, with the approval of the Lieutenant-Governor in Council, make and amend the by-laws which it deems necessary for securing health in industrial establishments, prescribed for by the fourth section of chapter second of title seventh of the Revised Statutes and relating to:

(a). The supply of drinking water; (b). Lighting; (c). The distance to be left between certain establishments and dwelling-houses, as well as the arrangement and details of the construction of the rooms; (d). Cubic space; (e). Aeration and ventilation; (f). Cleanliness and cleansing. (g). The expulsion and manner of disposing of dust, gas, vapor and waste produced in the course of work; (h). The system of drainage, including sinks, lavatories, urinals, privies or closets, and the method of disposing of waste liquids; (i). The temperature of the premises; (j). All other sanitary conditions which may arise in industrial establishments.

Dr. Lachapelle, who is a high santitary authority in the Dominion of Canada, writes as follows:

Montreal, 17th June, 1901.

Clark Bell, Esq., Secretary American Congress of Tuberculosis, New York.

Dear Doctor.—I have received your letter of the 5th inst.

Art. 50 of the Public Health Act 1901 makes the notification of advanced tuberculosis compulsory. Other articles of the same Act contain other provisions calculated to more or less directly deal with the spread of tuberculosis. I enclose a marked copy of the Act. Disinfection of the premises occupied by a tuberculous patient is provided for after his death by a provincial regulation which I enclose.

Yours Faithfully,

E. P. LACHAPELLE.

The provincial regulation to which Dr. Lachapelle refers is as follows:

The Board calls attention to the following by-law which is in force in the province since July 1900:

"25a. Any householder in whose household a death from pulmonary tuberculosis has occurred shall within forty-eight hours from said death notify the secretary-treasurer or the local board of health of the municipality in which the house is situated and upon such notification the municipality shall cause to be disinfected the apartments which it will deem to have been contaminated by the patient. Unless more precise and reliable indication be given, will be considered as contaminated the rooms the patient has occupied during his illness. (Are particularly recommended for these disinfections: the use of disinfectant solutions and sterilization by steam or the use of formaldehyde.)"

THE PROVINCE OF ONTARIO, DOMINION OF CANADA.

Dr. P. H. Bryce, Secretary of the Provincial Board of Health of Ontario, sends me in response to my letter.

1. A copy of an act respecting municipal sanatoria for consumptives, which became a law last year, [Chap. 57, Ontario Stat. 1900.] which is herewith submitted.

2. Copy of a circular letter issued by the committee on Epidemics of that Board to physicians and mebers of local boards of Health underd ate of June 5, 1900, from which the following selections are made:

Moved by Dr. Cassidy, Seconded by Dr. Bryce,

1st. That as Tuberculosis is a contagious and infectious disease, all inmates of Provincial Institutions who are affected with this disease should be isolated in wards set apart for such patients, and not to-be permitted to associate generally with other inmates.

2nd. That when rooms or wards, which have been occupied by consumptive patients, become vacant, they should be disinfected according to the methods set forth by the Provincial Board of Health in the pamphlet issued by it containing rules for checking the spread of contagious disease.

3rd. That an individual, affected with tuberculosis and living in a private family, should be isolated as much as possible from other members of the household, especial care being taken in the destruction of his expectorations.

4th. That when the room occupied by such patient becomes vacant, it should be thoroughly disinfected, and, as a matter of prevention, the whole dwelling should be disinfected according to the instructions in the pamphlet regarding disinfection issued by the Provincial Board of Health, and that such other precautions be taken as are provided in Section 101 of the Public Health Act (1897).

5th. That the Local Boards of Health be urged to establish rules for the notification of cases of tuberculosis to the Medical Health Officer or to the Secretary of the Local Board of the municipality.

Also rules and directions adopted for the benefit of consumptive patients to be enforced and sent out to make them known and cause them to be enforced.

This report is signed by Drs. J. J. Cassidy, P. H. Bryce and Wm. Oldright composing the Standing Committee on Epidemics of the Provincial Board of Health of that province.

The act referred to is as follows:

Her Majesty, by and with the advice and consent of the Legislative Assembly of the Province of Ontario, enacts as follows:

1. Subject to the provisions of this Act, any municipality, or any two or more municipalities in this Province may establish a sanatorium for the treatment of consumptives, and may for that purpose acquire lands and intersts therein and erect and equip buildings and other improvements thereon, and do such other things from time to time as may be necessary to complete, maintain and operate such sanatorium and carry out the objects and requirements of this Act.

2. Any municipality may procure or join another or others in procuring plans of proposed buildings and improvements for a sanatorium and estimate of the cost and such other information upon the subject (including a proposed site) as may seem desirable, and any two or more municipalities may confer together, by such repre-

sentatives as their councils may appoint, with a view to agreeing upon a basis for establishing a joint sanatorium, and they may enter into a provisional agreement respecting the same.

3. If one municipality only is establishing the sanatorium, a provisional by-law respecting the same shall be passed, and the plans. estimates, and the said provisional by-law, or said provisional agreement, as the case may be, and the proposed site (which may be anywhere within the Province) shall be submitted to the Provincial Secretary, who shall submit the same to the Provincial Board of Health for report. Upon receiving the report of the Board of Health, the Provincial Secretary may approve of the plans, estimates, provisional by-law or agreement, as the case may be, and the site; subject, however, to such modifications and alterations as he may think best.

Provided, that if a proposed site be not within the municipality or one of the municipalities proposing to establish the sanatorium, the Provincial Secretary shall, before approving of such site, transmit by post to the head of the municipality in which the proposed site is situate, notice of the application for approval for such remarks thereon as such municipality may desire to submit.

4. Upon the approval of the Provincial Secretary of the plans, estimates, etc., the council of the municipality, or of each of the municipalities concerned, as the case may be, may from time to time pass by-laws to raise the moneys proposed to be paid or contributed by such municipality in respect of the original cost of the sanatorium, or of the cost of the extensions, alterations and additions, and to issue debentures therefor. The provisions of The Municipal Act respecting by-laws creating debts and voting thereon by electors, and all other provisions of the said Act applicable thereto, shall apply.

5. Upon the said by-law or by-laws being passed as in the preceding section is provided for, the municipality or municipalities concerned may pass by-laws to establish the sanatorium, or to enter into the agreement to establish a joint sanatorium, as the case may be, in accordance with the approval given by the Provincial Secretary above provided for; and, upon by-laws being passed to raise the moneys proposed to be paid or contributed in respect of the cost of extensions, alterations and additions, the approval by the Provincial Secretary of the plans therof shall be obtained in the same way as provided for with respect to approval of the original plans, and upon such approval being given, the extensions, additions and alterations may be proceeded with by the municipality or municipalities concerned.

6. The by-law or agreement establishing a sanatorium or a joint sanatorium, as the case may be, shall provide for the appointment of a board of not less than five trustees to take charge of and manage the same. The qualifications, term of office, which shall not exceed five years, and quorum of the trustees, and the manner of appointing their successors or of filling vacancies, shall be declared in the said by-law or agreement, and the trustees appointed from time to time shall hold office until their successors are appointed. The agreement for a joint sanatorium shall state the proportion of the yearly cost of maintenance, operations and repairs to be borne by each municipality. The said by-law or agreement may also define the terms and conditions on which patients may be admitted into the sanatorium, and contain such other particulasr as may be thought best.

7. The trustees and their successors shall be a corporation under the name of "The Trustees of (here name the sanatorium)," and they shall be free from all personal responsibility for acts done within the scope of their authority as such trustees. They shall

have such powers and duties as are conferred by this Act, and such other powers and duties not inconsistent with this Act as may be conferred upon them by the said by-law or agreement as the case may be, or by any future by-law or agreement passed or entered into with the approval of the Provincial Secretary.

8. The trustees shall elect yearly one of their number to be chairman of the board, to hold office for one year thereafter until his successor as chairman is elected. A vice-chairman may also be similarly elected.

The lands and personal property acquired from time to time for the sanatorium shall be conveyed to and vested in the trustees for the uses and purposes thereof, and if proceedings for the expropriation of the site of a joint sanatorium become necessary such proceedings shall be taken on behalf of the municipalities.

DOMINION OF CANADA.

New Brunswick.

Dr. W. Bayard, of St. John, N. B., is a vice president of this Congress, and his reply to my communication is as follows:—

Dear Mr. Bell.—In answer to your note I regret to say that no laws have been enacted in this Province regarding sanatoria. Two years ago I brought the subject before the Provincial Board of Health, gave an address to the people of this city, at which the Governor and several of the members of councils were present. All promised support, but contigent upon my obtaining money to furnish a sanatoria. This I declined to do unless the government gave me a guarantee that they would support it. So the matter stands. I think such pressure will be brought upon the government that they will ultimately support it. Yours sincerely,

W. BAYARD.

Prince Edwards Island.

This Province of the Dominion of Canada is favorable for Sanitoria.

The most prominent physician there is Dr. R. MacNeill, of Charlottetown.

He takes a deep interest in the subject. His reply to my inquiry is as follows:

Charlottetown, P. E. Island, July 9, 1901.

Clark Bell, Esq,. Secretary.

Dear Sir.—I have to acknowledge the receipt of your esteemed favor this day, and in reply hasten to say that so far we have no laws upon our statute books respecting sanatoria or preventive legislation in re tuberculosis. No hospitals for consumptives have been established. Some time ago I called attention to this matter through our local press and pointed out that our Island was favorably situated. Although we have no high altitudes, we have pure sea air, and with properly arranged cottages, properly ventilated, great progress could be made for the relief of tubercular patients. Want of means is the great drawback. The island is most salubrious during the summer season and tourists are continually flocking to our shores. The long distance and the expenses attending a journey to New York prevented me from meeting with you, but anything I can do to help you along, so far as my feeble efforts are concerned, will be cheerfully done; and any information which you may require that I can procure will be given from time to time as you may require it. Wishing you every success in your laudable efforts, I remain,

Yours sincerely,

R. MacNEILL, M. D.

STIMULANTS IN FORENSIC MEDICINE.

A REVIEW OF

DRUG CONSUMPTION IN VERMONT.

BY DR. A. P. GRINNELL, BURLINGTON, VT.

I think an apology is due this society for offering any remarks upon such a hackneyed and threadbare subject as temperance, or upon the use or abuse of stimulants. And I crave your indulgence and hope that a measure of charity will be meted out to me for imposing upon you a paper, the title of which is sufficient to convey depression and distress to any one compelled to listen to it.

However, in spite of all that has been said or written upon the subject, I still have the temerity to assert that a few words can yet be added to the volumes already published which might convey to any thinking mind the possibility of our having erred in forming deductions, in basing opinions upon false premises, in forming conclusions dependent upon non-essential facts, and perhaps ignoring the most essential and important points that could be brought out in a discussion of the matter.

The so-called temperance reformer knows but little of the subject he attempts to discuss. The man who talks the most, who appears most in public print, who is most responsible for the legislative enactments regarding the sale of stimulants or narcotics,' who denounces the use and abuse of all things which he cannot use himself, has

Read before the NewYork Medico-Legal Society at April meeting, 1901 the most rudimentary knowledge of the actual effects ot these drugs or the evils they are likely to produce.

Few people are aware of the enormous consumption ot narcotics or stimulating drugs. With the development of pharmaceutical science and the consequent improvement and facility in preparing drugs and the alkaloids the market has grown accordingly. More wide-spread knowledge concerning the effects and special uses of opium, cocaine, quinine and Cannabis Indica, has further stimulated the demand for these drugs, until to-day the American people are confronted by a problem which is only equalled in magnitude by its terrible and appalling aspects.

When we pause to consider the fearful inroads the excessive or habitual use of these drugs has on the mentality, physical health and general existence of those addicted to them, we can easily appreciate what a serious menace to society a rapid increase of drug habitues must inevitably mean.

It is hardly necessary to speak of the results of the habitual and excessive use of narcotic drugs. Physicians more than any other class realize the fearful ravages made on the human system, and the large number of physical, moral and mental wrecks they are constantly meeting who owe their condition entirely to drug addiction tells eloquently how extensive and far reaching the drug evil has become. Every alienist is daily being brought face to face with the growing influence of certain drugs on psychic abnormalities and degenerations, and the insidious onset and progress of such conditions when so produced, can not fail to impress us with the medico-legal importance of the drug habit.

Opium and its alkaloids, particularly morphine, are used by far the largest class of drug habitues, and outside of cocaine their deleterious effects are most marked of all drugs. One has only to read DeQuincey's "Confessions of an English Opium Eater," or come in contact with a confirmed "morphine fiend," and note the craving, the fearful appetite, the terrible depravity which seeks only the gratification of the paramount desire—morphine—to realize that such a person is beyond the pale of sanity, some of the time, to say the least. The limits to which such a person will go to satisfy the appetite for the drug, and the marked decline of the mental faculties, particularly volitional, from its prolonged use, will ultimately make its forensic bearing of far greater importance than it is to-day.

For a great many years I have believed, and I know that the experience of every physician engaged in the practice of medicine will justify my belief, that every human being craves some artificial stimulant. Ask yourself what your stimulant is—what is mine—what is my neighbor's? We all have one, and after 30 years' experience in practice I can truthfully voice the opinion generally entertained by the medical profession that every human being craves and requires some artificial stimulation. By an artificial stimulant I mean something that will produce a condition or sensation which does not exist naturally. A person may select a stimulant that is either harmful or harmless, or one may be selected which is perfectly harmless in its immediate effects but quite disastrous when long continued or in its ultimate results. Again, a stimulant or drug may be selected that from the first can only mean destruction and death to one's self or a fearful legacy to one's progeny.

If you should ask any one of your neighbors—"What stimulant do you take?" and that person was an advocate of what is called prohibition in Vermont, which means the prohibition of alcohol, (the least of all in importance), he would probably say, "Nothing." But analyze his or her daily life; consider tea, coffee, tobacco, opium, cocaine, quinine or any of the various table condiments like tabasco sauce, or some of the special brands of catsup, the patent medicines called tonics and blood purifiers, and you will find that there is not one who can say that he does not take some one of the list, and would miss it if he did not. To some men alcoholic stimulant is everything they seem to need to satisfy their craving. What is a stimulant to one, however, may not be to another, consequently there is a great variation in the character and amount of the stimulants used.

One of the most noted post-prandial speakers this world ever produced never took anything with dinner but a glass of champagne; without it he felt lost; with it he could recall anything he ever heard in his life—and we waited for the morning paper to know what he said the night before. Another man whose utterances have a world-wide reputation, who has made speeches in France, England and Germany which electrified his hearers and reflected credit on us as a people, told me that his speeches were always prepared or delivered under the influence of black tea, and he ate nothing for some time before he was going to speak. Another man, who was largely responsible for the prohibitory law as it is called in Vermont, came to me for treatment. I told him under no circumstances to take acids. He said, "Do you mean to tell me that I can't eat pickles?" I told him certainly, that he had a disease of the kidneys and bladder which made the use of acids impossible. He said, "I have pickles three times a day, made out of everything that it is possible to make pickles from; I can't get along without pickles." And yet this man went to the state legislature and said, "I can't drink beer, therefore you shan't."

I firmly believe that an artificial stimulant is desired by or acceptable to everybody. The selection of that one stimulant depends upon the environment, occupation and peculiarity of the individual. And it is only such a person, capable of curbing his disposition and passion to an almost unheard of extent, who will say that every person is not in need of an artificial stimulant.

Let me tell you a little incident in regard to one of the most notable temperance lecturers that ever appeared in Vermont state. He was a temperance man and did a great deal of good. His wife said to me once, "Isn't it possible to stop my husband drinking so much coffee? The coffee pot is limited to four cups; he takes three of them with every meal." And yet this man would not be guilty of taking alcoholic stimulant. Another man, a public temperance speaker, told me that it was impossible for him to lecture upon temperance unless he was under the influence of compound tincture of gentian.

After seriously reflecting upon this matter, after watching the effect of the prohibitory law, (so called), in Vermont, and having a well grounded conviction that everybody indulged in the use of some artificial stimulant, I was led to make further investigation. Assuming that the law prohibiting the use of alcohol except for medicinal or mechanical purposes, was enforced, then it appeared to me reasonable that many persons might be driven to the selection of other stimulants or a substitute for alcohol.

For some time I had become interested in the subject of consumption of drugs by the people of Vermont, and in order to form an approximate estimate of the quantities being consumed, in the early part of January, 1900, I issued to all druggists in the state of Vermont, (130), this letter. I enclosed in it a stamped envelope directed to me, and requested replies to the questions. I will read the letter:

January, 1900.

My Dear Sir.

I am preparing a paper to be read before the State Medical Society upon the use of opium and other anodynes, and would respectfully request you to fill out the following blanks. I have no intention of making use of your name whatever, but simply desire to obtain information which will enable me to intelligently discuss the subject.

As far as can be estimated, what are your average monthly sales of:
Opium (gum or powder).
Morphine sulph. (powder or pills).
Dover powder.
Paregoric (Tinct. Opii. Camph.)
Laudanum (Tinct. Opii).
Cocaine.
Chloral.
Indian Hemp (Cannabis Indica),
Quinine (powder or pills).

Any further information you could offer in regard to this matter would be appreciated, and you would confer a favor by replying at your earliest convenience. Please find enclosed stamped envelope.

Thanking you in advance for your courtesy, I am,

Yours respectfully,

A. P. GRINNELL.

I sent 130 of these to the druggists in the State of Vermont, and received replies from 116. I also sent a letter to the stores called general stores, and by general stores is meant where all commodities are sold, and situated in villages and towns where no place exists devoted exclusively to the sale of drugs or medicines. There are 172 such stores in the state. I sent letters to them but did not get replies from all that were satisfactory. Many of them refused to reply and kept my stamped envelope. Some returned the letters, intimating they thought there was some investigation going on and did not not care to answer the questions. I did find out that of all the physicians in the State of Vermont, about 690, 90 per cent. dispensed their own medicines, and did not purchase them of the druggists in the place where they live, and if they did the druggist said that he did not include that in his sales given me. All the sales made were to ordinary customers.

I had trouble in getting anything from wholesale drug stores doing business with general stores in the state. They inferred that I was making illegitimate inquiries of them. I learned there were three concerns in the state of Vermont where they manufacture these things from crude drugs, viz.: paregoric, laudanum, essence of peppermint, wintergreen and valerian. They sell a great deal, (through the medium of pedestrian peddlers), but I was unable to procure their figures. Therefore, what I give you could be multiplied by five and be below consumption, because I gave you nothing in the composition of patent medicines or cough medicines; nothing dispensed by physicians; nothing that is dispensed by these three manufactories—simply the regular retail drug store business and the sales of the 160 general stores.

The amounts given in these instances were so large that I thought the druggist must have estimated by the year instead of by the month, and I sent the list of questions back with another stamped envelope, but they were all returned with the statement, "It is all right."

I do not wish to give any names of drug stores or individuals or places, but when I tell you that a place so small that it hardly appears upon the map sells every month 3½ lbs. of gum opium, 6 oz. morphine, 5 pints of paregoric, 5 pints of laudanum and 3 oz. of powdered quinine, it will be hard for you to believe it.

In another town where there are two drug stores, (one refused to give me any information, and in such cases where information was refused or no response was made I put it down as zero), this one store sold 3 lbs. of opium, one gallon of paregoric, three-quarters of a gallon of laudanum, 5 oz. powdered quinine, and 1,000 2 gr. quinine pills.

Another store situated in a city of over 10,000 inhabitants, with 10 other drug stores, sold only 5 oz. opium, 2 oz. morphine, 8 quarts laudanum, and 6 quarts paregoric—a retail drug store.

In a town of considerable importance, the druggist said he didn't sell very much of these things, so I put it down as zero on my list.

Another druggist said, "I could not tell you because I have no time to look over my books," so I put that down as zero. Another one said he sold 80 cents worth of a certain drug, and $2.50 worth of something else; all these I have put down as zero. Still another said, "My sales in these goods may amount to $25.00 a year." And another, "I am unable to state, but it is a very small quantity. I sell to only two or three persons, and they use small quantities." Not knowing the value of the drugs I could not estimate amount sold, and therefore included them in the list marked zero.

I am perhaps calling your attention to points you have not thought about, but we must think about them. Another incident: A druggist living on the border of the lake says: "Most of our customers go across the lake where it is cheaper." I put his sales down as zero.

Now, then, in the regular drug stores, and in 160 of the 172 general stores in the State of Vermont they sell every month 3,300,000 doses of opium, besides what they dispense in patent medicines, and besides what the doctors dispense, which gives one and one-half doses of opium to every man and woman in the State of Vermont above the age of 21 years, every day in the year. (By dose I mean one grain of opium, 1/8 grain morphine, one-half ounce paregoric and 20 drops of laudanum). And the amount consumed would average a half dose to every man, woman and child in the State of Vermont every day in the year.

The following table explains itself:

ONE MONTH'S SALE OF DRUGS IN VERMONT.

The statistics here given show the sales of opium, morphine, dover quinine in 69 towns of the state. The names of the towns were assured secrecy when they furnished

Opium.	Morphine pw's	MrphinePils	Dover Powder	Perogoric.	Laudanum.	Cocaine	Chlo	Ind hemp	Quinin pd	Quinine Pils
3 oz	1 oz			⅛ pt	½ pt		2 oz		½ oz	200 grs
		65 grs		½ pt	1 pt		½ oz	1 oz		1000 grs
small am't	4 oz		4 oz	1 pt	1 pt					1000 grs
				2 pts	1 pt				10 oz	
4 oz	7 oz	30 grs	2 oz	1 gal	4 pts	1 oz	6 oz		3 oz	5200 grs
2 lbs	1 lb 10 oz		5 oz	1 gal 1 qt.	2 gals 1 pt	2 oz	1 lb		10 oz	100 grs
2 oz		250 grs			1 pt	¼ oz	8 oz			2000 grs
12 oz	10 oz	500 grs	2 oz	3 qts	1 gal 1 qt	⅝ oz	14 oz		5 oz	1000 grs
1 lb 2 oz	15 oz		1 lb	1 gal	4 qts	3 oz	13 lbs		4 oz	1000 grs
1 oz		30 grs		1 pt	¼ pt					1300 grs
8 oz	8 oz	250 grs		½ pt	½ pt	½ oz	4 oz	4 oz	16 oz	1000 grs
4 oz		63 grs		½ pt	1 pt					2400 grs
4 lbs 2 oz	3 lbs	250 grs	4 lbs	6 gal	2 gals 1 pt	4½ oz	1 lb 3 oz	13 oz	1lb 7 oz	8000 grs
1 lb	2 oz		1 lb	1 qt	1 qt	¼ oz	4 oz		2 oz	
8 oz	5 oz		4 oz	½ pt	5 pts					
1 oz	1 oz	30 grs	2 oz	½ pt	¾ pt	½ dr	¼ oz	⅛ oz	½ oz	700 grs
3 oz		13 grs			3 pts		2 oz			1000 grs
2 oz	1 oz	33 grs	2 oz	1 pt	1 pt				1 oz	2000 grs
1 lb	3 oz		5 oz	½ pt	1 pt				5 oz	
1 lb 8 oz	10 oz		2 lbs	½ pt	½ pt				2 oz	400 grs
3 lbs	6 oz	125 grs	1 lb 8 oz	5 gal	5 gals	3 oz	1 lb 8 oz		8 oz	2000 grs
1 lb	4 oz		2 oz	1 qt	2 qts	1 dr	4 oz	2 oz	6 oz	
				1 pt	½ pt					200 grs
4 oz	1 oz	75 grs	4 oz	1 pt	2 pts	⅛ oz				1000 grs
2 oz	6 oz	60 grs	½ oz	3 pts	3 pts		3 oz			3000 grs
1 lb	20 oz	125 grs	8 oz	1 pt	1 pt					2500 grs
	4 oz		8 oz	2 pts	2 pts	¼ oz			2 oz	1000 grs
1 lb 1 oz	6 oz	6 grs	3 oz	½ pt	1 pt	20 grs	1 oz	4 oz	4 oz	200 grs
	1 oz		4 oz	¼ pt	1 pt					150 grs
small a mt	2 oz		4 oz	2 qts	2 pts		4 oz		4 oz	
4 oz	⅛ oz		2½ oz	⅓ pt	½ pt				10 oz	
8 oz	2½ oz	30 grs	6 oz	1¼ pts	1 pt		1 oz		6 oz	1000 grs
4 oz	¼ oz			¼ pt	1 pt		4 oz		4 oz	
4 oz	2 oz	50 grs		3 pts	1½ pts	1 oz			1 lb	800 grs
5 oz	5 oz		4 oz	½ pt	2 pts				5 oz	

powder, paregoric, laudanum, cocaine, chloral, indian hemp and are omitted as the druggists and proprietors of general stores Dr. Grinnell with the statement of their sales

8 oz	2 oz		⅛ oz	½ pt	½ pt					200 grs
1 lb	1 ⅔ oz	33 grs	6 oz	1 pt	2 pts	2 drs	3 oz		2 oz	60 grs
3 lbs		200 grs	2 lbs 8 oz	1 qt	3 gals					32 0grs
8 oz	3 oz			½ pt	2 pts				1 oz	
8 oz	5 oz		4 oz	2 pts	1 pt				5 oz	
1 lb 2 oz	7 oz	88 grs	12 oz	3¾ pts	5 qts 1½ pts	50 grs	2 oz	2 oz	5 oz	190 grs
2 oz	2 ¼ oz		4 oz	4 pts	2 pts	2 drs	1 oz		4 oz	1 00 grs
	1 oz	60 grs		1 pt	1 pt					4000 grs
1 lb	5 oz			2 pts	1 pt				5 oz	
3 oz	5 oz	50 grs	8 oz	1 pt	1 pt	40 grs	2 oz			150 grs
1 lb	2 oz		2 oz	2 pts	½ pt				2 oz	
	3 oz									100 grs
8 oz	5 oz			1½ pts	3 pts	1 dr			¼ oz	140 grs
	2 ½ oz	13 grs		2 qts	1 qt	¼ oz			7 oz	400 grs
small am't	3 oz		1 oz						2 oz	
4 oz		25 grs	1 oz	1 pt	2 qts		4 oz	1 oz		1 00 grs
1 lb 4 oz	11 oz	314 grs	4 oz	5 qts 2 pts	10 qts	1 oz			3 oz	12400 grs
1 oz	2 oz			½ pt	1 pt					300 grs
2 lbs 12 oz	7 oz	300 grs	4 oz	3 pts	1 qt 2½ pts	2¾ oz		4 pts	4 oz	1100 grs
2 oz	1 oz		1 lb	2 gals	6 qts	2 oz	2 oz		6 oz	
5 lbs	4 oz		2 lbs	1 gal	2 qts	2 oz			10 oz	
1 oz	3 oz			5 pts	2 pts				2 oz	400 grs
2 lbs	5 oz	250 grs	4 oz	1 pt	1 pt		4 oz		1 oz	2000 grs
2 oz	3 oz		1 oz	½ pt					1 oz	
5 oz	5 oz		8 oz	1 gal 3 qts					7 oz	200 grs
3 lbs 8 oz	6 oz		3 oz	5 pts	5 pts	½ oz	4 oz	½ oz	3 oz	
1 lb	4 oz		1 lb	2 qts	1 qt	¼ oz			8 oz	
					1 pt	1 dr	1 oz			
1 oz	2 oz		2 oz	4 pts	1 pt	1 dr	1 oz	½ oz	5 oz	
3 lbs	8 oz		4 oz	4 pts	4 pts	⅛ oz	2 oz		4 oz	
4 oz	3 oz		1 oz	2 pts	3 pts	'1 oz	1 oz			1000 grs
1 lb 11 oz	3 oz	20 grs	2 oz	4½ pts	2 pts	3 drs	1½ oz		6 oz	300 grs
½ oz	¼ oz		¼ oz	¼ pt	½ pt		4 oz	8 oz	7 oz	
5 oz	10 oz			1 gal	2 qts				10 oz	
47 lbs 12 oz	19 lbs 15 oz	3338 grs	25 lbs	32 gals 1 qt	32 gals 1 qt	27 oz 1 dr 30 grs	32lbs 4oz	37 oz	15lb10oz	74,200

Reported from 69 towns out of 244 towns, and from 116 drug stores out of 130. This does not include the amount sold in general stores.

Of the amount consumed as reported of other articles mentioned in my letter I was rather surprised, viz.: of chloral, Indian hemp and cocaine. I had been led to believe that the use of cocaine was largely on the increase, but evidently the drugs most preferred are opium and quinine. It may be urged that quinine is not a stimulant, but any physician will verify the statement that to many it is a great stimulant, and a two-grain quinine pill will flush the face as much as a drink of whiskey unless one is accustomed to its use. You can hardly find a man travelling that hasn't a bottle of quinine pills in his pocket; he says he is afraid he will have a cold and keeps them as a guard against such a misfortune. The amount of quinine consumed, considering one grain as a dose, is two grains a day to each man and woman in Vermont above 21 years of age, every day in the year, (assuming there are 320,000 population, that was the last census we have). The other items were not quite so much.

For several years I appointed medical examiners for life insurance companies doing business in Vermont and New Hampshire, and I was told that the companies took extra precaution to see if examiners had taken the "Keeley" or other "cures" since they had been graduated from college. The companies told me that the states where they had the most trouble with drunken doctors were prohibition states, and they showed me statistics in regard to it.

[*To be Continued.*]

THE INDETERMINATE SENTENCE IN NEW YORK

BY CLARK BELL, ESQ., LL. D., OF THE NEW YORK BAR.
PRESIDENT OF THE MEDICO-LEGAL SOCIETY,
HONORARY MEMBER OF THE MEDICO-
LEGAL SOCIETY OF FRANCE.

After a full period of discussion, it has been determined by the Legislature of the State to try the principle of the indeterminate sentence applied genrally to all criminals, who had been convicted of an offence punishable by imprisonment in a State prison:—

The Penal Code was amended by the Legislature of the State of New York, at the last session, by an act passed April 18, 1901, and which goes into effect September 1st, 1901.

The Act is as follows:—

LAWS OF NEW YORK, CHAP. 425. By Authority.

An act to amend the penal code relating to the sentencing of convicts to state prisons.

Became a law April 18, 1901, with the aproval of the Governor. Passed, a majority being present.

The people of the State of New York, represented in the Senate and Assembly, do enact as follows:—

SECTION 1. Title eighteen of the penal code is hereby amended by inserting a new section, to be known as section six hundred and eighty-seven a, and read as follows:—

687a. A person never before convicted of a crime punishable by imprisonment in a state prison, who is convicted in any court in this state of a felony, the maximum penalty for which exclusive of fines, is imprisonment for five years or less, and sentenced to a state prison, shall be sentenced thereto under an indeterminate sentence, the minimum of which shall not be less than one year; or in case a minimum is fixed by law, not less than such minimum, and the maximum of which shall not be more than the longest period fixed by the law for which the crime is, punishable, of which the offender is convicted. The maximum limit of such sentence shall be so fixed as to comply with the provisions of section six hundred and ninety-seven of penal code.

§ 2. This act shall take effect September first, nineteen hundred and one.

This is an important step in Criminology and will mark, as I think, a new era in the law of punishment of criminals in that State.

Contributed to the International Congress of Criminal Anthropology, Amsterdam, Holland, September Session, 1901.

It will b eobserved that it only applies to first offenders.

It is not intended, that its provisions shall apply to confirmed criminals.

A study of its provisions shows, that the Legislature intended it, as a general sweeping provision; because the class of confirmed criminals, who are outside of its provisions, is very small, when compared with the volume of crime and number of offenders in the State.

It embraces within its limits a great body of offenders.

The most serious objection that can now be raised against the administration of the present criminal law, is the inequality of punishment, as it is administered by the Judges.

There seemed to be no recognized standard at all among the judges who pass sentences.

One judge in one court has entirely different views as to the measure of punishment, from another in the same State.

The problem presented, of how to remedy this great evil, and to have an equalized standard or measurement of the degree of the punishment for the same class of offences, is one of the greatest social problems of the hour.

It used to be said in the Civil Courts, in the cases on the Equity side, that the conscience of the Court, was measured by the length of the Chancellor's foot.

In determining terms of sentence, and fixing the measure of punishment, the difference between the sentences of the Judge, who look at offenders, from the severest standpoint; and the one whose mind judicially is tempered with mercy; is as wide as the gulf, that separated the rich man and Lazarus in the parable.

If a National Symposium or Congress was called for a conference of the leading Judges of the country, to settle the proper punishment in degree, for each grade of crime in the abstract, it might result in bringing the judicial mind into a more uniform state.

The difficulty lies in making the judges feel willing to take part in such a conference and discussion.

It might be tried in a State, where a few prominent Judges could be brought together, and later, if thought advisable, extended to a conference for the nation and country.

The practical effect and workings of the new law in New York will be studied with great interest by the students of Criminology.

I believe, that one of its most beneficial results, will be to unconsciously bring the Judges of the Criminal Tribunals nearer each other in the application of this statute to the punishment of offenders.

A symposium of answers to questions by the leading Judges of the nation now on the Criminal bench on this subject, might be of great value, in initiating a discussion, that would arouse attention,—and pave the way to a system of equalization of punishment by statutory enactments.

The States that have tried the indeterminate sentences seem to regard this system as a public gain.

It is a study that involves the crime as well as the criminal, and students of Criminology may well consider the new departure in New York as a significant and interesting incident, in the philosophy of crime, in relation to and as affected by indeterminate punishment?

LAW AND MEDICINE FROM A LEGAL STANDPOINT.

BY HON. ABRAM H. DAILEY, OF BROOKLYN, N. Y., EX-PRESIDENT MEDICO-LEGAL SOCIETY, VICE PRESIDENT AMERICAN CONGRESS OF TUBERCULOSIS.

My theme in scope is far reaching, and more important than its title may indicate. I am impressed that this is an appropriate occasion for its presentation for consideration. It is primarily addressed to members of two great professions, but its ultimate object is to awaken thought and induce appropriate action regarding those matters to which it relates.

Man is the product of unfathomable causes, with a destiny certain, yet, taken as a whole, absolutely unknowable. That he came from his cradle and is going straight forward to his grave, he is assured from his knowledge of the unvarying course of all preceding life.

Perhaps, strictly within my theme, the cradle and the grave should mark its limitations. But it ranges before the first and after the other, for law and medicine may, and even do, deal with conditions preceding birth, and if, as most mankind assume, man is a dual being and in part survives the destruction of the body, then law and medicine may in their effects, extend further than the grave. Nature has wisely provided that all creatures desire to live and fear to die. Man naturally desires to live for the pleasures he hopes to realize. He is uncertain as to what is in store for him in another life, and so he had rather bear those ills he has, than to fly to others that he knows not of. Therefore, long life, comfortable surroundings, freedom from annoyances and from the ills that the flesh is heir to, are most devoutly to be desired.

There are three professions to which man naturally turns in his hours of distress, but which of the three depends upon the nature of his trouble. He finds that he is born possessed of certain faculties, and incident to these, are the appe-

Read before the American Congress of Tuberculosis in joint session with Medico-Legal Society, May 15-16, 1901.

tites and passions belonging to his nature. He is not chargeable with that which preceded his birth, but all that was precedent had everything to do with it. There is a vast amount of evidence which has accumulated as ages have rolled on, showing that prenatal conditions may materially affect succeeding generations; that heredity, like an heir loom, comes to children from their ancestors, affecting their natures both mentally and physically. How to improve that which is good, and eradicate that which is evil, or destroy it, is a problem with which law and medicine has been dealing, and may deal more rigorously with in the near future. Law and medicine are harmless enough in themselves; it is only in their application that wisdom is needed, and in that respect, each may become a bane or a blessing, according to the amount of wisdom exercised in its use. Nature is a law unto herself. Her decrees are inexorable unchangeable. Legislatures may enact and repeal their enactments, but the laws of nature are fixed and endure forever. To know her laws, to live and act in conformity with them, is an absolute essential to a perfect life. If we possessed the requisite knowledge, had the means to live accordingly, and would do so, there would be little need of medicines; but fate confronts us from our birth. Death is the dreaded executioner of one of the great laws of our nature. The house we live in, the tenement of the soul to which we are so closely related, through which we behold so much of the physical universe, and enjoy its numerous comforts and blessings, we find in the course of time, by its very nature, to be a temporary and unsubstantial affair, and liable to be made vacant at any moment, when its wonderful mechanism becomes so deranged that action ceases.

Every remedy for human ailments may be denominated medicine. Variation in the duration of life, tells the story of our frailties. A momentary glance at the tide of humanity which surges to and fro in the streets of our great cities, reveals the differentiation of mankind. From the perfect man and woman with stately yet graceful mien, to the deformed, diseased, disfigured, hobbling cripple, we behold the tide of humanity constantly passing before us. It is ever increasing in volume, but every one of its millions is on the journey from the cradle to the grave. To the vast majority the distance from the first to the last is exceedingly short.

When we look upon the sufferings to which so many are subjected, and consider that by far the greater part of it could have been avoided or prevented,—as humanitarians, as lawyers and as doctors,—we ask ourselves, what can we, and what should we do for the betterment of that race to which we belong? There is no man so low that he is not our brother, nor woman so degraded that she is not our sister. No matter what his complexion, or place his nativity, he still belongs to the great brotherhood of mankind. The ways of life have been traced from the moneron to man. We know that in the vast durations of time thousands of species in the animal kingdom have come, have inhabited the earth, and passed out of existence. We also know that nature in her dealings with life, is relentless. We know that no species came into being until the means for its sustenance was provided, and a dwelling place prepared for it, and that it disappeared when conditions became unfavorable to its continuance.

The erosions of the country through the valley of the John Day River, in the State of Washington, have revealed to the gaze of the geologist the fossil remains of animal life, to the depth of over 10,000 feet through solid rock, which tell a story of time, life and death upon the earth, antedating the coming of man, through ages of bewildering antiquity.

The undulations of continents and islands, the comings and goings of species in the seas, lakes and rivers, and upon the lands above the seas, have been occasioned by the operation of forces against which the might and power of man dwindles into significance. And yet,we are every day astounded at the majesty of the human mind in dealing with the unthinking forces of the universe. Man turns these forces to his own service in a thousand ways, and produces in vast abundance everything to meet his own ever increasing wants. It is an adage that, "history repeats itself." Why nations should die is a matter which concerns all living people. That they do, is an historical fact. Not only do nations die, but the places of their habitations become wildernesses. The Romans of the Caesars were unlike the Romans of to-day. The Egyptians of the Pharaohs and the Assyrians of the days of the great King Nebuchadnezzar were very unlike the Egyptians and Assyrians of our times. Modern explorers are recovering from the graves of the great cities, which once were the centers of splendor, of a great civilization, the literature of people who had lawyers, doctors and priests, as we have today. Why should nations culminate in their greatness, and fall into decay? Is it by reason of some unwritten, undiscovered law of nature, that, in its operation, disorganizes the fabrics of governments, and they fall apart; or is it because of the frailty of the people which make and unmake states? Could any wisdom of man have continued these nations in a healthful growth until now, increasing in population, containing cities, each numbering more than one hundred million souls, in the enjoyment of greater comforts, and possessing a civilization far surpassing that of the most enlightened people of our times? I ask, was such a condition possible? We are dealing with problems which must tend to answer these questions.

Indeed, we need not go to what we call the old world for evidence of the former existence, and the passing away of great nations. The antiquity of man may be traced to as remote a period in America as elsewhere. Within a few years I have examined the most convincing evidence, that at a very remote period of time, a numerous people, a race of dwarfs once inhabited our southern states; for their bones have been blasted out of lime rock at the depth of over 50 feet from the surface, with bones of animals whose species have long been extinct. Death has unquestionably been the immediate cause, but what has been the producing cause of the decline of those nations? Has it been the inception and spread of disease which could have been prevented or stayed by any wisdom of man?

This inclines us to look to causes beyond the control of man in the past and possibly so now. Among these are climatic changes, such as have been occasioned by changes of land elevations, and the establishment of new ocean currents, such as came at the time of the Flood when northern Siberia was changed from an almost torrid and temperate to a frigid zone.

No power of man could avail to prevent the catastrophe which followed, and the pestilence occasioned by the putrifaction of the dead bodies of men and beasts.

Man hitherto has been powerless to prevent sismic distubances whereby poisonous vapors and gases have escaped from subterranean chambers, producing pestilence, but I believe it possible for man to remove, in some degree, the causes of such disturbances. We cannot hope to successfully prevent famine occasioned by drought, or disasters from cyclones, tornadoes, floods and untimely frosts. But disasters from these causes have played a small part in producing the decline and disappearance of nations. Wars have done their part, and they are under the control of man. The making, and enforcement of a law preventing war and its attendant horrors, must be the work of nations so strongly combined as to command obedience to their decress. The fact that for many centuries there have existed laws of nations, established by the nations of the world, defining belligerent and neutral rights when two or more nations are at war, conclusively shows that it is quite possible for nations to combine and do away with such conflicts entirely. Already, in obedience to the dictates of common humanity, inhuman methods are condemned among all but barbarous people. Prisoners taken in battle are no longer put to death or tortured. The violation of the rule of honorable warfare is not common. The recent report that, in revenge for the slaughter of some Russians, the soldiers and sailors of the Czar put to the sword the entire people of a Chinese town numbering thousands of men, women and children, whose corpses choked the waters of a considerable river, shocked the world. Pestilence follows in the waks of decaying animal and vegetable matter. All the great plagues and pestilences which have visited the world, carrying away millions of people, have proceeded from preventable causes. To know the cause and the remedy, and be able to apply the remedy, has commanded the attention of physicians, lawmakers and governments for a considerable time.

When the plague visited London, the grass grew in her deserted streets. It found the city in an unsanitary condition, and its inhabitants for that reason, subject to the fatal attack. Miasmas and uncleanly habits are producing causes of bubonic plague, cholera and other pestilences. They originate in the far East, and spread rapidly, and often are exceedingly fatal in spite of extreme caution to bar the way of their progress. The fearful consequences accompanying the visitation of cholera or plague, have caused the people of all civilized countries to be watchful to prevent their coming, and be prepared in case they do come. But there has, as yet, never been, as there should be, any combined method of eradicating the cause of such diseases among those people where they originate. That methods may be devised for reaching the cause, I believe feasible, but it must be the combined work of nations to effect immediate results, or the slow work of a progressive civilization among a class of people who lack ambition to improve their condition and provide against danger.

There are no people who traverse the world more than our own. England carries her commerce everywhere, but the American, or, as we are called by foreigners, "the Yankee," is there to see what is going on, and the rapidity with which oceans and lands are traversed may bring at any unguarded moment, to our shores, the seeds of destructive disease.

There is a lack of proper regulation in foreign ports as to the condition of cargoes of outgoing vessels,—of the effects and health of sailors and passengers,—to prevent the importation of the germs of disease.

In our country we have had, and still have hotbeds of yellow fever, and its cause, eradication and cure, have had the attention of our ablest medical scientists. It had, long before our Civil War, been known. that malarial conditions, and a hot climate were most favorable for its development; and that clean streets, cleanly houses and habits, absence of stagnant water, removed, in a great degree, dangers to be apprehended from it.

We all know what precautions prevented its spread in New Orleans during that war, and the same precautions have, to a large extent, prevented its ravages in Havana, Santiago and other parts of Cuba since the occupation of those places by the American forces during the Spanish War. It is now claimed as a recent discovery, that the mosquitoes communicate the poison which infects and occasions the disease. It would be useless to legislate against mosquitos; but they evidently are of a different kind, or provide themselves with other poisons than those possessed by the Jersey pests. We can bar their way into our homes, with screens, and lessen the annoyance of the sound of their midnight revelries in our ears, and the sensations of their stings when they settle down to business. Their stings have sometimes produced fatal results; and why not? We have learned that it requires a microscope to discover some of the germs of diseases, and why may not the mandible of an insect communicate the poison from an infected body to a healthy one.

We are legislating in New York and New Jersey to protect from destruction the palisades which beautify the scenery of the Hudson River, and why not, by legislation, procure the filling of the marshes on the Jersey and Long Island shores, and around other cities in our country? Thus, in time, those dangerous marshes might be converted into useful and healthful grounds. In the Valley of the Housatonic River, in New England, from time to time during the last century, typhoid fever has ravaged with exceedingly fatal results. It has followed heavy summer freshets, when the waters have overflown the banks of the river, and settled in lowlands covered with thick vegetable growth, which has rotted in the stagnant waters, giving rise to sickening odors, unquestionably occasioning the fatal visitation. The expenditure of a very little labor would remove the cause of sickness and death in a large community, by draining the overflow into the river. The contamination of the waters we drink, as well as the air we breath, is a matter of so great importance that, when legislation is practicable, it should be resorted to to protect communities from it.

This leads me to speak of the disposition which should be made of our dead. We cannot but respect the tender regard we all feel for the bodies of our departed friends, but we know that they finally meet a common end—disintegration. They should not be allowed to contaminate air or water. It is a well known fact that poisonous matter affects the air above large grave yards and cemeteries, and contaminates the water drawn from wells in their immediate vicinity. Sentiment should give place to sense. The health of the living should not be imperiled by a misconception of duty, or respect to the dead. Speedy cremation, under the direction of, and at public expense, in all cases where burials cannot be speedily made, at places too remote to occasion danger, would be far better than the present method of burials. This line of suggestion could be greatly extended, but I must speak of other matters related to this subject.

What has been said, relates to it in its effects upon communities, and the world at large. There is less opposition to measures for the general good, affecting all alike, than there is to that which may be denominated "class or special legislation." We all surrender certain rights, and impliedly agree to conform to the laws of the country, and to support its government for the benefit it is supposed to give in return. But we are justifiably jealous of our freedom. We know that private property can, by the right of eminent domain, be taken for public purposes, but not without compensation for its value. Men forfeit their freedom by the commission of crime. Much which was formerly law is now obsolete. The deduction is, that the wiser men became, the less need there was of legal restraint. Practices of vice and immorality are restrained by law, or to state the fact, they are in violation of law. The restraint is only partial.

Although it is 105 years since Jenner introduced vaccination from the cow as a preventive of small pox, with the result of vastly lessening its severity, and in most instances, of preventing it altogether. And yet it has always met with strenuous opposition from many people for various reasons. To some the thought is repugnant, that a human being should be inoculated from the diseased part of an animal, and it is unquestionably true that in numerous instances pure blood has been contaminated and vicious disorders contracted by what is termed "impure vaccine matter." But the ratio of benefit is so great, that compulsory laws requiring vaccination are justified.

In many of our states restrictive legi:slation has obtained in regard to the practice of medicine. This has been bitterly combated, and there certainly is more than one side to the question, as to whether such legislation is justified to the extent that it has been carried. That which relates to measures to prevent contagion and the spread of disastrous diseases can easily be justified. And it is certainly the right of the medical profession that it should be, as far as practicable, protected against the imposition and injury which would follow from the assumption of unlearned persons to hold themselves as educated and skilled physicians when they are quacks, or even less than that. There are various schools of medicine, and methods of treatment, and it should be the individual right of every person of years of discretion, to make his or her own choice of physicians and remedies. But this certainly cannot be done if one class is proscribed by law from practicing. Anything which looks like "special or class legislation" is bound to be unpopular, and will eventually be overthrown.

For many years men learned in the medical profession, have contended that mesmerism and hypnotism had no existence in fact, and that those who attempted to practice it were fakes and frauds, and yet the fact remains, that this wonderful power is possessed by mankind, by some to a greater extent than by others, and that it can be advantageously resorted to to lessen pain, to actually prevent it, and to effect mental cures, without resort to any material medicines whatever. To what extent it may be ultimately carried we cannot say. But I do say that efforts to confine its practice to those holding medical certificates, is by no means right. I find a large number of the medical profession believe, that man is not a spiritual being, not having a soul or spirit surviving the destruction of the body. I regard this as an exceedingly unfortunate position, for it leads these learned men to frown upon all efforts to heal the sick, to cure the afflicted of what may be termed "mental maladies," through other means than drugs and surgical operations.

It seems to me that the wiser course would be, for all to hold their opinions in abeyance, and give others who claim to have the power to heal the sick or afflicted, by any other method than that resorted to by the ordinary practitioner, a fair opportunity to demonstrate the truth of his claim.

If the imagination does such wonderful things as is claimed by those who attribute to that the real secret of the cures effected by the Christian Scientists, what harm is done? If the cures are not imaginary, but are real, then a great wrong can easily be done by preventing the Scientist from practicing his method or treatment. And yet, on the other hand, it is plain to be seen from the utter failures to effect cures in many instances, that most painful and fatal results have followed, and the question arises, should there not be something done to remedy such consequences, if it is believed that other treatment would have resulted beneficially.

The efforts which were made through the Legislature of the State of New York, during it last session, to prohibit the practice of Christian Science and of clairvoyance, met with a deserved fate, to my mind, but I say this, because I did not favor the remedy proposed. If I may be permitted here to make a suggestion, it would be, that whoever is not a licensed physician, who attempts to heal the sick through method other than that used in the ordinary practice, should be held to strict responsibility for any evil consequences that flow from such acts. Such a measure might be very simple in its terms, but it would reach the evil complained of. In such an age as we are living in, when science is revealing so much that we have hitherto been ignorant of, particularly in regard to ourselves, when those who have given their attention for years to psychological studies are reporting astounding discoveries along their lines of research, and when we are told that the mental or spiritual forces of individuals may be projected for a long distance away, and impinge upon, and control or affect the mentality and actions of others, we may well hesitate to throw any barriers in the way of the prosecution of such investigation.

My friends, I have not forgotten that this is a congress to consider what shall be done to meet that great weapon of death, tuberculosis. I deem my theme appropriate to that, as well as to other matters affecting the health of mankind. The idea of inoculation as a preventative means, far antedated the discovery of Jenner. It was resorted to hundreds of years before his time. You have considered the propriety of inoculation as a specific or remedy for tuberculosis. Permit me to suggest, that you be not hasty of action in regard to compulsory inoculation as a remedy or otherwise. Although it is fatal if its progress is not stayed, it has not the terrors of a plague or pestilence, for in its action it usually moves slowly.

If you have discovered, or succeed in discovering, as every person hopes you have or may, a cure for this dreaded disease, make it speedily known, and the fact of the cure will speak more eloquently and forcibly than anything else. Establish your hospitals for the treatment of your patients, and, if you are seeking for money, your coffers will be filled with bankable money from those whom you have saved from their coffins; and, in addition to that, you will have what money cannot buy, the blessings of mankind.

I also desire to say a word in regard to the services of our physicians in our hospitals and charitable institutions. It is a fact, as every visiting physician knows, that people who are able to pay for services rendered, seek admission to these places, and receive benefits and superior care, medical and surgical attendance there afforded, in order that they may escape payment for value received.

What a man gives in charity should not be diverted from the purpose of the donor. He who obtains another's money without his consent is guilty of a wrong, and in many instances our laws would make it larceny. In the practice of my profession several instances have come to my attention, as in cases of accidents, where the injured have been taken to hospitals, who are well to do, and who seek and obtain recoveries in large sums for the injuries and having received the benefits of the best medical and surgical treatment, they then refuse to pay for such assistance. Nothing could be more unjust than this treatment of those who render such valuable services to the suffering in the hours of dire distress. It is the turning of charitable institutions to wrong purposes, to permit such persons to escape liability. They seem to suppose that because these institutions are wholly or semi-charitable they can command the services of the best physicians and surgeons in the country, without paying for them. I do not understand the law so to be, yet others differ from me in that respect, but at any rate, the liability should be declared by law, as a matter of justice to the medical profession.

The subject, "heredity" is addressed not only to the physician, but to every philanthropist, statesman and humanitarian in the land. The tracing of grains in order that the very best may be obtained, also the crossings essential to produce the most luscious fruits and beautiful flowers, show the wonderful working of Nature when aided by the knowledge and skill of man, in beautifying the earth, and filling the land with plenty. The same remarks apply to the breeding of stock, but, when we come to the human family, we stop, and the question arises, should the consideration which we have for the rights of man be carried to such an extent, that we will permit the workings of heredity as shown in disease and crime, to go unrestrained? Shall born criminals, epileptics and diseased persons be prevented from entering into the marriage relation, of begetting their own kind, as an act of humanity and justice to the race to which we belong. If the evils which flow from these sources can be readily prevented, then efforts should be made immediately in that direction, but if not, for one, I am in favor of radical measures. I will not pursue this course of thought further, but, in conclusion, wish to return to that line of thought and study which has occupied my attention more or less now for many years.

Permit me to say then, that too few persons realize that all forces are invisible. Because we are accustomed to deal with material objects, such as we can see, feel, hear and weigh, is no argument whatever against the existence and potency invisible things. We do not see the moving winds, yet they lash the sea into wild commotion, and devastate towns and forests. They move the clouds from place to place, and the cold which we do not see, congeals water to snow and ice; and the attraction of gravitation which we neither see nor seem to feel, brings the rain down from the skies to the earth, and holds worlds in their places. We do not realize, see, nor seem to feel the immense pressure upon us as we move about in our daily vocations. Let that pressure which is the weight of the atmosphere as drawn down upon us by the force of gravitation, be removed, and death would instantly follow. There are far too many learned men, many of whom are distinguished scientists, theologians, doctors, lawyers and jurists, who have made searching investigation into that branch of psychology which opens up the way for manifestations of invisible intelligence, with the result that they are convinced not only of its possibility, but of its being an accomplished fact, to justify a denial of it by those who have not made the same patient and careful investigations. This study opens a comparatively new field of research for men of all professions, for physicians as much as to any. I know the fact to be, that many physicians in difficult cases, apply to clairvoyants to assist them in locating and diagnosing diseases, and yet few will admit the fact. It is astonishing how few men have the courage of their convictions. The world is full of moral cowards. Few are daring enough to brave the current of public sentiment, even though they know that sentiment to be unjustified. Truth may sometimes be unpleasant, but it is always respectable, and is bound to win against ignorance and bigotry. Respectable lies have obtained, have flourished for a time, but wisdom, knowledge and established fact overthrow them eventually, and bury them beneath the mountains of truth which reach to the very heavens. Any enactment against the right of any person to rationally exercise any power or gift incident to his nature, and to give to others the benefit which he or she may be able to extend to them by reason of these powers or gifts, is an outrage against the freedom of thought, speech and action. And yet, that is just what is done in some places, and is attempted in others. But don't understand me as intimating that any gift or power may not be abused and used for bad purposes, and that when that is done the offender should not be punished. Legislation such as I am referring to has been mostly set on foot by religious fanatics, who think they are serving God, as did those who hung the witches at Salem. Let us remember with what zeal man has always adhered to that which seemed to be truth to him, particularly to that which he has regarded as pertaining to his spiritual welfare, and it is lamentable fact that the sword, the thumbscrew, implements of torture, and the fagot, instead of reason, forebearance and humanity, have often been the arguments with which man has met his brother, when he has differed with him upon matters of a spiritual nature. Law, religion and healing of the sick have come down the ages, and of the three, the doctor has been the most human. Let him continue so, not to the end, for there is no end to that which is of eternal duration. He has not, as a rule, sought to enact laws to enslave others, or deprive them of their rights. He has sought to assist nature in her work of healing the diseased and wounded. To do that is the most he can aspire to, and surely that is noble enough, for Nature's laws are God's methods, and man as a child of God must be the object of divine affection and love. He who serves God best, serves man most. If we do not seem to know much about the Divine, let us learn as much as possible of man, and all that we behold in the world in which we dwell. We shall find, my friends, later on, that man is a manifestation of the divine, and the more noble he becomes, the more Godlike he will be, and the more exalted will be his conceptions of Deity. Let us work together for the building up of the human race. Let manhood and womanhood in future ages be more noble because we have lived and helped to make them so. Let the number of their years be increased upon the earth, and let every man be worthy of freedom in all respects. Teach him to be master of himself, of all his passions and appetites, and let the ruling purpose of the lives of men and women be, to make this world the beginning of an unending paradise.

PROPHYLAXIS OF TUBERCULOSIS.

BY DR. E. P. LACHAPELLE,
President of the Board of Health of the Province of Quebec, Montreal, Canada—Vice President elect of the American Congress of Tuberculosis.

Mr. President, Gentlemen:—

In extending an invitation to address this meeting you have conferred upon me and the Province of Quebec, which I represent, an honor for which I am deeply indebted; allow me, therefore, to offer you my most sincere thanks. However, having to express myself in a language not my own, I feel it would be encroaching on your kindness and attention, were I not to limit myself to the time allotted. Therefore, while speaking on the prophylaxis of tuberculosis, I will briefly state how the question appeals to me, and what are my views upon the best means to insure the efficacy of its application.

The large number of cases of Tuberculosis, the fact of its frequent occurrence in infancy and childhood among children born of tuberculous parents, have led authors to classify this infection among hereditary diseases. Moreover, owing to the intimate nature of the disease remaining unknown for a long period the notion of hereditary transmission had become for several, almost one of absolute fatality. A child born of tuberculous parents was doomed before hand. Any trace of tuberculosis found in an individual was the means of immediately regarding the parents, direct or collateral, as also contaminated.

The study of tuberculosis guided by the light resulting from discoveries of Villemin, Pasteur and Koch, has brought out Pathology from the narrow circle in which it had heretofore been moving. It is no longer a disease of the nutrition, a consumption of the tissues, an ulceration of the organs from lack of vitality, brought upon a living being by hereditary influence, it is a germ disease, consequently trans-

Read at Medico-Legal Society and American Congress of Tuberculosis May 15th and 16th, 1901.

missible; common to man and beast, and usually communicated by direct contact. Both the medical and veterinary authorities agree upon this point basing their opinion on uncontestable proofs. As it happened with the soldiers of the Imperial Guard observed by Villemin, one may become tuberculous, despite a most healthy constitution and the absence of any trace of tuberculosis in the family history.

The simple aspiration of the dust of tuberculous sputum, or the deglutition of tuberculous food, is sufficient to contaminate.

No doubt there are predisposing causes. Contagion from infectious diseases is not necessarily more fatal than pathological heredity. Tuberculosis does not derogate from the law of infections in general; together with the virulence of the germ, the natural predisposition of the tissues must not be overlooked; this is what constitutes tubercular heredity. A child born of tuberculous parents does not of necessity, inherit the bacillus of Koch; this may be possible, but exceedingly rare; he becomes heir to a natural predisposition of tissues to tubercular invasion. Being a descendant from one or two organisms contaminated or weakened by Koch's bacillus, he grows with a modified nutrition, which makes him a fit prey and subject for tuberculosis. But the infection cannot break out without the presence of the pathogenic microbe, which, in most cases, comes from the exterior. He is contaminated in the same manner as those who are not born of tuberculous parents.

In tuberculosis, the constitution of the individual is an important factor; by hereditary predisposition, general debility, overwork, alcoholic intoxication, it facilitates tubercular invasion; it will also, to a great extent, influence the evolution of the disease, rendering it either more or less malignant with the possibility of recovery; or fatal from a progressive infectious course. For it is a well known fact, that tuberculosis can be cured, as well as the natural predisposition of the individual can be modified. Is it not by the treatment of the constitution that the efforts of the therapeutists are crowned with the greatest success? Do they not try to stamp out tuberculosis by hygienic treatment, that is, open air, overalimentation, rest, and in a word everything that can build up the general system?

From this scientific standpoint, it would be easy to come to an understanding upon the best means to establish a rational prophylaxis of tuberculosis. To be efficacious, such a prophylaxis should embrace the two recognized etiological principles, namely:

1. To keep the organism from debilitation, or to modify it, if there already exists a predisposition to tuberculosis.

2. To prevent contagion.

As a means of maintaining or improving health, that is to prevent or to eradicate the natural predisposition of the system to tuberculosis, we must resort to the following measures of paramount importance to the healthy child, to the predisposed one and to the adult:

1. To furnish the lungs of the child, always and everywhere, at home and at public and boarding schools, with a sufficient supply of fresh air; to give him but wholesome food of easy digestion and adapted to his age. To develop his physical strength by moderate exercise. To avoid muscular or nervous exhaustion and overwork.

2. If the child be predisposed to tuberculosis through heredity, scrofula and rachitis, greater care must be taken to apply the above measures and prescribe, if possible, a special hygiene, such as a sojourn in the country or near the sea.

3. In the case of adults, to oppose any special cause tending to diminish vitality and predisposing them and their descendants to the invasion of tuberculosis. such as alcoholism, overwork, bad nourishment, overcrowding and lack of ventilation. On this last point, to oversee in a special manner, the hygiene of dwellings, boarding schools, factories, warehouses, theatres, prisons, etc., so that each inhabitant should have the necessary cubic space.

As a safeguard against the transmission of the germ of tuberculosis, the following measures should be advocated:

1. The notification of tuberculous cases. Bringing thus the centres of infection to the knowledge of the sanitary authorities will enable the latter to take the necessary steps for the protection of the community, due consideration being always given to the interests of the patient and his family.

2. The struggle against the spread of the disease from the dessicated sputum of consumptives, and for that purpose, the disinfection of their places of abode, the prohibition of dry

sweeping and dusting, the formal defense of spitting upon floors, pavements and in public conveyances.

3. The struggle against the propagation of the germs of tuberculosis from infected food, and for this reason, the sterilization of milk, the inspection of meat, the regulation of dairies, abattoirs and butcher stalls.

4. The establishment of numerous popular sanatoria, where indigent tuberculous patients would be isolated, and learn to follow a treatment tending to their own possible cure and also to eliminate the danger of contagion to others.

But, as all the above precautionary measures which the sanitary authorities of Europe and America have succeeded in establishing, only after lengthy observations, cannot become truly effective without the voluntary co-operation of the patients and the public; to establish the prophylaxis of tuberculosis on a firm basis, it must be, above all, regarded as a question of conviction. The best means towards this end, is the education of the public. Enforce in all schools, the teaching of the prevention against contagious diseases, of tuberculosis in particular and within twenty years, you will have formed a generation with strong convictions and ready to give its most hearty support to the humanitarian efforts of physicians and hygienists.

And meanwhile, as the present generation cannot be neglected, increase for the dissemination of knowledge, the number of associations, public lectures, pamphlets, etc.

Thus by the demonstration of facts and by persuasion, will you gain the adherence of the masses, enact the necessary laws and regulations and prepare the golden age of Hygiene in America.

TUBERCULOSIS.

BY A. EUGENE AUSTIN, M. D., DELEGATE FROM ALASKA.

As a body of educated men standing on the threshhold of all that is best and good in this scientific morning of the twentieth century, we can not be indifferent, when we know and realize that the Great Physician said we were our brother's keeper. Our duty is not only to heal the sick but we must teach them so to live that their off-spring may be worthy citizens of the State. The fact that almost one-seventh of the entire mortality of the human race is the result of tuberculosis invests the etiology of the diseases with great importance. It attacks all races, it knocks at the door of the king and the serf alike, it snatches from our hearts the children which make our home so bright. It is not content with its wars against us, but attacks the warm blooded animals, most frequently the bovine. The great importance of the recognition of this statement lies in the fact that this class of animals supplies most of the meat and milk we consume as food.

Oftentimes the mother's love alone is not sufficient to rear her offspring, but we must call on these animals of the field for its food. Therefore, let us ask the legislature to give us a corps of men, so well educated that they will not need to use the tuberculin test, but, finding high ranges of temperature and hearing that cough once learned never forgotten and farther substantiating these symptoms by placing the trained ear over the lungs will not find it difficult to make the diagnosis.

After we have educated our patients to the danger of infecting others, should we not be backed by the State?

First. They should know through literature furnished by the State of the danger of occupying rooms in crowded hotels and public places. Proprietors should not be allowed to take consumptive guests should they gain entrance, the rooms after they are vacated should be made surgically clean.

Read before the American Congress of Tuberculosis, May 15, 1901.

We should ask the legislature to form committeess in well selected portions of the country where men with or without families could find compensating employment to be of such a nature and of such hours as would prove beneficial.

We should ask the legislature to form committees in well great cities cleaned at nights, also that the garbage, ashes and filth of the city be removed at the same time. That, we as citizens may not have thrown in our faces the dust coming from the street cleaners brush laden with the tubercle baccillus. This has been found very practical in some European cities. Cuspidors should be furnished by the State and placed in convenient places along the streets and in all public places. It should be an offense for any one to expectorate in the streets.

Let us deceive ourselves by thinking that we can help our patients with strong medicines and large doses, when those of us who have labored in the laboratories know that it is almost impossible to destroy them with high degrees of temperature. Rather let us call upon nature with her sunny climes and outstretched arms for the broken hearted patient to find rest and health. Let us give him carefully prepared diet lists, lessening the wear and tear of the system, as we find that even the Greeks gave it the name of Phthisis, which translated means a wasting disease. One of the first points of importance is to prevent all loss of weight. To accomplish this we improve the nutrition. We want to give such a diet as will give strength and build up the tissues with the least wear and tear of the system, therefore, pre-digested foods, notably zoolak, koumiss, etc., are especially good. In all diets pertaining to tuberculosis it is important to have the meals thoroughly balanced that there may be no excessive waste. Patients with temperature should be encouraged to take large quantities of water as possible, as the fever is calling the water from the tissues and thus destroy by burning them up. It also serves the double purpose, from a mechanical standpoint, of keeping the intestines flushed, thus preventing the intestine from excessive work in removing the waste.

Let us not alone feed a balanced diet to our stock, being careful to know the exact amount of protein and carbohydrates given per diem in the required proportions, but let us in this greatest beneficial movement give as much attention to human dietetics and hygiene.

THE CASE OF FREDERICK HAMMANN.

BY DR. CARLETON SIMON.

It affords me considerable pleasure to present the case of Frederick Hammann to this Congress, not alone because this young man has been snatched from an early grave, but as well to record the fact that he owes his salvation to the noble and philanthropic nature of Mr. William R. Hearst, of the New York Journal. It is now some six months since Mr. William R. Hearst noted the various good reports given from time to time in the various European Medical Journals, of the treatment for Tuberculosis, as prescribed by Dr. Adolf Hoff, of Vienna, and he resolved to send a patient to him to test this treatment, to hold out to the thousands of sufferers a ray of sunshine to dissipate the gloom, and to present to a suffering mass of humanity a cure.

The first object was to procure a suitable patient, one being in the incipient stage. Numerous agents sought all over New York City for a case that was typical, and at last one was procured from Dr. Daniel Cook, in the person of Frederick Hammann, 22 years of age, and the eldest son of a respectable, hard working family. About six years ago previous, he was attacked with pleurisy, followed later with bronchitis, leaving him in a debilitated condition. He was ambitious and returned to work as soon as possible. His earnings meant much to the family. He attributed his weakness to malaria, his cough to a cold, and his high temperature and rapidly beating heart to the fact that he was tired. Like thousands working in factories and stores, working on doggedly until the end, there came a time when he could work no more. Dr. Daniel Cook was then called in, and after making a bacteriological examination, and careful physical tests, pronounced the case one of Tuberculosis. His record case book gives the following:—

"Frederick Hammann, age 22, height 5 ft. 6 in.; weight, 117 pounds, blue-eyed, pale complectioned, occupation,

Read before the Medico-Legal Society and American Congress of Tuberculosis in joint session. May 15-16, 1901.

clerk; came to me for examination and treatment on September 21st, 1900. He complained of cough and pains under right scapular and had fever, had lost flesh and strength for three or four weeks, but had neglected his condition, because he had been ill the previous summer with malaria, and he saw no cause in his mind for alarm. Patient gives no family history of consumption. An examination of the lungs revealed subcrepitant rales over both lungs, the harsh breathing over large spaces due to consolidation around bronchial tubes, indicated a general tubercular infiltration, which was verified by microscopial examination. Temperature 99 1-2 F. pulse 88, chest measurement 32 1-2 in. expiration, and 34 in. full inspiration."

A specimen of the patient's sputum was sent to Dr. Maurice F. Schlesinger of New York City, for bacteriological examination, who promptly returned the report of the presence of large quantities of tubercle bacilli, five to eight each field.

Another specimen was sent to the Department of Health, of New York City, and in their laboratory report, No. 4911, testified to the finding of tubercle bacilli, and diagnosed the case one of pulmonary tuberculosis.

The patient was then taken to the Vanderbilt Clinic, New York City, and after very careful examination was found to be suffering from incipient tuberculosis. This diagnosis was based upon the fact that percussion showed a diminution of resonance and a rise in pitch at the right apex anteriorly, while osculation at the same place showed harsh inspiration, prolonged expiration and the presence of some few rales, heard after a spell of coughing, with presence of tubercle bacilli.

The patient was then taken to Dr. J. Mount Bleyer, of New York City, who made a physical and X-Ray fluoroscope examination, declaring that there was a slight haziness at the apex of the lung. From all the facts gathered, with the history, a bacteriological, laryngeological and physical examination of the case, he pronounced it to be one of early tuberculosis. He found the temperature to be 99 degrees, F., pulse 84; respiration 23, and discovered traces of an early pleuretic attack

Dr. Henry P. Loomis, of New York City, who next examined the patient, foud that the sputum contained tubercle

BEFORE.

AFTER.

bacilli, and declared the patient suffering from pulmonary tuberculosis.

There was no examination made that did not declare the patient suffering from tuberculosis. The New York Journal, being satisfied that there was no question, of the character of the malady and the correct diagnosis, the patient was placed aboard a steamer and sent to Dr. Adolf Hoff, in Vienna, for treatment.

Dr. Hoff, receiving the patient on December 26th, 1900, made a careful examination, and in his report stated the following:

"The so-called phthisical habit is emminently apparent. His eye, his small, slender, pale face, in connection with the circumstantial redness of the cheek bone, his stooping carriage, his narrow and almost sunken chest, and last, but not least, the apparent indifference with which he contemplates his suffering, fully confirm the opinion, even before a real examination, that the patient is afflicted with the suspected disease. I observe fatty excrescences from the glands in the neck. His chest is extremely flat. The depression above the collar-bones are singularly marked. The breathing is apparently done from both lobes of the lung. In breathing, the depression above the right collar-bone does not fill out so well as the one on the left side. There is nothing abnormal in the back, except that the shoulder blades stand rather away from the vertebral column. The hollowness of sound on the right side above the shoulder blade, from percussion is of greater area than on the left side, which corresponds to the examination as to the collar-bone. There is a pronounced rattling sound in the breathing observed in listening at the collar-bone and between the shoulder blades. Temperature 37.5 Celsius. I judge not alone from what the patient tells me, but as well from my own findings, that he has not had a hemorrhage for six weeks. The ailment is chiefly confined to the apex of the right lung. On the other hand the fever would show that the growth of the disease has not been arrested

On January 1st, 1901, I injected sputum from the patient into six guinea pigs. They at once began to show symptoms of tuberculosis. One of the six died at the end of the twelfth day, and all of them died of acute tuberculosis before

January 20th, which proved to me that the bacilli in Hammann's sputum were of extraordinary virulence."

The patient was immediately placed upon Dr. Hoff's treatment, which consisted of the following formula, called Hoff's Mixture:—

Acidi Arsenicis..............	0.1
Kali carbon. dep.............	0.2
Acidi cinnamylic.............	0.3
Aqua dist....................	5.0

Mix and dissolve by boiling until a perfect solution results, then add:

Cognac.....................	2.5
Ext. laudan. aquosi..........	0.3
Aqua dist....................	2.5

Sig. Take 6 drops after dinner on sugar or in a half a wine glass of water, the dose gradually increased until 22 drops are reached.

Week by week the drops were given, and gradually increased. Whenever the appetite failed the increase of drops was not enforced, nor increased later, this being considered the maximum dose. This was 18 drops. This maximum dose was given for a few weeks, and then reduced weekly by two drops until six drops were reached. After this a rest of eight days was given, and the treatment begun again as before. Tinct. Anodyni was at times added to reduce the cough and when combined with the arsenious acid did not seem to irritate the stomach.

With the medicine the patient had daily applications of cold packs, with subsequent rubbing of the chest and back after careful drying. Before retiring to bed a woolen jacket without sleeves was immersed in cold water, and put on next to the skin, the night shirt over this and allowed to remain on throughout the night. In the morning this jacket was removed and the patient was thoroughly rubbed down with cold water, then dried and allowed to dress.

This general treatment was kept up without any radical change. When, however, there was any febrile tendency which persisted, the following mixture was given, and which is called, Appolzer's Mixture:

Aqua Cinnamomi............70.0
Tinct. chinoidini............ 2.5
Chinin...................... 0.55
Elix. Acidi Halleri.......gtts. 10
Syr. Cinnamomi.............20.0

M. and Sig. Tablespoonful three time daily.

The above mixture being given by Dr. Hoff whenever there were symptoms of hectic fever, with invaribly good results, and the benefits were shown in a few days at the most.

Speaking of the efficiency of this later mixture, Dr. Hoff stated:

"The question arises—to what is the efficacy of Appolzer's mixture due? Not to the chinin. sulphate alone, but directly to the aquae and syrup cinnamomi, and refer to Chamberlain, Gadlic and others, who claim for cinnamon bacteriacidal properties.

"With the exception of Landerer's hetolin injections in tubercular infected rabbits, I am not aware of any experiment made with cinnamon on the living, hence will cite my experience.

Normally the blood of the mouse has no agglutinating power upon baccilli; if the serum of a phthisical patient is injected into the veins of a mouse or rabbit, the blood of these animals assumes property of agglutination. If instead of the serum aquae cinnamomi be injected, the same agglutination occurs, proving that aquae cinnamomi possesses all the properties of the serum full of antitoxin. This helps to prove Widall's explanation of agglutination."

At the end of the first week of treatment the patient's weight rose from 117 to 125 pounds, breathing difficulties of which he complained of previously had disappeared, there was freedom from night-sweats and fever. The appetite had improved and his general condition seemed much better. At the end of the fourth week, the slight cough was the only objective symptom, the patient having gained eight pounds. Seven weeks after the patient had entered upon the treatment under Hoff's direction, coughing had disappeared, there were no external manifestations of the disease, the phthisical look had disappeared, the appetite of the patient was excellent, amination no physical evidences of any active pulmonary there was no more troublesome night-sweats, and upon ex- trouble. Temperature being normal, and percussion right and left lung being without any noticable difference, that is, showing no perceptible trouble over right apex of the lung. In counter-distinction to the examination, of his sputum and the injection of the bacilli into guinea pigs when entering upon treatment, remains the fact that before leaving Vienna there were no bacteriological exidences of tuberculosis, nor did guinea pigs show any signs of infection after having some of the patient's sputum injected into them. The cough hàd entirely disappeared and no sputum was obtainable except in the morning after awakening.

Frederick Hammenn, on his return to New York, stopped at London to see Dr. Sylvester Willard and Sir William Broadbent, both of whom after careful examination found no evidences of any active disease present.

On his return to New York City, Dr. Daniel Cook, his physician, found no evidences of active tuberculosis, but determined that his breathing capacity had increased, general health much better, and consider him well and cured.

In a bacteriological examination by Dr. Maurice Schlesinger, no baccilli tubercle were found, he preparing four slides, and as a crucial test employed Bierdert's method, with the same negative results, proving conclusively the entire absence of the bacilli.

Another specimen was sent to the New York Post-Graduate Hospital, in the laboratory of Prof. Henry T. Brooks, and examined both by him and his assistant, Dr. B. F. Cline, without eliciting any evidences of tubercle baccilli.

Scheimer says in his work on "Creosote and Thiocol," "To speak of medical treatment of the dreaded disease, tuberculosis, in an age when sanitarium treatment leads to discussions of therepeutics in tuberculosis of the lungs, requires almost an apology. How little this apology is required and the positive interest with which even physicians of sanitariums regard any suitable new remedy, is proved by Dr. Pollak's treatise on 'Doutal, Phyramidon and Heroin.' This article proves conclusively that in spite of sanitarium treatment, it is the duty of the physician to make all the research possible for suitable remedies.

Dr. Hoff adopted the same line of treatment as that advanced by Dr. Pollak, in the use of the above mentioned remedies, assisted by suitable sanitary surroundings, with the difference, however, that Dr. Hoff substitutes Dionin for Heroin, Appolzer's Mixture for Phyramidon, Hoff's Mixture for Ductal.

All that it claimed for the Hoff mixture is the fact that it possesses a bacteriacidal power due to the cinnamon, being equal in agglutination power to anti-toxin. The arsenious acid being suspended thoroughly in solution, assists in this, acting as a febrifuge, bacteriocide, and has a direct action upon the hemoglobin, or respiratory pigment, increasing their number and the amount of cellular hematin.

In closing, I desire to note that the physicians engaged in the examination of this patient from time to time, were not alone eminent in their professional standing, but as well totally disinterested, financially, upon the result of the trial. There being no reason of any exaggeration in any detail of this case, because of no worldly compensation to any one engaged upon it, except that humane, charitable purpose which we as physicians are all engaged in, makes the cure of Frederick Hamman the more striking, as its circustances and the result as chronicled, eliminates any possible fraud or deception.

I desire to state that the New York Journal deserves all credit for the noble, generous and praise-worthy manner in which it has striven in the public interest to be a public benefactor.

BIOPLASM IN TUBERCULOSIS.

BY EDWIN F. BOWERS, M. D., OF N. Y.

This remedy is of value primarily as a vital incitant, and in a minor degree as an alterative. It is derived from the Saracenia Purpura, or Pitcher Plant, and exhibited in doses of 10 to 15 grains in powder or tablet form three times daily, after meals. It is anti-sudorific, promotes appetite, and increases assimilation.

The cardinal features in the treatment of tuberculosis, to my mind, are to support the organism, increase the digestive and assimilative capacity and meet symptoms as they present themselves. Chief among these as exhibiting the tendency to weaken the resisting powers are anorexia, night sweats, and cough. Loss of appetite is frequently the result of our over zealous habit of "stuffing' the patient to a point where sub-oxidation is an insured factor, and as a consequence toxins are formed in the alimentary canal, and auto-intoxication from intestinal absorption takes place. We lose sight of the fact that it is not the quantity of food consumed, but the amount assimilated which is the desideratum. Our efforts at this stage should be directed to thoro laxation, preferably by an hepatic stimulant. This condition relieved the appetite usually improves.

Failing, however, 10 grs. of Bioplasm, 1-2 hour before each meal tends to increase the digestive activity, and prevents a recurrence of the condition. Night sweats constitute another distressing feature which are entirely relieved or greatly ameliorated by a 15 grain dose of Bioplasm on retiring.

Reports in some fifty cases also show that the cough is relieved by this drug. To sum up briefly, Bioplasm is a valuable tonic and stimulant, promotes appetite and the capacity for assimilating food; relieves the night sweats, and soothes the cough. It is not contra indicated given with any other remedial agent, but on the contrary synergizes their action.

Read before the joint session of the American Congress of Tuberculosis and the Medico-Legal Society, New York, May 15-16, 1901.

SOME RESULTS OF CAMP AND OUTDOOR LIFE IN NORTHERN WISCONSIN.

BY THOS. BASSETT KEYES, M. D., OF CHICAGO.

Consumption.—Where shall the help come from. Best way is: Return to nature. Return to a natural diet, allow light and air to influence your system. Camp like the Israelites of old, camp in the balsam woods of Northern Wisconsin, living with nature, and thou shalt prolong thy days and have a goodly chance of recovery.

Men are the highest specimens of light air beings. Their life depends upon pure air and light. Water and food may strengthen their health and refresh their system, but light and air for men are the principal life producers and preservers. The best air for man is the air of the woods, full of fragrance of trees and herbs. Camp life in the Northern Woods of Wisconsin offers all opportunities for a genuine return to nature, a great and wonderful change takes place in the whole organism, digestion improves and all organs start an effective process of healing.

The wrtier has seen many patients pronounced to be beyond help, suffering from that dread disease, consumption, though thanks to "roughing it," many of these patients have recovered who apparently had not a "ghost of a show." It has been said by that astute physician, Dr. Chas. Gilbert Davis, that there is probably nothing which encourages exercise more, or no better exercise or recreation calculated to recuperate the nervous system, than life in a properly situated camp.

Who does not enjoy camp life, when there is good fishing and hunting and boating, and beautiful scenery. Life is worth living only when we are in condition to enjoy it. It is the mental pleasure which one receives, in camping, that greatly aids in the recovery of tuberculosis.

The danger of contracting cold is nil when proper clothing

Read before the American Congress of Tuberculosis in joint session with the Medico-Legal Society, May 15-16, 1901.

is worn, and patients soon become toughened to resist the atmospheric changes. At the Nordach Sanitarium in the Black Forests of Germany, which has gained more than a national reputation on account of the large number of consumptive patients cured, the patients are directed to exercise in the open air, they are not allowed to wear overcoats or to carry umbrellas, and the same exercise is kept up during rainy weather, and when wet to the skin they are not permitted to change their clothing. The percentage of cures are greater than in any other sanitarium in Germany.

In a well conducted camp, under the supervision of a physician, it is as easy to prescribe proper food for each individual patient here as in a sanitarium. In this case as at Camp Keyes, the food of each patient is prescribed and the physician eats with the patients. The principal article of diet here is goat's milk, and goat's milk Koumis, on account of its nutritive and curative effects. A selected herd of goats are kept for the camp. (The Goat's Milk Koumis Cure I have described in The Tubercle, Vol. V, No. 1.)

Under this wilderness cure when the patient returns to his former home he has been hardened, and is in good condition to resist the effects of confinement, and in many cases which I know of, no manifestation of the disease returns.

Dr. Alfred L. Loomis, of New York, called attention to camping out for consumptives (New York Medical Record, 1879). He says: "All these things, the breathing of pure air of the wilderness, the perfect rest, the wholesome food and the early hours combine to make tent life a powerful weapon in combating this dread disease."

Dr. Trudeau expresses himself strongly on this point, having faithfully tried tent life, and he adds: "Many of the risks supposed to attend out-of-door-life exist only in the minds of the timid." He believes that tent life, and a return to the invigorating, out-of-door existence of the savage, is nature's antidote for a disease which is almost an outgrowth of civilization.

Many persons think that "to camp is to rough it." This is not necessarily so. Camp life may under favorable circumstances be the most pleasant and luxurious imaginable, and consumptives are rapidly learning this, and that camp life, instead of being rough, is so smooth, so calm, so restful, that

life during the past ten years with patients from Maine to Flor-
life during the ast ten years with patients from Maine to Flor-
ida, and in California, Colorado, Texas and Mexico leads me to say that hospital and sanitarium life is a failure as compared with tent life in the wilderness. While I am well aware that great stress is laid upon fresh air, as a necessity in the treatment of tuberculosis, in most of the various sanitariums, especially those conducted upon the cottage plan, yet fresh air is not all that we obtain from camp life. It is the mental pleasure which it affords, and upon this I wish to lay the greatest stress. Camping in the backwoods country, in the land of the balsam trees, surrounded by lakes and forests of extreme beauty and grandeur, with the finest of fishing at one's command, encourages exercise, and the patient's muscles and nerve centers become accustomed to new habits, and there is probably nothing which answers the purpose so well as camp life. Camping tends to a greater degree than any other method to turn a man's thoughts away from his own condition, and then the patient is not bothered by that conventionalism which one finds at the sanitariums, there is no odor of the sick room.

What a joy to sleep in a canvas tent, in a backwoods country! For here the air is always as fresh as if out-of-doors, yet there is no draught, and such air, ladened with balsam fragrance, an impossibility to find in the city. After sleeping in a canvas tent, the best ventilated rooms will seem close and stuffy.

A person who is going to camp must decide upon a location. In the Adirondacks, which were among the first camping grounds for consumptives, partly owing to their proximity to New York city, it has become the custom for patients to camp there both winter and summer though the summer months are perhaps the most popular. My experience teaches me that the balsam wood belt of Northern Wisconsin is the best camping place for those patients suffering with catarrhal diseases, and statistics prove this to be one of the most healthful, if not the most healthful, summer climate in
the world for the climatic treatment of catarrh... diseases.
the world for the climatic treatment of catarrhal diseases.
soon come when this region will be the most popular of summer resorts. Here, too, would be the place for a stimulating ideal winter camp. The winter season is the most agreeable

part of the year, with plenty of blue sky, fine, bracing atmosphere, and very little rain. The ground is generally covered with snow. Coughs, colds and diseases of the lungs are very little known. The careful meteorological reports of the army surgeons prove the truth of these assertions.

Dr. J. Hunter, of Toronto, Canada, in an excellent article on the treatment of tuberculosis in the Canadian Journal of Medicine and Surgery, in recommending the climate of Ontario, Canada, for tubercular patients says that "the belief that certain climatic conditions exert a curative influence in tuberculosis is both so universal and so old as to challenge the most respectful consideration, however difficult it may be to find out what constitutes the basis of this faith" and "that we know now that many tubercular subjects endure the most inclement weather with impunity." "It is within the memory of most physicians, when the only change thought of was to send consumptive patients south. More accurate knowledge concerning the disease and wider experience have seriously questioned the wisdom of the advice hitherto given.

In North Central Wisconsin in the vicinity of Butternut, there is as great an abundance of benevolent influences, conducive to good health, body and mental vigor, and longevity, as can be found anywhere. Summer and winter are resplendent with sunshine, and the air during summer is kept pure and salubrious by occasional showers. As a climate for phthisical patients North Central Wisconsin has these points to recommend it.

Pure Air, kept pure by occasional showers, and its proximity to the great lakes, at the same time it is just far enough inland to temper and mellow the atmosphere.

Dryness of the Air. The hot sun produces a dryness of the air and ground. The sun always shines immediately after a shower, and in a few minutes everything is dry, and the air ladened with fragrance and ozone.

The sun's rays of Northern Wisconsin have great chemical power, and tan the skin very quickly, though at a high summer heat one seldom suffers from the heat, but if not careful at first one is apt to become badly sun burned. For instance one of my patients wished to show himself to his friends on his return to the city as being very much tanned, so he went rowing in a short sleeved shirt. After rowing about under the hot sun for about three hours his arms became quite red, and for the next three days he sat about his tent suffering from severe sun burns of his arms.

This chemical action of the sun is of great advantage to the phthisical patients for when the sun produces tan it seems to have a greater hemetonic effect, and since great good has been gained from the sun's rays in treating consumption, and killing germs, this becomes a most important feature.

Kime in the October, 1900, number of the Medical Record, N. Y., proves the power of penetration of reflected light. He fastened to a photographic dry plate, a transparency landscape picture and the two were placed upon the back between the shoulder blades of a well developed man weighing one hundred and fifty pounds, the transparency being placed next to the skin with the sensitive plate immediately behind it. Over these were placed black paper, black cotton wading, and some large black clothes and all were firmly bound down by means of a long black bandage. He was then taken to the light room of the photographer and exposed his chest to the rays of the reflector for fifteen minutes, with the results that a distinctive picture of the landscape was produced upon the photographic plate, thus proving that the rays of light went through the body.

He bases the therapy of light upon the fact that it is a powerful germicide, its bactericidal action being due to the violet and ultra violet rays, or so called chemical rays of the solar spectrum. 2nd. That "the chemical rays of light are irritant in their action, not only upon the skin but to all the tissues through which they pass. This irritant effect is noted in sun burn and is often seen even in mid-winter. Very strong electric light produces similar effects. Widmark, of Stockholm, has been able to demonstrate that this dermititis is due to chemical action and is independent of the heat rays, and that it is most not a burn. In the treatment of disease by this agent the improvement may at least in part be due to the irritant action arousing to greater activity the vital forces in the parts upon and through which the sun's rays are made to pass; in other words increased phagocytosis may play an important part in the therapy of light.

Part of the treatment for those who visit Northern Wisconsin should be to expose their bare chest and back to the rays of the sun with their powerful chemical action. In all my experience and in talking with others who have been exposed to the weather of all parts of the United States, they bear me out in the statement that the sun in the section of Northern Wisconsin, of which we are speaking, has a very powerful effect in producing tan.

As to the patients who will be benefited by a change of residence to Northern Wisconsin speaking broadly it would be supposed that those with a mild onset, slight temperature fluctuations,localized lesions, with bodily and mental vigor and a taste for outdoor life would be the one's who would derive the greatest benefit, and while this is true many cases of an acute nature have recovered. We believe that goat's milk koumis as part of this treatment has been a most powerful aid, and is certainly a great therapeutic agent.

During the summer of 1900 I sent seven patients to camp in the vicinity of Fifield. Six of these patients were in in-a taste for outdoor life would be the ones who would derive have improved. Of the remaining case I desire to report more in full. The case was a young lady twenty-three years of age, who had suffered from symptoms of tuberculosis for about one year, following child birth. Previous to marriage about two years ago, she nursed her mother with cancer of the uterous through a long spell of sickness, besides earning a living by sewing for both, and was no doubt very much overworked and run down. During the latter part of gestation she showed certain symptoms of tuberculosis, which gradually progressed and at the time when the journey to Northern Wisconsin was undertaken I had some misgivings and doubts as to the advisability of allowing the patient to take the trip, expecting death soon at hand, the symptoms being very acute, and the sputum containing lots of the tubercle bacilli. But how surprising were the results. The progress toward health was very slow during the first two weeks, but in another month she believed herself cured, having grown very strong, night sweats stopped, a good hearty appetite, with no bowel trouble. This patient now enjoys good health.

I believe that patients at Camp Keyes are under as favorable conditions to recover as anywhere else.

In order to get an expression of the value of North Central Wisconsin as a climate for phthisical patients I addressed a letter of inquiry to a number of the leading physicians of that section and received the following replies:

To the Editor of the Tubercle:
Chicago, Ill.

Dear Sir:—Yours of the 30th ult. received, in reply will state in June, 1896, I came here from Wisconsin because of my wife's heath. She had tuberculosis with a cavity the size of the palm of her hand in upper lobe of right lung, general health bad and continually failing under all treatments. I continued a nuclein and proto nuclein treatment during July and August, 1896, then resorted to God's great remedy, fresh air and exercise only. Since then she hasn't had one dollar's worth of medicine and is a picture of health. During the summer of '97 while she was in New York State she contracted a cold, but on returning a rapid recovery took place. I have, during the past four and one-half years, had but two cases of tubercular trouble. One inherited trouble, bad hygiene, slim purse, etc., results nil; the other, an imported case from Chicago in advanced stage. Came here during winter months, constitution all gone,. I sent him back home, poor fellow died in Union depot, Chicago.

I firmly believe that Northern Wisconsin will develop a field where very much good may be gained for these patients, especially if they come during the summer months and become acclimated.

(Signed) A. M. CORBETT, M. D.,
Rib Lake, Wis.

Marshfield, Wis., Nov. 11th, 1900.

Thos. Bassett Keyes, M. D.,
Chicago, Ill.

Dear Doctor: Yours of the 31st of October is received and contents noted, and in reply would say in regard to the climate of Northern Wisconsin for tubercular patients is good in the Pine regions and dry sandy soil. I believe that climatic changes have much to do in the cure of tuberculosis. I also think that climatic changes in the first stages with good care and little medicine is the physician's only dependence for the cure of his patients. I will say that First, No zone enjoys entire immunity from pulmonary consumption. Second, The popular belief that phthisis consumption is common in cold climates is fallacious, and the idea now so prevalent that phthisis is rare in warm climates is as untrue as dangerous. The disease causes a large proportion of deaths on the sea shore, the mortality diminishing with elevation up to a certain point. Altitude is inimically opposed to the development of consumption, owing chiefly to the greater purity of the atmosphere, and its freedom from organic matter in elevated situations, also its richness in ozone. This agrees with my own opinion that high and dry situations, especially rolling and consequently, dry pine lands are the best places to take up a residence in if one has to change at all. Moisture arising from a clay soil due to evaporation, is one of the most influential factors in its production.

Yours truly,
C. SMITH, M. D.

Plum City, Wis., Nov. 12, 1900.

Thos. Bassett Keyes, M. D,

Dear Doctor: Judging the few cases of tuberculosis which have come to my twenty years' of practice in central and mid-northern Wisconsin, I think my judgment would support my stating: That a doctor who would recommend this climate for a tubercular patient would do so from a pecuniary motive and not for the patient's good. This is on a yearly estimate of conditions of climate. In the warmer months I must admit that all cases appear to obtain good results. W. A. CURTIS.

Ashland, Wis., Nov. 11, 1900.

Thomas Bassett Keyes, M. D., Chicago, Ill.

Dear Doctor:—In reply to your letter of the 31st ult. asking for an expression of my views of the climate of northern Wisconsin for phthisical patients, I will say that this is a subject to which I have given much thought during the eleven years I have resided here, and take pleasure in complying with your request.

Everything considered we have little tubercular phthisis here, and that is largely among those who baev a predisposition to the disease. The Scandinavian people seem to have a tendency to anemia and its allied conditions, and are therefore often affected with tuberculosis.

Syphlis and tuberculosis are rapidly exterminating the Indians in Northern Wisconsin, due to their manner of living and intermingling and their universal unsanitary habits.

It is true the climate here is severe, but this is more than balanced by the dryness of both winter and summer.

From the middle of March until the middle of May we have our worst weather of the year. This is as a rule a rainy season and the frost in the ground and the ice in the bay and lakes, which remains late in April, gives the air a chilly penetrating character, not unlike that of Chicago in mild winter weather.

This is the season that phthisical patients should avoid. The remainder of the year is characterized by abundance of sunshine, and dry, pure air. In winter, when snow begins to fall, the air is cold and dry and the snow does not melt but continues to accumulate reaching a depth of from two to four feet. It is exceptional that it rains in winter. This climate has a peculiar stimulating effect which is noticeable in the capacity of residents for both mental and physical labor, and while this is true it cannot fail to develop in the body the elements of resistance to the subacute and chronic forms of disease.

In my opinion if we are ever to master tuberculosis it will be by increasing the resistance of the invaded body, and an invigorating climate will be better than a mild enervating one, especially in the first stage of the disease.

The shores of Lake Superior, and more especially the Apostle Islands, are destined to become an important health resort in the future for incipient phthisis for reasons given or implied in the foregoing. a more extended statement of which time does not now permit me to make. I shall be pleased to give more definite and complete information on this subject at some future time. and in the meantime wish your society and journal abundant success.

Fraternally,

(Signed) J. M. DODD, M. D.

The above papers were read before the Forum of Tuberculosis, Climatology and Hydrology, November 14, 1900, Chicago.

The paper was then discussed by Drs. Enoch Matcher, of Birmingham, Mich., Dr. T. C. Duncan, Dr. Sheldon Peck, Dr. F. A. Leusman, Dr. Replogle, Dr. McIntire, and Dr. Kellogg. Their discussion was as follows:

Enoch Mather, M. D., Ph. D., of Birmingham, Mich.:

Ladies and Gentlemen:—There is no model climate for all diseases, no state or portion of state can boast of being perfect in its tellural atmosphere and climatic conditions. It is true we have cases who come and go, season after season, place to place, for health. Consumption of the lungs is very prevalent, and patients are recommended to various places.

The climate of northern Wisconsin can be highly spoken of for its pure air. This is, of course, due to its proximity to the Great Lakes, its frequent showers, and its large tract of forest lands, at the same time the air is dry, for the sun is always shining immediately after a shower, so that we can call them sunshine-showers. It is also pleasant, for its air is ladened with the fragrance of the balsam woods.

In my estimation Northern Wisconsin will, before many years, become the one main place for patients suffering from consumption, or phthisical patients.

First. Because patients have to have pure air with sunshine, and lastly, good surroundings, pure food, good water; and all these are in northern Wisconsin.

Dr. T. C. Duncan, of Chicago, said:

That an acquaintance of his, Dr. Roberts, had sent a patient to northern Wisconsin with tuberculosis, and that the doctor reported the case thoroughly cured, and that he had known several who had been benefitted.

Dr. F. A. Leusman, of Chicago, said:

I think that Dr. Keyes and Dr. Kellogg deserve great credit for bringing to the attention of the society "Camp and Outdoor Life for Consumptives in Northern Wisconsin," and I believe that this will be ideal treatment in the near future. In literature I have noticed that many men with large capital advocate Sanitarium treatment, and claim that in camp life the proper treatment and examinations cannot be made, which is all nonsense, as it can be done as well in a regulated camp as in a sanitarium. And I to-day wish to raise a protest against this plea of the Sanitarium, where patients must pay all the way from twenty-five to fifty dollars a week. Now I do not object to the Sanitarium treatment nor the examinations of the blood, stomach contents, etc., two or three times a day, but what good comes from these blood counts? It is only to satisfy the scientific cravings of the physician and does the patient no good.

I only want to say that camp and outdoor life under the guidance of an experienced practioner, offers all the things that can be done at a sanitarium, and many more, in that, the mind of the patient can be better kept from his disease, and then all of these blood counts, stomach examinations, etc., can be made the same in a well regulated camp as at a sanitarium.

Under this form of treatment I believe that the patient has a better chance of recovery, and that in many cases the foci of tubercle inflamation becomes encapsulated and heals up.

I believe that outdoor life should be more generally advocated and that the laiety be made aware of it, for though this is the common property of the profession, it is not the general property of the profession.

Dr. B. S. McIntyre, of Chicago, was asked the relation of nervous diseases to tuberculosis and replied:

In answering a question of that kind I shall probably reply in the face of modern literature. It has been my opinion for a number of years that all chronic diseases have their origin in nervous causes. Now, as proof, we would all have tuberculosis were there not some undermining cause. In order that we may take on the disease tuberculosis, the system must be in a weakened condition. This, I believe, to be due to an enervation of the nervous system. Then if tubercular patients become nervous it is easy to account for the exceedingly nervous symptoms of all kinds. It is an outcry of the nervous system for more nutrition, and this accounts for the value of camp life, for the tubercular patients needs that which will occupy his mind and build up the nervous energy. Camp life does all this.

The camp treatment is the ideal treatment, and this should be done under a well regulated system, the patient being under the management of a physician.

At the close of the discussion the following motion was passed:

On motion by Dr. T. C. Duncan, the attention of the profession and public was called to the great success of the outdoor method of treatment for pulmonary and general tuberculosis, and we request the publication of the facts.

Meeting of The Forum of Tuberculosis, Climatology and Hydrology, November 14, 1900.

CONTRIBUTION TO THE TREATMENT OF TUBERCULOSIS BY MEANS OF STATIC ELECTRICITY, INHALATIONS OF COMPOUND OZONE AND IMMEDIATE ABSORPTION OF MEDICINES THROUGH THE SKIN.

BY F. T. LABADIE, M. D., OF N. Y.

I will not enter into any details about tuberculosis, its causes and ravages, as these are all well known to you. I want simply to speak of a treatment, relatively new. Since my last communication to the congress of Paris last year I have used this treatment with my confrere and collaborator, Dr. Noel, and it has given us both very satisfactory results. Up to date the treatments employed to cure tuberculosis have failed because almost all have had one purpose, namely: to kill the bacillus with substances more or less antiseptic, sometimes dangerous to the human system, and medicines,—always very bad for the patient's stomach. For my part, I think, as perhaps do some of my confreres, also, that the bacillus is only a secondary cause of tuberculosis, as this disease generally attacks poor people,—and by poor, I do not mean to say,—in the true sense of the word, those who are not well off,—but those suffering from poor health, overwork, malnutrition, alcoholism, excesses of all kinds, and the hereditary taint,—that is those who have inherited from their parents, not the bacillus, but the ground favorable to its development.

I think then that the treatment of tuberculosis, besides its prophylaxy, must have two points in view:

1st, to modify the ground in which the bacillus grows, viz: restore to the patient his lost strength, restoring the vitality and energy of the human cells in order that they can resist with advantage the invasion of the enemy.

Read before the American Congress of Tuberculosis in joint session with Medico-Legal Society, May 15, 16, 1901.

2nd. Fight this enemy and destroy the bacillus without danger to the human organism.

The treatment that I propose today has given us such good results that I deem it my duty to inform my confreres about it.

This treatment has been applied in Europe and in this country with most satisfactory results and answers the purpose at which we are aiming,—tonify the organism, destroy the bacillus and eliminate the toxines from the body.

This treatment is by means of Static Electricity, high frequency currents, inhalations of compound ozone and hot air treatments given with a special apparatus invented by Dr. Noel, which are extensively used in the Paris hospitals, and which I will show you here.

We know that the physiological effects of Static Electricity on the human body are the following: they regulate all the functions of the human system, improve appetite, digestion, sleep, pulse, temperature, oxidation, excretion, secretion, nervous irritability;—in one word, it increases metabolism. The sparks, by their mechanical disturbances, bring about a great molecular change and act like massage, vibration, etc., but in a very superior manner; in short, Static Electricity brings about a general progressive improvement.

This answers the first part of the treatment: Modification of the ground on which tuberculosis grows and, if it is true, as has recently been suggested by a physician in this country, that tuberculosis is a neurosis, there is one more reason to use Static Electricity.

Now, to destroy the bacillus I will say that electricity alone can do the work, as we have observed it. To confirm what I say, I will cite the communication of Dr. Doumer, of Lille, (France), to the Academy of Medicine, and published also in the "Gazette des Hopitaux," March 6th, 1900.

Dr. Doumer employs the high frequency currents and the large static machines give the same currents. The results are very remarkable, as in a few seances he obtained the disappearance of the night sweats and of the fever. The cough diminishes, becomes less painful, the expectoration changes its color, from purulent becomes mucous and, if the patient follows the treatment for sufficient time to obtain a cure, this comes with the disappearance of the bacillus in the sputa, after three, four or five months, according to the condition of the patient.

Dr. Mays, Professor of Diseases of the Chest in the Philadelphia Polyclinic, has used Static Electricity in tuberculosis with very good results.

We think we have obtained better results by improving the method and adding to it the static cataphoresis, the inhalations of compound ozone and the hot air baths which, besides their well known effects upon nutrition and metabolism, and so on, help immensely to eliminate the toxines.

The static cataphoresis is perfectly possible as the following short history will prove:

In 1747, Privati of Venice, conceived the idea that substances could be transported through the human body by means of Static Electricity, and was successful with it.

Later on, Mauduyct proved that in the treatment of amauosis and rheumatism the currents with the wooden points succeeded better than those obtained by the aid of metallic points.

In 1835, Becquerel, in his treatise on Electricity and Magnetism, speaks in a most scientific way of the transport of ponderable substances by electric discharges.

In 1838, Beckensteiner, physician in Lyons, France, and Parisal, chemist of the same city, made an experiment not less conclusive than the foregoing.

A patient being seated upon the insulated chair, has in one hand a small quantity of a starch solution. The operator having dipped the point of his electrode into iodine, approaches the same electrode to the patient's hand so as to obtain a spark and instantly the starch solution becomes blue, proving that iodine has been transported. A spark without iodine does not produce any change upon the solution.

Becquerel, conceived the idea of using different metals for his electrodes so as to obtain the transportation of the metallic salts into the human body, in order to treat and cure anaemia with iron, syphilis with mercury, etc.

In 1874, Dr. Etheridge, Professor of General Therapeutics at Rush Medical College, Chicago, translated into English the book of the French physician, A. Arthius, which speaks of static cataphoresis for the treatment of diseases.

In 1887, Dr. Huguet (of Vars) presented a report upon the static cataphoresis to the Academy of Sciences and the Academy of Medicine of Paris, France, and since then has employed the same method.

In 1891, Dr. Foveau de Courmelles, Secretary of the Association of Hygiene of France, has demonstrated that the electric transport of medicines into the human organism can be done not only by the continuous and interrupted galvanic current, but also and especially by Static Electricity.

In 1896, Dr. Imbert de la Touche, of Lyons, also made a communication upon the same subject to the Academy of Medicine of Paris, France, and stated that he has employed this method for several years to transport medicines directly to the seat of the disease.

To-day, several physicians employ the same method for the cure of tuberculosis, among them Drs. Riviere, Gautier, Conil in Paris, and others in this country.

I will speak now of inhalations of compound ozone, which we employ in connection with electricity.

Lender, in Germany, has studied the therapeutic effects of ozone since 1848, and he has demonstrated that the inhalations of ozones, at moderate doses, ameliorate very promptly anaemia and, in general, all the cute and chronic diseases due to insufficiency of tissue oxydation, and diminishes also reflex excitability.

Clemens, of Frankfort, has for a long time treated with success, pulmonary tuberculosis by oxonized oxygen, by means of the electric sparks. Oudin and Labbe, of Paris, also use ozonized oxygen for the same purpose. Desnos of the "Hospital de la Charite" uses the same method with good results, and I will state also that diabetis and albuminuris are also treated in the same way with success.

Ozone is also a powerful disinfectant as Schoenbein has demonstrated that the air containing 1-16,000 of its volume of ozone can disinfect 540 times its volume of air from putrified matter.

The special properties of ozone have been described by Drs. Regnier and Otto from Paris in the "Revue Internationale d'Electrotherapie" in July, 1898.

Dr. Mount Bleyer, of New York, speaks exclusively in one of his communications of the ozonification of the blood by means of the electric currents.

In the compound ozone which I use in collaboration with my friend, Dr. Noel, the ozone is mixed with medicated hot oxygen, that is oxygen passing through hot medicated solutions. We prefer the hot oxygen because its absorption is greater.

I also give these inhalations by means of the medicated static spray with a special brush electrode, according to the process of Riviere and Imbert de la Touche, and I use the electrodes made by Messrs. Waite & Bartlett, of New York.

We consider an important adjunct, in many cases, the dry hot air bath given in bed, with the special apparatus of Dr. Noel's invention, which can be given at the patient's house in his own bed.

This treatment is based on the hyperemia determined by the heat in the lungs which are always deficient in blood and tuberculosis always begins at the apex, perhaps for that reason.

According to Bier the treatment of articular tuberculosis by the hyperemia stagnation and the favorable action due to laparotomy in tuberculous peritonitis prove the good effects of hyperema in tuberculosis.

By increasing the quantity of blood in the apex, the conditions of nutrition are increased, the necrobiosis is diminished the organism is put in better condition to resist the infection, and the waste products and toxines are better eliminated. The mucous membranes of the lungs become less dry and the excretion of mucous is facilitated. The powerful physiological effects of this thermic process modify the constitution and give most beneficial results.

In conclusion I will say that by electricity we improve the general condition of our patients, we transport medicaments by cataphoresis, to avoid giving them by the mouth so as to prevent disturbances of the stomach.

By compound ozone we increase the blood oxidation, and disinfect the lungs, and by the thermal bath we facilitate the hyperemia of the lungs and at the same time, by the perspiration produced by the heat, we help the elimination of the toxines and waste products and assist the electricity to substitute new elements free of all morbid contamination.

I believe sincerely that these processes, employed with skill and judgment, according to circumstances and cases, are reliable in the treatment of all the diseases of the respiratory organs, and also in tuberculosis.

A REPORT ON THE CROTTE TREATMENT OF TUBERCULOSIS.

With a Full Description and Clinical History of the Cases that have Come under my Observation During a Period of One Year.

BY J. LEFFINGWELL HATCH,

B. Sc., M. D., F. R. M, S. (London), formerly Assistant Demonstrator of Morbid Anatomy and Lecturer on Bacteriology in the University of Pennsylvania; Pathologist to the Philadelphia Hospital; late Sanitary Inspector for the Port of Antwerp, Belgium, in the United States Marine Hospital Service, etc., etc.

The application of static currents of electricity has for a long time been used in medicine, so also has formaldehyde, but just as it took a Columbus to show the world how to make an egg stand upon its end, so also it took a Crotte to show us how to pass formaldehyde through the lungs by means of static currents of electricity of high and medium tension.

Ever since Koch discovered the tubercle bacillus in 1882 investigators all over the world have been trying to find a germicide that would be efficacious and at the same time be nocuous to the patient.

Granting that such a medicament could be found, another difficulty arose, viz., the anatomy of the tubercle which by its own growth throws out a wall of connective tissue around itself which is utterly impregnable to medicaments borne by the circulation.

Formaldehyde has been found to be a true germicide, but formaldehyde pure coagulates albumen, and consequently could not be passed directly into the blood current as it would coagulate the blood and cause immediate death by forming thrombi.

Crotte, after experimenting for a long time has been able to make a preparation of formaldehyde which he is able to pass into the lungs, through the tissues, in the form of a vapor by means of static currents of electricity.

Read before the American Congress of Tuberculosis in joint session with Medico-Legal Society, May 15-16, 1901.

In order to prove that the formaldehyde actually reached the lungs and that remarkable cures that he made were not due to electricity alone, he made experiments upon animals, and found the formaldehyde in the lungs after the animal had been subjected to the treatment.

In order to verify his own experiments he had other chemists present when he treated the animals, and allowed them also to test the tissues for the germicide transfused.

I here submit a report from Mr. A. S. Wolf, Medical Chemist and Toxicologist to the Woman's Hospital, 49th street and Fourth avenue:

New York, September 9th, 1899.

Dr. Francisque Crotte:

Dear Doctor:—"I removed the lungs and organs of the guinea pig you submitted to the formaline treatment, extracted same with distilled water, distilled the extract, treated the distillate with a drop of very dilute phenol and poured same over strong sulphuric acid. At the point of contact of the two fluids I observed a faint but positive pinkish coloration showing the presence of formaldehyde.

"The organs of this animal showed a marked form of preservation, not the slightest evidence of putrefaction being evident."

(Signed.) A. S. WOLF.

The above reference to the preserved condition of the specimen, after lying four days in a bottle without alcohol or other preservative, is another proof of the presence of formaldehyde, which prevents putrefaction.

New York, September 9th, 1899.

Dr. Francisque Crotte:

Dear Doctor:—"I received the lungs of the guinea pig you treated with the iodine; extracted same with distilled water and chlorine water, the same acidified and shaken with carbon disulphide; I obtained a marked violet red coloration, showing the presence of iodine."

(Signed.) A. S. WOLF.

Analysis of the viscera of a guinea pig submitted to the Crotte method of trnasfusion of medicaments.

In order to demonstrate the introduction into the organism of chemicals by means of the Crotte method of transfu-

sion by high tension static discharges, the following experiment was made:

A guinea pig was shaved on the surface of the abdomen and painted with a 10 per cent solution of Bichloride of Mercury ($HgCl_2$) and subjected immediately to proper electrical discharges for about one minute. The animal was killed after about two hours and the lungs, salivary glands and bladder with its contents, removed for examination as to their constituents.

I. Lungs and Salivary Glands.

The organs were reduced to a pulp with four times their weight of water and the liquid again separated by filtration. This submitted to the action of Hydrogen Sulphide H_2S yielded a black precipitate. This, upon separation and drying, proved to be insoluble in ammonium sulfhydrate (NH_4HS), Hydrochloric Acid (HCl) Nitric Acid (HNO_3.)

Partly soluble in boiling HNO_3 and entirely soluble in aqua regia, thus answering the tests to the presence of mercury in the filtrate.

II. Bladder and Contents.

The bladder was found to contain about one c. c. of urine of a rather dark color. This was diluted with one c. c. of H_2O, filtrated, and acidulated with one drop of HCl and in it was immersed a piece of zinc with some gold foil wound around it in such a manner as to leave exposed a few strips of zinc. Twenty-four hours afterwards this was removed from the liquid, the gold foil unwound, washed, dried and slowly heated in the closed end of a glass about 10 c. long. After a fraction of a minute a small amount of a whitish substance was seen to condense upon the upper and colder part of the tube; this, upon being examined with a magnifying glass, was found to be composed of minute globules of metallic mercury, thus proving the presence of this metal in the urine.

New York, February 6th, 1901.

M. Francisque Crotte:

Dear Sir:—I have the honor to submit to you the results of the following experiments that were carried out in your laboratory. Yours respectfully,

J. L. HATCH, M. D.

January 26th, 1901.

A guinea pig was shaved on the surface of the abdomen and made fast to a board and laid on the insulated table of a static machine. Next the positive pole of the machine was connected by means of a chain with the back of the animal and a sponge saturated with a solution of nascent iodine was fastened on the movable negative electrode. This sponge was brought in contact with the abdomen of the guinea pig, held there for a few minutes and then raised for a few inches, while sparks were allowed to pass from the sponge to the body

The animal was then chloroformed and an autopsy immediately made. The organs and intestines were tested with an acidulated starch solution and a characteristic blue reaction resulted, thus proving the presence of iodine, and also that it had been transfused through the tissues of the body by means of static currents of electricity of high tension.

J. L. HATCH, M. D.

January 24th, 1901.

Transfused a paper package and a thick muslin package both containing a paste of "facule de pommes du terre" with iodine, and on opening found the characteristic starch reaction.

I also performed the same experiment subsequently substituting an acidulated starch paste for the "facule de pommes du terre," and obtained the characteristic blue color reaction.

J. L. HATCH, M. D.

February 3rd, 1901. A guinea pig was shaved on the abdominal surface and fixed to a board as in the previous experiment, only in this case the head was covered with a thick cloth to keep the animal from respiring the substance to be transfused.

The connections with the machine having been established as before, a sponge saturated with a 4 per cent. solution of formaldehyde was attached to the movable negative electrode. There were also large sponges saturated with the same solution placed in the hollow brass cylinders at the two different poles on the machine from which the chains lead to the electrodes.

The sponge on the end of the negative electrode was placed against the abdomen and chest of the animal and the current turned on. The transfusion was kept up five minutes after which time the animal was chloroformed and an autopsy immediately made.

The different organs were put in separate vessels and allowed to macerate in distilled water. I took a small portion of the lungs, crushed it in the bottom of a test tube in a little distilled water with a glass rod, filtered the fluid and tested the filtrate with Henner's test for formaldehyde. I obtained a faint rose-violet ring thus proving the presence of formaldehyde.

Henner's Test.

To the suspected solution add the same quantity of a weak carbolic solution, pour this mixture upon concentrated sulphuric acid and if formaldehyde is present there will be formed at the point of junction of the two liquids a ring of rose-violet.

This test is very delicate—1 in 200,000.

I allowed the macerations to stand over night, and the next morning filtered and tested them seriatim. There were seven solutions in all, one from the lungs, one from the heart, one from the stomach, one from the liver, one from the kidneys, one from the intestines and one from the bladder.

In each and every instance I obtained the characteristic reaction, only the solution from the intestines gave the strongest reaction, while that from the heart gave the weakest.

This proves conclusively that formaldehyde can be transfused through the tissues, that is, transported to the internal organs, by means of static currents of electricity of high tension.

The voltage that was used was about 2,000,000 with a very low amperage, a fraction of 1.

J. L. HATCH, M. D.

Method of Transfusion.

The patient, stripped to the waist, sits upon an insulated platform and is connected with one pole of the static machine by means of a chain; to the other pole of the machine is attached an electrode that carries a sponge. The sponge is soaked in the solution of formaldehyde and the entire chest thoroughly wet with it while the current is passing through the sponge into the patient. This is kept up until the moist skin becomes dry, after which the sponge is removed and a metal ball attached in its place. A brisk massage is given with the ball in contact with the body, after which sparks are allowed to leap from the ball to the body.

This treatment is also applied to the back as well as the chest of the patient. from the apices of the lungs to their bases.

After this the patient inhales a mixture of formaldehyde gas and ozone from a sponge on the electrode.

Descending from the insulated platform, the patient's entire thorax is painted with a mixture of iodine and spirits of camphor.

The patient receives this treatment every day and it is remarkable to see the rapid improvement.

As soon as the activity of the bacilli is arrested, the fever decreases, and the night sweats lessen, the appetite improves, and the tonic of the electric bath gives the patient renewed vigor.

Of course, special symptoms require other therapeutic measures in connection with the treatment, and each case has to be watched carefully, but the great principle of Crotte's method is a simple one and is based upon electrical osmosis; that is to say, certain substances can be decomposed by electricity and their active principles carried along in the track of the electric current.

This principle is used in the arts, and in Germany there is a large factory for making wood proof against the attacks of the Marine Teredo by driving a preservative into it by means of the electric current.

The Crotte treatment appears to me to be the most successful of any that is known for Tuberculosis. Of course, it is not a worker of impossibilities and cannot replace lost lung tissue any more than it can replace an amputated leg, but that it does arrest the specific inflammation is a patent fact.

So much for the theory of the treatment and the laboratory experiments which prove it. Now let me add the weighty evidence of the clinical facts.

I am only going to take the cases that have come under my observation during the past twelve months, and will not select special cases favorable to the treatment, but take them all just as they come from the case book, seriatim.

Out of 53 cases I find the following results:

20 perfect cures.

9 partial cures (left before treatment was complete).

11 disappeared altogether.

7 died.

2 were refused.

4 under treatment at present and improving.

Subtracting the eleven that disappeared and the two refused, we have out of 40 patients treated

50 per cent. entirely cured.

32.5 per cent. partially cured and improving.

17.5 per cent. mortality.

OBSERVATION 1.—Mrs. Marie B., aged 32. Father is living in good health, mother died several years ago, does not know cause of death, but she had some sort of liver trouble for a long time before her death. Has had one brother and two sisters, all are dead, but she does not know the cause of death. She has two children the result of two difficult labors, both are in good health.

She was thin, and complexion of a muddy yellow color, when first examined. Weight 122½ lbs. Pulse 100. Temperature 100 degrees F. and Respiration 36.

She had fairly good appetite but was constipated.

She menstruates regularly.

She has coughed and expectorated for two or three years.

She had a pleurisy eight years ago the result of a cold.

Sputum analyzed shows the tubercle bacilli.

Both lungs are affected, crepitant rales throughout, and areas of congestion here and there.

Sputum has been tinged with blood, but never had any hemorrhages.

After four months treatment the bacilli entirely disappeared from the sputum. She does not cough. The lungs cleared up. no more rales or areas of congestion, and she gained 10 pounds in weight.

At the end of six months she was discharged cured.

I have seen her lately and she is in splendid health.

OBSERVATION 2.—Mrs. Angelina Murphy; aged 31; father died of Bright's disease; one sister died of cancer of the stomach; she has had two children, one died of a disease of the liver; the other died of intestinal trouble at the age of two months. Had bronchitis about six years ago, the origin of her present trouble. She had night sweats, coughed and expectorated a good deal, also had hemorrhages; she was emaciated and very nervous and impressionable. Microscopic examination of the sputum showed the tubercle bacilli. Number of respirations 24; pulse 100; temperature 99 degrees F.;

weighed 93 pounds; digestion impaired; menstruated regularly. consolidation of the left lung with crepitant rales; dullness on percussion over the upper lobe in front and in back. right lung dullness and consolidation in front and back of the upper portion.

After six months treatment the symptoms of night sweats and fever disappeared entirely and there were no more hemorrhages; patient gained ten pounds and then went away to the country. I have seen her since her return and she has had no recurrence of her previous symptoms, and is entirely cured.

Observation 3.—Miss Celia G.; aged 41; had one sister affected with tuberculosis (Mrs. Ida T.); had typhoid fever six years ago and pneumonia at the age of four; has suffered more or less with lung trouble since pneumonia; was pale and emaciated; weighed 103 pounds; pulse 90; temperature 100 degrees F.; very nervous and impressionable. appetite good; digestion fairly good, but had a tendency to constipation; menstruated regularly; coughed a good deal, especially in the morning; raised a good deal of sputum which on microscopic examination showed tubercle bacilli; on auscultation found a cavity at the apex of both lungs.

After eight months treatment all symptoms disappeared and she left a well woman for her home in Pennsylvania.

Observation 4.—Mrs. Ida T.; aged 35; one sister was tuberculous (Miss Celia G.); had been sick for ten years, was operated on five years previous for falling of the womb; had coughed for about six years; her aspect was fairly good; weighed 137 pounds but was nervous and impressionable; respiration 20; pulse 84; temperature 101.1 degrees F.. digestion good; after operation five years ago she had an uterine tumor, probably a fibroid which had increased to such an extent that her abdomen measured thirty-seven inches in circumference; menstruated regularly; she had numerous moist bronchial rales on the right side and her sputum on microscopic examination showed the tubercle bacilli.

At the end of eight months her abdominal measurement was reduced to thirty-three inches, cough and expectoration entirely disappeared, as well as the rales; she left with her sister Miss Celia G. for home a cured woman.

Observation 5.—Miss Marguerite H.; aged 33; brother died of heart disease; mother died at the age of 58, cause of death unknown; she had a very bad cold eight years ago which developed into pleuro-pneumonia, coughed ever since; never had night sweats or hemorrhages but had lost considerably in weight; aspect, emaciated and pale, very nervous; respiration 24; pulse 88; temperature 99.5 degrees F.; digestion good but was constipated; menstruation regular; sputum on microscopic examination showed tubercle bacilli.

Both lungs were affected, having a cavity at the apex on each side; moist rales to be heard everywhere over both sides.

After a period of eight months all symptoms disappeared and she was discharged cured.

OBSERVATION 6.—Mr. Arthur W.; aged 19; unmarried; father and mother living in good health; one brother and one sister also living in good health;one brother died of tuberculosis; had been sick for over a year result of a bad cold. had had hemorrhages, fever and night sweats; aspect, fairly good; respiration 20; pulse 80; temperature 100 degrees F.; digestion good; consolidation of the entire right lung with moist crepitant rales of the entire lung in front; consolidation of the left lung at the apex with tubular and crepitant rales.

After a period of eight months all his symptoms disappeared and he was discharged a well man.

OBSERVATION 7.—Mrs. A. D.; aged 23; father died from an accident; mother living in good health; also one brother living in good health; seven or eight years ago had a pleurisy on the left side; had coughed ever since. was in fairly good condition until she gave birth to a child two years ago; aspect, greatly emaciated; she had night sweats, fever and hemorrhages; respiration 30; pulse 140; temperature 102 degrees F.; bad appetite, indigestion and constipation; menstruation regular; right lung congested throughout; tubular souffle; cavity the size of an egg at the apex; sibilant and moist rales throughout in front and back. left lung, there was a souffle at the back; sibilant and moist rales at the front and back at the apex and sibilant rales at the base; on microscopic examination the sputum was found full of tubercle bacilli and pyogenic micro-organisms, also fibro-elastic tissue.

Patient improved greatly under treatment; at the end of four months was so much better that she went away to the country for a visit. While there took cold, had a relapse and was brought back to the city in a critical condition; was too weak to come to the office for treatment and died one week later.

Observation 8.—Miss Marguerite F.; aged 21. mother died of tuberculosis; one brother and one sister also died of tuberculous; for two or three months, she had lost flesh; felt tired, coughed and expectorated a little; never had hemorrhages or night sweats; aspect emaciated and pale; very nervous and impressionable; number of respirations 26; pulse 92. temperature 99.2 degrees F.; weight 104.5 pounds; appetite poor;constipated;menstruated regularly, but to an excess during a period of about five days; on microscopic examination the sputum showed a few tubercle bacilli; left lung, dullness on percussion in front and back at the apex: also some sibilant rales were heard in front and back at the center of the great bronchus; right lung, a little congested and consolidated at the upper third in front.

At the end of five months all these symptoms had disappeared and she was discharged cured.

Observation 9.—Mr. Walter G. B.; aged 24; unmarried; father and mother in good health, also a brother and sister in good health; about a year ago took a severe cold from exposure while bicycling; had never had hemorrhages but probably had bronchitis and pleurisy at the time he had cold. aspect, good; was nervous; number of respirations 20; pulse 92; temperature 99 degrees F.; digestion good; right lung, consolidated entirely in front and in back; left lung, some congestion in front and back.

After four months treatment he was very much improved but left before a radical cure had been made.

Observation 10.—Mr. Walter S.; aged 25; unmarried; father died of pneumonia at age of 56; mother still alive and in good health; had night sweats and fever; considerable pain at the center of the sternum and over the center of the large bronchus of the right lung; aspect, fairly good, but is very nervous and impressionable; number of respirations 18. pulse 104; temperature 98.5 degrees F.; weight 132 pounds; digestion good: left lung, dullness on percussion at the apex, with consolidation of the rest of the lung and a souffle was to be heard at the lower lobe; heart very irritable with a systolic murmur, action very rapid.

After three months treatment he was greatly improved, but left before entirely cured.

OBSERVATION 11.—Mr. M.; aged 40; for the last six years had had many hemorrhages; aspect, very pale; very nervous; wighed 142.5 pounds; number of respirations 28; pulse 112; temperature 99 degrees F.. right lung, completely affected, crepitant rales throughout. lung unable to perform its functions any longer; left lung,congested entirely at the base;there is dullness at the apex; on microscopic examination the sputum showed tubercle bacilli.

After being treated for two months there was much improvement but the patient left before being cured.

OBSERVATION 12.—Miss Annie L.; aged 25; father died of tuberculosis; mother, brothers and sisters living and in good health; two years ago had the grip; since that time had been more or less ill; spit blood; had night sweats and hectic fever; lost thirty-five pounds in one month. weighed on entrance 108.5 pounds; aspect, emaciated; vey nervous; respiration 24; pulse 92; temperature 99.3 degrees F.; digestion bad; constipated; menstruated regularly; right lung congested in front and there are some moist rales at the apex; left lung, there were crepitant rales at the center of the bronchus, also at the apex in front and back; microscopic examination of sputum showed numerous tubercle bacilli.

After five months treatment she was discharged entirely cured.

OBSERVATION 13.—Mrs. Victor S.; aged 34; father died of old age; Mr. S. believes that her mother died of consumption; seven or eight years ago had bronchitis; has been ill ever since; coughed and expectorated considerably; hectic fever but no night sweats; aspect, fairly good; very nervous and impressionable; number of respiration 20; pulse 80; temperature 99 degrees F.; digestion very good; menstruation had been irregular for seven months; right lung consolidated at base; dullness at apex with sibilant rales in the middle of the right bronchus which pass from front to back; left lung, respirations jerky; also had chronic pharyngitis and laryngitis; on microscopic examination the sputum showed tubercle bacilli.

After six months treatment all the symptoms disappeared and she was discharged cured.

OBSERVATION 14.—Mrs. M.; aged 40; had been ill for four years, the result of a bronchitic pneumonia; had profuse hemorrhages, night sweats and fever; coughed and spit a good deal; aspect, greatly emaciated and pale; very nervous and impressionable; respiration laborious and 30 in number; pulse 135; temperature 102 degrees F.; weighed 105 pounds; appetite bad, also digestion; vomited nearly everything taken into the stomach; both lungs congested, the left one consolidated, almost entirely and there were large cavities on both sides; on microscopic examination the sputum showed tubercle bacilli, also pyogenic forms and fibro-elastic connective tissue; she took two months treatment and was greatly improved but the weak condition of her stomach made it almost impossible for her to take nourishment, so that she became so weak that she could not come to the office for treatment; four months later she died.

OBSERVATION 15.—Mr. E. C.; aged 27; parents both living. four years ago had bronchitis; aspect, florid; impressionable but not very nervous; number of respirations 18; pulse 82; temperature 99 degrees F.; digestion fair; right lung, crepitant and sibilant rales at the apex in front, the entire base consolidated and at a point posteriorly, the evidence of an old pleurisy; at the apex of the left lung, there was a lesion which was the cause of the blood in the sputum; coughed a great deal and raised much thick sputum, which was occasionally tinged with blood; had night sweats and hectic fever.

After five months treatment he was greatly improved although not entirely cured when he left.

OBSERVATION 16.—Mr. W. B. S. R.; aged 43; father died of consumption at the age of 76; mother died of asthma at the age of 50; one brother died of consumption; had pleurisy seventeen years ago; aspect, decrepit; was nervous and impressionable; number of respirations 22; pulse, 100; temperature 99.5 degrees F.; digestion fair; right lung, apex consolidated and its functions greatly restricted; at the middle of the commencement of the right bronchus crepitant and sibilant rales could be heard; left lung, consolidated at the apex and base, also had very little action; there was atrophy of both lungs, enlargement of the liver, dilitation of the stomach, had pharyngitis and laryngitis; coughed and raised sputum slightly, no night sweats; tubercle bacilli were found in sputum.

Took one months treatment and then disappeared entirely.

OBSERVATION 17.—Mr. Frank B.; aged 26; mother died of tuberculosis; his brother is also affected; four years ago had pleurisy; night sweats and hectic fever and many hemorrhages; was greatly emaciated; coughed and raised a good deal; sputum showed tubercle bacilli; weighed 104 pounds; both lungs affected, crepitant and sibilant rales throughout.

He took treatment for two months when he took a bad cold which resulted in a congestion of the lungs and he died.

OBSERVATION 18.—Miss Gertrude W.; aged 21; brother of the mother died of galloping consumption; seven years ago took a bath while she was unwell, and had coughed ever since. Aspect, much emaciated; had night sweats, fever and hemorrhages; both lungs were affected; she was refused and death predicted in six weeks. Date of examination was June 16th and she died August 10th.

OBSERVATION 19.—Mr. R. E.; aged 29; tuberculosis of the third degree; took three months treatment and was very much improved; died of a hemorrhage on ferry boat going home from office.

OBSERVATION 20.—Mrs. P. S.; aged 31; one year ago took a severe cold followed by bronchitis; had night sweats and hectic fever, and an excited and irritable heart; both lungs are consolidated with crepitant and sibilant rales throughout; expectorated a good deal, sputum showing tubercle bacilli.

After three months treatment, she was greatly improved but left before entirely cured.

OBSERVATION 21.—Mr. M.; aged 23; father died of consumption four years ago; mother still living; was a consumptive of the third degree, both lungs affected; had had hemorrhages, night sweats and fever; was treated for four months, after which he was so greatly improved that he left and went to the country for a vacation. While there he caught a bad cold which finally resulted in his death.

OBSERVATION 22.—Mr. J. J. D.; aged 28; father and mother both living and in good health; three years ago had bronchitis; aspect, emaciated; had night sweats, fever and hemorrhages; both lungs were affected; had large cavity at the apex of the right lung.

Took three months treatment and then disappeared.

OBSERVATION 23.—Miss E. L.; aged 23; two aunts and one uncle died of consumption; mother died of typhoid fever, father still living; two years ago had pain in left side of chest; had pleurisy,, night sweats and cough; right lung consolidated at the apex and upper lobe; left lung congested in the upper lobe; has tuberculosis of the first degree.

Took two months treatment after which she was much improved but left before she was entirely cured.

OBSERVATION 24.—Mrs. C. O'N.; aged 24; father died of catarrh of stomach; mother of heart disease; one brother died of consumption. She was very emaciated, nervous and impressionable; both lungs were affected; had a cavity of the left lung and the entire substance seemed to be breaking down; took but one treatment and then disappeared.

OBSERVATION 25.—Mr. James S. O'N.; aged 28; had had hemorrhages for two years; very emaciated; both lungs affected: he also had one treatment and disappeared.

OBSERVATION 26.—Miss Eugenie M.; aged 13; mother is tuberculous; she was nervous and impressionable; had not yet menstruated; dullness on percussion at the apices of both lungs, consolidation at the base of right lung; tubercle bacilli in sputum.

After two months treatment she was greatly improved, but has disappeared.

OBSERVATION 27.—Mr. Percy L.; aged 31; father died with cancer of the tongue; mother died at age of 53, cause of death unknown; ten years ago had a severe cold followed by gastritis; two years ago had bronchitis and has coughed ever since with slight expectoration, no night sweats nor fever; right lung consolidated entirely from top to bottom; left lung congested from top to bottom, sputum showed tubercle bacilli.

After three months treatment was much better but left before entirely cured.

OBSERVATION 28.—Mr. Wm. A.; aged 22; had bronchitis on the right side four years ago; congestion on the left side in the upper lobe eight months ago; right lung showed bronchitis and there was dullness at the apex in front; left lung, on ausculation showed sibilant rales and there is a point of dullness at the apex; sputum showed tubercle bacilli on examination.

After four month's treatment was greatly improved but disappeared.

OBSERVATION 29.—Mr. D. J. O'L.: aged 32; five years ago had pleurisy on both sides at the base; had had hemorrhages, night sweats and fever; both lungs were affected; crepitant and sibilant rales throughout and cavities on both sides; it was a very grave case of the third degree accepted only for observation, but he disappeared after one month's treatment.

OBSERVATION 30.—Mrs. Mary E. B.; aged 43; six months ago had pleurisy of right side. slightly emaciated, very nervous and impressionable; had had severe hemorrhages, night sweats and fever; menstruated irregularly; right lung completely congested, moist and sibilant rales front and back; left lung completely consolidated with a tubular souffle at the apex. She had had five hemorrhages, three of which she had in one day, amounting to a liter; she also had cancer of the stomach.

After five months' treatment all the lung symptoms had disappeared and she gained in weight; she has been cured from her tuberculosis but still suffered from the cancer of the stomach; she has never had a hemorrhage since her first treatment.

OBSERVATION 31.—Mrs. R. B.; aged 27; father died of consumption; mother still living; about two years ago had bronchitis; since then she had had night sweats and fevers and coughed considerably; sputum showed tubercle bacilli; consolidation of right lung posteriorly and below, congestion above; left lung shows old pleuretic adhesions below with consolidation at base and congestion at apex; rales on left side during expiration.

After eight months' treatment she was entirely cured.

OBSERVATION 32.—Mr. John A. G.; aged 30; father died of consumption; had a bronchitis on the right side one year ago; right lung, there was dullness at apex front and back with sibilant rales; pleurisy on left side of base; the left lung, there was an obscure point at the apex which does not function; sputum showed tubercle bacilli.

After five months' treatment all symptoms entirely disappeared and he was discharged cured.

OBSERVATION 33.—Mrs. Sarah N. A.; aged 59; four years ago had bronchitis on the right side; also pleurisy; had coughed ever since; expectorates blood, had night sweats and fever; right lung was consolidated its entire length, moist crepitant rales with pleuretic adhesions at the base; left lung, crepitant rales at apex with consolidation at base and a tubular souffle; after four months treatment, was very much improved but left before entirely cured.

OBSERVATION 34.—Mrs. Theresa P.; aged 24; tuberculous case of the third degree, both lungs affected; took treatment for two months, was greatly improved and then disappeared.

OBSERVATION 35.—Mr. Harry W. E.; aged 24; a tuberculous patient of the third degree; took three months treatment, was much improved but finally disappeared.

OBSERVATION 36.—Mrs. M. D.; aged 34; a tuberculous case of the third degree; took treatment for two months, was much improved but disappeared.

OBSERVATION 37.—Mr. James A. T.; aged 34; mother living good health, father died of consumption; a case very far advanced in the third degree; cavities in both lungs and had tuberculosis of the intestines.

Took treatment for four months, made remarkable improvement,, but finally disappeared.

OBSERVATION 38.—Mrs. Martha F.; aged 25; father, one brother and two sisters living in good health; mother died of consumption; three or four years ago had bronchitis; since then she has had hemorrhages, night sweats and coughed and raised sputum which showed tubercle bacilli on microscopic examination; appetite and digestion good; six years ago was operated upon for tumor of the ovaries; since then has not menstruated; right lung entirely congested: left lung congested at the region of the bronchus, and there was an old lesion at the apex which was cicatrized.

She took treatment for four months, at the end of which time all the symptoms had disappeared and she was discharged cured.

OBSERVATION 39.—Miss Hayes W.; aged 23; brother of the mother died of galloping consumption; her sister, whom we refused to treat, died a month ago of consumption; about two months ago she took a bad cold which resulted in bronchitis and pleurisy, but the beginning of her trouble probably dates back two years ago when she took a bad cold, for she had coughed and expectorated ever since and had night sweats; right lung, there was dullness at the summit and it was congested; sibilant rales could be heard at the upper portion, and there was pleurisy at the base; left lung, small area of dullness at the apex; the sputum showed tubercle bacilli.

After four months treatment all these symptoms disappeared and she was discharged cured.

OBSERVATION 40.—Mr. John G.; aged 37; a very bad case of the third degree with heart complications.

Took treatment for two months, there was some improvement but he finally disappeared.

OBSERVATION 41.—Miss Ida W.; aged 16; one sister died of consumption and another is affected: four years ago she had a bad cold and had coughed and spit ever since; both lungs congested at the apex and there were sibilant rales; sputum showed tubercle bacilli; never had any hemorrhages but had had night sweats and fever.

After four months treatment all her symptoms disappeared and she was discharged cured.

OBSERVATION 42.—Mrs. Genevieve N.: aged 29; one sister died of consumption, two others are affected; two years ago had bronchitis; had coughed ever since: had no night sweats nor had she ever spit blood; dullness on percussion at the apices of both lungs; there were also sibilant rales; sputum showed tubercle bacilli.

After four months treatment, all symptoms disappeared and she was discharged cured.

OBSERVATION 43.—Mr. Ross L.; aged 23; grandfather on mother's side died of consumption; had pleurisy six years ago; since then he had had hemorrhages, night sweats and fever; was a very bad case of galloping consumption, both lungs being almost completely destroyed; he was refused treatment as a hopeless case.

OBSERVATION 44.—Mr. Horace B. B.; aged 50; mother died of consumption at 44; one sister also died of consumption at age of 18; three or four years ago had the grippe and bronchitis; since then he had coughed and expectorated a good deal; had had many hemorrhages; was nervous and impressionable; there were old pleuretic adhesions at the base of the left lung with dullness at the apex; right lung consolidated at the back for almost its entire length, in front crepitant rales could be heard. He also had a hypertrophic pharyngitis and enlargement of the sub-maxillary glands.

After six months treatment, all his symptoms had disappeared and he was discharged cured.

OBSERVATION 45.—Mrs. Marie K.; aged 28; mother had consumption, whom she had been nursing; claims that she was treated for Bright's disease when she was eighteen years old and cured; for the last six years had been troubled with a pain in the left side which she attributed to a pleurisy; also coughed and expectorated a good deal; there was dullness at the apex of the left lung and a slight wheezing sound was to be heard on expiration; sputum showed tubercle bacilli.

After four months treatment all her symptoms disappeared and she was discharged cured.

OBSERVATION 46.—Miss Grace S.; aged 21; father died of heart disease; mother living; mother had two or three cousins who died of consumption; seven years ago had a very bad cold on the chest, followed by swelling of the glands of the left side and neck; right lung had probably been affected ever since as there was a large cavity the size of an egg in the upper lobe; there were old pleuretic adhesions at the base; left lung greatly congested at apex; had had hemorrhages four years, night sweats, fever, cough and the sputum showed tubercle bacilli.

She took treatment for one month, was much improved but left before cured. Since writing the above have seen patient and find all her symptoms have disappeared. She has gained in weight and looks in splendid condition.

OBSERVATION 47.—Mrs. Ellen K.; aged 43; two years ago had bronchitis followed by pleurisy on both sides: had coughed and expectorated ever since: had had several hemorrhages; left lung consolidated from base to apex, cavity in upper lobe the size of an egg; right lung, entire upper lobe consolidated; crepitant and sibilant rales could be heard over entire area anteriorly and posteriorly.

After three months treatment she was greatly improved but left before she was cured.

OBSERVATION 48.—Mr. Wm. H. S.; aged 41: father and mother both living and in good health; had one brother die of consumption; one sister died of pneumonia at age of 32; about two years ago was taken with hemorrhages; had had night sweats ever since; had another hemorrhage last Summer and occasionally his sputum was tinged with blood; very nervous and impressionable; aspect, emaciated and pale; pulse 120; temperature 101 degrees F.; right lung, there was dullness of upper lobe. crepitant rales in front and above; there was consolidation of all the rest of the lung; left lung, there was dullness of upper lobe, with a souffle above and in front; there was a pleurisy of at least a year's standing on the left side below; he had tubercular laryngitis and pharyngitis.

After five months treatment was very much improved and is still under treatment.

OBSERVATION 49.—Mr. Harry A. P.; aged 38; father died at age of 67 of Bright's disease; mother living; mother had two aunts and one uncle die of consumption; seven years ago had a bronchitis; three years afterward had another attack; nervous and impressionable; right lung, there was dullness on percussion above and to the back; left lung, there was dullness on percussion above and to the back, souffle in front at the region of the large bronchus; sputum showed tubercle bacilli; had had no night sweats nor hemorrhages but some fever and cough.

After two months treatment all these symptoms entirely disappeared and he was discharged cured.

OBSERVATION 50.—Mr. George R.; aged 38; a very desperate case of galloping consumption, complete aphonia due to tubercular laryngitis.

Received two months treatment but was too far gone to do him much good and he died. Have found out since writing the above that he died from pneumonia, which he contracted by exposure to the weather.

OBSERVATION 51.—Mr. Charles B.; aged 28; a case of incipient phthisis; took one month's treatment, was very much improved but left before cured.

OBSERVATION 52.—Miss Hattie B.; aged 15; father and mother living; two sisters died of consumption; one sister, Lulu B., had consumption but was treated by Dr. Crotte two years and a half ago and cured. She was anaemic and frail; nervous and impressionable; had several attacks of bronchitis, and had not menstruated for five months; right lung, there was dullness on percussion at apex in front; consolidation of lower lobe to the front and side; sibilant rales to be heard all over; left lung, dullness on percussion in the upper and lower lobes; crepitant rales throughout; coughed and expectorated considerably; sputum showed tubercle bacilli.

She has been under treatment nearly three months and is a good deal better.

OBSERVATION 53.—Miss Dorothy D.; aged 36; father died of paralysis; mother died of consumption at age of 65; two brothers died of phthisis one having general tuberculosis.

had pleurisy about a year ago, coughed and expectorated a great deal ever since; had never had hemorrhages but had night sweats and fever; somewhat anaemic, poorly nourished, very nervous and hysterical; weighed 120 pounds when she entered; menses irregular; right lung, dullness on percussion at the lower lobe in front and back; left lung, dullness at the apex and a small area at the lower lobe in front and at the side; marked bronchial breathing; microscopic examination of the sputum showed tubercle bacilli strepto-cocci and staphylo-cocci, pus and fibro-elastic connective tissue.

She has now been under treatment about three months and her case is gradually yielding to the treatment. She has gained in weight and feels very much improved.

THE PREVENTION OF TUBERCULOSIS.

BY ELIZA HUBBARD M'HATTON, MACON, GA.

As a member of the Psychological Section of the Medico-Legal Society, I was put on the list for a paper on the prevention of Tuberculosis.

Knowing full well that the literature of the prevention of Tuberculosis is already very full, and contains many more suggestions than we can or are willing to carry out, I hesitate to add my mite, but the vital importance of the subject to humanity as shown by the fearful inroads being made on the people of all lands must stand as my excuse for re-telling what has already been told in many interesting papers.

It is now almost twenty years since Koch made his great discovery of the bacillus, and since then many eminent scientists have labored unceasingly to conquer this infinitesimal, though powerful foe, to the health and happiness of mankind. Great strides have been made in every line of treatment and cure of the disease, but the old saying that an "ounce of prevention is worth a pound of cure" holds good in this instance, and I feel it the duty of one and all to urge any and every method of prophylaxis.

It has been pretty plainly proved that Tuberculosis is not a disease that must exist in some form or other in all places—for there are many places where it is not known. In Spanish Honduras among the natives it is unknown. Dr.McHatton has made several trips into the interior of the country on mule-back and spent months among the people there, and has yet his to see his first case. It is practically unknown among all primitive people. Yet to-day our Indians are being decimated by the disease, though never having had it before contact with civilization. The death rate in all our large cities is fearful to contemplate, and in New York, the city with which I am most familiar, the deaths from Tuberculosis alone are more per week than from all the other con-

Contributed to the American Congress of Tuberculosis after the session of May 15, 16, 1901.

tagious diseases together, and I note in a very able article by Dr. J. E. Kinney, of Denver, Colorado, that was written for the meeting of the American Medical Association, June 5-8, 1900, that he gives the death rate for Tuberculosis as over 12 per cent. of all deaths. Dr. Kinney also is an advocate of paying strict attention to the diet and keeping the digestive tract in good order, believing that a bad digestion, or other intestinal disease, tends to the development of Tuberculosis, especially of the lungs, by impairment of the general health, rendering the system less able to throw off the Tubercular germs.

Arthur McDonald, of Washington, D. C., of the U. S. Bureau of Education, speaks of the special danger of contracting Tuberculosis at the age of Puberty. This is certainly so, and it is a wonder to me to see the ignorance shown by parents and teachers in regard to the physical conditions of the young in their care. Just at a time of life when they need all of their strength for proper development, the young are forced to overwork, often in over-crowded and badly ventilated rooms, and more often than not, improperly fed. Hence it is of importance in my mind that those in charge of the young should be educated themselves in the common causes of diseases and their prevention.

Any child with a marked predisposition to throat, nose and lung troubles, should certainly be removed from school life during the age of puberty, both for his or her own safety as well as the safety of others. I am shocked a dozen times a day by the crass ignorance displayed by educated intelligent people on most matters of common health and the ordinary workings of their organs. The false modesty practiced by most instructors of the young is to my mind also the cause of much disease of body, as well as of mind. I have found ignorance to be a great factor in both disease and crime.

Since I began this article I have made many inquiries among the people at large as to what they thought was a good method of preventing tuberculosis, and I find many do not even know what tuberculosis is, and when I explain, they say "Oh, that is consumption,—why you can't prevent that, it's inherited!"

The vast majority, however, have never given the matter a serious thought, so that in my mind if the people could be awakened to the importance of the subject and then instructed, it would prove a great factor in preventing the disease.

We should strive to give the community a knowledge of the true nature of the disease and the means necessary to control or cure it. The means to this end to be by publications of non-technical papers to be distributed in schools and other gatherings of the young and by proper instructions to the teachers or others in charge of the young or of institutions for the care of numbers of persons, old or young, and by constant efforts to induce all in influential positions to use their earnest efforts to prevent the spread of the disease and by trying to bring about any and all conditions whereby those in the early stages of the disease may be treated and cured, and for those too far advanced to be cured, to be cared for in such way as best calculated to prevent the infection of others. Dr. Guy Hinsdale has advocated much the same line as the above. In regard to legislation for the prevention of tuberculosis, it seems to me that the time is hardly ripe for much to be done in this way. We do not need laws that we cannot enforce, and at present the world at large is not educated up to the pitch where they recgnize the necessity for such laws. What is needed is practical instructions of the parents, teachers, nurses or others in charge of the young.

People must be taught the true status of the disease and the ways and importance of prophylaxis before we can expect much benefit from rigid laws. Then and not till then will legislation be of use. When the people are educated they will co-operate with law. All minor laws should be enacted and strictly enforced at present,—such as the ordinances against spitting in public places, the reporting of all cases of tuberculosis, etc.

I think it would be well to enact a law compelling all premises where a case is known to exist to be well cleansed and disinfected once a week or oftener in far advanced cases, and all rooms where a case has died to be as thoroughly disinfected as in any other case of contagious disease, the expense to be borne by the city if the people are not well off. A point to be considered is the choosing of a nurse for children. The family physician should in all cases oversee this matter and that a woman healthy in body and mind is procured. Some such supervision is used in regard to a wet nurse, but it is just as important to be sure of the health of the regular nurse or nursery governess, and to be sure that there is no active tubercular trouble in a nurse or others in the intimate relations existing between such persons and their young charges. Also great care should be used in the feeding of all young persons, especially seeing that they have the best and most nutritious food and plenty of it. Poorly or badly fed persons are much more prone to any disease. A grat factor in the spread of tuberculous disease of the air passages, is dust—so that it seems to me if the proper dampening of all streets in thickly settled places could be enforced, it would help greatly in its prevention. Also the floors and walls of all public buildings to be frequently washed with a disinfecting fluid and all public and private buildings to be built without sharp angles or corners as the most up-to-date hospitals are, thus reducing the places for germs anddust to lodge.

I am indebted to my friend, Professor Dudley Williams, of the Georgia State Academy for the Blind, for thought and attention that he has given to this subject, and he writes me: "For small communities it would be well to use drastic measures (as for instance in cities), but in larger fields of government, they would be of little use since the evasion of the law would be more possiblie. Thus education of the people seems to me to be the only sure and permanent mode of accomplishing final results. It appears to me that physicians, ministers, school teachers, and all other such persons as have an opportunity of catching the public ear can most certainly bring about the desired end. An appeal in all cases being made to the Ben Franklin side of human nature."

Another friend who has spent much time and thought on the betterment of humanity is Professor D. O. Abbott, for many years superintendent of the public schools of Bibb County, Georgia, and now filling the chair of mathematics in the State Normal School at Athens, Georgia. He advocates any and all methods, laws and education that can possibly be used to prevent diseases of all sorts, and writes: "Really, I go further in my thinking and would prevent by rigid and prohibitive legislation all marriages which had not a sound certificate of health for its basis. We owe it to posterity to reduce the percentage of the blind, the scrofuletic, the imbecile, the morally degenerate and the hereditary vicious. This may (nay must) be done by legislation—no matter what may be the amount of ignorance on the subject nor how unpopular it may be at first."

This opinion in regard to marriage I think applies perfectly to tuberculous subjects and if it is possible to prevent their marriage, I think it should be done. There can be very little true happiness in a home built on a foundation of possible, nay probable, tubercular disease in the parents or worse yet in the innocent child.

Long years of anxiety and nursing destroy all the pleasure of living and the constant dread of the sword falling on the head of the little ones renders life a burden. If, however, tuberculous subjects will either willfully or through ignorance marry,then I think that the innocent should be protected by not being allowed to be conceived. This opinion I know will be considered rank heresy,but I utter it only as a plea for the innocent. Is it not better to prevent than try to cure that which never should have been?

I read quite lately in the American Medical Journal an article by Dr. Bernheim on Pregnacy and Tuberculosis wherein he says "That advice as to marriages is difficult to give, but is very emphatic in stating that he would systematically prohibit maternity in all tuberculous patients, even in those recovered." This he advises on account of the danger to the woman of again developing the disease in the strain of pregnancy.

If it is to be prohibited for the mother's sake, why not for the innocent victim liable to be born with an inherent low vitality, a subject for almost sure infection of tuberculosis sooner or later.

Born only to be "tossed to hell" (or disease) like the "luckless Pots—marr'd in making" of the ancient Persian Poet.

TUBERCULOUS INFECTION.

BY J. I. GIBSON, STATE VETERINARY SURGEON,
DENISON, IOWA.

Speaking on the subject of tuberculous infection through dairy products, but more especially milk, J. I. Gibson, State Veterinary Surgeon of Iowa, asked the question, "How many sanitarians present own tuberculin tested cows or require that the cows from which they receive their milk for family use be tested?" In response three hands were raised. Continuing he said, "We are far advanced in sanitary preaching, but the practitioners of true sanitation are very few. In order to obtain the best results, the members of this congress should personally adopt certain rules of practice which would temporarily check and eventually eradicate this dread disease. In the history of veterinary practice we have many instances of direct infection from the use of milk from tuberculous cows, and as an example I wish to read to you a paragraph from a letter written to me by Dr. S. H. Johnston, of Carroll, Iowa, one of my assistants:

"'I hereby give you a brief report of a tuberculous cow which came under my notice three years ago, the cow presenting the following symptoms: Temperature, 103, dry, hacking cough, but otherwise apparently healthy. I advised the owner to have her tested with tuberculin, but he neglected to do it for about eight months, when my attention was again called to the case.

"Found the cow greatly emaciated, cough worse, sub-maxillary glands swollen, temperature 104. Again advised the tuberculin test, to which the owner consented. After injection I got a reaction of a degree and a half, on which I condemned the cow and recommended her destruction, to which the owner consented.

"Post mortem revealed extensive tubercular lesions of the lungs, intestines, and mammary glands.

Read at Medico-Legal Society and American Congress of Tuberculosis May 15th and 16th, 1901.

"I made inquiry as to the consumers of her milk, and found that three families had been supplied, with the following history: Three persons have died of tuberculosis and three others are thought to be infected with it There were two deaths in one family and one apparent infefction; one death in another family, and two other persons presenting symptoms. There is only one case that could be traced to any other source of infection.

"The patients exhibited the disease in the following forms: One lady aged forty, tuberculosis of the lungs; one man aged fifty, tuberculosis of the lungs, stomach, and intestines; one young man aged twenty-two, tubercular meningitis; one boy aged fourteen, tuberculosis of the throat. and two others believed to be suffering from tubercular infection.'

"Because of this very prolific source of infection, I insist that the members of this congress should refuse to use dairy products from any other than tested cows."

THE TUBERCULIN TEST.

BY LOUIS LEROY, B. S., M. D., STATE BACTERIOLOGIST, PROF. PATHOLOGY AND BACTERIOLOGY IN VANDERBILT UNIVERSITY ETC., NASHVILLE, TENN.

Mr. President and Members of the Congress:—

I desire to say that Dr. Lewis' paper is of the type which indicates careful thought, hard work, thorough investigation, and the scientific accuracy which makes for true progress. As to the action of the tuberculin test, I regard it as one of the most accurate and reliable of all diagnostic methods which we have at our disposal. It is true that care is necessary in its application, and that, for accurate results in all cases, especially those in which the reaction is not great, a certain amount of training is necessary. This however, is true of all laboratory work whose main requisite is exactness, and a careful exactness, which, to those unskilled in scientific manipulation, e'en though deeply schooled in classical works and empiricism is not only impossible but unappreciated and unthinkable. The ordinary technic is, of course, very simple, but this should not cause us to lose sight of the fact that there are cases requiring care. Again, there has been oftentime a tendency to claim the non-existence of tuberculosis in cases which gave a reaction and in which no gross leisons of the disease were manifest. I have seen two such cases within the past year or so. In many cases the infection is doubtless received through the respiratory tract and gains entrance through the bronchial tubes. Here, occasionally, the bacteria are intercepted by the peri-bronchial lymphatics and held in check for a varying length of time. In the two cases just referred to a satisfactory reaction was obtained in both cases by the tuberculin injection, but upon slaughtering the cattle no gross tubercular leisons were discoverable to the naked eye. There were, however, found upon microscopic examination several areas around the

Read before the joint session of the American Congress of Tuberculosis and the Medico-Legal Society, New York, May 15-16, 1901.

smaller bronchi, which showed beginning tubercles containing giant cells and in which I was able in parifine sections to demonstrate the tubercle bacilli.

This indicates that extreme care must be taken before we can declare the disease to be absent, especially so in cases where the tuberculin reaction has been present. I believe that had more careful search been made that a great many of the cases which are reported to have given the reaction, and subsequently found, upon post mortem examination to be devoid of tubercular leisons, would, under proper microscopic examination have demonstrated the presence of beginning disease. This, above all other times, is the period during which a diagnosis would be most valued, because the disease can be stopped before it has progressed sufficiently far to do much damage. At this stage the milk will not have been contaminated, and the cow will not have had calves so strongly predisposed to the disease, as would have probably have been the case had the disease been allowed to progress further. A large persentage of the cases of bovine tuberculosis are apparently transmitted directly from one animal to the other. This may be from bronchial secretions through drinking water, pails and otherwise, but it is certain that if the disease is recognized and the animal killed in this early stage before marked ulceration and destruction of tissue has occurred that the spreading of the disease will be practically stopped. It is not the part of wisdom to wait until the disease has progressed to such an extent in its ravages that every tissue and secretion of the body has become infected and the animal has become a fruitful source for the widespread dissemination of the infection, before we decide to make a diagnosis. I would most strongly advise the unhesitating and immediate destruction of all animals whatsover which gives a tuberculin reaction, for it will only be a question of time before the disease will have extended through the organism and before it may again be examined, countless numbers of animals and people will to a certainty have been exposed.

An interesting example of the probable transmission of the disease from man to cattle occurred in the case reported by Dr. W. J. McMurray, who is physician to the Confederate Soldiers' Home in Tennessee. This home had for its use a herd of cattle, some dozen or more, which remained for several years in splendid healthy condition and gave negative reaction to the tuberculin test. They were then allowed to graze for a part of the summer upon the large lawn on which the old soldiers were accustomed to wander and spend a good portion of their time. A large number of these men were tuberculous, in fact, Dr. McMurray informs me that 60 per cent. of the inmates of this institution die of the disease. Within a year from this time all of the herd were again examined and found to give the tuberculin reaction, were slaughtered, and upon autopsy, found to be in various stages of tuberculosis. This indicates that at least some care should be taken against the spreading of the disease from man to animal in institutions of this kind, lest they be spread again from animal to man, thus completing the vicious circle.

I would advise the compulsory examination of all cattle supplying milk or other products to all public institutions as we have no moral right to congregate individuals, whether it be against their will or not, and then supply them with the possible cause of death and suffering. Again, special care should be taken, not only to prevent the transmission of the disease from man to man, but to prevent cattle from grazing upon premises where tuberculous patients congregate or are liable to stay because it is practically an impossibility to make them realize the importance of the matter and refrain from expectorating in the open lawns, when they might be disposed to respect any sanitary regulation restricting the expectoration in their living quarters.

In answer to one of the previous speaker's questions, I will say that I have several times produced tuberculosis in guinea pigs by the injection into them of milk from tuberculous cattle, and it is but a comparatively simple experiment for any one to perform. In these cases I sedimented the milk in a centrifuge for an hour and injected about two cubic centimetres from the bottom of the tube. This shows that the bacilli in milk retain their virulence and are fully capable of engendering the disease. In a number of cases which I have had the opportunity of performing the autopsy upon, which had been diagnosed as death from "summer complaint" in children under two years of age, tuberculosis of the intestines was found to exist. In one of these cases, I remember especially, having traced the milk supply upon which the infant was fed to a couple of wandering, illkept cows, which were allowed to pick up a precarious existence along the roadways and suburbs of the town. These cattle gave every evidence of being tubercular, and although no tubercular test was made, nor autopsy held, I had the positive assurance of an excellent veterinary surgeon that they were tubercular, and, was told, that they died a year afterwards and that tubercular processes were found. I believe were the truth known, a large number of our cases of so-called "summer complaint" would in reality be found to be tubercular enteritis and that had we an adequate milk and cattle inspection, that the death rate from this cause would be reduced to the minimum, and that we, as physicians, as members of the various boards of health and as citizens, are, to an extent varying with our position, morally responsible for a large percentage of deaths which should be avoided. It is also inconceivable how men of alleged intelligence and enlightenment upon other subjects, can, for commercial reasons, local notoriety, mercenary reasons or other inconceivable motive, hamper or obstruct or oppose the necessary legislation in this direction. To my mind and to all practical purposes they might better be stealthily adding arsenic to a water supply for by so doing they would be only affecting the present generation, whereas by their present methods they are not only affecting the present but helping to lay the foundations for future generations of weaklings and degenerates, and in the present generation, are at least particeps-criminals to spreading one of the most terrible and loathsome deaths of which we know, and, in fact to nothing short of murder.

PRACTICAL SOLUTION OF THE QUESTION OF DEALING WITH THE CONSUMPTIVE POOR.

BY E. J. BARRICK, M. D., M. R. C. S., ENG., L. R. C. P. AND S., LONDON AND EDINBURGH.

VICE PRESIDENT AMERICAN CONGRESS OF TUBERCULOSIS.

The fight against Tuberculosis is primarily a campaign of popular education.

Before entering upon a campaign there are at least four points that should be well considered:—

1st. The numerical strength and destructive power of the enemy.

2nd. A comprehensive and well thought out plan of campaign.

3rd. The adoption of organized methods.

4th. Where the necessary funds are to come from to carry on the work.

With regard to the first, science tells us that the Bacilli of Tuberculosis, the enemy in this case are legion, their power of reproduction is phenomenal, millions are produced and thrown off each day in the sputa of a single patient in the advanced stages of the disease.

Statistics tell us that so great is the destructive power of this enemy that it is responsible for one-seventh of the deaths of the human race: that it causes more than twice as many deaths as diphtheria, scarlet fever, measles, whooping cough, typhoid fever and smallpox put together: that of all people who die between the ages of 15 and 60 no less than thirty-seven out of every hundred deaths are due to Tuberculosis: that of all deaths occurring between the ages of 25 and 35 nearly one-half are caused by this disease: that in industrial occupations it is the cause of nearly one-half of the mortality and more than half of the invalidism: that it kills each year in the Dominion of Canada about eight thousand of our people; and in your own country nearly 100,000.

Contributed to the American Congress of Tuberculosis after the session of May 15, 16, 1901.

Besides directly fighting this formidable enemy the apathy and indifference of the public has to be overcome and the following three popular errors reckoned with:—

1. That Consumption is hereditary and incurable.

2. That there is a mecca somewhere which is only to be reached to effect a cure.

3. That there is some particular medicine which, if only taken, a sure cure will be guaranteed.

I need not tell you that these three errors are deeply rooted in the public mind, and that it will require an active campaign of education for years to explode them.

In the explosion of the first no one need necessarily be hurt. The second is fanned and kept alive by interested individuals and private corporations for selfish purposes, and the explosion of this error will interfere with vested rights and opposition and obstruction may be looked for. The third is kept very much alive by manufacturers and vendors of the so-called sure and positive cures, by advertisements in the public press, religious as well as secular, and persistent opposition and obstruction may be counted upon.

When, however, the public mind becomes fully seized of the following facts, viz:—that consumption in the ordinary sense is not hereditary, is communicable, is preventible, is curable; that the mecca cry is a myth. that the so-called positive cures are a delusion; that apart from suitable medication, the three chief factors of cure are sunlight, fresh air, and nourishing food; that general sanitary measures must be observed in relation to quarantine, expectoration, public conveyances, places of public resort, factories, shops, offices and houses; and that there is urgent need of bringing a rural sanatorium within easy reach of each municipality with a wide open door to Consumptives in every condition of life, and in all stages of the disease, then we may confidently hope that the greatest enemy of the human race will be gradually overthrown, and Consumption will soon become as rare as Smallpox is to-day.

With these facts before us it would be utter folly to expect to defeat this enemy by any species of guerilla warfare, or by isolated efforts of individuals, or private corporations. Nothing short of a comprehensive, well considered plan of campaign and the adoption of organized methods, together with a well filled exchequer can satisfactorily arrest the ravages of this disease.

No plan of campaign is complete until ample provision is made for the care of the wounded, and in this case it is particularly so, because every wounded person in this fight becomes a factory in which the enemy is produced and turned out by the million each day.

I shall, therefore, confine my remarks to the practical solution of the question of caring for the Consumptive poor in rural sanitoria:—

To show that this question is capable of solution, and for the encouragement of other workers in this line, I shall give a brief outline of what has been done in the Province of Ontario and the City of Toronto. In a paper read before the Canada Medical Association in 1899, entitled, "How to deal with the Consumptive poor," I advocated the erection and maintenance of a rural Sanatorium in connection with each municipality or group of municipalities with a wide open door to the consumptives of said municipality in all conditions of life, and in all stages of the disease, not a free sanatorium, as such would tend to pauperism, but a sanatorium where those who were able to pay, should pay, where those able to pay only in part should do so, and where the absolutely poor would find an open door.

In the Province of Ontario there are about 40 counties One sanatorium in each would be 40 centres of education,and it must be remembered that suitable sanatoria are not only to be provided, but public opinion must be educated, so that the Consumptives will be willing to avail themselves of such provision.

Education, not compulsion, will have to be the watchword for many years to come.

To provide funds to carry out the foregoing, I advocated in the paper referred to, the co-operation of the Dominion Government, Local Legislatures, municipalities and philanthropic and charitable organizations and individuals, and submitted arguments to show why each of these factors should contribute and co-operate.

This plan has been endorsed by the Ontario Medical Association, Ontario Medical Council, and the Canada Medical Association. The Toronto Anti-Consumption League, which is a branch of the Canadian Association of which His Excellency Lord Minto is honorary president, waited upon the Ontario Government on the 7th of March, last year, laid the plan before the members and asked their co-operation.

Within one month a bill was framed entitled an "Act respecting municipal sanatoria for consumptives," which passed through all the stages and became law without a single opposing voice in the Legislature, and the first step in the plan was secured.

This legislation practically secures under certain conditions $4000 towards the erection of each municipal sanatorium, and $1.50 per week for each patient treated therein.

Last Autumn the League submitted the plan to the City Council and the question was referred by that body to the Medical Health Officer, who recommended co-operation in the shape of a by-law for $50,000 to be submitted to the qualified rate-payers, for land and building, and a grant of $2.80 per week for each poor patient for maintenance. This recommendation was unanimously endorsed by the Local Board of Health, and the By-Law will probably be submitted and carried at the municipal elections in January, 1902, and the second step in the plan completed. Local leagues have also been formed in four other county municipalities with the object of having by-laws submitted at an early date.

During the campaign necessary to accomplish the first two steps, the following facts should be made clear to the public:

1st. That no satisfactory progress can be made against the spread of consumption until adequate provision is made for the care of the poor suffering from this disease.

2nd. That the plan proposed rests upon an economically sound financial basis, and money expended in this direction will be a good investment to all concerned, a boon to the sick and protection from the disease to the well.

3rd. That the management and control being vested in a board of trustees, as provided by legislation, will be a guarantee that all funds placed in their hands will be strictly accounted for, and used in a way to produce the best results.

4th. That this is a movement of the people for the people, and governed and controlled by the people through their representatives in the municipal council, free from any party, sect, clique or personal aggrandisement.

The fololwing facts are applicable to the City of Toronto and in a modified form to every other city and municipality:

About 500 of our citizens die each year of consumption and other forms of Tuberculosis. That is a large financial loss to the state, the municipality and the community, and entails a further annual expenditure in caring for the orphans, and dependent persons produced thereby.

This municipality expends annually towards the care of the above and other sick poor through the hospitals, orphanages, homes and other charitable organizations about $90,000.

Philanthropy and charity expend probably as much more, and the Provincial Government perhaps half as much.

It is a regretable fact that while a very large proportion of this outlay is rendered necessary by the results of Tuberculosis, little or none of it goes to care for the consumptive poor, as the hospital doors are closed to them, and practically nothing is being done to check the spread of the disease.

The plan proposed strikes, directly at the root of the matter, by diverting the expenditures towards the prevention of the disease in providing Rural Municipal Sanatoria for the care of the poor, and others suffering from consumption, and will work out practically as follows:

LAND AND BUILDINGS.

The fund for the purchase of lands and erection of buildings to be provided for—

1st. Government grant of $4000.

2nd. By-Law $50,000.

This latter amount to be placed in the hands of the city treasurer, $25,000 of which shall be available when a similar amount has been procured from contributions, donations, bequests, legacies, &c. This will furnish accommodation for about 50 patients.

Another $5000 will be available when a similar amount has been received from the sources already mentioned, and further accommodation will be provided, and so on until provision is made for 100 patients.

MAINTENANCE.

The funds for maintenance will be drawn from the following sources:

1st. Government aid of a weekly allowance of $1.50 for each patient.

2nd. Municipal aid of a weekly allowance of $2.80 for each poor person.

3rd. Contributions, donations, bequests, legacies, &c., from the public generally.

4th. Contributions from patients.

5th. Contributions from churches, lodges, benefit and benevolent organizations on behalf of their sick members, who are unable to pay, or are entitled to sick dues.

The foregoing should recommend itself to every thoughtful person, and be followed by a generous response from the philathropic and charitably disposed, so that the Government and Municipal aid, may be supplemented both in the erection of buildings, and in the maintenance of the poor who seek relief.

What has been accomplished in Ontario may be done in every Province in the Dominion; and why, through the educating influence of this American Congress of Tuberculosis, should not the power of public opinion be brought to bear upon your Statesmen and Legislators until you see State after State enacting similar legislation, and until a rural sanatorium is brought within reach of every consumptive in each municipality of this great nation, and the annual destroyer of 100,000 of your fair sons and daughters is vanquished and driven from your midst.

HYGIENE IN BIBLE AND TALMUD AND SANITATION IN POST-RABBINICAL TIMES.

BY MORITZ ELLINGER, ESQ., OF NEW YORK.

Chemistry and Microscopy, which reached the highest development in the past century, have had the greatest share in the hygienic progress which enabled us to obtain an average higher longevity than ever before. Greater importance is given to the science of "macrobiotic," or living in agreement with the laws of nature as the best prevention of disease, as taught by Hufeland, than to the cure of diseases contracted by a disregard of the laws of hygiene. Older by far in laying down laws for the preservation of health and life are the hygienic laws laid down in the code of Moses. The religion taught by that great law-giver lays greatest stresss upon proper life-conduct as the means of prolonging life and the enjoyment of it. "You shall observe these laws," Moses taught "that you may live long." He did not command to believe this or that, nor did he point to reward and punishment in the life to come, but he laid down rules for conduct in this life and ordained punishment for the violation of these laws. Nor must we overlook the fact that religion as defined by the laws of Moses involved all laws for the government of man as individual, and as member and integral part of the state. All laws were promulgated in the name of God, the laws of days of rest and festivity as well as sanitary regulations.

The greater knowledge we have gained through our ability of deciphering the libraries of cuneiform tablets and hieroglyphic medicine-books convinces us that many of the sanitary laws contained in the Pentateuch have ben observed by the Egyptians, Babylonians, Assyrians and other Semitic nations previous to the existence of the Israelitish nation, but no nation has lived in such close conformity with these laws as the Jews, and by the overwhelming majority of them are

Read before the Medico-Legal Society and American Congress of Tuberculosis in joint session, May 15-16, 1901.

they strictly observed to this day. We know of "sciences that have been lost" and the knowledge of which seem irrecoverable. There can be no question that the ancients possessed a knowledge of laws that govern nature, which enabled them to form rules of conduct in conformity therewith. Whenever we find in the Mosaic code a law prohibiting the drinking or eating of blood of animals because blood is the *nephesh*, the life, we may assume that the law-giver knew the intrinsic essence and properties of blood, the rapid chemical change which takes place therein after death, the ptomaine poisoning of which it is the cause, the poison which it gathers from the deceased bodily organs and which are transferred to the human body when taken as animal food. We may safely assume, therefore, that the ritual mode of slaughtering practised by the Jews since time immemorial has been found the best safeguard against the transfer of disease from the meat of animals used for food, and which also accounts for their greater immunity from epidemics which decimated large poplations among whom they lived.

The fact is well established that tuberculosis, which is the greatest scourge of modern times, is largely due to the transference of the germ from the meat and milk of diseased animals. Before modern hygienic regulation ever insisted upon the introduction of any mode of inspecting the meat of animals previous to its offer in the public market for consumption, the Jews had made it obligatory upon those who were authorized to perform the slaughtering of animals to examine closely and carefully the carcass, to see whether the lungs were sound, whether the vital organs were free from disease, so that health was not endangered by the consumption. The slaughtering and inspecting of animals was not entrusted to the first comer. It was performed by persons trained and educated for the office; they had to pass an examination as to their knowledge of anatomy of animals and of the ritual laws prescribed for the performance of their duty. The Talmud, a work, the redaction of which has been completed some sixteen hundred years ago, contains extensive treatises on the subject and discloses a wonderful knowledge of the anatomy of the animal.

The mode of slaughtering consisted, or rather consists today, in severing completely the windpipe, the veins, the jugularies and *carotis communis* of the animal with one cut of the knife, which must be examined before the action as to its sharpness and freedom from the slightest dent. This mode inflicts a minimum of pain and causes a rapid out flow of the blood. It is well-known that the shock caused by pain induces coagulation of the blood, and effects a rapid chemical change of the blood, productive of ptomaine and for this reason the Jewish dietary law prohibits the flesh of animals killed by violence, such as blows, shooting with arrow or bullet. Such meat is "Trepha" the common name for violent death in the field. The further treatment of the meat by the Jewish housewife has the same point in view. The meat must be kept in water for a half hour, then thoroughly salted, after which it is subjected again to a thorough cleansing in water.

As much stress is laid in modern days upon the proper observance of a proper diet for the preservation of health as upon the use of drugs. The Jew who lived strictly in compliance with the dietary laws found in them protection against infection by many of the microbes and bacteriae which generate disease. Thus was not only a thorough inspection of the carcass of the bovine killed for the use of man required by the religious law but even fowls were examined and if any internal injury was found of a character that would have produced their natural death, the animal was declared unfit for food. As a protection against deleterious effect of microbes and bacteriae though not known by their technical names, it was commanded to thoroughly rinse berries, and all fruits, liguminous and other vegetables in water to purify them from all parasites and the dust particles which made them dangerous to health, before eating them when raw. It is only in modern days that we have discovered the trichinae in hog meat, which at least proves that some good reason existed in those ancient days for forbidding the use of swine flesh.

Another rule, probably of simple cleanliness, required the washing of hands before partaking of any meal and the rinsing of the mouth after rising from the table. The legislators evidently had a shadowy idea of the infinitesimal cocci, animalculae, spirillae and baccilae which float around and give the pathologists and biologists so much trouble. However, the rule was part of the hygienic system, and served well its purpose. A little story might not be out of place here, related in the Talmud in reference to the post-prandial ablution. A traveler arrived at a place on Friday and asked a man, whom he observed in the synagogue as one of the most devout and demonstrative worshippers, to entertain him over the Sabbath. The man agreed to receive him as a guest and took him to his house. Before dining the traveler handed the man a large bag of gold with the request the request to keep it for him over the Sabbath. The man put the bag in a locker. On Sunday morning the stranger requested the return of his treasure, but his pious host denied ever having received it. The man left in order to look for the rabbi, who was also the judge in those days. He did not find him at his house and walked about the city, when he met his host and observed some lentils on his flowing beard, evidently not having observed the ritual ablution. A thought struck him. He hurried to the house of his host and met the wife. He told her that her husband had sent him with the request to deliver him the bag put away for safe keeping in the locker. As a voucher for the truth of the message, he was to tell her that they had lentils for dinner. The wife deliverd and handed to him his property.

That many of the Mosaic commands had their *raison d'etre* in the sanitary safe guard, cannot be questioned. We find there the quarantine regulations against the spread of leprosy, the establishment of earth closets, the investigation of the priest as to the infectious character of disease. The strict regulations regarding ritual baths by women during the delicate period of their lives also belong to this character, which also had the effect of curbing sexual passion and influenced largely the purity of the Jewish family life which has become proverbial during the ages.

There is a peculiar law, which few people understand and which is ridiculed as superstitious. It is the defilement of the human body after death. The house in which a dead body lies becomes defiled, and all who were under the roof had to undergo a thorough cleansing with water or take a ritual bath; we known now and understand the infectious character of diseases which are more dangerous to health by infection from a dead body. They send forth deadly microbes and bacteriae, and we in modern time disinfect localities where death from zymotic diseases has occurred.

We are indeed apt to smile at ceremonies and customs practised in olden times, because we have lost knowledge of the motives underlying these practices. Of course many of them are obsolete enough, many of them are nothing but the last remnant of conceptions born in superstition. When we see a Jew to-day binding the phylacteries around his arm and his forehead, or don the praying scarf, we smile at him, but forget the great importance given to church vestments and the passionate dispute even in Protestant churches about ritualistic practices. They all rest upon the same belief. Bagehot says correctly that the binding cement of ancient people was the belief in certain customs and practices, the strict observance of which was the iron bond which kept nations intact, and that the progress of the world commenced when "discussion" took the place of iron laws. It may referentially be remarked here, that "discussion" was the great characteristic feature of the Jews. The Talmud, which records the disputes among the various schools of learning from the time of the great Sanhedrin to the year 600 of the present era, furnishes evidence of the constant flow of discussion on the most vital questions of life, of health and sickness, of religion and practices during that early period; and the "discussion" has ever flowed on to this day, so that opinions among the Jews as to the binding character of ceremonies and ritual practices differ and variegate more than ever.

Of course in a short paper like this I cannot enumerate the many laws which were enacted in Bible, Talmud and by post-Talmudical rabbis for the preservation of health. A close examination of these laws and their embodiment in a treatise would furnish many a valuable hint even for guidance in our days, and offer an explanation for the miracle of the preservation of the Jews through all the ages, with the full preservation of their energy and high intellecuality, and point to the strict observation of their ancient laws of hygiene.

THE TREATMENT OF CONSUMPTION

BY W. L. BULLARD, A. M., M. D., COLUMBUS, GA.,
VICE PRESIDENT AMERICAN CONGRESS OF TUBERCULOSIS.

The advance guard of progress seems never to move in even rank. As we look back over the past we are astonished at the uncertain lines of development. In some directions there is rapid progress while others of apparently equal importance seem to lag. But in this aspect of change there is no real ground for pessimistic view. Civilization taken in its entirety makes for the better—its fruit, on the whole is good. And so, while it seems strange that so little has been accomplished by science for the prophylaxis and care of tuberculosis, it is yet a matter of sincere congratulation that assemblages of learned men, such as this, are meeting or arranging to meet in all the great countries of the earth for the purpose of lessening by every means known to man the tragic and wasteful effects of this insidious and terrible disease. I will not attempt to discuss legislative means to this, much desired, end. The gentlemen learned in the law and practiced in the art of lawmaking will, I am sure, meet the question as fully and as satisfactorily as may be done with the light that is to be had on the subject. And while I feel that the burden of prevention and cure of tuberculosis must ever rest most heavily on the medical fraternity I am in no sense, I hope, oblivious to the great aid which may be expected from the legal profession and the State Boards of Health. To my mind prevention offers greater assurances than any known means of cure. Hygienic environment, cleanly habit, careful selection of food, abundance of open air exercise with free and assured exercise of lung under suitable climatic conditions, my judgment tells me, are of more

Read before the American Congress of Tuberculosis in joint session with Medico-Legal Society, May 15-16, 1901.

importance than all the medicines that have so far engaged the thought of physicians. I think the concensus of medical opinion bears me out in this view. Still the importance of the proper use of right drugs is not to be gainsaid; nor indeed would I so far forget myself as to neglect their consideration in the prevention, treatment and amelioriation of this dread scourge. So far as I know there has been no specific claimed by the scientific world. I have tried the various preparations of creosote I regret to say with little success. Local treatment seems largely out of the question, though the needle has been pressed into this service with I fear but indifferent success.

But there are many unhappy symptoms which obtain in tubercular cases that do yield to the timely administration of certain drugs. I may mention pain, fever, insomnia, gastric disturbances, profuse "night sweats" pleuritic phenomena and a host of others. Surely, it is the duty of the medical practitioner to relieve these, even if the relief per se be very far from cure.. When the highly excited condition of the nervous centres becomes manifest in the various phenomena of pyrexia, pain or profuse perspiration, treatment looking to removal of the basic cause of the disturbance is often best conserved by removal of symptoms of distress; but whether or no this be in strict accordance with the theory and logic of treatment, it is nevertheless assured by clinical experience.

That drug which tends by its physiological action on systemic metabolism to readjust the molecular interplay of nervous structure and re-establish the equilibrium of the organism, such is for instance the judicious administration of some such synthetic product of the coal tar derivatives as Pheno-Bromate, why beyond all question, that is the drug to receive our careful attention. For by the use of it we work along the lines of least resistance which is nature's habitual method and thereby conserve the vis vitae most happily. I mention this drug because in my hands in this class of cases I have secured most pronounced and favorable results.

There are yet many preconceived notions which we adhere to in the handling of cases of this kind and which should be excluded from practice. Too great reliance on drugs, is, in my opinion, a hindrance to the best interests of the patient which we seek to protect and favor. If we would place greater stress on the importance of hygiene, cleanly habit, wholesome food, lung gymnastics under conservative regulation, fresh air, moderate exercise and climatic conditions, we would, I think, find a much greater per cent. of cures and less reason for despair in the treatment of tubercular cases.

MEDICO-LEGAL SURGERY.

ASSOCIATE EDITORS.

Medical.

Granville P. Conn, M. D., Concord, N. H.
R. Harvey Reed, M. D., Wyoming.
Nicholas Senn, M. D., Chicago, Ill.
Webb J. Kelley, M. D., Galion, Ohio.

Legal.

Clarence A. Lightner, Esq., Detroit, Mich
Judge Wm. H. Francis, New York.
Prof. A. P. Grinnell, M. D., Burlington, Vt.

This department is conducted as the organ of the Section of the Medical Jurisprudence of Surgery of the Medico-Legal Society. Its officers for 1901 are as follows:

Chairman.

Chief Surgeon Charles K. Cole, M.D., of Helena, Montana.

LEGAL. Vice-Chairmen.

Clark Bell, Esq., of New York.
Judge W. H. Francis, of New York.
Hon. J. W. Fellows, of N. H.
Hon. W. C. Howell, of Iowa.
A. P. Grinnell, M. D., of Vermont.
Hon. A. R. Parmenter, of Troy, N. Y.
Hon. George R. Peck, of Illinois.
Hon. J. M. Thurston, of Nebraska.
Judge A. H. Dailey, of Brooklyn, N. Y.
Hon. Allen Zollers, of Indiana.

SURGICAL. Vice-Chairmen.

Ch. Surg W. A. Adams, of Ft. Worth, Tex.
Ch. Surg. F. H. Caldwell, M. D., of Fla.
Ch. Sur. Granville P. Conn, M. D., of N. H.
Ch. Surg. W. B. Outten, M. D., of Missouri.
Surgeon Geo. Chaffee, M. D., of Brooklyn.
Ch. Surg. B. F. Eads, M. D., of Texas.
Ch. Surg. John E. Owen, M. D., of Chicago.
Surg. Gen. R. Harvey Reed, M. D., of Wy.
Surg. Gen. Nicholas Senn, M. D., of Ill.
Ch. Surg. S. S. Thorne, M. D., of Ohio.

Secretary.

Clark Bell, Esq., 39 Broadway, N. Y.

Treasurer.

Judge Wm. H. Francis, New York City.
39 Broadway, N. Y.

Executive Committee.

Clark Bell, Esq., Chairman.

Surg. Thomas Darlington, M. D., of N. Y.
L. L. Gilbert, Esq., Pittsburg, Pa.
Ex-Ch. Sur. Geo. Goodfellow, M. D., Cal.
Surgeon J. N. Hall, of Denver, Colo.
Chief Surg. A. C. Scott, M. D., of Texas.
Judge A. H. Dailey, of Brooklyn, N. Y.
Sur. R. S. Parkhill, M.D., of Hornelsville, N. Y.
Sur. Fayette H. Peck, M. D., of Utica, N. Y.
Chief Sur. T. I. Pritchard, of Wis.
R. C. Richards, Esq., of Chicago, Ill.
Ch. Surg. F. A. Stillings, M. D., of N. H.
Ch. Surg. J. J. Buckley, Missoula, Montana

To Railway Surgeons and Railway Counsel:

We take occasion to advise you to unite with the Section of Medico-Legal Surgery, which can now be done by an annual subscription of $1.50, entitling each member to the *Medico-Legal Journal* free.

G. P. CONN, M. D.,
Ex-Chairman Section Med.-Leg. Surgery.

ABRAM H. DAILEY,
Ex-President Medico-Legal Society of New York.

SAMUEL S. THORN, M. D.,
Chief Surgeon T., St. L. & K. C. Railway Co., Ex-President National Association Railway Surgeons.

J. B. MURDOCH, M. D.,
Surgeon and Ex-President National Association of Railway Surgeons.

R. HARVEY REED, M. D.,
Surgeon General of State of Wyoming.

R. S. HARNDEN, M. D.,
Ex-President New York State Association Railway Surgeons. Ex-President Erie Railway Surgeons.

HUBBARD W. MITCHEL, M. D.,
Ex-President Medico-Legal Society of New York.

Members of the Section on Medico-Legal Surgery, who have not remitted their annual subscription to the Section, will please send same to Judge Wm. H. Francis, No. 39 Broadway, N. Y., and members will please not confound the Section Dues with the Annual Dues of the Society, which should be remitted to Caroline J. Taylor, Treasurer, Bridgeport, Conn. Members of the Society or Section will please propose names for membership in this Section.

It is proposed that members of the Society and Section each donate one bound volume annually to the Library of the Medico-Legal Society, by action of the Executive Committee.

The following new members of the Section are announced: J. P. Webster, M. D., Ex-Pres. Erie Railway Surgeons, Chicago, Ills.; W. L. Cuddebuck, M. D., Pres. Erie Railway Surgeons, Port Jervis, N. Y.; Dr. A. E. Ellingwood, Attica, N. Y.; Chief Surgeon J. J. Buckley, N. P. Ry. Co., Missoula, Montana.

THE NEW STATE ASSOCIATION OF RAILWAY SURGEONS.

This body will hold its annual meeting in the City of New York, at a two-days session, November 14th and 15th, 1901, under the Presidency of Dr. W. R. Townsend, of New York City.

The special topic of discussion on one day will be "Railway Sanitation," of which a detailed programme will be announced later. The second day will be devoted to a clinic, to be arranged and announced.

THE American Academy of Railway Surgeons announces its annual meeting to be held at the Auditorium in Chicago, Ill., on the 12th and 13th of September, 1901, with an attractive programme, under the Presidency of Dr. L. S. Fairchild, of Clinton, Iowa. We go to press without being able to present its work, but hope to give an extended notice of its transactions in our next issue.

INTERNATIONAL ASSOCIATION OF RAILWAY SURGEONS.

ANNUAL MEETING FOR 1901,
HELD AT MILWAUKEE, WIS., JUNE 10, 11 AND 12.

First Day:—

The association was called to order by Dr. Wm. Mackie, of Milwaukee, chairman of the committee of arrangements.

Mayor David S. Rose made an address of welcome.

Dr. George Ross, of Va., responded for the body.

The President, Dr. H. L. Getz, of Marshaltown, Iowa, then made his presidential address. At the close of which he made feeling allusions to the death of Dr. E. R. Lewis, the treasurer of the association.

The annual reports of the secretary and treasurer were made and received.

Dr. J. M. Salmon, of Ashland, Ky., read a paper entitled "Physical Examination of Railway Employes," which was discussed by Drs. Barr, Thorn, Geisendorfer, Milligan, Keller, Foxton, Ross, Jonas, Bowles, Jay, Keller, and the discussion closed by the author of the paper.

On motion the association adjourned until 2 p. m.

AFTERNOON SESSION, 2 P. M.

The nominating and judiciary committees were announced:

NOMINATING COMMITTEES.

Dr. J. A. Barr, Chairman, Pa.
Dr. C. Z. Aud, Kentucky.
Dr. George Ross, Virginia.
Dr. S. R. Miller, Tennessee.
Dr. A. F. Jonas, Nebraska.
Dr. Lester Keller, Ohio.
Dr. W. G. Jameson, Texas.

JUDICIARY COMMITTEE.

Dr. A. L. Peterman, Chairman, South Dakota.
Dr. J. M. Salmon, Kentucky.
Dr. H. N. Street, Mississippi.
Dr. W. C. Cox, Washington.
Dr. J. R. Hollowbush, Illinois.
Dr. Ben Thompson, Iowa.
Dr. W. D. Williamson, New Hampshire.
Dr. A. S. Geisendorfer, Oregon.
Dr. J. B. Hungate, Nebraka.
Dr. John D. Milligan, Penn'a.
Dr. C. R. Dickson Canada.
Dr. L. Worsham, Indiana.
Dr. W. W. Reed, Colorado.
Dr. S. B. S. Wilson, Kansas.
Dr. C. M. Lutterloh, Arkansas.

Dr. W. D. Middleton, of Davenport, Iowa, read a paper on "Abdominal Contusions," which was discussed by Drs. Jonas, McKnight, Barr, Worsham, Hungate, Clark, Hollowbush, Jay, Ross, Green, Brock, Beers, Warren, Milligan Bowles, Engle, and the discussion was closed by Dr. Middleton.

Dr. W. C. Cox, of Everett, Wash., read a paper entitled "Railway Spine, with Report of a Case." Discussed by Drs. Jay, Thorn, and, in closing, by the essayist.

Dr. Ben Thompson, of Tama, Iowa, read a paper on "Transverse Myelitis," which was discussed by Drs. Dougherty, McKnight, Thorn, Worsham, and the discussion closed by Dr. Thompson.

On motion, a paper by Dr. George Chaffee, of Brooklyn, N. Y., entitled, "Tuberculous Passengers on Railways," was read by title and referred to the committee on publication.

Dr. Bouffleur, of Chicago, made a brief verbal report in behalf of the executive board. He also reported verbally as chairman of the committee on transportation.

Drs. McKnight, Aud and Ross were appointed a committee on President's address.

Dr. A. F. Jonas, of Omaha, Neb., read a paper entitled "Union Pacific Emergency Association," the discussion of which was postponed until after the reading of the papers of Drs. Riordan and Dickson, Tuesday morning.

The President read a telegram from Dr. Drake, of Kansas City, announcing the death of the Treasurer, Dr. E. R. Lewis.

Drs. Stewart, of Minnesota, Hoy, of Ohio, and Ross, of Virginia, were named a committee to take suitable action on this death.

The President read a communication from the manager of the International Journal of Surgery, submitting a proposition to publish the proceedings of the Association, which was laid over till the morning of the succeeding day by the chair.

Dr. J. N. Warren, of Sioux City, Iowa, read a paper entitled "Report of a Case of Bilateral Neuritis of the Brachial Plexus."

Dr. C. R. Dickson, of Toronto, Can., read a paper on "First Aid at Home and Abroad."

The papers of Drs. Jonas and Dickson were then discussed jointly. The discussion was opened by Dr. Milligan, and continued by Drs. Riordan, Williams, Worsham, Allis, Barr, Hungate, Hoy, English, Ross, Thorn, and the discussion closed by the essayists.

After debate it was ordered that the report be published, if acceptable to a majority of the committee, that the work be accepted by the Association and be its property; that the work be endorsed by the body, but that no expense be incurred by the association in its publication, and that Dr.

Dickson be allowed a royalty of ten per cent. as compensation for the labor he has entered upon it.

Second Day, Afternoon Session:—

The committee on the recommendations of the President's address made a report:

1. Advising that the best interests of the society would be best served by holding its meeting at various cities.

2. Adverse to present action establishing a pathological museum.

3. That Section 2, Article 11, of the Constitution and By-Laws be amended by adding after word "Railway" in the second line the words "Mining and Manufacturing."

The report was read and adopted unanimously.

Dr. Bruce L. Riordan, of Toronto, Can., then read the report of the special committee on first aid to railway employes.

On motion of Dr. Ross the report was received.

The report was discussed by Drs. Thorn, Worsham, Warren, Hoy, McKnight, Dickson, Leipziger.

The secretary read the report of the auditing committee.

AUDIT OF TREASURER'S ACCOUNTS.

May 31, 1900, balance on hand		$1,348.75
Less error, allowed at Detroit		285.00
June 1, 1901, balance on hand		$1,063.75
Receipts—		
657 members, at $5.00	$3,285.00	
1 member at $2.00	2.00	
		$3,287.00
		$4,350.75
Expenses—		
Treasurer	$510.05	
Secretary and editor	695.00	
Executive board	73.54	
Reporter (stenographic)	100.00	
Printing	122.75	
Postage	155.00	
Expressage	1.00	
Fees returned	25.00	
Publisher	1,316.00	
		2,998.34
June 10, 1901, balance on hand		$1,352.41

(Signed)

A. I. BOUFFLEUR, Chairman,
C. W. P. BROCK,
H. L. GETZ,
B. L. RIORDAN,
R. GOODE,
W. D. MIDDLETON,
L. J. MITCHELL.

On motion of Dr. Barr, the report was received and filed.

Dr. John B. Murphy, of Chicago, then gave a talk on the subject of "Non-Union of Fractures." The discussion was opened by Dr. Thorn, and continued by Drs. Warren, Dougherty, Eddy, Sylvester and Jay, the debate being closed by the essayist.

Dr. W S. Hoy, of Wellston, O., followed with a paper entitled "The Cmmon-Sense Management of Fractures." Discussed by Drs. Eddy, Harper, Sylvester, Jay, Bowen, Lovett, Clark, Curry, Ross, Henderson, and Dougherty and the discussion closed by the author of the paper.

Dr. O. Johnson, of Quincey, Ill., read a paper entitled "Rare Fractures of the Upper Extremity, with Unusual Complications, and Synopsis of a Few Special Cases," which was discussed by Dr. Dougherty.

Dr. H. A. Leipziger, of Burlington, Ia., read a paper entitled "'Description of a Passenger Wreck and its Management," which was discussed by Drs. Ross, Hawes and Henderson.

The committee reported suitable resolutions of respect to the memory of Dr. E. R. Lewis, which were adopted, ordered spread on the minutes and a copy ordered sent to the family of the deceased.

June 12. Third Day, Morning Session:—

The society proceeded to the election of officers. The following officers were elected:

PRESIDENT, Rhett Goode, Mobile, Ala.

VICE PRESIDENTS, J. A. Barr, McKee's Rocks, Pa.; Walter M. English, London, Can.; Lester Keller, Ironton, Ohio; Bacon Saunders, Ft. Worth, Texas; S. R. Miller, Knoxville, Tenn.; Benj. Thompson, Tama, Iowa; A. L. Peterman, Parker, S. Dakota.

TREASURER, James A. Duncan, Toledo, Ohio.

SECRETARY, Louis J. Mitchell, 498 W. Adams St., Chicago.

EXECUTIVE BOARD—L. Worsham, Evansville, Ind., Chairman; D. S. Fairchild, Clinton, Iowa; J. N. Jackson, Kansas City, Mo.; W. S. Hoy, Wellston, Ohio; C. R. Dickson, Toronto, Can.; J. N. D. Shinkel, Friar's Point, Miss., and the ex-President, President, Treasurer and Secretary ex-officio.

After discussion the society decided by vote between St. Louis, Mo., and Put-in-Bay, O., that the former be selected as the place of meeting. A letter from Dr. W. B. Outten-Chief Surgeon M. R. R. R., was read strongly urging St. Louis as the place of meeting.

Dr. Goode, the President-elect, was introduced by Dr. Hoy in a bright speech, and made a graceful brief address.

The question of the proposition of the International Journal of Surgery then came before the body, and an exciting debate occurred on motions and amendments of various kinds, which were all finally reconsidered.

The proposition from the International Journal of Surgery to publish the proceedings, was submitted by the President, and it was without objection ordered referred to the executive committee with power.

Dr. McDonald, manager of the International Journal of Surgery, was then introduced and addressed the association in favor of the proposition he had made. At the close of his remarks it was moved and carried that the remarks of Dr. MacDonald be expunged from the minutes.

An informal discussion on the publication took place, in which Drs. Hoy, Geisenderfor, Ross, Warren, Dougherty, Riordan, Thompson, Plummer, Miller and Fairchild participated. At the close of this discussion Dr. Riordan moved that the Railway Surgeon be continued, and that the Executive Board be instructed that this is the sense of this association. This was seconded, and it was then moved and carried that Dr. Riordan's motion be laid on the table.

Dr. Getz, the retiring President, returned thanks to the members for their courtesy and loyalty.

Dr. Hoy moved thanks to Dr. Getz, which was carried.

Thanks were moved and carried to the committee of arrangements and the citizens of Milwaukee.

Dr. Hoy was placed on the Executive Committee to fill the place held by Dr. Getz, on the latter's motion.

The association adjourned sine die.

PSYCHOLOGICAL.

This Department is conducted with the following Associate Editors:

Judge Abram H. Dailey, Brooklyn, N. Y.	Wm. Lee Howard, M. D., Baltimore, Md.
Prof. A. A. D'Ancona, San Francisco, Cal.	R. J. Nunn, M. D., Savannah, Ga.
H. S. Drayton, M. D., N. Y.	A. E. Osborne, M. D., Cal.
M. Ellinger, Esq., N. Y. City.	Jas. T. Searcey, M. D., Tuscaloosa, Ala.
Dr. Havelock Ellis, London.	U. O. B. Wingate, M D., Milwaukee, Wis.
Thomson Jay Hudson, Esq., Wash., D. C.	Prof. W. Xavier Sudduth, Chicago, Ill.

as the organ of the Psychological Section.

The Psychological Section of the Medico-Legal Society has been organized, to which any member, Active, Corresponding or Honorary, is eligible on payment of an annual enrollment fee or dues of $1.50.

Any student of Psychological Science is eligible to unite with the Section without joining the Medico Legal Society on an annual subscription of $1.50, payable in advance and receive the MEDICO-LEGAL JOURNAL free. The officers for 1900 are as follows:

Chairman,

PROF. W. XAVIER SUDDUTH, OF CHICAGO, ILL.

LEGAL AND SCIENTIFIC.	*MEDICAL.*
Vice-Chairmen,	*Vice-Chairmen.*
Clark Bell, Esq., of New York.	T. D. Crothers, M. D., of Hartford, Conn.
Rev. Antoinette B. Blackwell, of N. Y.	F. E. Daniel, M. D., of Austin, Texas.
Harold Browett, Esq., Shanghai, China.	H. S. Drayton, M. D., of New York.
C. Van D. Chenoweth, Worcester, Mass.	Wm. Lee Howard, M. D., of Baltimore, Md.
Judge Abram H Dailey, of Brooklyn.	Henry Hulst, M. D., Grand Rapids, Mich.
Moritz Ellinger, Esq., of New York.	Prof. Thomas Bassett Keyes, of Chicago.
Rev. Phebe A. Hanaford, of New York.	R. J. Nunn, M. D., of Savannah, Ga.
Thomson Jay Hudson, Esq., Wash'n, D. C.	A. E. Osborne, M. D., of Glen Ellen, Cal.
Sophia McClelland, of New York.	Jas. T. Searcy, M. D., Tuscaloosa, Ala.
Mrs. Jacob F. Miller, of New York.	U. O. B. Wingate, M. D., Milwaukee, Wis.

Mrs. Mary Louise Thomas, of New York.

Secretary and Treasurer.

CLARK BELL, ESQ., OF NEW YORK.

Executive Committee.

CLARK BELL, ESQ., Chairman.

SAMUEL BELL THOMAS, OF NEW YORK CITY, Secretary.

M. Ellinger, Esq.	Judge A. H. Dailey.	Geo. W. Grover, M. D.
Carleton Simon, M. D.	Ida Trafford Bell.	H. W. Mitchell, M. D.

THE TREATMENT OF MELANCHOLIA.

BY CHARLER G. WAGNER, M. D., BINGHAMTON, N. Y.,
SUPT. BINGHAMTON STATE HOSPITAL.

Read at the annual meeting of the Lake Kenka Medical and Surgical Association held at Grove Springs, N. Y., August 13 and 14, 1901.

Viewed from the standpoint of the general practitioner there is probably no other form of mental derangement quite so important as melancholia. The reason for this is readily appreciated when it is remembered—first, that a large percentage of the acute and presumably recoverable cases of insanity that come under observation belong to this class, and second, that these are the patients for whom the family or friends most often desire treatment outside of asylums or hospitals for the insane. If the patient is in the opposite condition, that is, suffering from mania—noisy, boisterous, and violent in conduct, or if he is so demented that he has no appreciation of his surroundings—he is usually promptly certified as insane and taken to some institution where he may receive suitable care and treatment, but when the condition of melancholia develops, especially in its milder forms, the sympathies of the family and friends are usually more directly appealed to and the fact that insanity is developing or actually exists is often unappreciated until the disease has progressed for a considerable period of time.

Patients of this kind some times consult the physicians voluntarily with a feeling that something is wrong with them but without realizing the character of the trouble. They are apt to imagine themselves the victims of various habits, that they are suffering from incurable ailments of some of the vital organs or that they are to b emade to suffer for sins they have committed. The degree of mental disturbance varies from simple depression or hypochondriasis to the most profound melancholy, accompanied by delusions and hallucina-

Read at the Annual Meeting of the Lake Keuka Medical and Surgical Association held at Grove Springs, N. Y., August 13 and 14, 1901.

tions and more or less emotional excitement, or by stupor. When this profound melancholia exists or is even approximated there can be scarcely any question as to the desirability of hospital treatment in preference to home care but so long as only the milder degree of depression are observed the idea of care at home, or elsewhere, away from the hospital, may be properly considered. It is the treatment of these lesser cases which will be considered in this paper.

When insanity in any of its forms appears in a family, no matter how mild the attack, it is an occurrence of the gravest importance and the responsibility of the physician who is called upon to advise the afflicted ones as to the proper treatment for the patient can scarcely be over-estimated. On his advice oftimes depends not only the health of the patient and happiness of that family circle, but the very life of the sufferer who is under his care. It behooves him, therefore, to give the patient his best attention.. He should seek diligently to ascretain his life history, to acquaint himself with all his peculiarities and habits,and to find, if possible,the cause of his mental aberration, for upon the facts in this manner ascertained will depend largely his judgment as to the treatment to be followed. In obtaining this information the narrative given by the patient himself is of value as reflecting his views of his condition, but from his relatives and friends may be gathered much information that will prove more accurate and valuable to the physician. Many of these patients with mild melancholia or hyochondriasis suffering severely from their more or less imaginary troubles are in the borderland of insanity—scarcely insane within the meaning of the law, but almost certain to become so, unless the physician comes to the rescue and guides them safely back to health.

What then shall be done for these unfortunates? First as to environment. It is assumed that the patient or his friends wish, if possible, to avoid going to a hospital. It therefore immdeiately devolves upon the physician to determine what environment will be most favorable to recovery. First the patient should have a complete change of surroundings. The scenes amid which mental derangement developed are almost certain to exert a depressing influence on the sufferer and he must therefore be removed from them. The mrechant must be taken entirely away from his business, the professional man from the scenes of his professional labor, and the housewife from the immediate vicinity of her domestic care. Complete withdrawal from the society of the immediate family or near friends desirable for the reason that close relationship near friends is highly desirable for the reason that close relationship continually invites discussion of the more or less imaginary troubles that occupy the patient's mental field and such discussion always tends to intensify the malady. The best companion for such a case is an entire stranger, intelligent enough to enter sympathetically into new occupations, to engage the patient in conversation on new themes and to lead his ideas into new channels. Preferably such a companion should be a physician, of experience, qualified to regulate the diet, administer the medicines and attend to all of the patient's ailments, both real and imaginary. Quite often these melancholy patients, as well as those suffering from mania, will receive suggestions from a comparative stranger when they strongly resent such suggestions from their friends or relatives as an unwarranted interference with their private affairs. Such a companion, be he physician, nurse or attendant, should endeavor to gain the complete confidence of the patient and then endeavor to impress upon him that restoration to health is certain if he will but follow instructions and make some effort himself. Mental suggestion is a powerful influence in these cases and much may be done to lessen the force of delusive ideas by occasionally, firmly and positively declaring them to be without foundation, but care should be taken to avoid prolonged argument, as such disputation is apt to exhaust the patient and add to his depression. The great object to be attained is to excite interest in new matters, to the exclusion of old, painful ideas.

For some mild melancholy cases, travel and change of scene is desirable, but judgment must always be exercised in the selection of the means to effect this end. If the patient has shown the slightest suicidal tendency he must be kept out of the way of temptation, lest the sight of some means of effecting self-destruction should inspire a sudden impulse to end his career. This is especially important for the reason that it is well known fact that many insane persons have been moved to suicide by the mere sight of a body of water, a moving train, or a piece of rope, within easy reach. For these patients the sea voyage, railway journey, and mountain climbing, where the paths are at all dangerous, should be rigorously excluded. Their excursions should be in the form of walks or by carriage through some quiet, pleasant region, where means of self-destruction may be as remote as possible, rather than existing at hand and readily available.

In recommending travel, it is to be borne in mind that long, wearisome journeys are to be avoided. The fatigue, excitement and worry incident to laborious sight-seeing tend to increase melncholy and insomnia, and often excite new fears in the morbid mind of the sufferer.

In some foreign hospitals the dark room, seclusion, and rest in bed are favorite procedures in the treatment of melancholia, but the foremost alienists of our time do not countenance these methods. The open air, exercise and congenial companionship are almost essentials of treatmen, if we are to expect recovery.

Occupation is another factor that should not be overlooked. The patient will often firmly believe that he cannot do work of any kind and that he is no longer of any use in the world. A little effort on the part of the physician or nurse will often dispel this idea sufficiently to make a start. It matters little what the employment may be, so long as it necessitates some physical activity. Garden work, mechanical construction, painting, etc., are all valuable aids to treatment. When a start of this kind is once made, a long step toward recovery has been taken. Hope has been planted, where before there was only despair. In our hospitals special shops are provided for the express purpose of carrying out this idea. In them our patients are engaged in making clothing, boots and shoes, mattresses, brooms and brushes of all kind, and in the upholstery of furniture, and we are confident that in many cases improvement that has gone on to recovery has dated from the moment the patient first began to be interested in mechanical work.

Fully 90 per cent of melacholiacs present the condition and and appearance of bodily ill-health; the vital forces are subnormal, the appetite has failed, food has been taken in insufficient quantities and poorly digested, and there has been loss in weight, strength and muscular energy. Sometimes these patients eat but little through a mistaken notion that the stomach and bowels no longer preform their functions or that they act to but a little degree. Constipation is a common symptom and is often the foundation for more or less elaborate delusions. The physical condition at once indicates the proper treatment, for these patients will invariably be benefited by liberal ingestion of wholesome food. Feeding the melancholiacs is far more important than the administration of medicine—good, wholesome food, such as meats, eggs, and liberal quantities of milk are to be given, rather than the juices, extracts, and teas that are commonly found in the sick room. Persuade him, if possible, to take not only his regular meals, but eggs and milk between meals. Often the patient will object to this kind of diet and assert that in his deplorable condition it will do him harm, but this idea must be combated with firmness and persistence even to the extent of artificial feeding by means of the stomach tube, if necessary. Under the influence of a liberal diet with some mild laxative after meals the coated tongue, foul breath, and constipation will usually soon give place to a vastly improved state of bodily health and along with this betterment in the physical condition we may look for a better mental state. Indeed every pound gained in weight is an additional prop on which to base prognosis of recovery. Many of these patients do well with a moderate use of mild stimulants, malt liquors are acceptable to some, while others do best on a little Port or Burgundy wine.

Forcible feeding should be held as a last resort, to be used only after the utmost persuasion, either by the physician or by a trained nurse has failed. Sometimes patients who refuse food when it is brought to them will eat heartily if the food is left within reach while the attendant turns his attention to other matters and appears to take no notice—others will need to be fed with the stomach tube. It not infrequently happens that one feeding with the tube is followed by ready compliance when the request to eat is made.

Among tonics, strychnine sulfate is of value, especially in mild cases. It is a tonic to the whole system. It stimulates peristalsis and seems to have a selective action on the digestion. The appetite is improved and the bowels are aided in the preformance of their functions. It should be given in 1.60 to 1.30 grain doses before eating.

Iron is usually recommended in text-books, but practical experience demonstrates that generally it is not acceptable to the stomach in these cases. One form, however, the Elixir Calisaya ferri et strychninae, dose f zi to f zii is of value, as it is not so apt to derange digestion. If prescribed it should always be given guardedly and its effects closely observed.

A symptom to be looked for and carefully treated is constipatiou. In hospitals where facilities are to be had the daily enema of inspissated ox bilo, (mx) olive oil, (ziv) glycerine (ziv) or soap suds (oi) (given with a soft tube, twenty inches in length) is superior to any cathartic. If for any reason this is impractical, magnesium sulfate is a desirable alternative. If neither is possible, any cathartic, preferably the least irritating, should be given. The fluid extract of Cascara Sagrada, the pill of Aloin, Strychnine and Belladonna, and the officinal Mistura Rhei et Sodae are of great value.

Insomnia is an important symptom in many of these mild cases of melancholia. It appears early and often causes depression. These patients must be made to sleep. Sleep "that knits up the ravelled sleeve of care" is so essential to the refreshment of the whole nervous mass underlying consciousness, that without it we cannot hope for restoration of the normal mind. To induce sleep, in many cases, the hot bath at bed time will be found highly effective. The patient should enter the bath at 90 degrees. The temperature should then be gradually raised to 105 degrees.The bath should continue for about fifteen minutes, when the patient should be removed, given a glass of hot milk, rubbed thoroughly dry and placed in bed. If the patient is weak this treatmnet may properly be preceded by a little sherry wine, or whiskey and water, with advantage. He should sleep in a cool, quiet room, well aired.

With some patients a bowl of hot milk or gruel at bed time will suffice to induce sleep, others require drugs. But whatever remedy may be necessary, the patient must be made to sleep, if possible. To accomplish this end many drugs are available, but the most valuable is undoubtedly opium. Objection has been made to opium for various reasons, but the weight of experience is in favor of its use. We find its various forms effective with many patients, but especially with those advanced in years and physically feeble, for it relievs much of the mental pain during waking hours, besides inducing refreshing sleep through the night. Either the tincture or the solid opium should be administered,rather than the preparations of morphine, which are more apt to cause stomach or other nervous disturbances. Opium may be advantageously combined with chloral or hyoscyamus, both of which drugs often act very favorably in these cases. Other hypnotics, such as paraldehyd, sufonal, and trional are also of value and should be tried successively,if found necessary. The bromides, however, should be avoided, as they are apt to interfere with digestion and cause emaciation and increased depression. As to the time when hypnotics should be medicine no rule can be laid down. Some patients will require the medicine when about to retire, while others will fall asleep immediately on going to bed and awaken after an hour or two and remain restless the greater part of the night, unless some hypnotic be administered. Whatever hypnotic is given, care must be exercised to avoid excesses, and variety is to be preferred to the prolonged use of one drug.

In an ordinary case of simple melancholia without a definite history of suicidal tendencies what is the risk of suicide? In estimating this risk the first thing to be considered is the duration of the depression, if it has existed for several months is mild in type and comparatively stationary—if the patient has given no intimation of meditation on self-destruction, the risk is comparatively small; if, on the other hand, the duration of mental depression has been but a few weeks and the melancholy has been steadily increasing, if the patient is strongly inclined to avoid association with friends or other persons and to seclude himself, the risk is much greater. Immediately, on awaking from sleep, especially during the early morning hours, is often the period of greatest gloom and depression, and it is at this time that thought of self-destructioin is most likely to occur. In the great majority of cases melancholiacs are at their worst during the early hours of the day and at their best in the evening. It is, therefore, especially necessary to keep watchful eyes upon them during this period of dangre.

To briefly sum up the treatment of these cases the principal objects to keep in view are these—guard your patient carefully against either voluntary or involuntary accidents—see that he partakes of a liberal diet and induce sleep. Keep him in the open air as much as possible, and give him something to do. Often when our best efforts are spent to achieve these ends our patients will grow worse instead of better. The melancholia will become more and more profound, delusions and hallucinations will dominate the mental field and suicidal ideas will recur more and more frequnetly. When such conditions develop, all thought of home treatment should be abandoned and the patient at once taken to a hospital, where special facilities for safe and proper care are provided.

"RELATION OF MOSQUITOES TO MALARIA."

BY ARTHUR W. BOOTH, M. D., ELMIRA, N. Y.

The propogation of malaria by mosquitoes appears to be of some medico-legal interest. And at the suggestion of Mr. Clark Bell, it is a pleasure to submit an abbreviation of my paper recently read before "The Lake Keuka Medical and Surgical Association."

From the earliest medical writers, we learn that mankind, especially, that portion living in tropical and subtropical countries, suffered from malaria. Hippocrates recognized the disease and described the various forms, tertian, quartan, etc. He believed the fever was due to use of drinking water obtained from marshes.

Galen, in the 2nd century, taught the presence of a "marsh-poison." which contaminated the air.

Avicenna, an Arabian physician of the 10th century, is credited with referring the evil effects to the exhalations from vegetable decomposition in the water. A view that was popularly accepted and affected legislation in several European countries, in which the steeping of flax and hemp in springs, public reservoirs and ponds was prohibited under heavy penalties.

Indeed, for ages, this idea of a miasm has pervaded all thought upon the subject, as witness its name, malaria (bad air).

The idea that mosquitoes bear a casual relation to the spread of malaria appears to have been suggested in very early times. The Roman writers, Varro, Vitruvius and Columella commented upon the possibility. In Eastern Africa, malaria and the mosquito are called by the same name, Mbu.

In America, Dr. Nott, of New Orleans, in 1848, referred to the idea as a fact already known. And in 1883, Dr. A. L. A. King, of Washington, read a masterly paper before the Philosophical Society of Washington propounding the idea that mosquitoes transmitted malaria.

Read before Lake Keuka Medical and Surgical Association, August 13, 1901, and contributed to the Medico-Legal Journal.

His paper was received with general incredulity.

Our first definite knowledge of malaria dates from Laveran's discovery of his famous Plasmodium. This was announced in 1880, and was first seen by Laveran while examining the blood of French soldiers, suffering from malaria, stationed at Algiers.

For the past two decades, the medical profession has accepted Laveran's Plasmodium as the true germ of malaria. Although, it must be confessed, upon rather inadequate data. We simply knew that the germ was found usually in cases of the disease, and that it was not found in any other condition. Where the germ came from and how it entered the human body remained unsolved.

Before entering upon these questions, let us consider the behavior of the germ within the body, as observed by Laveran and his successors. Today, the term malaria is restricted to those intermittent and remittent fevers, characterized by periodic "chill, fever and sweat," and associated with some form of Laveran's Plasmodium in the blood. Each type of malaria is caused by a distinct species of plasmodia. They are not, so far as is known, interchangeable. The paroxysm of chill, fever and sweat occurs at a certain stage of development of the germ within the red blood corpuscle. This development varies with each species, thus in tertian malaria, it requires 48 hours to complete the life cycle. Tracing this 48 hour cycle we see the following: Within a red blood cell, we find a clear hyaline body, this bit of protoplasm possesses amoeboid movement and takes on various shapes. (amoebula stage).

Later, the amoebula becomes pigmented, it is devouring the blood cell. Then the pigment granules move about and begin to assume definite shape. The plasmodium then undergoes a remarkable change, lines of radiate striation appear, giving it a rosette-like figure composed of 12 to 20 parts. (segmentation) This proceeds until each segment becomes a spherule. The blood cell then bursts and the spherules escape into the blood current, after which they are called Sporocysts. These Sporocysts enter new blood corpuscles and begin a new cycle of corporeal life as young plasmodia. This asexual generation from sporocysts to adult plasmodia may continue indefinitely within the human body and this is the extent of our knowledge of malaria propogation until a very recent date.

In observing the above growth of a crop of plasmodia, it will be found that not all the cells undergo segmentation, some become pigmented and remain dormant and ultimately are devoured by the white blood corpuscles. However, if these same cells are removed to a warm stage and studied under the microscope, a still more marvelous change ensues. Some swell up while others throw out long thread-like arms, this is termed "Flagellation." The swollen ones represent the female and flagellated once the male. Nothing further would occur upon a warm stage, but under proper conditions, a true sexual generation follows.

This appropriate nidus is the stomach of a certain genus of mosquito. The Anopheles or so-called "malaria mosquito." Within the stomach of the Anopheles, the flagella of the male bodies detach themselves and seek the female parasite, they fuse, quite suggestive of the manner of spermatozoa and ovum. These fertilized females, called Zygotes, immediately work their way through the stomach of the Anopheles and lodge just within the outer muscular stomach wall. Rapid growth follows until they are 5 times their previous size. Clear zones appear, called Centromeres, and about the centromeres are seen innumerable very minute black lines. These under high magnification are found to be independent spindle-shaped cells. Eventually, the swollen Zygote bursts and the black spindle cells, called Blasts, invade the body of the mosquito. The blasts find their way to the salivary gland of the mosquito and are inoculated into the next human victim where they enter the blood current and develop into the amoebula stage already referred to in describing the corporeal life of a plasmodium.

Strictly speaking, a mosquito does not bite its victim, but rather aspirates a small quantity of blood used for food, but previous to the act of sucking, it injects a minute portion of an irritant under the skin to produce hyperaemia and cousequently a freer flow of blood. During this preliminary the blasts gain access to the blood of man.

The source of infection thus gravitates from man to mosquito and from mosquito to man. Man is the temporary host and the moquito is the definitive host of the plasmodium.

Only such Anopheles are infectious as have first obtained the germ from man.

Only one genus is capable of acting as extra-corporeal host, the genus Anopheles.

This in brief constitutes the so-called mosquito theory which is no longer a theory but a well established truth.

Earnest investigators abroad and in America have worked laboriously for years to complete the life history of the malaria germ. Their experiments have been checked by elaborate "controls." Unusual heroism has been displayed by many who subjected their ownselves, at the risk of death, to experimental inoculations from mosquitoes known to be infected by virulent malaria. The classic experiments conducted in the Roman Campagna and in India are too well known to require more than mention. The idea of extra-corporeal host for human parasites is not a new one, we have examples in the Tenia Echinococcus and Filiaria Sanguinis Hominis.

Allied forms of malaria in the lower animals present a similar alteration of generation between the animals and other genera of mosquitoes. In fact, the study of these lower forms of malaria contributed largely to the success of investigation of human malaria.

Our most familiar mosquito belongs to the genus Culex, a harmless variety as regards malaria. The Culex promptly digests human malarial parasites. The Culex breeds rapidly and everywhere in brackish water, stagnant pools, swamps and rain barrels.

The Anopheles selects rather more permanent still water, as it requires longer to hatch and develop. Such pools that support a luxuriant growth of Algae upon which the larvae feed.

The Anopheles differs in many respects from the commoner Culex.

The adult possesses palpi or feelers nearly as long as the probosis (beak), while the palpi of Culex are quite short.

The wings of Anopheles are spotted (dapple winged), while the wings of Culex are not. When resting on the ceiling of a room, the Anopheles holds its body nearly at right angles to the ceiling, while the Culex rests parallel thereto. The singing note of Anopheles (female) is lower than that of Culex. The sensation of the sting is not so severe as that of the Culex, this accounts for the frequent denial of malarial patients that they have suffered from any mosquitoes.

A curious fact about malaria mosquitoes is that only the female attacks man and usually at night.

At present, scientists are endeavoring to devise means to exterminate the mosquito. Among other measures advocated are spraying the breeding waters with petroleum, the oil clogs the respiratory apparatus of the larvae, and Dr. Doty, of New York, believes it also destroys the eggs. This method was in vogue at Cornell University some years ago.

Various other chemicals have been suggested, but none are so inexpensive as crude petroleum.

Introduction of voracious fish that feed upon the larvae.

It has been suggested to propogate certain dragon flies that feed upon the larvae. Systematic drainage will help solve the problem.

While we are waging war upon the mosquito, it might be well to bear in mind the very important fact that man, himself, is the real culprit. It is he who supplies the mosquito with the plasmodia. It is not unreasonable that society should demand of malarial patients proper isolation by suitable netting, so that the Anopheles may not acquire his malarial blood and thus be the means of infecting the neighborhood. Malaria ought to be regarded as an infectious disease. Some one has speculated upon the possibility of utilizing the Anopheles mosquito for criminal purposes. This is not fantastic in the least. Some types of malaria are quite virulent, and mosquitoes infected with this type could readily be liberated into sleeping rooms of intended victims, with very small chance of detection.

A large mass of valuable literature on the subject of malaria has appeared recently in the medical journals, and the lay press has attempted to explain in non-technical language the salient points.

However, from an extensive inquiry, I glean that the average individual has lost sight of the main points, viz.: That only the Anopheles transmits malaria and then only after having first obtained the germ from a human subject.

Among the articles recently published in English, the following deserve especial mention:

"Malaria According to the New Researches," Prof. Angelo Celli, Rome. English translation by John Joseph Eyre.

"Malaria and Certain Mosquitoes," L. O. Howard, Chief Entomologist, U. S. Agriculture Department. See Century Magazine, April, 1901.

"The Inoculation of Malaria by the Mosquito; A review of the Literature," Irving P. Lyon, M. D., Buffalo. N. Y. Med. Rec., Feb. 17, 1900.

EDITORIAL.

THE LONDON CONGRESS OF TUBERCULOSIS.

This gathering in the British capital possesses unusual interest throughout the civilized world, and will as a result increase and intensify the efforts now being considered and made among the foremost nations in the direction of the legalized suppression of tuberculosis.

The paper of Prof. Koch was certainly the more exciting, because its contents were so wholly unexpected. It has aroused a storm of criticism on both sides of the Atlantic.

To clearly understand the situation it is necessary to understand exactly what Professor Koch said. We quote from his paper entitled "The fight against Tuberculosis in the light of the Experience gained in the successful combat of other infectious diseases," a few of the more important sentences regretting that the space at our disposal does not permit) the full text of the most intensely interesting paper read before the body.

Under the heading "Tuberculosis a Preventable Disease," Prof. Koch said:

Strictly speaking, the fact that tuberculosis is a preventable disease ought to have become clear as soon as the tubercle bacillus was discovered, and the properties of this parasite and the manner of its transmission became known. I may add that I, for my part, was aware of the full significance of this discovery from the first, and so would everybody have been who had convinced himself of the causal relation between tuberculosis and the tubercle bacillus. But the strength of a small number of medical men was inadequate to the conflict with a disease so deeply rooted in our habits and customs. Such a conflict requires the co-operation of many, if possible of all, medical men, shoulder to shoulder with the State and the whole population. The moment when such co-operation is possible seems now to have come. I suppose there is hardly any medical man now who denies the parasitic nature of tuberculosis, and among the non-medical public, too, the knowledge of the nature of the disease has been widely propagated.

Speaking of "The Source of Infection," he says:

Now the question is whether what has hitherto been done, and what is about to be done, against tuberculosis, really strikes the root of tuberculosis, so that it must sooner or later die.

In order to answer this question it is necessary first and foremost to inquire how infection takes place in tuberculosis. Of course, I presuppose that we understand by tuberculosis only those morbid conditions which are caused by the tubercle bacillus.

In by far the majority of cases of tuberculosis the disease has its seat in the lungs, and has also begun there. From this fact it is justly concluded that the germs of the disease, that is, the tubercle bacilli, must have got into the lungs by inhalation. As to the question where the inhaled tubercle bacilli have come from, there is also no doubt. On the contrary, we know with certainty that they get into the air with the sputum of consumptive patients. This sputum, especially in advanced stages of the disease, almost always contains tubercle bacilli, sometimes in incredible quantities. By coughing, and even speaking, it is flung into the air in little drops, that is, in a moist condition, and can at once infect persons who happen to be near the coughers. But it may also be pulverized when dried, in the linen or on the floor, for instance, and get into the air in the form of dust.

In this manner a complete circle, a so-called circulus vitiosus, has been formed for the process of infection from the diseased lung, which produces phlegm and pus containing tubercle bacilli, to the formation of moist and dry particles (which, in virtue of their smallness, can keep floating a good while in the air), and finally to new infection, if particles penetrate with the air into a healthy lung and originate the disease anew. But the tubercle bacilli may get to other organs of the body in the same way, and thus originate other forms of tuberculosis. This, however, is considerably rarer. The sputum of consumptive people, then, is to be regarded as the main source of the infection of tuberculosis. On this point, I suppose, all are agreed. The question now arises whether there are not other sources too, copious enough to demand consideration in the combatting of tuberculosis.

Great importance used to be attached to the hereditary transmission of tuberculosis. Now, however, it has been demonstrated by thorough investigation that, though hereditary tuberculosis is not absolutely non-existent, it is nevertheless extremely rare, and we are at liberty, in considering our practical measures, to leave this form of origin entirely out of account.

Upon these topics no controversy will be found to exist among medical men of any extent or importance.

HUMAN SPUTUM THE MAIN SOURCE OF HUMAN TUBERCULOSIS.

So the only main source of the infection of tuberculosis is the sputum of consumptive patients, and the measures for the combating of tuberculosis must aim at the prevention of the dangers arising from its diffusion.

Upon the questions of "Differences Between Human and Bovine Tuberculosis" and the further question "Is Man Susceptible to Bovine Tuberculosis," which are the battle ground of the present conflict. Prof. Koch says of the former of these subjects:

But another possibility of tuberculosis infection exists, as is generally assumed, in the transmission of the germs of the disease from tuberculous animals to man. This manner of infection is generally regarded nowadays as proved, and as so frequent, that it is even looked upon by not a few as the most important, and the most rigorous measures are demanded against it. In this congress also the discussion of the danger with which the tuberculosis of animals threatens man will play an important part. Now, as my investigations have led me to form an opinion deviating from that which is generally accepted, I beg your permission, in consideration of the great importance of this question, to discuss a little more thoroughly.

Genuine tuberculosis has hitherto been observed in almost all domestic animals, and most frequently in poultry and cattle. The tuberculosis of poultry, however, differs so much from human tuberculosis that we may leave it out of account as a possible source of infection for man. So, strictly speaking, the only kind of tuberculosis remaining to be considered is the tuberculosis of cattle, which, if really transferable to man, would indeed have frequent opportunities of infecting human beings through the drinking of the milk and the eating of the flesh of diseased animals.

Even in my first circumstantial publication on the etiology of tuberculosis I expressed myself regarding the identity of human tuberculosis and bovine tuberculosis with reserve. Proved facts, which would have enabled me sharply to distinguish these two forms of the disease, were not then at my disposal; but sure proofs of their absolute identity were equally undiscoverable, and I therefore had to leave this question undecided. In order to decide it I have repeatedly resumed the investigations relating to it, but so long as I experimented on small animals, such as rabbits and guinea pigs, I failed to arrive at any satisfactory result, though indications which rendered the difference of the two forms of tuberculosis probable were not wanting. Not till the complaisance of the Ministry of Agriculture enabled me to experiment on cattle, the only animals really suitable for these investigations, did I arrive at absolutely conclusive results. Of the experiments which I have carried out during the last two years along with Professor Schutz, of the Veterinary College in Berlin, I will tell you briefly some of the most important.

A number of young cattle which had stood the tuberculin test, and might therefore be regarded as free from tuberculosis, were infected in various ways with tubercle bacilli takn from cases of human tuberculosis; some of them got the tuberculous sputum of consumptive patients direct. In some cases the tubercle bacilli or the sputum were injected under the skin; in others into the peritoneal cavity; in others into the jugular vein. Six animals were fed with tuberculous sputum amost daily for seven or eight months; four repeatedly inhaled great quantities of bacilli, which were distributed in water, and scattered with it in the form of spray. None of these cattle(there were nineteen of them) showed any symptoms of disease, and they gained considerably in weight. From six to eight months after the beginning of the experiments they were killed. In their internal organs not a trace of tuberculosis was found, only at the places where the injections had been made small supperative foci had formed, in which tubercle bacilli could be found. This is exactly what one finds when one injects dead tubercle bacilli under the skin of animals liable to contagion. So, the animals we experimented on were affected by the living bacilli of human tuberculosis exactly as they would have been by dead ones; they were absolutely insusceptible to them.

The result was utterly different, however, when the same experiment was made on cattle free from tuberculosis with tubercle bacilli that came from the lungs of an animal suffering from bovine tuberculosis. After an incubation period of about a week the severest tuberculous disorders of the internal organs broke out in all the infected animals. It was all one whether the infecting matter had been injected only under the skin or into the peritoneal cavity or the vascular system. High fever set in, and the animals became weak and lean; some of them died after a month and a half to two months; others were killed in a miserably sick condition after three months. After death extensive tuberculous infiltrations were found at the place where the injections had been made, and in the neighboring lymphatic glands, and also far advanced alterations of the internal organs,, especially the lungs and the spleen. In the cases in which the injection had been made into the peritoneal cavity the tuberculous growths which are so characteristic of bovine tuberculosis, were found on the omentum and peritoneum. In short, the cattle proved just as susceptible to infection by the bacillus of bovine tuberculosis as they had proved insusceptible to infection by the bacillus of human tuberculosis. I wish only to add that preparations of the organs of the cattle which were artificially infected with bovine tuberculosis in these experiments are exhibited in the Museum of Pathology and Bacteriology.

An almost equally striking distinction between human and bovine tuberculosis was brought to light by a feeding experiment with swine. Six young swine were fed daily for three months with the tuberculous sputum of consumptive patients. Six other swine received bacilli of bovine tuberculosis with their food daily for the same period. The animals that were fed with the sputum remained healthy and grew lustily, whereas those that were fed with the bacilli of bovine tuberculosis soon became sickly, were stunted in their growth, and half of them died. After three months and a half the surviving swine were all killed and examined. Among the animals that had been fed with sputum no trace of tuberculosis was found, except here and there little nodules in the lymphatic glands of the neck, and in one case a few gray nodules in the lungs. The animals, on the other hand, which had eaten bacilli of bovine tuberculosis had, without exception (just as in the cattle experiment), severe tuberculous diseases, especially tubercular infiltration of the greatly enlarged lymphatic glands of the neck and of the mesenteric glands, and also extensive tuberculosis of the lungs and the spleen.

The difference between human and bovine tuberculosis appeared not less strikingly in a similar experiment with asses, sheep and goats, into whose vascular systems the two kinds of tubercle bacilli were injected.

Our experiments, I must add, are not the only ones that have led to this result. If one studies the older literature of the subject and collates the reports of the numerous experiments that were made in former times by Chauveau, Gunther, Harms, Bollinger and others, who fed calves, swine and goats with tuberculous material, one finds that the animals that were fed with the milk and pieces of the lungs of tuberculous cattle always fell ill of tuberculosis, whereas those that received human material with their food did not. Comparative investigations regarding human and bovine tuberculosis have been made very recently in North America by Smith, Dinwiddie, Frothingham and Repp, and their result agreed with ours. The unambiguous and absolutely conclusive results of our experiments are due to the fact that we chose methods of infection which exclude all sources of error, and carefully avoided everything connected with the stalling, feeding and tending of the animals that might have a disturbing effect on the experiments.

Considering all these facts, I feel justified in maintaining that human tuberculosis differs from bovine, and cannot be transmitted to cattle. It seems to be very desirable, however, that these experiments should be repeated elsewhere, in order that all doubt as to the correctness of my assertion may be removed.

I wish only to add that, owing to the great importance of this matter, our government has resolved to appoint a commission to make further inquiries on the subject.

Upon the second proposition which is the crucial question of the hour, Prof. Koch says:

But, now, how is it with the susceptibility of man to bovine tuberculosis? This question is far more important to us than that of the susceptibility of cattle to human tuberculosis, highly important as that is, too. It is impossible to give this question a direct answer, because, of course, the experimental investigation of it with human beings is out of the question. Indirectly, however, we can try to approach it. It is well known that the milk and butter consumed in great cities very often contain large quantities of the bacilli of bovine tuberculosis in a living condition, as the numerous infection experiments with such dairy products on animals have proved. Most of the inhabitants of such cities daily consume such living and perfectly virulent bacilli of bovine tuberculosis, and unintentionally carry out the experiment which we are not at liberty to make. If the bacilli of bovine tuberculosis were able to infect human beings, many cases of tuberculosis caused by the consumption of alimenta containing tubercle bacilli could not but occur among the inhabitants of big cities, especially the children. And most medical men believe that this is actually the case.

In reality, however, it is not so. That a case of tuberculosis has been caused by alimenta can be assumed with certainty only when the intestine suffers first; that is, when a so-called primary tuberculosis of the intestines is found. But such cases are extremely rare. Among many cases of tuberculosis examined after death, I myself remember having seen preliminary tuberculosis of the intestine only twice. Among the great post-mortem material of the Charite Hospital in Berlin, 10 cases of primary tuberculosis of the intestine occurred in 5 years. Among 933 cases of tuberculosis in children at the Emperor Frederick's Hospital for Children, Baginsky never found tuberculosis of the intestine without simultaneous disease of the lungs and the bronchial glands. Among 3,104 post-mortem examinations of tuberculous children, Biedert observed only 16 cases of primary tuberculosis of the intestine. I could cite from the literature of the subject many more statistics of the same kind, all indubitably showing that primary tuberculosis of the intestine, especially among children, is a comparatively rare disease; and of these few cases that have been enumerated, it is by no means certain that they were due to infection by bovine tuberculosis. It is just as likely that they were caused by the widely propagated bacilli of human tuberculosis, which may have got into the digestive canal in some way or other; for instance, by swallowing saliva from the mouth. Hitherto nobody could decide with certainty in such a case whether the tuberculosis of the intestine was of human or of animal origin. Now we can make the diagnosis. All that is necessary is to cultivate in pure culture the tubercle bacilli found in the tuberculous material, and to ascertain whether they belong to bovine tuberculosis by inoculating cattle with them. For this purpose I recommend subcutaneous injection, which yields quite specially characteristic and convincing results. For half a year I have occupied myself with such investigations, but, owing to the rareness of the disease in question, the number of the cases I have been able to investigate is but small. What has hitherto resulted from this investigation does not support the assumption that bovine tuberculosis occurs in man.

Though the important question whether man is susceptible to bovine tuberculosis at all, is not yet absolutely decided, and will not admit of absolute decision to-day or to-morrow, one is nevertheless already at liberty to say that, if such a susceptibility really exists, the infection of human beings is but a very rare occurrence. I should estimate the extent of the infection by the milk and flesh of tuberculous cattle, and the butter made of their milk, as hardly greater than that of hereditary transmission, and I therefore do not deem it advisable to take any measures against it.

Prof. Koch concluded his paper with special consideration of the subjects of:

What is to be done in the direction of arresting the disease by preventing its diffusion through human infected spulm?

The foci of Tuberculosis infection especially in large cities; The need of hospitals for consumtives; Obligatory notification; Disinfection; Education of the public; Sanitoria, and concludes as follows:

If now, in conclusion, we glance back once more to what has been done hitherto for the combating of tuberculosis, and forward to what has still to be done, we are at liberty to declare with a certain satisfaction that very promising beginnings have already been made. Among these I reckon the consumption hospitals of England, the legal regulations regarding notification in Norway and Saxony, the organization created by Biggs in New York—the study and imitation of which I most urgently recommend to all municipal sanitary authorities—the sanatoria, and the instruction of the people. All that is necessary is to go on developing these beginnings, to test, and if possible to increase their influence on the diminution of tuberculosis, and wherever nothing has yet been done, to follow the examples set elsewhere.

If we allow ourselves to be continually guided in this enterprise by the spirit of genuine preventive medical science, if we utilize the experience gained in conflict with other pestilences, and aim with clear recognition of the purpose and resolute avoidance of wrong roads, at striking the evil at its root, then the battle against tuberculosis, which has been so energetically begun, cannot fail to have a victorious issue.

The copy of Prof. Koch's paper from which we quote, is from the Boston Medical and Surgical Journal of August 1, 1901, and we advise every student to read all of Prof. Koch's paper.

The conclusions to which the London Congress of Tuberculosis arrived may be best shown by the final resolutions adopted. The following resolution proposed by Dr. Hillier was adopted:

That this section is of opinion that a permanent international committee should be appointed (1) to collect and report upon measures that had been adopted for the prevention of tuberculosis in different countries; (2) to publish a popular statement of these measures; (3) to keep and publish periodically a record of scientific researches in relation to tuberculosis; (4) to consider and recommend measures of prevention for the guidance and information of the governments of states and local authorities.

This congress is further of opinion that such a committee should consist of representatives to be elected by the great national societies for the prevention of tuberculosis, and also of representatives nominated by various governments.

Prof. Delcprine, of Manchester moved the following resolution, which was adopted:

That in the opinion of the State section of the congress the statement made by Professor Koch, as to the danger of consuming tuberculous meat and milk, gives rise to serious administrative difficulties in this country. Such difficulties can only be removed by the confirmation or disapproval of Professor Koch's conclusions, and this section is therefore of opinion that the congress, as a whole, should appoint a deputation to wait upon the president of the Local Government Board and the president of the Board of Agriculture for the purpose of bringing these to their notice.

Mr. Hoffman, Statistican of the Prudential Life Insurance Company, proposed the following resolution, which was adopted·

That, whereas it is in evidence that the further reduction of mortality of tuberculosis is of the greatest financial importance to insurance companies, in the opinion of this section such companies should endeavor to give the greatest publicity to the most essential and easily comprehended facts as to the treatment and prevention of consumption.

Sir James Crichton Browne proposed the following resolution, which after considerable discussion and amendments proposed were defeated, was adopted unanimously:

That, in the opinion of this section, the provision of sanatoria is an indispensable condition for the treatment and diminution of tuberculosis, and that the duty of providing such sanatoria should devolve on the county councils.

PUNISHMENT.

Dr. C. A. Mercier, M. B., presented at the May meeting of the Medico Psychological Association of Great Britain a paper under the above heading of great interest.

We regret we cannot give it entire, but feel glad to make some quotations. Dr. Mercier said:

You will remember that the first time I brought the subject forward, it was in connection with the thesis that every lunatic is not necessarily to be considered exempt from punishment; that most lunatics ought properly to be punished for some of their wrongdoings; and that the practice in every asylum is to punish lunatics upon occasion. To this it was objected that although the fact was admitted that we do pursue towards lunatics the same course of conduct that is called punishment when applied to sane people, yet, when applied to lunatics, it is not punishment, because we dare not call it punishment.

Whatever pain is brought upon a man by his own conduct, of whatever description, in whatever department of activity, is, for him, punishment, and in this sense the punishment is a warning that, if he persists in that course of conduct, he will perish.

It has been maintained from the time of Beccaria and of Bentham that punishment is effectual, that is to say, deterrent, in proportion as it is certain and as it is prompt; but this is not the true statement of the deterrent element in punishment. The true statement is that punishment is deterrent in proportion to its known inevitableness, or, to put it otherwise, in proportion to the cohesion or closeness of association, in the mind of the punishee, between the conduct and the pain which is its consequence. It is possible for punishment to be both prompt and certain, and yet to have no deterrent effect whatever. It is possible for punishment to be neither prompt nor certain, nay, to be non-existent, and yet to be very efficiently deterrent.

My contention is that from the point of view of the punisher, punishment is primarily and essentially retaliatory. It is self-protective. It is a fundamental duty which every individual owes to himself, a duty the neglect of which is fatal. Punishment from this point of view is retaliation upon aggression,, and if we allow aggression to pass without retaliation we must perish in the end. It is contended by Lord Justice Fry that the fitness of punishment in sequence to transgression is a fundamental fact of human nature, a moral element incapable of further analysis; but I think that it is possible to reduce it to simpler terms. "Why," says Lord Justice Fry, "do we strive to associate pain with sin? The judge who pronounces sentence on the criminal tries to do this. The parent who punishes his child for a lie strives to do this."

It is a fundamental necessity for every organism that it must protect itself against injury or it must perish. Self preservation has been called the first law of nature, and although this statement is in my opinion erroneous, yet it may fairly be called the second obligation which lies upon every organism. Every organism must protect itself, on pain of death if it neglects the obligation. When we are threatened with injury, we are bound and obliged to take measures to prevent what is threatened. When we are actually in process of being injured we are bound and obliged to repel the injury, and more than this, we must, if we are to be safe, put the assailant into such a position that he cannot repeat his attack. If a man is after me with a revolver, it is not enough for me to dodge the bullets; I shall not be safe until I have deprived him of his weapon. So that it is clear that if retaliation upon injury is to be efficient, is to be preventive, some part of it must be subsequent in time to the actual injury. And then retaliation becomes punishment. From the point of view of the punisher, therefore, punishment is preventive retaliation. It is manifest that efficiency of retaliation upon injury has been, throughout the secular struggle for existence, a very powerful factor in securing the survival of the retaliator; and as all beneficial action will, if continued long enough, become fixed and embodied in an instinct, so has retaliatory action been thus embodied, and thus has been originated and preserved the habit of the pursuit of punishment, or what is called vengeance, that is to say, of pursuing retaliation after the cessation of the injury.

Dr. Mercier, in discussing the deterrent effects of punishment, and in illustration of Herbert Spencer's views, regarding the punishment of children, which he amplifies, says in criticism:—

Compare this system with the system by which our criminals are punished. Whatever the nature of the crime, the punishment is ingeniously devised so as to have no natural connection with it whatever. The man who habitually beats his wife, the man who strikes her in a fit of passion, the shop boy who takes money from his master's till, the vagrant who sleeps under a haystack, the jealous lover who shoots his mistress, the fraudulent trustee who converts trust funds to his own use, the solicitor who contumaciously clings to a document, the wife who poisons her husband, the cabby who gets drunk in his day's work, are all punished in precisely the same way, by precisely the same means, to precisely the same extent, save only in the duration of the punishment. Could anything be more unintelligent? It is the treatment of Dr. Sangrado applied to crime. And not the least of its defects is that it deprives the judge of the exercise of his ingenuity in devising a punishment that would fit the crime. Why should not the thief be compelled to make restitution? Why should not the wife beater be flogged? Why should not the homicide be compelled to work in slavery to support the family of his victim?

But it will be objected, what has this to do with insanity, and with the punishment of insane people? It has this to do with them—that so long as the mind of the lunatic is clear enough to be capable of forming a true and intimate connection between the wrong doing and the punishment which follows it, so long we are justified in inflicting upon him some punishment. I do not say, and I have never said—I have always protested against the position—that lunatics should be treated in the same way and punished with the same severity as sane people; but I still maintain, as I have always maintained, that of the conduct of most lunatics part is sane and part is insane; and that while they may not properly be punished for the insane part of their conduct, they may properly be punished, though with mitigated severity, for wrong doing which belongs to the sane part of their conduct.

The reading of this paper gave rise to a very interesting discussion and a remarkable one in respect to the legal gentlemen who took part in it.

We select from this discussion the remarks of some of those taking part, regretting that we cannot find room for all.

Mr. Montague Crackanthorpe, K. C., said:—

Dr. Mercier, whose argument was not the less cogent because it was concise, began by maintaining that punishment was, in its origin, retaliatory or vindictive, and that it remained so still. I agree with him on the first point; I venture to differ from him on the second. There are many conceptions and institutions now in vogue which are very different from what they were in their origin. Of such, punishment is, in my opinion, one. Dr. Mercier has quoted my friend Sir Edward Fry as an authority for the dictum that criminal punishment is, "suffering following upon sin." With the greatest respect both to Sir Edward and Dr. Mercier, I regard this dictum as of no value from the juridical point of view; and even from a moral standpoint I doubt its propriety, for are we not told in the Scripture, "Vengeance is mine, I will repay, saith the Lord." In this metropolis there is a great deal of unpunished and unpunishable sin. If the law were to deal with sin, as such, the criminal courts would be always open, and as for the unfortunate judges, they would never get a holiday. They have enough to do with dealing with those offences against society which are defined as criminal, and to mix up sin and crime is, to my mind, to obscure the issue.

The next observation I should wish to make is as to the object and end of punishment. I hold that its main object is a double one: (1) to deter others from doing likewise, (2) to restrain the original offender from repeating his offence while his sentence lasts. Its secondary object, which Dr. Mercier did not, I think, mention, is, in my view, to endeavor to reform the criminal. This I regard as a State duty. If the State shuts up a man in gaol for a number of months or years, it should take care not to turn him loose at the end of that time a worse or more helpless man than he was before he was convicted. Many in this room will probably agree that the effect of a long incarceration is to destroy rather than to strengthen the power of will and self-control, because the conditions of prison life are wholly artificial and differ from those of the outside world. Hence it is well to allow a man a certain amount of liberty at the end of his sentence that he may know how to order his own life and be able to grapple wih the difficulties he will have to encounter when he becomes a free man. Our present prison system for adults, in which there is no half-way house resembling that of our juvenile reformatories, leaves much to be desired in this respect.

With regard to the measure of punishment, it would be a great mistake (to use a hackeneyed phrase) to try to "fit the punishment to the crime" without reference to the individual offender. This is what we formerly did in England and what the Code Napoleon would be doing at the present day in France but for the introduction of "extenuating circumstances" which it is competent for the jury to find. Prisoners guilty of the same crime may be of very different kinds and may require very different treatment. All of them may be roughly classed under four heads:—(1) There are those who, in the opinion of experts like yourselves, are totally incapable of distinguishing right from wrong, and who are properly detained "until the pleasure of the Crown shall be made known." These are the insane. (2) There are those who have committed a single crime from passion—*un crime passionel*—as the French say—which they are never likely to repeat, but for which they must be punished by way of warning and example; (3) There are the habitual offenders, the men who steal again and again, or who give way again and again to drink which leads them into other criminal courses, and whose brain is below par, either from hereditary causes or by reason of their own acts of self-indulgence. For these a prison-asylum would be a more fitting place than a gaol as at present conducted. (4) There is the professionl criminal, the man who has several times been previously convicted, and who deliberately pursues the career of preying upon society for his own private ends. This class of person should (and here I agree with Dr. Anderson's recent article) be sequestrated for a considerable period, if not for life, but he, too, should, after a time, be allowed a certain amount of freedom. The element of hope should never be wholly shut out, but he should only be liberated, if at all, when the prison authorities have become satisfied that this may be done with reasonable safety to the community. In this respect he should be placed on the same footing as the inmate of a lunatic asylum who, after long confinement, is discharged as of sound mind. The "interminate sentence" resorted to in some of the States of America has not been without good results.

One other point with regard to the measure of punishment occurs to me. Some persons hold that an educated man who betrays a trust should be punished with a much longer sentence than a common thief who has frequently been convicted of larceny. This at first sight seems reasonable, but I am not sure that it may not sometimes work injustice. The educated man, who has lost the whole of his worldly prospects by reason of his misconduct, has been already punished severely, and it may be unfair to put him on the same level as the professional pickpocket, burglar, or blackmailer who has lost practically nothing, and to whom, in some cases, a prison affords as many material comforts as did the surroundings from which he has been forcibly removed. This matter has not, so far as I am aware, been considered by our judges in conclave. Would it not be well that they should come to some agreement about it, with the view of making their sentences more uniform?

Before sitting down let me again refer for a moment to the test of criminal responsibility known as the rule in MacNaughten's case. It was there laid down, in effect, that the crucial question for the jury was, Did the accused, at the time he committed the act charged, know that he was offending against morals? This test has been conclusively shown by Sir Fitzjames Stephen to be unsatisfactory. And so it is. Whether a jealous husband shoots down his wife's lover in order to vindicate his own honor, as sometimes happens in France, or a burglar stabs a policeman in order to prevent being arrested, as sometimes happens in England, each is, at the time of the act, incapable of distinguishing right from wrong. In the first case, the thirst for revenge; in the second, the desire for liberty, completely deadens all moral sense. If the test of momentary responsibility was applied without discrimination, a large percentage of sane persons must either be acqutted of crime or sent to Broadmoor. Here then, too, there is room for improvement of the law, and it would be for the benefit of the community if the rule in MacNaughten's case were authoritatively re-stated in clearer and more precise terms.

Sir Herbert Stephen said:—

I am glad to find myself in agreement with a good deal of what Dr. Mercier said in his paper. I agree with what I take to be his practical conclusion, namely, that some lunatics ought to be, and probably must be, punished when they do wrong, by those who have the control of them. I also agree that, historically speaking, the infliction of punishment by human beings upon each other was probably founded upon what has been called retaliation, but may perhaps as well be called revenge as anything else. That is to say, the principal sentiment in the minds of the persons who first inflicted punishment probably was, "You have hurt me, and I am going to hurt you." So far I agree, but I go much further. I think that this sentiment of revenge, or retaliation, is still, and will continue to be, the principal ground upon which punishment is based. I differ from those who hold that the idea of revenge in this connection is an archaic barbarism, that it has passed away from the minds of benevolent legislators and administrators of law, and that all that has to be considered in the proper infliction of punishment is, (1) an endeavor to reform or improve the character of the offender, and (2) what has been called its "deterrent" effect upon other persons likely to offend in the same manner. Let us test this opinion by reference to an actual case, and consider how it would work if judges were actually to take into consideration nothing but the improvement of the guilty person's conduct, and the desirability of preventing other people from behaving in the same way. Consider such a case as that of Jabez Balfour, which I specify only because its general features are probably within the recollection of every one present. Jabez Balfour was convicted of a number of frauds by committing which he deprived a great many people, some of them very poor, of all they had. For these crimes he was sentenced to a long term of penal servitude. What would have been the position of the judge who had to pass sentence upon him if he had not been allowed to give effect to any feelings except the wish to improve Balfour's character, and the wish to deter him and others from committing similar offences in future? He would probably have addressed him somewhat in this fashion:—You have been found guilty of extremely grave crimes, and in the ordinary sense of the words you may be considered to deserve severe punishment. But that is in itself no reason for sending you to penal servitude. I am not here to gratify any feelings of animosity, or to make you suffer because others have suffered through you. I have to consider, first, what course of treatment will have the most effect in reforming your character, and making you a useful citizen; and secondly, how I may best prevent you, and similarly evil-minded persons, from perpetrating similar frauds in future. First as to your character. It is manifest that at your age, and after the life you have lived, no punishment that I could inflict would have any effect upon that. It is impossible to suppose that, going into prison as bad a man as you are, you would come out any better. From that point of view, therefore, no punishment would be of any use. Next as to "deterring" you from doing the same things again. In your particular case, sending you to prison would have no such effect. You are not like the professional housebreaker, whose habits are so deeply ingrained that the only way to protect the public from his depredations is to lock him up. He will break into people's houses whenever he is at large, and it may be sometimes necessary to imprison him for a long period on his conviction of an offence trivial in itself. You, on the other hand, are rendered harmless by the mere fact of your conviction and disgrace. All your offences were founded upon the misplaced confidence of rash people, in your supposed intelligence and probity. Your name and character are now universally known, and nobody would be foolish enough to subscribe a shilling to a company of which you were known to be a promoter, nor would any sane person associate himself with you in any such enterprise. The only remaining reason that there could be for subjecting you to punishment would be that other wicked people might be afraid of following your example. The experience of mankind teaches that the fact that disgrace such as yours may culminate in imprisonment, probably has no such "deterrent" effect. Persons who steal on the enormous scale that you do are essentially gamblers. They always hope that things will go well, and that they will realize huge fortunes, and be able to meet all their obligations. They know from the beginning that if they fail they will be utterly ruined and lose all their property, their seats in Parliament, their social consideration, and so forth. That is the penalty which they dread and seek to avoid, and if that risk does not "deter" them from embarking on a course of crime, they will certainly not be "deterred" from the added risk of being sent to prison when they have failed and their offences are discovered. I should therefore serve no useful or humane purpose by sending you to prison, and my order is that you must be bound over in your own recognisance to come up for judgment when called upon.—Can any one suggest that such behavior on the part of the judge would have been anything but a flagrant and inconceivable dereliction of duty? Take again what has been described as the *crime passionel*—the case of a man who finds himself betrayed or disappointed in the master passion of his life, who watches for his successful rival, and kills him deliberately and with aforethought. Such cases are not very common, but they occur now and then, and if you are not angry with such a man for committing murder, why in the world do you want to punish him? It is futile to suggest that his character is likely to be effectively reformed by punishment. The probability is that he was a perfectly respectable and well-conducted person before the crime, but he was one of the few people who, once or twice at most in a lifetime, become so entirely engrossed in a personal affection, that for the moment no other considerations have any effect upon their minds in comparison, and that will continue to be his nature however much, or however little, you punish him. And as for deterring others, when a crime of this kind is committed the offender is, ex hypothesi, perfectly willing to take his chance of any kind of punishment in order to gratify the passion which wholly engrosses him.

In reference to the general question of the reformatory effects of punishment upon the character of adults, I was once making inquiries of a well-known prison official, who was at that time deputy governor of a prison with an average population of about one thousand convicted persons, and I asked him what proportion of that number were, in his opinion, persons with regard to whom there was any hope whatever of improving their characters or doing them any good. He answered, after consideration, "Perhaps four." I do not of course suggest that anything like this is true of what are called "juvenile offenders," but my own belief is that, among criminals twenty years of age and upwards, the hope of making any considerable number of them honest and respectable is chimerical.

In one point I must express total disagreement with Dr. Mercier, and that is in his wish for the introduction of what I may call fancy punishments, of the kind suggested by Bentham. Penal establishments can be conducted only by rule, on lines ascertained beforehand, and life is not long enough for the invention and execution of penalties supposed in each case to have some specific appropriateness to the circumstances of the offence.

It gave me great pleasure to gather from one or two speakers confirmation of an opinion I have lately formed—that we have got pretty well to the end of the old quarrel between you doctors and us lawyers as to the effects of insanity of legal criminal responsibility. I cannot see that there ought to be any quarrel at all. Whether a man is mad is a medical question, upon which we want your advice. Whether he is legally responsible is a legal question, upon which you are interested only in so far as you may be lawyers. The law is, and I believe you will agree that it ought to be, that some men are mad in such a manner as not to be legally responsible although they are mad. The tests actually accepted for distinguishing, in criminal cases, between these two classe are, in my opinion, susceptible of some slight improvement, but the more I see of them the more I am inclined to think that they supply a good working rule, which juries can and do apply with results that are satisfactory in the main. I have noticed of late years that medical witnesses on the Northern Circuit, especially at Liverpool and Manchester, seem to understand perfectly what is and what is not required of them, and to give their willing assistance in the application of the established legal principles to the facts of particular cases.

In conclusion, I wish to reiterate my opinion that the true and ultimate basis of all human punishment is retribution, or retaliation, or revenge, or whatever you like to call it, and that it will continue practicaly to be so whatever any of us may be able to persuade ourselves, or each other, to the contrary.

PRESS NOTICES OF THE AMERICAN CONGRESS OF TUBERCULOSIS.

The Vermont Medical Monthly, under the editorship of H. Edwin Lewis, M. D., is one of the brightest medical journals of New England, or of the country.

We copy from the June number of that journal a considerable portion of its account of the meeting of the American Congress of Tuberculosis. We omit, for want of space, extracts from some of the leading speakers, and cut down to our space much of what he says, but all we cut out is as good as that we quote:

It was a noticeable fact that while the members from away as well as the delegates to the Congress were prominent and representative members of their profession and locality, the members present from New York City, with a few important exceptions, were very far from representing the New York profession. The local leaders of the medical profession were indeed, conspicuous by their absence. That this was so cannot but be regretted for the presence of a goodly number of representative New York medical men was what was needed to make the meeting the most important assembly of scientific men the year 1901 will see. The meeting was a thorough success, just the same, and the men who were not identified with the Congress were the greatest losers.

As always happens in a meeting of scientific men, the ubiquitous crank was in evidence. In this particular instance he assumed the right of attacking all established medical facts. In a paper which could only emanate from an unsound and illogical mind, he denied the infectivity of tuberculosis, the contagiousness of small pox, and all accepted methods of their prevention and cure. Floods of vituperation and a tirade of recrimination for the shortcomings of the medical profession made up the substance of his paper, which by almost unanimous vote was relegated to the oblivion it deserved. But the poor man was more to be pitied than censured. Mental conditions as depicted by those of his class, are truly pitiable and should inspire sympathy rather than disgust. The "Yellow Journals" gave him an unenviable amount of free advertising, ready as they always are to exploit the opinions and actions of the perverted. But we shall not publish the name of the poor wretch for it would carry no weight and we do not care to assist in any way in pulling him from the depths of nonentity to which he properly belongs.

* * *

Several men stood out prominently in the various discussions of the meeting, among the leaders being Dr. Louis Leroy, of Nashville, Professor of Pathology in Vanderbilt University. Dr. Leroy although a young man, showed himself a thoroughly progressive scientific man, fully abreast of medical knowledge, and with an ease and method of expressing himself in public discussion that charmed and edified his hearers. He has a bright future before him.

Dr. H. D. Holton, of Brattleboro, Vt., as President of the Congress, made an admirable presiding officer. He steered the business and discussions of the various sessions with rare tact and skill and many expressions of approval were heard for his ability. Dr. Holton is recognized all over the country as one of the most solid members of the American medical profession. He truly represents the ideal medical man, finely equipped mentally, progressive in knowledge, conservative in expression, but above all an honest God-fearing gentleman.

Clark Bell, was of course, the moving spirit of the whole meeting. To him more than any other one man is due the great success of the American Congress of Tuberculosis. The enormous amount of labor which Mr. Bell threw into the project told in the results obtained. Every member, and delegate present felt the sincerest gratitude and admiration for the man whose executive ability and broad spirit of philanthrophy could bring to a successful focus an assembly of scientific men so laudable in its purposes and so far-reaching in its results.

Other men who left an imprint on the Second Annual Meeting of the American Congress of Tuberculosis were Dr. T. D. Crothers, who is known wherever the English language is spoken for his researches on inebriety: Dr. E. P. Lachapelle, of Montreal, President of the Provincial Board of Health, one of the foremost sanitary workers on the American continent; Dr. J. M. Emmert, of Atlantic, Iowa, a close student and an earnest speaker; Dr. J. Mount Bleyer, of New York City, who knows all that is worth knowing in regard to electricity and its use in disease; Dr. C. K. Cole, of Helena. Montana, a solid medical man: Hon. Moritz Ellinger, of New York, ex-coroner and corresponding secretary of the Medico-Legal Society; Dr. J. H. Pryor, of Buffalo, an earnest and convincing speaker; Dr. J. I. Gibson, of Denison, Iowa, State veterinarian and one of the best speakers and best informed men attending the meeting; Judge Abram H. Dailey, of Brooklyn, a jurist of note; and Dr. W. C. Woodward, of Washington, D. C., Health Officer of the District of Columbia, and a young man who is winning laurels in his chosen field of work.

* * * * *

The Banquet at the Hotel Majestic Thursday evening, May 16th, was a very enjoyable affair. A large number were present to partake of the ample repast, and much satisfaction was expressed for the tempting viands before the assembly. The post prandial exercises were thoroughly enjoyed and among those taking part were Dr. H. D. Holton, of Vermont, Dr. C. F. Ulrich, of West Virginia, Dr. A. N. Bell, of Brooklyn, Dr. C. K. Cole, of Montana, Dr. J. H. Donovan, of Montana, Dr. H. Edwin Lewis, of Vermont, Mrs. Mary Ellen Lease, of Nebraska and Brooklyn, Judge A. H. Dailey, of Brooklyn, and Dr. A. P. Grinnell, of Vermont. Hon. Clark Bell was the efficient Toastmaster.

* * * * *

Dr. A. P. Grinnell was the last speaker at the Banquet, and his remarks were easily the brightest and most amusing of the evening. Dr. Grinnell as a post prandial speaker is without an equal. His humor is delightful and his remarks, always incisive and pertinent, sparkle with pure wit. He invariably holds his audience intensely interested, and convulses them with flashes of genuine humor which have their principal charm in their spontaneity.

HUMAN AND BOVINE TUBERCULOSIS.

The discussion in the public press and in the London Congress has been very extended. It is impossible to give a tithe of the comments of either the lay or the medical press. It came upon the world like a blow and occasioned a mental shock. It was at first construed both in England and America as contradicting the generally received medical opinion of the civilized world upon the danger to man from Bovine Tuberculosis. If correct it would and should arrest proceedings under the arbitrary laws and regulations regarding tuberculous cattle; and by most of the Boards of Health it was felt that it would shake public confidence in sanitary legislation based on aggressive medical opinion. All must realize the overwhelming importance of this question. It is one that must be determined along carefully conducted scientific lines. The scientific world has rarely had a more important problem presented, and its solution bears directly upon all legislation to be presented for consideration.

In the London Congress the English scientists were unprepared for the consideration of such a question, but it was quite clear that the trend of opinion was to dissent from the conclusions of Prof. Koch as to the Bovine and Human Tuberculosis and the liability of man to take the infection from the animal.

Prof. Brouardell, of Paris, made an able address and put himself squarely on record against the views of Prof. Koch as to the communication of tuberculosis to man from bovine tuberculosis. He could not have been prepared for the question or rather could not have known it was to be thus presented, but he voiced the general feeling of dissent to the view of Prof. Koch in France.

In Germany the government was well aware of the experiments made by Prof. Koch with human and bovine tuberculosis, and it is asserted that at his request a government commission has been named there of experts to determine the question of which Virchow and Pollinger are members.

The Executive Board of the American Congress of Tuberculosis we trust will name a commission from among its members, who embrace the highest talent on this side of the Atlantic to make a careful examination and sicentific investigation of this subject, based on careful experiments and make their report at the session of 1902.

HOSPITAL FOR TUBERCULOUS CHILDREN.

It is reported that the King of Italy has donated $40,000 toward the founding of a Hospital for Children suffering from tuberculosis.

France and Germany both are recognizing the needs of special institutions for children predisposed; and near Paris there are already two institutions for such children, one with 120 beds, where the ages range from three to twelve years, and the other 250 beds, ranging from two to sixteen years of age.

The report of the German Central Committee for the suppression of tuberculosis calls attention to the importance of preventive means in large cities for children and the effect of summer outings in diminishing the death rate.

Our best medical educators should consider whether public attention should not be called to the needs of the children of the poor doomed to consumption without precautionary measures are taken for their protection.

THE MISSISSIPPI VALLEY MEDICAL ASSOCIATION

Holds its annual meeting at Put-in-Bay, under the Presidency of Dr. A. H. Cordier, of Kansas City. Dr. Frank Billings, of Chicago, will make the address on Medicine. Dr. Reginald Sayre, of New York, on Surgery.

ANTI TOXIN LABORATORY IN NEW YORK.

The new anti-toxin laboratory of the State Department of Health provided for by last year's legislature, has been opened and the work done in a part of the Bender Laboratory Building at Albany, under the supervision and direction of Dr. H. D. Pease, of the Sheffield Scientific School of Yale University, who will have five trained assistants.

Dr. Daniel Lewis, State Health Commissioner, is enthusiastic over the work and future of the movement. He will supply State institutions with anti-toxin free of cost and municipalities in the State who have no suitable provision for obtaining them. Dr. Blumer, who is director of the bureau of pathology and bacteriology of this department, will have especial charge of examination of sputum from consumptive patients. The announced intention of this State Department is to supply all the Health officers of the State with the same facilities for the investigation, diagnosis and treatment of infectious diseases as have heretofore been supplied to the profession in the City of New York.

We know of no legislation which promises more important results towards the suppression of infectious diseases than this.

THE SUPERVISING SURGEON GENERAL OF THE MARINE HOSPITAL SERVICE OF THE UNITED STATES NAVY.

The following letter was received from Surgeon General Wyman, after the paper "Sanitoria for Consumptives in the United States and the Canadas" had been forwarded to London, and after it was too late to make any notice of the facts stated in General Wyman's note. The author of the paper publishes the letter in the same number of the Journal, in which the article appears as the proper course to pursue.

Washington, August 16, 1901.

Clark Bell, Esq., L. L. D., 39 Broadway, New York, N. Y.

Sir.—In the advance sheets of your article on sanatoria for consumptives in the United States and the Canadas, you say, on page

1, "The question of Sanatoria for the General Government is under the charge of the War and the Navy Departments. These are for the benefit of the soldiers and sailors of the army and navy of the United States and are in charge of the surgeon-generals of the army and navy respectively," and further, on page 2, you say "Walter Wyman, M. D., Supervising Surgeon-General of the United States Marine-Hospital Service, at Washington, D. C., in response to my letter for information on the sanatoria of the Government in relation to tuberculosis in the Navy." From the above, you evidently believe that the Surgeon-General of the Marine-Hospital Service is under the Navy Department and is Surgeon-General of the Navy, which is a mistake; the Marine-Hospital Service is under the Treasury Department and is an entirely separate and distinct service from the Bureau of Medicine and Surgery of the Navy Department, of which Admiral Van Reypen is the Surgeon-General.

Respectfully,
WALTER WYMAN,
Surgeon-General, M. H. S.

TRI-STATE MEDICAL ASSOCIATION.

Physicians of Western Maryland, West Virginia and Wesrern Pennsylvania have organized an association under the above name. At its annual meeting at Cumberland, Md., the following officers were elected:

President—Dr. Wm. F. Barclay, Cumberland, Md.

Vice Presidents—Dr. Henry Hodgson, Cumberland, Md.; Dr. Frank L. Baker, Burlington, W. Va.; Dr. Bruce Lichty, Myersdale, Pa.

Secretary—Dr. Percival Lantz, Alaska, W Va.

Corresponding Secretary—Dr. Fred. W. Fochtman, Cumberland, Md.

Treasurer—Dr. E. B. Claybrook, Cumberland, Md.

SANATORIA.

MINNESOTA.

The Governor of this State has appointed a committee to look into the subject of Sanitoria for Consumptives and report to the next Legislature:

Dr. J. Longstreet Taylor, of St. Paul.

Dr. Geo. S. Waltan, of Warren, Minn.

Dr. Jas. L. Camp, Brainard, Minn.

We shall await their report and action with interest.

COUNTING THE WHITE CORPUSCLE IN BLOOD.

Kourloff in (Vratch) announces a new method of counting the white corpuscle.

It consist of drawing the blood into a graduated pipette, depositing a thin film on two cover glasses, whose surface is measured by a net work of lines.

The white corpuscles are then counted and the area measured by means of the moveable slage and eherlicles diaphragm.

This method does not require haste and can be verified at leisure.

Kourloff claims that he can count from one to two thousand more cells than by the Thomas Zeiss method, as the dilutent used in that process destroys or changes some of the white cells.

INTERNATIONAL ARBITRATION.

The committee on International Law of the American Bar Association report great progress in this work. All the Nations represented have ratified except China, Luxemburg and Turkey. The following countries have named judges of the International Court of Arbitration as provided by the convention:

Austria, Hungary, Belgium, Denmark, France, Great Britain, Italy, Japan, Netherlands, Portugal, Roumania, Russia, Servia, Siam, Spain, Sweden, Norway, Switzerland and the United States.

A code of rules for the court and the International conventions has been adopted.

The International Tribunal is at last organized and is substantially ready for work.

Each party may name two arbitrators from among the judges already selected, and these shall select an umpire. The Court will sit at the the Hague.

CORPORAL PUNISHMENT IN THE PUBLIC SCHOOLS OF THE STATE OF NEW YORK.

An impression has obtained in the public mind that corporal punishment in the public schools was in violation of law.

A rumor that State Superintendent, Hon. Chas. R. Skinner, had decided that teachers in the public schools could not chastise rebellant pupils went the rounds of the press.

Principal Gibbs, of the Spring Valley Union Free School, wrote to the Supreintendent, asking for the facts in the case, says the Montour Falls Free Press, and received the following reply:

"No instructions in regard to corporal punishment have been issued from this department. The law remains as it has been for many years, and while the school law is silent in regard to corporal punishment, section 223 of the penal code provides as follows: 'The use of force or violence upon or toward the person of another is not unlawful when committed by a parent or the authorized agent of any parent, or by any guardian, master, or school teacher in the exercise of a lawful authority to restrain and correct his child, ward, apprentice or scholar, and the force or violence used is reasonable in manner and moderate in degree."

THE ONTARIO MEDICAL ASSOCIATION.

The annual meeting was held June 19th, 20th at Toronto, and elected the following officers:

President—Dr. N. A. Powell, of Toronto.

Vice Presidents—1st, R. Ferguson, London, Ont.; 2nd, R. W. Garrett, Kingston; 3rd, L. C. Provost, Ottawa; 4th, R. L. Turnbull, Goderich.

Secretary—Dr. Harold C. Parsons, Toronto.

Assistant Secretary—Dr. Geo. Elliott, Toronto.

Treasurer—A. R. Gordon, Toronto.

POSTMASTER GENERAL'S MISTAKES.

The Hon. Mr. Madden, Third Assistant Postmaster General is making a crusade against those journals who offer premiums to subscribers.

He should reconstruct his ideas of what the relation of the Postoffice Department should be to publishers and the public.

Every encouragement the Government could make or give to the diffusion spread of and increase of the circulation of literature should be granted. A public officer who uses his position to suppress a journal for offering premiums of a tea sett for example to its subscribers, needs reconstruction as to what the duties of a public official should be; to the people, and especially to the diffusion of knowledge. Would Mr. Madden favor a tax on letters? Would he restrict that splendid position which journalism in the United States has attained? We protest against this action.

THE WHIPPING POST FOR WIFE BEATERS.

The public press of the country favor the *cat* as a proper penalty for wife beaters.

There seems to be quite good reasons for believing that if the wife beater was flogged the offense would cease.

Why public opinion should hesitate to justify the employment of any efficacious remedy to protect the weak and defenseless against the stronger arm is not apparent.

The maimed and bruised wife appeals quite as strongly to our humanitarian impulses as the bare back smarting under the rod of the husband who has beaten the mother of his children; the one he has sworn to love, cherish and protect.

The Chicago Record-Herald thus speaks of this offense editorially:—

MEDICO-LEGAL SOCIETY.

OPENING FALL SESSION.

The September session of the Medico-Legal Society is postponed. The first meeting of the Autumn will be held on the third Wednesday of October, 16th day.

Dr. Mihran K. Kassabian, M. D., of Philadelphia, Pa., will read a paper entitled "The X-Ray in Legal Medicine, with Illustrations of the X-Ray by Static Electricity."

The committee appointed to report to the London Congress of Tuberculosis, and the delegates who attended will make their report.

WHIPPING POSTS.

Tar and feathers, however, are too mild to make any impression upon a man who is enough of a brute to beat his wife.

The New York Herald publishes the remarks of its Chicago contemporary conspicuously on its editorial page, and says:—

True. What is neded is the old-fashioned whipping post, as you suggest. Tar will scrape off, but no man can get rid of ridicule who has been well lashed with a rawhide for beating the woman who does his cooking and gets his children ready for school every day.

It will be a forward and upward step in our civilization if the wife beater disappears with the advent of a punishment that can not be faced or borne, even by a drunken husband.

THE AMERICAN ASSOCIATION OF GENITO-URINARY SURGEONS.

The annual meeting was held at Old Point Comfort, Va., April 30, May 1, 2, 1901. The following officers were elected for 1901:

President—W. T. Belfried, of Chicago, Ill.

Vice President—Dr. Paul Thorndyke, of Boston.

Secretary—Dr. Jas. R. Hayden, of New York.

Member of Council—Dr. Wm. K. Otis, of New York.

The next meeting for 1902 was fixed at Atlantic City.

RESOLUTIONS BY THE MEDICO-LEGAL SOCIETY OF PHILADELPHIA.

The following resolutions were adopted at a recent meeting of this society:

Whereas, the advertising of abortionists and their drugs as well as other disreputable secret medicines has for years been a notorious disgrace to the newspaperdom of this city—an evil seemingly without redress, and

Whereas, The Philadelphia "Times" under its new ownership has declared for a high ethical plane, avoiding all sensationalism, while at the same time furnishing "all the news that is fit to print," excluding all medical and other questionable advertisements—so as to make it indeed a newspaper fit for the family circle, therefore be it

Resolved, that the Medico-Legal Society of Philadelphia highly approves of the advanced stand taken by "The Times," and urges upon the medical profession generally its active support in aiding to carry out that journal's elevated ideas.

Resolved, further, that the medical periodicals of this city be requested to publish the foregoing in their next issue and that, at the coming meeting of this organization, the Secretary report as to which of these, by printing it, have assisted in furthering so desirable a public movement.

THE AMERICAN MEDICAL ASSOCIATION.

The medical profession has honored the State of New York by the selection of its president, Dr. John A. Wyeth, of the City of New York, from that state, as well as Saratoga as its place of meeting. He is one of the leading surgeons of the nation, and worthily fills the position of honor in the National Medical Association.

His work on Surgery shows the honor well bestowed. The physicians of the Empire state have not been as prominent in that body of late as many felt they were entitled to.

Saratoga is an ideal place of meeting.

THE LONDON CONGRESS OF TUBERCULOSIS.

The following were named as delegates from the American Congress of Tuberculosis to the British Congress of Tuberculosis, held in London in July last:

Clark Bell, Esq., LL. D., of New York, General Secretary of the Amerilan Congress of Tuberculosis, Editor Medico Legal Journal.

H. Edwin Lewis, M. D., Editor Vermont Medical Monthly, Burlington, Vermont.

Augustus C. Bernays, M. D., of St. Louis, Mo., delegate appointed by Governor of Missouri.

Geo. Brown, M. D., of Atlanta, Ga., Military Surgeon on staff of Governor of Georgia.

The executive board empowered Clark Bell, Esq., the general secretary, to make additional appointments of delegates to the British Congress of Tuberculosis.

DELEGATES TO THE LONDON CONGRESS OF TUBERCULOSIS.

In addition to the delegates announced from the American Congress of Tuberculosis, the following were appointed delegates:

Dr. J. Leffingwell Hatch, M. D., of New York.

Dr. N. E. Aronstam, of Detroit, Mich.

Dr. John A. Robison, of Chicago, Ill.

Dr. J. C. Shrader, of Iowa City.

Up-to-date of our going to press, no report has reached the executive committee of the American Congress of Tuberculosis from any of the delegates in attendance.

THE ASSASSINATION OF THE AMERICAN PRESIDENT.

The act of the assassin brings us face to face with a profound conviction that our crimiual system is seriously at fault, when dealing with crimes of the magnitude of this one on the life of the President.

There can be no doubt whatever that as the law now stands, there is no punishment that could be awarded by a judicial tribunal at all adequate to the crime.

As at present arranged it is out of the power of the judiciary to "fit the punishment to the crime," as is commonly said to be the duty of the judge.

The punishment the law metes out to this criminal if McKinley had lived is a mere mockery.

It is difficult to imagine a suitable punishment for the horrible wretch now that McKinley is dead.

The death of the man who occupies the executive chair of a nation in its legal consequences, in the eye of the law as it now stands, is simply murder, no more so than if it was the coachman or the gardener of the President.

This is where our law needs reconstruction. The act was intended by the assassin wholly outside of the personality of the victim.

It was not in the slightest degree personal, nor in any sense due to any official act of the President nor from any personal feeling against him. It was a crime against our civilization as a people.

It was not even in condemnation of any act of Mr. McKinley's life in the high office he held.

It was a blow struck in the face of mankind, against any attempt to establish a form of government for the regulation of the rights of the citizens of a great nation.

It was the same spirit that smote the King of Italy, and the other members of ruling families, of the thrones of the Old World in recent crimes of a like character.

It was not in revenge for alleged wrongs, as the Nihilist threatens the rulers of Russia.

It was the outcome of that spirit of anarchy that is new to our day, not the killing of unjust rulers to redress public wrongs, but was an apparently concerted effort to prevent the existence of a government here, based on the will of the majority of the people, to govern the American nation under its written constitution.

How are we to meet this wonderful condition? The assassin of Lincoln acted from entirely different motives. Booth was not an Anarchist.

Guiteau, who slew President Garfield, was simply a lunatic, and the post-mortem examination of his brain by the committee of the Medico-Legal Society showed it to be physically diseased. It was the act of an insane mind.

It was fortunate for us that this was a demonstration, and not a mere opinion. It is an incontrovertible fact that Guiteau's act had not the slightest tinge of anarchy in either its design or execution.

This assassination of President McKinley is not the work of an insane mind.

It is apparently the culmination of a preconceived design and a carefully cemented plan.

In dealing with the wild beast or the deadly rattlesnake we consider, that the right to inflict death, as to an enemy of our race is an inherent right. Measured by every standard available to human reason, the Anarchist who decides to prevent the organization of human government by the assassination of him who has been chosen to act as the head of the government becomes the deadly enemy of the race, far more terrible than the hyena, the tiger or the rattlesnake.

It is not the question of the loss of a single life. Mr. McKinley disappears, in the magnitude of the crime against the rights of the American people.

Have the people, who are the real parties to this controversy, the right, to so reform their laws as to place the Anarchist on the same plane as the poisonous serpent or the deadly wild beast?

The movement to class an attempt at an assassination, by statute, with the same penalties as if it was successful, does not reach the case. The combination that slew the President may strike in the same deadly manner at his successor.

It is a stupendous question in our criminology how to prevent this crime. The death of the assassin is no adequate punishment for such a crime. The nation is now exposed to its repetition at every public function. We should consider whether our time honored custom of shaking the hand of the Executive should be continued. Apparently no precautions can prevent a recurrence if the custom continues.

TWO RISING SOUTHERN MEDICAL EDITORS.

M. M. SMITH, M. D., AUSTIN, TEXAS.

Dr. M. M. Smith was born in Travis county, Texas, November 20th, 1864, and was reared upon a farm; as a boy, he received his primary education in the country schools. He entered the Literary Department of the University of Texas, in the fall of 1883 and attended said institution for five years, receiving, therefrom, the degrees of B. Sc. and M. A. He attended the Jefferson Medical College, of Philadelphia, Pennsylvania, and graduated with M. D. from that institution in 1891; being elected President of the Graduating Class, a distinction that had not before gone South since the war between the States.

Dr. Smith, after graduation, at once began the practice of Medicine in Austin, Texas, where he still resides. He was Resident Physician of the City and County Hospital at Austin for four years. He has been Physician to the Texas State School for the Deaf for the past six years, Physician to the Texas Deaf, Dumb and Blind Asylum for Colored Youths for eight years. Member, Secretary and Treasurer of the Board of Medical Examiners for the State of Texas, member of the American Society for the Advancement of Science, member of the Medico Legal Society, member of the Texas Academy of Science, Texas Historical Association, American Medical Association, Mississippi Valley Medical Association, Texas State Medical Association, North Texas Medical Association, Central Texas Medical Association, South Texas Medical Association, Austin District Medical Society, and the Austin Academy of Science, and also ex-member of the Board of School Trustees for the City of Austin. He has been elected as one of the Vice Presidents of the American Congress of Tuberculosis for the State of Texas.

Dr. Smith has written a number of valuable papers for the different societies of which he is a member, notably among which might be mentioned: Paper on "Hypnotism," "The Prevention of Tuberculosis," "Public Hygiene," "The Public

Health and the State's Duty to Protect It," "Mental Therapy," etc., etc. He delivered the Alumni Address before University of Texas in 1894, it being entitled "Formative Influences." He delivered the Alumni Oration before the Texas State Medical Association in 1899, entitled "The Invisible Enemy and Our Methods of Defense.

Dr. Smith is the Managing Editor of the Texas Medical News, of Austin, Texas. He married in 1894, his wife being the daughter of Hon. A. W. Terrell, Ex-Minister to Turkey, under Mr. Cleveland. He is the proud father of two sons.

Dr. Smith has taken an aggresive stand in favor of a Medical Law regulating the Practice of Medicine in Texas (Law passed last Legislature) and the establishment of a State Board of Health having served on these committees from the Texas State Medical Association for years, etc., etc.

I. W. P. SMITHMEK, M. D.

Editor of the Southern Medical Journal, whose portrait is in a group of authors and officers of the American Congress of Tuberculosis, was born in Bertie county, North Carolina, in 1870, received his education at the public schools and Plymouth High School. Attended Trinity College and the University of North Carolina, and graduated in medicine from the University of Maryland in 1895. Spent one year in the University Hospital, since which he has been engaged in the practice of his profession, with excellent success. He contributed to the Carolina Medical Journal. In 1898 he founded the Southern Medical Journal, which has become firmly grounded among the profession of the states of Virginia and the two Carolinas. Is a member of the North Carolina State Medical Society and the Seaboard Medical Association, and Vice President of the organization for the Establishing of a Physicians' Orphans' Home. He is one of the Vice Presidents of the American Congress of Tuberculosis for the State of North Carolina; a young man of energy and tact, of literary tastes, and merit, and one of the rising men of the medical profession of his State. He takes a deep interest in the work of arresting the spread of consumption, and is a close and careful student of forensic medicine, to which he is giving much attention.

SAMUEL B. THOMAS,

Assistant Secretary Medico Legal Society.

Samuel Bell Thomas was born in July 6, 1869, in Kemper county, Mississippi. Parents emigrated to Texas when he was nine years of age. At the age of sixteen he entered the Southwestern University, Georgetown, Texas, and graduated with honor, with the degree of M. A., in 1889.

In 1890 he attended the law department of the State University of Texas, and was admitted to the Bar in August, 1892.

Located at Wichita Falls, Texas, and served one year as justice of the peace, filling out an unexpired term, and served also one year as city attorney.

In 1894 he moved to the City of Waco and began the practice of law. In 1896, was a candidate for State Senator, and on account of a split in the county convention, withdrew from the race and came to New York. Has taken quite an active interest in politics in New York city, and in 1900 was a strong advocate of the Democratic ticket, speaking in several states.

Is now connected with the firm of Waldo, Naylor & Linn, 290 Broadway, New York City. He is a member of The Thirteen Club, Democratic Club, Namioki Club, and Colonial Clubs, and Assistant Secretary of the Medico Legal Society, and has taken an interest in forensic medicine, and contributed to the literature of Medical Jurisprudence. He is an eloquent and graceful speaker, and has more than ordinary power as an advocate before a jury. He is a rising lawyer and a public spirited citizen.

JURY TRIAL IN THE INSULAR POSSESSIONS.

Judge Gear, of the Circuit Court at Honolulu, has held that the guarantees of the United States constitution relating to trial by jury are in full force in Hawaii, and he accordingly discharged two prisoners who had been convicted by a less than unanimous verdict of the twelve jurors who tried them. To the argument of the Attorney General that the decision would work a general jail delivery of prisoners convicted since the annexation of Hawaii, Judge Gear said:—

The Court finds that this defendant was not given his constitutional right to be held innocent until he had been declared guilty by twelve jurors, and, believing that to be the case, this Court has no option, under its oath before God to support the laws of the land, but to order his release.

This is one of the questions left in doubt by the recent decisions of the United States Supreme Court in the insular cases. It is not likely to be long, however, before that tribunal will be called upon to settle it, at least as far as Hawaii is concerned. In the Philippines no jury trial is provided for, either in civil or criminal cases, by the code of procedure prepared under instructions from Washington. Whether this omission is warranted under the constitution remains for the Supreme Court to say.—The New York Herald.

VICE PRESIDENTS OF THE AMERICAN CONGRESS OF TUBERCULOSIS.

The following vice presidents of the American Congress of Tuberculosis have been named by the executive officers, under the resolution authorizing the appointment of three vice presidents from each state, country or province:—

Dr. A. Eugene Austin, Alaska; E. T. Barrick, M. D., Toronto, Ont.; E. P. Benoit, M. D., Montreal; Hon. Alvin C. Brager, Milwaukee, Wis.; Dr. Barck, St. Louis, Mo.; Dr. H. M. Brackin, St. Paul, Minn.; W. O. Bridges, M. D., Omaha; E. J. Burkett, Esq., Lincoln, Nebraska; Charles J. Coster, M. D., Saint John, N. B.; Dr. C. S Caverly, Rutland, Vermont; John C. Clayberg, Esq., Helena, Montana; Dr. Francis Crosson, Santa Fe, New Mexico; Dr. Granville P. Conn, Concord, New Hampshire; Dr. H. C. Dunavant, Little Rock, Ark.; John A. Donovan, Butte, Montana; Dr. W. F. Drewry, Petersburgh, Va.; Dr. J. A. Egan, Springfield, Ill.; Dr. J. M. Emmert, Atlantic, Iowa; Hon. T. B. Fetter, Georgia; Hon. J. W. Fellows, Manchester, New Hampshire; R. Emmett Giffen, M. D., Lincoln, Neb.; Dr. J. J. Gibson, Dennison, Iowa; Judge J. W. Howe, Little Rock, Ark.; J. N. Hurty, M. D., Secretary State Board of Health, Indianapolis, Ind.; Peter Robinson Inches, M. D., Saint John, N. B.; Dr.

Paulus A. Irving, Secretary State Board of Health, Richmond, Va.; Geo. Ben Johnson, M. D., Richmond, Va.; Wyatt Johnson, M. D., Montreal; Judge Yancy Lewis, Austin, Texas; John W. Lacey, Esq., Cheyenne, Wyoming; Dr. C. S. Lindsley, New Haven, Conn.; Dr. Geo. T. MacCoy, Columbus, Ind.; Dr. H. McHatton, Macon, Ga.; Dr. J. B. McConnell, Montreal; Dr. Robert McNeill, Charlottetown, P. E. I.; Dr. J. D. Plunkett, Nashville, Tenn.; Hon. Fletcher Proctor, Proctor, Vt.; Gov. Rogers, Alaska; Judge L. Bradford Prince, Santa Fe, New Mexico; Dr. G. A. Ritchie, Wisconsin; Dr. R. Harvey Reed, Rock Spring, Wyoming; Dr. John A. Robison, Chicago, Illinois; Dr. M. M. Smith, Austin, Texas; Dr. J. W. P. Smithwick, La Grange, N. C.; J. Longstreet Taylor, M. D., St. Paul, Minn.; Flavius J. Van Vort, Esq., Indianapolis, Indiana; Dr. G. G. Verbryck, Cambria, Wyoming; Dr. Arthur A. Van Dyke, Atlanta, Ga.: Judge F. T. Winston, Windsor, N. C.; Dr. Wm. C. Woodward, Health Officer, Washington, D. C.; Dr. Irving A. Watson, Concord, N. H.; Dr. Moses J. White, Milwaukee; A. G. Young, M. D., Augusta, Maine; Dr. F. Montizambert, Director of Public Health, Ottawa.

The executive officers, in making these appointments, consulted with the delegates from each state, country or province.

In the Central and South American countries they are consulting with the presidents of the several republics, the ambassadors from each of these republics or ministers, and the American ambassadors and ministers to these countries.

It has been deemed wise to make single appointments as a nucleus of organization, in each country, province or state, before all three of these officials are selected.

It has been considered desirable, that if possible, one lawyer or layman be named in each country, province or state.

These preliminary appointments are announced, so as to show members and delegates that the work is progressing, and it is hoped that before our next issue the major part of these officials will be named.

NOTES ON TUBERCULOSIS.

Dr. H. Battey Shaw contributed an article to the British Medical Journal of June, 1901, on "Care of Malignant Disease of the Lungs with Pseudo Tuberculosis."

Dr. Thompson Campbell a paper to the same Journal on "The Pulse Rate in Pulmonary Tuberculosis," which is a valuable clinical contribution, based on an enlarged and valuable practical experience by the writer.

Dr. S. A. Knopf, of New York, contributed an important paper to the June 15th number of the Journal of the American Medical Association, which we will notice later, entitled "Relation of the Medical Profession in the 20th Century to the Tuberculosis Problem."

C. A. Ranns to the same journal one entitled "Variability of the Tubercle Bacillus."

LAKE KEUKA MEDICAL AND SURGICAL ASSOCIATION.

What the English lakes are to the Northwest of England, making what is known as the Lake Country of England, is that beautiful group of lakes in Southern Central New York, where the Iroquis dwelt in the early days. This group embraces Skaneatles, Cayuga, Seneca, Keuka, and Canandaigua lakes of the larger types, and some smaller ones near, Lake Keuka known as Wanita, and Lamoka, in the towns of Wayne and Tyrone, in Schuyler and Steuben counties.

No group of lakes in any land present more beauties than do these, but Lake Keuka, located almost in the centre of the group, is perhaps the more picturesque and beautiful of them all.

The counties surrounding these lakes are the richest in the state for fruit and agricultural purposes, and the medical men of all this region have united in an organization which holds its annual meeting as an outing, at Grove Springs Hotel, on the eastern shore of Lake Keuka.

It is composed of the counties of Broome, Cayuga, Chemung, Livingston, Monroe, Ontario, Schuyler, Steuben, Seneca, Tioga and Yates.

Its permanent organization was only effected last year, when its constitution and by-laws were adopted, and its officers formally elected, and a banquet of its members given at that hotel.

Its annual meeting of 1901 was held on August 13th and 14th, under the presidency of Dr. Henry Flood, of Elmira, N. Y., to whose great energy and executive ability must be awarded the signal success which attended its annual meeting.

Its officers for 1901 were:

President—Dr. Henry Flood, of Elmira, N. Y.

Vice President—Dr. Wm. B. Macy, of Willard, N. Y.

Secretary and Treasurer—Dr. W.W. Smith, of Avoca, N. Y.

The officers announced the following programme:—

1. President's AddressHenry Flood, M. D., Elmira, N. Y. Discussion opened by William Austin Macy, M. D., Williard, N. Y.

2. Affections of the Nervous System in Early and Late Syphilis—George Conderman, M. D., Hornellsville, N. Y. Discussion opened by W. Sylvester Cobb, M. D., Corning, N. Y.

3. Cerebro-Spinal Meningitis—Floyd S. Crego, M. D., Buffalo, N. Y. Discussion opened by Robert P. Bush, M. D., Horseheads, New York.

4. Treatment of Melancholia—Charles G. Wagner, M. D., Binghampton, N. Y. Discussion opened by G. D. Crandal, M. D., Blossburg, Pa.

5. Treatment of Lobar Pneumonia—Charles G. Stockton, M. D., Buffalo, N. Y. Discussion opened by C. L. Stiles, M. D., Owego, New York.

6. Relation of Mosquitoes to Malaria—Arthur W. Booth, M. D., Elmira, N. Y. Discussion opened by Veranus A. Moore, M. D., Ithaca, N. Y.

7. The Smallpox Problem, its Dissemination, Control and Attending Difficulties—Ernest Wende, M. D., Buffalo, N. Y. Discussion opened by H. D. Wey, M. D., Elmira, N. Y.

8. The Necessity of Proper Diet for Infants at the Beginning—Charles W. M. Brown, M. D., Elmira, N. Y. Discussion opened by Charles W. Hayt, M. D., Corning, N. Y.

9. Tetanus-Report of Three Cases—W. B. Clapper, M. D., Farmington, N. Y. Discussion opened by M. L. Bennett, M. D., Watkins, N. Y.

10. Appendicitis, When to Operate—A. L. Beahan, M. D., Canandaigua, N. Y. Discussion opened by C. S. Parkhill, M. D., Hornellsville, N. Y.

11. The Indications and Limitations of Surgical Intervention in Diseases of the Stomach—W. G. MacDonald, M. D., Albany, N. Y. Discussion opened by Lewis W. Rose, M. D., Rochester, N. Y.

12. Surgery of the Biliary Passages—John B. Deaver, M. D., Philadelphia, Pa. Discussion opened by Roswell Park, M. D., Buffalo, N. Y.

13. Asthma in its Relation to Nasal Disease—John O. Roe, M. D., Rochester, N. Y. Discussion opened by G. M. Case, M. D., Elmira, N. Y.

14. Concerning Purulent Ophthalmia—Lucien Howe, M. D., Buffalo, N. Y. Discussion opened by Sherman Voorhees, M. D., Elmira, N. Y.

15. Cancer of the Uterus—H. P. Jack, M. D., Canisteo, N. Y. Discussion opened by F. W. Ross, M. D., Elmira, N. Y.

16. Early Prophylaxis in Obstetrics—William A. Howe, M. D., Phelps, N. Y. Discussion opened by C. C. Harvey, M. D., Dundee, N. Y.

17. Pathology in the German University—A. T. Kunkel, M. D., Westfield, Pa.

18. Remarks on Leprosy—J. E. Walker, M. D., Hornellsville, N. Y. Discussion opend by H. R. Ainsworth, M. D., Addison, N. Y.

RECENT LEGAL DECISIONS.

CAN A PHYSICIAN REFUSE TO TREAT A CASE?

The Supreme Court of Indiana has recently passed upon this question, that he cannot.

The case was one where the doctor was called to attend a person dangerously ill, but refused to go, and the patient died, and it was alleged that no other physician could have been called in time to be of service.

The Court held in favor of the physician, that he is not liable for refusing to respond to a call, even though he may be the only one available.

In construing the Indiana statute regulating the practice of medicine, the Court said: "That in obtaining the State license to practice medicine, the State does not require, and the license does not engage, that he will practice at all or on other terms than those he may choose to accept."

There can be little doubt of the correctness of this decision.

We see no distinction or difference in such a case between the duty of the physician and the lawyer, and no one would hold that a lawyer could be compelled to take a case for a client unless he was willing to do so.

We can understand how all might feel that a physician who refused to take a case in an emergency, when no one else could be got in time and death resulted in consequence, would be generally censured; and the case would be a calamity, but that certainly would not establish a legal liability.

CHRISTIAN SCIENCE AND THE CHURCH.

THE WILL OF MRS. BRUSH.

Mrs. Brush made a will bequeathing the bulk of her property to the Christian Science Church.

The will was contested by relatives, on the ground of mental unsoundness and undue influence.

Surrogate Fitzgerald sustained the will. The language of his decision is as follows:

"Whether her determination not to give her fortune to her family was unwise, whether her residuary legatee herein has deserved the affection and gratitude which the testatrix has so bountifully given evidence of, are not questions for this Court to consider in arriving at its decision.

"The decedent, being of sound mind and free from restraint, had the right to do with her own as she pleased, and her will must therefore be admitted to probate."

The New York Herald in commenting on this case and decision says:

Surrogate Fitzgerald finds no proof of undue influence and holds that a belief in Christian Science is not of itself an evidence of insanity. This is equally true of Spiritualism or any other form of faith. As the Surrogate well says, "the truth or falsity of a religious belief is beyond the scope of a judicial inquiry." Religious mania, as is well known, is a common form of insanity. But this is not peculiar to any sect or denomination. It shows nothing as to the soundness or unsoundness of any creed or faith.

In declaring that it is not the business of a Court to determine whether a will is wise or unwise, just or unjust; that a testator has a right to do with his own as he pleases, and that the function of a judge is simply to decide whether thedocument is in due legal form and its author was of sound mind; Surrogate Fitzgerald simply affirms an established principle of the law, but one often overlooked by contestants and even judges themselves. The great number of wills contested in the courts and the deplorable consequences of the litigation are matters of common notoriety. In too many instances wills have been broken, and the purposes of the maker defeated on trivial technicalities, and often where they have been finally sustained, it has only been after the estate, long tied up, has been wasted by lawyers' fees and other costs. In this way many public benefactions have been either frustrated entirely, or their value greatly impaired.

Surrogate Fitzgerald's decision and the declarations we have quoted in the Brush case are well calculated to have a timely and salutary effect. Within a few simple limitations imposed by the law every man and every woman of testamentary capacity has a right to dispose by will of what they possess as they please. If the testator sees fit to devote his money to public or charitable uses instead of to relatives, to give to certain heirs, and disinherit others—in short, to dispose of his property according to his own judgment, wishes or even whims—that is his affair. The business of the courts is to see that his wishes are respected and carried out. Fortunately there has been a growing recognition of this vital principle on the part of judges, with the result that attempts at will breaking are neither so common nor so successful as formerly. It is to be hoped that the improvement will continue.

…RS OF THE AMERICAN CONGRESS
…LOSIS.

DR. U. O. B. WINGATE,
Milwaukee, Wis.

…RD LICEAGA,
…l Mexico.

DR. C. F. ULRICH,
Wheeling, W. Va.

DR. T. VIRGIL HUBBARD,
Atlanta. Ga.

TRANSACTIONS.

MEDICO-LEGAL SOCIETY FEBRUARY SESSION, 1901.

Presidency of lark Bell, Esq.

The February meeting of the :edico-Legal Society was held at the Hotel St. Andrews, Grand Bo evard and 72nd Street, New York City, on February 20, 1901, at diner at 7 o'clock P. M.

The President, Clark Bell, Esc in the hair, and Samuel Bell Thomas, Assistant Secretary in te absence of the Secretary.

The following were elected mebers on the recommendation of the Executive Committee:

Dr. N. E. Aronstam, 164 E. Igh Street, Detroit, Mich.

James R. Rogers, Esq., Counsllor at Law, 220 Broadway, New York.

The following papers were rea:

"Remarks on Suggestion of Hynotism in their Relation to Jurisprudence," by Baron De Schrenc-Notzing, of Munich.

"Amnesia," by L. J. RosenburgEsq., and N. E. Aronstam, M. D., of Detroit, Mich.

"Confessions of the Innocent," y W. H. S. Monck, Esq., of the Dublin bar, was laid over to the March meeting.

"Reminiscences of the Assassiation of Abraham Lincoln," by George L. Porter, M. D., of Bridsport.

The last paper was discussed b District Attorney Asa Bird Gardner and Hon. Jacob F. Miller.

A motion was made and carriedhat ie April meeting should be a joint session of the Society ar the ...ction on Medico-Legal Surgery.

The American Congress of Tuerculosis was announced to hold a two days' session May 15 and 1 1901.

The Society adjourned at a lat hour.

CLARK BELL,
President.

SAMUEL BELL THOMAS,
Assistant Secretary.

MARCH MEETING.

Presidency of lark Bell, Esq.

The March meeting of the Meico-Legal Society was held at a dinner given at Hotel St. Andrew New York City, March 20, 1901, at 7 o'clock P. M., Clark Bell, Prsident, in the chair, and Samuel Bell Thomas, Esq., Assistant Secrtary, in the absence of the Secretary.

VICE-PRESIDENTS AND PROMINET MEMBERS OF THE AMERICAN CONG OF TUBERCULOSIS.

DR JOHN A. ROBISON
Chicago, Ill

DR. U. O. B. WINGATE,
Milwaukee, Wis

DR. EDWARD LICEAGA,
City of Mexico.

DR. LOUIS LABAYLE
Leon, Nicaragua.

DR. C. F. ULRICH,
Wheeling, W. Va.

DR. LOUIS LEROY
Nashville, Tenn.

DR. T. VIRGIL HUBBARD,
Atlanta, Ga.

TRANSACTIONS.

MEDICO-LEGAL SOCIETY—FEBRUARY SESSION, 1901.

Presidency of Clark Bell, Esq.

The February meeting of the Medico-Legal Society was held at the Hotel St. Andrews, Grand Boulevard and 72nd Street, New York City, on February 20, 1901, at dinner at 7 o'clock P. M.

The President, Clark Bell, Esq., in the chair, and Samuel Bell Thomas, Assistant Secretary in the absence of the Secretary.

The following were elected members on the recommendation of the Executive Committee:

Dr. N. E. Aronstam, 164 E. High Street, Detroit, Mich.

James R. Rogers, Esq., Counsellor at Law, 220 Broadway, New York.

The following papers were read:

"Remarks on Suggestion of Hypnotism in their Relation to Jurisprudence," by Baron De Schrenck-Notzing, of Munich.

"Amnesia," by L. J. Rosenburg, Esq., and N. E. Aronstam, M. D., of Detroit, Mich.

"Confessions of the Innocent," by W. H. S. Monck, Esq., of the Dublin bar, was laid over to the March meeting.

"Reminiscences of the Assassination of Abraham Lincoln," by George L. Porter, M. D., of Bridgeport.

The last paper was discussed by District Attorney Asa Bird Gardner and Hon. Jacob F. Miller.

A motion was made and carried that the April meeting should be a joint session of the Society and the Section on Medico-Legal Surgery.

The American Congress of Tuberculosis was announced to hold a two days' session May 15 and 16, 1901.

The Society adjourned at a late hour.

CLARK BELL,
President.

SAMUEL BELL THOMAS,
Assistant Secretary.

MARCH MEETING.

Presidency of Clark Bell, Esq.

The March meeting of the Medico-Legal Society was held at a dinner given at Hotel St. Andrews, New York City, March 20, 1901, at 7 o'clock P. M., Clark Bell, President, in the chair, and Samuel Bell Thomas, Esq., Assistant Secretary, in the absence of the Secretary.

The minutes of the January and February meetings of 1901, were read and approved.

The following were elected members on the recommendation of the Executive Committee. Proposed by Hart Vance:

Eugent D. C. Bayne, Esq., 139 Kennan Street, Cleveland, O.

Proposed by Dr. di Moise, Francis L. Corrall, Counsellor at Law, 84 Elm Street, New York.

Dr. W. C. Abbott, Chicago, Ill; Dr. Waugh, of Chicago.

Proposed by Dr. A. N. Chevallier, of Belle, British Honduras.

The following papers were read:

Review of the recent "Bell View Hospital Homicide Trial," by R. L. Pritchard, of the New York Bar.

"A Case of Death by Electricity," by Prof. Dr. Lebrun, of Brussells, Belgium; translated by A. A. Jakobi, Esq., of the N. Y. Bar.

"Confessions of the Innocent," by W. H. S. Monck, Esq., of the Dublin Bar.

The papers were disucssed by J. R. Abarbanell, Esq., Carleton Simon, M. D., Judge A. H. Dailey, Hon. Jacob F. Miller, the president and others.

The announcement of the joint session of the Society with the American Congress of Tuberculosis on May 15 and 16 prox. was made and the President made a report on the progress of the work and the preliminary steps already taken.

The following announcements were ordered to be made:

There will be a joint session of the Section of Medico-Legal Surgery and this Society on the 3d Wednesday of April, 1901.

Contributions on subjects related to Medico-Legal Surgery for that occasion are requested. The titles of papers to be sent to the President.

The American Congress of Tuberculosis is announced to be held for two days' session, commencing on the third Wednesday of May, (15), in joint session with the Medico-Legal Society, at the Grand Central Palace.

A banquet will be given on the evening of May 15th, at 7o'clock, for Members and Delegates of the American Congress of Tuberculosis and of the Medico-Legal Society and its several Sections at $2 per plate.

The enrolling fee of the Congress has been fixed at $3 each, entitling the member to the Bulletin free.

The Governors of the American States and Canadian Provinces have been invited to name three or more delegates from each state and territory, all of those who hav replied, consent to do so. Invitations to contribute papens have been sent abroad and favorable responses are received.

The enrolling is progressing favorably.

Authors of papers for the Congress are requested to furnish titles of their papers to the Secretary of the Congresh, Mr. Clark Bell, Esq., 39 Broadway, N. Y. City.

The session will continue on Thursday. Detailed program will follow of both the April and May meetings in advance.

Members of both professions are invited to participate in this Congress of Tuberculosis.

Members unable to attend the Dinner on March 20th, are invited to come at 9 o'clock, when the papers will be read.

Members of both Sections are invited to attend and those wishing to secure seats will advise the officers in advance of the meeting.

The following have been elected Active Members of the Society: N. E. Aronstam, M. D., Detroit, Mich.; Frank Harvey Field, Esq., of Mechanics Bank Building, Brooklyn, N. Y.

The Society adjourned at a late hour.

CLARK BELL,
President.

SAMUEL BELL THOMAS,
Assistant Secretary.

APRIL SESSION.

Presidency of Clark Bell, Esq., L L D.

The Medico-Legal Society met pursuant to call and notice, April 19, 1901, in joint session with the Section of Medico-Legal Surgery, at a dinner given at the Hotel Piavano, West 35th Street, New York city. The President, Clark Bell, Esq., in the chair and Samuel Bell Thomas, Assistant Secretary, acting as Secretary. The minutes of the March meeting were read and approved.

The following new members were elected on recommendation of the executive committee:

C. Amende, M. D., 319 W. 45th Street, New York.

John Leffingwill Hatch, M. D., P. F. C., 865 Central Park W, New York City.

James R. Rogers, Esq., of the New York Bar.

The chair alluded to the death of the late Colonel E. C. James, of the Bar of New York, and paid a tribute to his active and useful professional life. Remarks were made by President Clark Bell, Hon. Jacob F. Miller, ex-Chief Justice L. Bradford Prince, of New Mexicó; Dr. A. P. Grinnell, of Burlington, Vermont.

It was moved and carried that the chair name a committee to prepare a suitable notice of the loss this body feels at the death.

The chair appointed as such committee Dr. A. P. Grinnell, of Burlington, Vermont, chairman; Hon. Bradford L. Prince, and Judge A. H. Dailey.

The Section on Medico-Legal Surgery then organized in joint session with the Medico-Legal Society.

In the absence of Chief Surgeon C. K. Cole, M. D., of Montana, Vice Chairman Clark Bell, Esq., LL D. took the chair.

The chair submitted circular letters which had been sent to members of the Section. It was received and ordered on file and read as follows:

New York, Jan. 17th, 1901.

Dear Colleagues.—We send you this reminder of the opening of a new century and we ask you to take up, each as one man, the advancement of the work of the Section and assist in its labors.

We send you a copy of the address of the late Chairman of this Section and now President of the Medico-Legal Society, presented to the International Medical Congress, is Paris last August. We call your attention to the work of the Section during the last year and to the papers in the December number of the Medico-Legal Journal.

We feel that if a mutual effort was made to bring the claims and benefits of our Section work to the notice of the profession it would result in a large increase in our membership, and extend the usefulness of our organization.

The field of Railway Surgery alone is now an enormous one. If you will bring the Section and its work to the notice of your friends who are not now members, and solicit their active co-operation, you will be doing a useful labor. It is now suggested that a joint session of this Section and the Medico-Legal Society be held on the third Wednesday of April, 1901; that officers and members be requested to submit short papers on subjects relating to the work of the Section, to be read on that occasion and that authors furnish the title of their communications to the Secretary as early as possible; that Chief Surgeon Granville P. Conn, Chief Surgeon W. B. Outten and Chief Surgeon F. H. Caldwell act in conjunction with the chairman and secretary of this Section in obtaining papers to be read, and as sub-committee of arrangements for the proposed meeting; and that members of the Section co-operate with this sub-committee of arrangements to make such a reunion a notable one in the annals of Medico-Legal Surgery.

When it becomes known that the Medico-Legal Journal is sent free to every member of this Section, and that the annual subscription to the Section is only $1.50 per annum, and that no initiation fee is required to secure a Section membership, many railway surgeons and railway lawyers will thank you for opening to them this door to the progress of railway surgery.

We enclose you a blank application for membership and ask that you bring in at least two or three new members, and that you promptly pay your Section dues, if you have not already done so, that the Journal can be sent to you.

Respectfully,
CHARLES K. COLE,
Chairman.

CLARK BELL, Secretary.
W. H. FRANCIS, Treasurer.

A paper was then read by Judge Wm. H. Francis, Vice Chairman Section Medico-Legal Surgery, entitled "Railway Surgeons and Hospitals."

Dr. George Chaffee, M. D., Vice Chairman of the Section of Medico-Legal Surgery, of Brooklyn, N. Y., read a paper entitled "First Aid and Transportation of the Injured."

A paper was then read by Chief Surgeon Webb J. Kelley, of Gallon, Ohio, entitled "Ankle Sprains—So Called."

A paper was then read by Dr. A. P. Grinnell, of Burlington Vt., Vice Chairman of the Section of Medico-Legal Surgery entitled "Stimulants in Forensic Medicine."

The annual report of the Section of Medico-Legal Surgery submitted at January meeting, 1901, was laid before the Section and on motion duly approved.

The Section then adjourned and the Medico-Legal Society resumed its session, the President Clark Bell, Esq., in the chair, and Samuel Bell Thomas, Assistant Secretary in the absence of the Secretary.

The President laid before the Society the preliminary work of the officers of the Society in relation to the proposed joint session of the Medico-Legal Society with the American Congress of Tuberculosis on May 15-16, 1901, and the call for the Congress; the action of the executive committee of the Medico-Legal Society, and the various letters addressed by the President to the Governors of the American States and the Canadian Provinces; the Presidents of the Central and South American Republics; their ministers at Washington, and the State and National Medical Societies, and made a statement of the progress of the work for such joint session. On motion tne action of Mr Clark Bell, President of tne Society was approved with the thanks of the body.

The President also announced the favorable responses made from a large number of eminent men of both professions, announcing their co-operation in the work.

Mr. Bell also gave notice of his paper proposed for that Congress, entitled "Tuberculosis and Legislation," asking for a symposium of replies from a large number of observers.

The Society adjourned at a late hour.

CLARK BELL,
President.
SAMUEL BELL THOMAS,
Assistant Secretary.

MEDICO-LEGAL SOCIETY—MAY SESSION, 1901.

Presidency of Clark Bell, Esq., L L D.

The Medico-Legal Society held its May meeting in joint session with the American Congress of Tuberculosis at the Hotel Majestic on May 15-16, 1901, Clark Bell, Esq., President, Samuel Bell Thomas, Assistant Secretary acting as Secretary.

The minutes of the April meeting were duly approved.

The following were duly elected active members on the recommendation of the Executive Committee. Proposed by Clark Bell.

Wm. Creighton Woodward, Esq., M. D., Health Officer, Washington, D. C.

U. H. McLaws, Esq., Counsellor at Law, Savannah, Ga.

Richard Petrilla, M. D., 1178 Sands St., Brooklyn, N. Y.

Henry D. Holton, M. D., Secretary State Board of Health, Brattleboro, Vt.

Charles F. Ulrich, M. D., Wheeling, W. Va.

George Brown, M. D., Atlanta, Ga.

T. Virgil Hubbard, M. D., Atlanta, Ga.

The President announced the receipt of a letter from Prof. D. P. Kossorotoff, of St. Petersburgh, Russia, Professor of Medical Jurisprudence at the Imperial Military Academy of Medicine; at the Military Academy of Jurisprudence; at the Imperial University of St. Peter's, Russia, returning thanks for his election as corresponding member, and announcing as an homage to the Society on his last work as a gift, "The Century of Imperial Military Academy of Medicine."

A. R. Grinnell, M. D., chairman of the committee to whom was referred the preparation of suitable resolutions on the death of Col. James, submitted the following:

Resolutions submitted to the Medico-Legal Society of New York, by the committee:

Whereas, it has pleased Divine Providence to take from among us Colonel Edward C. James, and although called away in the prime of life and in the midst of a most active and successful career as a lawyer, he has left behind him a record of usefulness, uprightness and devotion to his professional work, which fosters emulation and respect from his colleagues and constitutes an imperishable inheritance.

For many years he occupied an enviable position as an able lawyer in Northern New York, but after removing to New York city his unbounded ambition, his tireless devotion to labor, and his talents as a jurist found a field in which his intellectual merits and profound legal knowledge were recognized and appreciated. Colonel James was broad in his views, positive and pronounced in his opinions, aggresisve and courageous in trials of causes before the courts, and equally commendable were the social qualities manifested in his relations with men, and his wit and humor which pervaded his every-day life made him a most acceptable companion and friend. Therfore;

Resolved: That this Society expresses a deep felt sorrow in the loss of so ditinguished a member, and that we beg most sincerely to tender to his family our condolence. And be it further

Resolved, That this preamble and resolutions be spread upon the records of the Society, and an engrossed copy be transmitted to the family of the deceased.

A. P. GRINNELL,
A. H. DAILEY,
L. BRADFORD PRINCE,
Committee.

It was moved and carried that the June meeting of this Society be dispensed with, by reason of the extraordinary labor imposed upon the President of the Society, growing out of the work of the American Congress of Tuberculosis.

It was moved and caried that the President be empowered to name delegates to the British Congress of Tuberculosis. The International Congress of Criminal Anthropology, which meets in

Holland, and to all other foreign and home societies with which this body is in affiliation, for the ensuing year.

It was resolved that during the summer vacation the powers of the Executive Committee be conferred upon the Executive officers of the Society. The Society adjourned on May 16, 1901.

CLARK BELL,
President.
SAMUEL BELL THOMAS,
Assistant Secretary.

The following report of the transactions of the American Congress of Tuberculosis was presented to the London Congress of Tuberculosis at its session of July 23-25, in London:

New York, July 1, 1901.

To the British Congress of Tuberculosis of London, to be held July 22-25th, 1901.

The undersigned committee appointed under the action of the American Congress of Tuberculosis with instruction to report to your body so much of the transactions of the American Congress of Tuberculosis, held in the city of New York, May 15th and 16th, 1901, as can be printed in the time for your session, respectfully report:

We submit, (1) The transactions of the first and second days' proceedings herewith; the list of officers elected; the roll of delegates named by the Governors of States, in part; and by Societies, also only in part.

(2) So many of the papers read before the Congress in New York as have been published; the programme of the Congress; and regret that from the shortness of time, we are unable to append the completed Bulletin of the Congress, which when finished, will contain all the papers and transactions of the body.

Respectfully submitted,
H. EDWIN LEWIS, M. D., Chairman.
CLARK BELL,
JOHN A. ROBISON, M. D.,
J. MOUNT BLEYER, M. D.,
A. E. ARONSTAM, M. D.
Committee.

Attached to said report were the following papers:

1. Opening address of welcome to delegates, byClark Bell, Esq., President of the New York Medico-Legal Society.

2. Address by Dr. A. N. Bell, M. D., retiring president of the American Congress of Tuberculosis.

3. Transactions of first and second days' proceedings of the American Congress of Tuberculosis, with the programme of its papers and proceedings.

4. Pages 1 to 110 of the Bulletin of the American Congress of Tuberculosis, from advance sheets of the Medico-Legal Journal.

5. List of the officers of the American Congress of Tuberculosis chosen at the meeting of May 15-16, 1901.

6. Roll of the delegates named by the Governors of States in part.

7. Roll of delegates from foreign countries and scientific bodies in part, from advance sheets of the Medico-Legal Journal.

AMERICAN CONGRESS OF TUBERCULOSIS
IN JOINT SESSION WITH
THE MEDICO-LEGAL SOCIETY.

[Continued from June Number.]

THURSDAY, MAY 16, 1901, 10 A. M.
MORNING SESSION.
In the Chair:

For the Medico-Legal Society, Dr. A. P. Grinnell, of Vermont, supported by Dr. T. D. Crothers, of Hartford, Conn.

For the American Congress of Tuberculosis, Dr. Henry D. Holton, President, supported by Dr. J. C. Shrader, of Iowa.

The paper of Dr. E. T. Barrick, of Toronto, "Practical Solution of the Question of dealing with the Consumptive Poor," in the absence of the author was under the rule, read by title.

The paper of Dr. Heneage Gibbes, of Detroit, Mich., was then read in the absence of the author, by title, under the rule.

H. Edwin Lewis, M. D., of Burlington, Iowa, then read a paper entitled "The Development of Tuberculosis in the Individual."

This paper gave rise to an interesting discussion which was participated in by Dr. Oliver A. Blumenthal, of Syracuse, N Y.; by Dr. Wm. C. Woodward, of Washington, D. C.; Dr. Edwin F. Bowers, of Brooklyn, N. Y.; Dr. J. Mount Bleyer, of New York and Dr. Louis Leroy, of Nashville, Tenn. The debate was closed by the author of the paper.

Hon. Moritz Ellinger, Corresponding Secretary of the Medico-Legal Society, then read a paper entitled "Hygiene in Bible and Talmud and Sanitation in Post Rabbinical Times."

The paper announced by Dr. Wm. Jacobson, of New York, entitled "Childhood and Tuberculosis," in the absence of the author was then read by title.

Dr. Cressy L Wilbur, of Lansing, Michigan, then read a paper entitled "Recent Statistics of Tuberculosis in Michigan." The author asked leave to add some additional statistics, which was on motion granted.

A paper announced by Dr. C. C. Carroll, of New York, entitled "Tuberculosis as Shown in Human Blood," was at the request of the author read by title, the MSS to be sent later to the Secretary.

A paper by the same author was then read by title at the author's request entitled "Tuberculosis as Shown in the Female Generative Organs."

Dr. T. D. Crothers, of Hartford, Conn., moved that a committee of five be named by the chair on permanent organization and regulations for the session of next year. It was seconded and carried. The chair appointed as such committee: Dr. T. D. Crothers, of Conn., chairman; Dr. M. R. Crain, of Vermont; Dr. Clark Bell, Esq., of New York; Moritz Ellinger, Esq., of New York, with instructions to report at the afternoon session.

Dr. John H. Donovan, of Butte, Montana, moved the appointment of a committee by the chair to formulate the views of the Congress on the questions presented, so that the same could be discussed at the afternoon session at the close of the Congress. The resolution was on motion adopted. The chair named as such committee: Dr. J. H. Donovan, of Montana; Dr. Louis LeRoy, of Tenn.; Dr. H. Edwin Lewis, of Vermont; Dr. Wm. C. Woodward, of Washington, D. C., and Dr. Frederick C. Curtis, of Albany, N. Y.

Dr. T. D. Crothers, moved that a committee of three be appointed by the chair to arrange for an award of a suitable prize to the author of the most meritorious paper presented at the next year's session of this Congress, upon the "Prevention of Tuberculosis," which was seconded by Dr. H. Edwin Lewis and carried unanimously.

The chair appointed as such committee, Clark Bell Esq., LL D., of New York; Dr. J. Mount Bleyer, M. D., of New York and Dr. A. N. Bell, of Brooklyn.

It was moved and carried that at the end of the reading of papers any subject or paper presented should be open for discussion.

The Congress then took a recess until 2 P. M.

SECOND DAY, MAY 16, 2 P. M.

AFTERNOON SESSION.

In the Chair:

For the American Congress of Tuberculosis, the President, Dr. Henry D. Holton, supported by Dr. H. K. Emmett, of Iowa.

For the Medico-Legal Society, C. K. Cole, M. D. of Montana, supported by A. P. Grinnell, M. D., of Vermont.

Dr. Luis H. Labayle, M. D., delegate from Nicaragua, read a paper entitled "The Evolution of Tuberculosis in Tropical Countries."

Dr George Chaffee, of Brooklyn, N. Y. then read a paper entitled "Transportation of Tuberculous Passengers."

Dr. M. R. Leverson, of Brooklyn, N. Y., then read a paper entitled "Is Tuberculosis Infectious? Should it be Prevented by Legislation?" When the author had read fifteen minutes he was interrupted by the Chair who stated that the time he was entitled to the floor had expired, and the amount of business on the Secretary's desk was so great that he felt it his duty to enforce the rule limiting authors to fifteen minutes time.

The paper asserted that Tuberculosis was not at all infectious, and ridiculed the idea of preventing its spread by legislation. It reflected on the motives and conduct of medical men who believed it was infectious.

It pronounced vaccination as a humbug and fraud, and denounced in very strong and vehement language the medical profession and all who had supported legislation enforcing it, and characterized the motives and conduct of medical men who differed with the author in very offensive language.

Dr. C. K. Cole, of Montana, moved that the author be allowed to proceed and finish his paper. He said that while he was not in sympathy with one sentiment uttered by the writer, that he had found in his experience in life that when men of the stamp of this author sought to inflict their individual views, at variance with the general experience and belief of mankind, that it was the surest and most effective way to dispose of them by giving them full play, and he hoped that delegates would vote to allow the author to proceed. Over a strong protest from many members, Dr. Coles' motion was carried and Dr. Leverson finished the reading of his paper.

Dr. C. K. Cole then moved that the Congress decline to accept the paper, and that it should not be allowed to be published in the transactions.

Dr. C. A. Lindsley, of Conn., seconded Dr. Coles' motion and in very vigorous language said that in his opinion it was not proper in this day and age of the world to discuss medical axioms. That men, who sought to discuss the question of the infectious character of consumption, were still in the impenetrable night of ignorance.

That, for one, he believed the medical world united in the opinion that tuberculosis was infectious.

That the writer's assault upon the motives and actions of medical men was such an outrage, as in his opinion placed the speaker outside the pale of ordinary professional courtesy, and that the Congress could not, with self-respect, accept such a paper containing such sentiments.

Dr. Henry Mitchell, of the State Board of Health of New Jersey, spoke in support of Dr. Coles' motion concurring in Dr. Lindsley's remarks and denouncing in very forcible language the reflections made on medical men by the author, who differed with him in his views.

Dr. Frederick C. Curtis, of Albany, strongly supported the motion of Dr. Cole, and insisted that it was the duty of the Congress to put itself squarely on the record against the sentiments uttered by the reader of the paper.

Dr. Leverson spoke against the motion; strenuous objections were made to hearing him, but the chair allowed him to occupy five minutes that the rule allowed.

Dr. Cole closed the debate by stating that he was sorry to see such a spectacle presented by a medical man in such a place, but he was glad that the utmost latitude had been allowed the speaker to be heard, although, as he well knew, his statements and views were obnoxious to every member of the Congress.

The chair asked every person in the audience to vote on the question. Dr. Cole's motion was carried with only three dissenting votes; Dr. Leverson being the only member of the body who voted against Dr. Cole's motion.

Dr. Cole then moved, that as the sense of this Congress we entirely dissent from the views and statements of Dr. Leverson's paper.

On the motion being put it was carried unanimously, excepting the vote of Dr. Leverson and three persons in the large audience who were not members.

Dr. Leverson then asked the Secretary to return him the paper.

The Secretary stated to the Congress the demand, and moved that Dr. Leverson be allowed to withdraw the paper from the hands of the Secretary which was done and the incident closed.

The paper of Dr. John A. Robison, of Chicago, entitled "On the Need of a National Inter-State Society for the Prevention and Cure of Tuberculosis."

Dr. Carleton Simon, of New York, then asked that a paper entitled, "Milk in Its Relation to Tuberculosis," be read by title.

On his request he was allowed further time to complete it.

The Secretary then presented a paper from Maj. A. Havard, M. D., U. S. Army in Cuba, entitled: "Tuberculosis in Cuba."

The President asked leave to submit later a paper in time for the Bulletin and Journal to August 15, 1901, entitled:

"What Shall We Do to Prevent Tuberculosis in Rural Communities?" Leave was granted.

Dr. J. A. Fortich, delegate from Cartaginia, Colombia, S. A., Vice-President of the American Congress, then submitted a paper entitled, "Variety of Forms of Tuberculosis in the Mountains and Valleys of Colombia," and asked leave that it be read by title and he be allowed further time to August 15th, to complete it; granted on motion.

The secretary presented a request from Dr. Louis W. Spradling, delegate from Tennessee, that his paper entitled, "Why Not Educate Against Tuberculosis?" be read by title and that he would finish it later. Leave was granted on motion. The secretary presented to the body a large file of several hundred letters from home and abroad, including Great Britain and the Continent, too voluminous to be read.

It was on motion ordered that they be received and placed on file, and that the secretary be empowered and authorized to publish such of the same in the Bulletin as he believed to be of such public interest as would justify their publication.

The Medico-Legal Society then held a short session independent of the Congress; Clark Bell, President, in the chair, and S. B. Thomas acting as assistant secretary.

Dr. T. D. Crothers, chairman of the committee on permanent organization, submitted a report from the committee, recommending a constitution and by-laws. The report was discussed at length.

Mr. Clark Bell said that the body was made a permanent organization at the first session in February, 1900, and submitted its report and the officers then elected. He stated the relation of the organization to the Medico-Legal Society and how it had started. He presented the Part I of its Bulletin of 1900, and the report of a committee that had presented the same to the Paris International Congress of 1900.

He explained its present organization and autonomy of work, and advised that no action be taken that would interfere with its present status which would work smoothly.

He suggested that at the next year's session the subjects to which the main features of the report related could then be discussed and acted upon.

The report was also discussed by Dr. Louis Leroy, Dr. C. K. Cole, Dr. J. J. Gibson and Dr. C. K. Emmett, of Iowa; by Dr. John A. Donovan, of Montana; H. Edwin Lewis, of Vermont.

On the motion of Dr. C. K. Cole, of Montana, the report and the whole subject of the same was referred back to the committee with instructions to make a report at the next annual meeting.

The committee on organization through its chairman, Dr. John A. Donavan, of Montana, submitted as its report the following preamble and resolutions:—

Whereas, is is an established fact that tuberculosis is a highly communicable disease, being responsible for fully one-seventh of the total present death rate, and

Whereas, the majority of these cases might have been avoided by the observance of certain hygienic precautions.

Therfore, be it resolved by the American Congress of Tuberculosis, in New York assembled, May 16, 1901:

1. That it is the duty of the Governments to adopt measures to limit the spread of the disease.

2. That such measures should tend towards, (1). The education of the people through schools and dissemination of literature by the various Boards of Health. (2). By affording efficient and proper care of poor patients with the establishment of sanataria for such treatment.

3. A regular sanitary inspection of all public institutions, especially charities and correction.

4. An adequate inspection of all meats, milk, or food products, which may be diseased, or convey infection, or with a tendency to cause the disease.

5. A suitable control of the conduct of all tubercular patients to prevent the dissemination of the infectous materials.

Respectfully submitted,

JNO. A. DONOVAN, M. D., Butte, Mont.,
WM. C. WOODWARD, M. D., Washington, D. C.,
H. EDWIN LEWIS, M. D., Burlington, Vt.,
LOUIS LEROY, B. Sc., M. D., Nashville, Tenn.
H. F. CURTIS, M. D., Albany, N. Y.

The report was not discussed except by the Honorary President, Dr. A. N. Bell, who made a very strong plea against such action and thought it unwise and injudicious.

The report was unanimously adopted without a division.

The secretary read a letter from Dr. Malcolm Morris, General Secretary of the British Congress of Tuberculosis, to be held in London, July 22, 23, 24 and 25 next, inviting this Congress to send delegates to that body.

On motion the invitation was accepted and the executive officers or executive committee were authorized to name and appoint such delegates to that Congress and that the officers be instructed to name a committee to present to that Congress a resume of the work of this body.

Dr. C. K. Cole, of Helena, Montana, offered the following resolution, Resolved, That a select committee of fifteen be appointed by the chair to prepare and submit to the next meeting a comprehensive and detailed report, with recommendations to the Congress concerning the following: Federal and State legislation on the prevention and treatment of tuberculosis—including a hospital scheme for tubercular patients, with a map showing the tubercular belt, and the relatively immune districts in the United States," which was seconded and on motion adopted unanimously.

Dr. C. K. Cole moved, on the suggestion of the president, Dr. Henry D. Holton, "That a vote of thanks be extended by the whole body to the Hon. Clark Bell, Secretary of this Congress, for the energy, industry and great ability with which he had brought the session of this Congress to such a successful termination. The motion was carried unanimously.

The attention of members was called to the banquet in the evening, and the Congress adjourned sine die

HENRY D. HOLTON, M. D.,
President of American Congress of Tuberculosis.

CLARK BELL,
President Medico-Legal Society.

SAMUEL BELL THOMAS, Ass't Secretary Medico-Legal Society.

LAKE KEUKA MEDICAL AND SURGICAL ASSOCIATION.

ANNUAL MEETING HELD AT GROVE SPRINGS, AUGUST 13 AND 14, 1901.

11 A. M., AUGUST 13, 1901.

The Association met at the Pantheon of the Grove Springs Hotel, on Lake Keuka, N. Y., Dr. Henry Flood, of Elmira, N. Y., in the chair, and Dr. W. W. Smith, of Avoca, N. Y., Secretary, with a very large attendance of members and the following invited guests:

Dr. Roswell Park, Dr. Earnest Wende, Dr. Charles G. Stockton, of Buffalo; Dr. Charles G. Wagner, of Broome; Dr. John B. Deaver, of Philadelphia, Pa.; Dr. A. T. Kunkel, M. D., of Westfield, Pa.; Dr. MacDonald, of New York, editor of the International Journal of Surgery; Clark Bell, Esq., editor Medico-Legal Journal, of New York City and others.

The President called Dr. Bush, of Horseheads, to the chair and delivered his address, which was devoted to the danger of certifying lunatics, citing a case from his own practice when his associate and himself were prosecuted because of a legal error of the committing magistrate, but justified after a long and expensive trial by both Court and jury, though at great expense and loss of time and money.

The amount of fees to certifying physicians in lunacy cases was also discussed, which in some counties has been fixed in cases of indigent lunatics at $5, and in some at $10. The address was discussed by Dr. Howe, of Phelps; Dr. Ira B. Smith, of Bath, N. Y.; Dr. C. L. Stiles, of Owego, and Dr. Arthur W. Booth, of Elmira.

The next paper was read by Dr. George Conderman, of Hornellsville. It was a scholarly and able presentation of the subject and a brilliantly written analysis of Syphilis of the Brain. It was discussed by Dr. Stephens and by Dr. Frank Ross, of Elmira, N. Y.

Dr. Charles G. Wagner, Superintendent of the State Hospital for the Insane, at Binghampton, read a paper on "Melancholia," as to the treatment outside public institutions. It was discussed by Dr. Howe, of Phelps; Dr. A. W. Booth, of Elmira.

Dr. Charles G. Stockton, of Buffalo, read a paper on Lobar Pneumonia, which was discussed by Dr. C. L. Stiles, of Owego; Dr. Frank Ross, of Elmira; Dr. C. S. Parkhill, of Hornellsville; Dr. Carr, of Wayne.

Dr. Arthur W. Booth, of Elmira, read a paper (No. 6) on the programme, "Relation of the Mosquito to Malaria," which was discussed by Dr. Frank Ross, of Elmira.

Dr. Earnest Wende, of the Board of Health of the City of Buffalo, read a paper on "The Small-pox Problem," which gave rise to an extended discussion in which Dr. H. D. Wey, of Elmira, opening it was followed by Dr. C. L. Stiles, of Owego; Dr. Wm. A. Howe, of Phelps; Dr. C. S. Parkhill, of Hornellsville, and Mr. Clark Bell. The Association then took a recess until 9 o'clock, A. M. of the 14th.

The Chemung delegation entertained the members at a smoker at the Keuka Club House in the evening.

WEDNESDAY, AUGUST 14, 9 A. M.

The Association met with President Henry Flood, M. D., in the chair, and Dr. W. W. Smith, Secretary.

It was moved and carried that a committee of seven be named by the chair to consider a revision of the constitution and by-laws and all other matters before the body.

Dr. Charles W. M. Brown, of Elmira, read a paper on "The Necessity of Proper Diet for Infants at the Beginning," which was discussed by Dr. Wales, of Elmira; Dr. Wende, of Buffalo, and Dr. Stiles, of Owego.

Dr. Wm. A. Howe, of Phelps, read a paper "Early Prophylaxis in Obsterics," which was discussed by Dr. Ira B. Smith, of Bath; Dr. H. D. Wey, of Elmira; Dr. A. L. Beahan, of Canandaigua and Dr. C. W. M. Brown, of Elmira.

Dr. W. B. Clapper, of Farmington, N. Y., read a paper on "Tetanus," the discussion of which was opened by Dr. M. L. Bennett, of Watkins. Dr. Ira B. Smith gave details of cases of recovery in his practice. Dr. Frank Ross, of Elmira, reported a large number of cases, all fatal, and stated that he regarded the disease as always fatal. Dr. M. T. Babcock, Hammondsport, stated a large number of cases,—all fatal but one,— which he successfully treated with morphine.

Mr. Clark Bell stated the action of the Medico-Legal Society regarding the use of the anti-toxin of Tetanus, based on the report of the late Dr. Paul Gibier, and microscopical experiments of the microbe, report of the use of anti-toxins in the treatment of this disease, which resolutions made it the duty of every physician to use the anti-toxin in such cáses.

Dr. Roswell Park made an interesting statement of the successful use of the anti toxin in cases of tetanus, and advised that it be used freely and as early as possible. He advised its generous use in the disease as necessary and pronounced it successful if administered in time and in sufficient quantities.

The chair announced as the Committee on Revision of Constitution and By-Laws, and other matters:

Dr. A. L. Beahan, of Ontario; Dr. J. G. Kelley, of Steuben; Dr. Jonas Jacobs, of Chemung; Dr. M. L. Bennett, of Schuyler; Dr. Sherer, of Yates; Dr. Sharp, of Livingston, and Dr. C. L. Stiles, of Tioga.

Dr. Floyd then called to the chair Dr. Jack, of Canisteo, who presided.

Dr. John A. Roe, of Rochester, read a paper on "Asthma in its Relation to Nasal Disease," which was discussed by Dr. G. M. Case, of Elmira.

Dr. A. L. Beahan, of Canandaigua, read a paper on "Appendicitis and when to operate." It was discussed by Dr. C. S. Parkhill, of Steuben; Dr. Howe, of Phelps; Dr. Hubbs, of Addison, and Dr. J. B. Deaver, of Phil'a, was then called and made an eloquent powerful and brilliant address favoring early operation in cases of appendicitis. It was the most interesting feature of the session.

Dr. Deaver was most intense and enthusiastic, his earnestness of manner, complete knowledge of the subject and great experience, made all in all a scene rarely seen in a medical body. At least one hundred and fifty physicians were present. He spoke for about twenty minutes, and no one who heard him will ever forget it. He was full of the theme and gave full flow and vent to his convictions with great earnestness.

Dr. J. B. Deaver read a paper on "Surgery of the Billiary Passage," which was discussed by Dr. Stockton, of Buffalo; Dr. Philo K. Stoddard, of Prattsburgh, N. Y.; Dr. Brown, of Elmira, and Dr. Jack, of Canisteo.

Dr. H. P. Jack, of Canisteo, then called Dr. C. S. Stiles, of Owego, to the chair, and read a paper entitled "Cancer of the Uterus," which was discussed by Dr. Ross, of Elmira.

Dr. A. Kunkel, of Westfield, Pa., read a paper on "Pathology in the German Countries."

At this hour, Dr. Walker, of Corning, who was scheduled to read a paper on "Leprosy," stated that there was not time for its reading and discussion and asked leave to withold it, which was granted.

The chair had invited Mr. Clark Bell to present a resume of the transactions of the American Congress of Tuberculosis held in May, 1901, in New York city to the Association, if time permitted after the programme was finished, but the lateness of the hour and the time for the departure of the steamers forbade it, and the order of miscellaneous business was taken up, with Dr. Henry Flood, President, in the chair.

Dr. Jacobs, of Chemung, from the Committee of Seven, submitted a report from that committee nominating officers for the ensuing year:

For President, Dr. C. S. Parkhill, of Steuben.

For Vice-President, Dr. D. L. Allen, of Seneca.

For Secretary and Treasurer, Dr. W. W. Smith, of Steuben.

On motion the report was received and approved. On proceeding to the election the gentlemen recommended by the Committee were duly and severally unanimously elected.

Dr. Parkhill, President-elect, was introduced and made a short address. He complimented Dr. Flood whose administration had been so successful, on the success of his labor.

FFICERS, MEMBERS AND AUTHORS, TI
SURGICAL ASSO

oses T. Babcock, M. D.,
Hammondsport, N. Y.

Duncan S. Allen, Vice Pres.,
Seneca, N. Y.

r. Chas. E. Doubleday,
Penn Yan, N. Y.

C. S. Parkhil
Hornellsv

Chas. G. W
Bingha

Dr. Ro
Br

He accepted the honor with diffi nce because he knew how difficult it would be for him to equal t' work of his predecessor. He appealed to members to sustain hi in his efforts, and to contribute papers.

He thanked Dr. Alden, of Han ondsport, for his strong help in which he knew Dr. Flood wou join him, and proposed to do his utmost to make it a success.

A vote of thanks to the retiring (:cers was passed and the meeting adjourned.

The session was a great succe s point of numbers; outside the programme more than 200 attende during the session.

Only four of the announced pap s were not presented, and excuses were sent from those autho who were prevented from attendance by unexpected circumstai es.

A pleasant feature of the meeti was tha the Doctors brought their wives, many of them, and th e was an unusually large number of ladies present.

Dr. Robert Bell, of Monterey, Sc iyler County, now 86 years of age, hale and hearty, the oldest liv g practioneer in th e State still in active practice, may almost be ailed the nestor of the profession, was present. Dr. Moses T. abcock, of Hammondsport; Dr. Philo K. Stoddard, of Prattsburgh, . Y., and Dr. Ira B. Smith, of Bath, were present; all army irgeons in the War of the Rebellion in the early sixties; a still in harness and standing high in their work. It was a boc of physicians in general practice of which any section of the St e migh well have been proud, and its influence must be felt for ood, as well among the physicians themselves in encouraging a etter acquaintance and feeling, as in the community; which must h d in higher esteem a profession who thus use the summer vacatic and period of recreation for scientific inquiry for the advancement of medical :ience and the good of the race.

BIOGRAPHICA SKETCHES.

SWELL PARK, A. M., M. D., Pof. of Surgery, Director Medical Bureau Pan-American Exposition, Buffalo, N. Y.

r. Roswell Park was educated t Racine College and took his 'ee of M. D. at the Chicago M lical College—Medical Depart- ; of Northwestern University.

1877 he taught anatomy afte servi :e as instructor in Cook y Hospital.

vas first demonstrator of Ai tomy in the Woman's Medical ; then lecturer on Surgery . Rush Medical College, and in s offered the chair of Surg y in the University of Buffalo, e has since filled with honc to the college and himself.

lds the degree of A. M. fro Harvard, and of M. D. from rest University.

a graceful speaker and sta: s in the front rank of his pro- a the State.

FFICERS, MEMBERS AND AUTHORS, THE LAKE KEUKA MEDICAL AND SURGICAL ASSOCIATION.

OSES T. BABCOCK, M. D.,
Hammondsport, N. Y.

C. S. PARKHILL, President,
Hornellsville N. Y.

ROBERT BELL, M. D.,
Monterey, N. Y.

DUNCAN S. ALLEN, Vice Pres.,
Seneca, N. Y.

CHAS. G WAGNER, M. D.,
Binghamton, N. Y.

W. W. SMITH, Sec'y and Treas.,
Avoca, N. Y.

R. CHAS. E. DOUBLEDAY,
Penn Yan, N. Y.

DR. ROSWELL PARK,
Buffalo, N. Y.

W. A. HOWE, M. D.,
Phelps, N. Y.

He accepted the honor with diffidence because he knew how difficult it would be for him to equal the work of his predecessor. He appealed to members to sustain him in his efforts, and to contribute papers.

He thanked Dr. Alden, of Hammondsport, for his strong help in which he knew Dr. Flood would join him, and proposed to do his utmost to make it a success.

A vote of thanks to the retiring officers was passed and the meeting adjourned.

The session was a great success in point of numbers; outside the programme more than 200 attended during the session.

Only four of the announced papers were not presented, and excuses were sent from those authors who were prevented from attendance by unexpected circumstances.

A pleasant feature of the meeting was that the Doctors brought their wives, many of them, and there was an unusually large number of ladies present.

Dr. Robert Bell, of Monterey, Schuyler County, now 86 years of age, hale and hearty, the oldest living practioneer in the State still in active practice, may almost be called the nestor of the profession, was present. Dr. Moses T. Babcock, of Hammondsport; Dr. Philo K. Stoddard, of Prattsburgh, N. Y., and Dr. Ira B. Smith, of Bath, were present; all army surgeons in the War of the Rebellion in the early sixties; all still in harness and standing high in their work. It was a body of physicians in general practice of which any section of the State might well have been proud, and its influence must be felt for good, as well among the physicians themselves in encouraging a better acquaintance and feeling, as in the community; which must hold in higher esteem a profession who thus use the summer vacation and period of recreation for scientific inquiry for the advancement of medical science and the good of the race.

BIOGRAPHICAL SKETCHES.

ROSWELL PARK, A. M., M. D., Prof. of Surgery, Director Medical Bureau Pan-American Exposition, Buffalo, N. Y.

Dr. Roswell Park was educated at Racine College and took his degree of M. D. at the Chicago Medical College—Medical Department of Northwestern University.

In 1877 he taught anatomy after service as instructor in Cook County Hospital.

He was first demonstrator of Anatomy in the Woman's Medical College; then lecturer on Surgery in Rush Medical College, and in 1883 was offered the chair of Surgery in the University of Buffalo, which he has since filled with honor to the college and himself.

He holds the degree of A. M. from Harvard, and of M. D. from Lake Forest University.

He is a graceful speaker and stands in the front rank of his profession in the State.

His works "Lectures on Surgical Pathology," and "The History of Medicine," brought him prominently to public notice.

He is the editor and principal author of the "Text Book on American Surgery," a work now in its third edition.

He has doubtless acquired a higher public recognition by his selection as Director of the Medical Bureau of the Pan-American Exposition of 1901, a position he now holds. It was fortunate that Dr. Park was at hand at the assassination of President McKinley. He was the best qualified man that could have been selected for the position he filled in the surgical work of that case that could have been found.

We publish in another column his remarks, or an abstract of them, on tetanus, in the discussion of Dr. Clapper's paper on that subject, which is not yet ready for publication.

CHARLES GRAY WAGNER, M. D., Binghamton, N. Y.

Dr. Charles Gray Wagner was born at Minden, New York; fitted for college in the public schools of Utica; graduated from Cornell University in 1880, and from the College of Physicians and Surgeons, New York, in 1882. He served as interne in the New York City Presbyterian Hospital two years, from which he was made Assistant Physician in the State Hospital for Insane at Utica, where he served seven years and chose the position of an alchemist. In Assistant Physician in the State Hospital for Insane at Utica in 1884, where he served seven years. In 1889 he went abroad and spent some time in studying the foreign hospitals.

In 1891 he stood first in the competitive examination for advancement under Civil Service rules for positions in State institutions.

In 1892 he was appointed superintendent of the Binghamton State Hospital by the Board of Managers to succeed Dr. Armstrong, a position he has since held, and his service has been most successful, placing that institution in the front rank of the New York State institutions, and in many respects among the best of any country.

In 1896 he was President of the Broome County Medical Society. In June 1896 he was elected trustee for the Alumni of Cornell University, and he was re-elected to that position in 1901, which office he still holds.

Dr. Wagner is a disciple and follower of the non-restraint system in the care and treatment of the insane.

He put in practice in the Binghamton State Hospital, introduced the open door system, with great personal freedom to inmates, in 1893, which has been most successful there, so that Binghamton State Hospital may be now regarded as the most advanced in the open door system of any of the American asylums, and has no equal in Great Britain or upon the continent of Europe in this respect; mechanical restraint being entirely abandoned and not used for years.

He is of commanding presence, an eloquent and forcible speaker, a frequent contributor to the literature of mental medicine; universally respected, and occupies to-day a high position among American alienists.

MOSES T. BABCOCK, M. D., Hammondsport, N. Y.

Among the older members of the Lake Keuka Medical and Surgical Association stands the name of Dr. Moses T. Babcock, who stands high in all the Lake Keuka region not only in his profession but in the public estimation.

Dr. Babcock was born in Washington county, New York, April 30, 1825. He was educated at Franklin Academy, and was there a classmate of the writer; was successful as a teacher, studied medicine, and graduated at Geneva Medical College in 1852, and commenced practice at Hammondsport, New York, taking post-graduate courses at the Buffalo Medical College in 1855 and 1858.

In the war of the Rebellion he served with honor and distinction, entering the 141st New York as Assistant Surgeon in the fall of 1862, and served until the close of the war.

He was at the following battles of that war.

Suffolk, Va.; Wauhatchie, Lookout Mountain, Mission Ridge, Capville, Resaca, Dallas, Kenesaw Mountain, Marietta, Peach Tree Creek, siege of Atlanta, siege of Savannah, Bentonville and Raleigh.

He was complimented for his service by the chief of the 20th Army Corps, 1st Division, May 30th, 1865, and later by the Surgeon in charge of the 107th Regiment of Field Hospital, 1st Division, 20th Army Corp, in June 1865.

He has been a member of the State Medical Association since 1884, and has served as President of the Steuben County Medical Society.

He is an influential member of the Lake Keuka Medical and Surgical Association.

PHILO K. STODDARD, M. D.

Dr. Stoddard was born in Jerusalem, Yates County, New York, September 28, 1825. He is of Revolutionary stock. His ancestor settled in Danbury, Conn., and his grandfather served in the Revolutionary War.

Dr. Stoddard was educated at Franklin Academy, Prattsburgh, New York, after attending the common school of his youth in Yates County,. He was a teacher in the common school, and served one term as a teacher at Franklin Academy.

He studied medicine with Dr. Elisha Doubleday, of Italy Hill; later with Dr. Andrew Voorhees, of Prattsburgh. He was a student at Geneva Medical College in 1845-6, graduated from Buffalo Medical College in June, 1848, and commenced the practice of his profession at Prattsburgh, New York, where he has since resided.

For more than half a century he has been in active practice.

Although not as old as Dr. Robert Bell, of Monterey, he is without any competitor who has practiced for more than fifty-three years at one place.

He may be called one of the medical pioneers of Steuben county.

He volunteered in the war of the Rebellion as a volunteer surgeon after the second battle of Bull Run. In 1863 he was commissioned an Assistant Surgeon of the 161st New York, and served during the war with this regiment. He was at the battles of Mansfield, Pleasant Hill, Spanish Fort, at the capture of Mobile, and served at New Orleans, and at the Dry Tortugas, and at the hospitals of Vicksburgh, White River Landing.

Dr. Stoddard is a man of great personal courage, of splendid physique, of strong convictions, of strictly temperate habits, and has ever exercised a commanding influence in his section.

He wears his years splendidly, and at the session was strong, vigorous and energetic. He is one of the staunchest friends of the Society and has never missed a meeting.

IRA P. SMITH, M. D., of Bath, New York.

Ira P. Smith was born at Dansville, Steuben county, N. Y., Aug. 19th, 1835, of New England parentage. Was educated at the Rogersville Union Seminary, and at the University of Michigan. Read medicine wth Dr. Chas. S. Ackly, of Rogersville. Was graduated at Albany Medical College in1859. Began practice at Avoca, N. Y., where he remained two years, when he entered the military service as an acting assistant surgeon in the Regular Army, serving from August, 1862, to September, 1864, when he resigned and went to Bath, N. Y., where he has been in practice thirty-six years. He has served as coroner, as examiner for pensions on the Bath board. He has also ben health officer, president of County Medical Society, and president of County Bible Society; also an examiner for several life insurance companies. He was married in 1866 to Harriet A. Smith, daughter of John J. Smith, whose father came to Bath with Col. Williamson, the founder of the town.

W. W. SMITH, M. D., Avoca, N. Y.

Dr. W. W. Smith, the Secretary and Treasurer of the Lake Keuka Medical and Surgical Association, was born at Howard, Steuben county, New York, in 1846. His education was acquired in the district schools and at Lima Seminary. He studied medicine under Dr. A. B. Case, a man of great ability in his time, at Howard, New York; graduated at Bellvue Hospital Medical College in March, 1871.

Dr. Smith has been President of the Steuben County Medical Society, and has been a successful practioneer at Avoca, Steuben county, since his graduation.

He has a genius for the successful work of societies as secretary and treasurer.

He has served the Steuben County Medical Society in that capacity, and was the unanimous choice of the Lake Keuka Medical and Surgical Society for that position, in which he has served with great acceptability since its organization.

CHARLES E. DOUBLEDAY, M. D.

Dr. Charles E. Doubleday was born April 3, 1864, at Italy Hill, Yates county, New York. His father was Dr. Guy L. Doubleday, who was born, lived, practiced and died there in 1870, at the age of 43 years, just as he was entering upon a most successful professional career.

He is the grandson of Dr. Elihsa Doubleday, of Cortland county, New York, who came in an early day to Italy Hill, and who had an extensive and lucrative practice in the Lake Keuka region in Steuben, Yates and the adjoining counties, when the writer was a student at Franklin Academy, Prattsburgh, Steuben county, New York, and who died at Italy Hill universally respected and esteemed.

Dr. Charles E. Doubleday is then born and reared along medical lines, of a race of physicians.

He graduated in 1887 at the Medical College at Syracuse, N. Y. He then spent two two years abroad studying at foreign universities—Heidelberg and Vienna—under the ablest masters, and commenced practice on his return in 1890, at Penn Yan, New York, where he has built up a most successful practice.

He has taken a post-graduate course and keeps abreast of the times in the practice of his profession.

He was one of the Committee of Seven of the Lake Keuka Medical and Surgical Association, and is one of the rising young men of his county.

WILLIAM AUGUSTUS HOWE, B. S., M. D.

Dr. Howe was born at Phelps, N. Y., September 11, 1862, son of the late Dr. John Q. Howe, who practiced medicine continuously in Phelps for forty-seven years. He was graduated from the High School of his native place in 1882. In the fall of the same year he entered Hobart College, from which institution he was graduated in 1885. The next three years were spent by him in the College of Physicians and Surgeons, New York city, where he received the degree of M. D. in 1888.

Since his graduation he has been actively engaged in his profession at Phelps, N. Y., where he enjoys a large and substantial practice. The doctor is President of the Ontario County Medical Society, a member of the Central New York Medical Society, the Lake Keuka Medical and Surgical Association, the Rochester Academy of Medicine, and always takes an active part in the deliberations of these organizations. He has served two terms as coroner of his county, is a member of the U. S. Board of Pension Examiners at Canandaigua, is Health Officer of the village of Phelps, has been a member of the Board of Education for many years, and is public spirited and progressive in all of his ideas. He has devoted more or less time to literary efforts and is a clear and comprehensive writer.

ROBERT BELL, M. D.

Dr. Robert Bell may well be styled the Nestor of the medical profession in the Lake Keuka region of the State.

Born at Belfast, Ireland, August 15, 1815, he came as a lad to our shores, and has for more than two generations of man been identified with the material growth of our country, where he has come to be a physician of high standing, and a citizen of wealth and influence in his section.

He graduated at Geneva Medical College, January 20, 1845, and has been in active practice ever since.

induced to locate at Monterey, Schuyler County, on account of its favorable climate for his invalid wife, as the air of that valley has great value in cases of tuberculosis.

Perhaps the greatest triumph of his professional life is saving

His early life was spent in Elmira and other places, and he was

her life. She was with him at the session of the Society.

Dr. Bell, although at the great age of 86, is hale, hearty and vigorous, and still in an active practice, besides engaging in business and other pursuits.

He does not show his years. He has a beautiful home, and disburses a genial and generous hospitality, and may well be classed as one of the most accomplished men of his profession.

DUNCAN STEWART ALLEN, M. D., Vice President Lake Keuka Medical and Surgical Association, of Seneca, N. Y.

Dr. Allen was born in Amsterdam, N. Y. His early education was obtained in the common school. Then he entered Franklin Academy at Prattsburgh,N. Y., and later the Michigan University,at Ann Arbor.

He studied medicine first at the Buffalo Medical College, and later graduated in 1864 at Albany Medical College.

He commenced the practice of medicine in Branch county, Michigan, remained there three years, and in 1870 he removed to Seneca, N. Y., where he has since remained and built up a lucrative practice.

He has been President of the County Medical Society of his county is a member of the Medical Association of Central New York; a member and president of the Board of Examining Surgeons for Pensions of Ontario county.

He stands high in his profession; is held in high esteem by his associates; and was elected vice president of the Lake Keuka Medical and Surgical Asociation at its recent session.

CYRUS C. HARVEY, M. D., of Dundee, N. Y.

Dr. Cyrus C. Harvey is a native of Tompkins County, where he was reared on a farm. Born in 1848 he has been entirely the architect of his own fortunes and is wholly self-educated, and has the rare faculty of learning from books, of which he is a profound student. He graduated at the University of Buffalo in 1877, and commenced the practice of medicine in Dundee, New York, where he has not only built up a large and lucrative practice, but has acquired a snug fortune by careful and judicious investments, for which he has rare and wonderful adaptation.

While none of his medical brethren are more careful, painstaking and attentive to the sick than he, he has given large attention to public affairs, and he has a strong hold on the people of his section as a public leader.

He was elected Coroner of his county and served in that position twelve years. He has served as Pension Examiner for the Government ten years. He has served as a member of the Board of Education twelve years, and has recently been elected Supervisor of his town, a position he now holds. He is a prominent member of the Lake Keuka Medical and Surgical Association.

While Dr. Harvey is an excellent physician, and is an ideal family physician to the families he serves, his chief excellence in his profession is his rare skill as a surgeon, for which branch of the profession he has peculiar and splendid qualifications.

He is a member of the Medico-Legal Society of New York, and was selected by that body as a delegate to the Paris International Medical Congress of 1900, which he attended, taking part in the work of the Section on Legal Medicine, for which he has a strong inclination.

His career, both as a physician and a publicist, has just fairly opened; and he has a brilliant future before him if his life is spared.

THE AMERICAN ROENTGEN RAY SOCIETY.

The Second Annual meeting of this young Society was held at the Amphitheatre of the University of the City of Buffalo, on September 10th and 11th, 1901, with a very large attendance, under the Presidency of Dr. H. Robarts, of St. Louis, Mo. At the first day session, 2 p. m., the following papers were read:

TUESDAY, SEPTEMBER 10th, 2 P. M.

The Diagnostic value of the Roentgen Rays with special reference to their application in Medico-legal cases,
Dr. Mihran K. Kassabian, Philadelphia, Pa.

An Examining Frame and "One Minute" Localizer, with demonstrations; Dr. S. H. Monell, New York City.

How the induction Statistic Machine can be excited without a separate charger, Dr. John T. Pitkin, Buffalo, N. Y.

The X-Ray in country practice, Dr. Joseph C. Clark, Olean, N. Y.

What the X-Rays show in Actinomycosis,
Dr. G. E. Foseberg, Cedar Rapids, Ia.

X-Ray work in Great Britain, results of a trip,
Dr. G. P. Girdwood, Montreal, Canada.

TUESDAY, SEPTEMBER 10th, 8 P. M.

The President, Dr. Heber Robarts, delivered his Presidential address. There was a stereopticon display of instructive cases. Dr. Julius Silversmith, of Chicago, read a paper. H. Westbury, of Harrison, New Jersey, read a paper.

The following papers were read by title:

Brief remarks on the theapeutic value of the X-Ray and suggestion on a universal co-operation,
Dr. Constantin V. S. Boettger, Ottawa, Canada.

"Some Medico-legal X-Rays," illustrated,
Dr. F. Wesley Sells, Murray, Iowa.

Investigation of X-Ray problems,
Virgilio Machalo, Lisbon, Portugal.

Skiagraphy of the concretions in urine, especially cystine,
M. U. Dr. R. Jedlicka, Chirurgical Clinic, Prague, Bohemia.

WEDNESDAY, SEPTEMBER 11th, 10 A. M.

The following papers were read and discussed:

Why some mistakes are made in Radiography,
Dr. J. N. Scott, Kansas City, Mo.

Description of a simple and efficient form of Electrolytic Interruptor,
Dr. Elmer G. Starr, Buffalo, N. Y.

The treatment of Cutaneous Cancer by the X-Rays,
Dr. G. E. Pfhaler, Philadelphia, Pa.

Use of the X-Ray as a Therapeutic Agent, Illustrated, Demonstration,
Dr. H. P. Pratt, Chicago, Ill.

Some Light Rays in Tubeculosis,
Dr. J. Mount Bleyer, New York City.
X-Ray, an absolute necessity in Dental Surgery,
Dr. Frank Austin Roy, New York City.

A paper by Dr. J. Mount Bleyer was read by title. Dr. Roswell Park was introduced and made some interesting remarks regarding the use of the X Ray in the case of President McKinley.

WEDNESDAY, SEPTEMBER 11th, 2 P. M.

The following papers were read by title:

Development in Crookes Tubes in 1901,
H. Westbury, Harrison, N. J.
The Relative Efficiency of X-Ray Generators,
Dr. W. A. Price, Cleveland, O.
Turck's Gyromele and the X-Rays in diagnosis of the diseases of the Stomach. Demonstration. Illustrated,
Dr. J. Rudis-Jicinsky, Cedar Rapids, Ia.

The following officers were elected on recommendation of the nominating committee:

President—Dr. G. Girdwood, Montreal.
Secretary—Dr. James Bullitt, Louisville.
Treasurer—Dr. E. C. Florentine, Saginaw, Mich.

THE AMERICAN MEDICAL ASSOCIATION.

ANNUAL MEETING OF 1901.

Before the section on Materia Medica, Pharmacy and Therapeutics, under the chairmanship of N. S. Davis, M. D., of Chicago, and Frank Woodbury, M. D., Secretary, Philadelphia. The following papers were contributed at the afternoon session of the second day:

By Dr. S. E. Solly, "The Question of the Therapeutic Value of Residence in High Altitudes for Pulmonary Tuberculosis, and the Indications for this Treatment." The paper contrasts the high altitudes of Colorado with climates in other sections, and is an able examination of the effect on the blood of low and high temperatures.

Dr. Norman Bridge, of Los Angeles, Cal., contributed two papers: "The Adaptability of Southern California and Similar Climates to the Needs of Consumptives," and "The Proper Management of the Tuberculous Lung."

Dr. A. Burroughs, of Ashville, N. C., read a paper entitled "Nineteen Years Experience with Creosote in Tuberculosis." Dr. Burroughs favors large doses of 60 to 100 minims by the month in cod liver oil, whiskey or criane, three times a day, supplemented by inhalations of 15 to 20 minines daily in hydro carbon oil.

He commences with 20 minines daily of beech wood, creosote and runs it up to 80 with reports of many recoveries.

Prof. Arnold C. Klebs, of Chicago, read a paper on "Therapeutices in Pulmonary Tuberculosis." He reviewed briefly the various present methods of treatment, none of which were specific, but valuable with sanatarium methods, giving preference to the serum treatment. He questions the immigration theories which he regards as experimental. He favors sanitarium treatment and the inadvisability of relying on any drug, holding open air, hygiene and diet higher than drugs in treatment.

In the discussion that followed, Dr. S. C. Benney discussed the high altitude treatment and gave advice concerning it.

Dr. Miner, of Ashville, N. C., criticised Dr. Bridge's paper as not sufficiently definite as to "rest of the diseased lung."

Dr. Moon, of Nebraska, held that drugs and climate had little effect. That life in the open fresh air and sunshine were the most important of all curative agents.

Dr. S. C. N. Habberg discussed "Creosote," and attached great weight to its purity, and spoke of the manufacture and solubility.

He combatted Dr. Burrough's views as to large doses, and insisted that the greatest benefit could be obtained from small doses of 4 to 5,.or at most 10 Cg. given in capsules or pills, which would pass through the stomach into the intestines.

Dr. W. T. English, of Pittsburgh, read a paper before the Section on hygiene and sanitary science on "Pulmonary Tuberculosis." The element of fear in the patient was the subject, and he contended that a certain amount of fear should be instilled in the patient's mind as a curative agent to overcome that fearlessness which seems to be a concomitant of the adult patient.

MEDICAL EDITORS ASSOCIATION.

ANNUAL MEETING OF 1901.

The annual meeting held at St. Paul, June 3-5, 1901, was the most successful meeting held for fifteen years, both from point of attendance and the high standard of excellence of the papers presented. The paper by Dr. Burnside Foster, of St. Paul, entitled "Some Thoughts on the Ethics of Medical Journalism," was discussed by Doctors Lancater, Gould, Love and others. On motion of Dr. Foster, a committee consisting of Dr. Simmons, editor of the Journal of the A. M. A., Gould of American Medicine, and Foster of the St. Paul Medical Journal, was appointed to amend the constitution and by-laws of the association.

Other papers were those of Dr. John Punton, entitled "The Relative Value of Medical Advertising;" of Dr. Dudley S. Reynolds, entitled "Improvements in Medical Education;" Dr. Harold N. Moyer, "Relation of the Medical Editor to Original Articles."

Resolutions favoring the establishment of a psycho-physiological laboratory in the Department of the Interior at Washington, D. C., were adopted. A committee to draft a resolution requesting the Board of Directors of the Louisiana Purchase Exposition Co., in charge of the St. Louis World's Fair to recognize and commemorate in a suitable manner the great work done in medicine and surgery was appointed. The American Medical Journalist was selected as the official journal for publication of papers and proceedings.

The annual dinner of the association was held at the Metropolitan Hotel on the evening of June 3d, President Stone acting as toastmaster. The speakers of the evening were Doctors Love, Stone, Moyer, Matthews, Marcy, Fassett, Hall.

The officers for the ensuing year were elected as follows: President, Dr. Alex. J. Stone, of St. Paul; vice-president, Dr. Burnside Foster, of St. Paul; secretary and treasurer, Dr. O. F. Ball, of St. Louis.

The executive committee appointed for the ensuing year consisted of Doctors Gould, Matthews, Lillie, Fassett, Marcy.

The next meeting will be held at Saratoga Springs, N. Y., in June, 1902.

TETANUS.

Discussion of Dr. W. B. Clapper's paper on Tetanus by Dr. Roswell Park, of Buffalo, N. Y.

Tetanus is by no means a common disease. I do not suppose that I average more than two or three cases a year under my own observation. It should never be forgotten that tetanus is an infectious disease, no matter what clinical type it may assume, nor what may be the apparent source or origin. Tetanus of the newborn, for instance, is due to infection at the moment, and by the method of tying the umbilical cord with a dirty ligature. The so-called cephalic tetanus is simply a clinical type where the principal manifestations are confined to the head and face. That tetanus is, practically, a germ disease is now established beyond a doubt, and yet about the action of its peculiar germ there is still much of mystery. Some eleven years ago, I brought to this country, I think, the first cultures of the tetanus bacillus which ever came to this side of the ocean. I had been working with it in Koch's laboratory, more or less, with the assistance of Kitasato, who was one of the early investigators of the subject. One experiment which I used to repeat for demonstration, and often do now, is to inoculate a small animal at some point, say, at the root of the tail, with culture of the organism. Then, waiting five minutes by the watch, take the actual cautery and with it destroy completely the inoculated area, and burn to a reasonable distance all around it. Almost invariably it will be found that this does not protect the animal. In animals dying under these circumstances, as in other cases, it is seldom, if ever, possible to demonstrate the presence of the organism at a distance from the site of the inoculation, and it must be inferred from this that the peculiar poison is disseminated very rapidly.

The toxine of tetanus, by the way, is extremely potent; is perhaps the most virulent of the toxines that we know of, since 1-1,000,000 of a grain is enough to destroy a small animal.

The lesson to be learned from the experiment above detailed is this: Given a small wound where we fear infection from tetanus, it is hopeless to try to ward off the disease by mere local attention, although such attention must not be neglected, because symptoms of general infection might easily occur were such caution not taken.

The bacillus of tetanus seems especially to abound in rich black earth, and in those regions where horses abound. There is probably some real connection between the conventional stable floor, with its rusty nail, and the wounds in the feet of men and horses, which develop tetanus in both alike. It is said that the only cases of tetanus occurring on ship board occur on transports used for horses. It is especially among soldiers who lie for hours upon moist earth, after receiving disabling injuries, that the disease most often appears, and curiously enough, also among those who have been laid upon church floors in extemporized hospitals, where accumulated dust of years will probably explain the prevalence of the disease. It is a disease common to men and animals alike, though much less fatal in horses than in man. Veterinarians succeed in saving many horses, but physicians save few patients, or at least, they saved but few before the introduction of the anti-toxine.

In the treatment of the disease one must not lose sight of the necessity both for nutrition and elimination. A patient who has a convulsion every time anything is put to his lips may starve to death before he would die of the disease, and a patient whose elimination is completely neglected has added to his specific poisoning a general toxemia, which only serves to make it still worse. It is essential, therefore, not to neglect a patient in these respects. If chloroform be given, as it can be given, to control spasm, it is possible, at the same time, to pass a stomach tube and introduce nutrition, and a rectal tube, by means of which an enema can be given. Hot air baths are also strongly indicated in order to assist in elimination. I would not make light of drugs for control of certain symptoms of the disease, but I would say that there is no drug upon which any particular dependence can be placed. Out of many cases of tetanus which I have seen, I never succeeded in saving one until I used the anti-toxin.

A few years ago it was suggested to inject the anti-toxin through a trephine opening directly into the nerve centres. I made the first attempt of this kind that was made in this country in a case which I have never published, but in which I did the work some weeks earlier than has been reported in any of the published cases. This was a well developed case of tetanus when I saw it, where I trephined promptly, and injected a full dose of the antitoxin, with temporary amelioration of symptoms, but at the time I used all the supply at hand and could not get more in time to be of any use. The patient got worse again and died.

Last year I saw a case, in connection with Dr. Dorr, of Buffalo, a case of the ordinary "Fourth of July" variety, i e., a case due to infection of a dirty hand, by an explosive accident, with consequent ragged wounds. It was a young man, who developed tetanus within a few days. This case was seen early. We commenced using antitoxin, and used, during its continuance, some 23 vials of Parke, Davis & Co's tetanus antitoxin. Symptoms could be controlled by use of this material with almost the same certainty that morphine controls pain. Patient made a complete and most satisfactory recovery, but I am sure that if we had used it but once or twice, instead of more than 20 times, he would not have recovered. As I study the literature of these cases, I am convinced that the mortality of the disease has been reduced from nearly 100 per cent. to between 40 and 50 per cent. by means of this remedy; and I feel sure also that were it used early and much more liberally, and continued as long as any symptoms of the disease are present, the mortality of tetanus might be cut down to 10 or 15 per cent. I feel very strongly upon this subject, and am glad to have such an opportunity as this to express my views.

Discussion Continued by Dr. Ira P. Smith.

Dr. Ira P. Smith, of Bath, reported two cases of tetanus, one with pathetic sittings, it being in a young man from the battle field of the Second Bull Run. The doctor in going through his ward at Armory Square, in Washington, (it being near where the Fish Commission building now stands), at twilight heard a young man crying. On going to him he said nothing, pointed to his jaws, in an instant the case was clear. He had received a shot through the hand and it was followed by lock-jaw. He realized that far from home and friends he could not live but a few hours. Hence the tears. Death relieved him before daylight the next morning.

The second case was that of a man of thirty-five, who had the end of a finger crushed in the cogs of a wheel. Several days after he went to the funeral of a relative and was saturated by a cold rain. The next day he was seized by tetanus. Hydrate of choral was the chief remedy. After nine days he died. The doctor emphasized the fact of the tetanus being followed by the drenching which he thought bore the relation of cause and effect.

JOURNALS AND BOOKS.

ILLINOIS STATE BOARD OF HEALTH. Annual report for 1901.

This report contains a complete historical statement of the whole system and plan of operation adopted through a series of years for the purification of the waters of the Chicago River and of the plan adopted to drain the waters of Lake Michigan through the Illinois River, and the disposal of the sewage of Chicago by this output.

The report contains an article by James A. Egan, M. D, Secretary of the Illinois State Board of Health, on the "Pollution of the Illinois River as Affected by the Drainage of Chicago and Other Cities" Also Prof. John H. Long, of the Northwestern University Medical School, on "Chemical and Bacterial Examinations of the Waters of the Illinois River and Its Principal Tributaries."

Report by Prof. Robert Zeit, M. D, and Prof. Gustave Pütterer, M. D., on "The Identification of Bacteria Found in the Waters of the Illinois River and Its Principal Tributaries." Also a "Preliminary Survey of the Illinois River Drainage Basin," by Jacob A. Harman, Civil Engineer of Peoria.

This report is of enormous value not alone for the inhabitants of Chicago, but of the Valley of the Illinois River.

It demonstrates that the Illinois River, into which the entire sewage of Chicago is now turned, purifies itself through natural causes.

Prof. Long says: "Of the possible effect of the water of the Illinois River at its entrance into the Mississippi, I believe that it may be safely said that if the whole of the sewage of Chicago were to be excluded from the Illinois River, the condition at Grafton would remain unchanged, as far as organic contents and bacterial organisms are concerned.

"With the flow from Chicago excluded there would be a diminution in the harmless nitrates and chlorides only."

The operations at Chicago in passing the waters of Lake Michigan into the Illinois River have become an object lesson to the world, and those scientists who have doubted the self-purification of rivers will find in this report a scientific basis of facts that demonstrates the entire success of the trial made for the city of Chicago and the disposal of the sewage.

Indeed, the whole sewage of Chicago is less a cause of pollution than the waters of Lake Michigan, which for so many years has received the sewage of that city and retained it save as natural forces have purified it.

"WHERE TO LOOK FOR THE LAW." Lawyers' Co-Operative Publishing Co., Rochester, N. Y.

This is a small hand book for lawyers in which a list of all subjects and titles of legal questions in an index alphabetically arranged are placed, with a reference to what book the lawyer should refer to under each separate heading, which references go to elementary works and State reports of cases decided.

Most lawyers would regard this as a saving of time. Instead of going through the reports under a title for example, he goes at once to the title in this index and there finds the reference to the works that treat on the same or the report of cases decided upon the question desired to be examined.

HISTORY OF MEDICINE By Alexander Wilder, M. D. New England Eclectic Publishing Co., New Sharon, Maine. 1901.

The National Eclectic Medical Association on June 19, 1890, at its annual meeting at Niagara Falls passed a resolution requesting Dr. Alexander Wilder to prepare a history of medical reform during the earlier periods to be published with the sanction of that body.

The volume now published is the response and fulfilment of that request. It is doubtful if there was in the ranks of the Eclectic School of Medicine a man better armed and equipped for such a work than Dr. Wilder.

He has taken the ten years intervening to prepare a work of nearly 1,000 pages, which in all ways fully complies with the original resolution.

It may be claimed that Dr. Wilder has gone too exhaustively into the medical history of earlier periods. We do not, however, regard this as a vice. It is not a bad idea to have this done for us by such a scholarly pen as Dr. Wilder uses.

His chapters on "Archaic Medicine," "Medicine in Ancient Historic Periods," "Medicine in the Middle Ages," "Medicine in the Renaissence," "Medicine in the Seventeenth Century," "Medicine in the Eighteenth Century," "The Evolution of Modern Chemisty," and "The Former Years of the Nineteenth Century," will richly repay the student of medicine or the advanced practitioner of any school.

He devotes 400 pages of his book to these themes before he takes up "The Evolution of the American Practice of Medicine."

The remainder of his work is devoted to a critical and detailed history of the med cal conflicts that give rise to the school known as the Eclectic School. i

Dr. Wilder has been a writer on medical and philosophical themes of prominence and commanding ability.

He is a profound student of medical science and of social, scientific and psychological studies.

This work will be the great effort of his career, and it will, we feel sure, be regarded as a classic and a standard authority by the physicians of his school.

CYCLOPEDIA OF LAW AND PROCEDURE. By Wm. Mack and Howard P. Nash. Vol. I. The American Law Book Co., New York. 1901.

The embodiment of decisions in encyclopedic form seems now, that the report of cases are so enormous in number as to be beyond the reach of the busy lawyer, to be accepted by the profession as a necessity.

The well defined heads under which by common usage the bar has for years classified under titles, is resorted to in this work alphabetically arranged.

The plan of this work is to have each title preceded by an analysis and in distinct heads, with sub-divisions and references to pages, and to follow this under each title to cross references, also arranged alphabetically, in large type, so as to make each title completely indexed in all its sub-divisions and relations.

The citations to the authorities are made in small type, but with good clear type.

The plan of the work is to have men of learning and experience write the articles on titles with which they are familiar and best qualified to speak or write.

For example, in Vol. I, under the title "Abatement and Revival" the author's name is given, Archibald C. Boyd, Esq.

The subject is exhaustively treated and occupies 130 pages of the volume.

It is certainly the best treatise on this title that is anywhere accessible to the practicing lawyer, and is treated under six heads with elaborate sub-divisions, and the cross references are forty in number.

The title "Abduction" is by John Lehman, Esq., under three distinct headings, with extended sub-divisions and with eight cross references.

The title "Abortion" is edited by Wm. H. Hamilton, Esq., under eleven distinct heads, with elaborate sub-divisions, with cross references to titles involved and the title occupies 34 pages of the work.

"Abstracts of Title" as a subject is edited by Hon. John S. Wilkes, of the Supreme bench of Tennessee, under five heads.

"Accident Insurance" is edited by Thomas A. Moran, Esq., under sixteen heads and elaborate sub-divisions and complete cross references, and occupies seventy pages of the work.

"Accord and Satisfaction" as a title is edited by the well-known writer Seymour D. Thompson, under nine heads with ample cross references, and occupies forty-five pages of the work.

"Accounts and Accounting" is by John Lehman, and occupies 152 pages of the work.

"Acknowledgements" is edited by George Hoadly, under seventeen heads, and occupies 123 pages of the book, and is an able and entirely exhaustive treatment of this title.

The title "Actions," is by Joseph F. Randolph, and occupies 123 pages of the work.

Judge Charles C. Cole, of the Supreme Court of the District of Columbia, edits the title "Adjoining Landowners," covering thirty-seven pages of the volume.

The title "Admiralty" is edited by Isaac N. Huntsberger, and occupies 116 pages of the book.

The title "Adulteration" is edited by Judge Charles L. Lewis, of the Supreme Court of Minnesota, and "Adverse Possession," by W. A. Martin, Esq., who occupies 187 pages.

The volume of 1160 pages closes with the title "Affectatus," not finishing one-third of the letter A of the alphabet.

The value of such a work to the profession depends almost entirely upon the ability of the author of each important title and the manner in which he has prepared it and to what extent it is exhaustive and correct. The profession must feel that they can rely upon it without verifying its citations.

The last work of this character was the American Encyclopedia of Law, which had an enormous sale, but disappointed the profession because many of the subjects were not edited with that care and precision which skilled practitioners and legal specialists would have given to the subject.

The value of this work and the success of the enterprize will depend upon this element.

If men are selected to write on themes with which they are thoroughly familiar and such as are known to the profession and entitled to its confidence, regardless of the expense attending such an effort, it will receive the support of the profession, and when completed will be a monument of honor to its promoters, and we believe will be amply remunerative.

BOOKS, JOURNALS AND PAMPHLETS RECEIVED.

TRUMAN W. BROPHY, M. D., D. D. S., LL. D., Chicago. Surgical Treatment of Palatal Defects.

WM. BAYARD, M. D., St. John, N. B. Prevention and Cure of Consumption. 1899.
Provincial Board of Health, of New Brunswick: Resolutions of January 31, 1899.
The New Brunswick Association for the Prevention of Consumption. Advice from Board of Directors.

WM. M. WARREN, Publisher, Detroit. "The Doctor's Logic Limps."

MATTHEW M. SMITH, M. D., Austin, Texas. "Prevention of Tuberculosis." 1901.
"The Public Health and the State's Duty to Protect It." 1900.
"Alumni Address, University of Texas." 1894.
"The Invisible Enemy and Our Methods of Defence." Memorial to Governor and Legislature. 1899.
"Mental Therapy." 1896.
Hon. A. W. Terrell's Address, "Incorporated Monopoly." 1899.

T B. LACEY, M. D., Council Bluffs, Iowa. Annual Transactions of the American Academy of Railway Surgeons for 1900. Vol. 7. 1901.

C. F. ULRICH, M. D., Wheeling, W. Va. "The Mission and Duties of the True Physician." 1901.

A M. HOLMES, M. D., Denver, Colorado. Prospectus and Officers of The Rocky Mountain Industrial Sanitarium of Denver, Colorado. 1901.

STATE BOARD OF HEALTH OF WISCONSIN. Circulars as to Means of Prevention of Consumption. March, 1895.
Circulars as to Bovine Tuberculosis and the Public Health. 1898.

DR. F. H. HARRISON, New York City. "Antiphlogistine." 1901.

MUTUAL RESERVE FUND LIFE ASSOCIATION, Insane Department of Nebraska. Report on examination of Mutual Reserve Fund, Life. August, 1900.

R. MACDONALD, 42 White Street, New York. "Consumption Can be Cured by the Superheated Dry Air Process." 1900.

F. E. DANIEL, M. D., Austin, Texas. The New Medical Practice Law of Texas. 1901.

MAJOR V. HAVARD, Chief Surgeon U. S. A. "Sanitation and Yellow Fever in Havana." Report. February, 1901.

WALTER LYMAN, M.D., Supervising Surgeon-General, Marine Hospital Service. Official List of Commissioned and Non-Commissioned Officers of the Marine Hospital Service. 1901.

F. W. DRAPER, M. D., Boston, Mass. Fourth Annual Report of Massachusetts State Sanatorium at Rutland, Mass. 1900.
First Report of Massachusetts Hospital for Consumptive and Tuberculous Patients. 1897.
Second Annual Report of Massachusetts Hospital for Consumptive and Tuberculous Patients. 1898.
Supplement to Second Annual Report. 1898.

CRISWELL MACLAUGHLIN, Esq., Cornwall on Hudson. The School Master. May Number, 1901.

STATE BOARD OF HEALTH OF MAINE. Abstract of Health Law of State of Maine. 1895.

IRVING A. WATSON, M. D., Concord, N. H. New Hampshire Sanitary Bulletin, Vol. I, No. 8. Copy Act to Establish Sanatorium for Consumptives.

WALTER LINDLAY, M. D. The Idlewild Sanatorium Prospectus, San Jacinta Mountains.

HENRY P. STEARNS, M. D. Seventy-Seventh Annual Report of the Hartford Retreat for the Insane. 1901.

HON. J. B. SEXTON, President Board of Health, City of New York. Reports on Tuberculosis, Health Department, New York City. 1893.

Information for Consumptives. 1899.

The Use of Anti-Toxic Serum, by Herman M. Biggs, M. D., and Arthur R. Guerad, M. D. 1896.

Regulation of Tuberculosis, by Dr. Herman Biggs. 1900.

Circular of Information to Physicians. 1899.

Circular of Information to Physicians. 1897.

Bacteriological Examinations in Early Diagnosis. 1899

Report of Health Department to Mayor W. L. Strong. 1897.

Accompanying official letter to the American Congress of Tuberculosis of 1901.

LOUIS LEROY, B. S., M. D., Nashville State Bacterologist, Prof. of Path. and Bact. in Vanderbilt University. Small Pox, its Diagnosis, Treatment, Restriction and Prevention. Published by the Tennessee State Board of Health.

BENCH AND BAR, Vol. I, No. 6. New Law Journal, Chicago, Ill.

THE INTERNATIONAL STUDIO. Sept., 1901. Vol. XIV. No. 55. 67 Fifth Ave., New York. Charles Holme, Esq., Editor.

This journal is ably edited and beautifully illustrated. Its leading articles are "The Revival of Tempera Painting," by Almer Vallance; "The Glasgow International Exhibition," "Some Drawings by Patten Nelson," by Walter Shaw Sparrow. Studio talk is very interesting.

MAGAZINES.

THE "NEW" LIPPINCOTT MAGAZINE. Contents for August, 1901.

"The Lifting of a Finger," Ina Brevoort Roberts; "The Time of the Singing of Birds," Phœbe Lyde; "Philosophy 4," Owen Wister," "Found," Florence Riley Radcliffe; "A Goddess on a Pedestal," Maud Appleton Hartwell; "Raindrops," Agnes Lee; "Brother Pidgley Saves the Day," Cyrus Townsend Brady; "Conventionalities," Grace F. Pennypacker; "A Rose and a Thorn," Henry Collins Walsh; "The Intervention of Gran'pap," Ella Middleton Tybout; "Midnight," Mary Forney Thunder; "The Mortification of the Flesh," Paul Laurence Dunbar; "Books of the Month;" "Walnuts and Wine."

The number is unusually good. Out of a large number, we clip the following:

RESIGNED TO HIS FATE. In the early Indiana days, when both judges and attorneys literally "rode the circuit," a newly-elected Judge, noted for his lack of personal beauty, was plodding along on horseback between two county-seats one fine summer day. Passing through a piece of woods he was suddenly confronted by a hunter, who unslung his squirrel-rifle from his shoulder and ordered the horseman to dismount.

Somewhat startled by this peremptory command and the fact that the hunter was, if possible, even more deficient in facial symmetry than himself, the jurist began to remonstrate. He was quickly cut short, however, by the remark.

"It's no use talking. I long ago swore that if I ever met a homelier man than I am, I'd shoot him on sight."

The Judge was quick-witted, and, sizing up the situation, he promptly got off his horse. Folding his arms, he faced his assailant and said,—

"If I am any homelier than you are, for Heaven's sake, do shoot, and be quick about it!"

Then came a hearty mutual laugh, and a black bottle, produced from the Judge's saddle-bags, was duly investigated. After this came self-introductions, and the rising jurist gained an enthusiastic supporter for his future campaigns.—E. P. HOWE.

PHRENOLOGICAL JOURNAL. Fowler & Wells Co., New York.

The September number of this journal is received. The first article (with frontispiece) is on "Phrenology Manifested Through Character," and indicates the science and art of phrenology. "Heredity" is the subject of F. S. Western's article, which, when completed, will prove an exhaustive contribution. Several "People of Note" are described; Mrs. Mary H. Hunt, Superintendent of Scientific Instruction in Schools, and Editor of the School Physiology; and Edward H. Boyer, Principal of School 87. The Child Culture Department is particularly attractive this month. The half-tones are helpful in illustrating the context.

THE LEDGER MONTHLY. Robert Bonner's Sons, Publishers.

The July number, 1901, is No. 9, of Vol. 57. It is ptinted on excellent paper, profusely but elegantly illustrated, and edited along the lines that distinguished and characterized its founder, that Robert Bonner who created it by his genius and made it one of the foremost of the popular weeklies of his time.

It has increased in cost manyfold, but not in price—$1.00 a year still stands at its head lines—and it is still worth many times its subscription price to the public.

It was Mr. Bonner's pride and boast that the Ledger should never have anything unclean in its columns, and he insisted that it should be characterized by a high moral tone.

His sons who succeed him have not departed from the ideas of the founder.

It is entirely safe to be placed in any family in the land.

HARPER'S MAGAZINE. The September number of this journal perhaps as well as any of its later numbers, illustrates the splendid superiority of this journal in its illustrations.

Take for example the article on Prague, with the illustrations by Leucius Hitchcock.

H. Reuterdahl's drawings for H. W. Williams' "New German Navy" are nearly as good.

Joseph J. Thompson, of the Carmelite Laboratory, at Cambridge, England, contributes an admirable paper on "Cathode Rays," which is clearly explained

THE RAILWAY SURGEON. This journal announces that it has changed to a monthly and has enlarged its size, which detracts from its appearance and will make an unwieldy sized volume for the library.

It also announces that it has concluded arrangements to act as the official organ of the International Association of Railway Surgeons.

MEDICAL EXTRACTS AND SELECTIONS.

THE INTRAVENOUS INJECTION OF COLLARGOLUM. In his paper on "Silver as an External and Internal Antiseptic in Gynæcology," published in *Die Medicinische Woche*, Berlin, May 28 and June 3, 1901, Professor B. Crede pays especial attention to the administration of the soluble metallic silver by the intravenous method, and gives the following detailed directions for the intravenous administration of the Colloidal Silver:

"The intravenous injection of Collargolum, which has given me astonishingly good results, is most suitable for severe general sepsis, pyæmia, large abscesses, foudroyant gangrene, intractable articular rheumatism, and similar serious affections. It may be accomplished in simple manner by any physician with efficient lay help. Any convenient and prominent vein can be employed; the most suitable is the left cephalic, but varicose veins of the extremity, if present, can be used. The patient being recumbent, the arm is permitted to hang down for a minute, and a bandage or ligature is firmly tied about the upper arm. The arm is then allowed to hang down for one or two minutes more. By this method, which is a little different from that usually employed, I believe that the small veins are more tensely filled. The skin over the vein is then washed, rubbed down with ether, and a perforated needle at least the size of a thick pin is introduced into the vein. If the point is in the lumen of the vein, blood will flow out of it; if this does not occur, the needle must be reintroduced until it does. The syringe is then attached, the ligature on the arm removed, and the solution of Colloidal Silver injected slowly, and with frequent pauses If there should be much resistance, it is probably because the point of the needle has been projected into the opposite wall of the vein; it should then be gently retracted a little."

We call particular attention to Professor Crede's detailed directions for the intravenous injection of Collargolum. It is precisely by this method that Crede has seen the most astonishing results in severe general sepsis. The state of the patient's skin and his general condition may exclude the inunction of the silver ointment, and in such cases the more rapid method of intravenous injection of the soluble silver should be the method of election.

The exhaustive paper "On the Influence of Urotropin Upon Intestinal Decomposition," by Prof. W. F. Loebisch, Director of the Laboratory for Applied Medical Chemistry at the Imperial and Royal University of Innsbruck, shows a new field of usefulness for urotropin, since, as Professor Loebisch concludes, the drug will be useful for purposes of intestinal disinfection in the numerous cases in which the ordinary disinfectants, the phenols, the cresols, tribromphenol, etc, and purgative remedies, such as calomel and the salines, are inapplicable. He found that the urine of patients taking the drug contained little or no indican, and since the presence of this substance in the urine is one of the most accessible and reliable indications of bacterial intestinal decomposition, it led him to investigate the action of the drug upon these ordinary intestinal changes It was proved beyond doubt that in the healthy individual on a mixed diet the ingestion of urotropin in daily doses of thirty grains inhibits ordinary bacterial intestinal decomposition.—*Wiener Medicinische Presse*," *July 7th aud 14th, 1901.*

THE
MEDICO-LEGAL JOURNAL.

Published under the Auspices of the Medico-Legal Society of New York.

CLARK BELL, ESQ.,
EDITOR-IN-CHIEF.

ASSOCIATE EDITORS:

LEGAL.

Prof. W. L. BURNAP, Vermont.
Judge ABRAM H. DAILEY, Brooklyn.
Judge JOHN F. DILLON, New York.
T. GOLD FROST, Esq., New York.
Judge C. G. GARRISON, Camden, N.Y.
F. L. HOFFMAN, Esq., Newark, N. J.
SAMUEL BELL THOMAS, Esq. N.Y.
W. H. S. MONCK, Esq , Dublin.
A. WOOD RENTON, Esq., London.

MEDICAL.

Dr. HAVELOCK ELLIS, London.
Prof. Dr. J. T. ESKRIDGE, Denver.
W. W. IRELAND, M. D., Scotland.
Prof. HERMAN KORNFELD, M. D., Gleiwitz, Silesia.
GEORGE B. MILLER, M. D., Phila.
JULES MOREL, M. D., Belgium.
T. F. SUTHERLAND, M. D., Edinburgh, Scotland.
H. EDWIN LEWIS, M. D., Burlington, Vt.

SCIENTIFIC.

C. VAN D. CHENOWETH, Mass.
Prof. R. O. DOREMUS, New York.
MORITZ ELLINGER, Esq., N. Y.
Prof. W. B. MACVEY, Boston.
Prof. W. XAVIER SUDDUTH, Chicago.
Prof. VICTOR C. VAUGHAN, Mich.

RAILWAY SURGERY.

LEGAL.

C. H. BLACKBURN, Esq., Cincinnati.
Judge WILLIAM H. FRANCIS, N.Y. City
C. A. LIGHTNER, Esq., Detroit.
Judge CONWAY W. NOBLE, Cleveland.
Hon. J. M. THURSTON, Nebraska.

MEDICAL.

CHARLES K. COLE, M. D., Montana.
GRANVILLE P. CONN, M. D. Concord.
A. P. GRINNELL, M. D., Burlington, Vt.
DWIGHT J. KELLY, M. D., Ohio.
R. HARVEY REED, M.D., Rock Spring, Wy
NICHOLAS SENN, M. D., Chicago.

VOL. XIX.—No. 3.

DECEMBER.

NEW YORK:
MEDICO-LEGAL JOURNAL.
1901.

MEDICO-LEGAL SOCIETY.

OFFICERS FOR 1902.

President,
CLARK BELL, ESQ., of New York.

1st Vice-President,
A. P. GRINNELL, M. D., Burlington, Vt.

2nd Vice-President,
T. D. CROTHERS, M. D., of Conn.

Vice-Presidents for the States, Territories and Provinces.

Alabama—Judge Thos. W. Coleman, Montgomery.
Alaska—Clarence Thwing, M. D., Sitka.
Arizona—D. M. Purman, M. D., Phoenix.
Arkansas—H. C. Dunavant, M. D., Osceola.
Austria—Prof. R. Krafft-Ebing, Vienna.
Belgium—Dr. Jules Morel, Mons.
Brazil—Prof. Nina Rodrigues, M. D., Bahia.
British Honduras—Adam Chevaillier, M.D., Balize
California—A. E. Osborne, M. D., Glen Ellen.
Colorado—Prof. J. T. Eskridge, M. D., Denver.
Connecticut—Judge A. M. Tallmadge, Bridgeport.
China—Harold Browett, Esq., Shanghai.
Cuba—Chief Justice HechaVarria, of Santiago.
Dakota, N.—Dr. Dwight S. Moore, Jamestown.
Dakota, S.—John M. Harcourt, Steele.
Delaware—Judge Ignatius C. Grubb, Wilm'gt'n
Denmark—Prof. Godeken, Copenhagen.
District of Columbia—W. C. Woodward, M. D., Washington, D. C.
Dom. of Canada—Hon. A. G. Blair, Ottawa.
England—Dr. Fletcher Beach, London.
Ecuador—Senor J. M. P. Caminano, Wash D. C.
Florida—N. de V. Howard, M. D., Sanford.
France—Victor Parent, M. D., Toulouse.
Georgia—Richard J. Nunn, M. D., Savannah.
Germany—Dr. H. Laehr, Berlin.
Guatemala—Senor Rafael Montufar.
Hawaii—J. W. Waughop, M. D., Kalia Kanai
Hayti.—Genl. J. A. Bordes, Jeremie.
Holland—Dr. P. A. H. Sueens, Vucht.
Hungary—Staatsanwalt Em. V. Havas, BudaPesth
Illinois—J. E. Owens, M. D., Chicago.
India—P. S. Sivaswamy Aiyar, Madras.
Indiana—W. B. Fletcher, M. D., Indianapolis.
Indian Territory—I. H. Bailey, M. D., Dexter.
Iowa—Jennie McCowen, M. D., Davenport
Ireland—Conolly Norman, M. D., Dublin
Italy—Enrico Ferri, M. D., Rome.
Japan—Dr. J. Hashimoto, Tokio
Kansas—Judge Albert H. Horton, Topeka
Kentucky—F. H. Clark, M. D., Lexington.
Louisiana—J. J. Scott, M. D., Shreveport.
Maine—Judge L. A. Emery, Ellsworth.
Manitoba—D. Young, M. D., Selkirk.
Maryland—Wm. Lee Howard, M. D., Baltimore.
Massachusetts—Theo. H. Tyndale, Boston.
Mexico—Leon Lewis, M. D., Ozuluama.
Michigan—Clarence A. Lightner, Detroit.
Minnesota—C. K. Bartlett, M. D., Minneapol
Missouri—W. B. Outten, M. D., St. Louis.
Montana—C. K. Cole, M. D., Helena.
Nebraska—Hon. John M. Thurston, Omaha.
Nevada—S. M. Bishop, M. D., Reno.
New Brunswick—Dr. Wm. Bayard, St. John.
Newfoundland—Dr. K. D. McKenzie, St. John
New Hampshire—Gran. P. Conn, M.D., Concor
New Jersey—Judge C. G. Garrison, Camden.
New Mexico—Gov. Bradford L. Prince, Santa F
New South Wales—George A. Tucker, M. D.
New York—Mrs. M. Louise Thomas, N. Y. Cit
New Zealand—Prof. Frank G. Ogston, Dunedi
North Carolina—E. C. Smith, Esq., Raleigh.
Norway—Dr. Harold Smedal, Christiana.
Nova Scotia—Hon. Wm. S. Fielding, Ottawa.
Ohio—Judge H. C. White, Cleveland.
Oklahoma Ter.—A. H. Simonton, M. D., Okla. C
Ontario—Daniel Clark, M. D., Toronto.
Oregon—Ex-Chief Just. Hon. Wm. P. Lord, Sale
Pennsylvania—Geo. B. Miller, M. D., of Phila.
Peru—Senor F. C. C. Zegarro, Washington, D.
Portugal—Bettincourt Rodriguez, M. D., Lisbo
Quebec—Wyatt Johnson, M. D., Montreal.
Rhode Island—Judge P. E. Tillinghast, Provid
Russia—Prof. Dr. Mierzejewski, St. Petersburg
San Domingo—A. Wei Vos Gil, San Domingo.
Saxony—Judge de Alinge, Oberkotzon Hof.
Scotland—W. W. Ireland, Edinburgh.
Servia—Hon. Paul Savitch, Belgrade.
Sicily—Prof. Dr. Fernando Puglia, Messina.
Silesia—H. Kornfeld, M. D., Grotkau.
South Carolina—S. W. Babcock, M. D., Columbi
Spain—Sig. A. M. Alv. Taladriz, M.D., Valladoli
Sweden—Prof. Dr. A. Winroth, Lund.
Switzerland—Prof. Dr. L. Wille, Basle.
Tennessee—Michael Campbell, M. D., Nashvill
Texas—Dr. D. R. Wallace, Terrell.
Tonga—Dr. Donald McClennen, Tonga.
Utah—Frederick Clifft, M. D., St. George.
Vermont—Henry D. Holton, M. D., Brattlebo
Virginia—William F. Drewry, Petersburg.
Washington—Jas. C. Waugh, M. D., Mt. Verno
West Virginia—F. M. Hood, M. D., Weston.
Wisconsin—Dr. U. O. B. Wingate, Milwaukee.
Wyoming—R. Harvey Reed, M. D., Rock Sprin

Secretary,
SAMUEL B. THOMAS, Esq., of N. Y. City.

Corresponding Secretary,
MORITZ ELLINGER, Esq., of N. Y. City.

Assistant Secretary,
A. A. JAKOBI, of N. Y. City.

Pathologist,
WM. S. MAGILL, M. D., N. Y. City.

Treasurer,
CAROLINE J. TAYLOR, Bridgeport, Conn.

Chemist,
PROF. C. A. DOREMUS, M. D., N. Y. City.

Curator,
J. MOUNT BLEYER, M. D., New York.

Toxicologist,
PROF. W. B. McVEY, of Boston.

Librarian,
FRED. L. HOFFMAN, ESQ., of N. J.

Assistant Librarian,
THOS. G. FROST, ESQ., of N. Y.

Bacteriologist,
G. BETTINI DI MOISE, M. D., of N. Y.

Microscopist,
DR. ERNEST J. LEDERLE, of N. Y.

TRUSTEES:

Legal,
H. GERALD CHAPIN, Esq., of New York.
JUDGE WM. H. FRANCIS, Newark, N. J.
JUDGE A. J. DITTENHOEFER, of N. Y. City.

Medical,
R. W. SHUFELDT, M. D., of N. Y. Cit
P. M. WISE, M. D., of N. Y. City.
ISAAC N. LOVE, M. D., of N. Y. City.

COUNSELLORS,

For 3 years.

Legal.
HENRY WOLLMAN, Esq., of N. Y. City.
STILES JUDSON, Jr., of Bridgeport, Conn.
JUDGE FRED. E. CRANE, of Brookly, N. Y.

Medical.
C. C. CARROLL, M. D., of N. Y.
CARLETON SIMON M. D., of N. Y. Cit
J. LEFFINGWELL HATCH, M. D., of N. Y. Cit

PERMANENT COMMISSION:

For 3 years.

Legal,
JUDGE CHARLES G. GARRISON, of N. J.
JUDGE L. A. EMERY, of Maine.
CLARK BELL, ESQ., of New York.

Medical,
NICHOLAS SENN, M. D., of Chicago.
PROF. VICTOR C. VAUGHAN, of Ann Arbor, Mich
GEO. L. PORTER, M. D., of Bridgeport, Conn

THE FOLLOWING ARE THE EXCHANGE JOURNALS.

Archives Italian,
Archivie Giuridico,
Archives d'Anthropologie Criminale,
Alienist and Neurologist,
American Journal of Insanity,
American Law Register,
Archives of Pediatries,
Archives de la Psychiatrie Clinique et Legale et de Neurologie,
Academie de Medicine de Paris,
American Journal of Psychology,
American Chemical Journal,
American Law Review,
Atlanta Medical and Surgical,
Annales Medico-Psychologique,
Archivio di Psi Sci pen et antro crim.,
Archives de Neurologie,
Annales Societe Medico-Legal de Belge.
Albany Law Journal,
American Microscopical Journal,
Amer. Med. Review,
Annals Univ. Med. Science
Aerztliche Sachverstaendigen-Zeitung
American Medical Journalist,
Amer. Monthly Retrospect,
Amer. Journal of Med-Science,
Applied Microscopy,
American Economist,
American Lawyer,
Astrological Journal,
Amer Electro Therapeutry and X-Ray Era.
American X-Ray Journal,
Anglo American Magazine,
Annotated Cases,
Annals of Surgery
American Medicine,

Buffalo Medical Journal,
Boston Medical and Surgical Journal,
Bulletin Societe de Medicine Mentale Belgique.
Bulletin of the Iowa State Institutions,
Brooklyn Med. Journal,
Bombay Law Reporter,
Bulletin Medical de Quebec,
Bar, (W. Va.)
Bookseller

Case and Comment,
Canadian Practitioner,
Central Law Journal,
Connecticut State Board of Health,
Courier of Medicine,
Centralblat fuer Nerv.,
Canadian Law Times,
Charlotte Med. Journal,
Chicago Law Journal,
Chicago Legal News,
Columbus Med. Journal,
Canadian Journal Med. Surgery,
Cleveland Journal of Medicine,
Chicago Clinic,
Charities,
Colorado Med. Journal.
Chicago Legal News,
Calcutta Weekly Notes,
Canadian Law Review,
Chautauquan Magazine,

Der Irrenfreund,
Der Gerichtssaal,
Del Kongelige Sundhedskollegiums,
Davenport Acad. of Nat. Sci.
Detroit Legal News,
Dietetic and Hygiene Gazette,
Dunglisan Col. & Clin. Record.
Detroit Med. Journal,

English Lunacy Commission.
Exodus,
Eltka,

Fordhand Svensia Lakare Sallskapts,
Fort Wayne Med. Jour.,

Guy's Hospital Reports,
Gazette del Tribunal,
Giornale di Neuropatalogia,
Gerichtl Zeitung, Vienna,
Gazette des Hopitaux,

Hygiea,
Harvard Law Review,
Holstein Friestian Register
Hot Springs Med. Journal,
Hammondsport Herald,
Harper's Monthly,

Illinois State Board of Health,
International Journal of Surgery,
Index Medicus,
Iowa Law Bulletin,
Il Pisania Gazette Secula,
Indian Review,
Ideal Review,
Interstate Med. Journal
Interstate Med. Journal
Independent Thinker.

Johns Hopkins University,
Journal of Inebriety,
Journal of Medical Sci.,
Journal of Nervous and Mental Diseases,
Journal de Medicine,
Jahrbuecher fuer Psychiatrie
Journal of Electro Therapeutics,
Journal of Tuberculosis
Journal of Mental Science
Journal of Ass'n of Military Surgeons,
Journal American Medical Association,

Kansas City Med. Index
Kathiawas Law Reports

La. Psi. la Neurol e Sci.
Lippincott's Magazine.
L'Anthropologie,
London Lancet,
Littell's Living Age,
Law Quarterly Review,
La Progress Medicale,
Louisville Medical News
Lunacy and Charity.
Literary Digest,
Legal Intelligencer,
Lancet Pub. Co.,
La Habana Medica,
Law Students Journal,
Literature,
Legal Adviser,

Mass. State Board of Health,
Medico-Legal Society of Massachusetts,
Medical Review of Reviews,
Medical Annales

EXCHANGE JOURNALS—Continued.

Medical News.
Messeger of Neurology and Forensic Psycopathology. St. Petersburg.
Medicine,
Menorah Monthly.
Madras Law Journal,
Medical Fortnightly,
Medical Mirror,
Monatschrift fuer Unfallheilkunde.
Medical Herald,
Mind,
Medical Sentinel,
Med. and Surg. Bulletin,
Medical Bulletin,
Medical Register,
Medicus.
Medical Critic,
Maryland Med. Journal,
Magazine of Mysteries,
Medical Record,
Medical Times,
Metaphysical Magazine,
Medical World,

North American Review,
New Orleans Med. and Surg.,
New York Med. Record,
Nordisk Medicinski Arkiv
N. Amer. Journal of Diagnosis and Practice,
N. C. Med. Journal,
N. Y. Medical Journal,

Occidental Med. Times,
Our Animal Friends,
Optical Journal,
Ohio Archæological and Historical.
Our Dumb Animals,

Philadelphia Times and Register,
Pacific Medical Journal,
Pacific Record of Medicine and Surgery,
Personal Rights,
Phrenological Journal,
Psychological Review,
Penn Yan Democrat,
Pa. State Com. of Lunacy,
Public Opinion,
Psi and Nerve Path, Kharkoff, Russia,
Public Health Journal,
Printer's Ink,
Penny Magazine,
Perry's Magazine,
Providence Medical Journal,
Psychiatrische en Neuralgische Bladen,
Punjab Law Reporter,
Psychic and Occult Views and Reviews,
Pittsburg Legal Journal,
Progress Medicale,

Revue De Medicine,
Revue Medicale,
Repertorie de Pharmacie,
Review of Reviews,
Railway Surgeon,
Railway Age,
Revue de la Hypnotism
Revista Ciencas Medicas,
Revista Penale
Revista Medico-Legal,
Revista de Neuralogie, Psychiatre,
Revista de Antropologie, Criminella of Sciencias Medico-Legales,
Revista de Neurol, and Phy. (Lisbon),
Revista de Neurologie,
Revue de la Hypnotism,
Revista des Revistas,
Revista di Medicina Legale,

Scotch Board of Lunacy,
Sanitarian,
Sanitary Record,
Smithsonian Institute,
Societe Medicine Legale de France,
Society D'Anthropologie, Brussels,
Society for Psychical Research,
Society for Promoting the Welfare of the Insane,
Scienza Italiana,
St. Louis Courier of Med.,
Sei-I Kwai Med. Journal,
Spirit of the Times,
Suggestive Therapeutics,
Suggester and Thinker,
Spectator,
South African Law Journal,
Sind Sadar Court Reports,

The Southern Law Review,
The Journal of Mental Pathology,
The Southern Medical Journal,
The Hannemanian,
Tennessee State Board Health,
The Journal of Mi State Med. Ass.
The American Journal Psychology,
The Green Bag,
The Open Court,
The Freeman
The Arena.
The Monist,
The Cosmopolital Osteopath,
Texas Medical News
Turf, Field and Farm,
The Legal Adviser,
The Philistine,
The Sheep Breeder,,
The Therapist,
The Physician and Sugeon,
The Public,
The Texas Clinic,
The Flaming Sword,
The Coming Age,
The Stylus,
The Legal Gazette,
The Surgical and Dent News,
The Colorado Medi Journal,
The Journalist,
The Ladies Home Jounal,
The Forum,
The Law (Oklahoma)
The Century,
The Lawyer (Madras.)
The Monthly Cyclopedi

Union Industrial Dro: Penale,
Universal Med. Scien

Vermont Medical Monthl
Virginia Law Register,
Virginia Medical Semi Monthly,

Woman's Med. Journal,
Western Reserve La Journal,
Weekly Law Journal,
West Virginia Bar,

X-Ray Journal,

Yale Law Journal,
Youth's Companion,

Zeitschrift fuer Schweize Strafetcht.
Zeitchrift fuer Psychiatre,
Zeitschrift fuer Medizina Beamte.

HON. ALTON B. PARKER,
Chief Justice.

THE COURT OF APPEALS
OF THE
STATE OF NEW YORK.

[From advance sheets of the Supreme Courts of the States and Provinces of North America, in Medico Legal Journal]

Copyrighted, 1901, by Clark Bell, Esq.

HON. D 'BRIEN,
Assoc tice.

HON. ALBERT HAIGHT,
Associate Justice.

HON. JOHN CLINTON GRAY.
Associate Justice.

HON. IRVING G. VANN,
Associate Justice.

ghted, 1901, by Clark Bell, Esq.

HON. EDWARD T. BARTLETT.
Associate Justice.

HON. CELORA E. MARTIN.
Associate Justice.

HON. WM. E. WERNER.
Associate Justice.
Designated by the Governor.

HON. EDGAR M. CULLEN.
Associate Justice.
Designated by the Governor.

Copyrighted, 1901, by Clark Bell, Esq.

THE ROENTGEN RAYS IN FORENSIC MEDICINE.

BY MIHRAN K. KASSABIAN, M. D.,
In Charge of Roentgen Rays Laboratory and Instructor in Electro-Therapeutics in Medioo-Chirurgical College and Hospital, Philadelphia; Chairman Medico-Legal Committee of American Roentgen Rays Society.

Mr. President and the members of the Medico-Legal Society:

It is a great pleasure for me to read a paper before such a distinguished body of professional men, on a subject of such great importance in diagnosing obscure conditions, in relieving suffering humanity and in guiding physicians and jurymen in the right direction.

Since the discovery of the X-rays, many important medico-legal cases, both in this country and in Europe, have been decided by their aid. I have had a number of cases of a medico-legal nature, brought either by the physicians or lawyers, and it has also been my privilege to make X-rays diagnoses and skiagrams of more than 6000 patients who were brought to the hospital and to the clinics of the college during a period of five years, some of which subsequently took on a medico-legal aspect, requiring my presence in the courts as an expert witness, but space will not permit me to mention them here. The X-rays in this class of cases are of unquestionable value, first to the physician, in sustaining a doubted diagnosis; secondly, to the patient, who is suing for damages, and thirdly to the judge and jurymen, to whom medical nomenclature is

Read before the New York Medico Legal-Society on October 16, 1901.

unintelligible, and to whom "seeing is believing." The lawyers know very little about fractures and dislocations, but by this method they can acquire a clear understanding as to the character and extent of an injury, the amount of deformity, etc. By this means also the lawyers can decide whether a case should be compromised or taken to court. Very often skilled surgeons and physicians will be called as expert witnesses, and their opinions will be so conflictingt that a bad impression is left with judge, jurymen and laymen—they do not know who to believe. As a result of my large experience, I do believe that the information given by this method may be regarded as *absolutely* conclusive, although it may be a deliberate contradiction of the opinions of the best and most highly qualified observers. Any layman, with a skiagraph before him, can see what by any other means would be only a matter of probability or conjecture.

The court is generally glad to accept any scientific methods which will make clear the intricate questions brought before them, so that the use of the microscope in examining the blood, the photographing of criminals for identification, and many other scientific procedures are admissable in the court, among which and possibly foremost, is the evidence of the X-rays. However, there are wrong and prejudicial opinions in the minds of some surgeons and laymen as to the reliability of the X-rays diagnoses, and they claim that there are fallacies and errors and distortions referrable to this means of diagnosis. This may be true to a certain extent, but it is not the science that is at fault, but the incompetency of the persons entrusted with the work of making the X-rays examinations. The expert who has had a large experience never makes mistakes. He can see many truths that are invisible to the uneducated and untrained eye, In certain states the

X-rays evidence is admissable, while in other states only the fluoroscopic examination in the court room is accepted. We will look at the value of the X-rays from the standpoint of the patient, and of the physician, in case of malpractice.

PATIENT'S STANDPOINT.

The first question asked by the patient after an examination, is the result—what is the diagnosis?

It is often very difficult for the physician or surgeon to answer such a question as this. If a hesitating answer is given, it will cause suspicion and if a snap diagnosis is made, it is worse than telling the patient that you cannot answer at present, without studying the case. A doubtful answer or an uncertain diagnosis cannot be changed or corrected, and the patient may not come to the physician again and will go around telling people of this diagnosis made by Dr. ———, whereas in reality it was not a diagnosis, but an attempt to evade a direct answer.

THE PHYSICIAN'S STANDPOINT.

The medical profession, does not advertise, as the merchant or the business man, but each patient is a walking advertisement, and will recommend to fellow sufferers, a doctor who accomplished such good results for him. One mistake, or one moment's carlessness, may cost him his life-long and hard-earned reputation. Unfortunately when a young physician or surgeon begins to practice among so many fellow practitioners, his first patient may be one with a chronic disease, or one who has been treated by half a dozen other physicians; or it may be an accident case, a fracture of the elbow, which if improperly diagnosed and treated, may result in a stiff, deformed, useless joint; and if this happen in a small town, the physician will be constantly reminded of this unfortunate mistake, by meeting this deformed patient at every street corner, so that it would be better for this young physician to leave the town and begin elsewhere.

The physician should be extremely careful in his diagnosis treafment and in giving a prognosis. An early diagnosis, and proper treatment are interrelated and interdependent, the one to the other, in obtaining a good result. One point should be born in mind, namely: a patient should be warned of possible bad results following certain operations upon the joints.

MALPRATICE.

This may be defined according to Taylor (page 379.)—"The bad or unskillful practice on the part of the physician or surgeon, whereby the health of the patient is injured."

Negligent malpractice embraces those cases where there is no criminal intent or purpose, but merely negligence in bestowing the attention which the condition of the patient requires. *Ignorant* practice is an administration of medicines or the treatment of a disease or injury in a way calculated to do harm, and in a way unbecoming to a skilled and scientific medical man. It is a recognized fact that the numbers of claims for alleged malpractice, in recent years, is increasing, the majority of them being the work of black-mailers encouraged by a class of lawyers who are willing to champion a case for the chance of a fee. A suit for malpractice, even without foundation, is always an injury to the reputation of the physician. His intimate friends who know his innocence of the charge, may be unmoved by it, but the general public, and his enemies, may use it as a weapon, to do him harm and injury. So extreme care must be taken to avoid this kind of suit, if possible. Nearly all the suits of malpractice may be traced back to the following points;

DIAGNOSIS.

Failure to make an *early* and *correct* diagnosis of a case, which we may class as *neglect*. The symptoms of fractures are very often identical with the description in the text-book, and again they vary greatly, and are often mistaken, even by experienced surgeons especially, when occurring in the elbow, shoulder, and hip. I have seen many cases that were diagnosed as simple Colle's fracture and put in splints, and it was found afterwards that the condition was a simple sprain. And I have also seen the opposite mistake made.

TREATMENT.

The proper treatment of a case requires careful and earnest study on the part of the physician, and there are certain empiric and scientific laws, laid down in text-books, that must be followed. For instance, the direction of a fracture, whether oblique, transverse, or longitudinal, whether intra-capsular, intra-articular, or external injury, which will alter the treatment, and determine whether a limb must be put in a bandage or splint, and whether it requires extension. How often it happens, even in the practice of the most experienced surgeons, that a sprain is diagnosed, and after several weeks, shortening of the limb occurs, bearing witness to a wrong diagnosis. How often we notice stiff elbows, the result of being immobilized for a supposed fracture, when such treatment was entirely unnecessary. I will mention one out of many such cases that have come under my notice. Mr. S., age forty years, with a history of pain which started over the neck of the bladder, causing suffering for a period of five years, and for three years, intense pain, with frequent micturition, and all the symptoms indicating either the presence of a stone in the bladder or an enlarged prostate gland or cystitis. He had been treated by specialists who diagnosed his condition as enlarged, tubercular prostate gland. He had been in one hospital for three or four months, and in another for two months, being treated for neuresthenia. A sound was introduced with negative results. X-rays examination showed a phosphatic stone weighing four ounces which was removed by suprapubic cystotomy, the stone was encysted and behind the prostate gland. The patient recovered. Do you not call it malpractice, to allow this patient to suffer, and lose wages for this long period of time, due to wrong diagnosis? An X-ray examination, in this case, would have saved this man years of suffering, and much loss of time. Space will not permit me to mention similar cases, where failure to use this modern, authentic and reliable method of diagnosis resulted in suffering and death. Velpeau and Sir A. Cooper altogether made seven mistakes in diagnosing such large stones, they were excusable in their time, but, in the 20th century, such mistakes are not excusable.

Taylor says, physicians and surgeons are bound to give their patients their best judgment, but they are not liable for errors of judgment. If the errors of judgment, however, are so great as to be incompatible with reasonable care, skill and dilligence the physician or surgeon would be liable.

Prognosis.

After asking the first natural question, what is the diagnosis? the patient will ask a second and more difficult question, what is the *prognosis?* This is a more difficult question to answer. The answer must be given with care and caution. We surgeons and physicians neither guarantee nor assure a good and useful limb after a fracture or dislocation. It is always safe for the physician to answer in truth and explain all the posibilities, not promising good results, but telling the patient that he will do his best under the circumstances. The answer depends upon the diagnosis, the severity and variety of the diseased condition or injury, and the constitution and circumstances of the patient, and the mode of treatment. In some cases where the diagnosis is absolute, and the plan of treatment reasonably certain, the prognosis may be approximately given. In some cases we know that we cannot give a good prognosis, as in fracture of the elbow joint which is usually followed by deformity and loss of function; and in intracapsular fracture of the hip, where shortening of the limb is the general result. The prognosis will be favored by good general condition of the patient and lack ot complicating conditions. The treatment may be all right, but if the patient is subject to epileptic seizures, he may fall and displace the ends of a properly reduced fracture; in in such case, the physician or surgeon is not responsible. In medico-legal cases, the patient generally claims some of the following points: He may claim that the physician did not properly diagnose a fracture, or a dislocation, or the presence of a foreign body, etc.

2. He may claim that the physician delayed treatment in the reduction of an existing unrecognized dislocation or fracture, and that prolonged confinement in bed, with loss of wages resulted.

3. He may claim that the deformities have resulted from unreduced dislocation, or improperly set bones, or lost or impaired function of a joint, either temporary or permanent; ankylosis, neuritis, or palsies, due to the pressure upon or inclusion or inclusion by exuberent callus, cansed by too early removal of the splint or excessive massage.

4. He may claim the unnecessary amputation of a limb.

By use of the Roentgen rays, the foregoing claims may be modified either in the interests of the plaintiff or the defendant. The foregoing claims may be prevented, if the physician makes it a practice to have early and skillful skiagrams made of his cases, if he gives a guarded prognosis in all cases, and is careful, conscientious and scientific in his method of treatment, following the most approved method of treatment in each case. Taylor says, (page 380.) "If a physician or surgeon departs from generally improved methods of practice, and the patient suffers an injury thereby, the medical practitioner will be held liable no matter how honest his intentions or expectation was to benefit the patient." The use of the X-rays is so universally commended in the modern works on surgery and medicine, that if a surgeon fails to apply them in doubtful cases, he may justly be accused of negligent practice. In medico-legal cases, the X-ray diagnostician is likely to be asked the following questions:

1. Does the skiagram show fractures in all cases in which they exist? This question may be answered that not only will a fracture be shown in all cases, but the texture of the bone, and the relative densities of the surrounding parts will also be shown, and any disturbance in the texture will also be noticed. Rupture of ligaments and cartilages, tendons, diseased conditions of the bones, etc.

I present to your inspection a skiagram of a normal hand which shows ten separate layers of an arm namely, the upper surface of the sleeve of the coat, the upper surface of the shirt sleeve, the upper surface of the cuff, skin, muscle, two portions of bone, compact, cancelous, lower surface of shirt sleeve, lower surface of cuff, and lower surface of coat. This shows that the X-rays does not only show the shadow of the bone and muscle, but by skillful technique shows the different densities.

2. Does the skiagram show the callus formation? Yes, it may be seen in a period extending from the sixteen days after the fracture until the time of ossification, which may

be as late as three months from the time of accident. The duration of this callus formation, varies according to the age and health of the patient, and whether the fracture is simple or compound, and its location. When the bones are in perfect apposition, the callus formation will be hastened. Massage will also facilitate its production. It will be seen from the foregoing uncertain factors, that it is not always easy to predict how long it will be before callus will be strong to support the parts, but by skillful X-ray examinations, the amount and density of the callus may be determined.

2. Another question often asked is "Is the fracture united, or not?" The answer to this question will depend upon the age, general health, local complications, and mode of treatment. By means of the fluoroscopic examition, however, we can tell definitely whether union is firm, by pressing upon the bones and at the same time viewing through the fluoroscope; also by the skiagraph we can tell the amount of callus, which, to a certain extent determines the strength of the union or the causes of non-union, and by this revealation either protects the physician, or accuses him if he is in the wrong, preventing many malpratice suits, and many contrary statements of the experts.

4. In cases of deformity, we may be confronted by the question, was this deformity avoidable, or not? The avoidable cases are those resulting from an incorrect diagnosis on the part of the surgeon, or improper treatment. The unavoidable cases are those of oblique fracture where the over-riding of the bones cannot be prevented; extra or intra-capular fracture of the head of the femur in old age, where shortening is inevitable; in compound comminated fractures where it is necessary to wire the ends of the bones, which results in shortening; and in intra-articular fractures resulting very often in ankylosis of the joint.

Injuries to the epiphyses may also, cause atrophy of the joints and muscles.

Functional disability and degree of deformity do not bear a definite relation to each other, as the deformity may be great and the patient still have good use of the part, and vice versa. The avoidable causes are those in which the physician's diagnosis or treatment is at fault, while the unavoidable may be due to certain intra-articular fractures resulting in ankylosis, inclusion of nerves causing limited movement of the limbs, &c. Many cases of deformity and loss of function are permanent, while others may be improved by long continued treatment. In summing up the value of the X-rays in medico-legal cases, the patient will be benefitted by a correct diagnosis and proper treatment. The physician by this means will avoid the possibilities of claims of wrong diagnosis, and if they should be brought, he has a means of protecting himself. In addition, many suits may be discouraged, or compromises effected outside of court, by the ability to give a clear and definite statement of the condition of the injury.

Determination of Age by the X-rays.

It is sometimes necessary to tell the age of a person, or a dead body (for identification) or in case of rape where the age of a girl is in doubt, when all ordinary distinguishing marks are absent, and this is ascertained by the fact that the epiphyses of the bones are known to ossify at definite ages, and by making X-ray examinations of the bones, and knowing at what age ossification takes place, an approximate estimate of the age of the individual may be determined. The age of a fetus can also be discovered by this means. The hydrostatic test for the determination of still-born infants may be corroborated by the X-rays, as the lungs will appear opaque if they have never been inflated, whereas if the child has breathed they will be more transparent.

As an evidence of death the X-ray plays an important part. After death, the pulsation of the heart is invisible, and the organ presents a sharp outline. This will comfort those minds who are possessed of the time worn horror of premature burial.

POINTS ON THE TECHNIQUE OF MEDICO-LEGAL SKIGRAPHY.

The technique in these cases does not vary greatly from that in any X-ray examination, except that especial care should be taken to have good, clear negatives. It is most important to have a detailed report of the case, as to the time after the accident, course of treatment, and physical signs of the accident. Examine carefully first with the closed fluoroscope, in a darkened room, so that the patient himself, or his attendants, may not see the result of the examination. Place the plate in position, in the presence of witnesses and have a distinguishing mark upon it, such as a key or ring, for purpose of identification. Keep record of such details as the *time* of exposure, distance of the Crooks' tube, position of the tube and part, etc. Take negatives from different points of view, and if possible take the injured and normal parts upon the same plate, for the purpose of comparison.

INTERPRETATION.

Now study the negative, provided it is satisfactory as to technique. Compare with previous negatives you have taken of the same part of the body and also with the corresponding normal part of the same person, being careful, however, to ascertain whether the supposed normal part has ever been the seat of a fracture. Print several copies, light and dark, so you can choose the print that shows the condition the clearer. Write on the negative the names of the bones, and try to make the picture intelligible to any one who examines it. Also make a tracing on the card, which will facilitate a proper understanding of the picture to untrained eyes. Having now made a positive diagnosis, write your expert diagnosis in a clear manner. An X-ray diagnosis will carry more weight in court if made by a physician, than if made by a man who is merely a photographer or a manufacturer of X-ray apparatus.

When called to court as an expert witness in a medico-legal case, it is important for the X-ray diagnostician to prepare himself carefully on the anatomy and pathology of the parts, to take with him negatives and prints of his X-ray examination, together with a set of bones of the part under consideration. When on the witness stand, he should be careful and accurate as to his statements, remembering that the opposing party may also have an expert witness who would be likely to disprove his statements.

I cannot do better in conclusion than quote the sensible, manly advice given by Sir Wm. Blizard, of London. He says, "Be the plainest of men in the world in a Court of Justice. Never harbor a thought that if you do not appear positive you must appear little and mean. Give your evidence in as concise, plain and yet clear a manner as possible. Be intelligent, candid and just, but never aim at appearing unnecessarily scientific. State all the sources from and by which you have gained your information. If you can, make yonr evidence a self evident truth. Thus, though the court may at the time have a mean opinion of your judgment, they must deem you an honest man. Never be dogmatic or set yourself up for Judge and Jury. Take no side whatever but be impartial and you will be honest."

In conclusion again, I desire to say that I am of the belief that this distinguished body realize the importance of X-rays in forensic medicine, having already been of great aid in diagnosing and deciding complicated legal cases appearing before the courts.

By hearty co-operation of both the legal and medical men in the future, the X-rays diagnosis will furnish the most scientific and unerring evidence in such obscure cases.

STIMULANTS IN FORENSIC MEDICINE.

A REVIEW OF

DRUG CONSUMPTION IN VERMONT.

BY DR. A. P. GRINNELL, BURLINGTON, VT.

[*Concluded from September Journal.*]

The officer in command at Fort Ethan Allen three years ago told me he had had charge of United States troops in many military stations throughout the west, and where drinking saloons outnumbered other places of abode, and that he never had so many in the guard-house for drunkenness as he had in Vermont. "I can't understand it," he said, "but it is true." He had been in Oklahoma in charge of troops; he had never had any men in the guard-house there—but he had trouble here. When he allowed the men to go out for an evening they would come baek drunk.

However, I am not talking so much about alcohol as about other things. But in order to understand and comprehend the situation reference should be made here by way of comparison to the legitimate sale of alcohol in Vermont, as reported by the St. Albans Messenger of March, 1901, as follows:

In 71 towns of Vermont, being the only ones having legally authorized liquor agencies, there was sold during the last fiscal year $251,622.99 worth of liquor, or what was equivalent to $1.38 worth of liquor for every man, woman and child living in these 71 towns. Burlington, the largest city in the state and a town the popula tion of which is hardly more temperate or healthy than elsewhere in the state, was not included in the list. A little further calculation from the above figures will show that there was enough liquor sold in these 71 towns mentioned to supply every man, woman and child in the whole state of Vermont with 73 cents' worth of liquor for "medicinal, mechanical or chemical purposes." In some towns in the list the medicinal needs for liquor were quite large, as shown by the fact that nearly four dollars' worth was consumed per capita, while the average runs between this and one dollar, the majority being above two dollars. All in all, over one quarter of a million dollars' worth of liquor was legally required by a population of 182,356 people for medicinal purposes and the health reports show no epidemic or undue prevalence of disease!

I am astonished and amazed at the result of my investigation as given you. I have made no statement I can't prove, and the statements which I have made respecting the average amount of drugs consumed can be multiplied by five and then be below the actual consumption. Think of it! What will be the condition of our progeny? Should we not look upon all persons who have formed a drug habit with pity—not scorn and contempt, but as diseased, suffering and unfortunate mortals? Instead of censuring them, we should extend sympathy.

Not a word is ever said in our legislature regarding the uses and abuses of anything but rum. Look at what the United States government has done in the last eighteen month from reports by Atwater and Langworthy. Their book is one of the most wonderful productions I have ever seen. It represents an amount of labor in preparation which I can hardly conceive, in showing the amount of alcohol that is and will be absorbed by the human race to its benefit. Every kind of narcotics, also of foods, has been experimented upon by them, and if this report could be put before the legislature of any state it would open its eyes to the fact that there is something besides alcohol that can dwarf moral development and mental capacity.*

Following are some of their conclusions derived from prominent authorities and from their experiments: "Temporary drinking of alcohol in moderate doses, by those accustomed to it, increases the appetite and causes an improvement in the assimilation of the nitrogenous constituents of the food. The decomposition of protein in the body decreases strikingly under the influence of alcohol. Alcohol exercised no bad effect on digestibility even when 60 grams, (nearly 2¼ ounces of absolute alcohol) per day was consumed.

"The conclusion is reached that alcohol is a food and can take the place of fat as a protector of protein."

Sooner or later the reformers of the world have got to divert some of their feverish antipathy to alcoholic stimulants and consider calmly and intelligently the drug evil. The deleterious influence on the individual of all forms of drug addiction and the consequent effect on society and all relations of mankind, make its consideration in its sociological and criminal aspects of paramount importance.

The courts have never given much judicial importance to drug habits, but widespread development of drug addiction must surely, sooner or later, bring the matter into greater legal prominence.

Close students of psychology are beginning to realize the influence of drug habits on insane and criminal im-

*A Digest of Metabolism Experiments by W. O. Atwater, Ph. D., and C. F. Langworthy, Ph. D. Published by U. S. Dept. of Agriculture. Pages 52-53.

pulses, and to recognize the marked susceptibility of drug habitues to criminal suggestion, with suicidal or homicidal tendencies. The rapid increase of those addicted to drugs, and the growth of insanity during the last decade is more than a coincidence.

What, you will ask, is the solution of this problem? What can be done to control the appetites of persons craving artificial stimulants? What can be done to regulate the use or abuse of drugs? What man or body of men will assume the responsibility or exercise the right to establish rules for our guidance in the selection of the stimulants desired?

How much of the time during the sessions of any state legislature is occupied in the discussion of the liquor traffic, or how many bills are introduced in the interest of so-called reform!

It seems to be the vested right of every legislative body to enact laws attempting to control or regulate the sale of alcohol, and if this is right or acceptable why should these censors of public morals be confined in their beneficent labors to the correction or abatement of one evil ?

Why curtail the legislative reformers in the exercise of their duties in suppressing one vice or to the limitation or indulgence in one or two of the scores of drugs, narcotics or stimulants in common use?

When a legislative body has the right or power to say no man and woman shall marry who have by inheritance a tendency to tuberculosis, or whose ancestors exhibited a tendency to the commission of crime, or an individual who has acquired a drug or stimulant habit be prevented from mingling with others, thus establishing a barrier against procreation of moral perverts, then I shall think the millennium is at hand.

Very few appreciate the fact that most persons addicted to the use of stimulants or drugs have an insatiable thirst for them, and as a rule the uncontrollable desire for indulgence in them has a periodicity quite similar to the regular period of incubation of any contagious disease. When the inclination to partake of these stimulants takes possession of a person he struggles against the desire, exercising all the will power in his possession, but often without success, and the unfortunate victim is treated by his fellow men with derision and contempt and convicted of a crime for which he is no more responsible than as if he had contracted tuberculosis or small pox.

The late Duke of Norfolk is reported to have said:—"Next Monday, wind and weather permitting, I propose to be drunk." DeQuincey was accustomed to arrange for a debauch of opium, placing the intervals at three weeks, and methodically preparing for the event as though it was a public fete or social function.

The wisest men in every part of the civilized world have struggled with this problem, endeavoring to mitigate the evil and devise means for the relief or cure of the abuse of drugs or stimulants, and it would seem presumptuous for me to offer suggestions in criticism of their labors, or to assume an ability to substitute a plan of action superior to the ones already accepted. However, it must be acknowledged that no law has yet been enacted which meets the requirements or is satisfactory to the victim of the drug habit, to the reformer or the reformed.

I would make the use of all drugs and stimulants, including even tea, coffee and tobacco, so expensive to the consumer that they would be considered a luxury, (except when their employment in the treatment of disease was necessary and advised by a responsible physcian), and the revenue obtained be paid into the state treasury, to be applied in education and the care of the poor. The narcotic drugs and stimulants are useful and necessary, but their use cannot be safely left to the judgment or discrimination of persons who have lost the power of self restraint.

The average American citizen is too much imbued with the spirit of personal sovereignty to kindly submit to the dictation of anybody restricting the clothes he wears, the food he eats, or the liquids he imbibes, unless such indulgence or practice interferes with the comfort or existence of others. I doubt if any of us will receive with christian resignation and comply with the adage:

"You shall and you shan't,
You will and you won't.
You'll be damned if you do,
And be damned if you don't."

SHOULD PROSTITUTION BE REGULATED BY LAW?

T. CRISP POOLE, ESQ., BARRISTER-AT-LAW, BRISBANE, AUSTRALIA.

Much difference of opinion exists with respect to the answer which should be given to the above question, and that too among persons who cannot be suspected of being swayed by any personal immoral tendencies. It is on the one hand maintained that an attempt to restrict prostitution within legal limits gives at least a semblance of approval of the practice when carried on by persons not affected by venereal disease; that the periodical medical examination to which professional prostitutes may be subjected under the various contagious diseases acts, is degrading both to the medical examiner and to the female subjected to the examination, and tends to crush out the last vestiges of self-respect which may yet linger in the breasts of these unhappy women. On the other hand, the advocates of continuing the legal regulation of prostitution must not be assumed too readily to wish to perpetuate immorality. We may regret, they say, the presence of prostitution in our midst; if we could stamp the thing out of existence altogether we would gladly do so. Nevertheless we have to face the fact that there are females who will prostitute themselves; and since this is so, it is better to restrict the evil by only allowing undiseased women to practice prostitution, than to allow the spread of wholesale contagion, to the detriment not only of the present but of the unborn generation. The contagious diseases acts are therefore regarded as the most feasible way of dealing with an admitted evil. The object of this article is to consider whether such legislation is the only or best way of meeting the difficulty.

It may be freely conceded to start with, that legislators need not be credited with a wish to encourage vice, or to declare that they deem prostitution harmless when practiced un-

Read before the Medico-Legal Society, December 18, 1901.

der certain restrictions. The writer has heard a judge of the Queensland bench declare that there is no such thing in that country as a licensed prostitute. Certain females receive certificates from a medical officer (under circumstances detailed later on), that they are free from contagious diseases, which removes any legal restraint from practicing prostitution which they may have previously been under, and this is all. Nevertheless the system conveys to some minds an idea that the recipient of such a certificate pursues her avocation under the sanction of the law, and though the term may not be a correct one, it is not uncommon for these females to speak of themselves as "licensed prostitutes." An examination of some of the acts bearing on the subject will show more clearly what the position is which it is sought to discuss.

The English Act at present regulating prostitution is 29 Vic. c. 35 (The Contagious Disease Act 1866). This act was passed in substitution for the Contagious Diseases Prevention Act, 1864, (27-28 Vic. c. 85), which was only intended to be temporary. As this earlier act is now obsolete, it is not necessary to say more of it than that it seems to have been the first attempt to restrain prostitution by legislation. 29 Vic. c. 25 is headed "An act for the better prevention of contagious diseases at certain naval and military stations;" and it is clear from the provisions, both of this and of the earlier act, that their object was not so much to prevent the spread of contagious diseases generally as to do so among soldiers and sailors in Her (now His) Majesty's service. In each of these acts a schedule specifies the places to which its provisions are to apply, which upon inspection will all be found to be important military or naval stations. In each it is also provided that the expenses incurred in the execution of the act shall be defrayed under the direction of the Admiralty and of the Secretary of State for War, and it is to these officials also that power is given to appoint the officers and provide the institutions necessary to the working of the act. The provisions of the later act stated shortly, are to the effect that hospitals may be appointed for the reception of such females as have brought themselves within reach of its operation, by practicing prostitution within the prescribed localities. That upon an information being laid before a justice by a superintendent of police, that he has good cause to believe that a specified female resident within the limits of any place to which the act applies is a common prostitute, or being resident within five miles of those limits has been within the same for the purpose of prostitution within fourteen days before the laying of the information, that justice may, if he think fit, issue a notice to that female which is to be duly served upon her. Such a notice requires the female to appear either personally or by another person in her behalf, before a justice (who need not be the same as the justice who issued the notice), in order that the truth of the allegation may be inquired into. The female is, moreover, warned that if she do not appear, she may be ordered without further notice, to be subjected to periodical medical examination, and it is added that if she should prefer such a course, she may voluntarily submit herself to such periodical examination, in which case it will not be necessary for her to appear before the justice. It is next enacted that on the matter of the information being substantiated to the satisfaction of the justice, the female may be subjected to periodical medical examinations for any period not exceeding one year, for the purpose of ascertaining at the time of each examination, whether she is affected with a contagious disease; the time and place of the first examination to be specified. But any female, and not merely one against whom an information has been laid, in any place to which the act applies, may voluntarily submit herself to periodical medical examination for any period not exceeding one year.

Provision is not made for the detention in hospitals of any female with respect to whom such a procedure is deemed fitting, and it is enacted that any female found after examination to be affected with a contagious disease is liable to be detained in a hospital for treatment until duly discharged by the chief medical officer. No female, however, may be detained for a longer period than three months, unless the chief medical officer of the hospital in which she is detained, and the inspector of certified hospitals or the visiting surgeon for the place whence she came or was brought, conjointly certify that further detention for medical treatment is requisite, in which case she may be further detained. But no female may be detained under any one certificate for a longer term than six months. And there are further provisions that (1) any female under detention in a hospital who considers herself entitled to be discharged may, if the chief medical officer refuses to discharge her, require to be brought before a justice, who, if satisfied upon reasonable evidence that she is free from contagious disease, must order her discharge accordingly; and (2) every female on her discharge shall, if she so wishes, be sent to her place of residence without expense to herself.

It is next provided, that any female subjected to periodical medical examination by the order of a justice who attempts to evade the same by temporarily absenting herself from her dwelling, or who neglects or refuses to submit to the same, or who upon being ordered to be detained in a hospital quits the same without having been duly discharged, or who does not conform to the rules of the hospital, shall be liable to imprisonment, (details are omitted out of consideration for space); also that a female who, having received notice when leaving a certified hospital that she is still affected with a contagious disease is afterwards found in any place, (not merely a place to which the act applies), for the purpose of prostitution, shall be liable to imprisonment unless she had first received a certificate given (with certain formalities that she was then free from contagious disease. (This is probably the document these persons speak of when they call themselves "licensed prostitutes.") A female subjected to periodical examination and wishing to be relieved therefrom may, if she be not under detention in a certified hospital, make application to a justice for that purpose; who shall order her relief on its being shown to his satisfaction that she has ceased to be a common prostitute or if she enters into a recognizance with or without sureties to be of good behavior for three months. Such a recognizance is forfeited if the female to whom it relates conducts herself in any way as a common prostitute within the limits of any place to which the act applies. And the act concludes with enacting penalties against any person who, occupying or having the control over premises of any sort within the limits of the operation of the act, and believing a particular female to be a common prostitute and to have a contagious disease permits her to resort to those premises for the purpose of prostitution, and with some provisions as to procedure.

. Such is the law as it exists in Great Britain for the regulation of prostitution, evidently passed, as already observed, more for the protection of soldiers and sailors in the public service, than with any more extended object. The provisions of the English Contagious Diseases Act have, however, been adopted in Australasia with the wider view of preventing contagious diseases among the whole community. Four Australasian colonies (or states, as all with the exception of New Zealand should now be termed), have legislated with a view to regulating prostitution: namely, Queensland, New Zealand are in the main identical, and approximated more closely to the legislation of England, while that of Victoria and Tasmania, again in the main identical as between the two states, varies in some important particulars from the legislation of England, Queensland and New Zealand. The Queensland Contagious Diseases Act (31 Vict. No. 40 [1863]) and that of New Zealand (32-33 Vict. No. 52 [1869]) follow the English act in not being general in their applications, but declare that their provisions shall only be in force within such places or districts as their respective governors shall from time to time proclaim. The governor, however, is subjected to no restriction with respect to exercising his powers over any part of the territory within his jurisdiction; and the New Zealand act expressly adds that the proclamation of any particular district may be revoked, in which case the act will cease to operate within the district in question, unless reproclaimed; and that the expenses incurred in the execution of the act shall be borne by the Province, County or Borough within which the act shall be proclaimed. Provisions follow in both acts with respect to summoning females believed to be common prostitutes before a justice, giving the justice power, on the charge being substantiated to his satisfaction, to order the female to be subjected to periodical medical examinations; permitting the female, if she will, voluntarily to submit herself to such examinations; giving power to the visiting surgeon (the Queensland Act does not leave him any option) on a female being found to be affected with a contagious disease, to order her detention in a hospital (the New Zealand Act uses the word "reformatory") for treatment; together with provisions as to the rights, duties, and liabilities of females while subject to periodical examination, or under detention, or after their discharge from detention, and with respect to penalties incurred by a person within the limits of any place to which the act applies, who permits a female, believed to be a common prostitute and to have a contagious disease, to resort to his house for the purppse of prostitution, so similar to the provisions of the English Act (though there are slight variations), that it is not necessary to reiterate them. It may be noted, however, that the provision of the English Act that a female on her discharge from a hospital shall be sent to her place of residence, if she wishes it, without expense to herself, is not respected in either Queensland or New Zealand; and that an excellent provision of the English Act which is allowed in New Zealand is unhappily absent from the Act of Queensland; to the effect that adequate provision shall be made in any hospital (reformatory according to the New Zealand Act) where females are detained under the act for their moral and religious instruction while confined therein.

It has already been observed that the legislation of Victoria and Tasmania on this subject, almost identical as between the two states, differs in some important particulars from the legislation of England adopted in the main by Queensland and New Zealand. It is embodied in Victoria (where the term "syphilitic disease" is used rather than "contagious disease") in ss 142-152 of the Health Act of 1890 (54 Vict. No. 1098); and in Tasmania in the Contagious Diseases Acts 1879-1882 (42 Vict. No. 36; 43 Vict. No. 5; 45 Vict. No. 23; 46 Vict. No. 41). These acts apply indifferently over the whole area of the territories to which they respectively relate, and it is not left to the governor in council nor to any other person to specify particular towns or districts within which they shall be in force. They do not deal with the case of a female believed to be a common prostitute but not yet suspected of having any contagious disease, and are therefore silent on the question of periodical medical examinations of such females without detention of their persons. They provide that upon complaint made by an authorized official (details unimportant), that a particular female is or is reputed to be a common prostitute, or has within fourteen days previously been known to solicit prostitution, and that the official has been informed and has reason to believe that she is affected with venereal disease, a police magistrate may require the female in question to attend before him and prove by the evidence of a legally qualified medical practitioner that she is free from such disease. Should such proof not be forthcoming, the magistrate may direct the female to place herself in a specified hospital within a specified time for medical treatment. The fiact that the female is or is reputed to be a common prostitute must, however, be proven by credible witnesses, and no such direction may be given until the female is in a position, in the opinion of the magistrate, to procure the attendance and evidence of a legally qualified medical practitioner. A female thus directed to place herself in a hospital has at first the option of proceeding thither of her free will, but she may be apprehended and conveyed there should she fail to do so, and the same may be done to a female who fails to appear before the magistrate in the first instance after due notice. Provision is also made for permitting a female, desirous of so doing, to apply to a magistrate to be placed in a hospital for treatment of venereal disease, who may, upon proof that the female is so affected, order her to be detained in a hospital with the same consequences as though the order had been made after a notice to the female to appear before him. There is no limit in the Tasmania Acts to the time during which a female may be detained in a hospital, where it is declared that she must remain and be treated "until the medical officer in charge of such hospital shall give her a certificate in writing under his hand that she is cured of the said disease, and may safely be discharged from such hospital." (42 Vict. No. 36, sec. XI.) There is a similar provision in the Victorian Act, but three months is there fixed as the maximum time during which a female may be detained, and as no provision is made to meet the case of a female who is uncured at the end of that time, it is to be presumed that in such a case the whole procedure must be begun de novo. Both acts agree in making it an offense for a female detained in a hospital to refuse to submit to medical treatment while there or to quit the hospital without being lawfully discharged, for either of which she may be committed to gaol and be detained there for medical treatment until she has recovered from the disease. But a limit of six months has been fixed in Tasmania and of three in Victoria as the maximum time during which she may be detained in gaol. Certain misconduct while under detention in a hospital has also been made penal in Tasmania. There being no provision made in these acts for the case of a female being discharged from the hospital before she is cured (which is apparently a position not contemplated), there is consequently no penalty fixed for a female so discharged conducting herself as a common prostitute. These acts contain provisions similar to those found elsewhere with respect to a female under detention in a hospital being permitted to apply to a magistrate for her discharge, if this is refused by the medical officer in charge of the hospital, and impose penalties upon any person who permits a female who has venereal disease to reside in or resort to any premises of which he is occupier for the purpose of prostitution. The Victorian Acts, however, expressly declares that it shall be a defence if he can prove that he did not know that such female prostituted herself while in a state of disease.

[*To be Continued.*]

MEDICAL JURISPRUDENCE OF INSANITY.

LETTER FROM PROF. DR. MORITZ BENEDIKT.

The following letter has been received from Prof. Dr. Moritz Benedikt, of Vienna:

Prof. Dr. Benedikt, 1 Franziskaner Platz, 5 Vienna.

October 29, 1901.

My Dear Colleague.—I send you copies of a series of some of my recent brochures.

First, I recommend to you the open letter to Clifford Albut on tuberculosis. I foresee that there will be ag reat discussion upon this question in the Imperial Society of Surgeons at Vienna, at their next session. I have many things I wish to say on this subject and if this discussion does not take place I will, I think, publish an Epilogue in the form of an open letter to you (Epilogue to the London and American Congresses of Tuberculosis.)

A second paper which I send to you seems to me to have a special interest for Legal Medicine entitled "Neuropathies of Trauma." There are many misunderstandings and misdemeanors about this question which are beyond the comprehension of medical men.

The Juridicial letters will certainly interest you, and their legal relation to inebriety, as well as the smaller reports prepared or the International Congress of Criminal Anthropology held at Amsterdam. Accept, dear sir, the expressions of highest esteem from Yours faithfully,

M. BENEDIKT.

Clark Bell, Esq., President Medico-Legal Society and Secretary of the American Congress of Tuberculosis.

INSANITY AND CRIME.

BY PROF. DR. MORITZ BENEDIKT, OF VIENNA.

At a meeting of English Psychiatrists several years ago a member complained that the opinions of medical experts were not properly taken cognizance of in the courts. A committee was appointed to investigate the matter. It turned out that within the last 25 years not even a single case had occurred wherein an English judge had not respected the medical opinion. This was to some extent surprising and hardly could be applied to any other country in the world. It is not uninteresting to inquire whence this hearty, harmonious sympathy of the English judges with medical science originates. Continental education demands of the medical savant that he should know everything possible within the sphere of his study, which all his teachers know in their respective lines or think they know. The student during his early period of study is principally occupied with judicial dogmas, with the opinions of battles by celebrated and obscure teachers, with dialetical somersaults over paragraphs, sometimes backwards, at another time forwards, then again from right to left and again from left to right, and then under constant practice or exercise in all directions of the compass. He is stuffed with a lot of dogmatic knowledge, and therefore, many jurists carry with them through their lives a certain nausea for any further original study of fundamental pinciples.

In instruction, the starting point of the moral development of humanity, of pyschology, of the necessary social laws for the human race, and the frictions and necessary equalizations arising therefrom, is in most cases lacking; and frequently there is a want of motive or impulse to harmonize tecnical education with the perception of other sciences, and with the original problems of life.

Quite different is the education, American and English, which is based upon the principle, that a man prepared for

Contributed by the Author, and translated for the Medico-Legal Journal. Read before the Medico-Legal Society and Psychological Section, December 18, 1901.

student life passes a comparatively longer period of study in his early life, than in the university. It is peculiarly true of the English people, that there exists a powerful incentive, from the most learned to the illiterate, to form definite opinions and adopt fixed principles on public questions, regarding both private and public ethics, and it is by no means a rare spectacle; that by reason of grave arguments not only individual scholars and members of the erudite classes, but often a whole profession surrenders one fundamental principle or view and adopts another one. Even in political life we see Tories carrying out the principles of the Whigs, and vice versa. The English jurist remains always in touch with the intellectual currents, which flow outside of his own technical education, and which may be said to exercise an influence upon them in his life.

That the views of the English judges regarding medical opinion are so harmonious, must be considered as meritorious on the part of the latter. The eccentricities of continental medical men, which threatened jurisprudence in the misunderstood sense of progress, in the last decades by reason of their confused views on "Soundness of Mind," their British colleagues did not imitate and their good sense never was at fault in this respect. I was, therefore, happy to be able to cause to be announced at the Congress of Psychiatrists in Dublin (1894) that I concurred with them on all important questions, whereas my views were officially and academically combated or ignored at home.

With us there existed for a considerable time a certain aversion among the judges to have the mental condition of the accused investigated, to which the abuse of the lawyers contributed a good deal. To-day it is not likely that any judge in Austria would oppose such an investigation, even if it were only half way proved, and it would be difficult to establish that within the last few years, individuals had been tried or convicted who suffered from pronounced aberration of mind.*

*A case that happened some time ago I remember with sadness. At a resort in the neighborhood of Vienna I saw a lady whom I knew, promenading with a gentleman. I asked the physician in charge who the man was. He replied that he was the lady's husband. I had met him at the sick bed of his sister as a noble self-sacrificing man. Now he seemed entirely changed. I told the physician "that man is suffering from serious melancholia." He replied, "Will you give a certificate to that effect?" I asked what

The real cause of occasional judicial failures is the erroneous view that so-called moral insanity should exculpate for crime, and especially in the cases of sexual perverts, and particularly those difficult and obscure cases where the offense was due to alcoholic excesses.

I wish to lay particular stress upon the fact, that the origin and foundation of what may be styled moral degeneracy, or any departure from normal conditions, resulting in crimes, committed in periods of aberrations lead and point inevitably to the House of Correction. The proper treatment for moral insanity and the diffinitiation between the subjects of degeneracy before the Tribunals is the most important task in medical jurisprudence.

I will now briefly *mention the separate forms of insanity and their relation to Criminal Jurisprudence. Pronounced cases of "insanity" hardly escape the eye of the investigating judge in passing final sentence. These are the forms which arise either under the influence of ambition, or ideas of greatness, with increased general cheerfulness; or under the influence of melancholia and self-abasing thoughts, hallucinations or illusions which control the whole intellectual powers, and which increase in activity to violent acts. (delirium.) In like manner will secondary insanity develop itself from primary insanity and be liable to be overlooked by the judges. Under this secondary madness and influence, the power of insane ideas and hallucinations will certainly recede and diminish in degree.

They do not control any longer the life of the soul, with absolute power, and these mad ideas can recede so far that

*A more complete statement will be found in my book, "The Psychology of Man," as a pure experimental science. Leipsic, O. R. Reisland, 1895.

for. He replied "That the man was accused of participating in a fraudulent bankruptcy." I refused to do it, as I could not tell whether his insanity existed when the fraud was committed, and I did not wish to be used improperly in such a case. The man was tried. His associates were defended by three celebrated lawyers. This man sat silent through the trial, apparently caring for nothing that happened. This was attributed to remorse. This insane man, father of nine children, committed suicide immediately after the sentence. The public prosecutor, the judges and the lawyers did not observe his real mental suffering. The blame was primarily certainly not of the jurists who defended. It was a matter of negligence on the part of the family physician. A jurist, should however, possess a certain degree of acuteness to enable him to recognize such a case of insanity as here existed.

many combinations of thoughts and the general manner of acting can proceed undisturbed. Much less will this be possible when under observation this madness passes into confusion, in subsequent weakness of mind or imbecility; or the melancholic madness into stupor and stupidity.

Different and more difficult is the matter with the so-called primary—original insanity. Here one comes across individuals who often through their whole lives carry around their disease with them, and possess the art of hiding their hallucinations as much as possible. One can find such individuals in prisons, possessed with the most dangerous of hallucinations, and their dreadful and gruesome deeds often originate in such overlooked primary madness.*

But not only the difficulty of diagnosis in and by itself exists in primary insanity, but also the danger of mistaking certain extraordinary mental conditions. The most intimate relationship with primary madness is found in the mental condition of the fanatic. With him we find a more or less normal intelligence, mostly, however, below the average; further a superabundance of feeling combined with a heroic self-sacrifice, which, blended intimately with certain principles, induces these people with instinctive recklessness to commit acts of violence. By the terms recklessness and unwisdom, frenzy, eccentricity, perversity, flightiness, the public mind discriminates delicately many conditions of the mind from madness and insanity.

On the other hand experience shows that very frequently in revolts people suffering from primary insanity and alcoholists at the head of fanatics and others temporarily excited by these reckless persons frequently commit the misdeeds connected with such outbreaks.

*I had occasion to observe a case quite recently not less instructive. A few months ago there came to me a robust, good-looking man requesting me to examine him and give him a certificate of health. He stated that he "intended going

*This form of insanity was formerly called Monomania. But this improper designation caused much confuson. This is more true of the word Paranoia. "Whenever I hear this diagnosis I often ask myself, "who is more confused, the one that makes the diagnosis or the diagnosee?" I asked Psychiatrists this question at the international Congress in Rome,, and I had the satisfaction soon thereafter to hear at a congress of Psychiatrists at Dublin, that the British experts shared my opinion. We can quietly leave it to the non-German medical men, to find an appropriate expression for

to the East Indias, and his relatives tried to prevent it, fearing he was not strong enough to stand the rigors of a foreign climate. He conversed animatedly and coherently about his stay in the Transvaal and in London, and he gave me the impression of being an intelligent and enterprising man. As he proved upon being examined to be possessed of a very strong constitution,I issued the certificate without hesitation. Then I was informed by his relatives that he was to be medically examined on account of dementia. He had gone during the pevious summer from London to a German helath resort to obtain his uncle's consent to marrying his daughter. There, it seems, his insanity broke out in an acute manner. He thought himself persecuted by his uncle, misconstrued all conversation and gestures, and believed himself to be persecuted by his relatives and undue advantage taken of. The patient passed out of my sight and it was only during the last weeks that he came to me. He had been examined lately by a commission de lunatico inquirendo so that it should be determined whether a guardian should be appointed for him or not. The two medical men recognized the full condition of his intellect, only, however, when conversation turned upon the relationship to his family, he fell back in the former state

"original or primary insanity." I only advise them to look for it among the poets and in the treasure of the language of their own people. One of the most interesting cases I saw with Prins, the most prominent professor of Medical Jurisprudence in Brussels, who was at the same time Chief Inspector of Belgian prisons and endowed with great power,— in the prison at Louvain. I was shown a "celebrity in crime," whose name is familiar to every child in Belgium. He had murdered in one day three brothers. I was informed that he was very dangerous, and three prison attendants stood behind him in order to take hold of him should he be seized with one of his extreme paroxysms. The man had a head like that of Napoleon; this likeness produced in the man an illusion as to his personality and he fell at once into the most extreme rage when reminded of his real identity. He had already become a paralytic while in prison. I had quite a pleasant conversation with him; he complained of pain in the neck. I put my fingers in his mouth without hesitation, to examine him. Then I asked him if he was sometimes inclined to fall in a rage; he denied it good naturedly. I told him then that he must have been so several times during life. At this moment his face got livid and purple. He jumped up, exclaimed that he was not a Belgian but a Frenchman. The attendants caught at him at this dangerous moment and led him away. Prins who had the power to transfer every prisoner that was recognized as being insane, asked me whether he should do so. I advised him not to do it for reasons which I shall state at another time and place. He was then mentally unsound as he was at the time when arrested. He suffered from primary insanity and this was increased by his resemblance to the Emperor.

of his insanity of believing himself persecuted. The physicians stated very correctly that the man was suffering from partial dementia, while the presiding justice adjudged him to be composmentis and based his decision upon the testimony of laymen who formerly knew the man, who did not observe anything of insanity when conversing on business transactions. The court of review concurred in the opinion of the presiding judge. The man was set at liberty He was not satisfied with that. He came to me and requested to be confined for six months in a lunatic asylum in order to obtain a medical bill of health. He wanted, therefore, to obtrude upon the world a decision that his hallucinations were based upon sound reason, without having an occasion for it.

There is, therefore, no doubt that the man suffered from "primary verrucktheit"—dementia, and the ignoring of the medical opinion, by the judge and the court, may become fateful. Had science not distorted or caricatured the picture of his mental disturbance the medical men probably might have convinced the judge.

Another danger for certain individuals to be declared "verruckt" demented, exists for "cranks." This is not the place to dwell upon the psychology of the cranks. I only wish to state that as a rule, some secret physical abnormal defect, a vice that should be kept secret, a deed that must be kept secret, an event in life that should be kept from becoming public, a deep-seated difference of opinion and habits with those surrounding him, lead to the state of what may be called a "crank." This happens less frequently in criminal cases, oftener, however, where it is a question of capacity or ability of disposition, and experts as well as judges are easily liable to make a mistake. So levity and extravagance, when indulged in to a great extent, often seem to the normal man inconceivable, and often dementia is officially assumed at the expense of public morality, and those that are injured thereby when differently disposed, but not demented people are concerned. Justice only permits us to put such people under guardianship and to protect them and society as soon as their condition is known, from further consequences without holding them irresponsible for the past. In such cases, much "class justice," respectively "class injustice" is committed.

The "innate weakness of mind" deserves special consideration. Such a person who is as far as conception and association of ideas is concerned, intellectually abnormal, may be as regards moral relation and capacity of will power, fully normal. He is certainly an intellectual degenerate, but he can be likewise a degenerate in matters of morality and in his volition. If such an individual who is at the same time a moral degenerate, commits a criminal act, his eccentricities and power of will should be considered in themselves and the individual treated like a degenerate and not like one of the incendiaries suffer without a sufficient reason and from being intellectually and innately weakminded. But a weakminded incendiary should not be corrected through the insane asylum, but through prison, because other similarly weakminded persons have that moral endowment and development which will protect them rom committing the crime. A weakminded person may be a homo nobilis and a firm character.

Important forms of insanity are the so-called "psycho-epileptic attacks, or the so-called "psycho-epileptic equivalents." I shall devote a future letter to the relation of this form to-day.

Spcial mention deserves to be made of the so-called "paralysie generale (general paralysis), or paralytic dementia that has lately come into prominence. It represents, so to say, an abbreviation of that form, which from insanity leads to weakmindedness through dementia and illusion. Likewise melancholia combined with hallucinations, if it leads through stupor to weakmindedness, is commonly designated as paralytic weakmindedness. This disease is juridically very important in its beginning, as it is likely to be overlooked. Such persons are, for instance, apt to act quite rationally for a length of time upon the rostrum, in parliament, in court and in business life, and the intelligent expert is able to determine already the disease and its sad consequences. In the criminal courts this state is seldom undervalued, as usually the patient, if he has committed a criminal act, is already a pronounced and unmistakable insane person at the time when sentence is to be pronounced.

More important is the question in relation to the capacity or disposition of those people, who are placed under observation. It is to be remarked that a person can be already a paralytic and yet his capacity of disposition may remain intact for a series of normal acts of the will. I rendered a medical opinion in the case of an unmistakable paralytic, in which a million dollar inheritance was at stake, to the effect that the patient was of sound mind regarding his testamentry disposition, as these dispositions completely harmonized with the views and feelings which he had while in good health. No Austrian medical colleague wanted to countersign this opinion. It was done by a celebrated English physician of high social standing, and was recognized by the English courts. In another case against public morality, the charge through my expert intervention was with drawn, while the same patient in the same week without my intervention, but with my full scientific consent, had his power to dispose recognized in regard to the disposition of his estate.

There are certain forms of this disease that can be diagnosed years in advance, before there exists any mental derangement whatever, which could be proved. In my minutes many such cases may be found, in which I made the diagnosis for paralytic derangement of the mind years in advance, and the diagnosis was afterwards confirmed. Besides the forms of paralytic derangement of mind formerly mentioned, there are others which become juridicially significant; for instance those that emanate from senile changes in a slower or more rapid manner. Here, too, it is very difficult to determine at what period of the fixed attack of disease the capacity to dispose and the responsibility ceases.

In such cases a judge who merely judges according to the letter of the law, and who has at his side a not very shrewd or a biased expert, will draw conclusions that are diagonally opposed to true justice.

I will finally touch upon the questions of special institutions for insane criminals and criminals insane. To dwell thereon at considerable length would be to-day in Austria extravagance. Our criminal procedure is theoretically and practically upon such a low plane as hardly anywhere else in a civilized state, and the competent voices of a Zucker and a Mar-Kooich die away in the dissolute acts of our degenerate public life. The more intelligent and honest ones in Austria work now-a-days only under the supposition that a future happier generation may take up the discussion and realize it.

But in other civilized States this question of special institutions stands upon the height of discussion and practical accomplishment.

The environment of the criminal insane and of insane crimnals during the usual insane asylum life often leads to fatal mistakes. First because the latter might thereby become degraded and depraved or injured and the great humanitarian work and progress in the treatment of the unfortunate insane, the result of the work of a century be thereby arrested and prevented. For these insane criminals belong in the first instance mostly to the "celebrated" ones and their presence in insane asylums would deeply mortify or hurt those patients who still have the consciousness of their individuality and who would, for instance, see themselves treated on the same level as a notorius murderer.

Again, insane criminals, according to their nature, require an entirely different disciplinary treatment from the ordinary insane. It is more just to retain such individuals in prison perhaps in separate apartments, as long as there are no single self-independent so-called Mariconnii corminali, i. e, special institutions for criminal insane and insane criminals that have become insane.

There are still other grave reasons why criminals who were insane at the time of committing the deed, or who became such during the period of their confinement, should not be confined in the usual insane asylums.

I shall revert to this question in my next letters, which treat of the manner of separating the epileptic and the alcoholic criminals.

TOXICOLOGICAL.

POISONING BY ACONITE (THE CONDON CASE) IN NOTING PHYSIOLOGICAL ANALYSES OF ALKALOIDS.

BY WILLIAM S. MAGILL, A. M., M. D., NEW YORK CITY.

The subject for our consideration this evening involves an attempted poisoning with one of the most active of all known alkaloids—Aconitine.

The story of the case related by the prosecution runs as follows:

In April, 1897, at Springfield, Mass., Mrs. Condon, the defendant, was actively interested in stock speculation and found herself greatly embarassed by the Dean Co's failure which occurred about that time. Among her creditors—mostly women friends—a Mrs. Hunt was very insistent upon repayment of a few hundred dollars. She called upon Mrs. Condon for her money on Monday, and as a consequence of her insistence was promised full payment on the following Friday evening.

The day after this call (as shown by the prosecution) Mrs. Condon accompanied a cousin—a self-styled "Doctor"—to a local drug store, where he bought at her request and immediately gave to her, a two-ounce bottle full of tincture of aconite.

Friday afternoon the defendant purchased from a local liquor dealer, a pint of port wine, with this filled a two ounce flask which she sent to Mrs. Hunt that evening instead of the promised money.

In this wine was a more than fatal dose of aconitine.

As a cover to the crime, another portion of this wine was sent to a second woman friend. And this portion contained no poison.

The poisoned wine reached its intended victim so late in the evening, that, as she was about to retire, the gift was

Read before the Medico-Legal Society Nov. 20, 1901.

merely tasted and set upon a shelf. Saturday morning, on awakening, she felt quite badly and remembering the wine, took it from the shelf and at once drank half of its remaining contents. Continuing to feel ill, she lay down and soon became strangely worse. She felt very cold, numb and dizzy, unable to move, feeling throughout the muscles of her limbs a peculiar creepy sensation. Her vision grew obscure, and overcome by a feeling of despair and alarm, the victim, that all of this time had been alone in her apartment, struggled to the door and called for aid. Assistance came none to soon. A woman answering to her call found the sufferer already fallen and powerless. A physician was immediately called and responded most promptly. To him, Dr. Rice of Springfield, is due the entire credit of saving the woman's life. After three hours of untiring effort, Mrs. Hunt was out of danger and slowly recovering.

The evening of that same day (April 28th), what remained of the poisoned wine was delivered by the Chief of Police to Prof. E. P. Harris, of Amherst College, at whose request the writer was sent for and on his arrival at Amherst, associated with him for the toxicological work.

The chemical examination of the suspected liquid was pushed to its utmost and by specially devised analytical methods identified: first, an alkaloid poison, and second, that it was Aconitine; also that the wine sent to another woman contained no poison.

Minutely detailed notes of the entire work have been kept and may be consulted by those interested in such ultimate analyses of alkaloids, but they are too extensive for reproduction here.

Our chemical methods of qualitative analyses, conclusively proved that the port wine of the two ounce flask contained aconitine, but the quantity of the dose remained a most important problem.

It is firmly established in the minds of the investigators that no evidence of criminal poisoning shall be conclusive unless the poison be absolutely identified and its quantity determined. They are fully aware that no testimony as to the amount of alkaloid poison used in a criminal case has been offered where the toxicity of the alkaloid is sufficient to provoke death in a total absorption of some milligrammes. The reasons for this are obvious. For the total weight for determination in such a case approaches too closely the limits of error of chemical balances, thus invalidating gravimetric methods of quantitative analysis; the only means heretofore in use.

However, having succeeded in identifying an alkaloid which chemists in general confess their inabilty to do, it is proposed to determine its quantity by original methods of great precision whose absolute decisions shall be unquestioned.

Such methods in toxicology we propose as physiological analyses; in illustration of which are offered the details of animal experiments in the Condon case, with the following preliminary:

It has been for years the pretense of chemists that aconitine possessed no sufficiently characteristic chemical reactions to allow its qualitative determination and was so active a poison and used in so minute quantities that any quantitative analysis would be impossible.

That aconitine is easily and absolutely identified by qualitative chemical analysis has been amply demonstrated by the chemical part of our work. That this same poison, however minute its dose, can be quantitatively estimated by methods proven accurate to a variance of 6-1000ths of a milligramme is the result of the following report of experiments on the estimation of this poison by the graphic method applied to the observations of its effect on animals.

By such experiments, the means of detecting and accurately estimating minute quantities of poisons, and at the same time determining the most important factor of all, in a case of criminal poisoning, the toxicity are for the first time made public and have now established their legal admissibility and precedent (Commonwealth of Mass., Western District, Superior Court, 1898, Oct., sitting in re Commonwealth vs. Condon).

In devising this system of physiological analysis, the author wishes to acknowledge his indebtedness to the previous experimental work with animals, of his former teacher, Dr. Laborde, Director of the Laboratories of Physiology of the Medical Department of the University of Paris, and to the physiological studies of the toxicity of animal bloods and tissues, made by his master and teacher, Charles Richet, Professor of Physiology in the University of Paris.

Aside from the suggestion made by Dr. Laborde of the use of the graphic curves for the identification of the poison, there seems to be no record of any attempt at a quantitative physiological analysis in toxicology, and if so, the following experiments and their results constitute the pioneer steps of a method that would seem destined to become very important in all cases of criminal poisoning that involve small doses, or require careful differentiation.

ACONITINE:—Chemical, Clinical and Toxic Properties.

The alkaloid aconitine is the most violent of the vegetable poisons. Its chemical formula has been a subject of considerable discussion, but the study of the hydrolysis of aconitine leads to the conclusion that it is mono-benzoyl aconine —C 26, H' 40, (C 6, H 5, CO) NO II.

Two crystalline auro-chlorides are easily obtained and afford a satisfactory means of identifying the alkaloid, which may be recovered from them in a pure state.

One auro-chloride (C 33, H 45, NO 12, HAuCl 4) melts at 135.5 degrees C. The other with a formula C 33, H 45, NO 12, AuCl 3, melts at 129 degrees C.

There are two isomeric varieties of aconitine which may be distinguished as A and B. Both are obtainable in crystals of the same form and size and have the same chemical formula, but A aconitine melts between 182 and 184 degrees C., and has a toxicity only one-sixth of that of the B aconitine, which melts at 188.5 degrees C. (This great difference in the toxicity of the isomeres is a striking example of how much more the vitality of cells is affected by the form than by the composition of matter: a fact not sufficiently recognized by all toxicologists.)

The presence of a small trace of pseudo-aconitine makes it a very difficult matter to obtain the real aconitine in crystalline form, for it then has a tendency to be amorphous.

The most soluble salt is the nitrate of aconitine, and that is the usual salt of commerce, for aconitine is a weak base.

Its taste is slightly bitter, but very biting, irritating the mucus of the nose and throat oftentimes to a degree to provoke sneezing. Its contact with the tongue is said to cause a charcteristic tingling, numbing senastion, but several trials by the author and other chemists have utterly failed to give any such feeling. Duquesnel and Laborde report that this characteristic varies with the different kinds of aconitine, and in view of the combined negation of the constancy of this action it is evident that this particular sensation should not be looked upon as a characteristic of aconitine.

If an overdose of aconitine has been taken, the pricking and burning sensation extends from the tongue to the back of the throat, and is almost immediately followed by salivation, nausea, vomiting, dizziness, cardiac disturbances and syncope. There will be noticed a dilation of the pupils with troubled, or loss of sight, fibrillary muscular contractions, itching and creeping sensation of the skin about the face and extremities, which then become benumbed and paralysed. The head, lips and limbs seem to the patient to be of an excessive size. The pulse is irregular, a strong diarrhoea commences. There are clonic spasms, cold sweats. The body temperature falls, the voice fails; the breathing is more and more stertorous, and the end of death follows without great delay.

The intelligence, aside from a condition of syncope, remains intact to the last.

That recovery is sometimes possible is proven by a case reported by Chaudeleux and by the recovery of the victim of the attempt to poison herewith reported.

The physiological studies of Liegeois, Guilleaud, Laborde and others show that aconitine is a poison of the central nervous system, which it stimulates first to paralyze later. It likewise paralyzes the peripheric nervous system (sensory, motor and secretory nerves—see experiments), and finally attacks the sympathetic system, the muscles, the heart and the respiration through the bulbus.. Laborde insists upon the effects of the poison on the heart, which is accelerated, becomes irregular and finishes in tetanisation, an affect of the itermediation of the bulbo-spinal system.

POST-MORTEM:—The autopsy of a victim of aconite poisoning reveals an intense congestion of liver, kidney and spleen; hyperemia of the mucus of the mouth, oesophagus and stomach; the blood thick, of ad ark wine color or black; the heart in diastole and gorged with blood.

The poison will be found chiefly localized in the contents of the stomach, the intestines, kidneys, urine and blood.

Animals are very sensitive to the action of aconitine, one milligramme of which will kill a dog, one-fifth of a milligramme a rabbit, and one-tenth of a milligramme a frog.

The pigeon is perhaps the most delicate means of studying the action and determining the amount of this poison. But in all cases of physiological analysis, the greater the number and variety of the animals used for the experiments,the more precise and exact will be the results of the work.

In the human being acontine is the most poisonous of all known alkaloids, producing effects of a very decided nature in a dose of only one-tenth of a milligramme. One milligramme produces most severe symptoms of intoxication and three milligrammes could be fatal.

Cases of death resulting from aconite are not rare, but most of them were caused by suicidal intent or a mistake in the taking of medicine.

In the annals of crime, aside from the well-known "Lamson case" in England, little use of aconitine by poisoners is found. The few cases reported upon since that time are given at the end of this article, which reports the case of the Commonwealth vs. Condon, in which the poison and its amount are for the first time in Toxicology, positively determined.

The system of physiological analysis for the identification of alkaloids and the exact estimation of minute quantities, as well as the determination of relative toxicities is based upon the idea of intra-venous injection of a determined volume or weight of the suspected substance, in a series of animals.

The resulting symptoms, such as pulse beat, blood pressure, convulsions, paralysis, respiration, etc., are then careully tabulated by the graphic method of which the accompanying charts are illustrative.

Having identified chemically or clinically the alkaloids, a standard solution of the same is made up with perfectly pure water (or artificial serum) and the alkaloid salt. Of this solution, varying but always known quantities, are injected itravenously to animals as nearly identical physiologically as possible, to those of the series of experiments with the suspected substance. The resulting symptoms are then tabulated graphically, until, for each animal, a curve is found which most exactly corresponds to the curve previously found for the same animals injected with the suspected substance. When the curves correspond, that obtained with a known amount of the standard solution of the alkaloid salt gives us the exact dose of the poison, and thus determines the quantity in the suspected substance.

To test the accuracy of this physiological analysis, atfer determining by its aid, the amount of aconitine contained in the wine, a large accurately weighed portion of chemically pure nitrate of aconitine was made up in a dilute solution, the exact titration of which was known to the chemist alone —Professor Harris.

By purely physiological analysis the titration of this solution was then determined by the writer, using only 6 C. C. of the fluid. The quantity repeatedly reported by him, as found in no case varied from the quantity used by the chemist, more than 6-1000ths of a milligramme.

The auhtor made six careful experiments with rabbits; six with pigeons: two with cats; six with frogs; the notes of which are carefully presented, and which form the basis of the diagram, which occupy this paper.

By refernce to the reports of the experiments and the comparison of the graphic curves compiled therefrom, it will be seen that the quantity of aconitine requisite to duplicate in symptoms that contained in the poisoned wine is to be found in a solution, of which each C. C. contains 1-10th of a milligramme of aconitine.

By careful measurements of the contents of the flask when delivered to us, and from the evidence of its plenitude before th woman drank from it, it was determined that she took into her stomach at that time, a minimum of 34 C. C. of wine, of which each C. C. contained 1-10th of a milligramme of aconitine. The woman consequently swallowed 3.4 milligrammes of the pure alkaloid. Less than this would be a fatal dose and her survival is only to be attributed to the remarkably efficient and prompt assistance rendered by her physician. As it is, this is the second case known to toxicology, in which recovery from such a dose, known to have been taken into the system, has been possible.

At the trial of Mrs. Condon in October, 1897, after that the prosecution had closed its case, the nervous collapse of the defendant occurred. Her condition of health has ever since reained so precarious as to exclude all possibility of retrial.

In concluding the relation of our work on this case, aside from introducing to your consideration these methods of physiological analysis and insisting upon their great utility and precision in determining minute quantities of powerful poisons. While urging the great assistance afforded by these methods for the identification of alkaloids, we beg also to present to you the resource to be found here for the separation of combined alkaloids on account of the variation of time required for each of the poisons to pass through the animal system—a separation, so to speak, by "animal filtration."

To say, as has been done in New York in recent years, that the combination of alkaloids in a case of poisoning, renders toxicological evidence impossible, is worse than a pretense—it is ignorance.

Throughout a long series of experiments, we have yet to find any alkaloid, no matter how combined, the absolute identification and separation of which is not only possible, but precise and rapid, either by physiological methods alone or these in conjunction with methods of chemical examination and control.

PSYCHOLOGICAL.

This Department is conducted with the following Associate Editors:

Judge Abram H. Dailey, Brooklyn, N. Y.
Prof. A. A. D'Ancona, San Francisco, Cal.
H. S. Drayton, M. D., N. Y.
M. Ellinger, Esq., N. Y. City.
Dr. Havelock Ellis, London.
Thomson Jay Hudson, Esq., Detroit Mich.
Wm. Lee Howard, M. D., Baltimore, Md.
R. J. Nunn, M. D., Savannah, Ga.
A. E. Osborne, M. D., Cal.
Jas. T. Searcey, M D., Tuscaloosa, Ala.
U. O. B. Wingate, M. D., Milwaukee, Wis.
Prof. W. Xavier Sudduth, Chicago, Ill.

as the organ of the Psychological Section.

The Psychological Section of the Medico-Legal Society has been organized, to which any member, Active, Corresponding or Honorary, is eligible on payment of an annual enrollment fee or dues of $1.50.

Any student of Psychological Science is eligible to unite with the Section without joining the Medico Legal Society on an annual subscription of $1.50, payable in advance and receive the MEDICO-LEGAL JOURNAL free. The officers for 1900 are as follows:

Chairman,

PROF. W. XAVIER SUDDUTH, OF CHICAGO, ILL.

LEGAL AND SCIENTIFIC.

Vice-Chairmen,

Clark Bell, Esq., of New York.
Rev. Antoinette B. Blackwell, of N. Y.
Harold Browett, Esq. Shanghai, China.
C. Van D. Chenoweth Worcester, Mass.
Judge Abram H Dailey, of Brooklyn.
Moritz Ellinger, Esq., of New York.
Rev. Phebe A. Hanaford, of New York.
Thomson Jay Hudson, Esq., Detroit, Mich.
Sophia McClelland, of New York.
Mrs. Jacob F. Miller, of New York.

MEDICAL.

Vice-Chairmen.

T. D. Crothers. M. D., of Hartford, Conn.
F. E. Daniel, M D., of Austin, Texas.
H. S. Drayton, M. D., of New York.
Wm. Lee Howard, M. D, of Baltimore, Md.
Henry Hulst, M. D., Grand Rapids, Mich.
Prof. Thomas Bassett Keyes, of Chicago.
R. J. Nunn, M. D., of Savannah, Ga.
A. E. Osborne, M. D., of Glen Ellen, Cal.
Jas T. Searcy, M. D., Tuscaloosa, Ala.
U. O. B. Wingate, M. D., Milwaukee, Wis.

Mrs. Mary Louise Thomas, of New York.

Secretary and Treasurer.

CLARK BELL, ESQ, OF NEW YORK.

Executive Committee.

CLARK BELL, ESQ., Chairman.

SAMUEL BELL THOMAS, OF NEW YORK CITY, Secretary.

M. Ellinger, Esq.
Carleton Simon, M D.
Judge A. H. Dailey.
Ida Trafford Bell.
Geo. W, Grover, M. D.
H. W. Mitchell, M. D.

The following members have united with the Psychological Section since our last announcement:

A. G. Ellingwood, Attica, New York.
L. C. Brown, Esq., Baltimore, Md.
Edward Howard Carnohan, M. D., Meafort, Ontario.
Col. P. C. Rust, 128 Broadway, New York City.
Mary Katherine Wing, 140 St. Clair St., Toledo, Ohio.

ICE PRESIDENTS AND PROMINENT MEMBERS AND AUTHORS OF THE AMERICAN CONGRESS OF TUBERCULOSIS.

DR. HENRY B. BAKER,
Lansing. Mich.

DR. WM BAVARD.
St John, N. B.

DR. HENRY McHATTEN,
Macon. Ga.

N. E. ARONSTAM, E. D., Ph. G.
Detroit, Mich.

DR. CARLTON SIMON,
of New York City.

DR. R. HARVEY REED,
Surgeon Genl of Wyoming,
Rock Springs.

DR. ROBERT SANGIOVANNI,
of New York.

TUBERCULOSIS.

THE LONDON CONGRESS OF TUBERCULOSIS.

REPORT OF DELEGATES FROM THE MEDICO-LEGAL SOCIETY.

BY DR. H. EDWIN LEWIS, OF BURLINGTON, VT.

BURLINGTON, VT., October 11, 101.

Clark Bell, Esq., Secretary-General of the American Congress of Tuberculosis, New York City.

Dear Sir:—As a delegate from the American Congress of Tuberculosis to the British Congress for the study of the same disease, held in London, July 22 to 27, 1901, I am pleased to report that it was my privilege to attend and enjoy the meetings of this great international gathering.

The whole session was highly interesting, and in spite of the unwieldly size of the body, an admirable system throughout made possible the most ample discussion and consideration of a large number of valuable papers.

In the first place, however, the assembly was distinctively a British Congress. The many foreign delegates who were present were accorded every courtesy and attention,but it was plainly evident that the aim of the meeting was to impress the English laity and profession with the importance of British needs and British influence in combatting tuberculosis.

The Congress was held under the patronage of the King, the presidency of the Duke of Cambridge, and the co-operation of many distinguished members of both Houses of Parliament and the mayors of important cities. The Earl of Derby was president of the organizing council and presided at the enjoyable banquet given to the foreign delegates at the Hotel Cecil. The social arrangements for the entertainment of the members and foreign guests were many and bespoke the hearty hospitality of our English kindred. Receptions were given by the Lord Mayor of London and by the Earl and Countess of Derby. River and garden parties by Sir J. W. Ellis and the Duke of Northumberland, and still another by the Ladies' Committee, under the patronage of the Countess of Derby, at the Botanical Gardens in Regent Park.

The scientific work of the Congress was voluminous and of a high order. A great many valuable papers were read and discussed, but the real object and purpose of the Congress was completely overshadowed by an ill-proven communication from Dr. Koch, of Berlin. His paper promulgated the personal dictum that bovine and human tuberculosis are not intercommunicable. The slender grounds for warranting such a conviction and statement consisted in the negative fact that Koch was unable in a series of experiments on cattle to produce tuberculosis by inoculating them with material from human subjects. His deduction was that since human tuberculosis was not communicable by his methods to cattle, therefore conversely bovine tuberculosis was not communicable to human beings.

Although Dr. Koch as the discoverer of the tubercle bacillus had every claim to respect and attention and was given the same, it was the universal opinion of the meeting held in the mammoth St. James' Hall and attended by thousands of delegates from all over the civilized world, that his premise was "not proven." It was generally felt that his experiments were not sufficiently thorough nor conclusive, and that his deductions were in some respects illogical, and certainly not in accord with clinical facts.

It was a lamentable fact, however, that the able representatives of the profession in attendance were not sufficiently prepared to present the other side of the question. It was certainly not to the credit of the medical profession that the universal belief in the communicability of bovine tuberculosis to human beings should not have more readily presentable facts in its support and at the command of men like Lord Lister, Nocard, Bronardel, of Paris; Schrotter, of Vienna and others.

Dr. Koch's address was the sole theme of general discussion after its presentation. Uniform regret was felt at the premature character of his communication, and rather severe criticism was openly expressed that Koch should admit that further experiments were necessary to remove doubt as to the correctness of his assertions, and in almost the same breath make the unqualified statement in the presence of such doubt, that he did not deem it advisable to take any measures against infected meat or milk from tuberculous cattle!

Accordingly, just this stand was taken by the British Congress:

Until stronger evidence is produced to prove that bovine tubercle bacilli are entirely harmless, there is only one course to follow in the light of the numerous cases known to medical men where bottle fed babies born of healthy parents, have died of tubercular disease, and the source of contagion has been narrowed down to milk from tuberculous cows. That course is to maintain the most rigid and scrupulous avoidance of such possible source of danger.

Sputum from consumptive patients was recognized as the great source of infection, and recommendations were accordingly made to decrease promiscuous expectoration. But infected meat and milk were also considered occasional as well as possible sources of danger, and it was unanimously voted that until Koch's new theory was more conclusively proven, continued measures for obtaining pure food, particularly milk, were warrantable and highly advisable.

The discussion regarding the uses of tuberculin proved to be very interesting. In his remarks on this subject Dr. Koch also appeared to disadvantage, for he gave the impression of trying to evade many leading questions that were put to him. He and other advocates of tuberculin as a curative agent failed to present any new or convincing facts, and while its use was considered serviceable as a diagnostic procedure, the general consensus of opinion was against the therapeutic use of tuberculin.

As might be expected preventive treatment or prophylaxis was the keynote of most of the papers, but sanatoria and the methods possible in such institutions were generally recognized as offering the most favorable prospects for the successful treatment of consumptive patients.

I cannot close my report without referring to the Tuberculosis Museum in Queen's Hall. It was a remarkable collection of specimens demonstrating the pathology of tuberculosis and the life history of the tubercle bacillus and its allied forms. No such complete and comprehensive collection was ever brought together before, and it was in itself alone worth everything to those who had the opportunity of enjoying it. Great credit is due Dr. W. Jobson Harne, Hon. Secretary of the Museum Committee, for a splendid descriptive catalogue of the exhibits.

All in all the British Congress of Tuberculosis was a highly interesting meeting. The details were admirably carried out, and an especially satisfactory feature was the publication from day to day of comprehensive abstracts of the papers read. It is to be regretted that more American physicians were not present at this notable occasion.

In conclusion let me extend my sincere thanks to the American Congress of Tuberculosis for so kindly appointing me a delegate to this great international meeting. The experiences through which I passed as one of the representatives of our honored Congress will always remain fresh in my mind as some of the most enjoyable of my life. These experiences, however, have by no means detracted from my respect for dear old America and the American physician, nor lowered in any way the cherished hopes I hold for the future success of the American Congress of Tuberculosis.

THE LONDON CONGRESS OF TUBERCULOSIS.

REPORT OF DELEGATE DR. A. C. BERNAYS, OF ST. LOUIS, MO., U. S. A.

Vice-President of the American Congress of Tuberculosis.

St. Louis, October 1st, 1901.

Clark Bell, Esq., Secretary General A. C. T.

My Dear Sir:—The London Congress was a success. It brought together many of the men who are entitled by virtue of researches made in the past to be heard on the important subjects which were discussed.

Koch was of course the centre of attraction. Say what you will his work in tuberculosis is the greatest advance ever taken by one man during the past century. I am sure that since he has discovered the cause and demonstrated the etiology of tuberculosis, we can intelligently combat its spread among animals. Before Koch we labored in darkness, now we have a clear scientific basis upon which to work in our fight against this scourge of the human race. Koch's communication was received with respect, but it left us all in doubt; it was not convincing and must now pass through the hands of many investigators in many laboratories. Those who are now decrying his work have no right to do so. Let them investigate before they decide or criticise. Science knows no man's "ipse dixit" and authority has long been barred out from scientific discussions. Nothing but demonstrations has the floor.

I visited the Congress in order to apply to its transactions the measure of a practical surgeon. Much was said and done of interest to surgeons, but I can not so soon after the Congress presume to estimate the value of the work or even review it critically.

Much was done and all the foreigners were handsomely entertained by the Englishmen. The Congress was a success and will lead to much valuable work by the many investigators who were in attendance in large numbers.

A SYNOPTICAL REPORT OF THE PROCEEDINGS OF THE CONGRESS ON TUBERCULOSIS.

HELD IN THE CITY OF LONDON, ENGLAND,
JULY 22–25, 1901.

BY JOHN CLINTON SHRADER, A. M., M. D., LL.D.,
IOWA CITY, IOWA.

Vice-President and Delegate of the American Congress of Tuberculosis. Member and Ex-President of Iowa State Medical Society. Member of American Medical Association, and Ex-Vice-President, A. P. H. A. Member of British Congress of Tuberculosis. Member of British Medical Association, &c., &c.

Obesrvations made during my trip to England and the Continent of Europe, of the advances made in the study of Tuberculosis:—

A visit to any country other than our own has an indefinable charm for the observer, and especially is this so when such visit has for its object the pursuit of scientific study and research. Sanitarians the world over were attracted this last Summer to the great city of London,not that it is the metropolis of the world, but because the invitation had been sent out, that during the month of July, of the year 1901, there would be held in that city a meeting of the most learned men of the earth to consult together for the good of the people. Hoping and believing that by comparing views and discussing causes that produce the pestilence known as tuberculosis, that a means of staying its ravages and of its prevention; that by these and other means which might suggest themselves, that a cure might eventually be found to stop the ravages of the greatest destroyer of the human race that has ever existed. We have become so accustomed to its presence that it has ceased to cause alarm.

In pursuance of this object there assembled near 3,000 delegates—coming from all the civilized countries of the world.

Made to the Medico-Legal Society at the October meeting, 1901, and contributed to the Bulletin of the American Congress of Tuberculosis.

Among this vast number were learned doctors from the great universities, savants, judges of the highest courts, peers of the realm; divines who believe it their duty to save the bodies as well as the souls of their parishoners, editors of the great dailies and magazines, statesmen who believe in the brotherhood of man. Sanitarians all; all deeply imbued with the one object—the saving of the lives of the people from disease and death. What can be more ennobling than quenching the anguish of the nations of the earth from the fell destroyer—Death—seeking his victims from all ranks of society. The loving babe in its mother's arms, the beautiful maiden, the loving wife and mother, and the strongest athlete, all sink beneath the contagium of this dread disease—Consumption.

This great meeting was called to order by H. R. H. the Duke of Cambridge, H.-G., on behalf of His Majesty, the King, who fittingly spoke of the honor conferred upon the British nation by having a meeting of such vital importance to all the nations of the world held in the city of London.

After calling attention to the importance of the subject, and reviewing in a brief and terse manner, the ravages of consumption throughout the world and expressing his belief that great good would result from the conference now being inaugurated, he then introduced the Lord Mayor of London, who welcomed the delegates to the metropolis and tendered the usual hospitalities on such important occasions. He was followed by some of the most noted members of royalty and learned doctors of medicine, divinity and law; followed by one member from each country, who responded in a felicitous manner.

The further meetings of the Congress were divided into four sections, to meet each morning, as follows:

Section 1, State and Municipal; Section 2, Medical, including Climatology and Sanatoria; Section 3, Pathology, including Bacteriology; Section 4, Veterinary.

In addition, on each afternoon, a general meeting was held and addresses delivered, on some topic of common interest to the whole Congress. The meeting held on July 23rd was addressed by Prof. Robert Koch, of Berlin, on "The Fight Against Tuberculosis in the Light of Experience That Has Been Gained in the Successful Combat of Other Diseases." Prof. Koch said among other thisgs:

The task with which this Congress will have to busy itself is one of the most difficult; but it is also one in which labor is most sure of its reward. I need not point to the innumerable victims tuberculosis annually claims in all countries, nor to the boundless misery it brings on the families it attacks. You all know there is no disease which inflicts such deep wounds on mankind as this. All the greater, however, would be the general joy and satisfaction if the efforts that are being made to rid mankind of this enemy, which consumes its inmost marrow, were crowned with success. There are many who doubt the possibility of successfully combating this disease, which has existed for thousands of years, and has spread all over the world. This is by no means my opinion. This is a conflict into which we may enter with a surely founded prospect of success, and I will tell you the reasons on which I base this conviction. Only a few decades ago the real nature of tuberculosis was unknown to us; it was regarded as a consequence, as the expression, so to speak, of social misery, and, as this supposed cause could not be got rid of by simple means, people relied on the probable gradual improvement of social conditions, and did nothing. All this is altered now. We know that social misery does indeed go far to foster tuberculosis, but the real cause of the disease is a parasite; that is, a visible and palpable enemy, which we can pursue and annihilate, just as we can pursue and annihilate other parasitic enemies of mankind. Strictly speaking, the fact that tuberculosis is a preventible disease ought to have become clear as soon as the tubercule bacillus was discovered, and the properties of the parasite and the manner of its transmission become known. Success has been achieved in combating some other parasitic disease; why not this. We should draw valuable lessons from our experience in controlling other pestilences. We have learned that every disease must be treated individually and measures adopted according to its special nature and etiology. Take for an illustration the Plague, where formerly the patient was considered in the highest degree dangerous and a constant source of infection, but now our views have materially changed, and those patients only who are suffering from Plague pneumonia are considered dangerous. We know that the chief source of contagion are the ratas affected with this disease; and unless effective work is done in exteminating them, the chief etiological factor is not touched. By the course which has been pursued, the general spread of the disease has not been hindered in the least. Cholera, another disease affords an exaample of the individuality, for here the chief propagator of the contagion is water, and so it is the first thing to be considered. Hydrophobia is also instructive, for while inoculations are curative, they are not preventive of infection, and the only real way of combating this pestilence is by compulsary muzzling. Leprosy is closely akin to tuberculosis, and like it, spreads from man to man by close contact; so to combat it, it is necessary to prevent close communication of the well and sick, and so isolation is adopted.

We have wasted our energies—have not struck at the root of the evil. We must first understand how the disease is transmitted, and then we can hope to combat the pestilence. These parasites get into the lungs through the dried sputum of the patient, and, knowing this, we now know much better how to control the disease. The sputum in advanced stages, contains large quantities of the bacilli. Through coughing, and even speaking, the parasites are flung into the air in large quantities; they thus find ready ingress to the lungs from not only these methods, the most frequent, but by some others. We need not in these days, consider the hereditary element, for it is extremely rare, if it evists at all. It is generally regarded as proven, that tuberculosis is very frequently communicated from animal to man, and as the disease is so frequently found in animals—poultry and cattle—it seems that this should be true. But in the course of my investigations I am led to deviate from from this common belief. I have always from the first, looked upon this theory with doubt, and in the last two years, have performed many experiments to determine the truth of these statements. Let me give you some of the most important of these investigations. Prof. Schuts, of the Veterinary College in Berlin, assisted me. A number of young cattle which had stood the tuberculosis test, were infected in various ways with pure cultures of tubercule baccilli, taken from cases of human tuberculosis; some of them got the tuberculosis sputum direct. In some cases the tubercule baccilli or the sputum were injected under the skin, in others, into the peritoneal cavity, in others into the jugular vein. Six animals were fed with tuberculosis sputum for seven or eight months almost daily; four repeatedly inhaled great quantities of baccilli which were distributed in water and scattered with it in the form of spray. There were nineteen of these cattle, none showed any syptoms of the disease, and they gained considerably in weight. From six to eight months after the beginning of the experiments they were killed; in the internal organs not a trace of tuberculosis could be found—only in the places where injections had been made, small supperative foci had been formed—in which few tubercule vaccilli could be found.

These animals were infected by the living baccilli of human tuberculosis. They were absolutely insusceptible to them. The result was utterly different, however, when the same experiment was made on cattle free from tuberculosis, with tubercule baccilli that had come from the lungs of an animal suffering from bovine tuberculosis. After an incubation period of about a week, the severest disorders (of tuberculor nature) of the internal organs, broke out in all the infected animals. The result was the same where the infective material was introduced under the skin, into the peritoneal cavity of the vascular system. High fever set in, and the animal became weak and lean. Some of them died after a month and a half or two months. Others were killed in a miserably sick condition after three months. After extensive tubercular infilterations were found at the places where the injections had been made, and in the neighboring lymphatic gland and also far advanced alterations of the internal organs, especially the lungs and spleen; where the infective material had been injected into the peritoneal cavity—there these growths were found on the omentum and peritoneum. They were as susceptible to bovine tuberculosis, as they were insusceptible t human tuberculosis.

In experimenting with swine, I found the same conditions existing. Those fed with human sputum containing tubercule baccilli, remained healthy and grew lustily, while those fed with the bovine tuberculosis, became sickly, stunted, and hali of them dead. After three months the remainder were killed, and in those fed with sputum, no trace of tuberculosis could be found, except some small nodules in the lymphatic glands of the neck, and in one case, a few gray nodules in the lungs. While those fed with the bovine tuberculosis (as in the case of the cattle) had without exception, severe tubercular diseases—tubercular infiltration of the gland of the, neck, misentary, and extensive lesions of the lungs and spleen.

Experiments with asses, sheep and goats presented a like result; upon consulting some of the older writers, vis., Chauveau, Guenther, Harms, Bollinger and others, we find the same statments made, of unbelief in the identity of the two forms of the disease. Recently in America, Smith, Dinwidie and Frothingham, have taken the same view as to the non-identity of the two forms of tubercule baccilli. Considering all these facts, I feel justified in maintaining that human tuberculosis differs from bovine, and cannot be transmitted to cattle. But by far the most important question is, can bovine tuberculosis be transmitted to man? This question is more difficult to answer categorically, for the reason that we cannot experiment in the same direct way. This, however, we know, that the milk and other dairy products from tuberculous cattle contain millions of live, active tubercule baccilli and if they proved as virulent as is claimed by many, whole families would be destroyed. This milk is used as an article of food in hospitals for the care and treatment of sick children; they would soon be utterly destroyed; at the same time, we do not say that such infection does not exist, but that it is very rare, and is scarcely deserving our notice..

One argument to prove this statement of the infectiveness of dairy products, is that in these cases, the intestinal tract should be the first to show the tubercular lesion—whereas—Baginsky shows that in 933 autopsies in children, he never found tuberculosis of the intestines without simultaneous disease of the lungs. Of 3,104 post mortem in children, Beidert found only 16 primary cases of tuberculosis of the intestines.

Prof. Koch sums up his conclusions with these words: "Though the important question, whether man is susceptible to bovine tuberculosis at all, is not yet absolutely decided, and will not admit of absolute decision today, or tomorrow, one is nevertheless already at liberty to say, that if such a susceptibility really evists, the infection of human beings is but a very rare occurrence. I should estimate the extent of infection by the milk and flesh of tubercular cattle, and the butter made of their milk as hardly greater than that of hereditary transmission; and therefore do not deem it advisable to take any measures against it."

But notwistanding all this, Prof. Koch advises, as a matter of precaution, that all milk be pasteurized, where there is any reason to fear infection.

At the close of the address, Lord Lister, who was presiding, sprang to his feet to enter his protest to some of the statements made by Prof. Koch. The address was freely discussed by many members of the Congress, and many more desired to be heard. Lord Lister said it would be a serious thing to have this paper go out to the world as the expression of the belief of the delegates. He feared that it might lead to a relaxation of efforts being made at this time to provide a pure milk supply. He cited the instance of smallpox and cowpox, and stated that while smallpox could not often be inoculated from man to cows, it was possible to inoculate monkeys from man, and afterwards, cows from the monkeys; and we know the two diseases are identical. He urged further investigation, and while it could not be endorsed, he hoped it might be the means of doing good.

The third general meeting was addressed by Prof. Brouardel, of Paris, on "The Measures Adopted by Different Nations for the Prevention of Consumption." He referred to the havoc caused by the disease, and the general apathy among the people. The slowness in recognizing the dangers arising from damp, dark dwellings, and seventy years ago began the crusade for healthy homes. The grounds of prevention in all countries are identical. That is, that tuberculosis is preventable and curable. The great object is the education of the people; by means of legislation, the issuance of circulars of information by State Boards, and instruction by sanatoria. England has a National Association for the prevention of consumption. Germany has societies for building sanatoria and popularizing sanitary ideas. Belgium has a National League against tuberculosis. Norway has appropriated money for printing and disseminating a popular work on tuberculosis. France is taking the lead in this movement for imparting instruction to the people. They have selected those that are qualified to teach, and popular lectures are given, and, on every hand societies for the prevention of tuberculosis are springing up. Thus in all countries, the people are beginning to realize that by personal care and attention to cleanliness, pure air, sunlight, houses well ventilated, will do much to obviate contagion; and they are also learning that a comsumptive patient is dangerous only when necessary and proper precautions are not taken to protect friend and relatives from the great source of danger. the sputum. Spitting is a great danger, and when once this disgustink habit is suppressed the disease will rapidly diminish. In Sidney, New South Wales, a fine of 1 pd. is imposed for spitting in the streets. The sputum is not dangerous if put in antiseptic receptacles: not so dangerous in dry, light places, as in damp, dark and all ventilated alleys or houses, here it remains virulent a long time.

Dr. Brouardel dwelt at some length on the necessity for light, dry, well ventilated rooms and houses, both of a public or private character. In many of the countries of Europe, building societies have been established for the erection of healthy homes, especially for workmen and their families. Bad quarters exist in all towns: these must be sought out and remedied: for these are hot beds of disease, and especially tuberculosis. Intemperance is a potent factor in its production and dissemination: statistics prove an increased death rate in localities where inebriety exists.

In speaking of the care of weak, scrofulous children, he stated that France has erected fourteen sanatoria near the seashore, in healthy, salubrious localities, for their care and treatment. Good nutritious food is indispensible to success. Italy and Germany are moving in this direction also. Prevention is the remedy, and under this head he includes good food; the inspection of meat and milk—thinks private slaughter houses are a menace to public health. Milk from cows suffering from tuberculous mastites is reeking with germs, not only the tubercule vaccilli, but pus cells also in large quantities. In England, in the past fifty years, the mortality in adults has diminished 45 per cent.; the deaths in children have increased 47 per cent, which he attributes to the tuberculous milk fed to children. Now strict inspection is being made, and also is this true in Norway, Sweden and Denmark.

From an international standpoint it seems that consumption cannot be treated as some other of the infectious diseases, such as Plague, but much can be done by disinfection of railway carriages, steamboats, ships and hotels. In Germany every doctor who attends a case of pulmonary or laryngial tuberculosis, must report it in writing to the police, as soon as he has made his diagnosis. After death of a patient from tuberculosis, the room occupied and in which he died, must be disinfected, and all his belongings. Hotel proprietors, housekeepers, asylums, and in fact, all institutions, are compelled to notify the police at once of every case of tuberculous disease which arrives at their establishments.

The fourth general meeting was addressed by Prof. John McFadyean, on "Tubercule Baccilli in Cow's Milk, as a Possible Source of Tuberculous Disease in Man."

He summed up Prof. Koch's train of reasoning as follows: "First, That the baccilli found in cases of bovine tuberculosis were much more virulent in cattle and other domestic animals than the baccilli found in cases of human tuberculosis. Second, That this difference was so marked and so constant that it might be relied on as a means of distinguishing bacilli of bovine tuberculosis from those of the human disease, even assuming that the former might occasionally be found as a cause of the disease in man. Third, That if bovine baccilli were capable of causing the disease in man, there were abundant opportunities for the transferring of the baccilli from the one species to the other, and cases of primary intestinal tuberculosis from the consumption of tuberculous milk, ought to be of common occurrence, but post mortem examination of human beings proved that cases of primary intestinal tuberculosis were extermely rare in man, and, therefore, it must be concluded that the human subject was immuned against infection with the bovine baccilli, or was so slightly susceptible, that it was not necessary to take any steps to counteract the risk of infection in this way."

He thought one of these premises was ill founded and the others had but little bearing on the subject. He thought that even if bovine baccilli were more virulent to cattle, that it did not prove that the human bacillus had no deleterious effects; for it is known that bacteria common to all domestic animals, were pathogenic to man. He quoted from hospital statistics where milk was an article of diet, the great number of children proven to be tuberculous—post mortem. Prof. Koch claimed that the milk from tuberculosis cows was dangerous, only, when the udder was affected. He (Mr. McFadyean) showed that 30 per cent of the cows in Great Britian were tuberculous, while only 2 and 2-10 per cent had the udder affected. The milk from all tuberculous cows contained large quantities of the bacilli, while but few had painful or tender udders. He also spoke of the contamination of milk by dust and dirt. He recommended periodical inspection of herds at brief intervals by competent inspectors. Said compulsory notification of all tuberculous cattle, and the absolute interdiction of milk from all cows with diseased udders, and finally said this should apply to all suffering from tuberculosis.

There was an interesting discussion on the use and abuse of tuberculin. First, as a diagnostic agent, and second, as a curative one. Dr. Heron, who gave a history of it, thought it had fallen into disuse, owing to the too frequent use of it in unsuitable cases, its administration in too large doses, neglect of this rule—that a dose should never be given until the patient's temperature has been normal for the previous 24 hours at least, that the dose of tuberculin should never be increased, but rather diminished, when followed by a rise of temperature; that by following this rule much of the prejudice that has existed among medical men and patients would thereby be prevented; because of the severity of the symptoms which often follow its indiscriminate use. For diagnostic purposes, tuberculin was most valuable, making an early diagnosis possible when there was much better chances of recovery. Prof. Koch thought for diagnostic purposes it was valuable in the human subject when properly used, and was then without danger. The injections in weak subjects should be small enough—not more thaan 1-10 m. m.—to begin with, and not used again until the temperature was normal when the first injection gave but a weak reaction; the second, generally of the same amount, gave a decided reaction. Over 3000 cases had been observed by him and he felt justified in saying that the tuberculin test was almost absolute. In early, and uncomplicated cases, he thought as a therapeutic remedy it was of great value, and that complete cure frequently resulted. In cases of more advanced stages, the temperature should be normal before the injections are made. The treatment should be continued over a long period if necessary, with intervals of three or four months, until they gave no reaction.

Prof. Koch said the tuberculin was prepared from tubercule bacilli of human origin, but that the reaction was produced in both the human and bovine species, although the bacilli was different they possessed a common "group" reaction. There was much difference of opinion among the delegates about its curative qualities, but most all agreed to its harmlessness and its great value as a diagnostic test.

Climatology. In regard to the effect of climate as a curative agent there was a prolonged discussion; members from most countries of the earth believed there was much benefit to be derived from a proper climatic condition; that a fairly equable climate, one not subject to sudden changes of either moisture or temperature, at a moderate altitude, among the pines and where there is a great amount of sunshine necessary. All agreed these conditions to be a sine quo non to success; and further, each claimed that a certain portion of his "own" country, was the best for all purposes. I forgot to mention that some who had no mountains, thought a salubrious place near the sea, where the patient could inhale the salt laden breezes, was especially desirable. But all agreed that a damp climate with but little sunshine, or the dwelling in dark, damp rooms was very deleterious and should be avoided and shunned.

Many statistics were given which I have not time to repeat. There was much discussion on Sanitoria—their location, manner of construction, whether large, commodious structures, or, the cottage system gave the best results. The treatment by medicinal preparations, internally, by inhalations, etc., was carefully considered.

The X-Ray was deemed a great diagnostic instrument, showing clearly even small foci—consolidations and cavities. The movement of the diaphragm like a piston up and down was ordinarially equal on both sides of the chest, but in disease, was much less on the affected side, even when the disease was limited to one apex.

In the discussion on milk supplies, nearly every speaker took occasion to disagree with Prof. Koch; and expressed the opinion that tuberculous milk was dangerous to man as food. No animal could be declared free from tuberculosis, unless the tuberculin test had been applied.

At the last general meeting held on July 26th, the following resolutions were adopted:

1. That tuberculous sputum is the main agent for the conveyance of the virus of tuberculosis from man to man. Indiscriminate spitting should therefore be suppressed.

2. That it is the opinion of this Congress that all public hospitals and dispensaries should present every out patient suffering from phthisis with a leaflet containing instructions with regard to the prevention of consumption. and should supply, and insist upon the use, of a pocket spittoon.

3. That the voluntary notification of cases of phthisis, attended with tuberculous expectoration, and the increased preventive action which it has rendered practicable, has been attended by a promising measure of success, and that the extension of notification should be encouraged in all districts in which efficient sanitary administration renders it possible to adopt the consequential measures.

4. That the provision of sanatoria is an indespensable part of the means necessary for the diminution of consumption.

5. In the opinion of this Congress, in the light of the work that has been presented at its sittings, medical officers of health should continue to use all the powers at their disposal and relax no efforts, to prevent the spread of tuberculosis by milk or meat.

6. That in view of the doubts thrown on the identity of human and bovine tuberculosis, it is expedient that the government be approached and requested to institute an immediate inquiry into this question; which is of vital importance to the public health, and of great consequence to the agricultural industry.

7. That the educational work of the great national societies for the prevention of tuberculosis, is deserving of every encouragement and support; it is through their agency that a rational public opinion may be formed, the duties of public health officers made easier to perform, and such local and State legilation as may be required, called into existence.

8. That this Congress is of opinion that a permanent international committee should be appointed to collect evidence and report on the measures that have been adopted for the pervention of tuberculosis in different countries, to publish a popular statement of these measures, to keep and

publish periodically, a record of scientific research in relation to tuberculosis, and to consider and recommend measures of prevention.

This Congress is further of opinion that such a committee should consist of representatives to be elected by the great national societies formed for the suppression of tuberculosis, and also, representatives nominated by various governments.

It is further of the opimon that all international committees, and great national societies, whose object is the prevention of tuberculosis, should be invited to co-operate.

9. In the opinion of this Congress, overcrowding, defective ventilation, damp and general unsanitary conditions in the houses of the working classes, diminish the chances of curing consumption; and aid in predisposing and spreading the disease.

10. That while recognizing the great importance of sanitoria in combatting with tuberculosis in countries, the attention of governments should be directed towards informing charitable and philanthropic individuals and societies of the necessity for anti-tuberculous dispensaries, as the best means of checking tuberculous diseases among the industrial and indigent classes.

Dr. E. Maragliana, of Milan, said that the destructive action of the gastric juice, and the auto sterilization of the intestines, recently promulgated by Kohlbrugge, explàin the rarity of tuberculosis of the intestines from food infected by the tubercule bacillus, as well as from the bacilli in the sputa swallowed by the tuberculous patient. This argument has, therefore, little value as cited by Koch, to sustain his theory of the non-transmissibility of bovine tuberculosis to man. Maragliana says, that killed cultures of human tubercule, cause intense toxic phenomana in cows and goats; showing that these animals are susceptible to the toxins of human tuberculosis, and, therefore necessarially to its bacilli.

Michelozzi has recently published the results of study of the prolonged use of sterilized milk from tuberculous cows. He demonstrated that the milk from a tuberculous animal, even if the teats are intact, and no bacilli pop into the milk, it is yet extremely injurious, as the serum of the milk is injurious, being very toxic, even more toxic than that of the blood. The amount of toxins in the milk varies with the severity of the tuberculous process, but its toxic properties are unaltered, and are not affected by sterilizing the milk by heat.

A chronic intoxication of the organism ingesting the milk is determined in time. His experiments at Pisa indicate that the profound marasmus accompaning tuberculosis in man and animals, is the rseult of the action of the toxins resulting from the presence of the tubercule bacilli, thus confirming Maragliana's assertion, that "Tuberculosis" is preeminently a "toxicosis."

THE WORK OF THE LONDON CONGRESS OF TUBERCULOSIS AND DISCUSSION OF THE REPORT OF THE DELEGATES.

REMARKS BY FREDERICK L. HOFFMAN.

Ladies and Gentlemen:—I did not expect to be called upon for remarks, since I was not a delegate of the Society to the London Congress on Tuberculosis. I privately represented the Prudential Insurance Company of America and read a paper on the relation of Industrial insurance to the prevention of tuberculosis. I can only endorse what has been said by the preceding speakers, that our reception at London was exceedingly cordial and that the general arrangements for the work of the Congress were excellent. I feel satisfied that I voice the opinion of all who were present and I may add that there were more than 2,000 delegates from all parts of the world. that the work of the Congress will prove of an enduring character and represent a most important addition to our knowledge of the steps necessary for the successful combat of what has properly been called "The Great White Pleague." I cannot speak too highly of the arrangements made by the committee in charge of program in dividing the work of the Congress into four principal sections. This arrangement proved entiely adequate for the large amount of work to be done, and, while many who had expected to participate in the debates could not be accommodated for want of time, still the large majority who had taken proper steps in advance were given an opportunity to read their papers and discuss the remarks of others. It is also but proper for me to make acknowledgment of the generous hospitality extended to the delegates, which included a reception by the Lord Mayor and a very pleasant garden party at the seat of the Duke of Northumberland.

My own interest in the Congress was limited to the State and Municipal section, before which, as has been stated, I read a paper on the relation of Industrial insurance to the prevention of tuberculosis. The question which had been raised in the preliminary program was "Would it be to the interest of the Industrial Insurance Societies or other public bodies to contribute towards the erection and maintenance of sanatoria for consumptives?" As the result of a special investigation made in response to a request for data, I was able to demonstrate that it would be financially impossible for Industrial insurance companies, to undertake the erection and maintenance of sanatoria for policy-holders, since the average cash value of the reserve on Industrial policies would not be sufficient to meet the necessary expenses for proper treatment. The question was undoubtedly suggested to the committee on program by the frequent assertions made in the literature on the subject that insurance companies in Germany have been successful in providing such sanatoria, with a resulting profit to the companies. A careful investigation of these assertions, however, has made it clear to me that there exists no substantial foundation for this statement, since the erection of sanatoria in Germany has been entirely limited to the Government Insurance institutions, which naturally operate under entirely different conditions than private corporations, and as far as I have been able to learn, as the result of correspondence and personal investigation, no private life insurance company in Germany has ever undertaken the treatment of consumptive policy-holders in sanatoria, either owned by the company or operated by the State.

This brings me to a point which will always remain one of sincere regret, since I cannot but think that the best possible work of the Congress fell short of being attained in cousequence of the aggressive attitude of theGerman delegates.Not only was the Congress flooded with the literature of the German propaganda, in favor of sanatoria operated by the State or by Life Insurance Societies, but in particular the uncalled for remarks of Dr. Koch, did much to overshadow the most important work of the Congress.

I do not know how far I voice the sentiments of the speakers who have preceded me when I say plainly and emphatically that to my way of thinking Professor Koch took an undue and uncalled for advantage of the members of the Congress in making the statement which is now generally known, that tuberculosis of animals cannot be transmitted to man, or to be more accurate that tuberculosis of man cannot be transmitted to animals. I find nowhere in the general conditions governing the assembling of the Congress a warrant for the introduction of a matter of controversy of this kind, which by no stretch of the imagination can be connected with methods directly connected with successful efforts for the prevention of consumption. It was at its best a purely negative statement to the effect that the disease was in one particular way possibly not transmitted to man, but that was all. Even if true, which is very doubtful, nothing was gained, absolutely nothing resulted from this statement to further the work of the Congress, to increase public knowledge as to measures and means tending to successfully prevent the spread of tubercular diseases. Yet the statement was of such a character that it entirely overshadowed all the other work of the Congress, even though not, as I have already stated, in any way connected with the work of the Congress, that it is not going too far to say that an irreparable injustice was done to the more than two thousand delegates and the general causes of disease prevention by this uncalled for statement by Professor Koch. It was a statement which could have been made at any time before a scientific society in Germany or by communication to a medical publication; but the work of the Congress, the personal exchange of ideas on the part of over 2,000 delegates could not be performed in any other way than by the assembling of men from all parts of the world for a single week's work in one place. Instead of the public discussion being devoted to the general problems of the Congress, to a problem of such vast magnitude and importance that it is not likely that any other Congress or assembly of recent years will equal it in public value, it was largely given over to the all-absorbing question as to whether the works of hundreds and thousands of investigators had been useless, whether the conclusions of honest and painstaking men had been unwarranted and whether the services of probably half the sanitary organizations in England and other countries, that is the public inspection of milk and meat supplies, should be done away with. Now I cannot better illustrate the point which I would like to make clear to you than to suppose for a moment that an international meeting of bankers assembled for the purpose of discussing ways and means to improve the general condition of financial enterprises, the statement had been made by an invited guest, let us assume a bank examiner of international repute, that he had just found the Chemical Bank of New York City to be insolvent! You can readily imagine what little room would be left for other matters save this one, though not in the least connected with the objects for which the Congress had been called. It was just so with the Congress on Tuberculosis, an assembly which spite of the difficulty named and spite of the enormous hindrance to a free public discussion of the many problems presented, still produced an enduring record of a most excellent work. It is not the fault of either Professor Koch or of quite a number of his German associates that this was the case. I believe firmly, as time proceeds and as impartial investigations prove his assumptions to have been false, or at least not warranted by the inferences, that the harsh criticism I find it necessary to express will meet with general approval.

Pardon me for a moment longer if I call attention to the fact that among those who were present, at the Congress were Sir. Herbert Maxwell, Chairman of the State Section, who but a little more than two years ago, as Chairman of the Royal Commission appointed to inquire into "Administrative procedures of considering dangers through the use of food and milk of tuberculous animals," had deliberately expressed his opinion, endorsed by the members of his commission, that such dangers really existed, and that in other words, the disease of tuberculosis was liable to be transmitted to man directly through the use, as food, of the meat and milk of tuberculous animals. Now, if Professor Koch was right, then the Royal Commission of 1898 was wrong, yet this commission had availed itself of all the expert testimony furnished by the most competent and able practitioners in England. It was, therefore, not surprising that Lord Lister, for England, and Professor Brouardell, for France, publicly disavowed their belief in the new theory of Professor Koch, a theory which is as likely and almost certainly to be proven wrong, as other theories of Professor Koch have been in the past.

Will you allow me to make one further statement with reference to the remarks of Professor Koch, to which, as far as I know little public attention has been called, but which I incorporated in the introductory remarks in my address before the State Section. Professor Koch maintains that "The reason of the diminution in tuberculosis mortality was the dissemination of the knowledge that tuberculosis was an infectious disease." As I pointed out in my remarks before the Congress a more preposterous and more unwarranted statement was never made and attempted to be imposed upon an audience thoroughly familiar with fifty years of methods and results of sanitary science. Long before the theory of Professor Koch had been made public there had been a constant and remarkable decrease in the mortality from tuberculosis. As shown by the charts and diagrams exhibited by the Sanitary Officers of England and as corroborated by diagrams exhibited by me personally, for the large cities in this country, there has been a constant decline in the mortality from tubercular diseases for a period of almost half a century. For Professor Koch, therefore, to claim credit for the decline in the mortality from consumption as caused by the increasing knowledge that the disease was infectious rather than hereditary, is a claim for credit for himself and for a theory to which the larger amount of the decline in the mortality from tubercular diseases can certainly not be attributed. The disease has declined very largely in virtue of the general social progress which has been made during the past half century in cousequence of better living, better housing and a general higher standard of public morality. Yet it is not to be denied that an increasing public recognition of the disease being of a dangerous, infectious and communicable character will very materially aid public authorities and private enterprises in bringing about a further decrease in the mortality from tubercular diseases.

Mr. President and ladies and gentlemen, I thank you for your courteous attention.

ON THE QUESTION OF TUBERCULOSIS.

OPEN LETTER TO PROFESSOR CLIFFORD ALBUTT, (CAMBRIDGE.)

BY PROF. DR. MORITZ BENEDIKT OF VIENNA.

Esteemed Colleague.

I was greatly surprised to have been honored with an invitation to participate at the British Congress of Tuberculosis, to be held from the 22d to the 26th of July, this year, in London, under the protectorate of your King and the co-operation of so prominent men from all parts of Great Britain. I never took part in a discussion of this subject either publicly, or in writing or orally. I could only surmise that my international position on questions of patronage was the cause of my obtaining this honor. As I am unable to take part in the Congress, I feel that I should address you in a few words, of course with some hesitation, as I am afraid, I might say something that has perhaps been already passed upon by the profession.

I was one of the first among the physicians now living, who believed in the infection of tuberculosis. As a young physician I had several times made the observation that in conjugal cohabitation, be it blessed by the church or not, frequently the one who suffers from tuberculosis, can infect the other hitherto healthy one, so severely that the latter sooner succumbs to quick consumption than the one originally infected. I lived at that time in Italy and I was greatly astonished that this matter of fact was understood and recognized by the Italian people. One should not assume everything from the mouth of the people without criticism, but I recognize the advisability of paying attention to the sayings of the people; which through the wisdom of genial impressionists seizes truth and utters it, often sooner and more impressively than specialists would, whose manner of observation is often clouded by doctrinal prejudices.

When I communicated at that time my experience and conviction to my instructor, Mr. Oppolzer, he assumed an ingenious negative attitude. To-day the doctrine of infection of consumption is universally recognized and the recognition of it has even led to grave extremes.

There are certainly still other occasions of infection than conjugal cohabitation, and two thereof seem to me to be quite prominent, namely fashionable watering places which for a long time have been visited by numerous consumptives and homes for these invalids. It is for a physician one of the most painful matters to touch upon these questions of the institutions and Ibsen described in his "Volksfeind" (Enemy of the People) the difficulties and dangers of such exposure in the most emphatic manner.

My personal experiences which of course, are not authoritative, made me for many years afraid to send patients to such resorts and for a long time I have much frequented special watering places.

It seems to me the danger of infection through extended residence in these places has greatly increased, since we have latterly great epidemical and endemical influenza. It seems to me as if both of these microbes, far more dangerous and noxious in quarters where fewer well-to-do patients were to be crowded together, increase reciprocally their effect and where no attention is paid to hygiene.

A well frequented Austrian watering place is said to have been closed as such by the local authorities and now the truth about it will probably come to light. A prominent practitioner who practiced there some decades tells me, that for a long time he warned patients not to take up their residence in houses in which many patients reside every season, because he knew the infective qualities of these homes. He, likewise observed the terrible infectious effect upon the settled population. A physician who practised in a neighboring manufacturing town informed me, that the population hailing from the watering place was infected to such an extent, that the apparently healthiest workmen and working girls perished of consumption within a few years, so that the manufacturers did not any more employ workmen from the region of the watering place.

Even more dangerous might be an accumulation for many years of consumptives in large sanatorias. I beg to remind you of the terrible experience that was had in English Insane Asylums with tuberculosis. The sickly insane is prone to tuberculosis anyway, because the general decadence of vitality affects the nervous system of respiration, preventing a thorough ventilation of the lungs and, therefore, furthering and favoring the luxuriant growth of tuberculosis bacilli.

But if through a number of cases and years the institution is cumulatively infected then a local epidemic more readily appears by reason of the general predisposition and infected condition.

The moral of the matter is that the same principle should be applied to those affected with tuberculosis, as for the wounded and sick in war, to wit, the system of isolation, which was first proposed and carried out in the year 1859 by an Austrian Army Surgeon, Kraus.

The progressing hygiene might perhaps induce many a one nowadays, to believe that in great wars wounds could be aseptically operated upon and treated on the battlefield and the advanced field hospital. But for tuberculosis the matter stands worse inasmuch as we cannot bandage mouth and nose aseptically and the hands of the sick and their environs hardly could be kept aseptically clean. On the other hand of course, the infectious power of the tuberculosis bacillus is infinitely less than that of the suppuration coccees. There must be tuberculosis sputum in an extraordinary filthy state in order to infect. If, however, bed bugs and roaches are difficult to get out of old walls, so much less one will succeed with the invisible enemy bacilli. Great precaution will delay the danger, but not dispose of it.

As, doubtless, this question of tuberculosis will be taken in hand after the Congress has adjourned, in the United Kingdom by the State, the authorities and philanthropists, in grand style, it is to be hoped that no serious mistakes will be made. Nowhere else is philanthropy so prodigal as in Great Britain.

Do not build, for heaven's sake, any large, magnificent palaces, nor large sick hospitals, which in time will become palaces of bacilli. Proud portals, proud facades, luxurious appointments, are apt to throw sand in the eyes of high personages, weak women and the masses; but they do not serve the purpose. Well-to-do sick people may avoid the dangers to a certain degree; but the public care has principally to deal with those less favorably situated and the poor. Each tuberculosis sanitarium should be so laid out that it can be destroyed without great loss or burned down as soon as it can no longer be maintained free of bacilli. Therefore, a barrack system is preferable and the materials as far as possible, should be so chosen that they can be kept disinfected readily and can again be used for other invalid homes. Where large institutions cannot be avoided, the technical places, as kitchen, heating and illuminating centres, steam laundries, should be placed separately, while sleeping rooms and sitting rooms may be divided in small pavilions.

Very often the mistake is made—*exempla sunt odiosa*—that the ready money was spent in building and the means for proper provisions are wanting and there is no fund to take in the destitute.

One should not forget that philanthropy has many things to do in regard to the question of tuberculosis. If a sick one shall enter a home for tuberculous without hesitancy he should have the assurance that his family will be provided for while he is under treatment. I have often observed that the sick poor, who suffered from serious tuberculosis, declined to enter a sanitarium because they had to care for a poor mother, for a sick wife or for infant children and they worked and worked until they broke down past help. If a person affected with tuberculosis leaves the home as convalescent, his vitality and power of resistance are diminished and philanthropy must take care that he should not relapse or perish with his own. To such weaklings,who are not strong enough to take up the battle for their own and their families existence, too easily comes the demon alcohol as tempter, reducing and rapidly bringing on destruction.

Knowledge and treatment of tuberculosis do not require a specialist. Every physician is competent. The means of treatment are likewise relatively simple and, therefore, the sysetm of isolation can easily be carried out.

Small settlements at places free from dust and wind are preferable and a staff of well trained nurses can easily be obtained for this purpose.

Perhaps the system of dispersion may be partially carried out by placing light cases in the hands of private families for a proper compensation, at proper places, with definite instructions and under the charge of physicians. The danger of infection through single patients is not very great.

THE BASOPHILIC LEUCOCYTE VS. THE TUBERCLE BACILLI.

A Preliminary Report.

BY EDWIN LEONARD, JR., M. D., PATHOLOGIST TO THE MELROSE HOSPITAL.

It seems neither wise nor expedient at a meeting of this sort for me to occupy the time by giving figures and data pertaining to research along the line of antagonism of the basophilic leucocyte and the tubercle bacilli.

However, as the deductions seem to me to be of import both for future work along this line, as well as for the immediate treatment of the diseased condition, I will give you only a brief abstract together with my conclusions.

Ever since the days of Metchinkoff when he discovered the phagocytic properties of the white corpuscle, the leucocytes have figured more or less prominently in the treatment of diseases.

While the differentiation of the leucocyte into various classes and their transitional forms has aided us much in diagnosis, it remains for Neusser to bring out the coincideuces of the basophilic leucocyte as a resistant force in tuberculosis.

In this he has shown that whenever basophilia exists, as in gout or leukoemia, tuberculosis rarely occurs and that when tuberculosis does coexist with the uric acid diathesis, the tubercular process tends to cicatrize and heal. Simon in an extensive work upon the basophilia finds them in healthy individuals and this to me goes to prove that the resistant power of the individual against the tubercle lies in the basophilic leucocyte. When we find in from 25 to 50 per cent of our necropsies evidence of old tubercular lesions which have heal-

Read before the American Congress of Tuberculosis in joint session with Medico-Legal Society, May 15, 16, 1901.

ed, we know that nature in some way is able to combat the disease, for tuberculosis differs from many infectious diseases in that it tends to the production of marked and permanent anatomic changes in the tissues and organs involved, besides so far, we are able to produce little if any immunizing reactions in the organism.

Taking then Neusser's conclusions that whenever basophilia exists, tuberculosis rarely occurs and that this may be due to the presence of an excess of alloxan bases, I have taken those three products which not only have shown themselves to be distinct aids in the treatment of tuberculosis, but also one contains alloxan bases, while the other two, produce well marked leucocytosis namely, urea, sodium cinnamate and protonuclein and have tried to show their relation to the basophilia.

Harper has reported 9 cases in which he used pure urea, improvement followed in all and although he speaks of many recovered, tubercle bacilli were still found in the sputum of some. With sodium cinnamate or hetol, Landerer, Mann and others have published about 200 cases, showing some 70 per cent. with good results.

Canan reports 110 cases of all classes with some 75 per cent. of good results with the use of protonuclein.

The clinical picture of the first two, namely, the urea and sodium cinnamate is similar. A sensation like that of the so-called uric acid fatigue is observed and in several patients acute attacks of rheumatism and even gout occured.

Their reaction upon the blood causes a distinct leucocytosis although the leucocytosis caused by the urea was very slight.

No marked increase in basophilia was seen by giving urea, but further work, together with increase doses for a longer period may produce this result.

Sodium cinnamate produces both fever and a leucocytosis, and increase of eosinophiles as well as a slight increase of basophilies were noted.

Protonuclein showed a marked leucocytosis together with an increase of eosiniphiles and a moderate increase of basophiles.

Puther work may show that this increase of basophilia is dependent upon the increase in leucocytosis caused either by an ingestion of the nucleins or their by products.

To sum up we would state,

1st. Basophilia exists in healthy individuals.

2nd. Basophilia are increased in gout, uric acid diathesis and leukoemia.

3rd. That the resistance to the tubercle bacilli of persons having a uric acid diathesis and also those living upon a meat diet, may be due to the presence of basophilia.

4th. Clinically the giving of urea and sodium cinnamate causes a uric acid diathesis with attending blood symptoms.

5th. Protonuclein increases the basophilia without giving rise to unpleasant symptoms.

THE TREATMENT OF PULMONARY TUBERCULOSIS.

BY DR. E. LICEAGA,

President of the Supreme Board of Health of Mexico, Professor in the National School of Medicine, &c., and Vice President for Mexico of the American Congress of Tuberculosis.

Mr. President and Gentlemen:—The invitation to attend this Congress reached me so late, that it allowed me no time to procure an English translation of the different documents that the Superior Board of Health of Mexico has published in its efforts to establish a defense against Tuberculosis, or of those which I have myself written on this subject, or the preparation of fresh papers of my own.

With the permission of the Secretary, I now present an English translation of the paper which was read in my name in the 'Pan-American Medical Congress" that was held in Havana, in February of this year.

The paper which I am now about to read, is a summary of the methods that I have practiced for the last twenty-six years in the treatment of incipient Tuberculosis, and I beg to call your attention to the successful results which I have obtained with those methods.

The greater part of my observations relate to persons who arrive from Yucatan already sick. Some come from other parts of the Gulf Coast, whilst others, in a smaller number, come from the Pacific Coast, and many of my observations relate to patients in this Capital or other parts of the Central Table Land.

In almost all these cases, it has been proved that Tuberculosis existed amongst the ascendants of the patients; parents, grandparents, uncles or aunts, brothers, etc.; but as a general rule, the predisposition has come from the maternal or paternal side and really from both at the same time. It has not always been the case that the tuberculous patients who

Read before the American Congress of Tuberculosis in joint session with the Medico-Legal Society, May 15-16, 1901.

are the subject of this study, have lived under the same roof with their blood relations who were suffering from the same disease. The age has varied between 15 and 50 years. My observations cover a larger number of women than of men. The greater part of the patients have been of a weak constitution, although some presented a healthy and even robust appearance, the latter being specially observed amongst those who had the disease in its incipient state. Amongst the personal antecedents I have frequently found a series of previous attacks of intermittent fevers and I did not know whether to refer to paludism, which prevails endemically on our coasts or to premonitory manifestations of the tuberculosis itself.

Other patients have suffered from repeated attacks, at varied intervals, of gastric dyspepsia or diarrhoea. In many cases, I have discovered evident indications of anemia and in many young women, menstrual pertubations of Amenorrhea.

In a great number of cases, the commencement of the disease goes back to an attack of influenza; in others to a sudden chill: in some the first pulmonary symptoms have appeared after an attack of gastric dyspepsia or diarrhoea. Hemoptisis is very frequent in persons who take the disease on the coast, and is considered the starting point of the disease. It is very difficult to determine the age of the disease, but nevertheless, I consider that the apparent commencement is the period at which the patient discovers it himself through the simultaneous symptoms of cough, fever and loss of flesh, or else through the appearance of the first hemoptisis. In those cases which I have been able to observe from the beginning, I have also been able to discover variations in the pitch, rythm or tone of the respiration, as well as light but perceptible variations in the resonance of the thorax at the height of the diseased parts.

Cough is a symptom that is constant, but variable in its intensity, frequency or character. Some times it is dry, short and guttural; with greater frequency it forces up sputa that varies in its aspect, consistency, abundance, taste and smell. The coughs are separate even though they may be frequent, whilst at tims they appear in the form of fits of variable frequency, but whose intensity increases until they bring on vomitting, especially when the fit comes on after a meal.

Some times the expectorations are mixed with blood: at others, this phenomenon appears during the days following an attack of hemoptisis. This symptom is very common on the coast but uncommon in the patients who come from there to the Central Table Land; whilst it is very rare in those persons in whom the disease has been developed in these altitudes. A microscopical examination of the sputa has been made in almost all of the cases, but not always, resulting in the discovery of the Koch bacillus.

I will later on enter into an explanation of this fact, but for the moment I confine myself to the mere statement.

Dyspnoe is a symptom that is not frequently observed in the commencement, as can be easily understood, but it is one that generally accompanies the fits of coughing. These two symptoms present themselves and increase in intensity, when the patient lies on the diseased side. In all my observations, I have found that the fever takes an intermittent form. It generally commences between 10 a. m. and noon; increases during the afternoon and disappears during the first or latter part of the night, so that when the patients wake up, they have recovered their normal temperature, or even a few tenths lower. It commences with a feeling of cold rather than a chill, and terminates with the appearance of a sweat which is limited to the breast and hands; but more frequently to the head, and with less frequency to the whole body. Naturally, this only refers to incipient cases. The oscillations of temperature frequently vary in light cases or those which progress slowly, the variations reaching a few tenths above or below the normal temperature. During the successive invasions of the lungs, the temperature rises to 38 and 39 degrees and the secondary infections raise it to 39.5-40 degrees or more, apart from the real complications of bronchitis, pneumonia, pleurisy, etc. Intervals of apirexia are often seen that last for whole days and weeks. When the disease is about to be cured, the duration and intensity of the fever attacks diminish, and the fever keeps on decreasing in a continuous manner until the cure is complete. On the other hand, the invasion of fresh parts of the lung, the ulceration and the formation of cavities as well as the secondary infections raise the temperature more and more, augment the perspiration whilst the intermittency is no longer perceptible, or else is of short duration.

The denutrition is a phenomenon that I have constantly observed, and have always tried to estimate by the decrease in weight of the patient. This denutrition is continued as long as the disease advances; it is suspended whenever the disease remains stationary and the increase of weight, when combined with a diminished fever authorizes a good hope of cure.

My observations have in most cases shown me that the disease is confined to only one lung, generally the right one, rarely the left one, and still more rarely extending to both. The disease almost always takes its seat in the vertex of the lung, as stated by Louis, but the localization which I have been able to discover by percussion and an auscultation show the following order of frequency; the subclavial fossa on the right outside of the esternon; the space including between the vertebral column and the edge of the scapula those parts of the lung that correspond to the supra-spinal fossa; the internal part of the supra-spinal fossa; the external part outside of the focus that I mention on the right external edge. the axiliary region and the parts to which these lesions spread in the lower half of the same lung. In the left lung, the places that are invaded by the disease follow the same order as in the right lung.

I desire to call attention to the possibility of discovering by the means above indicated, comparatively small nuceli, between the internal edge of the scapula and the vertebral column; in the upper and internal part of the supra-spinal fossa and in the place that I have indicated outside of the esternon and below the clavicule. In this place the transmission of the heart beats contributes to the discovery of the hardening of the lung.

I have insisted on these details, because they have permitted me to make an early diagnosis of the tuberculosis, even when the analysis of the sputa had not shown the presence of any Koch bacillus.

I had intended to rectify the localization of the pulmonary lesions which have been shown by clinical observation, with the specimen of pathalogical anatomy that are collected in the San-Andres Hospital and with those that are preserved in the Museum of the National School of Medicine, I studied these and Doctor Huici, Curator of that Museum did me the favor to furnish me the corresponding memoranda as set down in his catalogue. I afterwards applied to Dr. Toussaint who has been kind enough to compare 585 post mortem examinations which he has made, extracting from them all the cases related to pulmonary tuberculosis, with which he has formed a table that I here present on account of its interest:

Right Lung Only—38 in the vertex and behind; 1 in lower lobe.

Not Ulcerous Left Lung Only—25 cases; 78 cases, more advanced in the vertices.

Right Lung—23 in vertex; 1 in middle lobe; 2 in lower lobe; 15 in the vertex.

Ulcerous, Left Lung—3 in lower lobe.

Both Lungs—26 in vertex alone. 18 in vertex and lobes.

The memoranda furnished me by Dr. Huici, are included in this table. A study of this table shows us that the lesion is more frequently found in the right than in the left lung, and oftener in the vertex than in other parts of the lung. These data prove my observations, but do not prove those which refer to the invasion of the two lungs, as I find such cases very rare, whilst the table shows them to be the most frequent. If the number of cases in which the lesion is observed in both lungs, is larger than the number of cases in each of the individual lungs, this difference is explained by the fact that my observations refer to incipient cases, whilst those which have been noted in the San Andres Hospital, related to patients who die of pulmonary phthisis, and precisely through the progress made by the disease, which in its last stages extends to both lungs.

I have already said that I would study the question of the Koch bacillus in the sputa of tuberculous patients, and I now proceed to give my opinion on that point. If a patient who for some months has been suffering from cough, dispnea, fever of the character I have above referred to, with a progressive loss of flesh and local indications of impermability to air in limited parts of the lung, as above mentioned, and if an examination of his sputa shows us the presence of the Koch bacillus, this patient is evidently suffering from tuberculosis. But if in the case of another patient who suffers from the same symptoms that I have just mentioned, an examination of his sputa does not show the Koch bacillus, we cannot for that simple reason declare that he is not suffering from Pulmonary Tuberculosis. The absence of the bacillus from the sputa, in such a case implies that the sputa does not come from the tuberculous focus either because it is closed or else because it proceeds from the bronchial tubes, that are not in communication with the focus. On the other hand, observation has taught me, that the Koch bacillus is frequently absent from the sputa of incipient cases, which are those to which I desire to call special attention. It is precisely in these cases, that we have to insist on the combination of characteristics I have above alluded to. Nevertheless, should any doubt exist, we can have the recourse of radiography, as I have done in some cases about which I felt no doubt,but on which my colleagues had doubts. After the discoveries made by Koch and when physicians familiarized themselves with the technique for discovering the bacillus, this proposition was laid down: that in order to declare a patient tuberculous, it is necessary to prove that his sputa contains the Koch bacillus. But observations began to multiply of patients who were unquestionably suffering from tuberculosis, and in whose sputa the bacillus could not be discovered, in spite of repeated and carefully made examinations. The case of granulia which rapidly ended in death and those in which the presence of tubercules in the lung was evident, without the bacillus being found in the sputa, proved, that that proposition could not be applied to all cases. The universality of this proposition was still further limited by the post mortem examinations of patients in whom the combination of circumstances above referred to, had established the diagnostic of pulmonary tuberculosis, even though their sputa did not appear to contain the bacillus. Pathological anatomy, by demonstrating that the bacillus could not appear in the sputa as long as the tuberculous focus did not communicate with a bronchial tube through the ulcerative process, furnished an explanation of those cases, in which all the indications pointed to the existence of the disease, even though the bacilli were absent from the sputa. Having established the fact that it is necessary for the tuberculous nucleus to ulcerate before it can discharge its bacilli into the bronchial tube from which they would be thrown out by a cough together with the mucus matter, we can understand how the presence of the bacillus in the sputa cannot be considered as a timely warning of the commencement of the pulmonary tuberculization. The enthusiasm that is always caused by discoveries, led people to think, that not only could the pulmonary tuberculization be demonstrated by the finding of the bacillus in the sputa, but also that their number, the formation of the groups and other characteristics, could serve as a basis from which to form an opinion as to the extent of the disease and its probable course. Subsequent studies that have been undertaken in many parts of the world and confirmed by autopsies, have come to demonstrate the errors committed by the first observers. These studies have lately been multiplied and I cannot do less than mention those that have lately been carried out amongst us by the modest and studious bacteriologist, Dr. Gonzales Fabela, which confirm the observations made in other parts, and I reserve another occasion, the interesting details that he has communicated to me on this point. I must here mention, that the data supplied to me by radiography run parallel with those supplied by percussion; thus whilst the latter shows us by the different tones of reasonance the degree of condensation that has been reached by the lung, so radiography indicates to us those same degrees of condensation, by the darker or lighter shade which is thrown by the tuberculous nucleus in the diseased lung.

Just as percussion is useful to show that the tuberculous nuclei are disappearing from the lung, so is radiography useful to show that the points of the lung which previously were more or less opaque, have now recovered their transparent qualities on a photographic plate.

In order to determine the antecedents of the person, the family, the sex and age of the patient as well as the site of the disease in one or other of the lungs and the points that were affected, I have taken advantage of the observations above stated, because they related to facts that had been proved by myself; but amongst these observations there are some relating to patients who have only once or twice consulted me, or only on very few occasions. I propose to take no account of these observations in my remarks, but rather of those cases in which I have been able to follow the course of the disease for a longer or shorter period, and which have enabled me to study its progress, form an opinion of the case, and see the results of the treatment.

Before going any further desire to state a fact that has tion which is the result of my observation, and confirms those of all the physicians who have studied this disease. Pulmonary tuberculization is curable in proportion to the promptitude with which the patients are attended towards the beginning of the disease. The probability of success depends, in the second place, on the previous state of health of the patient; on the effects of the present disease in a given case and time: on the hygienic conditions under which he lives: on his docility as regards treatment; his constancy in following directions, and the absence of complications that might disturb the natural course of the disease toward a cure.

There are some patients in whom a tendency to cure is observed from the commencement, whilst in others the disease remains stationary or advances, and then it is necessary to have great faith in the final success of the treatment, to continue it.

Before going any further I desire to state a fact that has been clearly proved by my observations and which is contrary to one of the conclusions reached by the Congress of Tuberculosis that was held in Berlin in the year 1899. It was there laid down as a rule, that to take consumptive patients to high altitudes, did not have a favorable influence on the cure of the disease. My observations of 26 years in Mexico have led me to form a contrary opinion. Through entirely special circumstances, the greater part of the patients whom I have had to treat, have come from the two coasts of the Republic: a few from the Pacific and many from the gulf, and more especially from the Peninsula of Yucatan, the greater part of these coming from the City of Merida. Well now, in almost all these cases, the mere fact of the patient coming from the coast to the Central Table Land, has brought about the commencement of a cure.

If therefore, all who have studied this important question are agreed that the earlier the treatment is undertaken, the greater are the probabilities of a cure, the necessity of making an early diagnosis becomes of immense importance. For the last ten years, Professor Grancher has energetically struggled to show the utility and possibility of making this early diagnosis. The utility of it is unquestionable, as the sooner we recognize the disease, the more promptly will we commence the treatment, watch over the patient and teach him to take care of himself as well of those that surround him. The possibility of making an early diagnosis has been demonstrated by the Professor I have just cited. He has combated the preconceived ideas with regard to the difficulties of the diagnosis of the disease during its initial stage, and has shown the way in which we can take advantage of all the data that leads to a suspicion that the patient is exposed to pulmonary tuberculosis: the family antecedents, the occupation of the patient, the medium in which he lives, the company of declared consumptives, the precursory dyspeptic-sufferings, the general state of emaciation: all these points have been studied in order to lead the physician to a suspicion that the patient before him is about to become tuberculous.

The certainty of the diagnostic is obtained by a minute and delicate exploration of those parts of the thorax in which I have shown that the first symptoms of the disease make their appearance. As a matter of fact, the methods for studying the modifications that take place in the sound of the respiration through those parts of the lung which are commencing to suffer, are already well described in the classic books. Afterwards come the changes, which the pulmonary lesions cause in the sounds produced by percussion; in the subclavial region we also have the transmission of the heart beats to the points in which the lung has become hardened. But this exploration must be made with the greatest care, and every physician can educate his senses so as to perceive the slightst modification produced by the entrance of the air, and by the methodical application of the percussion. Should any doubt remain as to the diagnostic, it can be entirely resolved by radioscopy and radiography, and even by the innoculation of animals.

As I have already said, the principal object of an early diagnosis, is the immediate establishment of a curative method. It is no longer necessary to demonstrate the curability of phthisis; the point on which it is now necessary to insist is, not only the possibility, but the probability of a cure, and its absolute certainty in some cases. Nothing can contribute more efficaciously to bring about this conviction than a specification of the terms of the problem. In all these studies I have kept before me one principal point of study: the chronic Tuberculization of the lungs in which the invasion by the bacillus is carried out through the respiratory channels; in which the bacillus invades a lobe of the lung and forms a limited initial lesion. that which Grancher has so happily compared with the initial chancre in the evolution of syphillis.

In other papers I have compared this initial lesion with the seed that is deposited on the ground, and the organism with the ground itself. This grain or seed may remain there —as has been shown by numberless observations—perfectly inoffensive and in repose, until something takes place to convert the organism into a soil adapted to the germination of that seed. If therefore, the mere existence of the germ is not sufficient but it is also necessary that the soil should be properly prepared, and if it is within our power to deprive this soil of its fertilizing properties, so that the grain will not germinaté, we will thus help the organism in the struggle that it spontaneously undertakes to free itself from the invading enemy.

If these images do not carry the precise meaning that I would like to give them, we still have these unquestionable facts: The tuberculization of the lungs in its incipient stage is confined to a limited and local lesion. The organism is not always prepared against the invasion. These two conceptions have been utilized in practice and dominate the treatment of tuberculosis.

The experience that always preceeds scientific explanation has shown me that if we improve the condition of the system, we oppose a barrier to the propagation of the existing tuberculosis and the first hygienic measures that present themselves for the realization of this end, are pure air, sunlight, good food, a comfortable dwelling, the abandonment of all business and the suppression of those pleasures which exhaust the system; an absolute rest for the patient, keeping his body properly sheltered, with a moderate exercise of his forces in the open air or under trees. These are the first resources that can be given the patient in order to place his system in an advantageous condition of defense. The ideal application of these means is to be found in sanatoria.

Our first efforts therefore, ought to be directed to advocating the establishment of these institutions. As I have said in another part of this paper, the sanitoria serve in the first place for the cure of patients and especially those who are suffering from incipient tuberculosis: they are really schools in which the patients are taught to live in an orderly maner; to remain quict or to be active, according to their condition, to eat at regular hours, to take their pleasure in a way that is suited to their strength and culture, to expectorate only in the cuspidor, to change their dress if it has been soiled with their own sputa and dejections, and generally to govern all their acts in such a manner as to contribute to the harmonious reestablishment of all their physical functions. The results that have been obtained in these sanitoria in the way of curing consumptive patients and especially those in the incipient stage, are facts that cannot now be questioned, as demonstrated by observation and statistics; but this is not the proper occasion for bringing up the figures that support my statement, but rather that of proving that the hygienic treatment given to them in the sanitoria is the ideal which we ought to try and copy.

But unfortunately, no sanitoria exist in my country, although tuberculous patients certainly do exist, and it is therefore indispensibly necessary that our treatment of these patients in the public and private hospitals or in our own dwellings, should imitate as far as possible the system that is adopted in the sanitoria. We ought specially to utilize the teaching of experience as adapted to our own territory, and induce the physicians who are practicing on our coasts, to advise their patients to go up on the Central Table Land, as soon as they have any reason to suspect the approach of tuberculosis, or discover its actual existence. In the second place, we should advise the patients who take the disease whilst living in the Central Table Land, to go to the more elevated points or to those whose hygienic conditions are better and whose climate is under more advantageous meterological conditions. Should the patients have the necessary means, it would be better to make them live in the country; but in any case, they should improve the conditions of their own private houses.

I always advise the patients whom I attend in the City, to select apartments on the second floor or at least at some height over the ground so that the floors can be ventilated underneath; that the room in which they live should preferable have a southern aspect and if this cannot be arranged, that it should be at least have an eastern aspect; that it should be ample, well ventilated and clean, with only the indispensible pieces of furniture; provided with long and comfortable chairs, that if necessary will permit the patient to rest the greater part of the day well wrapped up, with the windows open, except in bad weather; strongly recommending them also to arrange their meals, their hours of sleep and their amusements as if they were in a sanitorium. In one word, that each patient ought to imitate in his own house, the life that he would lead in one of those establishments.

The other solution of the problem that I have above referred to, is to combat the already existing disease by the means which are furnished to us by therapeutics. As my statements are founded on the study of my own personal observations I do not think I am under any necessity to enumerate all the measures that are employed in the medical treatment of pulmonary tuberculosis, but rather of those which I have utilized for reestablishing the health of my patients or for detaining the progress of the disease.

I am encouraged to communicate the means I have employed, by the numerous cures that I have been able to obtain, and whose exact number it would be impossible for me to give, not only because I have been unable to continue the numerical analysis of the observations that I have recorded, but also because I have not written up these observations for the first years of my practice, and I therefore cannot count the number of consumptive patients whom I have attended for over 26 years. But I am convinced that I have obtained many complete cures, of whom many were in the persons of residents of Mexico City, and I have therefore decided on this occasion to explain the methods that I have applied to cases of tuberculosis. My remarks will principally refer to patients in the incipient stage.

In a paper which I read in the International Congress that was held in Berlin in 1890, I stated in detail the series of considerations that suggested to me the therapeutic methods which I employ and which I have used since the time of my first practice as well as the systematic application of those methods which I have continued since 1874. As all that has already been published I will not trouble the meeting with a repetition of what I have already said.

As soon as the symptoms I have referred to in previous pages convince me that I have to deal with a tuberculous patient, I commence the exhibition of calomel, in doses of 1 centigram for each half hour. I continue the application of this medicine until the mercurial inflammation of the gums and diarrhoea set in, when I suspend that treatment and commence curing the inflammation of the gums or the colitis, however mild they may have been. At the same time I commence the application of fly blisters at the point at which the initial lesion has presented itself. I repeat this application every five or eight days, above, below and at the side of the one first placed. Should the lesion be also perceptible on the front wall of the thorax, I continue the application of the fly blisters as well as on the sides if the lesion extends so far. Should I observe any decided improvement, I delay the application of the blisters for even 10 or 12 days; but I continue it whatever may be the number that I may have to employ until the hardening of the lung has disappeared. As there are many persons in whom the renewal of the blisters brings on the formation of small pastules and even boils round the places where they were applied, I cure these accidents and substitute the blisters by the application of points of fire by means of the thermocautery. I put as many as 25 or 30 points with the needle of this apparatus. When I employ this method I repeat the operation every three or four days. In the case of very timid persons I substitute the above measures, by repeated applications of tincture of iodine or of an unguent with bi-iodide of mercury.

If at the time of commencing the treatment, the patient should be suffering from gastric or intestinal catarrh I always employ calomel, but I follow it up with the proper means to obtain the re-establishment of the digestive function, as their integrity is indispensibly necessary, both for the nourishment of the patient as well as for the application of the other medicines that I am now going to speak of.

Should the digestive organs be in good condition, I commence the exhibition of iodide of sodium in an aqueous solution of one-fifth, commencing with five drops and increasing every day with five more until I reach the limits of physiological toleration, when I re-commence with five drops. Should the iodide of sodium not be tolerated, I substitute it by that of strontium, and in this case I prefer to employ the Paraf-Javal solution. If the system will not stand the iodides I employ iodoform and if the patients cannot take it I employ tincture of iodine, which I slowly increase. I continue the application of iodine as well as of the blisters as long as there is any hardening in the lung; but I suspend this treatment as soon as any digestive disturbance appears, or to give place to another method of treatment that may be required by some of the complications that supervene in the courses of the principal disease.

For many years past I have used arsenic and strychnine simultaneously with iodine under the following formula:

Arseniatis sodici...............................	0.03 grams.
Sulphatis strychnic............................	0.06 grams
Extractis Gentiana rhubarb or quasia............	3 grams.

To be made up in 30 pills and one to be taken with each of the three meals. Since the use of cacodilate of soda has been introduced I have employed it in place of the arseniate with the same basis, in the above formula. In those cases in which the digestive organs will not tolerate the cacodilate I have commenced to make use of the same substance in subcutaneous injections with such success, that under its influence the temperature rapidly descends, and the fever often disappears. Since then I have suppressed the cacodilate in the formula above given and employ it exclusively in the form of hypodermic injection, which I repeat every third day until they have reached 15, when I suspend them, and after the lapse of 8 or 10 days I commence a fresh series.

From the very commencement of the treatment I lay down the hygienic rules that I have above mentioned. I insist on abundant and varied nourishment as far as possible; I recommend the patients who are accustomed to use milk as a food, to take it between meals as other persons do water, beer or wine, and I take the greatest care not to force the digestive organs, but arrange for a slow and progressive increase in the food.

Under the influence of this treatment the improvement makes itself felt after the first days. The temperature commences to descend and the attacks of fever are of less duration; the sweats diminish if there were any, the cough is improved as far as regards the duration of the attacks, their intensity and frequency; the appetite is renewed, strength comes back and the body gradually increase in weight, thus proving the improvement in the nutrition. At the same time, there are signs that the air penetrates with greater ease round the initial lesion of the lung. Should the relief continue, it will not be long before the percussions begin to show the improvement that has been indicated by auscultation.

Should everything go on favorably, at the utmost, we delay a little the application of the blisters, from time to time suspend the use of the iodide and of the strychnin., or delay the application of the injections of cacodilate.

There are patients in whom the favorable evolution of the disease is continuous and their health is re-established in two or three months. Even in these favorable cases, the hygienic and medicinal treatment must be continued for a long time. Should the patients come from the coast to Mexico, they should not be allowed to return home until the cure is certain and the physician can ascertain by a periodical inspection, that the patient has suffered no relapse. Should any doubt still remain, the physician can make use of radiography, which will allow him to make certain that the lung has recovered its transparency in those places in which its opacity indicated the presence of tuberculous nuclei.

But unfortunately things do not always go as above described. Either through infractions of hygienic precepts or because in spite of the treatment, the evolution of the tuberculosis advances, or because bronchitis or pleurisy supervene, either close to the focus or at some distance, or else through an attack of pneumonia, the cough reappears or increase in intensity, the temperature rises or the fever which was considered as overcome puts in a fresh appearance; the patient loses appetite and weight or else remains stationary, whilst generally, the physical means of exploration lead its the discovery of an extension of the local lesion which has caused the symptoms I have just spoken of, or else some of the complications to which I have just referred. In these cases I proceed as is generally done in the treatment of syphillis; I commence the treatment afresh but with the modifications I will now refer to. Should the symptoms be of as grave a character as those existing at my first visit to the patient, I administer as I did then, one centigram of calomel every half hour and I even have recourse to mercurial ointments in order to obtain a rapid saturation. Should the symptoms be of less intensity, I administer a centigram of calomel every half hour or even half a centigram, if the attack is milder. If for the second or third time I find fresh parts of the lung invaded, I again administer calomel but in smaller doses and at longer intervals. If the condition of the digestive organs prohibit the administration of calomel, or if the evidences of the new invasion are slow and torpid, I have recourse to a blue pill, in a dose of 5 centigrams per day, keeping it up for three or four weeks. I have seen cases in which I have had to repeat the application of mercury, even four times in the course of the disease.

Should limited pleurisy supervene, I apply repeated fly blisters to the places where the pleurisy has presented itself; but should bronchitis appear, I attend to it by the ordinary means. Should the bronchitis be of a fetid character I add to the ordinary resources, inhalations of compound benzoid tincture of the American pharmacopae in this form: I mix a teaspoon full of that substance with 100 parts of boiling water. I then place the mixture in a small porcelaain teapot to the spout of which I attach a rubber tube to protect the mouth of the patient and facilitate the application, recommending that the inhalations be repeated every six hours, for a period of a minute. Should the odor in the sputa continue I change these inhalationsfor others of a two per cent. solution of carbolic acid.

In all these cases I oblige the patients to keep to their rooms and remain in strict repose until the symptoms disappear, or until the disease has gone back to the favorable course which it presented before the aggravation set in.

Influenza is the most serious complication that can supervene in a tuberculous patient. The physician can think himself very fortunate if nothing worse happens than a temporary suspension of the cure, but as a general thing the original disease is aggravated and the explorations of the thorax discover fresh nuclei of pulmonary tuberculization; the fever reappears if not already existing, in which case it increases in strength; the cough becomes more frequent, more intense and takes the form of paroxysms whilst the appetite is lost and the strength of the patient visibly fails.

When the ulcerations have reached a certain extent, an examination of the sputa show the presence of estreptococi, estafilococi, which are some time mixed with the Pfeiffer bacillus. This complication may possibly give rise to a long delay in the cure. When the disease is further advanced or the attack of influenza has been serious, it may very possibly bring about a fatal termination.

I establish the treatment of influenza by the ordinary methods, and once that has been overcome I again undertake the treatment with calomel and repeated blisters; I recommend the patients not to leave their rooms, to protect themselves against all sudden changes of temperature and I combat all the complications that may present themselves.

If in spite of having employed all the means I have spoken of, the disease shows no disposition to withdraw, I employ the other therapeutical measures that are known, such as the arsenical drops of Dr. Hoff, of Vienna, creosote, gaiacol, etc.

As will be understood, I try to deal with the anaemia, dyspepsia, decrease of arterial tension, etc., by adequate means.

In conclusion, I would state that the treatment which I recommend, has been practiced by myself long and carefully; but if I could in any way doubt its efficacy in the patients who come from the coast to the Central Table Land, and in whom the simple change of climate is a favorable factor of improvement such doubt cannot be felt with regard to the persons who have contracted the disease here in the City of Mexico, and with whom the conditions have remained the same, both before and during the course of the disease, so that any relief they may obtain can only be attributed to the treatment that has been followed.

In the United States, where pulmonary tuberculosis is so frequently found, the physician will often find occasion to apply the methods above described to incipient cases, and I beg those of my colleagues who may see fit to adopt this method, to communicate to me the results obtained.

I sincerely hope that the present paper will contribute in some way to the curing of the tuberculous patients in your country.

Mexico, 6th of May, 1901.

PREVENTION OF TUBERCULOSIS.

BY J. A. M'NIVEN, M. D.,
VICE PRESIDENT AMERICAN CONGRESS OF TUBERCULOSIS.

How to prevent the rapid spread of tuberculosis is a question of no mean proportion. It is a serious problem, and one that is having the ear of the scientific world to-day. The inroads it has made within the past few years into localities where it was practically unknown, has startled the statistician to find that over one-sixth of all deaths are due to this dreaded disease in some form. It would seem that no country or section of country is immune from its ravages, and now, the mighty problem is, how is it to be dealt with? The physician and layman are alike aroused to the fact that some effort must be made to stop its pace if possible. The Medico-Legal Society of New York, prompted by the necessity of some plan of action, instituted what is known as the American Congress of Tuberculosis, composed of physicians and laymen, who met in joint session in New York city to look into the matter and arrive at some plan of procedure to call a halt in this rapidly spreading disease. About this time a similar call was made in London for a like purpose, and known as the London Congress of Tuberculosis, and like the American Congress, it proved to be a very instructive meeting and made up of the most noted professional men thoughout Europe. They took up their work along the same lines as did the American Congress, and to the British and American Congress of Tuberculosis chiefly, the country both here and abroad, owes a debt for the work they have done thus far in presenting to the world this troubled question in a shape that if followed up must result in some good.

To this end we have suggested to us two of the more feasible remedies, namely, "Education and Legislation," both of which are necessary. While education can do a great deal of good and we cannot afford to lose sight of its usefulness in

Contributed to the Congress on invitation of the officers.

this crusade, it is, however, in itself too slow for the general safety of the more fortunate, who are not afflicted with tuberculosis. Its most careful attention would have to be spread over at least one generation before we could hope to have any appreciable benefit therefrom.

Legislation, in my opinion, will yet be the solution of the problem. Isolation is the only remedy, and that would mean legislation in its fullest sense, in order to carry out the only sure and effective plan of campaign against this disease. Now how much legislation can we undertake with safety and what kind? A general law covering the entire field would be difficult if not impossible. It is going to take time to perfect a law that will meet all requirements in every particular. The utmost care and consideration would have to be exercised in preparing a bill for this purpose, as it would effect a very large portion of the population and all classes and phases of society. They are sensitive, and would be doubly so under a law providing for their isolation. They are citizens; they are free agents and have we the right to say they must colonize themselves in order that we might live? Is it removing a civil right and are we compelling them to make martyrs of themselves? These are a few of the perplexing questions with which our legislators would be confronted. If legislation is to be (as I have already stated that it is the surest and quickest way to reach a result that will be at all satisfactory), all these objections can and must be overcome. There are times within the life of every Government or individual, when one must be decided and firm in order to accomplish an end. There never was a law made that would meet the approval of all. Some of us must be disappointed in everything. We can only do that which is the greatest good for the greatest number. Therefore, we can with all safety, first strike at the root of what is by far the most dangerous source of tubercular infection, by making a law restricting the travel of consumptive persons. It has been my observation, and I believe statistics will support my belief, that tuberculosis is more prevalent among the well-to-do or moneyed classes than it is among the poor and neglected, not excepting those who inhabit the crowded quarters of large cities. They have means, and travel more. They come in contact with more people and are therefore more subjected to infection, notwithstanding they are as a rule more generally educated, intelligent, surrounded by (what is usually accepted to be) better hygienic conditions, and have a better understanding of things, yet, they are endangering their health at every turn and when they least expect it. It cannot be avoided with the present traveling accommodations offered, the object of which is comfort and no pretentions to the security of the public health. An accumulator is always a distributor, though it may be unconsciously. They contract more disease and must necessarily spread more. While the poorer people, who cannot afford to travel, seldom if ever, leave their home, and of course take less chances of being infected. Besides their afflicted with consumption are usually kept at home, and for the want of care, nourishment and proper surroundings die off more quickly, and with death ends the possibility of further infection from that source, consequently they spread less disease. The person with money and tuberculosis, the travelling consumptive is the greatest menace to the public health, and does more to sow broadcast the seeds of tuberculosis than come from all other sources combined. It is a well settled fact, conceded by the best authorities, that human tubercular sputum, when dried, powdered and blown about where it is easily inhaled, or in whatever way it gains entrance to the air passages, is the direct cause of tuberculosis in the human being and especially is this the case where it occurs in the otherwise healthy lung, where there is no predisposition or even tubercular history. The cause of this diffusion of the tubercle bacilli is clearly evident to anyone who will observe the consumptive who is touring the country for his health. It will be seen that he thoughtlessly expectorates anywhere a non-consumptive would, and not with any malicious intent to do injury to others, but that he does do injury to others is a fact well known to every one. From the very time he leaves his home and steps into the street or public conveyance, the health of the community in which he is, suffers from the influence of his condition in proportion to the severity of the case. He may have some definite place in view or he may not. If he has, so much the better. It is very seldom indeed that one will hear of a consumptive going to a sanitorium to remain for any length of time. Occasionally, one will find his way into some private hospital and this is usually because of his inability to further continue his travel, either from an aggravated condition of his case or for other reasons. The Western United States, particularly the Southern portion of it, and the dry mountain country more inland, is visited annually by a great number of consumptives, who present all phases of the disease, affording an excellent opportunity to study the danger of their mingling indiscriminately with the public. They may have a tubercular history only, or they may be in the earlier stages of consumption, or in the more advanced stages and a hopeless invalid. It, however, matters not. As soon as the seriousness of their condition is made known to them, they become alarmed and on the advice of their physician or on their own account, set out in search of a climate, that will check if possible the inroads, that is being made on them by this disease. Those of them, who are in the advanced stages are usually accompanied by a relative or friend, who nurses and cares for them, taking them to every health resort they can hear of in the country, giving them the benefit of every climate. This season they will try the sea level; next season the mountains; while they will spend the present winter in the South, thus making the rounds in a hope that they will yet find the place, that will cure them or at least give them relief. In this way they go about changing their locality, and intimately associating themselves with the healthy people, who must of necessity become contaminated to a greater or less degree.

They must cough and expectorate, and where? There is no place provided for them, and that means anywhere. The sleeping car, the hotel, the sidewalk, the drinking cup all come in for their share of infection, and so on they go, leaving in their wake the virus of disease for the healthy travelling public, who follow up to become infected, and they, in due time become the travelling consumptive. No more thoroughly scientific method of spreading this disease could be thought of, than is being done in this way, and needs first consideration, in our attempt to check the further spread of tuberculosis. It is not the fault of the individual referred to. It is the fault of the people, who have it in their power to correct the existing state of things.

It is not a case of legislating against the consumptive. It is a case of legislating for the protection of those, who are as yet uncontaminated with tuberculosis.

CRIME AND CRIMINALS; OR THE PROBLEMS PRESENTED BY ANTI-SOCIAL ACTS.

BY EDWIN C. WALKER, OF NEW YORK.

Herbert Spencer says: "In proportion as we love the truth more and victory less, we shall become anxious to know what it is which leads our opponents to think as they do. We shall begin to suspect that the pertinacity of belief exhibited by them must result from perception of something we have not perceived."

If I am not positive to-night, if I do not zealously advocate a theory and undoubtingly offer a panacea, it is because I realize, in the spirit of Spencer's thought, that there are many sides to and factors in this problem. But a very few of them can be examined, even in summary, at this time, and so I shall try to confine myself to the consideration of the question, "What shall be done with the men and women who commit deeds universally recognized in our civilization as anti-social, as criminal?

This is our most intricate and painful social problem, even when many of its economic, sumptuary and ethical parts are excised. My purpose is to deal only with the crimes of individuals, or very small groups of individuals, those acts which generally are accepted as invasive, inimical to personal safety, destructive of peace and security in society, for no advance toward a solution of the problem of social defense and the reformation of the criminal can be made while we are fundamentally divided as to what is crime and who is the criminal.

To this end, I wish to leave out of particular consideration on the present occasion, as causes of crime.

First.—The vast mass of industrial spoilation and the equally vast mass of blundering waste in the use of external nature. Each of these constitutes a great problem in itself,

Contributed to the Psychological Section of the Medico-Legal Society, Dec. 18, 1901.

and is receiving the attention of large numbers of persons. But neither of these evils, enormous as it is, is so complicated as is the other segment of the whole question, the segment which I wish you to help me to examine now.

Second.—So also we will leave to one side the thousands of offenses against the law which are created by prohibitory statutes, license regulations, Sunday edicts, tariff restrictions (from the last named comes smuggling and under-valuation of imports), and "moral" (sexual) enactments. Many of the victims of these various kinds of misdirected effort will be found in the classes of criminals which are under our present inspection, but now we need to consider them only as offenders against other individuals, not regarding their position as effects of removable causes, causes that may have started them toward the way in which they are now stumbling.

Third.—Neither shall I consider war, which is organized and wholesale appropriation and destruction of property, and infliction of torture and death, in connection with this question of personal crime. Until economic mal-adjustment and spoilation, until waste of natural resources, until paternal moral legislation, until war, are approximately as unpopular with the masses of the people as the anti-social acts of individuals are now, we shall not be in a position to calmly and improvingly examine our relations to criminals, in so far as their wrong-doing might be directly and consciously traced to monopoly, general ignorance, invasive legislation,and war. The best we can do, in a practical way, is to examine the position, influence and probable future of those who are designated criminals by the consensus of the people's voices, leaving to a more enlightened time the deeper probing for causes and a more accurate and just classification. Said in another way—While doing all we can to secure that deeper probing and that more just classification, we, as practical and humane men and women, have to face a very near and vital issue. What shall we do with, what shall we do for, how shall we guard ourselves against those individuals whom public opinion and the law agree in classing as criminals, as anti-social beings? We believe there will be an almost incalculable diminution in the number of these social offenders in the "sweet by-and-by," when there is more justice, more liberty among men, when War has sheathed his dripping sword, but we are living in the Now, and it is with the conditions of this day, not of the twenty-fifth century, that we must deal. So long as there is a great difference of opinion regarding monopoly, wastefulness, paternalism and war, so long as the people are herded into parties on such issues, so long as political campaigns are fought to determine which view shall prevail, the affirmative or the negative as to the unwisdom or criminality of monopoly, or paternalism, or war—so long will it be impossible to dispassionately and profitably discuss these matters as parts of the criminal problem. We must continue to regard them as general sociological problems, concerning which equally earnest and good men and women may differ. So long as this wide disagreement persists, each person can present his or her view, and the arguments in support of it, but until the controlling forces in society agree that a given act inveighed against by one or a hundred of us is a crime, an anti-social act, we can do nothing.

In other words, there are two stages in the study and treatment of crimes and criminals. In the first stage, we have to determine what is crime and who are criminals. In the second stage—having named our crimes and found our criminals—we proceed to discuss the questions: What shall we do with these criminals? How shall we stop the commission of these crimes? Manifestly, we cannot ask these questions in other than an academic way as regards the deeds of monopolists, of wasters of nature's riches, of paternal moralists, of warring nations. We have not yet educated the moving forces in society to look upon these actions as crimes, upon their doers as criminals.

Thus it comes to pass that I wish you to-night to confine your attention and remarks to the second stage of criminal study. Let us leave out of consideration for this time all partisan contentions as to what are crimes and who are criminals, and take cognizance only of those delinquencies about which there is practically no disagreement. Even when thus restricted, the subject is altogether too extensive and involved to be settled in a hundred years of serious and unimpassioned consideration.

There is substantial agreement that non-national killing is murder, is anti-social, is a crime; that non-legalized rape is a most serious offense; that arson, that train-wrecking, that kidnapping are atrocious wrongs; that theft, in its various forms, is a grave denial of the toiler's right to the products of his toil. No political parties exist to defend these actions; no political campaigns are conducted with these for issues. The race, as we know it here, has reached practical agreement that all these are anti-social acts, are crimes, and that the perpetrators are not mere political heretics, are not simply misdemeanants, but are criminals. As regards these actions, then, we are in the second stage of the study of criminology. Now we may legitimately ask: What shall be done with these offenders? What shall we do to reduce their capacity for harm, to protect other individuals against them, to reform them, to prevent other men and women being affected for evil by their example?

Having indicated the parts of the great social problem which it is not my intention to attempt to examine here and now, having shown, in the shortest possible way, the offenses which the people of our day and country generally agree in classing as criminal, having accepted as proper subjects of study those individuals whose anti-social acts are universally condemned, and without going "behind the returns" to ask what sort of lives these persons might have led in a different society, I recur to and repeat the real question of this hour: How shall we act toward these offenders against the property, persons and lives of others?

I have to confess to you that I do not know; that I do not pretend to know. My purpose is to counsel with you as serious, humane, candid men and women. Every scheme proffered as a solution proves, on fair and full examination, to be no solution, or, at best, but a partial solution of some small part of the problem. There are so many factors to be taken into account, so many moral, economic, psychological and passional elements to be considered and weighed, that, so far, it has been found impossible to reach a satisfactory conclusion, even a half-way or a merely tentative conclusion.

Even should we narrow this discussion still more by leaving out all reference to crimes caused by economic wrongs and ignorance of world statesmanship, and even should we ignore the "labor" difficulty found in the maintenance and employment of prisoners, and so find ourselves facing only the difficulties presented by the crimes of violence springing from envy, jealousy, revenge and other passions, and crimes such as embezzlement, forgery, malfeasance and the like, which are inspired by greed and avarice, by gambling on a large scale, by extravagance and love of display, we should still be at our wits' end to find a way to be at once effective in defense against and consistent and humane in our treatment of criminals.

Contrasting the present with the past, we see that enormous gain has been made in the direction of humanity in the treatment of social offenders. Even the worst prisons and the horrible convict camps of some of the states are almost immeasurably better than the best prisons of past centuries, and of some countries to-day. Physical torture—using the word torture in its chief sense, has vanished, except, perhaps, in sporadic cases, and in general prisoners are well fed and do not suffer from cold. There are exceptions, in some states and in some prisons in other states, but the strong and dominating tendency everywhere is toward the putting of all prisons on the level of the best.

But this is saying far less than we, with our rising ideals, wish we could say. What effect upon the future of convicts have our methods of restraint and care? The man who comes out of prison—what chance has he to remain out for the rest of his life? How does the public look upon the convict? What reception does it accord to him when he again stands among free men? More particularly and pertinently, what do you and I say and do if we come into immediate contact with him in the concrete and the singular? What effect have the associations of the prison upon the first-term prisoner?

The modern rationalist, the man of science, the student of anthropology, of psychology, realizes, in general terms of perception and admission, that every organism is the resultant of antecedent and contemporaneous forces which are operative outside itself as well as formative within itself; he knows that men are what their heredity, their early education and racial and climatic surroundings, and their present environment compel them to be. He knows that, given the same factors of formation and direction that the criminal had, he himself would be a criminal. The scientific man, I say, perceives this truth as a general, or abstract, proposition, but he does not always remember it when he is confronted by crime and the criminal in the concrete. He is sometimes no more ready than is the untaught rural lyncher to repudiate the idea of "punishment," to forego the gratification of vengeance.

It seems to me that there are six important rules of action which society should adopt in its handling of anti-social individuals:

a. Never for a moment should the offender be led by the actions or the utterances of the authorities or of teachers to believe that he is being "punished," in the sense that vengeance is being inflicted, that the treatment meted out to him is being made to "fit the crime," that, to illustrate, he is struck in order that he may suffer by a blow as the one he assailed suffered from his blows, on the savage principle of "an eye for an eye, a tooth for a tooth."

b. No irremediable penalties should be imposed, such as death or mutilation, because human senses are fallible in their testimony, because witnesses may falsify, and the man adjudged guilty today, tomorrow may be proven to be innocent. There are other reasons, which I shall refer to later.

c. No penalties, either of fine or imprisonment, should be inflicted when such punishment is likely to cause deprivation and suffering to those who are dependent upon the labor of the offender. The laws and the prison regulations should be such that the prisoner, if able-bodied, can earn sufficient to pay for his maintenance while in prison and to keep his dependents from suffering. He should also be enabled to save something with which to begin again the struggle of life when released. But this must be considered in connection with the next rule of action.

d. The prisoner should be taught always that society has but three objects in view in its dealings with him—The protection of uninvasive persons, restitution to his victim or victims, and his own return to the world as a self-sustaining, self-respecting individual. Of course the prisoner can not be so taught unless these are the objects of society.

e. While in prison the man or woman should not be idle, mentally, physically or emotionally. You can not make men and women better unless they are occupied with something in which they are interested. And all prisoners, at prescribed times, should be cheered, humanized, invigorated, inspired and kept sane by the unwatched visits of those who wish to see them and to whom they are attached.

f. The people should be told the truth, that they can not be excused from responsibility if they do not give released men a chance to redeem themselves, that these men are the products of efficient causes, just as is the man who was demented but is now sane, just as is the man who is physically deformed. If these sufferers are to be hooted at and shunned, as the savage or the untrained child hoots at or shuns the alien, the cripple, or the unconventionally dressed person, there is no hope for the released prisoner but in a return to crime and then to the shelter of the prison, and the criminal problem is indeed and forever insolvable.

I have said that it seems to me these six rules of action should guide the authorities and the people, but I know that each of these proposed principles of conduct is open to a multitude of objections, that the cases easily falling under each rule are no more numerous than the apparent exceptions, that in the way of the application of each there are mountains of difficulties, and this is why I said in the beginning that I am not here to enthusiastically propagate a theory, to undoubtingly offer a penacea, why I said later that I do not know what is to be done, that I come only to counsel with others.

[*To be Continued.*]

SPIRITISM AND MRS. LEONORA E. PIPER.

BY THOMSON JAY HUDSON, PH. D., LL. D.,
Author of "The Law of Psychic Phenomena," etc.

In constructing a title for this paper, I have not been impelled to use the name of Mrs. Piper because I imagine that her recent statement in the New York Herald has settled the question of spiritism adversely to the claims of that cultus. I have not so high an estimate of the value of her opinion. Nor do I agree with her spiritistic enemies in holding that her opinion is valueless because of the amnesia incident to trance. This, at most, would place her on a level with outsiders,—and this is their contention. It must be remembered, however, that not only was Mrs. Piper present at all her seances, but that she had the benefit of subsequent discussions of her phenomena by the able savants who had her in charge, and that she must have read their subsequent reports with much more than ordinary interest and intelligence. Moreover, we must not forget that she has been subjected, on two hemispheres, and during nearly a score of years, to a key-hole espionage by the ablest detectives of the London Society for Psychical Research: and that she has emerged triumphant, both at home and abroad,—not a shadow of a suspicion resting upon her character in any relation of life. Testimonials to this effect from all the leading members of the Society for Psychical Research have been numerous and voluminous, and almost hysterical in their insistence; so that she stands before the public to-day, secure in the possession of the highest possible credentials in proof of her absolute honesty, integrity and purity. It is also in evidence that she is liberally endowed with that rarest of all mental attributes—common sense—the inseparable concomitant of the cardinal virtues. It is idle to say that the opinion of a woman thus endowed, and thus fortified by all that

Read before the Psychological Section and the Medico-Legal Society in joint session, Dec. 18, 1901.

gives sanction to human testimony, and who necessarily knows more than any one else can know of the workings of her own inner consciousness, is not of greater value than the opinion of an outsider.

Nevertheless, as before remarked, her opinion does not settle the question: and in this respect she remains on a par with all who have opinions on the subject. It is not, therefore, because of her interpretation of her own phenomena that I use her name: but because the investigation of those phenomena by the Society of Psychical Research marks an epoch in the history of Spiritism. It is of that investigation that that I propose to offer a few remarks. In doing so I shall not attempt an exhaustive criticism of the methods of investigation employed by the members of that society. I shall merely attempt to point out briefly what I conceive to be the proper method of studying the phenomena in the light of their latest reports detailing the proceedings at the Piper seances.

Never before in the history of the scientific investigation of modern spiritism have the conditions been so favorable for the production of decisive results, one way or the other, as in this case. An ideal "medium," mentally, morally and psychically considered, is conceeded,—nay, strenuously insisted upon,—by all the investigators. She has been absolutely under their control during a long series of years, and necessarily free from the adverse influence of the Philistines. That the investigators are also all that can be desired will be as freely conceeded. They are all gentlemen of great ability, uncompromising integrity and vast learning. Best and most important of all, they have a thoroughly logical appreciation of what it is necessary to prove in order to establish the claims of spiritism. That is to say, they know that the one thing needful is proof of personal identity on the part of the *soi disant* "spirits" who "communicate." In this all-important attitude they stand in violent contrast to that long line of so-called "scientific investigators," on either side of the question, who have imagined, on the one hand, that the essential claims of spiritism can be established by verifying the physical phenomena; and, on the other hand, that those claims can be disproved by catching a trickster in the act of simulating psychical phenomena by legerdemain. In other words, they know that the purely physical phenomena of spiritism possess not the slightest evidential value, pending the settlement of the all-inclusive question of personal identity. They know, for instance, that if a piano should be levitated to the ceiling without physical contact or mechanical appliances, and all the rest of the household furniture should go into convulsions, the question would still remain whether the energy displayed proceeded from discarnate spirits, or was due to the "psychic force" (Crookes) of the medium. Hence they have wisely determined to ignore all physical phenomena, and to confine their attention to such mediums as Mrs. Piper, through whom, according to the spiritistic hypothesis, spirits can establish their identity by direct conversation with the sitter.

It is but simple justice to the British members of the S. P. R. to say that to them the credit is due for thus divesting the subject of all those irrelevant side issues which have heretofore served but to obscure the real question. It is, however, with a glow of patriotic pride that we recall the fact that they were compelled to come to this country for an honest medium, and to draw upon our universities for a man capable of conducting a spritistic propaganda in the highest style of the art. It is but a matter of common justice to say that Professor Hyslop is the ablest psychical researcher who has yet attempted a personal investigation of the Piper phenomena. He is the peer of the best in scholastic attainments; he is Professor of Logic in Columbia University; his honesty is transparent, and the report of his investigations covers 649 pages of the Proceedings of the Society for Psychical Research.

If therefore, he has failed to make a case for spiritism, one never can be made this side of the borderland; for there probably can never again be assembled under one roof such a combination of favorable conditions and instrumentalities. If there was an unsound element in the combination it did not reside with the medium, nor in the character or ability or attainments of the investigator. Nor do I see the slightest reason for distrusting his statements of fact. His deficiencies, therefore, if any are to be found, must be either in logic, or in the propaedeutics of psychic science, or in both.

The discussion of the subject will be conducted under two heads: 1, The issue that Professor Hyslop has defined; and 2, The issue that Prof. Hyslop has ignored.

Referring at large to the phenomena detailed in his report, Professor Hyslop says:

"The issue that is presented here is simply whether spiritism, or telepathy from living persons exclusively, is the more rational hypothesis to account for the facts."

It will thus be seen that the learned professor of logic assumes at the outset that the two hypotheses stand on an equal footing, thus forgetting for the moment the logical axiom that supermundane causes must never be assigned to phenomena so long as they or their cognates are explicable by reference to known natural causes.

To hold spiritism strictly to this rule, however, would be to end the discussion before it begins. for all admit that the "great bulk" (Myers) of the supernormally acquired knowledge of mediums is due to telepathy. It would, therefore, require demonstrative proof to overcome the logical implication that all such knowledge is not thus acquired; just as it would require the production and public exhibition of a "white crow" (James) to prove that crows are not all black. It would, however, require but one white crow for that purpose, and it would require but one demonstrated case of survival of personal consciousness after the death of the body to prove the essential claim of spiritism—a future life. But this one case has not yet been produced, and Prof. Hyslop is frank enough to admit that he has demonstrated nothing. (See note on p. 4 of his report.) The issue, therefore, as he has defined it, is conservative and legitimate.

To prepare one for an intelligent discussion of the question whether spiritism or telepathy is the more rational hypothesis to account for the phenomena produced by Mrs. Piper, it would seem that the essential prerequisite would be a knowledge (1) of the facilities and the difficulties, real or supposed, incident to communicating with spirits of the dead, and (2) of the methods, powers and limitations of telepathic communication between living persons. Unfortunately we can know nothing of the former except what spiritists tell us: and their stories are so contradictory that it is impossible for the layman to assign any certain limits to the difficulties or to the facilities. Thus, the old spiritists tell us that communication is always easy, providing we have a good medium and a harmonious environment. The late Prof. Hare, for instance, found no difficulty whatever in organizing a "convocation of spirits," of the ablest dead men he could think of, who cheerfully submitted to a prolonged catechism. To say that Prof. Hare learned from that "convocation," and others equally well posted, all that was worth knowing about the spirit land and other things, would be to unduly limit the scope of the acquired information. Judge Edmunds was equally fortunate in obtaining authentic information, not only of the geography and topography of the spirit land, but of its current philosophy; whilst Andrew Jackson Davis succeeded, without apparent effort, in tapping the philosophers of all the ages for material for upwards of thirty volumes of most remarkable literature. Thousands of others were equally fortunate in obtaining access to the inhabitants of all the spheres. Nor were the spirits themselves in the habit of complaining of lack of facilities, even when a Daniel Webster addressed his sitters in the language of a stevedore; or Noah Webster spelled Jehovah with a little g, or Lindley Murray split his infinitives into kindling-wood. The enemy might blaspheme, and to do them entire justice they did, but the spirits themselves were oblivious to all such degenerative implications. They did not complain of difficulties of communication, nor of the failure of "light," nor of infirmities due to their last illness of the body, nor of the failure of memory, nor of any of the multiform infirmities which afflict Mrs. Piper's familiar spirits when submitting to a scientific examination. It is true that there were occasional lapses of memory, as when Socrates forgot that he had been a Greek philosopher, and "thee'd" and "thou'd" like a Quaker when proudly recalling his career as a Roman Senator. This lapse, however, was afterwards explained by an erudite spiritist by saying that those "old fellows" have been dead so long that they have forgotten the "unimportant particulars" of their earthly lives. Satisfactory as this explanation is to spiritists, it does not explain the amnesia of another spirit at the same sitting who had forgotten his own middle name within a year after entering the spirit land. Nor does it explain the prompt response of "Cantharides, the Greek philosopher," when that coleopterous "personality" was summoned by a waggish Philistine. That, however, was easily explained by the statement that there are always spirits present at seances who delight in serving the cause of Truth by promptly "meeting fraud with fraud." In the logic of spiritism this formula has always occupied a foremost place, and it still performs yeoman's service whenever a fictitious personage responds with alacrity to a summons.

But then, as now, there were mediums and mediums. Some were ignorant, and others were educated. Some of them were destitute of the ability to acquire information by supernormal means; whilst others could at times correctly name the strangers present at their seances, and describe and name a long list of their friends, living or dead. At other times the same mediums would fail miserably. In a word, the same diversity of mediumistic powers prevailed then, as now; the same "harmonious conditions" were requisite; and supernormally acquired knowledge on the part of mediums was even more common than it is to-day. But there was one significant circumstance connected with early mediumship that does not prevail at this time; and that is that modern spiritism found a host of ready trained psychics in the mesmeric subjects of that epoch. Mesmerism was at the zenith of its popularity, mesmeric subjects were numerous, and under mesmeric methods telepathic powers were easily developed, and the exhibition of those powers was commonly the *piece de resistance* of the stage curriculum. But the significant part of it was that, not only was every mesmeric subject found to be a good medium, but the best of the mediums, that is to say, those who could demonstrate their possession of knowledge supernormally acquired, were for a long time drawn almost exclusively from those whose telepathic powers had been previously developed by mesmeric methods. This fact was noted at the time by the opponents of spiritism, and telepathy was thus shown to afford an easy explanation of all supernormally acquired information. Indeed, Dr. Dods, a noted mesmerist of that day, paralleled every phase of that class of spiritistic phenomena by the employment of mesmeric psychics and processes. With Dr. Dods it was but the a b c of mesmerism to develop telepathic powers in his subjects so perfectly that they could correctly describe events wholly unknown to the psychic or to any other person present. And this is all that the best mediums can ever do. It is all that spiritists claim can be done in proof of personal identity. It is true that in experimental telepathy the "dramatic play of personality" is necessarily lacking. Of this "dramatic play" Prof. Hyslop discourses exhaustively, seemingly oblivious of the fact that trance subjects are dominated by the inexhorable law of suggestion; and that any suggested character will always be dramatically personated, and with marvelous fidelity to the original,be it a dog or a philosopher, a spirit of health or a goblin damned.

This, however, is a digression. The point I wish remembered is that the alleged difficulties of communication by spirits seem to be widely variant; and that the facility in each case appears to be proportioned, not to the mental capacity of the spirit, but to the psychic powers of the medium. This, to say the least, is not what one would naturally expect, if the communications are from spirits. But we know that if the phenomena are to be explained by telepathy, the psychic powers of the medium must necessarily be the measure of limitation.

But, as before remarked, it is impossible to know what are the difficulties which beset communicators from other worlds than ours. One thing, however, appears to be beyond question, if we are to accept the testimony of spiritists. and that is that the spirits are as voluble as fishwives when they tell us something that can neither be verified nor disproved; but when subjected to anything like a scientific investigation their volubility is succeeded by a remarkable want of facility of clear and unequivocal expression, and they are troubled by a constantly recurring failure of "light." At critical moments their memory fails them, and they forget their own names and those of their nearest relatives. At other times, however, they have lucid intervals, the light is clear, and they can give names and dates with great facility, besides giving information that neither the psychic nor the sitters could have previously obtained through sensory channels.

These are some of the salient features of the limitation and of the power displayed by Mrs. Piper's spirits for the benefit of science and Professor Hyslop. And it must not be forgotten in this connection that special facilities were provided in his case for easy, free, and unlimited communication, without reference to the infirmities that might happen to afflict the particular spirits called for. To that end two great spirits were imported from England to act as amanuenses and advisors generally. They were specially well qualified by experience, having already acquired an international reputation by acting in the capacity of Familiars of the late W. Stainton

Moses. They were good, and wise, and great; and their names, respectively, were "Imperator" and "Rector,"—names well calculated to impress. That they were good is evidenced by their uniformly pious language and deportment. That were wise is shown by their refusal to reveal their own identity. That they were great is demonstrated by the fact that they had, before emigrating to America, evolved a system of spiritistic philosophy that converted an English orthodox clergyman from the error of his ways.

Manifestly the performance of such a feat must have required unlimited facilities for communication, plenty of light, a retentive memory, and an unfailing vocabulary. And it is in evidence that they had all these, and much more, under the mediumship of Stainton Moses. But it was all in violent contrast with the paralytic conditions prevailing under the Piper-Hyslop regime. I think that spiritists will agree with me that the contrast is due to variant mediumistic powers, rather than to varying facilities for knowing things, and communicating them, on the part of the same spirits. If, then, it is due to the variant psychic powers of the mediums, I have a right to assume, provisionally, at least, that the limitations, always most in evidence when personal identity is in question, are the limitations of telepathy between living persons.

This leads us to the second branch of our inquiry, namely, as to "the methods, powers and limitations of telepathic communications between living persons."

As I promised merely to suggest in this paper the proper method of studying Prof. Hyslop's report from a scientific standpoint, I shall, in pursuing this branch of the inquiry, cite but a few illustrative examples showing that the successes and the failures of his alleged "communicators" were just such as are incident to telepathic communications.

The following propositions are too well authenticated and understood by all intelligent psychical researchers to require proofs to sustain them:

(1) Telepathy is a power belonging exclusively to the subjective mind, or the "subliminal self," as it is frequently desiginated by the S. P. R. That is to say, the objective mind, or "supraliminal self," which is the mind of ordinary waking consciousness, is not necessarily aware of the content of the subjective mind. Hence the phenomenon of "latent

memory," as Sir William Hamilton designated it may years ago. That is, knowledge once acquired may remain latent in the subjective mind for an indefinite period. It may, however, be elevated above the threshold of normal consciousness in many ways, as by automatic writing, etc., or it may be reached by telepathy.

(2) Telepathic powers are best developed under abnormal conditions, as in trance, or in spontaneous or induced somnambulism.

(3) These powers vary in efficiency with different psychics, and in the same psychic they vary at different times, and under varying conditions which are not yet clearly defined.

(4) Rapport is, of course, always necessary; but the essential conditions of rapport are not yet clearly understood. It is known, however, that relatives and friends are either actually or potentially en rapport at all times.

These fundamental facts will not be disputed; and when they are considered in connection with the prodigious—if not perfect,—memory of the subjective mind, it will be seen that no limits can at present be assigned to the potentialities of telepathy. Its limitations, however, are more clearly defined and understood. Hence it is that, one who is acquainted with those limitations and their proximate causes, is better qualified to account for the failures of telepathy than any one can be to assign limits to its potentialities. But it so happens that even a knowledge of the causes of failure is of great value in enabling one to know to what class a particular phenomenon belongs.

The fundamental difficulty in telepathic communication consists in the fact that the power is not adapted to practical mundane uses. It seems,in fact,to be a means of communicating thoughts especially adapted to a disembodied existence; for it is never available here except under abnormal conditions. Even under the most favorable conditions the thoughts communicated must be interpreted, so to speak, in terms of our sensory experience. That is to say, the percipient must be caused to see something (visions) or hear something (clairaudience) that will enable her to grasp the idea sought to be communicated.

It will at once be seen that the inherent difficulties of telepathic communication are great, and in the conveyance of abstract ideas they are practically insuperable. It is true that if a psychic is clairaudient, and conditions are perfect, much may be conveyed in words. But clairaudience is a rare faculty, and perfect conditions hard to obtain; and when obtained they rarely last long enough for purposes of scientific investigation. We may, therefore, confine our attention to the most common methods of communicating telepathic information, which is by causing the percipient to see visions that convey the idea. I shall do this, not only because it is the most common method, but because it is, all things considered, the best that has yet been devised; and for further reason that it is evidently the one employed in the Piper seances.

It is obvious that intelligence communicated by means of visions must be extremely limited in scope and subject-matter. It is, in fact, just that kind of information that can be conveyed, in objective life, by a series of pictures; or, at best, by pantomime. Anything, therefore, that can be told by a picture, as for instance, a tragedy, can be very clearly reproduced by a good psychic, under good conditions. But abstract ideas cannot be thus represented. Symbolical visions, it is true, may sometimes convey such intelligence to a very limited extent; but its limitations are obvious. Again, under favorable conditions a vision may be very distinct; but those conditions are subject to frequent changes, and for no assignable cause; so that at one moment a psychic may be very lucid, and at the next be groping in the "dark.' This literally describes the situation when conditions fail;for telepathic visions, when the psychic's eyes are closed, come out of the darkness, with varying brilliancy, when conditions are favorable; and fade into it again, with varying indistinctness, when conditions fail. In a word, the lucidity of a telepathist is proportioned to the clearness of her visions; and the clearest of them are often evavescent, unstable, and "variable as the shade." Mrs. Piper's *soi disant* spirits, therefore, described an actual want, in literal terms, when they so often complained of the failure of "light." Again, it frequently happens that the fault is not in the psychic so much as in the sitter; for the clearness of a telepathic vision depends largely upon the power of visualization possessed by the subjective mind of the agent or sitter. This power varies in intensity in different individuals; and in the same person it fluctuates within very wide limits. The reasons for this are not yet clearly understood; but it seems to depend upon the passivity of the individual. Hence it is that trained psychics make the best sitters or agents; for they are habitually passive at seances, and their subjective minds are habitually active,--and that mind is the source of all information in telepathy. On the other hand, a novice often defeats the object of a seance by his over-anxiety, or want of passivity, to say nothing of his lack of subliminal training.

It should be here noted that telepathic messages cognized clairaudiently are subject to the same limitations of power and fluctuations of conditions. That is to say, a clairaudient psychic does not always hear clearly, any more than does a clairvoyant psychic always see clearly. Hence it happens that it either case, when conditions are imperfect or fluctuating, proper names are difficult to perceive. Some psychics, however, are both clairaudient and clairvoyant, to a limited extent, and thus have two strings to their bow. But even they are subject to the same uncertain conditions and limitations, and hence cannot always be certain of proper names; or, for that matter, of anything else. I mention proper names particularly because the failures in cognizing them, by even the best of psychics, are frequent in so-called spirit intercourse as well as in experimental telepathy, and presumably for thesame reasons.

One important fact remains to be noted, and that is that proper names, and sometimes other words, and even short sentences, are telepathically conveyed to clairvoyant psychics by means of visions of printed or written words, projected into the field of psychic vision. Obviously, the foregoing remarks relating to the varying conditions of telepathic lucidity, apply with peculiar force to phantasmic representations of words or phrases, and especially of proper names.

I have now stated a few of the salient powers and limitations of telepathy with especial reference to the difficulties habitually encountered in communicating intelligence by that means. They are among the propaedeutics of psychic science, without an understanding of which it is impossible to either appreciate the potentialities of telepathy, or to intelligently assign causes for its multiform failures and limitations. With an understanding of them we can at least judge, with proximate certainty, in any correctly reported case, whether the difficulties encountered are such as are incident to telepathy. If we find that they are, we have a right to assume telepathy to be the true explanation of the mysteries, at least until it is definitely shown to be either inadequate, or impossible, or both. Professor Hyslop has essayed the task of proving that it is both inadequate and impossible; but to do so he assumes the existence of difficulties that do not exist except in his imagination, as I shall attempt to show in its proper place.

First, however, I desire to suggest the proper method of analysing his report by citing a few illustrative examples, taken at random, showing beyond a reasonable doubt that telepathy affords an explanation of all the phenomena he describes. In doing so I shall assume, provisionally, that all the supernormally acquired information possessed by the medium existed, latent, in the subjective mind of the sitter. How so much of it got there is a question second to none in importance; but it must be deferred for the moment.

The first point to which I wish to invite attention relates to proper names. Those who have read the report (S. P. R. Proc. part XLI. Vol. XVI.) will remember the constant alternation of lucidity and amnesia on the part of somebody,—spirits or Mrs. Piper's subliminal—when the names of alleged communicators were called for. Often the name would be given with gratifying promptitude; but at other times—when the "light" failed—there would be groping, guess-work, "fishing" for clues, and sometimes total failure, followed by very voluble explanations that did not explain. Time and space forbids the citation of special examples; but they confront us almost everywhere in the report. Prof. Hyslop tells us that it is all due to the limitations of spirit power, first to remember the simplest facts of mundane experience, and, secondly, to communicate that knowledge through the best of mediums. Of these limitations we can know nothing, of course, except what Prof. Hyslop tells us. But, how does he know? He also informs us that the trouble is not due to the limitations of telepathy, because telepathy has no limitations. That is to say, he holds that the phenomena in question cannot be due to telepathy if telepathic knowledge is not "infinite," or "omniscient,"—which is a very easy, if not a logical, way of disposing of a difficulty. Of this, later on.

Nevertheless, anyone who knows anything at all of telepathy is aware that it is hedged about by just such difficulties in regard to names as were encountered in the Piper-Hyslop seances. Moreover, to suppose that those difficulties were due to the mental status of the spirits themselves, involves implications of degeneracy not warranted by current spritistic philosophy.

Again, there are many other phenomena detailed in the report which point clearly,—almost demonstrably,—to telepathy; as, for instance, when the medium—or the *soi distant* spirit—undertook to state the disease of which he, or someone else, died. In one instance it was incorrectly stated as typhoid fever; and in another it was correctly stated as throat disease. Obviously, typhoid fever could not well be represented by a phantasm. but a sore throat could be easily represented by a vision of a person with a bandaged throat.

Much stress has been laid upon the fact that a certain jack-knife, belonging to Prof. Hyslop's father, was correctly described, together with some of the uses for which it was employed during its late owner's lifetime, such as paring his nails, etc. I submit that it is not difficult to imagine the projection of a phantasmic jack-knife upon Mrs. Piper's field of psychic vision; nor would it seem to be difficult to guess at some of its uses, even without the aid of a phantasm.

Again,much of evidential value is attached,by Prof. Hyslop, to the fact that Mrs. Piper correctly described a skull-cap once worn by his father; but the name of the person with whom it was left was difficult to obtain. This very clearly illustrates the foregoing remarks relating to the comparative difficulty in obtaining names by telepathy.

I might cite many more examples of a similar character,—but time and space forbid. But they will serve to suggest to the student the proper method of analyzing the Piper phenomena as reported by Prof. Hyslop. All that is necessary is to bear in mind the methods of telepathy and its consequent limitations. When this rule is intelligently observed there will be found no difficulty in the telepathic explanation of all that seems so mysterious to Professor Hyslop.

As before remarked, I have thus far assumed that all the supernormally acquired knowledge of which Mrs. Piper was possessed, was not only obtained telepathically, but that it was obtained directly from the subjective mind of Professor Hyslop. This the learned Doctor would strenuously deny, on the ground that the great bulk of the information upon which he relies to prove his case for spiritism, was never known to him before he obtained it from Mrs. Piper,—but was, however, subsequently verified. And I freely admit that neither Professor Hyslop nor any other person present at the Piper-Hyslop seances was ever in conscious possession of any of the facts revealed by the trance personality of the medium, prior to the date of the seances.

The question now arises,—and this is the crucial question for spiritism,—how did Mrs. Piper obtain that wonderful fund of information which she so haltingly gave out at those famous seances?

Before attempting to answer this question from my own point of view I will state the position of Professor Hyslop.

To do entire justice to the intelligence of the learned Professor, he does not seriously deny the fact of the existence of telepathy as a possible factor in some cases. On the other hand, however, he holds that spiritism is the preferable hypothesis for the explanation of the Piper phenomena, for the reason that the telepathic theory necessarily presupposes "infinite knowledge" on the part of the psychic. It is, therefore, in his mind, "spiritism against omniscience," (page 134). No wonder that he "halts" on page 133, and becomes "suspicious" on page 136, and actually "gasps" on the same page "at the magnitude of the theories that are invented to sustain the case against spiritism." And well may skeptical science also "gasp," not to say, "throw up the sponge," if it has at last come to pass that the hypothesis of superstition can be disproved by no other argument than one that is based upon the presupposition that Mrs. Piper is "omniscient."

To do Professor Hyslop justice it must be said that he did not invent the theory. That he believes it, or thinks he does, is evinced by his constant reiteration of it; but he manages to throw the blame of it upon Dr. Hodgson. (p. 157.) In defense of Dr. Hodgson it should be stated that he is not wholly responsible; for Dr. Bovee Dods, in one of his lectures, gave utterance to a similar extravagance when undertaking to account for the supernormally acquired knowledge of his mesmeric subjects. (See his lecture on spiritism, pp 83-4). To his credit be it said, however, that his extravagant notions did not extend to implications of omniscience; and in further extenuation it must be remembered that he wrote fifty years ago, and knew nothing of the later development of experimental psychology. Nevertheless, he did develop telepathy in his subjects to such an extent that they came into possession of knowledge of facts not previously known to any one present. But, how to account for the fact, he knew neither more nor less than do the ablest spiritists of the S. P. R. spiritistic propaganda. He did know, however, that spirits of the dead had nothing to do with it.

The question now is, is it necessary to suppose that Mrs. Piper was possessed of "infinite knowledge" in order to account for her possession of information not previously existent in the normal consciousness of any one present? Is it necessary to suppose that she is either actually or potentially in communication with the "whole Universe of intelligence" in order to account for the facts? Is it even necessary to suppose that she was in telepathic communication with any one on earth, or in Heaven above, besides Professor Hyslop? I think not.

It seems to me that it is only necessary to suppose that Professor Hyslop was *en rapport* with the members of his own family, in order to account for his possession, subliminally, of all the knowledge that was in evidence at the Piper seances. Certainly there is nothing in the history of telepathic investigation to negative this proposition. Indeed, it may be confidentially asserted that if observation and experience teaches us anything at all in refernce to that mysterious power, it is that relatives and friends are always en rapport, and that they are always either actually or potentially, in communication. This is, perhaps, the most important induction possible in the case, and it certainly makes for the telepathic theory; for all of the "communicators," of evidential importance, were relatives of the sitter. But as yet we know little of the power of telepathic acquisition of knowledge; but all that we do know goes to show that it is enormous. The limitations apparently pertain wholly to the power of communicating the acquired intelligence, as I have already shown. It is also known that the great bulk of subliminal intelligence remains latent, indefinitely, and is never, except under abnormal conditions, elevated above the threshold of normal consciousness. It is also in evidence that subliminal memory is prodigious,—potentially, if not actually, perfect; so that what once enters that storehouse of memory is always available under favorable conditions.

These are a few of the inductions of modern psychological science pertinent in this case; and it cannot be successfully controverted that they afford a full explanation of the fact that the knowledge which Mrs. Piper obtained existed in the subjective mind of her sitter. I submit that it is a far call between "omniscience" and the conclusions derivable from the fundamental facts of psychic science.

The only question now remaining is whether the knowledge which, presumably, was thus telepathically acquired, was conveyed by the same means to Mrs. Piper's subliminal consciousness.

This is the issue which Professor Hyslop has seen fit to utterly ignore. And yet it is really the only pertinent issue in the case. To reduce it to its lowest terms, it is this:

Can information, telepathically acquired, be telepathically transmitted to a third person?

If it can, spiritism, considered as a scientific proposition, has not a leg to stand upon; for not a case has yet been recorded that cannot be telepathically explained if that simple proposition is true. There may be cases where the chain of telepathic transmission is difficult to trace. But so momentous a propsition as spiritism embraces cannot be logically sustained by an occasional failure of positive evidence against it. There are no logical presumptions in favor of a supermundane explanation of any phenomenon whatever. Indeed, the presumptions are all against it, even in the absence of evidence to disprove it; and when, as in this case, the great bulk of cognate phenomena are explicable by reference to known mundane causes,all supermundane hypotheses are summarily ejected from the court of logical inquiry.

The question, then, recurs,—"can telepathically acquired information be telepathically transmitted to a third person?" My proposition is this: A message transmitted from A to B, by any means of communicating human intelligence, can be transmitted, conditions being equal, from B to C by the same means.

If not, why not?

This is a very simple proposition, and its truth is self-evident. It is what Herbert Spencer wold denominate a "universal postulate;" for "its opposite is inconceivable"—unthinkable. Besides, it has been demonstrated, again and again, by experimental telepathy, that telepathy by three, or as the French call it, "*telepathle a troir*," is not only a possible, but a very common, phenomenon.

There is nothing left, therefore, for spiritism to do but to deny a self-evident proposition. for, if it is true, the telepathic hypothesis covers, not only every case cited by Professor Hyslop, but every case within the range of human conception.

In conclusion, I beg leave to say one word to both the friends and the foes of spiritism, in commendation of Professor Hyslop's report. The former will find it to be the ablest effort yet made to give spiritism a scientific status. If he has failed it is not for lack of zeal or ability. The latter will find in it a transparently honest report of the details of each seance. This is all that science can ask of a reporter of phenomena. It will take care of its own conclusions. If the internal evidence of the report overwhelmingly defeats the object of his argument, Professor Hyslop has not concealed the fact. Considered from any point of view—as a literary production, as a defense of spiritism, as an honest report of facts, or as an effort to obscure the vital issues involved, it is the ablest spiritistic document extant.

THE MUTUAL RELATIONSHIP IN HYPNOTISM, AND ITS BEARING ON TELEPATHIC AND SPIRITISTIC COMMUNICATION.

BY DR. JOHN DUNCAN QUACKENBOS, OF NEW YORK CITY.

Mr. Chairman, Members of the Medico-Legal Society—Section on Psychology:

You have asked me, through your honored President, Dr. Clark Bell, to express an opinion this evening regarding the nature of the communications reported in the proceedings of the Society for Psychical Research (Part XLI.) as having been received by Professor James H. Hyslop, of Columbia University, from Mrs. Piper, the spiritistic medium. It has occurred to me that an appropriate prelude to the inference which I shall draw might consist in a statement of the relationship apprehended by me to exist between the mind of an hypnotic operator and the subjective personality of the individual operated upon, through which relationship the minds in rapport are obnoxious to mutual impression. The conclusions which I have reached along this line of reciprocal communication are derived from some two thousand several experiences with hypnotized patients. These subjects sought my aid for almost every conceivable malady, mental and moral; some for ethico-spiritual, many for literary or dramatic inspiration. I have thus been brought into closest touch with the human soul, first objectively; subsequently, in the realm of subliminal life, where, practically liberated in the hypnotic slumber from its entanglement with a perishable body it has been open to approach by the objective mind in which it elected to confide, dynamically absorptive of creative stimulation by that mind, and lavish in dispensing to the personality in rapport the suddenly apprehended riches of its own higher spiritual nature.

To a reeent inquiry as to how it was possible for him to engage without injury to his physical and mental health so

Read before the Medico-Legal Society, Psychological Section, December 18, 1901.

unremittingly in his work as a suggestionist—a work that implies concentrated intellectual effort and is daily prosecuted on an average from 9 a. m. until midnight—the author of this paper made the reply: "Because I get something back from my patients; otherwise, I should be a nervous bankrupt." It is my purpose this evening to investigate the hypuotic procedure with a view to ascertaining what it is that the hypnotist who throws his soul into his work may receive in return from his subject; to offer a philosophical explanation of the spiritual exosmose and endosmose. Much has been written of the action of the operator and the passion of the subject. It is always what a suggestionist is doing to his mesmerizee, never what the mesmerizee is doing to his suggestionist. But the patient is as active subliminally as is the operator objectively; and the operator, where genuine rapport is established, realizes this activity.

It may be well for me to state at the outset that I understand hypnotic suggestion to be of the nature of inspiration; and the result of it is assumption of control either where control is relaxed or in fields where it has not before been exercised. Hypnotic suggestion is a summoning into ascendency of the true man; an accentuation of insight into life and its procedures; a revealing, in all its beauty and strength and significance, of absolute, universal, and necessary truth; and a portraiture of happiness as the assured outcome of living in consonance with this truth. It is not a mere pulling up of weeds by the roots as Horace Fletcher describes it in "Menticulture"; but it is a sudden overshadowing and starving out of character defects and mental weaknesses by a tropical growth of ethical energy which seeks immediate outlet in the activities of a moral life. The patient freely expresses his best self post-hypnotically, without effort, from a plane above that of the will—the plane of apprehension and of spontaneous command along lines of thought and action that are high and true. Thus is effected a perfect agreement between the law of right and the intelligent creature.

Such inspiration cannot be mere lip-work or rote-lesson. It implies a sincere belief in the suggestions offered; control by lofty, inflexible principles; an eloquent and incisive manner born of the courage of conviction; in short, it is a transfusion of personality. Perfunctory speeches are of no avail, for the mind of the mesmerizee is endowed with supranormal insight, instantaneously detects the disingenuous, and rejects the counsel of an uncandid or lukewarm guide.

The wear and tear of a continuous service in practical hypnotics, covering not only all phases of abnormal mental and moral attitudes, but involving as well inspirational work of the most difficult kind, is certainly out of the ordinary; the rapid recovery therefrom is phenomenal. There are grades of depression, time differences as regards the re-establishment of the operator's nervous balance, and degrees of subsequent uplift. Some patients are more exhausting than others, some mysteriously exalt, many are seemingly negative, all who in sincerity and faith seek moral or intellectual aid through hypnotic channels, in some way, immediately or remotely, refresh, exhilarate and nerve the mind that offers it. There is a more marked return in ethico-spiritual than in intellectual inspiration; little reciprocal benefit attends the treatment of mere physical conditions. Persons suffering from moral perversions and remorse consume more than the average amount of nervous energy, perhaps because they need a more generous quota of help. In certain instanstances it would seem as if the sufferer secured relief by casting upon the physician the whole burden of his imperative conception, self reproach, remorse, worry or fear. It may require hours or even days for one who extends aid subjectively to lift from his soul the dead weight of such an imposition. Coarse natures are especially trying; while refined minds ennoble and exalt from the earliest moment of contact. The more spiritual the work, the more marked the ascent, and the greater the consequent indifference of the operator to all worldly or purely material considerations. One seems sustained upon a higher plane where neither thought, nor passion, nor volition can intrude to ruffle the serene surface of his soul.

Some twelve months ago, in the up-rush of a violent nerve storm centering in a series of vicious assaults upon my integrity, there came into my life a spiritually-minded patient with the following request: "My deepest desire is consciously to realize my oneness with the Infinite God of Love. Impress upon me, as I sleep, the conviction that I have within me forces which, if I could but recognize them, would lift me to higher levels and open my soul to the illapse divine. Put into operation these spiritual powers, that I may lose myself in an acceptable service to others, and therein taste the perfect fruits of faith, aspiration, and love." Whereas I make no pretense to such power as would be implied in a literal response to the longings of this soul, and so explained my position to the petitioner, I do believe that by presentation of sovereign truth below the threshold of consciousness—that is, subliminal presentation—a soul may be made a hundred fold more intensely receptive than through mere objective exhortation. On this principle, I put the lady into a suggestible mind state, and as the inspiration proceeded, I felt myself elevated above the plane of the material and the transient, placed out of reach of worry thought and misgiving, and rendered incapable of irritation by the ingeniously contrived annoyances that had disturbed me hitherto. I realized a potency within me that was in every way adequate to the occasion; I became insensible to accusation and insult, I was made immune to the toxin of resentment. Association with pure souls in the realm of the subliminal has repeatedly proved similarly cheering and uplifting. Such uplift is to be carefully distinguished from the sense of self-congratulation that attends the doing of a kindness—from the gratification of that lively disinterested feeling which is a part of our animal nature, and which forever prompts us to make ourselves happy by making others happy first. It is marked by a peculiar erethismic thrill or shock, which would seem to accompany the touch of a soul. The inspiring suggestion blesses him that gives as well as him that takes.

But one must enter the ethico-spiritual field to experience the exaltation described in its perfection. In pure intellectual inspiration, in higher hypno-pedagogics, for instance, involving the exhibition to a sleeping subject of potential endowment and the post-hypnotic spontaneous expression of such endowment in the objective life—there is uplift of a different nature, similar, though specifically superior to the satisfaction accompanying felicitous objective instruction, persuasion or inspiration. The qualifying of a college student's subliminal for rigid examination; the symmetrical development of unbalanced mental faculties into harmoniously acting forces; the equipment of a talented woman for authorship or the stage—bring different degrees of intellectual compensation. In the creative communication that evolves a great actress, spiritual chords may be set in vibration as the true aim of dramatic art is pictured to be, not the mere representation of passion in itself, but of passion that leads to meritorious action—when tragedy is conceived of as poetry in its deepest earnest, and poetry as beauty plus spirituality. In the case of an actress inspired by me within the year and risen at a single bound to fame and fortune, the line of suggestion was as follows:

"You are now in a position to realize your talent and your power over its expression; and you are going on the stage in April—free from all agitation, having grasped in full the dramatic idea of the play whose heroine you are and confident in your own interpretation of the character of———. Your acting throughout will be consistent with this interpretation, sincere and natural in its tone. You will know intuiitively where the touch of nervousness is required to express the assumed emotion, when to affect a look of despair, how to manage the quick transition from real fright to apparent innocence. Your acting will be without artificiality, false to fact, but true to faith, your own conception. Realizing the efficiency within you, your whole being instinct with an intense vitality, you will naturally and unconstrainedly cast into your art all the magic that fascinates, all the control that holds an audience from first to last—your self-possession retained, but your self-consciousness all but submerged in your impersonation. So doing, you will impress without effort those who witness your acting with your masterly portraiture, with the superior quality of your representation, your truthfulness to nature, your heavy-handed realism. And you will be your own best automatic critic through it all, so confident in your talent and your spontaneous control over its utterance, that you will realize your elevation to a plane above necessity for sympathy from your audience. You have arisen in all the strength and fearlessness and majesty of your womanhood, and in all the glory of your genius, to assert yourself, and you can stand, if need be, unabashed before the world."

This gave the lady immediate insight into her endowment, with confidence in its expression, and she went before the footlights a consummate mistress of her art, to be curtained many times throughout the winter after the climax of the play.

To achieve this result, the lady in question was brought to a full realization of herself in her higher relationships; and wherever this is accomplished by the suggestionist, there is sure to be spiritual indemnification for the energy expended in awakening apprehension of the self at its best.

The reciprocal influence implied in hypnotic rapport is explicable on the principle of action and reaction, the third law of Sir Isaac Newton, viz: "To every action there is always an equal contrary reaction; a given body cannot press or attract another body without being itself pressed or attracted with equal force in an opposite direction." To carry this natural law into the world spiritual, no soul can impress another soul or personal intelligence without being reciprocally impressed. A soul errant in rapport experiences during the hour of impact with the mind of a pure-hearted suggestionist, a change in the direction of its aspirations or spiritual motions, and its total ethical energy is made actual. To the soul of the operator that stooped to point a way of escape to the sin-burdened spirit of the mesmerizee, is imparted a contrary upward motion and it rises to the heights of apprehension, spiritual insight and spontaneous yet absolute intellectual command. But in its ascent, it is not companionless; the emancipated soul is a factor in the rebound. Together the associated spirits enter the realm of pure mind life—the guiding spirit freed, by the intensity of its abstraction, from consciousness of a material environment; the spirit in rapport endowed, as incident to its subliminal state, with preternatural perception and thus become sensible of its measureless power over matter, its control of the vital functions of its objective body, as well as of its own intellectual attitudes and trends of thought. It realizes to the full the inherent dignity and worth of its higher nature, and discerns within itself a spiritual efficiency commensurate to its needs, whatever they may be—a power in reserve through the operation of which it may successfully parry the lance thrusts of disappointment, still the voice of remorse, quench the fires of passion, and break the clutch of crime. In the light of such apprehension, the so-designated heaven-left soul confidently assumes command of the forces conferred by its Creator for exploitation, and through the free and unconstrained operation of these natural forces, the objective life is spiritualized.

Ideal hypnotism thus implies on the part of one personality an expenditure of spiritual energy which, under the universal law of the conservation of force, cannot be destroyed, but which instantly materializes as ethical activity in the personality that is inspired. The energy that seemingly disappeared is transformed into a spiritual heat which warms the soul that kindled it, and creates reciprocally in that soul its full dynamic equivalent. If it be true that there are no forces in nature to which the law of energy does not apply, we have in this law an explanation of the reciprocal uplift in hypnotism, and we have in the fact itself an indicated way in which the souls of men may draw nearer to one another.

Do all persons who hypnotize other persons consciously receive from their subjects this lavish return for their investment of energy? Or are special qualifications required in the hypnotist? And if so liberal a dividend is assured, why should not all high-minded persons resort to hypnotism as a means of accentuating their own general receptivity and adding to their magnitude as moral stars? It were, indeed, a pity that the great mass of enlightened men and women who are striving for self-improvement or for the elevation of their kind should be debarred, through ignorance of its very existence, from so promising a field for their labors. The majority of hypnotists do mere perfunctory work; they do not sound the depths of the soul they seek to aid. There is a mere passing contact, a cold injunction to abandon demoralizing practice or secret sin; there is no outpour of sympathy, no encouragement of the stricken spirit to unbreast its woes. With what measure the hypnotist metes, it is measured to him again. If he be not an earnest and sincere believer in his suggestions; if he sees not a brother in the evil-doer; if he withholds that best gift one can offer to his neighbor, viz: himself—he can expect no return from the soul he addresses. A mesmerizee instinctively penetrates the veneer of indifference or deception, and revolts against rapport that is sought for selfish or sordid purposes. Further, the human soul delights in a realization of its own power, and responds sublimely to him who, in harmony with Paul, holds up before its subliminal vision that spiritual potency conferred on it by God as the means of accomplishing lofty purpose, as the way of escape (ekbasis) from temptation (1 Cor. x:3). The doctrine of the utter helplessness of man which is harped on so persistently by certain creeds, and which has for centuries unsouled the Christian, is taught neither by Jesus nor Paul. God does not turn out mere salework. He does not create souls without good in them; without power in themselves to help themselves—a mistaken philosophy which every blade of grass controverts, every sun, every diatom. The maximum efficiency of the human machine is illustrated in the life history of Job, that one conspicuous embodiment of purely human feeling and faith and potency at their best. The same spiritual energy that gave Job his victory, is potential in every human unit. There is no soul in which God is not; and what God hates is therefore intuitively hated by the human image of God, the superior spiritual self. Objective man is often sin-loving; subjective man is ever sin-hating. One fool hath said in his heart, "There is no God;" another fool, "There is no God in man"—and yet the Spirit beareth witness with our spirit that we are the children of God (Rom. VIII.). It is this spirit of ours, the pure pneuma, that deathless principle which dictates what is right, and whose attitude toward sin is by force of its very birth, one of repugnance and horror—it is this spirit that lusteth against the flesh,—all vicious appetites, wrong impulses, unmanly practices. So no sin-living man in the abstract is morally indifferent. He may smother his insensibility for a time, but he will always revolt and assert his manhood objectively when subliminally shamed into an apprehension of the blot upon his dignity as a man. In the conduct of his revolt, he is under obligation to make a competent use of the efficiency within him in an expression of willingness, perseverance, patience and moral energy, before appealing to the throne of grace. To the personality that apprises an apparently helpless soul of its own intellectual and moral powers and makes plain the possibility of conquest through self-help—the truth an enfamined world craves to-day—that soul flows out in a great tidal wave of recognition, gratitude and reciprocal stimulation. And the possibility of asserting a slumbering intellectual courage that clearly discerns, and a moral courage that grandly undercrests, is open to all who have lost sight of the god-like in their own lives. This is optimism at its climax, this making the man acquainted with himself.

Another fact—the thoughts, emotions, beliefs, aspirations and moral status of a suggestionist are undesignedly communicated most vividly to the subject, whose mind becomes mysteriously tuned in unison with that of the operator. I have been startled by hearing patients tell me days after hypnotization of feelings and incentives to action, of which I had suggested nothing but which I knew to be in the background of my consciousness at the time of treatment. An actress whom I was inspiring with confidence and preparing for her part, assured me a week after treatment that she had experienced a remarkable change in her disposition and her attitude as regards the purity of the stage. She would not entertain a propositition from a manager whose plays verged on the vulgar, and her newly adopted ideals were so exactly in conformity with my own that there could be no question regarding their source. In like manner, I have inadvertently communicated my love of nature and her wild life, my aesthetic sensibility, my facility with the pen, and even my faith. As one patient expressed it, "Your thoughts become my thoughts." The time has indeed come, as Maeterlinck predicted it would, when souls may know of each other without the intermediary of the senses. We have within us an immaterial principle entirely independent of sense organs and sense acquisition. Its pinion is not reconciled to earth. It represents a flight above the temporal, and hints of Heaven.

What light, if any, do these facts cast upon the principles of telepathic communication? The laws that govern such intercourse, the question as to the extent of its prevalence among the living, and its possible extension into the world of the dead, are of supreme concern to humanity. The fact that minds brought into hypnotic contact through the approximation of the physical bodies they tenant, can exchange thoughts, feelings, ideas, knowledge, convictions, suggests the possibility that minds temporarily separated and to all purpose discarnate in natural sleep or in hypnosis, or even in states of reverie—subliminal selfs free to traverse the world and its purlieus—may communicate without reference to space limitations, and are mutually impressed, exalted and refined.

Subliminal minds would seem to be attracted automatically 1. To their complements, each the other to strengthen, to instruct, to inspire; and 2. As mere almoners to other minds in need of help. Were the means of establishing such communication comprehended and under control, deliberate absent treatment for functional sickness or moral defect would be possible and in every way scientific.

Telepathy is the direct communication of one mind with another, at a distance, otherwise than through the normal operation of the recognized sense organs—that is, without the use of words, sounds, odors, looks, gestures or other material signs. It is a form of mystic perception and impression which inheres in animal nature and characterizes certain methods of brute communication. Recent experiments have proved moths and other insects to be capable of thought transference so far-reaching as to impress their fellows miles away with a knowledge of their existence and whereabouts. It is well known to whalers that a cetacean struck by a harpoon has power instantly to convey information of the presence of an enemy to a spouting school a mile distant, so that the individuals composing it immediately disappear below the surface. Every angler is aware that if one trout in a pool becomes conscious of his presence, the most deftly cast flies fall unheeded on the ripples. Some twelve years ago, the late Austin Corbin purchased 25,000 acres of farm and woodland in Sullivan County N. H., and stocked the estate liberally with cervidae. In 1897, it was predicted that the extinct carnivores whose natural food is venison would return to the region. Recently, Austin Corbin, Jr. reported the presence of a family of pumas, or mountain lions, in the Park, and other observers have discovered the lynx (both *rufus* and *canadensis*) in evidence. By what mysterious power of cognition did the great cat, a century vanished from this region, become aware of the presence of deer and elk in Blue Mountain Park? I suggest the theory of a telepathic communication—the radiation of subtle waves of cognizance from the mass of fear entertained for their traditional enemies by a community of 4000 animals of the deer tribe, to fugitive panthers in the Alleghanies or in remote areas of the Green and Adirondack Mountains. Similarly, intimations of intended movements having in view either my injury or my advantage, are frequently conveyed to me. I feel the thing in the air. If brutes possess this inscrutable power of communication, and exercise it for their benefit, it cannot seem marvelous that a professional trance-medium, in perfect training, should be able to project her subliminal indiscriminately or with method in her ecstasy, force her way subjectively into the penetralia of selected human minds, and so possess herself of information calculated to confuse, deceive, or otherwise impress her investigators. For has such a medium ever revealed anything that did not exist either in her own consciousness, or in the consciousness of some person present, or in the consciousness of some living human being not present at the seance? And yet I do not deny the possibility of impression by extra-human intelligences. Whence come the beautiful and practical thoughts that impress us as we sleep and clamor for utterance at the moment of our awaking, "the thoughts ye cannot stay with brazen chains." Granted, during the hours of rest, symposiums of kindred subliminal spirits having interests in common and free to combine and inter-penetrate, granted on such occasions unrestricted access on the part of every soul to the knowledge and experience and impulses and ideals cherished by every other soul, and thought impression during states of sleep is rationally explained through creative communication. The Gospel teaches the communion of saints, the spiritual fellowship, mystically in and through Jesus Christ, of all believers, dead as well as living, who are united in the Holy Catholic Church. But mystical communion does not necessarily imply communication between the living and the dead. The teaching of the New Testament as to the possibility of intercourse between embodied souls and discarnate spirits is negative; but it positively affirms the possibility of subliminal communication between uncarnate spirits and embodied souls. Intelligences not human, ill-wishing and well-wishing, would appear to influence man, and the *modus impressendi* must involve action on a receptive subliminal consciousness. In my higher work, I have at times felt myself seemingly thwarted by an intervening intelligence that opposed the strongest influence I could exert and for a time renderd futile all efforts at hypnotization. I may instance the case of Susie G., a bright little girl seven years of age, who was brought to me to be treated for an abuse taught in infancy by a nurse. The child realized that she was doing wrong and was desirous of cure; she trusted me implicitly, cheerfully came to my office, and had perfect faith in my ability to save her. She would enter the first stage of hypnosis with her hand confidingly in mine and her arm about my neck, when suddenly the trustful childish expression would desert her face and she would glare at me with a sullen, defiant, hunted look like an abandoned woman taken red-hand in the commission of a crime. For the nonce, further attempt to hypnotize failed. The revulsion was painful to me, and must have been to this unfortunate child. She described the interposing influence as that of Satan, who, she naively said, told her not to go to sleep for me, who regularly tempted her to do herself wrong, and whom, as she grew stronger, she was accustomed to refer to an adjoining house for a more promising victim. The alternative here is between an outside ill-wishing personality too strong for the simple child-nature, and a part of Susie's own personality. I have never seen anything so suggestive of possession in the cases of multiplex personality that have come under my own observation, although in a number of sexual perverts who have subjectively resisted hypnotism, something similar has seemed to occur. After three months, this interesting girl was brought to me again for treatment, and I easily succeeded in putting her into a placid and trustful sleep in which the redemptory suggestions were given without interruption. If the efforts at rescue were thwarted in the first instance by the intervention of a daimon, my subsequent success would seem to imply that extra-human intelligence may be as fugitive in their endeavors to deprave or ennoble, as are other intelligences clothed with human bodies.

The difficulty of discriminating is such a case as Susie's between an ill-wishing spiritual intruder and a separate personality of the individual under treatment, is obvious. No room for doubt exists in the case of Natalie W., another patient who passes daily from one personality to another without appreciable cause. In consequence of a nervous shock received in her eighth year, during convalescence from fever, the mind of Natalie W. remained a child's mind, while she gradually developed into physical womanhood in the thirty years that followed. In one personality she repeats aloud the petitions of the Prayer Book continuously for six hours, being constantly interrupted by the other personality whom she styles Miss W., and peremptorily orders out of her presence with emphatic gestures. In one personality, she is affectionate, confiding and tractable; in the other, she is cunning, suspicious and difficult to control. In one personality, this child woman loves me; in the other, she fears me.

Her mother believes her to be possessed. The psychology of this case of alternating personality is, however, clear.

But whether or not uncarnate daimons communicate through the instrumentality of suggestion, and whether or not disembodied souls reach, via the channel of the related selfs, those of us who are still in the flesh—one fact the writer regards as established by his experiments, viz: A Rational and Dignified Way is Open for Such Spiritual Communication Every Time We Lose Ourselves in Slumber, for There is no Difference as Regards Suggestibility Between Natural Sleep and the So-called Hypnotic Trance. In the latter, the sleeper is in rapport exclusively with the person who has induced the state; in the former, he may be in rapport with his own objective self, perhaps with a multitude of discarnate personalities who think and feel in common with him, and in case he be of superior parts, possibly with all well-wishing daimons. Iamblichus, the Neoplatonic philosopher, was right when he proclaimed the night-time of the body to be the day-time of the soul. The impressing outside personality, if it be operative at all, operates through the double consciousness fused in the single human mind, the superior spiritual self being obnoxious to the insinuation of a belief, impulse or thought, which may dominate the objective life. Spiritistic communication on this principle, implies a plane of meeting infinitely higher than that of the common seance, where soul and daimon are supposed to communicate through the mind of an entranced medium who chatters a confused mass of trivialities and irrelevancies. The human soul intuitively abhors an intermediary. In this life, the climax of soul communion is reached in the mutual embrace of the physical bodies—immediate relationship alone is acceptable and satisfactory. So if there be impression by disembodied souls, that impression, in the opinion of the speaker, is direct. The idea of intercourse with the dead through the machinery of the seance is repugnant to reason. Aside from the fact that if the communications be accepted as messages from the souls of the righteous departed, such a belief cannot be reconciled with an exalted conception of the powers of disembodied spirits, we are confronted with the equally significant fact that the intellectual status of all circles is low and disappointing.

Every hour of natural sleep is prolific of opportunity for communication with the departed, and who knows that it does not take place? It were pleasant to feel that a contingent of our better thoughts is inspired by those we have loved, who when they appear in visions we remember, always appear as living, and thinking, and acting personalities. Perhaps there is in this latter fact a suggestion of that immortality which psychic vision and psychic audition incontestably prove in that they illustrate the power of the soul to operate as a discarnate entity, as a spirit disentangled from the flesh.

The soul that exalts the operator in the hypnotic procedure is the same soul that is freed permanently at the moment of death. Why should it cease to project aspirations, modify attitudes, communicate ideas, uplift human natures, simply because it is forever done with the perishable body as an instrument of expression? If then, in the providence of God, disembodied pneumata are free so to do, assuredly they have it in their power to communicate directly with us through impression of the subliminal mind.

From my experience in subliminal inspiration, and from my knowledge of the reciprocal influence in psycho-therapy and of telepathic possibilities in general, I am inclined to accept the telepathic rather than the spiritistic hypothesis in explanation of the communications received by Professor Hyslop from Mrs. Piper.

(For the paragraphs quoted in the above from the author's article in Harper's Magazine for June, due acknowledgment is hereby made.)

TELEPATHY AND MRS. PIPER.

BY CLARK BELL, ESQ.

In reading the statement of Mrs. Leonora E. Piper as it appeared in the New York Sunday Herald recently, it seemed to me, that it was a clear duty to examine the evidence of the record of the communications which have been made by her in the trance state, to see how far they would sustain the view and position she assumes in her statement as announced in the New York Herald.

There can be no better place to look for that record, than in the proceedings of the Society for Psychical Research, and for this purpose we are justified in assuming their correct reproduction. They are certainly quite as reliable as the usual stenographic notes of the evidence of witnesses on a trial. It ought also to be assumed on entering this discussion, that no mere pride of opinion nor the change of views of observers, like Dr. Hodgson or Prof. Hyslop, should influence our analysis of the evidence.

It is only fair, to recall the fact that neither Dr. Hyslop nor Dr. Hodgson were avowed believers in the spiritualistic hypothesis, nor was the Society of Physical Research itself recognized as a body, that was committed to spiritualism at the time she commenced her labor for that society.

It is safe to say that both Dr. Hodgson and Prof. Hyslop were regarded as very skeptical indeed of what was then constantly exhibited as the phenomena of spiritualism, and in my own experience, I found Prof. Hyslop very adept, and quick, to detect frauds in the average mediumistic phenomena, which we some times saw together, and where we usually concurred as to the peculiar deceptions used.

To start with, neither Mrs. Piper, nor indeed the leaders of that body at the outset did not probably allege or indeed believe, that the phenomena was such as was then regarded as spiritistic phenomena.

Read before the Medico-Legal Society, Dec. 18, 1901.

So that it is but justice to Mrs. Piper to say, that so far as she is personally concerned, there is nothing in her statement that should be fairly classed as derogatory to either her integrity or veracity, or that was in contradiction of her views, at the time she commenced with the society work.

The fact that the gentlemen named have changed their views, even if that change had been based on the manifestations or her communications, should not alter the free discussion of the issue.

It is too extensive a subject, to consider in an exhaustive manner, on such an occasion,and I prefer to limit what I have to say to the evidence, and shall quote from the volumes of the proceedings of the Society of Psychical Research, and follow perhaps somewhat in the line of two members of that society, along lines which seem to me to be at the very root or heart of the discussion.

I shall refer to a paper by Mrs. Henry Sidgwick entitled "Discussion of the Trance Phenomena of Mrs. Piper."

Mrs. Sidgwick begins by referring carefully to the various papers relating to the phenomena as published in the proceedings, giving title, author, volume and page.

She assumes, and agrees, with Professor Newbold, at the outset, (Proceedings Vol. XIV, p. 7.) in the assertion, "I accept the conclusion arrived at by everyone so far as I know, who has studied the case at any length," "that it was not consciously got by Mrs. Piper during waking life and then fraudulently palmed off on the sitter as supernormal;" or as Dr. Leaf puts it (Proceedings Vol. VI., p. 559), "as to the first and most obvious question whether she consciously acquires knowledge with regard to her sitters with the intention of deceiving, I may say most positively, that I regard such a supposition as entirely untenable."

Mrs. Sidgwick, in searching for the real cause of the phenomena, assumed "That telepathy—in the sense of the impression of one living mind by another, otherwise than through the recognized channels of sense may be taken as provisionally established by the evidence collected by our society and other investigators."

Mrs. Sidgwick agrees with Prof. Lodge, "That thought transferrence is the most common place explanation to which it is possible to appeal in the case of Mrs. Piper." Proceedings Vol. Vi., p. 451.)

In such a discussion we should carefully consider and define telepathy, so that we might occupy a common ground in this respect, as it is now claimed by scientific men, and, concerning which we should not find or expect to find dissenting opinions.

Telepathy, as it is regarded by scientists who accept it as a fact, is some unknown sense or power of the human body, by which as a physical process, communication is held between brain and brain of the human organism. Some means by which the perceptions are reached in some manner analogous to the known and well-defined transmission of the electric current or the action of gravitation which we know exists, but we are as yet unable to comprehend how it acts, or to know its methods.

As yet the process of the action of telepathy is wholly undefined, but that it is a physical process is generally conceded by scientific workers.

Those who wish, like Mr. Hodgson, to extend this view of telepathy, so as to embrace communication between the living brain, and the spirit of the dead, through a living brain like that of Mrs. Piper, must be classed as in the region of controversy; such a view has not yet been demonstrated.

Mrs. Sidgwick is of the opinion that in no case has the spirits of deceased persons, known to the sitters used her organism to speak directly through her to the sitters wi h her voice or write for them directly with her hand. (Proceedings Vol. XV., part XXXVI, p. 19.)

Mrs. Sidgwick is of the opinion that the influence or intelligence operating through Mrs. Piper is frequently not Mrs. Piper, but some brain outside her own personality. She asserts the existence of two separate intelligences, one speaking and one writing at the same time, but insists that this condition frequently exists in hypnotic subjects, and throws no light on the subject of the controversy, quoting Mr. Gurney and Prof. Janet. (Peculiarities of Certain Past Hypnotic States. Proceedings Vol. 4, by Mr. Gurney, also Prof. Janet's work.)

She attaches little importance to the impressions of the sitter, regarding the personality of the communicating intelligence, because, when two or more minds are considering the same subject, one will often think it recognizes, and the other will on the same identical facts think otherwise. With Mrs.

Piper it was usually. Phinuit (Dr. P.) and he was speaking sometimes for others, and not for himself. This explains why the person who is directly communicating or attempting to do so, is not the person it claims to be, and which it often believes itself to be; but that it is in fact the trance personality of Mrs. Piper herself.

On no other theory can the inconsistencies, contradictions, errors, misstatements of known facts, concerning which the real person could not be in doubt or in error, which arise in communications through her, or in similar communications from or through other mediums of similar character be explained.

For example, Dr. Phinuit's description of himself as the spirit of a deceased Marseilles physician, is beyond all doubt, an incredible statement.

He cannot speak one word of French. He has not established even a fraction of a reputation for veracity, and so far as known none of his statements regarding incidents in his life on the earth, have ever been verified.

His testimony would not have a particle of weight before a court or jury if given in an action at law; and that this was Mr. Leaf's opinion of him, is clearly shown by Mr. Leaf's statement. (Proceedings Vol. VI, p. 60.)

Take the case of Mr. Stainton Moses (Proceedings Vol. XIII, pp. 407-412.) The spirit guides of Mr. Moses assumed several names, Imperator, Rector, Mentor, Doctor. As a group of witnesses, their statements regarding their own life on earth, about Mr. Moses himself, and their teachings to him, serve to discredit their evidence. It must be thrown out as evidence and would be in any court of justice.

They gave the names of the historical personages, they claimed to have been. Mrs. Piper wrote out these names. Investigation shows, those given not to have been correct. Wrong names were given. None right, but they are insisted upon for a time, and then corrected, and the names corrected to others, equally wrong.

The "Doctor" is Homer and "Mentor" is Ulysses, and he says that he often sees "Telemachus," and can't remember the name of the lady who is with him always, until his recollection is refreshed by Dr. Hodgson, when he recalls "Penelope."

It is perfectly safe to say, that these persons are not the personalities they claim to be; or that they are Mr. Stainton Moses Guides: or that they have actually used Mrs. Piper's hand as a writing machine to record the evidence of their misstatements of facts.

Mrs. Sidgwick cites an instance in point (Proceedings Vol. XIII, p. 348) where Mrs. M. records communications from her husband's aunt who had died in 1894, both through Phinuit and when she pretends to write herself, could never give her own name correctly, although Mrs. M. repeatedly tried to have her do so.

Mrs. Sidgwick cites the case of where Mr. Hodgson had given Mrs. Piper entranced a piece of Mss. Written by Dr. Wiltze to hold.

Shortly the spirit of Dr. Wiltze appeared, in person claiming to be dead and that his body was still in the water. Proceedings Vol. XXXVI, p. 25. Dr. Wiltze was at the time alive and well.

Is there any rational explanation of such an occurrence, other than to attribute it to an idiosyncracy of the trance personality of Mrs. Piper?

The conclusions which Mrs. Sidgwick reaches regarding the trance phenomena of Mrs. Piper are, that they are explainable in no other way, than that they are: consistent with the hypothesis that they may have originated with the trance personality of Mrs. Piper.

That it must be conceded that Mrs. Piper is in telepathic communication with the sitter, and that the sitter must play an important part in relation to the communication. We know so little of the methods of telepathic communication beyond the fact that it does exist, that it is only fair to suppose that the mind of Mrs. Piper in trance, may and probably does, have free access to the thoughts and subliminal consciousness of the sitter.

The mind of the sitter has its recollections of and its impressions of the deceased person. How far the trance personality of Mrs. Piper has access to these recollections and memories we do not quite know, nor as yet can we suppose them to be wholly unavailable or inaccessible.

If the dead could communicate with the living, it is not out of the question that the trance personality of Mrs. Piper could receive impressions from the spirit of the departed; but of this we have no positive evidence. On the whole evidence it is quite clear, or rather it is not sufficient, to raise even a conviction, that the trance phenomena of Mrs. Piper is in any sense due to the action of the spirits of the dead, on her trance personality, as to the communications made.

Andrew Lang contributes an article to the "Discussion of the Trance Phenomena of Mrs. Piper," called "Reflections on Mrs.Piper and Telepathy." Proceedings Vol XXXVI,at page 39 to 52, of considerable value. It is in the nature of a review of Dr.Hodgson's "Further Record of Observation and of Certain Phenomena of Trance," as published in Proceedings of Society of Psychical Research Vol. XXX, p. 406), in which he details at length the reasons which are conclusive on his mind, that the phenomena can not be regarded as having any true relation to communications from the spirit world or from the spirits of deceased persons. Mr. Lang criticises Dr. Phinuit, Mr. H. and G. P., and says that "if they were honorable spirits, they would say they don't know when they don't know. They would not give false information, 'natural enough,' easily guessed, but totally wrong."

He quotes Prof. Pierce, Mr. MacAlister, Mr. Marte, Dr. Weir Mitchell, Mr. Barkworth, Mr. Newbold, Mr. Podman, Prof. Trowbridge and others, but while he concedes that the facts would raise a strong presumption against the bona-fides of Mrs. Piper, he still says:

"On David Hume's theory a long set of impositions is the most legitimate explanation of Mrs. Piper's successes. For reasons given by Dr. Hodgson, I cannot accept the theory of imposture by Mrs. Piper in her normal state. For one thing she could not afford the expense of private inquiries which would more than swallow up the profits."

Mr. Lang says:

We are dealing here with a most imperfectly known agency, telepathy; with a better known agency, the secondary personality, and with another wholly unknown agency, spirits of the dead. The preference for any of these Laputan alternatives is apt to be decided by personal bias. But, to a faint extent, telepathy has the advantage of being a vera causa. The advocates of telepathy, attempting to explain Mrs. Piper's successes, may fall back, as Dr. Hodgson says, on "the hypothesis of telepathy from the living, that the subliminal consciousness of the sitters, and also of distant living persons, might be drawn upon the living." Thus, Mr. Pelham is doing something in Washington with a photograph of his son, G. P., and G. P. reports this at Boston through Mrs. Piper. The explanation (apart from guess or collusion), will be that Mrs. Piper

got at the subliminal consciousness of the remote Mr. Pelham, and so on in other similar cases. Such a telepathic explanation is "to the Greeks foolishness."

Mr. Lang continues in the discussion as follows:

Now the stretching of the telepathic hypothesis was almost forced on me (if I was to have any hypothesis), during Miss Angus' experiments with a glass ball? I presume that these experiments were "experimental," in Mr. Lodge's sense of the word, but I am not certain. (Making of Religion, Pp. 94-112.) There was in these experiments, apparently, a "selective and discriminative capacity in Miss Angus' percipient personality." But there was no room for the theory of the spirits of the dead, for all concerned were alive. To be sure the Polynesians explain all water-gazing by a theory of spirits, but Dr. Hodgson will not agree with the Polynesians. (Ellis, Polynesian Researches, II, p. 240.)

Again and again, Miss Angus, sitting with man or woman, described acquaintenances of theirs, but not of hers, in situations not known to the sitters, but proved to be true to fact. Now the "far-going" hypothesis of direct clairvoyance was here excluded (in most cases, not all), by conditions of time. In one instance Miss Angus described doings from three weeks to a fortnight old, of people in India, people whom she had never seen or heard of, but who were known to her "sitter." Her account, given on a Saturday, was corroborated by a letter from India which arrived next day, Sunday. In another case she described (about 10 P. M.), what a lady, not known to her, but the daughter of a matron present, (who was not the sitter), had been doing about 4 P. M. on the same day. What the person was doing was not a thing familiar, for I asked that question Again, "sitting" with one lady, Miss Angus described a singular set of scenes much in the mind, not of her "sitter," but of a very unsympathetic stranger, who was reading a book at the other end of the room. I have tried every hypothesis, normal and not so normal, to account for these and analogous performances of Miss Angus. There was, in the Indian and other cases, no physical possibility of collusion; chance coincidence did not seem adequate; ghosts were out of the question, so was direct clairvoyance. That Miss Angus, (who, by the way, was in the most normal and wide-awake condition), had got into touch with the absolute, and was making discriminating selection from the stores of omniscience, did not seem likely, because her crystal pictures appeared to be directed by the mind of a person present, not always the sitter. Nothing remained for the speculative theoriser but the idea of cross currents of telepathy between Miss Angus, a casual stranger, the sitters, and people far away, known to the sitters or the stranger, but unknown to Miss Angus. Unpublished examples of these things went on the same lines. Miss Angus picked up facts, unknown to the sitters, about people known to them but not to her.

Now suppose that Miss Angus instead of dealing with living people, by way of visions, had dealt by way of voice, or automatic handwriting, and had introduced a dead "communicant." Then she would have been on a par with Mrs. Piper, yet with aid from the dead. Her cases do not differ from Mrs. Piper's cases, except in copiousness, and in the circumstance that her condition was normal, and that she was new to all such exercises. Of course, like Mrs. Piper, she had failures. I asked her to try to see the room of a person known to me by correspondence only, a person whom I never met, (it was a room in Africa, though of course I did not say so), and she failed. It was trying her rather high. We did not seek to improve the result by exclaiming "Dear Tom, Dick or Harry, in Bengal, Edinburgh, or the Soudan, or the Red Sea, do try to appear more frequently in the glass," as Dr. Hodgson addresses the dead "communicators." We could not do that, because the essence of the game lay in Miss Angus' ignorance about Dick, Harry and Tom, who were kept private in mind of the sitters. Otherwise the performances of Mrs. Piper and Miss Angus were on a par (except for the deadness of the persons concerned), granting the difference of the methods of crystal gazing on one hand, and of trance-speaking, or automatic writing, on the other.

Not to rely solely upon Miss Angus, I take another instance. My friend Mr. Lesley is known to the world as a man of business, a golfer and a composer. He can see crystal pictures, but, (like most of my acquaintenances who possess the faculty, including my cook), has hardly any interest in the practice. One day Mr. Lesley and I had been talking about a lady, unknown to him, but known to me, though I had never seen her house. Mr. Lesley began to look into a glass water-jug, and described what he saw: the interior of a hall of a house, with a good deal of detail. Nenither of us recognized the house. I happened later to tell this to the lady of whom we had been talking; she said: "Why, that is my house," and on visiting it. I found that in all respects it answered to Mr. Lesley's description. It may be a common type of hall but I do not remember having seen one like it elsewhere, nor did Mr. Lesley know any such place.

Now suppose that the lady who occupied the house had been dead. And suppose that, instead of looking at a glass water-jug, Mr. Lesley had gone into a trance and announced that the dead lady was speaking with his voice. Suppose that when asked for a test she had described the hall in her house, (which was unknown to me and Mr. Lesley), with certain curious details. Would not Dr. Hodgson argue that this might be better explained by the hypothesis of communication through her spirit, than by telepathy between Mr. Lesley and anybody not present who knew the house? Yet, as its owner was and is alive, the theory of a spirit is wholly impossible, and if not telepathy a trois, then some other non-spiritualist theory must account for the facts, as for the facts in Miss Angus' cases.

Miss Angus' successes may not be due to cross-telepathy, nor may Mr. Lesley's success; very likely that is the wrong explanation. But of all known "supernormal" explanations, and that alone is viable, in these instances, and it is not, I think, incapable of application to Mrs. Piper's cases. Of course I do not reject the expianation by spirits, in Mrs. Piper's case; I only state the objections which occur to me, combined with the fact that Mrs. Piper is saturated with the animistic hypothesis, and has a dishonest secondary personality, if not dozens of such personalities. In Miss Angus' performances Mr. Podmore suggests (Part XXXIV., p. 130), my own provisional guess of telepathy a trois. It is a guess, even a wild Laputan conjecture. But we are here concerned with Laputan themes and speculations. Like Mr. Darwin, we are making "fools' experiments." Dr. Hodgson's hypothesis may be right; but in this region of dreams we ought to hold very lightly by all hypotheses; and, surely, we ought not to argue from one of them in favor of that old belief, the posthumous existence of the human spirit, and its power of communicating with the living, through a living organism. This is to base faith on a conjecture about conjectures. Moreover, in ordinary normal material, such as philogical or anthropological speculation, we often see how science overshoots her mark. remaining for a generation in sure confidence about a theory which the next generation explodes. We ought not to let our psychical theories affect our practical beliefs. To do that may be to prepare for ourselves, or for our successors, a cruel disappointment.

Mr. Lang concludes by saying, regarding experiments in thought transferrence:

"Twice my thought has (apparently and in the absence of any other hypothesis known to me), been 'picked up' by an experimenter, and in neither case was it my surface thought. These things bias one in favor of the belief that there is something here into which it may not be waste of time to inquire."

In experiments made by myself in the Ouicha board when I have endeavored to eliminate all possibility of collusion in the medium, and automatic collusion on my own part, I have had some experiences, that coincide with what seems to be Mrs. Piper's opinion respecting the phenomena she refers to.

1st. Example, an apparent intelligence describes itself as one S. B., whom I had well known in life, and knew by hearsay had been drowned on Lake Keuka, the details of which I did not know, but had been attributed to drink, to which S. B., a well known fisherman, was too much addicted.

There were two hands on the board, the other beside my own was a gentleman, and a spiritualist in belief, who has visited at that Lake and at a point where S. B. usually fished from, but was not conscious that he knew, or had ever seen or ever heard of S. B. I had fished the lake for years with S. B. and knew every foot of its bottom well, in that part where the transactions occurred near Grove Spring, Gibsons, and Keuka Landings.

S. B. spelling out his name gave me a complete detailed history of his drowning, fixed the hour at daybreak, or just before daybreak, when he was trolling for trout, the capsizing of his boat, and after many questions, stated that his body was then in the lake, with all his clothes on, precisely as he had died, lying with his face downward, and finally by questions referring to names and fishing grounds and places located the spot where his body then lay so exactly, that I could have dropped an anchor on it or within ten feet of it on what was known as the Barren ground among fishermen, in about 60 feet of water, almost exactly off the dock that was built there.

Subsequent investigation demonstrated that he was at the time of the communication to me, buried in the country grave yard near his home, and the whole statement drawn from either my imagination or that of my friend, the medium, who had given it full credence.

A peculiarity of this seance was that we were interrupted constantly by an intelligence who was most anxious to communicate with me, but who could not describe himself or even tell his name. After a long struggle he did at last spell out a name of Wm. S., also a fisherman on that lake, whom I knew well in his lifetime and who had been my client. He was a relation of Samuel B. and in life they were not the most intimate friends. He gave me information as to his state, his relations then to S. B. and to others of his old set, not worth repeating and not at all in accord with what is generally believed by the spiritualistic world—not of the slightest value, but it seemed simply to be a resolute, determined, and finally successful effort of a most obstinate and determined party to say "How do you do" to an old friend, but who had nothing whatever to communicate. The second hand on the board did not know this man in life, and has no consciousness of knowing him at all, but of course may have heard of him, as he was in his day the most prominent fisherman on the lake.

On another occasion, with a personal friend, a lady of high mediumistic powers, as the other of two hands on the board, I asked for and obtained the presence of D. B., a man of international reputation, known to the medium, and for whom I had acted professionally, and for whose estate I was then acting professionally. I had reason to believe that he had died possessed of real estate in a foreign city, but I had been unable to trace it through his relations, one brother knowing its whereabouts, but withholding it. We had been very intimate in life, and when he came, after some delay in finding him by the celestial messengers, he persisted in ignoring my questions, and devoting his whole talk to a description of his present plane and environment, and to explanations to me of his erroneous views of the future state in life (He had been an agnostic) and seemed most anxious to compel my attention to the erroneous views he had entertained in life

His description of his first view of me was remarkable, he said. Calling me by my first name, "I see you at an illimitable distance. I am farther from you than the fixed stars, yet, to my sense, the distance is annihilated, and I see you as conscious as if I was face to face on the earth." After a long struggle, with great difficulty, I brought him down from his high perch, and he answered my questions respecting this missing property. He gave me the name of the street, the number of the store, for he said it was a store in the business portion of a great city, and said that the store was and had been occupied as a liquor store for years.

This was wholly imaginary, and there was nothing in the interview to at all identify him to me, had he so desired to do—but his whole effort, of course due to the mentality of the medium, seemed to be to convince me of the truth of the spiritualistic phenomena, and especially to the immortality of the soul, and the future state for the spirits of the departed.

At the same seance, with the same medium, there came spelled out the name of Mr. J. G., a well known New York financier and railway operator, whom I had known well, and for whom I had acted professionally in various great corporations. The medium, did not know him personally in life, was intimately acquainted with stock operations in the enterprises, with which he was connected and I knew held, what was at that time a most unfavorable opinion of his character, life, motives and conduct. I shall not repeat what he said personal to himself, or relating to his life or his then present state, but he appealed to me as near as I can recall it now, in this wise:

"Whatever the world may say of me or of my past life, no one can truthfully speak one disparaging word, against my wife, or my children.

That which makes me suffer most now and here, is the reflection and the fear, that, the hatreds of those who classed themselves as my enemies, will visit their animosities upon my children. Appealing to me, he said: "You know this, as well as any one in New York. I introduced you to my oldest son. You know my oldest daughter. Use all your influence to prevent the animosities of those who hated me from reaching or harming my innocent children."

This did allude to a fact that had occurred in life between him and me, but it was within my consciousness, and is readily explainable by telepathy, and the medium, I think, also knew this fact and her mentality dominated the thought almost entirely. It did not impress me as a communication from the dead.

It was undoubtedly, both in my mind and in that of the medium.

I perhaps should say that after a most diligent search, extending over years, I have never had any communication that I believed to have come from the spirit of the dead.

Believing in the immortality of the soul, I would gladly welcome any voice from the beyond if it came. My mind is receptive to it, not antagonistic. The Bible plainly teaches it. Still it has as yet been unrevealed to my vision or consciousness.

A careful resume of the whole subject convinces me that Mrs. Piper's statement is entitled to weight and to credit.

It is in no sense a confession, and should not be so classed or regarded.

As I understand it the officials of the Society do not so regard it. They do not regard it as a violation of her engagement with the Society, and it is authoritatively stated that her relations are not severed with that body. Nor indeed should they be.

If she was now like Mr. Hodson, or Prof. Hyslop, an avowed spiritualist, it would not strengthen the value of her work with the members of that Society, who are for the most part not spiritualists, or not so regarded by the general public.

It claims to be a scientific workshop. Prof. James is not an avowed spiritualist; quite the reverse. Neither was Prof. Sidgwick; nor is it clear that Mr. Myers was.

The mission of spiritualism, if it is yet defined, should be to demonstrate

1. The immortality of the soul of man.
2. Its power to communicate with the living, by means incapable of being denied or refuted.

It is evidence that is needed. In the courts we establish what we call facts by human evidence.

Uncontradicted human evidence in a case is often accepted as a fact in a case, that in point of fact is not a fact at all.

Human evidence is full of weakness, yet in all the walks of life, we accept it, and we cannot consent to any plan or basis by which it is to be ignored.

A safe standard for our labor—one which must be considered by all to be conclusive—is Truth. We in determining as to the facts, or the law in a case before courts and juries, ask for the Truth. Science delights in demonstration, but in beliefs if demonstration is demanded, creeds must be written on a thumb nail, and not a half inch long. Let it be our motto to search only for the Truth, which is immortal and will live forever.

SPIRITISM AND MRS. LEONORA E. PIPER, AND DOCTOR THOMSON J. HUDSON'S THEORIES IN REGARD TO IT.

BY EX-JUDGE ABRAM H. DAILEY,

Ex-President of the Medico-Legal Society of New York.

In commenting upon a paper coming from the pen of so able a writer as Dr. Thomson J. Hudson has proved himself to be, in fairness to myself it is proper for me to say, that I would not undertake this task did I not feel it my duty to do so. A man placed as I am, who thinks he knows the truth, upon so important a matter as is here under discussion,—a truth affecting the entire human family,—and fails to speak the truth as he finds it, is cowardly, and does violence to a moral law which fair minded persons must recognize.

The subject is spiritism, and the recent utterances of a Mrs. Piper, who has been the instrument for spirit manifestations or otherwise, as the truth shall turn out to be,of many eminent persons for quite a number of years. I was not surprised to hear of her utterances to the effect, that she supposed that what she had said and done in an unconscious condition, could be accounted for by Telepathy; for long before that publication was made in the New York Herald, I had heard that she had stated, that she had no consciousness of what she had said or done in her trance conditions; that she did not know what it was that caused her to do those things. It seems that her utterances have turned out to be truthful, even though made in her unconscious condition, and though they relate to matters of which, in her normal condition, she does not know, and never did possess the slightest knowledge, excepting what she has been told concerning them since they were made. Her integrity is conceded by Dr Hudson. An explanation which does not explain, is no explanation.

Read before the Psychological Section of the Medico-Legal Society of New York, on the 18th day of December, 1901.

In my argument we shall apply the same rule to Dr. Hudson that he invokes in regard to the phenomena in question. I assume that he will be consistent in what he will say in his paper, to be read before the Psychological Section of the Medico-Legal Society, with his arguments contained in his various published works. He undertakes to explain the admitted phenomena, claimed to emanate from discarnate spirits upon the theory of Telepathy and Suggestion, and through the operation of the subjective mind of the psychic. He has invoked a rule in his favor, that the spiritual hypothesis cannot be accepted, if it can be accounted for upon any other natural theory. In other words, the presumption is always against a spiritistic source, and it amounts to this: that it must be proved that it could not possibly have originated from any other than a spiritual source, before it can be accepted.

You will see at the outset, that the poor ghost is at an eminent disadvantage. He is not entitled to even "the benefit of a reasonable doubt." The worst criminal arraigned in a court of justice is presumed to be innocent until he is proven guilty; notwithstanding the great volume of testimony that may be produced against him, if there is a reasonable doubt as to his guilt, he is entitled to the benefit of that doubt and must be acquitted. A man may travel around the world with letters of credit: he may be identified in various ways, so as to be received into the best society in distant countries, or anywhere on the civilized globe; but these letters of credit, or the usual methods of identification, would not be sufficient under the rule applied by Dr. Hudson, in dealing with the ghost, in his endeavors to identify himself to his friends and others, to whom he may desire to come for the benefit, not only of himself, but of the great humanity he has left behind. If he comes, as did Moses and Elias on the Mount of Tranfiguration to Jesus, and to some of his disciples; or as Jesus did to the two Marys at the door of the Sepulcher; or to the two disciples on their journey to Emmaus, and to other of his disciples, such appearances may not be accepted by scientists, because they might possibly be simulated; in other words, the testimony of all spiritual manifestations which has come down the ages, is subject to rejection, and must be rejected by scientists, if it could have been produced or accounted for on any natural hypothesis. To do Dr. Hudson no wrong, I quote from an article from his pen, contained in Harper's Monthly of August, 1900, and it reads:

"I will strenuously insist upon the recognition of the axiom of science, that we have no logical right to attribute any phenomena to supermundane agency, that can be accounted for on the principles of Natural Law." I am a lawyer, and claim to know something of legal principles, and also to have made some investigation into the claims of that great and ever increasing number of people denominated Spiritualists, who embrace within their doctrines the claim of the spiritual source of certain phenomena and manifestations. I don't know of any, who claims that anyone of these cannot be accounted for on the principles of natural law. I know of no persons who are such sticklers for the reign of Natural Law, as these much abused and little understood people. They now number among those, who accept the spiritual source of much of the phenomena, renowned scientists, professors, doctors of divinity, logicians and learned men and women all over the civilized world. I know of no great religion, embraced by the human family, that did not have its origin, to a greater or less extent in spiritual phenomena.

Dr. Hudson is a brave man; he has undertaken to account for a great part of this phenomena, certainly a very valuable part, upon the theory of telepathy, suggestion, auto-suggestion and hypnotism: anything but a spiritual source. This discovery strangely accounts for Abraham's faith, and the deep sleep which fell upon him, when the fortunes and misfortunes of his posterity were revealed to him. It is a strange way of accounting for the voice that called the child "Samuel, Samuel," awakening him from his sleep, and telling him what should befall the house of Eli, which revelation indeed, came true. It must be held to account for the source from which Micaich was able to tell Ahab so truthfully the fate that awaited him should he go out to battle with the king of Syria. If the sub-conscious mind and telepathy account for the numerous other communications in the Old Testament, then they account for the wonderful things given to the world recorded in the New Testamant.

It is long since man was first told to know himself, and certainly I agree with Dr. Hudson, that he has been a long time in attaining his present knowledge. According to Dr. Hudson, man has two minds; his objective mind and his subjective mind. and that as a rule, they are entirely unacquainted with each other. I have always believed, and still believe, that man has a natural and a spiritual body; that the spiritual body may be denominated the soul, the eternal principle of life, which gives the soul of man his spirit, and that, that spirit is immortal and indestructible. I have never believed, nor do I now, that man has two minds. I believe he has but one mind, and that which Dr. Hudson and other scientists denominate the "Sub-conscious Mind," or "Subliminal Consciousness," or the "Subjective Mind"—is part of the one mind, which has the capacity to observe more than one thing at a time, and that it may be used to do more than one thing at the same moment; and that while a man may centre his mind and reasoning faculties upon one thing, he is also conscious of numerous other things which are transpiring around him. They leave their impressions, and may be recalled but not so readily perhaps, as those objectively graven upon that part of the memory which is most in use. The different faculties of the mind are not uniformly developed in any one person. In some they are virtually atrophied for want of use, while others are abnormally keen and sensitive. Carried to its legitimate conclusion, Dr. Hudson's theory finds, that the Subconscious Mind is devoid of the power of reasoning synthetically; that it cannot reason inductively; that its processes are deducive or syllogistic. Therefore, the mind which he has used in writing his paper is the Objective Mind, possessed of the double power of reasoning inductively and deductively, and that this faculty has come from the necessities of pre-existing conditions, and possessing these powers man becomes morally responsible for his mistakes and errors. In the main I agree with him. He holds in his treatises, that "the Objective Mind, is merely the function of the physical brain, while the Subjective Mind, is a distinct entity, possessing independent powers and functions, having a mental organization of its own, and capable of sustaining an existence independent of the body. In other words, that it is the Soul." (Law of Psychic Phenomena, p. 30.) He also holds, "that man in his normal condition, is not controllable against reason, positive knowledge or the evidence of his senses by the suggestions of another." Also, "that the Subjective Mind of man in the hypnotic state, is unqualifiedly and constantly amenable to the power of suggestion," (i. d.) consequently, that the Subjective Mind always accepts as true every suggestion,and acts from that consideration,no matter whether true or false. He claims to sustain this by hypnotic experiments. I admit the facts he cites in support of his various theories, but not all of his conclusions.

He claims, and I agree with him, that we have cases of Auto-Suggestion or Self-Imposed hypnotic conditions, but we do not agree as to the extent to which it can be carried. This occasion does not afford the opportunity to answer many of the arguments advanced by Dr. Hudson, to maintain his theory that all of the phenomena of alleged supermundane sources, can be otherwise accounted for by telepathy and the wonderful operations of the Subjective Mind. If he fails in any one instance, then the rule he has invoked against the ghost will fail, and the ghost will be in evidence; for good rules work both ways; there are no exceptions.

The interesting feature in connection with Dr. Hudson's theory, which I shall here avail myself of, is that he has unquestionably demonstrated to his own satisfaction in his treatises, the existence and immortality of the soul of man, without resorting to any of the phenomena of the Spiritualists. It then follows, that this world since it became generative and life sustaining, has been producing and multiplying life in various forms, the physical part alone being visible. That life, soul and spirit, like all the potencies in the universe are invisible to us in our normal conditions, he must admit. The spiritual part of man he concedes, passed out of the body unobserved, and that it has an abiding place somewhere, he cannot and will not deny. That the Heavens or the Earth, and probably both, are the abodes of these spiritual beings, it seems to me must be admitted. That passing from the material world to the world of spirit, should destroy the identity of, or the affectionate nature of the spirit of man, he does not anywhere contend, but argues the reverse. (See laws Psychic Phenomena, p. 401, &c.) Therefore, the present population of this world is an insignicant number, compared with the countless hosts in the other world.

We start with these facts conceded. 1st. The existence of man, an embodied spirit, certain to become disembodied through death. 2nd. We will accept Dr. Hudson's scientific demonstration of the future life as established by his process of reasoning by inductive, deductive and synthetic methods, and that the soul of man lives on, and is "Over There," or somewhere, in constant evidence to those who are conscious of its presence, in the same sense that we are conscious of each other. Now, his position is, that his method is the scientific method, and the one method by which the existence of the soul of man after death can be demonstrated scientifically. I take issue with him. I deny that the other phenomena is devoid of evidential value. In his article contained in Harper's Magazine, he says: "A moment's consideration will reveal a clear line of demarcation between those phenomena such as rapping, table-tipping, levitation of ponderable bodies without physical contact or mechanical appliances, slate writing, et hoc genus omne. It is not, however, necessary either to doubt or deny that these phenomena are produced by super-normal means except for the purpose of assuming to be ultra- scientific; nor is it necessary to believe in their genuineness; for they all may be fraudulently produced; or they all may be veridical without affecting the question of spirit intercourse."

I would like to discuss fully his position as to this class of phenomena, but I shall refrain from doing so at this time.

I have in this paper assumed that Dr. Hudson will here take the same position, and advance the same or similar arguments contained in his contribution to Harper's Magazine of August, 1900. In this he assumes, First, the integrity of the medium, and Second, the medium believes the communications to be what they purport to be. Third, the medium is unconscious of having any part or lot in determining the contents or characters of the communication, or, of possessing any psychological power or attribute that would render unconscious participation possible. Fourth, that the medium normally possessing no dramatic power, often personates soi-distant spirits with wonderful accuracy, often imitating voice, gesture and mental idiosyncracies of the supposed personality. Fifth, the alleged spirit often manifests mental and normal characteristics, antipodal to those normally possessed by the medium, etc.

He then admits, that if unexplained, those statements, if true, go far towards establishing the validity of the claims o. the spiritists. He then says—and let all the world take note,—using his language: "It would be foolish to deny the facts since they can be so easily substantiated." But, he says, "in view of the discoveries of modern science, the spiritistic theory is no longer tenable. That is to say,—the phenomena can now be accounted for by reference to known psychological laws." He says we shall have no difficulty in finding a solution for all that is mysterious on principles of Natural Law, with which scientists are now well acquainted, principles which are perfectly consistent with the integrity of all concerned, which, "obviates all necessity for seeking a solution in the realms of the supermundane."

He then asserts, that the "solution of all this phase of spiritistic phenomena is found in the Law of Suggestion." That "this law is known to every psychological student, except perhaps a few scientists who are committed to the spiritistic hypothesis." For their benefit he explains what that law is. Briefly, it shows that if a person is hypnotised, the subject is under the control of the hypnotist; the hypnotist has control of the objective mind of the subject, he will have virtually dispossessed it and the subjective mind of the subject is amenable to the law of suggestion, and in that condition, the subject does all the wonderful things any spiritual medium ever did or can do, in addition to all the hypnotic subject has ever done. In aid of his theory of explanation he brings Telepathy and Clairvoyance. The first being the transmission of thought by mental processes alone, and the other the spiritual vision, of what he denominates, the Subjective Mind. I assume that he includes Clairaudience, which is the hearing of a spirit voice, not audible to others.

I find Dr. Hudson's theory admirably presented in his works: but he must admit that the whole of his argument is equally as consistent with the possibility of Spirit Suggestion, as it is to that of a mortal. He does not explain the conduct of the medium, nor the source of the communication, when there is no visible being present to suggest to the psychic the presence of the invisible one. What he attempts will be noted.

Now I will say frankly, that for nearly twenty-five years, I have lived in close relations with some of the best psychics in this country, and am now, and have been intimately acquainted with many from other countries, and Dr. Hudson does not account consistently and rationally for much of the phenomena I have witnessed. The rational and consistent method of reasoning upon which he relies, fails to bring me to his conclusions, for to my mind it has the fault of being neither. Let me give an instance which came under my observation. Something over twenty years ago, a lady of my acquaintance became conscious of some uncommon manifestations in her presence, and suddenly developed clairvoyant and clairaudient powers. In attempting to examine into the phenomena of the Spiritualists with a view to explain them, and explode the spiritistic hypothesis, I became convinced, by some of the most startling phenomena occurring in my presence, which I shall not here describe. I became convinced of its super-mundane source and that I was wrong, and like Paul, I asked, "Lord, what will Thou have me to do?" The answer came, "Wait, and it will be shown to you." Some days later this lady became entranced in my presence, by what claimed to be the spirit of a man, who in this life was a sailor; who during the early part of the Rebellion, had commanded a vessel in the government service; he said he died in the early Sixties, of asthmatic consumption, in the vicinity of New York, aged upwards of sixty wears. To certain questions which I put to him, he refused to give me answers, but as to the place of his nativity, his relatives, many of the incidents and hardships of his early life, of his going out to sea on a whaling ship from New Bedford when a little boy, of the brutality of his captain, of his leaving the ship in a foreign port and being taken up by another captain and taught navigation, and of numerous events in his life, he then told me. He said he had been brought to the lady medium by a daughter of mine, who had been then a good many years in the spirit world, having died in infancy. That he came for the purpose of taking charge of the young medium, of giving to me counsel and warnings insofar as he was able, and that thereby he would help me and advance himself spiritually. He made plain to me, what he required, but required that I should be as faithful to him as he would be to me. He required that I should be kind and charitable, that I should bear testimony to the truth as I found it to be. I have tried to do so, and I shall be astonished to find that I have been deceived and have been misleading others these many years.

Having now been for so many years living in the midst of convincing phenomena, and having thousands of times been wisely advised and deservedly censured and admonished by him, I did not take any steps to verify the truth of his statements as to his identity, or any of the incidents of his early life, until last September, when I went with this lady to New Bedford, Massachusetts, for that express purpose. We had neither of us ever been there, and had no acquaintances in the town. You will pardon me, I hope, for being a little explicit, for in this experience I am confirmed in my position, and meet the argument of Dr. Hudson and other supporters of the telepathic theory. Having alighted from the train, we stepped aside, and I then said: "Now, Captain, we are in your hands, and we want you to do what you can to verify your statement? He immediately replied through the medium: "Do you realize what you ask of me? Do you consider that it is ninety years since I lived here; that I went away when a little boy and seldom came back, and never to stay, and that I have been now away from here entirely, over sixty years; that all I ever knew here are dead long ago? Well, I will do the best I can. We lived in a place up back on the hill called Spruce Lane, now Spruce Street; go there." I went to a coachman and asked him if there was a street called Spruce Lane or Spruce Street in the city. He said, "yes, over back on the hill is a little street by that name." We went then to a hotel and got our dinner, and while there he told us of the name of a former owner, and of the changes that had been made in the hotel. All was true. We then took a coach and drove to Spruce Street. On our way he pointed out, and said through the medium, that where now are paved streets and blocks of houses, when he was a boy, there were open lots, criss-crossed with paths. When we drove into Spruce Lane, he found all was changed; the little house where he said he lived was gone. "Go," said he, "to the grave yards, first to the new one, and look at the tombstones. I will tell you the names before you go of some I knew and who are buried there." He gave us the full names of those persons and the relations they bore to each other. Some of these persons he had mentioned to me in Brooklyn, more than twenty years before. We entered the cemetery and found them as he had given them to us. "Now," said he, "go to the old Second St. cemetery where mother was buried." I asked the driver if there was such a cemetery and he said "yes." Now, twenty years before, in Brooklyn, he had told me of the sad life of his mother, and of her death in want, before poverty drove him to sea. He spoke of his devotion to her, and that when she died, a friend by the name of Spooner had given her a burial place in his family plot. That stones were erected in the plot with the name of Spooner inscribed thereon, but that only a piece of board with her name was placed at the head of his mother's grave. When we reached the old cemetery, we found it closed by a high fence, and the gate locked, but standing by the fence he pointed out to us, one hundred feet or more away, the place of his mother's burial, and we could read the name of Spooner, upon the stones in the plot he pointed to. On our way to the cemetery, he told us that his mother attended a little Mehodist church which we would pass, unless it too was gone. Directly we came to a new but small church, which had succeeded to the old one he had attended. Of that little church he had spoken many years before. We could only remain a few hours in New Bedford, and anticipate going there again to complete the identification of this spirit, whose name while here, was John Taylor. Taylor being a very common family name in New Bedford. The first time this spirit came to me I was alone with the medium, in Brooklyn. His existence was utterly unknown to us. To set the Law of Suggestion at work, there must be a suggester. Who was the suggester in this case? I claim to have obtained some evidence to corroborate his claim to having once lived in New Bedford. From whose subjective mind came the idea to this lady of a sailor by the name of John Taylor, who was born in New Bedford, and all this story of his life?

I have stated a case of facts known neither to the medium nor to any person present; those facts have, to a certain extent, been verified. Will the doctrine of telepathy account for it? If it does, from whence did the telepathic thoughts proceed? They must have originated in the mind of some absent or present person in mortal form, or from some absent or present being in invisible form. They could not have originated in either the mind of the medium or my own. In the absence of any other known method of communicating the name of this personality, and his having put in an appearance declaring his identity and means of determining it, is there any presumption raised that he is what he purports to be? It is true, the medium was not in her normal condition, when he first appeared. The question arises:—is that abnormal condition a manifestation that she is for the time being possessed of a separate intelligence? The fact that truthful statements come through her lips concerning matters of which neither she nor I ever had any knowledge, is very conclusive evidence that the communications are from some other intelligence. If they are not from such a personality, the question is presented: Is it possible that the communication could have originated from any other source? If so, from what source? Has Dr. Hudson anywhere explained? If he can't explain, then the argument is against him and his various theories fail.

I have noted with much interest, that he quotes in his article in Harper's Magazine, from Mr. W. F. H. Myers, recently deceased, saying there is a small percentage of messages apparently telepathic—containing,—that is to say, facts probably unknown to the autonomist, but known to some living person in his company or connected with him. He admits that Mr. Myers, after careful investigation, has committed himself to the spiritualistic theory, and says, he has so quoted him because, he is one of the ablest and fairest of the Psychical Researchers who have committed themselves to the spiritistic hypothesis; and because, he distinctly recognizes telepathy as the obvious explanation of one class of messages, and for the further reason,—using his own language,—"that inasmuch as I shall endeavor to make it clear that all that is mysterious in any of the above named classes of messages is easily explicable under the telepathic theory. I wish first to show definitely the point where our paths diverge. This parting of the ways occurs when the third class of communications is reached, namely, those containing facts known neither to the medium nor to any other person present." He then says that it is at this point that the issue is declared between the two hypothesis—the spiritistic and the telepathic. On one hand, spiritists decline to accept telepathy as a possible factor in the case, if anyone having knowledge of the facts related by the medium is actually present at the sitting. On the other hand, the advocates of the telepathic theory of explanation hold, that if any living person who is in telepathic rapport with any one present, has knowledge of the facts related, we are logically compelled to accept the telepathic hypothesis. This, of course, involves the denial on the one hand, and the affirmation on the other, that more than two persons may be concerned in the transmission of a telepathic message, and it is upon the settlement of this question that the whole controversy hinges. Reduced to its lowest terms, the question at issue may thus be stated affirmatively: "If A can by any known means of communication convey a message to B, B can convey the same message by the same means to C, other things, of course, being equal." He says, the truth of this proposition, seems to be self-evident. Therefore, the proposition advanced by Dr. Hudson amounts to this: that if Jones had known John Taylor in New Bedford ninety years ago; had told Smith about Taylor, and Smith had told Brown what Jones said to him about Taylor and Brown had told Greene what Smith said he had heard about Taylor, and Greene had told White what Brown had told him he had heard about Taylor, and Wite was acquainted with the medium, but had never told the medium what he had heard about Taylor, the doctrine of telepathy, would account for all that came through the lips of the medium, as purporting to come from John Taylor himself, in regard to the incidents of his early life, his career and death. You must bear in mind now, that suggestion apparently plays no part in producing the communication, because White, who knows the medium, is not present; is perhaps a thousand miles away,—knows nothing about what is transpiring, and consequently, cannot suggest to the medium that she should communicate even the name of John Taylor, or attempt to play the role of a sailor. But, in the case I have stated, even White is unknown to the medium, for no person has ever come in contact with her or me, who knew or heard of John Taylor.

Telepathy carried to its utmost, is only the transmission of thought from one intelligence to another. To account for all such communications, involves the necessity of there being several intelligences transmitting the successive statements to the medium, and the medium responding by giving expression in language to them, and they must all be incarnate, otherwise, the spirit hypothesis is involved. The most that all the experiments of the Psychical Research Societies have accomplished, is to establish the possibility of telepathic communication between one mortal and another. The moment it becomes the method of communication between a spirit and a mortal, the spiritistic theory is established and the ghost, becomes an important factor. Telepathy,—signifying thought—transference,—is inapplicable to express the interblending of minds in the manner suggested by Dr. Hudson. That is not thought transference. It becomes the commingling of the mentalities of several persons, whereby they become for the time being at least, common, while the mind of the psychic, like a burglar in a man's house, steals and carries away the secret and priceless jewels of his victim's life.. There is a little truth, and much error in the idea presented. There is a time coming, when man will no longer hide his sins. It is not now. Thought transference is a common language between discarnate spirits. It is possible to a very limited extent between mortals. It is greater between spirits and mortals, when the latter are in a receptive condition, as in moments of repose. Test mediums in an entranced condition, give by clairvoyant powers, and by the aid of discarnate spirits, communications from spirits, and often what only comes from clairvoyance, or soul seeing.

[*To be continued.*]

SPIRITISM, TELEPATHY AND MRS. PIPER.

The Hon. Luther R. Marsh, who had been invited to attend he December session of the Medico-Legal Society and its Psychological Section, was unable to be present, but sent his views in the form of a letter to the President of the Medico-Legal Society as follows:

10 Benton Ave., Middletown, N. Y.
December 16, 1901.

My Dear Mr. Bell.—You know my views on Spiritualism, and you know something of the years I have spent in investigating its phenomena; of the unusual advantage I have enjoyed for its study; and you know, too, of the unmixed desire and intent I have had to learn the real, absolute truth; and you know much of the qualifications I brought to the investigation.

I do not wish to discuss the Piper Episode. I have never regarded her as an uncommon psychic. I have never read any message through her, which seemed to me above the common-place. But she is perfectly honest, I have no doubt;—not the slightest. She believes what she says. When in a full trance she is utterly unconscious of what has been spoken through her; and when she comes to herself, she has no memory of what has taken place. It is natural that she should be incredulous. She cannot realize as true what she hears said as to what has been transmitted through her. I do not wonder at it at all; nor does her dissent, or her ignorance, have the slightest influence on me as bearing on the fact and truthfulness of her communications. That these messages have been given by a power outside of her own powers; that they are infused into her mind, or spoken to her inner ear, and that she has interpreted or delivered them, just as they were given to her, I do not permit myself to doubt. That all the proceedings with her, and by her, including the entire conduct of the learned savants, who have sought her mediumistic aid, have been carried on in perfect integrity, and with an earnest desire to learn the absolute truth; and to avoid all fallacies and phantoms, I have no manner of doubt or of suspicion

The lessons learned from these laborious and long continued experiments, are valuable, instructive and true, beyond any hesitation of mine to believe. And yet they seem to me to be lessons in the incipiency of the Science, Religion, or Philosophy, as you may choose to call it. To me, it is all three.

The experiments which I have seen; the messages I have received; the scenes I have witnessed; the lofty and divine communications vouchsafed to me, are,—and for many years have been—of an order so superior, so much loftier in thought, in eloquence, in expression, to any thing I have heard as coming through the lips of this lady, that I have not felt much interest in the experiments through her, except as valuable to beginners in the study of the great mystery.

The universal assault upon me by the unanimous press of this whole country and of Europe, some years ago, in my first attempt to disclose something of my teachings to the world;—a journalistic cyclone of abuse, vituperation, misrepresentation, derision and caricaturism—while it did not disturb me at all, nor ruffle a hair, has disinclined me to put before the public the results of my experiences.

All deep occult ratisocination, all profound suggestions,all doubts of scientists, and speculations of philosophers, all arguments of skeptics, are idle talk to me, in view of what mine eyes have seen, my ears heard, my fingers touched, my judgment approved. I have confidence in myself. I consider my education at the Bar, through more than half a century in investigating facts, in balancing proofs, in discriminating questions of principle,have given me confidence in judging of matters under my own personal cognizance. I do not ask anyone else to pin any faith in me. I am speaking of my confidence in my own capacity to judge for myself, and in my own pure integrity of purpose.

Science! I do not believe "Science is God," as I once heard a Spiritual lecturer declare. I honor science as highly as any one can. I acknowledge the countless blessings it has showered on humanity. But, after all, what is Science? It does not create. It is a mere observer. It takes account of phenomena, and classifies them. That's all.

If God had not created Nature, Science would have had nothing to observe, or operate upon. There are different kinds of science; real science, and science, as Bacon said, "falsely so-called."

A great deal is said about a scientific investigation of Spiritualism. Every man and woman who has eyes, ears, and common sense, is a Scientist in Spiritualistic manifestations. Why cannot the subject be treated like any other? Why assume that, while, in the common affairs of life, every thing is as it seems, yet, every thing of a Spiritual nature is to be presumed fraudulent? I am bold and audacious enough to believe that I am as good a judge of what I see, and hear, and know,—just as wise and reliable a scientist in that respect—as if I had spent years on years in a careful examination of weights and measures, or in the mysteries of astronomy, botany, mineralolgy, chemistry, mathematics, logic or any other science or art, known in the world. If I see a man, a woman, or know a fact, or witness a transaction, I do not need a learned student or professor to bring it clearly to my consciousness.

The proposition that seems to form the basis of Mr. Hudson's paper may seem justified to him, from the limited range of his inquiries and the lower order of his facts: from, indeed, the messages derived from Mrs. Piper, but, in my judgment it utterly fails in the vast experiences which have come to me.

His conclusion that all the messages received by sensitives has been telepathically acquired, and that, if the sensitive can telepathically impart it, it follows that "Spiritism, considered as a scientific proposition, has not a leg to stand upon; for not a case has yet been recorded that cannot be telepathically explained, if that simple proposition is true," is a statement utterly opposed, in all its parts, to my own experiences, my own convictions, my own knowledge. It cannot stand a moment. It is an assumption utterly unjustified.

Mr. Hudson's thesis is an evident attempt to maintain a pet theory; and though he sometimes seems to take an attitude of equilibrium, yet there constantly peeps out an animus of antagonism, and sneering insinuations, and unfair suggestions, that prove the partisan nature of his argument. I have not time, dear Bell, to point out the unjust and partial allusions, assumptions and implications, and to show how one-sided the article is; nor to specify the wholesale assertions, wholly unfounded, from which I, a Spiritualist, most emphatically dissent.

Mr. Hudson assumes that no information has ever been given by a medium which did not exist, already, in the mind of the sitter; an assumption he has no authority for making. Then he assumes that what is in the secret and unsuspected recesses of the sitter's mind,can be,without the sitter's knowing of it, telepathically conveyed to the mind of the medium; who reads it out as a spiritual communication. This seems a desperate effort to evade an obvious fact; obvious to every one but a scientific savant. The medium, some way, by a telepathic touch, stirs into activity the endless arcana of knowledge that somehow got into the sitter's mind,—nobody knows how,—and wholly unsuspected by him, and lo! there is unfolded to her vision the whole domain, natural or spiritual, of all that was ever known. This is science run mad! The sitter, it seems, has two minds in one body;—in one spirit or soul;—one, an outside or overcoat mind, of very limited powers and accumlations, fitted only for ordinary transactions; the other, an interior, hidden, subliminal, subjective mind, filled, chuck-full, with all things that have ever transpired in the world, and in the spirit sphere, and which, like holding certain writings to the fire, come out in bold relief, though unconsciously, and while keeping the owner in Egyptian darkness, illuminates the medium.

How the sitter,—who may pass for an ignorant, uneducated man, acquired, "unbeknownst" to himself, or to anybody else, these vast store-houses of knowledge;—having never bestowed a thought on the subject, in his waking moments, is a bewildering mystery. In the Piper case, she had, according to Hudson, an uncommon source of information in the well-stored subliminal mind of Prof. Hyslop, and, if so, some might wonder that she did not evoke some lofty spiritual thought, more worthy of record. Professor Hyslop didn't know how much he knew! why should he spend laborious days and weary nights, in studying, when he has only to tap,telepathically,his own exhaustless, subjective stores,open his concealed knowledge box; lift his subliminal knowledge "above the threshold of normal consciousness," bring his secret information out of his subjective cellar into the light, and flood the world!

Much attention seems to have been given to minor material details, such as jacknives, nails, skull-caps, relatives, diseases;—things which it might be supposed would not be carefully carried in the memory of a spirit introduced into a new world, of a wholly different character, and with new surroundings and associates;—where such little immaterial details of an abandoned earth-life were not of the slightest consequence, and not worth remembering.

Give a man a chance to assume what he wants; to lay down his own premises; to set up his own man of straw; and feeble must be his muscles if he cannot demolish it with a blow. So, Hudson fulminates his broad assertions, unsupported by any authority but his own assumptions. In his views, how crystal clear it all is! Hyslop, all the time, had this information in the secret chest of his subjective mind; Piper points a telepathic finger at the lock, and out comes the overflowing knowledges to enlighten mankind. Euclid's demonstrations are unsatisfactory in comparison!

My Beloved Clark Bell,—a wee bit of faith—a mere suspicion of it—a soupcon—would not, it seems to me, do any harm, in the consideration of spiritual themes. But that is a quality which, I perceive, is wholly discarded, by these great intellects, which, as they think, are sufficient unto themselves. He, from whom these intellects are derived, is an unknown factor, in their discussions; His messengers are disregarded, and everything is brought down to a purely natural plane. One would not suspect, throughout the whole debate, that there was any God, or any spiritual intuition. A very respectable thinker,—one of remarkable spiritual insight,—once said:

"The natural man receiveth not the things of the Spirit of God, for they are foolishness unto him, neither can he know them, because they are spiritually discerned."

I do not present my views to you, Dear Clark, as having any reference to the Piper manifestations, or the Hyslop report, for they all seem to me to be very inadequate, and not rising to the greatness of the theme, or the demonstrations of fact. And if Mr. Hudson had confined himself to an answer to them, I would not have troubled you with any expression or dissent of my own.

It is astonishing how ingenious men can confuse, distort and entangle the plainest facts. There seems to be nothing but what can be plausibly argued against. Specious arguments have been put forth, proving that Napoleon Bonaparte was a myth, never having had any real existence. But I have faith in the "Little Corporal;" and I have faith in the messages and manifestations I have received, through years, from the spirits of those who once lived on this earth plane in the flesh, and who now are residents of the spirit spheres. I see no explanation of them in telepathy, nor in the theory of subliminal consciousness, of subjective mind, of secret accumulations of knowledge, of strained and occult fancies, or bold assumptions, nor in the memory of the other mind, which, it is supposed, really exists, inside, outside, or along side, of what we have been accustomed to consider as our only mind.

Strange how people will puzzle their brains, and sit up nights, to study out some mode of avoiding, paddling around, or explaining, the clearest, plainest facts of consciousness, if, only, such facts have any relation to that life to which all mortals tend!

My Dear Clark, I opened your package, this evening, and, taking up the galleys of Mr. Hudson's article, read it, and sat immediately down to the table, and hastily wrote down the foregoing suggestions started by his screed.

I then took up your own galley, and, if I had read that before, I probably should not have written anything on the subject.

I must confess myself somewhat surprised at your unqualified avowal in regard to spiritual manifestations.

But I have experienced the futility of trying, by argument, to convince anybody in spiritual themes. Each looks through his own lens.

Yours ever and most decidedly,

LUTHER R. MARSH.

SPIRITISM, TELEPATHY AND MRS. PIPER.

BY H. C. WRIGHT, EDITOR OF ELTKA.

Mr. H. C. Wright, the editor of the Journal Eltka, who was invited to attend the meeting of the Psychological Section of the Medico-Legal Society in joint session with the parent body, unable to be present, responded as follows:—

Corry, Pa., Dec. 16, 1901.

Mr. Clark Bell, 39 Broadway, New York.

Dear Sir.—Your letter of invitation to attend the annual meeting of the Medico-Legal Society was duly received, and I wish to express my sincere appreciation of your kindness. I regret being obliged to state that it will be impossible for me to attend. The pressure of my work at present also makes it impossible for me to properly prepare a paper expressing my views and the evidence upon which they are based; this I would gladly have done had there been better opportunity. My conclusions have been arrived at as the result of personal experience and actual demonstration, rather than from book study; that is, I have endeavored to verify (or otherwise), all accounts before admitting them to my belief. I have studied and practiced hypnotism, in private, the past twelve years, and an important part of my experimental work has been with a "psychic" ("medium," sensitive," or whatever term you prefer) who is also unknown, in that capacity, to the general public (a gentleman, who, for sometime, was professor of Chemistry and Physics in the Meadville, Pa., High School). In our work we have reproduced, under absolutely satisfactory circumstances, practically all the phenomena mentioned in the paper by Camille Flamarion, which appeared in the December, 1897, Arena. Also have taken reports of the Society for Psychical Research, and in telepathic work have in some instances, we believe, improved upon them.

A part of my views might be briefly expressed as follows:

Either the theory of telepathy or the theory of spiritism will account for all the communications received by Mrs. Piper, and similar cases.

Telepathy, considered as communications between living brain, or action of the 'subjective mind," can account for all communications, even for that which gives facts "known" only to a deceased person, because the fact may have been telepathically communicated to the "subjective mind" of living persons before the decease of first person; the fact being later communicated telepathically from the person who is unconscious of being the holder of the knowledge to the "sensitive" who is able to make it known.

The view as entertained by many, that the "sub-conscious mind" is under control of, or susceptible to suggestion from the "conscious mind" is, I believe, in exact opposition to the facts. I hold that the "conscious mind" is completely under control of the "sub-conscious;" or, to get nearer to my meaning, the "conscious mind" is not a thing in itself, but merely a manifestation of the "sub-consciousness."

In regard to Spiritism:

I believe that existence is perpetual.

That the change which takes place at death is, to our present mind, inconceivable.

That we do not take with us, in its present form, our mind, intellect, emotions, etc., any more than we take with us our present body.

That we do merge into a universal "consciousness" (though here the word "consciousness" cannot express the idea.)

That this universal (which already includes us), may and does manifest itself through "Psychics," like Mrs. Piper (and everyone else); and this manifestation is limited only by our ability to comprehend.

I believe "mediums," in their highest development, cease to be "controlled" by a "personality." (I think this will eventually be the case with Mrs. Piper.)

I will be pleased in the future to send you reports of experiments which we conduct, when they are of such a nature as to be of interest to you; and should you find it convenient to send me a report of the proceedings of the present meeting I should be greatly indebted to you.

I regret that I have not been able to collect a more valuable letter for you. Thanking you once more for your kindness, I am

Yours sincerely,

H. C. WRIGHT.

MEDICO-LEGAL SURGERY.

ASSOCIATE EDITORS.

Medical.	*Legal.*
Granville P. Conn, M. D., Concord, N. H.	Clarence A. Lightner, Esq., Detroit, Mich
R. Harvey Reed, M. D., Wyoming.	Judge Wm. H. Francis, New York.
Nicholas Senn, M. D., Chicago, Ill.	Prof. A. P. Grinnell, M. D., Burlington, Vt.
Webb J. Kelley, M. D., Galion, Ohio.	

This department is conducted as the organ of the Section of the Medical Jurisprudence of Surgery of the Medico-Legal Society. Its officers for 1901 are as follows:

Chairman.

Chief Surgeon Charles K. Cole, M.D., of Helena, Montana.

LEGAL. Vice-Chairmen.	*SURGICAL. Vice-Chairmen.*
Clark Bell, Esq., of New York.	Ch. Surg W. A. Adams, of Ft. Worth. Tex.
Judge W. H. Francis, of New York.	Ch. Surg. F. H. Caldwell, M. D., of Fla.
Hon. J. W. Fellows, of N. H.	Ch. Sur. Granville P. Conn, M. D., of N. H.
Hon. W. C. Howell, of Iowa.	Ch. Surg. W. B. Outten, M. D., of Missouri.
A. P. Grinnell, M. D., of Vermont.	Surgeon Geo. Chaffee, M. D., of Brooklyn.
Hon. A. R. Parmenter, of Troy, N. Y.	Ch. Surg. B. F. Eads, M. D., of Texas.
Hon. George R. Peck, of Illinois.	Ch. Surg. John E. Owen, M. D., of Chicago.
Hon. J. M. Thurston, of Nebraska.	Surg. Gen. R. Harvey Reed, M. D., of Wy.
Judge A. H. Dailey, of Brooklyn, N. Y.	Surg. Gen. Nicholas Senn, M. D., of Ill.
Hon. Allen Zollers, of Indiana.	Ch. Surg. S. S. Thorne, M. D., of Ohio.
Secretary.	*Treasurer.*
Clark Bell, Esq., 39 Broadway, N. Y.	Judge Wm. H. Francis, New York City. 39 Broadway, N. Y.

Executive Committee.

Clark Bell, Esq., Chairman.

Surg. Thomas Darlington, M. D., of N. Y.	Sur. R. S. Parkhill, M. D., of Hornelsville, N. Y.
L. L. Gilbert, Esq., Pittsburg, Pa.	Sur. Fayette H. Peck, M. D., of Utica, N. Y.
Ex-Ch. Sur. Geo. Goodfellow, M. D., Cal.	Chief Sur. T. I. Pritchard, of Wis.
Surgeon J. N. Hall, of Denver, Colo.	R. C. Richards, Esq., of Chicago, Ill.
Chief Surg. A. C. Scott, M. D., of Texas.	Ch. Surg. F. A. Stillings, M. D., of N. H.
Judge A. H. Dailey, of Brooklyn, N. Y.	Ch Surg. J. J. Buckley, Missoula, Montana

To Railway Surgeons and Railway Counsel:

We take occasion to advise you to unite with the Section of Medico-Legal Surgery, which can now be done by an annual subscription of $1.50, entitling each member to the *Medico-Legal Journal* free.

G. P. CONN, M. D., *Ex-Chairman Section Med.-Leg. Surgery.*	ABRAM H. DAILEY, *Ex-President Medico-Legal Society of New York.*
SAMUEL S. THORN, M. D., *Chief Surgeon T., St. L. & K. C. Railway Co., Ex-President National Association Railway Surgeons.*	J. B. MURDOCH, M. D., *Surgeon and Ex-President National Association of Railway Surgeons.*
R. S. HARNDEN, M. D., *Ex-President New York State Association Railway Surgeons. Ex-President Erie Railway Surgeons.*	R. HARVEY REED, M. D., *Surgeon General of State of Wyoming,*
	HUBBARD W. MITCHEL, M. D., *Ex-President Medico-Legal Society of New York.*

Members of the Section on Medico-Legal Surgery, who have not remitted their annual subscription to the Section, will please send same to Judge Wm. H. Francis, No. 39 Broadway, N. Y., and members will please not confound the Section Dues with the Annual Dues of the Society, which should be remitted to Caroline J. Taylor, Treasurer, Bridgeport, Conn. Members of the Society or Section will please propose names for membership in this Section.

It is proposed that members of the Society and Section each donate one bound volume annually to the Library of the Medico-Legal Society, by action of the Executive Committee.

The following new members of the Section are announced: J. P. Webster, M. D., Ex-Pres. Erie Railway Surgeons, Chicago, Ills.; W. L. Cuddebuck, M. D., Pres. Erie Railway Surgeons, Port Jervis, N. Y.; Dr. A. E. Ellingwood, Attica, N, Y.; Chief Surgeon J. J. Buckley, N. P. Ry. Co., Missoula, Montana.

SELECTIONS AND EXCERPTS.

SMALLPOX AND VACCINATION.

We clip the following from the Monthly Bulletin of the State Board of Health of Connecticut for October. Dr. Lindsley is a high authority in sanitary science:

Several recent invasions of smallpox into the state, chiefly from New York and Canada, make the following correspondence of special interest:

Voluntown, Nov. 9th, 1901.

Dr. C. A. Lindsley, Secretary, &c.

Dear Sir:—As smallpox is in Moosup and Sterling, close by us, would you not think it advisable to vaccinate the school children and all others that need to be, provided the parents of the children are willing? And how would it do to ask the Selectmen to foot the bills for all those who are not able to pay the usual vaccination fee?

Yours truly,

W. R. DAVIS, Health Officer.

[The Response.]

Dr. W. R. Davis, Health Officer,

My Dear Doctor:—There is but one reasonable answer to your question.

There can be no doubt that it is the part of wisdom and prudence to have all the children in your town vaccinated who have not been already protected by that means. It is not wise to wait until your neighbor's house is on fire before you try to get your own insured.

I would suggest that you plainly lay the matter before your board of selectmen and ask them to offer free vaccination to all who feel that the expense will be a burden. It has always been observed that there are in every community a few who are abundantly able to pay the vaccination fee, but who will take advantage of the opportunity at the public charge. But even so, it is better and far cheaper for the general welfare, to tolerate the imposition than to suffer an epidemic of smallpox.

An epidemic of smallpox is impossible in a well-vaccinated community. Such is the undeviating experience of the last hundred years throughout the civilized world. Hoping your selectmen will see the wisdom of such a course, I remain very truly yours.

C. A. LINDSLEY, Secretary.

At no time since the discovery of the protective powers of vaccination has it been possible to do the operation with less risk of ill effects than at the present. Formerly there were two sources of trouble to which a vaccinated person might be exposed. One was the very rare introduction of a germ disease with vaccine virus taken from the human subject. The other was the contamination of the virus with septic matter and a more or less severe septic inflammation. Or the latter effect may have been caused by the careless exposure of the broken vaccine vesicle to septic contact. The first danger is avoided by the use of bovine virus, calves not being subject to diseases communicable to man.

The second risk is avoided by the extreme precautions which are taken to avoid septic contamination of the virus, by several well-known establishments engaged in the production of it. It only remains to protect the aseptic conditions in the application of it. The seriousness of the operation is not sufficiently appreciated by the public. The proper condition and preparation of the subject is highly important. It ought not, as too often heretofore, to be entrusted to parents, school teachers, or any conceited wiseacres, who think they can "do it well enough." Spurious vaccination with septic matter has been a potent influence in bringing discredit upon the practice. - It is an operation of too much consequence to the welfare of the subject and of the community to be trifled with.

Respectfully submitted,

C. A. LINDSLEY, M. D.,
Secretary of State Board of Health, and
Superintendent of Vital Statistics.

New Haven, November 15, 1901.

ARGENTAMINE is a more efficient, non-irritating and non-caustic substitute for silver nitrate, being a solution of that salt in ethylenediamine, which is a solvent of albumin and pus corpuscles.

It has the most vigorously penetrative properties of all the newer silver preparations, since the alkaline ethylenediamine prevents the precipitation of the silver by the chlorides and albumins, and permits the salt to unfold its full energy in the depths of the tissues.

Its bactericide power is greater than that of any other antiseptic, and it is thus the most reliable, active and innocuous of all the silver preparations.

Owing to its great affinity for the tissues, argentamine surpasses all other silver compounds in rapidity of action, and hence should especially be employed in every case of chronic gonorrhoea.

By Dr. Ludwig Kamen, Regimental Surgeon at Czernowitz in an article in Die Heilkunde, Vienna, June and July, 1899, said:

Argentamine is relatively the most powerful of all these antiseptics, more especially when its rapidity of action is taken into account.

Much has been said of the amount of silver contained in these various drugs, whose efficacy was supposed to depend thereon. Kamen's experiments prove to his satisfaction that Argentamine with 6.35 per cent. of metallic silver has a more energetic action than largin with 11 per cent. There must be another efficient factor in their action and such has indeed been noticed.

Schaffer found that Argentamine has a much greater affinity for the tissues than the nitrate of silver, and that, therefore, in an equal space of time it penetrates much more deeply into them. This was tested by placing cubes of rabbit liver of equal size in 1:2000 silver nitrate and Argentamine solutions, and allowing them to remain in a dark place. They were then placed in a dilute ammonium sulphide solution. The depth of the dark brown precipitate that formed was three times as great with Argentamine as with the nitrate. Stronger, such as ½ per cent. solutions, showed still greater differences, the Argentamine discoloration being five times more extensive.

Pezzoli has made similar experiments with human liver, the depth of the affected tissue being measured micrometrically. His figures are: Argentamine, 100; nitrate of silver, 66; largin, 58; and protargol, 38 microns.

Pezzoli has illustrated this by the following experiment: Four gelatin culture tubes were each inoculated with a drop of bouillon culture bacterium coli, shaken, and allowed to set. Then solutions of the four silver salts were poured on each, and the tubes preserved in the dark at the ordinary tempature. After three or four days it was found that no growth of the bacterium had taken place for a certain depth in each tube. The sterile zone was found to measure as follows: Argentamine, 16 mm.; silver nitrate, 4 mm.; largin, 10 mm.; and protargol, 5mm. There was also a cheesy deposit on the surface of the gelatin, which evidently influenced the imbibition of the drugs, and the depth of which was as follows: Argentamine, 1mm.; nitrate of silver, 6mm.; largin, 2mm.; and protargol, 3 mm.

Here also Argentamine proved itself superior to the other drugs.

Kamen has repeated Pezzoli's experiments exactly, using 1 per cent. solutions of Argentamine, argonin, largin, and protargol. In twenty-four hours the gelatin was thickly clouded, and contained some gas bubbles. The contact zones in the four tubes differed markedly in aspect.

With Argentamine the sterile zone measured 7mm., showed absolutely no growth, and the gelatin, was entirely clear.

With largin the sterile zone was 5mm. high.

With argonin it was also 5mm. high; but it was not quite transparent, and showed some signs of bacterial growth.

With protargol bacterial growth was only hindered, not stopped, in a zone, 5mm. broad.

So far as the nutrient gelatin goes, therefore, Argentamine showed the greatest and protargol the least penetrating power.

Dr. S. A. Buchanan, of Philadelphia, in a letter to the Editor of The Medical Summary, says:

"As regard the treatment of haemorrhoids, first we must relieve the constipation, and at the same time produce a shrinkage and retrogression of both the superficial and deep-seated veins, diminishing inflammatory action and markedly increasing the patient's comfort.

"I know that nothing has been more effective in producing the above results than Anusol Suppositories, which are a combination of zinc oxide, balsam Peru, bismuth with iodo-resorcin sulphonic acid, which seems to have a specific action upon the rectal mucosa.

"I have used the Anusol Suppositories in itching piles with most gratifying results."

Reynold W. Wilcox, M. D., Professor of Medicine and Therapeutics at the New York Post-Graduate Medical School and Attending Physician to the Hospital; Visiting Physician to St. Mark's Hospital, New York, writes under date January 9th, 1901:

"I have prescribed the bismuth iodo-resorcin-suppositories sold by you under the name of Anusol with excellent success for the pruritus ani so frequently encountered in gouty subjects. I presume it is generally admitted that this a most intractable symptom and relief by ordinary methods is not easy to obtain."

Dr. J. Williams, Kenesaw, Neb., writes under date of January 26th, 1901:

"I have used the Anusol Suppositories with entire satisfaction."

Personal experience and the testimony of many relieved sufferers has convinced us that actually marvelous benefit is derived from the use of Anusol in haemorrhoids. A trial will satisfy the most sceptical.—The American Therapist, September, 1900.

SELECTIONS.

HYDROLEINE.

In considering the value of any well-known remedy, like Cod-Liver Oil, in Tuberculosis, it is important to know how the medical profession regard it. Its usefulness is unquestioned, but in what form can it be presented to the victim of tuberculosis so as to overcome the loathing for fat food that so often accompanies that disease?

Dr. A. N. Bell, editor of the "Sanitarium" and honorary president of the American Congress of Tuberculosis, thus speaks of one of the prominent factors in overcoming these obstacles:

"Pancreatine, as an adjuvant to Cod-Liver Oil, is of much greater significance than Pepsin. But it must be borne in mind that its relation to acids is the reverse of that of pepsin. Pancreatine is, if unprotected by an alkali, neutralized by acids; hence, the particular utility of soda in the formula for Hydroleine. Pancreatine converts starch into sugar, dissolves albuminoids in an alkaline medium, and emulsifies fat so that the minute particles of it can be easily absorbed by the intestines."

And, speaking of the value of this remedy, says:

"Considering the properties, therapeutic value and uses of Cod-Liver Oil; the indigestion common to incipient tuberculosis, and the difficulty of rendering Cod-Liver Oil palatable and acceptable to the stomach under such conditions, and the process of digestion which should always be kept in view, as above briefly described: Hydroleine, in my opinion, combines in an eminent degree pure Cod-Liver Oil with such adjuvants as are best calculated to maintain its excellence, render it palatable and acceptable to the stomach, promotive of its favorable action in the treatment of tuberculosis and in cases of defective nutrition from other causes."

Such eminent names in the profession as James Tyson, M. D., Alfred Stille, M. D., William Gilman Thompson, M. D., Francis Delafield, M. D., Abraham Jacobi, M. D., have placed themselves on record as to the great value of Cod-Liver Oil as a food and efficient remedy in the treatment of Phthisis Pulmonalis. The problem has been, how can it be so prepared as to retain all its curative properties and overcome the repugnance of the patient?

The discoveries which have led to the production of Hydroleine, combining pancreatin, sodium carbonate, cod-liver oil, salicylic acid, with distilled water, in an emulsion, seem, in the general judgment of medical men, to have solved all the difficulties of this problem.

The C. N. Crittenton Co. are receiving testimonials from all sources—sufferers, as well as their physicians—as to the remarkable success of this remedy. One of the most convincing is a recent letter to them from Dr. Herbert L. Stebbins, of Syracuse, dated November 20th, 1901, in which he says:

"I consider Hydroleine the best flesh producer on the market. I used it four months and gained thirty-eight pounds."

TETANUS AND VACCINE VIRUS.

We insert with pleasure the following communication from Parke, Davis & Co:

Detroit, Mich., U. S. A., Dec. 6, 1901.

Clark Bell, Esq., Editor Medico-Legal Journal, 39 Broadway, New York City.

Dear Sir:—We ask a favor which we believe you can grant with perfect propriety in the columns of your valued periodical, and which will be a simple act of veracity and justice to us.

We respectfully ask you to apprise your readers, on the faith of our positive assurance to you, that not one of the recent tetanus fatalities following vaccination at Camden, Atlantic City, Bristol, Brooklyn, Cleveland and St. John, N. B., succeeded the employment of our Vaccine Virus. In not a single, solitary one of these cases was our Vaccine used. We incriminate no one's Vaccine, but we propose to assert the truth about our own. If we can prevent it, no physician or pharmacist shall labor under the false impression that a fatality has ever followed, either by coincidence or by cause and effect, the application of vaccine virus or serum bearing our name. Very respectfully yours,

PARKE, DAVIS & CO.

TRANSACTIONS.

MEDICO-LEGAL SOCIETY—OPENING FALL MEETING.

OCTOBER 18, 1901.

Society met at dinner at Hotel Plavano, 53 W. 35th Street, New York city. After the cloth was removed the Society met, the President, Clark Bell, Esq., in the chair, and Samuel Bell Thomas acting as Secretary.

On recommendation of the Executive Committee the following were duly elected members of the Society. On recommendation of Clark Bell, Esq.,

T. W. P. Smithwick, M. D., La Grang, N. C.
T. B. Lacey, M. D., Council Bluffs, Iowa.
John C. Clayberg, Esq., Helena, Montana.
Mr. Jivanlal V. Desai, Esq., B. A., Ahmedabad, India.
James A. Egan, M. D., Sec. State Board of Health, Springfield, Ill.
M. M. Smith, M. D., Austin, Texas.
Mihran K. Kassabian, M. D., 1808 Green Street, Philadelphia, Pa.
Charles G. Wagner, M. D., Supt. of State Hospital, Binghampton, New York.
Walter Lindley, M. D., 315 West 6th St., Los Angeles, Cal.
C. C. Carroll, M. D., 22 West 32d Street, New York City.
Edwin Reynolds, M. D., 129 Lafayette Avenue, Brooklyn, N. Y.
George Theodore Mundorff, M. D., 224 East 18th Street, N. Y. City.

The paper of the evening was read by Dr. Mihran R. Kassabian, of Philadelphia, entitled "The X-Ray in Forensic Medicine."

The paper was splendidly illustrated by Skiographs, which were passed and examined by the members.

The paper was discussed by Dr. J. Mount Bleyer, Judge Abraham H. Daily, F. L. Hoffman, Esq., and others.

Reports of delegates to the London Congress of Tuberculosis were made and read by Dr. A. Bernays, of St. Louis, Mo.; Dr. J. C. Shrader, of Des Moines, Iowa; Dr. H. Edwin Lewis, Burlington, Vt.; B. J. Leffingwell Hatch, New York, and F. L. Hoffman, Esq., of the Prudential Life Ins. Co., of Newark, N. J. The chair reported on the progress of the work of the American Congress of Tuberculosis. The Society adjourned at a late hour.

CLARK BELL,
President.

SAMUEL BELL THOMAS,
Acting Secretary.

NOVEMBER MEETING, 1901.

November 20, 1901, the Society met at dinner at Hotel Plavano, the President Clark Bell in the chair, and Samuel Bell Thomas, Esq., Assistant Secretary, acting as Secretary.

After dinner the chair called the Society to order. The reading of the minutes of October meeting was laid over.

On recommendation of the Executive Committee, the following were duly elected by unanmous vote of the body. Recommended by Clark Bell, Esq.:

ACTIVE.

Wm. S. Magill, M. D., of No. 1272 Boston Road, New York City.
Dr. Charles F. Sanborn, Assistant Physician at Willard State Hospital, Willard, N. Y.

CORRESPONDING.

Dr. August Fernandez Caro, Secretary General International Congress of Medicine, Faculte de Medicine, Madrid, Spain.
Proposed by Clark Bell, Esq.:
Dr. Julian Callega, Presidente XIV International Medical Congress of 1903, Madrid, Spain.
Dr. Alfred F. de Faria, editor Revista das Revistas, Porto, Portugal
Monsieur Vanden Fleavel, Minister of Justice, Brussels, Belgium.
Monsieur Francotte Member of the Chamber of Deputies, Brussels,
Monsieur Delbastee, Member of Chamber of Deputies, Brussels, Belgium.
Kanchiro Takagi, F. R. C. S., England, President Sei I Kwai Society, Tokio, Japan.
B. Tomatsuri, Esq., editor Sei-I-kwai Medical Journal. Tokio, Japan
Prof. Dr. Ch. Colombo, Editor Review International Therapis Physique, via Plinio, Rome, Italy.
Wm. Farr LL. M., President Oklahoma College of Law, Oklahoma City, Oklahoma.
W. W. Curran, M. D., Editor "The Medical Critic," 154 E. 72nd. Street, New York City.
Hon. Thomas A. Moran, LL. D., Dean of the College of Law, Chicago, Ill.
Hon. Howard N. Ogden, Ph. F., President Illinois College of Law, 112 Clark St., Chicago, Ill.
Hon. John N. Jewett, Dean of the John Marshall Law School, 107 Dearborn Street, Chicago, Ill.
Judge Owen T. Reeves, Dean Bloomington Law School, Bloomington, Ill.
Dr. Verniory, Prest. Med. Leg. Society of Belgium, Namur.
Dr. Van Bever, Vice-Prest., Antwerp, Belgium.
Prof. Dr. Strassman, Berlin, Germany.

HONORARY.

Hon. Luther P. Marsh, of Middletown, late of the Bar of N. Y.

The paper of the evening was read by Dr. Wm. S. Magill, entitled "Poison by Aconite." (The Conden Case), in noting the physiological analysis of alkaloids." It was discussed by Dr. J. Mount Bleyer, Esq., A. H. Daily, Henry Wollman, Esq., the chair and Dr. Bettini G. di Moise.

Nominations were in order and the following nominations were made for officers for the ensuing year:

MEDICO-LEGAL SOCIETY.

OFFICERS FOR 1902.

President,
CLARK BELL, Esq., of New York.

1st Vice-President,
A. P. GRINNELL, M. D., Burlington, Vt.

2nd Vice-President,
T. D. CROTHERS, M. D., of Conn.
J. MOUNT BLEYER, M. D., of N. Y. City.

Vice-Presidents for the States, Territories and Provinces.

Alabama—Judge Thos. W. Coleman, Montgomery.
Alaska—Clarence Thwing, M. D., Sitka.
Arizona—D. M. Purman, M. D., Phoenix.
Arkansas—H. C. Dunavant, M. D., Osceola.
Austria—Prof. R. Krafft-Ebing, Vienna.
Belgium—Dr. Jules Morel, Mons.
Brazil—Prof. Nina Rodrigues, M. D., Bahia.
British Honduras—Adam Chevaillier, M. D., Balize
California—A. E. Osborne, M. D., Glen Ellen.
Colorado—Prof. J. T. Eskridge, M. D., Denver.
Connecticut—Judge A. M. Tallmadge, Bridgeport.
China—Harold Browett, Esq., Shanghai.
Cuba—Chief Justice Hechavarria, of Santiago
Dakota, N.—Dr. Dwight S. Moore, Jamestown.
Dakota, S.—John M. Harcourt, Steele.
Delaware—Judge Ignatius C. Grubb, Wilm'gt'n.
Denmark—Prof. Godeken, Copenhagen.
District of Columbia—W. C. Woodward, M. D., Washington, D. C.
Dom of Canada—Hon. A. G. Blair, Ottawa.
England—Dr. Fletcher Beach, London.
Ecuador—Senor J. M. P. Cammano, Wash. D. C.
Florida—N. de V. Howard, M. D., Sanford.
France—Victor Parent, M. D., Toulouse.
Georgia—Richard J. Nunn, M. D., Savannah.
Germany—Dr. H. Laehr, Berlin.
Guatemala—Senor Rafael Montufar.
Hawaii—J. W. Waughop M. D., Kalia Kanai
Hayti.—Genl. J. A. Bordes, Jeremie.
Holland—Dr. P. A. H. Sueens, Vucht.
Hungary—Staatsanwalt Em. V. Havas, Buda Pesth
Illinois—J. E. Owens, M. D., Chicago.
India—P. S. Sivaswamy Aiyar, Madras.
Indiana—W. B. Fletcher, M. D., Indianapolis.
Indian Territory—I. H. Bailey, M. D., Dexter.
Iowa—Jennie McCowen, M. D., Davenport
Ireland—Conolly Norman, M. D., Dublin.
Italy—Enrico Ferri, M. D., Rome.
Japan—Dr. J. Hashimoto, Tokio.
Kansas—Judge Albert H. Horton, Topeka
Kentucky—F. H. Clark, M. D., Lexington.
Louisiana—J. J. Scott, M. D., Shreveport.
Maine—Judge L. A. Emery, Ellsworth.
Manitoba—D. Young, M. D., Selkirk
Maryland—Wm. Lee Howard, M. D., Baltimore.
Massachusetts—Theo. H. Tyndale, Boston.
Mexico—Leon Lewis, M. D., Ozuluama.
Michigan—Clarence A. Lightner, Detroit.
Minnesota—C. K. Bartlett, M. D., Minneapolis.
Missouri—W. B. Outten, M. D., St. Louis.
Montana—C. K. Cole, M. D., Helena.
Nebraska—Hon. John M. Thurston, Omaha.
Nevada—S. M. Bishop, M. D., Reno.
New Brunswick—Dr. Wm. Bayard, St. John.
Newfoundland—Dr. K. D. McKenzie, St. Johns.
New Hampshire—Gran. F. Conn, M. D., Concord.
New Jersey—Judge C. G. Garrison, Camden.
New Mexico—Gov. Bradford L. Prince, Santa Fe.
New South Wales—George A. Tucker, M. D.
New York—Mrs. M. Louise Thomas, N. Y. City.
New Zealand—Prof. Frank G. Ogston, Dunedin.
North Carolina—E. C. Smith, Esq., Raleigh.
Norway—Dr. Harold Smedal, Christiana.
Nova Scotia—Hon. Wm. S. Fielding, Ottawa.
Ohio—Judge H. C. White, Cleveland.
Oklahoma Ter.—A. H. Simonton, M. D., Okla. Cy.
Ontario—Daniel Clark, M. D., Toronto
Oregon—Ex-Chief Just. Hon. Wm. P. Lord, Salem.
Pennsylvania—Geo. B. Miller, M. D., of Phila.
Peru—Senor F. C. C. Zegarro, Washington, D. C.
Portugal—Bettincourt Rodriguez, M. D., Lisbon.
Quebec—Wyatt Johnson, M. D., Montreal.
Rhode Island—Judge P. E. Tillinghast, Provid'e
Russia—Prof. Dr. Mierzejewski, St. Petersburgh.
San Domingo—A. Wei Yos Gil, San Domingo.
Saxony—Judge de Alinge, Oberkotzon Hof.
Scotland—W. W. Ireland, Edinburgh.
Servia—Hon. Paul Savitch, Belgrade.
Sicily—Prof. Dr. Fernando Puglia, Messina.
Silesia—H. Kornfeld, M. D., Grotkau.
South Carolina—S. W. Babcock, M. D., Columbia.
Spain—Sig. A. M. Alv. Taladriz, M. D., Valladolid.
Sweden—Prof. Dr. A. Winroth, Lund.
Switzerland—Prof. Dr. L. Wille, Basle.
Tennessee—Michael Campbell, M. D., Nashville.
Texas—Dr. D. R. Wallace, Terrell.
Tonga—Dr. Donald McClennen, Tonga.
Utah—Frederick Clift, M. D., St. George.
Vermont—Henry D. Holton, M. D., Brattleboro.
Virginia—William F. Drewry, Petersburg.
Washington—Jas. C. Waugh, M. D., Mt. Vernon.
West Virginia—F. M. Hood, M. D., Weston.
Wisconsin—Dr. U. O. B. Wingate, Milwaukee.
Wyoming—R. Harvey Reed, M. D., Rock Springs

Secretary,
SAMUEL B. THOMAS, Esq., of N. Y. City.

Corresponding Secretary,
MORITZ ELLINGER, Esq. of N. Y. City

Assistant Secretary,
A. A. JAKOBI, of N. Y. City.

Pathologist,
WM. S. MAGILL, M. D., N. Y. City

Treasurer,
CAROLINE J. TAYLOR, Bridgeport, Conn.

Chemist,
PROF. C. A. DOREMUS, M. D. N. Y. City.

Curator,
J. MOUNT BLEYER, M. D., New York.
J. LEFFINGWELL HATCH, M. D., of N. Y.

Toxicologist,
PROF. W. B. McVEY, of Boston.

Librarian,
FRED. L. HOFFMAN, Esq., of N. J.

Assistant Librarian,
THOS. G. FROST, Esq., of N. Y.
R. L. PRITCHARD, Esq., of N. Y.
HON. FRANK MOSS, Esq., of N. Y.
MILES M. DAWSON, Esq., of N. Y.
JAMES R. ROGERS, Esq., of N. Y.

Bacteriologist,
G. BETTINI DI MOISE, M. D., of N. Y.

Microscopist,
DR. ERNEST J. LEDERLE, of N. Y.

TRUSTEES:

Legal,
H. GERALD CHAPIN, Esq., of New York.

Medical,
R. W. SHUFELDT, M. D., of N. Y. City.

COUNSELLORS,
For 3 years.

Legal.
HENRY WOLLMAN, Esq. of N. Y. City.

Medical.
C. C. CARROLL, M. D., of N. Y.

PERMANENT COMMISSION:
For 3 years.

Legal,
JUDGE CHARLES G. GARRISON, of N. J.

Medical,
NICHOLAS SENN, M. D., of Chicago.

The chair announced in feeling terms the death of Simon Sterne. Esq., of the New York Bar; Dr. Irving C. Rosse, Vice President of the Society for the District of Columbia, and Dr. Alfred S. Gihon, a corresponding member of the body of more than 25 years standing.

The chair called on Henry Wollman, who spoke feelingly of the life and career of Mr. Stern, and who at the close of his remarks moved the adoption of the following preamble and resolutions:

Simon Sterne belonged to that class of men who by nature are reformers. He despised wrong and had the courage to expose and fight it. He not only had the strength of vision to see the wrongs under which the public suffered, but had the skill to know how to correct them. He was not one of those men who pose as reformers either to attract attention, to subserve personal ambition or to obtain an office. He devoted himself faithfully and incessantly to the service of the people without ever askng, seekng or hoping for reward. No citizen of New York within the past thirty years, did more in the interest of the community than he. In every movement for the public good he was either a leader or among the leaders.

Simon Sterne was a clear and convincing writer. His works on Constitutional Law and other kindred subjects, are almost classics.

He was an upright, thorough and successful lawyer. He knew the law, and presented it clearly, luminously and convincingly. He was engaed in most important litigations all over this country, and almost from the moment of his admission to the bar, until the day of his death, had the profoundest respect of the judges all over the union.

He was always a student. He possessed the highest order of genius—intense industry, which was always exercised with such intelligence as to produce the most splendid results. By his death the people of this nation and the Bar of the entire United States have suffered a severe loss.

Be it Resolved by the Medico--Legal Society of New York, that this Society has heard with the deepest regret of the death of its member, Simon Sterne, an unselfish lover of his country, a loyal citizen, a great author, a profound lawyer, and above all, a true man.

The President submitted the action of the Executive Committee, approving of his recommendation upon Medico-Legal questions, to be submitted to a carefully selected committee on each question, who should take ample time to carefully consider and report upon the same to the Society for its approval or action.

First question or subject:—

The effect of traumatic or other injuries of the body in relation to the duration of human life, embracing injuries resulting in amputations or otherswise," on which the chair was instructed to name a committee and call upon members of the Society to furnish facts

Second subject:—The chair submitted the following letter from Dr. Robert Sangiovani, which he had laid before the executive committee:

New York, Nov. 11th, 1901.

To the President of the Medico-Legal Society of New York, 2240 First Avenue.

Dear Sir:—Since the deserving Medico-Legal Society of New York, of which you are, justly, the worthy President, leaves nothing untried by means of congresses and encouragements, to new discoveries, to the end to find rational means that might be efficacious in diminishing the spread of tuberculosis. I have the honor to ask the authorative patronage of this renowned Society, that I may execute, under its direction and control, some experiments that will make known the utility of my dietetic analeptic method of Iperalimentation, that, with facility and in a short time, say within one hundred days at the most, will cure the most dangerous form of the primary, essential or citogenic anaemia. That form is caused by inanition or dyspepsia, which is the most widely diffused among populations, and it is the unique, favorable fecund means for the life and multiplication of the bacillis of tuberculosis, and it is, therefore, the principal cause of the spread of this terrible disease.

This same analeptic method helps efficaciously the therapeutic cure of the chronic or acute exhausting disease, singularly the cure of tuberculosis, strengthening the organic resistence, so that one can obtain some recovery.

After the tenth day of this special cure of the primary anaemia, one observes already the initial progressive amelioration by means of augmentation of the red blood corpuscles, albumen, hemoglobine, forces appetite and weight of the body.

The solution of this important problem would be a positive progress of medicine, having the means of opposing the spread of tuberculosis, as you well understand.

I wish also that the public may be admitted to observe the course of these experiments. The receipts from the admission tickets will serve to defray the expenses of the other ulterior experiments which will be executed also upon some phthisical persons, affected from the first stage of this malady, because my method, by iperalimentation, helps efficaciously the therapeutical cure, so as to obtain some recovery.

I hope, rather I am sure, that my proposal will meet the approval of the honored Medico-Legal Society of New York.

Yours very respectfully,

DR. ROBERTO SANGIOVANI.

That the executive committee had resolved to accept the suggestion and offer of Dr. Sangiovani, and to hake a careful test of the same, if the same could be done without expense to this body, and authorized the chair to name a committee to take charge of the same with full power to add to their number, and to report the result of their labors to the Society.

That the chair had appointed as such committee, Ferd. L. Hoffman, of the Prudential Life Insurance Co., of Newark, Chairman; Dr. G. Bettini di Moise and Dr. J. Mount Bleyer, of New York city.

The President further reported as the further action of the executive committee, that he had been instructed to express to Frederick E. Crane, Esq., one of the members and officers of this Society, the pleasure and satisfaction felt by the members of the body without reference to partisan considerations, at his recent election as County Judge of Kings County, and to ask for his approval of some plan to commemorate that event in an appropriate manner at a general meeting of the Society, which instruction had been with great pleasure carried out by the chair.

Also the unanimous action of the executive committee directing the officers and members of the executive committee to unite in proposing and recommending Samuel B. Thomas, Esq., for appointment on the staff of Judge Wm. Travers Jerome, District Attorney-elect, as one eminently proper to be made, as well in the public interest as in that of the Society.

Also the further action of the executive committee recommending to the officers and executive committee of the American Congress of Tuberculosis, the importance of an early announcement of time and place of the session of 1902; assuring that organization of its deep interest in its labors; congratulating it on its splendid success in perfecting its organization, and recommending joint action of the executive committees of both organizations in preparations for the annual meeting of 1902. On motion the Society unanimously approved of the action of the executive committee.

Owing to the lateness of the hour the chair was authorized to appoint memorial committees on the life and career of Medical Director U. S. Navy, retired, Albert L. Gihon, M. D.; Dr. Irving A. Rosse, of Washington, D. C.; John H. Watson, James H. Calvin, M. D.; G. Graves, M. D., and other deceased members.

The chair named as such committee on Dr. A. L. Gihon—Dr. Isaac N. Love, Dr. A. N. Bell and the president.

On Dr. Irving C. Rosse—Dr. R. W. Shufeldt, Albert Bach, Esq., anu Dr. Woodward, of Washington, D. C.

The chair laid before the meeting a letter he had received from Prof. Dr. Morris Benedikt, of Vienna, and the several brochures which accompanied it in the German language, with a translation of the open letter to Dr. Malcomn Morris. On motion it was

Resolved, That the President be requested to express to Prof. Benedikt its high appreciation of his labors in Forensic Medicine, and to thank him in the inte.est of the science he has adorned and ornamented in his useful life, and invite him to contribute his contemplated open letter to the American Congress of Tuberculosis at the session of 1902, without regard to the discussion in Vienna to which his letter referred.

At the suggestion of the chair it was moved and carried that the Corresponding Secretary communicate to our Honorary member. Rudolph Virchow our congratulations at his continued health and vigor, and to express our hope for him still further usefulness to Forensic Medicine to be added as laurels to the crown which posterity must award him for his splendid labor. Society adjourned.

CLARK BELL,
President.

SAMUEL BELL THOMAS,
Assistant Secretary.

EDITORIAL.

THE CASE OF MRS. MAYBRICK.

The delay of the English authorities in ordering the release of this unfortunate American lady, occasions the deepest regret in all sections of our country, and severe criticisms have been made against what has seemed to be neglect, and by many is asserted to be inexcusable neglect, in not pressing upon His Majesty's ministers,the expediency, justice and propriety of her release, by those of her friends in America and England who have so long and persistently labored for this result.

A few words of explanation will suffice to show the very extraordinary circumstances surrounding the presentation of any new case to the new home minister, after the change in the English cabinet.

It must be remembered that the formation of a new ministry and the retirement of the home minister. before whom the memorial and application by the committee of the Medico-Legal Society was made, through the direction of President McKinley, by our American Ambassador, Mr. Choate, was announced very suddenly and quite unexpectedly, and before any decision had been announced to the government of the United States or the committee. upon the memorial laid before the home office.

The best legal advice consulted on both sides the Atlantic united in the opinion, that the superseding of the Rt. Hon. Matthew White Ridley as home minister, by a new official left the undecided application upon the memorial in a similar condition to a case in the law courts, which having been submitted and argued at length, had not been decided by the trial judge, before his term of office expired.

After a reasonable time it was agreed by all the friends of the prisoner, on both sides of the Atlantic to make a memorial by the same committee on 1. The points made in the first memorial, and the papers submitted therewith, by distinct reference to them all; 2. On the original letter of the Late Lord Chief Justice, the Earl of Killoween, and 3. On the stronger point that quite irrespective of and wholly outside of the question of the innocence or guilt of Mrs. Maybrick, she had already suffered sufficient punishment, and that the English government would be justified in ordering her discharge, without any reflection upon the administration of justice.

While the papers for this memorial were in process of preparation, the sudden death of Queen Victoria made a suspension of all action imperative.

No one can properly criticise the friends or counsel of Mrs. Maybrick for a complete and perfect silence during the exciting days following the death of her late Majesty, or the accession to the English throne of the present King.

Wbat his attitude was to be on the question of assuming the royal prerogative of pardon, which was vested in the crown by the constitution of England, could only be conjectured.

His mother, who had surrendered her prerogative when a young girl of 18, acting under the advice of her ministers and who had never once exercised the prerogative during her long reign, had consented, that the Home Secretary should exercise the powers vested by the British Constitution in the throne, and whether King Edward would follow her example, or exercise the prerogative in person, was wholly beyond the knowledge of any of her friends.

It was natural, that if any such change was under consideration, it would not be put in execution or might not be until after his coronation, and this with other strong and controlling reasons, made all the friends that had been consulted, unanimous in the opinion that the completion of a new memorial would be unwise and impolitic in the extreme.

There were also very strong and powerful reasons, which cannot well be stated, but which controlled action; on which very strong hopes were grounded, that the English government might, of its own motion, conclude,that the term of imprisonment had now reached a period that it could with self-respect consent to the almost universal prayer of the American people for the deliverance of their countrywoman, who while these events were thus progressing, still languished in an English prison, and to whom the Lord Chief Justice of England had said, both in the briefs he had filed with the Home Secretary urging her release, while Lord Chief Justice of England and his letter to her: "That her release ought to be granted. I feel as strongly as I have ever felt from the first that you ought never to have been convicted."

Then when so many weary months of delay, which brought no fruit to our hopes, had elapsed bringing up the question again, of whether the new application should be made, and transmitted again through President McKinley, by a fresh appeal for clemency, came the hand of the assassin and the powerful voice and interest of that great heart in her release ended forever, which put such a movement, at least for the present, out of further consideration. These considerations and reasons are given in response to the large number of anxious and earnest hearts of so many of her countrymen and women, who are asking the chairman of the Maybrick Memorial Committee, what tidings have you, or hopes do you entertain of her release?

When the letter of the Lord Chief Justice of England was published in England by the writer in September, 1900, on leaving London, some of the English provincial press pronounced it a forgery and denied its authenticity.

It was then photographed and the original placed in London where the American Ambassador could produce it on a day's notice for the inspection of the Home Secretary and a fac simile of that photograph reproduced and published in the Medico-Legal Journal, but it was too large, (being an exact reproduction of the original letter on the official paper of the High Court of Justice.) for reproduction in journals.

I am not aware that this reproduction was reproduced in England in any newspaper. I now reproduce that letter, reduced in size by photography so that it can be the more readily reproduced, and, to bring it to the eye of the people of England as well as of the civilized world, because I now as firmly believe as ever, that there is no country in Christendom who would be justified by its people in retaining in prison any one to whom the head of the judiciary had voluntarily and officially written, the words which the Earl of Killoween addressed to Mrs. Maybrick in this letter; after the fact had come officially and undeniably to the knowledge of the government.

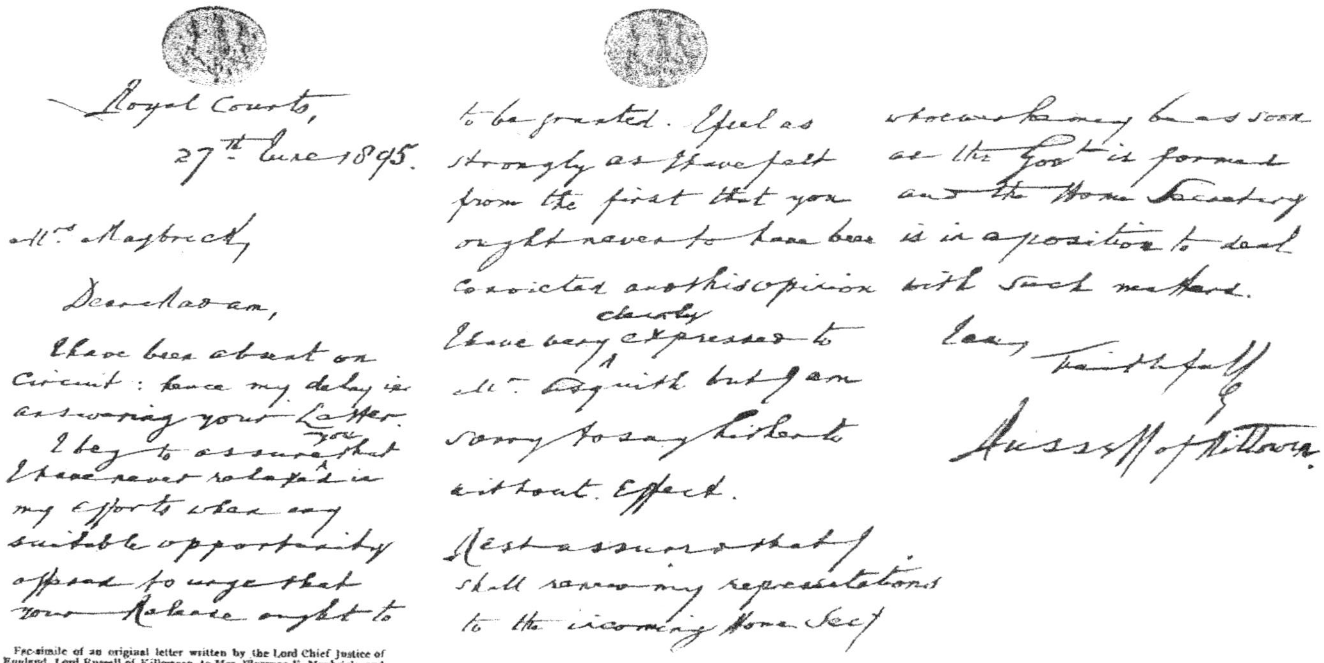
Royal Courts,
27th June 1895.

Mrs. Maybrick

Dear Madam,

I have been absent on Circuit: hence my delay in answering your Letter. I beg to assure you that I have never relaxed in my efforts when any suitable opportunity offered to urge that your Release ought to be granted. I feel as strongly as I have felt from the first that you ought never to have been convicted and this opinion I have very clearly expressed to Mr. Asquith but I am sorry to say hitherto without effect.

Rest assured that I shall renew my representations to the incoming Home Sec. whoever he may be as soon as the Govt is formed and the Home Secretary is in a position to deal with such matters.

Yours faithfully
Russell of Killowen.

Fac-simile of an original letter written by the Lord Chief Justice of England, Lord Russell of Killowen, to Mrs. Florence E. Maybrick, and placed by her in the hands of Clark Bell, Esq., as her attorney and counsel, photographed in London, and reproduced in New York.

THE BRITAIN AND THE BOER.

Mr. Broderick, the British Secretary for War, is reported to have said recently at the Carlton Club, referring to the determination of the English government to keep on in a policy that they call "wearing down the Boers," that "the country has set its teeth."

It is unfortunate for England, that the present English ministry, take credit to themselves for this "setting of the teeth," which it is to be hoped is more the feeling of the ministry than of the people of England.

How do the people of England really feel over this long protracted war, over the enormous sums expended, increasing the national debt? How about the terrible loss of life of the very flower of the English youth?

Is all now gained, or all that could be gained no matter what the result may in the future be, worth one tenth part of the treasure already spent or of the blood already spilled.

Is the Britain more obstinate than the Boer?

The Boer is descended from a race that carried on a war for many years with the most powerful nation of that date in all Europe. Shall we expect the extermination of the Boers in five years? How many years can Britain stand such a strain? Some means should be found and speedily to terminate this war.

Punch reflects English public sentiment in its cartoon, which represents Broderick and his conferees as blind.

This lockjaw of which Mr. Broderick speaks, may result in a fatal case of tetanus, to the present English ministry.

Two years more of such a war, at the cost of the past two years, would create such a reaction in England against the ministry as would be overwhelming.

The waste in money alone, leaving out of count, the blood of Englishmen is simply appalling. And the misery of it all is that it is a loss that is irreparable, and no matter what the result may be, can never be made good.

ENGLISH COMMITTEE ON TUBERCULOSIS.

His Majesty, King Edward, has appointed a commission to inquire into and report with regard to tuberculosis.

The commission is composed as follows:

Sir Michael Foster, Professor of Physiology at Cambridge University.

Dr. German Sims Woodhead, Professor of Pathology at Cambridge.

Dr. Sidney Harris Cox Martin, Professor of Pathology at University College, London.

Dr. John McFadyean, Principal of the Royal Veterinary College.

Dr. Robert William Boyer, Professor of Pathology at University College Liverpool.

The commission will inquire:—

1. Whether the disease in animals and men is one and the same.

2. Whether animals and man can be reciprocally infected with it.

3. Under what conditions, if at all, the transmission of the disease from animals to man takes place, and what are the circumstances favorable or unfavorable to such transmission.

THE NEW YORK COURT OF APPEALS.

The Medico-Legal Journal offers to the legal profession a fine large group of the present members of the Bench of the Court of Appeals as constituted in 1901, of a size suitable for framing, as an ornament to every lawyer's office at the price of $1.00 per copy.

The portraits are reproductions from photographs of the judges and have been prepared and grouped with great care and artistic effect.

The Journal offers to send free of charge to every new subscriber of the Journal, a copy of this fine group, to every member of the Bench or Bar, as a premium gratis.

MARINE HOSPITAL SERVICE.

Mr. Hepburn introduced a bill in the lower House of Congress providing for an increase of the efficiency of the service, and for a change of the name of that arm of the service to "The United States Health Service."

The bill was referred to the Committee on Interstate and Foreign Commerce.

THE TREASURY DEPARTMENT AND ITS CRITICS —IMMIGRATION OF CONSUMPTIVES.

The Secretary of the Treasury, under the advice of the supervising Surgeon-General of that department has decided that pulmonary tuberculosis is a dangerous contagious disease, and immigrants coming in suffering from this disease in advanced stages, are returned under the regulation adopted by the authorities.

This action has aroused the ire of some—and one obscure physician—in New York, who is the author of a work of conceded merit on the general subject, but who has not had, much of either experience or practice, has attacked the action of the Treasury Department as "unscientific and inhumane."

It is a way that some people have who desire notoriety, to gain it by assailing officers and public men, and thus seek to elevate themselves in the public estimation, by climbing up on the stairway of the reputations they seek to destroy.

The doctor in New York without a practice of any account or social position in his profession who fancies he will benefit himself by rushing into the lay press with accusations against Surgeon General Wyman and his want of humanity and assailing his scientific judgment, will hardly accomplish his purpose.

In the cases that have come up for review by the court, the department has been sustained in Brooklyn, but we learn that it will go on appeal to the United States court, where we do not doubt the judgment will be affirmed.

Surgeon-General Wyman is wise not to notice such an assault from such a quarter.

The regulations of his department do not encourage him in making a reply which was doubtless the object of the writer who assailed him.

A man may write a fairly good book and deserve the credit his work entitles him to on the general subject of tuberculosis and its treatment: and get a prize for it: but he may have very crude ideas of humanitarian legislation, and be all astray on questions of "scientific action or legislation."

As a rule so far as our observation goes, no solid enduring claim to public recognition in the profession—especially of medicine—can be practically gained by assaults against the scientific attainments of, the medical advisers of the Treasury Department, nor can the view of humanitarian subjects from such a source be of service to the Treasury Department, in regard to its regulations or to the courts in their enforcement.

The danger of extending the area of tuberculosis; the settled policy of the government, to prevent its spread by all legitimate legislation as a menace to the public health, is an imperative recognized duty.

It is much higher than any personal suffering in any isolated case or even in those where its workings might seem harsh.

Similar objections on so-called humanitarian grounds could be made, in cases of small-pox, cholera, yellow fever, leprosy, etc., but they should not be allowed to operate against the laws and regulations of the department based on the highest consideration of the public welfare.

THE CANTEEN IN THE AMERICAN ARMY.

Public sentiment seems much divided upon the question of the repeal of the recent act of Congress abolishing the canteen in the army.

Secretary Root took strong grounds in favor of its repeal,

which has been sustained by high medical authority and by what must be conceded to be a strong feeling among officers of the regular army, in favor of the repeal and the restoration of the canteen.

On the other hand the general of the army, in his annual report, strongly advises against the repeal of the act. Gen. Miles says:—

"It is believed that no injury has resulted thereby, and that the law has, in the main, been beneficial. The army is composed principally of young men, who have not formed the habit of using liquor, and although the majority of the enlistments actually occur in large cities, as the recruiting offices are principally located there, a large percentage of the men come from homes in the country and small towns and villages in every part of the United States. The prediction that the change would prevent enlistments and increase desertions has not been fulfilled. Since the law was approved, namely, February 2, 1901, the recruiting stations have been thronged with men seeking enlistment for the service, 25,944 men having enlisted since that date, and the percentage of desertions is now far less than in former years. Desertions most usually occur during the first six months of enlistment, and a much larger percentage of enlistments have been made during the last six months than heretofore. In many cases the men that have deserted belong to a class whose presence in the service was not desirable under any conditions, but whose real character was not known at the time of enlistment."

And his views are sustained by Generals Wheeler, Shafter, and Daggell.

The views of the English General Lord Roberts upon the subject must have great weight with members of our Congress.

In his "Forty-one Years in India," Lord Roberts writes:

My name appeared in the (Queen's) Jubilee Gazette (1887) as having been given the Grand Cross of the Indian Empire, but what I valued still more was the acceptance by the Government of India of my strong recommendation for the establishment of a club or institute in every British regiment and battery in India. In urging that this measure should be favorably considered, I had said that the British army in India could have no better or more generally beneficial memorial of the Queen's Jubilee than the abolition of that relic of barbarism, the canteen, and its supersession by an institute, in which the soldier would have under the same roof a reading-room, recreation-room, and a decently managed refreshment-room.

Lord Dufferin's Government met my views in the most liberal spirit, and, with the sanction of Lord Cross, "The Regimental Institute" became a recognized establishment, a fact which my colleagues in council referred to as a second Jubilee honor for me!

At a time when nearly every soldier could read and write, and when we hoped to attract to the army men of a bettter stamp and more respectable antecedents than those of which it was composed in "the good old days," it appeared to me a humiliating anachronism that the degrading system of the canteen should still prevail, and that it was impossible for any man to retain his self-respect if he were driven to take his glass of beer under the rules by which regimental canteens were governed. I believed, too, that the more the status of the rank and file could be raised, and the greater the efforts made to provide them with rational recreation and occupation in their leisure hours, the less there would be of drunkenness, and consequently of crime, the less immorality and the greater the number of efficient soldiers in the army.

Funds having been granted, a scheme was drawn up for the erection of buildings and for the management of the institutes. Canteens were reduced in size, and such attractions as musical instruments were removed to the recreation-rooms; the name "liquor bar" was substituted for that of canteen, and that there should be no excuse for frequenting the "liquor bar," I authorized a moderate and limited amount of beer to be served, if required, with the men's suppers in the refreshment-room—an arrangement which has been followed by the happiest results.

It is doubtful if Congress will consent to repeal the law, at least without a trial. The present size and needs of our army, its great strength, and the immediate work before it, will offer an opportunity to study the effects and results of the abolition of the canteen.

Congress is a conservative body. Reforms rarely move backward. The sober second thought of our people will be to wait and see how the law works.

It will be in time to repeal the act, when experience and trial have demonstrated, that these generals of the great armies now in action, are wrong in their judgment against the "canteen." It is prudent and conservative, now that we have the law in force to give it a fair trial.

ALCOHOLISM AND TUBERCULOSIS.

The ablest resume of the evolution of medical thought and opinion on both sides of the Atlantic regarding the influence of alcohol as a factor, both as a cause and a remedy, in cases of tuberculosis, is that printed by George F. Shrady, A. M., M. D., editor of the Medical Record in his issue of September 28th, 1901, which is so much in accordance with the views of the editor of this Journal that we reproduce it and shall ask permission of the Executive Committee of the American Congress of Tuberculosis to allow it to be incorporated as a contribution of public interest, in the Bulletin of the Congress of the work of that body, held in New York in May last, which is about to be published.

Dr. Shrady says:

The connection between alcoholism and tuberculosis has been and is still the cause of a wide diversity of opinion among medical men, and has given rise to copious discussion.

The physicians of a time gone by were generally implicit believers that alcohol was antagonistic to tuberculosis, and carried this belief into practice by dosing their patients with heroic quantities of spirit. Gradually, however, a change has come, leading to the rejection of this once popular view, and now many of the medical profession hold not only that alcohol is contraindicated as a therapeutic remedy in phthisical cases, but that the habit of alcoholism strongly predisposes to the contraction and propagation of tuberculosis.

Dr. Brouardel, of Paris, in his eloquent address delivered before the Congress on Tuberculosis, recently held in London, dwelt with special emphasis on this phase of the matter, and declared it to be his conviction that the relationship between alcoholism and consumption was very close. He said in part, "Alcoholism is the most potent factor in propagating tuberculosis. The strongest man who has once taken to drink is powerless against it."

Baudran of Beauvais has shown that the mortality from tuberculosis and that from alcoholism are nearly identical. Dr. Brouardel also drew attention to a mistake made too easily in the different countries of the world by ministers who have charge of the financial department of the State. They like to calculate the sum the State gets from the duty on alcohol, but they should deduct from it the cost to the community, of the family of the ruined drunkard, his degenerate, infirm, scrofulous and epileptic children, who must have shelter. The invasion of alcoholism ought to be regarded by everyone as a public danger, and this principle, the truth of which is incontestable, should be inculcated into the masses, that the future of the world may be in the hands of the temperate.

In the Edinburgh Medical Journal for September is an article by Dr. Kelynack, of Manchester, which follows the same line of argument. Dr. Kelynack puts the position, as regards the aspects from which the question is viewed by present-day scientific men, as follows: (1) That alcoholism is antagonistic to tuberculosis; (2) that alcoholism bears no special relationship to tuberculosis; (3) that alcoholism definitely predisposes to tuberculosis; and he gives the views of well-known physicians of various countries bearing on the point at issue.

Flint used alcohol freely, that is from 6 oz. to a pint of spirit daily, and appears to have had a firm belief in its efficiency in the treatment of tuberculosis. Chartens, writing in 1877, concerning the administration of whiskey to phthisical patients, says: "In private practice I order it to be taken ad libitum." Hermann Weber expressed himself in like terms, but Bell, of New York, as far back as 1859 opposed the view, then generally current, of the beneficial influence of large quantities of spirit on the course of pulmonary tuberculosis.

That alcoholism definitely predisposes to tuberculosis has of recent years received much support, and the theory would appear to be gaining ground at a rapid rate. Hector Mackenzie believes that alcoholism must be regarded as a powerful predisposing cause of tuberculosis. Osler refers to the subject thus: "It was formerly thought that alcohol was in some way antagonistic to tuberculous disease, but the observations of late years indicate clearly that the reverse is the case, and that chronic drinkers are much more liable to both acute and pulmonary tuberculosis. It is probably altogether a question of altered tissue soil, alcohol lowering the vitality, and enabling the bacilli more readily to develop and grow." Dr. Kelynack himself says that, having had exceptional opportunities of studying large numbers of cases among workhouse and hospital patients, he is convinced that the public house or saloon must be considered as one of the most serious obstacles to the speedy and effectual stamping out of tuberculosis.

Italians, Germans, and physicians of other countries who have studied the effects of alcoholism in connection with tuberculosis have arrived at similar conclusions. It is further contended by some that, in addition to a general impairment of vitality and pernicious environment, there is a special prejudicial influence arising from the action of the alcohol and its associates. This, as Dr. Kelynack points out, is very hard to prove, and at present, and until investigations have more clearly elucidated the matter, we must rest content with the knowledge already gained—that alcohol exerts little or no beneficial influence on the course of tuberculosis, but that on the contrary it tends to predispose to the malady those who consume it to any extent. Indirectly, of course, the fact is undeniable that alcohol is a prominent cause of tuberculosis, by lowering the vitality of its subjects. by inducing poverty and necessitating life in unhealthy surroundings, by causing degeneration of the individual and offspring, and by these means rendering the race more susceptible and prone to infection. Suppression of alcoholism should go hand in hand with that of tuberculosis.

Dr. A. N. Bell, the veteran editor of the Sanitarian, who is the Dr. Bell referredto in Dr. Shrady's article, to whom I wrote whether he entertains similar views, now says:

"I know that I have always approved whiskey in the treatment of tuberculosis, typhoid fever and diphtheria for which diseases it has been time agone, I hope forever, advocated by some distinguished practitioners.

THE CORONATION OF KING EDWARD.

The appointment of Hon. Whitelaw Reid as delegate to represent our Government at the formal coronation ceremonies of King Edward VII. of England, meets with universal commendation. No civilian could have been selected more completely fitted for this distinction than Mr. Reid.

It is a source of deep regret on this side the Atlantic, as it certainly will be on the other side, that General Miles, the head of our Army, and Admiral Dewey, of the Navy, have not been designated to be present on that occasion. The President would have been in full accord with popular sentiment at home had he named these splendid men to add lustre and credit to the American arms on land and sea to this ceremonial at the London capital.

SPIRITISM AND MRS. LEONORA A. PIPER.

The discussion of the subject of "Spiritism and Mrs. Piper's Statement" which was commenced at the December meeting will be continued at the February session of the Medico-Legal Society in joint session with the Psychological Section. Among those who are to take part will be Prof. W. Xavier Sudduth, Mary A. Lease, R. L. Parsons, M. D., Wm Lee Howard, M. D., H. S. Drayton, M. D., Cyrus Edson, M. D., Eleanor Gridley, Alex. Wilder, M. D., C. O. Sahler, M. D., T. D. Crothers, M. D., and others. All the papers will be presented in a brochure which will be sold at popular prices, issued by the Medico-Legal Journal in paper or muslin covers as desired, with portraits of the authors so far as the same can be ascertained. The papers read at the December meeting were by Thomson Jay Hudson, Dr. John Duncan Quackenbos, Clark Bell, Esq., Judge Abram H. Dailey, H. C. Wright, Esq., and Hon. Luther R. Marsh.

NOTICE TO MEMBERS OF AMERICAN CONGRESS OF TUBERCULOSIS.

Notice is also given to all new members who enrol in the American Congress of Tuberculosis of 1902, that Vol. 20, of the Medico-Legal Journal, and the remaining numbers of Vol. XIX will be sent to each and all who enroll in the Congress of 1902 at half price rates or $1.50 per volume.

The Governors of the American States, of the Canadian Provinces, the Central and South American States, and of all Medical societies or organizations of law or medicine will be invited to send delegates to this Congress, and to send the names of new members to enrol in the Congress, and it is announced that such delegates, or those who enrol, have the right to receive the Medico-Legal Journal at half price, so that the earlier publications can reach them before the official Bulletin is printed and issued.

CLARK BELL,
Secretary and Treasurer
American Congress of Tuberculosis.

Medico-Legal Society.

The FEBRUARY MEETING of the Medico-Legal Society will be held on WEDNESDAY, FEBRUARY 19th, 1902, at the Hotel St. Andrews 72d Street and Broadway, New York City, in joint session with the Pyschological Section of the Medico-Legal Society, at Dinner, at 7 o'clock P. M., sharp. You are invited to attend.

The order of business will be to continue the Discussion opened at the December Meeting, upon

"SPIRITISM AND MRS. LEONORA PIPER."

Papers are promised by the following contributors: Professor W. Xavier Sudduth, chairman of the Psychological Section of Chicago, Ill.; Dr. Henry S. Drayton; Dr. T. D. Crothers; Hon. Luther R. Marsh; R. L. Parsons, M. D.; Mary A. Lease; Alexander Wilder, M. D.; Cyrus Edson, M. D.; Eleanor Gridley; C. O. Sahler, M. D.; William Lee Howard, M. D.; the President and others, if time permits.

The price of seats at Dinner will be $1.75, exclusive of wine. Each member may bring one guest, on giving notice in advance to officers.

Members not intending to attend the Dinner will please come at 9 o'clock P. M., when the meeting will be called to order.

Oral discussion will be limited to five minutes each speaker.

Announcements will be made regarding the American Congress of Tuberculosis to be held May 14th, 15th and 16th, 1902, at the Hotel Majestic, and the local and other committees announced.

The following new member of the Psychological Section are announced: Prof. D. S. Abbott, Athens, Ga.; Joseph H. Dennis, 22 Weybosset street, Providence, Rhode Island; Eleanor Gridley, 67 South Clark street, Chicago; C. O. Rice, M. D., 235 Central Place, Pueblo, Colorado; Dr. A. Howard Young, 52 Mechanic Building, Pueblo, Colorado; Ernest Wende, M. D., 471 Delaware avenue, Buffalo, New York; Edward Howard Carnahan, Meaford, Ontario: L. C. Brown, Esq., Lock Box 85, Baltimore, Maryland; H. C. Wright, Esq., Corry, Pa.

A large attendance is expected and members will please apply for seats early.

Members who are in arrears for dues will please send to the Treasurer at once, on bills sent, as funds are needed for the vigorous prosecution of the Society work in regard to the American Congress of Tuberculosis for next May's session.

CLARK BELL,
President.

SAMUEL B. THOMAS,
Secretary.

GOVERNOR ODELL AND THE HOSPITALS FOR INSANE.

The Governor of New York has certainly been by a long way the most popular Governor the State has had for many years. Men of all creeds of political faith unite in admiring his intense, earnest and honest administration. That he is acting from high motives and for what he deems best for the public welfare, cannot for a moment be doubted or questioned. The evil he seeks to correct lies deeper than he has suspected.

The vice is in the law which gave any thing beyond advisory powers to the State Lunacy commission. There is no Board of Lunacy Commissions in the world except the single one in New York that gives arbitrary powers to the Lunacy Commisioners.

For nearly half a century the Earl of Shaftesbury was chairman of the English Lunacy Commission and he was not a physician. Under his wise, prudent and humane management all the great reforms in the Lunacy Statutes of England were worked out and secured. The corner stone of that Commission was that its action should be advisory only. He steadfastly opposed any legislation granting other than advisory powers to that Commission.

It exercises only such powers now; the same is true of the Scotch and Irish Commissions. It is true of the State Commission in Lunacy in every American state—save New York.

The change in New York was a step backward in lunacy legislation. It was mainly due to one man who expected to profit by it and limited its chairmanship to a class of which there was then not five eligible in the state.

Its practical working throws every state hospital into confusion in the state.

It was, as administered, a deplorable failure, and the chairman had to abdicate by universal consent.

Dr. P. M. Wise, of a large hospital experience and high standing among State superintendents, did much to allay the excitement and disaster that the act made necessary and unavoidable.

Governor Odell came into office with a vacancy in the office and a law so framed that he refused to proceed under it.

His action was wise, discreet and politic, but he did not look deep enough into either the law itself or the situation. His mistake was that he did not ask for the repeal of the whole law and not its most objectionable provisions.

The lunacy commission as now composed is beyond all question incompetent to carry out the ideals of the Governor.

Not a man in it has had previous hospital experience with the management of such hospitals as we now have.

The confusion that would follow if the plans of the Governor as we understand them were carried out, would be tenfold greater than those that followed Dr. Carlos MacDonald's administration. He antagonized every superintendent of every hospital in the State and every Board of Managers, and left office by general consent.

It is not too late for Governor Odell to restore a harmonious condition, and that is by repealing every provision of the law that confers powers other than advisory, upon the State Board of Lunacy Commission.

Its work by the experience of half a century in Great Britain and in our own country, should be, *visitation—inspection*, with accent on both, and *advice*. The experiment of arbitrary and not advisory powers in a State board has been demonstrated to be a failure by our experience in New York. The law in this respect is radically wrong and should be repealed in this regard.

The Superintendents of the State Hospitals for the Insane of the State of New York are among the most accomplished, able and experienced alienist of the insane hospitals of the world.

The boards of managers of the State hospitals are of the highest order of excellence.

Many of them, as at present composed, are far away superior to the State Board of Lunacy Commission as it is now composed in New York.

They deserve praise and thanks and commendation for a voluntary, unpaid service. To take any step that would compromise or in any way reflect upon their long and philanthropic labor, would be as unwise in Governor Odell as it would be cruel and unjust to their feelings and public reputation.

It is not so much a qustion between the Governor and the people of the State, as it is the welfare of the insane themselves.

The Earl of Shafterly in speaking to the British Parliament said that "he spoke for that unfortunate class who were unable to speak for themselves."

The welfare of the insane themselves is higher than all other considerations at this hour, and this large body of unfortunates, the wards of the State, would be the real sufferers should such a calamity occur as to place the State hospitals for the insane under the management of the State Lunacy Commission as it is at present organized.

JONATHAN HUTCHINSON, F. R. S., General Secretary of the New Sydenham Society, has requested Messrs. P. Blakiston's Son & Co., of Philadelphia, the American agents of the Society, to announce the publication of "An Atlas of Clinical Medicine, Surgery and Pathology," selected and arranged with the design to afford, in as complete a manner as possible, aids to diagnosis in all departments of practice. It is proposed to complete the work in five years, in fasciculi form, eight to ten plates issued every three months in connection with the regular publications of the Society. The New Sydenham Society was established in 1858, with the object of publishing essays, monographs and translations of works which could not be otherwise issued. The list of publications numbers upwards of 170 volumes of the greatest scientific value. An effort is now being made to increase the membership, in order to extend its work.

THE CONFLICT WITH TUBERCULOSIS IN CENTRAL AND SOUTH AMERICA.

It is not understood how extended the war against tuberculosis is being waged throughout the civilized world. One of our ablest public men abroad, as minister from the Government of the United States and the Argentine Republic is the Hon. Wm. P. Lord, late Governor of Oregon.

Addressing him as to the condition of affairs in relation to tuberculosis in that distant part of our Western American Hemisphere, and to aid our labors by the ablest men of that Republic, we received the following letter which discloses the efforts made by our brethren of the Latin American race in the countries of Central and South America which brings to light some of the splendid work doing there. These leagues are invited to co-operate with our movement in New York next May in support of the American Congress of Tuberculosis. Each of these leagues will be invited to send delegates and its members to contribute papers to be read on that occasion, as well as in each of these countries will the Presidents be requested to name both delegates and representative men to co-operate with the labors of this great body.

This letter throws so much light that we give it to the press with the request that members of this league in those countries may know and understand that we shall be glad of their aid, co-operation and assistance in our Congress to be held in the city of New York, May 14, 15 and 16, 1902.

Minister Lord replies as follows:

Legation of the United States of America,
Buenos Ayres, November 23, 1901.

Dear Sir:—In relation to your letter of September 4th last, I was instructed by the Minister to investigate the subject and secure the names of several doctors interested in the struggle against tuberculosis. At the "Departamento Nacional de Higiene" I was referred to the League or Society which has been formed here, and called the "Liga Argentina contra la Tuberculosis." Through the Secretary of this organization I secured an interview with one of its leading officers, who had also been its founder, and in a considerable talk with him I found out many facts in regard to the Society and its connections throughout South America, some of which may be of interest and help to the American Congress of Tuberculosis in its work.

At the second Latin-American Medical Congress held in Santiago de Chile last January an international commission was formed to combat the spread of tuberculosis, and this league is now in full operation, having representatives from all the Central and South American countries and from Cuba. This Commission has recommended the formation of local leagues in each of the countries embraced by it, and at the present writing nearly all have organized societies of conformity therewith.

On the 11th of May last was organized in this city by Dr. Emilio R. Coni, of Buenos Aires, the President of this International Commission, the "Liga Argentina contra la Tuberculosis." This "Liga" is under the patronage of the Minister of the Interior and has spacious offices in the building of the "Departamento Nacional de Higiene." It is a strong organization composed of leading members of the medical fraternity of Buenos Aires and has correspondents and branches in all the cities of the country It seems to be very zealous in its work, and indications point that much good will come from its labors.

The Society issues a monthly publication, containing original articles on the methods of fighting the dread disease, etc., extracts from papers and proceedings of like Societies throughout the world, and reports from the various countries included in the parent Latin-American organization. At present 2000 copies are printed every month and these are distributed gratuitously where they will do the most good. Every school, public and private, receives a copy, as do all the physicians of the city. Dr. Coni tells me that the number of copies will soon be increased and it is hoped to make this magazine or "revista" a powerful weapon of propaganda.

The league has also composed and printed a large poster entitled "Instruciones Populares sobre la Tuberculosis" (Popular Instructions Regarding Tuberculosis), which by order of the municipality is to be be fixed to the walls of all schools, railway stations and lodging houses throughout the capital. Owing to its labors, the municipality has decided to place the latest model hygienic and disinfected cuspidors in all railway stations and similar public places throughout its jurisdiction. It has at this moment a number of other sanitary and preventative measures before the authorities, and it is easily seen that this league, together with its connections throughout the whole of Latin America, is doing a noble work and deserves at least respectful recognition.

Dr. Coni showed great interest in the American Congress of Tuberculosis and expressed a great desire to enter into communication with that body. He gave me a complete set of the "Revista de la Tuberculosis," which I forward to you under separate cover, as well as copies of the poster, which I said above, was to be affixed in various places where people congregate and sanitary arrangements are apt to be bad. He promised to forward regularly to the American organization the "Revista," monthly as it appears, and voiced the hope that your Society would in return furnish the "Liga Argentina" with any periodicals or printed matter which it may issue from time to time.

Further particulars and details of the work of the "Liga Argentina" and of the "Comision Internacional" may be gathered from the publications forwarded to you, and the state of the disease in this country and necessity for action from the book "La Tuberculos dans la Republique Argentine," written by the President of the League, and which is also forwarded.

In view of the facts stated above, I would recommend you to communicate with the "Liga" as an organization, rather than with any of the officers as individuals; but that, of course, is a matter for your discretion. I can say through that I have no doubt all of the gentlemen composing the "Comicion," or Board of Managers would be glad to ally themselves with the American Congress of Tuberculosis, and I suggest herewith the names of three of the leading physicians interested who would, I feel, make worthy Vice Presidents of your organization:—

Doctor Emilio R. Coni, Calle Lavalle No. 859, President of the International Commission.

Doctor Samuel Gache, Calle Corrientes No. 729, President of the "Liga Argentina."

Doctor Francisco de Veyga, Calle Lavalle No. 859, Secretary of the "Liga Argentina."

I am, dear sir, very truly yours.

(Signed) CLARENCE L. THURSTON,
Secretary of Legation.

Clark Bell, Esquire, Secretary American Congress of Tuberculosis.
39 Broadway, New York City, U. S. A.

THE MUTUAL RESERVE FUND LIFE AND ITS ASSAILANTS.

President Burnham of the Mutual Reserve Fund Life Insurance Company is making it hot and lively for somebody who has been publishing libels against his company. In our opinion it is hardly worth the while of an insurance company to spend time or money on such people. If they were entirely unnoticed in the press it would be better for the companies.

President Burnham may be justified in prosecuting them criminally and civilly in the courts. They perhaps, should be tried and convicted, but the old saying still remains, "Sue a beggar and get a louse." Again the announcement of the arrest, the trial or even the conviction of these persons is of little consequence,—and it has this element in it,—it brings their calumnies into public notice which would otherwise be unknown.

President Burnham is a strenuous official. He smarts at the sting of these mosquitoes on the body of his company. The libeller is usually acting from motions of either cupidity or revenge. Experience and careful observation will convince any thoughtful mind that ventilation of even the punishment of calumnators and slanderers does little good, indeed it does harm, for it calls public attention frequently to the detriment of the injured. He might be justified in striking, but silence should go with the blow of the lash as a matter of prudence and policy.

BOVINE TUBERCULOSIS.

At the discussion on 19th December, 1901, of Dr. Theobald Smith's paper on the "Difference Between Bovine and Human Tuberculosis" before the New York Academy of Medicine, Vice President Herman Biggs, M. D., spoke at length we make extracts, for which we are indebted to the Medical News of New York city. Dr. Herman Biggs said:

That Koch's declaration has made the subject of human and bovine tuberculosis and their relation to each other and to disease in man of intense present-day interest. Koch's position as announced at the Congress involves two considerations—first, he claims that bovine and human tuberculosis and the bacilli which cause them are different, which positon is not proven, and, secondly, that the danger of infection of human beings by bovine tuberculosis may be ignored. There is no doubt that the main factor in the distribution of tuberculosis among human beings is human tuberculosis in those living near them. Health authorities realize how significant human contagion is because of the immense amount of tubrculosis which exists in tenement-house districts. As high as eighteen to twenty per cent. of the deaths among the population in certain parts of the city that are especially crowded are due to tuberculosis. In other parts of the city, where there are ample living space, light and air, the mortality is less than one-quarter of one per cent. The English statistics with regard to the origin of tuberculosis in human beings are very different from our own and also differ very strikingly from the Continental statistics. Sir Thorne Thorne, some two years ago in his lectures on the dangers of the spread of tuberculosis, collected statistics to show that ten per cent. of the deaths from tuberculosis in England take place from tabes mesenterica. He argues from this that the main source of infection is milk, though probably also meat infected with bovine tuberculosis has something to do with the spread of tuberculous disease, especially of the intestines. He pointed out, also,that while the general death-rate from tuberculosis was decreasing, the death-rate from the abdominal form of tuberculosis was on the increase.

AMERICAN STATISTICS.

Our statistics differ very materially from those of England in this matter Death from primary intestinal tuberculosis is very infrequent in this country and especially in this city,where proper examinations are made in order to determine the origin of the tuberculosis. The death-rate from tabes mesenterica is less than one per cent. Our statistics agree in this matter with those of Germany and of France. There is evidently some factor entering into the English statistics that makes them inapplicable to conditions in other countries. Our statistics from primary intestinal tuberculosis confirms Koch's position that the danger from bovine tubercle bacilli taken into the human system is so small that it can be practically ignored.

LIMITATION OF ANIMAL TUBERCULOSIS.

The question of the limitation of tuberculosis in animals is then not a human. sanitary problem, but an agricultural problem. The prevention of bovine tuberculosis is of extreme economic importance, but it must not be urged upon the community on the ground of danger to human beings because of the possibility of infection.

EXPERIMENTS UPON HUMAN BEINGS.

The inoculation of human beings with bovine tuberculosis is out of the question. Certain experiments in this line have been done in the past however. Baumgarten reports that Rokitansky inoculated with tuberculous material certain persons ,ten or twelve in number, who were suffering from cancer and were considered to be hopelessly ill. It had been obsrved that cancer patients did not suffer from tuberculosis. nor tuberculous patients from cancer. It was thought possible that the one disease might have some influence upon the other. Hence, the experiments were not entirely unjustified even from a humanitarian standpoint, as there seemed some faint hope ofthe rapeutic benefit The cancer patients were inoculated subcutaneously. Some local reaction took place, but no general infection occurred. At the autopsy no trace of tuberculosis could be found anywhere in the internal organs.

HUMAN SUSCEPTIBILITY.

Dr. William H. Park said that, while it cannot be predicated of any specific animal infection that it will infect any other kind of animal, it is well known that when an infectious material proves pathogenic for a number of classes of animals very few animals are immune to it. Infections that are virulent for many animals are usually pathogenic also for man. There are many anomalies, however ,in susceptibility. Rabies affects monkeys, but after it has passed through a series of monkeys the infectious material loses its virulence for dogs. On the other hand, rabbits are extremely susceptible to rabies ,but any number of passages of the virus through rabbits does not diminish its virulence for dogs. Tuberculosis is a most insidious disease. It is practically impossible to tell the exact time of its origin in any given case. Hence, the difficulty of determining what is the exact cause of a tuberculous process in any given individual. In order to determine whether human tubercle bacilli would affect cattle, Dr. Park has had four suckling calves fed on sputum from tuberculous patients. Among them was distributed all the sputum collected daily from the tuberculous patients under treatment at St. Luke's Hospital. After three months the animals gave a reaction to tuberculin, though there was no reaction just after birth. When killed, however, no trace of tuberculosis could be found in their tissues. It is possible that more careful search might have shown a very limited area of tuberculosis somewhere in the tissues as the result of the presence of which the tuberculin test became positive. In this series of experiments there seemed very good reason to think that the animals should suffer from the disease if they were at all susceptible. They were kept in a rather cold, dark room and were evidently not up to the usual standard of health as a consequence. Some human tubercle bacilli were also subcutaneously injected. These produced local abscesses, but no generalization of the infection. It would seem clear then that human tubercle bacilli do not infect cattle when ingested or injected under ordinary conditions.

DANGER OF BOVINE TUBERCULOSIS.

It is well recognized now by bacteriologists that for susceptible animals bovine tuberculosis is much more virulent than human tuberculosis. It is possible that even, though human tuberculosis does not affect cattle, bovine tuberculosis may prove serious for human beings. This would be especially true in young and delicate subjects and if, as is often the case in infants, because of lack of variety in the diet, a considerable number of tubercle bacilli found their way into the intestines at one time the danger might be very great. It seems clear, therefore, that we must not lessen our

precautions, though the question of the interchangeableness of human and bovine tuberculosis still remains open for discussion and is an extremely valuable field for study.

Dr. Herman Biggs' views will be regarded as of great interest and of more than ordinary value both by the general public and the medical profession.

This subject will attract great attention at the American Congress of Tuberculosis, May 14, 15 and 16 next in this city. The leading scientists of this country and of foreign countries will speak upon it on that occasion.

This subject will then be discussed under the Fourth Symposium, and will have one whole session assigned to its elucidation.

Aside from papers of a general or miscellaneous character the officers have formulated four symposiums—each to have a session assigned and towards which there is already a large number of contributors already announced. These symposiums are classified as follows:

1. Preventive Legislation, Embracing the Social, Municictpal and State Aspects of Tuberculosis.

[What aid should be expected from the State in the cure and prevention of Tuberculosis and how shall this be secured?]

2. Tuberculosis in its Pathological and Bacteriological Aspects.

3. The Medical and Surgical Aspects of Tuberculosis.

[Sanatoria; Climatic Conditions; Light and Electricity.]

4. The Veterinary Aspects of Tuberculosis.

ORGANIZATIONS TO PREVENT TUBERCULOSIS.

The Ohio Society for the Prevention of Tuberculosis formed under the leadership and by the splendid exertions of Dr. Probst, Secretary of the State Board of Health of Ohio, should be held up as an object lesson to the profession in other States. As a factor in arousing public sentiment and in its proper education, such labors will be of the very highest significance and value.

Dr. Probst has had the wisdom and forethought to secure the co-operation of some of the leading jurists of Ohio, and to have their names prominent on the list of its officers. He will give tenfold interest and value to his labors and reach the public confidence and attention much sooner and with greater force and weight.

In Canada, where the organization of similar bodies has been formed, notably in Ontario, at Toronto and in other Provinces; the great society of the Dominion of Canada all were formed along these lines, and their Vice-Presidents were selected largely from the Lt. Governors of the Provinces of the Dominion, officers, who are analagous in our country to the Governors of States. The Earl of Minto, Governor General, Lt. Governor Sir Oliver Mowatt, G. C. M. G., of Ontario, is a Vice-President of the Society formed for the Dominion of Canada as are others of like rank.

Senators and members of the Dominion Parliament are officers of the body. Sir. Wm. Hingston, member of the Senate from Montreal, moved the adoption of the most notable resolution in organizing the body; one of the most able, eloquent and influential men in the Dominion.

We hope to see Dr. Probst's work reproduced elsewhere, as it has been done in Vermont by Dr. Henry D. Holton and his colleagues; in Maine, in which the Governor of the State has taken a conspicuous part; in New Hampshire, where Dr. Watson and Dr. Fontaine have done so splendidly.

It is for this reason that the American Congress of Tuberculosis has asked public officials of the highest rank to act as its Vice Presidents, not only in the United States but in the Central and South American States, and in the Dominion of Canada, so that the public at large may come closer in touch with its labors, co-operating with those medical men who give attention to these subjects, a course also followed in England and other countries.

The American Congress of Tuberculosis.

THE Third Annual Session of this Congress is announced to be held on the **14th, 15th and 16th of May, 1902**, at the Hotel Majestic, 72d Street and Central Park, West, in the City of New York, in Joint Session with the Medico-Legal Society. There will be two sessions each day and no evening session, except on the 15th, when the Banquet will be given. This will enable delegates from distant States and countries to enjoy the amusements and attractions of the city.

Arrangements will be made with railway companies for a reduced rate of fare, the details of which will be announced to the Delegates.

In addition to the Vice-Presidents chosen at the sessions of May 15 and 16, 1901, the Executive Committee have authorized the appointment of three Vice-Presidents from each State, Country or Province, and an Honorary Vice-President from each Under this authorization about seventy additional Vice-Presidents have been named who have already accepted, but in some of the Countries and States all of them have not yet been named. Of the Honorary Vice-Presidents all but two of the Provinces of the Dominion of Canada have accepted already, and six from Governments. Among those who have accepted from the American States, already, five are Governors of States and others high public officers.

When completed, these officials will be all duly announced. There will be, aside from all papers of a miscellaneous nature, **four symposiums**, arranged each to occupy one session of the body, viz.:

1. **Preventive Legislation, Embracing the Social, Municipal, and State Aspects of Tuberculosis. (What aid should be expected from the State in the cure and prevention of Tuberculosis, and how shall this be secured?)**
2. **Tuberculosis in its Pathological and Bacteriological Aspects.**
3. **The Medical and Surgical Aspects of Tuberculosis. (Embracing Sanitoria and Climatic Conditions, Light and Electricity.)**
4. **The Veterinary Aspects of Tuberculosis.**

These will each be in charge of a Committee who will arrange for the opening papers, and for those who participate. These Committees will be arranged with great care and duly announced.

A large number of the enrolled members have already announced the titles of their papers for the Session of 1902, and a still larger number have sent their names to the Secretary, who will contribute papers and send the titles later.

The Presidents of the Central and South American Republics, and all Governments on the American Continents, have been invited to send Delegates and to name suitable persons to act as Vice-Presidents, and their men of Science requested to enroll and contribute to the work of the Congress, many of whom are already represented by delegates. No attempt will be made to classify and arrange these until the Programme can be announced, but, if thought advisable, a preliminary announcement will be made, one month before the Annual Meeting, of the titles of papers and names of authors.

Those who were named as delegates by the Governors of States, or Medical or Scientific bodies, for the Session of 1901, are cordially invited to enroll for the Congress of 1902. The enrolling fee will be $3, which will entitle the member to the Bulletin of the Congress of 1902.

All Medical Bodies, and Scientific or Legal Associations, or Associations of the Bar, are invited to send delegates to the Congress, who will be given the rights of the floor and a vote at the Session.

There will be named a local Committee for the Session, of strong names, who will do everything in its power to make the occasion one of great interest and pleasure to enrolled members.

The enrollment is open to members of both professions in every State, County or Province on the continents of America, in the western hemisphere, and in American waters, and papers are promised and will be solicited from all who are interested, in foreign countries.

For details and enrollment, address

CLARK BELL, Secretary,

39 Broadway, New York City.

MUSEUM OF THE AMERICAN CONGRESS OF TUBERCULOSIS.

The following announcement has been made by the officers of the Congress:—

Shall we have a museum at the May session of the American Congress of Tuberculosis in New York?

The great feature of the London Congress last June was its splendid museum. We have in our country material for such a museum, and one that can quite equal the splendid exhibit that our English cousins presented.

This will depend upon the co-operation which the profession of medicine gives to the effort of our committee.

The Executive Committee of the Medico-Legal Society has directed the appointment of a committee to organize such a museum, and a large number of the Vice-Presidents of the American Congress of Tuberculosis have strongly favored such action by the American Congress of Tuberculosis.

The Hotel Majestic, where the Congress will be held will provide a suitable room for the display on the floor above the parlors, near the session.

The delegates sent by the latter body to the London Congress speak in the highest terms of the exhibit presented in London.

Dr. H. Edwin Lewis, Editor of the Vermont Medical Monthly, of Burlington, Vermont, has consented to accept the chairmanship of a select committee to collect exhibits for such a movement.

He will be supported by a strong committee which is now being organized. The officers desire to know who will volunteer to co-operate in this labor and serve on this important branch of its work.

Those who will do so will please communicate with Dr. H. Edwin Lewis direct, or write Dr. Henry D. Holton, President of the American Congress of Tuberculosis, at Brattleboro, Vermont, or with Mr. Clark Bell, Secretary, 39 Broadway, New York city.

All curators of colleges and museums, or of medical schools or societies, and all members of the profession in the United States, the Canadas, or in South or Central American countries who are willing to loan or contribute specimens, drawings or contributions to such a collection for the use of that Congress, to be held at the Hotel Majestic, May 14 to 16, in the city of New York, will please at once communicate directly with Dr. H. Edwin Lewis, Chairman Committee on Museum, at Burlington, Vt., specifying contributions so that the same may be catalogued and the catalogue presented in advance of the session. The catalogue of the museum of the London Congress. occupied 200 pages of printed matter, and embraced drawings, maps, skiographs, photographs, engravings, charts, prints and contributions besides specimens, and illustrations of microscopic and biological work relating in any way to the subject.

If a favorable response is made to this appeal the collection will be a great public interest.

It is hoped that the laboratories of the Boards of Health of the cities and States of the Union and the medical colleges and schools will loan specimens of their work to this collection, and that the microscopists and students of biology, pathology and chemistry will enroll and co-operate in this laudable movement to extend the knowledge of the results attained by scientific endeavor in the great work of combating the spread of this great destroyer of mankind, Tuberculosis.

Very faithfully yours,

CLARK BELL, Secretary.

HENRY D. HOLTON, President.

AMERICAN CONGRESS OF TUBERCULOSIS.

OFFICERS FOR 1902.

Honorary President, A. N. Bell, M. D., Brooklyn, N. Y.; President, Henry D. Holton, M. D., of Vermont, Secretary State Board of Health, Brattleboro, Vt.; Vice Presidents, Henry B. Baker, M. D., Lansing, Mich.; E. T. Barrick, M. D., Toronto, Ont.; Wm. Bayard, M. D., St. John, N. B.; Ralcy Husted Bell, M. D., New York City; A. C. Bernays, M. D., St. Louis, Mo.; J. Mount Bleyer, M. D., New York City; Geo. Brown, M. D., Atlanta, Ga.; W. L. Bullard, M. D., Columbus, Ga.; Col. E. Chancellor, M. D., St. Louis, Mo.; C. K. Cole, M. D., Helena, Mont.; T. D. Crothers, M. D., Hartford, Conn.; Judge Abram H. Dailey, Brooklyn, N. Y.; Hon. Moritz Ellinger, New York City; Juan A. Fortich, M. D., Cartagena, Colombia, S. A.; R. F. Graham, M. D. Greely, Colorado; A. P. Grinnell, Burlington, Vt.; Major A. Harvard, U. S. A., Havana, Cuba; Thos. Bassett Keyes, M. D., Chicago, Ill.; Luis H. Labayle, M. D., Leon, Nicaragua; E. P. Lachapelle, M. D., Montreal, Canada; Louis Leroy, M. D., Nashville, Tenn.; Dr. Edouard Liceaga, City of Mexico; Dwight S. Moore, M. D., Jamestown, S. Dak.; Wm. H. Murray, M. D., Plainfield, N. J.; J. A. McNeven, of Idaho; A. E. Osborne, M. D., Glen Ellen, Cal.. John H. Pryor, M. D., Buffalo, N. Y.; J. C. Shrader, M. D., Iowa City, Iowa; J. H. Tyndale, M. D., Lincoln, Nebraska; C. S. Ward, M. D., Warren, Ohio; Prof. S. H. Weeks, M. D., Portland, Maine; Cressy L. Wilbur, M. D., Lansing, Mich.; U. O. B. Wingate, M. D., Milwaukee, Wis.; C. F. Ulrich, M. D., Wheeling, W. Va.; Secretary and Treasurer, Clark Bell, Esq., City of New York.

The executive officers or executive committee were directed to name Vice-Presidents from each State, Territory, Province or country, at least three from each, and selected as far as practicable from both professions of law and medicine. More than seventy-five of these have been already selected, and when all are filled will be announced.

The Executive Committee authorized and directed the selection of one or more Honorary Vice Presidents from each State, Province or country, and already a large number of these appointments have been made from the highest public officials in the Americans States, the Dominion of Canada and Central and South American countries, embracing the Governors of American States and the Provinces of the Dominion of Canada, and others in high official positions in sympathy with its labors.

The full list of officials, members and delegates named by the Governors of our States, and those of foreign countries, will be shortly published with the titles and authors of papers, of which a large number have already announced their names and title of contributions. They will be given in full in our next issue.

The meeting will be held, as before, in the Hotel Majestic, with whom arrangements have been made for reduced rates. Arrangements will be made with railways for reduced rates for delegates of which details will be announced later on.

The banquet will be given on the evening of the 15th of May, with price per plate at $2.00 each, exclusive of wine.

There will be a strong effort made to organize a museum, for which the Hotel Majestic will furnish a suitable room on the floor above the parlors.

Every medical society, every academy of medicine in the United States, in the Canadas and in the South and Central American States, and the Bar associations and legal societies, are invited to send delegates to this Congress to be held May 14, 15 and 16, at the Hotel Majestic, in the city of New York, and the Governors of all the States, Provinces and countries will be also invited to send delegates, so that the whole of both continents of the Western American Hemisphere may be represented in this work.

Those wishing to enroll can send their names to the Secretary, and the enrolling fee of $300, which will entitle them to all Bulletins of the Congress free.

HENRY D. HOLTON, President,
CLARK BELL, Secretary.

AMERICAN CONGRESS OF TUBERCULOSIS.

SEASON OF 1902.

The following letter has been sent to the delegates named by the Governors of the States and Provinces and to leading physicians and jurists throughout the Canadas, South and Central America and the United States:

Sir:—The Executive Committee of the American Congress of Tuberculosis at its meeting held December 18th. 1901, by the almost unanimous voice of its Vice-Presidents, scattered throughout the States, giving expression of their preference for the time and place of the Annual Meeting, have fixed upon the City of New York. and May 14, 15 and 16, 1902, as the time and place of the annual meeting of the Congress, to be held as last year, in joint session with the Medico-Legal Society.

All members of the legal and medical professions and all persons interested in the subject are invited to enroll in the Congress and to contribute a paper to be read at the annual meeting, and to send the title of such paper as early as possible to the officers to enable the same to be properly classified, and to devote one session to the discussion of each.

The Executive Committee have directed that three vice-presidents be named from each county, state and province upon the American Continent, both of North and South American, and that an honorary vice-president be also named for each.

A large number of these appointments have already been made and the officers of the Congress are now charged with the duty of filling such places which, when completed, will be announced in the regular programme of the annual meeting.

It has been proposed that four symposiums be arranged for the annual meeting, by appropriate committees, upon the following subjects:

1. Preventive Legislation embracing the Social, Municipal,

and State Aspects of Tuberculosis. (What aid should be expected from the State in the cure and prevention of tuberculosis, and how shall this be secured?)

2. Tuberculosis in its Pathological and Bacteriological Aspects.

3. The Medical and Surgical Aspects of Tuberculosis. (Embracing Sanitoria, and Climatic Conditions, Light and Electricity.

4. The Veterinary Aspects of Tuberculosis.

It is proposed to have the opening paper under each of these subjects prepared by either the chairman of the committee, or such prominent scientists as shall be selected by the committee to open the discussion.

Will you please indicate to the Secretary under which head you would prefer to be classified and give the title of your paper as early as possible? If unable to attend, your contribution can be forwarded and read in your name at the session.

Will you, in addition, furnish the officers with a list of the names and addresses of such persons in your country, state or province as you believe would enroll and take an active interest in the proceedings of the Congress, and also in those countries, states and provinces where the appointments have not yet been made of vice-presidents, will you kindly indicate to the officers suitable names to occupy the positions of vice presidents in your state, province or country?

This announcement is made early to enable responses to be received from the countries most distant in time to announce and prepare contributions for the annual meeting.

Every indication points to a large meeting and the interest is increasing beyond our most sanguine expectations. The enrollment fee is $3.00, which please remit to

Very faithfully yours,

CLARK BELL,
Secretary.

TUBERCULOSIS AND ITS MORTALITY.

The report of the Department of Public Health and Vital Statistics of San Francisco, is most complete and elaborate in detail of any that comes to our table. We give its comparative statement of deaths from pulmonary tuberculosis of a few leading cities:—

CITY.	MONTH.	Population.	Number of Deaths from Pulmonary Tuberculosis.	Total Deaths.
Baltimore,	July,	541,000	93	1,260
"	August,	518,000	86	893
Boston,	May,	560,892	110	929
"	June,	573 579	114	813
Chicago,	June,	1,758,025	198	1,805
"	July,	"	188	2,263
New Orleans,	July,	300,000	78	574
"	August,	"	57	457
New York City.				
Week ending	Aug. 24,	3,536,517	138	1,390
" "	" 31,		130	1,287
" "	Sept. 7,		128	1,418
" "	" 14,		146	1,411
			One month, 542	
Philadelphia.				
Week ending	Aug. 24,	1,293,697	50	491
" "	" 31,	"	37	410
" "	Sept. 7,	"	44	399
" "	" 14,	"	47	437
San Francisco,	July,	360,000		530
"	August,	"		470

The relative large death rate of Boston is worthy of notice. It seems greatly in excess of the other American cities.

INTERNATIONAL CONGRESS OF CRIMINAL ANTHROPOLOGY.

The Fifth International Congress of Criminal Anthropology was opened at Amsterdam on September 9th, with an address by M. Van Hamel, the President. Dr. Havelock Ellis, the English delegate, and Mr. Clark Bell, of New York, were appointed Vice Presidents. Professor Lombroso read papers on "Degeneration, the Practice of Tattooing by Criminals," and the "Remedial Possibilities of Symbiosis." Dr. Piepers read a paper on "The Idea of Crime." M. Scipio Sighele, of Brussels, delivered an address on "Collective Crime." He considered that the individuals composing crowds were not always responsible for their acts. On September 10th, the proceedings consisted mostly of a discussion on "Degeneration and Criminality," the speakers including M. Winkler, of Amsterdam; Dr. Garnier, of Paris. and Signor Ferri, of Rome. The afternoon sitting was presided over by M. Drill, Counsellor to the Minister of Justice in St. Petersburg, and the subject of discussion was "Juvenile Delinquency." Dr. Garnier, of Paris, said that offences committed by children, especially murder, were due to the abuse of alcohol by their ancestors, and expressed the hope that states would take measures against the abuse of alcohol. In the evening the members of the Congress were the guests of the students of the University.

On September 11th, the morning sitting was presided over by Colonel McHardy, Chairman of the Prison Commissioners for Scotland. Signor Ferri read a paper on "The Prevention and Repression of Crime" and on "The Symbiosis of Crime," or the utilization of the energies of criminals in such a way that least harm was done to the community at large. Part of the day was devoted to a visit to the lunatic asylum at Meerenberg, near Haarlem.

On September 12th, M. Drill, of St. Petersburg, spoke upon the responsibility of criminals. He contended that there existed neither a criminal type nor a born criminal, and was of opinion that crime could best be prevented by schools and education generally. Dr. Louise Rabinovitch, of New York, read a paper on the "Duty of States in Preventing the Propogation of Crime," which she said was mostly hereditary. Dr. Wallenbergh, of The Hague, made some recommendations with regard to penalties in the case of aged first offenders—that was to say, such as were above the age of 70 years.

On September 14th, the Congress resumed its discussion of The Physiological Action of Criminals, M. Treves, of Turin, Professor Benedikt, of Vienna, and M. Drill, of St. Petersburg, taking part. Mr. Clark Bell, of New York, contributed a paper entitled "The Indeterminate Sentence in New

York." Dr. Jules Morel, of Mons, Belgium, one entitled "On the Prophylaxis and Treatment of the Recidisist Criminal." A motion proposed by M. Albanel, of Paris, was then adopted. It recommended that children breaking the law should be examined before being brought into court and if found to be degenerate should be placed in special educational establishments. The Congress supported a proposition introduced by Mr. A. McDonald, of Washington, with regard to a combination of a psychical and physical laboratory with the Minister of Justice at Washington. Senor Falcon, of Cuba, delivered an address on "Interesting Features in Criminals." In his closing speech M. Van Hamel, the President, thanked the delegates to the Congress and observed that England was represented for the first time. It was decided that the next meeting should take place in Turin in 1906.—*From London Lancet.*

[The editor regrets his inability to make a review of the labors of this important Congress, because its officials have not sent him advance sheets from the published Bulletin, which is expécted daily. We hope to present a more detailed review in our March number.]

THE GERMAN PRINCE.

Prince Henry of Germany, is to visit our country in February; and he will receive a hospitable welcome. As the brother of the Emperor of Germany, this visit will tend to strengthen friendly feelings between the two countries.

The German Emperor shows great tact and discernment in arranging this visit.

He is sincere in his desire to foster and encourage reciprocal friendly relations.

His selection of an American builder for his private yacht helps because he caters to our National pride in giving us this proof of his belief in our superiority in ocean yacht building for speed, and he naturally hopes and expects his yacht to be as good as we can make it.

The young German Prince will receive a splendid welcome to our shores.

NEW YORK STATE HOSPITAL FOR CONSUMPTIVES.

The Governor of New York in his message to the Legislature for 1902, says on this subject:—

TUBERCULOSIS HOSPITAL.

The Commission designated by the Legislature has selected a site, and work upon this important undertaking will be begun in the spring. A tender of land by the Honorable Lucius N. Littauer, was received and declined because of the insufficiency of the land offered.

Perhaps no work yet undertaken by the State presents so many serious aspects as does this. It has been estimated that there are 65,000 persons in the State of New York who are afflicted with tuberculosis. It is our duty, of course, to furnish every protection possible for the health and happiness of our citizens. This departure, however, may lead to the establishment of other institutions, for which the State may be called upon to provide, and for which there may be the same claim advanced as by those who are stricken by this terrible scourge.

A policy should therefore be defined. Hopeless cases should not be received, and every locality should be interested to the extent of preventing the admission of such incurables to the hospital. This can only be done when each locality is interested through the expense which it may incur in the treatment of these cases. The policy of the State, therefore, should be to provide accommodations and to assess upon each county the actual cost for maintaining each patient from such locality, and it should be so enunciated by the Legislature. This would prevent the bringing into the hospital incurables and the creation thereby of an excessive tax, which could not be justified.

TO MEMBERS OF THE AMERICAN CONGRESS OF TUBERCULOSIS.

You are requested to send your enrolling fee for the Congress of May 14, 15 and 16, 1902, which entitles you to the Bulletin of that Congress free. The enrolling fee is $3.00 for the Congress of 1902.

It has been thought wise to delay the issuing of the Bulletin of the Congress of 1901 until it shall embrace all the papers read before the body or contributed to it, so that when issued it will be complete.

It will be a volume of more than 200 pages and will be illustrated with groups of its officers besides other illustrations.

As many of these papers have already been published in the Medico-Legal Journal and more will appear in the next number of this Journal, members of the Congress of 1901 have already received the June and September numbers of this Journal, and have thus had opportunity to read many of the papers as Nos. 1 and 2 of Vol. XIX were sent free of charge to all enrolled members of the American Congress of Tuberculosis.

To such delegates as were named by the Governors of States, by societies or by foreign Governments or societies, who did not enroll in the Congress of 1901, it is announced that an arrangement has been completed with the Medico-Legal Journal to supply the whole of Vol. XIX at half price, or for $1.50 to those who now remit before the session of May, 1902, so that all delegates can have this privilege who were appointed for the Congress of 1901.

The delegates to the Congress of 1901 appointed by the Governors of the United States of America, or by the Governments of other countries or provinces now on our roll, are invited and expected to enroll as members of the Congress of 1902, and the enrolling fee will be as before, $3 per annum, entitling each to the Bulletin of 1902 free, and to all publications free sent out by the Congress of 1902.

PERSONAL.

Professor Von Krafft-Ebing, Honorary Member of the Medico-Legal Society, Professor of Psychiatry in the University of Vienna since 1889, intends, as it is rumored, to resign his chair on April 1, 1902, and return to Graz where he formerly resided.

Professor Dr. P. Brouardel, Honorary Member of the Medico-Legal Society, has resigned his position as Dean of the Medical Faculty of Paris, a position he has held for fifteen years. We learn that his friends will present him with a medallion which is to be executed by the Artist Roty. His friends in America would feel it a privilege to be allowed to subscribe to this testimonial.

Dr. Ziemke, of Berlin, has been appointed Professor of Medical Jurisprudence in the University of Halle.

Prof. Dr. Rudolph Virchow. The action of the executive committee of the Medico-Legal Society, in regard to this illustrious man, an Honorary member recently taken, is as follows: At the suggestion of the President it was moved and carried that the Corresponding Secretary communicate to our Honorary member, Rudolph Virchow our congratulations at his continued health and vigor, and to express our hope for him still further usefulness to Forensic Medicine to be added as laurels to the crown which posterity must award him for his splendid labor. Distinguished honors have been shown him throughout the world of science. The Russian government has decided to establish a Virchow Institute in Moscow.

Charles T. Yerkes, another aggressive go-ahead American, is said to have overcome all the prejudices and obstinacy of the British managers of the Metropolitan Underground railway system, and introduced or is about to do so, the most advanced American ideas in the London Electric Railways.

J. Pierpont Morgan is one of the most enterprising and public-spirited of living Americans. He has contributed recently $25,000 to the Renovation Fund of Guys Hospital in London, and the same sum for the Electric installation of St. Paul's Cathedral in the English metropolis. He is charged by English journals with the intention of buying out English steamship lines, to stock those he contemplates putting under the American flag, rather than adopt the slower plan of building them.

Prof. Dr. Moritz Benedikt, of Vienna, writes the editor of this journal, that he will send an open letter to him as Secretary of the American Congress of Tuberculosis, in which he will give his views at length, as to the true mission and work of that body, and take up the discussion of some of the public questions which arose at the London Congress of Tuberculosis, and which will be discussed at Vienna in January and February of this year. The letter of Professor Benedikt that he sent to Prof. Clifford Albutt, of the London Congress, has been translated, into our tongue, for this journal, and appears in another column, as also some of the brochures, he has recently contributed to the Science of Medical Jurisprudence. Prof. Benedikt at this moment occupies the highest place among the medical legal jurists of his own country, and he has deserved the position, which he has attained by his talents and genius. His fame is world-wide.

Dr. Adolf Meyer. This gentleman has been appointed by the New York State Lunacy Commission, Director of the Pathological Institute of the State Hospital for the Insane in the State of New York in place of Dr. Ira Van Giesen. The appointment has been well received by the profession. Dr. Meyer is a graduate of the University of Zurich in the class of 1890. He was Pathologist of the Eastern Hospital for the Insane from 1893 to 1895 in the State of Illinois, and at the same time was lecturer on Neurology at the University of Chicago, Ill. He was then appointed Director of the Clinical Work and Laboratory of the State Hospital for the Insane at Worcester, Mass., where he has given great satisfaction. He is well equipped for the duty before him in his present position, and he has a high career of usefulness before him.

JOURNALS AND BOOKS.

PASSION AND CRIMINALITY, a Legal and Literary Study. By Louis Proal, one of the Presiding Judges at the Court of Appeal of Riom (Puy-de-Dome). Laureate of the "Institute." Translated into English by A. R. Allison, M. A. (Oxon.) Published by Charles Carrington, 13 Faubourg, Montmartre, Paris, France, 1901.

This very important, opportune and intensely interesting volume is a substantial octavo of nearly 700 pages, which includes a very able preface written by the translator.

One who is very familiar with the weight and standing of the author of this book has very truthfully remarked that "Judge Proal is a well-known authority on all questions connected with crime, its causes and motives, its various forms and manifestations, its frequency and distribution and its proper punishment, and the author of other valuable and interesting works, throwing light on these vitally important subjects. He holds a high position in the legal profession in France, being one of the Presiding Judges at a French Court of Appeal, and having previously held very responsible official and judicial appointments in other parts of the country, especially in the South. All this has afforded Judge Proal unrivalled opportunities of observation; and indeed the most cursory glance through his books must show what an enormous mass of invaluable information he has gleaned from many different sources—from cases in which he has acted as advocate or prosecutor, or presided as judge; from confidences made to him as 'Juge d'Instruction;' from reports of criminal trials; from official records of suicides, etc., etc. Moreover, this wealth of detail is marshalled in the most admirable order, each argument adduced and each conclusion arrived at being supported by a series of opposite facts in illustration, the whole set forth in that clearly ordered and lucid style that seems the birthright of every educated Frenchman."

Such is the reputation our author bears—a reputation which will surely be reflected in the remarkable book he has now given to the world. "No doubt the facts set forth in it," says a well-known English reviewer, "are often humiliating to our ideals of humanity, and throw lurid lights on some of the social conventions and the boasted civilization of modern Europe; but they are authentic. The impression is ever present of a writer of great original acumen and powers of observation, who is thoroughly acquainted with all aspects of his subject—a subject of enthralling interest to all concerned with the progress of mankind, and one displaying some of the most curious and little realized secrets of the human mind in health and still more in disease."

On these points the present reviewer desires by the way of supplement to say that the present volume is a book that should be on the shelves of every law office and in the library of every law court in the United States to be constantly used as a text-book in the class of cases with which it so fearlessly deals.

Judge Proal has published what, so far as I am aware, no American jurist would dare to give to the world, and that in words and terms that can have but one meaning, and upon which there can be placed but one construction. He has gone behind the scenes in the divorce cases of France, both those settled in and out of court; he stands, as it were, as a priest who, after a long and ripe experience, had violated all the secrets of the confessional; an old family solicitor who knew every bone in the skeleton in the closet in the case of scores of families, had he made a clean breast of all he knew, could not have said more. And information taken from all these sources, brought together, digested and the lessons they teach set forth in a legal and logical way, would form but a small part of what this book conveys to its readers. With all the dignity of a judge, with all the learning of a philosopher. with all the cogent reasoning of a jurist, with all the skill of the literary scholar, the author of this epoch-making book has described the complex workings of the human mind, and has demonstrated how terrible are the crimes which are being and which have been committed by men, women and even children where passion has alone been responsible and where lust has been the chief exciting cause.

Judge Proal has divided his book into fourteen chapters and some of the principal subjects he so forcefully deals with and liberally illustrates with actual cases are: "Suicide as Determined by Passion," "Double Suicide as Determined by Passion," "Hate an Incident of Love," "Seduction and Desertion," "Jealousy," "Adultery on the Part of the Wife and the Husband," "Suicide and Crime as Determined by the Contagion of Literature, of Novels of Passion and of Plays of Passion," "Responsibility in Cases of Crime Determined by Passion, and the Means of Diminishing Such Crimes"

In introducing his work, Judge Proal says: "It is no mere collection of crimes of passion I propose to compile; my subject is the psychology of the lover whom passion drives into crime, of the mistress whom desertion drives into despair, of the man whom jealousy or a mistaken sense of honor makes a murderer or disappointed love a suicide. These studies do but sum up the long series of observations I have made, both on the bench and in my chambers as a *Juge d'Instruction* and *Procureur de la Republique*, where I have enjoyed so many opportunities of cross-questioning those accused of crimes arising from passion, of studying their character and the motives of their aberrations; of reading the documents left behind by suicides, or composed by murderers in their own defence." * * * * * * *

"How comes it that affection may turn to hate, and lovers become the bitterest foes—that the transition is so easy from love to loathing, from the transports of the most exalted tenderness to the frenzies of the most savage anger? How is it so fond a feeling may grow so cruel and lead to the commission of so many barbarous murders by poison and strangulation, and the infliction of such appalling wounds Whence comes the cruelty of love and the ferocity of jealousy? Why does the jealous lover strike the very woman he adores? Why does he pierce with dagger thrusts the very bosom on which he has lain, and disfigure the very features he has just been covering with kisses? Why does the woman whom her lover has deserted burn out his eyes that moved her soul to love, and send a bullet through the heart she was fain but now to feel beating beneath her hand? How is it love may grow so venomous as to put knife and pistol into the hand of lovers and husbands, who, after having sworn eternal affection, tear each others' eyes out at the domestic hearth and in the very conjugal bed? Why does this passion, capable as it is of producing heroes, so often manufacture only cowards and murderers."

It is such questions as these and many of a kindred nature that Judge Proal attempts to answer for us in his *Passion and Criminality*. They are illustrated by instances culled from history of all ages; from every plane of society from shepherds and shepherdesses to kings and queens; and it is truly marvelous with what skill Judge Proal has employed this mass of subject-matter to demonstrate his classifications of crimes of this class and to solve the problems they give rise to in courts of law.

In many instances the present reviewer coincides in opinions with the learned jurist who has given this work to us, while in still others he finds that he is at utter variance with him. But to discuss these differences here would carry this notice far beyond the limitations of our space.

In concluding his chapter on ' Responsibility in Cases of Crimes Determined by Passion," our author states that "Crimes of passion falsely so called should not be allowed to benefit by the pity and indulgence inspired by crimes of love. Even love itself, though it may extenuate guilt, must never be suffered to justify crime. The victims of jealousy and amorous vengeance have as good a right to find protection in the law as those of greed or hate. Whether due to passion or not, crime is always crime." (p. 649.) In this opinion, couched in such conventional language and coming from the mind of a confirmed representative of the bench, the vast majority of jurists will concur. On the other hand there will be an army of dissenters and among these nearly all of our experts and students in insanity, psychology and psychopathia sexualis. Even Judge Proal might be inclined to change his opinion were he suddenly placed in the position that some of those men who have plead their cases before him have been placed. We are somewhat hasty when we throw all killings of men into the general category of crimes committed. In many instances fathers and brothers are often fully justified in slaying the wily and worldly seducer of an innocent and unsophisticated daughter or sister. The law neither recommends nor recognizes punishment at all adequate in many cases to punish the kind of a seducer I have in my mind as I write these lines.

Again, in the concluding chapter, I cannot agree with all that Judge Proal suggests in the way of the "Means of Diminishing Crime Determined by Passion." The general sentiment and trend of this chapter, however, is excellent; the high morality of its tone commands the respect of the reader of it; and the evidence of extensive research and careful thought it exhibits will win the esteem of both student and socialist alike, though some of this class may demur, nay, will demur, to the practicability of its suggestions.

I find myself to be utterly at variance with Judge Proal when he recommends the spreading and encouragement of the Christian religion and faith as an antidote to the crimes of passion. I fail to see how the perpetuation of superstition can ever prove to be an efficient cure for the various kinds of deeds and overt acts or crimes that Judge Proal discusses in his book. Nevertheless this is a work that can be read with infinite advantage by our Potters, and our Parkhursts, and our Jeromes, who scent vice and crime in every breath they draw in the streets of the city wherein they reside, while the means they employ to suppress this and encourage morality are enough in many instances to excite all sensible men and women to cry out in self defence. No epidemic of crime yet has been successfully snuffed out with a blanket, and in a great and very populous metropolis one of the best methods of putting crime on the increase and widely encouraging it is to keep up a constant howl in the press and pulpit that that metropolis is, from one end to the other, a perfect hotbed of immorality, wherein flourishes night and day every crime known in the calendar.

R. W. SHUFELDT, M. D.

STUDIES IN THE PSYCHOLOGY OF SEXUAL INVERSION. By Havelock Ellis. F. A. Davis & Co., Philadelphia. 1901.

This is the second edition of Dr. Havelock Ellis' first volume of his announced series of five volumes relating to the "Pcychology of Sex." The first edition was published in London five years ago, which produced a somewhat sensational trial. The late Sir Charles Hall, then Recorder of London, in a proceeding instituted against the publisher instigated by the police, made a decision that the work was not a scientific book and ordered it to be destroyed Our readers will recall that occurrence and will remember that the scientific men in all countries generally denounced that decision as absurd and aptly illustrating the ignorance of such men as occasionally by the mysterious dispensations of Providence come upon the bench. But Dr. Havelock Ellis properly held England responsible for the affront put upon him and immediately announced that he would not leave it in the power of any English judge to repeat the offence and that his works would be published in countries who would have a proper appreciation of his work and his motive.

He revised and enlarged the work, added new cases and made a few other changes, and the work appears with the imprint of F. A. Davis & Company as publishers.

It is a handsome volume of 272 pages, compressed into seven chapters, with five appendices, and will, we think, attract the attention of the medical profession and such jurists as have made any study of the subject.

Dr. Havelock Ellis in this work deals with facts as they are disclosed by careful observers.

The subject is gruesome, but the conditions exist and we can not eliminate them as proper subjects of scientific study and consideration.

It has been regarded as not quite the proper thing to discuss them, some say that we should be silent concerning them, because they relate to unnameable practices. In many countries the laws are strictly and closely set against them. In some no laws exist. It is no longer possible in the study of social problems to ignore actual facts and conditions. Their consideration can not be thus avoided.

If society, like the ostrich, hides its head so that it sees nothing, it does not change the environment.

In a literary way the work is more carefully written than either Krafft's, Ebbing's or Schrenck-Notzing's. The profession generally will regard this compilation as a valuable addition to our stock of knowledge.

The cases disclose, some of them present Medico-Legal questions of interest as to the legal views presented and as to the moral responsibility of the sexual invert. The subject is a disagreeable one, but it is admirably treated and shows a master hand in its production.

WARWICK OF THE KNOBS. By John Uri Lloyd. Dodd, Meade & Co., New York. 1901. pp. 305. Price $1.50.

If any one who read "*Stringtown on the Pike*" and had a faint heart as to its success, based on its sale only, they may have not taken into account the genius of John Uri Lloyd as a business man and a merchant.

In assiduous, constant, persistent and unremitting work we recognize the true genius of the man.

Faith without works is as bad an investment in book making and book selling as in religion.

John Uri Lloyd is both a genius and an artist.

He is a genius because he has discerned in this age of commercialism how to transform his manufactures into gold.

He has become a literary alchemist and he don't have to use the baser metals to replenish his coffers with golden ducats that have the genuine clink.

He is an artist because he is an apt disciple of William Morris, who finds his highest joy in his work and this gives his work a higher polish and greater value.

The world likes novelty and surprises, and his discovery has been to learn how to manage the press, in this money-making age, so as to make the dollars come out of the mill when he causes its wheels to go round.

His facility for artistic expression in the propogation of the gospel of faith in his own works, backed by a never-failing supply of good motive power, is a characteristic which may have been hidden and lain dormant in the past, but which must now be known and read of all men.

The author of "Mr. Brown, of New York," and of "Mr. Potter, of Texas," Mr. Archie Gunter, may have been tarred with the same stick. He may have placed a light in the way or a lamp for the path to guide and cheer the author of "Etidorpa" and "Warwick of the Knobs," but for a faith that could almost move mountains, and that splendid courage which displays the most admirable traits of Mr. Lloyd's character, that goes to the limit in a game whether he holds ace high or a pair of deuces, when he puts up his pile with the same calm courage as if he held a straight flush, presents Mr. Lloyd in a light which commands our highest admiration.

There have been generals, like Napoleon, who carried on wars wholly sustained by the gold and the treasuries of the enemies' country. They have aroused the wonder of the world by their victories, but what shall be said as to the genius and courage of him who carrie his conquests to triumphant financial results without such aids, and ground it out of the revolving cylinders of his advertising engines with a success that dazzles us all by its brilliancy?

His nerve has been grander than his triumph. What the world loves is the glamor of success.

Mr. Lloyd may have sat at the feet of Col. Richard Savage and may have learned of him, but we must acknowledge that he has held the enchanted wand which has had the talismanic power of transfusion and transmutation into gold.

Mr. Lloyd is a great chemist. He is more, he is an alchemist.

His publishers, Dodd, Mead & Co., must not be lost sight of in this matter. Other publishers might do well to study the methods by which Mr. Lloyd's books have come to the front. We commend this house to the authors of books who have ambition and faith.

Our advice to our readers is to take the good the gods give to you, buy "Warwick of the Knobs" and be happy.

The work is well written; it teaches good lessons; it shows that Mr. Lloyd has besides these qualities we have named literary ability of a high order. His literary success is no longer a problem. It is already a success.

THE INDIAN REVIEW. C. A. Natesan & Co., publishers, Madras, India. G. A. Nateson, Esq, B. A., Editor, Esplanade, Madras. Annual sub., 5 reals; $2.50.

The October number of this monthly, No. 10, Vol 2, is on our table. Sidney Webb, Esq., contributes an interesting article on "Twentieth Century Politics."

The editor contributes a big, able and masterly history of the reign of Abdur Rahaman, the Amee of Afghanistan, who has been for the past more than twenty years ruler of that country. The article gives a brief history of the British relations with Afghanistan since 1837, when Lord Auckland forced Shah Shuga on the Afghan throne against his rival, Dort Mahomed, resulting most disastrously to English interests in the Afghan war. Thousands of lives, millions of money, and the forced restoration of Dort Mahomed, the hatred of the Afghans toward England, which after his death in 1864 under the reign of his son and successor, Sher Ali; the treaty of May 26, 1879; followed almost immediately by the massacre of the British officers and residency; the invasion of the Kuram valley with a British force of 5,500 men; which was followed by the accession of the dead Amir to the Afghan throne. The article is an admirable translation of the rule of the dead Amir, his friendship for England, the details of his coming to the throne, and the social, moral and political situation and att'tude of Afghanistan, well worthy the study of those interested in the country and the subject.

The eldest son, Habibullah, succeeds the late ruler; Lord Curzon is the British Viceroy and the future of Afghanistan is one of the most intricate problems of Russian influence and interest and British policy in what is known as "The Central Asiatic Question."

K. M. Begbie contributes an able review of the character, genius and writings of the talented young American writer, Stephen Crane, in which full justice is done that lamented child of genius.

K. B. Ramanathan contributes a brief review which he entitles "A Literary Criticism in the Reign of Victoria."

He divides it into three parts: The era before her reign, the critics and writers of the Victorian era, and extracts from some of the ablest names, Ruskin, Shelly, Keats, Byron, Moore, J. A. Symonds, Matthew Arnold, as critics, the latter of the poets, Swinburne, Byron, Shelly, Chaucer, Dryden, Wordsworth; also as critics Water, Pater, Professor Raleigh, Colonel Lamb and de Quincy, and touches on the influence of the French critics and of Mr. Taine and Herbert Spencer.

The notes and other headings in the journal well worth review we shall reserve for future notice.

BENCH AND BAR. By Marshall Brown, Esq. 578 pp. T. H. Flood & Co., Chicago. 1899.

Mr. Marshall Brown, of the Pittsburgh Bar, the author of this work, contrasts wit and humor, and quotes some good sayings of Horace Smith, Dr. Fuller and Washington Irving, defining the difference between the humorous and the witty.

He also quotes Whipple, Herbert, Moliere, Rev. Isaac Barrow and Sidney Smith, as to the true significance and definition of wit.

The author has collected very many of the best stories, anecdotes and specimens of eloquence of our American bar, judges and lawyers, and has drawn on the standard works on the subject, from the English bench and bar.

The selections of sayings and stories are, many of them, new, and he embraces a large number of our prominent judges and lawyers. It would be quite impossible and invidious to quote even the best, for they are so many. Some of the best are given of Hon. Jos. H. Choate, our embassador to London.

J. Proctor Knott's speech on Duluth is given at length, and his view on the Schley and Sampson controversy. A fine extract is given from Mr. F. R. Coudert's address on "Success at the Bar." James T. Brady is remembered, but his brother, Judge John R., is forgotten. Samuel S. Cox, the soul of wit and the foremost humorist of the American Bar in Congress, is not mentioned.

A splendid example of the eloquence of Col. Robert Ingersoll is given. The great power of Wm. Fullerton, as a cross-examiner, is illustrated.

John G. Saxe's "Briefless Barrister" is given, as well as his "Early Rising." The selections from Daniel Webster are admirable, and Wirt's excellent letter of advice to Francis W. Gilmer is given at length.

Excellent stories of Sir Charles Russell, the Earl of Killoween, are told, and of Thomas B. Reed, S. S. Prentiss, George D. Prentice, Daniel O. Connell, Charles O'Connor, Thomas M. Marshall, and scores of others.

The selections of the stories of and by Abraham Lincoln are exceedingly fine.

The volume will be read by lawyers and judges with pleasure, and as a collection of humorous sketches, as well as eloquent selections, it is well worth a place on the shelves of any lawyer's library.

ARCHIVES DE NEUROLOGIE Paris. November. 1901. A. Joffroy, V. Magnan, F. Raymond, Directors; Dr. Bourneville, Editor-in-Chief; J. B. Charcot and J. Noir, Assistants.

The November number (71) contains an interesting paper by Ch. Fere, Physician at the Bicetre, entitled "L' Influence de Alcohol et du Tobac sur le Travail."

Dr. Fere insists that, from a hygienic standpoint, it is an act of extreme folly to drink the one or smoke the other.

He asserts that all physiologists agree that both these factors impair the energy of man. He presents an exhaustive array of facts, data and clinical experiments, in support of these propositions, and he quotes a long array of authorities, with very important and careful scientific tabulated records of the experimental work.

His article is elaborate and designed to be almost exhaustive of the theme, and is announced to be continued in following numbers

Dr. E. Marandon de Montyl, Physician at Ville Evrard, commenced also an elaborate and careful paper entitled "Contribution a l' etude des Reactions de la Pean ches les Aliennes."

The author claims that the subject has received too little attention, and says that Dr. Fere is the only one who has recently considered it in relation to the epileptic and hysterical, in his work in 1898, in which Mousa Lance took part. He cites the work of Cull, in 1859, and Zunker, in 1875, and alludes to the reports made by Michelson and Axenfeld, and alludes to the earlier work in which M. Laney assisted Dr. Fere in the demography of epileptics.

He explains the method adopted by himself, at his institution, with the aid of Dr. Capgras, based on an examination of 326 insane of all classes.

Their studies corrobborate Gull and Zunder, as well as Fere and Lance. Careful tables are given, and the subject is to be continued in succeeding numbers af the journal.

Under Mental Pathology, Dr. de Musgrave Clay reviews the presidential address of Dr. Fletcher Beach, before the British Medico-Psychological Association, of July, 1901, at London, as published in the *Journal of Mental Science*, and the same writer reviews eight articles in the October number, 1900 of that journal, and six articles in succeeding numbers.

The Editor, Dr. Bourneville, concludes his elaborate and careful report of the transactions of the 11th Congress of the Alienists and Neurologists of France and of Countries Speaking the French Language, held at Limoges, August 5th, 1901, under the presidency of Dr. Gilbert Ballit, reported by M. le Dr. H. Tagrut.

Dr. Paul Serieux contributes, under "Insane Asylums," notices of the 25th Annual Exercises of the Asylum at Ott-Scherbitz; also a resume of the Society for the Aid of the Insane, at Zurich, Switzerland, reviewing its 8th Annual Report; and the same writer gives a very interesting account of the Asylum for the Criminal Insane at Düren, in the Province of Ruenane, as also the report of Drs. Saoli and Danneman, of the German Alienists held at Frankfort in 1900; and he gives the Regulations adopted November 15, 1900, governing the internal administration of the Asylum of the Seine in France, containing 22 separate articles.

The announcement is also made, in this journal, of the then recent meeting of the "Concours de l' Internes," on December 2, 1901, at the Prefecture de la Seine.

THE BOMBAY REVISED REPORTS. Ahmedabad, India. Edited by Jivanlal V. Desai, Esq., B. A., and Manilal Harilal Vakil, B. A., LL. B, Vol. I.

The work is a studied, careful report of 72 cases decided between 1800 and 1820 These cases contain the corresponding references to those in Barrsdail's Reports, Vol. I. The work is full of interest, as the report is given quite at length, and the issue and reasons are good.

THE SOUTHERN MEDICAL JOURNAL. J. W. P. Smithwick, Editor· La Grange, N. C.

This Journal is making rapid strides in its general interest, due to the zeal and ability of its Editor, who has thrown so much of his personality into his work.

In looking over Vol. I, which closed with the June number, 1901, we find scarcely a notice that does not contain some original work by the Editor, usually clinical in character.

Dr. Smithwick is one of the most enterprising and industrious of the younger medical men of his State, and he has built up this Journal wholly by his own efforts.

ANTHONY'S PHOTOGRAPHIC BULLETIN FOR 1902. Vol. XIV. E. & H. T. Anthony & Co., N. Y. W. I. Scandlin, Editor.

Nowhere can we see a more complete record of the progress of Photography in Art than in the Annual Bulletins of the trade publishers of photographic reproduction.

The frontispiece is an example of very high artistic excellence, from a portrait taken by F. G. Shumacher, Los Angeles, and reproduced in photogravure by John Andrews & Son, of Boston, Mass., that would make Gutekunst, of Philadelphia, look to his laurels.

The Electric Light Engraving Co. present a fine photo-engraving of Senator Hanna's dinner party to President McKinley in 1896, in which the faces are good and the work creditable.

Such a volume shows as well the value and importance of artistic taste in the photographer, as in the reproduction by the photo-engraver.

The practical and the money making side is foremost and highest in this work. High executive excellence and advance seems not to have due weight. The reproductions are, few of them, of the first-class, in an artistic sense, and much finer work is done by amateurs than the bulk of these reproductions show.

Some of the best are by the Central City Engraving Co., of Syracuse, N. Y.; the Electric City Engraving Co., Buffalo; the Scientific Engraving Co. of N. Y., D. D. Spellman; Photochromotype Engraving Co., of Philadelphia.

The usefulness of the art in the progress of science, and the useful arts and trades, show the best work of this Annual.

The work of Scientific men, like Dr. R. W. Shufeldt, in photography from nature, illustrating plants, animals, shells, etc.; those of Chas. M. Taylor, Jr., illustrating scenes of Nature; W. H. Wamsley, in photomaeography, like his fig. 5 in maidenhair fern; and similar works in architecture, landscape, gardening and the trades, shows the vast scope and field of this department in publications.

There is an entire lack of high artistic ideas, æsthetic taste, or great artistic merit. Not one figure from the highest source of beauty, the human form, except the face, and in that not the progress we expected.

The beautiful, the exquisite, the æsthetic, is ignored too much, and the mercenary side is more prominent in the illustration of an art to which we must look for the elevation of artistic taste in the popular mind more than to all other sources combined,

Nothing can be more beautiful than the creations of nature, which the microscope reveals in plants, insects, and these creations too small for human unaided vision. Nothing that the miracle of photography reproduces can excel the exquisite beauty of these minutest forms of life, the eye, the wing, the organs of the minutest insects, and other infinitely smaller forms of animal life beyond our view. The whole field of the minute anatomy of the brain, of the blood, and of the substance that is thrilled by what we call life, is the true field and mission of this art of photography and its reproduction, and the highest form or expression of beauty and truth should be the goal and ambition of the most gifted of those who have, or should have, joy in the work of its artistic creation and reproduction.

Life of Lord Russell, of Killowen, by R. Barry O'Brian, of the Inner Temple, Barrister-at-Law. Smith Elder & Co., Publishers, 15 Waterloo Place, London. (1901.)

The work shows a rare devotion by the author to the late Chief Justice of England, and admiration for his genius and character. It deserves more than the passing notice we can give it here.

Its great interest lies in the first authorative published statement of facts concerning the case of Mrs. Maybrick that has come in any reliable way to the public knowledge, of his relations to the efforts he made for the release of the unfortunate lady, and in his persistent and long continued efforts with the Home Secretary of England for her release, which he carried on most steadily and persistently until the day of his death.

We quote from Mr. Bryan's work some selections, regretting that we can not give it more in detail. Mr. Bryan says under the heading:

THE MAYBRICK CASE.

To dwell on any of Russell's cases after the Parnell commission would be an anti-climax. Therefore, I shall pass lightly over them. The one which at the time excited the most interest was his defense of Mrs. Maybrick.

In the summer of 1889, Mrs. Maybrick was indicted at Liverpool for the murder of her husband (by arsenical poisoning), convicted and sentenced to death. The capital sentence was immediately commuted to penal servitude for life. For Russell's biographer the interest in the case is the characteristic persistency with which he assailed Home Secretary after Home Secretary, seeking as it were to carry his former client's freedom by storming the positions of those who kept the key to her prison house. Immediately after the trial he wrote to Mr. Mathews, then Home Secretary: "I am sorry to say it will be necessary for you to consider this case. Against her there was a strong case undoubtedly of the means being within her reach to poison her husband; but there was no direct evidence of administration by her. And further, but a small quantity of arsenic was discovered in the body after death, and none in the stomach, bile, heart, spleen, etc. The symptoms, all were agreed, were those of gastric enteritis; but while witnesses for the prosecution attributed it to arsenical poison, a very strong body of evidence was given for the defense that it was not so." In November, 1895, he wrote to Sir Matthew White Ridley, conveying his "strong and emphatic opinion that Florence Maybrick ought never to have been convicted, and that her continued imprisonment is an injustice which ought promptly to be ended. I have never wavered in this opinion. After her conviction, I wrote and had printed a memorandum which is, I presume, preserved at the Home Office. Lest it should not be, I herewith transmit a copy."

"As you know what happened was that Mr. Mathews after consultation with the present Lord Chancellor (Lord Halsbury), and Mr. Justice Stephen, and after seeing Dr. Stephenson, the principal crown witness, and also the late Dr. Tidy, respited the capital sentence on the express ground that there was sufficient doubt whether the death had been caused by arsenical poisoning, to justify the respite, and he ordered Florence Maybrick to be kept in penal servitude for life on the ground "that the evidence led to the conclusion that the prisoner administered arsenic and attempted to administer arsenic to the deceased with intent to murder him."

"It will be seen (1) that such a doubt existed as to the commission of the offence for which Florence Maybrick was tried as rendered it improper in the opinion of the Home Secretary and of his advisers that the capital sentence should be carried out, and (2) that for more than six years Florence Maybrick has been suffering imprisonment on the assumption of Mr. Mathews that she committed an offence, for which she was never tried by the constitutional authority, and of which she has never been adjudged guilty."

This in itself is a most serious state of things. It is manifestly unjust that Florence Maybrick should suffer for a crime in regard to which she has never been called upon to answer before any lawful tribunal. It is not obvious that if the attempt to murder had been the offense for which was arraigned, the course of the defense would have been different. I speak as her counsel of what I know. Read the report of the defense and you will see that I devoted my whole strength to and massed the evidence upon the point that the prosecution had misconceived the facts, that the foundation on which the whole case rested was rotten. For that, in fact, there was no murder; that on the contrary the deceased had died of death from natural causes. It is true, the incidental reference was made to certain alleged acts of Florence Maybrick, but the references were incidental only, the stress of my argument being that in fact no murder had been committed, because the evidence did not warrant the conclusion that the deceased had died from arsenical poisoning. On the other hand, had the crown counsel suggested the cause of attempt to murder by poison, it would have been the duty of counsel to address himself directly and mainly to the alleged circumstances which, it was argued, pointed to guilty intent. That these alleged circumstances were capable in part of being explained, in part of being minimized, and in part of being attacked as unreliably vouched, cannot, I think, be doubted by anyone who has with a critical eye scanned the evidence.

I do not deny that my feelings are engaged in this case. It is impossible they should not be. But I have honestly tried to judge the case, and I now say that if called upon to advise in my character of head of the Criminal Judicature of this country, I should advise you that Florence Maybrick ought to be allowed to go free."

In 1898, he returned to the subject, writing still more strongly to the Home Secretary: "I think it my duty to renew my protest against the continued imprisonment of Florence Maybrick. I consider the history of this case reflects discredit on the administration of the criminal law. I think my protest ought to be attended to at last. The prisoner has already undergone imprisonment for a period four times (or more) as long as the minimum punishment fixed by law for the commission of the crime of which she has never been convicted, or for which, indeed, she has never been tried, but of which she has been adjudged guilty by your predecessor in the office of Home Secretary."

In the very year of his death he made a fresh protest, and on February 6th, 1900, wrote a letter to the Home Secretary, from which I take the following extract: "I beg to thank you for your letter of the 3rd instant, which greatly distressed me. I saw the wretched woman last week while at Aylesbury. She looked wretched, although I believe she is not ill. In the ordinary sense I understand your view, but is it the right one? You say you regard her as a properly convicted murderer, undergoing a commuted sentence. Is this so? Your predecessor, Landaff, after inquiry, in which the Lord Chancellor and the Government Chemist assisted, publicly stated that there was room for doubt whether any murder had at all been committed, but that he came to the conclusion that the accused had attempted to commit murder. Nor was this view—that perhaps the man had not died of poison—other than most reasonable, because the quantity of poison revealed on analysis was infinitesimal, and such might well have been accounted for by the notorious arsenic eating habits of the man. The evidence of Sir James Pool, some time Mayor of Liverpool, established this: 'It is one of the faults of the summing up that the Judge failed to give due weight to this entirely reliable evidence. Nor did this evidence stand alone. It was strongly confirmed by that of a local chemist who had for years been in the habit of supplying the deceased with 'arsenical drinks.'" Mr. Bryan says further:

And so to the end, the fate of this unhappy woman occupied his thoughts, and he never ceased either in private or officially, as the opportunity occurred, to say that there had been a grave miscarriage of justice in the case, and that Florence Maybrick ought to be allowed to go free."

Lord Russell, of Killowen, felt himself under restraint as to speaking for publication, but his friends knew from him what he had done and was doing. He could not consider it proper for him to publish or to allow to be published what he had placed on the record at the office of the Home Secretary in support of the various briefs and arguments he from time to time made to that official urging her release. He repeated these statements to the Baroness de Roques, the mother of Mrs. Maybrick, and had no reserve in stating to her the arguments, reading some times copies of the language he had used with the Home Secretary, but never under conditions that would justify furnishing the language to the public. He frequently did the same to his personal friends. He expressed to many of these his strong belief in her innocence of th crime charged upon her, and to counsel connected with the efforts for her release.

Mr. Alexander W. MacDougall, barrister at law, was one of the counsel who gave a written opinion on the case with Mr. Reginald J. Smith, Q. C., and Sir Fletcher Moulton, Q. C., at the instance of the N. Y. World. The former told the writer that Lord Russell in the consultations with him respecting the case, and the opinions given, expressed to him, Mr. MacDougall, his belief in her innocence of the crime charged, and believed that she ought never to have been convicted, and that she should be released. That her imprisonment was an injustice which ought to be quickly ended.

There was an attempt after Lord Russell's death to libel his memory by the assertion that he doubted her innocence.

The letter he wrote her voluntarily in prison, while Lord Chief Justice, should let forever at rest such aspersions on his memory, and the direct statement to Mr. Bryan of his belief that "that there was no murder, and that on the contrary the deceased had died from natural causes,"—and "that the evidence did not warrant the conclusion that the deceased had died from arsenical poisoning"—should forever dispose of these slanders upon the name of Lord Russell, of Killowen.

The bar of public opinion is in accord with the general opinion of the Bar of all countries, and the great majority of the lawyers and judges who have examined the evidence, do not believe Mrs. Maybrick guilty of the crime for which she was indicted and tried.

But on one thing all men ought to be agreed; whether guilty or innocent, and outside that consideration, her twelve years in prison is punishment enough, and that the coronation of King Edward VII. should be signalized by the royal pardon of this long suffering lady.

EX-JUDGES SUPREME COURT OF OHIO.

HON. RUFUS P. SPALDING.
1848—1852.

HON. FRANKLIN J. DICKMAN.
1886—1896,

HON. JOHN McLEAN.
1815—1818.

HON. ALLEN G. THURMAN.
1852—1856.

HON. RUFUS P. RANNEY.
1850—1856. 1862—1864.

SOCIETY FOR PSYCHICAL RESEARCH VOL. XV. (1901).

KEEGAN. Paul, Trench & Trubner, London.

Vol. XV. of the work of this body, was issued in five separate parts, 36 to 40, both inclusive, and present an unusually large amount of new matter.

Part XXXVI contains, The Fire Walk, by Andrew Lang, which details accounts of eye witnesses and participants in some cases of the rite called Te Umu Ti, still practiced in Raiatea of the group of "Society Islands" as described by Miss Tchira Henry, and by Colonel Gudgeon, British Resident at Raretonga, where the rite was celebrated and where Dr. W. Craig, Dr. George Craig, Mr. Goodwin and Colonel Gudgeon walked with bare feet over the heated stones unharmed, followed by 200 Maoris. Other accounts,at other places, are given in an article by Andrew Lang, with details and authority cited.

The 2d paper is by Mrs. Henry Sidgwick entitled "Discussion of the "Trance Phenomena of Mrs. Piper."

Mrs. Sidgwick begins by referring carefully to the various papers relating to the phenomena as published in the proceedings, giving title, author, volume and page.

She assumes, and agrees, with Professor Newbold, at the outset, (Proceedings Vol. XIV, p. 7,) in the assertion, "I accept the conclusion arrived at by everyone so far as I know, who has studied the case at any length," "that it was not consciously got by Mrs. Piper during waking life and then fraudulently palmed off on the sitter as supernormal;" or as Dr. Leaf puts it (Proceedings Vol. VI., p. 559), "as to the first and most obvious question whether she consciously acquires knowledge with regard to her sitters with the inteution of deceiving, I may say most positively, that I regard such a supposition as entirely untenable."

Mrs. Sidgwick, in searching for the real cause of the phenomena, assumed "That telepathy—in the sense of the impression of one living mind by another, otherwise than through the recognized channels of sense may be taken as provisionally established by the evidence collected by our society and other investigators."

Mrs. Sidgwick agrees with Prof. Lodge, "That thought transferrence is the most common place explanation to which it is possible to appeal in the case of Mrs. Piper." Proceedings Vol. VI., p. 451.)

Mr. Andrew Lang contributes an interesting article on "The Trance Phenomena of Mrs. Piper," in which he discards all idea that Mrs. Piper's evidence is in any way on the evidence to be attributed to the interference of the spirits of deceased persons, and gives some very interesting experiences, respecting the working of telepathy, and in aid of the hypothesis of telepathy as an explanation of the phenomena.

A paper by Prof. Harlow Gale follows: Entitled, "A Study in Spiritualistic Hallucinations," giving very interesting details of Dr. E. S., of St. Paul, who believed he saw and conversed with Jesus Christ, as a maltreated spirit, and a very important communication on the whole subject of hallucinations being case No. 1 in the supplement.

Part 37, of Vol. 15, is devoted to the admirable presidential address of F. W. H. Myers, May 18, 1900, a most admirable presentation of the views of Mr. Myers, and a statement of the status of physical research from his standpoint, which must ever remain a classic in psychical literature.

Part XXXVIII of Vol. XV, issued in October, 1900, pp. 129 to 448, both inclusive, the greater part of which pp. 130 to 383, is devoted to the so-called divining rod, and is a valuable and most interesting report on the subject of finding water by this means.

The supplement contains a paper by F. W. H. Myerson, "Pseudo Possession," which is a discussion upon two books, the one by Dr. Janet, which deals with multiplex personality, and the work of Prof. Flourney and the subliminal mental accounts of remarkable cases, involving interesting observations and experiments in hypnotism.

Review of the the Pook of Petrovo Solovovo of St. Petersburg, by Walter Leaf; of a seance of S. A. Bezsonoff, and of Camille Flaminarion's work on L' Incounue and les problemes Psychiques," Paris 1900, by Frank Podmore,and of Lloyd Tuckey's work on "Treatment of Hypnotism," and suggestions by Dr. G. F. Rogers, and of "Psychism Analysis of Things Existing," by Paul Gibier, N. Y. Bulletin Pub. Co., 5th ed., no date.

Part 39, Vol. 15, is the beautiful memorial of Prof. Henry Sidgwich, by F. W. H. Myer, one of the loveliest and most beautiful tributes one man ever paid to the memory of another, and this part filled by the concluding No. 40 of the vol. 15, which announces the death of Mr. F. W. H. Myers, January 17, 1901, a paper by Dr. Morton Prince on a case of "Multiple Personality," and a list of the officers and members of the society.

BOOKS, JOURNALS AND PAMPHLETS RECEIVED.

PROFESSOR DR. MORITZ BENEDIKT, Viennna. Judicial Letters:
1. "Degeneration and Crime." 2. "Derangement of Mind and Crime." 3. "Epilepsy and Crime." 4. "Alcoholism and Crime." 5. Sexual Perversity and Criminal Law." 6. "On Reform of Legislation Relating to the Insane." 7. Board of Insane Asylums."

"On the Question of Tuberculosis." Open letter to Prof. Clifford Albutt, Cambridge.

"Traumatic Neurosis" Report made at the Scientific Session of the Medical Society of Vienna, held January 28, 1901.

"On the Question of Abstinence." Prologue pronounced at the last Anti-Alcoholism Congress at Vienna.

"Address" Read on same subject at above Congress.

"Report." Une formule fondamentale de Psychologie et ses relations av laec criminalite.

'Uranism."

"Les Crimes en Foule."

NOAH H. AARONSTAM, M. D., PH. D., Detroit. "The Modern Treatment of Tuberculodermata." October, 1901.

DR. MORITZ MAYER, Simmern. Royal County Surgeon. "Gunshot Wound of the Fossa Supraclavicularis." "Traumatic Hysterics with Contractions and Atrophy." Reprint from the Medical Expert-Gazette. (Aerz'liche Sachverständige-Zeitung.) No. 21, 1901.

Brochure II. "Division for Forensic Medicine." No. 32.

Reports made: 1. Mr. Emil Ungar, Bonn. "On the Influence of Putrefaction upon Lung Tests." 2. Mr. Moritz Mayer, Simmern. "On Poisonous Effects of Leucotactical Remedies." 3. Mr. Cassimir Stubenrath, Würzburg *a.* "Experimental Investigations of Cadaver Wax." *b.* 'Stereoscopical and Projective Exhibitions in the Service of Forensic Medicine." With demonstrations.

WILLIAM ALLEN PUSEY, A. M., M. D., Chicago. "Roentgen Rays in the Treatment of Diseases of the Skin." A review of recent literature and personal experience. Reprinted from the Journal of the American Medical Association.

M. J. ROSENAU, Passed Assistant Surgeon, U. S. Marine Hospital Service, Washington, D C. "Disinfection Against Mosquitos with Formaldehyd and Sulphur Dioxid." Bulletin No. 6 of the Hygienic Laboratory.

HAROLD N. MOYER, M. D., Chicago, Ill. "The Relation of the Medical Editor to Original Communications." Reprint from July number, Vol. XIV, Annals of Gynecology and Pediatry. Boston, 1901.

ENGLISH SOCIETY FOR THE STUDY OF INEBRIETY. Proceedings. No. 69. September, 1901.

C. H. HOPWOOD, Q C., M. B. "A Plea for Mercy to Offenders." 1894.

THE SOUTHERN MEDICAL JOURNAL. Vol. V. 1901.

J. V. DESAI, ESQ, B. A., Ahmedebad, India. "The Lawyer." Lawyer Co-operative Publishing Co. "Where to Look for the Law." 1901.

E. J. BARRICK, M. D., Toronto, Ontario. "Practical Solution of the Question of Dealing with the Consumptive Poor." 1901.

DR. WM. M. WARREN. 'The Doctor's Logic Limps." 1891.

TRUMAN W. BROPLY, M. D., D. D. S., LL. D., Chicago. "Surgical Treatment of Palatal Defects." 1901.

DR. E. LICEAGA, Mexico. Contribution: "A Study of the Cure of Phthisis."

"The Defence Against Tuberculosis." 1901. Translation by W. Thompson of "Defensa contra la Tuberculosis" 1901.

"Instructiones para las personas que Padeqeu del Pecho, y Para lasque les Rodeau." 1899.

"Le Plateau Central Mexique (Mesa Central) Consideri comme Station Sanitari pour les Phthiques."

MATTEEW W. SMITH, M. D., Austin, Texas. "Prevention of Tuberculosis." 1898.

"The Invisible Enemy and our Methods of Defense."

Doctor Emilio Conti, Buenos, Ayres, S. A. Revista de la Tuberculosis. Organs de la Liga Argentina contra la Tuberculosis. Buenos, Ayres. 1901.

Doctor Samuel Gache, Buenos, Ayres. La Tuberculose dans la Republique, Argentine. 1899.

La Lucha contra La Tuberculosis en la Republica Argentina. 1901.

John C. Dacosta, Jr., M. D. Clinical Hematology. P. Blakiston's Sons & Co., Philadelphia, Pa. 1902.

Eleventh Annual Report of the New York Kindergarten Association. June, 1900—June, 1901. 29 W. 42d St., N. Y.

William Davis Foster, M. D., Kansas City, Mo. Dermoid Tumors. 1901.

New Hampshire Sanitary Bulletin. Irving A. Watson, Editor. Vol. 1. Jan. 1902.

All Opinions of the United States Supreme Court. The Lawyers' Co-operative Publishing Company.

Dr. Charles Parnisetti, Alexandria, Italy. Anomelies du Polygone Arteriel de Willis chez Lez Criminels, en Rapport aux Alterations du Cerveau et du Coeur. J. H. de Bussy, Amsterdam. 1901.

G. A. Natesan & Co., Esplanade, Madras, India. The Indian Review. No. 10., Vol. 2. Oct., 1901.

Prof. F. Schuchardt, Rostock, Mecklenburg. Report on Psychiatric Literature in the year 1900. Supplement to Vol. 58 of the "Allgemeine Zeitschrift fuer Psychiatrie." Berlin. 1901.

Alphonse de Basschere, Conseiller a la Cour d' Appel de Bruxelles, Brussels, Belgium. La Legislation de Police Sanitaire. Oct., 1901.

Prof. Dr. I. J. Wising, Stockholm, Sweden. Hygiea. No. 10. Oct., 1901.

Sweet & Maxwell, L'td., 3 Chancery Lane, London. Bailments, by Wyatt Paine.

The Practice of the Privy Council in Judicial Matters. By Frank Safford and George Wheeler. Barristers.

Edwin C. Walker, N. Y. Vice: Its Friends and Its Foes. Oct. 1901.

Alf. F. de Faria, Editor. Porto, Portugal. Revista das Revistas. Nos. 62 and 63. Vol. 3.

William C. Sprague, Editor, The National Bankruptcy News and Reports. The Sprague Publishing Co., Detroit.

G. W. McCaskey, A. M., M. D., Professor of Clinical Medicine, Port Wayne College of Medicine. Physiology. The Basis of Clinical Medicines, A Plea for Scientific Methods; President's Address Before the State Medical Society at South Bend, Ind., May 16, 1901; Simple and Ethereal Sulphates: A Simple and Rapid Method for their Separate Determination—Thirty Minutes.

Dr. Jul. Morel, Medecin—directeur de l' Asile d' Alienees de l' Etat a Mons. La Prophylaxie et Le Traitment Du Criminel Recidiviste.

John Lawrence Farrell, of the New York Bar. The Divorce Question; Uniformity in Legislation.

Eugene C. Massey, Secretary and Treasurer Virginia State Board Association. Richmond, Va. Report of the Sixteenth Annual.

Charles Denison, A. M., M. D., Denver, Col. The Relation of Out-Door Life to High Altitude Therapy. Read before the Colorado State Medical Society, June, 1901; Devitalized-Air Toxaemia, a Prime Cause of Tuberculosis.

John F. Whitworth, Corporation Deputy, State Department, Pennsylvania. Taxations of Foreign and Domestic Corporations, Joint Stock Associations and Limited Partnerships in Pennsylvania, for State Purposes. Philadelphia. 1901.

Journal of The N. Y. County Medico-Pharmaceutical League, Nov., 1901. Vol. 6, No. 6. A Bi-monthly.

Henry D. Holton, A. M., M. D., Brattleboro, Vt. Scientific Aids to Diagnosis. Read before the Mississippi Valley Med. Association, at the annual meeting, held at Put-in-Bay, Ohio, Sept. 12, 13, 14, 1901.

H. Edwin Lewis, M. D., Burlington, Vt. Pulmonary Tuberculosis. Reprint from the Medical Mirror, for July, 1901.

Byron Robinson, B. S., M. D, Chicago, Ill. An X Ray and Dissection of the Ureter and Utero-Overian Artery; The Utero-Ovarian Vascular Circle. Taken from an article by Dr. Wm. E. Holland, in the American Journal of Surgery and Gyneaology.

Universal Naturalist's Gazette, central organ for the joint interests of Naturalists and Kindred circles. With two supplements. Carl Wenck, editor-in-chief, Berlin, South End. Year, No. 1. Berlin, Oct. 2, 1901.
Contents: 1 Introduction; 2 Communications from the Physical Institution of the High School at Sophia (P. Bachmetjew, On Anabiosis.) 3 Collective Reports from the whole department of the simple and applied Natural Sciences: *a* W. Kaufman, Goettingen, The Development of the Conceptions of the Electrones; *b* Francis Sachs, Berlin: New Investigations on Chemical Effects of Light; 4 Travels and Expeditions; 5 Personals; 6 Prize Essays; 7 Astronomical Weekly Review. Supplement.

October 5; 1 73rd Session of German Naturalists and Physicians in Hamburg, from 23d to 28th September, 1901; 3 Reception of the 73d Congress of German Naturalists and Physicians at the City Hall, at Hamburg by the Senate, on the 24th of September; 3 On Critical Data; 4 The theory of Tanning by Solarisation. (E. English, Stuttgard;) 5 Collective Reports from the whole department of the simple and applied Natural Sciences; I. G. Wolf and A. Fischel, on the regeneration of the Lens with Tritones and Salamanders; 6 Miscellaneous; 7 Personals; 8 Weekly Astronomical Review; the Constellation of the Planets.

MAGAZINES.

THE ALIENIST AND NEUROLOGIST, St., Souis, Mo. Prof. C. H. Hughes, Editor. The January number contains: ' The Acquirement of Nervous Health," by F. Savary Pearce, M.D.; "Manual Stigmata of Degeneration," by J. Elvin Courtney, M.D.; "Juvenile Female Delinquents," by E. S. Talbot, M. D., D. D. S.; "Clinical Observations on a New Hypnotic," by Dr. H. Schoenfeld; "Medical Aspects of the Czolgosz Case," "Medical Inquiry and the Guillotine Commended for Capital Crime," "A Psychological Opportunity Lost," by Charles Hamilton Hughes, M. D.; "Leon F. Czolgosz," "A Descriptive Analysis on the Basis of the Bertillon System," by Rev. August Drahms; "Consciousness and the Neural Structure," by James G. Kiernan, M. D; "Sexual Inversion Among Primitive Races," by O. G. Seligmann, M. D.; "Science and Christian Science," by Paul Paquin, M. D.; besides the regular Selections, Editorials, Book Notic s, Publishers' Department, Etc.

THE NEW "ARENA." The January number of "The Arena" begins the twenty seventh volume and the fourteenth year of that well-known review. It opens with a fine essay on "Anarchism," by the Rev. R. Heber Newton, D. D., in which the writer discusses the ethical, sociological, and political aspects of that burning question. "The English Friendly Societies," by Eltweed Pomeroy, A. M., is an interesting description of a recent visit to the scene of the "Rochdale experiment" in co-operation. Theodore F. Seward describes the "Spiritual Birth of the American Nation," and, in addition to his regular departments of "Topics of the Times" and "Books of the Day," Editor O. B. Flower contributes a luminous essay on "The Rise of Photography and its Service to Mankind." T. St. Pierre discusses "Responsibility in Municipal Government," and W. A. Curtis considers "Race Reversion in America." Other features are: "Corporations and Trusts," by Thomas Conyngton; "The Development of Brotherhood," by Prof. Eugenia Parham; "Ibsen's 'Peer Gynt,'" by Walter Leighton; "The Work of Wives," by Flora M. Thompson, and "What Shall it Profit?" a New Year's story by M. P. Stuart. Editor McLean announces that Dr. Newton will discuss the economic and religious causes of anarchism in the February number, which will contain many other valuable contributions. (25 cents, at news stands. The Alliance Publishing Company, Fifth Avenue, N. Y.)

LOS ANGELES SUNDAY TIMES. We are indebted to Mrs. N. Perrine for a copy of this journal, of date of October 20th. It is a superb production, admirably edited, and is a credit to its promoters.

SHOOTING AND FISHING, (weekly), 203 Broadway, N. Y. A. C. Gould, Editor. The Christmas number (December 12th, 1901), is a beautiful creation.

The leading article, "The Squirrels of the United States," is by Dr. R. W. Shufeldt, and is admirably illustrated by photographs from the life, nearly life-size, which are beautifully done, and present splendid specimens for scrap-book preservation. There is also a fine specimen of a woodcock, and some baby barred owls, by the same skilled hand, in this number.

The cover illustration is a Wild Turkey Hunting Scene, by Henry Hintermeister, (H. Schedler, engraver).

J. Bigier contributes a Newfoundland caribou, from life—snap-shot. W. A. Baille-Grohman, some old-time reminiscences of chamois shooting in the Tyrol. L. P. Brown overhauls his tackle and talks of fishing on the Slagle River in a way that makes the blood of a fisherman tingle in his veins. Joseph Bigier sends also, with his caribou, splendid hunting trophies from Newfoundland. Sherman Powell writes of elk hunting in Oregon, with fine views. J. S. Danforth writes reminiscences of Maine moose hunting and beaver killing with old Nahum, and of bass and jew fish capture in the St. Lawrence River, that are startling. A. Whitehead talks of "giving up fishing" in a most delightful article, and yet regretful manner, for those who have "given it up," and of forgiveness of Banker, who had "given it up," but fell a victim to temptation "beyond his strength." E. T. D. Chambers writes of moose and caribou in Northern Canada, and "Fly Rod" gives a delightful and well illustrated sketch of "The Woods and Lakes of Maine" with a view of Senator W. P. Frye's camp, and of "Climes," the home of an English actor and his wife, Mr. and Mrs. Charles J. Bainbridge Bell, formerly of this city, who have made a home in the wilderness, from which they come sometimes wheu "weary of the wilderness."

The American Lawyer's Monthly, H. Gerald Chapin, Esq., L. L. D., New York City, editor, Stumpf & Steurer, publishers. This enterprising journal concluded its ninth volume with the December number, 1901. The January number contains Sketch of the Late William M. Everts by, J. Hampden Dougherty, Esq., and one by Mitchell D. Follanshe, of the Chicago Bar, on The English Lawyer of To-day, read before the Law Club of Chicago, April 26, 1901. The Journal is ably edited aud full of interest to lawyers.

The Century. New York. The February Century is to contain two articles, with illustrations, on the new scheme for beautifying the City of Washington; aud another important feature in the same issue is "A Visit to Mount Vernon a Century Ago," containing conversations with General Washington as recorded in the diary of a Polish poet attached in this country to the suite of Kosciuszko. The present topographical arrangement of the City of Washington was designed under President Washington's supervision, and the new plans contemplate an enriching of this arrangement, the chief improvement being a superb avenue from the Capitol to the Washington Monument, the latter forming an axis, from which other avenues and vistas will open.

MEDICO LEGAL SOCIETY.

DECEMBER, 1901.

(*For List of Officers see page 6.*)

ACTIVE LIST.

Auld, Prof. J. M., M. D.
Adams, Geo. S., M. D.
Albutt, H. A., M. D.
Allen Theo. J., M. D.
Albin, John H., Esq.
Andriezen, W.Lloyd,M.D.
Annis, E. L., M. D.
Archibald, O. Welling ton, M. D.
Ancona, Prof. A. A. De
Arthur, Daniel H., M.D.
Augustine, Clark B.,Esq. (Life.)
Aiyar, P. S. Sivaswamy, Esq.
Adams, W. A., M. D.
Abarbanell Jacob R.,Esq.
Arthur, Judge Jesse
Adkin, Thos. F., Esq.
Allis, J. A., Esq.
Amende, C. M., M. D.
Aronstam, N. E., M. D.

Bach, Albert, Esq. (Life.)
Baily, J. H., M. D.
Baker, Henry B., Dr.
Barreto, Dr. Melio.
Barham, W. B., M. D.
Barker, W. S., M. D.
Bartlett, James W.,M D.
Bell, Clark, Esq. (Life.)
Benedict, S. C., M. D.
Benjamin, D., M. D.
Benson, V. S., M. D.
Blair, Hon. A. G.
Blair, F. L., Esq.
Burgess, F. J. W., M. D.
Browett, Harold, Esq.
Bruno, R. N., Esq. (Life.)
Burnap, Prof. W. H.
Burrell, D. R., M. D.
Burts, W. T., M. D.
Bell, Ida Trafford
Bleyer, J. Mount, M. D.
Buchanan, Surgeon,Capt. W. J.
Brush, Arthur C., M.D.
Burnside, S. H., M. D.
Bancroft, Charles P., M. D.
Bryant, D. C., M. D.
Banks, Chas. Lincoln, Esq.
Bartlett, Edwin J., M. D.
Beemer, N. H., M. D.
Burr, C. B., M. D.
Bordes, General J. A., Esq.
Bell, G. M., M. D.
Babcock, James W., M. D.
Beli, Robert, M. D.
Brown, Geo. W., M. D.
Beach, Fletcher, M. D.
Bennett, John E., Esq.
Bell, Ralcey Husted, M. D.
Blumenthal,Maurice Esq
Biddle, Hon. Clarence S.
Blodgett, Wm. H., Esq., M. D.
Buckley, J. J., M. D.
Bayne, Eugene D. C., Esq

Caldwell, Frank H.,M.D.
*Calvin, James H., M. D
Campbell, Michael, Dr.
Canfield, Charles Stewart, Esq.
Carpenter, Elon M., M. D.
Chaffee, George, M. D.
Chenoweth, C. Van D.
Clark, Daniel, M. D.
Clift, Frederick, M. D.
Cole, Charles K., M. D.
Coleman, Judge Thomas W.
Conn, Granville P., Dr.
Culbertson, H. Coe,Esq.
Coughtrey, Prof. Millen, M. D.
Conlan, Judge Lewis J.
Cowan, D. W., M. D.
Cowen, D., M. D.
Cowles, Ed., M. D.
Crane, Frederick E.,Esq
Crookshank, R. Perc M. D.
Currier, D. M., Dr.
Chevalier, Ada M., M.
Coxwell, Prof. J. E. G.
Cranmer, B. F., M. D.
Close, Jas. A., Esq., B., F. R. C. P.
Chapin, H. Gerald, Esq.
Crothers, T. D., M. D.
Crotte Francisque, Esq.
Cuddebuck, W. L., M. D.
Clark, J. Clement, M. D.
Caffey, Francis G. Esq.
Cassaro, Francis L., Esq.
Campbell, Donald, M. D.
Carroll, C. C., M D.
Carnahan, Edward Howard Esq.
Chittenden, Percy R., Esq.

Dailey, Judge Abram (Life.)
Davis, E. Webster, M.
Day, W. H., Esq.
DeKraft, William, M. (Life.)
Denhard, C. E., Dr.
DiMoise, G. Bettini, D. (Life.)
Dittenhoefer, Judge A.J
Dittenhoefer, Irving M. Esq.
Doremus, R. O., Prof.
Dormeus, Chas. A.,Pro
Dorsett, J. S., M. D.
Downs, F. B., M. D.
Drewry, W. F., M. D.
Dunavant, H. C., M. D
Duncan, Shelbey P.,Esq
Dupre, Ovide, Esq.(Life.
Dyer, Isidore, M. D.
Dawson, Miles M., M. D
Darlington, Thos.,M. D.
De Costa, Jose L, M. D.
Davis, N. S., M. D.

Del. Junco, Prof. Judge Emillio, Esq.
Densmore, Helen, M. D.
Davies, Samuel D., Esq.
Del Castro, Prof. Raymond.
De Jonge, A., M. D.
Desai, J. V. Esq.

Eads, B. F., M. D.
Ellinger, M., Esq.
Elliott, George F., Esq.
Ellis, Dr. Havelock.
Emery, Judge L. A.
Evans, Britton D., M. D.
Ewell, Prof. Marshall D. D.
Eyer, Alvin, M. D.
Edenharter, Geo. T., M. D.
Ellis, Howard, Esq.
Egan, James A., M. D.
Edson, Cyrus, M. D.

Fanning, James O., Esq.
Fast, F. R., Esq. (Life.)
Fellows, Joseph W., Esq.
Fennelly, E. M.
Finck, George, Esq.
Fischer, Charles S., Dr. (Life.)
Fitch, N. O., M. D.
Fleming, W. M., Dr.
Fletcher, W. B., M. D.
Ford, DeSaussure, M. D.
Francis, Judge William H.
Frost, Thomas G., Esq.
Fuller, F. B., M. D.
Fulton, A. L., M. D.
Fielding, Hon. Wm. S.
Fassett, Chas. Wood, Esq.
Foster, Eugene, M. D.
Foltz, Clara, LL. B.
Ferris, J. H., M. D.
Foley, John A., Esq.
Ferrer, F. Medina, M. D.
Fernandez, Dr. Santos.
Fennell, Thos. Garrett, Esq.
Field, Frank Harvey, Esq.

Garrison, Judge C. G.
Gerry, E. T., Esq. (Life.)
Gibbs, John Wilson, M. D.
Girard, Major A. C., M. D.
Girdwood, G. P., M. D.
Goodfellow, George, M. D.
Graham, J. T., M. D.
Grant, Gabriel, M. D.
Graves, G., M. D.
Grinnell, A. P., M. D.
Guernsey, R. S., Esq.
Guth, Morris S., M. D.
Gignoux, Robt., Esq.
Gunn, Robt. E., M. D.
Gilbert, L. L., Esq.
Grover, Geo. W., M. D.
Gil, Alexander Wos. Y.,
Gaston, Judge Louis.

Hall, J. N., M. D.
Hall, W. A., M. D.
Harrison, Daniel A., M.D.
Haviland, Willis H., Jr., M. D.
Hawes, Gilbert R., Esq. (Life.)
Hawkins, Jas. E., Esq.
Herold, Justin A. M., M. D.
Hill, H. B., M. D.
Hill, J. Lensey, M. D.
Hirschberg, Judge M. H.
Hirschfelder, J. O., M.D.
Horne, J. Fletcher, M. D
Horton, Judge O. H.
Hogg, Ex-Gov. James S.
Holliday, B. W., M. D.
Howard, John C., Dr.
Howard, N. de V., M. D.
Howard, Wm. Lee, M.D.
Heftt, G. Stanley, M. D.
Hirschl, Andrew J,. Esq.
Hoyt, Frank C., M. D.
Hubbs, M. B., M. D.
Hudson, Thomson Jay, Esq.
Hurt, G. M., M. D.
Huyer, R. P., M. D.
Hamm, Margherita A.
Hoffman, F. L., Esq.
Henderson, J. M., M. D.
Honan, Wm., M. D.
Hutton, Francis E., Esq.
Herdman, Prof. W. J., M. D.
Howell, Judge O. P., Esq.
Hardin, Alfred, Esq.
Hardwicke, Henry, Esq.
Hechavarria, Chief Justice Urbano Sanchez.
Hogg, F. Stanley, M. D.
Hilton. A. P., Esq.
Hatch, J. Leffiingwell, M. D.
Holton, Henry D., M. D.
Howard, N. de V., M. D.

Jackson, Francis M., Esq.
Jamison, W. T., M. D.
Jewett, Harry D., Esq.
Johnson, Wyatt, M. D.
Johnston, Alexander, M. D.
Jones, W. C., Esq.
Johnston, George Ben., M. D.
Judkins, E. H., M. D.
Judson, Stiles, Jr., Esq.
Jado, Judge Jose Varela.
Jakobi, A. A., Esq.

Keene, George F., M. D.
Kelley, Webb J., M. D.
Kellogg, T. H., M. D.
Kelly, W. J., Esq.
Kibler, C. B., M. D.
King, George W., M. D.
Kinkead, R. J., M. D.
Kinney, C. Spencer, M.D.
Klein, J. B., Esq.
Knapp, A. R., M. D.
Kratler, Prof. Julius, M. D.
Keyes, Thos. Basset, M D.
Kellogg, J. H., M. D.
Kelsey, R. C., M. D.
Kime, J. W., M. D.
Kindred, J. J., M. D.
Kirsten, Dr. A J.
Keisker, Dr. Laura
Kaufman, F. J., M. D.
Kassabian, Mihran K., M. D.

LaCourt, D., M. D.
Lee, Edward B., M. D.
Lee, Francis B., Esq.
Leet, N. T., M. D.
Legare, J. Cecil, M. D.
Lence, W. C., M. D.
Lewis, J. B., Dr.
Lewis, R. J., Esq.
Lightner, C. A., Esq.
Lindsay, J. L., M. D.
Loewy, Benno, Esq.
Lederle, Dr. Ernest J.
Lochner, John, M. D.
Lemen, L. E., M. D.
Leslie, C. F., M. D.
Lamanche, Judge Jose.
Levy, Abraham, Esq.
Letchworth, Hon. Wm. P.
Lawrence, W. O., M D.
Lease, Mary E.
Langan, Michael J., Esq
Love, I. N., M. D.

MEDICO LEGAL SOCIETY.

DECEMBER, 1901.

(*For List of Officers see page 6.*)

ACTIVE LIST.

Auld, Prof. J. M., M. D.
Adams, Geo. S., M. D.
Albutt, H. A., M. D.
Alien Theo. J., M. D.
Albin, John H., Esq.
Andriezen, W.Lloyd,M.D.
Annis, E. L., M. D.
Archibald, O. Wellington, M. D.
Ancona, Prof. A. A. De
Arthur, Daniel H., M.D.
Augustine, Clark B.,Esq. (Life.)
Aiyar, P. S. Sivaswamy, Esq.
Adams, W. A., M. D.
Abarbanell Jacob R.,Esq.
Arthur, Judge Jesse
Adkin, Thos. F., Esq.
Allis, J. A., Esq.
Amende, C. M., M. D.
Aronstam, N. E., M. D.

Bach, Albert, Esq. (Life.)
Baily, J. H., M. D.
Baker, Henry B., Dr.
Barreto, Dr. Mello.
Barham, W. B., M. D.
Barker, W. S., M. D.
Bartlett, James W.,M D.
Bell, Clark, Esq. (Life.)
Benedict, S. C., M. D.
Benjamin, D., M. D.
Benson, V. S., M. D.
Blair, Hon. A. G.
Blair, F. L., Esq.
Burgess, F. J. W., M. D.
Browett, Harold, Esq.
Bruno, R. N., Esq. (Life.)
Burnap, Prof. W. H.
Burrell, D. R., M. D.
Burts, W. T., M. D.
Bell, Ida Trafford
Bleyer, J. Mount, M. D.
Buchanan, Surgeon,Capt. W. J.
Brush, .rthur C., M.D.
Burnsid S. H., M. D.
Bancrof Charles P., M. D.
Bryant,). C., M. D.
Banks, Chas. Lincoln, Esq.
BartlettEdwin J., M. D.
Beemer,J. H., M. D.
Burr, CB., M. D.
Bordes, General J. A., Esq.
Bell, G.M., M. D.
Babcock James W., M. D.
Iell, Robt, M. D.
Brown, Co. W., M. D.
Beach, Flcher, M. D.
Bennett, hn E., Esq.
Bell, Raiy Husted, M. D.
Blumental,Maurice Esq
Biddle, Hn. Clarence S.
Blodgett,'m. H., Esq., M. D.
Buckley, J., M. D.
Bayne, Egene D. C., Esq

Caldwel Frank H.,M.D.
*Calvin, mes H, M. D.
Campbel Michael, Dr.
CantieldCharles Stewart, Eq.
Carpent, Elon M., M. D.
Chaffee,George, J
Chenowth, C. V
Clark, Daniel, /
Clift, Federic
Cole, Charles
Colemar Ja W.
Conn, G
Culberts
Cought M. D
Conle
Cow
Cowen, D., M. D.
Cowles, Ed., M. D.
Crane, Frederick E.,Esq.
Crookshank, R. Percy, M. D.
Currier, D. M., Dr.
Chevalier, Ada M., M. D.
Coxwell, Prof. J. E. G.
Cranmer, B. F., M. D.
Close, Jas. A., Esq., M. B., F. R. C. P.
Chapin, H. Gerald, Esq.
Crothers, T. D., M. D.
Crotte Francisque, sq.
Cuddebuck. W. L., M. D.
Clark, J. Clement, M. D.
Caffey, Francis G. Esq.
Cassaro, Francis L., Esq.
Campbell, Donald, M. D.
Carroll, C. C., M D.
Carnahan, Edward Howard, Esq.
Chittenden, Percy R., Esq.

Dailey, Judge Abram H. (Life.)
Davis, E. Webster, M.D
Day, W. H., Esq.
DeKraft, William, M. D. (Life.)
Denhard, C. E., Dr.
DiMoise, G. Bettini, D. (Life.)
Dittenhoefer, Judge A.J
Dittenhoefer, Irving M. Esq.
...mus, R. O., Prof.
...s, Chas. A.,Pro
J. S., M. D.
B., M. D.
. F., M. D.
H. C., M. D
Dun
Du

Del Junco, Prof. Judge Emillio, Esq.
Densmore, Helen, M. D.
Davies, Samuel D., Esq.
Del Castro, Prof. Raymond.
De Jonge, A., M. D.
Desai, J. V. Esq.

Eads, B. F., M. D.
Ellinger, M., Esq.
Elliott, George F., Esq.
Ellis, Dr. Havelock.
Emery, Judge L. A.
Evans, Britton D., M. D.
Ewell, Prof. Marshall D. D.
Eyer, Alvin, M. D.
Edenharter, Geo. T., M. D.
Ellis, Howard, Esq.
Egan, James A., M. D.
Edson, Cyrus, M. D.

Fanning, James O., Esq.
Fast, F. R., Esq. (Life.)
Fellows, Joseph W., Esq.
Fennelly, E. M.
Finck, George, Esq.
Fischer, Charles S., Dr. (Life.)
Fitch, N. O., M. D.
Fleming, W. M., Dr.
Fletcher, W. B., M. D.
Ford, DeSaussure, M. D.
Francis, Judge William H.
Frost, Thomas G., Esq.
Fuller, F. B., M. D.
Fulton, A. L., M. D.
Fielding, Hon. Wm. S.
Fassett, Chas. Wood, Esq.
Foster, Eugene, M. D.
Folts, Clara, LL. B.
Ferris, J. H., M. D.
Foley, John A., Esq.
Ferrer, [illegible] M. D.
Ferne
Fen
F
F

Good [illegible] orge, M. D.
Graha [illegible] M. D.
Grant [illegible] M. D.
Graves [illegible] D.
Grinn [illegible] M. D.
Guern [illegible] Esq.
Guth, [illegible] M. D.
Gigno [illegible] Esq.
Gunn, [illegible] M. D.
Gilber [illegible] sq.
Grove [illegible] M. D.
Gil, A [illegible] Vos. Y.,
Gaston, [illegible] cuis.

Hall, J. [illegible] D.
Hall, W. [illegible] D.
Harris [illegible] A., M. D.
Haviland [illegible] H., Jr., M. D.
Hawes, [illegible] e R., Esq. (Life.)
Hawkins, [illegible] as E., Esq.
Herold, J [illegible] n L. M., M. D.
Hill, H [illegible] D.
Hill, J. I ns M. D.
Hirschber [illegible] u e M. H.
Hirschfeld [illegible] O., M. D.
Horne, J. [illegible] et er, M. D.
Horton, J [illegible] ig O. H.
Hogg, Ex- [illegible] o James
Holliday, [illegible], M. D.
Howard, J hn C., Dr.
Howard, N [illegible] M. D.
Howard [illegible] m Lee, M. D.
Heftt, G [illegible] ny, M. D.
Hirschi, An [illegible] J., Esq.
Hoyt, Fr [illegible], M. D.
Hubbs, M. B M.
Hudson, Thoson Ja., Esq.
Hurt, G. M., M. D.
Huyer, R. P., M. D.
Hamm, Margerita A.
Hoffman, F. I Esq.
Henderson, J. M., M. D.
Honan, Wm., M. D.
[illegible] tton, Frank E., Esq.
[illegible] n, Prf. W. J.,

O. [illegible]

[illegible] wicke, [illegible] ry, Esq.
[illegible] rric, [illegible] ief Jus-
[illegible] anchez.
[illegible] y, M. D.

Jackson Francis M. Esq.
Jamison, W. T., M. D.
Jewett, Harry D., Esq.
Johnson, Wyatt, M. D.
Johnston, Alexander M. D.
Jones W. C., Esq.
Johnston, George Ben M. D.
Judkins, E. H., M. D.
Judson, St [illegible] E q
Jado, Judge Jose Vare'a [illegible] A [illegible] E

Keene, George F., M. D.
Kelley, Webb J., M. D.
Kellogg, T. H., M. D.
Kelly, W. J., Esq.
Kibler, C. B., M. D.
King, George W., M. D.
Kinkead, R. J., M. D.
Kinney C. Spencer, M. D.
Klein, J. B., Esq.
Knapp, A. R., M. D.
Kratler, Prof. Julius, M. D.
Keyes, Thos. Basset, M. D.
Kellogg, J. H., M. D.
Kelsey, R. C., M. D.
Kime, J. W., M. D.
Kindred, J. J., M. D.
Kirsten Dr. A. [illegible]
Keisker, D. [illegible]
Kaufman F. I. M. [illegible]
Kassabian, Mihran K. M. [illegible]

LaCourt, D., M. D.
Lee, Edward B., M. D.
Lee, Francis B., Esq.
Leet, N. T., M. D.
Legare, J. Cecil, M. D.
Lence, W. C., M. D.
Lewis, J. B., Dr.
Lewis, R. J., Esq.
Lightner, C. A., Esq.
Lindsay, J. L., M. D.
[illegible], Benno, Esq.
[illegible], Dr. Ernest J.
[illegible], M. D.
Lemen, [illegible]
Leslie, [illegible]
Lamanche, [illegible]
Levy, Abraham, [illegible]
Letchwort [illegible]
Lawrence

Lewis, H. Edwin, M. D.
Lacey, T. B., M. D.
Lindley, Walter, M. D.
Lawrence, W. O., M. D.

MacGuire, J. C., M. D.
Mackaye, H. Goodwin, M. D.
Maher, James E., M. D.
Marks, Solon, M. D.
Martin, J. C., M. D.
Mattison, J. B., M. D.
McCallum, J. M., M. D.
McClelland, Mrs. Sophia
McCorn, Alfred, M. D.
MacCowen, Jennie, M. D.
McCuaig, John E., M.D.
McGowan, J. T., M. D.
McFarland, W. G., M.D.
McIntyre, William H., Esq.
McKenzie, K. D., M. D.
McLennan, Donald, M.D.
McLeod, J. A., M. D.
McVey, Prof. W. B.

Mead, Julian A., M. D.
Menken, Percy, Esq.
Meyers, W. H., M. D.
Milbank, Robert, M. D.
Miller, George B., M. D.
Miller, J. F. Esq.
Mitchell, Hubbard W., M. D.
Mitchell, J. Murray, Esq.
Moore, Dwight Shumway, M. D.
Moore, George E., M.D.
Moore, George P., Esq.
Monday, W. H., M. D.
Morrow, W. B., M. D.
Murphy, P. L., M. D.
Murray, R. D., M. D.
McHatton, H., M. D.
Monck, W. H. S., Esq.
Moss, Hon. Frank
Markiewicz, M., M. D.
McQuesten, E. F., M. D.
McKibben, W. H., M. D.
Miller, J. B., Esq.
Manduley, Judge M. J.
Mulqueen, Michael J., Esq.
Marois, Prof. M. A., M. D.
Meachem, Lewis J., M. D.
McFarland, D. W., M. D.
Metz, Prof. A. L.
Maynard, Geo. V., Esq.
Messeter, Dr. Otto
Marie, August, M. D.

McLaws, U. H. W., Esq.
Moechel, Jean Robert, Dr.
Mundorff, Geo. Theo., M D.
Magill, S. Wm., M. D.

Nelson, William, Esq.
Newcomer, M. V. B., M. D.
Noble, Judge Conway W.
Nolan, John P., M. D.
Norbury, Frank P., M.D.
North, Judge Safford E.
Nugent, W. R., M. D.
Nunn, R. J., M. D.
Nye, C. A., Esq.
Neville, John James, M. D.
Nichols, Delancy F., Esq
Nicholson, Chancellor John R.
Noyes, Wm. B., M. D.

O'Connell, R. S., M. D.
O'Neil, E. D., Dr.
Orange, William, M. D., C. B.
Orme, H. L., M. D.
Osborne, A. E., M. D.
Outten, W. B., M. D.
Overholtzer, M. P., M.D.
Owens, J. E., M. D.
O'Hanlan, Philip F., M. D.

Paddock, Frank K., M. D.
Page, Samuel B., Esq.
Parsons, R. L., M. D.
Parmenter, R. A., Esq.
Peck, Fayette H., M. D.
Pfingsten, Gustav, M. D.
Phelps, R. M., M. D.
Platt, William Popham, Esq.
Poole, Thomas Crisp, M. D.
Porter, George L., M. D.
Prill, A. G., M. D.
Pritchard, J. F., M. D.
Pusey, Dr. A. L.
Pier, Kate H., M. D.
Piera, Senor Fidel G.
Potter, Florence Dangerfield, LL. B.
Pritchard, R. L., Esq., M. D.
Purman, D. M., M. D.
Payne, Robert E., D. D. L., M. D.

Pangborn, Major Z. Esq.
Porter, Ira W., M. D.
Pacquin, C. R., M. D.
Powers, Frederick, M. D.
Petrella, Richard, M. D.

Quimby, Isaac N., Esq.

Ransom, Judge R. S.
Raymond, Mrs. Henry
Reed, R. Harvey, M.
Reeve, J. T., M. D.
Regensberger, A. E., D.
Remondino, P. C., M.
Renton, A. Wood, E
Rice, C. A., M. D.
Richardson, A. B., M
Ritchie, I. A., M. D
Robinson, D. R., Esq
Roderigues, Prof. Nina
Rapmund, Otto, M. D.
Rogers, Prof. H. W.
Rosenthal, A. C., Es
*Rosse, Irving C., M.
Roeder, Rev. Adolph
Ransom, J. B., M. D.
Ross, Frank W., M.
Remy, W. O. B., M.
Ruland, F. B., M. D.
Robinson, Henry, Esq.
McGarry, J. G., Esq.
Raymond, Prof. F, M. D.
Ripley, E. F., Esq.
Robinovitch, Louise G., M.
Row, Sryanarain B, Esq.
Reynolds, Edwin, M. D.
Rogers, Jas. R., Esq.

Sauner, H. B., M. D.
Scott, A. C., M. D.
Scott, J. J., M. D.
Searcey, J. H., M. D.
Seeley, V. W., Esq.
Senn, Nicholas, M.
Shay, Thos. F., Esq.
Sander, W., M. D.
Shufeldt, R. W., M.
Smith, C. A., M. D.
Smith, E. C., Esq.
Smith, Prof. W. R.
Southall, James, M.
Stackpole, Paul A., M
Stanley, C. E., M. D.
Stern, Heinrich, Esq.
*Sterne, Simon, Esq.
Storer, David A., Esq

Stover, Judge M. T.
Strahan, S. A. K., M. D.
Strauss, Charles, Esq.
Sudduth, Prof. W. X.
Sullivan, M. B., M. D.
Sterne, A. E., M. D.
Simon, Carleton, M. D.
Sextus, Carl, Esq.
Sahler, C. O., M. D.
Stack, Thos. E., M. D.
Stewart, Cambrae, Esq.
Spratting, Edgar J., M. D.
Sutherland, J. F., M. D.
Schrenk-Notzing, F., M. D.
Seward, Fred. W., M. D.
Strassman W., Esq.
Smithwick, J. W. P., M. D.
Smith, M. M., M. D.
Sanborn, Chas. F., M. D.
Shasted, F. H., M. D.

Talcott, Selden H., M.D.
Talley, R. P., M. D.
Talmadge, Judge A. M.
Taylor, Caroline J.
Taylor, John F., Esq.
Taylor, Philip K., M. D.
Templeman, C., M. D.
Thomas, M. Louise
Thompson, A. A., M. D.
Thompson, Curtis, Esq.
Thorne, S. S., M. D.
Thurston, Hon. J. M.
Tighe, Judge James E.
Tomlinson, N. A., M. D.
Tompkins, Leslie J., Esq.
Towne, George D., M.D.
Tresider, John R., Esq.
Tripp, John J., Esq.
Trull, W. C., Esq.
Tucker, C P., Dr.
Tucker, Dr. George A.
Tranchida, Corrado, M. D.
Taber, Susan, J., M. D.
Tull, E. E., M. D.
Tillinghast, Judge Pardon, Esq.
Talioferro, E. T., Esq.
Thomas, Samuel Bell, Esq.
Tamburini, Prof. A., M. D.

Underhill, H. C., Esq.
Ulrich, C. F., M. D.

Valentine, John F., M D.
Valentine, W., Esq.
Vandeveer, M. D.
Vaughan, Prof. V. G.
Villneuve, Dr. George.
Volding, M. Nelson, M. D.
Vance, Hart, Esq.
Verela, Judge Jose
Valdeman, Mlle.
Voisin, Jules, M. D.
Valle, Prof. A., M. D.

Wait, A. S., Esq.
Wallace, D. R., M. D.
Ward, C. S., M. D.
Watson, Irving A., M.D.
Watson, J. H., Esq.
Watson, Wm. Perry, M. D.
Watson, W. S., M D.
Watts, Judge L. R.
Waughop, J. W., M. D.
Wedge, A. C., M. D.
Weed, Charles P., M.D.
Weisman, F. H., Esq.
Weldon, Hon. Charles B.
Wernberg, Jerry A., Esq.
Weston, A. T., M. D.
White, E. D., M. D.
White, Frank S., M.
*White, Moses C., M. D.
White, M. J., M. D.
White, Stephen M., Es
Whitney, Albert B., D.
Wilcox, J. V. Stanto M. D.
Williams, Homer J., D.
Williamson, A. P., M.
Wilson, J. T., M. D.
Winslow, L. Forbes,
Wingate, U. O. B., M.
Wolf, A. S., M. D.
Wood, W. R., D. M.
Worden, M. Etna, M.
Worsham, B. M., M.
Wright, Arthur W., Es
White, Prof. H. Cla Esq.
Wood, Edward S., M. D.
Waite, H F.. M. D.
Wade, J. P rcy, M. D
Wilder, Alexander, M D.
Wollman, Henry, Esq.
Williams, John G. Esq.
Walker A. T. M. D
Woodward Robert P., Esq.
Wise, P. M., M. D.
Wade, Judge M. J.
Woodward, Wm. C.
Wacholz Professor

Y rnell, Judge J. H.
Young, D., M. D.
Young, R. E., M. D.
Young, W. A., M D.
Yarrell Judge L D.
Y'barra, Fernaudez A. M., M. D.

***Deceased.**

THE

MEDICO-LEGAL JOURNAL.

Published under the Auspices of the Medico-Legal Society of New York.

CLARK BELL, Esq.,
EDITOR-IN-CHIEF.

ASSOCIATE EDITORS:

LEGAL.

Prof. W. L. BURNAP, Vermont.
Judge ABRAM H. DAILEY, Brooklyn.
Judge JOHN F. DILLON, New York.
T. GOLD FROST, Esq., New York.
Judge C. G. GARRISON, Camden, N.Y.
F. L. HOFFMAN, Esq., Newark, N. J.
SAMUEL BELL THOMAS, Esq. N.Y.
W. H. S. MONCK, Esq, Dublin.
A. WOOD RENTON, Esq., London.

MEDICAL.

Dr. HAVELOCK ELLIS, London.
Prof. Dr. J. T. ESKRIDGE, Denver.
W. W. IRELAND, M. D., Scotland.
Prof. HERMAN KORNFELD, M. D., Gleiwitz, Silesia.
GEORGE B. MILLER, M. D., Phila.
JULES MOREL, M. D., Belgium.
T. F. SUTHERLAND, M. D., Edinburgh, Scotland.
H. EDWIN LEWIS, M. D., Burlington, Vt.

SCIENTIFIC.

C. VAN D. CHENOWETH, Mass.
Prof. R. O. DOREMUS, New York.
MORITZ ELLINGER, Esq., N. Y.
Prof. W. B. MACVEY, Boston.
Prof. W. XAVIER SUDDUTH, Chicago.
Prof. VICTOR C. VAUGHAN, Mich.

RAILWAY SURGERY.

LEGAL.

C. H. BLACKBURN, Esq., Cincinnati.
Judge WILLIAM H. FRANCIS, N.Y. City
C. A. LIGHTNER, Esq., Detroit.
Judge CONWAY W. NOBLE, Cleveland.
Hon. J. M. THURSTON, Nebraska.

MEDICAL.

CHARLES K. COLE, M. D., Montana.
GRANVILLE P. CONN, M. D. Concord.
A. P. GRINNELL, M. D., Burlington, Vt.
DWIGHT J. KELLY, M. D., Ohio.
R. HARVEY REED, M.D., Rock Spring, Wy
NICHOLAS SENN, M. D., Chicago.

VOL. XIX.—No. 4.

MARCH.

NEW YORK:
MEDICO-LEGAL JOURNAL.
1901.

MEDICO-LEGAL SOCIETY.

OFFICERS FOR 1902.

President,
CLARK BELL, Esq., of New York.

1st Vice-President,
A. P. GRINNELL, M. D., Burlington, Vt.

2nd Vice-President,
T. D. CROTHERS, M. D., of Conn.

Vice-Presidents for the States, Territories and Provinces.

Alabama—Judge Thos. W. Coleman, Montgomery.
Alaska—Clarence Thwing, M. D., Sitka.
Arizona—D. M. Purman, M. D., Phoenix.
Arkansas—H. C. Dunavant, M. D., Osceola.
Austria—Prof. R. Krafft-Ebing, Vienna.
Belgium—Dr. Jules Morel, Mons.
Brazil—Prof. Nina Rodrigues, M. D., Bahia.
British Honduras-Ada M Chevaillier, M.D., Balize
California—A. E. Osborne, M. D., Glen Ellen.
Colorado—Prof. J. T. Eskridge, M. D., Denver.
Connecticut—Judge A. M. Tallmadge, Bridgeport.
China—Harold Browett, Esq., Shanghai.
Cuba—Chief Justice HechaVarria, of Santiago.
Dakota, N.—Dr. Dwight S. Moore, Jamestown.
Dakota, S.—John M. Harcourt, Steele.
Delaware—Judge Ignatius C. Grubb, Wilm'gt'n.
Denmark—Prof. Godeken, Copenhagen.
District of Columbia—W. C. Woodward, M. D., Washington, D. C.
Dom of Canada—Hon. A. G. Blair, Ottawa.
England—Dr. Fletcher Beach, London.
Ecuador—Senor J. M. P. Cammano, Wash. D. C.
Florida—N. de V. Howard, M. D., Sanford.
France—Victor Parent, M. D., Toulouse.
Georgia—Richard J. Nunn, M. D., Savannah.
Germany—Dr. H. Laehr, Berlin.
Guatemala—Senor Rafael Montufar.
Hawaii—J. W. Waughop M. D., Kalia Kanai.
Hayti.—Genl. J. A. Bordes, Jeremie.
Holland—Dr. P. A. H. Sneens, Vucht.
Hungary—Staatsanwalt Em. V. Havas, BudaPesth
Illinois—J. E. Owens, M. D., Chicago.
India—P. S. Sivaswamy Aiyar, Madras.
Indiana—W. B. Fletcher, M. D., Indianapolis.
Indian Territory—I. H. Bailey, M. D., Dexter.
Iowa—Jennie McCowen, M. D., Davenport.
Ireland—Conolly Norman, M. D., Dublin.
Italy—Enrico Ferri, M. D., Rome.
Japan—Dr. J. Hashimoto, Tokio.
Kansas—Judge Albert H. Horton, Topeka
Kentucky—F. H. Clark, M. D., Lexington.
Louisiana—J. J. Scott, M. D., Shreveport.
Maine—Judge L. A. Emery, Ellsworth.
Manitoba—D. Young, M. D., Selkirk.
Maryland—Wm Lee Howard, M. D., Baltimore.
Massachusetts—Theo. H. Tyndale, Boston.
Mexico—Leon Lewis, M. D., Ozuluama.
Michigan—Clarence A. Lightner, Detroit.
Minnesota—C. K. Bartlett, M. D., Minneapoli
Missouri—W. B. Outten, M. D., St. Louis.
Montana—C. K. Cole, M. D., Helena.
Nebraska—Hon. John M. Thurston, Omaha.
Nevada—S. M. Bishop, M. D., Reno.
New Brunswick—Dr. Wm. Bayard, St. John.
Newfoundland—Dr. K. D. McKenzie, St. Joh
New Hampshire—Gran. P. Conn, M.D., Concor
New Jersey—Judge C. G. Garrison, Camden.
New Mexico—Gov. Bradford L. Prince, Santa F
New South Wales—George A. Tucker, M. D.
New York—Mrs. M. Louise Thomas, N. Y. Cit
New Zealand—Prof. Frank G. Ogston, Dunedi
North Carolina—E. C. Smith, Esq., Raleigh.
Norway—Dr. Harold Smedal, Christiana.
Nova Scotia—Hon. Wm. S. Fielding, Ottawa.
Ohio—Judge H. C. White, Cleveland.
Oklahoma Ter.—A. H. Simonton, M. D., Okla.C
Ontario—Daniel Clark, M. D., Toronto.
Oregon—Ex-Chief Just. Hon. Wm. P. Lord, Sale
Pennsylvania—Geo. B. Miller, M. D., of Phila.
Peru—Senor F. C. C. Zegarro, Washington, D.
Portugal—Bettincourt Rodriguez, M. D., Lisbo
Quebec—Wyatt Johnson, M. D., Montreal.
Rhode Island—Judge P. E. Tillinghast, Provid
Russia—Prof. Dr. Mierzejewski, St. Petersburg
San Domingo—A. Wei Yos Gil, San Domingo.
Saxony—Judge de Alinge, Oberkotzon Hof.
Scotland—W. W. Ireland, Edinburgh.
Servia—Hon. Paul Savitch, Belgrade.
Sicily—Prof. Dr. Fernando Puglia, Messina.
Silesia—H. Kornfeld, M. D., Grotkau.
South Carolina—S. W. Babcock, M. D., Columbi
Spain—Sig. A. M. Alv. Taladriz, M.D., Valladoli
Sweden—Prof. Dr. A. Winroth, Lund.
Switzerland—Prof. Dr. L. Wille, Basle.
Tennessee—Michael Campbell, M. D., Nashvill
Texas—Dr. D. R. Wallace, Terrell.
Tonga—Dr. Donald McClennen, Tonga.
Utah—Frederick Clift, M. D., St. George.
Vermont—Henry D. Holton, M. D., Brattlebo
Virginia—William F. Drewry, Petersburg.
Washington—Jas. C. Waugh, M. D., Mt. Verno
West Virginia—F. M. Hood, M. D., Weston.
Wisconsin—Dr. U. O. B. Wingate, Milwaukee.
Wyoming—R. Harvey Reed, M. D., Rock Sprin

Secretary,
SAMUEL B. THOMAS, Esq., of N. Y. City.

Corresponding Secretary,
MORITZ ELLINGER, Esq., of N. Y. City.

Assistant Secretary,
A. A. JAKOBI, of N. Y. City.

Pathologist,
WM. S. MAGILL, M. D., N. Y. City

Treasurer,
CAROLINE J. TAYLOR, Bridgeport, Conn.

Chemist,
PROF. C. A. DOREMUS, M. D. N. Y. City.

Curator,
J. MOUNT BLEYER, M. D., New York.

Toxicologist,
PROF. W. B. McVEY, of Boston.

Librarian,
FRED. L. HOFFMAN, Esq., of N. J.

Assistant Librarian,
THOS. G. FROST, Esq, of N. Y.

Bacteriologist,
G. BETTINI DI MOISE, M. D., of N. Y.

Microscopist,
DR. ERNEST J. LEDERLE, of N. Y.

TRUSTEES:

Legal,
H. GERALD CHAPIN Esq., of New York.
JUDGE WM. H. FRANCIS, Newark, N. J.
JUDGE A. J. DITTENHOEFER, of N. Y. City.

Medical,
R. W. SHUFELDT, M. D., of N. Y. Cit
P. M. WISE, M. D., of N. Y. City.
ISAAC N. LOVE, M D., of N. Y. City.

COUNSELLORS,
For 3 years.

Legal.
HENRY WOLLMAN, Esq. of N. Y. City.
STILES JUDSON, Jr., of Bridgeport, Conn.
JUDGE FRED. E. CRANE, of Brookly, N Y.

Medical.
C. C. CARROLL, M. D., of N. Y.
CARLETON SIMON M D, of N Y. Cit
J. LEFFINGWELL HATCH, M D., of N. Y. Cit

PERMANENT COMMISSION:
For 3 years.

Legal,
JUDGE CHARLES G. GARRISON, of N. J.
JUDGE L. A EMERY, of Maine.
CLARK BELL, Esq, of New York.

Medical.
NICHOLAS SENN, M. D., of Chicago.
PROF. VICTOR C. VAUGHAN, of Ann Arbor, Mic
GEO. L. PORTER, M. D., of Bridgeport, Conn.

THE FOLLOWING ARE THE EXCHANGE JOURNALS.

Archives Italian,
Archivie Giuridico,
Archives d'Anthropologie Criminale,
Alienist and Neurologist,
American Journal of Insanity,
American Law Register,
Archives of Pediatries,
Archives de la Psychiatrie Clinique et Legale et de Neurologie,
Academie de Medicine de Paris,
American Journal of Psychology,
American Chemical Journal,
American Law Review,
Atlanta Medical and Surgical,
Annales Medico-Psychologique,
Archivio di Psi Sci pen et antro crim.,
Archives de Neurologie,
Annales Societe Medico-Legal de Belge.
Albany Law Journal,
American Microscopical Journal,
Amer. Med. Review,
Annals Univ. Med. Science
Aerztliche Sachverstændigen-Zeitung
American Medical Journalist,
Amer. Monthly Retrospect,
Amer. Journal of Med-Science,
Applied Microscopy,
American Economist,
American Lawyer,
Astrological Journal,
Amer Electro Therapeutry and X-Ray Era.
American X-Ray Journal,
Anglo American Magazine,
Annotated Cases,
Aunals of Surgery
American Medicine,

Buffalo Medical Journal,
Boston Medical and Surgical Journal,
Bulletin Societe de Medicine Mentale Belgique.
Bulletin of the Iowa State Institutions,
Brooklyn Med. Journal,
Bombay Law Reporter,
Bulletin Medical de Quebec,
Bar, (W. Va.)
Bookseller

Case and Comment,
Canadian Practitioner,
Central Law Journal,
Connecticut State Board of Health,
Courier of Medicine,
Centralblat fuer Nerv.,
Canadian Law Times,
Charlotte Med. Journal,
Chicago Law Journal,
Chicago Legal News,
Columbus Med. Journal,
Canadian Journal Med. Surgery,
Cleveland Journal of Medicine,
Chicago Clinic,
Charities,
Colorado Med. Journal.
Chicago Legal News,
Calcutta Weekly Notes,
Canadian Law Review,
Chautauquan Magazine,

Der Irrenfreund,
Der Gerichtssaal,
Del Kongelige Sundheds-kollegiums,
Davenport Acad. of Nat. Sci.
Detroit Legal News,
Dietetic and Hygiene Gazette,
Dunglisan Col. & Clin. Record.
Detroit Med. Journal,

English Lunacy Commission.
Exodus,
Eltka,

Fordhand Svensla Lakare Sallskapts,
Fort Wayne Med. Jour.,

Guy's Hospital Reports,
Gazette del Tribunal,
Giornale di Neuropatalogia,
Gerichtl Zeitung, Vienna,
Gazette des Hopitaux,

Hygiea,
Harvard Law Review,
Holstein Friestian Register.
Hot Springs Med. Jonal,
Hammondsport Heral
Harper's Monthly,

Illinois State Board Health,
International Journal Surgery,
Index Medicus,
Iowa Law Bulletin,
Il Pisania Gazette Se ula,
Indian Review,
Ideal Review,
Interstate Med. Journ
Interstate Med. Journ
Independent Thinker.

Johns Hopkins Unive sity,
Journal of Inebriety,
Journal of Medical Sci.
Journal of Nervous Mental Diseases,
Journal de Medicine,
Jahrbuecher fuer Psychiatr
Journal of Electro Ther peutics,
Journal of Tuberculosi
Journal of Mental Scien
Journal of Ass'n of itary Surgeons,
Journal American Me ical Association,

Kansas City Med. Inde
Kathiawas Law Report

La. Psi. la Neurol e Sci.
Lippincott's Magazine,
L'Anthropologie,
London Lancet,
Littell's Living Age,
Law Quarterly Review,
La Progress Medicale,
Louisville Medical News
Lunacy and Charity,
Literary Digest,
Legal Intelligencer,
Lancet Pub. Co.,
La Habana Medica,
Law Students Journal,
Literature,
Legal Adviser,

Mass. State Board of Health,
Medico-Legal Society of Massachusetts,
Medical Review of Reviews,
Medical Annales

EXCHANGE JOURNALS—Continued.

Medical News.
Messeger of Neurology and Forensic Psycopathology. St. Petersburg.
Medicine,
Menorah Monthly.
Madras Law Journal,
Medical Fortnightly,
Medical Mirror,
Monatschrift fuer Unfallheilkunde.
Medical Herald,
Mind,
Medical Sentinel,
Med. and Surg. Bulletin,
Medical Bulletin,
Medical Register,
Medicus.
Medical Critic,
Maryland Med. Journal,
Magazine of Mysteries,
Medical Record,
Medical Times,
Metaphysical Magazine,
Medical World,

North American Review,
New Orleans Med. and Surg.,
New York Med. Record,
Nordisk Medicinski Arkiv
N. Amer. Journal of Diagnosis and Practice,
N. C. Med. Journal,
N. Y. Medical Journal,

Occidental Med. Times,
Our Animal Friends,
Optical Journal,
Ohio Archæological and Historical.
Our Dumb Animals,

Philadelphia Times and Register,
Pacific Medical Journal,
Pacific Record of Medicine and Surgery,
Personal Rights,
Phrenological Journal,
Psychological Review,
Penn Yan Democrat,
Pa. State Com.of Lunacy,
Public Opinion,
Psi and Nerve Path. Kharkoff, Russia,
Public Health Journal,
Printer's Ink,
Penny Magazine,
Perry's Magazine,
Providence Medical Journal,
Psychiatrische en Neuralgische Bladen,
Punjab Law Reporter,
Psychic and Occult Views and Reviews,
Pittsburg Legal Journal,
Progress Medicale,

Revue De Medicinė,
Revue Medicale,
Repertorie de Pharmacie,
Review of Reviews,
Railway Surgeon,
Railway Age,
Revue de la Hypnotism
Revista Ciencas Medicas,
Revista Penale.
Revista Medico-Legal,
Revista de Neuralogie, Psychiatre,
Revista de Antropologie, Criminella of Sciencias Medico-Legales,
Revista de Neurol, and Phy. (Lisbon),
Revista de Neurologie,
Revue de la Hypnotism,
Revista des Revistas,
Revista di Medicina Legale,

Scotch Board of Lunacy,
Sanitarian,
Sanitary Record,
Smithsonian Institute,
Societe Medicine Legale de France,
Society D'Anthropologie, Brussels,
Society for Psychical Research,
Society for Promoting the Welfare of the Insane,
Scienza Italiana,
St.Louis Courier of Med.,
Sei-I Kwai Med. Journal,
Spirit of the Times,
Suggestive Therapeutics,
Suggester and Thinker,
Spectator,
South African Law Journal,
Sind Sadar Court Reports,

The Southern Law Review,
The Journal of Mental Pathology,
The Southern Medical Journal,
The Hannemanian,
Tennessee State Board Health,
The Journal of State Med. Ass.
The American Journal Psychology,
The Green Bag,
The Open Court,
The Freeman
The Arena,
The Monist,
The Cosmopolital Osteopath,
Texas Medical News
Turf, Field and Farm,
The Legal Adviser,
The Philistine,
The Sheep Breeder,,
The Therapist,
The Physician and Sgeon,
The Public,
The Texas Clinic,
The Texas Medical Journal
The Coming Age,
The Stylus,
The Legal Gazette,
The Surgical and Dent News,
The Colorado Medi Journal,
The Journalist,
The Ladies Home Jounal,
The Forum,
The Law (Oklahoma.)
The Century,
The Lawyer (Madras.)
The Monthly Cycloped

Union Industrial Dro Penale,
Universal Med. Scien

Vermont Medical Month
Virginia Law Register,
Virginia Medical Sem Monthly,

Woman's Med. Jou
Western Reserve La Journal,
Weekly Law Journal,
West Virginia Bar,

X-Ray Journal,

Yale Law Journal,
Youth's Companion,

Zeitschrift fuer Schweiz Strafetcht.
Zeitchrift fuer Psy histre,
Zeitschrift fuer Medizinal Beamte.

HONORARY VICE PRESIDENTS OF THE AMERICAN CONGRESS OF TUBERCULOSIS.

THE EARL OF MINTO,
Governor General of Canada,
Honorary Vice-President of the American Congress of Tuberculosis.

SIR OLIVER MOWATT, G. C., M. G,
Lt. Governor of Ottawa, Canada,
Honorary Vice-President of the American Congress of Tuberculosis.

HON. WM. W. STICKNEY,
Governor of Vermont.
Honorary Vice-President of the American Congress of Tuberculosis.

FRANK W. HUNT,
Governor of Idaho,
Honorary Vice-President of the American Congress of Tuberculosis.

INAUGURAL ADDRESS AS PRESIDENT OF THE MEDICO-LEGAL SOCIETY.

BY CLARK BELL, ESQ., LL. D., OF NEW YORK CITY.
Pronounced January 15th, 1902.

I have again to return thanks to the members of this body, for another re-election to the chair of this Honorable Society. I had hoped that some one else would have been chosen to fill this place, during the coming year, but it has doubtless been due to the position the Society now occupies in relation to the proposed meeting of the American Congress of Tuberculosis in May next, that has made the management so unanimous in refusing to change the present officers, and to override my personal wishes and feelings in that respect.

I submit to the general consensus of opinion among my associates, that a change at present would not be for the best interests of the body, and might prejudice its efforts, in one of the most important movements it has ever been connected with.

THE PAST.

It is now thirty years since I was elected to the chair you ask me now again to assume. I have not time to speak in detail of the work of the body in these eventful years, but must refer only to its later labors on which I touched in my last year's address.

THE PROGRESS OF THE SCIENCE.

During the year 1901 our labors in the field of Psychological Medicine, will be best understood and appreciated by the annual report of the Psychological Section, which accompanies this address, and should be considered as forming a part of it.

The same is true respecting the report of the section upon Medico-Legal Surgery.

A perusal of these reports, will best illustrate the ripe labors of this body, and show what such an energetic, resolute, and aggressive band of workers can accomplish who have united for a common purpose.

The recent events that have come to affect human destiny, especially in this nation and its environment, that have crowded upon us, in the past year, are of such enormous import, and so relate to and affect us, and our future, in the American nation as, to exceed in interest any and indeed all other years within our recent recollection.

The death of the Queen of England; the accession of King Edward to the throne of the British Empire, and his coronation next summer, have had, not only a very great influence in our country, but coupled with the tragic death of President McKinley, (the President most beloved of any by the American people since President Lincoln), have touched the hearts and aroused the keenest sensibilities of all peoples, who speak the language of our country, as they have never before been affected by human events. The accession of President Roosevelt to the chief seat in our nation, as the sequel of the terribly tragedy that placed the responsibility of this high place, with all its solemnities, upon him, seems to have united our people, with one mind to rally to his support, and to have lifted him to a higher sense of the great public interests and trusts, committed to his charge, and the spirit in which he received it, and the strong pledges he gave to the nation with such emotion and solemnity, to carry out the policy of the dead President, so clearly enunciated and defined, on the very day of his death, seems to have almost transferred to the new ruler, the great wealth of affection with which the American people had regarded the dead McKinley.

These tremendous events, so far-reaching in human destiny, and notably on the future of the American people on this continent, have caused an absolute suspension of all official action by the committee named by this society in respect to the anticipated release of Mrs. Maybrick for reasons, which are at once apparent, by reason of the change of rulers and ministers, so occurring as to make formal official action inappropriate and if not impossible, certainly impracticable.

Now that King Edward will shortly pass through the stately ceremonies of his coronation, it is believed that in accordance with what is belived to be public sentiment and opinion, that the occasion will be signalized by her release in accordance with a general conviction, that she who has languished more than twelve years in prison, will be pardoned, without reference to any question of her innocence or guilt. That especially when the late Lord Chief Justice of England has, while acting as the head of the English justiciary, placed himself on record, both in his voluntary letter to Mrs. Maybrick now in the hands of the committee of this body, and in various written papers, letters and briefs, on file in the office of the Home Secretary, "That she ought never to have been convicted. That she ought to be speedily released," and as stated by his late biographer in the recently published life of the Earl of Killowen, from the lips of the great jurist and from copies of his writings, about which there can be no doubt or question, not only of his profound conviction of her absolute innocence of the crime charged, but of his clear and undoubted belief, that she ought not to have been convicted upon the evidence, that the death of Mr. Maybrick was not due to arsenic, or any poison, and that from the day he took the oath as Chief Justice of England to the day of his death he never ceased to labor with one Home Secretary after another, with the greatest possible energy, persistentcy and ability, in urging the propriety and wisdom of her release by the English government.

For professional reasons this great jurist, while he never concealed his views and opinions from his personal friends, nor from the English Bar, would not either make them public himself, nor consent to giving them publicity, but the letter, he gave her voluntarily while Chief Justice, and written on the official paper of his high office was intended by him in the case of his death, to assure the world, of his belief in her innocence of the crime as charged in the indictment on which she was tried, and her continuance in prison, as contrary to his judgment on the evidence in the case.

THE LEGAL STRUGGLE WITH TUBERCULOSIS.

Since the organization of the Medico-Legal Society, indeed since the beginning of the last century, no such momentous question in forensic medicine, has ever been presented to the general judgment and verdict of the Professors of Law and of Medicine, as the one with which now all the civilized nations of the world are confronted, and with which all are now grappling in the question of legislation for its prevention and spread. How far can the ravages of consumption be arrested by legislation? Can any legal enactments or regulations sanctioned by law, arrest its devastating march upon, and its terrible destruction of human life?

It is the most momentous question of the hour, and last year our best effort was in inaugurating, organizing and rallying all the forces at our command upon this supreme question of medical jurisprudence.

THE AMERICAN CONGRESS OF TUBERCULOSIS.

While there had been an attempt to enlist the medical profession in the issue, in 1900, the labors of this society were initial and tentative, and only originated as a question of forensic medicine,which did not so deeply interest medical men outside the Medico-Legal Society, as it should have done; but the session of the American Congress of 1901, at the Hotel Majestic, on May 15th and 16th, 1901, was indeed splendidly successful in the organization of, and the real inauguration of a superb movement, international in scope and purpose, and based on the co-operation of not only the American States of our American Union, but on every state, province and country in the United States of America, in Mexico, and in the South and Central American Republics and in the Dominion of Canada. Both continents of the Western Hemisphere and all countries in American waters were intended to be embraced in its labors Governors of a large number of states of the American Union named delegates, and Mexico and the Central and South-American States were to some extent represented and the Dominion of Canada. The Bulletin of this work now nearly completed containing over 300 pages, which are a part only of its labor, will illustrate the great value and importance of its work and its value to the literature of the subject. The most important of all, however, was the organization of a strong body with a board of officers, selected from various parts of the states, provinces and countries of both continents upon the Western Hemisphere, the original officers of which have been announced to the world.

The plan proposed was to have three additional vice presidents chosen in each state, province and country, who would form the nucleus of work in each location, and this has progressed until these officials have been chosen and selected for at least half the American states, and in some of the Canadian provinces, Mexico, some of the Central and South American Republics and this branch of the work of organization is rapidly approaching completion.

The officials of that Congress have also appointed honorary vice-presidents, and are now making such appointments for each country, state and province, and these officials have been chosen and accepted for the Dominion of Canada, and in all its provinces from men of the very highest character and social position in the Dominion. This work is also progressing in the various states of the American Union and in Mexico and in all the Central and South American Republics and will soon be complete and ready for announcement. The delegates already appointed by the governors of the States of the American Union are over 160 in number exclusive of a considerable list of delegates from medical societies, academies of medicine, legal and other organizations.

The officers have announced the next general session of the Congress for the 14th, 15th and 16th of May, 1902, to be held in joint session with the Medico-Legal Society at the Hotel Majestic in the city of New York, with a public banquet on the evening of the 15th of May, in which all medical and legal societies are invited to co-operate and to send delegates, and medical and legal men are invited to contribute papers to be read. A programme will be prepared and announced later to embrace the issues of the hour, the discussion of which will enlist the ablest thinkers and talent in the profession of law and medicine, in both countries of the entire Western Hemisphere, and their dependencies.

A MUSEUM.

There will be a museum and a suitable room has been secured at the Hotel Majestic for this purpose, convenient to the assembly room and the preparation for the museum will be in the hands of a carefully selected committee, of which Dr. Edwin H. Lewis, of Burlington, Vermont, will be the chairman.

Prof. Dr. Moritz Benedikt, of Vienna, Austria, has announced his intention of contributing an open letter to this Congress, as he did to the London Congress of 1901.

RECEPTION AND ENTERTAINMENT.

These outlines seem to show the enormous labor that will devolve upon the officers of that Congress, and especially upon this Society, who will have to take the laboring oar in the work of the committee on reception and entertainment of our foreign visitors.

MEDICAL JURISPRUDENCE—QUESTIONS UNDER INVESTIGATION.

The subjects under investigation as announced last year, are still in charge of committees, and additional questions have been accepted by our executive officers and will be assigned to standing committees, the details of which will appear in our transastions, of which I shall allude to, a few only at this time.

It is more than probable that the enormous labors of the approaching Congress to be held in May, will divert and postpone to some extent the labors of the Select Committees on the subjects already referred to until later in the year, and perhaps until next autumn.

Death has cut down an unusually large number of our best names in the year that has passed.

Prof. Maschka, of Bohemia, I am informed by Prof. Dr. Morris Benedikt is no more. The details and sketch of his career will appear, I trust, later on.

Dr. Irving C. Rosse, of Washington,D.C.,one of our ablest neurologists and alienists has passed away, and appropriate action has been taken to his memory, as also Simon Sterne, of the New York bar; Judge David McAdam, of the Supreme Court of New York, who was one of the charter members of the society at its foundation; Ex-Medical Director Dr. Albert H. Gihon, who has for many years been identified with this society, and on whose life and career Dr. I. N. Love pronounced an eulogy at the January meeting.

The following are the present Honorary Members of this body:

Dr. Henry Maudsley, of London.
Prof. Dr. Brouardel, of Paris, France.
Prof. Dr. Krafft-Ebing, of Austria.
Hon. Noah Davis, of New York.
Prof. Dr. Rudolph Virchow, of Berlin.
Prof. Dr. Stanford E. Chaillee, of Louisiana.

Hon. Luther R. Marsh, of Middletown, N. Y.

I have the honor to recommend the election at this meeting as I assume the chair for the thirteenth time, the following gentlemen as Honorary members of this society.

Prof. Dr. Moritz Benedikt, of Vienna, one of the ablest of our colleagues in Vienna.

Prof. Dr. N. S. Davis, of Chicago, Ill., one of the most honored and able names among American physicians.

Judge Robert Earl, of Herkimer, N. Y., ex-Chief Justice New York Court of Appeals.

Prof. Dr. R. Ogden Doremus, ex-President of this society, and the nestor of American alienists.

Prof. Dr. Mierzejewski, of Russia, President of the Society of Psychiatry, of St. Petersburg, Russia.

Dr. A. Motet, Secretary Medico-Legal Society of France, and chairman of Section of Legal Medicine, Paris, Medical International Congress of 1900, of Paris, France.

Prof. Dr. Caesar Lombroso, of Italy, one of the most eminent criminologists of our time, for many years, a corresponding member of the society.

Prof. Dr. Charles H. Hughes, Editor of the Alienist and Neurologist, of St. Louis, Mo., and one of the foremost of American alienists.

A. N. Bell, the veteran editor of the Sanatarian, Honorary President of the American Congress of Tuberculosis.

Hon. Abraham R. Lawrence, who has sat upon the bench of the Supreme Court of the State of New York 28 years, and retired near the age limit on December 31, 1901.

Nicholas Senn, M. D., of Chicago, Surgeon General of the State of Illinois.

Pof. Dr. Axel Key, of Stockholm, Sweden, for years a corresponding member of this body, and one of the most eminent medical men in Sweden.

Judge L. A. Emery, a member of the Supreme Court of the State of Maine, who has for years been one of our active members and a devoted student of medical jurisprudence.

Members will recall that this is an honor which has been very bers will recall that this is an honor which has been very rarely bestowed. We are under our constitution limited to name only twenty Honorary members. I submit as an appendix to this address, a list of the Honorary members of this body, marking those with an asterisk who are deceased. Those now living are in the order of their appointment or selection:

I recommend that the constitution of the society be amended so that the word "twenty" be changed to "fifty" as the limit to our honorary membership.

The limitation in number was proper at the time of its adoption, but now that there are over fifteen hundred names on our various rolls of members; that the society has become national and international in character and labor; with many names of eminence in the professions of law, medicine, chemistry and science who are entitled to this high honor, and whom I desire to reccommend to you for this distinction, but am restrained by the constitution. I ask for its enlargement but I do not recommend lowering the high standard of excellence we have ever held for the position, and should prefer rather to elevate that than to lessen it in any degree.

During the past year we have lost by death 4; active members; by resignation, 5; members suspended for non-payment of dues, 2. New active members 56 have been elected, so that there was on January 1, 1902, 545 names on the the roll of active members. There are but seven names on the roll of honorary members.

On the roll of corresponding members 4 names have been vacated by death, and 20 have been elected. So that we have active members on January 1, 1902, 546 names; honorare members, 7, corresponding members, 568. Total 1120

Exclusive of members of Psychological Section......	172
Section Medico-Legal Surgery....................	104
	1396

Names on suspended list for non-payment of dues, about 360, making our total membership over 1700 names.

FINALLY.

The work devolving upon us in 1902 demands our greatest enthusaism, our highest energy and more personal sacrifice of time and unremunerative labor. I ask of the Fellows of the Society that splendid support that has so greatly encouraged me in the past, for the year before us.

SHOULD PROSTITUTION BE REGULATED BY LAW?

T. CRISP POOLE, ESQ., BARRISTER-AT-LAW, BRISBANE, AUSTRALIA.

[*Concluded from December Journal*]

Such being a general summary of the law as now existing in the territories mentioned on the subject of the regulation of prostitution, it will be seen that the legislation of Victoria and Tasmania possesses an advantage over that of Queensland and New Zealand (English legislation is disregarded here as being passed with a different object from that of generally checking the spread of contagious diseases), inasmuch as its operation is uniform and it is not left to the discretion of any person to limit its effect to towns or districts specially declared to be within its provisions, or even to make those provisions a dead letter by not proclaiming any such places at all. On the other hand, the Victorian and Tasmanian legislation is seriously defective, in that no female can be proceeded against in those states until she is at least believed to be suffering from a contagious disease, and in consequence a female against whom this cannot be proved may pursue a career of prostitution unchecked and spread much disease before the evidence is forthcoming by which it will be possible to restrain her. Whether the periodical medical examinations to which any female who practices prostitution may be subjected in Queensland and New Zealand, are the best means which can be devised of meeting the difficulty, is a question which will shortly be considered.

The writer has unfortunately been unable to discover whether there has been any legislation to regulate prostitution in Ameica, though he can see by the means at his disposal that legislation of some sort on prostitution exists in that country. But this will not be of so much consequence in an article intended for publication in America, and which will be principally read by American lawyers and physicians, nor is he without a hope that he may find, in consequence of this article, some information on this subject in the pages of the Medico-Legal Journal. But enough has been written at all events to give some idea of what has been done in England and Australasia in the direction of regulating prostitution, and we have materials enough to proceed to discuss the important question, whether such regulation is wise or necessary for the conservation of health.

It has already been observed that no lover of morality can regard the Contagious Diseases Acts in any more favorable light than as being the less of two alternate evils. The utmost that can be said in their favor is that it is better that none but undiseased females should be permitted to practice prostitution than that absence of all restrictions should spread venereal diseases not only among the guilty parties, but also among innocent persons coming into contact with them. But the evils which attend the execution of laws of the character above described are grave in the extreme. The degrading nature of the duties of the medical men who are appointed to conduct the periodical examinations, of the policemen who are required, if necessary, to compel the attendance of the females concerned at the appointed institutions, and of the magistrates and counsel who are concerned in conducting the investigations requisite under these acts, make up together a sum total of revolting obligations of which we cannot say, in the words of Shakespeare, that they are "much ado about nothing," but must pronounce to be much ado for the toleration of vice. Nor can we be so trustful in the firmness of human nature as to think it improbable that so much official contact with prostitution may sometimes tempt the participants into greater familiarity, and make vicious men of some who would otherwise have kept steadfast. We have further to consider the possibility that some who would otherwise avoid engaging the services of prostitutes through fear of contracting disease may be encouraged to do so on knowing that a particular female holds a certificate from medical practitioner guaranteeing that she is free from any contagious ailment. And with respect to the effect of the act upon the females themselves, to say nothing of the hardening process that such periodical examinations are likely to produce, the written certificate declaring her to be free from contagious disease is unquestionably looked upon by herself in many instances as an authority for her to certain the calling of a prostitute, and a recognition by law of her occupation as a lawful one. Nor is she mistaken in this supposition, for everything is lawful which is not prohibited, and a statute which declares that females of a particular class shall not be allowed to practice prostitution declares by implication that others not belonging to that class are at liberty to do so, and the darefulness of her pursuit is not altered by the fact that the law limits its recognition to bare toleration and will not aid the enforcement of any of her claims. Such are the weighty objections to the provisions of the Contagious Diseases Acts, and while we grant that it is necessary to have legislative protection against the promiscuous spread of contagious diseases, we must declare on the other hand that the protection given by these acts is bought at a very high price. There is only one satisfactory way of dealing with the evil which it is the design of the Contagious Diseases Acts to check, and the answer which the writer would give to the question which stands at the head of the article is "No." Prostitution should not be regulated by law, but wholly prohibited.

Let it not be objected that such a wholesale prohibition is not possible. It is assumed upon the passing of every Act that the law has power to enforce obedience to its own demands, and an act which declares that certain females shall be liable to punishment if they conduct themselves as prostitutes, presumably considers itself able to inflict those punishments as occasion arises. But if some females can be restrained from practising prostitution, why then is it not possible to restrain all? Why not make a general law that all females found practicing prostitution shall be liable to the same penalties as they now are under some of the Contagious Diseases Acts, if discharged from a hospital with notice that they are still affected with a contagious disease, and so do away at once with all the evils attending the system of periodical examination? If the question of expense be worth any consideration at all in so important a matter, the cost of enforcing such a law could hardly be greater than the cost of the present system with its retinue of medical officers and other functionaries. So far as the maintenance of hospitals for the cure of females affected with contagious disease is concerned, these could be continued under an act making all public prostitutions illegal, but as part of a penal establishment, and, as may be hoped, with less need of being utilized. Does any one object that such a law would be inefficient in working its purpose, and that there would be frequent violations of it, secret if not open? It can be answered that there is the same danger of secret violation under the present acts, and that it is no argument against a salutory law that there are to be found persons who will evade it. The same logic would prevent us from penalizing theft and murder because thieves and murderers exist, notwithstanding the penal nature of their acts. Nor can any tangible reason be formed why there should be greater difficulty in enforcing a law prohibiting all prostitution, than in enforcing that which already exists, unless it should be a melancholy fact that public morality is so low that it would not tolerate so general a restriction.

In conclusion the writer would emphasize the importance of society enforcing the penalty of social ostracism upon the male offender in the matter of sensual immorality equally with the female. Law after all can do but little when its enactments are in advance of the sentiment governing the people whom it professes to restrain. The history of duelling (a practice which has always been contrary to law) furnishes an example of this, for we know how in the days when it was popular the law was habitually evaded, and persons morally and legally guilty of murder permitted to escape, to be received after a brief interval of retirement into the arms of a society which regarded their homicides as acts necessary to the vindication of their honor as gentlemen. Where is the equity of branding the female who has unhappily slipped with the epithet of a "fallen woman," and regarding her as an outcast from society, while the man who has been the cause of her ruin may shine as a prominent star in the circles of fashion from which his selfish transgression has driven his victim Let it never be forgotten that it is the man who resorts to the prostitute that keeps prostitution alive, that without his concurrence no woman could support herself by such means, and that many a female has been almost impelled to such a career through inability to obtain more respectable employment, after having once fallen before the wiles of a heartless libertine. The article may appropriately conclude with a quotation from a writer of the eighteenth century, not so much read now as formerly, and who, amid much that is offensive to modern taste, has nevertheless left behind him many wise admonitions which his readers will be none the worse for remembering. In chapter V of book IX of Henry Fielding's novel "Amelia" will be found the following words:

"'Fie, child,' cries the doctor, 'do not make a conclusion so much to the dishonor of the great Creator. The nature of man is far from being in itself evil; it abounds with benevolence, charity, and pity, coveting praise and honor, and shunning shame and disgrace. Bad education, bad habits, and bad customs, debauch our nature, and drive it headlong as it were into vice. The governors of the world, and I am afraid the priesthood, are answerable for the badness of it. Instead of discouraging wickedness to the utmost of their power, both are too apt to connive at it. In the great sin of adultery, for instance, hath the government provided any law to punish it? or doth the priest take any care to correct it? on the contrary is the most notorious practice of it any detriment in the state, I had almost said in the church? is it any blot in his escutcheon? any bar to his honour? is he not to be found every day in the assemblies of women of the highest quality? in the closets of the greatest men and even at the tables of bishops? What wonder then if the community in general treat this monstrous crime as a matter of jest, and that men give way to the temptations of a violent appetite, when the indulgence of it is protected by law and countenanced by custom? * * * * * * and in a Christian society, which I no more esteem this nation to be than I do any part of Turkey. I doubt not but this very colonel would have made a worthy and valuable member.'"

CRIME AND CRIMINALS; OR THE PROBLEMS PRESENTED BY ANTI-SOCIAL ACTS.

BY EDWIN C. WALKER, OF NEW YORK.

[*Concluded from December Journal.*]

Now let us glance a little more in detail at these six proposed rules of conduct: It is objected to a and b that often men commit offenses which are best punished by bodily chastisement, as wife-whipping or petty theft. It is argued, and truly, that fining does little good as a deterrent in the case of the wife-whipper and merely takes food out of the mouth of the wife and children, while imprisonment has the same effect. It is said, too, that the wife is likely to get another beating in punishment so soon as the husband returns from prison, while, on the other hand, so salutary is the remembrance of the whipping, that he is far less apt to resort to violence again in revenge for her complaint than he would be had that complaint resulted in a less sharp punishment. That is to say, the whipping is a better deterrent than fining or imprisonment, does not take from the man money that should go to the support of the wife and children, and does not impose upon the people the burden of his support, as would imprisonment. To this argument comes the rejoiner that physical chastisement is degrading, alike to the receiver of it and to all who have to do with its infliction or witness or learn of its infliction. This is unquestionable, but it might be said again that those who impose fines and those who have prisoners in their care are not observed to become refined and elevated by their vocations. It is not possible that they should be so long as the existing ideals are in vogue. The moral tone of the physician or the attendant in a hospital for the insane is not necessarily degraded. This is because we are coming to take a scientific, a sane, view of the subject of insanity. In the ages when an insane person was looked upon as simply a tenement for devils those who in any way had charge of him were degraded by that work even more than are the keepers in the worst of our prisons today. The lesson is obvious.

Opponents of capital punishment encounter objections that can not be laughed out of court, objections which must be taken and carefully weighed in the scales against the considerations that impel us to antagonize the infliction of the death penalty.' What shall be done, it is asked, in the case of a man who deliberately sets fire to a crowded tenement house because he wishes to collect insurance or has a grudge against the owner of the building or the lessor or the janitor or a tenant, thus putting in deadly peril the lives of scores or perhaps hundreds of persons who have never injured him? Here was the Sandmere on Eighth Avenue the other night—set fire to and the vestibule doors carefully fastened to keep out the firemen as long as possible. This was not a murder, or an attempted murder, of sudden passion, a blow struck in a moment, but a carefully planned deed of wholesale destruction of property and life, in intention. Or here is a tramp or a discharged farm hand or a neighbor who sets fire to the barns where are scores of horses and cattle and other animals who die a cruel death in the flames. Or here is a man who wrecks a passenger train and so maims and kills many persons, and this for purposes of robbery or to get revenge on the road or an employe of it or a passenger. What is society to do with these men, if they are apprehended? Is not the prologation of their lives too great a risk and too onorous an expense, taking into consideration the cruel ruthlessness of their natures? Can they be transformed into useful and harmless members of the social body? We kill the rabid dog or cow without question, though they are less dangerous than such men and though they are as surely and completely the products of antecedent causes and present environments. It is answered that while we are unable to reason with and apply moral suasion to the animals named, we can reason with and apply moral suasion to the incendiaries and train wreckers. But, in the words of Dr. Frederick R. Marvin, is it not true that "there are paths of development behind the ape and there are men who tread them?" The difference seems to be that while, as a rule, we kill the rabid dog in a panic, but without attaching moral blame to it, we kill the men in anger, with all possible opprobrium, with accompaniments, frequently, of atrocious cruelty not dreamed of in the case of the dog. We think the dog has no mind and no will to do wrong, while the men have minds and they will to do wrong. This is a survival of the ancient delusion of an uncaused, a free will. Still the question remains, What is it best to do with these exceptionally destructive men? On what grounds shall we take the risk of their continued living? I see but two, the first of which is found under b, and is that we should inflict no irremediable penalties, lest we put beyond rescue an innocent life, and the second of which is that the deliberate taking of human life is a bad example for society to set and tends to keep alive the thirst for blood, especially in all who have immediately to do with the taking of human life by law.

Coming to c and d, we are confronted with "Labor's" strenuous denial of the right of prisoners to be engaged in productive labor. But I maintain there should not be an idle man or woman in any prison or reformatory, that is, if he or she is physically able to work, and that the rights of outside laborers are to be safeguarded in ways that will not utterly ruin the lives of the unfortunates who are behind the bars, just as I maintain that the wives of undeveloped men are to be protected by giving them more liberty, especially liberty to get away from their lash-wielding masters, instead of trying to protect them by putting a lash into the hands of a constable for application to the backs of the husbands. Idleness is prison, even more than idleness elsewhere, is destructive of moral, mental, and physical fiber, is worse for society than would be the summary execution of every man sentenced in court. And the work done in prisons must be done because it is a pleasure to work, not because work is supposed to be inflicted as a punishment. There are fewer men than we think who do not wish to do something, and the task of the men in charge of our prisons is to find in every case, if they can, what work the prisoner prefers to do, what work he is really interested in, and then provide that work for him, if possible. There is not another thing that can be done which will be so effective as this in turning loose on society men who are better fitted to lead useful lives and who will be more desirous of leading such lives than they were when arrested.

Let us determine that we want to increase the honest productive capacity of every person sent to prison, that we are no longer to be satisfied with the imposition of a task as a form of degradation, and that making a better man of the convict is not to be permitted to make a poorer man of the outside worker, and we shall surely find the ways and means whereby to put our determination into effect. The rights of the "free laborer" are not to be secured by further brutalizing the convict and by driving hope of better days out of his heart, but by wresting from the monopolist and the despot the privileges and powers which they have usurped.

I said under d that one of the three objects society should have in mind in dealing with anti-social persons is restitution. Vengeance is of the savage, and we should be done with it. The punishment of one to deter others from the commission of like offenses may be of some value sometimes but it bears too close a resemblance to vicarious atonement and its beneficent results are so hard to find when one is in a hurry, that we may be pardoned if we fail to see in it so much importance as many sociologists think it possesses. Restitution, however, is affirmative and while I am very far from claiming that its application is possible in even a majority of instances, I am inclined to think it should receive far more serious consideration than it has from moralist, lawmaker, and judge. Where is the economy, political or other, in sending a man to prison for a year because he has stolen property to the value of five dollars? The punishment is out of all proportion to the amount of plunder, and teaches the offender nothing except hatred for the power that is robbing him far more than he robbed the merchant or householder. He will come out of prison with about every chance in favor of his becoming a criminal in perpetuity or a homeless vagabond. But if society said to him, "See here, Brown, this is not a fair deal; Smith did not owe you anything and you should not have taken his property. Pay him five dollars and deposit the cost of collection and you may go about your business, and may it be a fairer business than this last enterprise of yours." My impression is that this would be fully as effective, to say the least, in restraining Brown from further depredations and in deterring others as would his imprisonment for a year, and it would be worlds cheaper for society, besides leaving Brown free to work for the support of his family. But, says the critic, suppose Brown has no money to pay Smith and the cost of collection?" That would mean that to the cost of collection would be added the item for his keep while he was earning the money. The impor-taant consideration is that it would be impressed upon him that society was not seeking vengeance, but trying to secure restitution to the wronged person. A man can not restore the life he has taken, do you say? True, but may it not be that he can, to some extent, take the place of his victim as a provider for the helpless? And if he steals much, disposes of what he has taken, and is too old to make much, if any, restitution through labor for the robbed, I do not see that the principle of restitution is invalidated through his inability to give back what he has taken. In the case of the murderer, no one is benefitted by his execution, save the tax-payer, and I doubt if even he is in the long run, while setting the murderer to help support the children of his victim is better for them than the legal killing of the murderer and may at once give back to the tax-payer a part at least of the expense incident to keeping the murderer alive, by reducing the taxpayer's bill for the support of pauper children.

I am not unaware that our courts today often make the return of stolen property the basis of clemency to the prisoner, but I do not think, so far as my observation goes, that the judge takes enough pains to impress the fact in its relation to the principle upon the understanding of the culprit. And assuredly the principle is not applied in the case of other crimes than larceny.

PSYCHOLOGICAL.

This Department is conducted with the following Associate Editors:

Judge Abram H. Dailey, Brooklyn, N. Y.
Prof. A. A D'Ancona, San Francisco, Cal.
H. S. Drayton, M. D., N. Y.
M. Ellinger, Esq., N. Y. City.
Dr. Havelock Ellis, London.
Thomson Jay Hudson, Esq., Detroit Mich.
Wm. Lee Howard, M. D., Baltimore, Md.
R. J. Nunn, M. D., Savannah, Ga.
A. E. Osborne, M. D., Cal.
Jas. T. Searcey, M. D., Tuscaloosa, Ala.
Prof. W. Xavier Sudduth, Chicago, Ill.
U. O. B. Wingate, M. D., Milwaukee, Wis.

as the organ of the Psychological Section.

The Psychological Section of the Medico-Legal Society has been organized, to which any member, Active, Corresponding or Honorary, is eligible on payment of an annual enrollment fee or dues of $1.50.

Any student of Psychological Science is eligible to unite with the Section without joining the Medico Legal Society on an annual subscription of $1.50, payable in advance and receive the MEDICO-LEGAL JOURNAL free. The officers for 1902 are as follows:

Chairman,
PROF. W. XAVIER SUDDUTH, OF CHICAGO, ILL.

LEGAL AND SCIENTIFIC.
Vice-Chairmen,
Clark Bell, Esq., of New York.
Rev. Antoinette B. Blackwell, of N. Y.
Harold Browett, Esq , Shanghai, China.
C. Van D. Chenoweth. Worcester. Mass.
Judge Abram H Dailey, of Brooklyn.
Moritz Ellinger, Esq., of New York.
Rev. Phebe A. Hanaford, of New York
Thomson Jay Hudson, Esq., Detroit, Mich.
Sophia McClelland, of New York.
Mrs. Jacob F. Miller, of New York.

MEDICAL.
Vice-Chairmen.
T. D. Crothers, M. D., of Hartford, Conn.
F. E. Daniel, M. D., of Austin, Texas.
H. S. Drayton, M. D., of New York.
Wm. Lee Howard, M. D , of Baltimore, Md.
Henry Hulst, M. D., Grand Rapids, Mich.
Prof. Thomas Bassett Keyes, of Chicago.
R. J. Nunn, M. D., of Savannah, Ga.
A. E. Osborne, M. D., of Glen Ellen, Cal.
Jas. T. Searcy, M. D., Tuscaloosa, Ala.
U. O. B. Wingate, M. D., Milwaukee, Wis.

Mrs. Mary Louise Thomas, of Pennsylvania.

Secretary and Treasurer.
CLARK BELL, ESQ., OF NEW YORK.

Executive Committee.
CLARK BELL, ESQ., Chairman.
SAMUEL BELL THOMAS, OF NEW YORK CITY, Secretary.

M. Ellinger, Esq.
Carleton Simon, M. D.
Judge A. H. Dailey.
Ida Trafford Bell.
R. W. Shufeldt, M. D.
H. W. Mitchell, M. D.

The following members have united with the Psychological Section since our last announcement:

Prof. D. S. Abbott, Athens, Ga.; Joseph H. Dennis, 22 Weybosset street, Providence, Rhode Island; Eleanor Gridley, 67 South Clark street, Chicago; C. O. Rice, M. D., 235 Central Place, Pueblo, Colorado; Dr. A. Howard Young, 52 Mechanic Building, Pueblo, Colorado; Ernest Wende, M. D., 471 Delaware avenue, Buffalo, New York; Edward Howard Carnahan, Meaford, Ontario; L. C. Brown, Esq., Lock Box 85, Baltimore, Maryland; H. C. Wright, Esq., Corry, Penn'a.

PSYCHOLOGICAL SECTION OF THE MEDCO-LEGAL SOCIETY.

ANNUAL REPORT, JANUARY 1, 1902.

TO THE FELLOWS OF THE PSYCHOLOGICAL SECTION AND OF THE MEDICO-LEGAL SOCIETY.

The following subjects are within the Domain of Studies pursued by the Section:

1. The Medical Jurisprudence of Insanity.
2. Inebriety, Heredity and Sociology.
3. Criminality and Criminal Anthropology.
4. Mental Suggestion, and especially of Physicians as to Clinical Suggestion and Therapeutic Hypnosis.
5. Experimental Psychology.
7. Clairvoyance.
8. Facts within the Domain of Physical Research, including investigation into so-called Modern Spiritism.

The work of the Section for the year, since the last Annual Report, may be summarized as follows:

The following papers, addresses and articles have been contributed to the Section during the year 1901:

1. Paper by Baron de Schrenck-Notzing, entitled "Suggestion and Hypnotism in Their Relation to Jurisprudence."

2. A large number of papers read before the Society and the American Congress of Tuberculosis by the following authors:—

By R. L. Pritchard, Esq., M. D., of New York.
C. F. Ulrich, M. D., of Wheeling, W. Va.
Heneage Gibbes, M. D.. of Detroit. Mich.
Noah E. Aronstam, M. D., of Detroit, Mich.
Wm. Bayard, M. D., of St. John. N. B.
Clark Bell, Esq., LL D., Tuberculosis and Legislation with a Symposium: By
Sir James A. Grant, M. D., of Ottawa, Canada.
E. P. Lachapelle, M. D, of Montreal, Canada.
T. D. Crothers, M. D., of Hartford, Conn.
Moritz Ellinger, Esq., of New York.
Papers on Tuberculosis by:
Prof. Schratter, of Vienna.
U. O. B. Wingate, M. D., of Wisconsin.
H. Edwin Lewis, M. D., of Vermont.
M. M. Johnson, M. D., of Hartford, Conn.
Dr. E. P. Lachapelle, of Montreal.
Judge Abram H. Dailey, of Brooklyn.
Prof. Thomas Bassett Keyes, M. D., of Chicago, Ill.
Dr. J. Leffingwell Hatch, M. D., of New York.
Dr. I. L. Gibson, of Iowa.
E. J. Barrick, of Toronto.
W. L. Bullard, M. D., of Georgia.
Dr. J. A. McNiven, M. D., of Idaho.
W. A. Hackett, of Michigan.

John A. Robinson, M. D., of Chicago, Ill.
H. H. Black, of Sheffield.
A. Eugene Austin, M. D., of New York.
Carleton Simon, M. D.
Dr. E. F. Bowers, of New York.
J. F. Labadie, M. D., of New York.
E. H. McHatton, M. D., of Macon, Ga.
Dr. Louis Leroy, of Tenn.
Moritz Ellinger, of New York.
Dr. E. Liceaga, of Mexico.

3. "Christian Science and the Law," by H. W. Mitchell, M. D., of New York.

4. "The Whipping Post and Its Deterrent Effect, by Edward Ben Jackson.

5. The same subject by the Editor.

6. "Sanitation and Progress," by Surgeon Gen. Walter Wyman, of the Marine Hospital Service.

7 "Sanatoria for Consumptives," by Clark Bell, Esq.

8. "Treatment of Melancholia," by Dr. Charles G. Wagner, of the Binghamton State Hospital.

9. "The Roentgen Rays in Forensic Medicine," by Mihran K. Kassabian, M. D., of Philadelphia.

10. "Insanity and Crime," by Prof. Dr. Moritz Benedikt, of Vienna.

11. Medical Jurisprudence of Insanity," by Prof. Dr. Moritz Benedikt, of Vienna.

12. Reports on London Congress of Tuberculosis by H. Edwin Lewis, M. D., of Vermont; A. C. Bernays, M. D., of St. Louis; John Charles Shrader, M. D., of Iowa; F. L. Hoffman, Esq, of New Jersey.

13. "Crime and Criminals," by Edward C. Walker, Esq., of New York.

14. "The Indeterminate Sentence in New York," by Clark Bell, Esq., of New York.

15. "Spiritism, Telepathy and Mrs. Piper," by Thomson J. Hudson, Esq.; Clark Bell, Esq.; John Duncan Quackenbos, M. D.; Judge Abram H. Dailey; Hon. Luther R. Marsh, and Wm. C. Wright, Esq.

The officers of the Section recommended for re-election for 1902 are as follows:

Chairman,

PROF. W. XAVIER SUDDUTH, OF CHICAGO, ILL.

Vice-Chairmen,

LEGAL AND SCIENTIFIC.

Clark Bell, Esq., of New York.
Rev. Antoinette B. Blackwell, of N. Y.
Harold Browett, Esq., Shanghai, China.
C. Van D. Chenoweth, Worcester, Mass.
Judge Abram H. Dailey, of Brooklyn.
Moritz Ellinger, Esq., of New York.
Rev. Phebe A. Hanaford, of New York.
Thomson Jay Hudson, Esq., Wash'n, D. C.
Sophia McClelland, of New York
Mrs. Jacob F. Miller, of New York.
Mrs. Mary Louise Thomas, of Penna.

Vice-Chairmen.

MEDICAL.

T. D. Crothers, M. D. of Hartford, Conn.
F. E. Daniel, M. D., of Austin Texas.
H. S. Drayton, M. D., of New York.
Wm. Lee Howard, M. D., of Baltimore, Md.
Henry Hulst, M. D., Grand Rapids, Mich.
Prof. Thomas Bassett Keyes, of Chicago.
R. J. Nunn, M D., of Savannah, Ga.
A. E. Osborne, M. D, of Glen Ellen, Cal.
Jas. T. Searcy, M. D, of Tuscaloosa, Ala.
U. O. B. Wingate, M. D., Milwaukee, Wis

Secretary and Treasurer,

CLARK BELL, ESQ., OF NEW YORK.

Executive Committee.

CLARK BELL, ESQ., Chairman.

SAMUEL BELL THOMAS, ESQ., OF NEW YORK CITY, Secretary.

M. Ellinger, Esq.
Carleton Simon, M. D.
Judge A. H. Dailey.
R. W. Shufeldt, M. D.
H. W. Mitchell, M. D.

The Standing Committees recommended for 1902 are as follows:

TELEPATHY, MODERN SPIRITUALISM, &c.—Judge Abram H. Dailey, Brooklyn, N. Y., Chairman; Thomson Jay Hudson, Esq., Detroit, Michigan; Sophia McClelland, New York; R. J. Nunn, M. D., of Savannah, Ga.; C. Van D. Chenoweth, Shrewsbury, Mass.

EXPERIMENTAL PSYCHOLOGY AND PSYCHICAL RESEARCH.—Prof. W. Xavier Sudduth, of Chicago, Chairman; Geo. W. Grover, M. D., Sheffield, Mass.; Prof. Harlow Gale, of Mineapolis, Minn.; Rev. A. Brown Blackwell, of N. Y.; Judge Abram H. Dailey, of Brooklyn, N. Y.; Mr. Clark Bell, of New York City; Percy R. Chittenden, Esq., of Brooklyn, N. Y.; J. Mount Bleyer, M. D., of New York City; Alexander Wilder, M. D., of N. J.

MORBID PSYCHOLOGY.—William Lee Howard, M. D., Baltimore, Md.; T. D. Crothers, M. D., Hartford, Conn.; Prof. C. H. Hughes, of St. Louis, Mo.; Carleton Simon, M. D., of N. Y.; E. Sanger Browne, M. D., Chicago, Illinois; W. S. Magill, M. D., of New York.

HYPNOTISM.—H. S. Drayton, M. D., New York City, Chairman; T. D. Crothers, M. D., Hartford, Conn.; Thomson Jay Hudson, Esq., Detroit, Mich.; Wm. Lee Howard, M. D., Baltimore, Md.; Thomas Bassett Keyes, of Chicago, Ill.; Clark Bell, Esq., New York City.

PSYCHO-THERAPEUTICS.—Prof. A. A. d'Ancona, Chairman, San Francisco, Cal.; Henry S. Drayton, M. D., N. Y. City.

The Woman's Committee of the Section is composed as follows:

COMMITTEE OF WOMEN.—Caroline J. Taylor, Chairman; M. Louise Thomas, C. Van D. Chenoweth, Rosalie Dailey, The Countess Bettini di Moise, Sophia McClelland, Ida Trafford Bell, Rev. Antoinette Browne Blackwell, Laura A. C. Miller, Rev. Phebe A. Hanaford, Florence Dangerfield Potter.

Every member of the Society is eligible to membership in the Section, as also the wives of members of the Society.

The annual Dues of the Section are $1.50, entitling the members to the Medico-Legal Journal free.

The Section is open to all Students of Psychological Science.

The only death during the year has been that of Dr. Irving Rosse, of Washington, D.C.

One member has resigned, two names stricken from the rolls for non-payment of dues, and fifteen members have been elected.

The following is the Roll of members of the Section:

ROLL OF MEMBERS—PSYCHOLOGICAL SECTION, MEDICO-LEGAL SOCIETY.

Dr. Raphael Asselta, 31 Prince Street, New York City.
Clarence A. Arnold, Esq., Colorado Springs, Colorado.
Rev. Dr. C. S. Arnold, Detroit, Mich.
Prof. A. A. d'Ancona, San Francisco, Cal.
Prof. D. S. Abbott, Athens, Ga.
Albert Bach, Esq., 115 Broadway, New York City.
Mrs. Helene S. Bell, 200 West 78th Street, New York City.
Clark Bell, Esq., Secretary, 39 Broadway, New York City.
Harold Browett, Esq., Yuen-Ming-Yuen Building,Shanghai,China.
Dr. Mary A. Brinkman, Brewsters, New York.
Major Paul R. Brown, M. D., U. S. A.
E. Sanger Browne, M. D., Chicago, Ill.
Dr. E. N. Buffet, Jersey City, N. J.
Ida Trafford Bell, Miller's Hotel, New York City.
Francis C. S. Burnham, Milburn, N. Y.
Mrs. A. C. Bunton, 173 West 133rd Street, N. Y.
Rev. Antoinette Brown Blackwell, 350 West 71st Street, New York City.
Prof. L. A. Baralt, Havana, Cuba.
John H. Buford, Oklahoma City, Oklahoma.
Samuel S. Buckley, College Park, Prince George Co., Md.
Prof. E.Boirac, 29 Rue de Berlin, Paris, France.
Dr. H. Baraduc, 191 Rue St. Honore, Paris, France.
Alice Berillon, 7 Rue de la Sorbonne, Paris.
Dr. Marcel Briand, Hospice de Ville de Juif, Paris.
Dr. Bourneville, 14 Rue des Carmes, Paris, France.
Mary Louise Benoit, M. ., State Central Asylum, Newark, N. Y.
L. C. Brown, Esq., Lock Box 885, Baltimore, Md.
Mrs. C. Van D. Chenoweth, Shrewsbury, Mass.
Edward W. Chamberlain, Esq., Counsellor-at-Law, 11 West 42nd Street, New York City.
D. M. Currier, M. D., Newport, N. H.
Henry Coe Culbertson, Esq., 44 West 46th Street,New York City.
T. D. Crothers, M. D., Hartford, Conn.
Prof. Dr. J. Crispin, 1 Rue de Soudan, Algiers.
Prof.Geo. Chase, New York Law School, 309 West 74th Street, New York City.
Dr. George W. Cook, Chicago, Ill.
Edward Howard Carnahan, Esq., Meaford, Ontario, Canada.
Thomas Darlington, M. D., Kingsbridge, N. Y.
F. E. Daniel, M. D., Texas Medical Journal, Austin, Texas.
Mary Randal Downs, Danbury, Conn.
Isidore Dyer, M. D., Tulane University, New Orleans, La.
Mrs. Judge Dailey, 451 Washington Avenue, Brooklyn, N. Y.
Judge Abram H. Dailey, ex-President Medico-Legal Society, 16 Court Street, Brooklyn, N. Y.
Miles M. Dawson, Esq., 157 West 103 Street, New York City.
Mrs. Ernest Dichman, Monroe, Orange Co., New York.
Dr. Helen Densmore, Brooklyn, N. Y.
Joseph H. Dennis, 22 Weybossett street, Providence, R. I.
Mlle. Dagnan, Iceland.
H. L. Drayton, LL B., M. D., 70 5th Ave., New York.
Havelock Ellis, M. D., Carbis Water, Lelant, Cornwall, England.
Prof. E. T. Eskridge, Denver, Colorado.

Moritz Ellinger, Esq., Surrogate's Office, New York City.
Sidney Flower. Esq., 211 Herald Building, Chicago, Ill.
Wm. S. Forest, Esq., Security Building, Chicago, Ill.
Mrs. Laura Dayton Fessenden, Happie-go-Luckie, Highland Park, Illinois.
Prof. John W. Farr, Jr., A. M. LL.B., Chattanooga, Tenn.
Dr. Frazer. Commissioner in Lunacy. Edinburgh, Scotland.
Dr. Wm. Cowpe Gardner, 121 West 71st Street, New York City.
Geo. W. Grover, M. D., Sheffield, Mass.
Prof. Harlow Gale, Chicago, Ill.
Eleanor Gridley, 67 South Clark street, Chicago, Ill.
Dr. Ganberide, San Panto, Brazil.
Mrs. Edloro W. Harrison, 31 Summit Ave., Jersey City, N. J.
B. W. Holliday, M. D., Cleveland, Ohio.
N. deV. Howard, M. D., Sanford, Fla.
Margherita A. Hamm, 83 Hicks Street, Brooklyn.
Rev. Phebe A. Hanaford, 201 West 88th Street New York City.
Alfred Dearing Harden, 135 William Street, New York City.
M. B. Hubbs, M. D., Addison, N. Y.
Dr. Wm. Lee Howard, 1126 North Calvert Street, Baltimore, Md
Prof. C. H. Hughes, Editor Alienist and Neurologist, St. Louis, Mo.
Thomson Jay Hudson, Esq., Washington, D. C.
Rev. R. Herbert Jones, Lawrence, S. C.
Col. Fred. Hamilton, 383 Seventh Avenue, Brooklyn.
Mrs. Frances Hutton, 209 West 70th Street, New York City.
Dr. Ella A. Hunt, Equitable Bldg., St. Louis. Mo.
Prof. E. Hiertstrom, Stockholm, Sweden.
A. Wilbur Jackson, M. D., 159 West 36th Street, New York City.
A. Laura Joscelyn, 309 Broadway, care Mutual Reserve Fund Life Insur., New York City.
Mrs. Geo. Jamieson, Bridgeport, Conn.
Judge Arthur T. Johnson, Gouverneur, St. Lawrence, N. Y.
Dr. Oscar Jennings, 17 Rue Vernet, Paris, France.
Mr. J. Louis Kellogg, 229 Broadway, New York City.
E. P. Kleingensmith, M. D., Blairsville, Pa.
F. Alice Kellor.
Charles W. Kimball, Esq., Ex-Dist. Att'y, Penn Yan, N. Y.
Laura Keisher, M. D., New York City.
Charles Benjamin Knowlton, Buffalo, N. Y.
Prof. Kossozotoff, Professor of Medical Jurisprudence, St. Petersburg, Russia.
Mrs. F. J. Lord, Brockwayville, Pa.
Clarence A. Lightner, Esq., Detroit, Mich.
Henry Lefuel, Cour de Appel., 15 Rue de l Universite, Paris.
Georges Leedru, Avocat la Cour de Appel, 42 Rue de Paradis. Paris.
Miss Alice F. Lewis, 93 Summit Ave., Jersey City, N. J.
Senor Rafael Montufar, M. D., Guatemala, S. A.
K. D. MacKenzie, M. D., St. Johns, New Foundland.
Mrs. Jacob F. Miller, 80 West 89th Street, New York City.
The Countess Bettini di Moise, New York City.
D. Gilbert McKoon, Esq., 291 Broadway, New York City.
Mrs. Sophia McClelland, 2114 West 103rd St., Tracy Ave., Chicago, Ill.
Dr. Bettini di Moise, New York City.
Hubbard W. Mitchell, M. D., 747 Madison Ave., New York City.
Wilson McDonald, Esq., Sculptor, 729 6th Ave., New York City.
J. McDonald, Jr., 106 Fulton Street, New York City.
J. B. Mattison, M. D., 188 Prospect Place, Brooklyn, N. Y.
Mrs. Madeline Morton, 223 West 22nd St., New York City.
I. A. Maryson, M. D., 194 East Broadway, New York.

Dr. Emile Mary, Thun, Switzerland.
Mrs. Matt. Morgan, Madison Ave., New York City.
Mrs. Mary Moore, 149 E. 31st Street, New York.
Miss Rosa Moore, 37 Leboutillier's Buildings, West 22nd Street, New York City.
Mrs. Eliza H. McHatton, Macon, Ga.
Mrs. Elizabeth T. McLaughlin, 47 Crescent Ave., Jersey City N. J.
Dr. Lucia Moramvitz, 5 Klollenhoff, Zurich.
Dr. A. Maire, 10 Rue St. Legare, Paris, France.
Prof. Dr. Meschede, University at Koenigsburg, Germany.
Dr. A. Marie, Supt. Ville Juif Asile, 20 Rue Cuvier, Paris, France.
Dr. Manheimer, 66. Rue Bonaparte, Paris.
D. V. Noel. 41 West 33rd Street, New York.
R. J. Nunn, M. D., Savannah, Ga.
Max Nordau, 34 Av. de Villiers, Paris, France.
A. E. Osborne, M. D., Superintendent, Glen Ellen, Cal.
Prof. Dr. Salvator Ottolenghi, University of Sienna, Italy.
T. S. Pyle, M. D., Canton, Ohio.
Robert E. Payne, Esq., New York City.
Caroline Pier, Counsellor-at-Law, Milwaukee, Wis.
Mrs. E. K. Pangborn, 63 Arlington Av., Jersey City, N. J.
Florence Dangerfield Potter, Attorney-at-Law, 137 Broadway, New York City.
Dr. Demetre Photakis. 7 Rue Broca. Athens, Greece.
Mrs. Isaac N. Quimby, 89 Summit Ave., Jersey City, N. J.
Prof. Nina Rodrigues, M. D., President Medico-Legal Society, Bahia, Brazil.
*Irving Rosse, M. D., Washington, D. C.
Hon. Henry Robinson, Concord, N. H.
Dr. Robert Reyburn, 714 13th St., Washington, D. C.
Dr. A. W. Van Reutergheen van Breistral, Amsterdam, Holland.
Col. P. C. Rust. 120 Broadway, New York.
Prof. Dr. E. Regis, University of Bordeaux. France.
Prof. Dr. Carlo Ruata, Perugia. Italy.
C. O. Rice, M. D., 235 Central Block, Pueblo, Colorado.
Alice J. Saunders. Woodlawn Park, Colorado.
James T. Searcey, M. D., Tuscaloosa. Ala.
Captain R. W. Shufeldt, M. D., 502 W. 142 street, New York.
P. W. Xavier Sudduth. 100 State Street, Chicago, Ill.
Dr. Agnes Sparks, 140 South Portland Avenue. Brooklyn, N. Y
Mrs. Alice May Scudder, 303 York St., Jersey City, N. J.
Dr. H. Sotolaroff. 251 East Broadway, N. Y.
Floyd Stewart. M. D., 124 Barronne St., New Orleans, La.
Dr. Carleton Simon, 114 E. 56th Street, New York City.
Dr. Robert Sheerin, Cleveland, Ohio.
Dr. B. Rosalie Slaughter. 19 Main St., Mount Holly, N. J.
Dr. Jules Socquet, 6 Boulevard Richard le Noir, Paris.
Dr. J. F. Sutherland, Deputy Commissioner in Lunacy, Edinburgh. Scotland.
Sir John Sibbald, 18 Great King St., Edinburgh, Scotland.
E. T. Talieferro, Esq., Temple Court, New York City.
Caroline J. Taylor, Bridgeport, Conn.
Mrs. M. Louise Thomas, Tacony, Penn'a.
Chas. Teubner, West Saticoy, Cal.
Dr. A. Tovarsky, Moscow. Russia.
Dr. Paul Tesdorpf, Thierschplatz 1. Munich, Bavaria.
Judge John A. Vance, Gouveneur, N. Y.
Mrs. Pauline Valentine, Hotel Balmoral, New York City.
Washington S. Valentine. Esq.. Produce Exchange, N. Y. City.
M. Nelson Volding, M. D., Supt. State Hospital, Cherokee, Iowa.
Mrs. Beatrice J. de Vol, 135 E. 16th St., New York.
Dr. de Val Court, 64 Boulevard St. Germain, Paris.

U. O. B. Wingate, M. D., Milwaukee, Wis.
A. B. Whitney, 148 West 77th Street, New York City.
Dr. Forbes Winslow, 33 Devonshire St., Portland Place, London.
A Leonora White, M. D., 151 W. 46th Street, New York City.
Harry Wellington Wack, Esq., London, England.
Simon A. White, Esq., 151 W. 46 Street, New York City.
Dr. Samuel B. Ward, Albany, N. Y.
Dr. T. R. Winde, Heustrasse 13, Munich.
Ernest Wende, M. D., 471 Delaware avenue, Buffalo, N. Y.
H. C. Wright, Esq., Corry, Pa.
A. Howard Young, M. D., 52 Mechanic Building, Pueblo, Colorado.
Total membership, 178.

January 1, 1902.

Respectfully submitted,
CLARK BELL,
Vice-Chairman and Secretary.

NOTE:—The officers recommended by the report were duly elected by the Executive Committee at January meeting, 1902:

WHY NOT EDUCATE AGAINST TUBERCULOSIS?

BY LEWIS W. SPRADLING. ATHENS, TENN.

Writing an article on the subject of tuberculosis at this day is considerably like "threshing old straw," notwithstanding, science has made some wonderful demonstrations upon the pathology of consumption, hitherto regarded as vague theories. But, the valedictory phrases devoted to treatment, are so different from the introductory of all writers on this disease that the fair field of inspiration is suddenly clouded with interrogation points! The ablest physician discounts his own confidence in therapeutics! His conscience gets sick, and he feels keenly that he has fallen short of being an all round benefactor.

The young doctor, as a rule, initiates himself into his chosen field of labor by accepting the medical care of one or more developed cases of tuberculosis, and he feels for the first time the stern decrees of nature. Thus he crosses the threshold of medicine with a modified opinion of his ability. Yet, he afterwards observes within his coliseum of practice, countless parallells of those past experiences. So nearly universal must be the above experience, that it seems to a casual observer of today, that long ere this there might have dawned upon the medical profession, a wave of energy to force before the world the importance of prophylaxis! Almost every other calamitous influence that has inflicted the world has been met by measures that have either destroyed it, or modified it to toleration.

To Koch, and others of his kind, is due the thanks of our intelligent observer for their voluntary investigations; which have thrown so much light upon the field of pathology. The great discoveries made, and that are being made, enables the present to bequeath to the future even a richer legacy than we can imagine was due us from the past. This age owes to its successor, the institution of measures for its protection

Contributed to the Bulletin of the American Congress of Tuberculosis.

against any foreseen threatened destruction. No word painting is necessary to impress on the minds of the profession the gravity of the situation.

There are countless instances in the minds of older doctors, and multitudes of buried memories, wherein had they possessed the knowledge of pathology now possible to acquire, many a bright light would yet be shining; many a happy circle yet unbroken; but, they like we, were forced to stand meekly by and helplessly see the passing of the world's brightest stars at their zenith. We have also watched the cursed halo fall upon other bright links of the same family chain, repeating one by one the tragic scenes of fate.

Realizing our almost utter helplessness to rescue a victim after the infection has developed symptoms serious enough to send him to us,should we not busy ourselves more in the promulgation of prophylactic measures?

The title of this paper was a question asked me by a college professor—a Master of Arts—while attending his afflicted daughter. She wore the indellible stamp of the great white plague. The question was so pertinent that it set me to thinking. His reasoning was so logical, so feasible, that I shall quote it in substance: "If tuberculosis is communicable, as science teaches, there certainly should be some universal educational measures adopted for the enlightenment of youth upon a subject of such vital importance to them. It does seem that this great problem might be simplified so that the young could and would understand it sufficiently well to avoid the open pitfalls all along the line of a students' life.

His logic reminded me of the fact that students especially, encounters the dangers of infection at a time when they were most likely to succumb. It also opened to me the idea that this knowledge so opportunely acquired, would, furthermore be at that epoch of life when impressions are most lasting. Thus caution would become habitual, and finally instinctive.

These educational measures might be inaugurated by legislative enactment of statutes calling for the production of a text book, to be taught in the public schools covering the esentials of the pathology of tuberculosis. This book ought to be the production of a committee composed of pathological teachers, and approved by a board of literary professors or the state board of public instruction. It ought to be so simple, and at the same time fascinating enough to be studied and asimilated by every common school pupil of the 5th to the 8th grade, and its teaching should be obligatory. A knowledge of this book should be required of every person seeking employment in any occupation. By this means the world would naturally absorb a knowledge of prophylaxis. Investigation would be broadened, sanitation and habits of life improved, the ubiquitous tenement houses annihilated and God's good sunlight shed into every dark, damp, and dusty corner of the earth.

It is the custom here in the south to educate the weakly or deformed members of the families so as to equip them for some of the professions. The only requisite being a reasonable degree of intelligence and a moderate education for the position of school teacher. Thus, the youth of our country while acquiring the knowledge to fit him for usefulness in life often imbibes from the fountain head the fatal drop that sooner or later shocks those interested by its development into an incurable malady. Schools of all kinds have a large percentage of tuberculous pupils, and are consequently a great factor in its distribution;hence,would it not be wisdom in this instance to apply a remedy directly to the diseased spot?Would not this system of reform be in keeping with the most approved precedents of reformation in the history of our country? What better or more permanent method could be applied to abort the conditions which threaten the future?

It is not our purpose to overlook in this paper the importance of perpetuating the sanitary war now waging against infection, which should be encouraged and carried so far that every American municipality and home espoused the cause with deserving zeal.

The world has demonstrated its interest in consumption, and its eagerness for light, by the reception tendered the last of Dr. Koch's sensations sprung at the British Congress of Tuberculosis on the much discussed bovine inoculation theory. Beyond this demonstration, the medical profession has probably not been benefitted to any extent.

TUBERCULOSIS, AS SHOWN IN THE HUMAN BLOOD.

BY C. C. CARROLL, M. D., PH. D., OF NEW YORK.

Tuberculosis is a disease of very ancient origin, co-existent with man as far as man's history has been handed down to us. What method of diagnosis was employed by the ancients to determine the case to be one of consumption (now known as tuberculosis), I am not apprised, but they certainly recognized the disease, as we find it recorded in the Jewish scriptures, of which mention is especially made in Leviticus 26:16., also in Deuteronomy 28:22, as one of the visitations that were to come upon that peculiar people, the Hebrews, for the violation of their law. There can be very little question that they regarded this disease, as all other diseases, as a visitation on them for their sins. This opinion may be a mooted question, notwithstanding what was believed, but that this, toggether with other diseases was the result of violated law, there could be little question. The state of health being the normal condition of the race in its primeval age, any departure from that was regarded by the Jews as a special visitation on account of sin. Such a hold had that doctrine or teaching upon the minds of that people, that they came, some thousands of years after this record of which we have made mention in Leviticus and Deuteronomy, to the Christ, with a man that was born blind, and they asked him the question—: "Master, who did sin, this man or his parents that he was born blind " The answer was: "Neither hath this man sinned nor his parents that he was born blind, but that the works of God may be made manifest in him." Without going into the theological import of that reply, we find its very purpose to be merely the refutation of the doctrine that —: "All disease is the result of sin." That it is the result of broken law undoubtedly is true. The law was not necessarily broken by the individual suffering, but may be by some

Read before the New York Medico-Legal Society and American Congress of Tuberculosis in joint session, May 15-16, 1901, by title and before the Medico-Legal Society, March 19, 1902.

progenitor dating far back, possibly some generations before the birth of the sufferer. In this way we have tuberculosis transmitted—not by heredity as a disease—but the tendency to the disease is imparted—like a narrow chest, a weak contracted lung, or a general constitutional weakness, that under favorable circumstances may develop tuberculosis. A father cannot directly transmit to his offspring tuberculosis, *per se*: that is, he cannot transmit the germ or bacilli of tuberculosis, but the mother can directly transmit her disease in utero.This disease,tuberculosis,in certain stages is easy of recognition. We have certain physical signs of tuberculosis which begin to manifest themselves generally, not in the first, but in what is understood as the second stage of the disease. I would classify the different stages of tuberculosis as,—first the irritative stage, secondly, the congestive stage, third, the inflammatory stage, and fourth, the suppurative or cavity stage. This classification is applicable to any organ that may be infected by the bacilli tuberculosis. Popularly understood, consumption has been regarded as a disease of the lungs. The medical profession in years past are responsible for that popular belief, overlooking possibly the fact that tuberculosis may be a disease of any organ. I hold that tuberculosis and cancer are blood diseases, and hence hematology furnishes a positive diagnosis. We owe to chemistry and the microscope the revelations pertaining to this and other diseases that produce an entire revolution in the science of medicine, if it be permissible to call empirical practice, a science. Science is defined to be "classified knowledge." To classify it is necessary to observe, compare, reflect, and record. This, the medical profession has been doing, as best they could, from the days of Esculapius down to the present time, with something of agreement on the part of the leading lights, as embodied in the text-books or treatises of experienced authors. Nevertheless, it is proverbial that doctors rarely agree, and they are honest in their disagreement. This fact of disagreement may be due to the standpoint of the observer. Disease or unhealth, if serious, has many complications presenting so many points of view, each of which might be taken as characteristic or pathognomic of a certain particular disease, hence Dr. Jones looking at a patient from a given point of observation and experience would be likely to have a different view from Dr. Brown, who looked at the same patient from another point of observation and experience. The microscope and chemistry, being revealers of exact science when the medical profession began to consult their aid, then true progress in classification began to be made, and now that the revelations of the microscope and chemistry are accepted as authoritive, medicine begins to assume something of a scientific aspect. It would seem as though we were on the threshold, as suggested before, of an entire revolution in diagnosis by the aid of the microscope, which is likely to work some change, if not a radical one, in therapeutics and the practice of medicine. It is now recognized that many of the ills that flesh is heir to, are traceable directly to fermentative processes induced by micro-organisms, which are fully described and classified by the leading investigators in the medical profession in this and other countries. The genesis, procreation, and habits of these micro-organisms are so well understood by original observers that there is no disagreement among them now, as to the office that they perform in the human economy.

In the human blood we have at least four forms of cell-life,—: 1st, The blood discs proper; 2d, The white blood corpuscles or leucocytes, or phagocytes as they are variously called, the haematoblasts, and the fourth form, called stationary cells. These cells which are found in protoplasm are to be differentiated from, and do not belong to the class of micro-organisms, or germs. The latter form of life are of vegetable origin, and are named according to their form or mode of proliferation, such as—: cocci, which means berry like, bacilli, meaning rod or hair like, and spirilli, or corkscrew bacteria. Some forms of bacteria are essential to health, and are called physiogenic bacteria, or germs. Other forms are injurious to health and are called pathogenic. Of these we have today to deal with the one form called the bacilli tuberculosis, which is a rod shaped fellow, with one or more neucleii. or spores. This bacillus, like others of its class, reproduce by fission, and that very rapidly, once every 30 seconds. A spore is generated from this rod, and each spore then becomes a parent of a new progeny, so that in a period of twenty-four hours we have the enormous multiplication of this bacillus into 16, 500, 000, an invading army that is staggering to contemplate. These bacilli are so minute that 100, 000 placed side by side, would measure less than an inch. When we learn that this one bacillus is the cause of consumption, or tuberculosis, it is not to be wondered at that consumption should be called the universal disease, or the great white plague that preys upon all animated existence, human and animal, in all countries, wherever the sun shines. It is not a matter of wonder and surprise that the disease is so universal, when we come to properly understand its nature, mode and rapidity of proliferation, and tenacity of life, but the wonder is that there is left upon the face of the globe, any living human being, when we realize from investigation how consumption is induced by this bacillus. Fortunately we have in the leucocytes a cell called phagocyte that feeds on this bacillus, and thus holds him somewhat in check. It is said that something must die, in order that something else shall live. This we find true through all the realm of nature, both in the animal and the vegetable kingdom. The phagocytes, or white blood corpuscles, come to our aid in fortifying us against this disease: at the same time assist greatly in the use of remedial agents to overcome this disease, called consumption, or tuberculosis. Now that we have discovered that this disease is caused by the bacilli tuberculosis, first isolated and discovered by Prof. Koch, the problem of cure consists of—: first the destruction of the bacillus that causes the disease, and second, of nutrition, or building up of the wasted form, broken down by this disease.

In order successfully to combat this very formidable and destructive disease it is essential that well regulated scientific measures shall be employed, that will embrace, first, prophylaxis, or preventive measures; second, rational therapeutic treatment after infection has taken place; third, stimulating the nutritive or metabolic processes to build and restore the wasted and broken down structures of the body, be it lung, liver, stomach, bowel or other organ that may be diseased: fourth, proper attention should be given to the development of wasted and atrophied organs, especially the chest, which has been contracted by the disease, should be methodically expanded to accommodate and give free play to expansion of the lungs, in order that deep, full and free breathing may be practical.

INFECTION.

Infection by the bacilli tuberculosis is shown in human blood, even in the first or irritative stage, by the presence of excess of fibrine, which under the microscope, by proper staining, is at once recognized by the expert, and affords a ready means of diagnosis of tuberculosis or consumption in the incipient stage, before any serious lesion of the organs has taken place. To this attention should be early directed where exposure to infection is known to exist. Exposure is imminent in all families, where a case of advanced tuberculosis, exists, and the members of the family should have their blood examined at frequent intervals by a conscientious capable hematologist, that infection by bacilli may be recognized, that prophylactic and curative means may immediately be employed, which can and has been done in many cases.

PROPHYLACTIC THERAPY.

The exudates from the lungs, and excretion from the bowels and glanular system of consumptives, manifest an alkaline chemical reaction, which suggests acid prophylactic and curative treatment. Following this suggestion, I formulated a very highly acid escharotic germicide, that I found destroyed bacilli tuberculosis almost instantly, even when subjected to ten per cent. solution of this acid preparation, and which, after carefully conducted experiments, I found I could pass it into the lungs, uterus, bowels or any other part of the body infected, without any inconvenience or injury whatever to the patient, resulting in the destruction of the bacilli tuberculosis, and after a few administrations of this germicide, in every case the bacilli began to disappear from the sputa obtained from the lungs, as well as from the excretions from the bowels and uterus of consumptives. The fibrine in the blood also soon begins to lessen, as shown under the microscope. As the result of administrations of this germicide, the patients, even in the far-gone cases, have made complete recoveries.

Now that the doctrine of infection by bacilli tuberculosis is accepted as the true cause of consumption by all the up-to-date thinkers and writers on this and the other side of the water, and that germicides afford a rational method for eliminating the bacilli from the infected patients, there follows as a sequence to the foregoing the query, "What can be done to prevent infection?"

The old adage, "An ounce of prevention is worth a pound of cure" is especially applicable to this subject. It is fitting that all the light possible should be thrown upon the prophylactic feature of our work. The great danger to the family in which an infected member resides, as well as the community, comes through the infection by sputa, both moist and dry. If the sputa contains living bacilli, it can readily be imparted by being carried through the air in fine particles of dust, or can be imparted by inoculation by moist sputa containing live bacilli.

The germicide to which I have referred positively does destroy the bacilli in the sputa, both in the body and out of the body, when it comes in contact with these bacteria, as has been many times demonstrated. This same germicide affords an efficient safeguard if the atmosphere in the apartment which the consumptive occupies is disinfected. This disinfection is immediately and easily accomplished by the use of an atomizer, spraying ten per cent. solution two or three times daily throughout the room, and will thus preclude the possibility of any one coming in the room being infected.

This feature of prophylactic therapy is of paramount interest and advantage, and marks an epoch in the consideration of tuberculosis that merits the careful, conscientious and thorough investigation by all to whom its merits are brought. This is no guesswork, but is based upon positive laboratory and clinical demonstration that is easily made and clearly understood by even a novice, to say nothing of the expert in chemistry and with the microscope.

I have found electricity to be a most beneficial aid as a therepeutic agent in stimulating nerve centers that are impaired by disease to perform their true office, that secures restoration of organic function.

The length of the present paper forbids the discussion at this time of my latest researches in the application of *electricity by high oscillation* in the treatment of diseases generally, and of tuberculosis especially, whereby instantaneous therapeutic results are shown in reduction of temperature, pulse and respiration, without the aid of the usual drugs that the employed for this purpose. As well by this means is the potency of the germicide carried to the liver, or other organs not usually reached direct by drug remedies, in a forcible positive and efficient manner by cataphoresis.

A logical deduction from the foregoing, based upon a large clinical experience in the treatment of tuberculosis through a series of years, constrains me to say in conclusion that, with a clear understanding of the nature and movement of tuberculosis, the medical profession should no longer, as in the past, hang its hands in an attitude of helpless surrender as it confronts the great white plague, tuberculosis, which has devastated the race from time immemorial down to the present time, but should, with the courage of its convictions, seize upon every means now at comamnd, and with one united effort, both lay and profesisonal, go forward from conquering to conquer, with victory emblazoned on its banner, until this terrible malady is stamped from the face of the earth, an event the accomplishment of which is destined to follow at no far distant day, the united, intelligent, co-operative work on the part of scientific, earnest, philanthropic men and women now seeking a solution of this great problem.

ICE PRESIDENTS OF THE AMERICAN CONGRESS OF TUBERCULOSIS.

IENRY O. MARCEY, A. M., M. D., LL. D.,
Of Boston, Mass.

WM. FAWCETT SMITH, M. D.
Sec'y Surgical Board of Health, Puerto Rico.

D E. REGENSBURGER, M D.,
San Francisco, Cal.

GEO. R. DEAN, M D.,
Spartansburgh, N. C.

B. D BOND, M. D.,
Hohala, Hawaii.

FRANCIS CROSSON, M. D.,
Santa Fe, New Mexico.

T. HENRY DAVIS M. D ,
Richmond, Ind.

THE USE OF LIGHT IN THE TREATMENT OF TUBERCULOSIS.

BY J. W. KIME, M. D., FORT DODGE, IOWA.

The manner in which I use light as a remedy in the treatment of tuberculosis is as follows:

A large reflector made of German plate mirror and blue glass, thirty-six inches in diameter and made of three concentric circles so arranged that all the light falling upon them is concentrated upon a surface about eight inches in diameter, is used to reflect the sunshine, and at the same time to separate the blue rays which are rich in actinic light from the red rays which contain a much higher percentage of the heat rays.

FIG. A.

In this manner the heat is rejected and the chemical rays are utilized. A powerful actinic light which is not sufficiently hot to be uncomfortable is thus obtained. This light passes entirely through the adult thorax. This is shown by the fol-

Read by title before the Medico-Legal Society, December 18, 1901, and contributed to the American Congress of Tuberculosis.

lowing photographs which have been taken through the body:

No. 1 is a scene in a valley in the Klondike, and No. 2 is the Fort Dodge City water tank. Both were taken by means of light which had been passed through the adult thorax from front to back, as more fully described in the author's paper on "Light as a Remedial Agent."

FIG. 1—Scene photographed through the body.

FIG. 2—Cut of water tank photographed through the body.

No. 3 is a small scene photgraphed through the writer's cheek, and No. 4 was taken through his right hand.

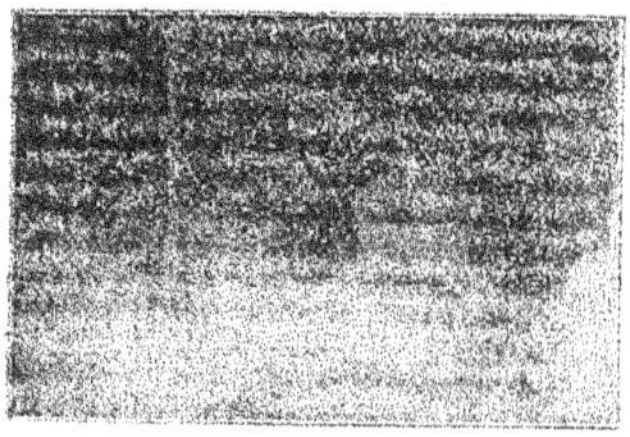

FIG 3—Photograph taken through the cheek

FIG. 4—Photograph taken through the hand.

Figure No. 5 shows the manner of using the light in the treatment of pulmonary tuberculosis. The same method is used in laryngeal and intestinal tuberculosis. The scene represents a treatment on the roof-garden. Treatment is given twice daily in half hour seances. During the winter months a solarium is made use of for this purpose.

FIG. 5—Treatment on roof garden.

That the light exercises some controlling influence cannot be doubted, as all cases, without regard to the stage of the disease, except when in extremis, are benefitted, and those even in advanced stages are materially improved.

What this influence may be I am at present unable to say; it may be the direct action of the light upon the bacilli; the effect of the light upon the surrounding tissues, or upon the blood which passes underneath the large area bathed in the strong actinic light, the blood itself accomplishing the results.

Imediate effects of the light are seen in the increased heart action. Ten minutes after beginning treatment the number of pulsations have increased ten per minute, and probably due to the irritant action of the rays upon the sympathetic ganglia of the heart; the pulse rate falls to its ordinary course half an hour after treatment.

This irritant effect of the light is seen upon the surface on which it is turned. The tegumentary capillaries become congested, many points being more engorged than others, giving a mottled appearnce of dark red and a red of lighter hue. In extremely tender skins slight petechiae have occasionally been observed.

Continued daily use of the light tans the skin to a dark reddish brown, which fades after one week's rest from treatment.

The special quality of the blue light is seen by a comparison of its effects with those of ordinary sunlight. Pure sunshine contains all the bands of the solar spectrum, including the red rays which are extremely irritating to the skin and which contain a high percentage of heat rays. But it is not the heat which produces the irritation, but the chemical quality of the red rays contained in pure sunlight.

This is shown by the following experiment:

A concentrated blue light of 120 degrees F. thrown upon the chest for one hour each day for two months produces no blistering of the skin. Ordinary sunshine falling upon the chest for thirty minutes at a temperature of 80 degrees F. produces extensive blistering of the skin. That is, white light, as ordinary sunshine, containing all the rays of the solar spectrum is very irritating to the skin while blue light which is concentrated to a much higher temperature produces no such effect.

I now have under treatment seven cases of pulmonary tuberculosis, all of which are much improved over the condition in which they were when admitted, and some of them will soon be returned to their homes as cured. I am able to present the histories of three cases which are to all appearauces permanently cured.

Case No. 1.—Miss B. W., Missouri Valley, Iowa, referred by Dr. E. A. Cobb, of Harlan, Iowa. The history of this case as given in a letter from her father, who is an unusually well infored man, under date of Oct. 1, 1900, is as follows:

"Our daughter B., age 17, was stricken with what the doctors call laryngo-pulmonary tuberculosis a year ago last April. It was thought she could not live until the next winter. I took her to Dr. E. Fletcher Ingals, of Chicago. He prescribed clove oil and nux vomica, but could give us no encouragement. Her pulse was 120 and temperature often 105. Other symptoms most distressing. Improved somewhat. Sent her to Boulder, Colorado, thirteen months ago. She changed clove oil to creosote carbonate in emulsion. Improved wonderfully. Gained twenty pounds in weight. Night sweats, expectoration, fever, cough wholly or almost entirely disappeared. Had robust appearance. In March tongue coated over badly, appetite became capricious, menses again disappeared or became irregular and she began to cough more and lose in weight.

She came home on the 15th of last May. Had lost all the weight she had gained. Slight expectoration, some fever, frequent nignt sweats, rapid pulse and increasing cough. Lungs are not worse than when Dr. Ingals saw her. She is not much hoarse either, but complains of her throat and has a weak voice. We fear an ulcer somewhere in that region."

The patient was examined Oct. 13, 1900. She was of good family history, no tuberculosis in near relatives. In addition to the information obtained from the father's letter, I learned that she had had two quite profuse hemorrhages about April 1, 1900, and that they occurred about one week apart. Menses absent and bacilli present. Weight 92 pounds. Percussion, left normal, right slightly dull at apex. Exaggerated respiratory murmur over left side; loose rales over upper part of right side. Is very weak and tires easily, complexion muddy. Respiration 35, pulse 120, and temperature

102. Her evening pulse and temperature from Oct. 13 to Nov. 11, were as follows:

October—13, temp. 100.8, pulse 120; 14, temp. 99.4, pulse 112; 15, temp. 100, pulse 108; 16, temp. 99.6, pulse 110; 17, temp. 100 pulse 110;18, temp. 100, pulse 110; 19, temp. 100.8, pulse 116; 20, temp. 101.6, pulse 106; 21, temp. 99.6, pulse 110; 22, temp. 100.4, pulse 106; 23, temp. 100, pulse 100; 24, temp. 100.4, pulse 106; 25, temp. 100, pulse 102; 26, temp. 100.8, pulse 106; 27, temp. 101, pulse 112; 28, temp. 102,pulse 110; 29, temp. 102, pulse 108; 30, temp. 102, pulse 110; 31, temp. 100, pulse 108.

November—1, temp. 102, pulse 112; 2, temp. 100.8, pulse 110; 3, temp. 101, pulse 112; 4, temp. 101, pulse 120; 5, temp. 100, pulse 106; 6, temp. 100, pulse 120; 7, temp. 100, pulse 106;8, temp. 100, pulse 120; 9, temp. 100.2, pulse 116; 10, temp. 100, pulse 100; 11, temp. 100, pulse 106

Patient was immediately put upon treatment as above outline and remained five weeks. Improvement was marked. Gained two pounds in weight, looked better and felt better, tongue comparatively clean. Appetite and digestion improved, pulse and temperature about the same as when admitted. Remained at home, living as much as possible in the open air, taking one dozen raw eggs and juice from a pound of beef per day, and following as closely as she could the line of treatment carried out while here, her father keeping me informed as to her condition.

Upon her arrival home he wrote me under date of Nov. 28: "We are surprised and delighted at the evident improvement the girl has made during the past five weeks. We are greatly encouraged and most grateful to you. We shall watch her closely, try to carry out as closely as possible the hygienic suggestions you have made and send her back if she does not succeed in holding her own here."

She returned for further treatment Jan. 24, 1901. Weight was then 95 pounds. Was considerably improved over the time of going home. Remained three weeks and during this time temperature did not reach 100 except when menses reappeared on Jan. 26, which have since remained normal and recurring each month.

On Aug. 28, 1901, she was sent to me for examination and for further treatment if thought best. No signs or symptoms of tuberculosis were found to be present. Temperature normal, respiration 20, pulse 85, weight 97. Feels perfectly well; no cough or expectoration and no bacilli. Advised taking up two studies at school.

Upon her return home her father wrote me: "B. returned home last night and seems as fresh this morning as though she had not had a long ride. Of course we are delighted to find our hopes confirmed by your judgment. We feel that we owe you a deep debt of gratitude."

No medicines were used at any time in the treatment of this case except as indicated for cough, night sweats, &c.

None of the so-called specifics were made use of.

On Sept. 29, Mr. W. writes: "B. walks down to the school house twice a day, five blocks, and back again after reciting. This return walk is up a gentle slope. She now weighs 100 pounds and seems to be doing well."

Case No. 2.—Miss H. J., Worthington, Minn., age 17, referred by Dr. F. E. Walker, of Worthington. This was an incipient case of pulmonary tuberculosis with very bad family history, a number of the immediate family having died of tuberculosis. There was slight dullness at right apex and some moist rales; slight cough and expectoration and bacilli were present. Temperature did not exceed 100 F. and was usually about 99 in the evening, while the mornig temperature was half a degree subnormal. Had night-sweats and was weak and listless, but suffered no loss in weight. Weight 133, menses regular. Had noticed she was failing for three months. Began treatment March 6, 1901, and remained until June 5.

Improved in every way, but still had an evening rise in temperature and pulse remained too high. Upon returning home she was referred back to Dr. Walker, under whose care she remained, carrying out the same treatment as here employed until Aug. 31, 1901.

On Sept. 10 Dr. Walker wrote me: "Have discharged Miss H. J. Aug. 31. At time of discharge no temperature, no sweat, splendid appetite, bowels regular, face full and of good color, spirits buoyant, sleeps good digestion perfect, pulse 70, respiration 18 and examination of chest nil. No cough or expectoration. She reported splendid health a few days ago. I am convinced she is permanently cured."

Case No. 3.—Miss M. J., Avoca, Iowa, referred by Dr. James Bisgard, of Harlan, Iowa. Examination July 31, 1901, age 28, two sisters dead of consumption at ages of 20 and 24. One sister not very strong. Two brothers healthy; mother insane since 1888. First noticed failure of health in April, 1901, soon after the death of a sister. Feels weak, night sweats and some cough, with slight expectoration. Bacilli present. Menses regular; present weight 123, former weight 140. Temperature a degree above normal since April, 1901. Tongue furred, appetite good. Slight roughness in murmur at right apex, small hemorrhage one month ago.

During her stay pulse and temperature have been a little above normal, but there has been persistent subnormal morning temperature which has now returned to the normal. Pulse has fallen from 86 to 79. Weight has increased from 123 to 146, or six pounds more than usual weight, making a gain of 23 pounds in 12 weeks. No bacilli. Discharged as cured Nov. 1, 1901. March 1, 1902, perfectly well and weighs 163 pounds.

To these cases which have been discharged as cured the following notes of cases still under my observation are added:

Case No. 4.—Miss L. D., Rock Rapids, Iowa; teacher, age 23, referred by Dr. H. H. Stoner of Rock Rapids, now of Highmore, S. D. Referred as a dernier resort, there being but little prospect of life being extended beyond more than a few weeks at most. Prognosis exceedingly grave; very weak and anaemic: unable to take but a few steps without exhaustion. Health began to fail three years ago. has two sisters dead at ages of 22 and 40 of tuberculosis; two brothers strong and healthy, and two in fair health. Cough very irritating and quite constant; appetite poor, night sweats severe, menses suppressed since January, 1901.

Examination made Jan. 26, 1901. Flatness over apices of both lungs, loud moist rales, pulse 120, temperature 102. Much expectoration and bacilli were present; tongue red and rough; weight 89 pounds, former weight 120. Has had usual treatment of creosote carbonate, guaiacol, etc. Began treatment Jan. 27, 1901. Temperature at evening has averaged until July, almost 101, and pulse 110. During July temperature 100.2; August, 99.9; Sept., 99.66; Oct., 99.55. Pulse now averages at evening 96. Weight has increased from 89 to 97.

Menses were re-established in August and have been normal since; night sweats disappeared in May; can now (Dec. 1, 1901), walk a mile without fatigue; cough is much improved and gives but little trouble; percussion sounds normal and no rales. Bacilli still found, though in small numbers. The mixed infection in this case is now practically nil and the patient is well advanced on the way to recovery.

Case No. 5.—Miss H. G., Odebolt, Iowa; referred by Dr. R. W. Selby, of Odebolt. Age 29; single; mother dead from tuberculosis at age of 48. also one brother at age of 16. Patient has never been strong; had meningitis at age of 1 1-2 years, and is slightly deaf and is also strabismic.

Three years ago began having cold abscesses on various parts of the body, several of which have been incised by the attending physicians. Incisions have been made below right breast, below left breast, inner side of left arm, on left forearm, over sacrum and on left leg. They have healed slowly and imperfectly. Now has open wound over head of sternum, with necrosis at its bottom, also has small abscess over outer end of right clavicle, which on incision was found necrosed. Has tuberculosis of the osseous system. Percussion sound normal both sides, and there are no rales. Former weight 130: present weight 103; temperature, 102 1-2; pulse, 116. Tongue clean, bowels constipated, menses suppressed since 1901, and never very regular; coughs, a great deal with but little expectoration. Bronchial breathing on right side, exaggerated murmur on left; respiration 32. This patient has been brought principally for removal of danger to other members of the family who fear infection. Practically all hope abandoned by friends. Temperature has ranged during stay at sanatorium. During August, average, a. m., 99.34; p. m., 100; Sept., a. m., 99.10; p. m., 100.-40; Oct., a. m., 98.40; p. m., 99.80. Pulse averaged August, 118; Sept., 110: Oct., 103. Weight at time of this report, 133 pounds, a gain of 30 pounds in twelve weeks. There is gradual decline in pulse rate and temperature, the former falling from 118 to 103, and the latter from 99.34 to 98.4 in the morning, and from 100 to 99.8 in the evening. This patient is getting well, has good color, good appetite, exercises freely and has made a very remarkable gain in weight. No necrosis at time of this report. March, 1902. Perfect health and all wounds healed.

Case No. 6.—Miss A. A., Fort Dodge, Iowa, admitted as private patient, age 27, domestic, mother died of tuberculosis at age of 59 and one sister at age of 19. Three brothrs and one sister healthy. Health began to fail March, 1901 (though probably much sooner.) Is very tired, has soreness of lungs and cough with expectoration. Many bacilli. Night sweats and fever. Evening temperature 102, morning temperature 100. Menses regular until April, 1901, since then suppressed. Former weight 120, present weight 113.

Flatness over left upper half lung, with bronchial breathing and loud moist rales; right normal. Began treatment June 27, 1901. There has been gradual amelioration of symptoms and at present she is doing well. Temperature range has been:

Average for July,a. m. 99.6, p. m. 101; Aug., a. m. 99.2, p. m. 100.7; Sept., a. m. 98.16, p. m. 100.2; Oct., a. m. 98.33, p. m. 99.8.

Weight has increased from 113 to 128. General condition in every way improved; no sweats or chills, and but little expectoration. Bacilli still found.

Case No. 7.—Miss C. B., Ackley, Iowa, referred by Dr. T. J. Symington, of Ackley. Family history free from tuberculosis. Patient has not had good health for past ten years, two of which were spent in Colorado. Menses have been irregular, but at no time suppressed. Tires easily and can walk but a very short distance. Has considerable dry cough and slight expectoration; night sweats and chills. Had pleurisy seven years ago, also one year ago. Weight 109. Bacilli present in small numbers. Dullness and bronchial breathing at apex of left lung, no rales. Normal, right. Evening temperature 99 3-5, pulse 88, respiration 28. Has had morphine habit for one year. Is hypochondriachal. No mixed infection in this case. Temperature has been practically normal during the entire stay at Sanatorium, but pulse has been a little rapid, averaging about 85 both morning and evening.

At time of this report still coughs some, a few bacilli present, no sweats. Some dullness and bronchial breathing at left apex. Menses normal, appetite good, bowels regular. Exercises freely.

Fibrosis is taking place in this case. Morphine habit cured. Now weighs 121 pounds, a gain of 12 pounds in 12 weeks.

A study of these reports will show that there is invariably an increase in the body-weight, a reduction of temperature and pulse rate and a gradual subsidence of all signs of mixed infection. And it is mixed infection that kills. Tuberculosis, per se, is not a malignant nor even a dangerous disease; it may lie dormant for many years and when once lighted up is with but little difficulty held in check by the tissue resistance; but let pyogenic infection once take place and the whole picture changes.

My observations lead me to conclude that it is the secondary infection that yields first and that the recovery from tuberculosis is a secondary step as well as of secondary importance.

SPIRITISM, HYPNOTISM, TELEPATHY AND MRS. LEONORA E. PIPER.

BY CLARK BELL, ESQ., LL. D., OF NEW YORK CITY.

The publication in the New York Sunday Herald of October 20th, 1901, of an extended written statement made by Mrs. Leonora E. Piper regarding her relation to the Society for Psychical Research and particularly declaring that in her relation to that body as a medium for so many years, she was of the opinion that the phenomena, so far as she could understand it, was due to causes allied to telepathy and hypnotism rather than to the influence of the so-called spirits of deceased persons; created a lively interest and deep feeling among the students of psychology and modern spiritism, to the study of which many members of the Psychological Section of the Medico-Legal Society had devoted much attention.

The scientific world had regarded the labors of the Society of Psychical Research on both sides the Atlantic with deep interest, and the persistency and courage, with which this body had pursued its labors, the character and high standing of the men, who had its work in charge, and the fairness, which had characterized its work and publications, had given great prominence to the evidence it had collected and published on many subjects. As a body the Society of Psychical Research was not understood to have accepted the phenomena, known as modern spiritualism, and while it was known that many who had such opinions were on its roll of membership, it was in the early days, at least, not regarded other than a purely scientific body, without any avowed opinions on these subjects, courageously pursuing the study along scientific lines of all the phenomena, and under favorable conditions and by impartial and unprejudiced observers.

Additional interest had been aroused in its work, from the fact, that Dr. Hodgson, who had the work of the society in charge in Boston, and Prof. Hyslop, of Columbia University,

Read at February session Medico-Legal Society in joint session with the Psychological Section of that body.

as the result of their studies and investigation, both recently, publicly embraced the spiritistic view as to the phenomena which had been conducted through Mrs. Leonora E. Piper, the medium who had been employed by the Society of Psychical Research for many years, and whose integrity and honesty had been quite generally accepted by all with whom she had come in contact.

The statement made by Mrs. Piper in the Herald, created a very extraordinary excited state of feeling, and a high pubilc interest was at once developed in the public mind.

I thought it wise and proper to bring the subject before the Psychological Section of the Medico-Legal Society for discussion.

At the December meeting, 1901, the discussion was opened by Thomson Jay Hudson, on my invitation, who contributed the opening paper, which was followed by contributions from Judge Abraham H. Dailey, Dr. John Duncan Quackenboss, Clark Bell, Esq., Hon. Luther R. Marsh, H. C. Wright, Esq., some of whom were only read by title, on account of the time at disposal, and the whole subject made a special order for discussion at the February meeting of the Medico-Legal Society in joint session with the Psychological Section.

It was deemed advisable, that the several contributions, should be printed in the form of a brochure, and the whole furnished as a volume, upon the subjects which the discussion involve. And that the language used by Mrs. Leonora E. Piper in the statement, published in her statement as published in the New York Herald, be carefully stated, so as to make the subject of discussion more exact I give the language of Mrs. Piper which was as follows:

"*I am inclined to accept the telepathic explanation of all of the so called pyschic phenomena, but beyond this I remain a student with the rest of the world.* * * * * * *

"*I must truthfully say that I do not believe that spirits of the dead have spoken through me when I have been in the trance state, as investigated by scientific men of Boston and Cambridge, and those of the English Physical Research Society, when I was taken to England to be studied. It may be that they have, but I do not affirm it.*"

"The world knows that among scientific men the opinions on psychic phenomena are many and varied. I have always maintained that these phenomena could be explained in other ways than by the intervention of disembodied spirit forces.

"The theory of telepathy strongly appeals to me, as the most plausible and genuinely scientific solution of the problem. To strengthen this opinion are many authentic experiences which have been satisfactorily, explained by means of the telepathic hypothesis.

[In the reprint where quotations are used from her letter or the opinions of men of science, the Journal will be named and credit given for all abstracts. Thanks are due the New York Herald and Ainslee's Magazine for courtesies in allowing extracts to be made from their publication and to Harper's Magazine for similar courtesy in the article contributed by Prof. John Duncan Quackenbos to the Medico-Legal Society.]

SPIRITISM AND MRS. LEONORA E. PIPER, AND DOCTOR THOMSON J. HUDSON'S THEORIES IN REGARD TO IT.

BY EX-JUDGE ABRAM H. DAILEY,

Ex-President of the Medico-Legal Society of New York.

[*Concluded from December Journal.*]

Let us glance for a moment, at the distinction between suggestion to a hypnotic subject and trance-communication. The hypnotic subject is first hypnotized. We will take Dr. Hudson's illustrations. The subject is told by the hypnotizer that he is President of the United States. He will act the part with wonderful fidelity to life. He is told that he is in the presence of angels; he will be profoundly moved to acts of devotion. If the presence of devils is suggested, his terror will be instant and painful to behold. He may be thrown into a state of intoxication, by being caused to drink a glass of water under the impression that it is brandy. He may be restored to sobriety by the administration of brandy, under the guise of an antidote for drunkenness. (p. 31) Law of Psychic Phenomena.

Without hypnotizing a subject first, he can be made to believe none of these things. There is no spirit medium in a normal condition who can be thus imposed upon; nor is the entranced medium subject to the Law of Suggestion. The partially entranced medium does not suppose nor believe himself or herself, to be other than what he or she actually is. If fully entranced, the medium is utterly unconscious of what is transpiring around her, but the entranced spirit reasons cogently, provided the medium is a fit subject for such purpose. It is a well known fact by investigators, that hypnotizing a person tends to aid in the development of mediumship as stated by Dr. Hudson in one of his treatises. It is also well known, that in numerous instances, a spirit will step in and take possession of the hypnotic subject, who thereafter becomes a spiritual medium, and will defy the hypnotist to hypnotize the subject thereafter. Such possession by the spirit does not come from any Law of Suggestion. It comes against the suggestion and desire of the hypnotizer; and the subject, knowing nothing of spirit phenomena, could not suggest, and would have been terrified at the thought of being possessed by a spirit. The hypnotizer is an embodied spirit —a man—and is visible. The spirit, is a disembodied man, and is invisible to the hypnotist and probably to the medium as well. He is on another plane of existence. If a man can hypnotize a subject, so he must do the strange things these subjects frequently do, it is quite rational to suppose, that a spirit, possessing a spiritual body, mental force and energy more potently now than when in earthly form, might actually entrance the subject, and become almost the personality he was in life, using the organism of the subject to give expression to his thoughts and acts. There is nothing imaginary about it. Because the hypnotist can delude his subject and make him the victim of practical jokes, as well as impractical ones, and can open up the powers of what Dr. Hudson calls the "Subjective Mind," bring back all the memories and impressions obtained in a lifetime, so that they can be used by the subject in playing the part assigned him, is no argument whatever, that the phenomena of entrancement and inspiration, can be accounted for upon that hypothesis.

Dr. Hudson's position, involves a telepathic linking of minds, in the same manner, measurably, as telegraphic lines are connected, and they thus encircle the world. But the forces at work are entirely unlike. In the one case, an inanimate substance vibrates the sounds of the transmitter's hammer or voice to the receiver at the other end of the line. There are only two mentalities engaged in communicating, one at each end of the wire. One knows just what the other transmits and no more. In the telepathic process, involving the connection of several distinct mentalities, in each instance, according to Dr. Hudson's theory, the psychic becomes in rapport with the subjective mind of each person, out of which he calls forth from the memory of each—and each containing millions upon millions of impressions and recollections,—that which now enables a psychic to give to the receiver and all others the name and history of John Taylor, the story of his life and death, and far more,—the names, vocations and relations of hosts of people to each other, who lived in the distant city when he was born. Those present having never heard of John Taylor, are astonished at his appearance, and after an acquaintance with him of over twenty years, in which time the psychic can hear his voice, and at times discern his spiritual presence, the telepathic theory of Doctor Hudson is submitted as overthrowing the spiritual hypothesis.

Quoting a familiar Latin phrase, it is "*reductio ad absurdam.*" But I recall more cases of personal experience, which I wish to relate, bearing directly upon the points in controversy. Fully twenty years ago, a spirit entranced this same medium, when she and I were alone, and announced himself as Dr. Morse, giving his full name, and stating to me that he had died a number of years before in the city of New Orleans, where he had lived and practiced his profession, and where he had a family still living. He said that he had been prominently connected with the hospitals in New Orleans, and had a very extensive practice, saying, that he probably had occasioned the death of some patients, but that he had assisted a great many, and had done the best he could. I was not well at the time, and the medium herself was in poor condition of health. He said that he had come to be of assistance to us, and while he did not propose to interfere unless it was necessary, with the treatment we were receiving, he would stand by and warn us of mistakes insofar as possible. He was very faithful in coming to us, and gave me very salutary advice in regard to my health. Upon one occasion the medium, whom I may say is my wife, was in a very weak condition. She had ascended a flight of stairs to her chamber, when I found her suddenly entranced of Dr. Morse, who directed me to give her a spoonful of brandy as quickly as possible, for she was on the point of passing out of her body. Her face was deathly pale and I hurriedly gave her the barndy. He directed me to place one of my hands upon her forehead, and the other upon the back of her head, while he would hold control until she had rallied. This was done, and in a short time she rallied, and her heart resumed its wonted action, he directing me to sense her pulse.

At the time of the Exposition in New Orleans, being in poor health, the medium and I went to that city and spent a few days. As we approached the city, she informed me that she felt the presence of Dr. Morse very strongly, and presently became quite interested in everything to be seen around us. She pointed out the locality in the city where Doctor Morse had lived, and said she could go directly to his house. Up to this time, I had taken no steps to verify what I have here stated. Arriving at our hotel, I visited a drug store, questioned the druggist as to whether such a person had ever lived in the city, as this Dr. Morse, and I received the fullest verification of all he had told me, even to the location of the house where he resided, which was in the section of the city indicated by the medium.

It is a fact well known to spiritualists, that through the personality or aura of a medium, the spirit can get in rapport with the medium, so that the spirit can see again upon the earth as if still in mortal form. Consequently, the opportunity was afforded Dr. Morse, he being in rapport with the medium, to look again upon the city and its surroundings, with which he had been so familiar many years before. The medium had this consciousness of his almost constant presence with her during our stay there. I regret to say that she became rather tired of it, and one day, while we were sitting outside the Exposition grounds on a settee, she arose and remarked: "I wish Dr. Morse would go away from me. I cannot take a step but I feel him stepping beside me, and it begins to annoy me." I instantly arose, considerably vexed at her remark, saying: "When you have been ill, Dr. Morse has been on hand to save you life. When I have been ill, I have had the benefit of his wisdom. I think you and I can both stand a good deal of Dr. Morse, and you should make no such remark as that." Immediately, the firm pressure, as of a hand, was upon my shoulder, and imagining somebody whom I had not seen was present, pushing me, I hurriedly turned, asking who pushed me but saw nothing; we were entirely alone insofar as I could see; but I knew what it meant, and I knew that the remark had deeply wounded our kind friend.

Telepathy, suggestion, clairvoyance and clairaudience are submitted as sufficient explanation of these remarkable manifestations. One other instance and I will finish my illustrations.

Some eighteen years ago the medium and I were quite intimately acquainted with a Dr. Howard, his wife and family. During our absence of a few weeks from the city, his wife had died, and had been some six weeks in the spiritual world, at the time the incident I am relating occurred. The medium was entranced of one, who had represented herself as the spirit of a little girl, whose name was Daisy Crandall. She had come to us many times, and is still part of our spiritual family. Several friends were present when she spoke hurriedly saying: "Why, here is Mrs. Howard. She says she has just come from the doctor's house; that the house is on fire, and that she was frightened, fearing that the old doctor would be burned up." It was a pat statement, and quite startling. I remarked: "I hope Daisy, you are not mistaken; for you know very well that the medium knows nothing of what you say, and if it turns out that there was no fire there, it would be very annoying to her." She became immediately indignant, and asked me if I supposed that Mrs. Howard would come there and tell a lie. I meekly replied ,'No, but I didn't know but that there might be a mistake." She reiterated that there was no mistake. She believed what Mrs. Howard said. I said nothing of the occurrence until after the company had gone. When I told the medium of what had been said through her lips, while she had been entranced, she became very much excited,—stamped her foot, and said that no control should put her in that position, for she did not believe there was a word of truth in the statement. She had hardly gotten the words from her mouth, before the spirit returned, seizing control of her, and sitting down, she burst into tears and said to me. "Tomorrow morning I want you to harness the horse and carriage, and take the medium down to Dr. Howard's house, and I will tell you just what you will find there. You will find that the fire engines were there, that they put water in through the house; that it came down through the ceiling; that the bedding was on fire, and that they threw the mattresses in the back-yard, and say to her when I am gone, that she must not question our truthfulness, for we do not lie." I did as requested. We drove down to Dr. Howard's; he lived in a brown stone house on Bedford avenue. As I drove up to the curbstone, there was no sign of fire in the front part of the building. The medium immediately exclaimed: "There, I told you so." I said, "Wait." I ran up the steps and rang the bell at the door. The call was answered by the doctor himself, and the moment the door was opened, the work of the flames and water was before me. The doctor at once stated that fire had broken out the night before, and he came near being burned up. I hurriedly ran through the hall of his house, looked out of the back window of the parlor, and the mattresses were still smouldering in the yard, and the ceilings were soaking with water.

I might multiply instances of similar occurrences, but I have stated sufficient, and Dr. Hudson and scientists who support his theory of explaining these remarkable phenomena, must present something more convincing as to the truth of their position, before I shall give up the happy consciousness in which I have lived so many years, that the spiritual world is around us, and our departed friends are not dead but can come to us.

It will be noted that Dr. Hudson has avoided entering into that domain of phenomena of a physical character, which he says may or may not be explained, as emanating from spiritual sources, but, because it can be duplicated by the application of known principles of natural law as evidence, the evidence that it emanates from a spiritual source is destroyed. I wish simply to say, that I have witnessed manifestations that cannot be duplicated through the application of any of the known principles of natural law, as I understand he desires to use that expression. As for myself, I regard the reign of natural law as supreme, and if God does not manifest himself through the laws of nature, then God,—if there be a God,—must be outside of nature's domain. I am a theist. I believe in God, but this is outside of the issue between us.

I note in his treatises that Dr. Hudson seems to endorse as truthful, the record of the remarkable powers possessed by Jesus, when he cast out evil spirits which had possessed some of the unfortunate psychics of those times. Dr. Hudson is a naturalist. I don't apprehend that he believes there are any spirits in the spiritual world, that have not come up through the processes which he has pointed out in his work, from the oversoul of the universe, having become first men and women, and then, through the process of death, spirits—angels. That some of the spirits passing from this to the other world are good and some are evil cannot be questioned, for death cannot be presumed to have changed the nature of a man nor the moral character of a person. If, therefore, the Master exorcised Mary Magdalen from the evil spirits possessing her, it necessarily follows that such spirits exist in the spiritual world, though invisible to mortals, and may work evil and good through them, as opportunity is afforded.

There are other features which clearly distinguish spirit control from hypnosis; and in passing it is important to state, that Prof. Carpenter, the famous hypnotist, mentioned by Doctor Hudson as assisting in his investigations, was a spiritualist. His wife was a medium, and I learned from his own lips, that his life-long study and practice of hypnosis, as well as his study of spirit phenomena, enabled him to unmistakably distinguish a case of spirit control from one of hypnosis.

The controlling spirit does not believe that he is the medium, or that the medium is the spirit; and in many instances in my experience, which is true in that of a thousand other investigators, the first time a spirit effects control, much difficulty is experienced. The medium will complain of strange sensations as she lapses into unconsciousness, frequently moans, and is ubject to convulsive action and is liable to fall from her chair. This is almost invariably preceded, by the symptoms of the condition of the spirit, just before and at the time of death. These manifestations are often painful to witness. They are never manifested in a case of hypnosis, nor of hypnotic suggestion, without the direct intervention of the mind of the suggestor, bringing about these conditions.

It is an exceedingly common occurrence, in the case of spirit control, for the spirit to express astonishment, at the strange circumstance in which he is placed; if it be a male spirit, talking through a lady medium; or, if the control is a female spirit, the same astonishment is expressed, that she is using the organism of a man to give utterance to her thoughts.

One may very naturally suppose, in the case I have mentioned, of our visit to New Bedford, that the return of the spirit to the place of his nativity, where the incidents connected with his early life transpired, many of which were exceedingly sad, would occasion emotions which would be thrown upon the medium. In this case, the medium retained her normal condition, and carried on a conversation with me, she giving utterance to what she clairaudiently received from him.

So strongly did she sense his emotions, that she became at times greatly agitated, as a sensitive naturally would, sensing the emotions of one revisiting the scenes of his childhood under such circumstances.

As we were turning out from Spruce Lane, she suddenly turned and exclaimed, "He says here is where old Aunt Margaret lived, who gave me a sup of milk, and a piece of bread and butter when I was hungry." She choked with emotion, and tears were flowing. Similar emotions were manifested at the grave-yard, when looking out upon the place of his mother's burial.

Before we entered the cemetery I have referred to, among the names mentioned by him, of people whom he had known in life, as being buried there, was one by the name of Benjamin Tripp. We found the tombstone containing this name of Benjamin Tripp, Jr., not far from the entrance, giving the date of birth as October 19, 1806, if I remember correctly, and the date of death, August 17, 1879. I cannot give all the names and incidents from memory, but I have a memorandum of them which is not at hand.

We supposed that the Benjamin Tripp whose grave we had found, was the one he referred to, but he corrected us and said, "No, this was the son of the man" he had known, and we presently found the grave of Benjajmin Tripp, who was the person whom he had known in his early life.

Most persons have experiences of their own of a telepathic nature. It is a common occurrence for the thought of a person to precede his coming into our presence. There is a cause for this. We are as lighted candles, giving off something of our being wherever we go, as a candle does light. The material objects which are so real to us, afford no barriers to the penetration of that strange, invisible something, which characterizes the personality of us all, and goes with, and precedes us through life.

Thoughts have been said to be things. At any rate, the language we use is the best method we have, though feeble indeed, of giving expression to our thoughts. I have been taught that telepathy—or thought transference,—is a common method by which spirits hold converse.

Your candle throws out a peculiar aura, which is known to your friends, which interblends with that of theirs, which immediately suggests to your friends your approach. A thought is born which is followed by your coming together. This illustrates in a general way one phase of what is denominated Telepathy.

The Society for Psychical Research, has experimented extensively to find to what extent thought transference could be carried. For instance, they place a subject in a room alone, with pencil and paper to draw or write as he may be impressed; the operators go into another room and concentrate their thoughts, perhaps upon a picture, and mentally suggest the picture to the subject, and it has frequently occurred that he has drawn a similar picture by himself. This is telepathic suggestion. A thought may be thus projected, but it has not been found possible thus to communicate a discourse to the recipient.

The organs of sight and hearing are simply nature's methods of communicating to our inner-consciousness, surrounding conditions, and the discoveries in regard to the response of these organs to the vibrations of light and sound, are adding to the wonders that are being unfolded in regard to our own being.

Clairvoyance and clairaudience, possessed by sensitives, and in certain conditions at times by numerous other persons, have demonstrated the possibility of discerning events transpiring in very distant places.

In my publication of the life of Mollie Fancher, I recorded numerous instances of her manifestation of these powers.

And if it be true, as demonstrated in her case, and in thousands of other instances, that the clairvoyant can see beyond the walls of her enclosed room, out into the street, and witness what is transpiring, she is also entitled to the credit of speaking truthfully when she declares, that she see the spiritual forms of her departed friends, as from time to time they present themselves to her, intangible though they be to the mortal touch, they are nevertheless there to her spiritual vision. She has the absolute consciousness of their presence. We may be sure that whatever transpires, either in this or in the Spiritual World, will take place in harmony with the principles of Natural Law. The great trouble with humanity is, that it is often ignorant of those principles, and hence this discussion.

If the illimitable linking of minds as claimed, is possible, so that they can be thus brought into harmonious connection then Telepathy will deserve to be called, Omniscience.

The mind may be capable, in the infinity of time which is before us, of unlimited comprehension, but that it is possible for individual minds to become so connected, that the knowledge possessed by each may become common, is something which cannot rationally be accepted.

If science is reduced to such straits to disprove the spiritistic theory, then science is in distress, and may be excused for grasping at straws.

In his argument, Dr. Hudson has combined truth with error, and asks us to accept his presentation of it as being wholly true. I have no doubt of the correctness of some of his conclusions; but his weak points are distinct.

The stone that the builders rejected has become the Head of the Corner, and the Temple of Spiritual Truth is becoming a mountain which shall fill the whole earth. (2nd ch. of Daniel.)

Great cowardice is manifested by most Christian teachers in ignoring that part of the teachings of Jesus, and of Paul and other early writers concerning spiritual gifts. If they read those passages, they avoid a sensible interpretation of their true meaning, and also of much that has come to us of what Jesus taught, and of what Paul and other of the apostles and disciples wrote.

The vile purpose to which psychic powers have been put, is no justification for condemning all psychics as unworthy persons, nor their communications as untrue.

The application of that rule to other matters would not be tolerated. None will claim, and neither do the controls themselves claim, that they are not liable to error. Truth will ever be attained under difficulties, and what is apparently true, must stand as true until proven otherwise.

We have before us a great realm for investigation, and we are wonderfully assisted, if we know we have co-operation on the "Other Side," to assist in opening communications between the visible and invisible realms.

The puerile character of many of the communications coming from trance mediums, as well as their untrustworthiness, being frequently by language, diction and thought totally unlike what might be expected from those from whom they purport to emanate, warrant the conclusions usually formed, that they are untruthful, and disgrace the cause so strenuously advocated by Spiritualists. These criticisms are warranted. and I shall say little to excuse or palliate them, no matter from what source they eminate. These conditions are not new (See II Chron. 18 c. 19-22.) I will quote one verse:

"And he said I will go out, and be a lying spirit in the mouth of all his prophets. And the Lord said, thou shalt entice him, and thou shalt prevail; go and do even so." (See Luke, 7 c 21 v.:8 c. 2 v.; I John, 4 c. 1 v.)

Who could expect to transmit through the undeveloped brain of an illiterate medium, the language and lofty inspirations of a Webster or Beecher? The communications usually are characterized by the personality of the mediums; and those ignorant of the laws of spirit control, at once condemn the whole as fraudulent. Not until the brain of the psychic is well developed, and can respond in appropriate language to the thoughts of the controlling spirit, will trance-mediumship attain the eminence to which it is destined. Testing the truthfulness of every spirit before giving it absolute credence, is always advisable.

For long periods of time, Jewish history teaches that the voice of prophets was still, and the people longed for one to rise, to whom they could go for consolation in distress, and for wisdom when perplexed with doubts. Joel said, "And it shall come to pass afterwards, that I will pour out my spirit upon all flesh; and your sons and your daughters shall prophesy, your old men shall dream dreams, and your young men shall see visions, and also upon the servants and handmaids in those days will I pour out my spirit." (Joel 2 c. 28-29 v.; also Acts 2 c. 17-18 v.) Following the crucifixion of Jesus, his disciples continued to manifest to the world the spiritual gifts which had been given them, but they were lost when the priesthood stoned and put the seers to death. How few clergymen will say to those who mourn for the dead, "I know there is no death to your loved ones. they live and can come again to you, and will abide with you if you prepare your heart and home to receive them." Christianity as taught by its founders is well, but it will never convert the world while ignoring a part of the commands of the Master. The Seance Room should be the Holy of Holies; the most sacred of places. Spiritualists have made it a dark chamber, rather than a place of sacred light. They have made the phenomena an idol, and have cast Christ out of their synagogues. They deny God, and have substituted Nature in His place, and present the world with a Soulless Universe. No wonder people ask, "Can any good come out of Nazareth?" Yet, for all this, there will a time come, when some one will rise up and separate the pure from the corrupt, and by Works, by Faith and Truthful Teachings, bring the religions of the world into accord, and the human family into a Universal Brotherhood, through the serene spirit of Christ, which was before the earth was formed, and will continue, when it ceases to be the habitation of man.

ERRATUM.

In my illustration of Dr. Hudson's theory, that telepathy would account for the medium's knowledge of John Taylor and the events in his life, I have supposed a case to the effect that some living person, with whom the medium is acquainted, has heard from some other persons whom she does not know, all that she has given as coming directly to her from John Taylor himself. This illustration fails to make clear the stretch of credence. Dr. Hudson demands, as he claims that if Jones knew John Taylor in his -life time, and Jones knew Smith, and Smith knew Brown, and Brown knew Green, and Green knew White and White knew the medium, this linking of minds would account for the correct statements by the medium of the facts given by her concerning John Taylor. Dr. Hudson's claim is in effect, that it is only necessary that the first named of all these persons—Mr. Jones—should have known John Taylor, and that the last named, Mr. White, should know the medium. As already stated, the medium knows of no person through whom this connection can be made.

A. H. D.

PSYCHIC PHENOMENA.

SPIRIT COMMUNICATION VS. MENTAL TELEPATHY.

BY ELEANOR GRIDLEY, OF CHICAGO.

Mr. Thomson Hudson, according to his standpoint, has closed the gate of investigation, research and information from the premise of Spirit communication by first stating that all psychic phenomena is physical manifestation; or rather that all occcult phenomena is but the prescience of "the subliminal self" as Myers puts it; the power of the ego or higher self to know all things.

If this be so and this subjective self is omniscient, then why limit its power, simply to that period of time, more or less, in which it dwells or is anchored to its earthly temple? Does it not strike the thoughtful individual that anything so powerful can be constituted so ephemeral?

The Society for Psychical Research, composed of learned men—scholars—who are wont to weigh well, deep questions, have just finished a series of psychical investigations with Mrs. Leonora Piper as the pricipal witness in the case. These men who have investigated with rare earnestness, subject to rigid methods, which left no loop hole for careless or unscientific research to creep in, have many of them been converted to the belief that much of the phenomena was genuine spirit communication.

In the first place, let us reason together and try to discover what this subliminal self, higher self, or human Ego is; for if it is omniscient, able to impart information and capable of discrimination and discovery, then it should know its constitution, purpose and ultimate end, either through self-knowledge or absorption from other entities or Egos.

Upon consulting standard works I find that Ego, the I, or the me, means "indviduality, personality." Individuality is defined as follows: "The quality or state of being distinct or individual. Sharply marked temperament. Personality im-

Contributed to the discussion of Mr. Thomson J. Hudson's paper read before the Psychological Section of the Medico-Legal Society.

plies particular characteristics; that which constitutes an individual, a distinct person; existence as a thinking being." I am overwhelmed with a cloud of witnesses and am obilged to accept the inevitable,for no matter,how much effort one makes to. avoid it, one cannot escape the reality of one's own egohood, or that which makes us say I.

The Ego, the real self, the I, is the individual as an object to his own reflective consciousness—the person as a distinct individual. the man reviewed by his own cognition, as the subject of all his mental phenomena, the agent of his own activities, the subject of his own feelings, and the possessor of his own faculties and his own characteristics.

Now let us consider this ego as to the possiblity or probability of both premises or either premise, the final extinction of that wonderful ego or the immortality of that supreme selfhood. Does it depend upon anatomical construction to be able to perform its activities, display and elaborate its characteristics? Are these extensive and subdivisible manifestations of the total self or Ego merely dependent on cerebral changes; thus purely material and absolutely subject to physical laws, and with the dissolution of the body ceases to be, ceases to exist? Is this powerful self a creation subordinate to its environment—to circumstances, to inheritance, to fate—and like its physical mate, the body, amenable also to the same natural laws and subject to the same fate—annihilation?

Is the Ego an indescribable and incomprehensible thing, susceptible to the opposite condition—and ascending is merged or absorbed into that from whence it came, no wiser, no happier, no better, a senseless, unknowing essence, its state or condition infinite bliss, eternal repose, in fact obliteration, a term synonymus to annihilation?

Or again, is the Ego independent of the body and does it possess the power to transmigrate into the bodies of other animals of a lower order thus descending the scale, or upon the other hand does the ego upon its release seek to live again in the old scenes and in order to do so, take up its habitation in a new human body, and therefore in one sense ascends the scale, because of its past experiences, and its return based upon the universal law of progress.

Or lastly, does not the Ego rise from out tne trammels and bondage of flesh, and asserting its omnipotence and eternal power, silently sweeping through realms of illimitable space, with the speed of the electric messenger, pausing now here, now there, to exchange greetings with other released egos, then rushing onward, to tell the story of its liberation, its freedom, to the loved ones still in bondage, know that

"When all shall stand transfigured like Christ, on Hermon Hill
And moving each to music, soul in soul and light in light,
Shall flash thro' one another in a moment as we will?"

Anything which is important for man to know can sooner or later be known by the power of inductive reasoning, either in physical or psychical laws, and a psychic fact is just as much a fact as any other fact, and science has no more right to ignore one than the other; in fact no fact in nature can be safely ignored, for no fact is wholly insignificant.

The right of the psychical or spiritual world to speak of its own phenomena is as secure as the right of the natural world to speak of itself.

By the observation of a series of physical phenomena we are able to predict with confidence that the law which produces a certain phenomena is as fixed and exact and absolute as any law of mathematics.

In the realm of psychic phenomena "We look not at the things which are seen, but at the things which are not seen; for the things that are seen are temporal, but the things which are not seen are eternal." The visible is the ladder up to the invisible; the temporal is but the scaffold of the eternal. The innumerable and marvelous phenomena of the powers and faculties of the Ego are so wonderful and complex that one pauses in sheer amazement and asks the question, What is its limit and where is its limit? We reply there is no limit for though harnessed to its vehicle of flesh, it even now has the power to do whatever it wills to do. The Ego in this state has the power to move ponderable bodies, otherwise known as levitation—simply by the exertion of will power. Will is the motive force, it chooses when stimulated by desire, and therefore its will is strong in proportion to its desire regarding any particular object. It has the power to dominate the will of other Egos and compel them to do its bidding. It also has the power to read the minds of other Egos—to see the thought of others (clairvoyance). the power to hear the thoughts of others (clairaudience), and to express its own thought as well as those of others by its physical apparatus either orally or through the medium of the pen. This Ego, steeped in all the delicate joy of tender emotions, thrills to the intensity and volume of song, expands in the joyous possession of freedom, revels in the ecstasy of love and in the embrace of tender compassion, sinks into that peace which passeth all understanding.

Now the intelligent investigator knows that the Ego has communicated facts of incidents hundreds of miles distant and to the receptive Ego or soul has given a clear and perfect statement of the events while this information may have been sent or projected at the moment of occurrence or deferred some hours. It has beheld the ego of the other individual and foretold its coming or visitation. It has sensed the alarm and disquietude of a loved one and with its undying and eternal power has calmed the fear and restored peace to the troubled soul.

The manifestations of this Ego are innumerable and the differentiations of its power are beyond conception to mortal ken. Now if this thinking, palpipating throbbing entity can transmute its intelligence when circumscribed by physical environment, then why cannot it display an equal if not superior intelligence when freed from bondage? And if not, why not? This conscious potentiality which has lived or existed in connection with its physical mate has always displayed an intense and passionate desire to retain its individuality, its self-preservation. Jesus expressed the strength and intensity of that desire when He said, "What shall it profit a man if he gain the whole world and lose his own soul?"

If this Ego, or man is indestructible and has really an eternal existence in its own right, it must be independent of form or limitation, and can therefore go or come as the desire leadeth. Without further question or argument, I shall only recognize the immortality and intelligent continuity of the Ego, and its power to communicate either directly to the individual, or through the circumscribed indivdiual. Now that this be so, let us take into consideration the constitution of the vehicle or instrument through which the disembodied intelligence communicates, and we shall no doubt have solved many perplexing questions and misgivings.

We are first met with the supposedly embarrassing statement that the intelligence has deteriorated since its advent into spirit life, because of the fact that the communications purporting to come from a former distinguished denizen of earth is below the intelligence of the ordinary man. And again it is discovered that other statements,—made by these supposedly disembodied entities are false, misleading, inaccurate or garbled. Granted to be true, all of these statements, and yet they can be accounted for simply through the law of conformity to the type. Whatever individuality is sought and used as the excarnate ego's vehicle of expression, thus by its free choice the Ego is obliged to conform to its selection, and the power of its thought, its quality and quantity and the language by which the thought is expressed, is now limited and circumscribed by the power of the medium to comprehend, to translate and to communicate.

The artist or the musician may be ever so great, even the greatest exponent of his special art that the world has ever known, and yet, with a low grade, imperfect instrument, or crude, ill-fashioned tools, this great master is utterly unable to produce that high standard of perfection which, under good conditions he is perfectly capable of achieving.

That false or unreliable statements are made by the medium is also another undisputed fact. Why should it be otherwise, for if the medium is untruthful, dishonest, unreliable or imaginary, how can the message be freed from this condition? A stream of water can rise no higher than its source—neither can the quality of thought be other than the constitution through which it flows. However purified the garment, or however whitened it may be it will become spotted, discolored and grimed by contact with soiled or blackened objects, and so with thought communication, it is also contaminated in its flight through poisonous channels.

We again are also told that the mediums or instruments through whom the intelligence is transmitted has never given any information other than the knowledge of that which resides in the mind of one or more present. That statement seems to me quite misleading for I could give hundreds of instances in which absolutely unknown and unknowable information was given to me. Many people have also made to me this same statement;but as that is only hearsay evidence (and not admissible in courts of justice and equity), I will confine my illustrations to my own personal knowledge. I have received prophetic information many times through spirit communication direct to self or through some other instrument.

This information was communicated to me, in many instances, as many as twenty years in advance of the actual occurrences. The details were minutely described, the persons named, in a number of instances then unknown to me. The results were so clearly and positively emphasized, that had I then been well grounded in the knowledge of spirit return, it seems to me I could have prevented the calamities which ensued and were enacted at the time and place so stated. In lieu of these experiences, I cannot argue that all psychic information is obtained or selected by the sensitive from some one at hand, or of not at hand, still present in the corporeal body of the material man who is somewhere on the earth plane.

I believe that spirit return is a demonstrated fact, but its value will be seen to be dependent upon its relation to other facts of equal importance. When we, hereupon the earth plane have developed to a high degree of intelligence and soul unfoldment, then will we not only attract those spirits who have achieved true immortality, but we will also be able to translate in purity of language and correct expression, their messages.

And such is the possibility open to those who are capable of understanding, and who are willing to receive and reveal the great and wonderful truths brought to earth by spirit man.

"It is God's promised blessing, set
Before the Coming race.
Our children's children's children yet
May see it face to face;
But we, the masters of To-day,
Must see the light and lead the way."

TELEPATHY, SPIRITISM, HYPNOTISM AND THE CASE OF MRS. ELENORA E. PIPER.

BY ALEXANDER WILDER, M. D., OF NEWARK, N. J.

The case of Mrs. Piper is comparatively simple, if we can fairly understand the premises. These belong unequivocally to the department of mesmerism. I prefer the use of this term instead of the one which has been dragged from the Greek language and misapplied, to evade giving due credit to the man who introduced the art and science to the notice of the world. The same reason which warrants the applying of the names of Volta, Galvani and Faraday to their discoveries, is entitled to equal force in the case of Anton Mesmer. It seems to me superlatively mean and base to pirate a man's work and refrain from giving him honest credit. This, to be sure, has been done in other departments of knowledge, nevertheless I think that for this once we can afford to do honorably.

It was early perceived in mesmeric experiments that the physical sensibility and even the reasoning faculty of the individual were more or less suspended,and that he became in a greater or less degree participant in the thoughts and perceptions of the mesmeriser. This occurred according as there was produced a partial or complete rapport between the two. In many instances there were such results as trance, intuition, somnambulism, clairvoyance, etc. In these cases we have had many wonderful disclosures which purported to come from other spheres of life. In the condition of trance, however, it was produced; this has been no uncommon occurrence. The works of Emanuel Swedenborg are significant evidences from the fact that he, while in a state of trance, received numerous communications which were imparted to him, as he declared, by spirits and angels in the invisible world. There exists no valid reason for doubting his veracity or clearness of perception in regard to his memorable relations, and we may enquire further.

Andrew Jackson Davis, now of Boston, and formerly known as "Poughkeepsie Seer," gave a fresh impulse to investigation in this direction by the production of "Nature's Divine Revelations." His disclosures were made while in the mesmeric trance in the presence of witnesses of different shades of religious belief, but generally intelligent and truthful. Dogmas of theology, problems of science, and matters beyond our common knowledge were treated as by one having competent learning and authority. One of these, I remember, was the announcement that there are two planets in our solar system not yet discovered. The star Neptune had only just come to our knowledge. This announcement was received in scientific and literary circles in silence or dismissed in language of derision. It might be true, but the revelation of a mesmeric clairvoyant could not be accepted. Yet not many weeks ago, the statement appeared that certain deflections in the course of other planets indicated the existence of two more worlds of similar nature in that far-off space. I do not, however, cite this with the expectation that such verification will be accepted in evidence. There exists a deep-seated Sadduceism in the so-called scientific world, that would not admit testimony even more unequivocal. But our quest is for truth, and we must let it find its own avenues.

The experimentation with Mrs. Piper under the auspices of the Society for Psychical Research has evidently resulted in establishing the fact that such avenues have actually been found. I place no importance upon her published disavowal. She was undoubtedly in the entranced state when making her replies to her magnetisers. We can not suppose her to be shamming. Her own character precludes this, and the members of the society having the matter in charge would have speedily detected any fraud if such had been attempted. I accept what the society has published as being true, and conscientiously declared. What, therefore, we have to consider is in relation to the disclosures themselves. I have no doubt that they rank with others of similar character obtained from other sources.

The question before us relates, as I understand it, to the nature of the communications, whether they were from some region beyond our common life, or to be explained by some theory of telepathy. It appears to me that both agencies possibly existed in the case. What I have noted in former examples has convinced me that there is a silent influence exerted by spectators, which we often do not suspect. This occurs in everyday life. The orator thus affects his audience and in turn the audience often inspires him. We are affected by every one with whom we have to do. The mesmerised person whose individuality is thus rendered dormant becomes more exquisitely sensitive to the aura and influence of those whose attention is concentrated upon him. Of course he is most susceptible to his magnetiser, sometimes evidently entirely so, but spectators have their share of influence. He will often reiterate what is in their thought, and they will take this for a special revelation. It is not necessary that they in each case are vividly conscious of such thinking, for our real thought is far beneath and beyond the sphere of our own consciousness. Only the superficial thinking is perceived by us. Hence we often operate on one another by our presence, by the concentrating of our attention through the silent energy of our will, and yet perhaps suppose that we are only passive.

It must be left to others to judge whether this in any degree explains the case of Mrs. Piper. Those who are personally cognisant may feel certain that it does not to any reasonable degree meet the conditions, and indeed it is proposed only as a partial explanation. The world of mind is too broad to warrant the including of such phenomena in a purview so narrow and circumscribed.

Our intelligence cognises a mode of being and a region of thought that are by no means comprehended within the sphere of material existence. It is neither logical nor philosophic to imagine that while there exists myriads of living beings in series between man and the monad, that beyond on the superior side it is blank, and devoid of life and sense. "We are compassed about with a great cloud of witnesses," declares an anonymous writer in the New Testament. "Millions of heavenly creatures walk the earth," the poet Milton assures us, and I am content to believe it. It is not to be assumed that they are not cognisant of our presence. If any of them are souls that have lived in the earth, they may have still an inclination to take some part in matters of this mundane life. They must possess enough still of our human quality to be able to make their wills operative upon those who are still living. Bunyan describes his Pilgrim followed by a wicked being who "whisperingly suggested many grievous blasphemies to him which he verily thought had proceeded from his own mind." It is reasonable to suppose that as we are compassed about with living essences, that they will be of a character substantially like our own, and that they are able to insinuate or rouse into activity thoughts in us which we will apprehend as our own. And if all this should in any way be objectified we might contemplate it as a spectacle before our face.

An individual in the mesmeric trance is dormant so far as the external senses are concerned. But the soul, the real self is as much awake as ever. It is then more susceptible to mental impression than in the wakeful period. As spectators by contemplating him intently may infuse their thoughts and emotions, so spiritual beings are capable of doing the same thing. Indeed, this is more likely to happen. They are more free to do so, and are naturally more eager and ready. The bars between the world of time and the vaster world beyond time, are in a great degree removed for the while, and communication opened as when a man is in conversation with a friend. Despite the fashionable skepticism that pervades such matters about with a dense wall of disbelief, and despite Mrs. Piper's own disavowals, I think this to be the true explanation of the case.

This is evidently suggested in the well-worn sentence of Shakespeare, which may be quoted appropriately once more:

"We are such stuff
As dreams are made on."

Visionary as it is common to term such things, they are actual entities in the region of mind, and our real self is the soul that undergoes such experiences, rather than the bodily fabric which it pervades and animates. If Shakespeare could produce the concepts which constitute the plot of the drama of "The Tempest," it appears to me unavoidably conclusive that such occurrences,in some manner and at some period of time must take place. What the mind conceives must be always a reality. In the case under consideration it is evident that Mrs. Piper, when in the mesmeric trance was made passive and susceptible to the mental and spiritual influences which her moral and physical condition attracted. These intelligences thus had an opportunity to utter their thoughts, and perhaps were in a manner constrained to do so, through a living human intermediary. Some of them may have been the minds of the magnetiser and spectators, but others were without doubt unbodied beings that desired to avail themselves of this means of communication. Of their individuality I am not so certain. Influence is reciprocal, and as a spirit may obsess a human being or an intermediary, it is reasonable to presume that a human being may obsess a spirit in turn. The eager fixed thought of a spectator at a sitting can so affect a spirit as to impel it to suppose itself the pesonality which the other has in mind. Swedenborg has described this occurrence in one of his works, *and it accounts for much of the drivel and absurdity which have been put forth as spiritual communications. Nevertheless to make such facts an argument for decrying all esoteric communion, and for rejecting all belief and confidence in the verity and importance of spiritual intercourse is the very reverse of candor and rationality. There is abundant reason for the belief that the wall or partition between the external world and that eternity which encompasses time is disappearing, or at least that there are individuals and agencies capable of penetrating the vail. We are at no infinite distance from that region in which all things are real.

---

*NOTE.—SWEDENBORG: *Spiritual Diary 2860–2861.*—"*That spirits may be induced who represent another person; and the spirit as also he who was known to the spirit cannot know otherwise than that he was the same.*

This has been many times shown to me: that the spirits speaking with me did not know otherwise than that they were the men who were the subject of thought; and neither did other spirits know otherwise; as yesterday and to-day some one known to me in life was represented by one who was so like him in all things which belonged to him, so far as they were known to me, that nothing was more like; wherefore, let those who speak with spirits beware lest they are those whom they have known, and that they are dead. For there are genera and species of spirits of a like faculty; and when similar things are called up in the memory of a man and are thus represented to them, they think that they are the same persons. Then all the things that are called forth from the memory which represent those persons, both the words, the speech, the tones, the gestures and other things besides, that they are induced to think thus when other spirits inspire them; for then they are in the fantasy of these, or think that they are the same.

THOUGHT TRANSFERENCE VERSUS SPIRITISM AS AN EXPLANATION OF MANY SO CALLED SPIRITISTIC PHENOMENA.

BY PROF. W. XAVIER SUDDUTH, A. M., M. D.,
Fellow of the Chicago Academy of Medicine.

In considering Mrs. Piper's disavowal of spirit control during her many years successful experience as a medium, it behooves us to lay down some definite principles to govern us in this discussion. In the first place, the testimony, post partem, of a medium or an hypnotic subject, should have no standing in a court of scientific inquiry for the reason that a person in a state of trance, or hypnosis, is not in the full possession of all his senses, consequently is not competent to pass judgment on the character of the conditions under which the revelations were made. At best his evidence would be based upon hearsay, and such testimony is always ruled out of court. Not only this, but as students of their own experiences during the trance state they are not to be trusted, for the further reason, that, just in proportion as they are good mediums, so are they incapacitated from analysing their own revelations.

The term medium is synonymous with "mouthpiece." A medium is a person who becomes the instrument of expression for the thoughts or messages of others, and just in proportion as he is honest and proficient in his chosen avocation, just so far does he lose his identity and individuality and assume the role of an automaton and voice the ideas of others.

Now, while Mrs. Piper is a trance medium and is supposed to receive messages only in that state, yet it is not absolutely necessary for an individual to lose consciousness in order to become sensitive to his environment and thus receive mes-

Read before the Medico-Legal Society and Psychological Section, February 19, 1902.

sages and reveal the so called, hidden mysteries of this world. In support of this last statement we have many successful "readings" of honest, competent psychometrists. All that is necessary for mediumistic revelations, is a condition of dissociation of consequences which permits the subjective perception to take cognizance of these subtle influences and raise them above the threshold of consciousness, thus bringing them into external relations where they may be "read," that is, perceived by us.

It matters not how this be brought about, whether by automatic writing, by planchette, or by the voice of a control speaking through the medium.

It is impossible for Mrs. Piper or any other medium, to say whether the opinions she holds at any time, are not the reflection of some other person's ideas upon the subject, telepathically or otherwise received.

In the present case, I have no doubt in my mind that her change of opinion regarding her past experiences is not the result of such influences. The thoughts received by her may have been my own, for ought I know, (sic) for notwithstanding the many years I have been studying spiritistic and hypnotic phenomena, I have never yet seen anything to lead me to believe other than Mrs. Piper has stated in her revocation of her so-called spiritistic control.

If thought transference (telepathy) is the source of her information as she now asserts, and as I firmly believe, she has proved herself to be a good medium for the reception and interpretation of thought vibrations, and as such vibrations are always on tap, so to speak, all that is necessary for her, or any other good medium to do in order to be able to receive and translate them into ordinary language, is to bring herself into a state of dissociation of consciousness. My explanation of the incoherent manner in which many of the messages have been received, is, that the medium was not always in the best physical or mental state to receive or interpret the thought vibrations that poured in upon her, or that she became weary from the forced attention required to keep in touch with a state of consciousness not normal to her. I know psychometrists, however, who work for hours daily, without any more apparent fatigue than would be manifest in any ordinary mental labor of the same duration. The fact that these incoherencies in Mrs. Piper's communications came just before the close of the sitting, seems to bear out this conclusion, that they were caused by fatigue of attention. It is possible that Mrs. Piper's own personality may have interjected these phenomena into the message. I have seen instances where such was the case. The medium assumed certain things to be essential to success. It has been very interesting to watch the outcroppings of these individual peculiarities of different mediums. In one of my own personal experiences, where I was studying a successful psychometrist, in the hypnotic state, I held in mind the image of my father, who had passed on some two years before. The subject had not known him personally, or in any manner. I have strong powers of visualization and can project thought images with great clearness, which I know help me in these experiments which I have been making for years along this line of observation.

In this instance the subject, a Mrs. E., very quickly caught the image and gave an accurate description of it. Now, she is not a spiritualist and strongly resents the idea of spirit control in her work which she generally carries on in the waking state. She deprecates anything that savors of spiritualism in relation to her work and consistently and conscientiously avoids it, and I made this a test of the genuineness of her protestations in this regard. Up to the time she had given the accurate description of my father not a word had been said as to his demise. The picture I held of him was one as I had last seen him alive and in the full enjoyment of health. Then I permitted my thought to naturally pass on to the final parting scene and the medium was visibly affected. She said "I do not understand this. I just saw the gentleman in perfect health, now he seems to be seriously ill." Her eyes were closed and she was in a perfect somnambulistic state, consequently could not have been affected by my own emotional state through the operations of the ordinary senses, but she was evidently influenced. I had purposely avoided saying anything up to this point, allowing the image to pass on to the next stage, the interment, and when I had fully regained my composure I very quietly asked, "Has he any message for me?" To my surprise she became greatly excited and said "I want you to wake me up." She had the idea that she could not waken without my consent. This also came from autosuggestion, I never having given her such suggestion. I tried in vain to quiet her and finally had to arouse her from the somnolent state. She arose from the couch, sat down in a chair and was very much overcome by her emotions. For a time I purposely avoided saying anything to her but carefully studied her every motion. Finally she said, "Doctor, I am willing you should study me, in fact I am anxious to know the source of my powers, but you must not try to make me the medium of spirit communications." My analysis of the experience is, that so long as I had a perfectly clear image in my mind, she could see it and give a verbal description, but when it came to asking her for something that did not exist in my mind she failed to answer my question and in her anxiety to do so became worked up into a high degree of excitement, and put up the excuse that she did not want to be made a medium of. I say 'put up' because in subsequent tests when I held thoughts "for her" of absent friends she did not rebel, but in many instances repeated them.

This same medium at another time, gave a successful reading of the contents of an hyperdermic vial of sulphate of morphia, not only describing the drug, but showing in her own person its physiological action. The vial was wrapped in paper until it made a very large package and every physical effort made to deceive her, but I held the drug and its action in my mind,studiously avoiding naming it mentally until she had shown the different symptoms—some of which are not known to the laity—and as she herself, afterward stated, not previously known to her, namely, that morphine in minute doses is a stimulant. She responded to the thought held in my mind, no word being spoken for some minutes. She flushed and showed every sign of increased heart action. Then she placed her hand to her head and finally on her stomach, blanched and showed marked symptoms of nausea. She was evidently "proving" the drug, as the homeopathist would say, without knowing that she held any drug in her hand.

Finally she read the name of the drug in my mind and exclaimed "Oh, it's a drug, take it away," and very ungraciously proceeded to throw the package at me, an act wholly out of keeping with her ordinary ladylike demeanor but fully justified by the circumstances. This test was not premeditated but was sprung on the medium in the presence of the Rev. Dr. Winbigler, of Philadelphia, after she had made quite a successful reading of a letter given her by him.

From these and hundreds of other tests made during the past twenty-five years, I am a firm believer in telepathy. The operation of an organic brain in the production of thought sets up vibrations which pass out into space, going on and on forever. The ether fairly teems with the vibrating thoughts of the bygone ages and all that is necessary to become possessed of this store of universal knowledge is to become sensitive to ether vibrations, and learn how to translate them into ordinary language. Without such ability they are as Greek to the illiterate.

Upon this same premise we may interpret the phenomena of death apparitions. A person in extremis may send out very intense thought vibrations which go on and on until they find a recipient. This is generally some near relative, who by reason of consanguinity has a similar vibratory note, consequently is enabled to receive and possibly translate the message into language. No ground is found however, on this theory to help spiritualists, for disembodied spirits are not possessed of organic brains and consequently cannot produce organic vibrations recognizable on this plane. The necessity for translation is absolute, otherwise the messages could not be made available. It is impossible to understand these indelible records of the past except we can translate them into object presentations and read them out loud, so to speak, in the language with which we are accustomed to think.

It is impossible to know the abstract except it be projected in terms of sense perception, in other words, except it be materialized. It is this very fact that makes it necessary for psychometrists and crystal gazers to have some object upon which to fix the attention. The controls, so universal with trance mediums, also serve the same purpose. namely, they objectively voice the subjective, and serve to bring it above the threshold of consciousness, thus making it "knowable."

The pen in the hand of the automatic writer,and planchette, are also of similar import.

In closing I wish to be understood as not disavowing belief in all spiritistic phenomena, or as discrediting the observations of the British Society for Psychical Research, nor the later work of Profs. James and Hyslop along these lines. Their investigations have seemed to promise light upon an hitherto dark subject.

To my mind the subject stands just where it did before Mrs. Piper made her disavowal.

When she avows her belief in telepathy, and puts that force forward as an explanation for the wonderful revelations she has made in the past, she is not explaining the character of the communication, or in anyway simplifying the subject, but the rather, making it the more complex.

What she has done however, has been to convict herself of incompetency to testify in a court of scientific inquiry, not because her former testimony was not true, but because her claim and her record show that she is possessed of mediumistic powers and is the mouthpiece for passing thought vibrations. Therefore she is not a competent judge of the phenomena, even though she be the medium of its manifestation.

The situation is not altered in the least by her confession. The question is still one for the Society of Psychical Research, and Profs. James and Hyslop have the floor.

SPIRITISM, TELEPATHY, HYPNOTISM AND THE CASE OF MRS. PIPER.

BY T. D. CROTHERS, M. D., OF HARTFORD, CONN.,
Vice President Medico-Legal Society.

To one who makes the mental phenomena of spirit and drug takers a study, a field of most bewildering psychic movements appear. The laws of dissolution become so sharply defined, as to bring into prominence laws of evolution, and signs of unknown psychic forces. Theories of explanation termed spiritism, telepathy, clairvoyance, subliminal consciousness, and so on, are illustrated by numerous examples in this field, which separately sustain widely different theories, but collectively bring confusion to the subiect. The persons in whom these examples occur are called border-liners, or those who live on the frontier of insanity, and whose mental health varies widely. As illustrative of some of the phenomena frequently noted, the following may be given: A spirit drinker after a prolonged attack believes he is about to die; the friends are gathered about the bedside; he talks of the spirit world, and describes the condition of friends over there. repeating their advice to the living. He is considered a medium of great power, and his communications are accepted as conclusive evidence of spiritism.

An opium smoker has similar periods of great mental and emotional exhaltation, during which he utters most startling predictions of coming events, and which occasionally happen as predicted. He is also a medium, and spirits talk and write through him to their friends here. He describes persons and events that seem beyond his knowledge and experience, and after a few hours of this mental ectasy, he sleeps awaking later a stupid, dull man. Other persons using spirits or drugs to excess will not infrequently have what is called deliriums of great mental exhaltation (of brief duration,) in which they will make statements and describe events that are unexplainable.

When these deliriums are extreme in wildness, there will occur flashes of good judgment and superior reasoning, that seem like intuition. Predictions of themselves and their friends; of what should be done, and the results that follow are most startling in accuracy. Instances like the following are not uncommon: A wife, mother, or other relative of an inebriate will be able to follow them in a large city; tell where they are at a certain time of day. The inebriate may not have been heard from directly in many days, and there can be no reason for locating them in any particular place, and yet we have been written to send a man to such a place to find him.

A father who was a drinking man came from San Francisco to find his son, who was also a drinking man and who had disappeared some months before, and supposed to have gone to Europe.

The father was confident that his son would reach New York on a certain day, and go to New Haven the day following. He came to Hartford to arrange for his son's admission to our hospital, then went to New Haven and found his son as expected twenty-four hours later. In this the father had no visible clue, or means of knowing the movements of his son. His habit was to drink to a semi-stuporous stage, and then tell where his son was, and what he was doing. The son was an extremely erratic, genteel tramp, who drank some all the time, but was seldom stupid. There seemed to be a certain affinity with the father after a certain stage in the drinking was reached, but before that they were mentally antagonistic. A man of some prominence in his profession, and highly cultivated, was a periodical drinker, and after he began to drink, he would dictate to his clerk several days in advance his movements and personal happenings, which would occur. This would be carried out literally, and the predictions of what would happen to him were equally exact and startling in fulfillment. The explanation by his friends included many theories of spiritism, clarivoyance and subliminal consciousness.

Opium and other drug delusional states bring out many mysterious facts of the movement of psychic forces, along the lines of dissolution. Several persons are confident that studies from this side are valuable, and that they will disclose many facts. From my own experience the phenomena manifested by the disordered brain, fails to support any one theory of spiritism, or telepathy, but rather points to forces and laws infinitely more complex and less simple. The very close resemblance of the mind reader, the medium, and the hypnotist, to those who live on the frontiers of insanity, suggest phases of dissolution, rather than evolution in the higher activities.

So much of the strange and mysterious in mental phenomena is due to physical causes, that the elimination of errors from this source is extremely difficult. Hence it follows that any credulous story of phenomena used to support a theory of psychic forces and laws, is open to question and doubt. As in observations of the heavens, both the observer, the means of observation, and the phenomena studied, all need verifying,and correction by others,before they can be accepted as facts, or even approximate facts. Mrs. Piper's manifestations and the critical study by Professor Hyslop should be received as probable evidence needing further study and examination, and while apparently supporting the theories of telepathy, are not conclusive.

Theories of mind reading and spirit influences of departed friends, clairvoyance and subliminal self, are too simple; the psychic forces and laws which govern brain action extend far beyond these narrow limits. The recent explanation of the great facts of electrical waves in wireless telegraphy give distinct hints of what is called physical forces, which may extend into the psychic, and perhaps is another form of force emanating from the brain, as well as from the generated electricity.

The form of transmission of thought depends on the propulsion of certain electrical waves whose vibrations are in exact rhythm,and strike on a receiver arranged to respond to the same rate of vibration. When the instrument to send the current, and the one to receive it, are timed or arranged on the same key, the transmission of the vibrations which are formed into words, go on irrespective of distance. These intangible shocks or waves of force, are read on receivers keyed to catch them. Thought may be projected and read by minds tuned to the same rhythm, regardless of space and physical obstacles.

For a long time the X-Ray, produced by an electrical current, was supposed to be a most wonderful light penetrating substance, and enabling us to see what was previously unknown. Recently this ray was found not to depend on machines for its production, but to exist in many substances in the earth, which can be demonstrated in the laboratory. It is called a crystallized solidified light, stored up from past ages, which from treatment in the laboratory can be made to give out its rays, furnishing a supply of light that is inexhaustible. Professor Thompson says a thousand grains of this illuminating earth on the ceiling of a room would furnish light for centuries. Yet this is nothing compared with the storing, reception, and emanating forces of the brain. The great waves of public opinion which dominate the years and ages, and the rise and growth of ideas and thought, are not accidents, but the operation of unknown forces. As in wireless telegraphy, and the X-Ray, there is something more than the course medium for the transmission of thought. The batteries of the brain, and the force generators and receivers, are yet to be discovered. The effort to make the phenomena explain and support a theory is not scientific. Mrs. Piper's ability to do what is unexplainable from our present limited knowledge, only deepens the mystery, and rouses keener interest to be informed of the laws and movements of thought. The Society for Psychical Research is approaching this realm on the side of exact science. It is in this field that medico-legal studies are most practical. The grouping of the exact facts, and their analysis and meaning, will show the laws which enabled Mrs. Piper to make answer to questions that seemed beyond her knowledge. The Scotch verdict of "not proven," can be urged with scientific accuracy to-day, and we wait for farther particulars necessary for conclusive evidence.

SPIRITISM AND MRS. LEONORA PIPER.

BY DR. WILLIAM LEE HOWARD, OF BALTIMORE, MD.

As Doctor Hudson states: "Never before in the history of the scientific investigation of modern spiritism have the conditions been so favorable for the production of decisive results; one way or the other, as in this case." In my opinion the investigations have resulted in weakening the spiritistic theory and strengthening the somatic, or telepathic. The various phenomena demonstrated in the Piper investigations —and all other alleged spiritistic phenomena—have their origin and activity in abnormal development or states of the psychic centers, and are part of every human being's mundane physiologic life.

Too many physiologic phenomena have been readily accepted as proofs of spiritism, and as "the wish is father to the thought" the scientific analysis of the facts have seldom been carried out. The pleasing and satisfactory acceptance of spiritistic evidence by individuals untrained in physiologic psychology, is not surprising to the neurologist who is daily brought in contact with cases of auto-suggestion,the unstable neurotic with fervid desires for the occult, and with the many half baked and half prepared intellects which can easily accept psychic phenomena as supernormal facts, but in whose untrained brains the physiologic conditions underlying psychic phenomena are laborious and difficult to comprehend.

Telepathy is the explanation, in my opinion, of all the phenomena witnessed by the conscientious observers in the Piper investigations. It is not necessary here for me to go into the evidence we have of telepathy being a normal—in a psychologic sense—attribute of sub-conscious activity. We have too many scientific facts to convince us of the mundane cause of telepathy, while we have not one single satisfactory

Read before the Medico-Legal Society and Psychological Section, February 19th, 1902.

fact to make us think for a moment of any supermundane explanation for the phenomenon. "It would require but one demonstrated case of survival of personal consciousness after the death of the body, to prove the essential claim of spiritism—future life." (Hudson.) No such single case has ever been known. That is, no case of evidential structure strong enough to withstand the cold, penetrating rays of science.

I relate the following incident as an example of the readily accepted evidence of supernormal existence. My valet, Bruno, is a young German who I brought from Berlin, and who has become, through a course of training, a remarkable psychic subject. He has been examined by a large number of eminent medical and scientific men who have been intensely interested in his remarkable susceptibility to suggestion. One evening in the presence of five gentlemen, two of whom were German, I hypnotized Bruno,and in a whisper inaudible to anyone but the subject, suggested he was Bismarck. This done, I sat down at the other end of the room, my mind passive. Then issued from the mouth of this delicate young man a wonderful speech. It was an oration teeming with Latin phrases, voluminous quotations and fiery denunciation. The tone was Bismarckian, the language scholarly,and the gestures vehement. The spectators were astounded;and wonderment was depicted on their countenances. When it was over, one asked Bruno if he saw the spirit of Bismarck, and he answered: "Yes, he comes in to me, that's all I know, Herr ——." With one exception the spectators were all religious men, pronounced churchmen, and trammeled by the training of early superstition. A lucidly written explanation sent the next day, has not convinced them of the satisfactory fact—satisfactory to minds trained by broad thinking —that all the phenomena they witnessed were just as certainly physiologic facts as are the variations of the pulse rate.

Doctor Hudson says in his able analysis of Professor Hyslop's report: "It is known, however, that relatives and friends are either actually or potentially en rapport at all times." I think this statement should be qualified; for while we know that many relatives and some dear friends are frequently en rapport, we do not know for a certainty—that is scientific certainty—to what extent the rapport exists, nor do we know much about the potential element existing in untried cases.

Professor Hyslop evidently wises to prove that the conditions and results were such as to eliminate telepathy; yet he gives us no satisfactory reasons or such an attitude, and, as said above we have never had ny scientific, or authentic, evidences at any time in the history of the world of any but somatic—or psychic—phenomena.

Psychic lucidity, or the memor and experience of the subliminal self, has its limitations; just such limitations as Mrs. Piper's subliminal self demonstrated. Hesitancy, inability to give names, maladroit explaations and oftimes failure, these are conditions found in sujects partially or completely autohypnotized, and due to the inability of the subconscious memory in the passive subect to completely submerge the conscious.

It is scarcely conceivable that spirit power, did such exist, would have the limitations just mentioned. If so, I hope I shall never be a spirit. I prefer to lie undisturbed.

Mrs. Piper has no self knowledge of what she, as percipient, gives to her investigators. She is a very sensitive psychic who seems ever en rapport with Prof. Hyslop; who, also, seems to have no self knowledge of his condition.

The assertion made by Professor Hyslop that spirits have but little power to remember mundane things—that is, that their memory is limited, while telepathy has no limitation, is certainly an extraordinary statement. Until Prof. Hyslop explains how he obtained such positive knowledge of the memory limits of spirits, I do not feel justified in further analyzing his report.

RESULTS OF PSYCHICAL RESEARCH.

BY REV. MINOT J. SAVAGE, D. D.

"It—the Society's work—is the most important work which is being done in the world—by far the most important."
—GLADSTONE.

The Society of Psychical Research was organized in England in the year 1882. Its first president was Professor H. Sidgwick, of Cambridge. It is well known that he is one of the greatest ethical writers of the age. He challenged the common sense, the intellect and the scientific knowledge of England by the statement that it was a "scandal" that such alleged facts should go so long without any serious attempt at investigation. He was president of the society from 1882 to 1884. He was followed by Professor Balfour Stewart, F. R. S., who held the position from 1885 to 1887. Then from 1888 to 1892 Sidgwick again took the presidency. In the year 1893, the Rt. Hon. A. J. Balfour, M. P., F. R, S., was

Contributed to the Medico-Legal Society and its Psychological Section by the author, through the courtesy of Ainslee's Magazine.

NOTE—By the Editor.

Rev. Minot J. Savage had accepted the invitation of the President of the Medico-Legal Society, for the December meeting, and his name was printed in the programme, but the state of his health and other causes prevented his coming, which he explained.

Later, when the discussion was resumed at the February meeting, he again wrote that he would be present and he was again announced to take part in the discussion. Again circumstances prevented his attendance, and he was so sure of attending that he gave no notice, and his seat was reserved till the end of the session.

The Society voted that his paper be printed as if he had attended, and the state of his health forbidding his attempting the preparation of a formal paper, he wrote suggesting that the Society accept the paper he had prepared on the subject for Ainslee's Magazine as a favor to him, which would appear in the March number of that magazine, or such extracts from it as would meet the editor's approval, with consent of that periodical.

Ainslee's Magazine, on learning of the situation, most kindly consented that the article by Dr. Savage might appear in the Journal, and its compilation of the papers on this theme by all the authors, and our members and readers are indebted to the courtesy of that magazine for the paper Dr. Savage contributes to the discussion.

president. He was succeeded by Professor William James, of Harvard, for the years 1894 and 1895. From 1896 to 1899, the position was held by Sir William Crookes, F. R. S., the inventor of the famous Crookes tube, which was the stepping-stone to the discovery of the X-rays. During the year 1900, Frederick W. H. Myers held the presidency. The present president is Dr. Oliver Lodge, F. R. S., a prominent member of the British Association for the Advancement of Science. These men are mentioned as indicating the kind of persons in England who have been willing to enter upon this work. The society in this country was organized in 1885. After a time it was found better to make the American society a branch of the English, so as to give its members the advantage of the work done on the other side of the sea.

One of the first, and as a preliminary, one of the most important results of the society so far has been to make the study respectable. Under the shadow of these great names a man can look into these things without having his sanity impeached. "Good society," to be sure, has as yet no place for it, and one's friends may regard him with a tolerant smile; but he can investigate as much as he pleases now, without being regarded as anything worse than "peculiar."

There are many reasons why these matters should be studied. There are thousands of people in the modern world, to speak within limits, who are accepting reports of such stories as true, and who are shaping their lives by the beliefs which are connected with them. It seems to me clear that the matter involved compels us to choose one of two alternatives. We are here face to face with the greatest truth of the universe, or else with the most lamentable delusion, one or the other; and I, for one, cannot conceive that there is any other problem more important to be decided upon.

The kinds of facts which constitute the subject matter of the society's investigation are not at all new.

Reports of happenings of this kind are inextricably bound up with the origin, the contents and the history of every religion on the face of the earth. Indeed, it is hardly too much to say that they are the visible roots out of which the religions have sprung. They are the credentials which have been offered to authenticate all the revelations. Every religion is full of them; every Bible is full of them. In making this statement, the Hebrew and Christian religions and Bibles are not excepted. Apparitions, visions, dreams, voices, spiritual and mental exaltations supposed to be connected with the communication of divine truth, transfigurations, levitations, annunciations, warnings—what are these but supposed facts woven into the very warp and woof of all the religions? They are of precisely the same kind as those alleged facts which are asserted to be taking place to-day, and which it is the object of the Society for Psychical Research to investigate. These alleged facts, then, are not new. Sporadic cases have been reported from all over the world and through all time.

The history of the world is full of reported apparitions or ghosts. Do such things as ghosts exist? I am perfectly certain that they do. This does not mean that I feel that I am ready to explain their origin or nature. I simply recognize the fact. Whether they are purely subjective or whether they represent some objective reality—this is a question to be settled in each particular case. I have many instances in my notes; but they must be omitted for the present.

There is one case, however, which is of a very extraordinary kind. It occurred about a couple of years ago here in the immediate vicinity of New York. There was a certain young man who had been studying abroad. He had been at Heidelberg University. He was of anything but an imaginative temperament. Tall and stalwart in build, he had a reputation as an athlete. His favorite studies were mathematical, physical and electrical. He had returned home from abroad, and so far as anybody knew, was in perfect health. He was at the summer home of his mother. It was his habit, after dinner, to go out on the piazza and walk up and down while smoking his pipe. One evening he came quietly in, and without talking with anybody, went up to bed.The next morning he went into his mother's room before she was up, and laid his hand on her cheek in order to awaken her quietly. Then he said, "Mother, I have something very sad to tell you. You must brace yourself and be strong to bear it." Of course she was startled and asked him what he was talking about. He said, "Mother, I mean just what I am saying. I am going to die, and very soon."

When his mother, startled and troubled, pressed him for an explanation, he said: "Last night, when I was walking up and down the piazza, smoking, a spirit appeared and walked up and down by my side. I have received my call, and am going to die." The mother, of course, was seriously troubled, and wondered whether anything might be the matter with him. She therefore sent for the doctor and told him the story. The doctor made a careful examination, said there was nothing the matter, treated the whole thing as a bad dream or an hallucination, and told them that within a few days they would be laughing at themselves for letting such a thing worry them. The next morning the young man did not seem quite as well as usual, and the doctor was sent for a second time. Again he said there was nothing the matter, and tried to laugh them out of their fears. The third morning the young man appeared in still poorer condition, and the third time the physician was summoned. He now discovered a case of appendicitis. The young man was operated on and died in a couple of days. From the time of the vision until his death not more than five days had gone by. Some time after this experience the mother visited a psychic here in New York. She made no previous appointment, but went as a perfect stranger and waited her turn. The son claimed at once to be present, and told his mother a whole series of very remarkable things, which by no possibility could the psychic ever have known. Then, in answer to the question, "Who was it that you saw that night?" (the question being purposely so framed as not to seem to refer to any one out of the body), he at once replied: "It was my father." The father had been dead for some years, and the mother had been married again.

Telekinesis is the technical term which psychical researchers have agreed to use as covering cases of the movement of physical objects, which seem to require as explanation some force other than muscular, or, indeed, any kind which is ordinarily recognized by science. Space will not permit my detailing experiences of this kind. I wish however, to note that they exist, and must be dealt with as a part of the problem.

I wish now to detail as briefly as possible, and yet with some clearness, a considerable number of typical cases which are generally classed as mental phenomena. My purpose in this is to place the intelligent reader in such a position that he may be able to make up his own mind as to what theory seems best fitted to account for the facts. The two theories which at present are rivals in the field will be presented and dealt with after the cases are outlined.

I prefer to deal chiefly with such occurrences as I have been personally familiar with. Almost all of them find their parallels in the published proceedings of the Society for Psychical Research; but in detailing cases which I have personally known there are two advantages. First, they are of course fresher and more vivid in my recollection; and, secondly, they will serve the purpose of re-enforcing and confirming the observations and experiences of others which have been already published.

First, I had sittings with Mrs. Piper years ago, before the society was organized or her name was publicly known. On the occasion of my first visit to her, she was, I think, in a little house on Pinckney Street, in Boston. At this time she went into a trance, but talked instead of writing. She described my father and my half-brother, neither of whom she had ever seen. She described the death of this half-brother which took place in Michigan long before. But details of this are omitted for lack of space.

Second. Mrs. Piper had moved from the West End of Boston to a house in Roxbury. My daughter made an engagement for a sitting with her. She did this through a friends who was living in Roxbury, having this friend write the letter making the appointment, and having the reply come to her house under an assumed name, at least two miles away from where I was then living. My daughter went to meet the appointment, of course utterly unknown. A friend had given her three locks of hair. She placed them in a book, one at the front, one at the back, and one in the middle, so that they should not come in contact with each other. She knew nothing about them, not even as to whether they had been cut from the heads of people living or dead. After Mrs. Piper had gone into a trance, these locks of hair were placed in her hand, one after another. She told all about them, gave the names, the name of the friend who had asked her to take them, told whose heads they were from, whether they were dead or living, and in regard to one of them, asked why they had cut it off at the extreme end of the hair where it was lifeless, instead of taking a lock nearer the head. My daughter, of course, did not know whether any of the names given or the statements made were correct or not. She made notes, however, and found that Mrs. Piper had been accurate in every particular.

Third. I have a lady friend who was the daughter of a New England clergyman, and whose husband in later years was also a minister. When she was a girl, this mediumistic power, whatever it may be, would take possession of her, not only without her will, but sometimes against it. She never sat for pay, but would occasionally oblige a friend who desired to witness experiments of this sort. One day a young German, apparently a "gentleman," whom she had never seen before, came and begged of her to give him a sitting. He said he had heard of her power, and had a very important reason for his request. She consented, and among other things, began, as she supposed, to jabber in the use of sounds which to her were without any meaning. When the influence had left her, she felt troubled and ashamed, and was going to apologize by explaining that she had seemed forced ot utter these sounds and was not able to control herself. The young German told her she need not apologize or explain. He said she had rendered him an incalculable service. He assured her that she had been speaking German, that his father had been talking to him. Then he went on to explain that this father had died suddenly, leaving his business affairs entangled so that they were utterly unable to straighten them out. This, he said, his father had now given him through her, and that the matter was perfectly plain. He wanted to pay her liberally for the service, but she declined. He afterwards sent her a valuable present as an expression of his gratitude.

Fourth. I now come to refer to a class of experiences of the most remarkable sort. To go into this with sufficient detail to make the whole matter perfectly clear, would necessitate the writing of a small volume. A few years ago there was a famous preacher to the poor in the City of Boston.

He and his wife both were particularly interested in those who had few other friends. They used to refer to these people as "my poor." In the old age of this minister he had a colleague. Both he and his colleague were intensely orthodox in their views, and naturally had nothing whatever to do with occult phenomena. After the minister's death, his former parishioners, these poor people, were naturally scattered in different parts of the city. Some of them in course of time moved to the suburbs, and even to other towns further away. It is a common objection brought against these manifestations that they seem matters only to amuse the curious, and never show an interest in any serious work of any kind. Now come some hints as to the nature of certain extraordinary facts. I asked the privilege of writing a small book detailing many of these experiences at length some years ago, but received a message purporting to come from the other side, forbidding my doing it. The reason given was that it would call attention to what was going on and interfere with the work. The work referred to was like this. For a series of years a loving labor of charity and help was carried on, involving no glory, no notoriety, no publicity, but the opposite. It cost effort and money to carry on this work, and nobody but two or three intimate friends were ever let into the secret. The widow of the colleague of this old clergyman was the "medium." She had never herself seen a medium in her life. She had had nothing whatever to do with ordinary spiritualism, did not believe in it, and, in fact, was opposed to it. She was, and is still, if living, not only orthodox, but intensely religious in her feelings. Such, then, was the situation. This old clergyman and his wife were the claimed agents in the unseen, who spoke through this widow of his former colleague, and made her the agent in their charitable undertakings. She lived in a town not far from the City of Boston. She would receive orders to go into town to such a street and such a number, and would be told that there she would find such and such a person or persons in such or such a condition, and she was to render them the service that was needed. Cases like this occurred over and over again. She would follow these directions, knowing absolutely nothing about the case except that which had thus been told her, and she said that there was never a mistake made. She always found the person and the condition as they had been described to her, and she did for them what their case required. In one instance she traveled to a city in another state under orders like these, knowing not even the name of the person she was to seek out, except that which had been told her. She found the case, however, as it had been reported, and rendered the called-for assistance. Not all of these were cases of mere physical need. Some of them were instances of rescue from moral peril, the description of which would read like a chapter in a sensational story. As a part of this general ministry, another happening is worthy of record. The daughter of this old minister received explicit orders claiming to come from her father, and through his colleague's widow as the medium, to enclose twenty dollars in an envelope and send it to another town, directing it to an address of which she had never heard. She hesitated about sending the money in this way, and wanted to wait and get a check so as to avoid risk of loss. She was peremptorily ordered, however, not to wait, as the matter was one of immediate and vital importance. She sent the money as thus directed, two ten-dollar bills. I have had the privilege of reading the letter acknowledging its receipt. It was written with difficulty, in the use of a lead pencil, and the grammar and spelling were poor. One could, however, almost hear the drip of tears as he read it. It told a story of abuse and desertion on the part of her husband. The forsaken wife had done all she could to keep her little family together. She had reached the end of her endeavor, had just pawned her last bit of decent furniture, and with the proceeds had bought some charcoal and was making preparations to go out of the world and take her children with her when the money arrived.

Fifth. There are cases of prophesy—I only note the fact; but cannot stop for special instances.

Sixth. (Under this head, I will only say that, at my request, the invisible intelligence has sometimes gone away for me, found out some fact unknown to any one present, then come back and told me about it.

Seventh. I have already referred to one case where the invisible intelligence goes at my request to find out something and report to me. This was in the city. I now refer to another illustration of the same kind, only more remarkable still. In this case the invisible intelligence went at my desire and reported occurrences taking place at the time in the State of Maine.

Eighth. I was having a sitting in my study with a friend, a psychic. During this sitting I held an hour's conversation with what was claimed to be a "dead" friend—as natural a conversation as I ever had with her living. The psychic did not know that such a friend had ever lived.

I was holding sittings with this friend, acting as psychic, once a week. Soon after this, at the very beginning of our next sitting, this same friend claimed to be present, and at once began to tell me of mental experiences and sufferings through which her sister in Maine was at that time passing. The psychic knew nothing whatever of this sister, and I was entirely ignorant of the existence of the troubles referred to. The communicator calling her sister by name, said, "She is passing through the greatest sorrow of her life. I wish I could make her know that I care. I wish you would write to her for me." When I asked her the nature of the trouble, there was a distinct and definite hesitancy about replying. The impression made on me was that I was treading on delicate ground, and that the question was being considered as to whether I had better be told. At last, as though no other way out of it was seen, she told me that the difficulty was caused by the unfaithfulness and cruelty of her sister's husband. I had never seen this husband but once, and had no way of knowing that the marriage was not perfectly happy. I wrote a letter of inquiry, however, asking whether any special trouble existed, and if the nature of it was such as to make it possible for me to be told what it was. I received a letter by return mail, confirming every word that had been told me, and begging me that the letter might be burned as soon as it was read. In this letter there was a little human touch that impressed me a good deal. What claimed to be the sister in the invisible, had said, "I wish I could make her know that I care." In the letter I received from Maine there was the same human feeling out after sympathy which had appeared on the invisible side. She wrote: "When my sister was alive I had some one to whom I could go in my troubles. Now I am all alone." I confess that this attempting to bridge the gulf by these corresponding outreachings for human sympathy seems to me most natural and very impressive. The peculiarity of this experience lies in the fact that here the intelligence in Boston, which has shown itself capable of telling where a person is and what she is doing two hundred miles way, now reaches beyond the external physical facts, and gets at the existence of secret sorrows of the heart and comes and tells me of them in the most natural and simple way in the world. And these were precisely such things as this friend would have come to me with had she been living and able to do so. At the same time, let me repeat, they were things of which the psychic by no possibility could have known anything, or of which I should have even dreamed or guessed, and that they came to me with a great shock not only of sorrow, but of surprise.

Ninth. I am now to detail a little experience which seems to me to have about it certain features which are very unusual, and therefore worthy of special remark. Never in my life, until my son died two years ago, did I attempt to get into communication with any special person at any sitting held with any medium. I have alweys taken the attitude of a student trying to solve the general problem involved. On two or three occasions, however, within the last two years, I have tried to see if I could get anything that appeared to be a message from my boy. He died two years ago last June at the age of thirty-one. I was having a sitting with Mrs. Piper. My son claimed to be present. Excluding for the moment all other things, I wish definitely to outline this one little experience. At the time of his death he was occupying a room with a medical student and an old personal friend, on Joy Street, in Boston. He had moved there from a room he occupied on Beacon Street since I had visited him, so that I never had been in his present room. I knew nothing about it whatever, and could not even have guessed as to anything concerning it which he might say. He said: "Papa (and this with a great deal of earnestness) I want you to go at once to my room. Look in my drawer and you will find there a lot of loose papers. Among them are some which I wish you to take and destroy at once." He would not be satisfied until I had promised to do this. Mrs. Piper, remember, was in a dead trance at the time, and her hand was writing. She had no personal acqaintance with my son, and, so far as I know, had never seen him. I submit that this reference to loose notes and papers which for some unknown reason he was anxious to have destroyed is something which would be beyond the range of guesswork, even had Mrs. Piper been conscious. Though my boy and I had been intimate heart-friends all our lives, this request was utterly inexplicable to me. It did not even enter into my mind to give a wild guess as to what he meant, or why he wanted this thing done. I went, however, to his room, searched his drawer, gathered up all the loose papers, looked through them, and at once saw the meaning and importance of what he had asked me to do. There were things there which he had jotted down and trusted to the privacy of his drawer which he would not have had made public for the world.

Tenth. Years ago, a world-famous naturalist came to Boston and delivered a course of lectures before the Lowell Institute. He had been trained in his youth as a clergyman of the Church of England. He told me that in his early life he had looked upon all these matters with contempt, but had been startled into making them a study by some personal experience. The result of it was that he and other friends organized a circle composed of sixteen people. They held sittings every week when they were in London, during a period of seven years. There was no one possessing mediumistic powers in this circle at the time when they began the sittings; but as they went on, psychic powers of every description were developed within the limits of their own membership. Among these sixteen are the names of people known all over the world, and who would be readily recognized if I should mention them. It would seem like a chapter out of the "Arabian Nights" if I should detail the things which this naturalist told me as having occurred at their sittings. What I have said is only an extraordinary introduction to one little incident which I wish to detail. This naturalist himself became an automatic writer. One member of the circle had a brother who was an officer in the army. They had talked over these things, and the brother had promised that if he died first he would try, if possible, to communicate. This gentleman came into the private room of the naturalist one day and said, "I wish you would see if you can get any writing." He did not feel like it, but as a matter of accommodation sat down and took paper and pen. Pretty soon his hand began to move, made certain meaningless scrawls at first, and then began to string letters together in the form of words. As, however, he looked on what he had written, it seemed to him without any meaning. He told me that if they were words at all, they were not words in any language with which he was acquainted. The friend asked him what he had obtained, and he remarked, carelessly, "Oh, nothing. It's nonsense; at any rate, it has no meaning to me." Whereupon, the friend himself came and looked over the paper, and started with surprise. He said, "Perhaps it has no meaning for you, but it has all the meaning in the world for me." And then he explained that this brother, who at this time was dead, had made up certain words out of his own head. They were not words in any language, but they were arbitrary arrangements of letters which appeared like words. He had given these to his brother, and had said, "If I can ever come to you I will bring these as a test. If I do not bring them, you need not believe that it is I." And here the naturalist, in absolute ignorance of these facts, had reproduced the identical combinations of letters which the officer years before had made as a proposed test for his brother.

[*To be Continued.*]

SPIRITISM AND MRS. PIPER.

BY RICHARD HODGSON, LL. D., OF BOSTON, MASS.

The secretary and treasurer of the American Branch of the Society for Psychical Research, was requested by the President of the Medico-Legal Society to make a short contribution to this discussion, so that his position and views might not be misunderstood, and that his personal knowledge of various subjects connected with the controversy, might be correctly stated and understood. His reply is as follows:—

Boston, Mass., March 6th, 1902

Dear Mr. Bell.—Concerning the statements attributed to Mrs. Piper in, and following, the various papers of October 20, 1901, it is quite clear that for a short time in the summer of 1901, Mrs. Piper thought, and was persuaded to allow the expression of her opinion to the effect, that her manifestations might be explicable on the hypothesis of telepathy from living persons.

What she really wished to say was that she did not make any claim that so-called discarnate spirits controlled her. She did not affirm that spirits controlled her, but, on the other hand, she was unwilling to commit herself to the view that spirits did control her. She wished it clearly understood that she made no claim one way or the other, and that she did not really know what the true explanation of her manifestations was.

The statement, which appeared in the New York Herald of Oct. 20th, and several other papers, was not drawn up by Mrs. Piper herself. It contains only a few fragments of statements made by her.

In my own view, Mrs. Piper's opinion, in any case, is of no value. She herself in past years has never had any opportunity of arriving independently at any definite conclusion by any investigation of her own, and she is, of course, not competent herself to deal with such a complicated problem. She herself has sometimes felt, owing to ignorance of her own work, and the reticence maintained by myself and other sitters, as if she would like to stop sitting altogether, and so put aside what to her has always seemed a mystery, which she herself had no hope of solving. There was never any agreement between Mrs. Piper and the Society for Psychical Research as such.

Her agreement for sittings since the beginning of 1897, was with the trance personality spoken of as "Imperator," and she has kept her agreement. She gave a sitting to myself on October 21st, 1901, in accordance with the injunctions given to her on the previous April by "Imperator." On October 21st, she received further instructions not to sit again for twelve weeks. She resumed her sittings on January 13th, and she has been sitting regularly ever since.

Mrs. Piper made some statements to reporters connected with the Boston Daily Advertiser and the Boston Morning Journal. I enclose you the cuttings from these papers in which the statements made by Mrs. Piper were re-produced.

Mrs. Piper's feeling in the summer that she would stop sitting altogether, represented merely a transient mood. The verbatim statements attributed to Mrs. Piper and myself in the Boston Morning Journal of October 29th, are given with substantial accuracy.

You can make any public use of this letter that you please, and of course you can use anything that appeared in the cuttings which I enclose.

Yours Sincerely,

R. HODGSON.

The extracts to which Dr. Hodgson refers, are as follow:

That from the Boston Morning Journal of October 29th, 1901, is as follows:

"MRS. PIPER AND DR. HODGSON REACH AN ARRANGEMENT."

Mrs. Leonora E. Piper, the medium, and Richard Hodgson, LL. D., Secretary of the Society for Psychical Research, have come to an understanding. Any differences that may have existed between them have been reconciled. Mrs. Piper will continue her sittings according to agreement, and the relations that have existed between her and the society will not be broken.

Yesterday Dr. Hodgson saw Mrs. Piper and talked with her about the statement which appeared in the New York Herald. Afterwards both, by appointment, were seen by a Boston Journal reporter and their statements agree as to future relations.

Dr. Hodgson feels that the incident is closed, and Mrs. Piper, as will be seen from her statement, holds the same view. She has been distressed by the criticism and publicity to which she has been subjected, and desires to let the whole matter drop from now on.

"EVERYTHING WILL GO ON."

(By Mrs. L. E. Piper.)

"Everything will go on just as it has previously, so far as I am concerned. I will continue my agreement with the trance personality Imperator.

"Regardless of whatever may have been said I will go on with the present arrangement with Dr. Hodgson and the society, as formerly.

"I do not deny that I said something to the effect that I would never hold another sitting with Mr. Hodgson, and that I would die first, to a New York Herald reporter last summer, when I gave the original interview, but last week I did not see a representative of the New York Herald and did not reply to Dr. Hodgson. That is a misrepresentation, and, furthermore, I am not responsible for many of the former statements that the Herald published as coming from me."

WILL KEEP AGREEMENT.

(By Dr. R. Hodgson.)

"Mrs. Piper has told me to-day that she proposes to keep her agreement with Imperator, and she also said that she made no statement last week such as appeared in the New York Herald on Thursday. That statement was taken from the old interview.

"When I left her to-day Mrs. Piper said: 'Of course I shall keep my agreement with Imperator.'"

The editor of Boston Morning Journal continues:

NOT "SPIRITISTIC."

The next sitting, according to arrangements, will not be held for about three months.

Mrs. Piper still holds and expresses her view that the manifestations are not spiritistic. In this opinion she differs from Dr. Hodgson, but agrees with Prof. James. She feels that the telepathic theory is more probable than the spiritistic hypothesis, and her opinion is derived from intelligent study of the reports of the Society for Psychical Research in addition to other literature.

There is no doubt of Mrs. Piper's perfect honesty in the matter. She is unwilling to have it appear that she believes herself capable of communicating with discarnate spirits, but she admits the mysterious power is not easily understood or accounted for.

The Boston Advertiser of the date of October 25th contained the following announcement to which Dr. Hodgson alludes in the following letter:

MRS. PIPER'S OWN DENIAL.

Boston Advertiser, Oct. 25, '01.

Arlington, Oct. 24.—Mrs. Leonora Piper dictated this statement to a representative of this paper tonight:—

"I did not make any such statement as that published in the New York Herald to the effect that spirits of the departed do not control me. The article says:

"I most truthfully say that I do not believe that spirits of the dead have spoken through me, when I have been in the trance state as investigated by scientific men of Boston and Cambridge and the English Psychical Research Society, when I was taken to England to be studied. It may be that they have, but I do not affirm it."

"I did not make that statement.

"My opinion is today as it was 18 years ago.

"Spirits of the departed may have controlled me and they may not, I confess that I do not know.

"I have not changed.

"I fancy a feeling of envy prompted this statement.

"I make no change in my relations."

This is Mrs. Piper's first statement about herself to any newspaper for years.

In the first clause the sensation which has stirred this country and Europe is punctured. In the last the allegation of severed relations with the Psychical Society is stripped of its fiction.

The same journal adds:—

Mrs. Piper, positively shrinks from publicity and shudders at notoriety and the thought of eyes prying into her own private, domestic life, which is sacred to her. For this reason she is very, very reluctant and chary about saying anything even in her own defense.

She is keenly sensitive to what is said. The appearance of the story published in New York, which was reaffirmed only yesterday as authentic, culminated in the dictated utterance given above, which breaks a long and trying silence, and pulls down on the heads of those who have made the mis-statements the whole fabric of their pens.

Mrs. Piper has been nearly prostrated. Newspaper men have flocked to her home during the past few days, but she felt obliged even under the exasperating circumstances to deny herself to all, until finally a statement seemed advisable.

She says it is all she has to say; not one single syllable more, not one syllable less. Envy and malice, it is said, are the key to the incident, first and last. Mrs. Piper is to-day, was yesterday and will be to-morrow, as she was 18 years ago. The publication of the New York story is perhaps due to what the Lydia Pinkham of the soul would term M. A. M.

Another root which has been growing in the public mind, that Mrs. Piper has been giving sittings to individuals outside of the Psychical Research Society, is also pulled out by her statements. Not even a fibre remains. She says she has not given a sitting to any one outside of the society.

People have asked her repeatedly, and besought her, but not a sitting has there been. Mrs. Piper stands by this assertion with great positiveness. There have been intermissions in her work for the society, but even in these there have been no sittings for others. A Rev. Mr. Free, Unitarian clergyman, is one who has been named as having been honored with a sitting. Investigation shows that he sought one, but was refused and all others have been refused.

The Journal also says:—

As a resident of Arlington Heights, as a member of the social and church life of the town, as a generous and delightful neighbor, as a wife, as a mother, as a matron in her own home, the life of Mrs. Piper is as near ideal as he is found here below.

She has lived in Arlington many years, about a decade, and there where she is known best, where she is seen day by day, among those who come in direct relationship with her, she is beloved the most.

Her life, her work, is in her own delightful home on Oakland ave., where the neighbors love to drop in, and where a most cordial welcome awaits all. There is no isolation by Mrs. Piper. She mingles as unaffectedly and warmly with her friends and neighbors as any woman. The care of her own home, which she has built on a most pleasant spot, and the attention of two young daughters who are attending school, are naturally the first to occupy her mind, and when she is not enveloped in her work for the Psychical Research Society, which demands her mornings, then, as any mother in a home, she moves among her friends and neighbors.

Often it has been rumored that she lived in a world of her own, and to this she says, yet in a kindly spirit:—

"I have had no intention of isolating myself, and have not intentionally done so. My duties have been such that they have confined me to my home during the past year or two. Up to that time I always went about, was friendly disposed to my neighbors, and they towards me, so far as I know."

Her neighbors know her, and speak of her as a representative American woman. Her neighbors say she contributes to charity, she attends their church, sends her children to their schools, and joins in their social diversions.

Psychical subjects are not tabooed, either. She as freely discusses them with those about her as with Prof. James or Dr. Hodgson. Oftentimes a neighbor will ask a question, and to all she has an intersting answer.

And concludes as follows:

She attends the meetings of the Woman's Club, goes to church fairs, and is an active member of the whist club, playing with a keen interest. As she talks with her neighbors about herself, when they have an inquiry to make, she says she does not know what the power is that she has. It came to her while a girl. She has never claimed to them, as they say, that she is a spiritualist.

She has frankly spoken of the power to tell of things that have occurred, but she never has claimed power to look into the future.

And here again her neighbors confirm her own remark about sittings. Not a neighbor has ever had a sitting. True, some admit they have sought them, but while many might have thought themselves called, not one has been chosen.

"Have you ever had a sitting with Mrs. Piper?" I asked a prominent resident, a neighbor, before I had seen Mrs. Piper herself, and he replied: "Not I, and I don't believe anyone else has."

Her neighbors say that all the mis-statements about Mrs. Piper have come from those who have been refused sittings.

Mrs. Piper has been sick a god deal, as many cares there are to worry her, but she pursues the even tenor of her way, quietly, happily, serenely, which is the way of her neighbors, and the regard and respect is mutually deep and sincere.

Dr. Hodgson of the Psychical Research Society visits her, as he has done almost daily this week as he has in the past, but outside of her own home her work never becomes "shop," talk.

SPIRITISM AND MRS. LEONORA E. PIPER.

BY PROF. J. H. HYSLOP.

I stated to Prof. J. H. Hyslop the situation our discussion occupied before the Medico-Legal Society and called his attention to the article in the New York Herald containing an alleged report of an interview recently published, as it appeared in the Herald, and in the same issue one with Rev. Dr. J. Minot Savage, and asked his permission to publish it as authorized by him as a part of the pending discussion.

He said he would correct the Herald's article, and send it to me as he corrected it for that purpose. The following is his letter containing the article in the Herald as corrected by him:—

Saranac Lake, N. Y., March 9th, 1902.

Mr. Clark Bell,

Dear Sir.—The interview in the Herald to which you call my attention is not accurate or complete. The first part of it is very inaccurate and some of it entirely false. The part of it which I enclose is more nearly what I said, though quite fragmentary, and in some features of it incomplete. I cannot at this date repeat it, and content myself with the statement that what I enclose of it may be good enough to represent my sentiments. What I have omitted in the rest of the interview may be considered as either wholly false or misleading. The incident about the oil lands in West Virginia is very incomplete, and does not show why I regarded it as an interesting case of chance. I mean some day to show this with a collection of like cases. The quotation of this interview by the New York Sun in the issue of March 3rd, is misleading. It quotes an incident as if I intended it to be spiritistic, while the Herald account does not indicate that I did so, and when I quoted it to the reporter I indicated it as a coincidence. Our poor newspaper editors are, as usual, as bemuddled on these matters as if they had been taking too much champagne.

"We pay no attention to what Mrs. Piper thinks of psychical phenomena or even regarding her own powers. We would be fools if we did so. Our task is simply to investigate the origin of the messages she transmits while she is an unconscious agent.

The following is from the Herald:

"I know of an instance of a man who called on a friend. While seated alone in a room he saw an apparition, the distinctive features of which was a standing collar on which two turned down points were visible, with a stringlike tie about it.

"When the friend entered the room the man asked him what he had been thinking about. He said he had been wondering whether he would wear a standing or a turn-down collar.

SUBJECT IS COMPLICATED.

"Well, what was that? You may call it mental telepathy or what you will. We are trying to learn how such matters originate. The subject, however, is more complicated than any other scientific one. The general public has no idea of the complications.

"Still, we have made some advances since the Society for Psychical Research was founded, in England, in 1882. We have gone so far as to be able to classify the subjects for investigation. We may never learn anything from our study of the subject, or it may be that one hundred or one thousand years may pass before any important discoveries are made. Still, it is, as Dr. Savage says, the only way, through the field of science, in which we may learn anything about a future life.

"We know at least that we ought to investigate the phenomena in order to determine whether such things are really spiritual manifestations or merely hallucinations. If we do that, and learn the origin of the mysterious happenings from the days of the Witch of Endor to our time, we will have accomplished something.

SHOULD UNDERSTAND MUCH.

"Nobody should engage in this work of psychic research who is not familiar with all forms of hallucination, insanity, secondary personality and all the methods of charlatanism.

"It is undoubtedly true that frauds and charlatans seek to impose on persons who believe in spiritual manifestations, but the experienced investigator can easily detect their tricks. Nor should the element of chance be overlooked in occurrences of this kind.

"Chance plays many curious tricks. I know of the case of a man who returned home hungry, but who fonud that his dinner was not ready. While waiting he picked up a book. While leaning against an open window the book fell from his hand. He caught it as it fell against the window sill. The edge of a page was turned up by striking the sill, and on looking at the page he saw a passage referring to a person who was waiting for a meal while hungry. That was mere chance.

"I once visited a so-called psychic, accompanied by two friends. The psychic told me that I had recently been interested in oil fields in West Virginia which had been involved in litigation, during which two men had perjured themselves.

"Now, those statements were true, but his words were merely a random shot. Nevertheless, it is the duty of the investigator and teacher never to let his pupils get ahead of him. He must inform himself on all matters whose origin is involved in doubt."

Very truly,

J. H. HYSLOP.

TELEPATHY, HYPNOTISM, SPIRITISM AND MRS. PIPER.

BY MRS. M. LOUISE THOMAS.

Mr. Clark Bell, Esq., Dear Mr. President:

I am glad that the subjects treating on soul and matter are entering upon the realm of pure science where they justly belong. It seems to me that the subject of spiritism is closely allied to the electric impulse; when the one becomes clear the other will be luminous. When Prof. Morse planned to bring together the two shores of the Atlantic it never occurred to him that it could be done without a visible line of cable from shore to shore. Marconi has accomplished the same thing without using anything, save the vibrations in the air about us. In the same way the soul sees, hears and speaks to those who open their consciousness to its workings. I think we are on the very eve of wonderful developments. I do not believe in passes and strokes, and staring into the eyes to obtain control over some mind weaker than that of the operator; that is the very lowest phase of the mighty science. I do not believe in it, and I would throw guards around it by the law to protect weak women from designing men. But, when such men as Judge Daily, Mr. Marsh, Mr. White, Prof. Sudduth, J. Minot Savage, Rev. Mr. Hepworth and others such as you have named, enter into the subject, we have no need to fear that it will be treated in any other, save a dignified and earnest manner.

If I live to return to my villa in Fordham, I shall hope to have some discussions on the subject held in my parlors, for with all earnestness I can declare that as the body fades away the soul takes on fresh strength and power. I am,

Sincerely your friend,

M. LOUISA THOMAS.

POSSIBILITIES.

BY REV. GEO H. HEPWORTH, OF NEW YORK.

The Rev. George H. Hepworth has had all the world as his audience for the sermons he preaches through the columns of the New York Herald.

In the issue of March 2, 1902, he took up the subject involved in the discussion going on before the New York Medico-Legal Society, under the heading "Possibilities," and by the kind permission of both the New York Herald and the author we give it here:

"*And it doth not yet appear what we shall be.*"—I John iii: 2.

It is a very curious and somewhat startling fact that we have just begun to believe that we have souls. Heretofore we have entertained vague and fantastic notions on the subject, admitting in a general way that a soul is better than a body because it lasts longer, but having no clear ideas as to its development or as to its future. This life was so frightfully real that any other possible life assumed the shape of a dream. But of late the soul has claimed the attention of science, and, although progress has been made with slow and hesitating steps, we have certainly advanced far beyond our fathers in acquiring a definite position.

Psychology has forced its way to the front, or at least toward the front, and half the world are asking questions concerning to-day and to-morrow which the other half are trying to answer. There is no reason why we should not make a great many discoveries in connection with that vital spark which at death leaves the physical man so much a wreck that its presence is no longer welcome. We give it back with many tears and an equal number of hopes to our mother earth. We are all looking with eager eyes into the Beyond, and if any one in authority has anything to say on the subject we listen with rapt attention. There is something almost painful in the pathos with which we demand new facts about a continued existence, for our affections cannot and will not be satisfied with the thought of extinction.

Almost every family has some legend or some memory of supernormal experience on the part of a dear one who was just crossing the threshold into the other life. In some cases the sight becomes phenomenally acute and the departed re-appear with outstretched hands to assist the newcomer in the passage to heaven. In others the ear is equally acute, and the overture of the angels is heard as a welcome to the brighter land. Death has thus been robbed of its terrors and made easy. These stories are floating in the air everywhere. Can it be that they mean nothing? And if they mean something, then, how much?

Science has a duty to perform in this large field. It has either ignored or simply looked on with the curiosity of indifference. But it is possible to gather verified facts enough to formulate a theory which may sometime solidify itself into a demonstrated faith. We cannot afford to "pass by on the other side," and the time is coming when skilful men will handle these things, some Darwin bold enough to follow the truth wherever it may lead, and tell us what we long to know. The hour is ripe, the attitude of the general mind propitious, and we have a right to look for startling discoveries in the near future.

Or again. When a man comes to me saying he has a message from the other world, I may be incredulous, but I cannot forget that the word "impossible" has become obsolete. I cannot help hoping that what he says is true, neither can I help believing that it is well within the limits of possibility. That Christ enjoyed this privilege, that the Old Testament is filled with instances of the kind, that St. Paul records a most remarkable experience along these lines, that in the life of every saint are similar occurrences cannot for a moment be doubted. Have all these been mistaken, and have we been deaming dreams when we put faith in these statements? Is the Bible to be trusted elsewhere and distrusted here? Is this universal longing to know about those who have gone through the church-yard to heaven a delusion and a snare, a bright promise of faith which simply "sets the children's teeth on edge?" A strange world, indeed, in which our thirst is never quenched, our hunger never satisfied! Why, then, the hunger and the thirst?

These matters are slowly coming within the range of scientific inquiry. The days of indifference have passed. With the future new glories will open to our surprised eyes, new truths will be discovered, and we shall find that the two worlds are so close together that as our prayers go forth to the gates the loved ones come to answer them and render assistance.

Before that time we ourselves may depart, but the way will be open to come back bringing the love of God, of Christ and of the risen ones into hearts and households.

SPIRITISM AND TELEPATHY.

BY C. VAN D. CHENOWETH, OF WORCESTER, MASS.

Among the most gifted members of the Psychological section is Mrs C. Van D. Chenoweth, of Worcester, Mass., one of the vice chairmen of the section, who is a thoughtful student of all psychological questions, to whom I wrote to take part in this discussion and who wrote me that circumstances and accident had prevented her from making any study of Mrs. Piper's phenomenal work, and who preferred on that account not to participate, but on my asking her for a few lines on certain aspects of the subject sent me the following:

Clark Bell, Esq. Worcester, Mass.

Dear Mr. Bell.—Any reader familiar with the published proceedings of the Society for Psychical Research in their relation to Mrs. Piper, must be deeply interested in the valuable papers upon the same subject contained in the Medico-Legal Journal for December, 1901.

With regard to telepathy, it is so much easier to believe than to disbelieve, that the great thought-producing power of man may have latent means of transmission not yet discovered, that I hold myself prepared for most interesting development in this direction.

I understand that telepathy recognizes the genuine interchange of thought, not necessarily confined to the humble symbols by means of which we are accustomed to express ourselves.

That thought, now so imperfectly transmitted through the medium of language, may be communicated in all its primal vigor and splendor by one intelligence to another, perfectly in accord, is rather an overpowering suggestion; but if I read my Wordsworth aright, that most mystical and emotional as well as most practical of English poets, this is precisely the view he indicates.

The wonderful mechanical devices of the day greatly foster the idea of poorly directed, as well as sadly wasted, mental energy; and I dare say that the time will come when we shall so clearly comprehend the carrying power of these good machines which we possess within us, that telepathy will seem less strange than wireless telegraphy.

If ever we get at facts touching the life beyond, I think we shall find telepathy between the living to have been the first step.

But life everlasting is such an inconceivably great thing that it seems to me the few years spent upon this earth might very well be the merest phase of being which could readily drop away from the wrapt consciousness of a soul strenuously bent upon higher development. An idea which would not preclude of future meeting when we too have attained.

As you know, I have never felt the slightest desire for any one to mediate between my beloved dead and me, and doubt, moreover, the ability of any one to do so.

The thought is distasteful.

I had the honor and privilege to be one of the somewhat early members of the Society for Psychical Research, and none values more highly the disinterested labor of this learned body.

The great names upon that roll command the world's respect and gratitude. I remain, my dear Mr. Bell,

Most sincerely yours,

C. VAN D. CHENOWETH.

TELEPATHY, SPIRITISM AND MRS. PIPER.

BY MARY ELIZABETH LEASE.

In discussing the question, "Are the occult manifestations given by Mrs.Piper before the Society for Psychical Research due (as recently alleged by her) to hypnotism, telepathy and clairvoyance rather than spiritism, it would materially limit and simplify the presentation of thought, were all required to speak to the question, "What do I know?"

It would certainly impress upon the mind that the mysteries which surround the life that now is, fully equal those of any life to come. While we grope after the hidden unknown, the material or supposedly known is as yet an unsolved riddle.

Physical science as interpreted by its foremost exponents, teaches that matter is not the final form of substantial existence, that it is composed of something which science cannot reach, and that being formed from that unknown invisible something, we may logically conclude that it will return to it again. Professor Tait, an acknowledged and eminent authority, declares that we do not know, and are possibly incapable of discovering what matter is, and that a true conception of it is certainly unlike anything which our reason or our sense can form.

The statement made by the eminent philosopher, Kant, must certainly be a gratification to the Christian and Mental Scientists, for he urges that, "We can only know phenomena, while noumenon, or the thing in itself, is forever beyond our ken."

Faraday advances the theory that all the properties of matter are attributes of motion, and that accurately speaking there is but one element in the universe, that element Force-Energy. Physical science supplements this theory by declaring that the realm of force or energy is the realm of causation.

The old Athenian philosopher, Plato, declares that there are two worlds, one a world of ideas or archetypal forms, the real world; the other the world of man's experience, the world which Mr. Hudson designates as the realm of objective sense, which is a world of appearance only, and consequently a vanishing and unreal world.

All the tendencies of scientific research point toward the conclusion that matter as known to chemistry and physics is but a modified form of universal ether. We may well ask "What is this universal ether that behaves toward matter as though matter did not exist?" And until this question is scientifically answered all our conclusions in regard to the phenomena of spiritism, hypnotism,telepathy or clairvoyance, are purely speculative.

Under the theory of advanced science it is no longer spirit that is vague, illusive and unreal, but matter. That which we have been accustomed to regard from the plane of externality as the real, is slipping away into modes of force, dissolving into activity, shading off into some great reality that is not material, and therefore must be spiritual. Not physic, but meatphysics is real, supreme, and on its triumpant banner is inscribed the word God.

It will not solve the question under discussion to declare the phenomena manifested through the personalty of Mrs. Piper are due to hypnotism, telepathy or clairvoyance, for we are still confronted with the question "Are not the phenomena of hypnotism, telepathy and clairvoyance due to spiritism?" We concede with Socrates that the mind is all there is of us and if the mind or enduring part of man, embodied in, or manifesting in the material form, can influence or dominate the mind of another, then is it not possible that the disembodied mind or that which we call the spirit can influence or dominate the minds of others.

That the so-called dead, the intelligence or enduring part of man yet continues to exist after the body has passed through the change called death, is not questioned or doubted by the great majority of thinking people whether in or outside the pale of the church. Can or do these so-called dead or disembodied intelligences influence or act upon the minds of the embodied living, That they can and do, is attested by thousands of good and wise men and women. To discredit or refuse to investigate the testimony of these men and women because the experiences which they relate have not become a part of our own exprience is to place a stigma upon human intelligence, make truth a bankrupt, and leave the signature of science to be protested. The mission of science is to study, to investigate, to test phenomena. Warned by the mistakes of the past we should not reject the most minute atom of evidence because the false is mingled with the true.

Only a short time ago hypnotism was pronounced an absurdity, mesmerism denounced as a fraud, telepathy was an outcast in the scientific world. Yet to-day they are recognized by jurisprudence as potent factors in human affairs. Does it not seem probable that hypnotism, telepathy, clairvoyance and kindred phenomena are evidences of spiritism? In any conclusion there is no word in human speech that we should use with more caution than the word "Impossible."

Longfellow echoes the seers and poets of all the ages when he says: "The spirit world lies about us, and its avenues are open to the unseen feet of phantoms that come and go, and we perceive them not, save by their influences, or when at times a most mysterious Providence permits them to manifest to mortal eyes."

BY THE EDITOR.

In closing this discussion I do not see how it would be at all justifiable in me to omit the statement made by Mrs. Piper as published in the New York Herald of October 20th, 1901, on which the controversy was initiated and on which it must of necessity largely hinge. The following is the statement as published by the Herald, who gives its permission to allow it to be published in this discussion, although copyrighted by the Herald, to whom we are also indebted for the portraits of Mrs. Piper, Prof. Hyslop and the contribution of the Rev. Geo. H. Hepworth.

The Medico-Legal Society and its Psychological Section are further indebted to the New York Herald for notices of some of the articles which have been contributed to this discussion by several of the authors, and the Medico-Legal Journal and its editor feel most grateful for the kind courtesy of the Herald in this regard.

The title of the article in the New York Herald was

MRS. PIPER'S PLAIN STATEMENT,

BY LEONORA E. PIPER.

The time having presented itself when it seems possible for me to be liberated from the Society for Psychical Research, I desire to state a few facts.

I will begin by saying that publicity has always been distasteful to me. My home duties have been and are the chief source of my greatest pleasure. But as my name has been before the public for fourteen years, while my case has been studied, and as the subject of psychic phenomena has, especially of late, aroused public attention, I believe it is right for me, in resigning from the service of the Psychical Research Society, to speak frankly to the public in my own individuality, in response to the request of the New York Herald.

NOTE BY THE EDITOR:

We have followed the Herald typographically, and have put in small capitals some sentences as they appeared in the New York Herald.

We have omitted some explanatory head notes which form no part of her statement.

In the service of the Society I have acted simply as an automaton, going into what is called a trance condition to be studied for purposes of scientific investigation, and also for the comfort and help of many suffering souls who have accepted the spiritistic explanation of the words which I unconsciously spoke while in this dreamy state.

It is undeniably true that many bereaved people have been at least temporarily comforted in sorrow. This is in itself a compensation for long devotion to this work. Apart from this, I do not feel that the world at large has derived a sufficient benefit from the many years' investigation of my case to warrant my continuing in it. Besides, personal circumstances are such that it would be impossible for me to do so.

After having given so many years of my life to this work. I now desire to become a free agent, and devote myself and my time to other and more congenial pursuits.

The world to-day knows that among scientific men the opinions on psychic phenomena are many and varied. I have always maintained that these phenomena could be explained in other ways than by the intervention of disembodied spirit forces.

The theory of telepathy strongly appeals to me as the most plausible and genuinely scientific solution of the problem. To strengthen this opinion are many authentic experiences which have all been satisfactorily explained by means of the telepathic hypothesis.

I am inclined to accept the telepathic explanation of all of the so-called psychic phenomena, but beyond this I remain a student with the rest of the world.

The lamented Phillips Brooks once said, after a sitting with me, when I asked him for his candid opinion on the subject:—

"It may be the back door to heaven, but I want to go in by the front door."

I also prefer to go in by the front door if I am fortunate enough to enter.

I must truthfuflly say that I do not believe that spirits of the dead have spoken through me when I have been in the trance state, as investigated by scientific men of Boston and Cambridge and those of the English Psychical Research Society, when I was taken to England to be studied. It may be that they have, but I do not affirm it.

In leaving the service of the Psychical Research Society I wish to state as clearly and definitely as possible my true position in regard to my relations with the society and my own views on the subject, which has aroused so much public attention during the last few years.

Only by the merest chance did I discover that I possessed a power wholly unexplainable to myself and mystifying to my family and friends. It was on account of my desire to understand the phenomenon and prove its nature that I gave myself up to scientific investigation and willingly placed myself in the hands of honored scientific men, who expressed the wish for me to do so, with the full understanding on both sides that I should submit to any form of test they might see fit to apply. In doing this, however, the thought of making it a remunerative occupation never once occurred to me, although since then I have as a matter of fact done so.

I must say that after having been associated with the society for about fourteen years I have no more definite knowledge concerning the subject than when I began.

During the experience of these fourteen years innumerable questions have been asked regarding my belief, some of which I will answer here and now:—

"Are you a spiritualist?"

No. I have never considered myself one.

"Have you never had any convincing proof of the possibility of spirit return?"

I cannot truthfully say that I have.

"Were you ever thrown in company with mediums or spiritualists before you took up this work?"

I never knew anything about mediums or spiritualism. In fact, the subject never had any attractions for me.

"Then why have you remained with the society so long?"

Because of my desire to ascertain if possible whether I were possessed or obsessed.

"What position do you consider that you have filled with the society?"

Simply that of an automaton.

"You say you are not a believer in spiritualism. What, then, is your opinion in regard to the utterances made by yourself while in a state of trance;"

I have often thought that if I could see myself as others see me, and hear my own utterances, I should be better able to form an opinion.

Many wise and good people have had sittings with me under the auspices of the Psychical Research Society, and some of them I have asked for an explanation when I came out of the condition. But I have never heard any explanation given, which seems to me conclusive.

For my own part, I cannot see how it can be scientifically proved that we can hold communication with the so-called spirit world.

As St. Paul says, spiritual things can only be spiritually discerned, much less handled.

On the other hand, I confidently feel that there is a grand, although mysterious, reality in the phenomenon which has arrested the attention of so many profound and brilliant intellects, and to which they have given so much time and thought. However this may be, I am glad that it has been of any comfort to people in sorrow.

But I believe that truth is a higher and deeper comfort than any such anodyne.

There have been many curious incidents connected with my sittings for the Psychical Research Society. They first heard of me in the simplest fashion. My home is in Arlington Heights, in what was once West Cambridge, not far from Harvard University. I was then living in Boston. My maid of all work told a friend who was a servant in the household of Professor William James, of Harvard, that I went into "queer sleeps," in which I said "many strange things." Professor James recognized that I was what is called a psychic, and took steps to make my acquaintance.

He at once expressed a wish for me to connect myself with the Psychical Research Society, and that is the way my work began.

At first when I sat in my chair and leaned my head back and went into the trance state the action was attended with something of a struggle. I always felt as if I were undergoing an anaesthetic, but of late years I have slipped easily into the condition, leaning the head forward. On coming out of it I felt stupid and rather dazed. At first I said disconnected things. It was all a gibberish, nothing but gibberish.

Then I began to speak some broken French phrases. I had studied French two years, but I did not speak it well.

After a while my automatic utterances announced the personality of one Dr. Phinuit, said to be a physician of France who died a long time ago. This so-called "control" returned for several years, and was the one consulted by many people and first studied by the Pyschical Research Society.

All at once this went. It was gone like the snapping of the fingers. Then for a time a literary man who had died—the one called "Pelham" in the reports of the Society for Psychical Research—was impersonated. Friends of his felt assured that he talked to them by using my voice, or by automatic writing, while I was in the trance state, and to many of them these experiences seemed a sacred revelation.

A Boston lady who had many sittings with me used to get answers not from Phinuit, but from a supposed spirit friend, who is called T. in the reports of the Society for Psychical Research. In her report for the society she said:—

"T. was a Western man, and the localism of using 'like' as a conjunction clung to him, despite my frequent correction, all his life. At my sitting on December 16, 1886, he remarked:—'If you could see it like I do.' Forgetful for the instant of changed conditions, I promptly repeated 'As I do.' 'Ah,' came tht response, 'that sounds natural. That sounds like old times.' "

Professor Peirce had a sitting with me some years ago, and he said that he received no testimony or impression to strengthen the theory of a communication with the departed. He never for one instant felt himself to be speaking with any one but me. He said that if he had seen or heard anything else he would gladly have borne testimony to it; because "a real communication with the glorious dead would surely be the greatest conceivable satisfaction to one who could not be many years separated from the state in which they abide."

After Professor Shaler saw me he wrote to the Society for Psychical Research that he was "curiously and yet absolutely uninterested." He also said "close observation of the medium made the impression on me that she is honest."

It was at a residence in Boston that I wrote automatically about a certain famous man called in the report Mr. Marte. I wrote under the so-called control of Pelham, saying, after a reference to this Mr. Marte:—

"That he, with his keen brain and marvellous perception, will be interested, I know. He was a very dear friend of X. I was exceedingly fond of him. Comical weather interests both he and I—me—him—I know it all. Don't you see I correct these? Well, I am not less intelligent now. But there are many difficulties. I am far clearer on all points than I was shut up in the prisoned body (prisoned, prisoning imprisoned you ought to say). No, I don't mean to get it that way. 'See here, H., don't view me with a critic's eye, but pass my imperfections by.' Of course I know all that as well as anybody on your sphere (of course). Well, I think so. I tell you, old fellow, it don't do to pick all these little errors too much when they amount to nothing in one way. You have light enough, I know, to understand my explanations of being shut up in this body, dreaming, as it were and trying to help on science."

I do not see how anybody can look on all that as testimony from a person in another world. I cannot see but that it must have been an unconscious expression of my subliminal self writing "such stuff as dreams are made of."

When I read over the reports of the Society for Psychical Research it all seems to me that there is no evidence of sufficient scientific value to warrant acceptance of the spiritistic explanation.

Andrew Lang contributed to the proceedings of the Society for Psychical Research for February, 1900, a criticism of the spiritist theory. He said that if students reject the idea that I am an impostor or in collusion with "Mrs. Howard," "we must try to produce some other hypothesis." Mr. Lang says he is inclined to explain the remarkable things that I say intrance, as well as the confused and muddled ones, by music reading or "telepathy a trois." He says he believes "there is something here into which it may not be a waste of time to inquire."

A physician reported for the Society for Psychical Research:—"At my first sitting with Mrs. Piper, Phinuit said, 'Get the medium to cut off a lock of your hair for me to examine and then prescribe some medicine for you.' This was done and the medicine sent to me and I used it for a time. I took a small vial of it in my pocket before visiting Mrs. Piper again, as I wished Phinuit to tell me what it was. I took it from my pocket during the trance and handed it to her, when she removed the cork and wet her finger, either from the cork or vial, and placed it to her forehead. Phinuit remarked that it was all right, corectly prepared.

"It contained among other things uva ursi and wild carrot. I now remember asking the question:—'Why was it necessary for you to have a lock of my hair to examine before prescribing for me when you had me right before you?' His answer was to the effect that the medicine might be examined by him after its preparation to see that it was all right. He then instanced a case he had prescribed for, where a wrong salt was used by the apothecary to the injury of the lady having the seance. I made no further experiment as to the seat of the sense of taste."

Of course it is understood that in speaking of "Phinuit" in this way it was merely for convenience, to indicate the seemingly distinct personality who talked while I was in trance.

At another time some onion was put into my mouth. It was reported by the Society for Psychical Research that "Dr. Phinuit seemed to taste the onion. The tongue moved about in the mouth and smacked on the lips for several seconds."

I had among other sittings when in New York one at the house of a doctor. The "control" was the one known as "George Pelham." An Italian lady was the sitter. It was in the report that Pelham gave the first names of both sitter and communicator, very uncommon names. The name of her dead sister was given. The Italian words for "It is well, patience, patience," were whispered by me at the end of the sitting.

I never called the people who came to me "my sitters" but "my clients." The upstairs room, my working room, where I used to see them in my own home, I always called the red room, because of the color of the wall paper and decoration. I also have there my little writing desk and my sewing machine.

My last impersonations were called "Imperator," "Rector" and "Pruden."

In deciding to release myself from "Imperator" I do not wish to antagonize any student of psychical phenomena, either here or in Europe, but I do not believe that the genuine spirit of science can be antagonized, nor any of those who humbly love science as Professor Agassiz loved it, ever ready to "appeal to nature," and like him, look through nature up to nature's God.

Because the spiritistic theory does not appeal to me after my experience I do not deny to any mortal a perfect right to accept it, if it seems consistent.

I have never heard of anything being said by myself while in a trance state which might not have been latent in (1) my own mind, (2) in the mind of the person in charge of the sitting, (3) in the mind of the person who was trying to get communication with some one in another state of existence, or some companion present with such person, or (4) in the mind of some absent person alive somewhere else in the world.

Not one of us present may have been conscious of any knowledge of facts stated, yet somewhere in my mysterious subliminal consciousness, which was in abnormal activity when I was in condition, the knowledge might have rested unknown to myself in my waking life. It might in the same manner have been latent in the mind of one of those present and have been transferred by unconscious telepathy from one of their minds to my own.

The wonders of wireless telegraphy and the use of the X-ray developed of late years in the realm of physical science make me feel that it would not be becoming, for me to say what may or may not be possible transferrence of thought in the subjective mind by laws not yet formulated. My reading has not shown me that all the laws of the objective mind are understood.

I have said that if the knowledge of facts stated by me while in the condition was not latent with me or with any of those present in the room with me at the time of a sitting, it might still have been in the mind of some other person alive somewhere in the world. It might have been latent, or it might have been active knowledge, and have been transferred to the mind of one of those in the room, then to my subjective mind, then automatically uttered or written by me. I do not find it is as hard to grasp this theory as that of a disembodied spirit telling the things.

If thought could be unconsciously transferred to me from a person in the room I do not see any reason why that person could not have received a thought message from somebody at a long distance and then telephoned it, so to speak, in thought, direct to me. If telepathy is possible between two people, why not among three, just the same as with telegraphy?

Everybody is familiar with the common coincidence of letters crossing between two people who had not written for a long time and who then wrote to each other at the same time. Distance does not seem to make any difference about such meetings, in, perhaps, the spirit; there are many instances of that sort of human wireless telegraphy; there are also instances of a third person learning by the same means of facts known to two other persons.

An interesting case of what seems like direct thought transference in the subjective mind was when I gave intelligible answers, in English, of course, while in the condition to questions asked of me by a sitter in Italian, a language I do not understand. All the communication seemed to be entirely between the subliminal thought of the sitter and myself. I sometimes think that may be the way we shall all talk to each other when in the future state.

It has sometimes happened that things I have said at a sitting were not at all consoling or important to those who were trying to satisfy their minds or hearts by these psychical experiments.

Once when an old Boston physician had a sitting with me it seems that I talked most about a pencil which was put into my hands, it having been the property of a deceased friend. When I came out of the condition he drew himself up in his chair and said, with excusable gruffness:—

"What made you talk about nothing but the top of an old pencil? Why didn't you talk about God and the angels;"

"What do you know about God and the angels?" I could not help retorting. He was good enough to smile, for of course the pencil was part of the scientific test and the other talk would not have been.

Once when another and still more famous Boston doctor came to see me, he said afterward that he "found Mrs. Piper huffy, but got on the good side of her by caressing her children."

A literary man said:—"I know Mrs. Piper is conscious, because she listened when the door bell rang." One sitter asked me if I had the face of my clock illuminated so that I could know when the hour was up, as I did not make it a practice to remain in the condition for more than an hour at a time. It has, however, at times been much longer.

Cultivated people have often been surprised at first meetings that I did not seem peculiar or unlike other women, and some of them expressed their wonder.

When I was taken to England the wife of one of the celebrated English men of science met me with the explanation to her husband:—

"Is this Mrs. Piper? You don't mean to tell me that this is Mrs. Piper!" Then to me:—"I thought you would be sure to be very fat, and like magneta color and wear friselettes!"

These words in her rich English voice made us both smile, but we afterward became good friends.

I have been so fortunate as to make good friends and pleasant acquaintances through my work. Some of them do and some do not believe that spirits have spoken through me. I do not think that even those who do have liked to see me mentioned in print, as I have been, as "the human telephone to the next world."

Such expressions were of course never used concerning me in the reports of the Psychical Research Society or in such articles as those of Mr. Lang, or of Professor Hyslop in the Literary Digest, the Arena, &c.; in Mrs. Katherine Tillman Bull's article in Harper's Magazine last year, or in any similar articles published at home or abroad. I am grateful for all thoughtful, profound or kindly intentioned articles. I am aware that I run the risk of the disapprobation of some people by voluntarily ceasing to be a "case" for study. But most students and lovers of science and humanity will, I hope, understand.

Phillips Brooks said in a public address:—"There is a belief in God which does not bring Him, nay, rather say, does not let Him come into close contact with our daily life. The very reverence with which we honor God may make us shut Him out from the hard tasks and puzzling problems with which we have to do. Many of us who call ourselves theists are like the savages who in the desire to honor the wonderful sun dial which has been given them built a roof over it. Break down the roof; let God in on your life!"

He also said:—"How every truth attains to its enlargement and reality in this great truth, that the soul of man carries the highest possibilities within itself."

LEONORA E. PIPER.

THE SUBJECT RESUMED.

The New York Herald, in addition to the statement of Mrs. Piper published the views of some other eminent gentlemen.

Among others the Herald published views from both Prof. Hyslop, Dr. Richard Hodgson and Dr. Thomson Jay Hudson, but as these gentlemen have contributed to the discussion the Herald's version of their views is not quoted here.

Prof. Wm. James, of Harvard, is quoted by the Herald in the same issue, as follows:—

Prof. Wm. James, Professor of Psychology at Harvard, said:—

"Taking everything that I know of Mrs. Piper into account, the result is to make me feel absolutely certain that she knows things in her trances that she cannot possibly have had knowledge of in a waking state and that the definite philosophy of her trances is yet to be found.

The Herald still further quotes Prof. James as follows:—

"As regards the spiritualistic hypothesis, I am still 'on the fence.' I said something about the alternatives to it in a notice of Hodgson's report on Mrs. P., which I wrote for the Psychological Review in 1898. WILLIAM JAMES.

"Silver Lake, N. H., Sept. 18, 1901."

"Mrs. Piper's trance memory then is no ordinary human memory, and we have to explain its singular perfection either as the natural endowment of her solitary subliminal self or as a collection of distinct memory systems, each with a communicating "spirit as its vehicle. The choice obviously cannot be made offhand. If I may be allowed a personal expression of opinion at the end of this notice, I would say that the Piper phenomena are the most absolutely baffling thing I know.

"Of the various applicable hypotheses, each seems more unnatural than the rest. Any definitely known form of fraud seems out of the question; yet undoubtedly, could it may be made probable, fraud would be by far the most satisfying explanation, since it would leave no further problems outstanding.

"The spirit hypothesis exhibits a vacancy, triviality and incoherence of mind painful to think of as the state of the departed; and coupled therewithal a pretension to impress one, a disposition to 'fish' and face round and disguise the essential hollowness which are, if anything, more painful still. Mr. Hodgson has to resort to the theory that, although the communications probably are spirits,

---

NOTE BY THE EDITOR:

For fear that questions might be raised as to the correctness of the New York Herald's report respecting the views of Professor James, I wrote him as to the accuracy of the Herald's report. Professor James replied that the Herald's report was substantially correct.

they are in a semi-comatose or sleeping state while communicating, and only half aware of what is going on, while the habits of Mrs. Piper's neural organism largely supply the definite form of words, &c., in which the phenomenon is clothed.

"Then, there is the theory that the subliminal extension of Mrs. Piper's own mind masquerades in this way, and plays these fantastic tricks before high heaven, using its preternatural powers of cognition and memory for the basest of deceits. Many details make for this view, which also falls well into line with what we know of automatic writing and similar subliminal performances in the public at large.

"But what a ghastly and grotesque sort of appendage to one's personality is this, from any point of view! The humbugging and masquerading extra-marginal self is as great a paradox for psychology as the comatose spirits are for pneumatology.

"Finally we may fall back on the notion of a sort of floating mind-stuff in the world, intra-human, yet possessed of fragmentary gleams of superhuman cognition, unable to gather itself together except by taking advantage of the trance states of some existing human organism and there enjoying a parasitic existence, which it proongs by making itself acceptable and plausible under the improvised name of a spirit control.

"On any of these theories our 'classic human life,' as we may call it, seems to connect itself with an environment so 'romantic' as to baffle all one's habitual sense of teleology and moral meaning. and yet there seems no refuge for one really familiar with the Piper phenomena—or doubtless with others that are similar—from admitting one or other, perhaps even all of these fantastic prolongations of mental life into the unknown.

"The world is evidently more complex than we are accustomed to think it, the absolute 'world ground' in particular being further off than it is the wont of either the usual empiricisms or the usual idealisms to think it."

The Herald also publishes the following statement by William S. Walsh, Esq.:—

"The woman in this case is an excellent and irreproachable character. She is Mrs. Piper, a resident of Arlington Heights, near Boston. Her husband is a tailor in very moderate circumstances. She has two children. Her age is about thirty-eight. She is an intelligent woman, but not what you would call an intellectual one. She is neither handsome nor homely, neither tall nor short, neither blonde nor brunette. She is just an average woman—a good wife and a good mother, as thank Heaven! the average woman of the United States has ever been.

"In 1882 or thereabouts she underwent a dangerous surgical operation. The physician who brought her through successfully was a spiritualist by belief. He detected in her spiritualistic possibilities. With her consent he made a medium of her, just the average, ordinary medium, who gives spiritualistic seances for a consideration.

"But, unlike many of her fellow workers, Mrs. Piper was absolutely honest. She had no explanation to offer of the strange powers with which she found herself endowed. She had no consciousness of what happened during the hypnotic trance. When she returned to her normal state she had no remembrance of what she had said or done, or what other forces had said or done through her agency.

"It was this transparent simplicity and ingenuousness of character, this lack of the hocus and mumbo jumbo of ordinary mediumship, that made Mrs. Piper conspicuous above the common herd of clairvoyants and similar charlatans.

"For fourteen years or more she has been under the close observation, first of Professor James, afterward of Dr. Hodgson and other competent persons.

"She and her husband have been shadowed by detectives. Her personal luggage has been searched, her correspondence read, her goings out and comings in closely watched. Yet, in all these years not the smallest circumstance has come to light reflecting in any way upon her honesty.

"Certainly no other medium has ever been subjected to so stringent an ordeal. And, in view of the fact that, under far more meagre supervision, Dr. Hodgson himself and other less competent inquirers have succeeded in bringing home the charge of dishonesty to many professional mediums, it is a fact entitled to much weight that this medium should have passed through the most searching and prolonged inquiries without even a rumor of exposure or the discovery of any suspicious circmustances.

"And so it was that she attracted an uncommon class of patrons. Educated and intelligent people flocked to her. Among the rest came Professor William James, of Harvard University.

"He hardly needs an introduction to our readers. Son of Henry James, the mystic; brother of Henry James, the novelist, and he himself the greatest of living American psychologists.

"It has been said of him and of his better known but no less eminent brother that the one writes psychology like a novelist and the other writes novels like a psychologist. In other words both are possessed of imagination as well as insight, but the imagination of the psychologist, though most restrained by scientific methods, is most in evidence.

"As one of the vice presidents of the Society for Psychical Research Professor James was naturally attracted to a case of mediumship which seemed to invite the serious attention of the society and its officers.

"In 1885-86 he visited Mrs. Piper about a dozen times and sent a large number of persons to her, making appointments himsef for most of these people, whose names were in no instance announced to the medium. His investigations convinced him that Mrs. Piper was a person of supernormal powers.

"As to the exact meaning and value of those powers, his attitude has been and is very frankly that of suspended judgment. Of one thing only is he certain—the suspicion of fraud in untenable. He almost wishes this was not so, for if this suspicion could be made plausible, 'fraud would be by far the most satisfying explanation; since it would leave no further problem outstanding.'

"But the fraud hypothesis being eliminated, bewildering problems remain waiting for an answer. He therefore called the attention of the society to this extraordinary case, with the hope that some light might be thrown upon the attendandt probems.

"These are the words with which he introduced Mrs. Piper:—'In order to disprove the assertion that all crows are black, one white crow is sufficient. My white crow is Mrs. Piper.'"

The Herald also quotes Dr. F. Wallace Patch of the Massachusetts General Hospital:—

"It is a pleasure for me to say that the Herald, replying to a question in regard to my acquaintance with Mrs. Piper, long known as the gifted instrument of the Society for Psychical Research, that she is a woman of rare sweetness of nature, fair minded, just and truthful. She has good mental qualities and is perfectly capable of exercising discretion in matters with which she may be connected.

"Her position of open mindedness on psychical matters is most refreshing to meet in one who has been through her peculiar experiences. This renders her work all the more valuable from a scientific standpoint, whether we see fit to accept or discard the once prevalent doctrine of Spiritualism.

"It would seem to one who has followed the discussions on this subject for many years that the spiritualistic theory utterly fails to account for the phenomena of so-called 'mediumship.' We can never hope to form a union between the individualities of Heaven and those of earth by any such finite means as those in question.

"It is probable that the phenomena of the trance state will yet be adequately explained—if, indeed they are not already so—along the well known lines of hypnosis, mental suggestion and telepathy. The seeming mystery will quietly melt away as the further light of modern research penetrates more deeply the mass of evidence now gathering."

CONCLUSION AND SUMMING UP OF THE DISCUSSION.

BY THOMSON JAY HUDSON, PH. D., LL. D.

Has spiritism no better method of refuting the arguments in favor of the telepathic theory than to exaggerate, distort and misrepresent it in order to find an excuse for answering it with a point-blank denial or a sneer? It seems not.

Dr. Hodgson, the official spiritistic propagandist of the S. P. R., set the pace some years ago, and the rest have obediently followed in his foot steps ever since. Thus, in his report on the Piper phenomena (See p. 394, Part XXXIII., Proc. S. P. R.), he tells us just what must be presupposed if we are to accept the telepathic explanation of said phenomena. To do the learned Doctor justice, he begins by candidly admiting that "if the information given at the sittings, both in matter and form, was limited to the knowledge possessed by the sitters, we should have no hesitation in supposing that it was derived from their minds, telepathically or otherwise." But, as some of the information given out was held not to be thus limited, he proceeds to say:

"We must then make the arbitrary suppositions that Mrs. Piper's percipient personality gets into relation with the minds of distant living persons, (1) who are intimate friends of the sitters at the time of the sitting, and (2) who are scarcely known, or not at all known, to the sitter. And many of these distant living persons had, so far as they knew, never been near Mrs. Piper. These cases then compel us to assume a selective capacity in Mrs Piper's percipient personality, and not only selective as to the occurrences themselves, but discriminative as to the related persons."

If all this were true, it must be confessed that the telepathic hypothesis would be hedged about with serious logical difficulties. Fortunately it is not true, as I shall show later on.

But this is nothing compared with the logical consequences involved in the telepathic hypothesis, which are, in part, set forth by Dr. Hodgson in words following, to wit:

"And I may add here that these arbitrary suppositions may be increased yet further to cover other forms of evidence that may be obtained hereafter, such as the giving of information supposed to be possessed by the dead alone, or the manifestation of knowledge not yet acquired by the human race, so far as we are aware, such as the existence of heavenly bodies previously unknown, or the customs of the inhabitants of other planets, verified, let us assume, in future years."

It will thus be seen that the learned Doctor has found no difficulty in frightening himself away from the telepathic hypothesis by the simple process of constructing a few "arbitrary suppositions." And it must be admitted that the "supposition" that the inhabitants of this earth can communicate telepathically with the inhabitants of "unknown" planets, is well calculated to frighten almost anybody who is not a spiritist, especially if he is told that he must believe it as a logical penalty for believing in the telepathic explication of Mrs. Piper's phenomena.

But, robust and strenuous as are Dr. Hodgson's suppositions, they are feeble in comparison with those of his pupil, Dr. Hyslop. As I have shown in my opening article, that gentleman holds that the telepathic explanation of the Piper phenomena is absolutely untenable except under the presupposition that that lady is "omniscient," or at the least is endowed with the ability to draw at will upon "the whole universe of intelligence." Thus believing, he is enabled to quiet his logical conscience when he ignores the real issue in the case.

Hon. Luther R. Marsh is another who finds a way to avoid the necessity for argument by the same general process. He tells us that the telepathic hypothesis requires the assumption that the sitter must be omniscient, or words to that effect. That is to say, his mind must be filled with "an endless arcana of knowledge,"—"chuck-full" of "all things that have ever transpired in the world, and in the spirit sphere."

This is a decided modification of the assumptions of Doctors Hodgson and Hyslop, who hold that the telepathic hypothesis requires us to assume that the medium is "omniscient." To do Mr. Marsh entire justice it must be said that his assumption is just as sensible, and just as near the truth, as that of Doctors Hodgson and Hyslop. They are both designed, apparently, to exaggerate the claims of their opponents for the purpose of denying them.

Judge Dailey presents another modification of the same polemical weapon. It is not so extravagant as those we have named; but the design is identical. I refer to what he says of my proposition relating to telepathy by three. He quotes the proposition and then proceeds to say that it means something that is obviously foreign to its plain import. (See Judge Dailey's article.)

And now comes the Rev. Dr. Savage, with still another modification of the same assumption, in which "unlimited powers" and "universal knowledge" is supposed to be necessary to enable the medium to do her work by the aid of telepathy. (See his article under the sub-head of "Telepathic Theory.")

Now, let us examine this question in the light of what is known of telepathic powers, and see if these extravagant assumptious are really a necessary part of the telepathic theory when it is invoked to account for spiritistic phenomena.

First, however, let us try to find a common ground of agreement, to the end that the issue may be more clearly defined. I think I may take it for granted that all intelligent spiritists, who know anything about telepathy, will admit that when a medium, acting under test conditions, states a fact that the sitter already knows, telepathy cannot be eliminated from the list of possible causes. Indeed, no scientific psychical researcher would for a moment consider the possibility of any other explanation. Why? Simply because he knows telepathy to be a *vera causa*, and he does not know anything about spirits. At least he is not certain about them; and most likely he is an adherent of the scientific axiom which Dr. Savage has given us, namely—"we must not explain the unknown by something else that is still more unknown." I have quoted Dr. Hodgson as an adherent to this principle, and F. W. H. Myers, in his "Science and a Future Life," (see p. 32), tells us that, forgotten or unforgotten, active or latent, "whatever has gone into the mind may come out of the mind." We may, therefore, safely assume that all are agreed that whatever the sitter knows must be presumed to be available to the medium. Nor will it be disputed that the sitter may obtain access to knowledge telepathically.

Now, if the exhaustive investigations of the S. P. R. count for anything at all, it must be admitted that they have demonstrated two things in regard to telepathy, namely, (1) that telepathy is a power belonging exclusively to the subjective mind, or subliminal consciousness; and that, consequently, information may be received from,or imparted to, another subjective mind, without the knowledge or consent of the objective mind of either. The evidence for this in the Society's reports is overwhelming. (2) It is also in evidence that relatives, friends and acquaintances are always *en rapport*, and that they are always either actually or potentially in communication. Of 830 cases reported in "Phantasms of the Living," only 36 were between strangers. But that number is sufficient to show that rapport, for telepathic purposes, is not exclusively confined to relatives or intimates.

We have, then, a basis of admitted facts and principles to start upon, namely, (1) that telepathy must be presumed whenever the sitter has prior knowledge of the fact communicated by the medium; (2) that subliminal knowledge may be acqüired telepathically, unconsciously to the percipient. The only point likely to be in dispute, therefore, is as to whatever telepathically acquired knowledge can be conveyed telepathically to the psychic or medium. If it can, we have an easy telepathic solution of all the phenomena of which we have been speaking.

To put the case in concrete form, so that my meaning may not be misunderstood or distorted, let us apply the principle to one of Dr. Savage's test cases, namely the communication supposed to be from his deceased son. All that is necessary is to suppose, (1) that Dr. Savage and his son were in telepathic rapport during the life time of the latter; and that, (2) for some reason, he desired to have his private papers taken care of by his father, his best friend,—his heart-to-heart confidant during all the years of his life. Thus far no one will dispute the assumptions. (3) Next we must suppose that the desire was conveyed from son to father by the only means available at the time, namely, by telepathy. No one who is conversant with the work of the S. P. R. can doubt this for a moment. Of the 830 cases cited in "Phantasms of the

Living," a large proportion were cases showing that the dying agents were endeavoring to acquaint their relatives or friends with some unsatisfied desire, or at least with the fact that they were in extremis. Indeed, it may be said that if the investigations of the S. P. R. render anything approximately certain, it is that dying persons make an effort to inform their relatives and friends of their condition, especially if there is any special object to be gained by so doing. If, then, the friend or relative toward whom the effort is directed happens to be edowed with psychic powers, the effort is successful; and the information conveyed to the subliminal consciousness is thereby elevated to the supraliminal. On the other hand, if the friend is not a psychic the information remains latent in the subliminal, and may never rise above the threshold.

But, in such a case, if the person afterwards becomes subjective from any cause, there is likely to ensue an uprush of the contents of the subliminal,and he thus becomes conscious of the information that had been telepathically conveyed to him originally. This phenomenon has been designated by Myers as "deferred percipience," several instances, some of them experimental, being cited in "Phantasms of the Living." (See pp. 56, 70-1, 201-2, 265, 325 and 519.)

These cases demonstrate that information telepathically conveyed, unconsciously to the percipient, reaches his subliminal consciousness nevertheless, and remains latent until an opportunity presents itself for elevating it above the threshold of normal consciousness. This may happen spontaneously, as when the percipient happens to attain the proper psychic conditions; or it may be brought about by the percipient coming in contact with a psychic who is endowed with telepathic powers, as in Dr. Savage's case.

This latter supposition, singularly enough, marks the parting of the ways. Why? I do not know why it should be denied that information telepathically received from one party can be telepathically conveyed to a third person, unless it is because the admission of the truth of the proposition would be equivalent to an abandonment of the spiritistic hypothesis, and an admission of the entire validity of the telepathic explanation.

Dr. Savage's case presents the issue in its simplest form. He will not deny that he was in telepathic rapport with his son. Nor will he deny that it was possible that the latter conveyed, telepathically, the information relating to his private papers to his father. But he will doubtless deny that it was possible for Mrs. Piper to obtain, telepathically, the content of that message from the mind in which it was lodged.

That would be *"telepathic a trois,"* or telepathy by three; and the average spiritist becomes hysterical whenever that subject is broached. Why? Is it because he sees that, if it is once admitted that information telepathically received can be telepathically transmitted to a third person, the claims of spiritism must be abandoned in favor of the telepathic hypothesis? I can imagine no other adequate cause for either the emotional and insensate denial of the proposition or for the studied attempt to ignore it. Much less can I see any other cause for the assertion that the telepathic hypothesis requires the presupposition of "omniscient" intelligence on the part of the medium. Be that as it may, the fact remains that, if "telepathy by three" is a telepathic potential, it does afford a full and complete explanation of every case yet reported where the psychic was shown to possess supernormally acquired knowledge not objectively in the possession of any one present. It affords, for instance, an easy explanati of each of the twelve cases reported by Dr. Savage, as well as of all the cases cited by Prof. Hyslop, It covers, in fact, every conceivable case of the kind.

It becomes important,therefore, to know whether telepathy by three is a telepathic potential. Fortunately for our present purposes, Dr. Clark Bell has quoted Mr. Lang on that subject, and he reports several cases of the kind. (See Dr. Bell's article.) It is, in fact, a very common phenomenon,although little attention has been paid to it, for the reason that its scientific value as bearing upon the subect of spiritism has not been fully appreciated by scientists until quite recently. In the cases cited by Mr. Lang spirits were out of the question, for nobody was dead; and numerous instances might be cited in experimental telepathy by means of hypnotism or mesmerism, where all concerned were alive and well.

It is true that in some cases the source of the telepathic message may be difficult to trace, as in the one reported by Judge Dailey. But no particulars possessing the slightest evidential importance in his case have been verified. A *soi disant* spirit comes to him and tells him that his name is John Taylor ;that he was born in New Bedford; that he ran away when a boy and went to sea; that he had a very checkered career, which he described with great particularity; that everybody that he ever knew in New Bedford was dead; for he had not visited his native place for over 60 years. All this Judge Bailey thinks he has "verified," "to a certain extent," by going to New Bedford and finding that "Taylor was a very common family name" in that city, (as it is in most other cities) that there were names on tomb-stones that Taylor had mentioned; that there were streets there that he had named, etc., etc. But not one item was verified that tended to establish the personal identity of John Taylor, or to show that any one of his numerous stories were true.

Now, Judge Dailey tells us that he is "a lawyer, and claims to know something of legal principles." But he does not say that he is an expert in weighing the value of evidence. If he is, what would he say of the weight of a witness' testimony should he claim to have witnessed a murder, and, in the absence of the *corpus delicti*, seek to verify his statement by showing a street in the city where the tragedy was alleged to have occurred, and by naming somebody whose patronymic could be found on a tomb-stone in the city cemetery? I may appear to be straining a point in Judge Dailey's favor when I say that I still have enough confidence in his legal ability to believe that he would summarily dismiss the jury and throw the case out of court, if that was the only evidence in the case. And yet it exactly parallels the evidence by which he seeks to establish the personal identity of John Taylor,and verify the history of his life as given through the medium in the case. Well may the learned Judge ask me who telepathed the personal history of John Taylor to the medium. I confess that I do not know. But I do know that all the facts bearing upon the case which the Judge learned on his scientific pilgrimage to New Bedford, could easily have been learned from a local history of that city.

As I remarked, it is sometimes difficult to trace the telepathic connections so as to say just where the information conveyed to the medium originated. But they are generally just such cases as that upon which Judge Dailey pins his faith; that is to say, cases that cannot be either verified or disproved. I confess that I am not sufficiently well versed in Judge Dailey's legal standard of evidential values to see clearly just how it is that an absence of facts tends to prove or to disprove, anything in an inductive investigation. Nor can I quite appreciate the logic of that attitude of mind which impels a hysterical shout of triumph from every spiritistic throat whenever a medium tells a long and weird tale that can neither be disproved nor verified. To the mind of the average spiritist such cases are the most convincing, for they can then triumphantly ask "How can telepathy account for this?" To which the obvious answer is that telepathy is not called upon to account for unverified statements.

This class of cases, however, are not the ones that present the real difficulties that may sometimes occur, although they are very rare. Let us suppose an extreme case: Suppose a *soi disant* spirit presents himself at a seance and announces himself as a stranger to all present; and then proceeds to relate facts entirely unknown to those present. Then suppose that those facts should be afterwards fully verified. Obviously, in such a case, it would be difficult to trace the telepathic connection. But would anybody but a spiritist imagine that the telepathic hypothesis had been disproved by an occasional failure to find the facts in such a case? I think not. And yet these are the cases upon which spiritists rely to establish their own theories and to "disprove" the telepathic hypothesis. In other words, it is the essence of the logic of spiritism to rely chiefly upon the absence of facts when conducting an inductive investigation. Is Judge Dailey's legal education responsible for this principle of his logic? If so, he would hang a man for murder simply for the want of evidence to establish either his guilt or his innocence.

Logically, the case stands thus: (1) There are sporadic cases where it is difficult to determine from what source a telepathic communication originated.

(2) On the other hand, there are innumerable cases where the telepathic connection is obvious, as in all of Prof. Hyslop's cases, in all of Dr. Savage's cases, and in most of those cited by Judge Dailey.

(3) In all cases where the facts are known, "telepathy by three" affords a complete telepathic explanation.

I submit that those few cases in which the facts are not known should not be allowed to weigh one hair against the great mass of cases where the telepathic connection is obvious; especially since the latter can all be explained on the telepathic hypothesis,—assuming, of course, that "telepathy by three" is a telepathic potential.

I re-submit my original proposition:—If A can, by any known means of communication, convey a message to B, B can convey the same message by the same means, to C, other things, of course, being equal.

If not, why not?

I have repeatedly submitted this proposition to spiritsts, and as repeatedly asked the same question. If it is not true there must be a valid answer to the proposition; but that answer has never been attempted otherwise than by the bare assertion, without argument, that "it is carrying telepathy too far." On the other hand, if the proposition is true, spirism, considered as a scientific proposition, is disposed of. Nor can this queston be successfully evaded by an attempt to ignore it, nor by substituting for argument such assertions as that the telepathic theory requires the presupposition of "omniscience" on the part of the psychic.

HONORARY MEMBERS OF THE MEDICO-LEGAL SOCIETY.

F. DR. MORITZ BENEDIKT,
Vienna, Austria.

DR. A. N BELL,
Editor Sanitarian, Brooklyn, N. Y

PROF. DR. R. OGDEN DOREMUS,
Ex-President Medico-Legal Society,
New York City

r. LUTHER R. MARSH,
Middletown, N. Y.

HON. ROBERT EARL,
Ex-Chief Justice New York Court of Appeals

ON THE RELATIONSHIP BETWEEN HUMAN AND BOVINE TUBERCULOSIS.*

BY J. G. ADAMI, M. D., OF MONTREAL,

Professor of Pathology, McGill University; Pathologist to the Agricultural Department, Dominion of Canada.

When in 1884 Koch published in the second volume of the Mittheilungen of the German Imperial Health Office, the classical account of his researches on the tubercle bacillus and the relationship of the same to different forms of tubercular disease in man and animals, he laid down with the greatest precision that there was but one form of tubercle bacillus, that grape disease (Perlsucht) in cattle, tubercular phthisis or pulmonary consumption in man, and tuberculosis in the domestic animals, are caused by one and the same micro-organism. This view was not based upon isolated observations—he studied 19 cases of miliary tuberculosis in man, 29 cases of pulmonary phthisis, tuberculosis ulcers of the tongue, tuberculosis of the womb, testicles, etc., 21 cases of scrofulous lymphatic glands, 13 cases of tuberculosis joints, 10 cases of tubercular bone affections, 4 of lupus—all these in man—and 17 cases of grape disease in cattle; while he made experimental inoculations with the bacilli obtained from all these cases into some 273 guinea-pigs, 105 rabbits and numerous smaller animals including rats, cats, dogs, pigeons, hens, etc. It was a most remarkable and exhaustive piece of work. And when he declared after all this prolonged study of years, that the organisms isolated from man and cattle were identical, it is not surprising that his view was almost universally accepted, although this was counter to the teaching of Virchow, who, since 1863, had laid down that tuberculosis in man and grape disease in cattle were two distinct diseases.

*Being a Portion of the Annual Report to the Department of Agriculture of the Dominion of Canada for the year 1901, about to be published, here printed by permission of the Minister of Agriculture.

From Virchow's address to the Berlin Medical Society July 27, 1901, (Berliner klinische Wochenschrift, August 5, 1901, p. 819) it would appear that at the Charite-Hospital in Berlin they have from time to time collected material from cases of human peritoneal tuberculosis showing massive tubercular growths quite unlike the ordinary tuberculosis of the abdominal cavity in man and resembling more those characteristic of the bovine disease, thus indicating, so far as I follow Virchow, that despite the general acceptance of the view enunciated by Koch and the disrepute into which his own earlier opinion had fallen, Virchow had, since 1884, still upheld that earlier opinion regarding the want of identity between the two diseases. But for years then Koch's conclusion was unreservedly accepted by pathologists in general, by veterinarians and those interested in hygiene, the view, namely, that one form of bacillus causes all forms of tuberculosis in the different species of animals.

The first check to these views came from Italy and France, when it was shown byMafucci (1899) and by Cadiot, Gilbert and Roger (1890) that the bacilli obtained from fowls, pheasants and other birds suffering from tuberculous disease, grow more readily and in their growth and in their action upon the animals of the laboratory differ markedly from the tubercle bacilli isolated from man, and in 1890 at the International Congress in Paris, Koch admitted these differences. As I have already pointed out (Report of the Minister of Agriculture for the Dominion for 1899) the researches of Nocard and Roux have clearly indicated that these differences in properties are not due to the existence of two absolutely distinct species of bacilli but to the fact that bacilli grown and passed from member to member of one species gradually assume characters different from those assumed by the bacilli of like origin, infecting and passing through members of another species of animal. The extreme example of this difference in the characters of different races of tubercle bacilli is to be met with in fish. It has been found by more than one observer that fresh water fish such as carp, fed for a long period with the sputum of human tuberculous patients, may eventually develop swellings of an inflamatory type from which tubercle bacilli can be obtained growing easily at the rodinary temperature on the usual media employed for this purpose (whereas tubercle bacilli obtained direct from man only gow at the body temperature and then only with difficulty). These piscine bacilli when inoculated into rabbits and guinea-pigs are found to be remarkably attenuated and lessened in their virulence. I learn that Professor Harrison of the Guelph Agricultural College has repeated and confirmed these experiments.

It is not surprising, therefore, that differences have been made out between the tubercle bacilli derived from cases of tuberculosis in man and cattle respectively. As a matter of fact, as already reported, Theobold Smith has more especially called attention to the differences in the cultures and the appearance of the bacilli, differences which we have been able fully to confirm (ibid. p. 139), while several observers have noted either that tuberculosis sputum from man, when fed to calves had no effect upon them, or that pure cultures of the bacilli isolated from lesions in man were similarly without effect, at most leading to a localised disturbance at the point of inoculation with little or no liability to lead to generalized disease. (Chauveau in France, Gunther and Harms and Bollinger (1894) in Germany, Sydney Martin (1895) in England, Frothingham (1897). Theobald Smith (1898), and Dinwiddie (1899) in the United States.)

We so fully accepted these results in 1899, that we only tested the matter upon one heifer, using large quantities of human tubercle bacilli and obtaining no result (ibid. p. 147.) The control heifer which received a like inoculation of bovine bacilli died of generalized tuberculosis in 42 days. One English observer, Crookshank, obtained positive results, but as I have previously noted (ibid.) and as Crookshank himself acknowledged at the London Congress, his case is peculiar, and is to be explained not as a pure tuberculor infection but as an example of a mixed infection, the suppurative disturbance and consequent lowered resistance in the calf favoring the mutiplication of the tubercle bacilli and the development of a generalised tuberclosis.

It may be noted here that in one of the capsule experiments in the calf, by my assistant, Dr. Higgins, in which the capsule containing the bovine bacilli ruptured, a few tubercles were found in the neighborhood. These were clearly arrested in their development.

Thus, previous to Koch's address, it was well known to those interested in the subject, that differences existed in the bacilli obtained from man and the cow; that human tubercle bacilli only occasionally and under special conditions are capable of causing tuberculosis in cattle, and that these do not cause nearly so virulent and rapid a development of the disease when inoculated into rabbits and guinea-pigs. The question had already been mooted as to whether bovine tubercle bacilli being more virulent for the lower animals, are also specially virulent for men, or whether the reverse was the case, so that passage of the tubercle bacilli through a series of cattle while leading these to be more dangerous for cattle and for animals of the laboratory, but will render them less capable of setting up infection in man.

In this connection before coming to deal directly with Koch's address it is but right that I should here note that in August, 1899, at the meeting of the Canadian Medical Association at Toronto, I delivered an address upon Bovine Tuberculosis and its significance, and upon the possibility of its eradication in Canada,* in which I cautiously drew attention to the fact that the evidence in favor of the view that bovine tuberculosis is transmissible to man, was not so strong as it was generally thought to be, that while cases did exist of such transmission, they were few in number; and I concluded therefore than inasmuch as it was with great difficulty that human tuberculosis was conveyed to cattle and vice versa, that therefore it was quite possible for us here in Canada to proceed to eradicate bovine tuberculosis from district to district of the Dominion, and this even when measures for eradicating human tuberculosis were either ineffective or not put into action. This paper was taken at the time by certain critics to mean that I did not believe that tuberculosis was transmitted from cattle to man: that I never stated, nor have I since then believed this to be the case. I believe that it is transmissible under certain favorable conditions, but that it is comparatively rarely transmitted. Throughout I was most careful to point out that this question of the transmissibility of the disease from one species to the other should not in any way lead to lessened restrictions or diminished endeavor to eradicate tuberculosis from cattle,

*Philadelphia Medical Journal, December, 1899.

but that on the contrary, as already stated, the less the extent of transmission from the one species to the other, the greater the hope of eradicating the disease from among our cattle, the greater the hope also of materially benefiting the Canadian farmer.

In discussing Dr. Koch's celebrated address it is but right in the first place to call attention to the fact that it was not directly but only incidentally upon this subject of the relationship of human and bovine tuberculosis, the full title given by him being "the combating of tuberculosis in the light of the experience that has been gained in the successful combating of other infectious diseases." The distinguished writer laid down in the first place that the most important lesson we have learnt from experiences is that it is a great blunder to treat pestilence uniformly. He pointed out that in the case of the plague, for example, we have learnt that human plague is dependent upon rat plague, that the real transmittors of the disease are rats, and that therefore to stamp out the disease we have to destroy the rats in a region; that with cholera the main propagator is water and that in combating this disease water is therefore the first thing to be considered. The compulsory muzzling of dogs has had remarkable effects in freeing Great Britain from hydrophobia, and leprosy has from early days been combated by isolation. Thus, to select the right means of eradicating tuberculosis, we must determine what is the root of the evil and must not squander for insuborinate ineffective measures, and, to arrive at a satisfactory result, we must, in the first place, enquire how infection takes place in tuberculosis.

He showed how we have abundant evidences that the disease is mainly set up by inhalation and that the sputum of consumptive people is to be regarded as the main source of the infection with tuberculosis. He took it that upon this point all were agreed. He next asked whether there were not other sources also copious enough to demand consideration in the combating of tuberculosis. Taking these into consideration he indicated that hereditary tuberculosis, while not absolutely non-existent, is so extremely rare that in considering practical measures we are at liberty to leave this form of origin entirely out of the question. It was at this point he discussed next the possibility of tuberculor infection from the transmission of the germs of the disease from tubercular infection from the transmission of the germs of the animals to man. Here it would be well to give his exact words.

"This manner of infection is generally regarded nowadays as proved, and as so frequent that it is even looked upon by not a few as the most important, and the most rigorous measures are demanded against it. In this Congress also the discussion of the danger with which the tuberculosis of animals threatens man will play an important part. Now, as my investigations have led me to form an opinion deviating from that which is genrally accepted. I beg your permission, in consideration of the great importánce of this question, to discuss it a little more thoroughly.

"Genuine tuberculosis has hitherto been observed in almost all domestic animals, and most frequently in poultry and cattle. The tuberculosis of poultry, however, differs so much from human tuberculosis that we may leave it out of account as a possible source of infection for man. So, strictly speaking, the only kind of animal tuberculosis remaining to be considered is the tuberculosis of cattle, which, if really transferable to man, would indeed have frequent opportunities of infecting human beings through the drinking of the milk and the eating of the flesh of diseased animals.

"Even in my first circumstancial publication on the etiology of tuberculosis I expressed myself regarding the identity of human tuberculosis and bovine tuberculosis with reserve.* Proved facts which would have enabled me sharply to distinguish these two forms of the disease were not then at my disposal, but sure proofs of their absolute identity were equally undiscoverable, and I therefore had to leave this question undecided. In order to decide it, I have repeatedly resumed the investigations relating to it, but so long as I experimented on small animals, such as rabbits and guinea-pigs, I failed to arrive at any satisfactory result, though indications which rendered the difference of the two forms of tuberculosis probable were not wanting. Not till the complaisance of the Ministry of Agriculture enabled me

*I have carefully read through Professor Koch's "first circumstantial publication" and found in it no signs of the reserve here mentioned. The impression given to the whole scientific world by that paper was that Koch had proved the identity of the two conditions and disproved the teaching of Virchow and others, who held their non-identity.

to experiment on cattle, the only animals really suitable for these investigations, did I arrive at absolutely conclusive results. Of the experiments which I have carried out during the last two years along with Professor Schutz, of the Veterinary College of Berlin, I will tell you briefly some of the most important.

"A number of young cattle which had stood the tuberculin test, and might therefore be regarded as free from tuberculosis, were infected in various ways with pure cultures of tubercle-bacilli taken from cases of human tuberculosis; some of them got the tuberculor sputum of consumptive patients direct. In some cases the tubercle-bacilli or the sputum were injected under the skin, in others into the peritoneal cavity, in others into the jugular vein. Six animals were fed with tubercular sputum almost daily for seven or eight months; four repeatedly inhaled great quantities of bacilli, which were distributed in water, and scattered with it in the form of spray. None of these cattle (there were nineteen of them) showed any symptoms of disease,and they gained considerably in weight. From six to eight months after the beginning of the experiments they were killed. In their internal organs not a trace of tuberculosis was found. Only at the places where the injections had been made small suppurative foci had formed, in which few tubercle-bacilli could be found. This is exactly what one finds when one injects dead tubercle-bacilli under the skin of animals liable to contagion. So the animals we experimented on were affected by the living bacilli of human tuberculosis exactly as they would have been by dead ones; they were absolutely insusceptible to them.

"The result was utterly different however, when the same experiment was made on cattle free from tubrculosis with tubercle-bacilli that came from the lungs of an animal suffering from bovine tuberculosis. After an incubation period of about a week the severest tubercular disorders of the internal organs broke out in all the infected animals. It was all one whether the infecting matter had been injected only under the skin or into the peritoneal cavity or the vascular system. High fever set in, and the animals became weak and lean; some of them died after a month and a half to two months, others were killed in a miserable sick condition after three months. After death extensive tubercular infiltrations were found at the place where the injections had been made, and in the neighboring lymphatic glands, and also far advanced alterations of the internal organs, especially the lungs and the spleen. In the cases in which the injection had been made into the peritoneal cavity the tubercular growths which are so characteristic of bovine tuberculosis were found on the omentum and peritoneum. In short, the cattle proved just as susceptible to infection by the bacillus of bovine tuberculosis as they had proved insusceptible to infection by the bacillus of human tuberculosis. I wish only to add that preparations of the organs of the cattle which were artifically infected with bovine tuberculosis in these experiments are exhibited in the Museum of Pathology and Bacteriology.

[*To be continued.*]

CREOSOTAL IN THE TREATMENT OF ACUTE NON-TUBERCULAR DISEASES OF THE RESPIRATORY ORGANS OF NURSLINGS AND CHILDREN.

BY DR. WILHELM MEITNER,
District Physician at Wostitz.

The author states that the simplicity and agreeable nature of Creosotal treatment makes it especially suitable for country practice, more particularly for children, and even for infants. Nothing more is required than occasional cardiac stimulation by small doses of wine.

The effect was noticeable both upon the etiological factor and the local disease focus; and the secondary affections that so frequently occur were either entirely absent or were far less severe.

He administered large doses of the non-poisonous remedy. The tissue fluids were saturated with creosote, and kidneys, skin, and lungs excreted it; but any excess was carried off by the bowels without any irritative symptoms.

The earliest Creosotal excretion occurs in the expired air, and hence Creosotal is very advantageous in respiratory affections. There is a constant creosote diffusion through the bronchial mucosa, which is in many cases the seat of disease; and the air spaces are filled with creosoted and disinfected air.

Antipyretics were needless. In acute laryngites, bronchites, and moderate bronchopneumonias the temperature gradually fell, so that in 12 to 36 hours the fever disappeared, exactly as occurs in fresh lobar pneumonia.

Dr. Meitner warns against the employment of too small doses. Children under 6 months old, seriously ill, should get 1 gram (15 grains); up to 1 year of age 1.5 grams (22½ grains); from 1 to 2 years, 2 to 2.5 grams (30 to 37½ grains); from 2 to 5 years, 2.5 to 4 grams (37½ to 60 grains); and from 5 to 10 years, 4 to 6 grams (1 to 1½ drams) daily. The number of doses into which these amounts may be divided is optional, but the drug should be given every 5 to 8 hours. Too great an interval should not take place without medication during the winter nights.

As the temperature falls, thirst, headache, dyspepsia, etc., become less; appetite often returns suddenly, so that it is difficult to keep the patients to a suitable diet. Nurslings can be permitted to satisfy their hunger freely.

Infants often swallow their expectoration; and here Creosotal, a most excellent intestinal antiseptic, prevents that tract from being damaged.

As soon as there is a decided local improvement the dosage may be diminished; but it should be continued for one day after mucus in the lungs has disappeared.

Dr. Meitner here appends a tabular list of 51 cases of bronchitis, 3 cases of bronchitis suffocativa, 10 bronchopneumonias, and 11 pneumonias treated with Creosotal. In some of them the disease was absolutely aborted. Complicated cases of measles get well almost as fast under Creosotal treatment as uncomplicated ones under no treatment at all. There were no sequellae of any seriousness. Even a severe case of pneümonia and enteritis, which was in a very serious condition when Meitner took hold of it, soon recovered under Creosotal.

In concluding Dr. Meitner points to the rapid action of Creosotal, in complications of measles, and states that anyone who has once treated such an epidemic with Creosotal will not be willing to do without it in the next series of cases that he meets.

MEDICO-LEGAL SURGERY.

ASSOCIATE EDITORS.

Medical.

Granville P. Conn, M. D., Concord, N. H.
R. Harvey Reed, M. D., Wyoming.
Nicholas Senn, M. D., Chicago, Ill.
Webb J. Kelley, M. D., Galion, Ohio.

Legal.

Clarence A. Lightner, Esq., Detroit, Mich
Judge Wm. H. Francis, New York.
Prof. A. P. Grinnell, M. D., Burlington, Vt.

This department is conducted as the organ of the Section of the Medical Jurisprudence of Surgery of the Medico-Legal Society. Its officers for 1902 are as follows:

Chairman.

Chief Surgeon Charles K. Cole, M.D., of Helena, Montana.

LEGAL. Vice-Chairmen.

Clark Bell, Esq., of New York.
Judge W. H. Francis, of New York.
Hon. J. W. Fellows, of N. H.
Hon. W. C. Howell, of Iowa.
A. P. Grinnell, M. D., of Vermont.
Hon. A. R. Parmenter, of Troy, N. Y.
Hon. George R. Peck, of Illinois.
Hon. J. M Thurston, of Nebraska.
Judge A. H. Dailey, of Brooklyn, N. Y.
Hon. Allen Zollers, of Indiana.

SURGICAL. Vice-Chairmen.

Ch. Surg W. A. Adams, of Ft. Worth. Tex.
Ch. Surg. F. H. Caldwell, M. D., of Fla.
Ch. Sur. Granville P. Conn, M. D., of N. H.
Ch. Surg. W. B. Outten, M. D., of Missouri.
Surgeon Geo. Chaffee, M. D., of Brooklyn.
Ch. Surg. B. F. Eads, M. D., of Texas.
Ch. Surg. John E. Owen, M. D., of Chicago.
Surg. Gen. R. Harvey Reed, M. D., of Wy.
Surg. Gen. Nicholas Senn, M. D., of Ill.
Ch. Surg. S. S. Thorne, M. D., of Ohio.

Secretary.

Clark Bell, Esq., 39 Broadway, N. Y.

Treasurer.

Judge Wm. H. Francis, New York City.
39 Broadway, N. Y.

Executive Committee.

Clark Bell, Esq., Chairman.

Surg. Thomas Darlington, M. D., of N. Y.
L. L. Gilbert, Esq., Pittsburg, Pa.
Ex-Ch. Sur. Geo. Goodfellow, M. D., Cal.
Surgeon J. N. Hall, of Denver, Colo.
Chief Surg. A. C. Scott, M. D., of Texas.
Judge A. H. Dailey, of Brooklyn, N. Y.
Sur. R. S. Parkhill, M.D., of Hornelsville, N.Y.
Sur. Fayette H. Peck, M. D., of Utica, N. Y.
Chief Sur. T. I. Pritchard, of Wis.
R. C. Richards, Esq., of Chicago, Ill.
Ch. Surg. F. A. Stillings, M. D., of N. H.
Ch. Surg. J J. Buckley, Missoula, Montana

To Railway Surgeons and Railway Counsel:

We take occasion to advise you to unite with the Section of Medico-Legal Surgery, which can now be done by an annual subscription of $1.50, entitling each member to the *Medico-Legal Journal* free.

G. P. CONN, M. D.,
Ex-Chairman Section Med.-Leg. Surgery.

ABRAM H. DAILEY,
Ex-President Medico-Legal Society of New York.

SAMUEL S. THORN, M. D.,
Chief Surgeon T., St. L. & K. C. Railway Co., Ex-President National Association Railway Surgeons.

J. B. MURDOCH, M. D.,
Surgeon and Ex-President National Association of Railway Surgeons.

R. HARVEY REED, M. D.,
Surgeon General of State of Wyoming,

R. S. HARNDEN, M. D.,
Ex-President New York State Association Railway Surgeons. Ex-President Erie Railway Surgeons.

HUBBARD W. MITCHEL, M. D.,
Ex-President Medico-Legal Society of New York.

Members of the Section on Medico-Legal Surgery, who have not remitted their annual subscription to the Section, will please send same to Judge Wm. H. Francis, No 39 Broadway, N. Y., and members will please not confound the Section Dues with the Annual Dues of the Society, which should be remitted to Caroline J. Taylor, Treasurer, Bridgeport, Conn. Members of the Society or Section will please propose names for membership in this Section.

It is proposed that members of the Society and Section each donate one bound volume annually to the Library of the Medico-Legal Society, by action of the Executive Committee.

SECTION OF MEDICO-LEGAL SURGERY—MEDICO-LEGAL SOCIETY.

ANNUAL REPORT—January 1, 1902.

To the Fellows of the Section of Medico-Legal Surgery and of the Medico Legal Society:

The domain and province of the Section is defined by the following standing resolution:

Resolved, That all questions in Medico-Legal Surgery are to be deemed within the scope and province of the Section on Railway Surgery, including, especially, military and naval surgery, and the broad domain of surgery in its relation to medical jurisprudence.

The Section is intended to embrace, besides naval, military, and railway surgeons and counsel railway managers, railway officials, whether lawyers or surgeons; many of whom have already united with the body, and who are eligible to membership under the statutes of the Society.

Three members of the Executive Committee constitute a quorum, and five of the Board of Officers of the Section.

The work of the Section during the preceding year has been devoted to the advancement of the science of the medical jurisprudence of surgery in all of its branches. The papers contributed upon these branches of science have been in part published in the Medico Legal Journal, which is the official organ of the Section.

The following is a *resume* of the work of the Section during the year:

1. Joint session of the Section with the Medico-Legal Society, April 19th, 1901.
2. Announcement of circular letter from the officers of the Section sent under date of January 17, 1900, to its members and others. (Printed on p 374 of Vol. XIX of the Journal..
3. Paper by Judge Wm. H. Francis, entitled "Railway Surgeons and Hospitals."
4. Paper by George Chaffee, M. D., entitled "First Aid and Transportation of the Injured."
5. Paper by Chief Surgeon Webb J. Kelley, of Galion, Ohio, entitled "Ankle Sprains." (So-called.)
6. Paper by Dr. A. P. Grinnell, of Burlington, Vt., entitled "Stimulants in Forensic Medicine."
7. Resolutions on the death of Col. Edward C. James (p 379, Vol. XIX Journal.)

The extraordinary time and space given to the American Congress of Tuberculosis interfered with and affected the work of this Section during all the year 1901.

The following are Associate Editors:

MEDICAL.

Granville P. Conn, M. D., Concord, N. H.
R. Harvey Reed, M. D., Wyoming.
Nicholas Senn, M. D., Chicago, Ill.
Webb J. Kelley, M. D., Galion, Ohio.
Prof. A. P. Grinnell, M. D., Burlington, Vt.

LEGAL.

Clarence A. Lightner, Esq., Detroit, Mich.
Judge Wm. H. Francis, New York.
Judge Abram H. Daile , Brooklyn.
Judge Charles G. Garrison, of N. Y.
Judge L. A. Emery, of Maine.

This department is conducted as the organ of the Section of the Medical Jurisprudence of Surgery of the Medico-Legal Society.

The following officers are recommended for re-election for 1902:

Chairman.

Chief Surgeon Charles K. Cole, M. D., of Helena, Mont.

LEGAL. Vice-Chairmen.

Clark Bell, Esq., of New York.
Judge W. H. Francis, of New York.
Hon. J. W. Fellows, of N. H.
Hon. W. C. Howell, of Iowa.
Prof. A, P. Grinnell, M. D., of Vermont.
Hon. A. R. Parmenter, of Troy, N. Y.
Hon. George R. Peck, of Illinois.
Hon. J. M. Thurston, of Nebraska.
Judge Abram H. Dailey, Brooklyn, N. Y.
L. L. Gilbert, Esq , of Pennsylvania.

SURGICAL. Vice-Chairman.

Ch. Surg. W. A. Adams, of Ft Worth, Tex.
Ch Surg. F. H. Caldwell, M. D., of Fla.
Ch. Surg. Granville P. Conn, M. D of N.H.
Ch. Surg. W. B. Outten, M. D., of St. Louis.
Surgeon Geo. Chaffee, M. D., of Brooklyn.
Surg. Thos. Darlington, M. D., of N. Y.
Ch. Surg. B. F. Eads, M. D., of Texas.
Surg. Gen. R. Harvey Reed, M. D., of Wy
Surg. Gen. Nicholas Senn, M. D., of Ill.
Ch. Surg. S. S. Thorne, M. D., of Ohio.

Secretary.

*Clark Bell, Esq., 39 Broadway, N. Y.

Treasurer.

Judge Wm. H. Francis, New York City.
39 Broadway. N. Y.

Executive Committee.

Clark Bell, Esq., Chairman.

Surg. Thomas Darlington, M. D., of N. Y.
Ex-Ch. Surg Geo. Goodfellow, M. D., Cal.
Chief Surg. A. C. Scott, M. D., of Texas.
Judge A. H. Dailey, of New York.
Sur. R. S. Parkhill M. D, of Hornelsville, N. Y.
Sur. Fayette H. Peck, M. D., of Utica, N. Y.
Claim Agt. R. C Richards, Esq., Chicago.
Ch. Surg. F. A Stillings, M. D., of N. H.

The following is the present

ROLL OF MEMBERS.

Surgeon H. B. Allen, Cloquet, Minn.
Surgeon E. L. Annis, M. D., La Porte, Ind.
Surgeon W. G. Branch, M. D., Bunkie, La.
Clark Bell, Esq., of New York.
Hon. C. H. Blackburn, of Cincinnati, Ohio.
Surgeon S. Grover Burnett, M. D., of Missouri.
Surgeon T. J. Bennett, M. D., of Austin, Texas.
Surgeon S. Belknap, M. D., Big 4 System, Niles, Mich.
Surgeon W. H. Burland, M. D., Punta Garda, Fla.
Charles L. Baxter, Esq., Atty El. R. R., Boston, Mass.
Chief Surgeon John J. Buckley, Missoula, Montana.
Surgeon George Chaffee, M. D., 226 47th St., Brooklyn, N. Y.
Surgeon D. W. Cowan, C. N. R. R. & S. P. & D., Hinckley, Minn.
Chief Sur. G. P. Conn, M. D., of Concord, N. H.
Chief Sur. Chas. K. Cole, M. D., of Helena, Mon.
Surgeon Martin Cavana, of Oneida, N. Y.
*Surgeon James H. Calvin, M. D., of Huron, O.
Chief Surgeon Chas. H. Caldwell (Plant System), Way Cross, Ga.
Surgeon R. Percey Crookshank, M. D., Rapid City, Manitoba.
Surgeon W. S. Cudebeck, Port Jervis, New York.
Judge A. H. Dailey, of Brooklyn, N. Y.
Surgeon J. M. Dinnen, of Fort Wayne, Ind.
Surgeon C. M. Daniel, M. D., of Buffalo, N. Y.
Surgeon H. W. Darr, M. D., of Caldwell, Texas.
Surgeon Thos. Darlington, M. D., N. Y. City.
Surgeon A. E. Ellingwood, Attica, New York.
L. E. Dickey, Esq., Birmingham, Ala.
Surgeon A. Eyer, M. D., of Cleveland, Ohio.
Chief Sur. B. F. Eads, M. D., of Texas.
Surgeon Jno. L. Eddy, Erie Ry. Surgeons, Olean, N. Y.
Hon. Joseph W. Fellows, of Concord, N. H.

Judge Wm. H. Francis, of No. 39 Broadway, N. Y.
Chief Sur. J. C. Field, H. & D., Denison, Texas.
Surgeon De Sassure Ford, M. D., of Augusta, Ga.
Chief Surgeon J. H. Ford, M. D., C. W. & M. Railway, Wabash,Ind.
Surgeon S. L. M. Foote, M. D., Argentine, Kansas.
Sur. William Govan, M. D., of Stony Point, N. Y.
*Surgeon G. Graves, M. D., Herkimer, New York.
Surgeon A. P. Grinnell, M. D., Burlington, Vt.
Chief Sur. Geo. Goodfellow, M. D., of California.
Surgeon W. N. Garrett, M. D., Forney, Texas.
Hon. William C. Howell, of Keokuk, Iowa.
Surgeon G. P. Howard, M. D., of Texas.
Surgeon R. S. Harnden, M. D., of Waverly, N. Y.
Surgeon J. L. Hall, M. D., Fairhaven, N. Y.
Surgeon M. B. Hubbs, M. D., Addison, N. Y.
Surgeon John E. Hannon, Jasper, Fla.
Col. Valery Havard, M. D., Med. Dept. U. S. A., Fort Monroe, Va.
Surgeon N. deV. Howard, M. D., Sanford, Fla.
Surgeon John H. Hurt, M. D., Big Springs, Texas.
Surgeon C. B. Herrick, M. D., Scy. N. Y. State Ass. Ry. Surgeons, Troy, N. Y.
Surgeon L. C. Hicks, M. D., Burlington, Wis.
Surgeon F. S. Hartman, M. D., 5 Blue Island avenue, Chicago, Ill.
Chief Surgeon W. T. Jameson, M. D., of Texas.
Dr. H. Johnson, Surg. at Hospital, Grandin, Mo.
W. J. Kelly, Esq., of New York.
Surgeon C. B. Kibler, M. D., of Corry, Penn.
Sur. A. P. Knapp, M. P. Railway, Leoti, Kansas.
Surgeon R. E. L. Kincaid, Bonham, Texas.
Chief Sur. N. Y. Leet, M. D., of Scranton, Pa.
Surgeon I.C. Legare, M. D., of Donaldson, La.
Surgeon J. A. Lightfoot, M. D., Texarkana, Ark.
Surgeon C. F. Leslie, Clyde, Kansas.
Surgeon F. T. Labadie, M. D., 122 W. 64th St., New York.
Surgeon W. H. Meyers, M. D., Myersdale, Penn.
Chief Surgeon Solon Marks, Milwaukee, Wis.
Chief Surg. W. H. Monday, M. D., Terrell, Tex.
Surgeon H. W. Mitchell, M. D., of New York.
Chief Surg. H. McHatton, M. D., of Macon, Ga.
Chief Surgeon John Mears, Kansas City.
Chief Surg. J. C. Martin, F. H. W. & W. Findlay, O.
Surgeon A. A. McLeod, M. D., of Michigan.
Surgeon William B. Morrow, N. Y. O. & W. R. R., Walton, Delaware Co., N. Y.
Surgeon W. H. Monday, Terrell, Texas.
Surgeons McCloud and Hodges, High Spring, Fla.
Judge J. G. McCarry, Walker, Minn.
Chief Surg. W. R. Nugent, M. D., Oscaloosa, Iowa.
Surgeon M. B. V. Newcomer, Tifton, Ind.
Chief Sur. W. B. Outten, of St. Louis, Mo.
Hon. George R. Peck, of Chicago.
Surg. R. S. Parkhill, M. D., of Hornellsville, N. Y.
R. A. Parmenter, Esq., Troy, N. Y.
Surg. T. P. Russell, M. D., of New Oshkosh, Wis.
Sur. General R. Harvey Reed, M. D., Wyoming.
Surgeon J. T. Reeve, M. D., of Appleton, Wis.
R. C. Richards, Esq., Claim Agent, N. W. Ry., Chicago, Ill.
Surgeon C. L. Stiles, M. D., of Oswego, N. Y.
Surgeon E. M. Schofield, M. D., of Jamestown, N. Y.
Chief Surgeon C. A. Smith, M. D., of Tyler, Texas.
Chief Surgeon F. A. Stillings, of Concord, N. H.
Sur-Gen. Nicholas Senn, M. D., of Chicago, Ill.

Surgeon H. B. Sauner, M. D., of Wisconsin.
Chief Surgeon A. C. Scott, G. C. & S. F. R., Temple, Texas.
R. W. Shufeldt, M. D., 502 West 142nd St., New York.
Surgeon Samuel D. Smoke, M. D., Fort White, Fla.
Hon. John M. Thurston, Omaha, Nebraska.
Chief Sur. S. S. Thorn, M. D., of Toledo, O.
Surgeon A. A. Thompson, of Waxaeaclin, Texas.
Judge L. R. Watts, of Portsmouth, Va.
Surgeon B. F. Wilson, M. D., of Slater, Mo.
Surgeon C. S. Ward, M. D., of Ohio.
Sur. H. J. Williams, M. D., of Georgia.
Chief Surgeon Webb J. Kelly, Sec'y, Galion, Ohio.
Surgeon J. R. West, M. D., Richmond, Ind.
Nelson W. Wilson, M. D., 53 7th St., Buffalo, N. Y.
Surgeon J. P. Webster, M. D., Chicago, Ill.
Judge Allen Zollars, Solicitor P. R. R., Fort Wayne, Ind.

Only one member has died. Three members have been elected during the year. Total 104 members. The report of Judge Wm. H. Francis, Treasurer, made January 15, 1902, showed:

Total Receipts	92.58
Total Disbursements	2.00
Cash on hand	$90.58

Respectfully submitted,

C. K. COLE, M. D., Chairman.

CLARK BELL, Chairman and Sec'y.

NOTE.—The officers recommended by the Committee, were duly elected by the Medico-Legal Society at January meeting, 1902.

FIRST AID TO THE INJURED.

TRANSACTIONS.

The Society for Instruction in First Aid to the Injured held its Annual Meeting February 27th, 1902, at the United Charities Building, No. 287 Fourth Avenue, New York City.

Charles H. Marshall presided, and presented a report regarding the work of the past year, which he considered very encouraging. Instruction had been given to forty-five classes, the students numbering 650 men and 256 women and girls. There were ten classes of policemen, 403 attending, and three of firemen, numbering 59 altogether.

Similar instruction was given in ten public schools, and out of 313 pupils, who took the examination, 301 took diplomas.

There were but seven pay classes, which were instructed at the Society's office.

The Society's expenditures for the year ending January 31, 1902, were about $3,000, and there is a balance on hand of some $1,800, the largest in its history.

The officers were re-elected, as follows:

President, Charles H. Marshall; Vice-President, Thomas H. Barber; Treasurer, Zelah Van Loan; Secretary, Henry H. Truman; Medical Director, Dr. E. L. Partridge.

The entire Board of Managers was re-elected also, except that Morris K. Jesup and Francis Lynde Stetson take the places of Gen. Fitz-John Porter and George Coppell, who have died since last election. The others are: James C. Carter, Dr. J. H. Emerson, Augustus C. Gurnee, Henry E. Howland, R. Somer Hayes, Dr. Charles Hitchcock, James J. Higginson, Charles H. Marshall, Peter Marie, James W. Pinchot, Philip Schuyler, F. Augustus Schermerhorn, James Speyer, Anson Phelps Stokes, Frederick Sheldon, Bayard Tuckerman, J. Kennedy Tod, Mrs. Julius Catlin, Miss Gertrude Hoyt, Mrs. Robert Hoe, Mrs. Henry A. Oakley, and Mrs. Henry Parish, Jr.

Mrs. Charles B. Wood was elected a life member of the Society.

TRANSACTIONS.

MEDICO-LEGAL SOCIETY—JANUARY MEETING, 1902.

PRESIDENCY OF CLARK BELL, ESQ.

The January meeting and annual dinner of the Medico-Legal Society for the installation of the officers elected for the year 1902 was held at the Hotel St. Andrew, Seventy-second street and Broadway, at a dinner at which Clark Bell, President, presided; Mr. Samuel Bell Thomas, Secretary, with a large attendance.

After the removal of the cloth the meeting was organized and the minutes of the December meeting were read and on motion approved as printed in the December number of the Medico-Legal Journal.

The following persons were duly elected on recommendation of the Executive Committee:

ACTIVE MEMBERS.

Proposed by Judge Tighe, of Brooklyn, Mr. Mitchell May, of 350 Fulton street, Brooklyn.

Proposed by Judge Abram H. Dailey, Mrs. May S. Pepper, No. 1062 Eddy street, Providence, Rhode Island.

The report of the Section on Medico-Legal Surgery was made to the meeting for the year ending December 31, 1901, with a board of officers recommended for election. On motion the report was received and the board of officers submitted were on motion approved and declared duly elected for the ensuing year.

The report of the Psychological Section was laid before the society and on motion the report was received and adopted and the board of officers as recommended for ensuing year were duly elected.

On motion both reports were received, placed on file and ordered printed in the Journal and sent to members of the Sections and the society's exchanges

President-elect Clark Bell, Esq., made his inaugural address, at the close of which he recommended the election of the following thirteen names as honorary members of this society. These names having received the approval of a quorum of the Executive Committee, were duly elected. They were as follows:

Prof. Dr. Moritz Benedikt, of Vienna, Austria; Prof. Dr. N. S. Davis, of Chicago, Ill.; Judge Robert Earl, of Herkimer, N. Y.; Prof. Dr. R. Ogden Doremus, of New York City; Prof. Dr. Mierzejewski, of Russia; Dr. A. Motet, of Paris, France; Prof. Dr. Cæsar Lombroso, of Italy; Prof. Dr. Charles H. H. Hughes, of St. Louis, Mo; A. N. Bell, Editor *Sanitarian*, of New York; Hon. Abraham R. Lawrence, Ex-Justice of the Supreme Court of New York; Nicholas Senn, M. D. of Chicago; Prof. Dr. Axel Key, of Stockholm, Sweden; Judge L. A. Emery, of the Supreme Court of Maine.

The Chair then declared the newly elected officers duly installed in the the offices to which they had been elected by the Society.

The recommendation, by the President, that the Constitution be so amended as to provide for fifty honorary members, instead of twenty, then came up and, on motion, was unanimously approved.

The Chair announced that, under the Constitution and By-Laws of the Society, notice of a motion to so amend the Constitution must be made at a prior meeting before it could be so acted upon.

FIRS AID TO THE INJURED.

TRANSACTIONS.

The Society for Instaction in First Aid to the Injured Meeting February 27tl 1902, at the United Charities Fourth Avenue, New ork City.

Charles H. Marshal presided, and presented a re work of the past year, hich he considered very encc tion had been given torty-five classes, the students and 256 women and gis. There were ten classes o tending, and three of temen, numbering 59 altoget

Similar instruction vas given in ten public s pupils, who took the eamination, 301 took diplom

There were but seve pay classes, which were in ty's office.

The Society's expenitures for the year ending about $3,000, and theris a balance on hand of in its history.

The officers were re-ected, as follows:

President, Charles H Marshall; Vice-Presid Treasurer, Zelah Van lau; Secretary, Henry rector, Dr. E. L. Partrge.

The entire Board of Muagers was re-electe K. Jesup and Francis Inde Stetson take t Porter and George Copell, o have died are: James C. Carter, r. Emerson, Howland, R. Somer Hye Charles H Charles H. Marshall, Ite e, James F. Augustus Schermer s Speye erick Sheldon, Bayard l, J. Ke Miss Gertrude Ho , M Hoe, M Henry Parish, Jr.

Mrs. Charles B. Woo ed a l

SOC

N

a

Memriam

OF

DAVID IcADAM,

EW YORK ITY, DECEASED.

PREME COIT OF NEW YORK STATE.

THE MEDI-LEGAL SOCIETY OF NEW YORK.

Y MR. CLAK BELL,

OF THE MEICO-LEGAL SOCIETY,

F THE MEDI-LEGAL JOURNAL,

A WARM PERNAL FRIEND.

The Secretary, Samuel B. Thomas, then gave notice that he now moved that Article III of the Constitution of the Society be amended so that the last clause of said article shall read as follows : "The number of honorary members shall be limited to fifty," instead of the clause as it now reads, and that he would renew the same motion at a future meeting.

The Chair held that this motion lie over until the February meeting, under the provisions of Article VIII of the Constitution, the Executive Committee having reported its approval of the amendment at this meeting.

Judge Abram H. Dailey moved that the President name and appoint committees, to act in conjunction with any and all committees to be appointed by the American Congress of Tuberculosis, for the annual meeting on May 14th, 15th and 16th, proximo.

It was also resolved that this body favors a committee to be named for a museum to be held with that Congress, and that the President be and hereby is authorized to organize such a committee, with a view of making it a joint committee of both organizations, and that the Chair be authorized to organize and appoint all committees to represent this body in that Congress, pursuant to the recommendation of the Executive Committee of this Society.

The Chair announced the death of Hon. David McAdam, one of the Justices of the Supreme Court of this State, resident in the City of New York, one of the charter members and founders of this Society, and paid a high tribute to the memory of the deceased.

Mr. Bell spoke of the long and useful life of Mr. Justice McAdam on the Bench and at the Bar of this city, before he rose to the Bench.

He dwelt upon his useful and upright life, his love of justice for justice's sake, his fearlessness and courage for that which he believed to be right, of the purity and cleanliness which had characterized his life as a citizen, a lawyer and a judge; of the interest he had taken in medical jurisprudence and in the early history of the Medico-Legal Society, and presented to the Society and to all the members and guests at the session a memorial that he had prepared, as a slight tribute of the regard and esteem he had ever felt for the deceased as a man, as a fellow-member and as a Judge of the high Court he had so adorned and illumined in his useful life.

Mr. Bell then introduced Mr. Justice Henry W. Gildersleeve, of the New York Supreme Court, one of the associates of the late Justice McAdam, a corresponding member of this Society, as one whom he had invited to speak on the occasion when this Society was called upon to mourn the loss his death had caused.

Judge Gildersleeve then paid the following tribute to the memory of Mr. Justice McAdam:

"David McAdam was born on the Island of Manhattan in 1838. His parents ranked among the humble people of the city. After receiving a necessarily limited education in the public schools, he entered upon the labor of life, as a bread-winner, at the age of ten years,—a time when most children begin to prepare themselves in institutions of learning for battle with the world. When first entering upon employment in the law office of his uncle, in the Inns of Court, 27 Beekman street, he displayed, as a boy, that tireless activity which, to the last, was his distinguishing characteristic. He early applied himself to the study of Blackstone and Kent and the Code of Procedure, committing the latter to memory. For years before his admission to the Bar, he was often seen in courts, trying cases and arguing motions.

"In 1856, at the age of about 19 years, David McAdam became managing clerk for Francis F. Marbury, at that time one of the most prominent lawyers at the New York Bar. There the young man did valuable work in important litigations conducted by his employer, in the course of which he was complimented by eminent lawyers, including the late Samuel J. Tilden. There was no typewriting in those days, and little, if any, stenography. The days were far too short for this energetic young

In Memoriam

OF

HON. DAVID MCADAM,

LATE OF NEW YORK CITY, DECEASED.

JUSTICE OF THE SUPREME COURT OF NEW YORK STATE.

ONE OF THE FOUNDERS OF THE MEDICO-LEGAL SOCIETY OF NEW YORK.

BY MR. CLARK BELL,

PRESIDENT OF THE MEDICO-LEGAL SOCIETY,

EDITOR OF THE MEDICO-LEGAL JOURNAL,

AND A WARM PERSONAL FRIEND.

managing clerk, and he spent large portions of the nights in drawing papers incidental to the law suits in which his office was interested.

"For several years prior to his majority, he had been recognized as a lawyer *de facto.* The long wished for twenty-first birthday came in 1859, and then he became a lawyer *de jure*, entitled to practice in all the courts of this State. Very soon after his admission to the Bar, the young practitioner opened an office in Wall street, and he also hired quarters on Eighth avenue, near his home, where, at night time, he could be found ready, at a moment's notice, to give advice to any client, rich or poor. The clients with little means frequented the latter office, and were by far the most numerous of those who sought his services. He was always a friend to the poor, and gave of his legal learning and hard earned money most freely and most generously. The two offices did not afford sufficient opportunity for work to this indefatigable spirit. After his clients had returned to their homes to rest for the night, this tireless man frequently worked in his library at home until the morning hours. An incident, narrated by the agent of a Benefit Association, strikingly illustrates David McAdam's passion for work and his unusually strong constitution. The agent in question called at his house for the purpose of enrolling the young lawyer as a member, but when he learned how incessantly David McAdam worked, while others slept, he declined to accept the risk, for the reason, as he said, that no man could stand such a strain for three months. However, keeping the young lawyer under surveillance, the agent, after about six months' observation, begged an application for membership, saying that nothing could kill a man who could work, as did David McAdam, at all hours, without showing signs of fatigue, and who had a joke on his lips when engaged even in the most serious occupation. He joined the Association, and, instead of being a bad risk, lived to see the death of the Society more than twenty years thereafter. Although not always taking an active part in the political campaigns of the day, he always felt a lively interest in politics, and was well posted on the questions raised and the situation generally. He was both feared and respected by political leaders, for the reason that the people were always with him David McAdam was distinctly and emphatically a man of the people. His latest achievement in the political field, and I believe one of the happiest incidents in the latter years of his life, was the election of his son to the Assembly of this State in the last campaign.

"In 1873 David McAdam was elected to the Bench of the Marine, now City, Court. He was re-elected to the same Court in 1876, and again in 1885. In the last-named year, through his efforts and influence, the name of the Court was changed to the City Court of the City of New York. During his long connection with this Court, of which he was Chief Justice for many years, he labored constantly, with marked ability, to increase its usefulness. His efforts were eminently successful. They resulted in raising the jurisdiction from actions involving five hundred dollars to those involving two thousand dollars, and otherwise adding to the dignity and power of the tribunal. He was the controlling spirit of the Court for many years, and the force of his personality was so great that he was appropriately called 'The Father of the City Court.' In 1890 Judge McAdam was elected to the Superior Court of the City of New York, and in 1896, on the merger of that Court within the Supreme Conrt, he became a Justice of the Supreme Court of the State of New York. His term of office wonld have ended on December 31st, 1904. The records of the courts, where he presided, and the official Law Reports, bear testimony to his untiring energy, extensive learning and sound judgment. He was also an author of high ability. *McAdam's Landlord and Tenant* is a most valuable contribution to the law libraries of the country. He was not a man of original research, seeking to develop and enforce new ideas. Principles that had been applied and approved were satisfactory to him. In ascertaining precedents and familiarizing himself with the rules of law, laid down in the leading cases, he was most industrious. He had more leading authorities at his immediate command than any one else with whom I have ever become acquainted. He was always ready to discuss questions of law with his associates and others, and cheerfully gave, to all, the benefit of his learning and experience. Although fully confident of his judgment upon the particular question of law under discussion, he never asked to have the statement of his views accepted as conclusive. His hands were speedily upon his books and the authority pointed out. He had no desire for display or for the surroundings that are the privilege of the rich. He was gifted, however, with musical talent and artistic tastes. His ambition was to lead, not to follow. He found his most congenial companionship among those whom he could instruct and dominate,—those who looked up to him as their superior. He was restless under discipline, and yielded an unwilling submission to the commands of others. Despite his long public life, his learning and prominence, he was a most companionable man. Life seemed easier and brighter after a conversation with Judge McAdam. He was prone to look upon the bright side, and keep his own troubles, if he had any, to himself. How often I have heard him in conversation in this connection repeat the following lines:

"'Laugh and the World laughs with you;
Weep, and you weep alone.
The dear old Earth enjoys our Mirth,
But has Sorrows enough of its own.'

"He was ever ready with anecdotes that brought smiles to the faces and rest to the hearts of his listeners. Though fond of humor, I never knew him to laugh aloud. Strenuousness and tenderness were commingled in his disposition. A determination which would stop at no obstacle was combined with child-like gentleness. He was quick to resent a wrong, but ever ready to forgive. His friendship was generous, loyal and abiding, and is now a rich treasure in the hearts of the friends who survive him. He was devoted to his wife and children, and was a model husband and father.

"His physical affliction, that resulted in his death, did not make its appearance until last summer, and it was not until December last that he was advised of its serious character. He employed the most skilled medical and surgical advice, and did as they bid him. We know the result. The details are too painful to dwell upon. When he turned his back upon the court house, but a few days before he died, he walked away with his customary vigor, and left no work unfinished behind him.

"It must be said that he was a man of originality of character and marked individuality. Observed from every point of view, his life was unusually brilliant and successful. He was stricken down with the harness on, and in the fullness of his powers, at a time in life of great usefulness to his fellow-men. His judicial work remains as a safe guide to those who follow in his footsteps. In his generous deeds and noble examples he still lives unseen, among us. He will be remembered, by those who were near him, with love and affection, and by all who knew him, with respect and admiration."

President Bell then introduced Mr. Justice Steckler, whom Governor Benjamin F. Odell had selected and appointed to fill the vacancy on the Bench of the Supreme Court, caused by the death of Mr. Justice McAdam.

Mr. Bell said that the Governor of the State, in filling this position and in the selection he had made to fill this vacancy, had chosen a man who had never been identified with the Republican party; that Mr. Justice Steckler's appointment had met with a favorable reception by the bar; that the Governor of the State, in sinking partisan political consideration and selecting a Democratic lawyer for the place, had shown great wisdom and sagacity, and he had heard only praise and commendation of the Governor's action.

He introduced Mr. Justice Alfred Steckler to speak of the great respect and reverence felt for the deceased jurist by the masses of the people of the city.

Judge Steckler returned thanks for the high honor shown him in allowing him the opportunity to speak, in this presence, of the virtues and merits of the really great jurist. whose untimely death had caused mourning among his associates on the Bench and the masses of the people of all ranks and classes in this city.

He said that Judge McAdam was an ideal Judge, who possessed in an extraordinary degree the supreme confidence of the people, especially of those whom Mr. Lincoln used to call the plain people; that if it were in his power to win a tithe of the success that had crowned Judge McAdam's judicial career, he should esteem himself the most fortunate of men; that he knew of no safer ideal to hold up in his mind, in the discharge of the duties devolving upon him, than the life which Judge McAdam led as a Judge, and the splendid success which had crowned that life and illumined his career; that he could only attempt to emulate it, and could not hope to excel or even equal him.

He complimented the Medico-Legal Society on its great work in the past, and spoke of the interest he felt in medico-legal questions. He predicted a high career of usefulness to the Society in its work, and especially in relation to the American Congress of Tuberculosis in May next to consider how to prevent and arrest the spread of this great scourge of the race.

Mr. Bell then alluded to the death of Dr. Albert L. Gihon, one of the oldest members, a corresponding member of nearly a quarter of a century's association in our labors, who had held the highest medical honors in the power of our Government to bestow, who had died universally respected and beloved, and called on Dr. Isaac N. Love, Editor of the *Medical Mirror*, late of St. Louis and now of New York City, an old and intimate friend of the deceased, to speak in his memory. Dr. Love paid a high tribute to the memory of Dr. Gihon.

Mr. Bell then spoke of the death of Dr. Irving Rosse, late of Washington, D. C., one of the leading neurologists and alienists of this country, and submitted the report of the Committee on his death, which was received and ordered placed on file.

It was moved and seconded that a copy of the action on the deaths above named be sent to the families of the deceased members and to those named by the President in his address.

The Society adjourned at a late hour.

CLARK BELL, President.
SAMUEL B. THOMAS, Secretary.

MEDICO-LEGAL SOCIETY—FEBRUARY MEETING, 1902.

PRESIDENCY OF CLARK BELL, ESQ.

February 19, 1902. Medico-Legal Society met pursuant to notice at dinner at the Hotel St. Andrew, 72nd street and Broadway, the president, Clark Bell, in the chair and Samuel Bell Thomas acting as secretary.

After dinner the minutes of the meeting of January were read and on motion duly approved.

The President announced the death of Prof. Dr. Axel Key, of Stockholm, Sweden, who had recently been elected an honorary member of this Society, and paid a high tribute to the memory of Prof. Key, and spoke of the loss which the Society, in common with the world of science, had sustained in the death of this eminent man, the notice of whose death had reached the President of this body recently from his bereaved family, and asked leave to present it in a more detailed state, later, for publication in the *Medico-Legal Journal* which was granted.

The President reported from the Executive Committee of the American Congress of Tuberculosis:

1. A list of the Vice-Presidents of the several states, provinces and countries, three from a state, under the authority of the Executive Committee of that body, up to this date.

2. The names of members of the Congress who had forwarded the titles of papers to be presented at the next session of the Congress, to be held May 14th, 15th and 16th, 1903, and the titles of the papers.

3. The names of enrolled members of the American Congress of Tuberculosis who had given notice that they desired to participate in the discussion of the papers to be presented to the said Congress, and under which of the four symposiums they desired to be enrolled to speak.

4. A general report as to the appointment of Honorary Vice-Presidents of the body, with a list of those who had thus far accepted that distinction.

5. The present state of the work of the Congress, preparatory to the next session, and the steps to open a museum and to open up the discussion of the subjects to be laid before the Congress, and the arrangements that had been concluded to hold the same at Hotel Majestic on May 14th, 15th and 16th, 1902, and for the banquet on the 15th, and to the progress of the work in the Central and South American States, in Mexico, the States and Provinces of the Dominion of Canada, and asked for further time to complete the appointment of committees, authorized to be appointed, as for the best interest of both bodies, and referred to the December number of the *Medico-Legal Journal* as containing the action of the Executive officers and the Executive Committee of that body. Leave was, on motion, duly granted.

The proposed amendment to Article III of the Constitution, regarding Honorary Members, was, by unanimous consent, laid over to the March meeting.

The Society then went into joint session with the Psychological Section In the absence of the Chairman of the Section, Prof. W. Xavier Sudduth, Mr. Clark Bell, Vice-Chairman, took the Chair.

The paper by Prof. Xavier Sudduth, entitled "Thought Transferrence vs. Spiritism as an Explanation of many so-called Spiritistic Phenomena," was read (after the Chairman, Clark Bell, Esq., had presented a short paper explaining the situation of the question and the issue before the Society) by Judge Abram H. Dailey, in the absence of the author.

The paper by T. D. Crothers, entitled "Spiritism, Telepathy, Hypnotism and the Case of Mrs. Piper," was then read by the Secretary, Samuel B. Thomas in the absence of the author.

Mr. Martin, of the Brooklyn Bar, then read a paper by Dr. Alexander Wilder, entitled "Telepathy, Spiritism, Hypnotism and the case of Mrs. Elenora E. Piper."

The hour of 10 p. m. having been reached, it was moved that the remaining papers be read by title, viz.:

By Eleanor Gridley, of Chicago, entitled "Psychic Phenomena—Spirit Communication vs. Mental Telepathy."

By Wm. Lee Howard, M. D., of Baltimore, entitled "Spiritism and Mrs. Elenora Piper."

All the other p pers were read in the same manner.

Discussion was then opened on the papers, in which the following speakers took part:

Mrs. Mary Lease, Mrs. Mary M. Pepper, Mrs. Lettie Reynolds, John Wilson MacDonald and Judge Abram H. Dailey.

The Chair read letters from Rev. M. J. Savage and Swami Abhedananda, promising to be present and apologizing for their absence.

The Chair closed the debate.

Mr. Bardwell and Mr. Martin of Brooklyn, and Mrs. Friedlander of New York, were among the guests.

The meeting was most enjoyable and the Society adjourned at a late hour.

CLARK BELL, President.
SAMUEL BELL THOMAS, Secretary.

MEDICO-LEGAL SOCIETY—MARCH MEETING, 1902.

PRESIDENCY OF CLARK BELL, ESQ.

At a meeting of the Medico-Legal Society, held at a Dinner given at the Press Club, New York City, on March 19th, 1902, the President, Clark

Bell, Esq., in the Chair, and Samuel B. Thomas, Esq., Secretary, the following business was transacted :

The minutes of the February meeting were read and approved.

Article III of the Constitution, and its amendments, came up on the motion of Samuel B. Thomas, renewing the motion of January meeting, made by him, that Article III of the Constitution be amended so that the last clause of said Article shall read as follows : "The Honorary members shall be limited to fifty," instead of the clause as it now reads.

Judge A. H. Dailey seconded the motion, and on being put to vote it was carried unanimously, and the Chair declared the amendment adopted.

The Report of the Executive Committee was read, recommending the election of the following active members :

Proposed by Clark Bell : Judge Alfred Steckler, of the Supreme Court of New York ; Prof. Wm. Farr, National College of Law. Nashville, Tenn.

Proposed by S. B. Thomas : Dr. A. S. Wood, of 32 Clinton St., Brooklyn, N. Y.

Proposed by Dr. C. C. Carroll : Dr. F. Von Ritz, 301 West 106th Street, N. Y. City.

The said persons were duly elected.

The Report of the Executive Committee was read, showing the recommendation of the election of the following gentlemen as Honorary members of the Society, pursuant to the recommendation of the President, of these names :

Prof Dr. Enrico Tomasio, of the University of Padua, Padua, Italy ; Prof. Dr. Enrico Ferri, Deputy of the Italian Parliament, Rome, Italy ; Prof. Dr. Augusto Tamburini, University of Turin, Turin, Italy ; Prof. Dr. Hermann Kornfeld, Privy Councillor, Gleiwitz, Germany ; Dr. V. Magnan, Superintendent Hospice for the Insane, St. Anne, Paris ; Prof. Dr. Vleminickx, Ex-President Medico-Legal Society of Belgium, Brussels ; Jules Morel, M D., Superintendent Medical Hospital of the Royal Society at Mons, Belgium ; Hon. H. M. Somerville, Ex-Justice of the Supreme Court of Alabama ; Hon. Charles G. Garrison, of the Supreme Court of New Jersey, Camden, N. J.; Hon. David J. Brewer, of the Supreme Court of the United States at Washington, D C.; Hon. L. L. Bleckley, Ex-Chief Justice of the Supreme Court of Georgia, Atlanta ; Hon. George B. Andrews, Ex Chief Justice of the Supreme Court of Connecticut ; Sir John Sibbald, M. D , Ex-Lunacy Commissioner, Edinburg, Scotland.

On balloting for these names they were unanimously elected.

The Chairman of the Women's Committee of the Psychological Section, Caroline J. Taylor, made a report in writing, which was received and placed on file, and, on motion, duly ratified and approved, and the thanks of this body made to the Chairman of that Committee for her action and report, The report was as follows :

"*To the Officers and Fellows of the Medico-Legal Society :*

"I have the honor to submit as a Report from the Women's Committee of the Psychological Section of the Medico-Legal Society, the following report :

"That, at the Annual Meeting of the National Legislative League, held at Washington, D. C., on the 25th of February, 1902, the following resolution, submitted by myself as one of the Vice-Presidents of that organization, was, after an interesting discussion, ananimously adopted.

"'*Resolved*, That without reference to any question of innocence or guilt, we are of the opinion that the release of Mrs. Florence E. Maybrick, an American woman, who has been confined more than twelve years in an English prison, in spite of the protest and petitions of many thousands of her countrywomen, and the intercession of the American Ministers and Secretaries of State, from Blaine and Lincoln to Hay and Choate, and the personal intercession of the late lamented President McKinley, would be such an act as would gladden the hearts of millions of her countrywomen, and in no wise detract from the dignity of the British Government, but would add additional lustre to the throne of King Edward VII.'

"All of which is respectfully submitted."

The following papers and contributions were read by title on the discussion of the Piper case, that had been before the Society at the December meeting of 1901 and February, 1902, which had been contributed to that discussion, viz.: Rev. Minot J. Savage, Prof. J. H. Hyslop, Richard Hodson, LL.D., M. Louise Thomas, Rev. Geo. H. Hepworth, Thomson Jay Hudson, various selections from the *New York Herald*, and others, and ordered printed in the Medico-Legal Journal, and in a brochure which should embrace the best of the said papers and contributions.

The President then laid before the Society:

1. A list of the additional Vice-Presidents named by the American Congress of Tucerculosis, to date, from the American States and other countries.
2. Honorary Vice-Presidents who have accepted the office.
3. Such delegates to the Congress of 1902 as had been already named for 1902 by Governors of States.
4. The Chair stated that Prof. Moritz Benedikt had sent him an extended paper to be laid before the American Congress of Tuberculosis—an open letter addressed to that Congress, to be held on May 14, 15 and 16 next.

The Chair was directed to have the same translated.

Letters of thanks for the honor of Honorary membership were announced and read by the Chair from Dr. Moritz Benedikt, Dr. Nicholas Senn, Dr. A. N. Bell, Dr. C. H. Hughes, Judge Robert Earle, and Judge Abraham R. Lawrence.

Dr. C. C. Carroll then read a paper entitled "*Tuberculosis in the Blood*," which was read by the author and illustratrd by clinical experiments.

The paper was discussed by Dr. H. Edwin Lewis, Dr. F. Von Ritz, Dr. A. S. Wood, Judge A. H. Dailey, Mrs. May Pepper and Dr. McKnne.

Dr. Lewis, Dr. Von Ritz and Dr. A. S. Wood were, on motion, selected to act as a committee to examine and report on the cases to this body.

The Society adjourned at a late hour.

CLARK BELL, President.
SAMUEL B. THOMAS, Secretary.

EDITORIAL.

AMERICAN CONGRESS OF TUBERCULOSIS.

PRELIMINARY ANNOUNCEMENT.

To the Members of the American Congress of Tuberculosis, and Fellows of the Medico Legal Society:

It is quite impossible to present in the March number of the Medico Legal Journal, so far in advance of the session of the Congress on May 14, 15 and 16 proximo, a complete list of the officers, thus far selected, who have accepted, in addition to the Board of Officers and Committees that were chosen at the session of May 15 and 16, 1901, which has been published, and it is still deemed wiser to wait until the complete list of officers from all the States, Provinces and Countries has been made and the programme prepared for the meeting.

Three vice presidents were directed to be named in each of the States of the American Union and the Dominion of Canada, as well as in Mexico and in each of the Central and South American States.

In eleven of the American States these officers have not yet been selected and in a few of the other States only two have yet been selected. Delay in filling these positions has occurred in some of the Central and South American States which is due to the great distance some of these States are from us, but correspondence with all is progressing.

Honorary Vice Presidents have been named for the Dominion of Canada and all the Provinces of that Dominion, but the three Vice Presidents of the several Canadian Provinces are not yet completed, except the Province of Quebec.

Honorary Vice Presidents have been named and accepted in a large number of the American States and in Central and South America, and these places will doubtless all be filled before May 1st, as well as the Vice Presidents; none however are announced even after names have been selected until the appointees accept the position.

It is also too early to announce the delegates appointed by the Executives of States, Countries, or Provinces in Canada, because the requests to make these appointments have but recently been sent out, and the same is true of Societies, Academies of Medicine or other organizations, as special invitations have not yet gone to these, only the general invitation contained in the announcement.

To show, however, the great interest taken in this work, especially in the distant states and countries, I announce the delegates that have already been named by a few of the Governors of the American States, each of whom had accepted the Honorary Vice Presidency of the body from their respective States.

Since our last announcement the following delegates have been appointed by the Governors of the States named:

ARIZONA.

By Hon. N. O. Murphy, Governor of the Territory of Arizona, and Honorary Vice President of the American Congress of Tuberculosis, for Arizona:

Dr. D. J. Brannen, Flagstaff, Arizona.
Dr. R. W. Craig, Phoenix, Arizona.
Dr. Thomas B. Davis, Prescott, Arizona.
Dr. William Duffield, Phoenix, Arizona.
Dr. Hiram W. Fenner, Tucson, Arizona.
Dr. Ancil Martin, Phoenix, Arizona.
Dr. Mark A. Rodgers, Tucson, Arizona.
Dr. Henry H. Stone, Phoenix, Arizona.
Dr. M. M. Walker, Clifton, Arizona.
Dr. John R. Walls, Prescott, Arizona.
Dr. William V. Whitmore, Tucson, Arizona.

IDAHO.

By Frank W. Hunt, Governor of Idaho, and Honorary Vice President of the American Congress of Tuberculosis, for Idaho:

Dr. D. P. Albee,
Oakley, Idaho.
Dr. George Collister,
Boise, Idaho.
Dr. J. L. Conant, Jr.,
Genesee, Idaho.
Dr. J. K. Dubois,
Boise, Idaho.
Dr. J. W. Givens,
Blackfoot, Idaho.
Dr. William R. Hamilton,
Silver City, Idaho.
Dr. T. R. Mason,
Wardner, Idaho.
Dr. F. P. Matchette,
Wardner, Idaho.
Dr. L. P. McCalla,
Boise, Idaho.
Dr. W. Newell,
Idaho City, Idaho.
Dr. R. L. Nourse,
Hailey, Idaho.
Dr. J. J. Plumer,
Hailey, Idaho.
Dr. D'Orr Poynter,
Montpelier, Idaho.
Dr. J. J. Pulse,
Denver, Idaho.
Dr. H. Schmalhausen,
Harrison, Idaho.
Dr. Wm. F. Smith,
Mountain Home.
Dr. W. D. Springer,
Boise, Idaho.
Dr. O. B. Steely,
Pocatello, Idaho.
Dr. C. S. Stone,
Wallace, Idaho.
Dr. R. T. Story,
Albion, Idaho.
Dr. G. M. Waterhouse,
Weiser, Idaho.
Dr. W. C. Whitwell,
Salmon City, Idaho.
Dr. J. M. Woodburn,
Rexburg, Idaho.

MONTANA.

By Hon. Jos. K. Toole, Governor of Montana, and Honorary Vice President of the Ameriran Congress of Tuberculosis, for Montana:

Dr. R. B. Alton,
Livingston, Montana.
Dr. J. B. Atchison,
Lewiston, Montana.
Dr. J. J. Buckley,
Missoula, Montana.
Dr. D. L. Carmichael,
Helena, Montana.
Dr. C. M. Chambliss,
Missoula, Montana.
Dr. Ernest Crutcher,
Great Falls, Montana.
Dr. J. H. Featherston,
Missoula, Montana.
Dr. I. D. Freund,
Butte, Montana.
Dr. R. W. Getty,
Philipsburg, Montana.
Dr. J. L. Johnston,
Butte, Montana.
Dr. S. G. Leard,
Livingston, Montana.
Dr. J. L. Leiser,
Helena, Montana.
Dr. Oliver Leiser,
Anaconda, Montana.
Dr. A. F. Longeway,
Great Falls, Montana.
Dr. James L. Jones,
Dillon, Montana.
Dr. M. A. Miller,
Dillon, Montana.
Dr. H. O. Miller,
Dillon, Montana.
Dr. W. P. Mills,
Missoula, Montana.
Dr. S. W. Minshall,
Missoula, Montana.
Dr. I. J. Murray,
Butte, Montana.
Dr. George T. McCullough,
Missoula, Montana.
Dr. F. W. McCrimmon,
Butte, Montana.
Dr. J. P. McKay,
Big Timber, Montana.
Dr. Charles A. Perrin,
Helena, Montana.
Dr. W. L. Renick,
Butte, Montana.
Dr. J. M. Sligh,
Anaconda, Montana.
Dr. J. F. Spelman,
Anaconda, Montana.
Dr. Fred. Treacy,
Lewiston, Montana.
Dr. J. A. Tremblay,
Big Timber, Montana.
Dr. Asa M. Willard,
Dillon, Montana.
Dr. E. M. Wilson,
Twin Bridges, Mont.

NORTH CAROLINA.

Hon. Charles B. Aycock, the Governor of North Carolina, has accepted the position of Honorary Vice President, and has named the following delegates, and says he may name others later:

Dr. W. L. Dunn,
Asheville, N. C.
Dr. Albert Anderson,
Wilson, N. C.
Dr. W. T. Pate,
Gibson, N. C.
Dr. S. W. Battle,
Asheville, N. C.
Dr. R. H. Lewis,
Raleigh, N. C.
Dr. J. L. Nicholson,
Richlands, N. C.
Dr. J. F. Miller,
Goldsboro, N. C.
Dr. James McKee,
Raleigh, N. C.
Dr. P. L. Murphy,
Morganton, N. C.

NEW MEXICO.

Hon. Miguel A. Otero, the Governor, is an Honorary Vice President of the American Congress of Tuberculosis. He is by profession a physician, and he takes an unusual interest in the aims, objects and work of the Congress. In his report as Governor of the Territory made September 14, 1901, for the fiscal year ending June 30, 1901, which is one of the most painstaking and carefully prepared reports that has been submitted in recent years to the Government, he contributed an article upon the Climatology of New Mexico, its general climatic conditions and its importance as a location for Sanitariums for the sufferers from pulmonary disorders, which is of the greatest possible value.

In his report he also gives some comparative climatic data between Santa Fe and the other principal cities of the United States, and it is in this report that the work of the General Hospital at Fort Bayard, in charge of Major D. M. Appel, is made, as well as the report of Surgeon F. M. Carrington, in charge of the Marine Hospital at Fort Stanton, for the year ending June 30, 1901, which has excited so much interest throughout the whole world.

Governor Otero has named twenty-three delegates and has given to each power of substitution. They are as follows:

Major D. M. Appel,
Surgeon U. S. A.,
Fort Bayard,
Dr. R. L. Bradley,
Roswell, N. M.
Dr. George C. Bryan,
Alamogordo, N. M.
Dr. F. M. Carrington,
Fort Stanton, N. M.
Dr. E. G. Condit,
Aztec, N. M.
Dr. P. G. Cornish,
Albuquerque, N. M.
Dr. J. M. Cunningham,
East Las Vegas, N. M
Dr. D. A. Clark,
Silver City, N. M.
Dr. G. G. Duncan,
Socorro, N. M.
Dr. R. C. Dryden,
Capitan, N. M.
W. G. Hope,
Albuquerque, N. M.
Dr. O. C. McEwen,
Farmington, N. M.
Dr. J. F. McConnell,
Las Cruces, N. M.
Dr. M. R.' McGrory,
San Marcial, N. M.
Dr. A. R. Smith,
Carlsbad, N. M.
Dr. S. D. Swope,
Deming, N. M.
Dr. E. B. Shaw,
East Las Vegas, N. M
Dr. H. M. Smith,
East Las Vegas, N. M
Dr. J. J. Shuler,
Raton, N. M.
Dr. J. H. Sloan,
Santa Fe, N. M.
Dr. W. R. Tipton,
East Las Vegas, N. M
Dr. E. L. Woods,
Silver City, N. M.
Dr. J. H. Wroth,
Albuquerque, N. M.

TEXAS.

By Hon, Joseph E. Sayers, Governor of Texas, and Honorary Vice President of the American Congress of Tuberculosis, for the State of Texas:

Dr. W. H. Allen,
Marlin, Texas.
Dr. J. C. Ellis,
Denison,
Dr. J. M. Inge,
Denton, Texas.
Dr. F. Paschal,
San Antonio, Texas.
Dr. J. P. Sessions,
Rockdale, Texas.
Dr. M. M. Smith,
Austin, Texas.
Dr. T. H. Stallcup,
Jefferson, Texas.
Dr. A. H. West,
Galveston, Texas.

VERMONT.

By Hon. Wm. W. Stickney, Governor of Vermont, and Honorary Vice President of the American Congress of Tuberculosis, for Vermont:

Dr. Charles S. Caverly,
Rutland, Vt.
Dr. Truman R. Stiles,
St. Johnsbury, Vt.
Dr. H. Edwin Lewis,
Burlington, Vt.
Dr. Don D. Grout,
Waterbury, Vt.
Dr. William N. Platt,
Shoreham, Vt.
Dr. William N. Bryant,
Ludlow, Vt.
Dr. C. W. Peck,
Dr. J. W. Copeland,
Brandon, Vt.
Lyndonville, Vt.
Dr. L. W. Hubbard,
Lyndon, Vt.
Dr. Edwin M. Brown,
Sheluon, Vt.

WEST VIRGINIA.

Hon. A. B. White, the Governor of West Virginia, has named the following delegates from West Virginia:

Dr. Hugh A. Barbee,
Point Pleasant, W. Va.
Dr. T. L. Barber,
Charleston, W. Va.
Dr. H. M. Brown,
Union, W. Va.
Dr. John W. Brown,
Wheeling, W. Va.
Dr. H. J. Campbell,
Glenwood, W. Va.
Dr. O. O. Cooper,
Hinton, W. Va.
Dr. William A. Cracraft,
Elmgrove, W. Va.
Dr. Frank T. Dare,
Wellsburg, W. Va.
Dr. N. L. Edwards,
Bluefield, W. Va.
Dr. C. S. Ford,
Wheeling, W. Va.
Dr. W. W. Golden,
Elkins, W. Va.
Dr. H. F. Gamble,
Charleston, W. Va.
Dr. A. S. Grimm,
St. Mary's, W. Va.
Dr. H. D. Hatfield,
Thacker, W. Va.
Dr. I. N. Houston,
Moundsville, W. Va.
Dr. Louise Jarvis,
Quiet Dale, W. Va.
Dr. S. L. Jepson,
Wheeling, W. Va.
Dr. Elbin J. Johnson,
Middlebourne, W. Va.
Dr. J. P. Johnson,
Wellsburg, W. Va.
Dr. W. S. Keever,
Parkersburg, W. Va.
Dr. G. W. Knapp,
Richlands, W. Va.
Dr. William M. Late,
Bridgeport, W. Va.
Dr. S. B. Lawson,
Logan, W. Va.
Dr. John Ligon,
Clover Lick, W. Va.
Dr. George Lounsberry,
Charleston, W. Va.
Dr. Robert L. Morrison,
Clarksburg, W. Va.
Dr. C. L. Muhleman,
Parkersburg, W. Va.
Dr. J. M. McGoughlin,
Addison, W. Va.
Dr. R. M. J. McGuffin,
Sewell, W. Va.
Dr. Jessie C. Norris,
Fairmont, W. Va.
Dr. D. R. Coale Price,
May Buery, W. Va.
Dr. Jos. L. Pyle,
Bearsville, W. Va.
Dr. Charles W. Riggs,
Cameron, W. Va.
Dr. W. Bolling Robertson,
Concho, W. Va.
Dr. I. R. Le Sage,
Huntington, W. Va.
Dr. W. H. Sands,
Fairmont, W. Va.
Dr. Herbert E. Sloan,
Clarksburg, W. Va.
Dr. Clifford Sperow,
Martinsburg, W. Va.
Dr. H. B. Stout,
Parkersburg, W. Va.
Dr. C. F. Ulrich,
Wheeling, W. Va.
Dr. Steptoe A. Washington,
Sewell, W. Va.
Dr. J. Y. Wharton,
Ceredo, W. Va.
Dr. G. R. White,
Williamson, W. Va.
Dr. Waitman T. Willey,
Morgantown, W. Va.
Dr. Zepha R. Wilson,
Pennsboro, W. Va.
Dr. John M. Yeager,
Marlinton, W. Va.
Dr. H. H. Young,
Charleston, W. Va.

As the appointments of delegates have just commenced to reach the Secretary, those from the other States will be announced in the programme of the Congress at its opening, or through the Lay, Legal and Medical Press from time to time, prior to the session, if deemed advisable.

It will, I think, prove of interest, to give copies of the letters received from some of the Governors of American States, as an indication of the real interest felt in our work in every part of the American Union. A few are submitted:

State of Utah, Executive Office, Salt Lake City.
February 15, 1902.

Mr. Clark Bell, Secretary and Treasurer, American Congress of Tuberculosis, 39 Broadway, New York.

Dear Sir.—Answering yours of the 8th instant, I accept with pleasure the appointment of Honorary Vice President for Utah, of the Congress of Tuberculosis, and will appoint delegates to the session of 1902 within a few days. I shall also endeavor to forward you a short letter, expressing my sympathy for the cause in which you are engaged.

Very respectfully,
HEBER M. WELLS, Governor.

Executive Office, Des Moines.
March 8, 1902.

Dear Sir.—I beg to acknowledge the receipt of your esteemed fa. I shall be glad to become an Honorary Vice President of your Society, and will within a short time appoint delegates from Iowa to the meeting of 1902. While I am not technically familiar with the subjects which you will consider, I have the deepest sympathy with every effort to ameliorate human suffering, and I sincerely hope that your profession which has contributed so much to the learning of the world, will in this field make another distinct advance.

Yours very truly,
ALBERT B. CUMMING, Governor.

Clark Bell, Sec'y.
39 Broadway, New York.

State of Vermont, Executive Department.
Ludlow, January 30, 1902.

Clark Bell, Esq., 39 Broadway, New York, N. Y.

Dear Sir.—I beg to acknowledge the receipt of your esteemed favor indicating that the American Congress of Tuberculosis had designated me as one of the Honorary Vice Presidents of that body from my State, and asking if I would accept the position.

I should be glad to do anything I am able to further the object of the Congress and will accept the appointment with pleasure. As to the other matters you write about I will commnuicate with you in reference to the same within a few days. I have the honor to be

Very truly yours,
WILLIAM W. STICKNEY, Governor.

State of Michigan, Executive Office, Lansing.
Lansing, March 7, 1902.

Mr. Clark Bell, Sec'y and Treas., New York City, N. Y.

Dear Sir.—In reply to yours of the 1st instant, it affords be pleasure to accept the appointment as Honorary Vice President for Michigan, to the American Congress of Tuberculosis. I sympathize strongly with the work this Congress is engaged in carrying on, and trust that in its battle against the ravages of this terrible disease it may win an unqualified victory.

Very respectfully,
A. T. BLISS, Governor.

State of New Hampshire, Executive Department.
Lancaster, January 25, 1902.

Clark Bell, Esq., Sec'y and Treas.

Dear Sir.—Your favor of the 23rd instant received. I think you have made a convert of me, or at least got me to the anxious seat. If it is thought that by the use of my name any one can be made better physically, mentally or morally,—it can be used.

Sincerely yours,
C. B. JORDAN, Governor.

Governor Beckham, of Kentucky, has expressed his great interest in the work of the body. His letter to the President of the Congress is as follows:

State of Kentucky, Executive Department, Frankfort.
J. C. W. Beckham, Governor. March 25, 1902.
Dr. Henry D. Holton, Pres. American Congress of Tuberculosis, 39 Broadway, New York.

Dear Sir.—I received some time ago your letter asking me for an expression of opinion upon the objects and purposes of the American Congress of Tuberculosis. It will be impossible for me to attend the convention to which you invite me, but I wish to assure you and the association of my hearty sympathy and encouragement in their efforts to reduce the ravages of the dread disease. I believe that by organized effort much good can be accomplished in that direction, and you gentlemen who are undertaking to accomplish it are entitled to much praise and credit. I hope that your meeting and all your efforts will be successful. Should you desire it I will appoint some delegates to the convention.

Very truly yours,
J. C. W. BECKHAM, Governor.

The Governor of West Virginia seems to have taken a deep interest in the work. Dr. C. F. Ulrich, of Wheeling, West Virginia, is one of the Vice Presidents of the American Congress of Tuberculosis. He has been working up the sentiment in that State.

West Virginia is certainly the banner state if we measure it by the number of delegates its Governor has appointed. He names 47 delegates. His letter is as follows:

Executive Department, Charleston, West Virginia.
March 25, 1902.
Clark Bell, Esq., Secretary, 39 Broadway, New York City, N. Y.

Dear Sir.—Your circular letter of March 1st, has just been called to my attention owing to repeated absences from the city.

Every intelligent effort for the suppression and cure of tuberculosis must command the sympathy and support of all thoughful people. It affords me great pleasure, in this campaign of education which you have inaugurated, to name a number of our leading and representative physicians, in accordance with the request of your circular letter. I enclose you herewith a list of persons appointed as delegates from this State. I regret that it will be impossible for me to attend your Congress.

In your efforts to arouse opinion in favor of remedial and preventive legislation you have my sympathy and best wishes for success.

Very respectfully yours,
A. B. WHITE, Governor.

The enclosed letter shows the interest felt in the Republic of Mexico, our nearest neighbor, and between whom and ourselves our commercial relations are now so enormously extending:

The Governor of the State of Vera Cruz, an Honorary member of the Congress, writes as follows:

Correspondencia Particular del Gobernador del Estado de Vera Cruz Llave. Xalapa, Mexico, February 28, 1902.

Clark Bell, Esq., Secretary American Congress of Tuberculosis, 39 Broadway, New York, U. S. A.

Sir.—I am in receipt of your esteemed favor of the twenty-eighth ultimo, informing me that I have been designated, by your Executive Officers, as one of the Honorary Vice Presidents of the American Congress of Tuberculosis from the State of Vera Cruz.

It is with much pleasure and with an appreciation of the honor conferred that I accept the appointment.

I am in hearty sympathy with and fully realize the great value of the work proposed by this organization, and am very pleased to become identified with it in the manner designated.

It would give me pleasure to act upon your suggestion to submit for the consideration of the Congress a statistical paper on Xalapa as a health resort, and I shall endeavor to have such a paper prepared for the meeting in May.

I should also be glad, in case I cannot be present at the meeting, if one or more of the leading physicians of this State could attend, as you suggest. The appointment of delegates to an international Congress, however, would be made by our Federal Government.

It is to be hoped that such co-operation will be given to this movement for the better understanding and treatment of tuberculosis as will effectively arrest the ravages of this dreadful enemy of mankind.

Permit me to hope that the meeting to be held next May, which I should be glad to be able to attend, will be productive of practical, beneficial results and will materially promote the important work undertaken by the Congress for the benefit of mankind. With great respect, I am

Your obedient servant,
THEODORO A. DEHESA, Governor.

THE NORTHWEST TERRITORIES OF THE DOMINION OF CANADA.

The Provinces of Alberta, Assiniboia, Athabaska, Sasskatchewan, Mackenzie, Unigau and Franklin all have their seat of government at Regina, and the Hon. A. E. Forget is the Lt. Governor of each and of all of them combined.

No man in Canada knows more of the sad effects of consumption in the Provinces and Territories over which he is placed, and no layman or public official in all Canada takes a deeper interest in the success of the measures this Congress is taking than does he. His letter, which explains why he cannot be present at the session, shows his profound interest in the subject. It is as follows:

Government House, Regina.
March 27th, 1902.

Sir.—I am in due receipt of your communication of the 1st inst., relating to the coming session of the American Congress of Tuberculosis to meet at New York on the 14th of May next. I thank you for your invitation to deliver an address on so important an occasion, and regret very much that it will not be possible for me to be present.

I fully realize the terrible nature of the foe against which you are fighting so bravely, and I think you are wise in making your efforts "a campaign of education." It is impossible the public can know too much about the question, and I have noticed with much interest the valuable information recently so widely disseminated by your organization and other associations with a kindred object in view. Great facts conveyed in simple language cannot fail to be effective, and I am pleased that the knowledge already imparted, not only traces the origin and causes of the disease, but indicates the best means individuals should adopt to prevent the spread of its ravages. When people once recognize the insinuating nature of the bacillus, its prevalence and fecundity, it seems to me that self-preservation, if not a general love for humanity, will prompt the application of the precautions, so simple and yet so efficacious, that are clearly indicated in the literature that has been sent broadcast, as the best means of thwarting the disease in its devastating march in every country on the face of the globe. The subject is one that appeals to everybody, and which scientists, philanthropists and legislators especially, should certainly take under their guidance.

For these reasons, the objects you have in view command my hearty sympathy, and I look forward with great hope to much practical good as a result of the deliberations at your Congress..

In regard to your request that I should send a delegate or delegates to the Congress, I may say that I have forwarded your communication to Premier Haultain, the head of my Government, and as he is an official of an organization with precisely similar objects in view as has The American Congress of Tuberculosis, I am sure a sympathetic consideration will be given to your proposals.

Yours truly,

A. E. FORGET, Lieutenant-Governor N. W. T.

Clark Bell, Esq., Secretary-Treasurer, American Congress of Tuberculosis, New York.

The Committees who will have charge of the Discussion of the four Symposiums cannot be well constituted at present but will be announced later.

Members or delegates who desire to take part in either of the Symposiums will please forward their names and indicate under which number they which to be classified, as soon as possible.

The Symposiums will be held, one at a session, to be announced on programme, and are as follows:

1. Preventive Legislation, Embracing the Social, Municipal, and State Aspects of Tuberculosis, (What aid should be expected from the State in the cure and prevention of Tuberculosis, and how shall this be secured,

2. Tuberculosis in its Pathological and Bacteriological Aspects.

3. The Medical and Surgical Aspects of Tuberculosis (Embracing Sanitoria and Climatic Conditions, Light and Electricity.)

4. The Veterinary Aspects of Tuberculosis.

REDUCTION OF FARE TO DELEGATES.

Last year we had more than one hundred delegates from distant States. We only had thirty-five who had carefully complied with the provisions of the regulations of the railways which entitled them to the return ticket at the reduced rate of one-third. As a result this neglect of delegates affected not only themselves, but their associates.

The contract was based on 100 tickets. Certificates from the agent who sells the ticket must in all cases be taken, as it is on this certificate that the return ticket is issued.

Delegates who are coming should advise the Secretary, so that we may know who will attend. They should get the certificate from the station agent, and buy the ticket for only one way. Those living near should purchase it, so as to increase the number beyond the requisite 100.

MUSEUM.

Dr. H. Edwin Lewis, M. D.., of Burlington, Vt., is the Chairman of the Committee on the Museum.

The other members of the Committee are Dr. Louis Le Roy, of Nashville, and the Secretary of the Congress.

The room at the disposal of the Committee is 40x45 and is on the floor above the parlors where the Congress meets. It is admirably adapted for a display of electrical, surgical and X-Ray instruments. Medical remedies and space will be let at reasonable prices for a display of all who wish to make exhibits.

Communications as to space can be made to the Chairman of the Committee or the Secretary of the Congress. Especial attention will be given to an exhibition of photographs, plans, specimens, drawings or exhibits from sanitariums throughout the whole American hemisphere.

ENROLMENT.

Those desiring to enrol should at once remit the enrolling fee to Clark Bell, Esq,. Secretary and Treasurer.

Titles of papers, outside the four symposiums should be sent as early as possible to the officers.

All papers offered will be submitted to a committee of censors, who will pass upon their acceptability and they should be in the Secretary's hands before the session.

Prof. Dr. Moritz Benedikt has sent an extended open letter to the Congress. It is written in German and is being translated by Hon. Moritz Ellinger, the Corresponding Secretary of the Medico-Legal Society.

Prof. Koch has been invited to contribute a paper to the Congress and to discuss the fourth symposium. The leading scientists in the United States and Canada, Mexico and the Central and South American States will be invited to participate in the discussion of the four symposiums.

The Congress is open to all persons interested in the prevention of the spread of tuberculosis by all lawful means.

A preliminary statement of titles of papers will accompany this statement.

HENRY D. HOLTON, M. D.,
President.
CLARK BELL,
Secretary.

AMERICAN CONGRESS OF TUBERCULOSIS.

The Secretary of this body makes the following announcements:

1. The officers of the Society, as chosen at the session of May, 1901, were as follows:

HONORARY PRESIDENT:

A. N. BELL, M. D., Brooklyn, N. Y.

PRESIDENT:

HENRY D. HOLTON, M. D., of Vermont,
Secretary State Board of Health, Brattleboro, Vt.

VICE PRESIDENTS-AT-LARGE:

HENRY B. BAKER, M. D., Lansing, Mich.
E. T. BARRICK, M. D., Toronto, Ont.
WM. BAYARD, M. D., St. John, N. B.
RALCY HUSTED BELL, M. D., New York City.
A. C. BERNAYS, M. D., St. Louis, Mo.
J. MOUNT BLEYER, M. D., New York City.
GEO. BROWN, M. D., Atlanta, Ga.
W. L. BULLARD, M. D., Columbus, Ga.
COL. E. CHANCELLOR, M. D., St. Louis, Mo.
C. K. COLE, M. D., Helena, Mont.
T. D. CROTHERS, M. D., Hartford Conn.
JUDGE ABRAM H. DAILEY, Brooklyn, N. Y.
HOM. MORITZ ELLINGER, New York City.
JUAN A. FORTICH, M. D., Cartagena, Colombia, S. A.
R. F. GRAHAM, M. D., Greely, Colorado.
A. P. GRINNELL, M. D., Burlington, Vt.
MAJOR A. HAVARD, U. S. A., Vice-Pres., Havana, Cuba.
THOS. BASSETT KEYES, M. D. Chicago, Ill.
LUIS H. LABAYLE, M, D., Leon, Nicaragua.
E. P. LACHAPELLE, M. D., Montreal, Canada.
LOUIS LEROY, M. D., Nashville, Tenn.
DR. EDOUARD LICEAGA, City of Mexico.
DWIGHT S. MOORE, M. D., Jamestown, N. Dak.
WM. H. MURRAY, M. D., Plainfield, N. J.
J. A. MCNEVEN, Gibbonsville, Idaho.
A. E. OSBORNE, M. D., Eldridge, Cal.
JOHN H. PRYOR, M. D., Buffalo, N. Y.
J. C. SHRADER, M. D., Iowa City, Iowa.
J. H. TYNDALE, M. D., Lincoln, Nebraska.
C. F. ULRICH, M. D., Wheeling, W. Va.
C. S. WARD, M. D., Warren, Ohio.
PROF. S. H. WEEKS, M. D., Portland, Maine.
CRESSY L. WILBUR, M. D., Lansing, Mich.
U. O. B. WINGATE, M. D., Milwaukee, Wis.

SECRETARY AND TREASURER:

CLARK BELL, Esq., City of New York.

The following gentlemen constitute the Executive Committee of the American Congress of Tuberculosis:

Clark Bell, Esq.. LL.D., President of the Medico-Legal Society, Secretary of the American Congress of Tuberculosis, Chairman, 39 Broadway, New York City.

Henry B. Baker, M. D., Secretary State Board of Health, Lansing, Michigan.

T. D. Crothers, M. D., Editor of *The Journal of Inebriety*, Hartford, Connecticut.

Hon. Abram H. Dailey, Ex-Surrogate Kings County, N. Y., Ex-President Medico-Legal Society, Brooklyn, N. Y.

Hon. Moritz Ellinger, Corresponding Secretary Medico-Legal Society, Ex Coroner of New York City, of New York, Secretary.

E. P. LaChapelle, M. D., Secretary Provincial Board of Health for the Province of Quebec, Montreal, Canada.

John C. Shrader, A. M., M. D., of the State Board of Health of Iowa Member of British Congress of Tuberculosis, of Iowa City, Ia.

EX-OFFICIOS :

A. N. Bell, M. D., Honorary President, Brooklyn, N. Y.

Henry D. Holton, M. D., President, Brattleboro, Vt.

FOREIGN DELEGATES TO THE AMERICAN CONGRESS OF TUBERCULOSIS.

Hon. Powell Clayton, the American Ambassador at Mexico, called the attention of the officers of the American Congress of Tuberculosis to the propriety of asking the recognition, sympathy and aid of the Government of the United States to the aims and purposes of the Congress by instructions to our own representatives abroad, and to the American Republics upon both the American Continents of the Western Hemisphere, stating that without advices from our Government, American representatives would not feel free to lend their full aid to the movement. Similar advice was given by the American representatives in other countries, and Foreign Ministers resident in Washington, also felt some restraint as to how far the Government of the United States was interested in, and in sympathy with the efforts this body was making to arrest and prevent the spread of the terrible disease.

The Secretary of the American Congress of Tuberculosis laid the subject before the American Government and asked for such an expression of its sympathy and co-operation as would not only remove these objections, but enlist the active co-operation of the Governments of the Republics of Mexico, Central and South America, and of our representatives abroad, whose co-operation we had sought and which had been extended by the American Minister in the Argentine Republic, Hon. Wm. P. Lord, with the results made apparent in the last number of this Journal, of gaining the cooperation of the Ligua Argentina Contra Tuberculosis, a body working in the Latin-American States with whom we hope to be in perfect sympathy and accord, and which organization we hope will be represented on the floor of the American Congress of Tuberculosis.

Dr. Emilio H. Coni is the President of the International Permanent Commission for the prevention of Tuberculosis in Latin America, which has been formed to combat tuberculosis and prevent its spread in the Latin-American Republics in the Western Hemisphere on both continents of North and South America, an organization that is accomplishing a great work with purposes akin to the aims of this body.

The action of the American Government is of the most gratifying character.

The following letter from the office of the Honorable, the Secretary of State, shows that the warmest sympathy exists in our Government for the success of the efforts of the Congress, and we hope will result in each country being represented by delegates named by the Governments:

Department of State, Washington.
April 4, 1902.

Clark Bell, Esq., Secretary American Congress of Tuberculosis, 39 Broadway, New York City.

Sir.—I have to acknowledge the receipt of your letters of the 25th and 28th ultimo, in regard to the session of the American Congress of Tuberculosis, which is to be held at the Majestic Hotel in New York City in May next.

In compliance with the request which you make, the Ambassador to Mexico, and the Ministers to the Central and South American States, have been instructed to express to those Governments the pleasure with which that of the United States would learn that they found it convenient to be represented in the Congress. I am Sir,

Your obedient servant,

DAVID J. HILL,
Assistant Secretary."

As a result Dr. Emilio H. Coni, of Buenos Ayres, in the Argentine Republic, has accepted the position of Honorary Vice President of the American Congress of Tuberculosis, and Dr. Samuel Gache, Dr. Francisco de Veyga, have accepted the positions of Vice Presidents of the Congress for that Republic.

At the session of 1901 of the American Congress of Tuberculosis the Government of Guatemala was represented by Dr. Joaquin Yela, the Consul General of Guatemala, who presented credentials from that Government. Honduras, Ecuador and Nicaragua were duly represented by Dr. Luis Debayle, who presented credentials from the Governments of those countries, and who was made one of the Vice Presidents of the body.

Mexico was represented by Dr. Eduoard Liceaga, President of the supreme Board of Health, who presented a paper that is published in the Bulletin of that Congress, and the Republic of Colombia was represented by Dr. J. A. Fortich,of Cartagena; both Dr. Liceaga and Dr. Fortich were elected Vice Presidents of the Congress of 1901, and now hold that position.

The Government of the Dominion of Canada and the Provincial Governments of that Dominion had early, and with great energy, announced the deepest interest and solicitude in the subject.

His Excellency, the Earl of Minto, Governor General of the Dominion, had presided at the convention from all parts of Canada, which had as result organized "The Canadian Society for the Prevention of Consumption."

He consented to accept an Honorary Presidency in it, and the Lieutenant-Governors of the Provinces with scarcely an exception, had accepted the position of Vice Presidents therein.

In the American Congress of 1902 the sympathy and cooperation of the leading men in the Dominion was warm and outspoken, and Dr. E. P. Lachapelle, of the Provincial Board of Health of Quebec; Dr. Peter H. Bryce, of the Provincial Board of Health of Ontario; Dr. E. T. Barrick, of Toronto; and Dr. Wm. Bayard enrolled and accepted prominent official positions in this organization.

The Governor General, his Excellency the Earl of Minto, accepted the position of Honorary Vice President of this Congress from that Dominion, as did Dr. F. Montizambert, Director of the Public Board of Health of that country.

The Lieutenant-Governors of the several Provinces, with scarcely an exception, also accepted the same distinction. Hon. Henry G. Joly de Lotbiaiere, of British Columbia; Hon. Sir Oliver Mowatt, G. C. M. G., Lieut.-Governor of Ontario; Hon. A. Forget, Lieutenant-Governor of the North West Territories; the Hon. A. C. Jones, Lieutenant-Governor of Nova Scotia, and Prof. J. G. Adami, one of the highest, if not the highest leading authority on our side the Atlantic, accepted the Honorary Vice Presidency of the body.

His Excellency, the Earl of Minto, has advised the Secretary that the delegates who will represent the Dominion of Canada will shortly be announced, as soon as they are selected,and has forwarded his portrait for reproduction,which appears in this number of the Journal, as does that of Sir Oliver Mowatt, Prof. Dr. Moritz Benedikt, of Vienna, who contributes an open letter to the American Congress of Tuberculosis, which will be read before the body and is an extended article; also Dr. Coni, of the Argentine Republic, and a large number of Governors and other officials who have accepted Vice Presidencies in the Congress.

The Secretary of the American Congress of Tuberculosis applied to the State Department requesting that similar action be taken by our Government in respect to the Dominion of Canada and that of New Foundland, to that already announced with the Latin American Republics in the Western Hemisphere, and the following letter has been received from the American Government, and the delay in the issue of the Journal enables us to announce it in the current number.

Department of State, Washington.

April 10, 1902.

Clark Bell, Esq., Secretary and Treasurer American Congress of Tuberculosis, 39 Broadway, New York City.

Sir:—I have to acknowledge the receipt of your letter of the 5th instant and to inform you that in compliance with the request therein made, the British Embassador has been asked to make known to the Governments of Canada and Newfoundland the value which the American Congress of Tuberculosis sets upon representation by those Governments at the forthcoming session of the Congress at New York City in May next, and the hope of this Government that they may find it to their interest to be represented by delegates. I am, Sir,

Your obedient servant,

DAVID J. HILL,
Assistant Secretary.

The distance of some of the Republics named, and the time required to obtain replies from letters is so great that announcement of delegates named by foreign governments could not be made at all complete in the current number of the Medico-Legal Journal, but these will be announced through the legal and medical press from time to time as the announcements reach the Secretary of the American Congress of Tuberculosis.

NOTICE TO OFFICERS, MEMBERS AND DELEGATES OF THE CONGRESS OF TUBERCULOSIS.

To enable you to obtain the reduction of fare, it is necessary for you to notify the agent at the railway station where you purchase your ticket, and obtain from him the usual certificate which will entitle you to receive the return ticket here at the Congress at the reduced rate.

An agent of the railway lines will attend the Congress and on your certificate that you have bought your ticket as a delegate give you your return transportation at the reduced rates.

To insure the reduced rate at least 100 tickets must be sold to delegates, so that all are earnestly requested to (1) notify this office that you intend to come; (2) obtain the proper certificate from the railway station agent when you do come, and (3) those living near New York will greatly help those who are distant by also purchasing the delegate ticket and obtaining the return certificate even if the fare is small, because this will help to make the necessary number to entitle the delegate from the Pacific coast, or the frontier of Mexico to his reduction, with the same effect as if he lived in Connecticut or New Jersey, where the amount of the fare is small.

This notice is sent because last year more delegates neglected to obtain the necessary certificate from the railway station agent than those who paid it, and there was not enough who did obtain it to entitle our delegates to the reduced rate, and great dissatisfaction ensued.

The Secretary appeals to all to take the necessary steps to secure your reduced rate and show the station agent your certificate of enrollment if he requires it.

CLARK BELL,
Secretary.

REDUCED RATES OF TRANSPORTATION.

We make the following suggestions to Secretaries of meetings in instructing their members respecting a reduction of fare on the Certificate plan for delegates. I enclose copy of the instructions sent me by the Trunk Line Association:

DR. CLARK BELL, New York City:

A reduction of fare and one-third, on the Certificate plan, has been secured for those attending the Meeting of American Congress of Tuberculosis, New York City, May 14–16.

The following directions are submitted for your guidance:

1. Tickets at full fare for the going journey may be secured within three days (exclusive of Sunday) prior to and during the first two days of the meeting. The advertised dates of the meeting are from May 14 to 16, consequently you can obtain your ticket not earlier than May 10, nor later than May 14, except from stations where it is possible to reach place of meeting by noon of May 15; tickets may be sold for morning trains of that date. Be sure that, when purchasing your ticket, you request a Certificate. Do not make the mistake of asking for a receipt.

2. Present youself at the Railroad Station for ticket and certificate at least thirty minutes before departure of train.

3. Certificates are not kept at all stations. If you inquire at your station you will find out whether certificates and through tickets can be obtained to place of meeting. If not, agent will inform you at what station they can be obtained. You can purchase a local ticket thence, and there take up a certificate and through ticket.

4. On your arrival at the meeting, present your certificate to Dr. Clark Bell.

5. It has been arranged that the special agent of the Trunk Line Association will be in attendance to validate certificate on May 15. You are advised of this because if you arrive at the meeting and leave for home again prior to the special agent's arrival, you cannot have the benefit of the reduction on the home journey. Similarly, if you arrive at the meeting later than May 15, after the special agent has left, you cannot have your certificate validated for the reduction returning. No refund of fare will be made on account of failure to have certificate validated.

6. So as to prevent disappointment, it must be understood that the reduction on return journey is not guaranteed, but is contingent on an attendance of not less than 100 persons holding certificates obtained from ticket agents at starting points, showing payment of full first-class fare of not less than 75 cents on going journey; provided, however, that if the certificates presented fall short of the required minimum and it shall appear that round-trip tickets are held in lieu of certificates, they shall be reckoned in arriving at the minimum.

7. If the necessary minimum is in attendance, and your certificate is duly validated, you will be entitled up to May 20 to a continuous passage ticket to your destination by the route over which you make the going journey, at one-third the limited fare.

AUTHORS WHO HAVE ALREADY CONTRIBUTED TITLES OF PAPERS FOR AMERICAN CONGRESS OF TUBERCULOSIS FOR 1902.

Prof. Dr. Moritz Benedikt, of Vienna, "An Open Letter on Tubercuosis."

Dr. Wm. Livet, of Paris, France, "La Baccillinine; dans le Treatment de le Tuberculose."

Clark Bell, New York, "Preventive Legislation."

Dr. Wm. F. Drewry, M. D., Petersburg, Va.

Dr. George Brown, Atlanta, Ga., "The British Congress of Tuberculosis, Who Composed It and an Epitome of Its Transactions.

Frederick L. Hoffman, Esq., Newark, N. J., "Life Insurance, Its Relation to the Prevention of Tuberculosis."

Charles F. Ulrich, M. D., Wheeling, W. Va., "The Hygienic Treatment of Tuberculosis."

J. W. P. Smithwick, M. D., La Grange, N. C., "Tuberculosis Among the Negro Race Before and Since Emancipation."

William Lee Howard, M. D., Baltimore, Md., "Preventive Legislation."

Martha Hughes Cannon, M. D., Salt Lake City, "Some Inter-Mountain Sections Favorable to the Cure of Tuberculosis."

Dr. J. Rudis-Jicinsky, Cedar Rapids, Iowa, "The Importance of the Early Diagnosis of Tuberculosis."

Matthew M. Smith, M. D., Austin, Texas, "The New Life Saving Service, or the Prevention of Consumption."

Dr. J. W. Bell, Minneapolis, Minn., "The Early Diagonis of Pulmonary Tuberculosis."

G. Lenox Curtis, M. D., New York, "The Influence of Electric Ozonations Upon Tuberculosis."

Dr. H. McHatton, Macon, Ga., "Tuberculosis and Environment."

Dr. Helen Densmore, Long Beach, Cal., "The Anti-Pyretic Treatment in the Cure of Tuberculosis."

Hon. Judge Abram H. Dailey, Brooklyn, N. Y., "Some Suggestions by a Lawyer to the Medical Profession."

Dr. Louis Le Roy, "A Consideration of the Various Biological Products Advanced for the Cure of Tuberculosis."

Dr. Augustus C. Bernays, St. Louis, Mo., "Tuberculosis and Its Relations to Other Infections."

Dr. Francis Crosson, Albuquerque, New Mexico, "Climatic and Sanatorium Treatment of Tuberculosis."

N. E. Aronstam, M. D., Ph. G., Detroit, Mich., "Genito-Urinary Tuberculosis."

Dr. Mihran K. Kassabian, Philadelphia, Pa., "Diagnosis of Pulmonary Tuberculosis by Roentgen X-Ray Method."

Dr. T. Henry Davis, Richmond, Ind., "Preventive Legislation."

Ira A. Donovan, M. D., Butte, Montana, "The Treatment of Tuberculosis by Nebulization."

The Hon. Theo. A. Dehea, Governor of Vera Cruz, Mexico, "Xalapa as a Health Resort."

Dr. John R. Walls, Prescott, Ariz., "The Climate of Arizona in Relation to Tuberculosis."

Benjamin Lee, M. D., Phiadelphia, Pa., "The Highlands of Jamaica as Appropriate Localities for Sanitoria for Consumptives."

Dr. M. Markiewicz, New York City, "The Obligation of the State in Reference to Hereditary and Acquired Tuberculosis of Children."

P. C. Remondino, M. D., San Diego, California, "Climate, Race and Tuberculosis."

Dr. F. Paschal, San Antonio, Texas, "On the Death Rate From Consumption in Some of the Health Resorts in This Country."

Dr. L. H. Warner, New York City, "Latest Scientific Research as to the Etiology and Treatment of Tuberculosis."

Dr. J. Mount Bleyer, of New York, "Demonstration by Electrical Vivisection of the Direct Sterilization of the Blood in Tuberculosis by Means of Electricity," with remarks upon the recent researches of Prof. Low's recent discoveries.

THE VISIT OF PRINCE HENRY.

The reception extended to the representative of the German Emperor on his recent visit to our shores, is understood to be peculiarly gratifying to that monarch and to the German people.

In the City of New York the most distinguished function was the banquet of the German Society of New York City, at the Hotel Waldorf-Astoria, which was in all respects the most notable, complete and splendid ever given in the Metropolis and reflected great credit on George Boldt as proprietor of that hotel and the Committees who had the details in charge.

A close second to it was that of the representative Captains of American industry, in which J. Pierpont Morgan took a conspicuous part. A more elegant, unique and recherche affair could not be well imagined, or carried out in any capital of the world than were these two functions in honor of Prince Henry.

Maurice Grau greatly distinguished himself and excelled any prior effort of his life that we can now recall, by the reception given at the Metropolitan opera house, and if any citizen of this country was to be singled out for decoration by the German Emperor for what was done by our people no one man would deserve it as much as Maurice Grau.

The banquet by the Press in New York while it was a large affair could hardly be called a representative banquet by the American Press, in honor of the Prince.

The Press of America had it arranged a representative banquet would have presented quite a different and more splendid affair.

This was unfortunately forestalled by the business manager of the greatest and most successful German newspaper in America.

Oswald Ottendorfer before his death, with the aid of his talented wife had made the Staatz Zeitung famous as a journal in New York and through it he had amassed a fortune. This corporation belonging to that estate, through the enterprise of its publisher and business manager, forestalled any movement in the interest of the Press, by obtaining generally permission to allow that newspaper, to tender the Prince a banquet, to which the leading publishers of the daily Press were invited with a sprinkling of the representative journalists of the Nation.

It was carried out on a large scale and the affair reflects great credit on the brilliant coup of the manager who absorbed to himself and the journal he represented the credit of an entertainment of great magnitude and merit.

The German Prince was graciously received by the President of the United States and by the people in the American cities he visited. It is doubtful if he ever will be called upon to receive such an overwhelming exhibition of popular good feeling as that which he met every where.

Emperor William has greatly advanced in the American mind as a wise and sagacious ruler. The visit was most timely and most fortunate in all ways. It is idle to attempt to conceal the fact that a strong anti-German feeling had been engendered in America, largely due to events at Manilla, which had created a feeling in the breast of Admiral Dewey, shared in by both our army and navy, and which had reached the better classes of our people, that Germany had been unfriendly to our flag in that war. The most important fruit of the work of the German Emperor in planning this visit, has been to allay, and in a great way dispel this feeling, and to place the friendship of the two countries on a more solid and enduring basis.

CECIL RHODES.

The career of this remarkable man has ended and his great merits and faults are now matters of history.

No one can give a satisfactory explanation which would from any ethical standpoint justify the Jameson Raid.

It was doubtless necessary from this point of view, and it no doubt was the most important single factor in the progress of those events, that led to the Boer War, and the disintegration of the South African Republics.

In finance Mr. Rhodes' conceptions and operations were collossal and immense. His gains were on as large a scale as his conceptions.

That he was a dreamer is clear from Mr. Stead's exposition of a world federation of the English speaking countries, or rather the millionaires of those countries.

He was a broad, a free and a progressive thinker, and as an Englishman he had entirely outgrown all insular methods of conventional lines.

In his contempt of conventionalities as to thought and action he was quite unique and free. Human life did not enter into his plans, and to reach his ends, he did not for one moment hesitate, because the pathway would be crimsoned with human blood.

The star that was most dazzling to Cecil Rhodes was the "Star of Empire."

If England were to catalogue her colonial possessions, what an enormous extent in South Africa must be put to the credit of the name of Cecil Rhodes, who as has been said, has added almost another India to the British flag and nation.

To the mind of Rhodes "territory" was the primal thought, and towards its acquisition he bènt all his efforts.

It may be and is undoubtedly true that Rhodes' motives and reasons were not wholly based upon any love of America; her greatness, her future, or those characteristics which no matter how we admire or praise them as factors in our development, are not held in veneration in English minds.

It may be that Cecil Rhodes sought to create a force and an energy among American men who having been educated at Oxford would crystalize in a body who by their education had been Anglicised in feeling, and would form the nucleus in America of a school of thought reflecting Oxford views and ideas which would have great weight, at least by the end of the century, in aid of a movement in favor of that federation of American and English opinion which was the dream of his life.

With all his faults there was a commanding magnetism that bound all South Africans to him, because he stood as the ideal of progress and development in those vast, new and wonderfully endowed countries.

That his great heart reached to America and our work is made clear by the last act of his life, when he took steps to make the greatness of his soul an eternal monument in America.

His will is the most unique and remarkable document of modern times. It grapples with a question and devotes an enormous sum to the development of a thought, so far reaching that it will occupy generations of men to measure its full importance or effect. In this respect we think that the mind of Rhodes has been influenced and moulded by an American whom we honor and revere—by the life and character and work of Andrew Carnegie.

Without anything in common, between two natures as far apart as the poles, the American Democrat has influenced the Anglo-African statesman. Rhodes, disregarding Carnegie's advice as to realizing his plans in one's own life time, has felt the great heart throbs of Carnegie's heart by that unknown and untranslated telepathy, that knows no distance, and in which space is unrecognizable; and has hurriedly and in the darkning shadows of his last days, prepared his scheme of co-cducation of the American and the Englishman, with a trace of the old Saxon on lines so broad and comprehensive, and so far reaching; that the genii of the destiny of our country in preparing an inscription for the monument posterity will raise for him on American soil, will at least find room in enduring and immortal letters for Cecil Rhodes.

GOVERNOR ODELL AND THE LUNACY STATUTES

The pressure of the work of preparation for the session of the American Congress of Tuberculosis has been so great and the correspondence so immense that we have not found time to refer to it in the manner its importance demands.

We shall defer it until we have time for a more careful and critical discussion. That the Governor has lost ground in the public mind by his radical changes by which he has thrown his own personality into the scale may be true.

But it seems to us that he has been active for what seemed to him a public good. He may have had bad advisers, or he may have recognized what he regarded to be deeply seated evils, and may have determined to eradicate them by radical surgery, and take up the arteries after the operation.

Beneath it all is the vice to which he seems blind, of giving anything but advisory powers to a lunacy commission.

In no country in the world has this power ever been entrusted to such a commission. New York stands alone and it is an object lesson for the students of alienisim everywhere in Christendom.

It may all prove for the good and throw a light upon our path for future action. We shall meanwhile await the result of this revolutionary legislation. Without relinquishing our confidence in the integrity of the Governor, let us wait and see what lessons can be learned of the present conditions, and ask those who now condemn the Governor to suspend sentence for the present.

GENERAL GEORGE M. STERNBERG, SURGEON GENERAL OF THE UNITED STATES ARMY.

A bill has been introduced and a strong movement is on foot to promote this officer to be a Major General prior to his approaching retirement on the age limit.

We give it our hearty support. It would be a well merited distinction to a splendid officer, as crowning a life long work devoted to the welfare of the Army and the good of the service.

He won high econiums for eminent and distinguished service in the war with Spain in Cuba, and his whole career has been one that reflects great credit upon him. His work in the progress and advance in Medical Science has entitled him to the recognition, and we sincerely trust that the bill will pass.

The Harvard Law Review makes an announcement which will be of interest to all members of the profession, under date of Feb. 15, 1902:

"GENTLEMEN:—We have just published a pamphlet of 86 pages of the same size and print as the *Harvard Law Review*, containing the text of the NEGOTIABLE INSTRUMENTS LAW as recommended by the Conference of Commissioners on Uniform State Laws, together with a reprint of the following articles: "The Negotiable Instruments Law," by Professor James Barr Ames, Dean of the Harvard Law School, reprinted from the *Harvard Law Review*, Dec., 1900; "A Defense of the Negotiable Instruments Law," by Hon. Lyman D. Brewster, President of the Boards of Commissioners, from the *Yale Law Journal*, Jan., 1901; "The Negotiable Instruments Law—a Word More," by Professor Ames, from the *Harvard Law Review*, Feb., 1901; 'The Negotiable Instruments Law—A Rejoinder to Dean Ames," by Judge Brewster, from the *Harvard Law Review*, May, 1901 Supplementary "Notes" have been added by the same writers upon Tolman *v.* the American Bank, 48 Atl. Rep. 1180, and Jeffry *v.* Rosenfeld, 61 N. E Rep. 49.

"We belive that the text of the Act in this convenient form will be most useful, and that the comments and criticism of these eminent writers, throwing light not only upon the merits and defects of the Act, but also upon the interpretation of many doubtful sections, ought to prove especially valuable to the profession and to students, both where the Act has been adopted and where it has not

"The price of the pamphlet sent postpaid is *thirty cents*."

PERSONAL.

Dr. Wyatt Johnson, of Montreal, Canada, will deliver the annual address before the American Medico Psychological Association, to be held June 17th, 18th, 19th and 20th, at Montreal. Dr. Johnson is lecturer on Medical Jurisprudence at McGill University. The title of his address is: "The Medico Legal Appreciation of Trauma in its relation to Abnormal Mental Conditions."

NOTES ON TUBERCULOSIS.

IN SWEDEN.

The city physician of Gothensberg, Sweden, reports that of the 131,000 inhabitants, 1,700 suffer from consumption, and that 350 die annually from this malady.

The total deaths from tuberculosis in 1901 are reported at 454, of which 352 were from pulmonary tuberculosis.

TUBERCULOSIS IN THE PROVINCE OF INDIA.

The Recorder of Vital Statistics of the Province, Dr. Paul E. Provost reports the deaths in that Province from tuberculosis in 1897, 3,079 persons; in 1898, 2,876; in 1899, 3,085; in 1900, 3,015.

IN QUEBEC.

The only sanitarium in the Province of Quebec for consumptives is the sanitarium at St. Agatha des Morits, under ths charge of Dr. Arthur J. Richer, of Montreal, and legislation is sought in the Provincial Legislature for aid in the care of consumptives.

SANITARIUMS IN NEW JERSEY.

The New York Herald announces that a bill is before the legislature of New Jersey for the creation of a State Hospital for Consumptives. This powerful journal strongly favors the passage of the bill, which it asserts has the endorsement of the medical profession and is backed by a strong public sentiment favoring the movement.

Professor Dieulafoy contributes to the Semaine Medical of Nov. 20, 1901, an interesting paper on "How shall we determine whether an acute serofibrinous pleurisy is or is not tuberculosis.

IN GERMANY.

Sprengel reports in the Berliner Klinische Wochenschrift in a paper on "Sanatorium Treatment for Surgical Tuberculosis."

Prof. Rob't Koch contributes to the Deutsche Medenische Wochenschrift an important paper entitled "The Agglutination of Tubercle Bacilli and the Importance of this Agglutination."

In this paper he announces another method in making cultures which he describes in minute detail, and gives the results he has attained by its use as a test fluid. An abstract of this paper condensed may be found in the March 22, 1902, number of the Philadelphia Medical Journal.

IN PENNSYLVANIA.

Dr. Lawrence F. Flick, of Philadelphia, has contributed to the Philadelphia Medical Journal of March 22, 1902, an elaborate paper entitled "The Implantation of the Tubercle Bacillus."

Dr. Flick claims: That it is now demonstrated that animal tuberculosis of one species can be inoculated into animals of other species; and that same can be also conveyed to other animals by feeding. That in man tuberculosis can be inoculated into animals of different species; and that it can be conveyed into animals of other species by feeding and by inhalation. That it has been demonstrated by accidental inoculation that animal tuberculosis can be inoculated into human beings. That up to the present time it has not been demonstrated that animal tuberculosis can be conveyed to human beings by feeding or by inhalation.

He says: "That there are a number of observations on record which strongly point to the conclusion that animal tuberculosis can be conveyed to human beings by feeding, and some of these observations are as convincing as they can be, short of demonstration, but they lack the one essential element, namely, absolute exclusion of human seed supply, (quoting Kepp from Am. Medicine Oct. 6th and Nov. 2nd, 1901), and claims that the above is the same of our knowledge of inter-transmissibility of human and animal tuberculosis.

Dr. Flick discusses the subject of the source of human tuberculosis, which he classifies 60 per cent. due to a human source. Of the remaining 40 per cent. he attributes 25 per cent. to association with other consumptives, of the remaining 15 per cent. he deducts all cases of tubercular sputem in saloons, cars, churches, school, streets, &c., and he divides this with the food supply from meat, milk, butter and cheese.

Dr. Flick attacks the commonly received opinion that the tubercle bacilli is usually carried into the system through the lungs, and occasionally through the alimentary canal, and quite rarely through the skin, on scientific grounds.

SELECTIONS.

A REMARKABLE TRIBUTE TO THE LIVING AGE.

The Rev. John M. Marsters, of Cambridge, Mass., recently wrote, in a letter to the publishers of The Living Age:

"I wish to say to you that I have just finished reading your 230 volumes. I have been at it almost continuously for two and one-half years. I have not read the novels or smaller pieces. I have read over 6,200 articles; and in common print this would make some 440 volumes. Needless to say, my reading has been wholly delightful * * * You may wish to know what is my judgment as to the value of the magazine. My answer is this: I do not believe that in the periodical literature of the world there is its equal. For style, eloquence, interest in particulars, and depth and variety it leads all its associates. It is a beautiful mine of learning * * * These 230 remarkable volumes should be in every library, public and private, of the English-speaking race. Lastly, I would say that the new numbers are quite on a par with the old. I have averaged in reading over 20 articles in each volume. But in the last half dozen the average has been 40."

THE RIDPATH LIBRARY OF UNIVERSAL LITERATURE,

Comprising 25 Volumes, gleaned from more than 2,000 great authors, is beautifully illustrated and is indeed a compendium of Poetry, History, Biography, Romance, Science, Drama, Theology, Oratory, Philosophy, Humor, Exploration, and Journalism.

Dixon & Cary, Publishers, 91–93 Fifth Avenue, N. Y., announce the work in three different styles of binding: Art Vellum Buckram, $4.00; Half Leather, $5.00, and Full Leather, $6.00 per volume.

As a reference for men of the professions, for quick work on all the subjects, and especially for journalists, it will be found an invaluable aid in the speedy preparation of articles, and the student who takes it up will find it hard to lay it down. We quote some of its references:

I have received a set of your publication entitled "The Ridpath Library of Universal Literature." I began to investigate the character of the work and found it very interesting. The soundest literary discrim-

-ination has been exercised by Dr. Ridpath in the selections which he produces and in the condensation of matter, so as to put the largest possible qnantity of information in reach of the inquirer. The illustrations are abundant, and of a high order of art. The mechanical execution of the work, the type, the binding, the embellishments, etc., exceed any publication within my knowledge. The work is bound to prove a favorite on the shelves of libraries, and to be of great assistance to brain workers in the higher fields at critical points, and where assistance could not be otherwise obtained. T. J. SIMMONS,
Chief Justice Supreme Court of Georgia, Atlanta.

I have carefully examined "The Ridpath Library of Universal Literature" with great satisfaction, and am convinced that to every home and family and to every thinking reading man and woman, these books are invaluable. The history of famous authors and selections from their best writings will never grow old or be put out of date, hence the permanency of such works. The pleasure of having selections from the best work of all the great men of the past, of the great poems and essays, and stirring orations which have influenced the work is incomparable. The handy size of the volumes, the large clear type and superior binding add immensely to the value of these works. No other work can be so instructive and valuable and widely educational in the best sense, and it is safe to predict a sale equal to Webster's Dictionary, as any other wide sought for work of the age.

I find that its value increases with acquaintance and that it is essentially a busy man's library which can be taken up at odd moments and read with great pleasure.

The skill in condensing and giving in brief space a clear conception of the writer and his best thoughts are apparent on every page. In one sentence it seems clear that this is the great library of the age for both the professional and business men of today. T. D. CROTHERS, M. D.
President Walnut Lodge Hospital, Hartford, Conn.

JOURNALS AND BOOKS.

THE AMERICAN MEDICAL COMPEND, Toledo, Ohio. W. W. Grube, A. M., M. D., Editor. Monthly.

The February number of this journal contains an able and interesting article, by Dr. J. A. Wright, of Toledo, Ohio, on the question of the right of a medical man to relieve the mother, in extreme cases of nausea and vomiting in pregnancy, by instrumental abortion.

It involves the issue of whether the physician has the right to take the life of the child before quickening, even in the extreme case, if it should occur, to save the life of the mother.

Dr. Wright shows that the duty of the physician is to treat the mother for the nausea, and not to kill the fœtus.

That the lethal form, resulting in death, rarely occurs.

That it is doubtful if it should be recognized as fatal in any case, and that in those cases so sometimes regarded, a careful examination would disclose gastric ulcer, malignant growths, tuberculosis, peritonitis, or some other cause, as producing death.

That instrumental abortion should not be resorted to, in such cases; it is unscientific, unjustifiable and unwarrantsd, "except as a desperate chance to save her from certain death."

While Dr. Wright does not define, with precision, the cases to which his exception refers, he says, in another part of his paper: "From the days of Hypocrates to the present time the attitude of the profession has been one of strenuous hostility and outspoken opposition to the practice of abortion for any purpose but that of saving the mother from certain and speedy death."

It is doubtful if any combination of circumstances could occur, or be surmised, that would justify a physician in killing a quickened, unborn child, to save the life even of the mother.

On an indictment against a physician, for the destruction of a living fœtus, it would hardly be a legal defense to set up that it was done to save the life of the mother.

It is the very exceptions that Dr. Wright makes, that the law now denies to the physician.

The question of whether the killing of the child would save the mother's life, would always be too much a matter of opinion and doubt, to quote in defence of the crime of killing, which would of course have to be a premeditated act.

Now that science has discarded the old idea of "quickening," as applied to fœtal life, as it was formerly construed by the courts, and while science teaches that fœtal life exists in the embryo, *ab initio*, the difficulties surrounding the legal justification of abortion, in any case whatever, increase.

The true role of the physician is to save life, not to take it; and it is doubtful if the courts of to-day would justify any such exercise of discretion or action, in a physician, as even in the exception specified in the able essay of Dr. Wright.

While we quite agree with Dr. Wright in the position he assumes, we doubt the force of the exception. We can conceive of no case where the killing of the child would be justifiable, on the lines of the exception Dr. Wright makes, "even of saving the mother from certain and speedy death."

NEW YORK IN BONDAGE. By John D. Townsend, of the New York Bar. Published by Margaret Townsend Tagliapietra. 1901.

John D. Townsend was a prominent lawyer, and is said to have successfully defended forty-five men indicted for murder. His friends claim that only one man whom he defended was ever executed, and that was Pellicier, who killed Senor Oleso.

Mr. Townsend died Christmas night, 1896, very suddenly, in the midst of an active practice, at the very zenith of his professional powers, at the age of sixty-one years.

He wrote a book which contains more details of the inner working of the Tweed ring and regime than has seen the light, and he carried it up to the contest of 1894, the Committee of Seventy, and the campaign in which Dr. Parkhurst bore such a conspicuous part.

It gives the names of the Respectable citizens who backed the Tweed ring, and it is interesting reading to see names behind that ring who do not now care to have these subjects discussed.

It is boldly written—fearlessly so. The death of Mr. Townsend prevented its earlier publication.

Madame Tagliapietra, who publishes the book, is a daughter of Mr. Townsend. It was published by subscription It should have been placed in the hands of a great publisher, and would have had a large sale. It is only to be obtained, now, by application to her, at her address, No. 343 West 34th Street, New York City.

For reference to documents, dates, data, and list of the men who backed the rings, there is no better work of reference accessible.

All who would like to see what John D. Townsend, the famous criminal lawyer, wrote concerning the Tweed ring and its work, and the later City management and the control of the Committee of Seventy, should send for this book. The price is only $2 00.

THE UTILITARIAN PRINCIPLES OF TAXATION AND THEIR RELATION TO ALTRUISM. By R. S. Guernsey, of the New York Bar. The New York *Sanitarian*. 1901.

The *Sanitarian*, of New York City, has been publishing, during 1901, and is still running, a series of articles under the general head of "The Utilitarian Principles of Taxation and Their Relation to Altruism," by Mr. R. S. Guernsey, of the New York Bar, whose writings, relating to Medico-Legal subjects, are well known, the first one being a paper read before the New York Medico-Legal Society, in November, 1872, on the accession of Mr. Clark Bell to the presidency of that association.

The transactions of that Society show several other papers by Mr. Guernsey, since that time. They all evince much originality of thought and are out of the usual line of writers.

The foundation of his manner of considering and treating the subject of taxation, sufficiently appears in the articles already published to show how municipal taxation may be directed and extended to effect beneficial reforms. He claims and discusses those questions from the standpoint of a system which has the maxim of "the greatest good to the grearest number," with which term all readers of Bentham and Spencer are familiar. He argues that these utilitarian principles of taxation have the same starting point that all moral and enlightened municipal laws have: that taxation and revenue from it shonld be to conserve individuals in life, liberty and the pursuit of wealth, and the enjoyment that arises from it, should be applied, appropriately, to the particular conditions existing, or to which it is aimed. Without some humanitarian end in view in the law imposing taxes, there is no check to the operation of legislation in its efforts to obtain revenue for public uses. The distribution of the greatest amount of happiness may be considered to be for the general welfare and greatest good of a community—permanent good, as distinguished from momentary pleasure. The prime necessaries of life, those of the most common and extensive use, should be taxed at the minimum, and luxuries at the maximum. The tax on land and dwelling places, and on food water and clothing, should be made as little as conditions will allow. Public improvements should also be made with the end in view of "the greatest good to the greatest number." The few should not be taxed for the benefit of the many, nor the many for the benefit of the few.

Among the dozen subjects already discussed are "Taxation for Protection of Human Life," "Taxation of Water," "Taxation and the Tenement House Problem," and sanitary appliances, generally, in connection with food, light, air, and their effect on health, longevity, and the development of man.

Many of our well-known writers on taxation blandly assert and claim that there is no system of taxation, and there can be none. Their conclusions are evidently drawn from isolated examples and attempts to force upon a community a plan of spasmodic taxation that was not appropriate to the conditions to which it was applied, without any consideration of the comparative difference in social conditions in other communities. They still rely upon the teachings of a class of writers on political economy that emanated from Adam Smith, without taking into consideration the change in the economic conditions in modern modes of production, transportation, diversity of occupations, and the demands of modern life.

The utilitarian principles of taxation, Mr. Guernsey asserts, can be applied in as complete a system as can the science of government, both of which should be in harmony with the economic needs and social conditions of a community or state, and the system applied to a community with an appropriate end, in view with a regard to its effects—other than economic; that there is a natural law in the business world as well as in the physical and moral world; that in each case these laws will follow the line of the least resistance, and will be oppressive, when not appropriate.

This mode of treating the subject is wide and original, and will, sooner or later, awaken much attention among thinkers, much more than it has heretofore, because confined only to one-sided legislation.

Banks & Co., of Albany, N Y., announce the following new editions for 1902 in press: "Pocket Code of Civil Procedure," 1902, 1 vol., with all amendments, $3.50. "Criminal and Penal Code," 1902, 1 vol., with all amendments, $3.50. "Miscellaneous Corporation Laws," 1902, 1 vol., with all amendments, in paper $1.50, buckram $2.00. "Insurance Corporation Laws," 1902, 1 vol., with all amendments, in paper $1.50, buckram $2.00. "Railroad Corporation Laws," 1902, 1 vol., with all amendments, in paper $1.50, buckram $2.00. "Banking Laws," 1902, 1 vol., with all amendments, in paper $1.50, buckram $2.00. "Cumming and Gilbert's Religious Corporation Law," 1902, 1 vol., with all amendments, in sheep $3.00, buckram $2.50. "Waugh's Religious Corporation Law," 1902, 1 vol., with all amendments, in sheep $2.00, buckram $1.50. "Hamilton's Tax Law," 1902, 1 vol., with all amendments, in paper 50 cents. "Balch's Manual Board of Health," 1 vol., with all amendments, in cloth $1.50. "Code of Civil Procedure—as it is," 1902, 1 vol., with all amendments, in sheep $2.50.

They are sending out the Amendments to the Code of Civil Procedure, which can be pasted in the volume, and will do the same for the Criminal and Penal Codes.

The Alienist and Neurologist. St. Louis, Mo.

The April number, 1902, of this interesting journal, contains, among others, the following original articles: "Outlines of Psychiatry and Clinical Lectures," by Prof. Wernicke. "Gall's Special Organology," by P. J. Moebius, M. D. "Puberty and Genius," by Cesare Lombroso, M. D. "Juvenile Female Delinquents," by Eugene S. Talbot, M. D. The number contains the usual Editorials, Selections, Book Notices, Reviews, Publisher's Notices, etc.

BOOKS, JOURNALS AND PAMPHLETS RECEIVED.

DR. ERNESTO QUESADA, C· De La Academia Espanola. Resenas y Criticas. Buenos Aires. 1893.

La Epoca de Rosas su verdadero Caracter Historico.

La Iglesia Catolica y La Cuestion Social.

La Cuestion Femenina.

Nuestra Raza.

Discurso Pronunciado En El Banquete Dado a Los Periodistas Brasilianos El Sabado 27 de Octubre de 1900.

Bismarck Y Su Epoca.

Los Privilegios Parlamentarios Y La Libertad De La Prensa.

Comprobacion De La Reincidencia.

La Politica Argentina Respecto De Chile, (1895–1898).

La Politica Chilena En El Plata.

FESTIVAL REPORT, dedicated to Privy Councillor Prof. Dr. Richard Baron v. Krafft-Ebing, on the celebration of the completion of his thirty years services as Professor of the University by the Society for Psychiatry and Neurology at Vienna. 1872–1902.

FLOYD S. MUCKY, M. D., C. M. Hay Fever and Asthma. A Permanent Cure by Means of Nasal Surgery. Reprint from Northwestern Lancet, 1902.

DR. HARRY HAKES, Wilkesbarre, Pa. "Quackery." A paper read before the Society March 6, 1901. Reprint from the proceedings of the Luzerne County Medical Society.

REV. GEORGE C. LORIMER, D. D. "The Puritan and his Mission." Annual Sermon preached before the New England Society in the City of New York, December 22, 1901.

DR. G. ASSELIN, Medecin de l'Armee Coloniale. "L'Etat Mental des Parricides." Paris, 1902.

TIDSSKRIFT FOR SUNDHEDSPLEJE. Forste Raekke. Jacob Lunds Boghandel, Copenhagen, Denmark.

"LA FRANCE." March, 1902. Boston, Mass.

DR. CH. CLOMBO. Rome. "Revue Internationale De Therapie Physique." February, 1902.

Psychiatrische en Neurologische Bladen, January and February, 1902. Amsterdam.

AMERICAN MEDICAL COMPEND. March, 1902. Toledo, Ohio.

LEGAL LITERATURE. February, 1902. Sweet & Maxwell, Limited, 3 Chancery Lane, London, W. C.

G LENOX CURTIS, M. D., New York. "The Influence of Electric Ozonation Upon Disease." Reprint from the New York Medical Journal for January 18 and February 1, 1901.

SOFUS B. NELSON, D. V. M. "The Relation of Tuberculosis in Domesticated Animals and Man." Reprint from the Journal of Comparative Medicine and Veterinary Archives, August, 1900.

THIRD BIENNIAL REPORT OF THE STATE VETERINARIAN, of the State of Washington to the Governor and Legislature, for the years ending August 31, 1899, and August 31, 1900.

EDWARD P. THOMPSON, M. E., New York. "Patent and Technical Services for Distant and Local Clients."

THE AMERICAN JOURNAL OF NURSING. March, 1902. Vol. II, No. 6. J. B. Lippincott Company, Philadelphia, Pa.

THE HUMANE REVIEW. January, 1902. Ernest Bell, 6 York Street, Convent Garden, London.

THE INTERNATIONAL MONTHLY. A Magazine of Contemporary Thought. April, 1902. Vol. V, No. 4.

WORLD'S FAIR, St. LOUIS, 1903. Commemorating Purchase of Louisiana Territory, 1803. Official Classification of Exhibit Department.

CLARENCE D. ASHLEY, LL D., Dean of the School of Law, New York University. "Legal Education and Preparation Therefor." A paper read before the Section of Legal Education of the American Bar Association, at its Annual meeting held at Denver, Col., August 23, 1901.

H. D. GEDDINGS, Passed Assistant Surgeon, U. S. Marine Hospital Service, Washington, D. C. "Sulphur Dioxide as a Germicidal Agent." 1902.

GEORGE J. SEABURY, New York. "The Constructive and Reconstructive Forces that are Essential to Maintain American International Commercial Supremacy." and that "Universal Commercial Reciprocity Treaties and Tariff Revision are Premature."

JOURNAL OF THE NEW YORK COUNTY MEDICO-PHARMACEUTICAL LEAGUE. March, 1902.

CLINICAL EXCERPTS. Vol. VII, Nos. 11, 12.

EIGHTEENTH ANNUAL REPORT of the Northern Pacific Beneficial Association for the Fiscal Year ending June 30, 1900. St. Paul. H. M. Smith Printing Co.

R. S. GUERNSEY, of the New York Bar. "Taxation of Water. What Municipal Ownership Has Done and What it Should do. New York City as an Object Lesson." From the Sanitarian for October, 1901.

H. EDWIN LEWIS, M. D., Burlington, Vt. "Pulmonary Tuberculosis, a Brief Consideration of its Etiology, Symptomatology, Diagnosis and Treatment." Reprint from the Medical Mirror for July, 1901.

REPORTS of the Trustees and Superintendent of the Butler Hospital, presented to the Corporation at its Fifty-Eighth Annual Meeting, January 22, 1902. Providence, R. I.

THE LAW MAGAZINE AND REVIEW. A Quarterly Review of Jurisprudence. Vol. XXVII, No. 323, February, 1902. London.

AMERICAN MEDICAL JOURNALIST. Vol. VI, March, 1902. No. 90 William Street, New York.

H. EDWIN LEWIS, M. D., Burlington, Vt. "The Development of Tuberculosis in the Individual, with some Remarks on the Tubercle Bacillus and certain Allied Forms of Bacilli." Reprint from the Journal of Tuberculosis

EDWIN C. WALKER, New York. "Vice: Its Friends and its Foes." 1901.

LE BULLETIN DE L'AFAS, No. 101, March, 1902. Paris.

REPORT of the Governor of New Mexico to the Secretary of the Interior. 1901.

IRVING A. WATSON. "New Hampshire Sanitary Bulletin." Apr., 1902.

L. J. ROSENBERG, LL. B., and N. E. ARONSTAM, M. D., Detroit, Mich. "A Contribution to the Study of Suicide." Reprint from the Medical Age, January 10, 1902.

HON. CHARLES A. FOULEIR, M. C., of New Jersey. Speech to maintain the Gold Standard.

PING AB LAW REPORTER, Lahore, India. Announcement of new Indexes.

MEDECINA PUBLICA REONTA DE LA TUBERCULOSIS. Dr. Emilo R. Coni, Editor, Beunos Aires. February, 1902. Vol. I to No. 9.

MAGAZINES.

New Series—The Law Digest and Recorder. Vol. No. 1. January, 1902. Printed at Madras, India. S. Sundarisa Ayar, Publisher.

This is an experimental venture to place before the Bar of India the latest intelligence respecting the action of the Courts. It has three original articles by prominent Indian Barristers, with a decision as to Notes, Reviews, Summary of Leading English Cases, Index of Cases, Digest of Indian Reported Decisions, and Reports of Current Cases.

With it appear two supplements :

1. Supplement to the New Series of The Law Digest and Recorder. Vol. January, 1902. Issued by the Government of India. Rules, Regulations, Notifications and Orders relating to India and Burma.

2. Supplement Relating to the Criminal Part, which contains four heads :

a. Digest of Reports of Indian Decisions.
b. Index to Reported Indian Cases.
c. Summary of Leading English Cases.
d. Reports of Current Cases.

The Indian Review. March No. 1902, (No. 3). Edited by G. A. Nalesan, B. A , Madras, India.

The March number contains some interesting articles :

"Eastern and Western Ideals." By John M. Robertson.
"The Anglo-Japanese Agreement." By Dr. Lim Boon Keng.
"The Philosophy of Maeterlinck." By E Labouchere Thomlin, I.C.S.
"University Education in India." By Prof. S. Sathianadhan, M. A., L. L. M.
"Kim." A Review.
"Valenki and Shelley." By M. V. Shrinivasa Aiyangar.

It is an interesting number.

The Century Magazine. MacMillen & Co., Publishers, New York and London.

The May number of this capital Magazine is out in advance, with a fine table of contents.

Its leading article, "The Great Southwest," is illustrated by two full page pictures in colors, the one of the Irrigating Canal and the other of the Desert with the distant mountains.

"Is the Moon a Dead Planet?" is the title of an interesting paper by Prof. Wm. H. Picking, of Harvard.

The photographs of the moon are finely executed, and indeed the illustrations of the whole journal are very fine.

The Forum. J. M. Rice, Editor, New York.

The May number is out as we go to press.

Prof. Ladd, of Yale, contributes a paper entitled "The Degradation of the Professional Office." Dr. H. D. Chapin one on "The Problem of Pure Milk Supply," and Prof. Chas F. Thwing, President of the Western Reserve University, writes on the "Collegiate Conditions of the United States."

The Metaphysical Magazine contains some interesting articles in its April number, 1902.

Dr. R. S. Clymer, Ph. D., M. S., M D., writes on "Occultism, Man's Grandest Duty.

Henry Frank, in the Department of Independent Thought, on "Tolstoi." "The German Prince and what he may Teach us."

Ernst Crosby, on "Religion and Humanity." "Atoms found to be Divisible," is the editorial heading of the statement of the theory of the divisibility of the atom, with a definition of the "Electron," and it is by contrast made much smaller than the bacillus; but is all this demonstrated by Science, or are we looking for the evidences of it?

Professor Loeb, Dr. J. Mount Bleyer and the writers in the Electrical Review, go into detail as to the "Infinitesimalism of the Electrons and their Groupings."

"Is it Demonstrated that the Atom is Divisible?"

"Beyond the Lowest Depth, is there Another Deep?"

INDEX--MEDICO-LEGAL JOURNAL, 1901-1902.

VOLUME XIX.

ERRATA.

At page 601, 1st line of Dr. A. N. Bell's quotation, for "approved" read "opposed."

SUPPLEMENT.

HON. ROBERT B. WARDEN.

SUPREME COURT OF OHIO.

1854.

Robert Bruce Warden was born at Bardstown, Nelson County, Ky., January 18, 1824. He was the son of Robert and Catherine Lewis Warden. When about three years of age he, with his parents, removed to Cincinnati, Ohio. He was educated at the Athenæum, a Roman Catholic college in Cincinnati. His attendance, however, was very irregular—but his very studious nature enabled him to round out his education to a very high degree. When twelve years old his father died and the boy was forced to seek employment and aided in the support of the family.

He commenced the study of the law in Cincinnati in 1840, under the tuition of Judge Reed, in the office of Morris & Reardon. Afterward he had Judge Timothy Walker, author of "Walker's American Law," for his legal teacher and friend. At the age of seventeen he became deputy clerk of the Court of Common Pleas of Hamilton County, (Cincinnati), Ohio, and two years later the clerk of that court, with charge of the Court House desk. This office he held until 1845, when at the age of twenty-one he was admitted to the bar. Early in 1850, having barely attained the legal age, he was elected by the Legislature President Judge of the Common Pleas Court, Cincinnati. In 1851 he was elected by the people one of the co-equal judges of that court. In the same year he became reporter of the Supreme Court of the State of Ohio, and in 1854 he was commissioned one of the Judges of the Supreme Court of Ohio.

His practice in Ohio was extensive, his legal services having been engaged in cases on trial in various parts of the state. He was well known as an eloquent and forceful speaker, both before the courts and in political campaigns. In politics he was decidedly too independent and fearless to permit the "machine" to influence his course, and this quality denied him the close affiliation with either of the great political parties.

While Presiding Judge of the Cincinnati Court he assigned Mr. Hayes, later the President of the United States, to his first case—the defense of Nancy Farrar (supposed to be insane) on trial for murder.

In January, 1873, Judge Warden removed to Washington, D. C., being at the time engaged in writing "An Account of the Private Life and Public Services of Salmon Portland Chase," which work was published in Cincinnati in 1874. This work was written at the request of Chief Justice Chase, who furnished Judge Warden with his private diaries and papers, and who died while the work was in progress. These men had for years been very warm personal friends. This work was never properly published, and though in demand could not be obtained.

Judge Warden's legal practice in Washington was chiefly before the Supreme Court of the United States, and the Court of Claims. Also prosecuting important matters before the State and Treasury Departments.

In 1877 Judge Warden was appointed by President Hayes a member and attorney of the Board of Health of the District of Columbia. This board was an important organization upon which, by laws of Congress, were imposed duties of broad scope, involving the consideration of questions of great scientific importance and action for the protection of the health of the National Capital. Judge Warden continued a member and attorney of this board until it was abolished by the law which provided a permanent form of government for the District of Columbia, and which established a government by commissioners, to whom was given the authority to appoint, in lieu of the Board of Health, a physician as Health Officer, whose duty it was, under directions of the said commissioners, to enforce all laws and regulations relating to the public health and vital statistics, including those made and established by the Board of Health.

Judge Warden did much writing for the press. Among his literary works were "A Familiar Forensic View of Man and Law," written in Columbus, Ohio, in 1859; "A Voter's Version of the Life and Character of Stephen Arnold Douglas," written in Columbus, Ohio, in 1860; "An Account of the Private Life and Public Services of Salmon Portland Chase," written in Washingtonand published in Cincinnati in 1874. Another of his literary productions was a drama, entitled, "Ardvoirlich," and subsequently entitled "Was it Fate?"

At the age of nineteen years he married Catherine R. Kerdolff, who died in Washington in 1884. Judge Warden survived his wife four years, his death occurring in Washington on December 3, 1888. He left two children and a niece (an adopted daughter), namely: Lucy A. Warden (now Mrs. Clifford Warden), and Charles G. Warden, both residing in Washington, D. C., and Emma Becking, (now Mrs. Atherton Thayer), of Wyoming, Hamilton County, Ohio.

OZIAS BOWEN.

SUPREME COURT OF OHIO.
1856–1866.

Judge Bowen was born at Augusta, Oneida County, New York, July 21, 1805. When he was fifteen years of age his family removed to Ashtabula County, from Fredonia, New York, where he worked in a printing office. He studied law at Canton; was admitted to the bar 23d of September, 1828, at Canton, and he commenced the practice at Marion, Ohio.

On February 7, 1838, he was elected by the legislature president judge of the second judicial circuit of the state for seven years; was re-elected, and served until the new constitution ousted him from office, when he resumed his law practice. In 1856 he was appointed by Governor Chase to fill the vacancy caused by Judge C. C. Convers' resignation, and he was elected to fill the unexpired term at the succeeding election.

In 1860 he was one of the Ohio presidedtial electors.

He retired from the bench in 1866. He held a high position on the bench and with the bar.

He died at Marion, Ohio, September 26, 1871.

HON. JOSIAH SCOTT.

SUPREME COURT OF OHIO.
1856–1872.

Judge Josiah Scott was born on the 1st day of December, 1803, in Washington County, Pa., near Cannonsburg, the seat of Jefferson College, where he was educated under Matthew Brown, and his religious teachings under the celebrated Doctor McMillen. He graduated in 1823 from Jefferson College; taught two years in the Academy at Newton, Bucks County, then taught two years in a classical school in Richmond, Va., and commenced the study of the law. He was then made a tutor in Jefferson College, one year, continuing his legal studies.

He visited in Mansfield, Ohio, in the spring of 1829, the Hon. Thos. Bartley, who had been his pupil in college.

He was admitted to the bar, and located, in June, 1829, at Bucyrus, Crawford County, Ohio, when the town was a mere hamlet in the wilderness, where he soon obtained prominence in his profession.

In 1840 he was elected to the general assembly from Crawford, Marion and Delaware Counties.

In 1851 he removed to Hamilton, Butler County, and continued an enlarged practice, meeting such opponents as John Woods, Lewis D. Campbell. Thos. Milliken and William Bebb.

In October, 1856, he was elected a judge of the Supreme Court for the term commencing February 9, 1857. Shortly after his election he was appointed by Governor Chase to fill the vacancy caused by the resignation of Judge Ranney, and held under that appointment until February 9, 1857, when his term commenced. He was twice re-elected, and continued on the bench until the 9th of February, 1872, declining a nomination for another term.

On leaving the bench he returned to Bucyrus and resumed the practice of law, and in January, 1876, he was appointed by Governor Hayes a member of the Supreme Court Commission of the state, on which he served until its expiration, in February, 1879, and shortly after this he was stricken with a malignant disease, from which he died June 15, 1879, in the 76th year of his age, but still in his intellectual prime.

He is thus described by his law partner and personal friend: "His knowledge and skill in mathematics were astonishing. No mathematical problem capable of solution baffled him. It may safely be asserted that he was absolute master of algebra and geometry.

"While he was a profound scholar and linguist, yet his greatest triumphs were at the bar.

"He had a leading practice in all the counties in his part of the state, and rarely was an important jury case tried but he conducted one side of it.

"In his arguments he was ordinarily mild, eloquent and persuasive before a jury, but when occasion required, he would pour out a torrent of invective that was overwhelming, like that of Curran's celebrated denunciation of Flood in the Irish Parliament."

His published judicial opinions are found in the Ohio Reports, Vols. 5 to 21, and the first series of volumes containing the decisions ot the commission.

NOTE.—Hon. S. R. Harris, Esq., of the bar of Bucyrus, presented to the Ohio State Bar Association a sketch of the life and character of Judge Scott, to which I am indebted for the data of this biography.

MILTON SUTLIFF.

SUPREME COURT OF OHIO.
1858–1863.

Judge Sutliff was born in Vernon, Trumbull Co., Ohio. Oct. 16, 1806.

When seventeen years of age he went South and taught school; returning to Ohio he graduated at the Western Reserve College in 1833. After graduating he became an agent of the Western Reserve Anti-Slavery Society, and traveled at his own expense promulgating the anti-slavery doctrine of Garrison and Phillips.

In 1834 he was admitted to the bar at Warren, O.; in 1850 he was elected to the Ohio Senate by the Free

Soil party and assisted in electing Benj. F. Wade to the United States Senate.

In 1857 he was elected Supreme Judge of Ohio by the Republican party and held that position five years.

In 1872 he supported Horace Greely for President, and was the Democratic nominee for Congress in opposition to General Garfield. He died in Warren, O., April 24, 1875.

(NOTE.—This sketch was taken from Howe's Historical Collection of Ohio.)

WILLIAM YATES GHOLSON.

SUPREME COURT OF OHIO.
1859-1863.

BY EDWIN GHOLSON, OF CINCINNATI, O.

Judge William Yates Gholson was born in Southampton County, Virginia, December 25th, 1807. His father, Thomas Gholson, Jr., was a member of Congress from Virginia, and though only thirty-six years of age at the time of his death, July 14th, 1816, was then serving his fifth consecutive term in that office.

His mother was a daughter of William Yates, Lieutenant Colonel of the Virginia State Line during the war of the Revolution, and a grand-daughter of Rev. William Yates, one of the early Presidents of William and Mary College.

He graduated from "Nassau Hall," at Princeton, New Jersey. He returned to Virginia, studied law under Chancellor Creed Taylor, was admitted to the bar, and entered upon the practice of his profession. He married in 1827 Anne Taylor, niece of Chancellor Taylor and daughter of Samuel Taylor, then one of the most prominent lawyers of the State. From this time until 1831, he resided in

Brunswick county. Early in 1834 he removed to Mississippi, locating in Pontotoc in that State, where he speedily acquired a considerable practice. He was one of the organizers of, and one of the earliest trustees of the University of Mississippi.

Judge Gholson was not in sympathy with the Southern people on the question of human slavery, and although in the enjoyment of a lucrative practice, and recognized as one of the leaders of the bar, he decided to leave Mississippi, and he removed to Cincinnati, Ohio in 1844.

There again his ability was shortly recognized, and he was soon in an active practice. Two years later he was appointed city solicitor. In 1854 he was elected as one of the three judges of the Superior Court of Cincinnati, then just organized. From 1859 to 1863 he was a justice of the Supreme Court of Ohio, having been first appointed by the governor to fill an unexpired term, and afterwards elected for a full term. In 1863, on account of failing health, he resigned the office and returned to the practice of law at Cincinnati, where for a time he seemed to find a renewal of his vigor. His mind, indeed, failed not, but his feebler body succumbed. He died at his home in Avondale, near Cincinnati, September 21st, 1870.

He had married, secondly, in 1839, Elvira Wright, daughter of Hon. Daniel W. Wright, one of the early judges of the Supreme Court of Mississippi, who survived him many years.

As an estimate of the character of Judge Gholson, I can do no better than to quote the language of one who was intimately associated with him at the bar and upon the bench:

As a man of great intellectual power, cultivated to a high degree by incessant activity, furnished with all that laborious labor could impart; of a well balanced temperament, uniting in just proportion the qualities of a sound judgment with an active and subtle perception; cautious in conclusions; ingenious in reasoning, he was remarkable, not more for the depth and reach of his abilities, than for his intellectual integrity and the courage of his convictions. His moral nature was equally harmonious, and in all that constitutes probity and honor, he was without stain. His self-respect invariably preserved a dignity that was natural and easy; his respect for others made his demeanor a model of urbane courtesy. At the bar his superiority was never felt as an oppression. On the bench he was kind, patient, free from prejudice and partiality, respecting not persons, regarding only law, justice and reason. He loved jurisprudence as a systematic science, for its logic, but never forgot that it was vitalized by the spirit of justice, and was not an end for itself, but only a means to something higher. His life was one of unremitting professional labor. His diligence and well directed industry was unexcelled. He amused his hours of leisure with the labors of authorship, and his judicial opinions rank high for learning and accuracy.

HORACE WILDER.

SUPREME COURT OF OHIO.
1863-1865.

Judge Horace Wilder was born in West Hartland, Conn., August 29th, 1802. He graduated at Yale College in 1823, and commenced the study of the law with the Hon. Elisha Phelps, of Simsbury. In 1824 he went to Virginia as a teacher, continuing his study of the law, where he was licensed to practice in the courts of Virginia; returned to Hartland in the fall of that year, but he removed to Ohio in the spring of 1827, and located at East Ashtabula; was admitted to the bar at the August Term of the Supreme Court of Ohio in 1828; In October, 1823, he was elected prosecuting attorney of Ashtabula County, and in the fall of 1854 was elected to the state legislature. In 1837 he removed to Conneaut, Ohio; in 1855 he was elected judge of the court of common pleas, in the third subdivision of the ninth judicial district, to fill a vacancy, and in 1856 he was elected to the same position for the full term of five years. In 1862, after his time expired, he was appointed draft commissioner for Ashtabula County; on the 1st of January 1863, he removed to Ashtabula, Ohio, and on

December 12th, 1863, he was appointed by Governor Todd a judge of the Supreme Court, to fill a vacancy occasioned by the death of Judge Gholson, and in the fall was elected for the balance of Judge Gholson's term

His opinions will be found in volumes 14 and 15 Ohio State Reports.

He died at Red Wing, Minn., December 26th, 1889, at the advanced age of 87 years and four months.

HOCKING H. HUNTER.

SUPREME COURT OF OHIO.

1864-....

Hocking H. Hunter was born in the year 1801, in the Hocking Valley, to which his father, Captain Joseph Hunter, emigrated from Kentucky in the year 1798. His father was a native of Virginia and his mother, Dorothy Berkshire, was born in Maryland. Hocking H. Hunter was the first white child born within the present corporate limits of Lancaster, Ohio; his education was obtained in the common schools and at the Lancaster Academy, under the instruction of Prof. Whittlesy; studied law with Judge W. W. Irvin, and was admitted to the bar in 1824.

In 1827 he was made prosecuting attorney for Fairfield County, Ohio, and held the position until 1836. He was elected judge of the Supreme Court in 1864, but for business reasons never took his seat upon the bench.

He was, during a long life, one of the great lawyers of his state, and may well be said to have been an ornament to the Lancaster Bar. He was a man of commanding eloquence, unquestioned integrity, and while a man of strong passions and impetuous nature, was one of the most brilliant men of the state. He died on the (?)

WILLIAM WHITE.

SUPREME COURT OF OHIO.
1868–1884.

Judge William White was born in England, January 28th, 1822. His parents dying early he was brought to Springfield, Ohio, by his uncle, James Dory, in 1831, where he was indentured as an apprentice for nine years to a cabinet maker. He studied also at the Springfield High School, under Rev. Chandler Robbins, and entered the law office of Wm. A. Rogers, at Springfield; he was admitted to the bar in 1846, and entered the law firm of his preceptor. He was chosen prosecuting attorney of Clark County in 1847. In 1856 he was elected to the bench of the common pleas, and was re-elected in 1861.

On the resignation of Judge Hocking H. Hunter, Judge White was appointed by Governor Brough a judge of the Supreme Court, to fill the vacancy, in February, 1864; in October of the same year he was elected to the unexpired term, and he was re-elected in 1868, and also in 1873, and in 1878.

LUTHER DAY.

SUPREME COURT OF OHIO.
1865–1875.

SUPREME COURT COMMISSION.
1876–1879.

Judge Luther Day was born in Washington county, New York July 9th, 1813.

In September, 1838, he entered the law office of R. P. Spalding, Esq., at Ravenna, Ohio, as a law student, and on October 1840 he was admitted to the bar, and formed a partnership with Elias Darius Lyman. In 1853 he was made prosecuting attorney for Portage County.

In 1851 he was elected judge of the Court of Common Pleas for that district which office he held for six years. In 1863 he was elected to the state senate from the counties of Portage and Snmmit.

In 1864 he was elected judge of the Supreme Court and took his seat in 1865; in 1869 he was re-elected to that position and during his term was for four years the active chief justice. In April 1875 he was appointed by Gov. Allen, one of the three judges to revise the statute laws of Ohio. In 1876 he was appointed by Governor Hayes as one of the first Supreme Court Commission on which he served for three years.

The result of his judicial labors extended through fifteen volumes of the state reports. He was the father of Hon. Wm. R. Day, Secretary of State under President McKinley, and now one of the judges of the United States Circuit Court of Appeals for the sixth circuit of Ohio. He died at Ravenna, Portage County, Ohio, on March 8th, 1885, in the seventy-second year of his age.

On the occasion of his death the Supreme Court ordered a commission to be appointed to present a suitable memorial of his life and public services. The committee submitted a report which was ordered to be approved and printed in Volume 42 of the Ohio State Reports.

JOHN WELCH.

SUPREME COURT OF OHIO.
1868–1874.

Judge John Welch was born in Harrison County, Ohio, October 29th, 1805. His father was of English and his mother of Irish birth, and were early pioneers of Ohio.

At 18 years of age he commenced to educate himself, and taught school to defray expenses. He entered Franklin College in 1823, and worked his way through by teaching in part, and graduated in 1828.

In January, 1829, he commenced the study of the law with Hon. Joseph Dana, at Athens, Ohio, and in 1833 he was admitted to the bar, and commenced the practice at Athens, Ohio.

In 1845 he was elected to the state senate, and in 1850 he was elected to Congress; he was a delegate to the Baltimore Convention that nominated Gen. Winfield Scott for President; was a presidential elector in 1852, and cast a vote for General John C. Freemont.

In 1862 he was elected a judge of the common pleas; in 1865, on the resignation of Judge Rufus P. Ranney, he was appointed judge of the Supreme Court, and was re-elected and served until 1874.

His opinions are found in volumes XVI to XXVI, and some in XXIX.

GEORGE W. McILVAINE.

SUPREME COURT OF OHIO.
1871-1876.

Judge George W. McIlvaine was born in Washington County, Pennsylyania, on the 14th day of July, 1822.

He eommenced the study of the law in the office of Seth T. Hurd, of the bar of that county, and was admitted to the bar in 1845. A year later he removed to New Philadelphia, Ohio, where he commenced the practice of the law, and where resided during the remainder of his life. In 1861 he was elected judge of the court of common pleas, for the eighth judicial district, and at the expiration of his term he was re-nominated and re-elected without opposition. At the fall election of 1870 he was elected a judge of the Supreme Court, and took his seat on the 9th fo February, 1871. He was re-elected in 1875, and again in 1880. In 1885 he was re-nominated for a fourth term, but was compelled to decline the nomination on account of his failing health. His judicial service was continuous for a term of twenty-five years: ten upon the bench of the common pleas, and fifteen upon the bench of the Supreme Court. He died December 23d, 1887, at New Philadelphia, Ohio. After his death the Supreme Court appointed a committee to prepare a memorial of his life and public service, which was approved by the Court, and ordered printed in Volume 65, Ohio State Reports as a tribute to his memory.

WILLIAM H. WEST.

SUPREME COURT OF OHIO.
1871-1872.

Judge West was born at Millsborough, Washington County, Pennsylvania, February 7, 1824.

His paternal ancestor settled in the Penn's colony in 1682 on the Delaware.

Jonathan West, his grandfather, settled in Ohio about 1798 in Washington County; his father, Thomas West, returned to Fredericktown, Pa., but Wm. H. West came to Millsborough after his majority, and in 1830 settled in Knox County.

In 1844 he entered the academy at Martinsburg, and teaching school to pay expenses, he entered Jefferson College in 1844, and graduated in 1846.

He taught at Lexington, Kentucky, from graduation till 1848, when he was chosen tutor in Jefferson College, and in 1849 was chosen adjunct professor in Hampden-

Sydney College, Va. In 1850 he entered on the study of the law at Bellefontaine, Ohio, and was admitted to the bar in 1851.

In 1852 he was elected prosecuting attorney; in 1857 he was elected to the legislature, re-elected in 1861; in 1863 was chosen senator; in 1865 was elected attorney general, and re-elected in 1867. In 1869 General Grant appointed him consul to Rio Janeiro, which he declined. In 1871 he was elected to the Supreme Bench, and after serving one year he resigned. In 1873 he was a member of the constitutional convention; in 1877 he was the Republican nominee for governor, and in 1860 he was a delegate to the Chicago Convention which nominated Abraham Lincoln.

WALTER F. STONE.

SUPREME COURT OF OHIO.
1872–1874.

Judge Walter F. Stone was born the 18th of Nov., 1822, at Wooster, Wayne County, Ohio. His parents had emigrated from Vermont. He studied law at Pittsburg, Pennsylvania, and afterward at Cleveland; was admitted to the bar in 1845, and in 1846 removed to Sandusky, where he resided the remainder of his life.

In 1865 he was elected to the bench of the common pleas, and re-elected in 1870; in 1872 he was appointed by Governor Noyes one of the Supreme Court judges, to fill the vacancy caused by the resignation of Judge West, and was elected to fill that vacancy, and re-elected to a full term. He served till August, 1874, when he resigned for reason of ill health.

His opinions are in the twenty-third and twenty-fourth Ohio Reports.

His health failed, and he visited California to improve, but in vain, and he died December 23, 1874.

GEORGE REX.

SUPREME COURT OF OHIO.
1874-1877.

George Rex was born in Canton, Stark County, Ohio, on the 25th of July, 1817. He completed his education at the Capital University, at Columbus, and afterwards taught school in the public school of Canton for three years. He studied law with Hon. John Harris, of Canton. and on the 10th of Octeber, 1842, was admitted to the bar.

In February, 1843, he removed to Wooster, and commenced the practice of the law, where he continued to reside until his death. He continued in the practice of his profession except when interrupted by the duties of professional positions.

In the fall of 1847 he was elected prosecuting attorney of Wayne County, and was re-elected in October, 1849, serving four years; in October, 1851, he was chosen to the senate of Ohio for the district ot Wayne and Holmes Counties. He was elected president pro tem. of that body. In October, 1859, he was again elected prosecuting attorney, and was re-elected in 1861.

At August term, 1864, of the court of common pleas, he was appointed prosecuting attorney of the county to fill a vacancy. At the October election, in 1867, he was elected a second time senator of the state, for the district composed of the counties of Wayne, Holmes, Knox and Morrow, serving the full term.

Whilst a member of the senate, he was a leading member of the committee on common schools, and took a deep interest in, and rendered efficient aid in the establishment of our present school system.

On the 11th of September 1874, he was appointed by Governor Allen judge of the Supreme Court of the state, to fill a vacancy occasioned by the resignation of Judge Stone; and afterward, at the October election, was elected for the unexpired term of Judge Stone, and served until his term of office expired, on the 9th of February, 1877. In the fall of 1876 he declined to be a candidate for re-election. His health was seriously impaired by the labors of the bench, and although, on retiring from that position, he resumed the practice of his profession, yet his health never became re-established. He died at Wooster, March 27, 1879, leaving his widow and a daughter surviving him.

Judge Rex was distinguished for his public spirit; was a man of strong convictions, and indefatigable and fearless in the discharge of duty. He left a spotless private character, and his official career is without reproach. His judicial opinions are found in volumes 24, 25 and 26 of the Ohio State Reports.

[NOTE.—The above sketch was inserted by the direction of the judges of the Supreme Court, as a just tribute to the memory of the deceased, in volume 34 of the Ohio State Reports.]

WILLIAM JAMES GILMORE.

SUPREME COURT OF OHIO.

1874-1880.

William James Gilmore was the son of Dr. Eli Gilmore and Clara Moseby Clayton Gilmore, and was born in Liberty, Bedford county, Va., April 24, 1821. His father moved to Preble county, Ohio, in 1825, settled in Israel township, and continued in the practice of his profession, of which he was a very prominent member, until his death.

He began reading law in 1844, in the office of Hon. Thomas Millikin, at Hamilton, Ohio, and completed his studies in the office of J. S. & A. J. Hawkins, in Eaton,

Ohio. While prosecuting his studies he supported himself by teaching school, clerking, and as farm laborer. He was admitted to the bar by the Supreme Court at Columbus, December 8th, 1847, his examination having been conducted by Henry Stanbery, Noah H. Swayne and Aaron F. Perry. He practiced law for a short time in Hamilton, Ohio. in partnership with Col. Thomas Moore, and then removed to Eaton, Ohio, where, in 1849, he formed a partnership with J. S. Hawkins, which continued until the death of Mr. Hawkins in 1852. In 1862 he went into partnership with Judge J. V. Campbell, which continued until 1867. While his office was located in Eaton during this time, his practice called him to all the surrounding counties, where he was known as a successful lawyer. At the expiration of his term of service as one of the judges of the Supreme Court of Ohio, in 1880, he opened a law office in Columbus, and continued in practice there up to the time of his death, August 9th, 1896. One son survives him, Clement R. Gilmore, who is a practicing lawyer at Eaton, Ohio.

The public offices which Judge Gilmore held were all in the line of his profession. He was Prosecuting Attorney of Preble county for four years, from 1852 to 1856; in 1857 he was appointed by the Governor and subsequently elected to fill a vacancy on the Common Pleas Bench of the First Subdivision of the Second Judicial District, his term expiring in 1862; in 1866 he was again elected to the same position and re-elected in 1871, serving until he entered upon his term as one of the judges of the Supreme Court of Ohio in 1875, serving in that position until 1880.

His decisions are reported in Vols. 25, 26, 29, 31, 34 and 35 of the Ohio State Reports. He was one of the original members of the Ohio State Bar Association and its President for the year 1885–86. He was appointed in 1871, by the Governor, a Trustee of Miami University, and held the position until his death. He was also a Trustee of the Ohio State Archæological and Historical Society for a number of years, under appointment from the Governor.

NOTE BY THE EDITOR.—The foregoing sketch was furnished by his brother, James A. Gilmore, Counsellor-at-law, of Eaton, Ohio, and is in part a transcript of a memorial prepared by a committee of the Franklin County Bar Association at the time of Judge Gilmore's death. The excellent portrait was also furnished by his brother, Jas. A. Gilmore.

WASHINGTON W. BOYNTON.

SUPREME COURT OF OHIO.
1876–1882.

Judge Boynton was born in Russia Township, Loraine County, Ohio, January 27, 1833. In 1855 he was made one of the board of school examiners of Loraine County. He taught school and studied law.

In 1856 he was admitted to the bar; in 1859 he was appointed prosecuting attorney, and re-elected twice; in 1865 he was elected to the general assembly; in 1869 he was elected to the common pleas and re-elected.

He was elected to the Supreme Bench 1876, and served until 1882.

JOHN WATERMAN OKEY.

SUPREME COURT OF OHIO.
1878–1886.

Judge Okey was born near Woodsfield, Monroe County, Ohio, January 3, 1827. His grandfather, Leven Okey, was an associate judge of Monroe County.

He was educated at Monroe Academy and by private tutors. He was admitted to the bar in 1849. In 1853 he was made probate judge, and twice re-elected.

Ohio. While prosecutingiis studies he supported himself by teaching school, clerkig, and as farm laborer. He was admitted to the bar by te Supreme Court at Columbus, December 8th, 1847, his examination having been conducted by Henry Stanber, Noah H. Swayne and Aaron F. Perry. He practiced lar for a short time in Hamilton, Ohio. in partnership with Col. Thomas Moore, and then removed to Eaton, Ohio, were, in 1849, he formed a partnership with J. S. Hawkis, which continued until the death of Mr. Hawkins in 1852. In 1862 he went into partnership with Judge JV. Campbell, which continued until 1867. While his offie was located in Eaton during this time, his practice caled him to all the surrounding counties, where he was knwn as a successful lawyer. At the expiration of his tern of service as one of the judges of the Supreme Court of Oio, in 1880, he opened a law office in Columbus, and cntinued in practice there up to the time of his death, Augst 9th, 1896. One son survives him, Clement R. Gilmore who is a practicing lawyer at Eaton, Ohio.

The publi offices whic Judge Gilmore held were all in the line of his professin. He was Prosecuting Attorney of Preble county for far years, from 1852 to 1856; in 1857 he was appointed by he Governor and subsequently elected to fill a vacancy on ie Common Pleas Bench of the First Subdivision of the Seond Judicial District, his term expiring in 1862; in 186 he was again elected to the same position and re-electe in 1871, serving until he entered upon his term as oe of the judges of the Supreme Court of Ohio in 1875, serıng in that position until 188

His decisions are reportd in Vols. 25, 26, 29, 31, 3 35 of the Ohio State Repors. He was one of the members of the Ohio StateBar Association and dent for the year 1885–86. He was appointed the Governor a Trustee of [illegible] and held the position until his death. [illegible] Trustee of the Ohio State Academy [illegible] number of years under appoint[illegible] the Governor.

Note by the Editor: The [illegible] sketch was furnished by his brother, James A. [illegible] of [illegible] part a transcript of a memorial paper [illegible] County Bar Association at the time of Judge [illegible] death. The excellent portrait was also furnished [illegible]

WASHINGTON [illegible]

SUPREME COUR[illegible]

[illegible]

Judge Boynton was born in [illegible] Township, Lorain County, Ohio, January [illegible], 18[illegible]. In 18[illegible] he was made one of the board of school examiners of Lorain County. He taught school and studied la[illegible]

In 1856 he was admitted to the bar. In 18[illegible] he was appointed prosecuting attorney, and re-elected twice. In 18[illegible] he was elected to the general assembly. In 18[illegible] he was elected to the common pleas and re-elected.

He was elected to the Supreme Bench 18[illegible], and served until 1882.

JOHN WATERMAN OKEY

SUPREME COURT OF OHIO.

18[illegible]

Judge Ok[illegible] born [illegible]dsfield, Monroe County, Ohio, Ja[illegible] [illegible] Okey, wa[illegible]

In 1856 he was elected judge of the court of common pleas, in the Belmont District, and re-elected in 1861, when he removed to Guerney County.

In 1865 he resigned the judgeship and removed to Cincinnati, and entering the law office of W. W. Gholson, engaged in preparing the "Ohio Digest;" later he prepared "Okey and Miller on Municipal Law," published in 1869.

In 1875 he was appointed by Governor William Allen one ot the commissioners to codify the general laws of the state, and in 1877 he was elected to the Supreme Bench of the state, and served until 1886.

WILLIAM WARREN JOHNSON.

SUPREME COURT OF OHIO.
1880–1886.

Judge Johnson was born near Chandersville, Ohio, on the 26th ot August, 1826. In the fall of 1849 he commenced the study of the law in the office of the Hon. Charles C. Conway, then speaker of the Ohio Senate, and afterwards a judge of this court. He was admitted to the bar in 1862, and began the practice at Ironton, Lawrence County, Ohio. In 1858 he was elected judge of the court of common pleas for the seventh judicial district, and served until the fall of 1876; two years later he returned to that bench. and remained there until 1872, when owing to ill health he retired. In 1876 he was appointed one of the judges of the Supreme Court Commission, and served during the life of that Commission. In the fall of 1879 he was elected judge of the Supreme Court, and took his seat February 9th. 1880. He was re-elected on October 4th, 1884, but resigned on account of ill health, November 9th, 1886. He had a period of judicial service of nearly twenty years. He died March 2d, 1887. The Supreme Court appointed a committee of the bar to prepare a suitable memorial of his public service, which was ordered to be inserted in volume forty-four of the Ohio State Reports.

NICHOLAS LONGWORTH.

SUPREME COURT OF OHIO.
1881-1883.

Judge Nicholas was born in the city of Cincinnati, on the 16th day of June, 1844. He was the son of Joseph Longworth, and grandson of Nicholas Longworth, citizens of distinction of the city.

He graduated at Harvard University with high honors, in 1856; he studied law with his uncle, Rufus King, in the city of Cincinnati, and was admitted to the bar in the spring of 1869. He was elected a judge of the court of common pleas of Hamilton County, and entered upon his duties in the early part of 1867; he served with ability and distinction until 1881, when he was elected to the bench of the Supreme Court of Ohio. The failing health of his father, of whom he was the only surviving son, devolving upon him the care of the estate of his father and grandfather, led to his resignation and his retirement from the bench on March 8th, 1883. On retiring from the bench he formed a partnership with Thomas McDougal in the practice of the law in Cincinnati, but on the death of his father, near the close of the year 1883, he retired permanently from the practice of the law, and devoted his entire time until his death to the management of the great estate left by his father, and to affairs of a public and private nature. His intellectual gifts were of a high order; he had a marvellous memory, clear and quick perception; he was of a generous disposition, attracted men to him, and formed warm friendships with those with whom he was intimate. He became one of the most prominent citizens of his native city, and occupied a high social position. He died universally respected on the 18th day of January, 1890.

The Supreme Court appointed a committee of members of the bar of that Court to prepare and submit a memorial of his life and public services; their action was approved, and their memorial ordered to be inserted in volume forty-seven of the Ohio State Reports.

JOHN H. DOYLE.

SUPREME COURT OF OHIO.
(1883-)

Judge John H. Doyle was born April 23d, 1844, in Perry County, Ohio, and has lived nearly all of his life at Toledo, Ohio.

He was educated at the public schools of Toledo, and at Dennison University, Granville, Ohio.

He was admitted to the bar at Toledo on the 23d of April, 1865. He was elected judge of the Court of Common Pleas in the district comprising Cleveland and Toledo and in the intermediate counties in 1879. He way nominated by acclamation in the Republican State convention in 1882 for judge of the Supreme Court, in which year the Republican party was defeated. He was appointed judge of the Supreme Court by Governor Foster, to fill the vacancy caused by the resignation of the Hon. Nicholas Longworth, in January 1883, and served the balance of Judge Longworth's term. He was again nominated by the Republican convention in 1883 for the full term of the Supreme Court, but the Republican party was again defeated and Judge Doyle resumed his practice at the bar at Toledo in 1884.

He was 35 years of age when he took his seat upon the bench of the Court of Common Pleas; and 38 years of age when he took his seat upon the Supreme Court Bench. He is still in active practice in the City of Toledo and occupies a high and prominent position at the bar of the state.

MARTIN DEWEY FOLLETT.

SUPREME COURT OF OHIO.
1884–1886.

Judge Follett was born at Grosburg, Vt., October 8, 1826. He was the son of the John F. Follett who removed to Ohio in 1836.

He graduated at Marietta College in 1853. He taught school after graduation, and in 1856 was elected Supt. of Public Schools of Marietta and served two years. He studied law and was admitted to the bar in 1859, and commenced the practice of the law at Marietta, Ohio. He was a Democrat and was a member of the National Convention that nominated Gen. McClelland for the presidency. He ran for congress on the Democratic ticket in 1861 and 1868 and was defeated.

In 1884 he was made justice of Supreme Court and served two years.

GIBSON ATHERTON.

SUPREME COURT OF OHIO.
1885-

Judge Gibson —therton was born in Newark Township, Licking County, Ohio, January 19th, 1831. His boyhood was spent on a farm. He entered Denison University at

Grandville, Ohio, and remained until 1851, when he entered Miami University, at Oxford Ohio, where he graduated in 1853. The next year he took charge of the academy at Osceola, Mo.; in 1854 he returned to New York continuing his legal studies in the office of the Hon Luccius Case and was admitted to the bar in 1855. In 1857 he was elected prosecuting attorney of Licking county, Ohio, and was re-elected in 1859 and 1861. He was elected mayor of the city of Newark, O., and re-elected in 1862. He was nominated by the Democratic party for state senator in 1863 for the 16th senatorial district but was defeated. In 1866 he was nominated by the Democratic party in his judicial district for the bench of the Common Pleas but was defeated. In 1878 he was nominated and elected to congress from the 14th Ohio district. In 1880 he was re-nominated and re-elected from the 13th congressional district, the lines of which had been changed in the meantime. On August 20th, 1885, he was nominated for the vacancy upon the bench of the Supreme Court occasioned by the death of Judge Okey, and on the same day was appointed to fill the vacancy pending the election. He failed of eleetion, and hence his term of service on the bench was limited being from August 20th, 1885, to December 16th, 1885, when he again resumed the active practice of the law. He was stricken with paralyis, and it resulted in his death on the 10th of November, 1887.

His opinions, necessarily few, appear in the 43d volume of the Ohio State Reports. The Supreme Court on the occasion of his death appointed a committee to prepare and submit a memorial on his life and services. Their report was approved by the court and ordered to be inserted in volume 45 of the Ohio State reports as a tribute to his memory.

Lightning Source UK Ltd.
Milton Keynes UK
UKHW011813070119
335139UK00009B/377/P

9 781528 432498